IN CRIMINOLOGY

Social Structure Approaches

Social Disorganization

1920 **Thomas and Znaniecki** Displaced immigrants

1920s-1930s **Park & Burgess** Social ecology, social pathology, concentric zones (Chicago School)

1929 **Shaw & McKay** Cultural transmission (Chicago School)

1982 **James Q. Wilson & George L. Kelling** Broken windows, defensible space, criminology of place

1987 **Rodney Stark** Theory of deviant neighborhoods

Culture Conflict

1927 **Frederic Thrasher** Gangs and gang typologies

1938 **Thorsten Sellin** Conduct norms, primary conflict, secondary conflict

1943 **William F. Whyte** Subcultures

1955 **Albert Cohen** Gangs, reaction formation

1957 **Sykes & Matza** Techniques of neutralization

1958 **Walter B. Miller** Focal concerns

1960s **Cloward & Ohlin** Illegitimate opportunity structure, delinquent subcultures

1967 **Ferracuti & Wolfgang** Violent subcultures

Strain Theory

1938 **Robert Merton** Anomie, conformity, innovation, ritualism, retreatism, rebellion

1982 **Blau & Blau** Relative deprivation, frustration, distributive justice

1992 **Robert Agnew** General Strain Theory

1994 **Messner & Rosenfeld** American Dream

Social Process Theories

Social Learning Theory

1939 **Edwin Sutherland** Differential association

1960 **Daniel Glaser** Differential identification theory

1966 **Burgess & Akers** Differential association-reinforcement

Social Control Theory

1950s **Walter Reckless** Containment theory, inner and outer containment

1969 **Travis Hirschi** Social bond and self control: attachment, commitment, belief, involvement

1970s **Howard Kaplan** Self degradation

1990 **Hirschi & Gottfredson** Social bonds and self control

1995 **Charles Tittle** Control-balance, control surplus, control deficit

Labeling Theory

1938 **Frank Tannenbaum** Tagging, dramatization of evil

1951 **Edwin Lemert** Primary deviance, secondary deviance

1963 **Howard Becker** Outsiders, moral enterprise

1997 **John Braithwaite** Reintegrative shaming, stigmatic shaming

Dramaturgy

1960s **Erving Goffman** Dramaturgy, impression management, discrediting information, total institutions, disculturation

Social Conflict Theories

1848 **Karl Marx** The Communist Manifesto

1916 **Willem Bonger** Class struggle

1938 **Thorsten Sellin** Culture conflict

1939 **Rusche & Kircheimer**

Radical Criminology

1958 **George Vold** Political conflict between groups, conflict is normal

1959 **Ralf Dahrendorf** conflict is normal, destructive change

1969 **Austin Turk** Social order= pattern of conflict, laws serve to control

1970s **William Chambliss** Power gaps, crime reduces surplus labor

1974 **Richard Quinney** Contradictions of capitalism, socialist principles

Feminist Criminology

1975 **Adler & Simon** Gender socialization

1977 **Carol Smart** Gender bias in criminology

1988 **Daly & Chesney-Lind** Androcentricity, crime may not be normal

1989 **John Hagan** Power-control theory

Peacemaking Criminology

1986 **Pepinsky & Quinney** Restorative justice, participatory justice

1989 **Lozoff & Braswell** New Age principles

Left-Realist Criminology

1973 **Taylor, Walton and Young** The New Criminology

1980s **Young & DeKeseredy** Social justice, reality of crime

Welcome to the fifth edition!

The following pages introduce what's new in the
fifth edition, as well as the hallmark features that have made
Criminology Today: An Integrative Introduction one of the
most respected criminology textbooks in America today.

What's New

New Boxes throughout the Text

New "Who's to Blame" Boxes

Author-created hypothetical cases and critical thinking questions help to focus on the theme of the text (social problems vs. social responsibility).

New "Profiles in Crime" Boxes

These Profiles offer insights into the lives and criminal motivation of notorious offenders, such as Ted Kaczynski (the "Unabomber").

New Sections in the Text

- **Convict Criminology** (in Chapter 9)
- **Child Sexual Abuse/Sexual Offenses Against Children** (in Chapter 10)
- **Prostitution** (in Chapter 13)
- **Human Trafficking and Human Smuggling** (in Chapter 15)

Theme

Social Problems vs. Social Responsibility

The theme of the text is at the core of today's thinking about crime. It draws on the distinction between those who believe that crime is a matter of individual responsibility, and those who emphasize that crime is a manifestation of underlying social problems.

The Theme of This Book

This book builds on a social policy theme by asking questions about the sources of crime and criminality, and by asking what we can do to control crime. Our theme contrasts two perspectives now popular in American society and in much of the rest of the world (see Figure 1–3). One point of view, termed the **social problems perspective**, holds that crime is a manifestation of underlying social problems like poverty, discrimination, inequality of opportunity, the breakdown of traditional social institutions, the low level of formal education among some disadvantaged groups, pervasive family violence experienced by some during the formative years, and inadequate socialization practices that leave too many young people without the fundamental values necessary to contribute meaningfully to the society in which they live. Advocates of the social problems perspective, while generally agreeing that crime and violence are serious social problems, advance solutions based on what is, in effect, a public health model. Adherents of that model say that crime must be addressed in much the same way as public health concerns like AIDS, herpes, or avian flu.

Proponents of the social problems perspective typically foresee solutions to the crime problem as coming in the form of large-scale government expenditures in support of social programs designed to address the issues that are perceived to lie at the root of crime. Government-funded initiatives, designed to enhance social, educational, occupational, and other opportunities, are perceived as offering programmatic solutions to ameliorate most causes of crime.

The social problems approach to crime is characteristic of what social scientists term a *macro* approach because it portrays instances of individual behavior (crimes) as arising out of widespread and contributory social conditions that enmesh unwitting individuals in a causal nexus of uncontrollable social forces.

A contrasting perspective lays the cause of crime squarely at the feet of individual perpetrators. This point of view holds that individuals are fundamentally responsible for their own behavior and maintains that they choose crime over other, more law-abiding courses of action. Perpetrators may choose crime, advocates of this perspective say, because it is exciting, because it offers illicit pleasures and the companionship of like-minded thrill seekers, or because it is simply personally less demanding than conformity. This viewpoint, which we shall call the **social responsibility perspective**, has a close affiliation with what is known in criminology as rational choice theory (discussed in detail in Chapter 4). Advocates of the social responsibility perspective, with

social problems perspective
The belief that crime is a manifestation of underlying social problems, such as poverty, discrimination, pervasive family violence, inadequate socialization practices, and the breakdown of traditional social institutions.

■ **Thematic Question**
What are the assumptions inherent in the social problems perspective on crime?

social responsibility perspective
The belief that individuals are fundamentally responsible for their own behavior and that they choose crime over other, more law-abiding courses of action.

Questions for Review/Questions for Reflection

The theme of the book is carried through the end of the chapter within the Questions for Review and Questions for Reflection. They are tied directly to the learning objectives at the start of the chapter.

QUESTIONS FOR REVIEW

1. What are the four definitional perspectives in contemporary criminology? What is the definition of *crime* that the authors of this textbook have chosen to use?

2. What is crime? What is the difference between crime and deviance? How might the notion of crime change over time? What impact does the changing nature of crime have on criminology?

3. What is the legalistic approach to the study of crime? How can it be used to decide what forms of behavior are criminal?

4. What do criminologists do? Provide a list of employment opportunities available in the field of criminology.

5. What are the various definitions of criminology presented in this chapter? Which is the one chosen by the authors of this textbook? Why?

6. How does contemporary criminology influence social policy? Do you think that policymakers should address crime as a matter of individual responsibility and accountability, or do you think that crime is truly a symptom of a dysfunctional society? Why?

7. What is theme of this textbook? What are the differences between the social problems and the social responsibility perspectives on crime causation?

8. Describe the various participants in a criminal event. How does each contribute to an understanding of the event?

9. In what way is contemporary criminology interdisciplinary? Why is the sociological perspective especially important in studying crime? What other perspectives might be relevant? Why?

QUESTIONS FOR REFLECTION

1. This book emphasizes a social problems versus social responsibility theme. Describe both perspectives. How might social policy decisions based on these perspectives vary?

2. Do you think you might want to become a criminologist? Why or why not?

3. What do crimes such as doctor-assisted suicide tell us about the nature of the law and about crime in general? Do you believe that doctor-assisted suicide should be legalized? Why or why not?

4. Are there any crimes today that you think should be legalized? If so, what are they and why?

5. Can you think of any advances now occurring in the social or physical sciences that might soon have a significant impact on our understanding of crime and criminality? If so, what would those advances be? How might they impact our understanding of crime and criminal behavior?

The Recent Rise in Crime Rates

Compared to 2005, homicides and robberies are increasing in dozens of cities.

Crime in the News

Author Faced Prison for Insulting Turkishness

ISTANBUL—One of Turkey's leading authors was acquitted on September 20, 2006 of "insulting Turkishness"—a crime Western-looking Turks view as an embarrassment and one of the biggest obstacles to joining the European Union.

The speedy court decision was seen as a step toward securing greater freedom of speech, but critics said until the law is abolished, Turkey will remain a place where authors are regularly put on trial.

A nationalist demonstrator gestures at a poster of Turkish writer Elif Shafak during a protest outside of a courthouse in Istanbul, Turkey, in 2006. A Turkish court acquitted Shafak, one of Turkey's leading authors, saying there was no evidence that she had "insulted Turkishness" in a novel she had written.

Source: AP/Osman Orsal

"The fact remains that (Turkey's courts) established a restrictive interpretation of article 301 of the penal code which is not in line with the European Court of Human Rights and European standards of freedom of expression," EU spokeswoman Krisztina Nagy warned after the decision.

But the government is reluctant to change the law—which makes it a crime to insult Turkey, "Turkishness" or the government—because it has broad nationalist support.

EU officials counter the real damage to Turkey's image comes from putting writers like Elif Shafak on trial—a case brought by nationalist lawyers because of words spoken by the novelist's fictional characters.

The court ruled to acquit about an hour-and-a-half into the trial on the grounds there was "no evidence" Shafak had insulted Turkishness.

"I hope that the absurdity of this case—we're talking about fictional characters—will encourage people that it's time to act," said Joost Lagendijk, a senior European Parliament member who attended the trial and is a vocal supporter of Turkey's EU bid.

Lagendijk called on Turkey's pro-EU Prime Minister Recep Tayyip Erdogan, who has himself spent time in jail for reciting an Islamist poem in 1999, to intervene and change the law.

"Each court case that is started is a victory for those who don't want Turkey in the EU, and a defeat for me and those in the EU who are in favor of Turkey's accession," Lagendijk said.

But nationalist lawyers said they will continue to bring legal action against anyone who insults Turkey and vowed to appeal the Shafak decision.

Fiercely opposed to Turkey joining the EU and hostile to any foreign intervention, the lawyers spent most of the trial trying to eject non-Turkish observers—especially Lagendijk—from the packed Istanbul courtroom.

Multiculturalism

The book promotes an understanding of the differences in crime from a multicultural perspective.

FBI Crime Reporting

The text recognizes the importance of the National Incidence-Based Reporting System (NIBRS), which is becoming the standard data format for FBI crime reporting.

NIBRS: The New UCR Data Format

Recently, the Uniform Crime Reporting Program has undergone a number of significant changes, and more are scheduled to be implemented shortly as a new, enhanced, incident-driven crime-reporting system, funded in part by the federal Crime Identification Technology Act of 1998,[10] is phased in. The new system, the National Incident-Based Reporting System (NIBRS), revises the definitions of a number of offenses for reporting purposes, but its incident-driven nature is its most important feature. "Incident-driven" means that the FBI will use the new system to collect detailed data on the circumstances surrounding each serious criminal incident. The NIBRS data-collection format focuses on each single incident and arrest within 22 crime categories, with incident, victim, property, offender, and arrestee information being gathered when available. The 22 NIBRS crime categories are, in turn, made up of 46 specific crimes called "Group A offenses" (as compared with only eight major offenses on which the old UCR Program

■ Lecture Note
Numerous scholars of criminology have commented that the FBI's UCR/NIBRS reports are a better measure of police behavior than of crime. Illustrate the merit (or lack of merit) of this statement through discussion of the UCR/NIBRS Program.

■ Lecture Note
Mention that media reporting of crime statistics is dominated by UCR/NIBRS statistics. Explain to students how much the public's

Technology

Technology and Crime

Keeping pace with current events, the book includes expanded coverage of all the latest technological crimes, with close attention paid to identity theft.

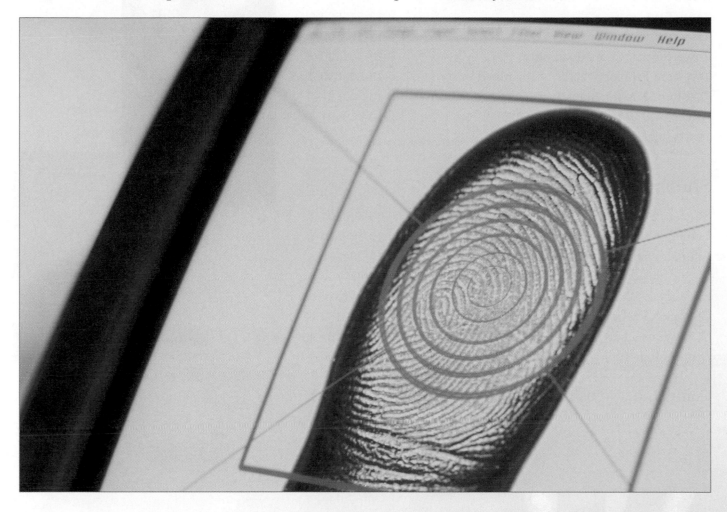

Library Extras

Found in every chapter, these useful tools provide the latest direct links to specific Internet articles and scholarly papers about criminology.

Web Extras

Found in every chapter, these valuable links take students to Websites relevant to the study of criminology.

Supplements

Instructor Supplements

Instructor's Resource Manual	0-13-513502-8
Instructor's Resource Manual* (download only)	0-13-502135-9
Instructor's Resource CD with PowerPoints and TestGen	0-13-513503-6
TestGen* (download only)	0-13-513500-1
PowerPoints* (download only)	0-13-502136-7
Test Item File for WebCT* (download only)	0-13-503040-4
Test Item File for BlackBoard* (download only)	0-13-503187-7
ABC News Video Library on DVD (1–5)	0-13-513497-8

*File also available at the Instructor's Resource Center, www.prenhall.com/irc

Student Supplements

Student Study Guide	0-13-513501-X
Careers in Criminal Justice CD-ROM	0-13-119513-1
Ethics in Criminal Justice CD-ROM	0-13-204398-X
CJ Simulations CD-ROM	0-13-225222-8
CJ Student Writer's Manual, 4/e	0-13-231876-8
CJ Pocket Dictionary	0-13-192132-0
CJ Systems Chart Poster	0-13-170161-4
Criminology Interactive DVD	0-13-513504-4

Companion Website—www.prenhall.com/schmalleger

CRIMINOLOGY TODAY
AN INTEGRATIVE INTRODUCTION

STUDENT EDITION

FIFTH EDITION

FRANK SCHMALLEGER, Ph.D.

Distinguished Professor Emeritus, The University of North Carolina at Pembroke

PEARSON

Prentice
Hall

Columbus, Ohio
Upper Saddle River, New Jersey

Library of Congress Cataloging in Publication Data

Schmalleger, Frank.
    Criminology today : an integrative introduction/Frank Schmalleger.—5th ed.
    p. cm.
        ISBN-13: 978-0-13-513031-5
        ISBN-10: 0-13-513031-X
    1. Criminology. 2. Criminology—United States. I. Title.
HV6025.S346 2009
364—dc22

2007030308

Editor in Chief: Vernon R. Anthony
Senior Editor: Tim Peyton
Development Editor: Elisa Rogers
Editorial Assistant: Alicia Kelly
Project Managers: Barbara Marttine Cappuccio, Stephen C. Robb
Production Coordination: Emily Bush, S4Carlisle Publishing Services
Art Director: Mary Siener
Interior Design: Robert Aleman
Cover Design: Robert Aleman
Cover Image: Fotosearch and Getty Images
Photographer: (Getty) Shooting Star
Operations Supervisor: Patricia A. Tonneman
Director, Image Resource Center: Melinda Patelli
Manager, Rights and Permissions: Zina Arabia
Manager, Visual Research: Beth Brenzel
Manager, Cover Visual Research & Permissions: Karen Sanatar
Senior Image Permission Coordinator: Cynthia Vincenti
Photo Researcher: Jerry Marshall/Truitt and Marshall
Director of Marketing: David Gesell
Marketing Manager: Adam Kloza
Marketing Coordinator: Alicia Dysert

For Nicole and Jason

This book was set in Melior by S4Carlisle Publishers Services. It was printed and bound by Courier Kendallville, Inc. The cover was printed by Phoenix Color Corp.

10 9 8 7 6
ISBN-13: 978-0-13-513031-5
ISBN-10: 0-13-513031-X

Brief Contents

Contents

Preface

The twenty-first century began with momentous events in the United States, including the destruction of the World Trade Center and an attack on the Pentagon by Islamic terrorists, a steep decline in equity markets, and corporate scandals that cost Americans billions of dollars in lost investments.

The crimes committed by terrorists set a tone for the start of the new century unlike any in living memory. Homeland security became an important buzzword at all levels of American government, while pundits questioned just how much freedom people would be willing to sacrifice to enhance security. Americans felt both physically and economically threatened as stock market losses were traced to the unethical actions of a surprising cadre of corporate executives who had previously been held in high regard in the business world and in the communities where they lived. Soon the media were busily showing a parade of business leaders being led away in handcuffs to face trial on charges of crooked accounting.

Added to the mix by the beginning of 2008 were shocking acts of criminality that emanated from all corners of the world—including the depravities of sex tourism involving human trafficking, sex acts with minors streamed across the Internet in real time, claims of successful human clonings by a fringe religious sect, stem cell controversies involving Korean scientists said to be in league with Russian organized crime, and the thefts of hundreds of thousands of personal identities—the latter constituting a very intimate crime that can literally cause a person to face the loss of his or her social self in a complex culture that increasingly defines one's essence in terms of an economic, educational, and ever-more complex social nexus.

Criminologists found themselves wondering what new laws might be enacted to control the potential misuse of emerging computer and biotechnologies that, while they seemed to hold amazing promise to cure disease and reshape humanity's future, threatened the social fabric in a way not seen since the birth of the atomic bomb or the harnessing of electricity. Similarly, climate changes, including violent storms such as Hurricane Katrina, and the impact of global warming on human populations, combined with our nation's desperate need for alternative energy sources and instability in the Middle East to contribute to a growing awareness that the challenges facing criminologists in the twenty-first century are unlike any they have previously faced.

It was against this backdrop that the need for a comprehensive revision of *Criminology Today* emerged. This new edition addresses the poignant question of how security and freedom interface in an age of increasing globalism. Chapter 15, in particular, provides substantially enlarged coverage of terrorism and cyberterrorism, including an overview of many types of terrorist groups, such as nationalist, religious, state-sponsored, left-wing, right-wing, and anarchist groups. The findings and recommendations of special committees and government bodies that have focused on terrorism in recent years are also discussed, and online links to the full text of their reports are provided. Included here are the reports of the 9/11 Commission, the Gilmore Commission, the three-phased report of the U.S. Commission on National Security in the 21st Century (also known as the Hart-Rudman Commission); and the National Commission on Terrorism (also known as the Bremmer Commission).

In the past few years, crime and criminals have changed in ways that few had previously imagined would occur, and these changes hold considerable significance for each one of us and for our nation as a whole. It is my hope that this new edition will help today's students understand the nature of the changes that have occurred and that it will help them find a meaningful place in the social world that is to come.

Frank Schmalleger, Ph.D.
Distinguished Professor Emeritus
The University of North Carolina at Pembroke

What's New in This Edition

The fifth edition of *Criminology Today: An Integrative Introduction* continues to offer students a clear, contemporary, and comprehensive introduction to criminology that encourages critical thinking about the causes of crime and crime prevention strategies. The text's hallmark thematic approach of social problems versus social responsibility (is crime a matter of individual responsibility or a symptom of a dysfunctional society?) prompts students to think critically about the causes of crime and helps them see the link between crime theories and crime policies.

New Features in the Fifth Edition

"Who's to Blame—Society or the Individual?" boxes provide author-created hypothetical case studies and critical thinking questions to help students focus on the book's overall theme of social problems versus social responsibility.

"Criminal Profiles" boxes provide insights into the lives and criminal motivation of notorious offenders such as Theodore John "Ted" Kaczynski (The Unabomber), Sanyika Shakur (aka Monster Kody Scott), Mohammed Atta, and Dennis Rader (The BTK Killer).

"Questions for Reflection" at the end of each chapter encourage students to think critically about the criminological issues addressed in that chapter.

Chapter 15 on globalization and terrorism combines the study of comparative/international criminology with a comprehensive investigation into the nature, origin, and control of terrorism—domestic, international, and transnational. Chapter 15 also now addresses the challenges that human smuggling, human trafficking, and illegal immigration represent to homeland security.

The topic of social policy is now integrated throughout the text, rather than addressed only in one chapter, associating social policy issues more closely with the criminological perspectives that underpin them. Chapter opening stories, part opening narratives, many photos, and all news boxes, tables, figures, and statistics have been updated.

Start-of-chapter learning objectives have been made consistent with major chapter headings and with the end-of-chapter discussion questions throughout the text.

A series of Library Extras within each chapter now matches the Web Extras features found in previous editions. Web Extras take students to Web sites of relevance to the study of criminology, while Library Extras provide direct links to specific articles and papers on the Internet of relevance to the topics under discussion. All links are maintained by Frank Schmalleger, ensuring their availability throughout the life of the edition.

Chapter 2: The NIBRS data format is discussed in more detail, and its history and development are explained. Recent upward trends in crime data for the United States are explored and explanations are suggested.

Chapter 3: A description of the Academy of Experimental Criminology has been added, along with a description of the new Stockholm Prize in Criminology, and recent prize recipients.

Chapter 9: This chapter, "Social Conflict Theories," now contains a new section on convict criminology, which is a perspective on crime, crime causation, and the justice system provided by degreed offenders, credentialed former offenders, and their associates who are actively involved in producing a new body of criminological literature.

Chapter 10: A new and comprehensive section on child sex abuse has been added to this chapter. As the National Institute of Justice notes, "few criminal offenses are more despised than the sexual abuse of children, and few are so little understood in terms of incidence (the number of offenses committed), prevalence (the proportion of the population who commit offenses), and reoffense risk." A comprehensive typology of child sexual abusers is provided, and each of the types is provided.

Chapter 13: This chapter, "Public Order and Drug Crimes," contains a new section on prostitution. The chapter describes the legal status of prostitution and sex workers in various parts of the world, and pays special attention to prostitution in the United States, including the various types of prostitutes and their motivation. Feminist perspectives on prostitution are included.

Chapter 15: What is essentially a new chapter on globalization and terrorism combines the study of comparative/international criminology with a comprehensive investigation into the nature, origin, and control of terrorism—both domestic and international. Transnational crimes are also discussed. This chapter now also contains a comprehensive new section on human smuggling, human trafficking, and illegal immigration. Not only is immigration an important social and political issue today, but illegal immigration, human smuggling, and human trafficking represent important challenges to homeland security.

Epilogue: A book-concluding epilogue, new to this edition, focuses on the future of criminology and describes the techniques of future research as they are applicable to the study of crime and crime control.

The Endpapers: The inside back covers now contain a comprehensive description of annotated links from the Prentice Hall Cybrary of special relevance to the study of criminology.

Acknowledgments

A book like *Criminology Today* draws upon the talents and resources of many people and is the end result of much previous effort. This text could not have been written without the groundwork laid by previous criminologists, academics, and researchers; hence, a hearty thank you is due everyone who has contributed to the development of the field of criminology throughout the years, and especially to those theorists, authors, and social commentators who are cited in this book. Without their work, the field would be that much poorer. I would like to thank, as well, all the adopters—professors and students alike—of my previous textbooks, for they have given me the encouragement and fostered the steadfastness required to write this new edition of *Criminology Today*.

The Prentice Hall team members, whom I have come to know so well and who have worked so professionally with me on this and other projects, deserve a special thanks. The team includes Robin Baliszewski, Alicia Dysert, JoEllen Gohr, Alicia Kelly, David Gesell, Adam Kloza, Craig Marcus, Tim Peyton, Stephen Robb, Elisa Rogers, Mary Siener, Santos Shih, and Pat Tonneman. I would especially like to thank Barbara Cappuccio at Prentice Hall and Emily Bush at S4Carlisle Publishing Services for their commitment and attention to this project. My thanks also to cover designer Vicki Kane, interior designer Wanda España, and photo researchers Alexandra Truitt and Jerry Marshall, whose efforts have helped make *Criminology Today* both attractive and visually appealing.

My friends and professional colleagues Ellen Cohn at Florida International University, Cassandra Renzi at Keiser University, Debra Kelley at Virginia's Longwood University, and Karel Kurst-Swanger at Oswego State University helped in many ways. Dr. Kelley's assistance in developing the annotated instructor's material showed her understanding of instructors' needs. Dr. Cohn graciously used her deep personal creativity in enhancing the supplements package. Thanks to Carolyn Dennis for developing the Companion Website and Venessa Garcia for developing the PowerPoint Slides. I am especially thankful to Ellen Cohn for the quality products she has created and for her exceptional ability to build intuitively upon concepts in the text. Thanks also to Bob Winslow at California State University–San Diego for insight and encouragement on a number of important issues and to Jack Humphrey at St. Anselm College and Stephen J. Schoenthaler for their valuable suggestions in the preparation of this new edition.

This book has benefited greatly from the quick availability of information and other resources through online services and in various locations on the Internet's World Wide Web. I am grateful to the many information providers who, although they are too numerous to list, have helped establish such useful resources.

I am thankful as well for the assistance of Bill Tafoya and Nancy Carnes, both with the Federal Bureau of Investigation (Bill is now retired); William Ballweber at the National Institute of Justice; David Beatty, director of public affairs with the National Victim Center; Kris Rose at the National Criminal Justice Reference Service; Marilyn Marbrook and Michael Rand at the Office of Justice Programs; Mark Reading at the Drug Enforcement Administration; and Barbara Maxwell at *USA Today*.

Manuscript reviewers who have contributed to the development of *Criminology Today* include:

Rood Adams, East Carolina State University
Michael P. Brown, Ball State University
Gregg Buchholz, Keiser University
Bryan D. Byers, Ball State University
Dianne Carmody, Old Dominion University
Steven M. Christiansen, Joliet Junior College
Myrna Cintron, Texas A&M University
Patrick G. Donnelly, University of Dayton
Ronald D. Hunter, State University of West Georgia
Steven Johnson, Eastern Arizona College
Daniel D. Jones, University of Washington
John Kirkpatrick, University of New Hampshire
Joan Luxenburg, University of Central Oklahoma

M. Joan McDermott, Southern Illinois University
William McGovern, Sussex County Community College
Darrell K. Mills, Pima Community College (East Campus)
Robert Mutchnick, Indiana University of Pennsylvania
Michael Pittaro, Lehigh Valley College
Glen E. Sapp, Central Carolina Community College
Jennifer L. Schulenberg, Sam Houston State University
Louis Shepard, West Georgia Technical College
John Siler, Georgia Perimeter College
Tamson L. Six, Lock Haven University
Dianne Williams, North Carolina A&T State University
Jeffrey Zack, Fayetteville Technical Community College
Anthony W. Zumpetta, West Chester University

Finally, but by no means least, I am indebted to a small but very special group of contemporary criminologists who have laid the foundation for our discipline's presence on the Internet. Among them are Cecil Greek at Florida State University, whose online lecture notes (www.criminology.fsu.edu/crimtheory) are massively informative; Tom O'Connor of Austin Peay State University, whose Megalinks in Criminal Justice (http://www.apsu.edu/oconnort) provide an amazingly comprehensive resource; Matthew Robinson at Appalachian State University, whose Crime Theory Links (www.appstate.edu/~robinsnmb/theorylinks.htm) allow visitors to vote on what they think are the causes of crime; Bruce Hoffman, whose Crime Theory site (http://crimetheory.com) at the University of Washington offers many great insights into the field; and Regina Schekall, volunteer Webmaster for the Santa Clara Police Department, whose organized crime page (formerly www.crime.org) provides a valuable resource for both students and educators. All of these excellent resources are referred to throughout this book—and it is to these modern-day visionaries that *Criminology Today* owes much of its technological depth.

About the Author

Frank Schmalleger, Ph.D., is professor emeritus at the University of North Carolina at Pembroke, where he also was recognized as Distinguished Professor. Dr. Schmalleger holds degrees from the University of Notre Dame and Ohio State University, having earned both a master's (1970) and a doctorate in sociology (1974) from Ohio State University with a special emphasis in criminology. From 1976 to 1994, he taught criminal justice courses at the University of North Carolina at Pembroke. For the last 16 of those years, he chaired the university's Department of Sociology, Social Work, and Criminal Justice. As an adjunct professor with Webster University in St. Louis, Missouri, Schmalleger helped develop the university's graduate program in security administration and loss prevention. He taught courses in that curriculum for more than a decade. Schmalleger has also taught in the New School for Social Research's online graduate program, helping build the world's first electronic classrooms in support of distance learning through computer telecommunications. An avid Web user and site builder, Schmalleger is also the creator of award-winning World Wide Web sites, including one that supports this textbook (www. crimtoday.com).

Frank Schmalleger is the author of numerous articles and many books, including the widely used *Criminal Justice Today: An Introductory Text for the 21st Century* (Prentice Hall, 2009), now in its tenth edition; *Juvenile Delinquency* (with Clemmens Bartollas; Allyn & Bacon, 2008), *Criminal Justice: A Brief Introduction,* seventh edition (Prentice Hall, 2008); *Criminal Law Today,* third edition (Prentice Hall, 2006); *Crime and the Justice System in America: An Encyclopedia* (Greenwood Publishing Group, 1997); *Trial of the Century: People of the State of California vs. Orenthal James Simpson* (Prentice Hall, 1996); *Career Paths: A Guide to Jobs in Federal Law Enforcement* (Regents/Prentice Hall, 1994); *Computers in Criminal Justice* (Wyndham Hall Press, 1991); *Criminal Justice Ethics* (Greenwood Press, 1991); *Finding Criminal Justice in the Library* (Wyndham Hall Press, 1991); *Ethics in Criminal Justice* (Wyndham Hall Press, 1990); *A History of Corrections* (Foundations Press of Notre Dame, 1983); and *The Social Basis of Criminal Justice* (University Press of America, 1981). Schmalleger is also founding editor of the journal *Criminal Justice Studies* (formerly *The Justice Professional*).

Schmalleger's philosophy of both teaching and writing can be summed up in these words: "In order to communicate knowledge we must first catch, then hold, a person's interest—be it student, colleague, or policymaker. Our writing, our speaking, and our teaching must be relevant to the problems facing people today, and they must—in some way—help solve those problems."

1 PART

The Crime Picture

> Society secretly wants crime, needs crime, and gains definite satisfactions from the present mishandling of it! We condemn crime; we punish offenders for it; but we need it. The crime and punishment ritual is part of our lives!
>
> —Karl Menninger[iv]

CHAPTER 1 What Is Criminology?

CHAPTER 2 Patterns of Crime

CHAPTER 3 Where Do Theories Come From?

Over the years, social commentators have observed that people are simultaneously attracted to and repulsed by crime—especially stories of highly gruesome crimes involving extreme personal violence. The popularity of today's TV crime shows, Hollywood-produced crime movies, true-crime books and magazines, and Web sites devoted exclusively to the coverage of crime supports that observation. In late-2006, for example, Internet sites were abuzz with news of the impending auction of personal items belonging to Nathaniel Benjamin Levi Bar-Jonah, a sexual predator with a 30-year history of extremely violent crimes involving young boys. Bar-Jonah, a short-order cook who is reputed to have served neighbors pot pies and hamburgers made from human flesh, had been described as evil incarnate after creating, encrypting and hiding a recipe for "little boy stew" among his chef's notebooks.[i] The auctioned items, which some termed "murderabilia," included Bar-Jonah's handwritten letters, shoes, bifocals, artwork, and even lockets of his hair. Similarly, in 2007, one of the most widely-viewed YouTube videos showed a real-life schoolyard attack by three teenage Suffolk County (New York) girls on an eighth grade classmate. The video was also posted on the community Website MySpace and repeatedly shown on nationally televised news shows.[ii]

One of the things that fascinates people about crime—especially violent crime—is that it sometimes seems so inexplicable. How, for example, can the actions of Amish schoolhouse shooter Charles Carl Roberts IV, a Pennsylvania milkman who held a schoolroom full of young Amish children hostage and shot ten of the girls in 2006, be explained? Roberts, a father of three, called his wife shortly before he killed the children to tell her that he wouldn't be coming home, and then shot himself. Strangely, Roberts left a note for his daughter telling her "I want you to know that I love you, and I'm sorry I couldn't be here to watch you grow up."[iii] While it is true that some crimes are especially difficult to understand, we nonetheless seek to find some reason for the unreasonable. We search for explanations for the seemingly unexplainable.

But people wonder not only about spectacular crimes. Even "everyday" crimes like robbery, drug use, assault, vandalism, and computer intrusion need explaining. Why do people fight? Does it matter to a robber that he may end up in prison? How can so many people sacrifice love, money, careers, and even their lives for access to illegal drugs? What motivates a terrorist to give up his own life to take others? Why do gifted techno-savvy teens and preteens feel the need to devote themselves to hacking seemingly secure sites on the Internet?

While this text may not answer all these questions, it will examine the multitude of causative factors that come into play when a crime is committed, and it will help you appreciate the challenges of crafting effective crime control policy. In the first two chapters of this book, however, we will focus primarily on examining the nature and extent of crime and deviance. In Chapter 3 we will learn where theories come from; we will explore the historical basis for the scientific study of crime; and we will review the research methods that criminologists use today.

[i]Mark Memmott, "Killer's Effects for Sale on Internet," *USA Today*, December 5, 2006, p. 3A; and Kim Skornogoski, "Bar-Jonah Puts 'Murderabilia' Up for Auction," *Great Falls Tribune* (Montana), December 4, 2006, http://www.greatfallstribune.com/apps/pbcs.dll/article?AID=/20061204/NEWS01/612040302.

[ii]"L.I. Officials: Help Available in Wake of Web Video Attack," WNBC.com, January 16, 2007, http://www.wnbc.com/news/10766168/detail.html.

[iii]William M. Welch, "Pa. Gunman Intent on Massacre, 911 Tapes Show," *USA Today*, October 10, 2006, p. 3A.

[iv]Karl Menninger, *The Crime of Punishment* (New York: Viking, 1968).

What Is Criminology?

Outline

Crime is the only way to get ahead, Duke. You'll never have anything if you live your life within the law.

—Dialogue from the NBC TV movie *Beyond Suspicion*[1]

Much is already known about the phenomenon of crime. Further development in theoretical criminology will result primarily from making sense out of what we already know.

—George B. Vold and Thomas J. Bernard[2]

The objective of criminology is the development of a body of general verified principles.

—Edwin Sutherland and Donald Cressey[3]

The whole paraphernalia of the criminal law and the criminal courts is based on the need of the upper class to keep the lower class in its place.

—Jay Frost[4]

Learning Outcomes

After reading this chapter, you should be able to

- List the four definitional perspectives found in contemporary criminology, and relate the definition of *crime* used in this textbook
- Recognize the difference between acts that are criminal and those that are deviant, and explain how some forms of behavior can be both
- Understand the legalistic approach to the study of crime and explain how it can be used to decide what human activity is criminal
- Describe what criminologists do

- Offer an informed definition of *criminology*
- Explain how contemporary criminology sometimes influences social policy, especially in the area of crime control
- Describe the theme of this text, and be able to distinguish between the social problems and social responsibility perspectives on crime causation
- Describe the social context within which crime occurs, and identify the people and groups that are most affected by it
- Explain the interdisciplinary nature of criminology, while identifying reasons for the primacy of sociological approaches in the field today

Introduction

Now entering its sixth season, the CBS-TV megahit *CSI: Miami* has achieved heights that most other shows can't even dream of. With 50 million regular viewers in more than 55 countries, it's currently the most popular television show in the world.[5] But *CSI* programming extends well beyond it's Miami-based series, and the CSI franchise, which now includes shows featuring New York City and other locales, is available to a global audience of nearly 2 billion viewers in 200 countries around the globe.[6]

The popularity of prime-time television crime shows is not limited to *CSI*, as other widely followed series demonstrate. Included here are shows like *Criminal Minds* (CBS), *Without a Trace* (CBS), *Numb3rs* (CBS), *The Unit* (CBS), *The Sopranos* (HBO); *The District* (CBS); *The Shield* (FX); *The Wire* (HBO); *Cold Case* (CBS), *CIS* (CBS), *Prison Break* (Fox), and *Law and Order* (NBC)—along with the *Law and Order* spin-offs, *Law and Order: Criminal Intent* and *Law and Order: Special Victims' Unit*. Social commentators note that the plethora of crime shows bombarding the airwaves today reveals a penchant among American TV viewers for crime-related entertainment and a fascination with criminal motivation and detective work.

The public's interest in real-life stories of criminal victimization, revenge, and reformation has given birth to reality TV crime shows, including *America's Most Wanted* (which premiered on Fox in 1988), *COPS* (Fox), *Crime and Punishment* (NBC), and *World's Wildest Police Videos* (SPIKE). Similarly, video magazine shows like *60 Minutes* (CBS), *20/20* (ABC), and *Nightline* (ABC) frequently focus on justice issues, and any number of movies—including films like *SWAT, Training Day, 2 Fast 2 Furious, The Green Mile, Runaway Jury,* and *Minority Report*—play off the public's fascination with crime and the personal drama it fosters.

WEB
Extra
Like this textbook, many of today's television shows deliver content across a variety of media. View the online CSI crime labs at **Web Extra 1–1** and see some real-life crime prevention links sponsored by *Law and Order: SVU* at **Web Extra 1–2**.

What Is Crime?

Of course, not all television shows depict actual crimes, no matter how dramatic or convincing the actors' performances may be. And, although a few people may find it surprising, the investigative activities undertaken by some actors and the legal snares set for some suspects may not be entirely realistic. Hence, before we begin the discussion of criminology in earnest, we need to consider just what the term *crime* means. Crime can be defined in a variety of ways, and some scholars have suggested that at least four definitional perspectives can be found in contemporary criminology. These diverse perspectives see crime from (1) legalistic, (2) political, (3) sociological, and (4) psychological viewpoints. How we see any phenomenon is crucial because it determines the assumptions that we make about how that phenomenon should be studied. The perspective that we choose to employ when viewing crime determines the kinds of questions we ask, the nature of the research we conduct, and the type of answers that we expect to receive. Those answers, in turn, influence our conclusions about the kinds of crime control policies that might be effective. Hence, when we study crime, it is vital to keep in mind that there are differing viewpoints within the field of criminology as to the fundamental nature of the subject matter itself.

Seen from a legalistic perspective, **crime** is *human conduct in violation of the criminal laws of a state, the federal government, or a local jurisdiction that has the power to make such laws.* This is the definition of crime that we will use in this textbook because without a law that circumscribes a particular form of behavior, there can be no crime, no matter how deviant or socially repugnant the behavior in question may be.

crime

Human conduct in violation of the criminal laws of a state, the federal government, or a local jurisdiction that has the power to make such laws.

The notion of crime as behavior[7] that violates the law derives from earlier work by criminologists like Paul W. Tappan, who defined crime as "an intentional act in violation of the criminal law . . . committed without defense or excuse, and penalized by the

A still image from the highly popular CBS-TV show *CSI: Crime Scene Investigation*. Cast members appearing in this image from the "Lab Rats" episode are Hodges (Wallace Langham, far left) Archie (Archie Kao, far right), Henry (Jon Wellner), Mandy (Sheeri Rappaport) and Wendy (Liz Vassey). Why do many people like to watch TV crime shows like *CSI*?

Source: CBS/Ron Jaffe/Landov © 2007 CBS Broadcasting, Inc. All Rights Reserved.

state as a felony or misdemeanor."[8] Edwin Sutherland, regarded by many as a founding figure in American criminology, said of crime that its "essential characteristic . . . is that it is behavior which is prohibited by the State as an injury to the State and against which the State may react . . . by punishment."[9]

A serious shortcoming of the legalistic approach to crime is that it yields the moral high ground to powerful individuals who are able to influence the making of laws and the imposition of criminal definitions on lawbreakers. By making their own laws, powerful but immoral individuals can escape the label "criminal." Although democratic societies like the United States would seem to be immune from such abuses of the legislative process, history demonstrates otherwise. While we have chosen to adopt the legalistic approach to crime in this textbook, it is important to realize that laws are social products. As a consequence, crime is socially relative in the sense that it is created by legislative activity. Without a law defining it, there can be no crime. Hence, as sociologists are fond of saying, "crime is whatever a society says it is." In Chapter 9, we will explore this issue further and will focus on the process of criminalization, which is the method used to **criminalize** some forms of behavior—or make them illegal—while other forms remain legitimate.

Another problem with the legalistic perspective is its insistence that the nature of crime cannot be separated from the nature of law, as the one explicitly defines the other. Not always recognized by legalistic definitions of crime, however, is the social, ethical, and individual significance of fundamentally immoral forms of behavior. Simply put, some activities not contravened by **statute** nonetheless still call out for a societal response, sometimes leading commentators to proclaim, "That ought to be a crime!" or "There should to be a law against that!"

The legalistic definition of crime also suffers from its seeming lack of recognition of the fact that formalized laws have not always existed. Undoubtedly, much immoral behavior occurred even in dimly remembered historical epochs, and contemporary laws probably now regulate most such behavior. English common law, for example, upon which much American **statutory law** is based, judged behavior in terms of traditional practice and customs and did not make use of written statutes. Although all American jurisdictions have enacted comprehensive legal codes, many states still adhere to a common law tradition. In such "common law states," individuals may be prosecuted for violating traditional notions of right and wrong, even though no violation of written

criminalize

To make illegal.

statute

A formal, written enactment of a legislative body.

statutory law

Law in the form of statutes or formal, written strictures made by a legislature or governing body with the power to make law.

Crime in the News

Snoop Dogg Arrested—Again!

For the third time in as many months, Snoop Dogg has been arrested on weapons charges. On Tuesday night (November 28, 2006), the rapper, 35, whose real name is Cordozar Calvin Broadus, Jr., was arrested as he left the Los Angeles studios for NBC's *Tonight Show with Jay Leno.* Police say they found a gun and drugs after searching his car and home.

The series of brushes with the law aren't the rapper's first dealings with police. His arrest record dates back to 1990 with drug and weapons violations, and he had at least one year-long stint in jail. He also made headlines in 1993 when he was involved in a murder trial.

Snoop Dogg spent about seven hours with police late Tuesday when he was booked for investigation of being a convicted felon in possession of a firearm and cocaine, transporting marijuana and having a false compartment in his car, officials say.

After posting $60,000 bail, he was released Wednesday morning and was scheduled to be arraigned on January 11, 2007.

Snoop's Rap Sheet

- *November 28, 2006:* Arrested on weapons charges. Outcome: Undecided.
- *October 26, 2006:* Arrested at Bob Hope Airport in Burbank, Calif., on suspicion of drug and gun possession after police searched his car. Outcome: Undecided.
- *September 27, 2006:* Arrested on suspicion of weapons charges after a police baton is found in his luggage at John Wayne International Airport in Santa Ana, Calif. Outcome: Undecided.
- *August 2003:* Named by police in an affidavit claiming he lured underage girls in New Orleans to take off their shirts for a video by offering them marijuana and Ecstasy. Outcome: Settled (and sealed) in July 2004.
- *October 2001:* After searching his tour bus, Ohio police charge the rapper with possession of marijuana and drug paraphernalia. Outcome: In 2002, he pleads no contest. Sentence: Fines totaling $398.30 and a suspended 30-day jail sentence.
- *May 1998:* Charged with misdemeanor marijuana possession in Los Angeles. Outcome: Fines totaling $370.
- *August 1993:* Charged with accomplice to murder in the L.A. shooting death of Phillip Woldemariam. Outcome: In 1996, a jury found him not guilty of murder charges and deadlocked on voluntary manslaughter charges.
- *July 1993:* L.A. police find a firearm in his car during a traffic stop. Outcome: In 1997, he pleads guilty to one count of handgun possession. He must record three public service announcements, pay a $1,000 fine and serve three years' probation.
- *June 1990:* Arrested for selling cocaine to an undercover L.A. officer. Outcome: He is convicted and serves one year in jail.

Source: Karen Thomas, "Snoop Dogg Arrested Again: One Rapper's Rap Sheet Just Keeps Growing," *USA Today*, November 29, 2006. Reprinted with permission. For the latest crime and justice news, visit www.crimenews.info.

Rap performer Snoop Dogg arrives at Pasadena Superior Court on April 11, 2007, for arraignment on two felony charges related to a prior arrest for gun and marijuana possession. The 35-year-old singer, whose real name is Cordozar Calvin Broadus, Jr., faced up to four years in prison before pleading "no contest" and being sentenced to five years of probation and 800 hours of community service. The charges stemmed from an October 2006 incident at Burbank's Bob Hope airport when police discovered marijuana in Snoop's vehicle while confronting him about a parking violation. Why do many rap musicians seem to get into trouble with the law?
Source: AFP PHOTO/Hector Mata

Discussion Questions

1. Why is the media (and the public) so interested in possible law-violating behavior involving well-known people like Snoop?

2. How might Snoop explain his history of criminality? In other words, what might he say has led him to be involved in crime-prone situations and settings?

3. Use the social problems versus social responsibility theme of this text to analyze Snoop's behavior and arrests. Might Snoop's proximity to criminal activity be the consequence of underlying social problems? If so, what might those "problems" be?

4. Can we expect Snoop to become more socially responsible? Why or why not?

law took place. Such prosecutions rarely occur, and when they do, they are not often successful.[10] Common law is discussed in more detail in Chapter 4. You can also learn more about common law at Web Extra 1–3.

WEB
Extra
▪▪▪▪

Changes in the laws will undoubtedly continue to occur, perhaps even legitimizing former so-called crimes where fundamentally moral or socially beneficial forms of behavior have been unduly criminalized. Over the last few years, for example, state legislatures along with members of the general public have debated the pros and cons of same-sex marriages and certain forms of biomedical research—especially those involving human cloning and the use of human stem cells.

A second perspective on crime is the political one, which places the process of law creation and criminalization on center stage. From a political point of view, crime is the result of criteria that have been built into the law by powerful groups and are then used to label selected undesirable forms of behavior as illegal. Those who adhere to this point of view say that crime is a definition of human conduct that is created by authorized agents in a politically organized society. Seen this way, laws serve the interests of the politically powerful, and crimes are merely forms of behavior that are perceived by those in power as direct or indirect threats to their interests. Thus, the political perspective defines crime in terms of the power structures that exist in society and asserts that criminal laws do not necessarily bear any inherent relationship to popular notions of right and wrong.

The political processes that create criminal definitions, however, are sometimes easier to comprehend in totalitarian societies than in democratic ones. Nonetheless, the political perspective can also be meaningfully applied to American society. John F. Galliher, a contemporary criminologist, summarizes the political perspective on crime when he writes, "One can best understand crime in a class-structured society such as the United States as the end product of a chain of interactions involving powerful groups that use their power to establish criminal laws and sanctions against less powerful persons and groups that may pose a threat to the group in power."[11] It is important to realize, Galliher points out, that since legal definitions of criminality are arrived at through a political process, the subject matter of criminality will be artificially limited if we insist on seeing crime solely as a violation of the criminal law.

Some criminologists insist that the field of criminology must include in its concerns behaviors that go beyond those that are defined as crimes through the political process. Not doing so, they say, restricts rather than encourages inquiry into relevant forms of human behavior.[12] Adherents of our third perspective, the sociological one, would likely agree with this statement. Also called the "sociolegal viewpoint," the sociological perspective sees crime as "an antisocial act of such a nature that its repression is necessary or is supposed to be necessary to the preservation of the existing system of society."[13] Some criminologists have gone so far as to claim that any definition of crime must include all forms of antisocial behavior.[14] Ron Claassen, a modern-day champion of restorative justice (discussed in more detail in Chapter 9), suggests, for example, that "crime is primarily an offense against human relationships, and secondarily a violation of a law—since laws are written to protect safety and fairness in human relationships."[15] A more comprehensive sociological definition of crime was offered by Herman Schwendinger and Julia Schwendinger in 1975. It says that crime encompasses "any harmful acts," including violations of "the fundamental prerequisites for well-being, [such as] food, shelter, clothing, medical services, challenging work and recreational experiences, as well as security from predatory individuals or repressive and imperialistic elites."[16] The Schwendingers have challenged criminologists to be less constrained in what they see as the subject matter of their field, saying that violations of human rights may be more relevant to criminological inquiry than many acts that have been politically or legally defined as crime. "Isn't it time to raise serious questions about the assumptions underlying the definitions of the field of criminology," ask the Schwendingers, "when a man who steals a paltry sum can be called a criminal while agents of the State can, with impunity, legally reward men who destroy food so that price levels can be maintained whilst a sizable portion of the population suffers from malnutrition?"[17] Jeffrey H. Reiman, another contemporary criminologist, asks similar questions. "The fact is that the label 'crime' is not used in America to name all or the worst of the actions that cause misery and suffering to Americans," says Reiman. "It is primarily reserved for the dangerous actions of the poor." Writing about unhealthy and unsafe workplaces, Reiman asks, "Doesn't a crime by any other name still cause misery and suffering? What's in a name?"[18] While a sociolegal approach to understanding crime is attractive to many, others claim that it suffers from wanting to criminalize activities that cause only indirect harm. In other words, it is easier for most people to appreciate the criminality involved in, say, a holdup, a rape, or a murder than in cost-cutting efforts made by a businessperson, even when those efforts result in injuries to workers or consumers.

Finally, from a psychological (or maladaptive) perspective, "crime is a form of social maladjustment which can be designated as a more or less pronounced difficulty that the individual has in reacting to the stimuli of his environment in such a way as to remain in harmony with that environment."[19] Seen this way, crime is problem behavior, especially human activity that contravenes the criminal law and results in difficulties in living within a framework of generally acceptable social arrangements. According to Matthew B. Robinson, "The maladaptive view of crime does not require any of the [traditional] elements . . . in order for an act to be a crime: no actual harm to others; no prohibition by law before the act is committed; no arrest; and no conviction in a court of law. Any behavior which is maladaptive—i.e., which stands in the way of an individual developing to his or her fullest potential—would be considered crime. If criminologists adopted this view of crime," says Robinson, "the scope of criminology would be greatly expanded beyond its current state. All actually or even potentially harmful behaviors could be examined, analyzed, and documented for the purpose of gaining knowledge about potentially harmful behaviors and developing strategies to protect people from all harmful acts, not just those that are called 'crime' today."[20]

As this discussion shows, a unified or simple definition of crime is difficult to achieve. The four points of view that we have discussed here form a kind of continuum, bound on one end by strict legalistic interpretations of crime and on the other by much more fluid behavioral and moralistic definitions.

Crime and Deviance

Sociologically speaking, many crimes can be regarded as deviant forms of behavior—that is, as behaviors that are in some way abnormal. Piers Beirne and James Messerschmidt, two contemporary criminologists, define deviance as "any social behavior or social characteristic that departs from the conventional norms and standards of a community or society and for which the deviant is sanctioned."[21] Their definition, however, does not count as deviant any sanctionable behavior that is not punished. Hence, we prefer another approach to defining deviance. The definition of **deviant behavior** that we will use in this book is as follows: *Deviant behavior is human activity that violates social norms.*

deviant behavior

Human activity that violates social norms.

Abnormality, deviance, and crime are concepts that do not always easily mesh. Some forms of deviance are not violations of the criminal law, and the reverse is equally true (see Figure 1–1). Deviant styles of dress, for example, although perhaps outlandish to the majority, are not circumscribed by criminal law unless (perhaps) decency statutes are violated by a lack of clothing. Even in such cases, laws are subject to interpretation and may be modified as social norms change over time.

A little over a decade ago, for example, Patricia Marks, a New York State county judge, overturned the convictions of ten women who had been arrested for publicly displaying their breasts. The women, known as the Topfree Ten, had been arrested after baring their chests during a picnic in a city park. At the time, New York law forbade women from displaying their breasts in public—unless they were breast-feeding or performing onstage. The women claimed that the law discriminated against them and argued that if men have the right to appear in public without a shirt, then the same right should apply to women. Judge Marks agreed and, in reversing the convictions, ruled that the New York statute was sexist and gender biased because "male and female breasts are physiologically similar except for lactation capability."[22] The judge relied in part on the testimony of experts

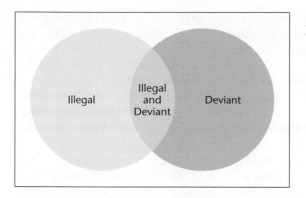

FIGURE 1–1

The Overlap between Deviance and Crime

who articulated their belief that "community standards have changed and women's breasts are no longer considered a private or intimate part of the body."

The Topfree movement soon spread across the country and into Canada. The Florida public nudity conviction of Kayla Sosnow was overturned by Florida's Eighth Circuit Court of Appeals. Sosnow, who had been arrested for not wearing a shirt in the Osceola National Forest, is a member of the Florida Topfree Ten. She was supported in her appeal by the National Organization for Women, the American Civil Liberties Union (ACLU), the Human Rights Council of North Central Florida, the Florida Coalition for Peace and Justice, and the Gainesville (Florida) Women's Health Center. After the court's ruling, Sosnow spoke with reporters, telling them that the court's action removed one more obstacle to equal rights for women. "Who decides that women's breasts are more obscene than men's?" she asked. "By going topfree, we are rejecting the criminalization of our breasts and reclaiming control of our bodies."[23]

The Topfree movement highlights the role that societal interpretation plays in defining a criminal offense. Even if appellate courts are correct and no noteworthy physiological differences exist between the breasts of men and women, American society (and many other societies) nonetheless appears to have turned relatively minor differences of size and shape into a major distinguishing factor between the sexes. In other words, what some might say is a relatively insignificant biological difference has traditionally been endowed with a great deal of social significance, and laws regulating various styles of dress (or undress) have evolved based largely on subjective perceptions rather than on objective considerations.

Some types of behavior, although quite common, are still against the law. Speeding on interstate highways, for example, although probably something that most motorists engage in at least from time to time, is illegal. Complicating matters still further is the fact that certain behaviors are illegal in some jurisdictions but not in others. For example, commercialized gambling, especially that involving slot machines and games of chance, is against the law in most parts of the United States—but has been legitimized in Nevada, on some Indian reservations, on cruise ships operating outside of U.S. territorial waters, and on some Mississippi riverboats. Even state governments, seeking to enhance revenues, have gotten into the gambling business through state lotteries—which now operate in 38 states; and many states have laws specifically forbidding participation in online gambling, due largely to their interest in protecting their own lottery revenues. Similarly, prostitution, which is almost uniformly illegal in the United States, is an activity that is fully within the law in parts of Nevada as long as it occurs within licensed brothels and as long as those engaged in the activity meet state licensing requirements and abide by state laws that require condom use and weekly medical checkups.

What Should Be Criminal?

As you have probably realized by now, the question "What is crime?" is quite different from the question "What should be criminal?" Although most people agree that certain forms of behavior, such as murder, rape, burglary, and theft, should be against the law, there is far less agreement about the appropriate legal status of things like drug use, abortion (including the use of "abortion pills" like RU-486 or Mifeprex), gambling, and "deviant" forms of consensual adult sexual behavior.

While the question "What should be criminal?" can be answered in many different ways, the social and intellectual processes by which an answer is reached can be found in two contrasting points of view: (1) the consensus perspective and (2) the pluralist perspective. The consensus viewpoint holds that laws should be enacted to criminalize given forms of behavior when members of society generally agree that such laws are necessary. The consensus perspective (described in greater detail in Chapter 9) is most applicable to homogeneous societies, or those characterized by shared values, norms, and belief systems. In a multicultural and diverse society like the United States, however, a shared consensus may be difficult to achieve. In such a society, even relatively minor matters may lead to complex debates over the issues involved. Not long ago, for example, a Chicago municipal ordinance banned giving wine to a dog and provided that anyone who did so could be arrested and jailed.[24] While the ordinance may have seemed reasonable to those who enacted it (after all, dogs sometimes need to be shielded from their owners' indiscretions, and there are plenty of precedents in the form of laws already on the books that are intended to protect animals), others felt that the law was silly and unnecessary. Still others insisted that adult dogs should have a right to imbibe just as do humans who are of drinking age. The ordinance pitted wine connoisseurs, collectors, growers, and sellers, as well as some animal rights activists, against animal protectionists and some city council members. Those favoring repeal of the ordinance argued that it was old-fashioned and reflected badly on an acceptable consumer product, which was also a staple of certain ethnic diets (French and Italians frequently drink wine with meals, and their descendants living in Chicago, because of the "bad press" associated with the law, might find their lifestyles negatively affected). Eventually, the ordinance was repealed, and the hubbub it had inspired ended. The debate, however, shows just how difficult it is to achieve a consensus over even relatively minor matters in a society as complex as our own.

The second perspective, the pluralist view of crime (also described in more detail in Chapter 9), recognizes the importance of diversity in societies like ours. It says that behaviors are typically criminalized through a political process only after debate over the appropriate course of action. The political process often takes the form of legislation and may involve appellate court action (by those who don't agree with the legislation). After the horrific shootings that occurred on the campus of Virginia Tech University in 2007, for example, legislatures at both the state and federal level began to reexamine gun laws to see if new laws were needed to keep guns out of the hands of potential mass killers. Given the diversity of perspectives that characterize our society, however, agreement was not easy to reach—and gun control proponents vigorously debated those who sought to protect existing laws supporting gun ownership, and making the purchase of guns relatively easy for most Americans. Learn more about both sides of the gun control debate via **Web Extras 1–4** and **1–5** at crimtoday.com.

WEB
Extra
▪ ▪ ▪ ▪

What Do Criminologists Do?

criminologist

One who is trained in the field of criminology. Also, one who studies crime, criminals, and criminal behavior.

criminalist

A specialist in the collection and examination of the physical evidence of crime.

A typical dictionary definition of a **criminologist** is "one who studies crime, criminals, and criminal behavior."[25] Occasionally, the term *criminologist* is used broadly to describe almost anyone who works in the criminal justice field, regardless of formal training. There is a growing tendency, however, to reserve application of the term *criminologist* to academics, researchers, and policy analysts with advanced degrees who are involved in the study of crime and crime trends and in the analysis of societal reactions to crime. Hence, it is more appropriate today to describe specially skilled investigators, crime laboratory technicians, fingerprint experts, crime scene photographers, ballistics experts, and others who work to solve particular crimes as criminalists. A **criminalist** is "a specialist in the collection and examination of the physical evidence of crime."[26] Police officers, corrections professionals, probation and parole officers,

Who's to Blame—The Individual or Society?

Should Polygamy Be a Protected Religious Practice?

Taeler Leon, a member of the Fundamentalist Church of Jesus Christ of Latter Day Saints, an ultraconservative offshoot of the Mormon church, was arrested in a rural area outside of Salt Lake City, Utah, and charged with polygamy and the rape of a child. The charges came after the parents of a 13-year-old girl, whom Leon had "married" in a ceremony performed by a church elder, complained to the Utah State Bureau of Investigation (SBI) that Leon was holding their daughter against her will. SBI agents visited Leon's compound and learned that six of Leon's wives and 16 of his children were living at the compound. The compound, which consisted of four houses and a communal building containing a small school, chapel, and dining and meeting areas, was set in a secluded location well off the main road.

A follow-up investigation revealed that the children's births had been officially registered at the county courthouse, and that the needed home-schooling papers had been filed with the state board of education for each of the school-aged children living at the compound—meaning that they were exempt from required attendance at public schools.

Polygamy is a criminal offense in Utah and is banned under the state's constitution. It has been officially repudiated by the mainstream Mormon Church since 1890. After determining that Leon was married concurrently to multiple women, SBI agents took him into custody, and interviewed each of his wives. Each told much the same story of how they had been promised by their parents to Leon at an early age, how they had been married in small ceremonies, and how they had borne Leon's children. What surprised investigators, though, was the women's agreement that their way of life, while it might not be common in the wider society, was a matter of choice—and that they should be left alone to practice their faith. "Taeler's committed no crime in the eyes of God," said Adaleen, Leon's first wife, speaking for the others. "We should be free to practice our religion just like others are," she said.

Hendy, another of the wives, pointed out that members of the American Indian Church have been allowed to use peyote in their religious ceremonies, even though it is a banned drug, unavailable to non-Native Americans. "If they can smoke peyote, then why can't we get married and live the way we want to?" she asked. "It's our religion, and it's supposed to be a free country."

Think about it:

1. Not all women involved in polygamous unions would agree with Hendy and Adaleen, and those who oppose polygamy argue that not only is it illegal, but that it degrades women, devalues the family, and victimizes young women who are forced into arranged unions. Nonetheless, there are those who would agree with Hendy and Adaleen that the practice should be allowed based on constitutional guarantees of freedom of religion. Which perspective makes the most sense to you? Why?

2. Do a bit of historical research and see if you can learn the legal history of the practice of polygamy in the United States. When did it become illegal? Why?

3. What rights, if any, should members of minority faiths have when they advocate or engage in behavior that goes beyond social norms or violates the law? Give some examples.

4. Would the rights you identified above extend to the practice of polygamy? Why or why not?

Polygamist Warren Steed Jeffs is pictured on an FBI Ten Most Wanted poster prior to his arrest in 2006. Jeffs, the fugitive leader of a polygamist Mormon sect, was wanted in Utah and Arizona on charges linked to allegations of arranging marriages between men and underage girls. He was arrested and convicted on those charges in 2007. Why is the practice of polygamy a violation of the criminal law? Should it be?
Source: FBI/AP Wide World Photos

judges, district attorneys, criminal defense attorneys, and others who do the day-to-day work of the criminal justice system are best referred to as criminal justice professionals.

Academic criminologists and research criminologists generally hold doctoral degrees (Ph.D.'s) in the field of criminology or criminal justice from an accredited university. Some criminologists hold degrees in related fields like sociology and political science but have specialized in the study and control of crime and deviance. Most Ph.D. criminologists teach either criminology or criminology-related subjects in institutions of higher learning, including universities and two- and four-year colleges. Nearly all criminology professors are involved in research or writing projects by which they strive to advance criminological knowledge. Some Ph.D. criminologists are strictly researchers and work for federal agencies like the National Institute of Justice (NIJ), the Bureau of Justice Statistics (BJS), and the National Criminal Justice Reference Service (NCJRS) or for private (albeit often government-funded) organizations with such names as RAND and the Search Group, Inc.

The results of criminological research in the United States are generally published in journals like *Criminology* (the official publication of the American Society of Criminology), *Theoretical Criminology, Justice Quarterly* (the Academy of Criminal Justice Sciences), *Crime and Delinquency,* the *American Journal of Criminal Justice* (the Southern Criminal Justice Association), the *Journal of Qualitative Criminology, Social Problems,* and *Victimology.*[27] International English-language journals are numerous and include the *Canadian Journal of Criminology,* the *Australian and New Zealand Journal of Criminology,* and the *British Journal of Criminology.* Read some of these journals and visit the organizations that sponsor them at **Web Extra 1–6**.

WEB
Extra
■ ■ ■ ■

People who have earned master's and bachelor's degrees in the field of criminology often find easy entrance into police investigative or support work, probation and parole agencies, court-support activities, and correctional (prison) work. Criminologists also work for government agencies interested in the development of effective social policies intended to deter or combat crime. Many criminologists with master's degrees also teach at two- and four-year colleges and schools.

Private security provides another career track for individuals interested in criminology and criminal justice. The number of personnel employed by private security agencies today is twice that of public law enforcement agencies, and the gap is widening. Many upper- and mid-level private managers working for private security firms hold criminology or criminal justice degrees. The same may soon be true for the majority of law enforcement personnel, especially those in managerial positions.

Anyone trained in criminology has many alternatives (see Table 1–1). Some people with undergraduate degrees in criminology or criminal justice decide to go on to law school. Some teach high school, while others become private investigators. Many criminologists provide civic organizations (such as victims' assistance and justice advocacy groups) with much-needed expertise, a few work for politicians and legislative bodies, and some appear on talk shows to debate the pros and cons of various kinds of social policies designed to "fight" crime. Some criminologists even write books like this one! For more thoughts on the role of criminologists in the twenty-first century, read **Library Extra 1–1** at crimtoday.com.

LIBRARY
Extra
■ ■ ■ ■

What Is Criminology?

The attempt to understand crime and deviance predates written history. Prehistoric evidence, including skeletal remains showing signs of primitive cranial surgery, seems to indicate that preliterate people explained deviant behavior by reference to spirit possession. Primitive surgery was an attempt to release unwanted spiritual influences. In the thousands of years since, many other theoretical perspectives on crime have been advanced. This book describes various criminological theories and covers some of the more popular ones in detail.

Before beginning any earnest discussion, however, it is necessary to define the term *criminology.* As our earlier discussion of the nature of crime and deviance indicates,

TABLE 1–1	**What Do Criminologists Do?**

The term criminologist *is usually applied to credentialed individuals, such as those holding advanced degrees in the field, who engage in the study of crime, criminal behavior, and crime trends. The word* criminalist *is used to describe people who specialize in the collection and examination of the physical evidence associated with specific crimes. Others working in the criminal justice system are called* criminal justice professionals. *This table lists the activities of all three.*

The activities of criminologists include but are not limited to

Data gathering	Public service
Data analysis	Analysis of crime patterns and trends
Theory construction	Scholarly presentations and publications
Hypothesis testing	Education and training
Social policy creation	Threat assessment and risk analysis
Public advocacy	

Jobs in the field of criminalistics include but are not limited to

Forensics examiner	Crime scene photographer
Crime laboratory technician	Polygraph operator
Ballistics expert	Fingerprint examiner
Crime scene investigator	

Jobs in the field of criminal justice include but are not limited to

Law enforcement officer	Judge
Probation or parole officer	Defense attorney
Correctional officer	Prosecutor
Prison program director	Jailer
Computer crime investigator	Private security officer
Juvenile justice worker	Victims' advocate

not only must criminologists deal with a complex subject matter—consisting of a broad range of illegal behaviors committed by frequently unknown or uncooperative individuals—but also they must manage their work under changing conditions mandated by ongoing revisions of the law and fluctuating **social policy**. In addition, as we have already seen, a wide variety of perspectives on the nature of crime abounds. All this leads to considerable difficulties in defining the subject matter under study.

There is some evidence that the term *criminology* was coined in 1889[28] by a Frenchman, Paul Topinard, who used it to differentiate the study of criminal body types within the field of anthropology from other biometric pursuits.[29] Topinard, while he may have coined the term, did little to help define it. As with the concept of crime, various definitions of *criminology* can be found in the literature today. A little more than a decade ago, criminologist Joseph F. Sheley wrote, "There seem to be nearly as many definitions of *contemporary criminology* as there are criminologists."[30]

One straightforward definition can be had from a linguistic analysis of the word *criminology*. As most people know, *ology* means "the study of something," and the word *crimen* comes from the Latin, meaning "accusation," "charge," or "guilt." Hence, linguistically speaking, the term *criminology* literally means "the study of criminal accusations,"—that is, "the study of crime." In addition to this fundamental kind of linguistic definition, three other important types of definitions can be found in the literature. They are (1) disciplinary, (2) causative, and (3) scientific. Each type of definition is distinguished by its focus. Disciplinary definitions are those that, as their name implies, focus on criminology as a discipline. Seen from this viewpoint, criminology is a field of study or a body of knowledge. Some of the earliest criminologists of the past century, including

social policy

A government initiative, program, or plan intended to address problems in society. The "war on crime," for example, is a kind of generic (large-scale) social policy—one consisting of many smaller programs.

Edwin H. Sutherland, who is often referred to as the "dean of American criminology," offered definitions of their field that emphasized its importance as a discipline of study. Sutherland, for example, wrote in the first edition of his textbook *Criminology* in 1924 that "[c]riminology is the body of knowledge regarding the social problem of crime."[31] Sutherland's text was to set the stage for much of American criminology throughout the rest of the twentieth century. Reprinted in 1934 with the title *Principles of Criminology,* it was to become the most influential textbook ever written in the field of criminology.[32] Although Sutherland died in 1950, his revered text was revised for many years by Donald R. Cressey and later by David F. Luckenbill. By 1974, Sutherland's classic definition of *criminology* had been modified by Cressey to read "Criminology is the body of knowledge regarding delinquency and crime as a social phenomenon. It includes within its scope the processes of making laws, of breaking laws, and of reacting toward the breaking of laws."[33] Causative definitions emphasize criminology's role in uncovering the underlying causes of crime. In keeping with such an emphasis, contemporary criminologists Gennaro F. Vito and Ronald M. Holmes say that "[c]riminology is the study of the causes of crime."[34]

Finally, there are those who point to the scientific nature of contemporary criminology as its distinguishing characteristic. According to Clemens Bartollas and Simon Dinitz, for example, "Criminology is the scientific study of crime."[35] Writing in 1989, Bartollas and Dinitz seemed to be echoing an earlier definition of criminology offered by Marvin E. Wolfgang and Franco Ferracuti, who wrote in 1967 that "[c]riminology is the scientific study of crime, criminals, and criminal behavior."[36]

Sutherland suggested that criminology consists of three "principal divisions": (1) the sociology of law, (2) scientific analysis of the causes of crime, and (3) crime control.[37] Another well-known criminologist, Clarence Ray Jeffery, similarly sees three components of the field: (1) detection (of the offender), (2) treatment, and (3) explanation of crime and criminal behavior.[38] In like manner, contemporary criminologist Gregg Barak writes that criminology is "an interdisciplinary study of the various bodies of knowledge, which focuses on the etiology of crime, the behavior of criminals, and the policies and practices of crime control."[39]

One of the most comprehensive definitions of the term *criminology* that is available today comes from the European Society of Criminology (ESC) which, in its constitution

A criminalist at work. Crime scene investigators, like the person shown here, can provide crucial clues needed to solve crimes. How does the work of a criminologist differ from that of a criminalist? Would you like either kind of work?

Source: Corbis/Sygma

defines criminology as "all scholarly, scientific and professional knowledge concerning the explanation, prevention, control and treatment of crime and delinquency, offenders and victims, including the measurement and detection of crime, legislation, and the practice of criminal law, and law enforcement, judicial, and correctional systems."[40] The ESC's emphasis is on *knowledge*, and even though it mentions the "practice" of what many would call criminal justice (that is, policing, courts, and corrections), it is the study and knowledge of such practice that forms the crux of the ESC perspective.

For our purposes, we will use a definition somewhat simpler than that of the ESC, but one which brings together the works of previous writers and also recognizes the increasingly professional status of the criminological enterprise. Throughout this book, then, we will view **criminology** as *an interdisciplinary profession built around the scientific study of crime and criminal behavior, including their manifestations, causes, legal aspects, and control.* As this definition indicates, criminology includes consideration of possible solutions to the problem of crime. Hence, this text (in later chapters) describes treatment strategies and social policy initiatives that have grown out of the existing array of theoretical explanations for crime.

Our definition is in keeping with the work of Jack P. Gibbs, a notable contemporary criminologist, who writes that the purpose of criminology is to offer well-researched and objective answers to four basic questions: (1) "Why do crime rates vary?" (2) "Why do individuals differ as to **criminality**?" (3) "Why is there variation in reactions to crime?" and (4) "What are the possible means of controlling criminality?"[41]

As a field of study, criminology in its present form is primarily a social scientific discipline. Contemporary criminologists generally recognize, however, that their field is interdisciplinary—that is, it draws upon other disciplines to provide an integrated approach to understanding the problem of crime in contemporary society and to advance solutions to the problems crime creates. Hence, anthropology (especially cultural anthropology or ethnology), biology, sociology, political science, psychology, psychiatry, economics, ethology (the study of character), medicine, law, philosophy, ethics, and numerous other fields all have something to offer the student of criminology, as do the tools provided by statistics, computer science, and other forms of scientific and data analysis (see Figure 1–2).

The interdisciplinary nature of criminology was well stated by Jim Short, past president of the American Society of Criminology, who said, "The organization of knowledge by traditional disciplines has become increasingly anachronistic, as the generation of knowledge has become more interdisciplinary. From its earliest beginnings, when philosophers grappled with relationships between human nature and behavior and

criminology

An interdisciplinary profession built around the scientific study of crime and criminal behavior, including their forms, causes, legal aspects, and control.

criminality

A behavioral predisposition that disproportionately favors criminal activity.

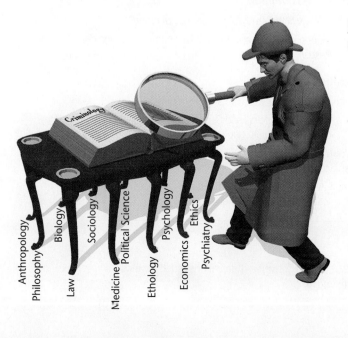

FIGURE 1–2

Criminology's Many Roots

Anthropology
Philosophy
Biology
Law
Sociology
Medicine
Political Science
Ethology
Psychology
Economics
Ethics
Psychiatry

Theory Versus Reality

Varying Perspectives on Crime and Criminology

What is crime? What is criminology? Throughout the years, writers have offered contrasting definitions of these terms. This box contains a number of definitions of both terms. Note that the definitions used in this book appear at the beginning of the table.

Crime	Criminology
Our Definition	**Our Definition**
"Human conduct in violation of the criminal laws of a state, the federal government, or a local jurisdiction that has the power to make such laws."	"An interdisciplinary profession built around the scientific study of crime and criminal behavior, including their manifestations, causes, legal aspects, and control."
Legalistic Definition	**Linguistic Definition**
"Crime is a violation of law."	"The study of (*ology*) crime (*crimen*)."
—Edwin H. Sutherland, *Criminology* (Philadelphia: Lippincott, 1924), p. 18	Note: The Latin term *crimen* literally means "accusation," "charge," or "guilt."
Crime is "an intentional act in violation of the criminal law (statutory and case law), committed without defense or excuse, and penalized by the state as a felony or misdemeanor."	**Disciplinary Definition**
—Paul W. Tappan, "Who Is the Criminal?" *American Sociological Review,* Vol. 12 (1947), pp. 96–102	"Criminology is the body of knowledge regarding the social problem of crime."
Political Definition	—Edwin H. Sutherland, *Criminology* (Philadelphia: Lippincott, 1924), p. 11
"Crimes are acts [that are] perceived by those in power as direct or indirect threats to their interests" and that are defined as criminal through a political process.	"Criminology is the body of knowledge regarding delinquency and crime as a social phenomenon. It includes within its scope the processes of making laws, of breaking laws, and of reacting toward the breaking of laws."
—Joseph F. Sheley, *Criminology: A Contemporary Handbook* (Belmont, CA: Wadsworth, 1991), p. 40	—Edwin H. Sutherland and Donald R. Cressey, *Criminology,* 9th ed. (Philadelphia: Lippincott, 1974), p. 3
Sociological Definition	"Criminology . . . is the study of crimes, criminals, and victims."
Crime is "an anti-social act of such a nature that its repression is necessary or is supposed to be necessary to the preservation of the existing system of society."	—Stephen Schafer, *Introduction to Criminology* (Reston, VA: Reston Publishing, 1976), p. 3
—Ezzat Fattah, *Introduction to Criminology* (Burnaby, British Columbia: School of Criminology, Simon Fraser University, 1989)	**Causative Definition**
Psychological Definition	"Criminology is the study of the causes of crime."
"Crime is a form of social maladjustment which can be designated as a more or less pronounced difficulty that the individual has in reacting to the stimuli of his environment in such a way as to remain in harmony with that environment."	—Gennaro F. Vito and Ronald M. Holmes, *Criminology: Theory, Research, and Policy* (Belmont, CA: Wadsworth, 1994), p. 3
—Ezzat Fattah, *Introduction to Criminology* (Burnaby, British Columbia: School of Criminology, Simon Fraser University, 1989)	**Scientific Definition**
	"Criminology is the scientific study of crime."
	—Clemens Bartollas and Simon Dinitz, *Introduction to Criminology: Order and Disorder* (New York: Harper & Row, 1989), p. 548
	"Criminology is the scientific study of crime, criminals, and criminal behavior."
	—Marvin E. Wolfgang and Franco Ferracuti, *The Subculture of Violence* (London: Tavistock, 1967)

Discussion Questions

1. Which definition of *crime* most appeals to you? Why?

2. Which definition of *criminology* seems most useful? Why?

3. Why might varying definitions, such as those shown here, be instructive?

biologists sought to relate human physiology to behavior, criminology's concerns have reached across virtually all disciplines that focus on the human condition. Additionally, much of the impetus for criminology has come from concerns that crime be controlled. Criminology thus cuts across professions as well as disciplines."[42]

It is important to note that although criminology may be interdisciplinary as well as cross-professional, few existing explanations for criminal behavior have been successfully or fully integrated. Just as physicists today are seeking a unified field theory to explain the wide variety of observable forms of matter and energy, criminologists have yet to develop a generally accepted integrated approach to crime and criminal behavior that can explain the many diverse forms of criminality, while also leading to effective social policies in the area of crime control. The attempt to construct criminological theories of relevance is made all the more difficult because, as discussed earlier, the phenomenon under study—crime—is very wide ranging and is subject to arbitrary and sometimes unpredictable legalistic and definitional changes.

Not only must a successfully integrated criminology bring together the contributions of various theoretical perspectives and disciplines, but also it must—if it is to have any relevance—blend the practical requirements of our nation's judicial system with emotional and rational calls for morality and justice. Is the death penalty, for example, justified? If so, on what basis? Is it because it is a type of vengeance and therefore deserved? Can we say that it is unjustified because many sociological studies have shown that it does little to reduce the rate of serious crime, such as murder? Just what do we mean by "justice," and what can criminological studies tell us—if anything—about what is just and what is unjust?

The editors of the relatively new journal *Theoretical Criminology*,[43] which began publication in 1997, wrote in the inaugural issue that "criminology has always been somewhat of a haphazardly-assembled umbrella-like structure which nevertheless usefully shelters a variety of theoretical interests that are espoused and employed by different disciplinary, methodological and political traditions." Such a structure, they said, "has obvious advantages, notably that it facilitates an interdisciplinary and inclusivist formation rather than supposing an exclusive but contentious 'core.' But one of its weaknesses is that its inhabitants, many of whom shuttle backwards and forwards between it and their parent disciplines, tend to communicate honestly and meaningfully only with those who speak the same theoretical language."[44] In other words, while the field of criminology can benefit from the wide variety of ideas available via a multiplicity of perspectives, all of which seek to understand the phenomenon we call "crime," successful cross-disciplinary collaboration can be quite difficult.

As our earlier definition of *criminology* indicates, however, it is more than a field of study or a collection of theories; it is also a profession.[45] More than a decade ago, in his presidential address to the American Society of Criminology, Charles F. Wellford identified the "primary purposes" of the criminology profession. Wellford said, "Controlling crime through prevention, rehabilitation, and deterrence and ensuring that the criminal justice system reflects the high aspiration we have as a society of 'justice for all,' characterize the principal goals that in my judgment motivate the work of our field."[46]

Notably, criminology also contributes to the discipline of **criminal justice,** which emphasizes application of the criminal law and study of the components of the justice system, especially the police, courts, and corrections. As one author stated, "Criminology gives prominence to questions about the *causes of criminality,* while the *control of lawbreaking* is at the heart of criminal justice."[47] Learn more about the interdisciplinary nature of criminology via **Web Extra 1–7.** Read a few articles describing the nature of contemporary criminology at **Library Extras 1–2, 1–3, and 1–4** at crimtoday.com.

criminal justice

The scientific study of crime, the criminal law, and components of the criminal justice system, including the police, courts, and corrections.

WEB
Extra
■ ■ ■ ■

LIBRARY
Extra
■ ■ ■ ■

Theoretical Criminology

Theoretical criminology, a subfield of general criminology, is the type of criminology most often found in colleges and universities. Theoretical criminology, rather than

Criminology examines the causes of crime and seeks ways to prevent or control it. Criminal justice examines the criminal justice system, including police, courts, and corrections. How do the two disciplines complement one another?

Source: D. Greco, The Image Works

theory

A series of interrelated propositions that attempt to describe, explain, predict, and ultimately control some class of events. A theory gains explanatory power from inherent logical consistency and is "tested" by how well it describes and predicts reality.

general theory

A theory that attempts to explain all (or at least most) forms of criminal conduct through a single, overarching approach.

unicausal

Having one cause. Unicausal theories posit only one source for all that they attempt to explain.

integrated theory

An explanatory perspective that merges (or attempts to merge) concepts drawn from different sources.

simply describing crime and its occurrence, posits explanations for criminal behavior. As Edwin Sutherland stated, "The problem in criminology is to explain the criminality of behavior. . . . However, an explanation of criminal behavior should be a specific part of [a] general theory of behavior and its task should be to differentiate criminal from noncriminal behavior."[48]

To explain and understand crime, criminologists have developed many theories. As we shall see in Chapter 3, a **theory,** at least in its ideal form, is made up of clearly stated propositions that posit relationships, often of a causal sort, between events and things under study. An old Roman theory, for example, proposed that insanity was caused by the influence of the moon and may even follow its cycles—hence the term *lunacy.*

Theories attempt to provide us with explanatory power and help us understand the phenomenon under study. The more applicable a theory is found to be, the more generalizable it is from one specific instance to others—in other words, the more it can be applied to other situations. A **general theory** of crime is one that attempts to explain all (or at least most) forms of criminal conduct through a single, overarching approach. Unfortunately, as Don M. Gottfredson, past president of the American Society of Criminology, observes, "Theories in criminology tend to be unclear and lacking in justifiable generality."[49] When we consider the wide range of behaviors regarded as criminal—from murder, to drug use, to white-collar and computer crime—it seems difficult to imagine one theory that can explain them all or that might even explain the same type of behavior under varying circumstances. Still, many past theoretical approaches to crime causation were **unicausal,** while attempting to be all-inclusive. That is, the approaches posited a single, identifiable source for all serious deviant and criminal behavior.

An **integrated theory,** in contrast to a general theory, does not necessarily attempt to explain all criminality but is distinguishable by the fact that it merges (or attempts to merge) concepts drawn from different sources. As noted criminologist Gregg Barak states, "An integrative criminology . . . seeks to bring together the diverse bodies of knowledge that represent the full array of disciplines that study crime."[50] Hence, integrated theories provide potentially wider explanatory power than narrower formulations. Don C. Gibbons, professor of sociology at Portland State University, notes, "The basic idea of theoretical integration is straightforward; it concerns the combinations of single theories or elements of those theories into a more comprehensive argument. At the same time, it would be well to note that in practice, integration is a matter of degree: some theorists have combined or integrated more concepts or theoretical elements than have others."[51]

Both theoretical integration and the general applicability of criminological theories to a wide variety of law-violating behavior are intuitively appealing concepts. Even far more limited attempts at criminological theorizing, however, often face daunting challenges. "As we shall see," notes Gibbons, "criminologists have not managed to articulate a large collection of relatively formalized arguments in a general or integrated form."[52] Hence, although we will use the word *theory* in describing the many explanations for crime covered by this book, it should be recognized that the word is only loosely applicable to some of the perspectives we will discuss.

As we shall learn in Chapter 3, many social scientists insist that to be considered theories, explanations must consist of sets of clearly stated, logically interrelated, and measurable propositions. The fact that only a few of the theories described in this book rise above the level of organized conjecture—and those offer only limited generalizability and have rarely been integrated—is one of the greatest challenges facing criminology today.

Before leaving this brief discussion of theory, we should mention that a particular aspect of criminology, called *experimental criminology*, consists of the effort to use social scientific techniques to test the accuracy of theories about crime and criminality. Experimental criminology is discussed in more detail in Chapter 3.

Criminology and Social Policy

Of potentially broader importance than theory testing are social policies based on research findings. Some policy implications, such as those relating to the physical environment, may be readily agreed upon and easy to implement—such as the installation of brighter lighting in crime-prone areas in an effort to reduce criminal activity.[53]

Other policy innovations, especially those involving calls for cultural or social changes can be far more complex and difficult to implement, even when there is strong evidence for them. In 2007, for example, an editorial in the highly-regarded British magazine, *New Scientist*, asked "why are we so reluctant to accept that on-screen violence is bad for us?" The article, entitled "In Denial," noted that "by the time the average U.S. schoolchild leaves elementary school, he or she will have witnesses more than 8,000 murders and 100,000 other acts of violence on television." If the child has access to computer games and cable TV, the article noted, the numbers will be far higher. Scientific studies have consistently demonstrated the detrimental effects of media violence, according to the article, "yet every time a study claims to have found a link between aggression, violence, educational, or behavioral problems and TV programs or computer games, there are cries of incredulity. . . ."

A number of professional groups—including the American Medical Association, the American Academy of Pediatrics, the American Psychological Association, and the American Academy of Child and Adolescent Psychiatry—have all said that that violence in television, music, video games, and movies leads to increased levels of violent behavior among children.[54] A joint statement issued by those organizations says that "the effects of violence in the media "are measurable and long-lasting." The groups reached the conclusion "based on over 30 years of research . . . that viewing entertainment violence can lead to increases in aggressive attitudes, values and behaviors, particularly in children." Moreover, "prolonged viewing of media violence can lead to emotional desensitization toward violence in real life." Similarly, some years ago the Federal Trade Commission (FTC) issued a report[55] on teenage violence, which concluded that "Hollywood aggressively markets violent movies, music and electronic games to children even when they have been labeled as appropriate only for adults."[56] The complete 116-page FTC report *Marketing Violent Entertainment to Children* is available at **Web Extra 1–8**.

WEB Extra

Even after all the studies that have been done, however, policymakers have been reluctant to curtail the production of violent media, and violence on TV and in video games is still a way of life in the United States. *New Scientist* notes that the profit motives of media vendors interfere with policies aimed at crime reduction, and says that "any criticism of a multibillion-dollar business is bound to provoke a sharp rebuttal."[57]

Professional criminologists are acutely aware of the need to link sound social policy to the objective findings of well-conducted criminological research. A meeting of the American Society of Criminology (ASC), for example, focused on the need to forge just such a link. At the meeting, ASC President Alfred Blumstein, of Carnegie Mellon University, told criminologists gathered there that "an important mission of the ASC and its members involves the generation of knowledge that is useful in dealing with crime and the operation of the criminal justice system, and then helping public officials to use that knowledge intelligently and effectively."[58] Blumstein added, "So little is known about the causes of crime and about the effects of criminal justice policy on crime that new insights about the criminal justice system can often be extremely revealing and can eventually change the way people think about the crime problem or about the criminal justice system."[59]

Social Policy and Public Crime Concerns

Although American crime rates declined steadily for more than a decade beginning in the mid-1990s, concern over national security, crime, and terrorism remains pervasive in the United States. About 25 years ago, crime was the number one concern of Americans voicing opinions in public polls. In the interim, concern over crime came to be replaced with economic and other worries. Following a spate of seemingly random violence, however, including widely publicized shootings, cult-based violence, gang-related drive-by shootings, terrorist attacks, and highly visible inner-city crime, fear of violence and concern over personal safety has once again moved to the forefront of national issues.

A recent Gallup poll, for example, found that 67% of respondents believed that crime in the United States is more prevalent than it was a year earlier, and 49% rated the problem of crime in the United States as "extremely serious" or "very serious." While some issues, such as immigration, racial integration and wars, have come and gone from the list of concerns identified by pollsters, others—including crime, education, and the economy—appear to be enduring worries.[60] See **Web Extra 1–9** for recent public opinion polls about crime, concerns about crime, and fear of crime.

WEB
Extra
▪▪▪▪

Even though crime rates have declined, concern over crime remains an important determinant of public policy. Hence, political agendas promising to lower crime rates or to keep them low, as well as those that call for changes in the conditions that produce crime, can be quite successful for candidates or incumbents who promote them in an environment where concern over crime remains high.[61] For more information about measuring the fear of crime, read **Library Extra 1–5** at crimtoday.com.

LIBRARY
Extra
▪▪▪▪

According to pollsters, crime remains one of the American public's top concerns. Given recent statistics showing falling crime rates, is such concern justified?

Source: H. Darr Besiner, USA Today

The Theme of This Book

This book builds on a social policy theme by asking questions about the sources of crime and criminality, and by asking what we can do to control crime. Our theme contrasts two perspectives now popular in American society and in much of the rest of the world (see Figure 1–3). One point of view, termed the **social problems perspective,** holds that crime is a manifestation of underlying social problems like poverty, discrimination, inequality of opportunity, the breakdown of traditional social institutions, the low level of formal education among some disadvantaged groups, pervasive family violence experienced by some during the formative years, and inadequate socialization practices that leave too many young people without the fundamental values necessary to contribute meaningfully to the society in which they live. Advocates of the social problems perspective, while generally agreeing that crime and violence are serious social problems, advance solutions based on what is, in effect, a public health model. Adherents of that model say that crime must be addressed in much the same way as public health concerns like AIDS, herpes, or avian flu.

Proponents of the social problems perspective typically foresee solutions to the crime problem as coming in the form of large-scale government expenditures in support of social programs designed to address the issues that are perceived to lie at the root of crime. Government-funded initiatives, designed to enhance social, educational, occupational, and other opportunities, are perceived as offering programmatic solutions to ameliorate most causes of crime.

The social problems approach to crime is characteristic of what social scientists term a *macro* approach because it portrays instances of individual behavior (crimes) as arising out of widespread and contributory social conditions that enmesh unwitting individuals in a causal nexus of uncontrollable social forces.

A contrasting perspective lays the cause of crime squarely at the feet of individual perpetrators. This point of view holds that individuals are fundamentally responsible for their own behavior and maintains that they choose crime over other, more law-abiding courses of action. Perpetrators may choose crime, advocates of this perspective say, because it is exciting, because it offers illicit pleasures and the companionship of like-minded thrill seekers, or because it is simply personally less demanding than conformity. This viewpoint, which we shall call the **social responsibility perspective,** has a close affiliation with what is known in criminology as rational choice theory (discussed in detail in Chapter 4). Advocates of the social responsibility perspective, with

social problems perspective

The belief that crime is a manifestation of underlying social problems, such as poverty, discrimination, pervasive family violence, inadequate socialization practices, and the breakdown of traditional social institutions.

social responsibility perspective

The belief that individuals are fundamentally responsible for their own behavior and that they choose crime over other, more law-abiding courses of action.

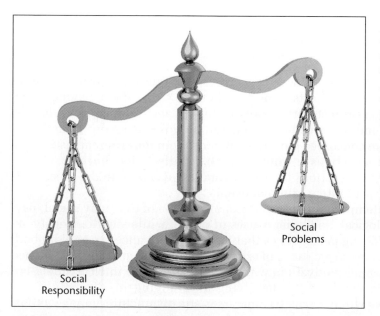

Social Responsibility

Social Problems

FIGURE 1–3

The Theme of This Book: Social Problems versus Social Responsibility

At the core of today's thinking about crime exists a crucial distinction between those who believe that *crime is a matter of individual responsibility* (the social responsibility perspective) and those who emphasize that *crime is a manifestation of underlying social problems* beyond the control of individuals (the social problems viewpoint)

their emphasis on individual choice, tend to believe that social programs do little to solve the problem of crime because, they say, a certain number of crime-prone individuals, for a variety of personalized reasons, will always make irresponsible choices. Hence, advocates of the social responsibility approach suggest highly personalized crime reduction strategies based on firm punishments, imprisonment, individualized rehabilitation, increased security, and a wider use of police powers. The social responsibility perspective characteristically emphasizes a form of *micro* analysis that tends to focus on individual offenders and their unique biology, psychology, background, and immediate life experiences.

Over time, the social responsibility perspective has substantially influenced national crime control policy. Examples of conservatism in our nation's approach to criminals abound. The Violent Crime Control and Law Enforcement Act of 1994, for example, which is discussed in detail later in this text, expanded the number of capital crimes under federal law from a handful of offenses to 52.[62] The law also made billions of dollars available to municipalities to put 100,000 new police officers on the streets, and it allocated billions for states to build and operate prisons and incarceration alternatives like boot camps. Prison funding was intended to ensure that additional prison cells would be available to put—and keep—violent offenders behind bars. A subchapter of the 1994 Violent Crime Control and Law Enforcement Act created a federal "Three Strikes and You're Out" law, mandating life imprisonment for criminals convicted of three violent federal felonies or drug offenses. Similarly, the law increased or created new penalties for over 70 federal criminal offenses, primarily covering violent crimes, drug trafficking, and gun crimes. Since the 1994 federal legislation was passed, many states have moved to toughen their own laws against violent criminals. Violent juveniles and repeat offenders have been especially targeted, while the USA PATRIOT Act— enacted in 2001 and renewed with modifications in 2006—targets terrorism and crimes committed in support of terrorist activity. The PATRIOT Act has been criticized by many for going too far in limiting individual freedoms and restricting personal choice, although its supporters argue that its provisions are needed to effectively fight the war on terrorism. The PATRIOT Act and the crime of terrorism are discussed in more detail in Chapter 15.

A note about wording is in order: Although the social responsibility perspective might also be termed the *individual responsibility perspective* because it stresses individual responsibility above all else, we've chosen to use the term *social responsibility perspective* instead, as it holds that individuals must be ultimately responsible to the social group of which they are a part and that they should be held accountable by group standards if they are not. In short, this perspective is characterized by societal demands for the exercise of individual responsibility.

The Social Context of Crime

Crime does not occur in a vacuum. Every crime has a unique set of causes, consequences, and participants. Crime affects some people more than others, having a special impact on those who are direct participants in the act itself—offenders, victims, police officers, witnesses, and so on. Crime, in general, provokes reactions from the individuals it victimizes, from concerned groups of citizens, from the criminal justice system, and sometimes from society as a whole, which manifests its concerns via the creation of new social policy. Reactions to crime, from the everyday to the precedent-setting, may color the course of future criminal events.[63]

In this book, we shall attempt to identify and examine some of the many social, psychological, economic, biological, and other causes of crime, while simultaneously expounding on the many differing perspectives that have been advanced to explain both crime and criminality. Popular conceptions of criminal motivation are typically shaped by media portrayals of offender motivation, which often fail to take into consideration the felt experiences of the law violator. By identifying and studying this diversity of perspectives on criminality, we will discover the characteristic disjuncture among victims, offenders, the justice system, and society as to the significance that each assigns to the behavior in question—and often to its motivation. It will not be unusual to find, for example, that sociological or psychological initiatives with which the offenders themselves do not identify are assigned to offenders by theorists and others.

Another example of misattribution can be seen in the 15-year-old case of Damian Williams, the African American man sentenced in December 1993 to ten years in prison for beating white truck driver Reginald Denny during riots in Los Angeles. Most reporters and many attorneys assumed that Williams was motivated during the beating by his knowledge of verdicts of innocence that had been returned earlier that day in the state trial of California police officers accused of beating African American motorist Rodney King—an incident captured on videotape that galvanized the nation. An infuriated Williams, the media supposed (and reported), attacked Denny in response to frustrations he felt at a justice system that seemed to protect whites at the expense of African Americans. Williams, however, told a reporter at his sentencing that he knew nothing about the verdicts at the time he attacked Denny and that he was just caught up in the riots. "Maybe other people knew about [the King verdict], but I wasn't aware of it until later. . . . I was just caught up in the rapture," Williams said.[64] Williams served four years in prison and was released. In an interesting footnote to the Denny beating, however, Williams was convicted in 2003 for the alleyway shooting death of 43-year-old Grover Tinner, a South Central Los Angeles drug dealer. Williams was sentenced to 30 years to life in prison for the murder and to an additional 21 years in prison for firearm theft and related charges.[65]

Making Sense of Crime: The Causes and Consequences of the Criminal Event

This book recognizes that criminal activity is diversely created and variously interpreted. In other words, this book depicts crime not as an isolated individual activity but as a *social event*.[66] Like other social events, crime is fundamentally a social construction.[67] To say that crime is a social construction is not to lessen the impact of the victimization experiences that all too many people undergo in our society every day. Nor does such a statement trivialize the significance of crime prevention efforts or the activities of members of the criminal justice system. Likewise, it does not underplay the costs of crime to individual victims and to society as a whole. It does, however, recognize that although a given instance of criminal behavior may have many causes, it also carries with it many different kinds of meanings—at least one for offenders, another (generally quite a different meaning, of course) for victims, and still another for agents of the criminal justice system. Similarly, a wide range of social interest groups, from victims' advocates to prisoner "rights" and gun control organizations, all interpret the significance of lawbreaking behavior from unique points of view, and each arrives at different conclusions as to what should be done about the so-called crime problem.

For these reasons, we have chosen to apply the concept of **social relativity** to the study of criminality.[68] Social relativity means that social events are interpreted differently according to the cultural experiences and personal interests of the initiator, the observer, or the recipient of that behavior. Hence, as a social phenomenon, crime means different things to the offender, to the criminologist who studies it, to the police officer who investigates it, and to the victim who experiences it firsthand.

Figure 1–4 illustrates both the causes and the consequences of crime in rudimentary diagrammatic form. In keeping with the theme of this textbook, it depicts crime as a social event. The figure consists of a foreground, describing those features that immediately determine the nature of the criminal event (including responses to the event as it is transpiring), and a background, in which generic contributions to crime can be seen along with interpretations of the event after it has taken place. We call the background causes of crime *contributions* and use the word *inputs* to signify the more immediate

social relativity

The notion that social events are differently interpreted according to the cultural experiences and personal interests of the initiator, the observer, or the recipient of that behavior.

Crime in the News

Teenager Sentenced to 26 Years for Killing Playmate

EPHRATA, Wash. (AP)—A boy convicted as an adult of stabbing a playmate to death when he was 12 years old was sentenced Monday to the maximum 26 years in prison.

A jury convicted Evan Savoie, now 15, of first-degree murder for the 2003 stabbing death of 13-year-old Craig Sorger, who was developmentally disabled.

Savoie's attorneys have said they will appeal the verdict.

Savoie has repeatedly proclaimed he is innocent. He said Craig fell from a tree while they were playing and that he left him injured—without a pulse—on a trail but didn't kill him.

The prosecution said the victim had been beaten and had 34 stab wounds.

Prosecutors alleged Savoie had planned the killing. They told jurors he had blood on his clothes, access to knives, and lied to investigators, at one point deliberately leading searchers away from Sorger's body but later admitting that.

Savoie showed no reaction as the sentence was read, but he smiled when he was led from the courtroom in handcuffs.

"Somebody is going to have to figure out how a 12-year-old can be so violent so young," Grant County Superior Court Judge Ken Jorgensen said as he imposed the maximum sentence.

The Sorger family had pushed for the maximum sentence.

"In your worst nightmare, you never believe this could happen to you," the victim's mother, Lisa Sorger, wrote in a letter read to the court.

The key to the prosecution's case was the testimony of Jake Eakin, another playmate who pleaded guilty last year to second-degree murder by complicity. He is serving 14 years in prison.

Eakin led investigators to the murder weapon and identified Savoie as the killer. On the witness stand, he described the brief attack in wrenching detail, saying Sorger repeatedly cried out: "Why are you doing this to me?"

Discussion Questions

1. How would you answer Sorger's sad question, "Why are you doing this to me?" In other words, why did Savoie kill Sorger?

2. This chapter says that "popular conceptions of criminal motivation are typically shaped by media portrayals of offender motivation, which often fail to take into consideration the felt experiences of the law violator." What does that statement mean?

3. Explain this story in light of Figure 1–4 (see page 26). How does the criminal event described here hold different meanings for the four parties identified in the figure? In this story, who are those parties, and what might those "meanings" be?

Lisa Sorger and son, Keith, listen as Lisa's written statement about her murdered son, Craig, is read during the sentencing of Evan Savoie. Savoie was only 12 years old when he stabbed 13-year-old Craig Sorger to death. As he imposed the maximum legal sentence on Savoie, Judge Ken Jorgensen said "somebody is going to have to figure out how a 12-year-old can be so violent so young." How would you answer the judge's question?

Source: Don Seabrook, The Wenatchee World/*AP Wide World Photos.*

Source: "Washington Teen Sentenced for Killing Playmate," *USA Today*, July 10, 2006. Copyright 2006 The Associated Press. Used with permission of The Associated Press Copyright © 2007. All rights reserved.

For the latest crime and justice news, visit www.crimenews.info.

Theory Versus Reality

The Murder of John Lennon

At 10:50 P.M. on December 8, 1980, Mark David Chapman, 25, killed famous musician and former Beatle John Lennon. Lennon, who was returning home from a recording session with his wife, Yoko Ono, died in a hail of bullets fired from Chapman's .38-caliber pistol. As a musical luminary, John Lennon was well known to the world. Even his private life—from his residence in the exclusive Dakota Apartments in New York City to his dietary preferences and investment portfolios—was the subject of popular news stories and media exposés.

Following Lennon's death, the public generally assumed that Chapman had chosen his murderous course of action due to innate, albeit perverted, needs fed by a twisted rationale—specifically, to become famous by killing a celebrity. In similar assassination attempts involving Gerald Ford, Ronald Reagan, and others, the media have assumed much the same type of motivation. News stories have communicated to the public the image of would-be assassins sparked by the desire to make headlines and to see their names become household words. To assign such motivation to the killers of famous people is understandable from the media's perspective. Many of the people encountered by newscasters and writers in their daily work have an obvious interest in seeing their names in print. Constant experiences with such people do much to convince byline authors and narrators that the drive for glory is a major motivator of human behavior.

Such "pop psychology," however, probably does not provide an accurate assessment of the motivation of most assassins. We know from recent conversations with Chapman that he, at least, was driven by a different mind-set. In an interview ten years after the killing (the first one he gave since the shooting), Chapman related a story of twisted emotions and evil whisperings inside his own head. Just before the shooting, the unemployed Chapman, living in Hawaii, had gotten married. Faced with a difficult financial situation and rising debts, he became enraged by what he perceived as Lennon's "phoniness." Lennon, he reasoned, had become rich singing about the virtues of the common person, yet Lennon himself lived in luxury made possible by wealth far beyond the reach of Chapman and others like him. According to Chapman, "He [Lennon] had told us to imagine. . . . He had told us not to be greedy. And I had believed!" In effect, Chapman shifted responsibility for his own failure onto Lennon. For that, he reasoned, Lennon must pay. In preparation for the killing, Chapman recorded his own voice over Lennon's songs, screaming such things as "John Lennon must die! John Lennon is a phony." Once a born-again Christian, Chapman turned to Satanism and prayed for demons to enter his body so that he could have the strength to carry out the mission he had set for himself.

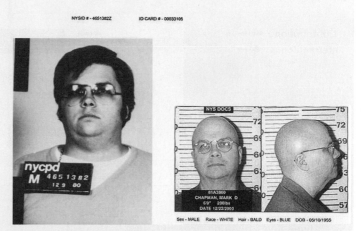

Mark David Chapman shown in an NYPD mugshot (left) killed well-known musician John Lennon in 1980. Chapman, also shown in a recent department of corrections photo (right) has repeatedly been denied parole. What can crimes like Chapman's tell us about criminal motivation?
Source: eyevine/ZUMA Press

Today, says Chapman, he has changed. Much of his time behind bars is spent writing religious tracts and other stories, with inspiration drawn from verses Lennon made famous. In an interview that Chapman gave shortly before his first parole eligibility date in September 2000, the now-repentant killer indulged in psychological self-analysis and blamed the killing on a father who never showed love. "I think the main problem," said Chapman, "was that my father never talked about life or problems . . . and I guess the more I look back on it, I didn't feel any love from him. Perhaps I was getting back, killing John Lennon, ruining my life as well." Parole officials were unimpressed with Chapman's self-assessment and denied his bid for parole. To date, he has been denied parole four times—in 2000, 2002, 2004, and 2006. Read Chapman's 2002 parole board interview at **Web Extra 1–10**, and learn more about him and his crime at **Web Extra 1–11**.

WEB
Extra
■ ■ ■ ■

Discussion Questions

1. Why did Chapman kill Lennon? Will we ever be sure of his true motivation? How can we know when we have uncovered it?

2. Was Chapman insane at the time of the killing? What does insanity mean in this context? How can it be determined?

3. Should Chapman be paroled? Why or why not?

Sources: "In-Depth: Mark David Chapman," Court TV online. Web posted at http://www.courttv.com/onair/shows/mugshots/indepth/chapman.html (accessed June 14, 2007); Jack Jones, "Decade Later, Killer Prays to Be Forgiven," *USA Today,* December 3, 1990, p. 1a; and "John Lennon's Killer Blames His Own Father," Reuters wire service, September 26, 2000.

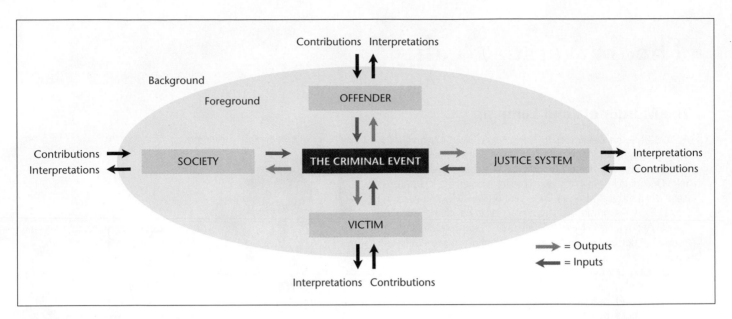

FIGURE 1–4

The Causes and Consequences of Crime

propensities and predispositions of the actors involved in the situation. Inputs also include the physical features of the setting in which a specific crime takes place. Both background contributions and immediate inputs contribute to and shape the criminal event. The more or less immediate results or consequences of crime are termed *outputs,* while the term *interpretations* appears in the diagram to indicate that any crime has a lasting impact both on surviving participants and on society.

As Figure 1–4 shows, the criminal event is ultimately a result of the coming together of inputs provided by the

- offender
- justice system
- victim
- society

Offenders bring with them certain background features, such as personal life experiences, a peculiar biology (insofar as they are unique organisms), a distinct personality, personal values and beliefs, and various kinds of skills and knowledge (some of which may be useful in the commission of crime). Background contributions to crime can be vitally important. Recent research, for example, tends to cement the existence of a link between child-rearing practices and criminality in later life. Joan McCord, reporting on a 30-year study of family relationships and crime, found that self-confident, nonpunitive, and affectionate mothers tend to insulate their male children from delinquency and, consequently, later criminal activity.[69] Difficulties associated with the birthing process have also been linked to crime in adulthood.[70] Birth trauma and negative familial relationships are but two of the literally thousands of kinds of experiences individuals may have. Whether individuals who undergo trauma at birth and are deprived of positive maternal experiences will turn to crime depends on many other things, including their own mixture of other experiences and characteristics, the appearance of a suitable victim, the failure of the justice system to prevent crime, and the evolution of a social environment in which criminal behavior is somehow encouraged or valued.

Each of the parties identified in Figure 1–4 contributes immediate inputs to the criminal event. Foreground contributions by the offender may consist of a particular motivation, a specific intent (in many cases), or a drug-induced state of mind.

Like the offender, the **criminal justice system** also contributes to the criminal event, albeit unwillingly, through its failure to (1) prevent criminal activity, (2) adequately identify and inhibit specific offenders prior to their involvement in crime, and (3) prevent the release of convicted criminals who later become repeat offenders. Such background contributions can be seen in prisons (a central component of the justice system) that serve as "schools for crime," fostering anger against society and building a propensity for continued criminality in inmates who have been "turned out." Similarly, the failure of system-sponsored crime prevention programs—ranging from the patrol activities of local police departments to educational and diversionary programs intended to redirect budding offenders—helps set the stage for the criminal event. On the other hand, proper system response may reduce crime. A study by Carol W. Kohfeld and John Sprague, for example, found that police response (especially arrest) can, under certain demographic conditions, dramatically reduce the incidence of criminal behavior.[71] Additionally, Kohfeld and Sprague found that arrest "constitutes communication to criminals in general," further supporting the notion that inputs provided by the justice system have the power to either enhance or reduce the likelihood of criminal occurrences. Immediate inputs provided by the justice system typically consist of such features of the situation as the presence or absence of police officers, the ready availability (or lack thereof) of official assistance, the willingness of police officers to intervene in precrime situations, and the response time required for officers to arrive at a crime scene.

Few crimes can occur without a victim. Sometimes the victim is a passive participant in the crime, such as an innocent person killed on the street outside of his or her home by random gunfire from a drive-by shooting. In such cases, the victim is simply in the proverbial wrong place at the wrong time. Even then, however, merely by being present the victim contributes his or her person to the event, thereby increasing the severity of the incident (that is, the random shooting that injures no one may still be against the law, but it is a far less serious crime than a similar incident in which somebody is killed). Sometimes, however, victims more actively contribute to their own victimization by appearing defenseless (perhaps because of old age, drunkenness, or disability), by failing to take appropriate defensive measures (leaving doors unlocked or forgetting to remove the key from a car's ignition), by unwisely displaying wealth (flashing large-denomination bills in a public place), or simply by making other unwise choices (walking down a dark alley off of Times Square at 3 A.M., for example). In a study of Canadian victimization, Leslie W. Kennedy and David R. Forde found that violent personal victimization "is contingent on the exposure that comes from following certain lifestyles."[72] This was especially true, they found, "for certain demographic groups, particularly young males."

Although lifestyles may provide the background that fosters victimization, a more active form of victimization characterizes "victims" who initiate criminal activity, such as the barroom brawler who picks a fight but ends up on the receiving end of the ensuing physical violence. Victim-precipitated offenses are those that involve active victim participation in the initial stages of a criminal event and that take place when the soon-to-be victim instigates the chain of events that ultimately results in the victimization.

Finally, the general public (termed *society* in Figure 1–4) contributes to the criminal event both formally and informally. Society's formal contributions sometimes take the form of legislation, whereby crime itself is defined. Hence, as we shall discuss in considerable detail in Chapter 15, society structures the criminal event in a most fundamental way by delineating (through legislation and via statute) which forms of activity are to be thought of as criminal.

Society's less formal contributions to crime arise out of generic social practices and conditions like poverty, poor and informal education, various forms of discrimination by which pathways to success are blocked, and the **socialization** process. Socialization has an especially important impact on crime causation because it provides the interpretative foundation used to define and understand the significance of particular situations

criminal justice system

The various agencies of justice, especially the police, courts, and corrections, whose goal it is to apprehend, convict, punish, and rehabilitate law violators.

socialization

The lifelong process of social experience whereby individuals acquire the cultural patterns of their society.

in which we find ourselves, and it is upon those interpretations that we may (or may not) decide to act. Date rape, for example, can occur when a man concludes that his date "owes" him something for the money he has spent on her. That feeling, however inappropriate from the point of view of the victim and the justice system, probably has its roots in early learned experiences—including values communicated from television, the movies, and popular music—about gender-related roles under such circumstances. In other words, society, through the divergent values and expectations it places upon people, property, and behavior under particular conditions, may provide the motivational basis for many offenses.

The contributions society makes to the backgrounds of both offender and victim and to the structure of the justice system and the influences each, in turn, has upon the general social order provide for a kind of "feedback loop" in our vision of crime (even though the loop is not shown in Figure 1–4 for fear of unnecessarily complicating it). Through socialization, for example, individuals learn about the dangers of criminal victimization; but when victimization occurs and is publicized, it reinforces the socialization process, leading to an increased wariness of others and so on. An example can be seen in the fact that children throughout the United States are routinely taught to avoid strangers and to be suspicious of people they do not know. A few decades ago, stranger avoidance was not ordinarily communicated to children; it entered cultural awareness following a number of horrendous and well-publicized crimes involving child victims. It is now a shared part of the socialization process experienced by countless children every day throughout the United States.

The contributions made by society to crime are complex and far reaching. Some say that the content of the mass media (television, movies, newspapers, popular music, etc.) can lead to crime by exposing young people to inappropriate role models and to the kinds of activity—violence and unbridled sexuality, for example—that encourage criminality.

Society's foreground contributions to crime largely emanate from the distribution of resources and the accessibility of services, which are often the direct result of economic conditions. In a study of the availability of medical resources (especially quality hospital emergency services), William G. Doerner found that serious assaults may "become" homicides when such resources are lacking but that homicides can be prevented through the effective utilization of capable medical technology.[73] Hence, societal decisions leading to the distribution and placement of advanced medical support equipment and personnel can effectively lower homicide rates in selected geographic areas. Homicide rates will be higher in areas where such equipment is not readily available. In Doerner's words, "The causes of homicide transcend the mere social world of the combatants."[74]

The moments that immediately precede any crime are ripe with possibilities. When all the inputs brought to the situation by all those present coalesce into activity that violates the criminal law, a crime occurs. Together, the elements, experiences, and propensities brought to the situation by the offender and the victim, and those that are contributed to the pending event by society and the justice system, precipitate and decide the nature, course, and eventual outcome of the criminal event. As one well-known criminologist explained, "An understanding of crime and criminality as constructed from the immediate interactions of criminals, control agents, victims, and others, and therefore as emerging from a tangled experiential web of situated dangers and situated pleasures, certainly refocuses theories of criminal causality on the criminal moment."[75] While focused on the criminal event as it unfolds, however, it is important to note that some of the inputs brought to the situation may be inhibiting; that is, they may tend to reduce the likelihood or severity of criminal behavior.

As mentioned earlier, the causes of crime, however well documented, tell only half the criminological story. Each and every crime has consequences. Although the immediate consequences of crime may be relatively obvious for those parties directly involved (for example, the offender and the victim), crime also indirectly impacts society and the justice system over the longer term. Figure 1–4 terms the immediate effects of crime *outputs*. As with the causes of crime, however, the real impact of such outputs is mediated by perceptual filters, resulting in what the figure terms *interpretations*. After a crime has taken place, each party to the event must make sense out of what has transpired. Such interpretations consist of cognitive, emotional, and (ultimately) behavioral reactions to the criminal event.

Interpretations are ongoing. They happen before, during, and after the criminal event and are undertaken by all those associated with it. In an interesting and detailed study of the interpretative activity of criminal justice system personnel, James F. Gilsinan has documented what happens when callers reach the 911 operator on police emergency lines.[76] Because many prank calls and calls for information are made to 911 operators, the operator must judge the seriousness of every call that comes through. What the caller says was found to be only a small part of the informational cues that the operator seeks to interpret before assigning the call to a particular response (or nonresponse) category. Honest calls for help may go unanswered if the operator misinterprets the call. Hence, quite early on in the criminal event, the potential exists for a crucial representative of the justice system to misinterpret important cues and to conclude that no crime is taking place.

Other interpretative activities may occur long after the crime has transpired, but they are at least as significant. The justice system, taken as a whole, must decide guilt or innocence and must attempt to deal effectively with convicted offenders. Victims must attempt to make sense of their victimizations in such a way as to allow them to testify in court (if need be) and to pick up the pieces of their crime-shattered lives. Offenders must come to terms with themselves and decide whether to avoid prosecution (if escape, for example, is possible), accept blame, or deny responsibility. Whatever the outcome of these more narrowly focused interpretative activities, society—because of the cumulative impact of individual instances of criminal behavior—will also face tough decisions through its courts and lawmaking agencies. Society-level decision making may revolve around the implementation of policies designed to stem future instances of criminal behavior, the revision of criminal codes, or the elimination of unpopular laws.

Our perspective takes a three-dimensional integrative view of the social event termed *crime.* We will (1) attempt to identify and understand the multiple causes that give rise to criminal behavior, (2) highlight the processes involved in the criminal event as it unfolds, and (3) analyze the interpretation of the crime phenomenon, including societal responses to it. From this perspective, crime can be viewed along a temporal continuum as an emergent activity that (1) arises out of past complex causes; (2) assumes a course that builds upon immediate interrelationships among the victim, offender, and social order that exist at the time of the offense; and (3) after it has occurred, elicits a formal response from the justice system, shapes public perceptions, and (possibly) gives rise to changes in social policy.

The advantages of an integrative perspective can be found in the completeness of the picture that it provides. The integrative point of view results in a comprehensive and inclusive view of crime because it emphasizes the personal and social underpinnings as well as the consequences of crime. The chapters that follow employ the integrative perspective advocated here to analyze criminal events and to show how various theoretical approaches can be woven into a consistent perspective on crime. For a different point of view, one that describes crime in terms of the five dimensions of (1) law, (2) offender, (3) target and/or victim, (4) location, and (5) time of the incident, read **Library Extra 1–6** at crimtoday.com.

LIBRARY
Extra
▪▪▪▪

The Primacy of Sociology?

This book recognizes the contributions made by numerous disciplines to the study of crime and crime causation, including biology, economics, psychology, psychiatry, physiology, and political science. It is important to recognize, however, that the primary perspective from which many contemporary criminologists operate is a sociological one. Hence, a large number of today's theoretical explanations of criminal behavior are routinely couched in the language of social science and fall within the framework

A makeshift memorial in Nickel Mines, Pennsylvania, October 8, 2006, for the girls slain in an Amish school shooting that took place just down the road. Charles Carl Roberts IV, a milkman known in the community, stormed the Amish schoolhouse killing five girls and critically wounding five others before turning the gun on himself. Is it possible to understand the thinking or motivation of those who commit such horrific crimes?

Source: AP Photo/Carolyn Kaster

of sociological theory. The social problems versus social responsibility theme, around which this book is built, is in keeping with such a tradition.

Many, however, would disagree with those who claim that the sociological perspective should be accorded heightened importance in today's criminological enterprise. Those who argue in favor of the primacy of sociology emphasize the fact that crime, as a subject of study, is a social phenomenon. Central to any study of crime, they say, must be the social context of the criminal event because it is the social context that brings victims and criminals together.[77] Moreover, much of contemporary criminology rests upon a tradition of social scientific investigation into the nature of crime and criminal behavior that is rooted in European and American sociological traditions that are now well over 200 years old.[78]

One of sociology's problems, however, has been its apparent reluctance to accept the significance of findings from other fields, as well as its frequent inability to integrate such findings into existing sociological understandings of crime. Another has been its seeming inability to demonstrate conclusively effective means of controlling violent (as well as other forms of) crime. As Diana Fishbein, professor of criminology at the University of Baltimore, says, "Sociological factors play a role. But they have not been able to explain why one person becomes violent and another doesn't."[79]

While sociological theories continue to develop, new and emerging perspectives ask to be recognized. The role of biology in explaining criminal tendencies, for example, appears to be gaining strength as investigations into the mapping of human DNA continue. Charles F. Wellford, past president of the American Society of Criminology, explained the current state of affairs, saying: "I strongly believe that the future development of causal theory is dependent upon our movement toward integrated theories that involve biological, social, and cultural dimensions. Our failure to achieve much in the way of understanding the causal sequences of crime is in part a reflection of our slowness in moving toward multidisciplinary, integrated theoretical structures. The fact is that for two-thirds of this century, as criminology developed, we remained committed to a small number of sociological models for which there is extensive proof of their important but limited value. Fortunately in the last 20 years, this has begun to change. Today we see under way substantial research efforts that are based upon models of explanation that far exceed the traditional sociological approaches."[80]

Nonetheless, whatever new insights may develop over the coming years, it is likely that the sociological perspective will continue to dominate the field of criminology for some time to come. Such dominance is rooted in the fact that crime—regardless of all the causative nuances that may be identified in its development—occurs within the context of the social world. As such, the primary significance of crime and of criminal behavior is fundamentally social in nature, and any control over crime must stem from effective social policy.

SUMMARY

At the start of this chapter, the term *crime* was simply defined as a violation of the criminal law. Near the end of this chapter, we recognized the complexity of crime, calling it an "emergent phenomenon." In the process, crime was effectively redefined as a lawbreaking event whose significance arises out of an intricate social nexus involving a rather wide variety of participants. As we move through the early decades of the twenty-first century, contemporary criminologists face the daunting task of reconciling an extensive and diverse collection of theoretical explanations for criminal behavior. All these perspectives aim to assist in understanding the social phenomenon of crime—a phenomenon that is itself open to interpretation and that runs the gamut from petty offenses to major infractions of the criminal law. At the very least, we should recognize that explanations for criminal behavior rest on shaky ground insofar as the subject matter they seek to interpret contains many different forms of behavior, each of which is subject to personal, political, and definitional vagaries.

KEY TERMS

crime, 4

criminalist, 10

criminality, 15

criminalize, 5

criminal justice, 17

criminal justice system, 27

criminologist, 10

criminology, 15

deviant behavior, 8

general theory, 18

integrated theory, 18

socialization, 27

social policy, 13

social problems perspective, 21

social relativity, 23

social responsibility perspective, 21

statute, 5

statutory law, 5

theory, 18

unicausal, 18

QUESTIONS FOR REVIEW

1. What are the four definitional perspectives in contemporary criminology? What is the definition of *crime* that the authors of this textbook have chosen to use?

2. What is crime? What is the difference between crime and deviance? How might the notion of crime change over time? What impact does the changing nature of crime have on criminology?

3. What is the legalistic approach to the study of crime? How can it be used to decide what forms of behavior are criminal?

4. What do criminologists do? Provide a list of employment opportunities available in the field of criminology.

5. What are the various definitions of criminology presented in this chapter? Which is the one chosen by the authors of this textbook? Why?

6. How does contemporary criminology influence social policy? Do you think that policymakers should address crime as a matter of individual responsibility and accountability, or do you think that crime is truly a symptom of a dysfunctional society? Why?

7. What is theme of this textbook? What are the differences between the social problems and the social responsibility perspectives on crime causation?

8. Describe the various participants in a criminal event. How does each contribute to an understanding of the event?

9. In what way is contemporary criminology interdisciplinary? Why is the sociological perspective especially important in studying crime? What other perspectives might be relevant? Why?

QUESTIONS FOR REFLECTION

1. This book emphasizes a social problems versus social responsibility theme. Describe both perspectives. How might social policy decisions based on these perspectives vary?

2. Do you think you might want to become a criminologist? Why or why not?

3. What do crimes such as doctor-assisted suicide tell us about the nature of the law and about crime in general? Do you believe that doctor-assisted suicide should be legalized? Why or why not?

4. Are there any crimes today that you think should be legalized? If so, what are they and why?

5. Can you think of any advances now occurring in the social or physical sciences that might soon have a significant impact on our understanding of crime and criminality? If so, what would those advances be? How might they impact our understanding of crime and criminal behavior?

WEB QUEST

Learn what criminologists do by visiting some of the professional associations they have formed. The American Society of Criminology (www.asc41.com) and the Academy of Criminal Justice Sciences (www.acjs.org)—each with over 2,000 members—are among the oldest and most established of such organizations and are easily accessible via the Internet. Regional associations include the Northeastern Association of Criminal Justice Sciences (www.neacjs.org), the Southern Criminal Justice Association (www.scja.net), and the Western Society of Criminology (www.sonoma.edu/cja/wsc/wscpages/default.htm). Many state organizations exist as well, and most can be found on the Internet. The European Society of Criminology (www.esc-eurocrim.org) is relatively new, having formed in 2000 to bring together European criminologists.

You might also want to visit some forensic Web sites, including the American Academy of Forensic Sciences (www.aafs.org), the American College of Forensic Examiners (www.acfe.com), and the British Forensic Science Society (www.forensic-science-society.org.uk). Hundreds of other criminology-related professional associations can be found by searching Prentice Hall's Cybrary (www.cybrary.info), using search terms like *association, academy, society,* and so on. The Cybrary also contains an "Associations" category that you can use to speed your search.

If asked to do so by your instructor, visit the Web sites listed here and write a brief description of what each contains. Include in your descriptions the mission statement for each organization that you visit.

NOTES

[1] Air date: November 22, 1993.

[2] George B. Vold and Thomas J. Bernard, *Theoretical Criminology,* 3rd ed. (New York: Oxford University Press, 1986).

[3] Edwin Sutherland and Donald Cressey, *Principles of Criminology,* 9th ed. (Philadelphia: Lippincott, 1973), p. 3.

[4] Jay Frost, *The English* (London: Avon Press, 1968).

[5] CTV Global Media, "CSI: Miami," http://www.ctv.ca/servlet/ArticleNews/show/CTVShows/1064338847511_59746366 (accessed March 10, 2007).

[6] Gerard Gilbert "*CSI:* The Cop Show that Conquered the World," *The* (London) *Independent,* December 19, 2006, http://www.findarticles.com/p/articles/mi_qn4158/is_20061219/ai_n17081057 (accessed March 10, 2007).

[7] From the standpoint of the law, the proper word is *conduct* rather than *behavior* because the term *conduct* implies intentional and willful activity, whereas *behavior* refers to any human activity—even that which occurs while a person is unconscious, as well as that which is unintended.

[8] Paul W. Tappan, "Who Is the Criminal?" *American Sociological Review,* Vol. 12 (1947), pp. 96–102.

[9] Edwin Sutherland, *Principles of Criminology,* 4th ed. (New York: Lippincott, 1947).

[10] In 1996, for example, euthanasia advocate Dr. Jack Kevorkian was arrested and unsuccessfully prosecuted in Michigan on charges of violating the state's common law against suicide.

[11] John F. Galliher, *Criminology: Human Rights, Criminal Law, and Crime* (Upper Saddle River, NJ: Prentice Hall, 1989), p. 2.

[12] C. D. Shearing, "Criminologists Must Broaden Their Field of Study beyond Crime and Criminals," in R. Boostrom, ed.,

Enduring Issues in Criminology (San Diego, CA: Greenhaven, 1995).

[13] Ezzat Fattah, *Introduction to Criminology* (Burnaby, British Columbia: School of Criminology, Simon Fraser University, 1989).

[14] Hermann Mannheim, *Comparative Criminology* (Boston: Houghton Mifflin, 1965).

[15] Ron Claassen, "Restorative Justice: Fundamental Principles," http://www.fresno.edu/pacs/rjprinc.htm (accessed May 5, 2007).

[16] H. Schwendinger and J. Schwendinger, "Defenders of Order or Guardians of Human Rights?" in I. Taylor, P. Walton, and J. Young, eds., *Critical Criminology* (London: Routledge and Kegan Paul, 1975).

[17] Ibid.

[18] Jeffrey H. Reiman, *The Rich Get Richer and the Poor Get Prison,* 4th ed. (Boston: Allyn & Bacon, 1997).

[19] Fattah, *Introduction to Criminology.*

[20] Matthew Robinson, "Defining 'Crime,'" http://www.appstate.edu/~robinsnmb/smokeharms.htm (accessed November 4, 2006).

[21] Piers Beirne and James W. Messerschmidt, *Criminology* (San Diego, CA: Harcourt Brace Jovanovich, 1991), p. 20.

[22] "Topless Standard," *Fayetteville* (NC) *Observer-Times,* November 14, 1991, p. 7A.

[23] Air Capital Naturist Society, "Bare Breasts Not Illegal Says Judge," http://www.aircapital.org/mainsite/topfree.htm (accessed February 18, 2005).

[24] See The Wineman at http://www.thewineman.com/strangelaw.htm (accessed March 11, 2007).

[25] *The American Heritage Dictionary* on CD-ROM (Boston: Houghton Mifflin, 1992).

26 *The American Heritage Dictionary of the English Language,* 3rd ed. (Boston: Houghton Mifflin, 1996).

27 This list is not meant to be exclusive. There are many other journals in the field, too many to list here.

28 Piers Beirne, *Inventing Criminology* (Albany: State University of New York Press, 1993).

29 See also Paul Topinard, *Anthropology* (London: Chapman and Hall, 1894).

30 Joseph F. Sheley, *Criminology: A Contemporary Handbook* (Belmont, CA: Wadsworth, 1991), p. xxiii.

31 Edwin H. Sutherland, *Criminology* (Philadelphia: Lippincott, 1924), p. 11.

32 "Sutherland, Edwin H.," *Encyclopedia of Criminology,* http://www.fitzroydearborn.com/chicago/criminology/sample-sutherland-edwin.asp (accessed November 15, 2007).

33 Edwin H. Sutherland and Donald R. Cressey, *Criminology,* 9th ed. (Philadelphia: Lippincott, 1974), p. 3.

34 Gennaro F. Vito and Ronald M. Holmes, *Criminology: Theory, Research, and Policy* (Belmont, CA: Wadsworth, 1994), p. 3.

35 Clemens Bartollas and Simon Dinitz, *Introduction to Criminology: Order and Disorder* (New York: Harper & Row, 1989), p. 548.

36 Marvin E. Wolfgang and Franco Ferracuti, *The Subculture of Violence: Towards an Integrated Theory in Criminology* (London: Tavistock, 1967).

37 Sutherland, *Principles of Criminology,* p. 1.

38 Clarence Ray Jeffery, "The Historical Development of Criminology," in Herman and Mannheim, ed., *Pioneers in Criminology* (Montclair, NJ: Paterson Smith, 1972), p. 458.

39 Gregg Barak, *Integrating Criminologies* (Boston: Allyn & Bacon, 1998), p. 303.

40 European Society of Criminology, Constitution, Section 1 (d), http://www.esc-eurocrim.org/constitution.shtml (accessed July 10, 2007).

41 Jack P. Gibbs, "The State of Criminological Theory," *Criminology,* Vol. 25, No. 4 (November 1987), pp. 822–823.

42 Jim Short, "President's Message: On Communicating, Crossing Boundaries and Building Bridges," *The Criminologist,* Vol. 22, No. 5 (September/October 1997), p. 1.

43 Available through Sage Publications, Thousand Oaks, CA.

44 Piers Beirne and Colin Sumner, "Editorial Statement," *Theoretical Criminology,* Vol. 1, No. 1 (February 1997), pp. 5–11.

45 There are, however, those who deny that criminology deserves the name "discipline." See, for example, Don C. Gibbons, *Talking about Crime and Criminals: Problems and Issues in Theory Development in Criminology* (Upper Saddle River, NJ: Prentice Hall, 1994), p. 3.

46 Charles F. Wellford, "Controlling Crime and Achieving Justice: The American Society of Criminology 1996 Presidential Address," *Criminology,* Vol. 35, No. 1 (1997), p. 1.

47 Gibbons, *Talking about Crime and Criminals,* p. 4.

48 Sutherland, *Principles of Criminology.*

49 Don M. Gottfredson, "Criminological Theories: The Truth as Told by Mark Twain," in William S. Laufer and Freda Adler, eds., *Advances in Criminological Theory,* Vol. 1 (New Brunswick, NJ: Transaction, 1989), p. 1.

50 Barak, *Integrating Criminologies,* p. 5.

51 Don C. Gibbons, "Talking about Crime: Observations on the Prospects for Causal Theory in Criminology," *Criminal Justice Research Bulletin* (Sam Houston State University), Vol. 7, No. 6 (1992).

52 Ibid.

53 Not all studies support such a policy, however. See, for example, P. R. Marchant, "A Demonstration that the Claim that Brighter Lighting Reduces Crime Is Unfounded," *British Journal of Criminology,* Vol. 44, No. 3 (2004), p. 441.

54 Congressional Public Health Summit, *Joint Statement on the Impact of Entertainment Violence on Children,* July 26, 2000.

55 Federal Trade Commission, *Marketing Violent Entertainment to Children* (Washington, DC: U.S. Government Printing Office, 2000).

56 Sue Pleming, "U.S. Report Says Hollywood Aims Violence at Kids," Reuters wire service, September 11, 2000.

57 *New Scientist,* "Editorial: In Denial About On-screen Violence," April 21, 2007, http://www.newscientist.com/channel/opinion/mg19426003.600-editorial-in-denial-about-onscreen-violence.html (accessed August 1, 2007).

58 Alfred Blumstein, "Making Rationality Relevant: The American Society of Criminology 1992 Presidential Address," *Criminology,* Vol. 31, No. 1 (February 1993), p. 1.

59 Ibid.

60 Lydia Saad, "Crime Tops List of Americans' Local Concerns," Gallup Organization, June 21, 2000, http://www.gallup.com/poll/releases/pr000621.asp (accessed February 20, 2004).

61 For an especially good discussion of this issue, see Theodore Sasson, *Crime Talk: How Citizens Construct a Social Problem* (Hawthorne, NY: Aldine de Gruyter, 1995).

62 Public Law 103–322.

63 For a good overview of this issue, see Wesley G. Skogan, ed., *Reactions to Crime and Violence: The Annals of the American Academy of Political and Social Science* (Thousand Oaks, CA: Sage, 1995).

64 "Denny Beating," Associated Press wire service, December 8, 1993.

65 "Reginald Denny Beating Defendant Sentenced in Murder Case," NBC TV News, http://www.nbc4.tv/news/2686224/detail.htm (accessed August 28, 2007).

66 For an excellent discussion of crime as a social event, see Leslie W. Kennedy and Vincent F. Sacco, *Crime Counts: A Criminal Event Analysis* (Toronto: Nelson Canada, 1996).

67 For a good discussion of the social construction of crime, see Leslie T. Wilkins, "On Crime and Its Social Construction: Observations on the Social Construction of Crime," *Social Pathology,* Vol. 1, No. 1 (January 1995), pp. 1–11.

68 For a parallel approach, see Terance D. Miethe and Robert F. Meier, *Crime and Its Social Context: Toward an Integrated Theory of Offenders, Victims, and Situations* (Albany: State University of New York Press, 1995).

69 Joan McCord, "Family Relationships, Juvenile Delinquency, and Adult Criminality," *Criminology,* Vol. 29, No. 3 (August 1991), pp. 397–417.

70 Elizabeth Candle and Sarnoff A. Mednick, "Perinatal Complications Predict Violent Offending," *Criminology,* Vol. 29, No. 3 (August 1991), pp. 519–529.

71 Carol W. Kohfeld and John Sprague, "Demography, Police Behavior, and Deterrence," *Criminology,* Vol. 28, No. 1 (February 1990), pp. 111–136.

72 Leslie W. Kennedy and David R. Forde, "Routine Activities and Crime: An Analysis of Victimization in Canada," *Criminology,* Vol. 28, No. 1 (February 1990), p. 137.

73 William G. Doerner, "The Impact of Medical Resources on Criminally Induced Lethality: A Further Examination," *Criminology,* Vol. 26, No. 1 (February 1988), pp. 171–177.

74 Ibid., p. 177.

75 Jeff Ferrell, "Criminological *Verstehen:* Inside the Immediacy of Crime," *Justice Quarterly,* Vol. 14, No. 1 (1997), p. 11.

76 James F. Gilsinan, "They Is Clowning Tough: 911 and the Social Construction of Reality," *Criminology,* Vol. 27, No. 2 (May 1989), pp. 329–344.

77 See, for example, Miethe and Meier, *Crime and Its Social Context.*

78 For a good discussion of the historical development of criminology, see Leon Radzinowicz, *In Search of Criminology* (Cambridge: Harvard University Press, 1962).

79 As quoted in W. Wayt Gibbs, "Trends in Behavioral Science: Seeking the Criminal Element," *Scientific American,* Vol. 272, No. 3 (March 1995), pp. 100–107.

80 Wellford, "Controlling Crime and Achieving Justice," p. 4.

Outline

"I had," said he, "come to an entirely erroneous conclusion which shows, my dear Watson, how dangerous it always is to reason from insufficient data."

—Arthur Conan Doyle[1]

Once I've done a crime, I just forget it. I go from crime to crime.

—Serial killer Henry Lee Lucas, 1984

If you wish to make a big difference in crime, you must make fundamental changes in society.

—James Q. Wilson[2]

I hate this "crime doesn't pay" stuff. Crime in the United States is perhaps one of the biggest businesses in the world today.

—Peter Kirk, professor of criminalistics, University of California, 1960

Learning Outcomes

After reading this chapter, you should be able to

- Explain the history of statistical crime data collection and analysis and understand the usefulness and limitations of crime data
- Recognize the various methods currently used to collect and disseminate crime data
- Describe the three major shifts in crime rates since record keeping began, and identify the likely direction of coming changes in such rates
- Describe the nature of the crime problem in America today, and explain how we can assess its extent

- List the major crimes on which data is gathered, and describe the extent of each
- Provide an overview of the FBI's Part II offenses, and describe the extent of such crimes
- Describe sources of crime data that are available in the United States in addition to FBI and NCVS statistics
- Discuss how criminologists gather information on unreported crimes, and explain what is meant by the "dark figure of crime"
- Define and discuss the social dimensions of crime, including key demographic factors

Hear the author discuss this chapter at **crimtoday.com**

Introduction

Ninety-eight-year-old Wesley "Pop" Honeywood knows little about statistics, but he is familiar with crime. Over the years, Honeywood, who lives in Jacksonville, Florida, has been arrested 46 times. Five of those arrests were for felonies. Honeywood has been imprisoned on eight occasions since 1946, serving sentences in Philadelphia, Baltimore, Tampa, Orlando, and Jacksonville.[3]

Honeywood's troubles with the law began at the close of World War II, when he and a couple of friends stole a bomber and flew it over Italy for fun. After landing, Honeywood was arrested by military police, did a brief stint in jail, and received a dishonorable discharge from the army.

Not long ago, the geriatric career criminal stood before a Florida judge, awaiting sentencing after pleading guilty to charges of armed assault and possession of a firearm by a convicted felon. The incident grew out of Honeywood's liking for grapes, which he had watched ripen in his neighbor's yard at the end of the summer. Finally, unable to resist the temptation any longer, Honeywood helped himself to bunches of the fruit. When confronted by the neighbor, Honeywood pulled a gun and threatened the man.

Because of all the crimes he'd committed, Honeywood faced sentencing as a habitual offender and could have been sent to prison for 60 years. Worse, Honeywood was on probation for the attempted sexual battery of a seven-year-old girl when he was arrested for the grape theft. And age hasn't mellowed him. Honeywood admits shooting a man in the buttocks in 1989 but claims self-defense. The case never went to trial.

Honeywood said he is not afraid of a prison sentence. "I can do it," he smiles. "I've been locked up a whole lot of times here, but they turn me loose every time."

As things turned out, the judge sentenced him to three years in prison. Honeywood survived the time behind bars and returned to his Jacksonville home upon release. It may be, however, that we haven't heard the last from Pop Honeywood. His father lived to be 113.

A History of Crime Statistics

Pop Honeywood is a statistical anomaly. Few people are involved in crime past middle age. Fewer still ever reach Honeywood's stage in life. Statistical data from the *Sourcebook of Criminal Justice Statistics*[4] show that the likelihood of crime commission declines with age. People 65 years of age and older, for example, commit fewer than 1% of all crimes, and the proportion of crimes committed by those over age 90 is so small that it cannot be meaningfully expressed as a percentage of total crime.

Although the gathering of crime statistics is a relatively new phenomenon, population statistics have been collected periodically since pre-Roman times. Old Testament accounts of enumerations of the Hebrews, for example, provide evidence of Middle Eastern census taking thousands of years ago. In like manner, the New Testament describes how the family of Jesus had to return home to be counted during an official census, providing evidence of routine census taking during the time of Christ. The *lustrum,* which was a ceremonial purification of the entire ancient Roman population after census taking, leads historians to conclude that Roman population counts were made every five years. Centuries later, the *Doomsday Book,* created by order of William the Conqueror in 1085 to 1086, provided a written survey of English landowners and their property. Other evidence shows that primitive societies around the world also took periodic counts of their members. The Incas, for example, a pre-Columbian Indian empire in western South America, required successive census reports to be recorded on knotted strings called *quipas.*

Although census taking has occurred throughout history, inferences based on statistical **demographics** appear to be a product of the last 200 years. In 1798, English economist **Thomas Robert Malthus** (1766–1834) published his *Essay on the Principle of Population as It Affects the Future Improvement of Society,* in which he described a worldwide future of warfare, crime, and starvation. The human population, Malthus predicted, would grow exponentially over the following decades or centuries, leading

demographics

The characteristics of population groups, usually expressed in statistical fashion.

to a shortage of needed resources, especially food. Conflict on both the interpersonal and the international levels would be the result, Malthus claimed, as individuals and groups competed for survival. View contemporary U.S. demographic data from the U.S. Census Bureau at Web Extra 2–1.

WEB
Extra
▪▪▪▪

Adolphe Quételet and André Michel Guerry

As a direct result of Malthusian thought, investigators throughout Europe began to gather "moral statistics," or social enumerations, which they thought would prove useful in measuring the degree to which crime and conflict existed in societies of the period. Such statistics were scrutinized in hopes of gauging "the moral health of nations"—a phrase commonly used throughout the period. One of the first such investigators was **André Michel Guerry** (1802–1866), who calculated per capita crime rates throughout various French provinces in the early 1800s.

In 1835, Belgian astronomer and mathematician **Adolphe Quételet** (1796–1864) published a statistical analysis of crime in a number of European countries, including Belgium, France, and Holland. Quételet set for himself the goal of assessing the degree to which crime rates vary with climate, sex, and age. He noticed what is still obvious to criminal statisticians today—that crime changes with the seasons, with many violent crimes showing an increase during the hot summer months and property crimes increasing in frequency during colder parts of the year. As a consequence of these observations, Quételet proposed what he called the "thermic law." According to the thermic law, Quételet claimed, morality undergoes seasonal variation—a proposal that stimulated widespread debate in its day.[5]

The first officially published crime statistics appeared in London's *Gazette* beginning in 1828 and in France's *Compte generale* in 1825. Soon comparisons (or what contemporary statisticians call "correlations") began to be calculated between economic conditions and the rates of various types of crime. From a study of English statistical data covering the years 1810 to 1847, Joseph Fletcher concluded that prison commitments increased as the price of wheat rose. In like fashion, German writer Georg von Mayr, whose data covered the years 1836 to 1861, discovered that the rate of theft increased with the price of rye in Bavaria.

The work of statisticians like Guerry and Quételet formed the historical basis for what has been called the **statistical school** of criminology. The statistical school foreshadowed the development of both sociological criminology and the ecological school, perspectives that are discussed in considerable detail later in this book. Learn more about contemporary social statistics in the area of criminology at Web Extra 2–2.

statistical school

Criminological perspective with roots in the early 1800s that seeks to uncover correlations between crime rates and other types of demographic data.

WEB
Extra
▪▪▪▪

Crime Statistics Today

The government-sponsored gathering of crime statistics for the nation as a whole began in the United States around 1930. Before then, most police departments kept arrest records and sometimes tabulated them. Courts kept records of cases heard, trial transcripts were often maintained, and county offices, churches, and newspapers kept records of various goings-on. Most crime information was anecdotal, however, and spread either by word of mouth, or printed in local newspapers (or both). Early news records are useful even today, and in 2001, for example, historian Douglas Eckberg studied homicide accounts from newspapers to match against county coroner records in an effort to calculate the exact number of murders that occurred in Charleston, South Carolina, between 1877 and 1878.[6]

But it wasn't until the Uniform Crime Reporting (UCR) Program was begun by the FBI in 1929 that official crime data gathering programs covering the entire United States came into being. The UCR Program developed out of a national initiative undertaken by the International Association of Chiefs of Police (IACP), whose goal it was to develop a set of uniform crime statistics for use by police agencies and policymakers throughout the country. In 1930, the U.S. Congress enacted Title 28, Section 534, of the U.S. Code,

**National Crime
Victimization Survey
(NCVS)**

A survey conducted annually by the
Bureau of Justice Statistics that
provides data on surveyed
households that report they were
affected by crime.

**Uniform Crime Reporting
Program (UCR)**

A Federal Bureau of Investigation
summation of crime statistics tallied
annually and consisting primarily of
data on crimes reported to the
police and on arrests.

**National Incident-Based
Reporting System (NIBRS)**

A new and enhanced statistical
reporting system that will collect
data on each single incident and
arrest within 22 crime categories.

which authorized the attorney general of the United States to begin gathering crime information. The attorney general designated the FBI to serve as a national clearinghouse on crime statistics, and police agencies around the country began submitting data under the UCR Program. In its initial year of operation, 400 police departments, representing cities and towns in 43 states, participated in the program.

Today's official U.S. crime statistics come from the Bureau of Justice Statistics (BJS), which conducts the annual **National Crime Victimization Survey (NCVS);** and from the Federal Bureau of Investigation (FBI), which publishes yearly data under its summary-based **Uniform Crime Reporting (UCR) Program** and its more detailed incident-driven **National Incident-Based Reporting System (NIBRS).** As we will discuss in more detail later in this chapter, NIBRS data provide a more complete picture of crimes reported and committed. Because the UCR Program is currently undergoing a transition in format that involves more complete use of NIBRS data, we refer to UCR information that is cited in this chapter as UCR/NIBRS data.

NCVS data appear in a number of annual reports, the most important of which is *Criminal Victimization in the United States.* FBI data take the form of the annual publication *Crime in the United States.* Numerous other surveys and reports are made available through the Bureau of Justice Statistics. Such surveys not only cover the incidence of crime and criminal activity in the United States but also extend to many other aspects of the criminal justice profession, including justice system expenditures, prisons and correctional data, probation and parole populations, jail inmate information, statistics on law enforcement agencies and personnel, and information on the activities of state and federal courts. These and other reports are generally made available free of charge to interested parties through the National Criminal Justice Reference Service (NCJRS), which is located in Rockville, Maryland.[7] Visit the Bureau of Justice Statistics via **Web Extra 2–3.** NCJRS is available via **Web Extra 2–4** at crimtoday.com.

The largest collection of statistics about all aspects of American crime and criminal justice is BJS's *Sourcebook of Criminal Justice Statistics,* which is compiled yearly by the Bureau of Justice Statistics and made available in various formats. The *Sourcebook* consists of approximately 800 tables, covering crime and criminal justice in the United States. *Sourcebook* information is a compilation of statistics from many different places and includes much of the data found in the aforementioned publications, *Crime in the United States* and *Criminal Victimization in the United States.* Under sponsorship of the BJS Utilization Project, the *Sourcebook* is available online through collaboration with the Hindelang Criminal Justice Research Center School of Criminal Justice of the University at Albany (SUNY), in Albany, New York. The *Sourcebook,* which is continually updated, may be accessed online via **Web Extra 2–5** at crimtoday.com. View the latest version of BJS's *Criminal Victimization in the United States* at **Library Extra 2–1;** and read the FBI's most recent uniform crime reporting data at **Library Extra 2–2.**

Other crime-related and criminal justice information sources include the National Archive of Criminal Justice Data, operated by the Interuniversity Consortium for Political and Social Research (ICPSR) in Ann Arbor, Michigan (which is described in greater detail in the Web Quest section at the end of Chapter 3); the Justice Statistics Clearinghouse (part of BJS); the Justice Research and Statistics Association; the Bureau of Justice Assistance Clearinghouse; the Police Executive Research Forum (PERF); the Police Foundation; the Data Resources Program of the National Criminal Justice Reference Service; and the SEARCH Group, Inc. These and other sites can be easily located on the Web via the Prentice Hall Cybrary at www.cybrary.info.

WEB
Extra
■ ■ ■ ■

LIBRARY
Extra
■ ■ ■ ■

Programmatic Problems with Available Data

This chapter will describe crime in the United States, or what some authors call "the crime picture" in America, using information derived from the latest BJS and FBI reports. It is important to realize at the outset, however, that the nature of the information provided by these two agencies differs significantly. In recognition of these difficulties, a Uniform Crime Reporting program release begins with these words: "Data users are

New York City resident Brynn Jarosh helps light candles during a commemorative ceremony marking the destruction of the World Trade Center on September 11, 2001, by Islamic terrorists. Terrorism is a criminal act and may involve mass murder, arson, destruction of property, kidnapping, hijacking, conspiracy, and other offenses. How might criminologists help prevent future acts of terrorism?

Source: AP Wide World Photos

cautioned against comparisons of crime trends presented in this report and those estimated by the National Crime Victimization Survey (NCVS), administered by the Bureau of Justice Statistics. Because of differences in methodology and crime coverage, the two programs examine the nation's crime problem from somewhat different perspectives, and their results are not strictly comparable. The definitional and procedural differences can account for many of the apparent discrepancies in results from the two programs."[8]

The UCR/NIBRS and the NCVS each use their own specialized definitions in deciding which events should be scored as crimes. Sometimes the definitions vary considerably between programs, and none of the definitions used by the reporting agencies are strictly based on federal or state statutory crime classifications.

The UCR Program

Early UCR data were structured in terms of seven major offense categories: murder, rape, robbery, aggravated assault, burglary, larceny, and motor vehicle theft. These crimes, called **Part I offenses,** when averaged together and compared with the country's population, formed the FBI's Crime Index. The Crime Index provided a crime rate that could be compared over time and from one geographic location to another. Rates of crime under the UCR/NIBRS Program are generally expressed as "x number of offenses per 100,000 people." The 2006 rate of criminal homicide, for example, was 5.7 murders for every 100,000 people in the U.S. population.

In 1979, Congress mandated that arson be added to the list of major crimes offenses. Unfortunately, the inclusion of arson as an eighth index offense made it difficult to compare pre- and post-1979 Crime Indexes. For this and other reasons, the FBI officially discontinued use of the term *crime index* beginning with its report of crime data for 2005.[9]

In today's UCR/NIBRS reports, Part I offenses are subdivided into two categories: violent personal crimes (consisting of murder, rape, robbery, and aggravated assault) and property crimes (consisting of burglary, larceny, motor vehicle theft, and arson). Table 2–1 lists Part I offenses, showing the number of crimes reported to the police in 2006. UCR/NIBRS trend data since 1960 are shown graphically in Figure 2–1.

Part I offenses

The crimes of murder, rape, robbery, aggravated assault, burglary, larceny, and motor vehicle theft, as defined under the FBI's Uniform Crime Reporting Program.

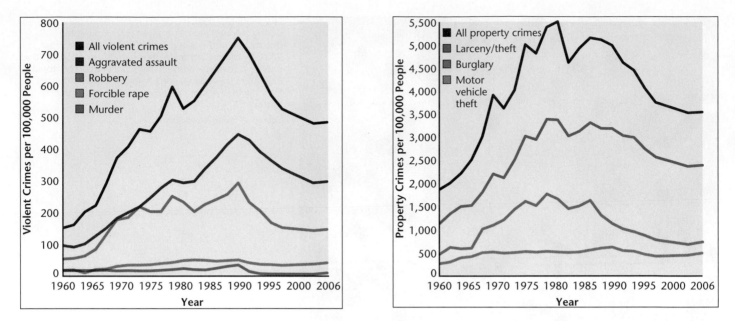

FIGURE 2–1

Recorded Rates of Major Crimes, 1960–2006 (UCR/NIBRS)

Source: Federal Bureau of Investigation, *Crime in the United States.*

TABLE 2–1	Major Crimes Known to the Police, 2006 (UCR/NIBRS Part I Offenses)

Offense	Number	Rate Per 100,000	Clearance Rate (%)
Personal/Violent Crimes			
Murder	17,034	5.7	60.7
Forcible rape	92,455	30.5	40.9
Robbery	447,403	149.4	25.2
Aggravated assault	860,853	287.5	54.0
Property Crimes			
Burglary	2,183,746	729.4	12.6
Larceny	6,607,013	2,206.9	17.4
Motor vehicle theft	1,192,809	398.4	12.6
Arson	69,055	26.8	18.0
U.S. total	**11,470,368**	**3,834.5**	

Note: Totals include arson, an offense not normally shown in official FBI totals of Part I offenses.
Source: Federal Bureau of Investigation, *Crime in the United States, 2006.*

Each year, when the FBI issues its annual report, *Crime in the United States,* it includes information within each Part I offense category on the percentage of crimes that have been "cleared." *Cleared crimes* are those for which an arrest has been made or for which the perpetrator is known but an arrest is not possible (as when the offender is deceased or is out of the country). Cleared crimes are also referred to as "solved," although clearances as counted by the FBI have nothing to do with successful in-court prosecution. Hence, those charged with a crime that is scored as cleared by the FBI may not yet have been adjudicated. In official UCR/NIBRS terminology, a Part I offense is regarded as cleared or solved when (1) "a law enforcement agency has charged at least one person with the offense" or (2) "a suspect has been identified and located and an arrest is justified, but action is prevented by circumstances outside law enforcement control." Clearance rates are reported for each Part I crime category. A **clearance rate** is the proportion of reported or discovered crimes within a given offense category that are solved.

clearance rate

The proportion of reported or discovered crimes within a given offense category that are solved.

Problems with the UCR Program

The most significant methodological feature of the Uniform Crime Reporting Program is indicated by its name. It is a *reporting* program. In other words, only crimes that are reported to the police (or that are discovered by the police or by others who then report them to the police) are included in the statistics compiled by the program. Unless someone complains to the police about a criminal incident, it will go unreported and will not appear in UCR Program reports. Most complaints are made by victims.

Because UCR/NIBRS data are based on *reported* crime, the program has been criticized for seriously underestimating the true incidence of criminal activity within the United States—a measurement that would also include unreported crimes. Unreported and underreported criminal activity has been called the **dark figure of crime.** Some experts say, for example, that rape is the most underreported crime in the FBI data, with four to five times as many rapes occurring each year as are reported. Reasons for not reporting a crime like rape are numerous and include (1) fear of the perpetrator; (2) shame, which may carry over from traditional attitudes about sexual behavior and a woman's role in sexual encounters; (3) fears the victim may have of not being believed; and (4) fear of further participation in the justice system, as when a victim is required to go to court and testify against the offender, thereby exposing herself to potentially embarrassing cross-examination and public scrutiny.

dark figure of crime

The numerical total of unreported crimes that are not reflected in official crime statistics.

Although rape is indeed seriously underreported (a conclusion drawn from comparison of NCVS and UCR/NIBRS rape statistics), many other crimes are underreported as well. The most seriously underreported crime may be larceny because the theft of small items may never make it into official police reports.

NIBRS: The New UCR Data Format

Recently, the Uniform Crime Reporting Program has undergone a number of significant changes, and more are scheduled to be implemented shortly as a new, enhanced, incident-driven crime-reporting system, funded in part by the federal Crime Identification Technology Act of 1998,[10] is phased in. The new system, the National Incident-Based Reporting System (NIBRS), revises the definitions of a number of offenses for reporting purposes, but its incident-driven nature is its most important feature. "Incident-driven" means that the FBI will use the new system to collect detailed data on the circumstances surrounding each serious criminal incident. The NIBRS data-collection format focuses on each single incident and arrest within 22 crime categories, with incident, victim, property, offender, and arrestee information being gathered when available. The 22 NIBRS crime categories are, in turn, made up of 46 specific crimes called "Group A offenses" (as compared with only eight major offenses on which the old UCR Program gathered data). In addition to Group A offenses, there are 11 Group B offense categories for which only arrest data are reported. The goal of NIBRS is to make data on reported crime more useful by relating them more completely than the old system did to other available information, such as victim and offender characteristics.[11]

NIBRS reports are much more detailed than those previously provided under the UCR Program. Under the older summary-based UCR Program, for example, whenever an aggravated assault occurred, the police department under whose jurisdiction it came recorded merely one instance of aggravated assault. Under NIBRS, however, that same department is now asked to collect (1) information about the offense (including the type of location where it occurred, whether a weapon was involved or used, whether the perpetrator was under the influence of drugs or alcohol, and whether there was a racial, religious, or gender-based motivation behind the offense), (2) information about the parties involved (including such demographics as sex, age, and race of both victim and offender; any known relationship between victim and offender; and circumstances that might have motivated the crime, such as an argument), and (3) information about the property (if any) involved (including the value of any property damaged, seized, or stolen as a consequence of the offense).

The Justice Research and Statistics Association (JRSA) has identified the many advantages of incident-based crime-reporting systems over summary-based crime-reporting systems:[12]

- Data collection is not restricted to a limited number of offense categories.
- Offense definitions can meet local, state, and national reporting needs.
- Details on individual crime incidents (offenses, offenders, victims, property, and arrests) can be collected and analyzed.
- Arrests and clearances can be linked to specific incidents or offenses.
- All offenses in an incident can be recorded and counted (in contrast, with the hierarchy rule used in the FBI Uniform Crime Reports, only the most serious offense that occurs during a criminal incident is counted—regardless of what other crimes may have been committed).
- Additional crime-scoring categories, such as crimes against society, can be created.
- Distinctions can be made between attempted and completed crimes.
- Linkages can be established between variables for examining interrelationships among offenses, offenders, victims, property, and arrestees.
- Detailed crime analyses can be made within and across law enforcement jurisdictions.
- Regional law enforcement agencies can share information easily.
- Strategic and tactical crime analyses can be made at the local and regional levels.

WEB
Extra

Learn more by visiting JRSA at Web Extra 2–6.

Although the FBI began accepting crime incident data from state reporting agencies in NIBRS format in 1989, the transition process toward full NIBRS reporting is not moving as quickly as planned. The NIBRS was originally scheduled to be fully in place by 1999. However, delays continue to occur in some areas. According to recent FBI press releases, NIBRS will be implemented "at a pace commensurate with the resources, abilities, and limitations of the contributing law enforcement agencies."

A sample of NIBRS data can be viewed at Web Extra 2–7. To learn more about the effects of NIBRS on crime statistics, including comparisons of older FBI crime data with NIBRS data, see Web Extra 2–8. Table 2–2 shows how NIBRS offense definitions differ from traditional UCR definitions, and you can learn more about such definitional differences at Web Extra 2–9 at crimtoday.com. Finally, the Bureau of Justice Statistics provides an NIBRS information page, which is accessible via Web Extra 2–10.

WEB
Extra

Hate Crimes

hate crime

A criminal offense in which the motive is hatred, bias, or prejudice based on the actual or perceived race, color, religion, national origin, ethnicity, gender, or sexual orientation of another individual or group of individuals.

An important recent change in the UCR Program involves the collection of **hate crime** statistics, and was mandated by the U.S. Congress with passage of the Hate Crime Statistics Act of 1990.[13] Under the law, the FBI is required to serve as a repository for data collected on crimes motivated by religious, ethnic, racial, or sexual orientation prejudice. The Violent Crime Control and Law Enforcement Act of 1994[14] mandated the addition to the hate crimes category of crimes motivated by biases against people with disabilities, and the UCR Program began reporting such crimes in 1997.

According to the Bureau of Justice Statistics, hate crimes, also called "bias crimes," are crimes characterized by "manifest evidence of prejudice based on race, religion, sexual orientation, or ethnicity, including where appropriate the crimes of murder, non-negligent

TABLE 2–2	**Definitional Differences Among the Traditional UCR, UCR/NIBRS, and NCVS**		
Offense	**Traditional UCR**	**UCR/NIBRS**	**NCVS**
Murder and nonnegligent manslaughter	The unlawful killing of a human being.	The willful (nonneligent) killing of one human being by another.	NA
Forcible sex offense	NA	Any sexual act directed against another person, forcibly and/or against that person's will; or not forcibly or against the person's will where the victim is incapable of giving consent. Forcible rape, forcible sodomy, sexual assault with an object, and forcible fondling are included in this category.	NA
Forcible rape	The carnal knowledge of a female, forcibly and against her will.	The carnal knowledge of a person, forcibly and/or against that person's will; or not forcibly or against the person's will where the victim is incapable of giving consent because of his/her temporary or permanent mental or physical incapacity or because of his/her youth.	Carnal knowledge through the use of force or threat of force, including attempts. Rape includes victimization of both males and females.
Sexual assault	NA	NA	A wide range of victimizations, separate from rape or attempted rape. These crimes include attacks or attempted attacks generally involving unwanted sexual contact between victim and offender. Sexual assaults may or may not involve force and include such things as grabbing or fondling. Sexual assault also includes verbal threats.
Robbery	The unlawful taking or attempted taking of property that is in the immediate possession of another by force or threat of force or violence and/or by putting the victim in fear.	The taking of or attempting to take anything of value under confrontational circumstances from the control, custody, or care of another person by force or threat of force or violence and/or by putting the victim in fear of immediate harm.	Completed or attempted theft, directly from a person, of property or cash by force or threat of force, with or without a weapon.
Assault	An unlawful attack by one person upon another.	An unlawful attack by one person upon another.	An attack without a weapon resulting either in minor injury or in undetermined injury requiring less than two days' hospitalization, including attempted assault without a weapon and verbal threats of assault.
Aggravated assault	The unlawful attack by one person upon another for the purpose of inflicting severe or aggravated	The unlawful attack by one person upon another wherein the offender uses a weapon or displays it in a threatening	An attack or attempted attack with a weapon, regardless of whether or not an injury occurred, and an attack

(*continued*)

TABLE 2–2 *(Continued)*

Offense	Traditional UCR	UCR/NIBRS	NCVS
	bodily injury; this type of assault usually is accompanied by the use of a weapon or by means likely to produce death or great bodily harm.	manner, or the victim suffers obvious severe or aggravated bodily injury involving apparent broken bones, loss of teeth, possible internal injury, severe laceration, or loss of consciousness. This also includes assault with disease (as in cases when the offender is aware that he/she is infected with a deadly disease and deliberately attempts to inflict the disease by biting, spitting, etc.).	without a weapon when serious injury results.
Burglary	The unlawful entry of a structure to commit a felony or a theft (excludes tents, trailers, and other mobile units used for recreational purposes).	The unlawful entry of a structure with intent to commit a felony or a theft (excludes tents, trailers, and other mobile units used for recreational purposes).	The unlawful or forcible entry or attempted entry of a residence, garage, shed, or other structure on the premises, usually but not always involving theft.
Larcency-theft	The unlawful taking or attempted taking, carrying, leading, or riding away of property from the possession or constructive possession of another. Motor vehicles are excluded.	The unlawful taking or attempted taking, carrying, leading, or riding away of property from the possession or constructive possession of another. Motor vehicles are excluded.	Completed or attempted theft of property or cash without personal contact.
Motor vehicle theft	The theft or attempted theft of a motor vehicle. *Motor vehicle* is defined as a self-propelled vehicle that runs on land surface and not on rails. This offense category includes the stealing of automobiles, trucks, buses, motorcycles, motor scooters, snowmobiles, etc. It does not include farm equipment, bulldozers, airplanes, construction equipment, or motorboats.	The theft of a motor vehicle. *Motor vehicle* is defined as a self-propelled vehicle that runs on land surface and not on rails. This offense category includes the stealing of automobiles, trucks, buses, motorcycles, motor scooters, snowmobiles, etc. It does not include farm equipment, bulldozers, airplanes, construction equipment, or motorboats.	The stealing or unauthorized taking of a motor vehicle, including attempted thefts.
Arson	The burning or attempted burning of property with or without intent to defraud.	NA	NA

NA = Not Applicable

Source: Ramona R. Rantala, *Effects of NIBRS on Crime Statistics* (Washington, DC: Bureau of Justice Statistics, 2000).

manslaughter, forcible rape, aggravated assault, simple assault, intimidation, arson, and destruction, damage, or vandalism of property."[15]

Based on FBI statistics on hate crimes, 7,489 hate crime incidents were reported in 2006.[16] These incidents involved 9,100 victims, with 70% of the incidents involving a single victim. Since a single incident may involve multiple offenses, it is important to state also that the 7,489 reported incidents accounted for a total of 8,715 chargeable offenses. Slightly more than one-half of these incidents were motivated by racial bias (52.5%), 16.4% by religious bias, 16.4% by bias based on sexual orientation, and 14.2% by bias based on ethnicity or national origin. Crimes against the person represented 63.3% of all reported offenses, with intimidation being the most commonly reported personal offense at 49.7%, followed by simple assault at 32.7%. In the crimes-against-property category, vandalism or destruction of property was the most frequently occurring type of hate offense. Murder accounted for only 0.1% of all hate crimes; a total of 13 people were killed in 2006 because the offender was motivated by hate.

The Role of Hate Groups

Hate groups like the Ku Klux Klan (KKK), the Aryan Nations, the National Alliance, and the Identity church movement have existed for many years and have long been associated with acts of violence. It is easy to classify groups within the hate-group category when their fundamental purpose is grounded in prejudice. In the case of some other groups, however, classification is not as easy. Are all militia groups hate groups? Given its anti-Semitic position, for example, does the Nation of Islam, led by Louis Farrakhan, qualify as a hate group? The Anti-Defamation League seemed to think so when, some years ago, it officially protested Farrakhan's appearance on the TV show *Meet the Press.* In an interview with NBC's Tim Russert, Farrakhan blamed Jews for controlling and oppressing blacks, saying, "They are the greatest controllers of Black minds, Black intelligence." Following the interview, Abraham H. Foxman, national director of the Anti-Defamation League, wrote a letter to Bob Wright, president of the National Broadcasting Corporation, complaining that "interviews such as yesterday's give unwarranted status to Farrakhan as a Black leader while offering him an opportunity to propagate his message of hate which we have all heard before."[17]

We might ask, however, whether hate groups are a necessary feature of hate crimes. Citing a wide array of research studies, James B. Jacobs and Kimberly A. Potter found that "the vast majority of reported hate crimes are not committed by organized hate groups and their members, but by teenagers, primarily white males, acting alone or in a group."[18] Visit the National Criminal Justice Reference Service's "Hate Crime Resources" page via **Web Extra 2–11** and the Anti-Defamation League's "Combating Hate" page at **Web Extra 2–12** to learn more about hate crimes. View the latest FBI statistics on hate crimes via **Library Extra 2–3** at crimtoday.com.

WEB
Extra

LIBRARY
Extra

Data Gathering under the NCVS

Another major national crime statistics-gathering program, the NCVS, began collecting data in 1972. It differs from FBI-supported programs in one especially significant way: Rather than depending on reports of crimes to the police, the data contained in the NCVS consist of information elicited through interviews with members of randomly selected households throughout the nation. Hence, the NCVS uncovers a large number of crimes that may not have been reported, and it is therefore regarded by many researchers as a more accurate measure of the actual incidence of crime in the United States than the UCR/NIBRS. NCVS data are gathered by U.S. Census Bureau personnel who survey approximately 42,000 households consisting of about 76,000 people age 12 and older. Interviews are conducted at six-month intervals, with individual households rotating out of the sample every three years. New households are continually added to the sample to replace those that have been dropped.

NCVS interviewers collect individual and household victimization data from anyone 12 years old or older at residences within the sample. Questions are about the incidence of rape, personal robbery, aggravated and simple assault, household burglary,

Students at Guilford College in North Carolina rally against bigotry following an attack on three Palestinian students. How do law enforcement officials identify hate crimes?

Source: Lynn Hey/News & Record/ Library

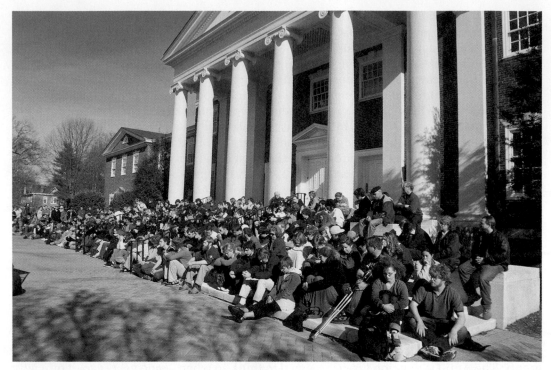

personal and household theft, and motor vehicle theft as they have affected household members during the past six months. Information is gathered on victims (including sex, age, race, ethnicity, marital status, income, and educational level), offenders (sex, age, race, and relationship to the victim), and crimes (time and place of occurrence, use of weapons, nature of injury, and economic consequences of the criminal activity for the victim). Questions also cover self-protective measures employed by victims, the possibility of substance abuse by offenders, and the level of previous experience victims may have had with the criminal justice system. Finally, interviewed victims are asked to describe and assess law enforcement response to victimizations that were reported to the police. Unlike the UCR/NIBRS, the NCVS does not measure criminal homicide, arson, or crimes against businesses (such as shoplifting, burglaries of stores, robberies of gas stations and convenience stores, and credit card and commercial fraud). Similarly, the NCVS does not attempt to uncover, nor does it report, crimes against children under 12 years of age.

The NCVS instrument is well designed, and data gatherers are thoroughly schooled in interviewing techniques. NCVS interviewers are trained, for example, not to inadvertently lead, or "coach," respondents into supplying doubtful information and not to spend an excess amount of time making small talk with respondents. Questions used by the survey, however, are designed to elicit information about crimes that may not be in the forefront of the respondent's mind. Following are a few typical survey questions:

- Was anything stolen from you while you were away from home, for instance at work, in a theater or restaurant, or while traveling? (If "yes," how many times?)

- (Other than any incidents you've already mentioned) was anything (else) at all stolen from you during the last six months? (If "yes," how many times?)

- Did you find any evidence that someone *attempted* to steal something that belonged to you (other than any incidents already mentioned)? (If "yes," how many times?)

- Did you call the police during the last six months to report something that happened to *you* which you thought was a crime? (Do not count any calls made to the police concerning the incidents you have just told me about.) (If "yes," what happened?)

- Did anything happen to *you* during the last six months which you thought was a crime but did *not* report to the police (other than incidents already mentioned)? (If "yes," what happened?)

The number of victimizations counted by the NCVS for any single reported criminal occurrence is based on the number of people victimized by the event. Hence, a robbery may have more than one victim and will be so reported in NCVS data. Although this distinction is applied to personal crimes, households are treated as individual units, and all household crimes are counted only once, no matter how many members the household contains.

NCVS Findings

The next few sections of this chapter present data from the UCR/NIBRS, and NCVS in narrative form. Some of the more general findings from recent NCVS reports, however, reveal a number of consistent and interesting patterns:[19]

- About 16 million violent and property victimizations occur annually throughout the United States, including about 12.1 million property crimes and 3.7 million violent crimes.
- Approximately 16 million households (16% of the total) experience one or more violent or property crimes each year.
- A violent crime against a person age 12 or older occurs in 3% of U.S. households every year.
- Overall, violent victimization and property crime rates are currently among the lowest recorded since the inception of the NCVS in 1973 and are about half of what they were in 1993.
- Males suffer violent victimization significantly more often than females, and rates of violent victimization for both males and female adults decline with age.
- Females are most often victimized by someone they know, while males are more likely to be victimized by a stranger.
- About 440,000 cases of intimate partner violence occur annually.
- African American residents experience higher rates of violent victimization than do persons identifying themselves as Hispanic, while whites experience the lowest rates of violent victimization.
- Generally speaking, rates of violent victimization decline as household income rises, and members of lower-income families are more likely to become victims of violent crimes than are members of middle- and upper-income families.
- About 7% of violent crime victims face an offender armed with a firearm.
- The chance of violent criminal victimization is significantly higher among young African American men than among any other segment of the population.
- Though all social groups experienced significant decreases in property crime over the past few decades, some groups experienced greater rate declines than others. Households that rent showed smaller declines than households that own homes, and households with annual incomes greater than $50,000 experienced larger drops in property crime rates than did households with lower incomes.
- Urban residents experience the highest rates of crime, while lower crime rates characterize suburban areas, and rural residents face still lower rates.

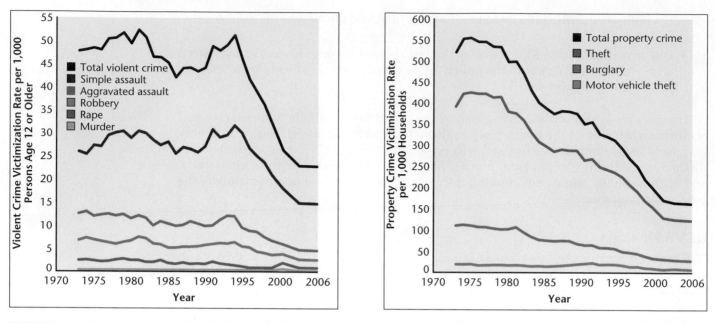

FIGURE 2–2

Major Crime–Rates from the NCVS, 1973–2006

Source: Bureau of Justice Statistics, National Crime Victimization Survey (various years).

- Victims report about half of the violent crimes and about 40% of the property crimes that they experience to the police.

- Violent crimes against females are more likely to be reported to police than those against males, and African American females are the most likely of all to report violent victimization when it occurs.

It is important to note that NCVS-reported rates of violent victimization declined significantly in all categories beginning around the mid-1990s and that rates of property crime began declining even earlier. NCVS victimization rates for both violent crimes and property crimes throughout the United States for the years 1973 through 2006 are shown in Figure 2–2.

The decline in victimization rates noted by the NCVS in recent years is especially noteworthy because it contrasts with continuing high concern about crime among the general public, as reported in Chapter 1. Increased levels of public concern about crime may, however, be explained by four factors: (1) a persistent media focus on stranger-precipitated violent crime and random acts of violence and on the seeming inability of the criminal justice system to protect innocent victims; (2) a continuation of the "war on drugs" and the ongoing publicity associated with drug arrests; (3) the sense that crime rates are just "taking a breather" and that they retain explosive potential, which could manifest should American neighborhoods drop their guard; and (4) an increased fear of terrorism and terrorism-related crimes.

Critique of the NCVS

Just as the UCR/NIBRS has been criticized for underestimating the actual incidence of criminal activity within the United States, the NCVS can be criticized for possible over-reporting. No comprehensive attempt is made to verify the actual occurrence of any of the crimes reported to NCVS interviewers. Hence, no reliable measure exists of the number of crimes that might be falsely reported or of the number of crimes that might be underreported in NCVS data. Although the proportion is not known, it is likely that some individuals, when approached by NCVS interviewers, may be unable to resist embellishing crime reports pertaining to their households and may even concoct criminal incidence data for purposes of self-aggrandizement or in an attempt to please the interviewer by providing copious amounts of data.

As previously noted, NCVS data-gathering efforts began in 1972. Hence, the program is much newer than the FBI's UCR Program, and comparisons of officially reported crimes with levels of self-reported victimization are unavailable for the years before 1973. As with the UCR/NIBRS, definitions of crimes measured by the NCVS do not necessarily correspond to any federal or state statutes or to definitions used for other purposes, making comparisons with other state and federal crime records difficult. Complicating matters still further, changes in NCVS categories have resulted in the inability to easily compare NCVS findings of even a decade ago with current NCVS data.[20]

Patterns of Change

Since official crime statistics were first gathered beginning around 1930, there have been three major shifts in crime rates. The first occurred during the early 1940s and was due to the outbreak of the Second World War. This was a time when crime decreased sharply due to the large number of young men who entered military service. Young males make up the most "crime-prone" segment of the population, and their removal to the European and Pacific theaters of war did much to lower crime rates at home. From 1933 to 1941, the Crime Index declined from 770 to 508 offenses per every 100,000 members of the American population.[21]

The second significant shift in offense statistics was a dramatic increase in most forms of crime that began in the 1960s and ended in the 1990s. Many criminologists believe that this shift also had a link to World War II. With the end of the war and the return of millions of young men to civilian life, birth rates skyrocketed between 1945 and 1955, creating a postwar baby boom. By 1960, baby boomers were entering their teenage years. A disproportionate number of young people in the U.S. population produced a dramatic increase in most major crimes.

Other factors contributed to the increase in reported crime during the same period. Modified reporting requirements, which reduced victims' stress associated with filing police reports, and the publicity associated with the rise in crime sensitized victims to the importance of reporting. Crimes that may have gone undetected in the past began to figure more prominently in official statistics. Similarly, the growing professionalization of some police departments resulted in more accurate and increased data collection, making some of the most progressive departments appear to be associated with the largest crime increases.[22] Finally, the 1960s were tumultuous years, punctuated as they were by the Vietnam War, a vibrant civil rights struggle, the heady growth of secularism, dramatic increases in the divorce rate, diverse forms of "liberation," and the influx of psychedelic and other drugs. As a consequence, social norms were blurred, and group control over individual behavior declined substantially. The "normless" quality of American society in the 1960s was also a likely contributor to the rise in crime. According to the FBI, from 1960 to 1980, crime rates rose from 1,887 to 5,950 offenses per every 100,000 members of the U.S. population.

Crime rates recorded by the FBI continued their upward swing, with the exception of a brief decline in the early 1980s, when postwar boomers began to "age out" of the crime-prone years and American society emerged from the cultural drift that had characterized the previous 20 years. About the same time, however, an increase in drug-related criminal activity led crime rates to soar once again, especially in the area of violent crime. Crime rates peaked about 1991 and have since shown a third major shift, with decreases in the rates of most major crimes being reported since that time. Between 1991 and 2006, the crime rate decreased from 5,897 to 3,835 offenses per every 100,000 citizens, sending it down to levels not seen since 1975.

Decreases in crime since the mid-1990s may have been largely due to an "aging out" of the post–World War II baby-boomer generation (members of which are now mostly too old to continue active criminal lifestyles), new strict laws, expanded justice system and police funding, changes in crime-fighting technologies, and economic factors, as well as to the advent (and widespread implementation) of family-planning practices beginning around 1900.

Such practices include development of the birth control pill and the legalization of abortion, which kept birth rates relatively low among members of the boomer generation and may have especially affected birth rates among members of economically disadvantaged groups.[23] Economists John J. Donohue and Steven D. Levitt, in a detailed study of the effects of legalized abortion on rates of offending, found that legalized abortion contributed significantly to recently observed reductions in crime.[24] Donohue and Levitt noted that "crime began to fall roughly 18 years after abortion legalization." They found that "the 5 states that allowed abortion in 1970 experienced declines earlier than the rest of the nation, which was legalized in 1973 with *Roe* v. *Wade.* States with high abortion rates in the 1970s and 1980s experienced greater crime reductions in the 1990s. In high abortion states, only arrests of those born after abortion legalization fall relative to low abortion states." According to Donohue and Levitt, "Legalized abortion appears to account for as much as 50 percent of the recent drop in crime." Their findings are disputed by some who find them suggestive of a conspiracy of oppression targeted at the socially disadvantaged.

The most significant contributors to crime's decline, however, may have been economic and demographic factors that were largely beyond the control of policymakers. In a cogent analysis of the factors contributing to the crime drop of the 1990s, for example, Canadian criminologist Marc Ouimet notes that both the United States and Canada experienced similar downward trends in the rates of major crimes during the 1990s.[25] From 1991 to 1999, for example, homicide rates declined by 42% in the United States and 43% in Canada; cases of reported sexual assault decreased by 23% and 31%, respectively; robbery decreased by 22% and 23%; and burglary rates dropped by 38% in the United States and 35% in Canada.

The criminal justice policies and practices of the two countries during the period could hardly have been more different. In striking contrast to the United States, which dramatically increased spending on policing and correctional services, Canada was budgeting about the same number of dollars for justice system activities at the end of the 1990s as it had at the start of that decade. In fact, says Ouimet, "the growth in the budget of [Canadian] justice-related organizations was below the level of inflation." As a consequence of such differences in spending, the number of police officers in the United States increased by 20% between 1991 and 1999, while it fell by 3% in Canada. Similarly, because Americans passed ever-tougher criminal legislation, while Canadians did not, the incarceration rate climbed by 42% in the United States during the period, while it went down by 3% in Canada.

Two things that the United States and Canada *did* have in common during the 1990s were economic expansion and a significant shift in demographics caused by an aging of the population. During the period, unemployment decreased by 36% in the United States and 27% in Canada, while the number of people aged 20 to 34 declined by 18% in both countries. Ouimet concludes that the ready availability of jobs combined with demographic shifts in the population—and not the official efforts of policymakers—to produce a noteworthy decrease in crime during the 1990s.

While the more than ten-year decline in crime that took place beginning in 1991 is noteworthy, it did not even begin to bring the overall rate of crime in this country anywhere close to the low crime rates characteristic of the early 1940s and the 1950s. From a long-term perspective, even with recent declines, crime rates in this country remain more than seven times what they were in 1940.

Recent evidence seems to indicate that the decline in crime is ending, and that we may be on the cusp of a new cycle of increased crime. Some criminologists think that recent economic uncertainty, an increased jobless rate among unskilled workers, the growing number of ex-convicts who are back on the streets, the recent growth in the teenage population in this country, the increasing influence of gangs, copycat crimes, and the lingering social disorganization brought on by natural disasters like Hurricane Katrina in 2005 may lead to sustained increases in crime.[26] "We're probably done seeing declines in crime rates for some time to come," says Jack Riley, director of the Public Safety and Justice Program at RAND Corporation in Santa Monica, California. "The question," says Riley, "is how strong and how fast will those rates [rise], and what tools do we have at our disposal to get ahead of the curve."[27] Learn more about changing crime rates and how crime rates are measured via **Library Extra 2–4** at crimtoday.com.

LIBRARY
Extra
■ ■ ■ ■

Crime in the News

Dozens of U.S. Cities See a Jump in Violent Crime

WASHINGTON—Less than a month after the FBI reported that violent crime rates rose across the nation in 2005, there is fresh evidence that homicides and robberies are continuing to increase in dozens of cities.

A review of 55 cities' crime data from the first six months of this year indicates the overall number of homicides rose by 4.2% compared with the same period in 2005, according to the Police Executive Research Forum, a police advocacy group. In a report Thursday, the group also said robberies rose nearly 10% and that aggravated assaults were up slightly.

The report is the latest turn in a debate over whether the U.S. government has neglected local law enforcement needs by directing tens of millions of dollars to anti-terrorism initiatives. The police executives' group has been among those pressing for more police funding to counter rising numbers of violent incidents involving gangs and drugs. Among other things, the group has cited the FBI's report last month that detailed a 1.8% increase in the nation's murder rate in 2005, after a two-decade low in 2004.

Chuck Wexler of the police group said Thursday's report is an "early warning" that many cities could be at "the front end of a tipping point of violent crime."

While emphasizing the need to prevent terrorism, the Justice Department has acknowledged that crime is continuing to rise in some cities this year. However, Deputy Attorney General Paul McNulty and other officials say it is too soon to tell whether the increases are a significant departure from the historically low crime rates of the past decade.

Of the 55 cities surveyed by the police group, 10 had double-digit percentage increases in homicides. More than 40 cities reported jumps in robberies. Among them:

- Orlando had 30 homicides in the first six months of the year, up from seven during the same period in 2005. Orlando police Sgt. Barbara Jones says about 60% of this year's slayings have been linked to drugs.

- In Memphis, homicides rose 43.6%, robberies were up 35% and aggravated assaults rose 7.4% in the first six months of 2006, compared with the same period last year. Tom Kirby of the Memphis and Shelby County Crime Commission cites gangs that have had turf battles and preyed on immigrant communities.

U.S. Rep. Frank Wolf, R-Va., chairman of the House Appropriations panel that oversees the Justice Department, called Thursday's report "staggering." He urged Robert Portman, head of the Office of Management and Budget, to meet with police officials "to better understand their needs."

Homicides have declined in some cities in 2006, the report said. Among them: Dallas, Chicago, Kansas City, Milwaukee, Norfolk and Washington, D.C.

Discussion Questions

1. Why did the FBI report show an apparent rise in violent crime in some cities, but not in others? What differences between cities might account for the observed differences in crime rate changes?

2. What does it mean to say that the report cited here is an "early warning" that many cities could be at "the front end of a tipping point of violent crime"? How will we know when and if that "tipping point" has been reached?

Los Angeles Sheriff's Department deputies and Compton Fire Department personnel work at the scene of a shooting in Compton, California. Crime statistics have shown an upsurge in violent crime over the past two years. What do you think accounts for the increase?

Source: Bob Riha, Jr., USA Today

Source: Kevin Johnson, "Dozens of Cities See Jump in Murders, Robberies," *USA Today,* October 12, 2006, http://www.usatoday.com/news/nation/2006-10-12-violent-crime_x.htm. Reprinted with permission.

For the latest crime and justice news, visit www.crimenews.info.

The Crime Problem

Some people find it more meaningful to speak of the crime *problem* rather than the crime *rate*. They ask, Do crime rates provide an accurate measure of the extent of the crime problem in the United States? To answer this question, we might ask another one: Are U.S. crime rates really on the decline? While official statistics would seem to say yes, it is important to realize that official rates are based only on a highly select group of crimes chosen by the FBI and the Bureau of Justice Statistics. Drug offenses, for which arrests continue to increase (see Figure 2–3), are not included in the FBI's crime rate calculations and play no direct role in NCVS-reported victimization rates. A significant and ongoing increase in drug-related arrests, combined with widely popular "get tough on crime" initiatives (discussed in Chapter 15), has accounted for a substantial increase in our country's correctional populations (see Figure 2–4). This increase in correctional populations has been all the more surprising for many because it has occurred during a time of officially declining rates of crime. As a consequence, some criminologists question whether the size of our nation's correctional populations, rather than our traditional emphasis on crime rates, might not provide a truer picture of the crime problem in the United States.

FIGURE 2–3

Arrests for Drug Abuse Violations by Age, 1970–2006

Source: Federal Bureau of Investigation, *Crime in the United States.*

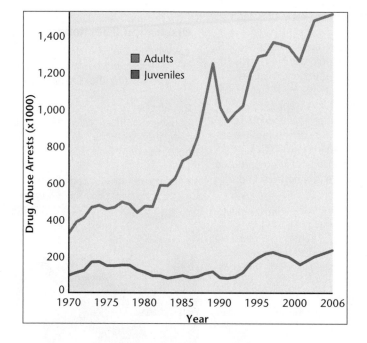

FIGURE 2–4

Adult Correctional Populations in the United States, 1980–2006

Source: Bureau of Justice Statistics, *Correctional Populations in the United States,* (Washington, DC: U.S. Government Printing Office, various years).

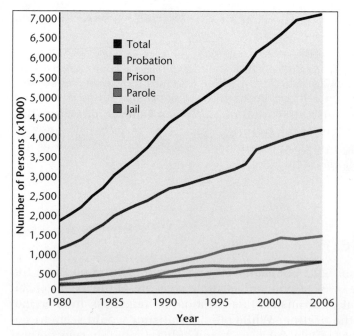

Crime in World Context

Crime rates, no matter how they are figured, might not provide an accurate assessment of the actual extent of the crime problem in any society, especially if rates are computed without regard to an international context. Noted criminologist **Elliott Currie,** for example, says that while Americans seem smugly satisfied that crime rates are going down, a close examination of international crime rates reveals that the United States remains a "far more violent place than the rest of the advanced industrial world."[28] Moreover, says Currie, America's rate of violent crime "is still out of the ballpark by comparison with every other industrial democracy." Even when measured against our own historical standards, Currie points out, "the recent declines [in crime rates] are not exactly what they are sometimes described as being." While the media often portray crime's decline as "a sudden fall from a plateau, which appears quite spectacular," Currie says, the fact is that the data merely "represent a falling-off from an extraordinary peak." Levels of violence in the United States, he argues, despite recent declines, are still unreasonably high. The decline of the last decade, Currie notes, "merely puts us back at close to the very high endemic levels of violence we've been suffering for thirty-odd years."

According to Currie, we Americans have hidden our crime problem, not beaten it. The real issue, says Currie, is that "public discourse about crime rarely counts the people behind bars as part of our crime problem. Instead they are usually counted as part of the solution, if they are counted at all." Hence, when we assess the degree of the crime problem in the United States, we usually do so by looking at crime rates, and "we fail to include that part of the problem that's represented by the people currently behind bars." Says Currie, the "problem is that we measure our crime rate without factoring in the reality that we've simply shifted some of the total 'pool' of criminals in our society from one place to another. We haven't stopped producing. We've just moved them." Instead of measuring the crime rate, suggests Currie, we should be measuring the criminality problem in our society. This error, concludes Currie, is "like measuring the extent of some physical illness in our society while systematically excluding from the count all those people who are so sick we've had to put them in the hospital." While nobody would do that in the public health field, Currie says, "we do it all the time in the field of criminology." Currie's ideas can be summarized by a formula representing the **criminality index** (that is, the actual extent of the crime problem) in any society, as follows:

$$\text{criminality index} = \text{actual crime rate} + \text{latent crime rate}$$

where the **latent crime rate** refers to a rate of crime calculated on the basis of crimes that would likely be committed by those who are in prison or jail or otherwise incapacitated by the justice system. It is important to note that the latent crime rate does not count the criminal activity of anyone on probation or parole, since probationers and parolees, by virtue of the fact that they are not behind bars, are capable of committing crimes that contribute to the actual crime rate.

The formula shown here permits calculation not only of a general index of criminality but also of criminality indexes for specific crimes. The criminality index for robbery, for example, can be computed by adding the reported rate of robberies and the estimated robbery rate that would have been generated by incarcerated individuals had they been free. In 2006, for example, approximately 447,500 robberies were reported. If 140,000 persons were in prison in 2006 for robbery and if the average number of robberies committed by a "typical" robber in any given year is known to be around 5,[29] we can then calculate that 700,000 were prevented by imprisonment. On this basis, we can conclude that the total number of potential robberies in the United States in 2006 would have been 1,147,000—for a composite robbery index of approximately 400 robberies per 100,000 residents. Such calculations reveal a potential U.S. robbery *problem* that is more than twice that shown in official crime statistics, which count only the actual number of robberies reported to the police or to survey interviewers.

criminality index

The actual extent of the crime problem in a society. The criminality index is computed by adding the actual crime rate and the latent crime rate.

latent crime rate

A rate of crime calculated on the basis of crimes that would likely be committed by those who are in prison or jail or who are otherwise incapacitated by the justice system.

Major Crimes in the United States

Criminal Homicide

During his third year at an Illinois medical school in the early 1980s, Dr. Michael Swango was nicknamed "Double-O Swango" by his classmates after five patients under his care died. The nickname was a reference to movie legend James Bond's "license to kill." Swango worked at several hospitals across the United States and in Africa for 15 years following graduation from medical school. Wherever he went, patients died under mysterious circumstances.[30]

In 1983, Swango entered a neurosurgery internship at Ohio State University Medical Center, and patients who seemed to be getting better started dying. One patient, Rena Cooper, was recovering from back surgery when a student nurse saw Swango put something into her IV line. A few minutes later, Cooper turned blue and began convulsing. Cooper recovered and told university police that Swango had tried to kill her. Her hospital roommate corroborated her story, and Swango left the hospital. Four deaths had occurred during the five weeks Swango spent at Ohio State—all of them suspicious.

In 1984, Swango took a job as a paramedic in Quincy, Illinois, and was soon arrested and convicted of battery for poisoning the iced tea and donuts of his coworkers, all of whom recovered. As a result of the conviction, Swango was sent to prison, where he spent two years. Upon release, he applied to work at the Veterans Affairs Medical Center in Northport, New York. Once hired, patients started dying. When hospital officials found that he had falsified his hiring papers, Swango was asked to leave. Fearing a continuing investigation, he fled to Africa. Soon Zimbabwe officials ordered him taken into custody for intentionally causing the deaths of five patients in a hospital there, and he fled back to the United States, where he was arrested for fraudulently obtaining a federal position.

Following conviction, Swango was sentenced to three to five years in federal prison. While still in prison, he was indicted for killing three patients at the Northport VA hospital, and in 2000, he pled guilty to murder and was sentenced to life in prison without the possibility of parole. Swango is suspected in the deaths of as many as 60 patients and several colleagues, and his activities are the subject of the book *Blind Eye: The Terrifying Story of a Doctor Who Got Away with Murder,* by Pulitzer Prize–winning author James B. Stewart.[31] When asked for a motive that might explain Swango's actions, Assistant U.S. Attorney Gary Brown, who served as the principal federal prosecutor in the case, said, "Basically, Dr. Swango liked to kill people."[32]

The terms *homicide* and *murder* are often used interchangeably, although they are not the same. Homicide is the willful killing of one human being by another, whereas murder is an unlawful homicide. Some homicides, such as those committed in defense of oneself or one's family, may be justifiable and therefore legal. The term used by most courts and law enforcement agencies to describe murder is **criminal homicide.** In legal parlance, *criminal homicide* means the causing of the death of another person without legal justification or excuse.

Jurisdictions generally distinguish among various types of murder. Among the distinctions made are **first-degree murder,** also called "premeditated murder"; **second-degree murder;** and third-degree murder, or **negligent homicide.** First-degree murder differs from the other two types of murder in that it is planned. It involves what some statutes call "malice aforethought," which may become evident by someone "lying in wait" for the victim but can also be proved by a murderer's simple action of going into an adjacent room to find a weapon and returning with it to kill. In effect, any activity in preparation to kill that demonstrates the passage of time, however brief, between formation of the intent to kill and the act of killing itself is technically sufficient to establish the legal requirements needed for a first-degree murder prosecution.

Second-degree murder, on the other hand, is legally regarded as a true crime of passion. It is an unlawful killing in which the intent to kill and the killing itself arise almost simultaneously. Hence, a person who kills in a fit of anger is likely to be charged with second-degree murder, as is one who is provoked into killing by insults, physical

criminal homicide

The illegal killing of one human being by another.

first-degree murder

Criminal homicide that is planned or involves premeditation.

second-degree murder

Criminal homicide that is unplanned and that is often described as "a crime of passion."

negligent homicide

The act of causing the death of another person by recklessness or gross negligence.

abuse, and the like. For a murder to be second degree, however, the killing must follow immediately upon the abuse. Time that elapses between abuse or insults and the murder itself allows the opportunity for thought to occur and hence for premeditation.

Both first- and second-degree murderers intend to kill. Third-degree murder is different. It is a term that varies in meaning between jurisdictions but often refers to homicides that are the result of some other action that is unlawful or negligent. Hence, it is frequently called "negligent homicide," "negligent manslaughter," "manslaughter," or "involuntary manslaughter." Under negligent homicide statutes, for example, a drunk driver who causes a fatal accident may be charged with third-degree murder, even though that person had not the slightest intent to kill.

Some jurisdictions have created a special category of **felony murder,** whereby an offender who commits a crime during which someone dies (or caused to die) can be found guilty of first-degree murder, even though the person committing the crime had no intention of killing anyone. Bank robberies in which one of the robbers is shot to death by police, for example, or in which a bank patron succumbs to a fear-induced heart attack may leave a surviving robber subject to the death penalty under the felony murder rule. Hence, felony murder is a special class of criminal homicide whereby an offender may be charged with first-degree murder when that person's criminal activity results in another person's death.

felony murder

A special class of criminal homicide in which an offender may be charged with first-degree murder when that person's criminal activity results in another person's death.

Murder Statistics

Statistics discussed in this section are derived from the FBI's UCR/NIBRS Program because the NCVS does not gather information on criminal homicide. UCR/NIBRS statistics count only the number of murders committed, not attempts to murder, because attempts are scored as aggravated assaults. Likewise, the UCR/NIBRS Program does not count cases of negligent manslaughter among murder statistics.

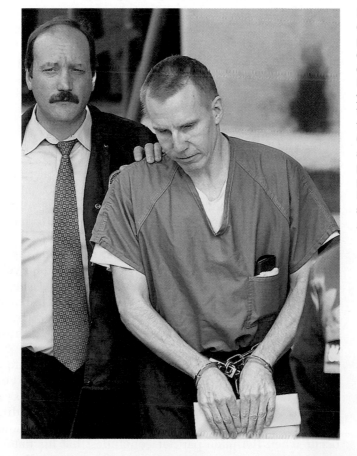

Dr. Michael Swango, suspected of having killed at least 35 people under his care. Swango continued practicing medicine on two continents while eluding law enforcement officials for 10 years. In 2000, he pled guilty to the murders of three patients at the Veterans Affairs Medical Center at Northport, New York, and was sentenced to life in prison without the possibility of parole. What does Swango's long string of crimes say about security in the professions?
Source: AP Wide World Photos

According to the UCR/NIBRS, 17,034 murders were committed throughout the United States in 2006.[33] The 2006 rate of criminal homicide was 5.7 people murdered for every 100,000 individuals in the U.S. population.

Age is no barrier to murder. In 2006, for example, 203 murder victims were under the age of 1, while 263 were 75 years old or older. Sixty-five murders were committed by offenders over 75, while 12 murders were committed by those aged 9 to 12. Of the murder victims in 2006, 79% were male, and 50% were African American (47% were white, and the remainder were of other races).

As in other recent years, the typical murder offender in 2006 was a young African American man. Of all murder arrestees, 89.1% were male. Seventy-one percent of all murder arrestees in 2006 were between the ages of 17 and 34 years old, and 51% were African American (47% were white, and the remainder were of other races). Although African Americans make up only 13% of the American population, they typically account for almost 50% of all people arrested for murder.

FBI statistics reveal a plethora of other information about the crime of murder. Approximately one-half of all murder victims in 2006, for example, were either related to (11.9%) or acquainted with (23.1%) their assailants. Only 12.7% of murders were committed by strangers, and the relationship between killer and victim was undetermined for 44% of all reported murders.

Murder is primarily an intraracial crime. In 2006, 82% of white victims were killed by other whites, whereas 92% of African American victims died at the hands of African American killers. As in other years, handguns were the weapon of choice in most murders, with 52% of all murder victims dying of handgun-inflicted injuries. Another 3% were killed with shotguns and 3% with rifles. Knives (or other sharp instruments) were used in 12% of murders and blunt instruments (clubs, hammers, and so on) in 4%. Hands, fists, and feet were listed as murder weapons in those 6% of all murder cases in which victims were punched and kicked to death.

Various circumstances lead to murder, although in 2006 arguments were the most common cause of such crime. Twenty-six percent of all murders resulted from arguments, and 16% were the consequence of other felonious activity like robbery, rape, and arson. Murderous arguments may arise over sexual claims, jealousy, money, personal honor, or anything else that may lead to anger or bring offense.

Of all reported or discovered criminal homicides in 2006, 61% were cleared—the highest rate of clearance for any of the major crimes. Small cities reported the highest clearance rates (72%), while large cities had the lowest rates of clearance (56%).

Forcible Rape

UCR/NIBRS reports, as currently structured, distinguish among three categories of **rape:** (1) forcible rape, (2) statutory rape, and (3) attempted forcible rape. Some jurisdictions draw a distinction between **forcible rape** with the use of a weapon and forcible rape without the use of a weapon, and data collected under the newer NIBRS format now encorporate such distinctions.

Other types of rape include spousal rape, gang rape, date rape, and same-sex rape. **Spousal rape,** or the rape of one's spouse, is a relatively new concept, having entered the law of many state jurisdictions only in recent years. Just a few decades ago, it was believed that a woman entering into marriage implicitly gave her consent to sexual intercourse at the behest of her husband. In today's more enlightened times, wives may prosecute their spouses under rape statutes if their husbands force them to have nonconsensual intercourse.

Date rape, which is often defined as unlawful forced sexual intercourse with a woman against her will that occurs within the context of a dating relationship, has also received much attention in recent times, although it is undoubtedly a phenomenon that has existed as long as the institution of dating. According to recent studies, date rape is much more common than previously believed. Some authors suggest that date rape may occur when the male partner concludes that his date "owes" him something for the

rape (NCVS)

Carnal knowledge through the use of force or the threat of force, including attempts. Statutory rape (without force) is excluded. Both heterosexual and homosexual rape are included.

forcible rape (UCR/NIBRS)

The carnal knowledge of a female forcibly and against her will. Assaults or attempts to commit rape by force or threat of force are also included in the UCR/NIBRS definition; however, statutory rape (without force) and other sex offenses are excluded.

spousal rape

The rape of one spouse by the other. The term usually refers to the rape of a woman by her husband.

date rape

Unlawful forced sexual intercourse with a woman against her will that occurs within the context of a dating relationship.

Who's to Blame—The Individual or Society?
Pro-Choice, Right to Life, and Criminal Protest

In early 2008, Tom Clarkson participated in a demonstration that turned ugly at a downtown women's clinic well-known for its policy of offering to finance abortions for young women as an alternative to motherhood.

As the demonstration began, 12 protestors, including Clarkson, stood across the street from the clinic carrying placards and shouting antiabortion slogans at people entering or leaving the center. Soon, however, a small group of abortion supporters arrived and began heckling the demonstrators. A scuffle ensued, and in the melee bricks were pulled from the parking area in front of the clinic and thrown through the building's windows. One of the bricks hit a nurse inside the building who was helping a patient prepare for an examination. Although she wasn't seriously hurt, police officers called to the scene arrested Clarkson and other demonstrators and charged them with rioting, aggravated assault, and destruction of private property.

Clarkson was also charged with violating the federal Freedom of Access to Clinic Entrances Act. But the most serious charge facing Clarkson, he soon learned, was a state charge of riot in the first degree. Relevant state law reads: "A person is guilty of riot in the first degree when (a) simultaneously with ten or more other persons he engages in tumultuous and violent conduct and thereby intentionally or recklessly causes or creates a grave risk of causing public alarm, and (b) in the course of and as a result of such conduct, a person other than one of the participants suffers physical injury or substantial property damage occurs."

At his arraignment Clarkson pled not guilty and was allowed to make a statement. He told the presiding judge that he was bound by a higher loyalty than man-made laws. "The laws of man are short-sighted," he said. "I'm trying to save lives, and that's all that matters. I have committed no crime in the eyes of God Almighty."

Think about it:

1. Do you agree with Clarkson that there are "higher laws" than those made by the legislature? If so, how do we know what they are? If not, are there nonetheless any "bad" laws that most of us would be better off not following?

2. How do our understandings of right and wrong influence our perspectives on the just handling of criminal offenders?

3. Should Clarkson be punished for what he did? If so, what might be an appropriate punishment?

4. If Clarkson is imprisoned and later released, can he be expected to follow statutory law in the future?

5. How might Clarkson be rehabilitated? What would "rehabilitation" mean in his case?

---

money he has spent on her.[34] Many women apparently do not report the crime, and their hesitancy exists for a variety of reasons. Sometimes they feel responsible for some aspect of the social relationship that led to the rape; in other instances, they may feel some concern for the offender and not wish to have him become the target of a criminal prosecution—even one that is deserved.

Same-sex rape, although not punishable as rape in all jurisdictions, is more widely recognized today than in the past. Many states and a number of foreign countries now provide for the prosecution of men who force other men to have sex with them, as happens especially in prison. In 1994, the English House of Lords, for example, passed an amendment to the British Criminal Justice Bill[35] replacing the offense of "non-consensual buggery of men," which carried a ten-year sentence, with the crime of "male rape," which is punishable by life imprisonment.

Although rape statutes have evolved to the point where many jurisdictions prosecute cases of same-sex rape, gender bias still characterizes most rape laws. No jurisdictions, for example, effectively prosecute husbands raped by their wives, and lesbian rape (the rape of one woman by another) is never prosecuted as such. On very rare occasions, however, a female individual may be charged with the rape of a male individual. In 1993, for example, Jean-Michelle Whitiak, 24, a Fairfax County, Virginia, swimming coach, pleaded guilty to one count of statutory rape resulting from an affair with a 13-year-old boy.[36] Whitiak also admitted to having sex with two of the boy's friends.

The motivation of rapists has been the subject of frequent study. Contemporary social scientific wisdom, supported by the research of scholars like A. Nicholas Groth,[37] holds that rape is primarily a crime of power and that most rapists seek self-aggrandizement via the degradation of another human being. Rapists, this school of thought maintains, demean their victims in order to feel important and powerful. Hence, the rape of elderly and physically unattractive women by virile and powerful young men can be explained as a crime of power rather than one of sex. Some scholars, however, have cast doubt on power as the primary motivation of rapists, returning to an emphasis on sexual gratification as the root cause of sexual assault.[38]

Rape Statistics

UCR/NIBRS statistics on rape, as currently reported, include both forcible rape and attempted forcible rape. Statutory rape and other sex offenses are excluded from the count of rape crimes. In 2006, 92,455 rapes were reported nationwide under the UCR Program, a slight increase over the previous year. The rate of reported forcible rape was officially put at 30.5 rapes per 100,000 people. However, the rape rate for females is effectively twice that figure because any realistic tally of such crimes should compare the number of women raped with the number of female individuals in the overall population (rather than with a count of the entire population, which includes males). When such a comparison is made, the rate of reported rape is 61 per 100,000 for women in large cities, 60 per 100,000 for women in small towns, and 49 per 100,000 for women in rural counties. The hot summer months generally show the highest rate of reported forcible rape. The year 2006 was no exception, with the month of August showing the largest number of reports.

In 2006, 41% of all reported forcible rapes were cleared by arrest or exceptional means (such as the death of the suspected offender), with rural and suburban county law enforcement agencies reporting slightly higher clearance rates than city law enforcement agencies. The nationwide number of reported rapes decreased 1.5% over the previous year.

NCVS data paint a somewhat different picture of rape than the UCR/NIBRS statistics. According to the NCVS, 272,350 rapes and sexual assualts occurred in 2006.[39] The NCVS calculates a rape/sexual assault rate of 220 per 100,000 females ages 12 or older.

The NCVS reports that rapes by strangers are almost twice as common as those by nonstrangers. Of rapes involving strangers, 50% occur between 6 P.M. and midnight, while only 38% of nonstranger rapes occur during those hours. The NCVS also records the location of criminal events, including parking lots or garages, commercial buildings, school property, school buildings, apartments, yards and parks, public transportation, and so forth. Most rapes (17.9%) are described as occurring "on the street not near own or friend's home." However, of the rapes involving nonstrangers, 50% occur within the victim's home. Only 17.2% of rapes recorded by the NCVS involved the use of weapons, although weapons were employed in 34.6% of all rapes committed by strangers.

The NCVS also collects data on self-protective measures taken by victims. Of the rape victims responding to NCVS interviewers, 80% reported the use of some type of self-protective measure. These measures included "resisting" (20.8% of all such measures reported), persuading or appeasing the offender (18.7%), running away or hiding (13%), scaring or warning the offender (13%), raising an alarm (11%), and screaming (8.9%). Only 6% of rape victims reported attacking their victimizers, and fewer than 1 in 100 attacked the offender with weapons.

Many rape victims (51%) reported that the self-protective measures that were taken helped the situation, although 17% believed the measures made their situation worse. Another 14% said such measures had no effect on the situation. Twenty percent of rape victims reported economic costs due to time lost from work as a result of victimization.

As mentioned earlier, NCVS data score only victimizations of household residents who are 12 years of age or older. Some BJS studies, however, have found that many victims of rape are quite young. A 1994 study, for example, of 11 states and the District of Columbia, found that 10,000 girls under the age of 18 were raped in reporting jurisdictions—about half of all the rapes that were reported in those areas.[40] Investigators found that at least 3,800 victims were children under the age of 12. As a result of these figures, the study's authors concluded that "the rape of young girls is alarmingly commonplace." When young women and girls are raped, however, the crimes often go unreported because they frequently involve family members or friends. The survey found that although girls under the age of 18 make up 25% of the nation's female population, they account for 51% of all rape victims.

Even researchers were surprised by the number of young girls who reported having been raped. As Patrick A. Langan, one of the authors of "Child Rape Victims, 1992," said, "The [finding] that one in six of the reported rapes were girls under 12 was startling. You would think that the number would have been minute. But it's not tiny. . . . It's a substantial part of the picture."

Robbery

The crime of robbery is regarded as a personal crime because it is committed in the presence of the victim. **Robbery** is defined by the UCR/NIBRS Program as "the unlawful taking or attempted taking of property that is in the immediate possession of another by force or threat of force or violence and/or by putting the victim in fear." The NCVS definition is similar and also involves *attempts.* Although some individuals mistakenly use the terms *robbery* and *burglary* interchangeably (as in the phrase "my house was robbed"), it should be remembered that robbery is a personal crime and that individuals are robbed, not houses (which are burglarized).[41]

A number of terms are used to describe subtypes of robbery. *Highway robbery,* for example, simply refers to any robbery that occurs in a public place, generally outdoors. It is also called "street robbery" by the FBI. *Strong-arm robbery* means that the robber or robbers were unarmed and took the victim's possessions through intimidation or brute physical force. Strong-arm robbery is often perpetrated by a group of robbers working in consort, as when a gang preys upon one or two unwary victims. The term *armed robbery* signifies that a weapon was used—most often, a gun. Armed robberies usually occur when banks, service stations, convenience stores, and other commercial establishments are robbed.

robbery (UCR/NIBRS)

The taking of or attempting to take anything of value from the care, custody, or control of a person or persons by force or threat of force or violence or by putting the victim in fear.

Robbery Statistics

UCR/NIBRS data for 2006 show that 447,404 robberies came to the attention of authorities across the nation that year, meaning that the rate of robbery was 149.4 per every 100,000 people in the United States. Cities are the places where most robberies occur, with large metropolitan areas recording a robbery rate of 380 per 100,000 inhabitants in 2006, while rural areas reported a mere 17 robberies per 100,000.

In 2006, according to the FBI, 33% of robberies were committed using strong-arm tactics, and firearms were the weapon of choice in 35% more. Knives were used in 7%, with a variety of other dangerous weapons used in the remainder.

Robberies generally occur most frequently in December, probably reflecting an increased need for money and other goods around the holiday season. Most robbery (approximately 45%) takes the form of highway robbery, and robberies of businesses account for approximately 22% of all such crimes, while 2% of robberies are bank robberies.

Estimated losses due to robberies throughout the United States in 2006 totaled $567 million. However, as the FBI concludes, "The impact of this violent crime on its victims cannot be measured in terms of monetary loss alone. While the object of a robbery is to obtain money or property, the crime always involves force or threat of force, and many victims suffer serious personal injury."[42] In addition to monetary loss and possible physical injury, many robbery victims suffer lasting psychological trauma.

The nationwide clearance rate for robberies reported by the Uniform Crime Reporting Program in 2006 was 25%. The highest clearance rate was 43% in rural counties, and the lowest rate of clearance for robberies was found in the nation's cities. Youths under the age of 18 accounted for offenders arrested in 28% of all robberies counted as cleared, and nearly two-thirds of all people apprehended for robbery were under 25 years of age. The offenders were males in 88% of all robberies, and African Americans accounted for 56% of those arrested (42% were white, and the remainder were members of other racial groups).

NCVS statistics show a much higher number of robberies than do UCR/NIBRS data. NCVS interviewers uncovered approximately 711,570 robberies in 2006, which the BJS report broke down as two-thirds completed and one-third attempted. NCVS data show that one in every two completed robberies (and one in every three attempted robberies) resulted in injuries to the victim. By far the most robbery-prone segment of the population is the 12- to 15-year-old age group, and males are robbed almost twice as frequently as females. African Americans report a robbery victimization rate three times higher than that of whites, and the incidence of robbery declines as family income rises. Members of the poorest families interviewed by NCVS field researchers (families with incomes of less than $7,500) were the most frequently robbed (8.1 per 1,000 people), while members of families with yearly incomes above $75,000 reported the lowest incidence of robbery (1.8 per 1,000 people). Income and educational levels tend to be correlated. Hence, as the NCVS report concluded, the more educated people are, the less chance they have of being robbed.

NCVS data reveal that victims took some type of protective action in 63% of all robberies and that "a robbery . . . committed by an offender who was known to the victim was significantly more likely to result in physical injury than a robbery . . . that was committed by a stranger."[43] Eleven percent of all robbery victims incurred medical expenses as a direct result of victimization, and 12% of all robberies caused the victim to miss time at work.

NCVS survey data reveal that only 56.9% of all robberies are reported to the police. Women are far more likely to report robberies (64%) than are men (42%), although men are only slightly more likely to resist robbery than are women.

Aggravated Assault

aggravated assault (UCR/NIBRS)

An unlawful attack by one person upon another for the purpose of inflicting severe or aggravated bodily injury.

simple assault (NCVS)

An attack without a weapon, resulting either in minor injury or in undetermined injury requiring less than two days of hospitalization.

The UCR Program defines **aggravated assault** as "the unlawful attack by one person upon another for the purpose of inflicting severe or aggravated bodily injury." If a weapon is used or if serious bodily injury requiring hospitalization results, the UCR/NIBRS is likely to count the offense as an aggravated assault. The NCVS definition of aggravated assault is essentially the same, although the NCVS also reports on the crime of **simple assault,** which it defines as an "attack without a weapon resulting either in minor injury or in undetermined injury requiring less than two days of hospitalization." Hence, under both the NCVS and the UCR/NIBRS, an assault with a deadly weapon would be scored as aggravated assault, although UCR/NIBRS data are far more likely to score any assault that results in hospitalization as "aggravated." Under all programs, assaults that cause serious bodily injury are scored as aggravated assaults, even without the use of a weapon. If an assault results in death, however, the offense becomes a homicide, rather than an assault, for statistical-reporting purposes.

Assault Statistics

According to the FBI, 860,853 aggravated assaults were reported to police agencies across the nation in 2006, producing an aggravated assault rate of 288 for every 100,000 people in the country. A total of 1,354,750 aggravated assaults were reported to NCVS interviewers in 2006, which translates into an aggravated assault rate of 550 per every 100,000 people aged 12 or over. Rates of aggravated assault were highest in metropolitan areas and lowest in rural areas.

The greatest number of aggravated assaults is usually recorded during the hot summer months, with July typically showing the highest incidence of such crimes. When cross-regional comparisons are made (always difficult as populations vary between regions), the southern states accounted for the most aggravated assaults (43%), while the western states provided 25% of the total, the midwestern region 18%, and the northeastern states 14%. Assault rates were higher in the South than elsewhere in the country.

During 2006, 34% of aggravated assaults reported to the police were committed with blunt objects, meaning that the offender probably grabbed whatever was at hand to commence or continue the attack. Hands, feet, and fists were used in 25% of all aggravated assaults, firearms were employed in 22%, and knives or other cutting or stabbing instruments were used in 19%.[44] Like most other major crimes, aggravated assault has shown a steady yearly decrease. The number of aggravated assaults reported nationwide has decreased by almost 20% over the past five years.

Because victims often know the people who assault them, the clearance rate for aggravated assault (which stood at 54% in 2006) is relatively high. As with most crimes, city police agencies report a lower rate of clearance for aggravated assault than other law enforcement departments, while rural areas have the highest rate of clearance.

Burglary

The UCR/NIBRS Program defines **burglary** as "the unlawful entry of a structure to commit a felony or a theft." The definition goes on to say that "the use of force to gain entry is not required to classify an offense as burglary." Burglaries, as scored by the NCVS and the UCR/NIBRS, generally fall into three subclassifications: (1) forcible entry, (2) attempted forcible entry, and (3) unlawful entry where no force is used. Forcible entries are those burglaries in which some evidence of breakage, prying, or other evidence of forceful entry is found. A broken window, a jimmied door, a loosened air-conditioning duct—all may provide evidence of forcible entry. Attempted forcible entries (that is, attempted burglaries) are another form of burglary reported by the UCR/NIBRS. Attempted forcible entry also shows evidence of force, although the perpetrator may not have achieved actual entry. The third type of burglary, unlawful entry where no force is used, occurs when a burglar enters an unlocked residence uninvited, stealing items found there.

burglary

By the narrowest and oldest definition, the trespassory breaking and entering of the dwelling house of another in the nighttime with the intent to commit a felony. Also, the unlawful entry of a structure to commit a felony or a theft.

Although most burglaries are, strictly speaking, property crimes, the potential for personal violence is inherent in many such crimes. Nighttime burglary, for example, which is more severely punished in some jurisdictions than daytime burglary, holds the possibility of violent confrontation between offender and homeowner. Assault, rape, and even murder may be the outcome of such encounters. On the other hand, sometimes burglars themselves are injured or killed by irate residents.

According to the laws of most jurisdictions and to the UCR/NIBRS and NCVS definitional categories, burglary has not occurred unless it was the intent of the unlawful entrant to commit a felony or a theft once inside the burglarized location. Other forms of illegal entry may simply be counted as trespass.

Burglary Statistics

The FBI recorded 2,183,746 reported burglaries in 2006, a slight increase over the previous year. Burglary has shown a steady decrease over the past decade, with the 2006 burglary rate approximately 20% lower than five years earlier. The UCR/NIBRS rate of reported burglary in 2006 was 729.4 per 100,000 inhabitants. As with most other Part I offenses, cities had the highest rate of burglary (758 per 100,000), whereas rural areas had the lowest (555 per 100,000).

Of reported burglaries in 2006, 62% involved forcible entry, 31% were the result of unlawful entries in which no force was used, and 6.3% were attempts. Two of every three reported burglaries were of residences (the remainder were commercial burglaries or burglaries committed on government property).

The average amount lost per burglary in 2006 was set at $1,834 by the FBI, although the loss was slightly lower for residential property than for nonresidential property. The total loss suffered by all burglary victims in 2006 was estimated at approximately $4 billion.

Of all arrestees for the crime of burglary in 2006, 86% were men, 30% were under the age of 18, and 69% were white. African Americans accounted for 29% of burglary arrestees, and members of other races made up the remaining 2%.

Because burglaries are typically property crimes, the clearance rate for burglaries is quite low. Only 12.6% of all burglaries were cleared in 2006. As with other crimes, rural law enforcement agencies cleared a higher proportion of burglaries (16%) than city departments (14%).

In contrast to UCR/NIBRS reports, NCVS statistics on burglary paint quite a different picture. In 2006, the NCVS reported 3,539,760 household burglaries and attempted burglaries—nearly 90% more than UCR/NIBRS estimates.[45] Rates of burglary were generally higher for African American households than for white households, regardless of family income levels, although wealthy African American families had far lower burglary rates than did low-income white families. The same was true for locality. Hence, African American people living in cities were more likely than whites to have their houses burglarized, while African Americans living in rural areas were also more likely than their white neighbors to become burglary victims, although wealthy African Americans in either locale were less likely than poor whites to experience burglary. NCVS data also show that the longer a respondent lives at a particular residence, the less likely that person will be to report having been burglarized. Hence, a residence of six months or less was associated with a burglary rate of 151 per 1,000 households versus a rate of only 38 per 1,000 households when those living at the reporting address had been there for five years or more.

Larceny

In 2003, Gordon McWhorter, 27, of Salt Lake City, Utah, was sentenced to five years in federal prison for attempting to sell stolen U.S. property on the Internet.[46] The property in question consisted of moon rocks that had been stolen from NASA's Johnson Space Center in Houston a year earlier. The stolen rocks had been brought to earth by the Apollo moon mission in 1969. Fellow conspirators Tiffany Fowler, 26; Thad Roberts, 26; and Shae Saur, 20, all pleaded guilty to conspiracy to commit theft and interstate transporation of stolen property. Fowler, Roberts, and Saur had worked at NASA when the theft occured.

larceny-theft (UCR/NIBRS)

The unlawful taking, carrying, leading, or riding away of property (other than a motor vehicle) from the possession or constructive possession of another. Attempts are included.

Larceny is another name for theft. Sometimes the word *larceny* is used by itself in published crime reports, and at other times, *larceny-theft* is used. Both mean the same thing. The UCR/NIBRS defines **larceny-theft** as "the unlawful taking or attempted taking, carrying, leading, or riding away of property, other than a motor vehicle, from the possession or constructive possession of another" person. The NCVS definition is similar, except that it further subdivides larceny into categories of "household larceny" and "personal larceny." Crimes of larceny do not involve force, nor do those who commit larceny intentionally put their victims in fear, as do robbers.

Differences exist between the NCVS and the UCR/NIBRS in the way subtypes of larceny are categorized. The UCR/NIBRS, for example, currently scores both purse snatching and pocket picking as larceny-theft, whereas the NCVS calls such crimes "personal larceny with contact." Similarly, the UCR/NIBRS scores shoplifting and thefts from coin-operated machines as larceny, but the NCVS does not gather data on commercial thefts and so excludes all such incidents from larceny counts. With these provisos in mind, larceny data in the NCVS and the UCR/NIBRS can be compared.

Larceny Statistics

The UCR/NIBRS Program counted 6,607,013 reports of larceny in 2006, for a rate of 2,207 such crimes per every 100,000 people in the population. The larceny rate increased slightly from the previous year, but as in other years, reported larcenies were most common during the summer. Most items reported stolen had been taken from motor vehicles (26%), meaning that packages, money, and other goods were stolen from parked cars. Of all larcenies reported, 10% were of motor vehicle accessories like tires, "mag" wheels, cellular phones, CD players, and radar detectors. Another 13% of the total reported number of larcenies were from buildings, 13% were due to shoplifting, and 4% were of bicycles. Purse snatching, pocket picking, and thefts from coin-operated machines each accounted for less than 1% of the total number of larcenies reported to the police in 2006.

The average reported value of property stolen per larceny incident was $855 in 2006. This figure, however, is open to interpretation because reports to the police that estimate the dollar value of stolen or destroyed property are likely to be exaggerated. Some victims hope to receive a high return from insurance companies for stolen goods (even though such hope may be unfounded), some are unsure of the value of missing items, and others honestly overestimate the worth of lost goods because they do not realistically allow for depreciation. In addition, false claims are sometimes filed by people seeking to bilk insurance companies. Hence, in instances of larceny, burglary, auto theft, and arson, it is difficult to know with certainty the true value of lost or stolen items.

NCVS data on larceny estimate 14,275,150 cases of larceny in 2006, with the largest category involving the theft of items worth between $50 and $249. NCVS estimates put the figure for larceny far above the number of thefts officially reported to the police and recorded by the UCR/NIBRS. NCVS trend data, however, show that all forms of larceny have been on the decline since peaking around 1978 and 1979.

Motor Vehicle Theft

Motor vehicle theft is defined by the UCR/NIBRS for reporting purposes simply as "the theft or attempted theft of a motor vehicle." The FBI adds that "this offense category includes the stealing of automobiles, trucks, buses, motorcycles, motorscooters, snowmobiles, etc." Excluded from the UCR/NIBRS count of motor vehicle theft is the stealing of vehicles like airplanes, boats, trains, and spacecraft (which would be counted as larcenies). The taking of a motor vehicle by a person having lawful access to that vehicle is similarly excluded. This designation often includes spouses, who are sometimes reported as having stolen a vehicle owned by their marriage partners. In most jurisdictions, however, married people effectively own most types of property jointly, even though titles, deeds, receipts, and so forth may not specifically list both parties. Hence, a wife who tells her husband that he may not drive her car will not be taken seriously if she calls the police when he disobeys.

Carjacking, a much more serious crime than motor vehicle theft, involves the stealing of a car while it is occupied. Hence, although carjacking involves theft, it is akin to robbery or kidnapping. Often, the theft occurs at gunpoint, and in many carjacking cases, the victim is either injured or killed. Carjacking, almost unheard of two decades ago, increased rapidly in the early 1990s, when thieves targeted vehicles that could be sold easily for valuable parts.

Motor Vehicle Theft Statistics

The NCVS definition of *motor vehicle* is quite concise: "an automobile, truck, motorcycle, or any other motorized vehicle legally allowed on public roads and highways." Both the NCVS and the UCR/NIBRS include attempts in counts of motor vehicle theft. Because of the similarity of definitions and because most motor vehicle thefts are reported for insurance purposes, NCVS and UCR/NIBRS statistics on motor vehicle theft are in close agreement. A total of 1,192,809 vehicles were reported stolen in 2006 by the FBI, while NCVS data estimate that 993,910 were illegally taken. The rate of motor vehicle theft in 2006 was 398 vehicles per 100,000 people, according to the FBI, and the value of motor vehicles stolen that year totaled about $7.9 billion nationwide.

August is usually the prime month for motor vehicle thefts, and most thefts in any given month occur in the nation's cities. As a result, the UCR/NIBRS Program calls motor vehicle theft "primarily a large-city problem."

Law enforcement agencies reported a 12.6% clearance rate for motor vehicle thefts nationwide in 2006, although 62% of all stolen vehicles were recovered. Hence, although many stolen vehicles were eventually returned to their rightful owners, relatively few arrests of car thieves were made.

Arson

On February 18, 2003, 26-year-old Yolanda Dubose lost an appeal of her criminal conviction when Connecticut Supreme Court justices upheld a lower court's finding that Dubose had committed arson.[47] The case began in 1995, when Dubose, then an 18-year-old single

motor vehicle theft (UCR/NIBRS)

The theft or attempted theft of a motor vehicle. According to the FBI, this offense category includes the stealing of automobiles, trucks, buses, motorcycles, motorscooters, and snowmobiles.

carjacking

The stealing of a car while it is occupied.

mother, purchased a small home in a poor section of New Haven. After living there for only a short while, Dubose became concerned with drug activity and crime in the neighborhood. Her residence was repeatedly broken into, and Dubose also discovered that the plumbing and sewage systems in the home weren't working properly. In 1996, she visited the City of New Haven's Office of Housing and Neighborhood Development and applied for a rehabilitation loan. City officials told her that she could not obtain such a loan without first securing insurance on the property, so Dubose obtained the needed coverage. Nonetheless, her loan application was refused, and the bank that held the mortgage on the property began foreclosure proceedings. Not long afterward, the house burned down, and fire investigators later determined that the fire had been started intentionally. Two eyewitnesses told investigators that on the night of the fire they had seen Dubose park her car near the house and that she carried what appeared to be a container of gasoline into the home. A few minutes later, they said, she drove off, and smoke and fire started coming from the house. Dubose was arrested, and in 2000, a trial jury returned a verdict of arson in the first degree against her. She was sentenced to up to 12 years in prison.

arson

The willful or malicious burning or attempt to burn, with or without intent to defraud, of a dwelling house, public building, motor vehicle or aircraft, personal property of another, and so on.

The UCR/NIBRS reporting program defines **arson** as "any willful or malicious burning or attempt to burn, with or without intent to defraud, a dwelling house, public building, motor vehicle or aircraft, personal property of another, etc." The FBI adds that "only fires determined through investigation to have been willfully or maliciously set are classified as arsons." The NCVS does not report arson statistics.

Arson occurs for a variety of reasons. Some arsonists are thrill seekers who set fires for the excitement it brings. Others are vandals, wanting only to accomplish a random sort of destruction. Such people, sometimes called "pyromaniacs," may suffer from psychological problems that contribute to their fire-setting activities. Sometimes arson is a vengeful act, in which a former employee may strike back at an employer or an aggrieved former spouse may attempt to settle past scores. A few arsonists are called "vanity pyromaniacs." They are people, often in some official or responsible role, who place themselves in position to take credit for putting out fires that they secretly start. A handful of security guards, firefighters, and others in similar positions of trust have been involved in this kind of behavior.

In many other instances, arson is used to disguise other felonies, like murder or burglary. Buildings containing the bodies of murder victims, for example, may be burned to cover the evidence of homicide or to make the victim's death appear to have been caused by the fire itself. Most instances of arson, however, appear to be intended to defraud insurance companies into paying for property that the owners no longer want but that they haven't been able to dispose of legally (through sale, transfer, or other means).

Arson Statistics

Under the UCR/NIBRS Program, 69,055 instances of arson were reported in 2006, with an average property loss per instance of approximately $13,325. Of the total number of arsons reported, 25% involved residences, 28% were of motor vehicles, 4% were of commercial buildings, and 2.9% involved storage facilities. Public buildings were targeted by approximately 5% of all reported arsons.

Nationally, the clearance rate for arson was only 18%, with the highest rates of clearance being reported in small towns (those with populations of less than 10,000). Of all arson arrests in 2006, 52% involved juveniles—a higher percentage than for any other major crime. Seventy-six percent of arson arrestees were white, and 83% were men.

Part II Offenses

Part II offenses

Less serious offenses as identified by the FBI for the purpose of reporting arrest data.

The traditional UCR Program also reports the number of arrests made by police for various crimes referred to as **Part II offenses.** Part II offenses are generally less serious than Part I offenses, and some are classified as misdemeanors in many jurisdictions. Only arrests are recorded because many Part II offenses, by virtue of both their semisecret

TABLE 2–3 **UCR/NIBRS Part II Offenses, 2006**	
Offense Category	**Number of Arrests**
Simple assault	1,305,757
Forgery and counterfeiting	108,823
Fraud	280,693
Embezzlement	20,012
Stolen property (receiving)	122,722
Vandalism	300,679
Weapons (carrying)	200,782
Prostitution and related offenses	79,673
Sex offenses (statutory rape, etc.)	87,252
Drug-law violations	1,889,810
Gambling	12,307
Offenses against the family (nonsupport, etc.)	131,491
Driving under the influence	1,460,498
Liquor-law violations	645,734
Public drunkenness	553,188
Disorderly conduct	703,504
Vagrancy	36,471
Curfew/loitering	152,907
Runaways	114,179
All other violations of state and local laws (except traffic-law violations)	4,022,068
Total	**12,228,550**

Source: Federal Bureau of Investigation, *Crime in the United States, 2006.*

nature (some might be regarded as "victimless" or "social-order" offenses) and their lesser degree of seriousness, are not reported to the police and are discovered only when an arrest occurs.

A list of Part II offenses and the 2006 incidence of each are provided in Table 2–3. Total arrests for Part II offenses in 2006 were estimated at 12.2 million, with arrests for driving under the influence (1.46 million), simple assault (1.3 million), and drug-law violations (1.9 million) leading the list. When Part I offenses are added to the total, the overall arrest rate for the United States in 2006 was measured at 4,832 arrests per 100,000 people, with arrests of residents of small cities (6,343 per 100,000) showing the highest rate.

Part II offenses reported by the FBI do not identify arrestees and make no attempt to distinguish offenders who were arrested once from those who have been arrested many times. Hence, some frequently arrested individuals may have contributed significantly to the overall incidence of Part II crime statistics.

Other Sources of Data

Many other programs and surveys provide crime data on a regular basis. Of special interest to students of criminology might be campus crime statistics, which colleges are required to report to the federal Department of Education under the Crime Awareness and Campus Security Act of 1990.[48] Congress enacted the law following the brutal rape and murder of 19-year-old Jeanne Cleary in her dormitory room at Lehigh University in Bethlehem, Pennsylvania, in 1986. It was only after Cleary died that her parents learned that 38 violent crimes had occurred on the Lehigh campus in the previous three years but had not been made public.[49]

The Campus Security Act amended Section 485 of the Higher Education Act (HEA) of 1965 by adding campus crime statistics and security-reporting requirements for all colleges and universities that receive any form of federal funding. The security provisions were amended in 1992 by the Campus Sexual Assault Victims' Bill of Rights to require that schools develop policies to deal with sexual assault on campus and that they provide certain assurances to victims. Under the provisions of the act, all prospective students and employees are entitled to a copy of a school's crime statistics for the three most recent calendar years and a copy of the school's security policies. Current students and employees are to be given this information automatically.

Under a 1998 amendment to the HEA,[50] the federal Office of Postsecondary Education was authorized and funded by Congress to create the Campus Security Statistics Web site (CSSW). The site provides a direct link to reported criminal offenses for over 6,700 colleges and universities in the United States. Colleges and universities are required to report their crime statistics to the Office of Postsecondary Education for posting by October 1 of each year. Schools can be fined up to $25,000 for each crime they fail to report. Visit the CSSW via **Web Extra 2–13.**

WEB
Extra
▪▪▪▪

Unreported Crime

Many crimes are not reported, leading criminologists to talk about the "dark figure of crime."[51] As we learned earlier in this chapter, this term refers to the large number of unreported crimes that never make it into official crime statistics. Crime's dark figure is sometimes glimpsed through offender self-reports, also known as offender **self-report surveys,** in which anonymous respondents without fear of disclosure or arrest are asked to report confidentially any violations of the criminal law that they have committed. Unfortunately for researchers, self-reports of crime are too often limited to asking questions only about petty offenses (such as shoplifting or simple theft), are usually conducted among young people like high school or college students (and hence may not provide results that are representative of the wider population), typically focus on juvenile delinquency rather than adult criminality, and cannot guarantee that respondents have told the truth. Limitations aside, some criminologists believe that "the development and widespread use of the self-report method of collecting data on delinquent and criminal behavior was one of the most important innovations in criminological research in the 20th century."[52]

Early self-report surveys were conducted in the 1940s, and researchers found that respondents were often ready and willing to make self-reports of their delinquency and criminal behavior.[53] In 1943, Austin L. Porterfield provided the first published results from a self-report survey on crime.[54] Porterfield analyzed the juvenile court records of 2,049 delinquents from the Fort Worth, Texas, area and identified 55 offenses for which those juveniles had been adjudicated delinquent. He then surveyed 200 men and 137

self-report survey

A survey in which anonymous respondents, without fear of disclosure or arrest, are asked to confidentially report any violations of the criminal law that they have committed.

Young men displaying signs of gang membership. Self-report surveys of cross sections of the American population provide an alternative to the data-gathering techniques used by many other crime-reporting programs. What kinds of offenses might self-report surveys be especially adept at uncovering?

Source: A. Lichtenstein, Corbis/ Sygma

women from three colleges in northern Texas to determine if and how frequently they had committed any of the same kinds of offenses. He found that every one of the college students had committed at least one such offense. The offenses committed by the college students were equally as serious as those committed by the adjudicated delinquents, although not as frequent, yet few of the college students had come into contact with legal authorities.[55]

Inspired by Porterfield's methodology, James S. Wallerstein and Clement J. Wylie sampled a group of 1,698 adult men and women in 1947 via mailed questionnaires containing 49 offense categories.[56] The researchers requested self-reports of delinquent behavior committed before the age of 16. Almost all respondents reported committing at least one delinquent act, and 64% of the men and 29% of the women admitted committing at least 1 of the 14 felonies that had been included on the checklist.

Although the contributions of Porterfield and of Wallerstein and Wylie were significant developments in the self-report methodology, the work of James F. Short and F. Ivan Nye[57] revolutionized ideas about the feasibility of using survey procedures with a hitherto taboo topic and changed thinking about delinquent behavior itself. What distinguished Short and Nye's research from previous self-report methods was their attention to methodological issues and their clear focus on the substantive relationship between social class and delinquent behavior.[58]

Short and Nye collected self-report data from high school students in three western communities varying in size from 10,000 to 40,000 people; from three midwestern communities varying across rural, rural-urban fringe, and suburban areas; and from a training school for delinquents in a western state. A 21-item list of criminal and antisocial behaviors was used to measure delinquency. Focusing on the relationship between delinquent behavior and the socioeconomic status of the adolescents' parents, Nye, Short, and Virgil Olson found that among the different socioeconomic groups, relatively few differences in delinquent behavior were statistically significant.[59]

Some of the more recent and best-known self-report surveys include the **National Youth Survey (NYS)** and the **Monitoring the Future** study. Begun by Delbert S. Elliott, David Huizinga, and Suzanne S. Ageton in 1976, the NYS surveyed a national sample of 1,725 youths between the ages of 11 and 17.[60] Members of the group (or "panel") were interviewed each year for five years between 1977 and 1981 and later at three-year intervals. The survey, which was last conducted in 1993, followed the original respondents into their thirties. Self-report data were compared with official data over time, and data were gathered on a wide variety of variables, including the demographic and socioeconomic status of respondents and their parents and friends, neighborhood problems, education, employment, skills, aspirations, encouragement, normlessness, attitudes toward deviance, exposure to delinquent peers, self-reported depression, delinquency, drug and alcohol use, victimization, pregnancy, abortion, use of mental health and outpatient services, violence by respondents and acquaintances, use of controlled drugs, and sexual activity. Among other things, researchers found that (1) females were involved in a much higher proportion of crime than previously thought, (2) race differentials in crime were smaller than traditional data sources (that is, the UCR/NIBRS) indicated, and (3) violent offenders begin lives of crime much earlier than previous estimates provided by official statistics indicated. The NYS also found a consistent progression from less serious to more serious acts of delinquency over time.

Monitoring the Future[61] is an ongoing national self-report study of the behaviors, attitudes, and values of American secondary school students, college students, and young adults. The study began in 1975, and each year, a total of almost 50,000 eighth-, tenth-, and twelfth-grade students are surveyed. (Twelfth graders have been surveyed since 1975, eighth and tenth graders since 1991.) In addition, annual follow-up questionnaires are mailed to a sample of each graduating class for a number of years after their initial participation.

Findings from the Monitoring the Future survey have provided a primary source of information on trends in drug use among young people in this country for the last 25 years. For 2006, for example, the Monitoring the Future study found that substance abuse among young teens had begun to stabilize—reversing a decline that surveyors had

National Youth Survey (NYS)

A longitudinal panel study of a national sample of 1,725 individuals that measured self-reports of delinquency and other types of behavior.

Monitoring the Future

A national self-report survey on drug use that has been conducted since 1975.

WEB
Extra
■ ■ ■ ■

LIBRARY
Extra
■ ■ ■ ■

seen since the early 1990s. The 2006 survey found that 31.5% of high school seniors reported using marijuana within the past 12 months (versus 24% in 1992), 25.2% of tenth graders reported such use (versus 17% in 1992), and past-month marijuana use rose from 8% of eighth graders in 1992 to 11.7% in 2006. Even though it is based on self-reports, the survey may underestimate the amount of drug use among teens because it is unable to poll school dropouts and because students completing the survey may fear official reprisals even in the face of assurances to the contrary. Learn more about the Monitoring the Future study via **Web Extra 2–14.** Read more about self report surveys as measures of crime and criminal victimization at **Library Extras 2–5** and **2–6** at crimtoday.com.

The dark figure of crime can be at least partially estimated through analysis of data from the NCVS. According to NCVS analysts, the majority of crimes measured by the NCVS were not reported to the police.[62] More specifically, according to the NCVS:[63]

- Only 49% of violent victimizations and 38% of property crimes were reported to the police.
- Violent crimes were most likely to be reported to the police; personal thefts were the least likely crimes to be reported.
- Eighty-one percent of motor vehicle thefts were reported to the police, making this the most highly reported of crimes. Larcenies, at 32%, were least likely to be reported.
- Women were more likely to report violent victimizations to the police than were men, and some evidence suggests that this was also the case for crimes of theft.
- The reporting rates for violent crimes committed against whites and African Americans were similar.
- Violent crimes committed by strangers were no more likely to be reported to the police than violent crimes committed by persons known to the victims.
- Homeowners were significantly more likely than those who rented to report household crimes to the police.
- Generally, as the value of loss increased, so did the likelihood that a household crime would be reported.

Victims have many reasons for not reporting crimes:

- Fear of future victimization by the same offender
- Embarrassment over the type of victimization (as with some sex crimes) or over the fact of victimization (as with some cases of fraud where the victim is embarrassed to admit having fallen for a fraudulent scheme)
- The view that the police are likely to be ineffective in solving the crime
- Feelings of hostility toward the police and the justice system
- The belief that the matter is a private affair, perhaps one that should be settled personally without police involvement
- The view that the incident is too trivial or too common to require reporting
- The fear that involvement in court proceedings may entail a considerable degree of personal inconvenience
- The belief that the incident is not, or should not be, a crime (as might be the case in some drug offenses, employee thefts, and traffic violations)

An interest in recovering property or in receiving insurance payments motivated many victims of property crimes who reported their victimization to the police. The two most common reasons for not reporting violent victimizations were that the crime was a personal or private matter and that the offender was unsuccessful and the crime was only attempted.

The Social Dimensions of Crime

What Are "Social Dimensions"?

Crime does not occur in a vacuum. It involves real people—human perpetrators and victims, just like you and me. Because society defines certain personal characteristics as especially important, however, it is possible to speak of the "social dimensions of crime," that is, aspects of crime and victimization as they relate to socially significant attributes by which groups are defined and according to which individuals are assigned group membership. Socially significant attributes include gender, ethnicity or race, age, income or wealth, profession, and social class or standing within society. Such personal characteristics provide criteria by which individuals can be assigned to groups like "the rich," "the poor," "male," "female," "young," "old," "black," "white," "white-collar worker," "manual laborer," and so on.[64]

We have already alluded briefly to the fact that the UCR/NIBRS and NCVS structure the data they gather in ways that reflect socially significant characteristics. The UCR/NIBRS, for example, provides information on reported crimes that reveals the sex, age, and race of both victims and perpetrators. NCVS statistics document the race, age, and sex of crime victims and the incomes of households reporting victimizations.

The social dimensions of crime are said by statisticians to reveal relationships or correlations. A **correlation** is simply a connection, or association, that is observed to exist between two measurable variables. Correlations are of two types: positive and negative. If one measurement increases when another, with which it is correlated, does the same, then a positive correlation, or a positive relationship, is said to exist between the two. When one measurement decreases in value as another rises, a negative, or inverse, correlation has been discovered. NCVS data, for example, show a negative relationship between age and victimization. As people age, victimization rates decline. Hence, although some elderly people do become crime victims, older people as a group tend to be less victimized than younger people. UCR/NIBRS data, on the other hand, show a positive relationship between youth and the likelihood of arrest—specifically, between young adulthood and arrest. Young adults, it appears, commit the most crimes. Hence, as people age, they tend to be both less likely to be victimized and less likely to become involved in criminal activity.

A word of caution is in order, however. Correlation does not necessarily imply causation. Because two variables appear to be correlated does not mean that they have any influence on each other or that one causes the other to either increase or decrease. Correlations that involve no causal relationship are said to be "spurious." A study of crime rates, for example, shows that many crimes seem to occur with greater frequency in the summer. Similarly, industry groups tell us that food retailers sell more ice cream in the summer than at any other time. Are we to conclude, then, from the observed correlation between crime rates and ice cream sales that one in some way causes the other? To do so on the basis of an observed correlation alone would obviously be foolish.

Even if two variables appear to be related, it may be difficult to determine the actual nature of the relationship. Some criminologists have observed, for example, that in the past, as the number of prison cells increased, so did the crime rate. While this relationship no longer seems to hold, the implication at the time was that building more prisons would somehow cause more crime. Others have noted how the rather remarkable growth in the number of criminal defense attorneys over the past three or four decades has almost precisely paralleled the observed rate of increase in violent crime—with similar implications. Of course, it would seem logical to conclude that swelling crime rates have led to increases in the number of both attorneys and prison cells.

Some observed correlations do appear to shed at least a little light on either the root causes of crime or the nature of criminal activity. It is to these that our discussion now turns.

correlation

A causal, complementary, or reciprocal relationship between two measurable variables.

Age and Crime

If arrest records are any guide, criminal activity is associated more with youth than with any other stage of life. Every year, UCR/NIBRS data consistently show that young people, from their late teens to their early and mid-twenties, account for the bulk of street, property, and predatory crime (that is, Part I offenses) reported in this country. Although young people between their thirteenth and eighteenth birthdays make up about 6% of the population, they account for approximately 30% of all arrests for major crimes and 18% of total arrests in the United States in a given year.

During the 1990s, a number of well-known criminologists, among them **Alfred Blumstein,**[65] **John J. DiIulio, Jr.,**[66] **James Alan Fox,**[67] **Joan Petersilia,**[68] and **James Q. Wilson,**[69] alerted policymakers to a coming demographic shift that they believed would combine with an increased level of youth violence to produce alarming rates of violent crime by 2010. James Fox, for example, noted that within a few years, "the number of teens, ages 14–17, will increase by 20 percent, with a larger increase among blacks in this age group (26 percent)."[70] This fact, said Fox, is especially worrisome because over the past ten years, "the rate of murder committed by teens, ages 14–17, [has] increased 172 percent." Indicative of what he saw as a significant trend, Fox said that "black males aged 14–24," although constituting only 1 percent of the population, "now constitute 17 percent of the victims of homicide and over 30 percent of the perpetrators." Also, claimed Fox, "the differential trends by age of offender observed for homicide generalize to other violent offenses." During the five years prior to his sounding the alarm, Fox noted that "the arrest rate for violent crimes (murder, rape, robbery and aggravated assault) rose over 46% among teenagers, but only 12% among adults." Joan Petersilia, a former American Society of Criminology (ASC) president, lent her weight to the belief that an avalanche of youth-spawned violence would soon inundate American society. Petersilia believed that there was very little that anyone could do to avert it. She cited James Q. Wilson's sage advice: "Get ready."[71]

Like other writers who have warned of a coming crime wave, Alfred Blumstein, another past president of the ASC, notes that "[p]articularly relevant to future crime, and to consideration of prevention and intervention strategies, is the size of the current teenage population. The age **cohort** responsible for much of the recent youth violence is the smallest it has been in recent years. By contrast, the cohort of children ages 5 to 15, who will be moving into the crime-prone ages in the near future, is larger."[72]

The predicted tidal wave of criminal violence, however, has not yet materialized, although some argue that we may now be seeing initial warning signs of it on the horizon. At this point, no one is sure, and the data seem to be conflicting. Shifting demographics will soon result in an increase in the percentage of the American population that is made up of young people in the "crime-prone years,"[73] but recent FBI statistics appear to show that many forms of juvenile crime have actually been declining.

Crime waves come and go—and no one stays young forever. Involvement in crime appears to decrease consistently, beginning at approximately age 25. The same is true for Part II offenses, with the exception of vagrancy, public drunkenness, gambling, and certain sex crimes—declines in these types of criminal involvement are more likely to begin around age 30. Even though crimes of all kinds appear to decline with age and even though chronic repeat offenders commit fewer crimes as they grow older, criminologists have found that differences in offense rates remain much the same throughout the life cycle.[74] In other words, proportionate differences in rates of offending are unchanged between social groups like males and females, the rich and the poor, whites and African-Americans, and so on, even as members of those groups age.

Although most forms of criminality decrease with age, which is sometimes referred to as the **desistance phenomenon,** even old age is no bar to criminal involvement. According to UCR/NIBRS statistics, around 560,000 people aged 50 or over are arrested every year throughout the country. Of those, nearly 60,000 are past the age of 65. Figure 2–5 provides a graphic comparison of people arrested by age for all reported Part I offenses, and Figure 2–6 shows violent crime victimization rates by age.

cohort

A group of individuals having certain significant social characteristics in common, such as gender and date and place of birth.

desistance phenomenon

The observable decrease in crime rates that is invariably associated with age.

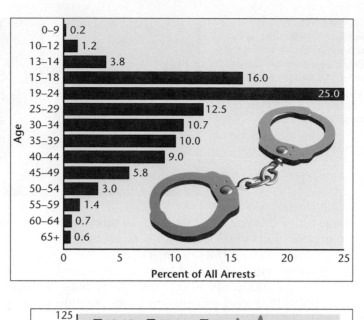

FIGURE 2–5

Arrests by Age for Part I Offenses, 2006

Source: Federal Bureau of Investigation, *Crime in the United States, 2006.*

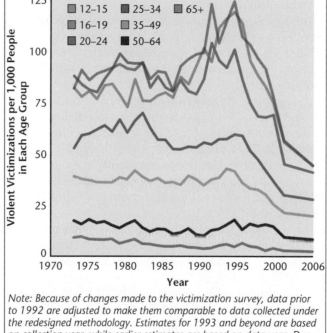

Note: Because of changes made to the victimization survey, data prior to 1992 are adjusted to make them comparable to data collected under the redesigned methodology. Estimates for 1993 and beyond are based on collection year, while earlier estimates are based on data year. Due to changes in the methods used, these data differ from earlier versions. Violent crimes included are homicide, rape, robbery, and both simple and aggravated assault.

FIGURE 2–6

Violent Victimization Rates by Age of Victim, 1973–2006

Source: Bureau of Justice Statistics.

Recently, crimes of the elderly, or geriatric criminality, have sparked much interest among criminologists and the popular media. Movies like *The Over the Hill Gang* have depicted the exploits of aged criminals. Although in the minority, real-life elderly criminals are not hard to find. The case of J. L. Hunter "Red" Rountree, a 92-year-old bank robber, is illustrative.[75] Rountree, who made something of a reputation for himself as a bank robber, turned to crime quite late in life—after he was divorced from his second wife. He was arrested and convicted, and died in prison in 2004 at the age of 93.

Why do older people commit crimes? One author explains it this way: "The reasons older people turn to crime are varied. Some people never retire—from trouble. Others find that retirement gets them into trouble. Boredom and unstructured leisure, fear of the future, frustration over limited finances, family neglect or stress—the same conditions that contribute to teenage crime—can lead seniors to commit desperate or foolish acts."[76]

Melvena Cooke, 79, was identified by authorities as the bank robber shown in this photo holding up a Bank of America branch in Chicago in 2005. Do the motivations of older offenders differ from those of younger ones?

Source: Courtesy of Bank of America via the FBI, Chicago Division

Some older criminals use their age to advantage. Few people, for example, suspect older people of criminal intent. Hence, potential victims are less likely to be on their guard against crime in the presence of an older offender. Similarly, experience gained from previous criminality, and from life in general, can be turned into an asset in the criminal arena. As the old adage goes, "Knowledge is power," and whereas social convention holds that wisdom comes with age, so does increased criminal opportunity for those so inclined.

Although street crime may be the bailiwick of the young, the indications are that older offenders are overrepresented in other forms of crime, including those that require special skills and knowledge. Many of these crimes are job-related and involve fraud, deception, or business activities that are criminal. Such crimes are discussed in detail in Chapter 12.

Although the elderly are less likely to be victimized than other groups, statistics show many more elderly victims than geriatric criminals. The NCVS defines *elderly* to include everyone aged 65 or older living in the United States.[77] NCVS data show that "persons age 65 or older are the least likely of all age groups in the nation to experience crime,"[78] and victimization rates among the elderly have been declining since 1974—about the time NCVS data gathering began. According to the NCVS, the rates for personal theft and household crime among the elderly are now the lowest ever recorded in the history of NCVS.[79]

Even so, nearly 2 million criminal victimizations of the elderly occur in the United States every year.[80] Table 2–4 shows NCVS victimization rates for various age groups. A recent report by the NCVS makes the following observations about elderly crime victims:[81]

- The violent crime rate is nearly 50 times higher for people under 25 than for people 65 and over (see Table 2–4).
- As with personal crime victimizations, people 65 and over are significantly less likely to become victims of all forms of household crime than are members of younger age groups.
- Personal larceny with contact (purse snatching and pocket picking) is an exception. Those who are 65 and older are about as likely as those under age 65 to be victims of personal larceny with contact.

TABLE 2–4   Number of Victimizations by Age (per 1,000 People)

Age	Violent Crime
16–19	52.3
35–49	20.0
50–64	13.1
65 and over	3.5

Source: U.S. Department of Justice, *Criminal Victimization 2006* (Washington, DC: Bureau of Justice Statistics, 2007).

- Injured elderly victims of violent crime are more likely than younger victims to suffer a serious injury.
- Elderly victims of violent crime are more likely than younger victims to face assailants who are strangers.
- Elderly victims of violent crime are almost twice as likely as younger victims to be raped, robbed, or assaulted at or near their homes.
- Elderly victims act to protect themselves during a violent crime less often than do younger victims.
- Elderly victims of robbery and personal theft are more likely than younger victims to report those crimes to the police.

One crime against the elderly that is often not reported is elder abuse. The physical and emotional abuse of the elderly by family members, caregivers, and others has been called a "national tragedy,"[82] involving as it does an estimated 1.5 million cases per year. Recent hearings before the House Subcommittee on Human Services, Select Committee on Aging, revealed that 1 of every 25 Americans over the age of 65 suffers from some form of abuse, neglect, or exploitation.[83] Subcommittee members also concluded that elder abuse is increasing. Unfortunately, however, cases of elder abuse rarely come to the attention of authorities. The desire shared by many elderly citizens for privacy, the fear of embarrassment at having abuse at the hands of loved ones revealed, and the relatively limited ability of elderly citizens to access law enforcement services all contribute to the problem.

To address the concerns of the elderly, the 1994 Violent Crime Control and Law Enforcement Act provides, under Title 24, Protections for the Elderly, monies for the development of local community partnerships between senior citizen groups and law enforcement agencies designed to combat crimes against older Americans. The act also provides monies to assist with funding a Missing Alzheimer's Disease Patient Alert Program, which, in the words of the legislation, "shall be a locally based, proactive program to protect and locate missing patients with Alzheimer's disease and related dementias." Finally, the act increases penalties for telemarketing fraud directed against

Police from Maryland's Prince George's County Anti-Gang Unit question and detain the girlfriend of a Mara Salvatrucha 13 (MS-13) gang member in Langley Park, Maryland. The girl, who is 18 years old, has three children by different MS-13 members and is in government counseling and tattoo removal programs. What is the attraction that gangs hold for young people?

Source: Robert Nickelsberg/Getty Images

the elderly and requires criminal justice agencies to assist in providing background information on caregivers with felony convictions who are being considered for employment in nursing homes and long-term care facilities.

Gender and Crime

Gender appears to be so closely linked to most forms of criminal activity that it has been called "the best single predictor of criminality."[84] Table 2–5 shows the degree of involvement in each of the major crimes by gender. The columns in the table do not show the total number of crimes reported but, rather, represent the proportion of male-female involvement in each Part I offense. For example, of all murders in this country in a given year, approximately 90% are committed by men and 10% by women.

The apparently low rate of female criminality has been explained by some as primarily due to cultural factors, including early socialization, role expectations, and a reluctance among criminal justice officials to arrest and prosecute women. Others have assumed a biological propensity toward crime and aggression among men, which may be lacking in women. Although these and other issues are addressed in later chapters, it is important here to note that the rate of female criminality has changed very little over time—a fact much in contrast to assumptions made years ago by some criminologists who insisted that the degree of female involvement in crime would increase as women assumed more powerful roles in society.

Even when women commit crimes, they are more often followers than leaders. One study of women in correctional settings, for example, found that women are far more likely to assume "secondary follower roles during criminal events" than "dominant leadership roles."[85] Only 14% of women surveyed played primary roles, but those who did "felt that men had little influence in initiating or leading them into crime." African American women were found to be more likely to play "primary and equal crime roles" with men or with female accomplices than were white or Hispanic women. Statistics like these dispel the myth that the female criminal in America has taken her place alongside male offenders—in terms of either leadership roles or the absolute number of crimes committed.

Turning to victimization as it is associated with gender, women are victimized less frequently than men in most crime categories. NCVS data show that crimes of violence reported by American women reflect victimization rates of 23 per 1,000 female individuals aged 12 and older versus 27.3 for males. As with the population in general, the rate of female victimization for all crimes decreases with age, leading NCVS authors to

---

TABLE 2–5   Male-Female Involvement in Crime

UCR Part I Offense	Percentage of Arrests by Gender	
	Males (%)	Females (%)
Murder and nonnegligent manslaughter	89.1	10.9
Rape	98.7	1.3
Robbery	88.7	11.3
Aggravated assault	79.3	20.7
Burglary	85.5	14.5
Larceny-theft	62.3	37.7
Motor vehicle theft	82.3	17.7
Arson	83.0	17.0
Average, all crimes	**76.3**	**23.7**

Source: Federal Bureau of Investigation, *Crime in the United States, 2006.*

conclude that (1) white women aged 65 and older have the lowest violent crime rates and (2) African American women aged 65 and older have the lowest personal theft rates.[86] Two significant exceptions are rape and spousal abuse. Rape is a crime of special concern to many people because official reports to the police of rape have continued to show relatively stable rates of victimization, even as reports of many other types of crimes have declined substantially.[87]

Chapter 10 provides a detailed description of the victimization of women in general and of the crime of rape in particular. That chapter also provides recent information from the annual National Violence against Women (NVAW) survey. The NVAW survey is supported under the Violence against Women Act (VAWA),[88] which was recently reauthorized by Congress, and is sponsored by the National Institute of Justice and the Centers for Disease Control and Prevention. The first NVAW survey solicited telephone responses from 8,000 women and 8,000 men throughout the United States. Selected survey results released in July 2000 showed that nearly 25% of women and 7.5% of men were raped and/or physically assaulted by a current or former spouse, cohabiting partner, or date at some time over the course of their life.[89] Women, however, bore the brunt of the violence, with the NVAW survey finding that women are significantly more likely than men to report being victims of rape, physical assault, or stalking. The survey also found that rates of intimate partner violence vary significantly among women according

Theory Versus Reality

Adolescent Motherhood and Crime

A study by the Office of Juvenile Justice and Delinquency Prevention has identified a significant relationship between adolescent motherhood and crime. The study found that children born to teenage mothers had a considerably higher likelihood of turning to crime than those born to older mothers. Following are edited excerpts from the study.

> Nearly 1 million American teenagers (about 10% of all 15- to 19-year-old girls) become pregnant each year. About 33% abort their pregnancies, 14% miscarry, and 52% bear children—72% of them out of wedlock. Of the half million teens who give birth, approximately 75% are first-time mothers. More than 175,000 are 17 years old or younger.

> These young mothers and their offspring are especially vulnerable to severe adverse social and economic consequences. More than 80% of these young mothers end up in poverty and on welfare, many for the majority of their children's critically important development years.

> One study looked at the higher engagement in crime by male children of adolescent mothers and found that the sons of adolescent mothers are 2.7 times more likely to be incarcerated than the sons of mothers who delayed childbearing until their early twenties. Nationally, about 5% of all young men were behind bars over a 13-year period. This is well below the 10.3% rate of observed incarceration for young

men born to adolescent mothers and slightly above the 3.8% rate for young men born to mothers who began their families at age 20 or 21.

Roughly half of the observed difference for young men born to adolescent versus older childbearers is accounted for by observable differences in the demographic and background characteristics of offspring of both groups of mothers. Still, if these adolescents postponed childbearing until age 20 or 21, it would, by itself, reduce the incarceration rate for the affected children by 13% (from 10.3% to 9.1%).

Even the relatively small fraction of the higher incarceration rate that is directly attributable to adolescent childbearing costs society dearly. A delay in childbearing until the age of 20.5 would reduce the national average incarceration rate by 3.5%, for an annual savings of about $1 billion in correctional costs and a potential savings of nearly $ 3 billion in total law enforcement costs. These results are, of course, long-range. Even if all prospective adolescent mothers were to delay their childbearing as of tomorrow, the incarceration rates would not fall as predicted for approximately 20 years—the earliest age at which young offenders start going to jail in any substantial numbers.

Thus, policies that successfully address adolescent childbearing could lead to additional cost savings for the nation.

Source: Rebecca A. Maynard, Ph.D., and Eileen M. Garry, *Adolescent Motherhood: Implications for the Juvenile Justice System* (Washington, DC: Office of Juvenile Justice and Delinquency Prevention, January 1997), citing "Crime: The Influence of Early Childbearing on the Cost of Incarceration," in Rebecca A. Maynard, ed., *Kids Having Kids: Economic Costs and Social Consequences of Teen Pregnancy* (Washington, DC: Urban Institute Press, 1996).

to ethnicity. Asian and Pacific Islander women and men reported lower rates of intimate partner violence than did men and women from other minority backgrounds. Similarly, socioeconomic status was associated with violence, with poor women experiencing the highest rates of violence.

Violence among intimates may lead to other forms of crime. The National Clearinghouse for the Defense of Battered Women, one of the few national organizations that collect data on the relationship between violence against women and women's involvement in illegal activity, reports that more than half of all women in detention had been battered or raped before being incarcerated. Other studies have similarly uncovered a link between the victimization of women and their criminal behavior.[90]

Race and Crime

Several years ago, Professor Lani Guinier of the University of Pennsylvania School of Law was interviewed on *Think Tank,* a PBS show. Guinier was asked by Ben Wattenberg, the program's moderator, "When we talk about crime, crime, crime, are we really using a code for black, black, black?" Guinier responded this way: "To a great extent, yes, and I think that's a problem, not because we shouldn't deal with the disproportionate number of crimes that young black men may be committing, but because if we can't talk about race, then when we talk about crime, we're really talking about other things, and it means that we're not being honest in terms of acknowledging what the problem is and then trying to deal with it."[91]

Crimes are committed by individuals of all races. The link between crime—especially violent, street, and predatory crimes—and race, however, shows a striking pattern (see Table 2–6). In most crime categories, arrests of African American offenders equal or exceed arrests of whites. In any given year, arrests of African Americans account for more than 50% of all arrests for violent crimes. African Americans, however, comprise only 12% of the U.S. population. When *rates* (which are based upon the relative proportion of racial groups) are examined, the statistics are even more striking (see Figure 2–7). The arrest rate for murder among African Americans, for example, is six times that of whites. Similar rate comparisons, when calculated for other violent crimes, show that far more African Americans than whites are involved in other street crimes, such as assault, burglary, and robbery. Related studies show that 30% of all the young African

---

TABLE 2–6   Arrest Rates by Race (per 100,000 People) and Relative Rates of Arrest for Selected Offenses, 2006

Offense	African Americans	Whites	Rate of Arrest, African American vs. White
Murder	13	2	6.5:1
Rape	19	6	3.2:1
Robbery	119	16	7.4:1
Aggravated assault	321	100	3.2:1
Burglary	163	65	2.5:1
Larceny	725	251	2.9:1
Motor vehicle theft	118	28	4.2:1
Weapons	123	33	3.7:1
Drug abuse	1,086	331	3.3:1
Prostitution	68	16	4.2:1

Source: Derived from FBI, *Crime in the United States, 2006*; and Population Estimates Program, Population Division of the U.S. Census Bureau, *Resident Population Estimates of the U.S.,* January 1, 2007.

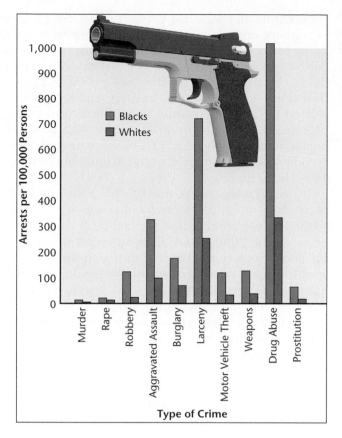

FIGURE 2–7

Relative Arrest Rates by Race and Type of Crime for Selected Offenses, 2006

Sources: Derived from FBI, *Crime in the United States, 2006*; and Population Estimates Program, Population Division of the U.S. Census Bureau, *Resident Population Estimates of the U.S.*, January 1, 2006.

American men in the United States are under correctional supervision on any given *day*—a far greater percentage than for members of any other race in the country.[92]

The real question for anyone interested in the justice system is how to explain such huge race-based disparities.

Some authors maintain that racial differences in arrest and imprisonment rates (see Figure 2–7) are due to the differential treatment of African Americans and other minorities at the hands of a discriminatory criminal justice system.[93] Marvin D. Free, Jr., for example, says the fact that African Americans are underrepresented as criminal justice professionals results in their being overrepresented in arrest statistics.[94] Some police officers, says Free, are more prone to arrest African Americans than whites, frequently arrest African Americans without sufficient evidence to support criminal charges, and overcharge in criminal cases involving African American defendants, which leads to unfair statistical tabulations that depict African Americans as responsible for a greater proportion of crime than is, in fact, the case.

Other writers disagree. In *The Myth of a Racist Criminal Justice System,* for example, **William Wilbanks** claims that while the practice of American criminal justice may have been significantly racist in the past and while some vestiges of racism may indeed remain, the system is today by and large objective in its processing of criminal defendants.[95] Using statistical data, Wilbanks shows that "at every point from arrest to parole there is little or no evidence of an overall racial effect, in that the percentage outcomes for blacks and whites are not very different."[96] Wilbanks claims to have reviewed "all the available studies that have examined the possible existence of racial discrimination from arrest to parole." In essence, he says, "this examination of the available evidence indicates that support for the 'discrimination thesis' is sparse, inconsistent, and frequently contradictory."[97]

Wilbanks is careful to counter arguments advanced by those who continue to suggest that the system is racist. He writes, for example, "Perhaps the black/white gap at arrest is a product of racial bias by the police in that the police are more likely to select and arrest black than white offenders. The best evidence on this question comes from the National Crime Survey which interviews 130,000 Americans each year about crime victimization. . . . The percent of offenders described by victims as being black is generally consistent with the percent of offenders who are black according to arrest figures."[98] Such data are complemented by annual surveys conducted by the Centers for Disease Control and Prevention (CDC), which consistently find that people treated at hospital emergency rooms for nonfatal gunshot wounds related to crime are mainly male, black, and young. A recent CDC study, for example, found that men comprise almost 90% of those treated for firearm injuries connected to crimes and that 59% of those treated are black. According to the CDC, "The racial breakdown for crime-related [gunshot] wounds [is] 59% black, 19% white, and 14% Hispanic."[99]

However, observes Wilbanks, "the assertion that the criminal justice system is not racist does not address the reasons why blacks appear to offend at higher rates than whites before coming into contact with the criminal justice system. . . . It may be," he suggests, "that racial discrimination in American society has been responsible for conditions (e.g., discrimination in employment, housing, and education) that lead to higher rates of offending by blacks, but that possibility does not bear on the question of whether the criminal justice system discriminates against blacks."[100] Marvin Free, Jr., agrees, suggesting that blacks are still systematically denied equal access to the societal resources that would allow for full participation in American society, resulting in a higher rate of law violation.[101] In a work that considers such issues in great detail, John Hagan and Ruth D. Peterson attribute higher crime rates among ethnic minorities to (1) concentrated poverty, (2) joblessness, (3) family disruption, and (4) racial segregation.[102] Table 2–7 lists factors identified by recent research that appear to contribute to minority overrepresentation in the juvenile justice system.

A fundamental critique of Wilbanks's thesis comes from **Coramae Richey Mann,** who says that his overreliance on quantitative or statistical data fails to capture the reality of racial discrimination within the justice system.[103] White victims, says Mann, tend to overreport being victimized by African American offenders because they often misperceive Hispanic and other minority offenders as African American. Similarly, says

---

TABLE 2–7   Underlying Factors Contributing to Minority Overrepresentation in the Juvenile Justice System

Socioeconomic Conditions	Educational System
Low-income jobs	Inadequate early childhood education
Few job opportunities	Inadequate prevention programs (early dropouts)
Urban density/high crime rates	Inadequate education quality overall
Few community support services	Lack of cultural education, cultural role models
Inadequate health and welfare resources	

The Family	Juvenile Justice System
Single-parent homes	Racial/ethnic bias
Economic stress	Insufficient diversion options
Limited time for supervision	System "labeling"
	Barriers to parental advocacy
	Poor juvenile justice system/community integration

Source: Adapted from Patricia Devine, Kathleen Coolbaugh, and Susan Jenkins, *Disproportionate Minority Confinement: Lessons Learned from Five States* (Washington, DC: Office of Juvenile Justice and Delinquency Prevention, 1998).

Mann, African American victims are sometimes reluctant to report victimization—especially at the hands of whites. And, says Mann, the fact that far more whites than African Americans live in the United States means that they will naturally account for a greater percentage of victims, which explains the seeming overvictimization of whites by African Americans.

Although Mann cites the need for the greater use of qualitative measures, most available data on race and crime are statistical. According to such data, African Americans not only appear to commit street crimes at a rate disproportionate to their representation in the population, but also are disproportionately victimized by such crimes. Two authors asserted that "black-on-black crime is the true face of crime in America."[104] No less a figure than American civil rights leader Jesse Jackson has identified black-on-black crime as "the most important issue of the civil rights movement today."[105] If such assertions are even partially correct, although unpopular, then, many suggest, it is incumbent upon policymakers to admit and realistically assess the degree of overinvolvement in street crime that characterizes a disproportionately large segment of the African American population in the United States today.

Such overinvolvement may be a sign of a sinister form of racism. U.S. District Judge Robert L. Carter, for example, points out that although American society seems prepared to tolerate the conditions that produce high crime rates among blacks, it is unlikely that it would if whites were committing as many crimes. In a speech, Judge Carter said that two of every three black men in the United States aged 20 to 29 are in prison, awaiting trial, or on probation, and he noted that "everyone in this room knows that if white men were in this situation or in danger of being so placed, there would be a nationwide howl of protest."[106] The fact that no such protest can be heard, said Carter, "is outrageous and constitutes unmitigated racism. Instead of seeking remedies," observed the judge, "the nation is spending billions of dollars for new prison facilities, apparently gearing up to be able to soon house half the 20- to 29-year-old black men."

At the very least, it would seem that the existing relationship between race and most forms of street crime is one source of continuing divisiveness in American society. In a recent report, the National Criminal Justice Commission, a project of the National Center on Institutions and Alternatives (NCIA), noted that "the fact that so many minority men are in the criminal justice system raises profoundly disturbing questions." The commission concluded, "To the extent that racial disparities in prison are the result of racial bias, then that bias must be rooted out of the criminal justice system. To the extent that they are the result of higher African-American crime, then the underlying causes of that crime must be addressed. Failure to do so puts the nation at risk of social catastrophe."[107]

High rates of crime and of criminal victimization within the African American community have led to a heightened fear of crime among African Americans. One report by the Bureau of Justice Statistics, which was based on data from the American Housing Survey (conducted by the Department of Housing and Urban Development), found that "black households are nearly three times more likely than white ones to fear crime in their neighborhoods."[108] The survey showed that fear of neighborhood crime rose almost twice as much among blacks as whites between the mid-1980s and mid-1990s. In black central-city households, neighborhood crime was cited as residents' primary concern. Study findings are said to "mirror the incidence of violent crime, which victimizes blacks more than whites and central city residents more than those in suburbs or rural areas."[109]

Finally, in any discussion of race and crime, one caveat that was alluded to earlier needs to be stressed. It has to do with the fact that racial identity is not always well defined and is frequently subject to personal and social interpretation. This appears to be especially true in the case of so-called mixed-race individuals, for whom the concept of "race" itself may have lost all meaning. Hence, as the American population becomes more biologically and culturally homogeneous, categorizing offenders on the basis of race may prove far less meaningful for analytical purposes.

Social Class and Crime

Prior to 1960, criminologists generally assumed that a correlation existed between social class and crime. They believed that members of lower social classes were more prone to commit crime, and they thought that this propensity applied to all types of criminal activity. In the early 1960s, however, studies of the relationship between social class and crime, which made use of offender self-reports, seemed to show that the relationship between social class and criminality was an artifact of discretionary practices within the criminal justice system.[110] Such studies, especially of teenagers, found that rates of self-reported delinquency and criminality were fairly consistent across various social classes within American society. Similar studies of white-collar criminality (which is discussed in more detail in Chapter 12) seemed to show that although the nature of criminal activity may vary between classes, members of all social classes have nearly equal tendencies toward criminality. Hence, the apparent penchant for crime among members of the lower social classes was explained away as a consequence of discretionary decisions by police officers, prosecutors, and judges—decisions that discriminated against those with lower social status and that resulted in such individuals being arrested, found guilty, and sentenced to imprisonment much more frequently than members of other classes.

In 1978, a comprehensive reevaluation of 35 previous studies of the relationship between social class and crime concluded that previously claimed links were nonexistent.[111] Publication of the 1978 report fueled further study of the relationship between social class and crime, and in 1981, a seminal article by Australian criminologist **John Braithwaite**—who summarized the results of 224 previous studies on the subject—concluded rather convincingly that members of lower social classes were indeed more prone to commit crime.[112] In contrast to earlier studies, Braithwaite found that "socioeconomic status is one of the very few correlates of criminality which can be taken, on balance, as persuasively supported by a large body of empirical evidence."

Many of the difficulties surrounding research into the relationship between social class and crime appear to stem from a lack of definitional clarity. In the many different studies evaluated by Braithwaite, for example, neither *crime* nor *class* was uniformly defined. Margaret Farnworth, Terence P. Thornberry, Marvin D. Krohn,[113] and others have similarly suggested that earlier studies may have been seriously flawed by their near-exclusive focus on young people and by their conceptualization of crime in terms of relatively minor offenses (truancy, vandalism, and so on). Hence, a lack of concise definitions of the subject matter, combined with inadequate measurement techniques, may have led to misleading results.

More recent data provided by the National Youth Survey[114] and analytical techniques that define *class* based on a status-attainment model using indicators of sustained underclass status[115] and that define *delinquency* as repeated involvement in more serious street crimes[116] have led researchers to conclude that a fairly significant correlation between certain forms of criminality and social class exists.[117] Therefore, although it would be grossly unfair to conclude that all, or even most, members of lower social classes are criminals, careful statistical analysis of available information appears to show that street crimes, including crimes of violence, theft, and drug abuse, are more likely to be perpetrated by individuals with low socioeconomic status.[118] Such findings have led to the introduction of the "underclass" concept as a way of helping to explain the criminality of those with low social standing.

SUMMARY

Crime statistics have been gathered in one form or another for at least 150 years. Although early data about crime may have been used to assess the moral health of nations, modern-day crime statistics programs provide a fairly objective picture of crime in the United States and elsewhere. Statistics often form the basis for social policy, and innovative crime control strategies like the "Three Strikes and You're Out" initiative that began in the 1990s are frequently based on an understanding of crime patterns provided by such information.

Today, two large-scale government programs collect crime data in the United States. One, the National Crime Victimization Survey, is run by the Bureau of Justice Statistics and provides yearly reports on the criminal victimization of households and individuals. The other, the Uniform Crime Reporting Program (which is undergoing modification via the incorporation of data from the National Incident-Based Reporting System, or NIBRS), is administered by the Federal Bureau of Investigation and collects information annually on crimes reported to the police and on arrests throughout the country.

As discussed, the social correlates of crime in the United States include age, gender, race, and social class. Although crime statistics do not tell the whole story and other forms of crime need to be recognized, it appears from the best information available that young African American men are especially overrepresented in American street crime statistics. While some people see this as an indictment of American society, a number of criminologists feel that recognizing the reality of such involvement could help our society secure a safer future for all of its citizens and could enhance effective crime prevention efforts.

Other than age, gender, and ethnicity, social class can be a significant indicator of the likelihood of criminal involvement. Suffice it here to say that crimes are committed by members of all social classes. As we will see in later chapters, however, powerful classes make the laws and are therefore less apt to have a need to break them, while at the same time they are probably more committed to preserving the status quo. Hence, many offenders, especially those arrested for street, property, and predatory crimes, come from the lower social classes.

Some people argue that crime statistics do not justify the degree of concern that Americans express about crime. Others suggest that these statistics are misleading and that they do not provide a true measure of the extent of the crime problem in America. Nonetheless, even though the actual incidence of crime is difficult to measure, crime statistics can provide us with an appreciation for the extent of the problems facing victims of crime, social policymakers, and the criminal justice system today.

KEY TERMS

aggravated assault, 60

arson, 64

burglary, 61

carjacking, 63

clearance rate, 41

cohort, 70

correlation, 69

criminal homicide, 54

criminality index, 53

dark figure of crime, 41

date rape, 56

demographics, 36

desistance phenomenon, 70

felony murder, 55

first-degree murder, 54

forcible rape, 56

hate crime, 42

larceny-theft, 62

latent crime rate, 53

Monitoring the Future, 67

motor vehicle theft, 63

National Crime Victimization Survey (NCVS), 38

National Incident-Based Reporting System (NIBRS), 38

National Youth Survey (NYS), 67

negligent homicide, 54

Part I offenses, 39

Part II offenses, 64

rape, 56

robbery, 59

second-degree murder, 54

self-report survey, 66

simple assault, 60

spousal rape, 56

statistical school, 37

Uniform Crime Reporting (UCR) Program, 38

KEY NAMES

Alfred Blumstein, 70

John Braithwaite, 80

Elliott Currie, 53

John J. DiIulio, Jr., 70

James Alan Fox, 70

André Michel Guerry, 37

Thomas Robert Malthus, 36

Coramae Richey Mann, 78

Joan Petersilia, 70

Adolphe Quételet, 37

William Wilbanks, 77

James Q. Wilson, 70

QUESTIONS FOR REVIEW

1. How did the gathering of crime data begin in the United States? How has it evolved since that time?

2. What are the major differences among the NCVS and UCR/NIBRS? Can useful comparisons be made between these two programs? If so, what kinds of comparisons might be made?

3. What major shifts in crime rates have occurred since record keeping began in the United States? What future direction are crime rates likely to take?

4. What is the nature of the crime problem in the U.S. today? How can we best measure it?

5. What are the major crimes on which data is gathered today? How prevalent is each?

6. How do Part II offenses, reported by the FBI, differ from Part I offenses? How common are Part II crimes today?

7. What are the major available sources of contemporary crime data in the United States? What other sources exist?

8. What resources and techniques exist for gathering information about crimes that are not reported to the police? What is the "dark figure of crime"?

9. What is meant by the "social dimensions of crime"? Which social dimensions does this chapter discuss?

QUESTIONS FOR REFLECTION

1. This book emphasizes a social problems versus a social responsibility theme. Which perspective is best supported by a realistic appraisal of the "social dimensions" of crime discussed in this chapter? Explain.

2. This chapter says that African Americans appear to be overrepresented in many categories of criminal activity. Do you believe that the statistics cited in this chapter accurately reflect the degree of black and white involvement in crime? Why? How might those statistics be inaccurate?

3. What does it mean to say that the traditional UCR was summary-based, while the newer NIBRS is incident-based? When NIBRS is fully operational, what kinds of data will it contribute to the UCR Program? How will this information be useful?

4. What is a crime rate? How are rates useful? How might the NCVS and the UCR/NIBRS make better use of rates?

5. Why don't victims report crimes to the police? Which crimes appear to be the least frequently reported? Why are those crimes so rarely reported? Which crimes appear to be the most frequently reported? Why are they so often reported?

WEB QUEST

A rich repository of crime and justice information on the World Wide Web can be found at the National Criminal Justice Reference Service (NCJRS). NCJRS makes an excellent starting point for Web exploration in the field of criminology because it is essentially a collection of clearinghouses supporting all bureaus of the U.S. Department of Justice, the Office of Justice Programs and its programs' offices, the National Institute of Justice, the Office of Juvenile Justice and Delinquency Prevention, the Bureau of Justice Statistics, the Bureau of Justice Assistance, and the Office for Victims of Crime. It also provides direct links to the Office of National Drug Control Policy, the home of our nation's cabinet-level "drug czar." The NCJRS documents database (available under Publications/Products and Library/Abstracts) is one of the most extensive sources available anywhere of online information about crime statistics, crime prevention, and research and evaluation in the area of crime control. The database is fully searchable, and the complete text of many documents is directly available on the Web.

NCJRS provides a wealth of services to an international community of policymakers and professionals in the criminology field. You can be among them by pointing your browser to the NCJRS home page: www.ncjrs.gov. When you arrive at the NCJRS home page, you will find it arranged by topical areas, each of which is "clickable." The site contains links organized under the following key headings:

- Corrections
- Courts
- Crime
- Crime Prevention
- Drugs
- Justice System
- Juvenile Justice
- Law Enforcement
- Victims

Choices listed near the top right of the home page, and in the right-hand margin allow users to conduct keyword searches of all topics on the site, to review and subscribe to the

NCJRS e-mail newsletter, and to see a listing of upcoming events in the crime and justice field.

If your instructor asks you to, explore some of NCJRS's features. Conduct a document search on a topic of interest to you, and create an annotated bibliography of selected documents available from NCJRS. Enhance the bibliography with the Internet addresses of Web sites related to the topic you selected.

NOTES

[1] Arthur Conan Doyle, "The Adventure of the Speckled Band," *The Strand,* February 1892.

[2] James Q. Wilson, *Thinking about Crime* (New York: Basic Books, 1983), p. 251.

[3] Some of the information in this story comes from Chuck Shepherd's News of the Weird, http://www.newsoftheweird.com/cgi-bin/search/newsweird.cgi (accessed June 15, 2007).

[4] Ann L. Pastore and Kathleen Maguire, eds., *Sourcebook of Criminal Justice Statistics Online,* http://www.albany.edu/sourcebook (accessed January 5, 2007).

[5] A number of contemporary criminologists continue to study the effect of weather on crime. See, for example, Ellen G. Cohn, "The Effect of Weather and Temporal Variations on Calls for Police Service," *American Journal of Police,* Vol. 15, No. 1 (1996), pp. 23–43; Ellen G. Cohn, "The Prediction of Police Calls for Service: The Influence of Weather and Temporal Variables on Rape and Domestic Violence," *Environmental Psychology,* Vol. 13 (1993), pp. 71–83; Ellen G. Cohn, "Weather and Crime," *British Journal of Criminology,* Vol. 30, No. 1 (1990), pp. 51–64; and Derral Cheatwood, "Is There a Season for Homicide?" *Criminology,* Vol. 26, No. 2 (May 1988), pp. 287–306.

[6] Douglas Eckberg. "Stalking the Elusive Homicide: A Capture-Recapture Approach to the Estimation of Post-Reconstruction South Carolina Killings." *Social Science History,* Vol. 25, No. 1, (2001), pp. 00–91.

[7] NCJRS may be reached at 800–851–3420, or write to National Institute of Justice, National Criminal Justice Reference Service, Box 6000, Rockville, MD 20850.

[8] Federal Bureau of Investigation, *Crime in the United States, 1992* (Washington, DC: U.S. Government Printing Office, 1993), p. vi.

[9] See FBI, "About the UCR Program," http://www.fbi.gov/ucr/05cius/about/about_ucr.html (accessed July 10, 2007).

[10] Public Law 105–251.

[11] See Association of State UCR Programs, "NIBRS News," http://www.asucrp.org/news/index.html (accessed March 30, 2007).

[12] JRSA Incident-Based Reporting Resource Center, http://www.jrsa.org/ibrrc/more_about/index.html (accessed March 22, 2006).

[13] 28 U.S.C.A. § 534.

[14] Public Law 103–322.

[15] Bureau of Justice Assistance, *Addressing Hate Crimes: Six Initiatives That Are Enhancing the Efforts of Criminal Justice Practitioners* (Washington, DC: U.S. Department of Justice, 2000).

[16] FBI, *Crime in the United States, 2003* (Washington, DC: U.S. Government Printing Office, 2004).

[17] http://www.adl.org/frames/front_islam.html (accessed December 5, 2000).

[18] James B. Jacobs and Kimberly A. Potter, "Hate Crimes: A Critical Perspective," in Michael Tonry, ed., *Crime and Justice: A Review of Research* (Chicago: University of Chicago Press 1997), p. 19.

[19] Bureau of Justice Statistics, *Criminal Victimization, 2006* (Washington, DC: U.S. Dept. of Justice, 2004); and Patsy A. Klaus, *Crime and the Nation's Households, 2003* (Washington, DC: BJS, 2004).

[20] For further information, see Ronet Bachman and Bruce Taylor, "The Measurement of Family Violence and Rape by the Redesigned National Crime Victimization Survey," *Justice Quarterly,* Vol. 11, No. 3 (September 1994); Bureau of Justice Statistics, "National Crime Victimization Survey Redesign," *BJS Fact Sheet,* October 19, 1994; and BJS, "Questions and Answers about the Redesign," October 30, 1994.

[21] The President's Commission on Law Enforcement and Administration of Justice, *The Challenge of Crime in a Free Society* (Washington, DC: U.S. Government Printing Office, 1967). The President's Commission relied on Uniform Crime Reports data, and the other crime statistics reported in this section come from UCRs for various years.

[22] Frank E. Hagan, *Research Methods in Criminal Justice and Criminology,* 5th ed. (Boston: Allyn & Bacon, 2000).

[23] See, for example, Jackie Cissell, "Health Commentary: When Birth Control Could Lead to Race Control," *Milwaukee Times Internet Edition,* September 16, 1999, http://www.milwtimes.com/articles/oped/09031999/oped25409031999.htm (accessed December 5, 2000).

[24] John J. Donohue and Steven D. Levitt, "Legalized Abortion and Crime," Stanford Law School, Public Law and Legal Theory Working Paper No. 1 (2000), http://papers.ssrn.com/paper._taf?abstract_id=174508 (accessed January 10, 2005).

[25] Marc Ouimet, "Explaining the American and Canadian Crime 'Drop' in the 1990s," *Canadian Journal of Criminology,* Vol. 44, No. 1 (January 2002), pp. 33–50.

[26] John J. DiIulio, Jr., "The Question of Black Crime," *Public Interest* (fall 1994), pp. 3–12.

[27] Quoted in Dan Eggen, "Major Crimes in U.S. Increase: 2001 Rise Follows Nine Years of Decline," *Washington Post,* June 23, 2002, p. A1.

[28] All of the references to the work of Elliott Currie in this section are from Elliott Currie, "Reflections on Crime and Criminology at the Millennium," *Western Criminology Review,* Vol. 2, No. 1 (1999), http://wcr.sonoma.edu/v2n1/currie.html (accessed February 13, 2007).

[29] Some researchers have attempted to estimate the number of crimes that would otherwise be committed by incarcerated individuals. See, for example, Jose A. Canela-Cacho, Alfred Blumstein, and Jacqueline Cohen, "Relationship between the Offending Frequency of Imprisoned and Free Offenders," *Criminology,* Vol. 35, No. 1 (1997), pp. 133–175.

[30] "Life in Prison for Poison Doctor," CBS News, September 6, 2000, http://www.cbsnews.com/stories/2000/07/12/national/main214413.shtml (accessed June 8, 2006).

[31] James B. Stewart, *Blind Eye: The Terrifying Story of a Doctor Who Got Away with Murder* (Carmichael, CA: Touchstone Books, 2000).

[32] David Woods, "U.S. Doctor May Have Killed 60," BMJ Publishing Group, September 16, 2000, http://bmj.bmjjournals.com/cgi/reprint/321/7262/037.pdf (accessed June 8, 2005).

[33] This and other UCR statistics in this chapter are taken from FBI, *Crime in the United States, 2006.*

[34] Frank Schmalleger and Ted Alleman, "The Collective Reality of Crime: An Integrative Approach to the Causes and Consequences of the Criminal Event," in Gregg Barak, ed., *Varieties of Criminology: Readings from a Dynamic Discipline* (New York: Praeger, 1994).

[35] "British Law Lords Recognize Male Rape," United Press wire service, Northern edition, July 12, 1994.

[36] "Swim Coach Guilty of Statutory Rape," *USA Today,* August 13, 1993, p. 3A.

[37] A. Nicholas Groth, *Men Who Rape: The Psychology of the Offender* (New York: Plenum, 1979).

[38] See, for example, Schmalleger and Alleman, "The Collective Reality of Crime."

[39] This and most other NCVS data are taken from the Bureau of Justice Statistics, *Criminal Victimization in the United States, 2006* (Washington, DC: U.S. Department of Justice, 2007), and other years.

[40] Patrick A. Langan and Caroline Wolf Harlow, *Child Rape Victims, 1992* (Washington, DC: Bureau of Justice Statistics, 1994); and Pierre Thomas, "Rape of Girls Too Common, Study Finds; Half of All Victims Are under Age 18," *Washington Post* wire service, June 23, 1994.

[41] The occupants of houses may be robbed by someone who comes to their door. Hence, household robbery is a crime distinguishable from household burglary.

[42] FBI, *Crime in the United States, 1992,* p. 27.

[43] BJS, *Criminal Victimization in the United States, 1990* (Washington, DC: U.S. Department of Justice, 1991), p. 68.

[44] Numbers may not total 100% because of rounding.

[45] This is true even though the NCVS does not record burglaries of businesses or commercial properties.

[46] "Man Jailed for Selling Stolen Moon Rocks," Associated Press News Service, August 27, 2003, http://www.pda.ananova.net/news/story/sm_813426.html?menu=news.story (accessed June 10, 2006).

[47] Details for this story come from *Connecticut* v. *Yolanda Dubose* (AC 21999, February 18, 2003).

[48] 20 U.S.C. § 1092.

[49] Diana Jean Schemo, "Colleges Rushing to Compile Crime Statistics for the Web," *New York Times,* October 18, 2000, http://www.nytimes.com/2000/10/19/national/19CRIM.html (accessed March 1, 2001).

[50] H.R. 6, Higher Education Amendments of 1998, Public Law 105–244.

[51] The coining of the term *dark figure of crime* is sometimes attributed to Michael Gottfredson. See Michael Gottfredson, "Substantive Contributions of Victimization Surveys," in Michael Tonry and Norval Morris, eds., *Crime and Justice: An Annual Review of Research,* Vol. 7 (Chicago: University of Chicago Press, 1986).

[52] Terence P. Thornberry and Marvin D. Krohn, "The Self-Report Method for Measuring Delinquency and Crime," *Criminal Justice 2000* (Washington, DC: National Institute of Justice, 2000), p. 34.

[53] See Austin L. Porterfield, "Delinquency and Outcome in Court and College," *American Journal of Sociology,* Vol. 49 (November 1943), pp. 199–208; and J. S. Wallerstein and C. J. Wylie, "Our Law-Abiding Law-Breakers," *Probation,* Vol. 25 (1947), pp. 107–112.

[54] Porterfield, "Delinquency and Outcome in Court and College."

[55] Some of the wording in this section is adapted from Thornberry and Krohn, "The Self-Report Method for Measuring Delinquency and Crime."

[56] Wallerstein and Wylie, "Our Law-Abiding Law-Breakers."

[57] J. F. Short, Jr., and F. I. Nye, "Reported Behavior as a Criterion of Deviant Behavior," *Social Problems,* Vol. 5 (1957), pp. 207–213; J. F. Short, Jr., and F. I. Nye, "Extent of Unrecorded Juvenile Delinquency: Tentative Conclusions," *Journal of Criminal Law and Criminology,* Vol. 49 (1958), pp. 296–302.

[58] Some of the wording in this section is adapted from Thornberry and Krohn, "The Self-Report Method for Measuring Delinquency and Crime."

[59] F. Ivan Nye, James F. Short, Jr., and Virgil Olson, "Socioeconomic Status and Delinquent Behavior," *American Journal of Sociology,* Vol. 63 (January 1958), pp. 381–389.

[60] See, for example, Delbert S. Elliott, David Huizinga, and Suzanne S. Ageton, *Explaining Delinquency and Drug Use* (Newbury Park, CA: Sage, 1985).

[61] National Institute on Drug Abuse, *Monitoring the Future: National Results on Adolescent Drug Use—Overview of Key Findings, 2006* (Rockville, MD: U.S. Department of Health and Human Services, 2007).

[62] Shannon M. Catalano, *Criminal Victimization, 2006* (Washington, DC: BJS 2007).

[63] Ibid.

[64] For an excellent overview of the social dimensions of crime, see John Hagan and Ruth D. Peterson, *Crime and Inequality* (Stanford, CA: Stanford University Press, 1995); and James W. Messerschmidt, *Crime as Structured Action: Gender, Race, Class and Crime in the Making* (Thousand Oaks, CA: Sage, 1997).

[65] Alfred Blumstein, "Violence by Young People: Why the Deadly Nexus?" *National Institute of Justice Journal,* No. 229 (August 1995), pp. 3–9.

[66] John J. DiIulio, Jr., "The Question of Black Crime," *Public Interest,* Vol. 117, No. 3 (fall 1994), pp. 3–12.

[67] James Alan Fox, *Trends in Juvenile Violence: A Report to the United States Attorney General on Current and Future Rates of Juvenile Offending* (Boston: Northeastern University Press, 1996); and Gary Fields, "Youth Violent Crime Falls 9.2%," *USA Today,* October 3–5, 1997, p. 1A (quoting James Fox).

[68] James Q. Wilson and Joan Petersilia, *Crime* (San Francisco, CA: Institute for Contemporary Studies Press, 1995).

[69] Ibid.

[70] Fox, *Trends in Juvenile Violence.*

[71] Wilson and Petersilia, *Crime.*

[72] Blumstein, "Violence by Young People."

[73] Council on Crime in America, *The State of Violent Crime in America: A First Report of the Council on Crime in America* (Washington, DC: New Citizenship Project, 1996).

[74] Travis Hirschi and Michael Gottfredson, "Age and the Explanation of Crime," *American Journal of Sociology,* Vol. 89 (1983), pp. 552–584.

[75] "Elderly Man Sentenced to More than 12 years for Bank Robbery," Associated Press wire service, January 24, 2004.

[76] Edna Buchanan, "You're under Arrest," *New Choices for Retirement Living,* June 1994, p. 61.

[77] U.S. Department of Justice, *Elderly Crime Victims* (Washington, DC: Bureau of Justice Statistics, March 1994).

[78] Ibid.

[79] Patsy Klaus, et al., *Age Patterns in Violent Victimizations, 1976–2000* (Washington, DC: U.S. Department of Justice, 2002).

[80] For an excellent review of homicide and the elderly, see James Alan Fox and Jack Levin, "Homicide against the Elderly: A Research Note," *Criminology,* Vol. 29, No. 2 (May 1994), pp. 317–327.

[81] U.S. Department of Justice, *Elderly Crime Victims.*

[82] Mel E. Weith, "Elder Abuse: A National Tragedy," *FBI Law Enforcement Bulletin,* February 1994, pp. 24–26.

[83] U.S. Congress, House Subcommittee on Human Services, Select Committee on Aging, *Elder Abuse: An Assessment of the Federal Response,* 101st Congress, 1st Session, June 7, 1989.

[84] Stephen E. Brown, Finn-Aage Esbensen, and Gilbert Geis, *Criminology: Explaining Crime and Its Context,* 2nd ed. (Cincinnati: Anderson, 1996), p. 198.

85 Leanne Fiftal Alarid et al., "Women's Roles in Serious Offenses: A Study of Adult Felons," *Justice Quarterly*, Vol. 13, No. 3 (September 1996), p. 431.

86 U.S. Department of Justice, *Elderly Crime Victims*, p. 4.

87 NCVS data show that the rate of rape has dropped somewhat over the past two decades, even though the number of such crimes reported to the police has increased. Generally, UCR data are probably more reliable than NCVS data where rape is concerned because the NCVS's use of a redesigned questionnaire has thrown the reliability of NCVS rape data into question. For 1992, the number of rapes reported to the police (UCR data) exceeded the number of estimated rape victimizations (NCVS data) for the first time since record keeping began. See Kathleen Maguire and Ann L. Pastore, eds., *Sourcebook of Criminal Justice Statistics, 1993* (Washington, DC: U.S. Superintendent of Documents, 1994), Table 3.26, for additional information.

88 The Violence Against Women Act (VAWA) is Title IV of the Violent Crime Control and Law Enforcement Act of 1994 (Public Law 103–322). It was reauthorized by Congress in 2005, and signed into law by President George W. Bush in 2006.

89 Patricia Tjaden and Nancy Thoennes, *Extent, Nature, and Consequences of Intimate Partner Violence: Findings from the National Violence against Women Survey* (Washington, DC: National Institute of Justice, July 2000).

90 Beth E. Richie, Kay Tsenin, and Cathy Spatz Widom, *Research on Women and Girls in the Justice System* (Washington, DC: National Institute of Justice, September 2000).

91 Reprinted in "For the Record," *Washington Post* wire service, March 3, 1994.

92 Marvin D. Free, Jr., *African-Americans and the Criminal Justice System* (New York: Garland, 1996).

93 For a good overview of the issues, see Dee Cook and Barbara Hudson, *Racism and Criminology* (Thousand Oaks, CA: Sage, 1993).

94 Free, *African-Americans and the Criminal Justice System*.

95 William Wilbanks, *The Myth of a Racist Criminal Justice System* (Monterey, CA: Brooks/Cole, 1987).

96 William Wilbanks, "The Myth of a Racist Criminal Justice System," *Criminal Justice Research Bulletin* (Sam Houston State University), Vol. 3, No. 5 (1987), p. 2.

97 Ibid., p. 5.

98 Ibid., p. 3.

99 Jim Abrams, "Gun Crimes," *Associated Press* wire service, April 12, 1997.

100 Wilbanks, "The Myth of a Racist Criminal Justice System," p. 2.

101 Free, *African-Americans and the Criminal Justice System*.

102 Hagan and Peterson, *Crime and Inequality*.

103 Coramae Richey Mann, "The Reality of a Racist Criminal Justice System," in Barry W. Hancock and Paul M. Sharp, eds., *Criminal Justice in America: Theory, Practice and Policy* (Upper Saddle River, NJ: Prentice Hall, 1996), pp. 51–59.

104 Paul Glastris and Jeannye Thornton, "A New Civil Rights Frontier: After His Own Home and Neighborhood Were Invaded by Street Punks, Jesse Jackson Dedicated Himself to Battling Black-on-Black Crime," *U.S. News and World Report*, January 17, 1994, p. 38.

105 Ibid.

106 Robert L. Carter, "The Criminal Justice System Is Infected with Racism," *Vital Speeches of the Day*, Vol. 62, No. 10 (March 1, 1996), pp. 290–293.

107 Steven R. Doonziger, ed., *The Real War on Crime: The Report of the National Criminal Justice Commission* (New York: Harper Perennial, 1996), p. 128.

108 Michael J. Sniffen, "Crime Fear," *Associated Press* wire service, Northern edition, June 20, 1994.

109 Ibid.

110 For a good review of the issues involved, see John Hagan, *Structural Criminology* (New Brunswick, NJ: Rutgers University Press, 1989).

111 Charles R. Tittle, Wayne Villemez, and Douglas Smith, "The Myth of Social Class and Criminality: An Empirical Assessment of the Empirical Evidence," *American Sociological Review*, Vol. 43, No. 5 (1978), pp. 643–656; see also Charles R. Tittle, "Social Class and Criminality," *Social Forces*, Vol. 56, No. 2 (1977), pp. 474–502.

112 John Braithwaite, "The Myth of Social Class and Criminality Reconsidered," *American Sociological Review*, Vol. 46, No. 1 (1981), pp. 36–57.

113 Margaret Farnworth, Terence P. Thornberry, and Marvin D. Krohn, "Measurement in the Study of Class and Delinquency: Integrating Theory and Research," *Journal of Research in Crime and Delinquency*, Vol. 31, No. 1 (1994), pp. 32–61.

114 The National Youth Survey (NYS), begun in 1976, first reported results in 1977. It is headquartered at the University of Colorado.

115 See, for example, Delbert S. Elliott, "Serious Violent Offenders: Onset, Developmental Course, and Termination—The American Society of Criminology 1993 Presidential Address," *Criminology*, Vol. 32, No. 1 (1994), pp. 1–21; and Delbert S. Elliott and Suzanne S. Ageton, "Reconciling Race and Class Differences in Self-Reported and Official Estimates of Delinquency," *American Sociological Review*, Vol. 45, No. 1 (1980), pp. 95–100.

116 As in the research conducted by Farnworth, Thornberry, and Krohn, "Measurement in the Study of Class and Delinquency."

117 International studies are similarly supportive. See, for example, Per Olof H. Wikstrom, "Housing Tenure, Social Class and Offending: The Individual-Level Relationship in Childhood and Youth," *Criminal Behaviour and Mental Health*, Vol. 1, No. 1 (1991), pp. 69–89; and William R. Smith, *Social Structure, Family Structure, Child Rearing, and Delinquency: Another Look* (Stockholm: University of Stockholm, 1991).

118 See also Nicole H. Rafter, "Crime and the Family," *Women and Criminal Justice*, Vol. 1, No. 2 (1990), pp. 73–86; and Margaret Farnworth, *Social Background and the Early Onset of Delinquency: Exploring the Utility of Various Indicators of Social Class Background* (Albany, NY: Hindelang Criminal Justice Research Center, 1990).

Where Do Theories Come From?

Outline

Theories are nets to catch the world, to rationalize, to explain and to master it.

—Karl Popper[1]

It is a capital mistake to theorize before one has data. One begins to twist facts to suit theories, instead of theories to suit facts.

—Sherlock Holmes, fictional detective created by Sir Arthur Conan Doyle. (Sir Arthur Conan Doyle was born on May 22, 1859).

The cardinal principle of experimentation is that we must accept the outcome whether or not it is to our liking.

—Abraham Kaplan[2]

Science must be theoretical and our theories must be scientific. Science and theory cannot be divorced.

—John H. Laub[3]

Learning Outcomes

After reading this chapter, you should be able to

- Recognize the role of criminological research in theory development and display an understanding of various types of research designs
- Appreciate the relevance of criminological theory to the study of crime and criminals
- Discuss the role of research and experimentation in theory building

- Explain the differences between quantitative and qualitative methods in the social sciences
- Recognize the ethical considerations involved in conducting criminological research
- Identify the impact of criminological research and experimental criminology on the creation of social policy
- Describe the process of writing a research report and identify common sources for publishing research findings

Introduction

Carolyn Risher, the 61-year-old Pentecostal mayor of Inglis, Florida, believes in an unusual crime-reduction strategy.[4] In 2002, she issued an official proclamation banning Satan from Inglis and rendering him powerless over its 1,400 citizens. In the proclamation, issued on official town stationery, Risher wrote, "We exercise our authority over the devil in Jesus' name. By that authority . . . we command all satanic and demonic forces to cease their activities and depart the town of Inglis." While the mayor was undoubtedly well intentioned, Mitchell Billups, the town's police chief, says that crime did not decrease after the mayor took action.[5] Vandalism spiked when someone removed the four hollowed-out wooden posts containing copies of the proclamation that had been placed at town entrances. Following a threatened lawsuit by the American Civil Liberties Union, which accused the mayor and town council of violating our nation's hallowed principle of separation of church and state, the town later rescinded its proclamation and moved the wooden posts, which had been rebuilt and sunk into the ground with concrete, onto private property.[6] The mayor later reimbursed the town for the use of the stationery on which they had been written.[7] Risher was reelected as the town's mayor in 2003, a post she still holds today.[8]

The goings-on in Inglis reminded me of the first criminology class that I taught years ago at a small southern college in the heart of what was then referred to as the Bible Belt. Many of my students were devoutly religious and thoroughly churched in such hallowed concepts as good and evil, sin, salvation, and redemption. When the three-month course was nearly over and a detailed discussion of biological, psychological, and sociological theories of crime causation had ended, I decided to take a survey. I wanted to see which of the theories we had discussed most appealed to the majority of my students. On the last day of class, I took a brief survey. After explaining what I was about to do, I started with the question "How many of you think that most criminal behavior can be explained by the biological theories of crime causation we've studied?" Only one or two students raised their hands. This was a very small number, for the class, a popular one, held 131 students and was taught in a small auditorium. "How many of you," I continued, "think psychological theories explain most crime?" Again, only a handful of students responded. "Well, then, how many of you feel sociological theories offer the best explanation for crime?" I asked. A few more hands went up. Still, the majority of students had not voted one way or the other. Fearing that my teaching had been for naught and not knowing what else to ask, I blurted out, "How many of you believe that 'the devil made him do it' is the best explanation for crime that we can offer?" At that, almost all the students raised their hands.

I realized then that an entire semester spent trying to communicate the best thoughts of generations of criminologists had had little impact on most students in the class. They had listened to what I had to say, they considered each of the perspectives I presented, and then they dismissed all of them out of hand as so much idle conjecture—assigning them the status of ruminations sadly out of touch with the true character of human nature and lacking in appreciation for the true cosmic temper of human activity.

That class held a lesson for me greater than any that the students had learned. It taught me that contemporary criminological theory cannot be fully appreciated until and unless its fundamental assumptions are comprehended. Until students can be brought to see the value of scientific criminology and unless they can be shown why today's criminologists think and believe the way they do, it is impossible to convince them that the criminological enterprise is worthy of serious attention.

The lesson I learned that day was given voice by noted criminological researcher Lawrence W. Sherman, who, upon realizing that even the best scientific evidence the field has to offer is rarely accorded the significance that it deserves by policymakers, wrote: "The mythic power of subjective and unstructured wisdom holds back every field and keeps it from systematically discovering and implementing what works best. . . ."[9]

This chapter describes how criminologists make use of contemporary social scientific research methods in the development of criminological theories and **evidence-based**

evidence based

That which is built on scientific findings; and especially practices and policies founded upon the results of randomized controlled experiments.

In hopes of keeping crime at bay, the mayor of Inglis, Florida, issued a proclamation in 2002 aimed at keeping Satan and his legions out of town. But Bob Farnan, owner of the Port Inglis Restaurant, isn't convinced that drug dealing and burglary have declined. His restaurant, behind him in this February 20, 2004, photo, has been broken into three times in less than a year. Did the proclamation impact the town's crime rate? Did it keep crime from rising? How can we know?

Source: AP Wide World Photos

policies and practices. It is my way of showing to those now embarking upon the study of criminology why the modern-day science of criminology has both validity and purpose—that is, to show how it is applicable to the problems and realities of today's world. Were it not, the study of criminology would be pointless, and the criminological enterprise would be fruitless and irrelevant. Because contemporary criminology is built on a social scientific approach to the subject matter of crime, criminology—especially what some call **experimental criminology**—has much to offer as we attempt to grapple with the problems of crime and crime control now facing us. For criminology to bear the fruit of which it is capable, however, it must do more than use good social scientific techniques. To realize its ultimate promise, criminology must become accepted as a policy-making tool, consulted by lawmakers and social planners alike, and respected for what it can tell us about both crime and its prevention. Learn more about research methods in the social sciences at **Web Extra 3–1** at crimtoday.com.

experimental criminology

A form of contemporary criminology that makes use of rigorous social scientific techniques, especially randomized controlled experiments and the systematic review of research results.

WEB
Extra
■ ■ ■ ■

The Science of Criminology

In his seminal 2003 presidential address to the American Society of Criminology, John H. Laub used the framework of life course theory (discussed in Chapter 8) to describe the history of criminological thought.[10]

Laub identified three eras that he says have characterized the field of criminology over the past 100 years. The first era, said Laub, covered the years 1900 to 1930 and can "be thought of as the 'Golden Age of Research.'" It was a time when data on crime and criminal behavior were largely gathered and evaluated independent of any particular ideational framework.

The second era, the period from 1930 to 1960, Laub calls the "Golden Age of Theory" and describes it as a time when intellectual theorizing "dominated the scene." Strangely, says Laub, during this second period, "there was no systematic attempt to link criminological research to theory."

Era three extended from 1960 to 2000 and was "characterized by extensive theory testing of the dominant theories, using largely empirical methods." In other words, the third era identified by Laub was a time of scientific examination of the accuracy of criminological theories that had been previously advanced

Although he didn't address it directly, Laub indicated that the current era (that is, twenty-first-century criminology) is heir to the first three eras and contains "all possible offspring" of what came before.

As Laub's remarks show, criminologists over the past century have undertaken the task of building a scientific or evidence-based criminology, as distinguished from what had been the "armchair criminology" of earlier times. Armchair criminologists offered their ideas to one another as conjecture—fascinating "theories" that could be debated (and sometimes were) ad nauseam. Although the ruminations of armchair criminologists may have achieved a considerable degree of popular acclaim through (1) the involvement of distinguished lecturers, (2) the association of such ideas with celebrated bastions of higher learning, and (3) their publication in prestigious essays, they were rarely founded on anything other than mere speculation.

The ideas of armchair criminologists followed in the intellectual tradition of medieval Christian theologians who sometimes busied themselves with debates over questions like how many angels could fit on the head of a pin or whether Noah had forgotten to take certain types of insects on board the ark. They were the kinds of things one could probably never know with certainty, no matter how much the ideas were debated. And the ideas being debated were rarely amenable to real-world tests. Under such circumstances, one person's theory was another's fact and still another's wishful thinking.[11]

Although it is easy to dispense with armchair criminology as the relaxed musings of carefree intellectuals undertaken almost as sport, it is far more difficult to agree on the criteria necessary to move any undertaking into the realm of serious scientific endeavor. Present-day criminology is decidedly more scientific, however, than its intellectual predecessor—which means that it is amenable to objective scrutiny and systematic testing. The drive to make criminology "scientific" has been a conscious one, beginning with many of the approaches discussed in Chapter 5.

A variety of criteria have been advanced for declaring any endeavor "scientific." Among them are these:[12]

- The systematic collection of related facts (as in the building of a database)
- An emphasis on the availability and application of the scientific method
- "The existence of general laws, a field for experiment or observation . . . and control of academic discourse by practical application"
- "The fact that it has been . . . accepted into the scientific tradition"
- An "emphasis on a worthwhile subject in need of independent study even if adequate techniques of study are not yet available" (as in the investigation of paranormal phenomena)

Probably all the foregoing could be said of criminology. For one thing, criminologists do gather facts (Laub's "Golden Age of Research"). The mere gathering of facts, however, although it may lead to a descriptive criminology, falls short of offering satisfactory explanations for crime. Hence, most contemporary criminologists are concerned with identifying relationships among the facts they observe and with attempting to understand the many and diverse causes of crime. This emphasis on unveiling causality moves criminology beyond the merely descriptive into the realm of conjecture and theory building. A further emphasis on measurement and objectivity gives contemporary criminology its scientific flavor.

Theory Building

In 2007, inspector Andy Parr, of the Sussex Police Department in England, reviewed crime statistics for the town of Brighton and found that violent crime was higher on nights when the moon was full.[13] "I compared a graph of full moons and a graph of last year's violent crimes and there is a trend," Parr told the United Kingdom's *Telegraph*

Crime in the News

Do Violent Video Games Make Kids Kill?

LOS ANGELES (Reuters)—Do video games kill? The jury is still out on whether violent video games lead to violent behavior in children, but a new study asserts that killer games do not make killer kids.

University of Southern California sociologist Karen Sternheimer, who has been researching the topic since 1999, said blaming video games for youth violence fails to take into account other major factors.

"A symphony of events controls violence," said Sternheimer, who began her research after some experts blamed the video game *Doom* for the gun rampage at Columbine High School in Colorado in which two students killed 13 people and then themselves.

"It was a tragic and, very fortunately, rare event and it was discouraging to see that the conversation often started and stopped at video games."

Sternheimer's article, "Do Video Games Kill?," will appear in the American Sociological Association's *Contexts* magazine as the European Union weighs outlawing certain violent games and harmonizing national penalties for retailers caught selling such products to under-age children.

Her research, which involved analyzing newspaper coverage and FBI statistics detailing trends on youth crime, found that in the 10 years after the release of *Doom*—and many other brutal-sounding titles—juvenile homicide arrest rates in the United States fell 77%.

Students have less than a 7 in 10 million chance of being killed at school, Sternheimer found.

"If we want to understand why young people become homicidal, we need to look beyond the games they play . . . (or) we miss some of the biggest pieces of the puzzle," she said, listing community and family violence, suburban alienation and less parental involvement as other possible factors.

Sternheimer said violent video games have come to carry the baggage of social anxieties over youth violence as the industry has grown into a $10 billion-plus behemoth that rivals Hollywood box office sales.

This also provides a quick fix for when the public demands an explanation for why middle-class children become murderers.

In the United States, the video game industry is self-regulated and retailers decide whether or not to sell M-rated games for mature audiences to minors. These games carry content deemed appropriate for people aged 17 and older.

Sternheimer said putting the blame on video games exonerated the environment in which the child was raised and also removed the culpability of the criminals.

"It's a complicated problem that merits more than a simple solution," she said.

Discussion Questions

1. Do you think that violent video games can have an impact on a player's emotions and influence his or her view of the world? Might they also influence his or her real-life behavior? If so, how?

2. Do you believe that legislation is needed to restrict the access of minors to violent video games? Why or why not?

Source: "Study: Violent Video Games Don't Make Killer Kids," *USA Today,* March 3, 2007. Reprinted by permission.

For the latest crime and justice news, visit www.crimenews.info.

Amy Brady, right, and Allyson Craghead, left, play Ghost Recon Action War Fighter at the UBI Soft booth at the Electronic Entertainment Exposition in Los Angeles on May 11, 2006. Some say that violent video games can make young people act out their violent fantasies. The studies cited in this article, however, seem to show that that is not the case. What do you think?

Source: AP Wide World Photos/Kevork Djansezian

newspaper. "People tend to be more aggressive" when the moon is full, Parr concluded. His findings were supported, he said, by his patrol experience. "When you try to reason with people on a full moon they become more aggressive and less rational," he told reporters. "When you try to reason with them on a full moon they become more argumentative."

Ultimately, the goal of research in criminology is the construction of theories or models that allow for a better understanding of criminal behavior and that permit the development of strategies intended to address the problem of crime. Simply put, a theory consists of a set of interrelated propositions that provide a relatively complete form of understanding. Hence, even if we find that crime is higher when the moon is full, we must still ask why. Is it because the light from full moons makes it possible for those who want to commit a crime to see better at night? If so, then we would expect crime to be higher in areas where there is no cloud cover than in areas where clouds obliterate the full moon's light. Likewise, cities should show less of a rise in crime during full moons than rural areas and small towns, as city lights effectively minimize the impact of the light of the moon. In any event, a complete lunar theory of crime causation would contain specific propositions about the causal nature of the phenomena involved.

There are many ways to define the word *theory*. One cogent definition comes from Don M. Gottfredson, a well-known criminologist of modern times, who writes, "Theories consist of postulates [assumptions], theoretical constructs, logically derived hypotheses, and definitions. Theories can be improved steadily through **hypothesis** testing, examination of evidence from observations, revisions of the theory, and repetitions of the cycle, repeatedly modifying the theory in light of the evidence."[14] Another well-known methodologist describes theories this way: "A theory is a set of related propositions that suggest why events occur in the manner that they do. The propositions that make up theories are of the same form as hypotheses: they consist of concepts and the linkages or relationships between them."[15]

These definitions both have something to offer; in fact, the definition of the term *theory* that we choose to use in this book combines aspects of both. For our purposes, then, a **theory** is *a series of interrelated propositions that attempt to describe, explain, predict, and ultimately control some class of events.* Theories gain explanatory power from inherent logical consistency and are "tested" by how well they describe and predict reality. In other words, a good theory provides relatively complete understanding, and it is supported by observations and stands up to continued scrutiny.

Theories serve a number of purposes. For one thing, they give meaning to observations. They explain what we see in a particular setting by relating those observations to other things already understood. Hence, a simple example of a theory of physics explains the behavior of light by saying that light has the properties of both waves and particles. Such a theory is immediately useful, for although we may have trouble conceptualizing light's essence, we can easily grasp ideas like wave and particle, both of which we experience in everyday living.

Theories within criminology serve the same purpose as those within the physical sciences, although they are often more difficult to test. Few people, for example, can intuitively understand the motivation of "lust murderers" (a term developed by the Federal Bureau of Investigation and popularized by the media)—that is, men who sexually abuse and kill women, often sadistically. Most people, after all, are not lust murderers and therefore lack an intellectual starting point in striving to understand what goes on in the minds of those who are. Some psychiatric theories (discussed in Chapter 6) suggest that lust murderers kill because of a deep-seated hatred of women. Hate is something that most minds can grasp, and a vision of lust murder as an extreme example of the age-old battle between the sexes provides an intellectual "handle" that at least some people can comprehend. Hence, theory building disposes of the old adage that "it takes one to know one," instead bringing at least the possibility of understanding within the reach of all. Note, however, that although such limited explanations as the one discussed here may provide a degree of understanding, they must still be tested to determine whether they are true.

Theories provide understanding in a number of ways. Kenneth R. Hoover identifies four "uses of theory in social scientific thinking":[16]

1. Theories provide patterns for the interpretation of data. Population density, for example, tends to be associated with high crime rates, and maps showing high population density tend to be closely associated with diagrams that reflect rates

---

hypothesis

An explanation that accounts for a set of facts and that can be tested by further investigation.

---

theory

A series of interrelated propositions that attempt to describe, explain, predict, and ultimately control some class of events. A theory gains explanatory power from inherent logical consistency and is "tested" by how well it describes and predicts reality.

of crime. Hence, some theorists are quick to suggest, overcrowding increases aggression and therefore crime. "People," says Hoover, "like to think in terms of images, analogies, and patterns; this helps to simplify complex realities and to lighten the burden of thought."

2. Theories link one study with another. Some years ago, for example, a case study of women's prisons in California found the existence of artificially constructed "families" around which women's lives centered. A similar but later study of a Chinese prison also found that the female inmates there had created family-like groups, prompting some theorists to suggest that women feel a need to nurture and to be nurtured by aspects of social structure and that they carry this need with them into prison. The fact that cross-cultural support was found for the suggestion provided a linkage between the two studies, which tended to lend further support to the suggestion itself.

3. Theories supply frameworks within which concepts and variables acquire special significance. The death penalty, for example, although especially significant to individuals condemned to die, acquires special significance when seen as a tool employed by the powerful to keep the powerless under their control.

4. Theories allow us to interpret the larger meaning of our findings for ourselves and for others. Hence, the death penalty has become a moral issue for many Americans today, shrouded as it is in ethical considerations and images of national identity and ultimate justice.

Learn more about the nature of modern social scientific thought and theory construction at Web Extras 3–2 and 3–3.

WEB
Extra
■ ■ ■ ■

The Role of Research and Experimentation

More important than the claims made by theories and by the theorists who create them are findings of fact that either support those claims or leave them without foundation. Hence, theories, once proposed, need to be tested against the real world via a variety of research strategies, including experimentation and case studies. This is equally true whether the proposed theory is relatively simple or dauntingly complex.

In 2005, for example, attention turned to the "mean world syndrome"—a phrase coined by TV violence researcher George Gerbner. Gerbner's death late that year at the age of 86 caused a resurgence of interest in his idea that televison had more of a socializing impact on children than did their parents, teachers, or local community. Gerbner had been dean of the Annenberg School for Communications at the University of Pennsylvania for 25 years and spent 30 years studying the effects of television on people. "You know," he once said, "who tells the stories of a culture really governs human behavior. It used to be the parent, the school, the church, the community. Now it's a handful of global conglomerates that have nothing to tell, but a great deal to sell."[17] Gerbner's research led him to conclude that people who watch a lot of TV come to think of the world as an unforgiving and scary place—from which he coined the phrase "mean world syndrome." Violence on television, he said, had a powerful effect on the world views of those who watched it.

The mean world syndrome is certainly an interesting concept—and could provide a useful hypothesis for further research. As with any theoretical construct, an idea gains credence if activity based on it produces results in keeping with what the idea would predict. Hence, if research were conducted which demonstrated a link between TV viewing and fear levels, the mean world syndrome would find scientific support. As Bernard P. Cohen, a seminal thinker on the subject of social scientific theory construction tells us, "scientific knowledge is theoretical knowledge, and the purpose of methods in science is to enable us to choose among alternative theories."[18]

Knowledge is inevitably built on experience and observation. Hence, the crux of scientific research is data collection. Data collection occurs through a variety of techniques, including direct observation, the use of surveys and interviews, participant observation, and the analysis of existing data sets—all of which will be discussed shortly.

Research can be defined as the use of standardized, systematic procedures in the search for knowledge.[19] Some researchers distinguish between applied research and non-applied, or pure, research. **Applied research** "consists of scientific inquiry that is designed and carried out with practical application in mind."[20] In applied research, the researcher is working toward some more or less practical goal. It may be the reduction of crime, the efficient compensation of victims of crime, or an evaluation of the effectiveness of policies implemented to solve some specific aspect of the crime problem. **Pure research**, on the other hand, is undertaken simply for the sake of advancing scientific knowledge. It "does not carry the promise or expectation of immediate, direct relevance."[21]

Another type of research, secondary research or secondary analysis, can be distinguished from primary research.[22] **Primary research** "is characterized by original and direct investigation,"[23] whereas **secondary research** consists of new evaluations of existing information that has already been collected by other researchers.

Scientific research generally proceeds in stages, which can be divided conceptually among (1) problem identification, (2) the development of a research design, (3) a choice of data-collection techniques, and (4) a review of findings, which often includes statistical analysis.

Experimental criminology, which uses the techniques of the social sciences in theory testing, is helping today to produce a growing body of evidence-based findings. When used in this context, the word *evidence* refers to scientific findings, and *not* to the kind of evidence gathered by the police or used in criminal trials. Experimental criminology is given voice today by the Academy of Experimental Criminology, which is based at the University of Pennsylvania, and by a number of important new journals, including the *Journal of Experimental Criminology,* which is the first journal in the field of criminology to focus directly on experimental methods.[24] You can reach the Website of the Academy of Experimental Criminology via **Web Extra 3–4** at crimtoday.com.

research

The use of standardized, systematic procedures in the search for knowledge.

applied research

Scientific inquiry that is designed and carried out with practical applications in mind.

pure research

Research undertaken simply for the sake of advancing scientific knowledge.

primary research

Research characterized by original and direct investigation.

secondary research

New evaluations of existing information that had been collected by other researchers.

WEB
Extra

Problem Identification

Problem identification, the first step in any research, consists of naming a problem or choosing an issue to study. Topics may be selected for a variety of reasons. Larry S. Miller and John T. Whitehead, for example, say that "the choice of what criminologists study is influenced by political decisions,"[25] meaning that the availability of government grant monies frequently determines the focus of much contemporary research in the area of crime. It may also be that private foundation monies have become available to support studies in a specific area. Or perhaps the researcher has a personal interest in a particular issue and wants to learn more, or maybe a professor or teacher has assigned a research project as part of the requirements for a class. Whatever the reason for beginning research, however, the way in which a research problem is stated and conceptualized will help narrow the research focus and will serve as a guide to the formulation of data-gathering strategies.

Although some criminological research undertaken today is purely descriptive, the bulk of research in criminology is intended to explore issues of causality, especially the claims made by theories purporting to explain criminal behavior. As such, much contemporary research is involved with the testing of hypotheses.

The *American Heritage Dictionary* defines the word *hypothesis* in two ways:

1. "An explanation that accounts for a set of facts and that can be tested by further investigation"
2. "Something that is taken to be true for the purpose of argument or investigation"

Within the modern scientific tradition, a hypothesis serves both purposes. Some criminologists, as mentioned earlier, have observed what appears to be a correlation, or relationship, between the phases of the moon and the rate of crime commission. Such observers may propose the following hypothesis: The moon causes crime. Although this is a useful starting hypothesis, it needs to be further refined before it can be tested. Specifically, the concepts contained within the hypothesis must be translated into measurable variables. A **variable** is simply a concept that can undergo measurable changes.

Scientific precedent holds that only measurable items can be satisfactorily tested. The process of turning a simple hypothesis into one that is testable is called **operationalization**. An operationalized hypothesis is one that is stated in such a way as to facilitate measurement. It is specific in its terms and in the linkages it proposes. We might, for example, move a step further toward both measurability and specificity in our hypothesis about the relationship between the moon and crime by restating it as follows: Rates of murder, rape, robbery, and assault rise when the moon's fullness increases and are highest when the moon is fullest. Now we have specified what we mean by *crime* (that is, murder, rape, robbery, and assault), rates of which can be calculated. The degree of the moon's fullness can also be measured. Once we have operationalized a hypothesis and made the concepts it contains measurable, those concepts have, in effect, become variables.

Once the concepts within our hypothesis are measurable, we can test the hypothesis itself. That is to say, we can observe what happens to crime rates as the moon approaches fullness, as well as what happens when the moon is full, and see whether our observations support our hypothesis. As our dictionary definition tells us, once a hypothesis has been operationalized, it is assumed to be true for purposes of testing. It is accepted, for study purposes, until observation proves it untrue, at which point it is said to be rejected. As two renowned research methodologists have stated, "The task of theory-testing . . . is predominantly one of rejecting inadequate hypotheses."[26]

variable

A concept that can undergo measurable changes.

operationalization

The process by which concepts are made measurable.

Research Designs

Research designs structure the research process. They provide a kind of road map to the logic inherent in one's approach to a research problem. They also serve as guides to the systematic collection of data.

Research designs consist of the logic and structure inherent in any particular approach to data gathering.

A simple study, for example, might be designed to test the assertion that the consumption of refined white sugar promotes aggressive or violent tendencies. One could imagine researchers approaching prison officials with the proposal that inmate diets be altered to exclude all refined sugar. Under the plan, cafeteria cooks would be instructed to prepare meals without the use of sugar. Noncaloric sweeteners would be substituted for sugar in recipes calling for sugar, and sweetened beverages and carbonated drinks containing sugar would be banned. Likewise, the prison canteen would be prohibited from selling items containing sugar for the duration of the experiment.

To determine whether the forced reduction in sugar consumption actually affected inmates' behavior, researchers might look at the recorded frequency of aggressive incidents (sometimes called "write-ups" in prison jargon) occurring within the confines of the prison before the experiment was initiated and compare such data with similar

research design

The logic and structure inherent in an approach to data gathering.

The full moon rising over a sandy shoreline. Are phases of the moon correlated with changes in the rate of occurrence of certain crimes? It is the job of researchers to determine the validity of such claimed relationships—and of theorists to explain why such relationships hold.

Source: Chad Ehlers/The Stock Connection

information on such incidents following the introduction of dietary changes. A research design employing this kind of logic can be diagrammed as follows:

$$O_1 \times O_2$$

Here "O_1" (termed a *pretest*) refers to the information gathered on inmate aggressiveness prior to the introduction of dietary changes (which themselves are shown as "X," also called the *experimental intervention*), and "O_2" (termed the *posttest*) signifies a second set of observations—those occurring after dietary changes have been implemented. Researchers employing a strategy of this type, which is known as a "one-group pretest-posttest" design, would likely examine differences between the two sets of observations, one made before introduction of the experimental intervention and the other after. The difference, they may assume, would show changes in behavior resulting from changes in diet—in this case, the exclusion of refined white sugar.

Although this basic research design well illustrates the logic behind naïve experiments, it does not provide a good research structure because it does not eliminate other possible explanations of behavioral change. For example, during the time between the first and second observations, inmates may have been exposed to some other influence that reduced their level of aggression. A new minister may have begun preaching effective sermons filled with messages of love and peace to the prison congregation; television cable service to the prison may have been disrupted, lowering the exposure inmates received to violent programming; a new warden may have taken control of the facility, relaxing prison rules and reducing tensions; a transfer or release of especially troublesome inmates, scheduled at some earlier time, may have occurred; a new program of conjugal visitation may have been initiated, creating newfound sexual outlets and reducing inmate tensions; and so on. The possibilities for rival explanations (that is, those that rival the explanatory power of the hypothesis under study) are nearly limitless. Rival explanations like these, called by some researchers "competing hypotheses" and by others **confounding effects**, make the results of any single series of observations uncertain.

confounding effects

A rival explanation, or competing hypothesis, that is a threat to the internal or external validity of a research design.

Achieving Validity in Research Designs

Confounding effects, which may invalidate the results of research, are of two general types: those that affect the **internal validity** of research findings and those that limit the ability of researchers to generalize the research findings to other settings—called **external validity**. Often, when external validity is threatened, researchers do not feel confident that interventions that "worked" under laboratory-like or other special conditions will still be effective when employed in the field. Hence, researchers achieving internal validity may be able to demonstrate that diets low in refined white sugar lower the number of instances of overt displays of aggressiveness in a single prison under study. They may not feel confident (for reasons discussed in the paragraphs that follow), however, that similar changes in diet, if implemented in the general nonprison population, would have a similar effect. Most researchers consider internal validity, or the certainty that experimental interventions did indeed cause the changes observed in the study group, the most vital component of any planned research. Without it, considerations of external validity become irrelevant. Factors that routinely threaten the internal validity of a design for research are said to include[27]

- **History:** specific events that occur between the first and second observations, which may affect measurement. The examples given in the prison study described earlier (the arrival of a new minister or a new warden, for example) are all applicable here.

- **Maturation:** processes occurring within the respondents or subjects that operate as a result of the passage of time. Fatigue and decreases in response time due to age are examples.

- **Testing:** the effects of taking a test upon the scores of a later testing. When respondents are measured in some way that requires them to respond, they tend to do better (that is, their scores increase) the next time they are tested. In effect, they have learned how to take the test or how to be measured, even though they may not have acquired more knowledge about the subject matter that the test intends to measure.

- **Instrumentation:** changes in measuring instruments, or in survey takers that occur as a result of time. Batteries wear down, instruments need to be recalibrated, interviewers grow tired or are replaced with others, and so on—all of which can change the nature of the observations made.

- **Statistical regression:** a return to more average scores. When respondents have been selected for study on the basis of extreme scores (as may be the case with personality inventories), later testing will tend to show a "regression toward the mean" because some extreme scores are inevitably more the result of accident or luck than anything else.

- **Differential selection:** built-in biases that result when more than one group of subjects is involved in a study and when the groups being tested are initially somehow different. The random assignment of subjects to test groups greatly reduces the chances that such significant differences will exist.

- **Experimental mortality:** a differential loss of respondents from comparison groups, which may occur when more than one group is being tested (for example, one group loses members at a greater rate than another group, or certain kinds of members are lost from one group but not from another).

Threats to external validity include

- **Reactive effects of testing:** sensitizing effects of initial tests. A pretest may sensitize subjects in such a way that they especially respond to the experimental intervention when it is introduced. Nonpretested subjects (such as those in other locations) may not respond in the same way.

internal validity

The certainty that experimental interventions did indeed cause the changes observed in the study group.

external validity

The ability to generalize research findings to other settings.

- **Self-selection:** a process whereby subjects are allowed to decide whether they want to participate in a study. Self-selected subjects may be more interested in participation than others, and they may respond more readily to the experimental intervention or treatment.
- **Reactive effects of experimental arrangements:** sensitizing effects of the setting. People being surveyed or tested may know that they are part of an experiment and therefore may react differently than if they were in more natural settings. Even if they are not aware of their participation in a study, the presence of some investigative paraphernalia (such as observers, cameras, and tape recorders) might change the way in which they behave.
- **Multiple-treatment interference:** interaction of multiple exposures or treatments. Sometimes more than one study is simultaneously conducted on the same person or group of people. Under such circumstances, "treatments" to which subjects are exposed may interact, changing what would otherwise be the study's results. Multiple-treatment interference may also result from delayed effects, as when a current study is affected by one that has already been completed.

Experimental and Quasi-Experimental Research Designs

controlled experiment

An experiment that attempts to hold conditions (other than the intentionally introduced experimental intervention) constant.

To have confidence that the changes intentionally introduced into a situation are the real cause of observed variations, it is necessary to achieve some degree of control over factors that threaten internal validity. In the physical sciences, controlled experiments often provide the needed guarantees. **Controlled experiments** are those that attempt to hold conditions (other than the intentionally introduced experimental intervention) constant. Some researchers have defined the word *experiment* simply as "controlled observation."

Whereas constancy of conditions may be possible to achieve within laboratory settings, it is far more difficult to come by in the social world, which by its very nature is

A high school science fair booth pays homage to the scientific method. What is evidence-based criminology? How does it make use of the scientific method?

Source: AP Photo/Orlin Wagner

in an ongoing state of flux. Hence, although criminologists sometimes employ true experimental designs in the conduct of their research, they are more likely to find it necessary to use quasi-experimental designs, or approaches to research that "are deemed worthy of use where better designs are not feasible."[28] **Quasi-experimental designs** are especially valuable when aspects of the social setting are beyond the control of the researcher. The crucial defining feature of quasi-experimental designs is that they give researchers control over the "when and to whom" of *measurement,* even though others decide the "when and to whom" of exposure to the experimental intervention.

Sometimes, for example, legislators enact new laws intended to address some aspect of the crime problem, specifying the kinds of crime prevention measures to be employed and the segment of the population to receive them. Midnight basketball, intended to keep young people off the streets at night, provides an example of a legislatively sponsored intervention. During debate on the 1994 Violent Crime Control and Law Enforcement Act, midnight basketball became a point of contention, with senators asking whether money spent in support of such an activity would actually reduce the incidence of serious street crime in our nation's inner cities. Unfortunately, no good research data that could answer the question were then available. Now, however, federally funded midnight basketball programs, which have existed for a number of years, might be studied by researchers. Hence, although criminologists were not politically situated so as to be able to enact midnight basketball legislation, they are able to study the effects of such legislation after it has been enacted.[29]

Whether criminologists decide on experimental or quasi-experimental designs to guide their research, they depend upon well-considered research strategies to eliminate rival explanations for the effects they observe. One relatively powerful research design that criminologists frequently employ can be diagrammed as follows:

$$\text{Experimental group} \quad O_1 \times O_2$$

$$\text{Control group} \quad O_3 \quad O_4$$

The meaning of the notation used here is similar to that of the one-shot case study design discussed earlier. This approach, however, called the "pretest-posttest control group design," gains considerable power from the addition of a second group. The second group is called a **control group** because it is not exposed to the experimental intervention.

Critical to the success of a research design like this is the use of randomization in the assignment of subjects to both the experimental and the control groups. **Randomization** is the process whereby individuals are assigned to study groups without biases or differences resulting from selection. Self-selection (when some individuals volunteer for membership in either the experimental or the control group) is not permitted, nor are researchers allowed to use personal judgment in assigning subjects to groups.

Control over potential threats to internal validity is achieved by the introduction of a properly selected control group because it is assumed that both experimental and control groups are essentially the same at the start and that any threats to internal validity will affect both groups equally as the experiment progresses—effectively canceling out when final differences between the two groups are measured. If some particular historical event, for example, affects the experimental group and modifies the measurable characteristics of that group, that event should have the same impact on the control group. Hence, in the previous design, when O_4 is subtracted from O_2, the remaining observable *net effects* are assumed to be attributable to the experimental intervention.

In the prison study discussed earlier, randomization would require that all inmates be systematically but randomly divided into two groups. Random assignments are typically made by using a table of random numbers. In this simple study, however, something as easy as the flip of a coin should suffice. Members of one group (the experimental group) would no longer receive refined white sugar in their diets, while members of the other (the control group) would continue eating as before. Because, with this one exception in diet, both groups would continue to be exposed to the same environment, it can be assumed that any other influences on the level of violence within the prison will cancel out when final measurements are taken and that measurable

quasi-experimental design

An approach to research that, although less powerful than experimental designs, is deemed worthy of use when better designs are not feasible.

control group

A group of experimental subjects that, although the subject of measurement and observation, is not exposed to the experimental intervention.

randomization

The process whereby individuals are assigned to study groups without biases or differences resulting from selection.

differences in violence between the two groups can be attributed solely to the effects of the experimental variable (in this case, removal of sugar from the diet).

According to Shawn Bushway and David Weisburd at the University of Maryland, criminology is the only field within the social sciences to "show a marked increase in the use of experimental designs over the past 40 years."[30] And the movement has powerful friends. No less an authority than Lawrence W. Sherman, professor and chair of the Department of Criminology and Criminal Justice at the University of Maryland and the former director of research at the Police Foundation, says that the use of experimental design in the field of criminology is the "gold standard" to which evaluations of both theory and practice should be held.[31]

Techniques of Data Collection

It is the combination of (1) hypothesis building, (2) operationalization, and (3) systematic observation in the service of hypothesis testing that has made modern-day criminology scientific and that has facilitated scientific theory building within the field. Hence, once a research problem has been identified, concepts have been made measurable, and a research design has been selected, investigators must then decide on the type of data to be gathered and the techniques of data gathering they wish to employ. Ultimately, all research depends on the use of techniques to gather information, or data, for eventual analysis. Like research designs, which structure a researcher's approach to a problem, data-gathering strategies provide approaches to the accumulation of information needed for analysis to occur.

Many first-time researchers select data-gathering techniques on the basis of ease or simplicity. Some choose according to cost or the amount of time the techniques require. The most important question to consider when beginning to gather information, however, is whether the data-gathering strategy selected will produce information in a usable form. The kind of information needed depends on the questions to be answered. Surveys of public opinion as to the desirability of the death penalty, for example, cannot address issues of the punishment's effectiveness as a crime control strategy.

Five major data-gathering strategies typify research in the field of criminology: surveys, case studies, participant observation, self-reporting, and secondary analysis.

Surveys

Survey research typically involves the use of questionnaires. Respondents may be interviewed in person or over the telephone or queried via e-mail or fax. Mail surveys are common, although they tend to have a lower response rate than other types of social surveys. The information produced through the use of questionnaires is referred to as "survey data." Survey data provide the lifeblood of polling companies like Gallup, CNN, and Roper, which gather data on public opinion, voting preferences, and so forth. Similarly, U.S. Census Bureau data are gathered by survey takers who are trained periodically for that purpose. Survey data also inform the National Crime Victimization Survey (NCVS) and result in such publications as *Crime and the Nation's Households, Criminal Victimization,* and other NCVS-related reports produced by the Bureau of Justice Statistics. Surveys have also been used in criminology to assess fear of crime and attitudes toward the police and to discover the extent of unreported crime.

survey research

A social science data-gathering technique that involves the use of questionnaires.

Case Studies

Case studies are built around in-depth investigations into individual cases. The study of one (perhaps notorious) offender, the scrutiny of a particular criminal organization, and the analysis of a prison camp may all qualify as case studies. Case studies are useful for what they can tell us to expect about other, similar cases. If study of a street gang, for example, reveals the central role of a few leaders, then we would expect to find a similar organizational style among other gangs of the same kind.

When one individual (a "single subject") is the focus of a case study, the investigation may take the form of a life history. Life histories involve gathering as much historical data as possible about a given individual and his or her experiences during early socialization and adulthood. Most life histories are quite subjective because they consist primarily of the recounting of events by the participants themselves. Life histories may also be gathered on groups of individuals, and similarities in life experience that are thereby discovered may provide researchers with clues to current behavior or with points at which to begin further investigations.

Case studies, although they may suffer from high levels of subjectivity in which feelings cannot be easily separated from fact, provide the opportunity to investigate individual cases—an element that is lacking in both survey research and participant observation.

Participant Observation

Participant observation "involves a variety of strategies in data gathering in which the researcher observes a group by participating, to varying degrees, in the activities of the group."[32] Some participant researchers operate undercover, without revealing their identity as researchers to those whom they are studying, whereas others make their identity and purpose known from the outset of the research endeavor. As one criminologist states, participant observation "means that criminologists must venture inside the immediacy of crime."[33]

One of the earliest and best-known participant observers in the field of criminology was William Foote Whyte, who described his 1943 study of criminal subcultures in a slum district that he called "Cornerville" this way: "My aim was to gain an intimate view of Cornerville life. My first problem, therefore, was to establish myself as a participant in the society so that I would have a position from which to observe. I began by going to live in Cornerville, finding a room with an Italian family. . . . It was not enough simply to make the acquaintance of various groups of people. The sort of information that I sought required that I establish intimate social relations. . . . This active participation gave me something in common with them so that we had other things to talk about besides the weather. It broke down the social barriers and made it possible for me to be taken into the intimate life of the group."[34]

It is possible to distinguish between at least two additional kinds of participant observation: (1) the participant as observer and (2) the observer as complete participant. When researchers make their presence known to those whom they are observing, without attempting to influence the outcome of their observations or the activities of the group, they fit the category of participants who are observers. When they become complete participants in the group they are observing, however, researchers run the risk of influencing the group's direction. As Whyte explains, "I made it a rule that I should try to avoid influencing the actions of the group. I wanted to observe what the men did under ordinary circumstances; I did not want to lead them into different activities."[35] Even researchers who make their presence known, however, may inadvertently influence the nature and direction of social interaction because people tend to act differently if they know they are being watched.

Another problem facing the participant observer is that of "going native," or of assuming too close an identification with the subjects or the behavior under study. Like undercover police officers who may at times be tempted to participate in the illegalities they are supposed to be monitoring, participant researchers may begin to experience feelings of kinship with their subjects. When that happens, all sense of the research perspective may be lost, and serious ethical problems may arise.

On the other hand, some researchers may feel disgust for the subjects of their research. Data gatherers with a particular dislike of drug abuse, for example, may be hard put to maintain their objectivity when working as participant observers within the drug subculture. Hence, as noted social science researcher Frank Hagan observes, "The researcher must avoid not only overidentification with the study group, but also aversion to it."[36]

participant observation

A strategy in data gathering in which the researcher observes a group by participating, to varying degrees, in the activities of the group.

Self-Reporting

Another subjective data-gathering technique is one that uses self-reports to investigate aspects of a problem not otherwise amenable to study. When official records are lacking, for example, research subjects may be asked to record and report rates of otherwise secretive behavior. Self-reports may prove especially valuable in providing checks on official reports consisting of statistical tabulations gathered through such channels as police departments, hospitals, and social service agencies.

Self-reports may also be requested of subjects in survey research, and it is for that reason that self-reporting is sometimes considered simply another form of survey research. However, many self-reporting techniques require the maintenance of a diary or personal journal and request vigilant and ongoing observations of one's own behavior by the subject under study. Hence, sex researchers may ask subjects to maintain an ongoing record of their frequency of intercourse, the variety of sexual techniques employed, and their preference in partners—items of information that are not easy to come by through other means or that cannot be accurately reconstructed from memory.

Self-reporting enters the realm of the purely subjective when it consists of introspection, or personal reflection. Introspective techniques, or those intended to gather data on secretive feelings and felt motivation, are often used by psychologists seeking to assess the mental status of patients. Criminologists, however, have at times used introspective techniques to categorize criminal offenders into types and to initiate the process of developing concepts more amenable to objective study.

Secondary Analysis

Not all data-gathering techniques produce new data. Secondary analysis, for example, purposefully culls preexisting information from data that have already been gathered and examines it in new ways. Secondary analysis can be thought of as the secondhand analysis of information that was originally collected for another purpose. The secondary analysis of existing data and the use of previously acquired information for new avenues of inquiry are strategies that can save researchers a considerable amount of time and expense.

One important source of data for secondary analysis is the National Archive of Criminal Justice data located in the Institute for Social Research at the University of Michigan. In the words of the U.S. Department of Justice, the archive's sponsoring agency, "The Archive continually processes the most relevant criminal justice data sets for the research community,"[37] maintaining information on victimization, various aspects of the criminal justice system, and juvenile delinquency. Access to archive data is by request, and data sets are available to individual researchers. Visit the archive via **Web Extra 3–5**.

The use of secondary data rarely alerts research subjects to the fact that they (or the data they have provided) are being studied, although they may have been so aware when the data were first gathered. Hence, secondary analysis, which constitutes one form of unobtrusive research, is said to be "nonreactive." Although unobtrusive measures include other forms of data collection, the use of archival records in data analysis constitutes a virtual "goldmine of information waiting to be exploited."[38] Nonetheless, it is important to keep in mind that secondary analysis usually involves the use of information that was collected for a purpose outside of the interests of the current researcher.

Problems in Data Collection

Scientific data gathering builds on observations of one sort or another. Observation is not unique to science. Individuals continuously make observations and draw a plethora of personal conclusions based on what they see or hear. Scientific observation, however, generally occurs under controlled conditions and must meet the criteria of intersubjectivity and replicability. **Intersubjectivity** means that for observations to be valid, independent observers must report seeing the same thing under the same circumstances. "Do you see what I see?" is a question that highlights the central role of intersubjectivity in scientific observation. If observers cannot agree on what they saw, then the raw data necessary for scientific analysis have not been acquired. **Replicability** of observations means that, at least in the field of scientific experimentation, when the same conditions

WEB
Extra
▪ ▪ ▪ ▪

intersubjectivity

A scientific principle that requires that independent observers see the same thing under the same circumstances for observations to be regarded as valid.

replicability

A scientific principle that holds that valid observations made at one time can be made again later if all other conditions are the same.

exist, the same results can be expected to follow. Hence, valid experiments can be replicated. The same observations made at one time can be made again at a later time if all other conditions are the same.

In the physical sciences, replicability is easy to achieve. Water at sea level, for example, will always boil at 100° Celsius. Anyone can replicate the conditions needed to test such a contention. When replicability cannot be achieved, it casts the validity of the observation into doubt. Some years ago, for example, a few scientists claimed to have achieved nuclear fusion at room temperature. Their supposed accomplishment was dubbed "cold fusion" and was hailed as a major breakthrough in the production of nuclear energy. However, when scientists elsewhere attempted to replicate the conditions under which cold fusion was said to occur, they could find no evidence that the initial experimenters were correct. Replicability and intersubjectivity are critical to the scientific enterprise for, as one researcher states, "science rests its claim to authority upon its firm basis in observable evidence."[39]

It is important to recognize, however, that some observations—even those that stand up to the tests of intersubjectivity and replicability—can lead to unwarranted conclusions. For example, spirit possession, an explanation for deviance that was apparently widely held in primitive times, must have appeared to be well validated by the positive behavioral changes that became apparent in those who submitted to the surgery called for by the theory—a craniotomy intended to release offending spirits from the head of the afflicted person. The actual cause of behavioral reformation may have been brain infections resulting from unsanitary surgical conditions, slips of the stone knife, or the intensity of pain endured by those undergoing the procedure without anesthetics. To the uncritical observer, however, the theory of spirit possession as a cause of deviance and cranial surgery as a treatment technique would probably appear to have been supported by the evidence of induced behavioral change.

Some methodologists note that "theories are as much involved in the determination of fact as facts are in establishing a theory."[40] Theories are intimately involved in the process of data collection. They determine what kinds of data we choose to gather, what we look for in the data, and how we interpret the information we have gathered. In short, theories determine what we see, as well as what we ignore. In the late 1700s, for example, when a meteor shower was reported to the French Academy of Sciences, observers reported that some fragments had struck the ground, causing tremendous explosions. The learned scientists of the academy quickly dismissed these accounts, however, calling them "a superstition unworthy of these enlightened times."[41] Everyone, they said, knows that stones don't fall from the sky.

Social science research within a correctional setting. Inmate surveys may increase our knowledge of crime causation. Specifically, what might such surveys tell us?

Source: Rick Friedman, Black Star

Data Analysis

Some data, once collected, are simply archived or stored. Most data, however, are subject to some form of analysis. Data analysis generally involves the use of mathematical techniques intended to uncover correlations between variables and to assess the likelihood that research findings can be generalized to other settings. These are statistical techniques, and their use in analyzing data is called "statistical analysis." Some theorists, for example, posit a link between poverty and crime. Hence, we might suspect that low-income areas would be high-crime areas. Once we specify what we mean by "low-income" and "crime," so that they become measurable variables, and gather data on income levels and the incidence of crime in various locales, we are ready to begin the job of data analysis.

Statistical techniques provide tools for summarizing data. They also provide quantitative means for identifying patterns within the data and for determining the degree of correlation that exists between variables. Statistical methods can be divided into two types: descriptive and inferential. **Descriptive statistics** are those that describe, summarize, or highlight the relationships within the data that have been gathered. **Inferential statistics**, on the other hand, attempt to generalize findings by specifying how likely they are to be true for other populations or in other locales.

Descriptive statistics include measures of central tendency, commonly called the "mean," "median," and "mode." *Mode* refers to the most frequently occurring score or value in any series of observations. If, for example, we measure the age of all juvenile offenders held in a state training facility, it may be that they range in age from 12 to 16, with 15 being the most commonly found age. Fifteen, then, would be the modal age for the population under study.

Median defines the midpoint of a data series. Half of the scores will be above the mean and the other half will be below. It may be, for example, that in our study of juveniles, we find equal numbers in each age category. The median age for those offenders would then be 14.

The mathematical average of all scores within a given population is the *mean.* The mean is the most commonly used measure of central tendency. It is calculated by simply adding together all the scores (or ages, in our example) and dividing by the total number of observations. Although calculations of the mean, median, and mode will often yield similar results, such will not be the case with populations that are skewed in a particular direction. If our population of juveniles, for example, consisted almost entirely of 16 year olds, then the mode for that population would inevitably be 16, while other measures of central tendency would yield somewhat lower figures.

Other descriptive statistics provide measures of the standard deviation of a population (that is, the degree of dispersion of scores about the mean) and the degree of correlation or interdependence between variables (that is, the extent of variation in one that can be expected to follow from a measured change in another). As discussed in Chapter 2 (where the term *correlation* is defined), although the degree of correlation may vary, the direction of correlation can also be described. We say, for example, that if one variable increases whenever another, upon which it is dependent, does the same, a positive correlation, or positive relationship, exists between the two. When one variable decreases in value as another rises, a negative, or inverse, correlation exists.

Another statistical technique, one that provides a measure of the likelihood that a study's findings are the results of chance, is commonly found in criminological literature. **Tests of significance** are designed to provide researchers with confidence that their results are, in fact, true, and not the result of sampling error. We may, for example, set out to measure degree of gun ownership. Let's say that the extent of gun ownership in the area under study is actually 50%. (We have no way of knowing this until our study is complete.) We may decide to use door-to-door surveys of randomly selected households because cost prohibits us from canvassing all households in the study area. Even if we have made our best survey effort, however, some slight probability remains that the households we have chosen to interview may all be populated by gun owners. Although it is very unlikely, we may, by chance, have excluded those without guns.

descriptive statistics

Statistics that describe, summarize, or highlight the relationships within data that have been gathered.

inferential statistics

Statistics that specify how likely findings are to be true for other populations or in other locales.

test of significance

A statistical technique intended to provide researchers with confidence that their results are, in fact, true and not the result of sampling error.

Assuming that everyone interviewed answers truthfully, we would come away with the mistaken impression that 100% of the population in the study area is armed!

The likelihood of faulty findings increases as sample size decreases. Were we to sample only one or two households, we would have little likelihood of determining the actual incidence of gun ownership. The larger the sample size, however, the greater the confidence we can have in our findings. Hence, a positive correlation exists between sample size and the degree of confidence we can have in our results. Even so, in most criminological research, it is not possible to study all members of a given population, and so samples must be taken. Statistical tests of significance, expressed as a percentage, assess the likelihood that our study findings are due to chance. Hence, a study that reflects a 95% confidence level can be interpreted as having a 5% likelihood that the results it reports are mere happenstance. In other words, for every hundred such studies, five yield misleading results. The problem is that it would be impossible to know (without further research) which five that would be!

Learn more about statistics and statistical methods from the American Statistical Association and the American Association for the Advancement of Science via **Web Extras 3–6** and **3–7**. Read about statistical tools on the World Wide Web via **Library Extra 3–1**.

WEB
Extra
■ ■ ■ ■

LIBRARY
Extra
■ ■ ■ ■

Quantitative versus Qualitative Methods

Years ago, during the Clinton administration, then–Attorney General Janet Reno addressed researchers, criminologists, and professors gathered at the annual meeting of the American Society of Criminology in Miami, Florida. "Let's stop talking about numbers," Reno exhorted the crowd, "and start talking about crime in human terms." With her admonition, Reno placed herself squarely on the side of those who feel that there has been a tendency in American criminology over the past half century to overemphasize **quantitative methods** or techniques—that is, those that produce measurable results that can be analyzed statistically. To be sure, as such critics would be quick to admit, a considerable degree of intellectual comfort must be achieved in feeling that one is able to reduce complex forms of behavior and interaction to something countable (as, say, the frequency of an offense). Intellectual comfort of this sort derives from the notion that anything expressible in numbers must be somehow more meaningful than that which is not.

It is crucial to realize, however, that numerical expression is mostly a result of how researchers structure their approach to the subject matter and is rarely inherent in the subject matter itself. Such is especially true in the social sciences, where attitudes, feelings, behaviors, and perceptions of all sorts are subject to quantification by researchers who impose upon such subjective phenomena artificial techniques for their quantification.

One highly quantitative study, for example, reprinted in the journal *Criminology*, reported on the relationship between personality and crime.[42] The study found that "greater delinquent participation was associated with a personality configuration characterized by high Negative Emotionality and Weak Constraint." It may seem easy to quantify "delinquent participation" by measuring official arrest statistics (even here, however, official statistics may not be a good measure of delinquent behavior, as many law violations go undiscovered), but imagine the conceptual nightmares associated with trying to make measurable such concepts as "Negative Emotionality" and "Weak Constraint." In such studies, even those replete with numerical data derived through the use of carefully constructed questionnaires, questions still remain of precisely what it is that has been measured.

Not everyone who engages in social science research labors under the delusion that everything can and must be quantified. Those who do, however, are said to suffer from the "mystique of quantity." As some critics point out, "The failure to recognize this instrumentality of measurement makes for a kind of *mystique of quantity;* which responds to numbers as though they were repositories of occult powers. . . . The mystique of quantity is an exaggerated regard for the significance of measurement, just because it is quantitative, without regard either to what has been measured or to what can subsequently

quantitative method

A research technique that produces measurable results.

Crime in the News

Idaho Town Arming Itself

The Town Council in Greenleaf, Idaho, is considering a recommendation that all households keep and maintain guns because of the crime that might come with the encroaching growth from nearby Boise.

To date, violent crime is nearly unheard of in Greenleaf, population 890, admits City Councilman Steve Jett, who proposed the ordinance the council will take up Tuesday. Even so, Jett says it's only a matter of time.

"The biggest thing I was looking at is preparation," Jett says.

When asked about violent crime in Greenleaf, which doesn't have its own police force, Albert Erickson, police chief of neighboring Wilder, says, "I don't remember any."

Erickson, whose department covers Greenleaf, finally recalled a domestic-violence complaint there last year. "But I don't even know that it went to court."

Alan Weinacht, pastor of Greenleaf Friends Church, in Greenleaf, Idaho, owns a gun but opposes the plan to recommend that all of the town's "heads of households" own at least one. Does gun ownership help to reduce criminal opportunity?
Source: Paul Hosefros/The New York Times

Boise is not exactly a hotbed of violence. Its violent crime rate last year was 383 per 100,000 people, below the national average of 469 but higher than Idaho's rate of 257 per 100,000, according to the FBI Uniform Crime Report.

Greenleaf's proposal is not surprising, especially in the West, says David Kopel of the Denver-based Independence Institute, a free-market think tank.

Kopel, author of The Samurai, the Mountie, and the Cowboy: Should America Adopt the Gun Controls of Other Democracies?, ranks Montana as the state with the strongest gun rights, closely followed by Idaho and Wyoming.

"These laws are more suggestive of culture and attitude than a real attempt to arm everybody," says Gary Marbut, president of the Montana Shooting Sports Association.

The Montana Legislature routinely considers resolutions urging residents to own guns. Aumsville, Ore., considered, but rejected, an ordinance similar to Greenleaf's proposal in 2001, a year after the tiny southern Utah town of Virgin passed one.

In a nod to Greenleaf's Quaker roots—it takes its name from Quaker abolitionist and poet John Greenleaf Whittier—Jett says his proposal is merely a recommendation, not a requirement like Virgin's. The wording exempts convicted felons, others prohibited from owning guns and those who object to gun ownership.

The ordinance is modeled on a 1982 law in Kennesaw, Ga., a town that, like Greenleaf, found itself becoming a suburb to a sprawling state capital. "It was basically the law heard 'round the world," says Kennesaw Mayor Leonard Church. He says he has received inquiries from as far away as Australia about Kennesaw's measure.

Although the law is largely a formality—"We don't go door to door, saying, 'Show me your gun'"—Church says studies show enactment of the law coincides with a marked drop in burglaries and violent crime.

Peter Hamm, spokesman for the Brady Campaign to Prevent Gun Violence, says the group doesn't oppose Greenleaf's proposal.

"There aren't too many rural towns in Idaho where everybody doesn't already have a gun," he says. "And we fully support the right of law-abiding citizens . . . to own a firearm for self-defense, or hunting, or sporting purposes."

Discussion Questions

1. Do you agree or disagree with the possible recommendation by the Greenleaf town council that community residents be required to own guns? Why or why not?

2. Can you envision an experiment that might be conducted to determine whether gun ownership actually reduces the incidence of serious crime in a community? If so, how might that experiment proceed?

3. What other types of social policies might the council consider if it wishes to keep crime at bay?

Source: Gwen Florio, "Councilman to Idaho Town: Get Your Guns," USA Today, October 2, 2006, p. 3A. From USA TODAY, a division of Grannett Co., Inc. Reprinted with Permission.

For the latest crime and justice news, visit www.crimenews.info.

be done with the measure."[43] The mystique of quantity treats numbers as having intrinsic scientific value. Unfortunately, this kind of thinking has been popular in the social sciences, where researchers, seeking to make clear their intellectual kinship with physical scientists, have been less than cautious in their enthusiasm for quantification.

Qualitative methods, in contrast to those that are quantitative, produce subjective results, or results that are difficult to quantify. Even though their findings are not expressed numerically, qualitative methods provide yet another set of potentially useful criminological research tools. Qualitative methods are important for the insight they provide into the subjective workings of the criminal mind and the processes by which meaning is accorded to human experience. Introspection, life histories, case studies, and participant observation all contain the potential to yield highly qualitative data.[44]

> **qualitative method**
>
> A research technique that produces subjective results, or results that are difficult to quantify.

Consider, for example, how the following personal account[45] of homicidal motivation conveys subjective insights into the life of a Los Angeles gang member that would otherwise be difficult to express:

> Wearing my fresh Pendleton shirt, beige khakis, and biscuits [old men's comfort shoes, the first shoe officially dubbed "Crip shoe"], I threw on my black bomber jacket and stepped out into the warm summer night. I walked up Sixty-Ninth Street to Western Avenue and took a car at gunpoint. Still in a state of indecision, I drove toward the hospital.
>
> I intentionally drove through Sixties'hood. Actually, I was hoping to see one of them before I had made it through, and what luck did I have. There was Bank Robber, slippin' [not paying attention, not being vigilant] hard on a side street. I continued past him and turned at the next corner, parked and waited. He would walk right to me.
>
> Sitting in the car alone, waiting to push yet another enemy out of this existence, I reflected deeply about my place in this world, about things that were totally outside the grasp of my comprehension. Thoughts abounded I never knew I could conjure up. In retrospect, I can honestly say that in those moments before Bank Robber got to the car, I felt free. Free, I guess, because I had made a decision about my future.
>
> "Hey," I called out to Robber, leaning over to the passenger side, "got a light?"
>
> "Yeah," he replied, reaching into his pants pocket for a match or lighter. I never found out which.
>
> I guess he felt insecure, because he dipped his head down to window level to see who was asking for a light.
>
> "Say your prayers, muthaf. . . ."
>
> Before he could mount a response I blooted him thrice in the chest, started the car, and drove home to watch *Benny Hill.* Bangin' was my life. That was my decision.

The passage was written by Sanyika Shakur, once known as "Monster Kody" to fellow South Central Los Angeles Crips members. Monster, named for his readiness to commit acts of brutality so extreme that they repulsed even other gang members, joined the Crips at age 11. Sent to a maximum security prison while still in his teens, Monster learned to write, took on the name Sanyika Shakur, and joined the black nationalist New Afrikan Independence Movement. Shakur's prison-inspired autobiography, *Monster,* provides a soul-searching account of the life of an L.A. gang member. The purpose of the book, says Shakur, is "to allow my readers the first ever glimpse at South Central from my side of the gun, street, fence, and wall."

Although Shakur's book is a purely personal account and may hold questions of generalizability for researchers, imagine the difficulties inherent in acquiring this kind of data through the use of survey instruments or other traditional research techniques. Autobiographical accounts, introspection, and many forms of participant observation amount to a kind of phenomenological reporting in which description leads to understanding and intuition is a better guide to theory building than volumes of quantifiable data.

Jeff Ferrell of Texas Christian University uses the term **verstehen** to describe the kind of subjective understanding that can be achieved by criminologists who immerse themselves in the everyday world of the criminals they study. Criminological *verstehen,* a term derived from the early writings of sociologist Max Weber, means, says Ferrell, "a researcher's subjective understandings of crime's situational meanings and emotions—its moments of pleasure and pain, its emergent logic and excitement—within the larger process of research." Ferrell adds, "It further implies that a researcher, through attentiveness and

> **verstehen**
>
> The kind of subjective understanding that can be achieved by criminologists who immerse themselves in the everyday world of the criminals they study.

An 18-year-old Los Angeles gang member. Some researchers doubt that quantitative methods can adequately assess the subjective experiences of certain kinds of offenders. What is the nature of such "subjective experiences"?

Source: Jim Tynan/James Tynan Photography

WEB
Extra
▪ ▪ ▪ ▪

LIBRARY
Extra
▪ ▪ ▪ ▪

participation, at least can begin to apprehend and appreciate the specific roles and experiences of criminals, crime victims, crime control agents, and others caught up in the day-to-day reality of crime."[46] Learn more about *verstehen* at "Max Weber's Home Page" via **Web Extra 3–8.** You can learn more about the techniques of social science research at **Library Extra 3–2** at crimtoday.com.

Values and Ethics in the Conduct of Research

Research, especially research conducted within the social sciences, does not occur in a vacuum. Values enter into all stages of the research process, from the selection of the problem to be studied to the choice of strategies to address it. In short, research is never entirely free from preconceptions and biases, although much can be done to limit the impact such biases have on the results of research.

The most effective way of controlling the effects of biases is to be aware of them at the outset of the research. If, for example, researchers know that the project they are working on elicits strong personal feelings but necessitates the use of interviewers, then it would be beneficial to strive to hire interviewers who are relatively free of biases or can control the expression of their feelings. Potential data gatherers might themselves be interviewed to determine their values and the likelihood that they might be tempted to interpret the data they gather or to report them in ways that are biased. Similarly, data gatherers who are prejudiced against subgroups of potential respondents can represent a threat to the validity of the research results. The use of such interviewers may "turn off" some respondents, perhaps through racial innuendo, personal style, mannerisms, and so forth.

Of similar importance are ethical issues that, although they may not affect the validity of research results, can have a significant impact on the lives of both researchers and research subjects. The protection of human subjects from harm, privacy, the need for disclosure of research methods, and **data confidentiality**—which embraces the principle of protecting the confidentiality of individual research participants, while simultaneously preserving justified research access to needed information provided by them—are all critical ethical issues.

To address these and other concerns, the Academy of Criminal Justice Sciences (ACJS) has adopted an official code of ethics. Concerning confidentiality issues, for example, the ACJS Code of Ethics says that researchers "should seek to anticipate potential threats to confidentiality." The code goes on to say, "Techniques such as the removal

data confidentiality

The ethical requirement of social scientific research to protect the confidentiality of individual research participants, while simultaneously preserving justified research access to the information participants provide.

of direct identifiers, the use of randomized responses, and other statistical solutions to problems of privacy should be used where appropriate. Care should be taken to ensure secure storage, maintenance, and/or destruction of sensitive records."[47]

The ACJS code also says, "Confidential information provided by research participants should be treated as such by members of the Academy, even when this information enjoys no legal protection or privilege and legal force is applied. The obligation to respect confidentiality also applies to members of research organizations (interviewers, coders, clerical staff, etc.) who have access to the information. It is the responsibility of administrators and chief investigators to instruct staff members on this point and to make every effort to insure that access to confidential information is restricted."[48]

Informed consent is a strategy used by researchers to overcome many of the ethical issues inherent in criminological research. **Informed consent** means that research subjects are informed as to the nature of the research about to be conducted, their anticipated role in it, and the uses that will be made of the data they provide. Ethics may also require that data derived from personal interviews or the testing of research subjects be anonymous (not associated with the names of individual subjects) and that raw (unanalyzed) data be destroyed after a specified time interval (often at the completion of the research project).

Federal regulations require a plan for the protection of human subjects as part of grant proposals submitted to federal agencies. The National Institute of Justice, for example, a major source of grant support for researchers in the area of criminology, has this to say:[49]

> All National Institute of Justice (NIJ) employees, contractors and grant recipients must be cognizant of the importance of protecting the rights and welfare of human subject research participants. In this period of expanding research on criminal justice issues and growing concerns for personal privacy, the protection of human subjects in our research endeavors is extremely important. All research conducted at NIJ or supported with NIJ funds must comply with all Federal, U.S. Department of Justice (DOJ), Office of Justice Programs and NIJ regulations and policies concerning the protection of human subjects and the DOJ confidentiality requirements.

Learn more about NIJ requirements for confidentiality and the protection of human subjects at Web Extra 3–9.

Some universities, research organizations, and government agencies have established institutional review boards tasked with examining research proposals to determine whether expectations of ethical conduct have been met before these proposals are submitted to funding organizations. Institutional review boards often consist of other researchers with special knowledge of the kinds of ethical issues involved in criminological research.

Participant observation sometimes entails an especially thorny ethical issue: Should researchers themselves violate the law if their research participation appears to require it? The very nature of participant observation is such that researchers of adult criminal activity may at times find themselves placed in situations where they are expected to "go along with the group" in violating the law. Those researching gang activity, for example, have sometimes been asked to transmit potentially incriminating information to other gang members, to act as drug couriers, and even to commit crimes of violence to help establish territorial claims important to members of the gang. Researchers who refuse may endanger not only their research but also themselves. Compliance with the expectations of criminal groups evokes other kinds of dangers, including the danger of apprehension and prosecution for violations of the criminal law. As one criminologist explains, "Criminological (and other) field researchers cannot conveniently distance themselves from their subjects of study, or from the legally uncertain situations in which the subjects may reside, in order to construct safe and 'objective' studies. Instead criminological field research unavoidably entangles those who practice it in complex and ambiguous relations to the subjects and situations of study, to issues of personal and social responsibility, and to law and legality."[50]

informed consent

The ethical requirement of social scientific research that research subjects be informed as to the nature of the research about to be conducted, their anticipated role in it, and the uses to which the data they provide will be put.

WEB
Extra
■ ■ ■ ■

Although the dilemma of a participant observer, especially one secretly engaged in research, is a difficult one, some of the best advice on the subject is offered by Frank E. Hagan, who says, "In self-mediating the potential conflicting roles of the criminal justice researcher, it is incumbent on the investigator to enter the setting with eyes wide open. A decision must be made beforehand on the level of commitment to the research endeavor and the analyst's ability to negotiate the likely role conflicts. Although there are no hard and fast rules . . . *the researcher's primary role is that of a scientist.*"[51]

Hagan also suggests that a code of ethics should guide all professional criminologists in their research undertakings. This code, says Hagan, would require the researcher to take the following personal responsibilities:[52]

- Avoid procedures that may harm respondents.
- Honor commitments to respondents and respect reciprocity.
- Exercise objectivity and professional integrity in performing and reporting research.
- Protect confidentiality and the privacy of respondents.

Hagan's admonition to "exercise objectivity and professional integrity" became especially important in the mid-1990s, when supporters of Project D.A.R.E. blocked publication of research results that showed the program to be ineffective.[53] D.A.R.E., a widely popular antidrug program that is common in the nation's schools, is a favorite of educational administrators because of the funding it provides. The study, a review of most prior D.A.R.E. research, was conducted by the Research Triangle Institute, a respected research firm in North Carolina, and was paid for by the National Institute of Justice (NIJ).[54] When results showed that D.A.R.E. programs did not significantly reduce drug use among student participants, however, NIJ decided not to publish the findings. "We're not trying to hide the study," said NIJ's Ann Voit. "We just do not agree with one of the major findings."[55] In contrast, Research Triangle Institute researcher Susan T. Ennett proposed that results of the study should be used to decide how to spend drug-education money. Other studies have since supported the finding that D.A.R.E. does not have a significant impact on actual drug use, drug-related outcomes, or attitudes toward drugs.[56] Learn more about the D.A.R.E. study via Library Extra 3–3 at crimtoday.com.

LIBRARY
Extra

Scientific research which demonstrates that popular, and often widely-supported programs, are ineffective, will inevitably fuel controversy. Such was the case in 2006, when a group of Italian researchers published findings purporting to show that the 12-step method used by Alcoholics Anonymous to prevent future problem drinking doesn't work. The researchers concluded that "no experimental studies unequivocally demonstrated the effectiveness of A.A. or professional 12-step theory for reducing alcohol dependence or problems."[57] The research left some people claiming that A.A. worked for them, and others saying that more (and better) studies were needed.

Because criminological research can affect social policy, which often involves the expenditure of public funds, the ethical code of the ASC mandates that criminologists be "committed to enhancing the *general well-being* of societies and of the individuals and groups within them." Thus, says the ASC code, "criminologists have an obligation not to recreate forms of social injustice such as discrimination, oppression, or harassment in their own work."[58]

Learn more about ethics in criminological research directly from the ASC and the ACJS via Web Extras 3–10 and 3–11. To read a comprehensive code of ethical standards for general survey research, visit the Council of American Survey Research Organizations via Web Extra 3–12.

WEB
Extra

Social Policy and Criminological Research

Ideally, research results in the field of criminology should have a significant impact on public crime control policy. Faye S. Taxman of the University of Maryland's Center for Applied Policy Studies explains it this way: "[T]he normative educative model assumes

Project D.A.R.E. participants. A decade ago, studies of Project D.A.R.E. questioned its effectiveness, but government officials decided not to publish the results. How can the objectivity of social scientific research be ensured?

Source: Mark Burnett/Stock Boston

that a rational use of data by policy makers, practitioners, and scientists . . . will be of value to the field."[59] In other words, the results of scientific studies in the field of criminology should have practical implications that can guide daily practice in relevant areas. Sometimes they do. For example, after studies showed that arrests (rather than mere warnings) of domestic violence perpetrators proved effective in reducing the likelihood of reoffending, many police departments across the country began advising their officers to make such arrests, and some state legislators advocated passage of mandatory arrest laws.[60]

Unfortunately, however, publicly elected officials are often either ignorant of current criminological research or do not heed the advice of professional criminologists, seeking instead to create politically expedient policies. The extent to which seemingly good research has been ignored by policymakers has led some to proclaim the "irrelevance" of criminology. James Austin of George Washington University, for example, bemoans the lack of attention that politicians give to the results of research in criminology. "Despite the annual publication of hundreds of peer-reviewed articles and textbooks proudly displayed at our annual conventions," he writes, "policy makers are paying little if any attention to us. When Congress or state legislatures debate new crime bill legislation or the effectiveness of past actions, their first question is not, 'What do the criminologists think?' I would venture," says Austin, "that one would be hard pressed to cite another discipline that has been so ignored for such a long time."[61]

Research findings may be ignored because they are at odds with public sentiment. A realistic appraisal must recognize that criminologists are as much to blame for the current situation as anyone else. As Robert M. Bohm explained in his 1993 presidential address to the ACJS, "[M]uch of our work is simply ignored because it is not politically expedient or does not serve the dominant ideology. At the same time, others among us are more than willing to do the bidding of politicians and criminal justice officials in order to feed at the trough of political largess. I don't know whether these people actually believe in what they are doing, or maybe they still believe in the myth that their work is objective or value-neutral. In either case, these apologists for the status quo legitimize and perpetuate . . . short-sighted, counterproductive, detrimental policies . . . and do a disservice to our discipline."[62]

One year later, at the 1994 annual meeting of the ASC, then–Attorney General Janet Reno appealed to the nation's assembled criminologists for urgent assistance in dealing with some of the major crime and criminal justice issues facing the country. Her address to conventioneers identified 12 important problem areas, and she challenged ASC members to translate existing research findings into useful recommendations that could benefit practitioners and policymakers throughout the nation who routinely confront issues of crime and justice.

Following her presentation, the ASC National Policy Committee formed 12 task forces—one to investigate each issue identified by the attorney general. Task force members distilled research findings into policy recommendations that could meaningfully contribute to public debates that were then raging (and many of which are still continuing) over how best to deal with problems of crime, juvenile delinquency, prison overcrowding, and so on. In 1997, after all 12 task forces had submitted final reports, the documents were published by the National Institute of Justice and were made available through the National Criminal Justice Reference Service under the title *Critical Criminal Justice Issues: Task Force Reports from the American Society of Criminology.* At the time of publication, Jeremy Travis, then-director of the NIJ, termed the reports a "remarkable contribution to improving our understanding of the issues of crime and the challenge of justice." The task force reports, which have contemporary applicability as well as historical relevance, can be viewed at the *Criminology Today* Web site crimtoday.com, where the 132-page publication *Critical Criminal Justice Issues* is available in its entirety as **Library Extra 3–4**.

LIBRARY Extra

Three-strikes laws, which became popular with legislatures across the country near the end of the last century, provide an example of the kind of dilemma facing criminologists who would influence social policy on the basis of statistical evidence. Three-strikes laws require that felons receive lengthy prison sentences (often life without the possibility of parole) following their third felony conviction. Such laws are built on the commonsense notion that "getting tough" on repeat offenders by putting them in prison for long periods should reduce the crime rate. Logic seems to say that lengthy prison sentences for recidivists will reduce crime by removing the most dangerous offenders from society.

A study of the three-strikes laws in 22 states, however, concluded that such legislation typically results in clogged court systems and crowded correctional facilities and encourages three-time felons to take dramatic risks to avoid capture.[63] A wider-based study,[64] dubbed "the most comprehensive study ever of crime prevention,"[65] found that "much of the research on prisons was inadequate or flawed, making it impossible to measure how much crime was actually prevented or deterred by locking up more criminals." More significant, the central finding of the massive study, which was sponsored by the federal Office of Justice Programs and was carried out by researchers at the University of Maryland's Department of Criminology and Criminal Justice, was that current government-sponsored crime prevention initiatives—totaling over $3 billion annually—are often poorly evaluated, leading to uncertainty over whether funded programs actually work. The study, a **meta-analysis** (that is, a study of other studies), reviewed more than 500 impact evaluations of local crime prevention programs and practices throughout the nation. Researchers concluded that due to largely ineffective evaluation efforts that are often only loosely tied to funded programs, "the current [government-sponsored research] plan does not . . . provide effective guidance to the nation about what works to prevent crime." Hence, although the three-strikes laws remain popular with the voting public and lawmakers have been quick to seize upon get-tough crime prevention policies in the interest of getting votes, solid and consistent research support showing the efficacy of such laws continues to be elusive.

meta-analysis

A study of other studies about a particular topic of interest.

One important repository of crime and justice-related literature today can be found at the Campbell Crime and Justice Coordinating Group, a subsidiary project of the Campbell Collaboration. The Campbell Collaboration, named in honor of the noted social science methodologist Donald T. Campbell, focuses on what works in the areas of education, social welfare, and criminal justice. The Campbell Collaboration began in 2000 to make systematic reviews of research on the effects of social interventions accessible. You can access the Collaboration via **Web Extra 3–13** at crimtoday.com. The Campbell Collaboration Crime and Justice Coordinating Group, which provides a number of the Library Extras referenced throughout this book, can be reached via **Web Extra 3–14**.

WEB Extra

Theory Versus Reality

The Stockholm Prize in Criminology

On June 5, 2007, American criminologist Alfred Blumstein and British social science researcher Terrie E. Moffitt stepped to a podium outside of the city hall in Stockholm, Sweden, to be recognized at the awards ceremony of the International Stockholm Criminology Symposium as corecipients of the 2007 Stockholm Prize in Criminology. The symposium met on the campus of Stockholm University, but the awards ceremony, conducted by Her Majesty, Queen Silvia of Sweden, was held at city hall to allow greater participation of political decision makers, the Swedish citizenry, and the media.

Blumstein, of Carnegie-Mellon University in Pittsburgh, Pennsylvania, and Moffitt, a professor at the University of London, became the prize's second corecipients. The prize, which was first awarded in 2006, recognizes outstanding achievements in criminological research or in the practical implementation of research findings in order to combat crime and promote human rights. It carries a cash award of 1.3 million Swedish kronor (about $140,000). Blumstein and Moffitt were recognized for their discoveries about the development of criminal behavior over the life-course, including their pioneering studies of the patterns of onset, persistence, frequency, severity, and desistance in criminal acts. Moffitt's identification of "adolescent-limited" versus "life-course persistent" offenders in a New Zealand birth cohort (see Chapter 8), led to a great deal of research on patterns of offending. Blumstein's analysis of variations in the frequency of offending among the career criminals in the United States has contributed significantly to the devleopment of life-course criminology (see Chapter 8).

The Stockholm Prize is financed by the Jerry Lee Foundation in the United States with support from the Japanese Correctional Association, the Hitachi Mirai Foundation, and the Söderberg Foundation of Sweden. The prize intends to promote:

- improved knowledge on causes of crime on an individual and structural level
- more effective and humane public policies for dealing with criminal offenders
- greater knowledge of alternative crime prevention strategies inside and outside the judicial system
- effective policies for helping victims of crime
- better ways to reduce the global problem of illegal or abusive practices that may occur in the administration of justice

Recipients of the 2006 prize were John Braithwaite of the Australian National University, and Friedrich Lösel of Cambridge University in the United Kingdom. The jury selecting the winners of the first Stockholm Prize took special note of Braithwaite's influential theories of "reintegrative shaming" and "responsive regulation" (see Chapter 8), and of Lösel's systematic reviews of empirical evidence on the effectiveness of correctional treatment. Lösel, a German citizen, began his career at the University of Erlangen-Nuremberg in Germany, where he conducted studies showing that repeat offending can be reduced by providing prison rehabilitation programs for convicted offenders.

Visit www.criminologyprize.com for further information about the prize and the award recipients, and to learn more about the annual Stockholm Criminology Symposium.

American criminologist Alfred Blumstein and British social science researcher Terrie E. Moffitt step to the podium in Stockholm, Sweden, to receive the 2007 Stockholm Prize in Criminology. Awarding the Prize is Queen Silvia of Sweden. What accomplishments does the prize recognize?

Source: Dr. Laura Dugan, PhD

Sources: "The Stockholm Prize in Criminology: About the Prize," http://www.criminologyprize.com/extra/pod/?id=12&module_instance=3&action= pod_show&navid=12 (accessed May 7, 2007); and "The Stockholm Prize in Criminology," awards announcement (pamphlet), prize office (Stockholm, Sweden).

Writing the Research Report

Following the research and the analysis of data, findings are typically presented in the form of a report or paper in which suggestions for further study may be made. Policy issues, or strategies for addressing the problems identified by the researcher, are also frequently discussed. Charts, graphs, and tables may be included in the body of a research report. Most reports are professional-looking documents prepared on a word processor with a grammar and spelling checker and printed on a laser or ink-jet printer. Some are eventually published in professional journals, and a few become staples of the field—frequently cited works that illustrate fundamental criminological or methodological principles.

Most research reports follow a traditional format, which has been developed over the years as a generally acceptable way of presenting research results. Following are the component features of professional reports.

- **Title page.** The title page contains the names of the report's authors, their institutional or professional affiliations, the date of the report, and, its title. Many report titles consist of a main title and a subtitle. Subtitles generally give additional information about the report's subject matter. Although some report titles seem all-inclusive, such as

  "The Impact of Family Structure and Quality on Delinquency: A Comparative Assessment of Structural and Functional Factors"[66]

  others are relatively straightforward and to the point, such as

  "Comparing Criminal Career Models"[67]

- **Acknowledgments.** Often, the author wishes to express appreciation to individuals and organizations that facilitated the study or without whose help the study would not have been possible. Sources of grant support, including funding agencies and foundations; individuals and organizations who either participated in the study or were themselves studied; and people who facilitated various aspects of the study or the production of the report are all frequently acknowledged.

- **Table of contents.** Reports of any length (say, beyond ten pages) often contain a table of contents. A table of contents helps readers quickly find the needed material and provides structure to the report itself. A good table of contents will reflect section headings within the body of the report.

- **Preface (if desired).** The purpose of a preface is to allow the author to make observations, often of a personal nature, which might not be appropriate within the body of the report. Reasons for choosing the subject of study, observations about the promise held by the field of study, and wide-ranging statements about the future of criminological research are all frequent topics of prefaces found in research reports.

- **Abstract.** An abstract is a brief (usually one-paragraph) summation of the report's findings, allowing readers to gauge, without reading the entire report, whether the subject matter will be of interest to them. In this day of electronic information retrieval, abstracts serve the additional function of providing a quick synopsis that can readily be made available to those searching large databases containing many research articles. Reproduced here is a concise and well-written abstract from Greg Pogarsky's study entitled "Projected Offending and Contemporaneous Rule-Violation: Implications for Heterotypic Continuity," which appeared in the February 2004 issue of *Criminology*.[68]

  This study integrated two methodologies, the vignette-based survey and the randomized laboratory experiment, to investigate the relationship between projected and actual offending behavior. Findings indicate that respondents' estimates of the likelihood they would drive drunk in a hypothetical vignette were positively correlated with whether they simultaneously cheated on a laboratory task to earn a cash bonus. Implications are discussed for both the prospective measurement and heterotypic continuity of criminal and antisocial behavior.

- **Introduction.** Most authors write an introductory section as part of their research report. The introduction describes the aim and purpose of the study and provides a general statement of the problem studied. It also furnishes a general conceptual framework for the remainder of the report. The introduction may outline issues that are related to the problem under study and issues that could benefit from further investigation.

- **Review of existing literature.** Most research builds on existing knowledge and makes use of previous findings. To cite a few proverbial observations, although it is not true that "there is nothing new under the sun" when conducting research, it is also not necessary to "reinvent the wheel." In other words, the relevant works of other researchers should be discussed in any report, and the bearing previous studies have upon the present one should be explained. Sometimes researchers who are engaged in literature reviews discover that the questions they wish to study have already been answered or that someone else has found a more concise way of stating their concerns. Hence, new investigators can avoid concept development that is merely repetitive and even data gathering that has already been undertaken.

- **Description of existing situation.** Sometimes a description of the existing situation is combined with a report's introduction. If not, then it is appropriate to elaborate on the problem under study by providing details that describe the conditions existing at the beginning of the study.

- **Statement of the hypothesis.** Research etiquette in criminology frequently requires the statement of a hypothesis to be tested. Most researchers have an idea of what they expect to find. Often, they have set out to test a theory or a proposition derived from a theory. Researchers may, for example, wish to test whether the Brady Law, which limits handgun sales, has effectively met its goal of reducing the number of deaths by firearms. A hypothesis should be a clear and concise statement of what the study purports to test. As mentioned previously, hypotheses useful in guiding research are always operationalized, or expressed in terms that are in some way measurable. Descriptive studies, on the other hand, are not designed to prove or disprove assumptions (although they may not be free of them), and such studies may not contain hypotheses.

- **Description of the research plan.** The research design, data-gathering strategies, and plans for statistical analysis should all be described. This section, although it may be elaborate and lengthy, simply provides an overview of the methodology employed by the researcher and explains how the problem was investigated and why particular research strategies were chosen.

- **Disclaimers and limitations.** All research is subject to limitations. Shortages of money, time, personnel, and other resources impose limitations on research undertakings, as do shortcomings in statistical techniques and restrictions on the availability of data. Limitations should be honestly appraised and presented in the research report so that readers will be able to assess their impact on the results that are reported.

- **Findings or results.** Along with an overview of the research as it was actually conducted, the "findings" section provides a statement of research results. Many regard it as the heart of the report. The manner in which results are presented can be crucial for ease of understanding. Some researchers choose to employ tables containing raw numbers when pictorial forms of representation like charts and graphs would better facilitate comprehension. Bar charts and pie charts are probably the most commonly employed types of diagrams, although the type of data collected will determine the appropriate format for its presentation.

- **Analysis and discussion.** Once findings have been presented, they should be discussed and analyzed. Not all analysis need be of a quantitative sort. However, much of today's criminological literature is replete with statistical analyses, some of it quite sophisticated. Unfortunately, however, poorly conceptualized research cannot be helped by later analysis, no matter how sophisticated that analysis may be. It is therefore of crucial importance to the success of any research endeavor that early planning—including conceptual development, strategies for data collection, and research designs—be undertaken with an eye toward producing data that will lend themselves to meaningful analysis after data gathering has been completed. The analysis section should also focus on whether the data, as analyzed, support the study's guiding hypothesis.

- **Summary and conclusions.** The summation section encapsulates the study's purpose and findings in a few paragraphs. It may also contain discussion of suggested improvements or recommended solutions to the problem studied based on the evidence produced by the report. Policy implications are also discussed (if at all) in the conclusion of the report because they are simply broad-based solutions to problems that have been identified.

- **Endnotes.** Either endnotes or footnotes may be used to reference quoted sources or to refer readers to supporting documents. Sometimes a combination of footnotes and endnotes is employed. Endnotes, as their name implies, appear at the conclusion of a report (often after the summary but before the appendixes), whereas footnotes are found at the bottom of the pages containing the referenced material.

- **Appendixes.** Not all reports contain appendixes. Those that do may place sample questionnaires, accompanying cover letters, concise exhibits from literature reviews, detailed statistical tables, copies of letters of support, detailed interview information, and so forth near the end of the document. Appendixes should be used only if they serve the purpose of further explicating the report's purpose, methods, or findings. Otherwise, appendixes may appear to "pad" the report and can discredit the researcher's efforts in the eyes of readers.

- **List of references.** No report is complete without a bibliography or other list of references used in planning the study and in preparing the document. Although all items listed in the bibliography may not be referenced within the body of the report, source material should still be listed if it was reviewed and served some purpose in study development. Literature that is examined, for example, may guide the researcher to other material or may provide useful insights during the study's overall conceptual formation.

Writing for Publication

Criminologists often seek to publish the results of their research to share them with others working in the field. The primary medium for such publication consists of refereed professional journals. Refereed journals are those that employ the services of peer reviewers to gauge the quality of the manuscripts submitted to them. Although thereview process can be time-consuming, it is believed to result in the publication of manuscripts that make worthwhile contributions to the field of criminology and in the rejection of those of lesser quality.

Perhaps the best-known professional journals in the field of criminology today are the *American Journal of Criminal Justice,* the *British Journal of Criminology, Crime and Delinquency, Crime and Social Justice, Criminal Justice and Behavior, Criminal Justice Ethics,* the *Criminal Justice Policy Review,* the *Criminal Justice Review, Criminology, Criminology and Public Policy, Critical Criminology,* the *Journal of Contemporary Criminal Justice,* the *Journal of Crime and Justice,* the *Journal of Criminal Justice Education,* the *Journal of Criminal Law and Criminology,* the *Journal of Quantitative Criminology,* the *Journal of Research in Crime and Delinquency, Justice Quarterly,* and *Theoretical Criminology.*[69] For a comprehensive list of journals in the field of criminology, including some that are Web-based, visit **Web Extra 3–15** at crimtoday.com.

WEB
Extra
∎ ∎ ∎ ∎

Each journal has its own requirements for manuscript submission. Some require a single copy of a manuscript; others ask for multiple copies. A few journals request manuscript files on disk along with hard copies, and still others are moving toward electronic submission via the Internet. An increasing number of journals have established submission fees, usually in the $10 to $20 range, to help defray the costs associated with the review process.

Submission etiquette within the field of criminology demands that an article be sent to only one journal at a time. Simultaneous submissions are discouraged and create difficulties for both authors and editors when articles are accepted by more than one publication. Given the complexities of the review and publications processes, it is

Who's to Blame—The Individual or Society?

Is Criminology Really Just a Form of Academic Excuse Making?

Three teenage boys were arrested in the small town of Hillsboro, Maine, and charged with beating a homeless man to death with a baseball bat in an underground parking garage on a cold January evening. A surveillance camera captured the beating and the youngsters were identified by residents who watched the video clip on local TV news.

Because the boys were juveniles, a storm of controversy swarmed around a local judge's decision to charge them as adults and to bind them over for trial in criminal court—something that state law allows for serious crimes if the suspected offenders were over 14 years of age at the time of the alleged offense.

Soon opinions were being heard from many quarters, and the news media arranged to interview a criminology professor, Dr. Roy Humbolt, at a local college to see if he might be able to shed some light on the boys' behavior.

The first question came from a reporter holding a digital voice recorder out toward Professor Humbolt. "What happened here? How do you explain this kind of senseless killing?"

"Well," Humbolt began, "it's not senseless. Crime is a social event, not just an isolated instance of individual activity. And in much youth crime we see patterns of co-offending."

Humbolt felt as though he was hitting his stride, and started lecturing as though he was in the classroom with his undergraduates, "Criminal behavior is often attributable to social failings rather than to

individual choice. Consider, for a moment, the backgrounds of these young men. Were they subjected to physical abuse while they were growing up? Was violence what they learned at the hands of older siblings or parents? Were they, in this instance, involved in some adolescent rite of passage, maybe even an initiation into a gang? Did they feel forced to behave this way because of peer pressure? Was it something that they saw on television, or in video games that they might have played, and then decided to re-enact?"

"Dr. Humbolt" the reporter asked, bringing the professor back from his reverie "Even if you find that some of those things are true, isn't criminology just an exercise in excuse-making for criminals?"

Think about it:

1. What do you think of the explanations offered by Professor Humbolt for the boy's behavior? Which of his explanations, if any, make the most sense? How can we know for sure if those explanations are accurate?

2. What do you think of the reporter's stinging criticism of the professor? Is the reporter right, that criminology is "just an exercise in excuse-making for criminals"? Explain your answer.

3. Generally speaking, does understanding absolve responsibility? In other words, if we can understand why someone does something, then should we hold him or her less responsible for doing it? Why or why not?

---

probably best to write the editor of any journal to which submission is being contemplated to inquire as to that journal's particular expectations.

Most journals require that manuscripts be prepared according to a particular style, meaning that citations, capitalization, footnoting, abstracts, notes, headings, and subheadings are all expected to conform to the style of other articles published in the same journal. Two of the most prevalent styles are the American Psychological Association (APA) style and the American Sociological Association (ASA) style.

Most criminological journals, however, utilize a modification of one of these styles. When considering the submission of a manuscript for publication review, it is advisable to write to the editor of the journal in question requesting a style sheet or general style guidelines. Style guides are also available from the APA[70] and the ASA, with third-party publishers making style guides available through university and special-purpose bookstores.

If a research report is not intended for publication, other styles may be acceptable. Answers to general questions about report writing and style can be found in publications like William Strunk and E. B. White's *The Elements of Style*[71] and Mary-Claire van Leunen's *A Handbook for Scholars.*[72]

SUMMARY

Criminology—like its sister disciplines of sociology, psychology, geography, and political science—is a social science that endeavors to apply the techniques of data collection and hypothesis testing through observation and experimentation. Successful hypothesis testing can lead to theory building and to a more complete understanding of the nature of crime and crime causation. Experimental criminology, in particular, offers

the promise of building a valuable collection of evidence-based knowledge that can be of service to policymakers and individuals concerned about the fight against crime.

Although the scientific framework and its techniques have largely been inherited from the physical sciences—such as chemistry, astronomy, and physics—in which they have been well established for centuries, criminology has been accepted into the scientific tradition by all but the most hard-nosed purists. Even so, criminologists are still game to study aspects of the field that are in need of study, even where adequate resources (funding) or techniques (for example, the complete mapping of all human chromosomes) are not yet available.

Another component of scientific criminology, the detailed description of crime and related phenomena even where meaningful hypotheses are lacking, is also very much with us. In one descriptive area alone, that of crime statistics (discussed in Chapter 2), so much data have already been gathered that it is unlikely they will ever be completely analyzed.

The fondest hope of many criminologists today is that effective research into the causes of crime, coupled with meaningful evaluations of crime prevention efforts, will one day significantly influence social policy mandates, resulting in legislation and government-sponsored initiatives built on programs shown to be effective.

KEY TERMS

applied research, 94
confounding effects, 96
control group, 99
controlled experiment, 98
data confidentiality, 108
descriptive statistics, 104
evidence-based, 88
experimental criminology, 89
external validity, 97
hypothesis, 92
inferential statistics, 104

informed consent, 109
internal validity, 97
intersubjectivity, 102
meta-analysis, 112
operationalization, 95
participant observation, 101
primary research, 94
pure research, 94
qualitative method, 107
quantitative method, 105
quasi-experimental design, 99

randomization, 99
replicability, 102
research, 94
research design, 95
secondary research, 94
survey research, 100
test of significance, 104
theory, 92
variable, 95
verstehen, 107

QUESTIONS FOR REVIEW

1. What is the role of criminological research in theory building?

2. How can theories help us to understand criminal behavior? To design strategies intended to control such behavior?

3. What role do research and experimentation play in theory building in criminology? How might a good research design be diagrammed? What kinds of threats to the validity of research designs can you identify? How can such threats be controlled or eliminated?

4. What are the differences between quantitative and qualitative methods in the social sciences? What are the advantages and disadvantages of each method?

5. What are some of the ethical considerations involved in conducting criminological research? How can researchers make sure that such considerations are met?

6. How do criminological research and experimental criminology impact social policy?

7. What sections might a typical research report contain? Where are research findings in criminology published?

QUESTIONS FOR REFLECTION

1. This book emphasizes a social problems versus social responsibility theme. How might a thorough research agenda allow us to decide which perspective is most fruitful in combating crime?

2. What is a hypothesis? What does it mean to operationalize a hypothesis? Why is operationalization necessary?

3. What is a theory? Why is the task of criminological theory construction so demanding? How do we know if a theory is any good?

4. What is a meta-analysis? For what purposes might a meta-analysis be conducted?

5. List and describe the various types of data-gathering strategies discussed in this chapter. Is any one technique "better" than another? Why? Under what kinds of conditions might certain types of data-gathering strategies be most appropriate?

6. In 2007, the Bureau of Justice Statistics announced findings that male military veterans were less than half as

likely as nonveteran men of the same age to be in prison (the rates reported were 630 versus 1,390 per 100,000 male prisoners, respectively). Does this mean that we can say with confidence that military service decreases a man's

likelihood of committing a criminal offense? What other influences might be operating to lower the likelihood of crime commission by military veterans? (See the full BJS report at www.justicestudies.com/pubs/veterans.pdf.)

WEB QUEST

Visit the world's largest archive of computerized social science data at the Interuniversity Consortium for Political and Social Research (ICPSR) at www.icpsr.umich.edu. The ICPSR is based at the Institute for Social Research at the University of Michigan. The three goals of ICPSR's criminal justice data archive are to

- Provide computer-readable data for the quantitative study of crime and the criminal justice system through the development of a central data archive that disseminates computer-readable data

- Supply technical assistance in selecting data collections and the computer hardware and software for analyzing data efficiently and effectively

- Offer training in quantitative methods of social science research to facilitate secondary analysis of criminal justice data

ICPSR brings together the data collections of over 370 member colleges and universities in the United States and abroad. It also routinely receives data from the BJS, the NIJ,

the Office for Juvenile Justice and Delinquency Prevention, and the FBI. As a consequence, the consortium is able to provide access to voluminous amounts of information. UCR/NIBRS and NCVS data are available through ICPSR, as is information on capital punishment, adult and juvenile correctional facilities, and jails; state and federal court statistics; expenditure and employment data for the criminal justice system; and surveys of law enforcement and other criminal justice agencies.

Much of ICPSR's available information takes the form of data sets, which are ready for analysis through software packages such as the Statistical Package for the Social Sciences (SPSS) and SPSS PC-plus. Important criminology-related data sets are available through the National Archive of Criminal Justice Data (NACJD), which can be accessed directly at www.icpsr.umich.edu/NACJD.

If your instructor asks you to do so, access the NACJD page at ICPSR and read the Frequently Asked Questions (FAQs) section under the "Access Data" subheading. Prepare a summary of each question and answer that's contained within the FAQs.

NOTES

[1] Karl Popper, *The Logic of Scientific Discovery* (Vienna: Springer, 1934).

[2] Abraham Kaplan, *The Conduct of Inquiry: Methodology for Behavioral Science* (San Francisco: Chandler, 1964), p. 145.

[3] John H. Laub, "The Life Course of Criminology in the United States: The American Society of Criminology 2003 Presidential Address," *Criminology,* Vol. 42, No. 1 (2004), p. 19.

[4] "Florida Town Casts Out Satan," CNN, January 29, 2002, http://cnn.com/2002/US/01/29/town.satan (accessed June 3, 2007).

[5] Mike Schneider, "Mayor Bans Satan from Florida Town," Associated Press wire service, April 15, 2002.

[6] Alex Leary, "ACLU Action Lands Satan on Inglis Meeting Agenda," *St. Petersburg Times* online, January 25, 2002, http://www.sptimes.com/2002/01/25/TampaBay/ACLU_action_lands_Sat.shtml (accessed May 7, 2007).

[7] "Inglis, Florida," *Wikipedia,* http://en.wikipedia.org/wiki/Inglis,_Florida (accessed May 7, 2007).

[8] The Carpetbagger Report, "An Interesting Update on Inglis, Fla., and its Campaign against Satan," March 15, 2004, http://www.thecarpetbaggerreport.com/archives/1403.html (accessed May 7, 2007).

[9] Lawrence W. Sherman, *Evidence-Based Policing* (Washington, DC: Police Foundation, 1998), p. 4.

[10] Laub, "The Life Course of Criminology in the United States."

[11] As discussed by Piers Beirne and Colin Summer, "Editorial Statement," *Theoretical Criminology: An International Journal,* Vol. 1, No. 1 (February 1997), pp. 5–11.

[12] Mannheim, *Comparative Criminology,* p. 20.

[13] Details for this story come from Paul Stokes "Extra Police Put on the Beat for Full Moon," *The Telegraph,* June 7, 2006, http://www.telegraph.co.uk/news/main.jhtml?xml=/news/2007/06/06/nmoon106.xml (accessed July 12, 2007).

[14] Don M. Gottfredson, "Criminology Theories: The Truth as Told by Mark Twain," in William S. Laufer and Freda Adler, eds., *Advances in Criminological Theory,* Vol. 1 (New Brunswick, NJ: Transaction, 1989), p. 3.

[15] Kenneth R. Hoover, *The Elements of Social Scientific Thinking,* 5th ed. (New York: St. Martin's, 1992), p. 34.

[16] Ibid., p. 35.

[17] George Gerbner's Cultivation Theory online, http://www.colostate.edu/Depts/Speech/rccs/theory06.htm (accessed May 22, 2007).

[18] Bernard P. Cohen, *Developing Sociological Knowledge: Theory and Method,* 2nd ed. (Chicago: Nelson-Hall, 1989), p. 13.

[19] Ibid., p. 71.

[20] Susette M. Talarico, *Criminal Justice Research: Approaches, Problems and Policy* (Cincinnati: Anderson, 1980), p. 3.

[21] Ibid.

[22] For a good review of secondary research, see J. H. Laub, R. J. Sampson, and K. Kiger, "Assessing the Potential of Secondary Data Analysis: A New Look at the Glueck's Unraveling Juvenile Delinquency Data," in Kimberly L. Kempf, ed., *Measurement Issues in Criminology* (New York: Springer-Verlag, 1990), pp. 241–257; and Robert J. Sampson and John H. Laub, *Crime in the Making* (Cambridge: Harvard University Press, 1993).

[23] Sampson and Laub, *Crime in the Making*, p. 3.

[24] David Weisburd, "Editor's Introduction," *Journal of Experimental Criminology*, Vol. 1 (2005), p. 3.

[25] Larry S. Miller and John T. Whitehead, *Introduction to Criminal Justice Research and Methods* (Cincinnati: Anderson, 1996).

[26] Donald T. Campbell and Julian C. Stanley, *Experimental and Quasi-Experimental Designs for Research* (Chicago: Rand-McNally, 1966), p. 35.

[27] As identified in ibid., p. 5, from which many of the descriptions that follow are adapted.

[28] Ibid., p. 34.

[29] According to Denise C. Gottfredson, "[M]idnight basketball programs are not likely to reduce crime." Gottfredson cites research (J. G. Ross et al., "The Effectiveness of an After-School Program for Primary Grade Latchkey Students on Precursors of Substance Abuse," *Journal of Community Psychology*, OSAP Special Issue [1992], pp. 22–38) showing that such programs may actually increase the risk for delinquency by increasing risk-taking and impulsiveness. See Denise C. Gottfredson, "School-Based Crime Prevention," in Lawrence W. Sherman et al., *Preventing Crime: What Works, What Doesn't, What's Promising* (Washington, DC: National Institute of Justice, 1998), http://www.ncjrs.org/works/chapter5.htm (accessed June 15, 2004).

[30] Shawn Bushway and David Weisburd, "Acknowledging the Centrality of Quantitative Criminology in Criminology and Criminal Justice," *The Criminologist*, Vol. 31, No. 4 (2006), p. 1.

[31] Lawrence W. Sherman, David P. Brandon, C. Welsh, and Doris L. Mackenzie, *Evidence-Based Crime Prevention* (New York: Routledge, 2002).

[32] Frank E. Hagan, *Research Methods in Criminal Justice and Criminology*, 6th ed. (New York: Allyn and Bacon, 2003).

[33] Jeff Ferrell, "Criminological *Verstehen*: Inside the Immediacy of Crime," *Justice Quarterly*, Vol. 14, No. 1 (1997), p. 11.

[34] William Foote Whyte, *Street Corner Society: The Social Structure of an Italian Slum* (Chicago: University of Chicago Press, 1943), pp. v–vii.

[35] Ibid., p. vii.

[36] Hagan, *Research Methods in Criminal Justice and Criminology*.

[37] Nicole Vanden Heuvel, *Directory of Criminal Justice Information Sources*, 8th ed. (Washington, DC: National Institute of Justice, 1992), p. 145.

[38] Hagan, *Research Methods in Criminal Justice and Criminology*.

[39] Hoover, *The Elements of Social Scientific Thinking*, p. 34.

[40] Kaplan, *The Conduct of Inquiry*, p. 134.

[41] As reported in ibid.

[42] Avshalom Caspim et al., "Are Some People Crime-Prone? Replications of the Personality-Crime Relationship across Countries, Genders, Races, and Methods," *Criminology*, Vol. 32, No. 2 (May 1994), pp. 163–195.

[43] Kaplan, *The Conduct of Inquiry*, p. 172.

[44] As with almost anything else, qualitative data can be assigned to categories, and the categories can be numbered. Hence, qualitative data can be quantified, although the worth of such effort is subject to debate.

[45] Sanyika Shakur, *Monster: The Autobiography of an L.A. Gang Member* (New York: Penguin, 1993), pp. 45–46.

[46] Ferrell, "Criminological *Verstehen*," p. 10.

[47] Academy of Criminal Justice Sciences, *Code of Ethics*, Section 18.

[48] Ibid., Section 19.

[49] National Institute of Justice, *Protecting Human Subjects*, http://www.ojp.usdoj.gov/nij/humansubjects (accessed June 16, 2007).

[50] Ferrell, "Criminological *Verstehen*," p. 8.

[51] Hagan, *Research Methods in Criminal Justice and Criminology*.

[52] Ibid.

[53] See Dennis Cauchon, "Study Critical of D.A.R.E. Rejected," *USA Today*, October 4, 1994, p. 2A.

[54] See Susan T. Ennett et al., "How Effective Is Drug Abuse Resistance Education? A Meta-Analysis of Project DARE Outcome Evaluations," *American Journal of Public Health*, Vol. 84, No. 9 (September 1994), pp. 1394–1401.

[55] Susan T. Ennett et al., "Long-Term Evaluation of Drug Abuse Resistance Education," *Addictive Behaviors*, Vol. 19, No. 2 (1994), pp. 113–125.

[56] Donald R. Lynam and Richard Milich, "Project DARE: No Effects at 10-Year Follow-Up," *Journal of Consulting and Clinical Psychology*, Vol. 67, No. 4 (August 1999), pp. 590–593.

[57] Kevin Helliker, "The Case for Alcoholics Anonymous: It Works Even if the Science is Lacking," *Wall Street Journal*, October 17, 2006, p. D1.

[58] American Society of Criminology, *Draft Code of Ethics*, Section II, paragraph 7 (unpublished manuscript).

[59] Faye S. Taxman, "Research and Relevance: Lessons from the Past, Thoughts for the Future," *Criminology and Public Policy*, Vol. 3, No. 2 (March 2004), p. 170.

[60] Julian Leigh, "Mandatory Arrest Laws Can Reduce Domestic Violence," in Tamara L. Roleff, ed., *Domestic Violence: Opposing Viewpoints* (San Diego, CA: Greenhaven Press, 2000).

[61] James Austin, "Why Criminology Is Irrelevant," *Criminology and Public Policy*, Vol. 2, No. 3 (July 2003), pp. 557–564.

[62] Robert M. Bohm, "On the State of Criminal Justice: 1993 Presidential Address to the Academy of Criminal Justice Sciences," *Justice Quarterly*, Vol. 10, No. 4 (December 1993), p. 537.

[63] The Campaign for an Effective Crime Policy, *The Impact of Three Strikes and You're Out Laws: What Have We Learned?* (Washington, DC: CECP, 1997).

[64] Sherman et al., *Preventing Crime*.

[65] Fox Butterfield, no headline, *New York Times News Service* online, April 16, 1997.

[66] Patricia Van Voorhis et al., "The Impact of Family Structure and Quality on Delinquency: A Comparative Assessment of Structural and Functional Factors," *Criminology*, Vol. 26, No. 2 (May 1988), pp. 235–261.

[67] David F. Greenberg, "Comparing Criminal Career Models," *Criminology*, Vol. 30, No. 1 (February 1992), pp. 133–140.

[68] Greg Pogarsky, "Projected Offending and Contemporaneous Rule-Violation: Implications for Heterotypic Continuity," *Criminology*, Vol. 42, No. 1 (February 2004), pp. 111–135.

[69] This list of journals is representative at best. For a much more complete list, see Michael S. Vaughn et al., "Journals in Criminal Justice and Criminology: An Updated and Expanded Guide for Authors," *Journal of Criminal Justice Education*, Vol. 15, No. 1 (spring 2004), pp. 61–192.

[70] American Psychological Association, *Publication Manual of the American Psychological Association*, 5th ed. (Washington, DC: APA, 2001).

[71] William Strunk, Jr., and E. B. White, *The Elements of Style*, 4th ed. (New York: Longman, 2000).

[72] Mary-Claire van Leunen, *A Handbook for Scholars*, rev. ed. (Oxford: Oxford University Press, 1992).

2
PART

Crime Causation

> **Men have always loved to fight. If they didn't love to fight, they wouldn't be men.**
>
> —General George S. Patton, Jr.[i]

> **The only way to get out is to die.**
>
> —Eric Norah, 11, after attending the funeral of classmate Robert Sandifer, killed in a gang shooting in Chicago as police sought him on murder charges[ii]

CHAPTER 4 **Classical and Neoclassical Thought**	**CHAPTER 6** **Psychological and Psychiatric Foundations of Criminal Behavior**
CHAPTER 5 **Biological Roots of Criminal Behavior**	

The need to know *why* people commit crimes is central to criminology. Our need to understand criminal *motivation* differs, however, from our ability to describe crime *causation*. The causes of crime may vary substantially from the reasons a particular offender had in mind when breaking the law. Crime causation involves a wide array of factors, including the shaping of personality by early childhood experiences like poor parenting, conscious and unconscious attempts at peer group emulation, the impact of poverty on people whose lives might be destitute were it not for the opportunities provided by crime, the values and lifestyles learned from those around us, and, quite possibly, fundamental and profound biological and genetic influences on the choices that we make.

At the same time, it is important to consider barriers that might prevent crime, even in the face of strong criminal motivation and in situations where the causes of crime seem firmly rooted in social, economic, and other conditions. Barriers to crime are those aspects of a setting that limit criminal opportunity and prevent offending.

Barriers cause would-be criminals to reconsider their intention to violate the law, or simply deny them the opportunity to follow their plans through to completion. Some barriers can be found in the physical arrangements of the external environment, while others are more abstract and consist of the threat of severe punishment or the internal strictures by which people limit their own freedom of action, even in the face of strong temptation.

In this part, we consider various theoretical approaches to crime causation, including biological theories (Chapter 5) and psychological approaches (Chapter 6). As we move through these chapters, we will be examining aspects of the human organism and its surroundings, as well as the contents of individual consciousness—and we will always be looking for clues as to what leads to crime. We begin our consideration of theoretical perspectives with Chapter 4, "Classical and Neoclassical Thought"—a chapter rich in historical subject matter that takes us back to the early days of criminological theorizing.

---

[i] As cited in David Jones, *History of Criminology: A Philosophical Perspective* (Westport, CT: Greenwood Press, 1986), p. 1
[ii] "So Young to Kill, So Young to Die," *Time*, September 19, 1994, p. 54.

Chapter 4

Classical and Neoclassical Thought

Outline

> Nature has placed mankind under the governance of two sovereign masters, pain and pleasure.
>
> —Jeremy Bentham[1]

> The more promptly and the more closely punishment follows upon the commission of a crime, the more just and useful will it be.
>
> —Cesare Beccaria[2]

> Classical criminology is grounded in the tenets of free will rationality, and hedonism.
>
> —M. Lyn Exum[3]

> People make choices, but they cannot choose the choices available to them. Nor can they be sure what chain of events will follow from their choices, including choices made by others.
>
> —Marcus Felson[4]

Learning Outcomes

After reading this chapter, you should be able to

- Identify the major principles of the Classical School of criminological thought
- Explain the philosophical bases of classical thought
- Discuss the Enlightenment and describe its impact on criminological theorizing
- Identify modern-day practices that embody principles of the Classical School
- Explain the role of punishment in classical and neoclassical thought
- Discuss the policy implications of the Classical School
- Assess the shortcomings of the classical approach

Hear the author discuss this chapter at **crimtoday.com**

Introduction

In 2004, Richard Schmidt, a 61-year-old former teacher from Baltimore, Maryland, was arrested by federal authorities when he returned to the United States from Cambodia and the Philippines.[5] Officials charged Schmidt under a new federal law aimed at eliminating the practice of child sex-tourism. According to an indictment filed in the case, Schmidt, who had previously served 13 years in a Maryland prison for the rape of a 13 year-old boy, molested eight boys while overseas. Today, Schmidt sits in a federal prison where he is serving a 15-year sentence for molesting Cambodian boys as young as ten.[6]

Sex-tourism, which involves traveling to foreign countries to engage in sexual relations for hire, is especially rampant in Third World countries, where young children may be forced into the sex trade by parents or by others anxious to reap the potentially lucrative financial rewards that are available. Child sex-tourism largely depends upon the relative wealth that Westerners seeking such services are able to bring to less developed parts of the world.

Although official enforcement activities in Third World countries are sometimes lacking, it has become commonplace for employees and members of charities and religious groups who are based overseas to watch for Americans, Europeans, and others seeking to have sex with children. These civilian monitors then hand over names, photographs, and needed evidence to authorities in the United States and the travelers' home countries.

The new American law, which resulted from pressure by child advocacy and religious groups to fight the sexual exploitation of children worldwide, is similar to one passed in Canada in 1997. Canada's sex-tourism law makes it possible to prosecute Canadians in Canada if they sexually abuse children while outside the country.[7] The Canadian law targets acts such as child prostitution, child sexual exploitation, indecent acts with children, child pornography, and incest that Canadians commit in other parts of the world.[8] Officials in both the United States and Canada are also targeting the owners of Web sites and travel services promoting sex tours, especially when the services offered involve providers under the age of 18.

These relatively new sex-tourism laws result from lawmakers' beliefs that the decision to travel to foreign countries in search of child sex partners is a highly rational one involving detailed planning, explicit itineraries, and collaboration on the part of travelers and information providers who let them know what services are available and where. In the face of stiff legal penalties, legislators concluded, travelers would avoid unlawful activity while overseas. Hoping to capitalize on such rationality, the U.S. State Department recently gave World Vision, an organization working to stamp out child sexual exploitation, a $500,000 grant to design pop-up advertisements on travel Web sites telling travelers of the consequences of the new law. The law is also being explained in brochures handed out at airports by child-welfare groups and on billboards paid for by advocacy organizations.

The belief that at least some illegal activity is the result of rational choices made by individuals seeking various kinds of illicit rewards forms the basis for the perspectives on crime causation that are discussed in this chapter.

Major Principles of the Classical School

This brief section summarizes the central features of the Classical School of criminological thought. Each of the points listed in this discussion can be found elsewhere in this chapter, where they are discussed in more detail. The present cursory overview is intended to provide more than a summation; it is meant to be a guide to the rest of this chapter.

Most classical theories of crime causation make the following basic assumptions:

- Human beings are fundamentally rational, and most human behavior is the result of free will coupled with rational choice.
- Pain and pleasure are the two central determinants of human behavior.

- Punishment, a necessary evil, is sometimes required to deter law violators and to serve as an example to others who would also violate the law.
- Root principles of right and wrong are inherent in the nature of things and cannot be denied.
- Society exists to provide benefits to individuals that they would not receive in isolation.
- When men and women band together for the protection offered by society, they forfeit some of the benefits that accrue from living in isolation.
- Certain key rights of individuals are inherent in the nature of things, and governments that contravene those rights should be disbanded.
- Crime disparages the quality of the bond that exists between individuals and society and is therefore an immoral form of behavior.

Forerunners of Classical Thought

The notion of crime as a violation of established law did not exist in most primitive societies. The lack of lawmaking bodies, the absence of formal written laws, and loose social bonds precluded the concept of crime as law violation. All human societies, however, from the simplest to the most advanced, evidence their own widely held notions of right and wrong. Sociologists call such fundamental concepts of morality and propriety "mores" and "folkways." *Mores, folkways,* and *law* are terms used by **William Graham Sumner** near the start of the twentieth century to describe the three basic forms of behavioral strictures imposed by social groups upon their members.[9] According to Sumner, mores and folkways govern behavior in relatively small primitive societies, whereas in large, complex societies, they are reinforced and formalized through written laws.

Mores consist of proscriptions covering potentially serious violations of a group's values. Murder, rape, and robbery, for example, would probably be repugnant to the mores of any social group. **Folkways,** on the other hand, are simply time-honored customs, and although they carry the force of tradition, their violation is less likely to threaten the survival of the social group. The fact that American men have traditionally worn little jewelry illustrates a folkway that has given way in recent years to various types of male adornment, including earrings, gold chains, and even makeup. Mores and folkways, although they may be powerful determinants of behavior, are nonetheless informal because only laws, from among Sumner's trinity, have been codified into formal strictures wielded by institutions and created specifically for enforcement purposes.

Another method of categorizing socially proscriptive rules is provided by some criminologists who divide crimes into the dual categories of *mala in se* and *mala prohibita.* Acts that are **mala in se** are said to be fundamentally wrong, regardless of the time or place in which they occur. Forcing someone to have sex against his or her will and the intentional killing of children are sometimes given as examples of behavior thought to be *mala in se.* Those who argue for the existence of *mala in se* offenses as a useful heuristic category usually point to some fundamental rule, such as religious teachings (the Ten Commandments, the Koran, and so on), to support their belief that some acts are inherently wrong. Such a perspective assumes that uncompromisable standards for human behavior rest within the very fabric of lived experience.

Mala prohibita offenses are those acts that are said to be wrong for the simple reason that they are prohibited. So-called victimless or social-order offenses like prostitution, gambling, drug use, and premarital sexual behavior provide examples of *mala prohibita* offenses. The status of such behaviors as *mala prohibita* is further supported by the fact that they are not necessarily crimes in every jurisdiction. Prostitution, for example, is legal in parts of Nevada, as is gambling. Gambling, mainly because of the huge revenue potential it holds, is rapidly being legalized in many areas, while it remains illegal in others.

mores

Behavioral proscriptions covering potentially serious violations of a group's values. Examples include strictures against murder, rape, and robbery.

folkways

Time-honored customs. Although folkways carry the force of tradition, their violation is unlikely to threaten the survival of the group.

mala in se

Acts that are thought to be wrong in and of themselves.

mala prohibita

Acts that are wrong only because they are prohibited.

Demons torment a man in this historical rendition. Crime and other social evils have always begged for explanation. What would today's criminologists think of the claim that "the devil made him do it"?

Source: Corbis/Bettmann

The Blue Devils ___!!

The Demonic Era

Since time began, humankind has been preoccupied with what appears to be an ongoing war between good and evil. Oftentimes evil has appeared in impersonal guise, as when the great bubonic plague, also known as the "black death," ravaged Europe and Asia in the fourteenth century, leaving as much as three-quarters of the population dead in a mere span of 20 years. At other times, evil has seemed to wear a human face, as when the Nazi Holocaust claimed millions of Jewish lives during World War II.

Whatever its manifestation, the very presence of evil in the world has begged for interpretation, and sage minds throughout human history have advanced many explanations for the evil conditions that individuals and social groups have at times been forced to endure. Some forms of evil, like the plague and the Holocaust, appear cosmically based, whereas others—including personal victimization, criminality, and singular instances of deviance—are the undeniable result of individual behavior. Cosmic-level evil has been explained by ideas as diverse as divine punishment, karma, fate, and the vengeful activities of offended gods. Early explanations of personal deviance ranged from demonic possession to spiritual influences to temptation by fallen angels—and even led to the positing of commerce between human beings and supernatural entities like demons, werewolves, vampires, and ghosts.

Archaeologists have unearthed skeletal remains that provide evidence that some early human societies believed outlandish behavior among individuals was a consequence of spirit possession. Carefully unearthed skulls, dated by various techniques to approximately 40,000 years ago, show signs of early cranial surgery, or **trephination,** apparently intended to release evil spirits thought to be residing within the heads of offenders. Such surgical interventions were undoubtedly crude and probably involved fermented anesthetics along with flint-cutting implements.

trephination

A form of surgery typically involving bone, especially the skull. Early instances of cranial trephination have been taken as evidence of primitive beliefs in spirit possession.

Early Sources of the Criminal Law

The Code of Hammurabi

Modern criminal law is the result of a long evolution of legal principles. The **Code of Hammurabi** is one of the first known bodies of law to survive and be available for study

Code of Hammurabi

An early set of laws established by the Babylonian king Hammurabi, who ruled the ancient city from 1792 to 1750 B.C.

today. King Hammurabi ruled the ancient city of Babylon from 1792 to 1750 B.C. and created a legal code consisting of a set of strictures engraved on stone tablets. The Hammurabi laws were originally intended to establish property and other rights and were crucial to the continued growth of Babylon as a significant commercial center. Hammurabi law spoke to issues of theft, property ownership, sexual relationships, and interpersonal violence. As well-known criminologist Marvin Wolfgang has observed, "In its day, 1700 B.C., the Hammurabi Code, with its emphasis on **retribution,** amounted to a brilliant advance in penal philosophy mainly because it represented an attempt to keep cruelty within bounds."[10] Prior to the code, captured offenders often faced the most barbarous of punishments, frequently at the hands of revenge-seeking victims, no matter how minor their transgressions had been. Learn more about the Code of Hammurabi at **Web Extra 4–1.**

Early Roman Law

Of considerable significance for our own legal tradition is early Roman law. Roman legions under Emperor Claudius I (10 B.C.–A.D. 54) conquered England in the middle of the first century, and Roman authority over Britannia was further consolidated by later Roman rulers who built walls and fortifications to keep out the still-hostile Scots. Roman customs, law, and language were forced upon the English population during the succeeding three centuries under the Pax Romana—a peace imposed by the military might of Rome.[11]

Early Roman law derived from the **Twelve Tables,** which were written around 450 B.C. The Tables were a collection of basic rules regulating family, religious, and economic life. They appear to have been based on common and fair practices generally accepted among early tribes, which existed prior to the establishment of the Roman Republic. Unfortunately, only fragments of the tables survive today.

The best-known legal period in Roman history occurred during the reign of Emperor Justinian I (A.D. 527–565). By the end of the sixth century, the Roman Empire had declined substantially in size and influence and was near the end of its life. In what may have been an effort to preserve Roman values and traditions, Justinian undertook the laborious process of distilling Roman laws into a set of writings. The Justinian Code, as these writings came to be known, actually consisted of three lengthy legal documents: (1) the Institutes, (2) the Digest, and (3) the Code itself. Justinian's code distinguished between two major legal categories: public and private laws. Public laws dealt with the organization of the Roman state, its Senate, and governmental offices. Private law concerned itself with contracts, personal possessions, the legal status of various types of people (citizens, free people, slaves, freedmen, guardians, husbands and wives, and so forth), and injuries to citizens. It contained elements of our modern civil and criminal law, and it influenced Western legal thought through the Middle Ages. Learn more about early Roman law at **Web Extra 4–2.**

Common Law

Common law forms the basis for much of our modern statutory and case law. It has often been called *the* major source of modern criminal law. **Common law** refers to a traditional body of unwritten legal precedents created through everyday practice in English society and supported by court decisions during the Middle Ages. Common law is so-called because it was based on shared traditions and standards rather than on those that varied from one locale to another. As novel situations arose and were handled by British justices, their declarations became the start for any similar future deliberation. These decisions generally incorporated the customs of society as it operated at the time.

Common law was given considerable legitimacy in the eleventh century upon the official declaration that it was the law of the land by Edward the Confessor, an English king who ruled from 1042 to 1066. The authority of common law was further reinforced by the decision of William the Conqueror to use popular customs as the basis for judicial action following his subjugation of Britain in A.D. 1066.

Eventually, court decisions were recorded and made available to barristers (English trial lawyers) and judges. As criminologist Howard Abadinsky wrote, "Common law

retribution

The act of taking revenge upon a criminal perpetrator.

WEB
Extra
▪ ▪ ▪ ▪

Twelve Tables

Early Roman laws written circa 450 B.C., which regulated family, religious, and economic life.

WEB
Extra
▪ ▪ ▪ ▪

common law

Law originating from usage and custom rather than from written statutes. The term refers to nonstatutory customs, traditions, and precedents that help guide judicial decision making.

involved the transformation of community rules into a national legal system. The controlling element [was] precedent."[12] Today, common law forms the basis of many of the laws on the books in English-speaking countries around the world. Learn more about common law at **Web Extra 4–3**.

The Magna Carta

The Magna Carta (literally, "great charter") is another important source of modern laws and legal procedure. The Magna Carta was signed on June 15, 1215, by King John of England at Runnymede, under pressure from British barons who took advantage of John's military defeats at the hands of Pope Innocent III and King Philip Augustus of France. The barons demanded a pledge from the king to respect their traditional rights, and they forced the king to agree to be bound by law.

At the time of its signing, the Magna Carta, although 63 chapters in length, was little more than a feudal document[13] listing specific royal concessions. Its original purpose was to ensure feudal rights and to guarantee that the king could not encroach on the privileges claimed by landowning barons. Additionally, the Magna Carta guaranteed the freedom of the church and ensured respect for the customs of towns. Its wording, however, was later interpreted during a judicial revolt in 1613 to support individual rights and jury trials. Sir Edward Coke, chief justice under James I, held that the Magna Carta guaranteed basic liberties for all British citizens and ruled that any acts of Parliament that contravened common law would be void. Some evidence suggests that this famous ruling became the basis for the rise of the U.S. Supreme Court, with its power to nullify laws enacted by Congress.[14] Similarly, one specific provision of the Magna Carta, designed originally to prohibit the king from prosecuting the barons without just cause, was expanded into the concept of due process of law, a fundamental cornerstone of modern legal procedure. Because of these later interpretations, the Magna Carta has been called "the foundation stone of our present liberties."[15]

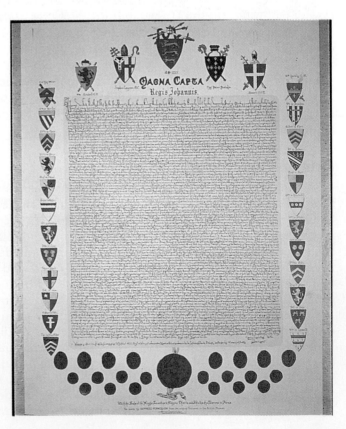

The Magna Carta, an important source of modern Western laws and legal procedure. What are some other important sources of modern criminal law?

Source: Corbis/Bettmann

The Enlightenment

The **Enlightenment,** also called the Age of Reason, was a highly significant social movement that occurred during the seventeenth and eighteenth centuries. The Enlightenment built upon ideas developed by thinkers like Francis Bacon (1561–1626), Thomas Hobbes (1588–1679), John Locke (1632–1704), René Descartes (1596–1650), Jean-Jacques Rousseau (1712–1778), and Baruch Spinoza (1632–1677). Because of their indirect contributions to classical criminological thought, it will be worthwhile to spend a few paragraphs discussing the writings of a few of these important historical figures. Learn more about the Enlightenment and the intellectual figures who gave it life at **Web Extra 4–4.**

Enlightenment

A social movement that arose during the eighteenth century and that built upon ideas like empiricism, rationality, free will, humanism, and natural law.

WEB
Extra

Thomas Hobbes (1588–1679)

English philosopher **Thomas Hobbes** developed what many writers regard as an extremely negative view of human nature and social life, which he described in his momentous work, *Leviathan* (1651). Hobbes described the natural state of men and women as one that is "nasty, brutish, and short." Fear of violent death, he said, forces human beings into a **social contract** with one another to create a state. The state, according to Hobbes, demands the surrender of certain natural rights and submission to the absolute authority of a sovereign, while offering protection and succor to its citizens in return. Although the social contract concept significantly influenced many of Hobbes's contemporaries, much of his writing was condemned for assuming an overly pessimistic view of both human nature and existing governments.

John Locke (1632–1704)

In 1690, English philosopher **John Locke** published his *Essay Concerning Human Understanding,* in which he put forth the idea that the natural human condition at birth is akin to that of a blank slate upon which interpersonal encounters and other experiences indelibly inscribe the traits of personality. In contrast to earlier thinkers, who assumed that people are born with certain innate propensities and even rudimentary intellectual concepts and ideas, Locke ascribed the bulk of adult human qualities to life experiences.

In the area of social and political thought, Locke further developed the Hobbesian notion of the social contract. Locke contended that human beings, through a social contract, abandon their natural state of individual freedom and lack of interpersonal responsibility to join together and form society. Although individuals surrender some freedoms to society, government—once formed—is obligated to assume responsibilities toward its citizens and to provide for their protection and welfare. According to Locke and other writers, governments should be required to guarantee certain inalienable rights to their citizens, including the right to life, health, liberty, and possessions. A product of his times, during which the dictatorial nature of monarchies and the Roman church were being much disparaged, Locke stressed the duties that governments have toward their citizens, while paying very little attention to the inverse—the responsibilities of individuals to the societies of which they are a part. As a natural consequence of such an emphasis, Locke argued that political revolutions, under some circumstances, might become an obligation incumbent upon citizens.

social contract

The Enlightenment-era concept that human beings abandon their natural state of individual freedom to join together and form society. In the process of forming a social contract, individuals surrender some freedoms to society as a whole, and government, once formed, is obligated to assume responsibilities toward its citizens and to provide for their protection and welfare.

Locke also developed the notion of checks and balances between divisions of government, a doctrine that was elaborated by French jurist and political philosopher **Charles-Louis de Secondat Montesquieu** (1689–1755). In *The Spirit of Laws* (1748), Montesquieu wove Locke's notions into the concept of a separation of powers between divisions of government. Both ideas later found a place in the U.S. Constitution.

Jean-Jacques Rousseau (1712–1778)

Swiss-French philosopher and political theorist **Jean-Jacques Rousseau** further advanced the notion of the social contract in his treatise of that name (*Social Contract,* 1762). According to Rousseau, human beings are basically good and fair in their natural state but historically were corrupted by the introduction of shared concepts and joint activities like property, agriculture, science, and commerce. As a result, the social contract emerged when civilized people agreed to establish governments and systems of education to correct the problems and the inequalities brought on by the rise of civilization.

natural law

The philosophical perspective that certain immutable laws are fundamental to human nature and can be readily ascertained through reason. Human-made laws, in contrast, are said to derive from human experience and history—both of which are subject to continual change.

Rousseau also contributed to the notion of **natural law,** a concept originally formulated by Saint Thomas Aquinas (1225–1274), Baruch Spinoza (1632–1677), and others to provide an intuitive basis for the defense of ethical principles and morality. Natural law was used by early Christian church leaders as a powerful argument in support of their interests. Submissive to the authority of the church, secular rulers were pressed to reinforce church doctrine in any laws they decreed. Thomas Aquinas, a well-known supporter of natural law, wrote in his *Summa Theologica* that any human-made law that contradicts natural law is corrupt in the eyes of God. Religious practice, which strongly reflected natural law conceptions, was central to the life of early British society. Hence, natural law, as it was understood at the time, was incorporated into English common law throughout the Middle Ages.

Rousseau agreed with earlier writers that certain immutable laws are fundamental to human nature and can be readily ascertained through reason. Human-made law, in contrast, he claimed, derives from human experience and history—both of which are subject to continual change. Hence, human-made law, also called "positive law," changes from time to time and from epoch to epoch. Rousseau expanded the concept of natural law to support emerging democratic principles, and he claimed that certain fundamental human and personal rights were inalienable because they were based on the natural order of things.

Natural Law and Natural Rights

natural rights

The rights that, according to natural law theorists, individuals retain in the face of government action and interests.

Thomas Paine (1737–1809), an English-American political theorist and the author of *The Rights of Man* (1791 and 1792), defended the French Revolution, arguing that only democratic institutions could guarantee the **natural rights** of individuals. At the Second Continental Congress, Thomas Jefferson (1743–1826) and other congressional representatives—many of whom were well versed in the writings of Locke and Rousseau— built the Constitution of the United States around an understanding of natural law as they perceived it. Hence, when Jefferson wrote of inalienable rights to "life, liberty, property," he was following in the footsteps of his intellectual forebears and meant that such rights were the natural due of all men and women because they were inherent in the social contract between citizens and their government.

Natural law and natural rights have a long intellectual history and are with us today in a number of guises. In a *National Review* article subtitled "If Natural Law Does Not Permit Us to Distinguish between Men and Hogs, What Does?" Harry V. Jaffa, director of the Claremont Institute's Center for the Study of the Natural Law, called an 1854 speech given by Abraham Lincoln "the most moving and compelling exhibition of natural-law reasoning in all political history."[16] In that speech, Lincoln argued in favor of freedom for slaves by succinctly pointing out that there is no difference between people, whatever their color. In Lincoln's words, "Equal justice to the South, it is said, requires us to consent to the extending of slavery to new countries. That is to say, inasmuch as you do not object to my taking my hog to Nebraska, therefore I must not object to your taking your slave. Now, I admit this is perfectly logical, if there is no difference between hogs and Negroes." Lincoln's point, of course, was that there is a huge difference between human beings and animals by virtue of their nature and that such a difference cannot be denied by logic.

Other commentators have cited the "crimes against humanity" committed by Nazis during World War II as indicative of natural law principles. The chilling testimony of Rudolf Hess,[17] Hitler's deputy, during the 1945 war crimes trial in Nuremberg, Germany, as he recalled the "Fuehrer's" order to exterminate millions of Jews indicates the extent of the planned "final solution." Hess testified, "In the summer of 1941, I was summoned to Berlin to Reichsfuehrer SS Himmler to receive personal orders. He told me something to the effect—I do not remember the exact words—that the Fuehrer had given the order for a final solution of the Jewish question. We, the SS, must carry out that order. If it is not carried out now then the Jews will later on destroy the German people. He had chosen Auschwitz on account of its easy access by rail and also because the extensive site offered space for measures ensuring isolation."[18] Who could argue against the premise, natural law supporters ask, that Hitler's final solution to the Jewish "question" was inherently wrong?

Although the concept of natural law has waned somewhat in influence over the past half century, many people today still hold that the basis for various existing criminal laws can be found in immutable moral principles or in some other identifiable aspect of the natural order. The Ten Commandments, "inborn tendencies," the idea of sin, and perceptions of various forms of order in the universe and in the social world have all provided a basis for the assertion that natural law exists. Modern-day advocates of natural law still claim that it comes from outside the social group and that it is knowable through some form of revelation, intuition, or prophecy.

The present debate over abortion is an example of the modern-day use of natural law arguments to support both sides in the dispute. Antiabortion forces, frequently called "pro-lifers" or "right-to-lifers," claim that an unborn fetus is a person and that he or she is entitled to all the protection that we would give to any other living human being. Such protection, they suggest, is basic and humane and lies in the natural relationship of one human being to another and within the relationship of a society to its children. Antiabortion advocates are striving for passage of a law, or for a reinterpretation of past Supreme Court precedent, that would support their position. Advocates of the present law (which allows abortion upon request under certain conditions) maintain that abortion is a right of any pregnant woman because she is the only one who should be in control of her body. Such "pro-choice" groups also claim that the legal system must address the abortion question but only by way of offering protection to this natural right of women.

Perhaps the best-known modern instance of a natural law debate occurred during confirmation hearings for U.S. Supreme Court Justice Clarence Thomas. Thomas, who was confirmed in 1991, once wrote an opinion in which he argued from a natural law point of view. That opinion was later challenged by Senate Judiciary Committee members who felt that it reflected an unbending judicial attitude. Learn more about natural law at **Web Extra 4–5**.

WEB
Extra
■ ■ ■ ■

Thomas Paine (1737–1809), an important contributor to the concept of natural law. What are the central tenets of natural law?

Source: Corbis/Bettmann

The Classical School

As many authors have pointed out, the Enlightenment fueled the fires of social change, leading eventually to the French and American Revolutions and providing many of the intellectual underpinnings of the U.S. Constitution. The Enlightenment—one of the most powerful intellectual initiatives of the last millennium—also inspired other social movements and freed innovative thinkers from the chains of convention. As a direct consequence of Enlightenment thinking, superstitious beliefs were discarded, and men and women began to be perceived, for the first time, as self-determining entities possessing a fundamental freedom of choice. Following the Enlightenment, many supernatural explanations for human behavior fell by the wayside, and free will and rational thought came to be recognized as the linchpins of all significant human activity. In effect, the Enlightenment inspired the reexamination of existing doctrines of human behavior from the point of view of rationalism.

Within criminology, the Enlightenment led to the development of the **Classical School** of criminological thought. Crime and deviance, which had previously been explained by reference to mythological influences and spiritual shortcomings, took their place in Enlightenment thought alongside other forms of human activity as products of the exercise of free will. Once people were seen as having control over their own lives, crime came to be explained as a particularly individualized form of evil—that is, as moral wrongdoing fed by personal choice.

Classical School

A criminological perspective of the late 1700s and early 1800s that had its roots in the Enlightenment and that held that humans are rational beings, that crime is the result of the exercise of free will, and that punishment can be effective in reducing the incidence of crime, as it negates the pleasure to be derived from crime commission.

Cesare Beccaria (1738–1794)

Cesare Beccaria (his Italian name was Cesare Bonesana, but he held the title Marchese di Beccaria) was born in Milan, Italy. The eldest of four children, he was trained at Catholic schools and had earned a doctor of laws degree by the time he was 20.

In 1764, Beccaria published his *Essay on Crimes and Punishments.* Although the work appeared originally in Italian, it was translated into English in London in 1767. Beccaria's *Essay* consisted of 42 short chapters covering only a few major themes. Beccaria's purpose in penning the book was not to set forth a theory of crime but to communicate his observations on the laws and justice system of his time. In the *Essay,* Beccaria distilled the notion of the social contract into the idea that "laws are the conditions under which independent and isolated men united to form a society."[19] More than anything else, however, his writings consisted of a philosophy of punishment. Beccaria claimed, for example, that although most criminals are punished based on an assessment of their criminal intent, they should be punished instead based on the degree of injury they cause. The purpose of punishment, he said, should be deterrence rather than retribution, and punishment should be imposed to prevent offenders from committing additional crimes. Beccaria saw punishment as a tool to an end, not an end in itself, and crime prevention was more important to him than revenge.

To help prevent crimes, Beccaria argued, adjudication and punishment should both be swift, and once punishment is decreed, it should be certain. In his words, "The more promptly and the more closely punishment follows upon the commission of a crime, the more just and useful it will be." Punishment that is imposed immediately following crime commission, claimed Beccaria, is connected with the wrongfulness of the offense, both in the mind of the offender and in the minds of others who might see the punishment imposed and thereby learn of the consequences of involvement in criminal activity.

Beccaria concluded that punishment should be only severe enough to outweigh the personal benefits to be derived from crime commission. Any additional punishment, he argued, would be superfluous. Beccaria's concluding words on punishment are telling. "In order," he said, "for punishment not to be, in every instance, an act of violence of one or of many against a private citizen, it must be essentially public, prompt, necessary, the least possible in the given circumstances, proportionate to the crimes, [and] dictated by the laws."

Beccaria distinguished among three types of crimes: those that threaten the security of the state, those that injure citizens or their property, and those that run contrary to the social order. Punishment should fit the crime, Beccaria wrote, declaring that theft should be punished through fines, personal injury through corporal punishment, and serious crimes against the state (such as inciting revolution) via application of the death penalty. Beccaria was opposed to the death penalty in most other circumstances, seeing it as a kind of warfare waged by society against its citizens.

Beccaria condemned the torture of suspects, a practice still used in the eighteenth century, saying that it was a device that ensured that weak suspects would incriminate themselves, while strong ones would be found innocent. Torture, he argued, was also unjust because it punished individuals before they had been found guilty in a court of law. In Beccaria's words, "No man can be called guilty before a judge has sentenced him, nor can society deprive him of public protection before it has been decided that he has in fact violated the conditions under which such protection was accorded him. What right is it then, if not simply that of might, which empowers a judge to inflict punishment on a citizen while doubt still remains as to his guilt or innocence?"

Beccaria's *Essay* also touched upon a variety of other topics. He distinguished, for example, between two types of proof: "perfect proof," where there was no possibility of innocence, and "imperfect proof," where some possibility of innocence remained. Beccaria also believed in the efficacy of a jury of one's peers but recommended that half of any jury panel should consist of peers of the victim, whereas the other half should be made up of peers of the accused. Finally, Beccaria wrote that oaths were useless in a court of law because accused individuals will naturally deny their guilt even if they know themselves to be fully culpable.

Beccaria's ideas were widely recognized as progressive by his contemporaries. His principles were incorporated into the French penal code of 1791 and significantly influenced the justice-related activities of European leaders like Catherine the Great of Russia, Frederick the Great of Prussia, and Emperor Joseph II of Austria. Evidence suggests that Beccaria's *Essay* influenced framers of the U.S. Constitution, and some scholars claim that the first 10 amendments to the Constitution, known as the Bill of Rights, might not have existed were it not for Beccaria's emphasis on the rights of individuals in the face of state power. Perhaps more than anyone else, Beccaria is responsible for the contemporary belief that criminals have control over their behavior, that they choose to commit crimes, and that they can be deterred by the threat of punishment. Learn more about Cesare Beccaria at **Web Extra 4–6**.

WEB
Fxtra
■ ■ ■ ■

Jeremy Bentham (1748–1832)

Jeremy Bentham, another founding personality of the Classical School, wrote in his *Introduction to the Principles of Morals and Legislation* (1789) that "nature has placed mankind under the governance of two sovereign masters, pain and pleasure."[20] To reduce crime or, as Bentham put it, "to prevent the happening of mischief," the pain of crime commission must outweigh the pleasure to be derived from criminal activity. Bentham's claim rested upon his belief, spawned by Enlightenment thought, that human beings are fundamentally rational and that criminals will weigh in their minds the pain of punishment against any pleasures thought likely to be derived from crime commission.

Bentham advocated neither extreme nor cruel punishment—only punishment sufficiently distasteful to the offender that the discomfort experienced would outweigh the pleasure to be derived from criminal activity. Generally, Bentham argued, the more serious the offense is the more reward it holds for its perpetrator and therefore the more weighty the official response must be. "Pain and pleasure," said Bentham, "are the instruments the legislator has to work with" in controlling antisocial and criminal behavior.

Bentham's approach has been termed **hedonistic calculus** or **utilitarianism** because of its emphasis on the worth any action holds for an individual undertaking it. As Bentham stated, "By the principle of utility is meant that principle which approves or

hedonistic calculus

The belief, first proposed by Jeremy Bentham, that behavior holds value to any individual undertaking it according to the amount of pleasure or pain that it can be expected to produce for that person.

utilitarianism

Another term for Jeremy Bentham's concept of hedonistic calculus.

Jeremy Bentham (1748–1832), whose work is closely associated with the Classical School of criminology. What are the key features of the Classical School?
Source: Corbis/Bettmann

disapproves of every action whatsoever, according to the tendency which it appears to have to augment or diminish the happiness of the party whose interest is in question; or, what is the same thing . . . to promote or to oppose that happiness." In other words, Bentham believed that individuals could be expected to weigh, at least intuitively, the consequences of their behavior before acting so as to maximize their own pleasure and minimize pain. The value of any pleasure, or the inhibitory tendency of any pain, according to Bentham, could be calculated by its intensity, duration, certainty, and immediacy (or remoteness in time).

Bentham claimed that nothing was really new in his pleasure-pain perspective. "Nor is this a novel and unwarranted, any more than it is a useless theory," he wrote. "In all this there is nothing but what the practice of mankind, wheresoever they have a clear view of their own interest, is perfectly comfortable to. An article of property, an estate in land, for instance, is valuable, on what account? On account of the pleasures of all kinds which it enables a man to produce, and what comes to the same thing the pains of all kinds which it enables him to avert." Bentham's ideas were not new, but their application to criminology was. In 1739, David Hume distilled the notion of utilitarianism into a philosophical perspective in his book *A Treatise of Human Nature*. Although Hume's central concern was not to explain crime, scholars who followed Hume observed that human behavior is typically motivated more by self-interest than by anything else.

Like Beccaria, Bentham focused on the potential held by punishment to prevent crime and to act as a deterrent for those considering criminal activity. In any criminal legislation, he wrote, "the evils of punishment must . . . be made to exceed the advantage of the offence." Bentham distinguished among 11 different types of punishment:

- **Capital punishment,** or death
- **Afflictive punishment,** which includes whipping and starvation

Crime in the News

Man Arrested 226 Times

LINCOLN, Nebraska (AP)—Kevin Holder's rap sheet is 43 pages long, dating back to 1980, and he just got another entry—his 226th arrest.

Police say they caught him Sunday morning after a brief chase and found burglar tools in his possession.

"He's very well-known to Lincoln police officers," Police Chief Tom Casady said.

Holder's convictions include criminal mischief, marijuana possession, violation of a protection order, assault, resisting arrest, assault on an officer, possession of cocaine. Many were misdemeanors, but he also has been sentenced to at least three prison terms for felonies, including a four-year stretch starting in 1996.

"Your average Nebraskan thinks after a prisoner has committed a certain number of crimes (he or she) will be put away for a long period of time. That doesn't happen," Casady said.

Lancaster County Attorney Gary Lacey said Holder was charged Tuesday with felony possession of burglar tools, and prosecutors will urge a judge to treat Holder as a habitual criminal. With another felony conviction, that could result in a sentence of up to 60 years. Holder remained behind bars Tuesday afternoon.

Holder's list of arrests doesn't come close to setting a record for Lincoln-Lancaster County. He's only No. 40, police spokeswoman Katherine Finnell said Tuesday.

A number of people have more than 500 arrests in Lincoln, a city of 226,000 people. The record is held by Edward Rooks, who died in 2004, with 652 arrests.

Discussion Questions

1. How does arrest differ from conviction? How is it that a person who has been arrested 226 times can still be free? How often was Holder convicted of a crime?

2. Should people like Holder be subject to habitual offender statutes that would require lengthy imprisonment following a set number of convictions? If so, how might such a law work?

3. This chapter says that punishment that is swift and certain can deter crime. Why hasn't punishment worked in Holder's case?

A police department mugshot of Kevin Holder—one of many that authorities have taken over the past 27 years. Holder made headlines nationwide in 2006, when he was arrested for the 226th time. Why hasn't the threat of criminal punishment deterred Holder?
Source: Courtesy Lincoln Police Department

Source: "Man Arrested for 226th Time: Nebraska Record Safe," Associated Press, August 15, 2006. Used with permission of The Associated Press Copyright © 2007. All rights reserved.

For the latest crime and justice news, visit www.crimenews.info.

- **Indelible punishment,** such as branding, amputation, and mutilation
- **Ignominious punishment,** such as public punishment involving use of the stocks or pillory
- **Penitential punishment,** whereby an offender might be censured by his or her community
- **Chronic punishment,** such as banishment, exile, and imprisonment
- **Restrictive punishment,** such as license revocation or administrative sanction
- **Compulsive punishment,** which requires an offender to perform a certain action, such as to make restitution or to keep in touch with a probation officer
- **Pecuniary punishment,** involving the use of fines

- **Quasi-pecuniary punishment,** in that the offender is denied services that would otherwise be available to him or her
- **Characteristic punishment,** such as mandating that prison uniforms be worn by incarcerated offenders

Utilitarianism is a practical philosophy, and Bentham was quite practical in his suggestions about crime prevention. Every citizen, he said, should have their first and last names tattooed on their wrists for the purpose of facilitating police identification. He also recommended the creation of a centralized police force focused on crime prevention and control—a recommendation that found life in the English Metropolitan Police Act of 1829, which established London's New Police under the direction of Sir Robert Peel.

Bentham's other major contribution to criminology was his suggestion that prisons be designed along the lines of what he called a "Panopticon House." The **Panopticon,** as Bentham envisioned it, was to be a circular building with cells along the circumference, each clearly visible from a central location staffed by guards. Bentham recommended that Panopticons be constructed near or within cities so that they might serve as examples to others of what would happen to them should they commit crimes. He also wrote that prisons should be managed by contractors who could profit from the labor of prisoners and that each contractor should "be bound to insure the lives and safe custody of those entrusted to him." Although a Panopticon was never built in Bentham's England, French officials funded a modified version of such a prison, which was eventually built at Lyons, and three prisons modeled after the Panopticon concept were constructed in the United States.

Bentham's critics have been quick to point out that punishments often seem not to work. Even punishments as severe as death appear not to have any effect on the incidence of crimes like murder (a point we will discuss in greater detail later in this chapter). Such critics forget Bentham's second tenet, however, which is that for punishment to be effective, "it must be swift and certain." For any punishment to have teeth, Bentham said, it not only must mandate a certain degree of displeasure but

Panopticon

A prison designed by Jeremy Bentham that was to be a circular building with cells along the circumference, each clearly visible from a central location staffed by guards.

An architect's rendering of Jeremy Bentham's Panopticon design for a prison. What did Bentham mean when he said that for punishment to be effective "it must be swift and certain"?

Source: University College London (Bentham papers 119a/119)

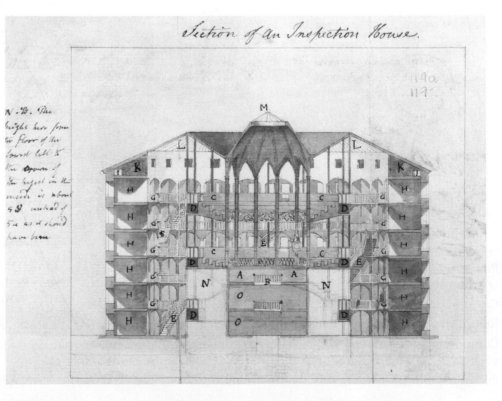

also must follow almost immediately upon its being decided, and there must be no way of avoiding it. Learn more about Jeremy Bentham from the Bentham Project via Web Extra 4–7.

WEB Extra

Heritage of the Classical School

The Classical School was to influence criminological thinking for a long time to come. From the French Revolution and the U.S. Constitution to today's emphasis on deterrence and crime prevention, the Classical School has molded the way in which thinkers on the subject of crime have viewed the topic for more than 200 years. The heritage left by the Classical School is still operative today in the following five principles, each of which is a fundamental constituent of modern-day perspectives on crime and human behavior:

- **Rationality.** Human beings have free will, and the actions they undertake are the result of choice.
- **Hedonism.** Pleasure and pain, or reward and punishment, are the major determinants of choice.
- **Punishment.** Criminal punishment is a deterrent to unlawful behavior, and deterrence is the best justification for punishment.
- **Human rights.** Society is made possible by individuals cooperating together. Hence, society owes to its citizens respect for their rights in the face of government action and for their autonomy insofar as such autonomy can be secured without endangering others or menacing the greater good.
- **Due process.** An accused should be presumed innocent until proved otherwise, and an accused should not be subject to punishment before guilt is lawfully established.

Neoclassical Criminology

By the end of the 1800s, classical criminology, with its emphasis on free will and individual choice as the root causes of crime, had given way to another approach known as "positivism." **Positivism,** which made use of the scientific method in studying criminality, is discussed in much greater detail in Chapter 5. For the purposes of this chapter, however, it is important to realize that positivism, in its original formulation, was based upon an acceptance of **hard determinism,** or the belief that crime results from forces that are beyond the control of the individual. Hence, as we shall see later in this book, the original positivists completely rejected the notion of free will and turned their attention instead to the impact of socialization, genetics, economic conditions, peer group influences, and other factors that might determine criminality. Acceptance of the notion of determinism implied that offenders were not entirely (if at all) responsible for their crimes and suggested that crime could be prevented by changing the conditions that produced criminality (see Figure 4–1).

While positivism remains an important component of contemporary criminology, many of its assumptions were undermined in the 1970s by studies that seemed to show that offenders could not be rehabilitated no matter what was tried, by a growing and widespread public fear of crime that led to "get tough on crime" policies, and by a cultural reaffirmation of belief in the rational nature of human beings. The resulting resurgence of classical ideals, referred to as **neoclassical criminology,** focused on the importance of character (a kind of middle ground between total free will and hard determinism), the dynamics of character development, and the rational choices that people make as they are faced with opportunities for crime. The neoclassical movement appears to have had its start with a number of publications produced in the

positivism

The application of scientific techniques to the study of crime and criminals.

hard determinism

The belief that crime results from forces that are beyond the control of the individual.

neoclassical criminology

A contemporary version of classical criminology that emphasizes deterrence and retribution, with reduced emphasis on rehabilitation.

FIGURE 4–1

Classical Criminology versus Positivism— The Role of Free Will

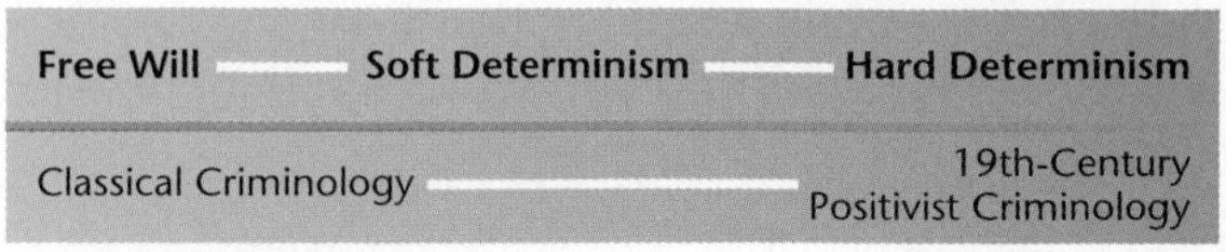

| Free Will ———— Soft Determinism ———— Hard Determinism | | |
| Classical Criminology ———————— | | 19th-Century Positivist Criminology |

nothing-works doctrine

The belief popularized by Robert Martinson in the 1970s that correctional treatment programs have little success in rehabilitating offenders.

three-strikes legislation

Criminal statutes that mandate life imprisonment for criminals convicted of three violent felonies or serious drug offenses.

1970s. One of these was Robert Martinson's national survey of rehabilitation programs.[21] Martinson found that when it came to the rehabilitation of offenders, nothing seems to work, as most resume their criminal careers after release from prison. The phrase "Nothing works!" became a rallying cry of conservative policymakers everywhere, and the **nothing-works doctrine** received much public attention. Many conservative politicians and some criminologists began calling existing notions of crime prevention and rehabilitation into question amidst claims that enhanced job skills, increased opportunities for employment, and lessened punishment did nothing to stem what was then a rising tide of crime. In 1975, Harvard political scientist James Q. Wilson wrote *Thinking about Crime,* in which he suggested that crime is not a result of poverty or social conditions and cannot be affected by social programs.[22] Wilson

Theory Versus Reality

Three-Strikes Laws

Throughout the 1990s, many states joined the "get tough on crime" bandwagon and adopted the justice model in their approach to crime control legislation. In the spring of 1994, for example, California legislators passed the state's now-famous "three strikes and you're out" law. Amid much fanfare, then-Governor Pete Wilson signed the **three-strikes** measure into law, calling it "the toughest and most sweeping crime bill in California history." California's law, which is retroactive (in that it counts offenses committed before the date the legislation was signed), requires a 25-year-to-life sentence for three-time felons with convictions for two or more serious or violent prior offenses. Criminal offenders facing a "second strike" can receive up to double the normal sentence for their most recent offense. Under the law, parole consideration is not available until at least 80% of an offender's sentence has been served.

In 2003, in two separate cases, the U.S. Supreme Court upheld the three-strikes California convictions of Gary Ewing and Leandro Andrade.[i] Ewing, who had four prior felony convictions, had received a 25-year-to-life sentence in a California courtroom following his conviction for felony grand theft of three golf clubs. Andrade, who also had a long record, had been sentenced to 50 years in prison for two petty-theft convictions.[ii] In writing for the Court in the *Ewing* case, Justice Sandra Day O'Connor noted that states should be able to decide when repeat offenders "must be isolated from society . . . to protect the public safety," even when nonserious crimes trigger the lengthy sentence. In deciding these two cases, both of which were based on Eighth Amendment claims, the Court found that it is *not* cruel and unusual punishment to impose a possible life term for a nonviolent felony when the defendant has a history of serious or violent convictions.

In 2004, Californians voted down Proposition 66, a ballot initiative that would have changed the state's three-strikes law so that only specified serious or violent crimes could be counted as third strikes. Passage of the proposition would also have meant that only previous convictions for violent or serious felonies, brought and tried separately, would have qualified for second- and third-strike sentence increases.

California's three-strikes law remains firmly in place today. In its current form, it punishes anyone who commits a third felony, regardless of its severity, with a mandatory sentence of 25 years to life if the first two felonies were violent or serious. Learn more about crime control policy at the Center for Law and Social Policy via **Web Extra 4–8**.

WEB Extra ■ ■ ■ ■

Discussion Questions

1. Some people suggest that three-strikes sentences should be imposed only on offenders who commit violent crimes, such as murder, rape, armed robbery, and certain types of arson. What do you think?

2. How is three strikes legislation in keeping with the spirit of the justice model described in this chapter?

[i] *Ewing* v. *California,* 583 U.S. 11 (2003); *Lockyer* v. *Andrade,* 583 U.S. 63 (2003).

[ii] Under California law, a person who commits petty theft can be charged with a felony if he or she has prior felony convictions. The charge is known as "petty theft with prior convictions." Andrade's actual sentence was two 25-year prison terms to be served consecutively.

argued, instead, for the lengthy incarceration of offenders and for the elimination of criminal opportunity. Also in 1975, David Fogel, who was then director of the Illinois Law Enforcement Commission, published a book called *We Are the Living Proof: The Justice Model of Corrections.*[23] Fogel's **justice model,** predicated on the growing belief that prisons do not rehabilitate or cure and that criminal offenders *deserve* punishment because of the choices they make, was proposed to the Illinois state legislature as a model for prison reform. Fogel argued that for the criminal justice process to work, offenders must be treated "as responsible as well as accountable, that is, volitional."[24]

justice model

A contemporary model of imprisonment in which the principle of just deserts forms the underlying social philosophy.

Rational Choice Theory

Rational choice theory, a product of the late 1970s and early 1980s, mirrors many of the principles found in classical criminology. The theory rests upon the belief that criminals make a conscious, rational, and at least partially informed choice to commit crime. It employs cost-benefit analysis, akin to similar theories in the field of economics, which view human behavior as the result of personal choice made after weighing both the costs and the benefits of available alternatives. Rational choice theory is noteworthy for its emphasis on the rational and adaptive aspects of criminal offending. It "predicts that individuals choose to commit crime when the benefits outweigh the costs of disobeying the law. Crime will decrease," according to such theories, "when opportunities are limited, benefits are reduced, and costs are increased."[25]

rational choice theory

A perspective that holds that criminality is the result of conscious choice and that predicts that individuals choose to commit crime when the benefits outweigh the costs of disobeying the law.

Two varieties of rational choice theory can be identified. One, which builds on an emerging emphasis on victimization, is called **routine activities theory (RAT).** A second, which is largely an extension of the rational choice perspective, is called **situational choice theory.**

Routine activities theory (also termed **lifestyle theory**) was proposed by **Lawrence Cohen** and **Marcus Felson** in 1979.[26] Cohen and Felson suggested that lifestyles contribute significantly to both the volume and the type of crime found in any society. The two believed that changes in the nature of American society during the 1960s and 1970s—specifically, increased personal affluence and greater involvement in social activities outside the home—brought about increased rates of household theft and personal victimization by strangers. Central to the routine activities approach is the claim that crime is likely to occur when a motivated offender and a suitable target come together in the absence of a capable guardian. A **capable guardian,** simply put, is one who effectively discourages crime. Hence, a person who has taken crime prevention steps is less likely to be victimized. As Cohen and Felson observe, "The risk of criminal victimization varies dramatically among the circumstances and locations in which people place themselves and their property."[27] For example, a person who routinely uses an automated teller machine late at night in an isolated location is far more likely to be preyed upon by robbers than is someone who stays home after dark. Lifestyles that contribute to criminal opportunities are likely to result in crime because they increase the risk of potential victimization.[28] Although noncriminal lifestyles at a given point in one's lifetime are partly the result of unavoidable social roles and assigned social positions, those who participate in a given lifestyle generally make rational decisions about specific behaviors (such as going to a given automated teller machine at a certain time). The same is true of criminal lifestyles. Hence, the meshing of choices made by both victims and criminals contributes significantly to both the frequency and the type of criminal activity observed in society. Learn more about the routine activities approach, including its implicatons for crime control via **Library Extra 4–1** at crimtoday.com.

routine activities theory

A brand of rational choice theory that suggests that lifestyles contribute significantly to both the volume and the type of crime found in any society.

situational choice theory

A brand of rational choice theory that views criminal behavior "as a function of choices and decisions made within a context of situational constraints and opportunities."

lifestyle theory

Another term for the routine activities approach of Lawrence Cohen and Marcus Felson.

capable guardian

One who effectively discourages crime.

LIBRARY
Extra

In a later work, Felson suggested that a number of "situational insights" might combine to elicit a criminal response from individual actors enmeshed in a highly varied social world. Felson pointed out that "individuals vary greatly in their behavior from

---

TABLE 4–1   Twenty-Five Techniques of Situational Crime Control, with Examples

Increase the Effort	Increase the Risks	Reduce the Rewards	Reduce Provocations	Remove the Excuses
1. Harden targets • steering column locks and immoblizers • Anti-robbery screens • Tamper-proof packaging	*6. Extend guardianship* • take routine precautions: • go out in group at night, • leave signs of occupancy, carry phone • "cocoon" neighborhood watch	*11. Conceal targets* • off-street parking • gender-neutral phone directories • unmarked bullion trucks	*16. Reduce frustration and stress* • efficient queues and polite service • expanded seating • soothing music/muted lights	*21. Set rules* • rental agreements • harassment codes • hotel registration
2. Control access to facilities • entry phones • electronic card access • baggage screening	*7. Assist natural surveillance* • improved street lighting • defensible space design • support whistleblowers	*12. Remove targets* • removable car radios • women's refuges • pre-paid public phone cards	*17. Avoid disputes* • separate enclosures for rival fans • reduce crowding in pubs • fixed cab fares	*22. Post instructions* • "No parking" • "Private property " • "extinguish camp fires"
3. Screen exits • tickets needed for exit • export documents • electronic merchandise tags	*8. Reduce anonymity* • taxi driver ID's • 'how's my driving?' decals • school uniforms	*13. Identify property* • property marking • vehicle licensing and parts marking • cattle branding	*18. Reduce emotional arousal* • controls on violent pornography • enforce good behavior on sports field • Prohibit racial slurs	*23. Alert conscience* • roadside speed display signs • signatures for customs declarations • "shoplifting is stealing"
4. Deflect offenders • street closures • separate bothrooms for women • disperse pubs	*9. Utilise place managers* • CCTV for double-deck buses • two clerks for convenience stores • reward vigilance	*14. Disrupt markets* • monitor pawn shops • controls on classified ads. • license street vendors	*19. Neutralize peer pressure* • 'idiots drink and drive' • 'it's OK to say NO' • disperse troublemakers at school	*24. Assist compliance* • easy library checkout • public lavatories • litter bins
5. Control tools/weapons • "smart" guns • disabling stolen cell phones • Restrict spray paint sales to juveniles	*10. Strengthen formal surveillance* • red light cameras • burglar alarms • security guards	*15. Deny benefits* • ink merchandise tags • graffiti cleaning • speed humps	*20. Discourage imitation* • rapid repair of vandalism • v-chips in TVs • censor details of modus operandi	*25. Control drugs/alcohol* • breathalysers in pubs • server intervention • alcohol-free events

Source: Center for Problem Oriented Policing. Web available at http://www.popcenter.org/25techniques.htm.

---

one situation to another" and said that criminality might flow from temptation, bad company, idleness, or provocation.[29] Convenience stores, for example, create temptations toward theft when they display their merchandise within easy reach of customers. Other authors have defined the term *situation* to mean "the perceptive field of the individual at a given point in time" and have suggested that it can be described "in terms of who is there, what is going on, and where it is taking place."[30]

soft determinism

The belief that human behavior is the result of choices and decisions made within a context of situational constraints and opportunities.

Situational choice theory provides an example of **soft determinism**. It views criminal behavior "as a function of choices and decisions made within a context of situational constraints and opportunities."[31] The theory holds that "crime is not simply a matter of motivation; it is also a matter of opportunity."[32] Situational choice theory suggests that the probability of criminal activity can be reduced by changing the features of the environment. **Ronald V. Clarke** and **Derek B. Cornish,** collaborators in the development of the situational choice perspective, analyze the choice-structuring properties of a potentially criminal situation. They define *choice-structuring properties* as "the constellation of opportunities, costs, and benefits attaching to particular kinds of crime."[33] Clarke and Cornish suggest the use of situational strategies like "cheque guarantee cards, the control of alcohol sales at football matches, supervision of children's play on public housing estates, vandal resistant materials and designs, 'defensible space' architecture, improved lighting, closed-circuit television surveillance,"[34] and the like as effective crime prevention additions to specific situations—all of which might lower the likelihood of criminal victimization in given instances.

In brief, rational choice theorists concentrate on "the decision-making process of offenders confronted with specific contexts" and have shifted "the focus of the effort to prevent crime . . . from broad social programs to target hardening, environmental design or any impediment that would [dissuade] a motivated offender from offending."[35] Twenty-five techniques of situational crime control can be identified, and each can be classified according to the five objectives of situational prevention. The five objectives are to (1) increase the effort involved in crime, (2) increase the risks associated with crime commission, (3) reduce the rewards of crime, (4) reduce the provocatons that lead to criminal activity, and (5) remove the excuses that facilitate crime commission. Table 4–1 outlines the 25 techniques and provides examples of each.[36]

Although rational choice theory is similar to classical deterrence theory, earlier approaches focused largely on the balance between pleasure and pain as the primary determinant or preventative of criminal behavior. Rational choice theory tends to place less emphasis on pleasure and emotionality and more on rationality and cognition. Some rational choice theorists distinguish among the types of choices offenders make as they move toward criminal involvement. One type of choice, known as "involvement decisions," has been described as "multistage" and is said to "include the initial decision to engage in criminal activity as well as subsequent decisions to continue one's involvement or to desist."[37] Another type of choice, event decisions, *relates* to particular instances of criminal opportunity, such as the decision to rob a particular person or to let him or her pass. Event decisions—in contrast to involvement decisions, which may take months or even years to reach—are usually made quickly. Learn more about rational choice theories via **Web Extra 4–9.** You can read about the use of environmental design techniques to reduce crime at **Library Extra 4–2.** Learn more about crime prevention in general via **Library Extra 4–3** at crimtoday.com.

WEB
Extra
■ ■ ■ ■

LIBRARY
Extra
■ ■ ■ ■

Steve Coogan in the movie, *The Parole Officer.* Rational choice theory says that offenders make a conscious, rational choice to commit crimes. Might some crimes also be irrational?

Source: Stephen Morley/DNA Films– Picture Desk, Inc./Kobal Collection

The Seductions of Crime

One criminologist who focuses on the relationship between the decision to commit crime and the rewards that such a decision brings is **Jack Katz.** In the book *Seductions of Crime,* Katz explains crime as the result of the "often wonderful attractions within the lived experience of criminality."[38] Crime, Katz says, is often pleasurable for those committing it, and pleasure of one sort or another is the major motivation behind crime. Sometimes, however, the kind of pleasure to be derived from crime is not immediately obvious. Moreover, as Katz points out in the following paragraph, criminologists have often depicted crime as something to be avoided and have failed to understand just how good crime *feels* to those who commit it:[39]

> The social science literature contains only scattered evidence of what it means, feels, sounds, tastes, or looks like to commit a particular crime. Readers of research on homicide and assault do not hear the slaps and curses, see the pushes and shoves, or feel the humiliation and rage that may build toward the attack, sometimes persisting after the victim's death. . . . How adolescents manage to make the shoplifting or vandalism of cheap and commonplace things a thrilling experience has not been intriguing to many students of delinquency. . . . The description of "cold-blooded, senseless murders" has been left to writers outside the social sciences. Neither academic methods nor academic theories seem to be able to grasp . . . how it makes sense to them to kill when only petty cash is at stake. Sociological and psychological studies of robbery rarely focus on the distinctive attractions of robbery, even though research has now clearly documented that alternative forms of criminality are available and familiar to many career robbers.

For criminal offenders, crime is indeed rewarding, Katz says. It is exciting; it feels good, he tells his readers. "The particular seductions and compulsions [which criminals] experience may be unique to crime," he says, "but the sense of being seduced and compelled is not. To grasp the magic in the criminal's sensuality, we must acknowledge our own."[40] Katz describes the almost sexual attraction shoplifting held for one young offender. As the thief said, "The experience was almost orgasmic for me. There was a buildup of tension as I contemplated the danger of a forbidden act, then a rush of excitement at the moment of committing the crime, and finally a delicious sense of release."[41]

Katz's approach, which stresses the sensual dynamics of criminality, says that for many people, crime is sensually compelling. As one writer notes, "Jack Katz argues for a redirection of the criminological gaze—from the traditional focus on background factors such as age, gender, and material conditions to foreground or situational factors that directly precipitate criminal acts and reflect crimes' sensuality."[42] Learn more about the seductions of crime at **Web Extra 4–10.**

WEB
Extra

Situational Crime Control Policy

Building upon the work of rational and situational choice theorists, Israeli criminologist David Weisburd describes the advantages of a situational approach to crime prevention. Weisburd points out, "Crime prevention research and policy have traditionally been concerned with offenders or potential offenders. Researchers have looked to define strategies that would deter individuals from involvement in crime or rehabilitate them so they would no longer want to commit criminal acts. In recent years, crime prevention efforts have often focused on the incapacitation of high-rate or dangerous offenders so they are not free to victimize law-abiding citizens. In the public debate over crime prevention policies, these strategies are usually defined as competing approaches."[43] However, Weisburd says, "they have in common a central assumption about crime prevention research and policy: that efforts to understand and control crime must begin with the offender. In all of these approaches, the focus of crime prevention is on people and their involvement in criminality."

"Although this assumption continues to dominate crime prevention research and policy," says Weisburd, "it has begun to be challenged by a very different approach that seeks to shift the focus of crime prevention efforts." The new approach developed in large part as a response to the failures of traditional theories and programs. The 1970s, in particular, saw a shattering of traditional assumptions about the effectiveness of crime prevention efforts and led to a reevaluation of research and policy about crime prevention. For many scholars and policymakers, this meant having to rethink assumptions about criminality and how offenders might be prevented from participating in crime. Others suggested that a more radical reorientation of crime prevention efforts was warranted. They argued that the shift must come not in terms of the specific strategies or theories that were used but in terms of the unit of analysis that formed the basis of crime prevention efforts. This new crime prevention effort called for a focus not on people who commit crime but on the context in which crime occurs.

This approach, which is called **situational crime prevention,** looks to develop greater understanding of crime and more effective crime prevention strategies through concern with the physical, organizational, and social environments that make crime possible.[44] The situational approach does not ignore offenders; it merely places them as one part of a broader crime prevention equation that is centered on the context of crime. It demands a shift in the approach to crime prevention, however, from one that is concerned primarily with why people commit crime to one that looks primarily at why crime occurs in specific settings. It moves the context of crime into central focus and sees the offender as but one of a number of factors that affect it. Situational crime prevention is closely associated with the idea of a "criminology of place," which is discussed in the Theory versus Reality box in Chapter 7.

Weisburd suggests that a "reorientation of crime prevention research and policy from the causes of criminality to the context of crime provides much promise." Says Weisburd, "At the core of situational prevention is the concept of opportunity." In contrast to offender-based approaches to crime prevention that usually focus on the dispositions of criminals, situational crime prevention begins with the opportunity structure of the crime situation. By "opportunity structure," advocates of this perspective are not referring to sociological concepts like differential opportunity or anomie but, rather, to the immediate situational and environmental components of the context of crime. Their approach to crime prevention is to try to reduce the opportunities for crime in specific situations. This may involve efforts as simple and straightforward as **target hardening** or access control.[45]

The value of a situational approach lies in the fact that criminologists have found it difficult to identify who is likely to become a serious offender and to predict the timing and types of future offenses that repeat offenders are likely to commit. And, as Weisburd says, "legal and ethical dilemmas make it difficult to base criminal justice policies on models that still include a substantial degree of statistical error." Moreover, Weisburd adds, "if traditional approaches worked well, of course, there would be little pressure to find new forms of crime prevention. If traditional approaches worked well, few people would possess criminal motivation and fewer still would actually commit crimes."

Situational prevention advocates argue that the context of crime provides a promising alternative to traditional offender-based crime prevention policies.[46] They assume that situations provide a more stable and predictable focus for crime prevention efforts than do people. In part, this assumption develops from common-sense notions of the relationship between opportunities and crime. Shoplifting, for example, is by definition clustered in stores and not residences, and family disputes are unlikely to be a problem outside of the home. High-crime places, in contrast to high-crime people, cannot flee to avoid criminal justice intervention, and crime that develops from the specific characteristics of certain places cannot be easily transferred to other contexts.

Another example can be found in robberies, which are most likely to be found in places where many pedestrians stroll (such as bus stops and business districts), where there are few police or informal guardians (for example, doormen), and where a supply

situational crime prevention

A social policy approach that looks to develop a greater understanding of crime and more effective crime prevention strategies through concern with the physical, organizational, and social environments that make crime possible.

target hardening

The reduction in criminal opportunity for a particular location, generally through the use of physical barriers, architectural design, and enhanced security measures.

of motivated offenders can be found nearby or at least within easy public transportation access.[47] Similarly, such places are not likely to be centers for prostitution, which would favor easy access of cars (and little interference by shopkeepers who are likely to object to the obvious nature of street solicitations), or flashing, which is more likely to be found in the more anonymous environments of public parks.

In short, situational crime control works by removing or reducing criminal opportunity. Felson and Clarke remind us that "accepting opportunity as a cause of crime also opens up a new vista of crime prevention policies focused upon opportunity-reduction."[48] Such policies, they say, "do not merely complement existing efforts to diminish individual propensities to commit crime through social and community programs or the threat of criminal sanctions. Rather, the newer policies operate on circumstances much closer to the criminal event and thus have a much greater chance to reduce crime immediately."

If we accept that opportunity is a cause of crime that is equal in importance to the personal and social characteristics that other researchers point to as causes, then, say Felson and Clarke, we have a "criminology that is not only more complete in its theorizing, but also more relevant to policy and practice." If Felson and Clarke are correct in what they say then much of the crime prevention work that is already being done by police agencies, private security, and businesses aimed at reducing criminal opportunity directly impacts the basic causes of crime.

WEB
Extra
▪▪▪▪

Learn more about situational crime prevention and target hardening via **Web Extra 4–11.**

Critique of Rational Choice Theory

Rational and situational choice and routine activities theories can be criticized for an overemphasis on individual choice and a relative disregard for the role of social factors in crime causation, such as poverty, poor home environment, and inadequate socialization. In one study, for example, Laura J. Moriarty and James E. Williams found that the routine activities approach explained 28% of property crimes committed in socially disorganized (high-crime) areas of a small Virginia city and explained only 11% of offenses committed in low-crime areas.[49] In the words of the authors, "This research demonstrates more support for routine activities theory in socially disorganized areas than in socially organized areas."[50] Hence, although one could argue that the kinds of routine activities supportive of criminal activity are more likely to occur in socially disorganized areas, it is also true that the presence (or absence) of certain ecological characteristics (that is, the level of social disorganization) may enhance (or reduce) the likelihood of criminal victimization. As the authors state, "Those areas characterized by low socioeconomic status will have higher unemployment rates, thus creating a larger pool of motivated offenders. Family disruption characterized by more divorced or separated families will result in more unguarded living structures, thus making suitable targets more available. Increased residential mobility will result in more non-occupied housing, which creates a lack of guardianship over the property and increases the number of suitable targets."[51]

Similarly, according to M. Lyn Exum of the University of North Carolina at Charlotte, rational choice theory does not adequately consider the impact of emotional states on cognitive ability and the role of psychopharmacological agents in decision making.[52] Exum studied the effects of alcohol and anger on aggression and found that "alcohol diminishes individuals' perceptions of the costs associated with aggression and, in some instances, actually increases the perceived benefits." Similarly, high arousal levels, such as those associated with anger and other emotions, appear to impair judgment. Hence, when acting under the influence of alcohol or when experiencing strong emotions, "the individual's capacity to anticipate gratification and aversion, success and failure, and cost is diminished."[53] As Exum notes, other studies show that approximately 40% of offenders are under the influence of alcohol when committing the crimes for which they are arrested. Exum suggests that future research involving the rational

Theory in Perspective

The Classical School and Neoclassical Thinkers

The Classical School is a criminological perspective developed in the late 1700s and early 1800s. It had its roots in the Enlightenment and held that men and women are rational beings and that crime is the result of the exercise of free will and personal choices based on calculations of perceived costs and benefits. Hence, punishment can be effective in reducing the incidence of crime when it negates the rewards to be derived from crime commission.

Classical Criminology

The application of Classical School principles to problems of crime and justice

Period: 1700s–1880

Theorists: Cesare Beccaria, Jeremy Bentham, others

Concepts: Free will, deterrence through punishment, social contract, natural law, natural rights, due process, Panopticon

Neoclassical Criminology

- The modern-day application of classical principles to problems of crime and crime control in contemporary society, often in the guise of get-tough social policies.

Period: 1970s–present

Theorists: Lawrence Cohen, Marcus Felson, Ronald V. Clarke, Derek B. Cornish, Jack Katz, many others

Concepts: Rational choice, routine activities, capable guardians, situational crime prevention, target hardening, just deserts, determinate sentencing, specific deterrence, general deterrence

choice perspective should include the role of emotions and the potential impact of psychopharmacological agents such as drugs or alcohol.

Rational choice theory, in particular, seems to assume that everyone is equally capable of making rational decisions when, in fact, such is probably not the case. Some individuals are more logical than others by virtue of temperament, personality, or socialization, whereas others are emotional, hotheaded, and unthinking. Empirical studies of rational choice theory have added scant support for the perspective's underlying assumptions, tending to show instead that criminal offenders are often unrealistic in their appraisals of the relative risks and rewards facing them.[54] Similarly, rational and situational choice theories seem to disregard individual psychology and morality with their emphasis on external situations. Moral individuals, say critics, when faced with easy criminal opportunities, may rein in their desires and turn their backs on temptation.

Finally, the emphasis of rational and situational choice theories upon changing aspects of the immediate situation to reduce crime has been criticized for resulting in the **displacement** of crime from one area to another.[55] Target hardening,[56] a key crime prevention strategy among such theorists, has sometimes caused criminals to find new targets of opportunity in other areas.[57]

displacement

A shift of criminal activity from one location to another.

Punishment and Neoclassical Thought

Punishment is a central feature of both classical and neoclassical thought. Whereas punishment served the ends of deterrence in classical thought, its role in neoclassical thinking has been expanded to support the ancient concept of retribution. Those who advocate retribution see the primary utility of punishment as revenge.

If a person is attracted to crime and chooses to violate the law, modern neoclassical thinkers argue, then he or she *deserves* to be punished because the consequences of crime were known to the offender before the crime was committed. Moreover, the criminal *must* be punished, such thinkers propose, so that future criminal behavior can be curtailed.

In 1994, the "caning" of an American teenager in Singapore provided an example of just this kind of thinking. In that year, 18-year-old Michael Fay from Dayton, Ohio, was ordered to receive six lashes from a four-foot-long, half-inch-thick split-bamboo rod called a *rotan.* Fay's caning was to be his punishment for five charges of vandalism, mischief, and keeping stolen property—crimes committed while he lived in Singapore with his parents and to which he pleaded guilty. Fay, along with other teenagers, had spray-painted and thrown eggs at parked cars. At the time of the offenses, Fay was probably unaware that Singapore law mandates caning in cases of vandalism when an indelible substance is used. The law was originally passed in the 1960s to curtail the use of political graffiti. Caning is no simple punishment. It has been described as making "pieces of skin and flesh fly at each stroke."[58] Singapore law requires that those who faint be revived by a doctor, so that the caning can continue.[59]

Before Fay's caning, his parents begged Singapore's courts for leniency, pleaded for intervention from the International Red Cross, beseeched Singapore President Ong Teng Cheong for clemency, and asked then–President Bill Clinton for help—all to no avail. Although many Americans expressed dismay at the severity of the punishment, the Singapore Embassy in Washington, DC, along with newspapers and television stations throughout the United States, received thousands of letters and phone calls from American citizens supporting the punishment and saying that the U.S. judicial system could learn something from the crime reduction strategies used in Singapore.

Notions of revenge and retribution are morally based. They build on a sense of indignation at criminal behavior and on the sense of righteousness inherent in Judeo-Christian notions of morality and propriety. Both philosophies of punishment turn a blind eye to the mundane and practical consequences of any particular form of punishment. Hence, advocates of retributive philosophies of punishment easily dismiss critics of, say, the death penalty, who frequently challenge the efficacy of court-ordered capital punishment on the basis that such sentences do little to deter others. Wider issues, including general deterrence, become irrelevant when a person focuses narrowly on the emotions that crime and victimization engender in a given instance. Simply put, from the neoclassical perspective some crimes cry out for vengeance, while others demand little more than a slap on the wrist or an apology from the offender.

Just Deserts

just deserts model

The notion that criminal offenders deserve the punishment they receive at the hands of the law and that punishments should be appropriate to the type and severity of crime committed.

The old adages "He got what was coming to him" and "She got her due" well summarize the thinking behind the **just deserts model** of criminal sentencing. Just deserts, a concept inherent in the justice model, refers to the concept that criminal offenders deserve the punishment they receive at the hands of the law and that any punishment imposed should be appropriate to the type and severity of crime committed. The idea of just deserts has long been a part of Western thought, dating back at least to Old Testament times. The Old Testament dictum of "an eye for an eye, and a tooth for a tooth" has been cited by many as divine justification for strict punishments. Some scholars believe, however, that in reality the notion of "an eye for an eye" was intended to reduce the barbarism of existing penalties, whereby an aggrieved party might exact the severest of punishments for only minor offenses. Even petty offenses were often punished by whipping, torture, and sometimes death.

One famous modern-day advocate of the just deserts philosophy was Christian thinker C. S. Lewis, who wrote[60]

> The concept of desert is the only connecting link between punishment and justice. It is only as deserved or undeserved that a sentence can be just or unjust. I do not here contend that the question: "is it deserved?" is the only one we can reasonably ask about a punishment. We may very properly ask whether it is likely to deter others and to reform the criminal. But neither of these two last questions is a question about justice. There is no sense in talking about a "just deterrent" or a "just cure"—we demand of a deterrent not

whether it is just but whether it will deter. We demand of a cure not whether it is just but whether it succeeds. Thus when we cease to consider what the criminal deserves and consider only what will cure him or deter others, we have tacitly removed him from the sphere of justice altogether.

According to the neoclassical perspective, doing justice ultimately comes down to an official meting out of what is deserved. Justice for an individual is nothing more or less than what that individual deserves when all the circumstances surrounding that person's situation and behavior are taken into account.

Deterrence

True to its historical roots, **deterrence** is a hallmark of modern neoclassical thought. In contrast to early thinkers, however, today's neoclassical writers distinguish between deterrence that is specific and that which is general. **Specific deterrence** is a goal of criminal sentencing that seeks to prevent a particular offender from engaging in repeat criminality. **General deterrence,** in contrast, works by way of example and seeks to prevent others from committing crimes similar to the one for which a particular offender is being sentenced.

Following their classical counterparts, modern-day advocates of general deterrence frequently stress that for punishment to be an effective impediment to crime, it must be swift, certain, and severe enough to outweigh the rewards that flow from criminal activity. Unfortunately, those who advocate punishment as a deterrent are often frustrated by the complexity of today's criminal justice system and by the slow and circuitous manner in which cases are handled and punishments are meted out. Punishments today, even when imposed by a court, are rarely swift in their imposition. Swift punishments would follow quickly after sentencing. The wheels of modern criminal justice, however, are relatively slow to grind to a conclusion, given the many delays inherent in judicial proceedings and the numerous opportunities for delay and appeal available to defense counsel. Similarly, certainty of punishment is anything but a reality. Certain punishments are those that cannot be easily avoided. However, even when punishments are ordered, they are frequently not carried out—at least not fully. In contemporary America, offenders sentenced to death, for example, are unlikely to ever have their sentences finalized. For those who do, an average of nearly 12 years passes between the time a sentence of death is imposed and the time it is carried out.[61] Death row inmates and their lawyers typically barrage any court that will hear them with a plethora of appeals designed to delay or derail the process of justice. Often, they win new trials. If they are able to wait long enough, some inmates may find their sentences overturned by blanket U.S. Supreme Court rulings that find fault with some aspect of a state's trial process. Those who are able to delay even longer may die of natural causes before the machinery of the state grinds its way to a conclusion.

If the neoclassicists are correct, criminal punishments should ideally prevent a repetition of crime. Unfortunately, as high rates of contemporary recidivism indicate, punishments in America rarely accomplish that goal. **Recidivism** means, quite simply, the repetition of criminal behavior by those already involved in crime. Recidivism can also be used to measure the success of a given approach to the problem of crime. When so employed, it is referred to as a **recidivism rate,** expressed as the percentage of convicted offenders who have been released from prison and who are later rearrested for a new crime, generally within five years following release. Studies show that recidivism rates are high indeed, reaching levels of 80% to 90% in some instances, meaning that 8 or 9 of every 10 criminal offenders released from confinement are rearrested for new lawbreaking activity within five years of being set free. Such studies, however, do not measure the numbers of released offenders who return to crime but who are not caught, and they ignore those who return to crime more than five years after release from prison. Were such numbers available, recidivism rates would likely be even higher.

One reason American criminal justice seems so ineffectual at preventing crime and reducing recidivism may be that the punishments that contemporary criminal law provides are rarely applied to the majority of offenders. Statistics show that few lawbreakers

deterrence

The prevention of crime.

specific deterrence

A goal of criminal sentencing that seeks to prevent a particular offender from engaging in repeat criminality.

general deterrence

A goal of criminal sentencing that seeks to prevent others from committing crimes similar to the one for which a particular offender is being sentenced.

recidivism

The repetition of criminal behavior.

recidivism rate

The percentage of convicted offenders who have been released from prison and who are later rearrested for a new crime, generally within five years following release.

FIGURE 4–2

The Crime Funnel

Note: Includes drug crimes.

Source: Statistics derived from the Bureau of Justice Statistics, *Sourcebook of Criminal Justice Statistics,* 2006 (Washington, DC: National Institute of Justice, 2007).

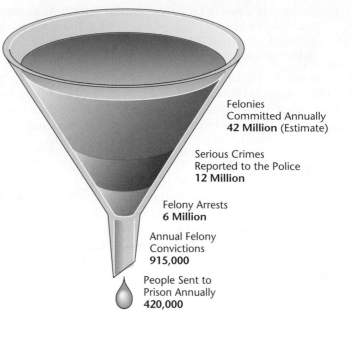

Felonies
Committed Annually
42 Million (Estimate)

Serious Crimes
Reported to the Police
12 Million

Felony Arrests
6 Million

Annual Felony
Convictions
915,000

People Sent to
Prison Annually
420,000

are ever arrested and that of those who are, fewer still are convicted of the crimes with which they have been charged. After a lengthy court process, most offenders processed by the justice system are released, fined, or placed on probation. Relatively few are sent to prison, although short of capital punishment, prison is the most severe form of punishment available to authorities today. To represent this situation, criminal justice experts often use a diagram known as a "crime funnel." Figure 4–2 shows the crime funnel for 2002. As the figure shows, fewer than 1% of criminal law violators in America can be expected to spend time in prison as punishment for their crimes.

Exacerbating the situation is the fact that few people sent to prison ever serve anything close to the sentences that have been imposed on them. Many inmates serve only a small fraction of their sentences due to early release made possible by time off for good behavior, mandated reentry training, and the practical considerations necessitated by prison overcrowding.

The Death Penalty

Notions of deterrence, retribution, and just deserts all come together in **capital punishment.** The many different understandings of crime and crime control, along with arguments over free will and social determinism, combine with varying philosophies of punishment to produce considerable disagreement over the efficacy of death as a form of criminal sanction.

Opponents of capital punishment make ten kinds of claims, as follows: (1) Capital punishment does not deter crime; (2) the death penalty has, at times, been imposed on innocent people, and no workable system is currently in place to prevent the accidental execution of innocents; (3) human life is sacred, even the life of a murderer; (4) state-imposed death lowers society to the same moral (or amoral) level as the murderer; (5) the death penalty has been (and may still be) imposed in haphazard and seemingly random fashion; (6) the death penalty is imposed disproportionately upon ethnic minorities; (7) capital punishment goes against the most fundamental precepts of almost every organized religion; (8) the death penalty is more expensive than imprisonment; (9) internationally, capital punishment is widely viewed as inhumane and barbaric; and (10) there is a better alternative (usually said to be life in prison without

capital punishment

The legal imposition of a sentence of death upon a convicted offender.

possibility of parole). Read more about arguments against the death penalty at Library Extras 4–4 and 4–5 at crimtoday.com.

LIBRARY Extra

Advocates of capital punishment generally discount each of these claims, countering abolitionist arguments with the proposition that death is *deserved* by those who commit especially heinous acts and that anything short of capital punishment under certain circumstances is an injustice in itself. Some people, the claim is made, deserve to die for what they have done. Such arguments have evolved from a natural law perspective, are sometimes supported on religious grounds, and are based on the notion of just deserts, as discussed earlier.

Strong feelings on both sides of the issue have generated a plethora of studies of the efficacy and fairness of capital punishment as a criminal sanction. Although one might expect study results to have produced some agreement, just the opposite seems to have happened—and a relative impasse exists as to how those death penalty studies that have been conducted should be interpreted. The extent to which the death penalty acts as a general deterrent, for example, has been widely examined. Some researchers[62] have compared murder rates between states that have eliminated the death penalty and those that retain it, finding little variation in the rate at which murders are committed. Others have looked at variations in murder rates over time in jurisdictions that have eliminated capital punishment, with similar results.[63] A now-classic 1988 Texas study provided a comprehensive review of capital punishment by correlating homicide rates with the rate of executions within the state between 1930 and 1986.[64] The study, which was especially important because Texas has been quite active in the capital punishment arena, failed to find any support for the use of death as a deterrent.

Regardless of studies to the contrary, many death penalty advocates remain unconvinced that the sanction cannot be an effective deterrent. As with other punishments, a death penalty that is swift and certain, they point out, is likely to deter others. As noted earlier, however, modern-day capital punishment rarely meets these requirements because offenders sentenced to death are unlikely to ever have their sentences finalized.[65] Even if the threat of death does not effectively deter others, advocates of capital punishment say, it will ensure that the people who are put to death will never commit another crime. Learn more about how capital punishment is seen in contemporary America from the Death Penalty Information Center at Web Extra 4–12. Read about the current state of the death penalty at Library Extra 4–6 at crimtoday.com. A balanced approach to the subject can be read at Library Extra 4–7.

WEB Extra

LIBRARY Extra

Capital Punishment and Race

According to the Washington-based Death Penalty Information Center,[66] the death penalty has been imposed disproportionately on racial minorities throughout most of American history. Statistics maintained by the center show that "since 1930 nearly 90% of those executed for the crime of rape in this country were African Americans. Currently, about 50% of those on the nation's death rows are from minority populations representing 20% of the country's population." The center, a fervent anti–capital punishment organization, claims that "evidence of racial discrimination in the application of capital punishment continues. Nearly 40% of those executed since 1976 have been black, even though blacks constitute only 12% of the population. And in almost every death penalty case, the race of the victim is white." In 1996 alone, according to the center, "89% of the death sentences carried out involved white victims, even though 50% of the homicides in this country have black victims. Of the 229 executions that have occurred since the death penalty was reinstated [in 1972]," says the center, "only one has involved a white defendant for the murder of a black person."

A 1994 congressional report by the Subcommittee on Civil and Constitutional Rights[67] reached much the same conclusion. The report, entitled *Racial Disparities in Federal Death Penalty Prosecutions 1988–1994,* had this to say about race and capital punishment under federal law: "Racial minorities are being prosecuted under federal death penalty law far beyond their proportion in the general population or the population of criminal offenders. Analysis of prosecutions under the federal death penalty

Twenty-four-year-old Ronell Wilson, right, is escorted past a corrections officer in New York City. Wilson was convicted in 2007 of shooting two undercover police officers during a buy-and-bust drug operation that took place in 2003. A Brooklyn jury recommended that Wilson be sentenced to die by lethal injection—making him the first person in more than 50 years to be sentenced to death in a federal case in New York State. Why is the number of death sentences being handed out in the United States declining?

Source: AP Wide World Photos/Ed Betz

provisions of the Anti-Drug Abuse Act of 1988 reveals that 89% of the defendants selected for capital prosecution have been either African-American or Mexican-American. Moreover, the number of prosecutions under this Act has been increasing over the past two years with no decline in racial disparities. All ten of the recently approved federal capital prosecutions have been against black defendants. This pattern of inequality adds to the mounting evidence that race continues to play an unacceptable part of the application of capital punishment in America today." The report was prepared with the assistance of the Death Penalty Information Center.

On the other hand, capital punishment advocates say that the real question is not whether ethnic differences exist in the rate of imposition of the death penalty but whether the penalty is *fairly* imposed. They argue, for example, that if 50% of all capital punishment–eligible crimes were committed by members of a particular, but relatively small, ethnic group, then anyone anticipating fairness in imposition of the death penalty would expect to see 50% of death row populations composed of members of that group—no matter how small the group. In like manner, one would also expect to see the same relative ethnicity among those executed. In short, they say, if fairness is to be any guide, those committing capital crimes should be the ones sentenced to death— regardless of race, ethnicity, gender, or other similar social characteristics.

Although evidence may suggest that African Americans and other minorities in the United States have in the past been unfairly sentenced to die,[68] the present evidence is not so clear. For an accurate appraisal to be made, any claims of disproportionality must go beyond simple comparisons with racial representation in the larger population and must somehow measure both the frequency and the seriousness of capital crimes between and within racial groups. Following that line of reasoning, the Supreme Court, in the 1987 case of *McCleskey* v. *Kemp*,[69] held that a simple showing of racial discrepancies in the application of the death penalty does not amount to a constitutional violation.

In order to reduce the likelihood that capital punishment decisions will be influenced by a defendant's race, the Washington-based Constitution Project[70] recently recommended that "all jurisdictions that impose the death penalty should create mechanisms to help ensure that the death penalty is not imposed in a racially discriminatory manner."[71] The project said that two approaches are especially appropriate in building such mechanisms: (1) the gathering of statistical data on the role of race in the operation of a jurisdiction's capital punishment system and (2) the active involvement of members of all races in every level of the capital punishment decision-making process. Read the entire report of the Constitution Project at Web Extra 4–13.

WEB
Extra
■ ■ ■ ■

Is the System Flawed?

In 1996, researchers at the Institute for Law and Justice in Alexandria, Virginia, published *Convicted by Juries, Exonerated by Science,* a report funded by the National Institute of Justice.[72] The study provided a detailed review of 28 cases in which postconviction DNA evidence conclusively exonerated defendants who had been sentenced to lengthy prison terms. The 28 cases were selected on the basis of a detailed examination of records, which indicated that the convicted defendants actually might have been innocent. The men in the study had served, on average, seven years in prison, and most had been tried and sentenced prior to the widespread availability of reliable DNA testing—although eyewitness testimony and other forensic evidence had led to their convictions. In each case, the DNA results unequivocally demonstrated that the defendants had been wrongfully convicted, and each defendant was ultimately set free. Although the study did not specifically involve the death penalty, *Convicted by Juries* showed just how fallible the judicial process can be.

More recent studies have focused on claimed injustices inherent in the sentencing process that leads to imposition of the death penalty, as well as on the seemingly inequitable application of capital punishment. In 2000, for example, a nonprofit group, the Texas Defender Service, examined hundreds of capital trials and appeals, including every published death penalty decision handed down by the Texas Court of Criminal Appeals (the state's highest criminal court) since 1976.[73] The study found, among other things, that (1) poor clients routinely received bad representation by court-appointed attorneys, (2) race has a pervasive influence on the administration of capital punishment because prosecutors are far more likely to ask for imposition of the death sentence in cases in which the victim is white as opposed to black, and (3) blacks and Hispanics are often excluded from capital juries. The report also identified instances in which prosecutors intentionally distorted truth in order to win convictions, cases involving the use of courtroom testimony from disbarred psychiatrists, and examples of the use of unreliable "jailhouse informers" in capital cases.

A year-2000 U.S. Department of Justice (DOJ) study found significant racial and geographic disparities in the imposition of federal death sentences.[74] The study revealed that 80% of the 682 defendants who have faced capital charges in federal courts since 1995 have been black. Perhaps even more significant, U.S. attorneys in only 49 of the nation's 94 judicial districts have prosecuted defendants for capital crimes. Critics of the study noted that such numbers are meaningless unless compared with the actual proportion of minority defendants qualifying for capital prosecution. Similarly, the absence, in some jurisdictions, of crimes that might qualify for prosecution as capital offenses may explain the lack of death penalty prosecutions rather than the supposed exercise of prosecutorial discretion.

A potentially more significant study was conducted by Columbia University Law School professors James Liebman and Jeffrey Fagan and published at about the same time as the DOJ review. Liebman and Fagan examined 4,578 death penalty appeals during the years 1973–1995[75] and found that most cases were seriously flawed—with many having to be retried. A state or federal court threw out the conviction or death sentence in 68% of the cases analyzed. This means that appellate courts found serious, reversible errors in almost 7 out of every 10 cases involving capital sentences. Eighty-two percent of defendants whose death sentences were overturned by state appellate courts due to serious error were found to deserve a sentence less than death, and 7% were found to be innocent of the capital crime with which they had been charged. According to the study's authors, "Our 23 years worth of findings reveal a capital punishment system collapsing under the weight of its own mistakes."

FIGURE 4–3

Death Row Prisoners Exonerated and Freed since1973.

Source: Death Penalty Information Center.

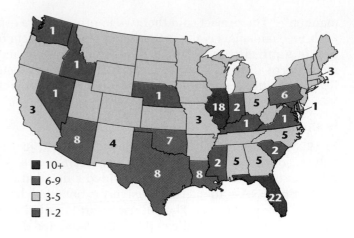

According to the Death Penalty Information Center, 114 people in 25 states were released from death rows across the United States between 1973 and mid-2004 after proof of their innocence became available.[76] Figure 4–3 shows such releases on a state-by-state basis.

Studies like the ones cited here have led to official rethinking of the death penalty in some parts of the country, contributing to what some have called a moratorium movement focused on reform of capital punishment laws.[77] In January 2000, for example, Illinois Governor George Ryan suspended executions in his state after DNA results showed conclusively that 13 death row prisoners were innocent. Ryan appointed a commission to study capital punishment in Illinois and to determine what reforms, if any, could ensure a fair and impartial capital punishment system. In 2002, after 24 months of discussions, the governor's commission concluded that "if capital punishment is to continue to be imposed in Illinois, achieving a higher degree of confidence in the outcomes will require a significant increase in public funding at virtually every level, ranging from investigation through trial and its aftermath." The commission's report contained 85 recommendations intended to reform what the members of the commission saw as a broken system.[78] Recommendations included videotaping all police questioning of a capital suspect and revising procedures for police lineups intended to lead to eyewitness identification. The commission also recommended limiting applicability of the death penalty to "cases where the defendant has murdered two or more persons, or where the victim was either a police officer or a firefighter; or an officer or inmate of a correctional institution; or was murdered to obstruct the justice system; or was tortured in the course of the murder." Finally, the commission recommended that "the death penalty be barred in certain instances because of the character of the evidence or the defendant." Capital punishment, said the commission, should not be available when a conviction is based solely upon the testimony of a single eyewitness or on evidence provided by an in-custody informant.

On May 9, 2002, Maryland became the second state to declare a moratorium on executions on order of Governor Parris N. Glendening after the governor decided that "reasonable questions have been raised in Maryland and across the country about the application of the death penalty."[79] Glendening wanted to have an opportunity to consider the results of a two-year University of Maryland study (which was about to be released) examining the effects of racial and jurisdictional factors on the imposition of capital punishment before deciding on a future course of action.

In May 2000, the New Hampshire legislature voted in favor of abolishing the death penalty. In doing so, it became the first state legislature to cast such a vote since the U.S. Supreme Court's 1976 decision in *Gregg* v. *Georgia*,[80] which invalidated the manner in which capital punishment was imposed in a number of jurisdictions. New Hampshire's governor subsequently vetoed the legislation.

Crime in the News

U.S. Death Sentences Drop to 30-year Low

The number of death sentences handed out in the United States dropped in 2006 to the lowest level since capital punishment was reinstated 30 years ago, reflecting what some experts say is a growing fear that the criminal justice system will make a tragic and irreversible mistake.

Executions fell, too, to the fewest in a decade.

"The death penalty is on the defensive," said Richard Dieter, director of the Death Penalty Information Center, a Washington organization that looks at problems with the capital punishment system.

Death sentences fell in 2006 to 114 or fewer, according to an estimate from the group. That is down from 128 in 2005, and even lower than the 137 sentences the year after the U.S. Supreme Court reinstated the death penalty in 1976. It is also down sharply from the high of 317 in 1996.

A total of 53 executions were carried out in 2006, down from 60 in 2005. Executions over the past three decades peaked at 98 in 1999.

Among the many causes given by prosecutors, lawyers, and death penalty critics: the passage of more state laws that allow juries to impose life without parole; an overall drop in violent crime; and a reluctance among some authorities to pursue the death penalty because of the high costs of prosecuting a capital case.

But above all, many said, is the possibility of a mistake, made dramatically clear in recent years. Since the death penalty was reinstated, 123 people have been freed from death row after significant questions were raised about their convictions—14 of them through DNA testing, according to the Death Penalty Information Center.

"The fact is they've gotten a lot of the wrong guys," said Deborah Fleischaker, director of the American Bar Association's Death Penalty Moratorium Implementation Project. "There's no question that has, in the public, created a lot of doubt about how the death penalty is working."

The turn away from the ultimate punishment also reflects a changing sentiment among juries and prosecutors, too, said Arthur Green, district attorney in Bessemer County, Ala., outside of Birmingham. He said he considers the risk of executing an innocent person in deciding whether to pursue the death penalty.

"That's one reason I don't do it, except in very, very rare circumstances—one, that I'm convinced he or she did it, and number two, it's a horrible crime," Green said. He has sought and won two capital cases since becoming district attorney in 2001.

Thirty-seven of the 38 states that have the death penalty on their books now also allow for life without parole. Texas enacted such a law in 2005. Life-without-parole laws give another option to jurors who fear that the death penalty is the only way to keep a killer from getting out on the streets again.

The death penalty has also received more scrutiny from lawmakers around the country and the courts.

Illinois is in the seventh year of its moratorium on executions, and executions are effectively halted in New York because of a 2004 court ruling.

Also, questions about whether lethal injection is inhumane have put executions on hold in nine states—Arkansas, California, Delaware, Florida, Maryland, Missouri, New Jersey, Ohio and South Dakota—and in the federal system.

This week in New Jersey, a special commission recommended that the state become the first to abolish the death penalty legislatively since 1976, citing "increasing evidence that the death penalty is inconsistent with evolving standards of decency."

Backers of capital punishment say support for the death penalty remains strong, despite the drop-off in death sentences.

"It's a refinement. I don't think it's an abandonment of the death penalty, but a recognition that the death penalty should be reserved for the worst of the worst," said Joshua Marquis, district attorney in Clatsop County, Ore., and a vice president of the National District Attorneys Association.

"From prosecutors, there's a more discriminating attitude about which cases to bring," he said. "Juries have been much more picky about allocating the death penalty and I think that's an appropriate thing to do."

A Gallup poll in May 2006 found that two-thirds of Americans 18 and older support the death penalty. But when asked which is the better penalty for murder, roughly half said life without parole and about half said the death penalty.

Discussion Questions

1. What are your feelings about capital punishment? Provide reasons to support the way you feel.
2. What do you think are the most significant arguments against the death penalty?
3. What do you consider to be the most convincing arguments in favor of it?

Police officer Sadie Darnell pauses at a graffiti wall memorializing five students slain at the University of Florida in Gainesville in 1990. The victims were all slashed and stabbed with a hunting knife. Their killer, Danny Harold Rolling, wanted to be remembered as a "superstar" among criminals. Rolling, a police officer's son, was executed on October 25, 2006. Did he deserve to die?

Source: John Raoux/AP Wide World Photos.

Source: Robert Tanner, "U.S. Death Sentences Drop to 30-year Low," Associated Press, January 4, 2007.

For the latest crime and justice news, visit www.crimenews.info.

Not all state governors are convinced that the death penalty should be abolished. Instead, some, like Massachusetts Governor Mitt Romney, believe that capital punishment should be revived. Massachusetts has long been one of the 12 states where capital punishment is not a sentencing option for the crime of murder. The state abolished the death penalty in 1984 and has not carried out an execution since 1947.[81] In 2003, however, Governor Romney, after having campaigned in favor of the death penalty, established the Governor's Council on Capital Punishment in an effort to restore the death penalty in his state. Romney told constituents that he was seeking to avoid the problems that have cast the death sentencing systems of other states into doubt. The council's report, issued in 2004, included a recommended requirement that physical or scientific evidence like DNA be used to corroborate guilt during the sentencing phase of trial. Jurors would also be informed of the demonstrated fallibility of human evidence and eyewitness testimony. Were the state to follow the council's recommendations, jurors would be told that, in order to impose a sentence of death, they must find that there is "no doubt" about the defendant's guilt—a much higher standard of proof than the reasonable doubt standard used elsewhere. The council's complete report is available as **Library Extra 4–8** at crimtoday.com. Finally, in 2006, the New Jersey legislature voted to suspend use of the death penalty until a state task force made its report on whether capital punishment is fairly imposed.[82]

LIBRARY
Extra
▪ ▪ ▪ ▪

In 2004, in recognition of the power that DNA testing holds to exonerate the innocent, President George W. Bush signed the Innocence Protection Act[83] into law. The Innocence Protection Act provides federal funds to eliminate the backlog of unanalyzed DNA samples in the nation's crime laboratories[84] and sets aside money to improve the capacity of federal, state, and local crime laboratories to conduct DNA analyses.[85] The act also facilitates access to postconviction DNA testing for those serving time in state[86] or federal prisons or on death row and sets forth conditions under which a federal prisoner asserting innocence may obtain postconviction DNA testing of specific evidence. Similarly, the legislation requires the preservation of biological evidence by federal law enforcement agencies for any defendant under a sentence of imprisonment or death.

Not all claims of innocence are supported by DNA tests, however. In 2006, for example, DNA test results confirmed the guilt of Roger Keith Coleman, a Virginia coal miner who had steadfastly maintained his innocence until he was executed in 1992. Coleman, executed for the rape and murder of his sister-in-law, Wanda McCoy in 1981, died declaring his innocence and proclaiming that he would one day be exonerated. His case became a cause celebre for death penalty opponents, who convinced Virginia Governor Mark Warner to order DNA tests on surviving evidence. Coleman's supporters claimed that the tests would provide the first scientific proof that an innocent man had been executed in the United States. Results from the tests, however, conclusively showed that blood and semen found at the crime scene had come from Coleman.[87] View more than 1,000 capital punishment-related Web links at **Web Extra 4–14** at crimtoday.com.

WEB
Extra
▪ ▪ ▪ ▪

Policy Implications of the Classical School

A few years ago, Lawrence W. Sherman of the University of Pennsylvania described four paradigms of justice, shown in Figure 4–4.[88] As the figure illustrates, each form of justice can be described in terms of whether it presumes either a rational or an emotional basis for crime and either a rational or an emotional societal response to criminality. According to Sherman, two types of justice, one rational (that is, focused on deterrence) and the other emotional (that is, focused on retribution), "have competed for primacy" since the dawn of the modern era. Combining those two perspectives on justice with notions of either a rational or an emotional offender yields the four paradigms in the figure.

The first paradigm, which Sherman terms *expressive economics,* assumes that crime is a rational act, but that the justice philosophy that undergirds it uses "punishment as a symbolic *expression* of the emotions of anger and outrage by the state and society at the act of a criminal." Expressive economics, then, finds an emotional society using the

FIGURE 4–4

Lawrence W. Sherman's Paradigms of Justice

	Offender Rational	Offender Emotional
Law Emotional	Expressive Economics	Expression
Law Rational	Rational Economics	Emotional Intelligence

Source: Lawrence W. Sherman, "Reason for Emotion: Reinventing Justice with Theories, Innovations, and Research: The American Society of Criminology 2002 Presidential Address," *Criminology*, Vol. 41, No. 1 (2003), pp. 1–37. Reprinted with permission.

criminal law and the justice system as a combined means of expressing its feelings and inflicting retribution on offenders who have made the decision to violate the law. This, says Sherman, is the "paradigm that dominates current practice." It is also, he says, the reason that so many people come away from the justice process feeling unfulfilled. "Few of us," says Sherman, "expect much justice from an expressive state that dramatizes its outrage at a rational offender who coolly calculates costs and benefits."[89] It was, says Sherman, Beccaria's attacks on expressive punishment as immoral that led to abolition of the death penalty in many European countries.

Another important justice paradigm is a kind of *rational economics,* under which an assumed-to-be-purposeful offender encounters a justice system based on rational—rather than emotional—principles. Such a system employs punishment to make the economics of crime more favorable to law-abiding than to lawbreaking behavior. This kind of rational economics favors deterrence and most closely mirrors the principles of classical and neoclassical thought that we have been discussing in this chapter.

During the past 30 years or so, a mixed American justice philosophy of expressive and rational economics has led to the advent of such seemingly rational punishment practices as determinate sentencing and truth in sentencing and to such emotional consequences as long prison terms and a rebirth of interest in the use of capital punishment.

Determinate sentencing is a strategy that mandates a specified and fixed amount of time to be served for every offense category. Under determinate sentencing schemes, for example, judges might be required to impose seven-year sentences on armed robbers, but only one-year sentences on strong-armed robbers (who use no weapon). Determinate sentencing schemes build upon the twin notions of classical thought that (1) the pleasure of a given crime can be somewhat accurately assessed and (2) a fixed amount of punishment necessary for deterrence can be calculated and specified. **Truth in sentencing** requires judges to assess and make public the actual time an offender is likely to serve, once sentenced to prison, and many recently enacted truth-in-sentencing laws require that offenders serve a large portion of their sentence (often 80%) before they can be released.

Partially as a result of the widespread implementation of determinate sentencing strategies and the passage of truth-in-sentencing laws during the last quarter century, prison populations today are larger than ever before. By mid-2006, the nation's state and federal prison population (excluding jails) stood at 1,556,518 inmates, a figure that represented an increase of more than 700% over 1970. Figure 4–5 shows the U.S. prison population growth rate from 1924 to 2006.

Imprisonment is one component of a strategy of incapacitation. **Incapacitation,** simply put, is the use of imprisonment or other means to reduce the likelihood that an offender will be capable of committing future offenses.

Proponents of modern-day incapacitation often distinguish between selective incapacitation, in which crime is controlled via the imprisonment of specific individuals, and collective incapacitation, whereby changes in legislation and/or sentencing patterns lead to the removal from society of entire groups of individuals judged to be dangerous. Advocates of selective incapacitation as a crime control strategy point to

determinate sentencing

A criminal punishment strategy that mandates a specified and fixed amount of time to be served for every offense category. Under the strategy, for example, all offenders convicted of the same degree of burglary would be sentenced to the same length of time behind bars.

truth in sentencing

A close correspondence between the sentence imposed upon those sent to prison and the time actually served prior to prison release.

incapacitation

The use of imprisonment or other means to reduce the likelihood that an offender will be capable of committing future offenses.

FIGURE 4–5

Growth in U.S. Incarceration Rate, 1924–2006

Source: From Correctional Forum: A Publication of the Pennsylvania Prison Society, by Alfred Blumstein, p. 10, December 2005. Reprinted with permission from Alfred Blumstein, Heinz School, Carnegie Mellon University.

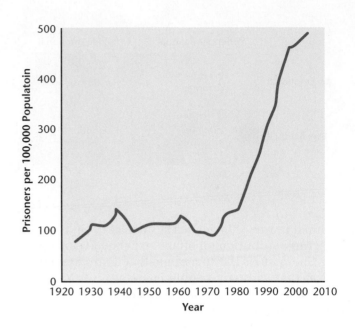

studies that show the majority of crimes are perpetrated by a small number of hard-core repeat offenders. The most famous of those studies, conducted by University of Pennsylvania Professor Marvin Wolfgang, focused on 9,000 men born in Philadelphia in 1945.[90] By the time this cohort of men had reached age 18, Wolfgang was able to determine that 627 "chronic recidivists" were responsible for the large majority of all serious violent crimes committed by the group. Other, more recent studies have similarly shown that a small core of criminal perpetrators is probably responsible for most criminal activity in the United States.

Such thinking has led to the development of incapacitation as a modern-day treatment philosophy and to the creation of innovative forms of incapacitation that do not require imprisonment—such as home confinement, the use of halfway houses or career training centers for convicted felons, and psychological and/or chemical treatments designed to reduce the likelihood of future crime commission. Similarly, such thinkers argue, the decriminalization of many offenses and the enhancement of social programs designed to combat what they see as the root causes of crime—including poverty, low educational levels, a general lack of skills, and inherent or active discrimination—will lead to a much reduced incidence of crime in the future, making high rates of imprisonment unnecessary.

Before leaving our discussion of Sherman, however, it should be pointed out that the figure implies the existence of two other justice paradigms. One of these, which he terms quite simply *expression,* results from the combination of an emotional offender and an emotional society. In this particular interface—of emotion upon emotion—says Sherman, "the state is morally obliged to take an explicitly *emotional* stance towards a presumably emotional offender, without regard for harm to the state's self-interest in the effects of its action on the offender's future behavior."[91]

It is the fourth paradigm, however—that of *emotional intelligence*—in which Sherman places the most hope for the future. Under such a paradigm, actors within the criminal justice system would control their emotions and would work with offenders and victims to bring about a reasonable resolution of the situation that would repair the harm caused by the crime. Sherman cites the 32% drop in executions that occurred nationwide following the growing availability of DNA evidence that helped to exonerate those wrongfully convicted of capital crimes as evidence of how intelligence and reason can ameliorate emotions in even the most egregious crimes.

Who's to Blame—The Individual or Society?

The Excitement of Crime

Following his arrest for the theft of a police car, Moonbeam Kittaro met with one of his friends in the visiting area of the local jail. Here's what he said:

> I stole a cop car and s***, was it exciting!
>
> I mean, the thing was just sitting there running in the parking lot with the keys in it. Who wouldn't take it?
>
> I've never been so high on pure adrenaline. It was an adrenaline rush being behind the wheel of that f***ing car.
>
> It turned my girlfriend on too.
>
> I drove over to her place with the lights and siren on, and as soon as she saw the car she wanted to go for a ride.
>
> We must have hit 140 on the Interstate!
>
> Then we pulled into a rest stop and made love in the back seat.
>
> It was the whole illegal thing that got her so excited.
>
> But that's when we got arrested.
>
> The cops surrounded the car, guns drawn and all that s***.
>
> We didn't even hear them coming.

Think about it:

1. Why did Kittaro steal the car? Do you think that he knew, before he stole it, that the theft would lead to so much excitement?

2. Can the desire for excitement explain crimes like Kittaro's? Can the same desire explain other kinds of crimes? If so, what might they be?

3. If excitement explains crime commission, then why doesn't everyone commit crime for the excitement that it brings?

4. What kinds of crime prevention programs might be based on the principles illustrated here?

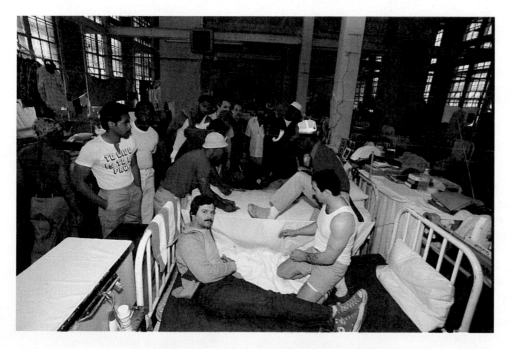

Rahway (New Jersey) State Prison. Today's "law and order" approach has led to dramatically overcrowded prisons. How can overcrowding be reduced?

Source: J. P. Laffont, Corbis/Sygma

A Critique of Classical Theories

Classical and neoclassical thought represents more a philosophy of justice than it does a theory of crime causation. As Randy Martin, Robert J. Mutchnick, and W. Timothy Austin have observed, for example, "The true test of Beccaria's essay can be judged by the influence it has had over time on our justice system."[92] The influence of Beccaria, the Enlightenment, and classical thinkers can be found today in the U.S. Constitution, in existing get-tough approaches to crime, and in a continuing emphasis on individual

Profiles in Crime

Gary Stephen Krist

Born in Aberdeen, Washington, in 1945, Gary Steven Krist was raised in a small fishing village called Pelican in Alaska's Alexander Archipelago off the western coast of Canada. Krist's father was a salmon fisherman, and Krist himself described his mother as "a well-intentioned scatterbrain."[i] The Krist's fishing business kept his parents at sea, and the financial return was not impressive.

During his parents' absence, Gary and his brother, Gordon, were left in the care of others. As a preteen, Gary showed a propensity for violence when, on one occasion, he fired a shotgun over his babysitter's and brother's heads because the babysitter made him angry by being too bossy. In an article for *Life* magazine, Krist later wrote that this incident illustrated his "absolute hatred for authority."

Examination of this period of Krist's life by prison officials in Georgia revealed that he was known throughout the tiny Pelican community as a troublemaker. A striking discovery, however, was his parents' attitude towards the reports of theft, vandalism—including blowing up an empty oil drum—and repeated reports of frequent intercourse with an 11-year-old town girl. Krist's parents seemed to view this behavior as simply displays of typical youthful exuberance.

As he entered his teens, Krist's delinquency bloomed into full-fledged criminality. At the age of 14, Krist was arrested with a friend for a series of burglaries, various sexual conquests, and much drinking. He later wrote in a memoir that their "crimes arose, I believe, more from an overpowering hungry curiosity coupled with excess physical energy than from any defined hostility or malice toward others."

While on probation for these offenses, Krist stole a car. This offense got him sent to a reform school in Ogden, Utah, where he earned straight A grades as a student in the local public school. He also unsuccessfully tried to escape on two different occasions, yet later recalled that he was "happy" in this reform school because he was "accepted."

After being released in 1961, Krist served a series of short jail terms for crimes such as auto theft. In 1965, he married, then was arrested a year later, again for auto theft. Eight months into a five-year sentence, he engineered an escape during which guards shot his accomplice to death. Since California law permitted capital punishment when an escape led to someone's death, Krist worried that he'd get the gas chamber if he were found. So he moved his young family to Boston and created a new identity as George Deacon, an aspiring scientist.

The undeniably intelligent Krist obtained a job as a lab technician at MIT. This led, in September 1968, to his participation in a marine science expedition where the still-married Krist began an affair with a student named Ruth Eisemann Schier. Before the expedition was over a month later, Krist confessed his true identity and criminal past to her, and they formed a plan to run off to Australia.

To finance their planned new life together, Krist and Eisemann Schier plotted to kidnap Emory University student Barbara Jane Mackle, the daughter of a prominent Miami family, and bury her in a homemade box, where she would remain until they received a $500,000 ransom.

Krist and Eisemann Schier did abduct and bury Mackle, who ultimately survived 83 hours underground before police, informed by Krist of the burial site, were able to find and release her. The kidnappers were subsequently caught and tried in Decatur, Georgia, in May of 1969.

Before his trial, Krist's intellect was evaluated by a psychiatrist as "if not at the genius level, then certainly in the near genius category." But the doctor also declared him fit to stand trial, and classified Krist as "having a sociopathic character disorder with no evidence of psychosis." Found guilty, the 23-year-old Krist received a life sentence.

Paroled after ten years, Krist set about lobbying for a complete pardon, which he eventually obtained in 1989. He then enrolled in a medical school in the West Indies, and completed his M.D. degree. Several states denied him a medical license before the state of Indiana finally granted him a probationary license in 2001.[ii] That license was revoked two years later when Krist's past criminal record and allegations of sexual assaults on patients surfaced.[iii]

In January 2007, 61-year-old Gary Krist, who once described himself as the "Einstein of crime," was on his way back to prison to serve a five-year, five-month sentence. A federal sting operation busted Krist and his 41-year-old stepson in early 2006 for conspiracy to bring cocaine and illegal aliens into the United States.[iv]

A bearded Gary Steven Krist is escorted from an elevator by a DeKalb County (Georgia) deputy sheriff en route to jail in 1969. Krist had been found guilty for his part in the kidnapping of Barbara Jane Mackle, and was sentenced to life in prison. Paroled after 10 years, he entered a new life of crime. Why didn't he reform?

Source: © Bettmann/CORBIS All Rights Reserved

Notes:
[i] Steve Fennessy, "The Talented Dr. Krist." Atlanta Magazine Online, http://www.atlantamagazine.com/article.php?id=299, (accessed May 21, 2007).
[ii] *Cincinnati Enquirer,* The Enquirer Online Edition, "Doctor Found to Have Been Imprisoned for Kidnapping," November 16, 2002, http://www.enquirer.com/editions/2002/11/16/loc_in-felondoc16.html (accessed July 10, 2007).
[iii] Wishtv.com, "Doctor's License Revoked," August 29, 2003, http://www.wishtv.com/Global/story.asp?S=1423007 (accessed May 21, 2007).
[iv] MSNBC, "Georgia Man in 1960s Buried Alive Case Gets 5 Years in Drug Case," http://www.msnbc.msn.com/id/16710294/ (accessed May 21, 2007).

Theory Versus Reality

Assessing Dangerousness

Dangerousness is a difficult concept to comprehend. Indicators of dangerousness have yet to be well defined in the social scientific literature, and legislators who attempt to codify any assessment of future dangerousness often find themselves frustrated. On the individual level, however, dangerousness might be more easily assessed. What follows is a description of the criteria one judge, Lois G. Forer, used in deciding whether an offender needed to spend a long time away from society.

I had my own criteria or guidelines—very different from those established by most states and the federal government—for deciding on a punishment. My primary concern was public safety. The most important question I asked myself was whether the offender could be deterred from committing other crimes. No one can predict with certainty who will or will not commit a crime, but there are indicators most sensible people recognize as danger signals:

- First, was this an irrational crime? If an arsonist sets a fire to collect insurance, that is a crime but also a rational act. Such a person can be deterred by being made to pay for the harm done and the costs to the fire department. However, if the arsonist sets fires just because he likes to see them, it is highly unlikely that he can be stopped from setting others, no matter how high the fine. Imprisonment is advisable even though it may be a first offense.
- Second, was there wanton cruelty? If a robber maims or slashes the victim, there is little likelihood that he can safely be left in the community. If a robber simply displays a gun but does not fire it or harm the victim, then one should consider his life history, provocation, and other circumstances in deciding whether probation is appropriate.

- Third, is this a hostile person? Was his crime one of hatred, and does he show any genuine remorse? Most rapes are acts of hostility, and the vast majority of rapists have a record of numerous sexual assaults. I remember one man who raped his mother. I gave him the maximum sentence under the law—20 years—but with good behavior, he got out fairly quickly. He immediately raped another elderly woman.
- Fourth, is this a person who knows he is doing wrong but cannot control himself? Typical of such offenders are pedophiles. One child abuser who appeared before me had already been convicted of abusing his first wife's child. I got him on the second wife's child and sentenced him to the maximum. Still, he'll get out with good behavior, and I shudder to think about the children around him when he does. This is one case in which justice is not tough enough.
- By contrast, some people who have committed homicide present very little danger of further violence—although many more do. Once a young man came before me because he had taken aim at a person half a block away and then shot him in the back, killing him. Why did he do it? "I wanted to get me a body." He should never get out.

Discussion Questions

1. How are public safety and criminal punishment related?

2. Do you agree that the criteria used by Judge Forer to identify dangerousness are useful? Why?

3. Do you believe that offenders who are identified as "dangerous" should be treated differently from other offenders? If so, how?

4. What elements of classical or neoclassical thought are apparent in Judge Forer's writing?

Source: Lois G. Forer, "Justice by the Numbers; Mandatory Sentencing Drove Me from the Bench," *Washington Monthly,* April 1992, pp. 12–18. Reprinted with permission from The Washington Monthly. Copyright by The Washington Monthly Company, 1611 Connecticut Ave., N.W., Washington, D.C. 20009; 202–462–0128. Web site: www.washingtonmonthly.com.

rights. Martin and colleagues conclude that the Classical School "has left behind a legacy that we see in almost every aspect of our present-day justice system."[93]

As we observed in Chapter 3, any perspective gains credence if actions taken on the basis of its assertions appear to bear fruit. Not surprisingly, advocates of today's neoclassical approaches to crime control take much of the credit for the recent drop-off in crime rates. After all, following the implementation of "get tough on crime" policies like the determinate sentencing schemes called for by the just deserts model, official rates of crime have shown substantial declines. As discussed in Chapter 2, however, the extent of crime's decline may not be as substantial as many people think; publicized statistical declines may be largely an artifact of the measuring process or may be due to demographic changes in the American population.

Critics charge that classical and neoclassical thought lacks comprehensive explanatory power over criminal motivation, other than to advance the relatively simple claim that crime is the result of free will, the personal attractions of crime, and individual choice.

dangerousness

The likelihood that a given individual will later harm society or others. Dangerousness is often measured in terms of recidivism, or the likelihood of new crime commission or rearrest for a new crime within a five-year period following arrest or release from confinement.

Such critics point out that classical theory is largely bereft of meaningful explanations as to how a choice for or against criminal activity is made. Similarly, classical theory lacks any appreciation for the deeper fonts of personal motivation, including those represented by aspects of human biology, psychology, and the social environment. Moreover, the Classical School, as originally detailed in the writings of Beccaria and Bentham, lacked any scientific basis for the claims it made. Although neoclassical writers have advanced the scientific foundation of classical claims (via studies like those showing the effectiveness of particular forms of deterrence), many still defend their way of thinking by referring to what are purely philosophical ideals, such as just deserts.

SUMMARY

The Enlightenment, a social and cultural renaissance that occurred throughout the late seventeenth and early eighteenth centuries, proved to be a highly liberating force in the Western world. Enlightenment thinkers established many of the democratic principles that formed the conceptual foundations of the American and French Revolutions. Their ideas are still alive today and significantly shape our understanding of human nature and human behavior. The twin conceptual prongs around which this textbook is built—social responsibility and individual rights—both have their roots in Enlightenment thought and in the belief in free will it engendered. Notions of deterrence as a goal of the justice system and of punishment as a worthy consequence of crime owe much of their contemporary influence to the Classical School of criminology. Although we live in the twenty-first century, we carry with us an intellectual heritage far older than we may realize.

KEY TERMS

capable guardian, 139

capital punishment, 148

Classical School, 132

Code of Hammurabi, 126

common law, 127

dangerousness, 159

determinate sentencing, 155

deterrence, 147

displacement, 145

Enlightenment, 129

folkways, 125

general deterrence, 147

hard determinism, 137

hedonistic calculus, 133

incapacitation, 155

just deserts model, 146

justice model, 139

lifestyle theory, 139

mala in se, 125

mala prohibita, 125

mores, 125

natural law, 130

natural rights, 130

neoclassical criminology, 137

nothing-works doctrine, 138

Panopticon, 136

positivism, 137

rational choice theory, 139

recidivism, 147

recidivism rate, 147

retribution, 127

routine activities theory (RAT), 139

situational choice theory, 139

situational crime prevention, 143

social contract, 129

soft determinism, 140

specific deterrence, 147

target hardening, 143

three-strikes legislation, 138

trephination, 126

truth in sentencing, 155

Twelve Tables, 127

utilitarianism, 133

KEY NAMES

Cesare Beccaria, 132

Jeremy Bentham, 133

Ronald V. Clarke, 140

Lawrence Cohen, 139

Derek B. Cornish, 140

Marcus Felson, 139

Thomas Hobbes, 129

Jack Katz, 142

John Locke, 129

Montesquieu, 129

Thomas Paine, 130

Jean-Jacques Rousseau, 129

William Graham Sumne, 125

QUESTIONS FOR REVIEW

1. What were the central concepts that defined the Classical School of criminological thought?

2. Name the various preclassical thinkers identified in this chapter. What ideas did each contribute to Enlightenment philosophy? What form did those ideas take in classical criminological thought?

3. Identify the central figures in the Classical School, and explain the contributions of each.

4. What form does classical thought take today? What implications does such thought hold for crime control policy?

5. What role does punishment play in classical and neoclassical thinking about crime and crime prevention? According to this way of thinking, what kinds of punishment might work best to prevent crime?

6. What are the policy implications of the Classical School? What kinds of crime prevention and crime control programs might be based on classical principles?

7. What are the shortcomings of the Classical School? Of neoclassical thinking about crime and crime control?

QUESTIONS FOR REFLECTION

1. This book emphasizes a social problems versus social responsibility theme. Which perspective is most clearly supported by classical and neoclassical thought? Why?

2. Define *natural law*. Do you believe that natural law exists? If so, what types of behaviors would be contravened by natural law? If not, why not?

3. What is meant by the idea of a social contract? How does the concept of a social contract relate to natural law?

4. What were the central concepts that defined the Classical School of criminological thought? Which of those concepts are still alive? Where do you see evidence for the survival of those concepts?

5. Define *recidivism*. What is a recidivism rate? Why are recidivism rates so high today? What can be done to lower them?

WEB QUEST

Few debates encompass the issues raised in this chapter better than the one now raging over the death penalty. Visit some of the death penalty sites on the Internet to explore arguments on both sides of the debate and to identify the individual rights and law and order issues involved. Here are a few such sites:

ACLU Death Penalty Page (www.aclu.org/capital/index.html)

Amnesty International Death Penalty Campaign (www.web.amnesty.org/pages/deathpenalty-index-eng)

Campaign to End the Death Penalty (www.nodeathpenalty.org)

Capital Defense Network (www.capdefnet.org)

Cornell Law School Death Penalty Project (www.lawschool.cornell.edu/lawlibrary/death/default.htm)

Justice for All (www.jfa.net)

Pro-Deathpenalty.com (www.prodeathpenalty.com)

Other sites representing both sides of the capital punishment debate can be found by searching the Prentice Hall Criminal Justice Cybrary (www.cybrary.info). If your instructor asks you to, visit each of the sites listed here, along with others of your choosing. Then write a brief summary of the philosophy represented by each site that you view.

NOTES

[1] Jeremy Bentham, *An Introduction to the Principles of Morals and Legislation* (London: T. Payne, 1789).

[2] Cesare Beccaria, *Essay on Crimes and Punishments,* translated by Henry Paolucci (New York: Bobbs-Merrill, 1963).

[3] M. Lyn Exum, "The Application and Robustness of the Rational Choice Perspective in the Study of Angry Intentions to Aggress," *Criminology,* Vol. 40, No. 4 (2002), p. 932, citing Allen E. Liska and Stephen F. Messner, *Perspectives on Crime and Deviance,* 3rd ed. (Upper Saddle River, NJ: Prentice Hall, 1999).

[4] Marcus Felson, "Linking Criminal Choices, Routine Activities, Informal Control, and Criminal Outcomes," in Derek B. Cornish and Ronald V. Clarke, eds., *The Reasoning Criminal: Rational Choice Perspectives on Offending* (New York: Springer-Verlag, 1986), p. 127.

[5] Details for this story come from Donna Leinwand, "Having Sex with Kids Overseas Illegal for Travelers, Ads Warn," *Tennessean,* February 21, 2004, http://www.tennessean.com/nation-world/archives/04/02/47210431.shtml (accessed January 21, 2007).

[6] U.S. Department of State, "Operation Global Pursuit: In Pursuit of the World's Most Dangerous Fugitives and Terrorists," http://www.state.gov/m/ds/rls/53171.htm (accessed March 10, 2007).

[7] Bill C-27. Known as the Child Sex Tourism Bill, it became law in May 1997.

[8] Greg Joyce, "Police Looking at 'Sex-Tourism' Law in Arrest," CNews Canada, February 15, 2004, http://cnews.canoe.ca/CNEWS/ Canada/2004/02/15/349327-cp.html (accessed January 3, 2007).

[9] William Graham Sumner, *Folkways* (New York: Dover, 1906).

[10] Marvin Wolfgang, "The Key Reporter," *Phi Beta Kappa*, Vol. 52, No. 1.

[11] Roman influence in England had ended by A.D. 442, according to Crane Brinton, John B. Christopher, and Robert L. Wolff, *A History of Civilization*, 3rd ed., Vol. 1 (Upper Saddle River, NJ: Prentice Hall, 1967), p. 180.

[12] Howard Abadinsky, *Law and Justice* (Chicago: Nelson-Hall, 1988), p. 6.

[13] Edward McNall Burns, *Western Civilization*, 7th ed. (New York: W. W. Norton, 1969), p. 339.

[14] Ibid., p. 533.

[15] Brinton, Christopher, and Wolff, *A History of Civilization*, p. 274.

[16] Harry V. Jaffa and Ernest van den Haag, "Of Men, Hogs, and Law: If Natural Law Does Not Permit Us to Distinguish between Men and Hogs, What Does?" *National Review*, February 3, 1992, p. 40.

[17] Referred to in official transcripts as Rudolf Franz Ferdinand Hoess.

[18] International Military Tribunal, "One Hundred and Eighth Day, Monday, 4/15/1946, Part 03," in *Trial of the Major War Criminals before the International Military Tribunal, Volume XI. Proceedings: 4/8/1946–4/17/1946* (Nuremberg: International Military Tribunal, 1943), pp. 398–400.

[19] The quotations attributed to Beccaria in this section are from Beccaria, *Essay on Crimes and Punishments*.

[20] The quotations attributed to Bentham in this section are from Bentham, *An Introduction to the Principles of Morals and Legislation*.

[21] R. Martinson, "What Works: Questions and Answers about Prison Reform," *Public Interest*, No. 35 (1974), pp. 22–54.

[22] James Q. Wilson, *Thinking about Crime* (New York: Vintage, 1975).

[23] David Fogel, *We Are the Living Proof: The Justice Model of Corrections* (Cincinnati: Anderson, 1975).

[24] Conrad P. Rutkowski, "Fogel's 'Justice Model': Stop Trying to Reform. Punish, but Treat All Alike," *Illinois Issues*, February 1976.

[25] Felton M. Earls and Albert J. Reiss, *Breaking the Cycle: Predicting and Preventing Crime* (Washington, DC: National Institute of Justice, 1994), p. 49.

[26] L. E. Cohen and Marcus Felson, "Social Change and Crime Rate Trends: A Routine Activity Approach," *American Sociological Review*, Vol. 44, No. 4 (August 1979), pp. 588–608. Also see Marcus Felson and L. E. Cohen, "Human Ecology and Crime: A Routine Activity Approach," *Human Ecology*, Vol. 8, No. 4 (1980), pp. 389–406; Marcus Felson, "Linking Criminal Choices, Routine Activities, Informal Control, and Criminal Outcomes," in Derek B. Cornish and Ronald V. Clarke, eds., *The Reasoning Criminal: Rational Choice Perspectives on Offending* (New York: Springer-Verlag, 1986), pp. 119–128; and Ronald V. Clarke and Marcus Felson, eds., *Advances in Criminological Theory: Routine Activity and Rational Choice* (New Brunswick, NJ: Transaction, 1993).

[27] Cohen and Felson, "Social Change and Crime Rate Trends," p. 595.

[28] For a test of routine activities theory as an explanation for victimization in the workplace, see John D. Wooldredge, Francis T. Cullen, and Edward J. Latessa, "Victimization in the Workplace: A Test of Routine Activities Theory," *Justice Quarterly*, Vol. 9, No. 2 (June 1992), pp. 325–335.

[29] Marcus Felson, *Crime and Everyday Life: Insight and Implications for Society* (Thousand Oaks, CA: Pine Forge Press, 1994).

[30] Gary LaFree and Christopher Birkbeck, "The Neglected Situation: A Cross-National Study of the Situational Characteristics of Crime," *Criminology*, Vol. 29, No. 1 (February 1991), p. 75.

[31] Ronald V. Clarke and Derek B. Cornish, eds., *Crime Control in Britain: A Review of Police and Research* (Albany: State University of New York Press, 1985), p. 8.

[32] Ronald V. Clarke, "Situational Crime Prevention—Everybody's Business." Paper presented at the 1995 Australian Crime Prevention Council conference, http://barney.webace.com.au/~austcpc/conf95/clarke.htm (accessed December 2, 2000).

[33] See Derek B. Cornish and Ronald V. Clarke, "Understanding Crime Displacement: An Application of Rational Choice Theory," *Criminology*, Vol. 25, No. 4 (November 1987), p. 933.

[34] Clarke and Cornish, *Crime Control in Britain*, p. 48.

[35] Werner Einstadter and Stuart Henry, *Criminological Theory: An Analysis of Its Underlying Assumptions* (Fort Worth, TX: Harcourt Brace, 1995), p. 70.

[36] For a history of the development of the concept of situational crime prevention, see Clarke, R.V. ed., *Situational Crime Prevention: Successful Case Studies* (2ed) (New York: Harrow and Heston, 1997); Clarke, R.V. and Eck, J., *Become a Problem-Solving Crime Analyst* (London: Jill Dando Institute of Crime Science, University College London, 2003); and Wortley, R., "A Classification of Techniques for Controlling Situational Precipitators of Crime," *Security Journal*, Vol. 14 (2001), pp. 63–82.

[37] Daniel J. Curran and Claire M. Renzetti, *Theories of Crime* (Boston: Allyn & Bacon, 1994), p. 18.

[38] Jack Katz, *Seductions of Crime: Moral and Sensual Attractions in Doing Evil* (New York: Basic Books, 1988), p. 8.

[39] Ibid., p. 3.

[40] Ibid., p. 76.

[41] Ibid., p. 71.

[42] Bill McCarthy, "Not Just 'for the Thrill of It': An Instrumentalist Elaboration of Katz's Explanation of Sneaky Thrill Property Crimes," *Criminology*, Vol. 33, No. 4 (1995), pp. 519–538.

[43] The quotations attributed to Weisburd in this section are from David Weisburd, "Reorienting Crime Prevention Research and Policy: From the Causes of Criminality to the Context of Crime," *NIJ Research Report* (Washington, DC: National Institute of Justice, June 1997).

[44] See P. Brantingham and P. Brantingham, "Situational Crime Prevention in Practice," *Canadian Journal of Criminology* (January 1990), pp. 17–40; and R. V. Clarke, "Situational Crime Prevention: Achievements and Challenges," in M. Tonry and D. Farrington, eds., *Building a Safer Society: Strategic Approaches to Crime Prevention, Crime and Justice: A Review of Research*, Vol. 19 (Chicago: University of Chicago Press, 1995).

[45] Weisburd, "Reorienting Crime Prevention Research and Policy."

[46] See, for example, J. E. Eck and D. Weisburd, eds., *Crime and Place: Crime Prevention Studies*, Vol. 4 (Monsey, NY: Willow Tree Press, 1995).

[47] See L. Sherman, "Hot Spots of Crime and Criminal Careers of Places," in J. E. Eck and D. Weisburd, eds., *Crime and Place: Crime Prevention Studies*, Vol. 4 (Monsey, NY: Willow Tree Press, 1995); and L. Sherman, P. R. Gartin, and M. E. Buerger, "Hot Spots of Predatory Crime: Routine Activities and the Criminology of Place," *Criminology*, Vol. 27, No. 1 (1989), pp. 27–56.

[48] Marcus Felson and Ronald V. Clarke, *Opportunity Makes the Thief: Practical Theory for Crime Prevention* (London: British Home Office, 1998), p. 33

[49] Laura J. Moriarty and James E. Williams, "Examining the Relationship between Routine Activities Theory and Social Disorganization: An Analysis of Property Crime Victimization," *American Journal of Criminal Justice*, Vol. 21, No. 1 (1996), pp. 43–59.

[50] Ibid., p. 43.

[51] Ibid., p. 46.

[52] Exum, "The Application and Robustness of the Rational Choice Perspective in the Study of Angry Intentions to Aggress."

[53] Dolf Zillman, *Hostility and Aggression* (Hillsdale, NJ: Lawrence Erlbaum, 1979), p. 279.

[54] Kenneth D. Tunnell, "Choosing Crime: Close Your Eyes and Take Your Chances," *Justice Quarterly,* Vol. 7 (1990), pp. 673–690.

[55] See R. Barr and K. Pease, "Crime Placement, Displacement and Deflection," in M. Tonry and N. Morris, eds., *Crime and Justice: A Review of Research,* Vol. 12 (Chicago: University of Chicago Press, 1990).

[56] For a good summation of target hardening, see Ronald V. Clarke, *Situational Crime Prevention* (New York: Harrow and Heston, 1992).

[57] For a good summation of studies on displacement, see R. Hesseling, "Displacement: A Review of the Empirical Literature," in R. V. Clarke, ed., *Crime Prevention Studies,* Vol. 3 (Monsey, NY: Willow Tree Press, 1994).

[58] Carol J. Castaneda, "Not All Urging Mercy for Teen Facing Flogging," *USA Today,* April 4, 1994, p. 3A.

[59] The number of lashes Fay received was reduced to four, and he spent an additional month imprisoned in Singapore before being released and returning to the United States.

[60] C. S. Lewis, "The Humanitarian Theory of Punishment," *Res Judicatae,* Vol. 6 (1953), pp. 224–225.

[61] Tracey L. Snell, *Capital Punishment, 1999* (Washington, DC: Bureau of Justice Statistics, 2000), p. 12.

[62] See, for example, W. C. Bailey, "Deterrence and the Death Penalty for Murders in Utah: A Time Series Analysis," *Journal of Contemporary Law,* Vol. 5, No. 1 (1978), pp. 1–20; and William Bailey, "An Analysis of the Deterrent Effects of the Death Penalty for Murder in California," *Southern California Law Review,* Vol. 52, No. 3 (1979), pp. 743–764.

[63] See, for example, B. E. Forst, "The Deterrent Effect of Capital Punishment: A Cross-State Analysis of the 1960s," *Minnesota Law Review,* Vol. 61 (1977), pp. 743–764.

[64] Scott H. Decker and Carol W. Kohfeld, "Capital Punishment and Executions in the Lone Star State: A Deterrence Study," *Criminal Justice Research Bulletin* (Criminal Justice Center, Sam Houston State University), Vol. 3, No. 12 (1988).

[65] Snell, *Capital Punishment, 1999.*

[66] From the Death Penalty Information Center's site on the World Wide Web: http://www.deathpenaltyinfo.org (accessed December 15, 2007).

[67] *Racial Disparities in Federal Death Penalty Prosecutions 1988–1994:* Staff Report by the Subcommittee on Civil and Constitutional Rights, Committee on the Judiciary, 103rd Congress, Second Session; prepared with the assistance of the Death Penalty Information Center, March 1994.

[68] As some of the evidence presented before the Supreme Court in *Furman* v. *Georgia,* 408 U.S. 238 (1972), suggested.

[69] *McCleskey* v. *Kemp,* 481 U.S. 279 (1987).

[70] Formerly known as the National Committee to Prevent Wrongful Executions.

[71] The Constitution Project, *Mandatory Justice: Eighteen Reforms to the Death Penalty* (Washington, DC: The Constitution Project, 2001).

[72] Edward Connors, Thomas Lundregan, Neal Miller, and Tom McEwen, *Convicted by Juries, Exonerated by Science: Case Studies in the Use of DNA Evidence to Establish Innocence after Trial* (Washington, DC: National Institute of Justice, 1996).

[73] Texas Defender Service, *A State of Denial: Texas Justice and the Death Penalty* (Houston, TX: TDS, 2000), www.texasdefender.org/study (accessed January 5, 2005).

[74] U.S. Department of Justice, *The Federal Death Penalty System: A Statistical Survey—1988–2000* (Washington, DC: U.S. Department of Justice, 2000).

[75] James S. Liebman, Jeffrey Fagan, and Valerie West, "A Broken System: Error Rates in Capital Cases, 1973–1995," Columbia Law School, 2000, http://www.law.columbia.edu/instructionalservices/liebman (accessed September 10, 2007).

[76] *"Released"* in this context means exonerated or determined to be innocent. The definition of *innocence* used by the Death Penalty Information Center in placing defendants on the list is that they had been convicted and sentenced to death and that subsequently either (a) their conviction was overturned and they were acquitted at a retrial or all charges were dropped or (b) they were given an absolute pardon by the governor of the relevant state based on new evidence of innocence.

[77] Jeffrey L. Kirchmeier, "Another Place beyond Here: The Death Penalty Moratorium Movement in the United States," *University of Colorado Law Review,* Vol. 70, No. 1 (2002), pp. 1–116.

[78] Governor's Commission on Capital Punishment, *Report of the Governor's Commission on Capital Punishment* (April 2002), from which material in this paragraph is taken, http://www.idoc.state.il/us.ccp.ccp/reports/commission_report (accessed January 21, 2007).

[79] Governor's Press Office, State of Maryland, "Governor Glendening Issues a Stay of Execution in the Case of Wesley Eugene Baker," May 9, 2002, http://www.gov.state.md.us/gov/press/2002/may/html/baker.html (accessed January 30, 2005).

[80] *Gregg* v. *Georgia,* 428 U.S. 153 (1976).

[81] "Massachusetts Panel Offers Limited Death Penalty Plan," *Criminal Justice Newsletter,* May 17, 2004, p. 1.

[82] "New Jersey Suspends Death Penalty Pending a Task Force Review," *Criminal Justice Newsletter,* January 17, 2006, p. 8.

[83] Title IV of the Justice for All Act of 2004.

[84] At the time the legislation was enacted, Congress estimated that 300,000 rape kits remained unanalyzed in police department evidence lockers across the country.

[85] The act also provides funding for the DNA Sexual Assault Justice Act (Title III of the Justice for All Act of 2004), and the Rape Kits and DNA Evidence Backlog Elimination Act of 2000 (42 U.S.C. 14135), authorizing more than $500 million for programs to improve the capacity of crime labs to conduct DNA analysis, reduce non-DNA backlogs, train evidence examiners, support sexual assault forensic examiner programs, and promote the use of DNA to identify missing persons.

[86] In those states that accept federal monies under the legislation.

[87] The Clark County (Indiana) Prosecutor's Office, "Roger Keith Coleman," http://www.clarkprosecutor.org/html/death/US/coleman175.htm (accessed May 20, 2007).

[88] Sherman, "Reason for Emotion."

[89] Ibid., p. 8.

[90] Marvin Wolfgang, Thorsten Sellin, and Robert Figlio, *Delinquency in a Birth Cohort* (Chicago: University of Chicago Press, 1972).

[91] Sherman, "Reason for Emotion," p. 7.

[92] Randy Martin, Robert J. Mutchnick, and W. Timothy Austin, *Criminological Thought: Pioneers Past and Present* (New York: Macmillan, 1990), p. 17.

[93] Ibid., p. 18.

Biological Roots of Criminal Behavior

Outline

Biological explanations shaped criminology at its inception, and today they are reemerging with fresh vigor and increased potential.

—Nicole Rafter[1]

The evidence is very firm that there is a genetic factor involved in crime.

—Sarnoff A. Mednick[2]

At one time, the influence of biological factors on crime was a taboo subject for criminologists . . . it was assumed that

crime was caused by nonbiological factors: society, culture, subcultures, families, schools, peers, and so on. Happily, things have changed. Leading criminologists now believe that a comprehensive theory of crime must include biological factors as well as the usual suspects.

—David C. Rowe[3]

Investigators of the link between biology and crime find themselves caught in one of the most bitter controversies to hit the scientific community in years.

—*Time*[4]

Learning Outcomes

After reading this chapter, you should be able to

- Identify the fundamental assumptions made by biological theories of crime causation
- Explain the relationship between human aggression and biological determinants
- Describe the research linking genetics and crime

- Explain the contribution of sociobiology to the study of criminality
- List some of the constitutional factors cited in this chapter as contributing to criminality
- Identify modern-day social policies that reflect the biological approach to crime causation
- Assess the shortcomings of biological theories of criminal behavior

Hear the author discuss this chapter at **crimtoday.com**

Introduction

At a recent annual meeting of the American Neurological Association, Russell Swerdlow and Jeffrey Burns, neuroscience researchers at the University of Virginia Medical School, reported on the case of a man with no history of pedophilia who began molesting children after developing an egg-sized brain tumor.[5] According to Swerdlow and Burns, friends of the man told investigators that the 40-year-old married teacher had never previously exhibited abnormal impulses but suddenly started visiting prostitutes, making sexual advances toward children, and spending time on Web sites selling child pornography. Soon, they reported, his wife left him and he was arrested and convicted on child molestation charges. Although he entered a treatment program for pedophiles, he propositioned women at the facility and was expelled from treatment. About the same time, he began having headaches and went to a hospital emergency room where he reported experiencing strong sexual urges and said that he feared he would rape his landlady. Attending neurologists noticed other symptoms indicative of neurological problems, such as poor balance and the inability to copy simple drawings. An MRI scan conducted at the hospital showed that the man had a large tumor in the right frontal cortex of his brain. The tumor was removed and the man's abnormal urges disappeared. Later, however, they reoccurred, and another scan showed that the tumor had returned. Once again it was removed, and the man's behavior returned to normal.

Swerdlow and Burns reported that the tumor was located in the part of the brain associated with social judgments and self-control, and they speculated that it was the cause of the man's pedophiliac urges. "We're dealing with the neurology of morality here," said Swerdlow. The case was reminiscent of the 1966 University of Texas bell tower sniper shootings, which left 14 students dead and many others injured. An autopsy conducted on Charles Whitman, the shooter, after he had been killed by police officers who stormed the tower, revealed that he had a tumor in the amygdale—a portion of the brain involved with controlling emotions.[6]

Can a brain tumor cause crime? Many biological theories have been advanced to explain criminality. Abnormalities of the brain,[7] brain damage,[8] head trauma,[9] genetic predispositions, vitamin deficiencies, an excess of hormones like testosterone, hypoglycemia (low blood sugar), fetal alcohol syndrome (FAS),[10] a relative lack of neurotransmitters like serotonin in the brain, and blood abnormalities are among the many biological explanations of crime available today.

The field of criminology has been slow to give credence to biological theories of deviant behavior. One reason for this, as noted in Chapter 1, is that contemporary criminology's academic roots are firmly grounded in the social sciences. As well-known biocriminologist **C. Ray Jeffery,** commenting on the historical development of the field, observes, "The term *criminology* was given to a social science approach to crime as developed in sociology. . . . Sutherland's (1924) text *Criminology* was pure sociology without any biology or psychology; beginning with publication of that text, criminology was offered in sociology departments as a part of sociology separate from biology, psychology, psychiatry and law. . . . Many of the academicians who call themselves criminologists are sociologists."[11]

The cancellation of a previously scheduled 1992 National Institutes of Health–sponsored conference focusing on biology and crime made clear the strong bias against biological explanations for crime that then existed. The conference was canceled after critics charged that the meeting would, by virtue of its biological focus, be racist and might intentionally exclude sociological perspectives on the subject.[12] Dr. Peter Breggin, director of the Center for the Study of Psychiatry in Bethesda, Maryland, and leader of the opposition to the conference, argued that "the primary problems that afflict human beings are not due to their bodies or brains, they are due to the environment. Redefining social problems as public health problems is exactly what was done in Nazi Germany."[13] Three years later, when the conference was finally held at a site selected to discourage demonstrations, C. Ray Jeffery pointed out that "when ideology replaces rational thought there is little hope for a better understanding of human problems."[14]

A mother reads to her child. Are the choices that people make determined more by their biology or by what they have learned? This question forms the essence of the "nature versus nurture" controversy.

Source: J. Carini, The Image Works

Critics of biological investigation into the root causes of crime fail to recognize that the advance of science has never been impeded by objective consideration of alternative points of view. Most researchers today would argue that narrow-minded criticism, made before all the facts are in, does little to advance human understanding. Open inquiry, as C. Ray Joffery notes, requires objective consideration of all points of view and an unbiased examination of each for its ability to shed light on the subject under study.

Society shies away from biological explanations for criminality and disordered behavior because of phrases like "genetic determinism," which have come to be synonymous with inevitability. Hence, people tend to believe that "biological" equals "hopeless"[15]—since the physical makeup of a person is hard to change. Yet, as this chapter will show, genes may be more facilitators than determinants of behavior. Moreover, biologically based interventions may be some of the easiest to implement, and new possibilities in the treatment arena are emerging daily.

Major Principles of Biological Theories

This brief section summarizes the central features of most **biological theories** of crime causation. Each of these points can be found elsewhere in this chapter, where it is discussed in more detail. This cursory overview, however, is intended to provide more than a summary; it is meant to be a guide to the rest of this chapter.

Biological theories of crime causation make certain fundamental assumptions:

- The brain is the organ of the mind and the locus of personality. In the words of C. Ray Jeffery, "The brain is the organ of behavior; no theory of behavior can ignore neurology and neurochemistry."[16]

- The basic determinants of human behavior, including criminal tendencies, are, to a considerable degree, constitutionally or genetically based.

biological theory

A theory that maintains that the basic determinants of human behavior, including criminality, are constitutionally or physiologically based and often inherited.

- Observed gender and racial differences in rates and types of criminality may be at least partially the result of biological differences between the sexes and between racially distinct groups.

- The basic determinants of human behavior, including criminality, may be passed on from generation to generation. In other words, a penchant for crime may be inherited.

- Much of human conduct is fundamentally rooted in instinctive behavioral responses characteristic of biological organisms everywhere. Territoriality, condemnation of adultery, and acquisitiveness are but three examples of behavior that may be instinctual to human beings.

- The biological roots of human conduct have become increasingly disguised, as modern symbolic forms of indirect expressive behavior have replaced more primitive and direct ones.

- At least some human behavior is the result of biological propensities inherited from more primitive developmental stages in the evolutionary process. In other words, some human beings may be further along the evolutionary ladder than others, and their behavior may reflect that fact.

- The interplay among heredity, biology, and the social environment provides the nexus for any realistic consideration of crime causation.

Biological Roots of Human Aggression

In 1966, **Konrad Lorenz** published his now-famous work *On Aggression*.[17] It was an English-language translation of a 1963 book entitled *Das Sogenannte Bose: Zur Naturgeschichte der Aggression (The Nature of Aggression)*, which had originally

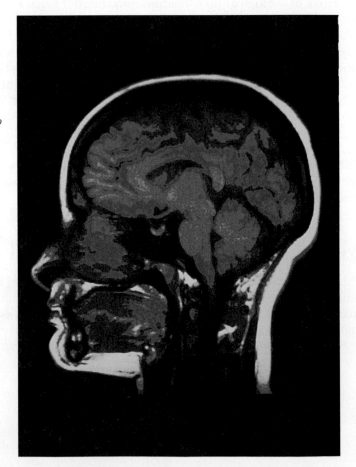

The brain is indeed "the organ of the mind," as early criminologists claimed. Here a computer-enhanced image shows areas of activity within the brain. Do you think biology may play a significant role in crime?

Source: Scott Camazsine, Photo Researchers, Inc.

Charles Darwin (1809–1882), founder of modern evolutionary theory. How might evolutionary theory relate to criminality?

Source: Julia Cameron, Corbis, Bettmann

appeared in German. In his writing, Lorenz described how aggression permeates the animal kingdom and asked, "What is the value of all this fighting?" He wrote, "In nature, fighting is such an ever-present process, its behavior mechanisms and weapons are so highly developed and have so obviously arisen under the . . . pressure of a species-preserving function, that it is our duty to ask this . . . question."[18]

Lorenz accepted the evolutionary thesis of nineteenth-century biologist **Charles Darwin** that intraspecies aggression favored the strongest and best animals in the reproductive process, but he concluded that aggression serves a variety of other purposes as well. Aggression, said Lorenz, ensures an "even distribution of animals of a particular species over an inhabitable area"[19] and provides for a defense of the species from predators. Human aggression, he claimed, meets many of the same purposes but can take on covert forms. Lorenz described the drive to acquire wealth and power, which was so characteristic of Western men at the time of his writing, as part of the human mating ritual whereby a man might "win" a prized woman through displays of more civilized forms of what could otherwise be understood as intraspecies aggression.

Lorenz's greatest contribution to the study of human behavior may have been his claim that all human behavior is, at least to some degree, "adapted instinctive behavior." In other words, much of human conduct, according to Lorenz, is fundamentally rooted in instinctive behavioral responses characteristic of biological organisms everywhere and present within each of us in the form of a biological inheritance from more primitive times. Even rational human thought, claimed Lorenz, derives its motivation and direction from instinctual aspects of human biology. The highest human virtues, such as the value placed on human life, "could not have been achieved," said Lorenz, "without an instinctive appreciation of life and death."[20]

Building upon the root functions of aggression, Lorenz concluded that much of what we today call "crime" is the result of overcrowded living conditions, such as those experienced by city dwellers, combined with a lack of legitimate opportunity for the effective expression of aggression. Crowding, from this perspective, increases the likelihood of aggression, while contemporary socialization simultaneously works to inhibit it. In the words of Lorenz, "In one sense we are all psychopaths, for each of us suffers from the necessity of self-imposed control for the good of the community."[21] When people break down, said Lorenz, they become neurotic or delinquent, and crime may be the result of stresses that have been found to typically produce aggression throughout the animal kingdom.

At first blush, Lorenz's explanations, like many of the biologically based theories we will encounter in this chapter, appear to be more applicable to violent crime than to other forms of criminal offense. However, it is important to recognize that modern frustrations and concomitant manifestations of aggression may be symbolically, rather than directly, expressed. Hence, a stockbroker who embezzles a client's money, spurred on by the need to provide material goods for an overly acquisitive family, may be just as criminal as a robber who beats his victim and steals her purse to have money to buy liquor.

Early Biological Theories

criminal anthropology

The scientific study of the relationship between human physical characteristics and criminality.

Numerous perspectives on criminal biology predate Lorenz's work. Some of the perspectives fall into the category of criminal anthropology. **Criminal anthropology** is the scientific study of the relationship between human physical characteristics and criminality. Criminal anthropology probably derives from earlier subjective feelings, prominent for millennia, that unattractiveness, deformity, and disfigurement are somehow associated with evil, spiritual malaise, and general uncleanliness. Physiognomy, or the "science" of reading personality characteristics from facial features, can be traced to ancient Greece. Greek culture espoused the notion that the mind and body were closely interconnected—a belief that implied that a twisted mind would reside in a deformed body. "Aristotle confirmed this view in his *Metaphysics* when he reasoned that the essence of the body is contained in the soul."[22]

phrenology

The study of the shape of the head to determine anatomical correlates of human behavior.

One of the earliest criminological anthropologists was **Franz Joseph Gall** (1758–1828). Gall hypothesized, in his theory of **phrenology** (also called "craniology"), that the shape of the human skull was indicative of the personality and could be used to predict criminality. Gall's approach contained four themes:

- The brain is the organ of the mind.
- Particular aspects of personality are associated with specific locations in the brain.
- Portions of the brain that are well developed will cause personality characteristics associated with them to be more prominent in the individual under study, whereas poorly developed brain areas lead to a lack of associated personality characteristics.
- The shape of a person's skull corresponds to the shape of the underlying brain and is therefore indicative of the personality.

Gall was one of the first Western writers to firmly locate the roots of personality in the brain. Prior to his time, it was thought that aspects of personality resided in various organs throughout the body—a fact reflected in linguistic anachronisms, which survive into the present day (as, for example, when someone is described as "hard-hearted" or as having "a lot of gall" or as thinking with some organ other than the brain). Greek philosopher Aristotle was said to believe that the brain served no function other than to radiate excess heat from the body. Hence, Gall's perspective, although relatively primitive by today's standards, did much to advance physiological understandings of the mind-body connection in Western thought.

Although Gall never tested his theory, it was widely accepted by many of his contemporaries because it represented something of a shift away from the theological perspectives prevalent at the time and a move toward scientific understanding—a trend that was well under way by the time of his writings. Phrenology also provided for systematic

Theory in Perspective

Types of Biological Theories

Biological Theories

adhere to the principle that the basic determinants of human behavior, including criminality, are constitutionally or physiologically based and inherited.

- *Early Positivism.* These biological approaches, built upon evolutionary principles, were the first to apply scientific techniques to the study of crime and criminals. Early positivistic theories saw criminals as throwbacks to earlier evolutionary epochs.

  Period: 1880s–1930

  Theorists: Franz Joseph Gall, Johann Gaspar Spurzheim, Cesare Lombroso, Charles Buckman Goring, Earnest A. Hooton

  Concepts: Phrenology, atavism, born criminals, criminaloids

- *Constitutional Theories.* These biological theories explain criminality by reference to offenders' body types, inheritance, genetics, or external observable physical characteristics.

  Period: Modern constitutional theories, 1960s–present; classical constitutional theories, 1930s–1940s

  Theorists: Ernst Kretschmer, William H. Sheldon, Richard Louis Dugdale, Arthur H. Estabrook, Henry Herbert Goddard

  Concepts: Somatotyping, mesomorph, ectomorph, endomorph, XYY supermale, twin studies, behavioral genetics, heritability

- *Body Chemistry.* These biological theories utilize chemical influences, including hormones, food additives, allergies, vitamins, and other chemical substances, to explain criminal behavior. The impact of weather is included.

  Period: 1940s–present

  Theorists: Various, including Ellen G. Cohn and James Rotton

  Concepts: Weather and crime, hypoglycemia, vitamins, food allergies, seratonin, PMS, MAOA

- *Sociobiology.* This theoretical perspective developed by Edward O. Wilson includes "the systematic study of the biological basis of all social behavior," which is "a branch of evolutionary biology and particularly of modern population biology."

  Period: 1975–present

  Theorist: Edward O. Wilson

  Concepts: Altruism, tribalism, survival of the gene pool

WEB Extra

evaluation of suspected offenders and was intriguing for its ease of use. One of Gall's students, **Johann Gaspar Spurzheim** (1776–1853), brought phrenological theory to America and, through a series of lectures and publications on the subject, helped to spread its influence. Phrenology's prestige in America extended into the twentieth century, finding a place in classification schemes used to evaluate newly admitted prisoners. Even Arthur Conan Doyle's fictional character Sherlock Holmes was described as using phrenology to solve a number of crimes. It is still popular today among palm readers and fortune-tellers, some of whom offer phrenological "readings"—although a few states have outlawed such activities. Learn more about phrenology at **Web Extra 5–1**.

The Positivist School

One of the best-known, early scientific biological theorists—nineteenth-century Italian army prison physician **Cesare Lombroso** (1836–1909)—coined the term **atavism** to suggest that criminality was the result of primitive urges that, in modern-day human throwbacks, survived the evolutionary process. He described "the nature of the criminal" as "an atavistic being who reproduces in his person the ferocious instincts of primitive humanity and the inferior animals."[23]

At about this time, Charles Darwin was making a substantial impact on the scientific world with his theory of biological evolution. Darwin proposed that human beings and other contemporary living organisms were the end products of a long evolutionary process governed by such rules as natural selection and survival of the fittest. Lombroso adapted elements of Darwin's theory to suggest that primitive traits survived in present-day human populations and led to heightened criminal tendencies among individuals who harbored them. Darwin himself had proposed this idea when he wrote, "With mankind some of the worst dispositions which occasionally without any assignable

atavism

A term used by Cesare Lombroso to suggest that criminals are physiological throwbacks to earlier stages of human evolution.

cause make their appearance in families, may perhaps be reversions to a savage state, from which we are not removed by very many generations."[24]

The atavistic individual, said Lombroso in his now-classic work *L'Uomo delinquente* (1876), was essentially a throwback to a more primitive biological state. According to Lombroso, such an individual, by virtue of possessing a relatively undeveloped brain, is incapable of conforming his or her behavior to the rules and expectations of modern complex society. Lombroso has been called the father of modern criminology because he was the first criminologist of note to employ the scientific method—particularly measurement, observation, and attempts at generalization—in his work. Other writers have referred to him as the "father of the Italian School" of criminology in recognition of the fact that nineteenth-century positivism began in Italy.

Positivism, as mentioned in Chapter 4, built upon two principles: (1) an unflagging acceptance of social determinism, or the belief that human behavior is determined not by the exercise of free choice but by causative factors beyond the control of the individual, and (2) application of scientific techniques to the study of crime and criminology. The term *positivism* had its roots in the writings of Auguste Comte (1798–1857), who proposed use of the scientific method in the study of society in his 1851 work *A System of Positive Polity*.[25] Comte believed that a new "positive age" was dawning during which both society and human nature would be perfected, and his writings were an attempt to bring that age to fruition. Positivism holds that social phenomena are observable, explainable, and measurable in quantitative terms. For a strict positivist, reality consists of a world of objectively defined facts, which can be scientifically measured and—ultimately—controlled.[26]

Lombroso's scientific work consisted of postmortem studies of the bodies of executed offenders and deceased criminals, measuring the bodies in many different ways. The body of one such well-known criminal, named Vilella, provided Lombroso with many of his findings and reinforced his belief that most offenders were biologically predisposed toward criminality. When he examined Vilella's brain, Lombroso found an unusual depression, which he named "the median occipital fossa." Lombroso identified features of Vilella's brain as being similar to those found in lower primates. Study of another offender, an Italian soldier whom Lombroso calls "Misdea" in his writings[27] and who "attacked and killed eight of his superior officers and comrades," supported his conclusions.

In addition to his examination of Vilella, Lombroso conducted autopsies on another 65 executed offenders and examined 832 living prison inmates, comparing physical measurements of their body parts with measurements taken from 390 soldiers. As a result of his work, Lombroso claimed to have found a wide variety of bodily features predictive of criminal behavior. Among them were exceptionally long arms, an index finger as long as the middle finger, fleshy pouches in the cheeks "like those in rodents," eyes that were either abnormally close together or too far apart, large teeth, ears that lacked lobes, prominent cheekbones, a crooked nose, a large amount of body hair, a protruding chin, large lips, a nonstandard number of ribs, and eyes of differing colors or hues. Lombroso went so far as to enumerate characteristics of particular types of offenders. Murderers, whom he called "habitual homicides," have, in Lombroso's words, "cold, glassy eyes, immobile and sometimes sanguine and inflamed; the nose, always large, is frequently aquiline or, rather, hooked; the jaws are strong, the cheekbones large, the hair curly, dark, and abundant; the beard is frequently thin, the canine teeth well developed and the lips delicate."[28]

Atavism implies the notion that criminals are born that way. Lombroso was continuously reassessing his estimates of the proportion, from among all offenders, of the born criminal population. At one point, he asserted that fully 90% of offenders committed crimes because of atavistic influences. He later revised the figure downward to 70%, admitting that normal individuals might be pulled into lives of crime. In addition to the category of the born criminal, Lombroso described other categories of offenders, including the insane, "criminaloids," and criminals incited by passion. The insane were said to include mental and moral degenerates, alcoholics, drug addicts, and so forth. **Criminaloids,** also called "occasional criminals," were described as people who were pulled into breaking the law by virtue of environmental influences. Nevertheless, most criminaloids were seen by Lombroso as exhibiting some degree of atavism and hence

criminaloids

A term used by Cesare Lombroso to describe occasional criminals who were pulled into criminality primarily by environmental influences.

Theory versus Reality

Positivism: The Historical Statement

In 1901, Enrico Ferri, one of the fathers of positivist criminology, was invited to deliver a series of lectures at the University of Naples. Ferri used the occasion to admonish classical criminologists and to advance the principles of positivism. This box contains excerpts from those lectures.

Let us speak of this new science, which has become known in Italy by the name of the Positive School of Criminology. . . . The 19th century has won a great victory over mortality and infectious diseases by means of the masterful progress of physiology and natural science. But while contagious diseases have gradually diminished, we see on the other hand that moral diseases are growing more numerous. . . . While typhoid fever, smallpox, cholera and diphtheria retreated before the remedies which enlightened science applied by means of the experimental method, removing their concrete causes, we see on the other hand that insanity, suicide and crime, that painful trinity, are growing apace. And this makes it very evident that the science which is principally, if not exclusively, engaged in studying these phenomena of social disease, should feel the necessity of finding a more exact diagnosis of these moral diseases of society, in order to arrive at some effective and more humane remedy. . . .

The science of positive criminology arose in the last quarter of the 19th century. . . . [T]he positive school of criminology arises out of the very nature of things, the same as every other line of science. It is based on the conditions of our daily life. . . .

The general opinion of classic criminalists and of the people at large is that crime involves a moral guilt, because it is due to the free will of the individual who leaves the path of virtue and chooses the path of crime, and therefore it must be suppressed by meeting it with a proportionate quantity of punishment. . . .

And the illusion of a free human will (the only miraculous factor in the eternal ocean of cause and effect) leads to the assumption that one can choose freely between virtue and vice. How can you still believe in the existence of a free will, when modern psychology armed with all the instruments of positive modern research, denies that there is any free will and demonstrates that every act of a human being is the result of an interaction between the personality and the environment of man?

And how is it possible to cling to that obsolete idea of moral guilt, according to which every individual is supposed to have the free choice to abandon virtue and give himself up to crime? The positive school of criminology maintains, on the contrary, that it is not the criminal who wills; in order to be a criminal it is rather necessary that the individual should find himself permanently or transitorily in such personal, physical and moral conditions, and live in such an environment which become for him a chain of cause and effect, externally and internally, that disposes him toward crime. This is our conclusion . . . and it constitutes that vastly different and opposite method, which the positive school of criminology employs as compared to the leading principle of the classic school of criminal science.

Discussion Questions

1. Why does Ferri link control over contagious diseases with the study of crime?

2. If Ferri was asked to define "positive criminology," what kind of definition do you think he would offer?

3. How are notions of moral guilt and free will associated in Ferri's line of thought?

Source: Ernest Unterman, trans., *The Positive School of Criminology: Three Lectures Given at the University of Naples, Italy,* on April 22, 23, and 24, 1901, by Enrico Ferri (Chicago: Charles H. Kerr, 1912).

were said to "differ from **born criminals** in degree, not in kind." Those who became criminals by virtue of passion were said to have surrendered to intense emotions, including love, jealousy, hatred, or an injured sense of honor.

Although he focused on physical features, Lombroso was not insensitive to behavioral indicators of criminality. In his later writings, he claimed that criminals exhibited acute sight, hearing abilities that were below the norm, an insensitivity to pain, a lack of moral sensibility, cruelty, vindictiveness, impulsiveness, a love of gambling, and a tendency to be tattooed.

In 1893, Lombroso published *The Female Offender.*[29] In that book, he expressed his belief that women exhibited far less anatomical variation than do men, but he insisted that criminal behavior among women, as among men, derived from atavistic foundations. Violence among women, although a rarity in the official statistics of the late 1000s, was explained by the **masculinity hypothesis,** or the belief that criminal women exhibited masculine features and mannerisms. Lombroso saw the quintessential female offender, however, as a prostitute. The prostitute, said Lombroso, is "the genuine typical representative of criminality" among women.[30] Prostitutes, he claimed, act out

born criminal

An individual who is born with a genetic predilection toward criminality.

masculinity hypothesis

The belief that, over time, men and women will commit crimes that are increasingly similar in nature, seriousness, and frequency. Increasing similarity in crime commission was predicted to result from changes in the social status of women.

Thirty-seven-year-old Joseph Smith, left, arrested in the 2004 Florida disappearance of 11-year-old Carlie Brucia, whose makeshift memorial is shown at right. Smith had been arrested at least 13 times in Florida since 1993 and was caught on camera leading the girl away prior to the discovery of her body. In statements reminiscent of early phrenological theories, some commentators suggested that Smith's facial features made him look like a throwback to primitive man. Would you agree? If so, does Smith's case lend any credibility to early biological theories of criminality?

Source: Steve Nesius/AP Wide World Photos

WEB
Extra

atavistic yearnings and, in doing so, return to a form of behavior characteristic of humankind's primitive past. Learn more about Lombroso and the theory of atavism via **Web Extra 5–2**.

Evaluations of Atavism

Following in Lombroso's positivistic footsteps around the turn of the twentieth century, English physician **Charles Buckman Goring** (1870–1919) conducted a well-controlled statistical study of Lombroso's thesis of atavism. Using newly developed but advanced mathematical techniques to measure the degree of correlation between physiological features and criminal history, Goring examined nearly 3,000 inmates at Turin prison beginning in 1901. Enlisting the aid of London's Biometric Laboratory, he concluded that "the whole fabric of Lombrosian doctrine, judged by the standards of science, is fundamentally unsound."[31] Goring compared the prisoners with students at Oxford and Cambridge Universities, British soldiers, and noncriminal hospital patients and published his findings in 1913 in his lengthy treatise *The English Convict: A Statistical Study.*[32] The foreword to Goring's book was written by Karl Pearson, who praised Goring for having no particular perspective of his own to advance. Goring could, Pearson said, therefore objectively evaluate the ideas of others, such as Lombroso.

A similar study was conducted between 1927 and 1939 by **Earnest A. Hooton,** a professor of anthropology at Harvard University. In 1939, Hooton published *Crime and the Man,*[33] in which he reported having evaluated 13,873 inmates from ten states, comparing them along 107 physiological dimensions with 3,203 nonincarcerated individuals who formed a control group. His sample consisted of 10,953 prison inmates, 2,004 county jail prisoners, 743 criminally insane, 173 "defective delinquents," 1,227 "insane civilians," and 1,976 "sane civilians."

Hooton distinguished among regions of the country, saying that "states have favorite crimes, just as they have favorite sons." He reported finding physiological features characteristic of specific criminal types in individual states. For example, "Massachusetts criminals," he said, "are notable for thick beards, red-brown hair, dark brown, green-brown, and blue-gray eyes, whites of eyes discolored with yellow or brown pigment flecks, rayed pattern of the iris of the eye, external and median folds of the upper eyelids, broad, high nasal roots and bridges, concave nasal profiles, thick nasal tips, right deflections of the nasal septum, thin integumental lips, thin upper membranous lip and thick lower lip, absence of lip seam, some . . . protrusion of the jaws, pointed or median chins, much dental decay but few teeth lost, small and soldered or attached ear lobes, and right facial asymmetries."[34] He went on to say that through a sufficient degree of statistical manipulation, "we finally emerge with differences between the offense groups which are not due to accidents of sampling, are not due to state variations, and are independent of differences between the ages of the offense groups. Thus, in the case of first-degree murder we find the members of that offense group deficient in persons with abundant head hair, deficient in individuals with narrow nasal bridges, presenting an excess of persons with pointed or median chins, and with compressed cheek bones."[35] He also found that first-degree murderers were more "square-shouldered" than other criminals and had larger earlobes. From findings like these, he was drawn to the conclusion that "crime is not an exclusively sociological phenomenon, but is also biological."[36]

In writing "it is impossible to improve and correct environment to a point at which these flawed and degenerate human beings will be able to succeed in honest social competition,"[37] Hooton made it clear that he did not believe that rehabilitation programs could have much effect upon most offenders, and he suggested banishing them to a remote location. Hooton concluded that criminals showed an overall physiological inferiority to the general population and that crime was the result of "the impact of environment upon low grade human organisms."[38] Learn more about the life and work of Earnest Hooton at Web Extra 5–3.

WEB
Extra
■■■■

Hooton, an example of whose work is provided in Figure 5–1, was quickly criticized along a number of dimensions. Stephen Schafer, a well-known contemporary criminologist, says, "The major criticisms were that his criminal population was not a representative sample of all criminals, that his control group was a fantastic conglomeration of noncriminal civilians, . . . that he emphasized selected characteristics and disregarded others, that he gave no convincing evidence that the criminal's 'inferiority' was inherited,

OLD AMERICAN CRIMINALS

Mosaic of Cranial, Facial, Metric and Morphological Features

MASSACHUSETTS

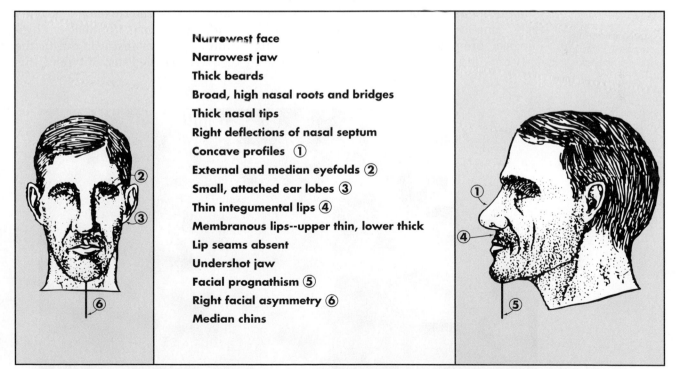

Narrowest face
Narrowest jaw
Thick beards
Broad, high nasal roots and bridges
Thick nasal tips
Right deflections of nasal septum
Concave profiles ①
External and median eyefolds ②
Small, attached ear lobes ③
Thin integumental lips ④
Membranous lips--upper thin, lower thick
Lip seams absent
Undershot jaw
Facial prognathism ⑤
Right facial asymmetry ⑥
Median chins

FIGURE 5–1

Earnest A. Hooton's "Massachusetts Criminal"

Source: Reprinted by permission of the publishers from *Crime and the Man* by Earnest Albert Hooton, Cambridge, MA: Harvard University Press. Copyright © 1939 by the President and Fellows of Harvard College, renewed 1967 by Mary O. Hooton.

and that he failed to explore other important data that were available."[39] Perhaps even more significant, Hooton failed to recognize that members of his noncriminal control group may, in fact, have been involved in crime but had managed to elude capture and processing by the criminal justice system. In other words, it may have been that the most successful criminals did not appear in Hooton's study group of inmates because they had eluded the law, thereby making their way into his supposedly noncriminal control group. His study may have simply demonstrated that "inferior" criminal specimens are the ones who get caught and end up in prison.

Nonetheless, claims that physical abnormalities may be linked to crime persist into the present day. In a study of 170 teenage boys reported in 2000, for example, Canadian researchers L. Arseneault and Richard E. Tremblay conducted hormonal, anthropometric, psychophysiological, neuropsychological, and psychiatric evaluations of 1,037 boys who had attended kindergarten in 1984 in a socially and economically disadvantaged area of Montreal.[40] Using evaluations provided years later by parents, teachers, classmates, and the children themselves, Arseneault and Tremblay concluded that subtle physical abnormalities, including minor abnormalities in the shape of the ears, tongue, and teeth, were associated with an increased risk of behavioral and psychiatric problems. The researchers suggested that such minor physical abnormalities might have resulted from genetic problems or prenatal insults associated with exposure to toxins. They concluded that "both the total count of minor physical anomalies and the total count of minor physical anomalies of the mouth were significantly associated with an increased risk of violent delinquency in adolescence, beyond the effects of childhood physical aggression and family adversity." Arseneault and Tremblay recognized, however, that abnormalities of the type they identified might be associated with neurological deficits and that abnormalities of the mouth could lead to feeding problems in the first months after birth, which might somehow cause problems in development or socialization.

constitutional theory

A theory that explains criminality by reference to offenders' body types, inheritance, genetics, or external observable physical characteristics.

somatotyping

The classification of human beings into types according to body build and other physical characteristics.

Body Types

Constitutional theories are those that explain criminality by reference to offenders' body types, genetics, or external observable physical characteristics. A constitutional, or physiological, orientation that found its way into the criminological mainstream during the early and mid-twentieth century was that of body types. Also called **somatotyping,** this

Endomorphs on the march. A group of would-be actors line up to audition for roles in the movie *Fat Chance.* How might body type relate to criminal activity?
Source: AP Wide World Photos

perspective was primarily associated with the work of **Ernst Kretschmer** and **William H. Sheldon.** Kretschmer, a professor of psychiatry at the German University of Tubingen, proposed a relationship between body build and personality type and created a rather detailed "biopsychological constitutional typology." Kretschmer's somatotypology revolved around three basic mental categories: cycloids (also called "cyclothymes"), schizoids (or "schizothymes"), and displastics. The **cycloid** personality, which was associated with a heavyset, soft type of body, according to Kretschmer, vacillated between normality and abnormality. Cycloids were said to lack spontaneity and sophistication and were thought to commit mostly nonviolent property types of offenses. **Schizoids,** who tended to possess athletic, muscular bodies but, according to Kretschmer, could also be thin and lean, were seen as more likely to be schizophrenic and to commit violent types of offenses. **Displastics** were said to be a mixed group described as highly emotional and often unable to control themselves. Hence, they were thought to commit mostly sexual offenses and other crimes of passion.

Influenced by Kretschmer, William H. Sheldon utilized measurement techniques to connect body type with personality.[41] Sheldon felt that Kretschmer had erred in including too large an age range in his work. Therefore, he chose to limit his study to 200 boys between the ages of 15 and 21 at the Hayden Goodwill Institute in Boston. Sheldon concluded that four basic body types characterized the entire group. These types, described partly in Sheldon's words, are as follows.

- The **endomorph,** who is soft and round and whose "digestive viscera are massive and highly developed" (that is, the person is overweight and has a large stomach)
- The **mesomorph,** who is athletic and muscular and whose "somatic structures . . . are in the ascendancy" (that is, the person has larger bones and considerable muscle mass)
- The **ectomorph,** who is thin and fragile and who has "long, slender, poorly muscled extremities, with delicate, pipestem bones"
- The balanced type, a person of average build, without being overweight, thin, or exceedingly muscular

Individuals were ranked along each of the three major dimensions (the balanced type was excluded), using a 7-point scale. A score of 1–1–7, for example, would indicate that a person exhibited few characteristics of endomorphology or mesomorphology but was predominantly ectomorphic. Sheldon claimed that varying types of temperament and personalities were closely associated with each of the body types he identified. Ectomorphs were said to be "cerebrotonic," or restrained, shy, and inhibited. Endomorphs were "viscerotonic," or relaxed and sociable. The mesomorphic, or muscular, body type, however, he said was most likely to be associated with delinquency or "somatotonia," which he described as "a predominance of muscular activity and . . . vigorous bodily assertiveness." Sheldon's work was supported by constitutional studies of juvenile delinquents conducted by Sheldon Glueck and Eleanor Glueck and reported in 1950.[42] The Gluecks compared 500 known delinquents with 500 nondelinquents and matched both groups on age, general intelligence, ethnic-racial background, and place of residence. Like Sheldon, the Gluecks concluded that mesomorphy was associated with delinquency. Learn more about early theories of body types via **Web Extra 5–4.**

Early biological theorists like Sheldon, Lombroso, and Gall provide an interesting footnote in the history of criminological thought. Today, however, their work is mostly relegated to the dustbins of academic theorizing. Modern biological theories of crime are far more sophisticated than their early predecessors, and it is to these that we now turn.

Chemical and Environmental Precursors of Crime

Recent research in the area of nutrition has produced some limited evidence that the old maxim "You are what you eat" may contain more than a grain of truth. Biocriminology has made some significant strides in linking violent or disruptive behavior to

cycloid

A term developed by Ernst Kretschmer to describe a particular relationship between body build and personality type. The cycloid personality, which was associated with a heavyset, soft type of body, was said to vacillate between normality and abnormality.

schizoid

A person characterized by schizoid personality disorder. Such disordered personalities appear to be aloof, withdrawn, unresponsive, humorless, dull, and solitary to an abnormal degree.

displastic

A mixed group of offenders described by constitutional theorist Ernst Kretschmer as highly emotional and often unable to control themselves. They were thought to commit mostly sexual offenses and other crimes of passion.

endomorph

A body type originally described as soft and round or overweight.

mesomorph

A body type described as athletic and muscular.

ectomorph

A body type originally described as thin and fragile, with long, slender, poorly muscled extremities and delicate bones.

WEB
Extra
■ ■ ■ ■

eating habits, vitamin deficiencies, genetic inheritance, and other conditions that affect the body. Studies of nutrition, endocrinology, and environmental contaminants have all contributed to advances in understanding such behavior.

One of the first studies to focus on chemical imbalances in the body as a cause of crime was reported in the British medical journal *Lancet* in 1943.[43] The authors of the study linked murder to **hypoglycemia,** or low blood sugar. Low blood sugar, produced by too much insulin in the blood or by near-starvation diets, was said to reduce the mind's capacity to reason effectively or to judge the long-term consequences of behavior. More recent studies have linked excess consumption of refined white sugar to hyperactivity and aggressiveness. Popular books like *Sugar Blues* provide guides for individuals seeking to free themselves from the negative effects of excess sugar consumption.[44]

To some degree, even courts have accepted the notion that excess sugar consumption may be linked to crime. In the early 1980s, for example, Dan White, a former San Francisco police officer, was given a reduced sentence after his lawyers used what came to be known as the "Twinkie Defense."[45] They argued that White's night-long binge on large numbers of Coca-Colas and Twinkies before he murdered San Francisco Mayor George Moscone and City Councilman Harvey Milk, was evidence of White's unbalanced mental state. The consumption of junk food was presented as evidence of depression since White was normally very-health concious. Some have also suggested that the consumption of large amounts of refined white sugar increases excitability and lowers the ability to make reasoned decisions.

More than ten years later, however, a well-conducted 1994 study reported in the *New England Journal of Medicine* seemed to contradict the notion that sugar may lead to hyperactivity.[46] Similarly, neither sugar nor artificial sweeteners were shown to have any link to an increase in learning disabilities. In the study, researchers at Vanderbilt University and the University of Iowa varied the diets of supposedly sugar-sensitive youngsters from a diet that was high in sugar to a diet that was low in sugar but that contained the artificial sweetener aspartame. A third experimental diet contained very little sugar but had added saccharin. After surveying parents, teachers, and babysitters and testing the study group for changes in memory, concentration, and math skills, the researchers concluded, "We couldn't find any difference in terms of their behavior or their learning on any of the three

hypoglycemia

A medical condition characterized by low blood sugar.

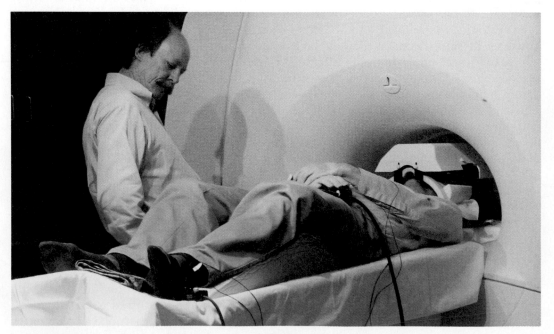

A man undergoes an MRI scan of his brain. Some companies like No Lie MRI, which currently offers testing services in Tarzana, California, have developed guilty knowledge tests using MRI brain scans. Trained operators are said to be able to identify lies by looking for areas of the brain that are known to undergo enhanced activity when subjects are lying. What might such scans tell us about truth or falsehood? What do they say, if anything, about the biological basis of morality?

Source: Mary Ann Chastain/AP Wide World Photos.

diets."[47] Hence, to date, the evidence concerning sugar's impact on behavior is less than clear.

While dietary levels of refined sugar may or may not affect behavior, studies done using positron-emission tomography (PET), in which scans of the prefrontal cortex of subjects' brains were analyzed, show interesting results. PET scans can be used to measure the "uptake" of glucose by the brain. In a study conducted by Adrian Raine in 1994, PET scans of the brains of 22 murderers (including some who had only attempted murder) revealed that the murderers showed much lower levels of glucose uptake in the prefrontal cortex than did the controls.[48] "The differences were not related to age, gender, handedness, ethnicity, motivation, history of head injury, or presence of schizophrenia. In addition, no subjects were taking psychoactive drugs at the time of the test."[49] Raine and his colleagues say that their data strongly suggest that "deficits localized to the prefrontal cortex may be related to violence" in some offenders. Raine also notes that "frontal damage is associated with impulsivity, loss of self-control, immaturity, lack of tact, inability to modify and inhibit behavior appropriately, and poor social judgment." The researchers explain, however, that prefrontal cortex dysfunction must be evaluated in terms of how individuals who exhibit the condition interact with environmental conditions, including social and psychological influences. Because prefrontal cortex dysfunction may result in failure in school, the inability to hold a job, problems in relationships, and so forth, it may not be a direct cause of crime but might, rather, predispose those afflicted with the condition to "a criminal and violent way of life."[50]

Allergic reactions to common foods have been reported as the cause of violence and homicide by a number of investigators.[51] Some foods—including milk, citrus fruit, chocolate, corn, wheat, and eggs—are said to produce allergic reactions in sensitive individuals, leading to a swelling of the brain and the brain stem. Involvement of the central nervous system in such allergies, it has been suggested, reduces the amount of learning that occurs during childhood and may contribute to delinquency as well as to adult criminal behavior. Such swelling is also thought to impede the higher faculties, reducing a person's sense of morality and creating conditions that support impulsive behavior.

Some studies have implicated food additives, such as the flavor enhancer monosodium glutamate, dyes, and artificial flavorings, in producing criminal violence.[52] Other research has found that coffee and sugar may trigger antisocial behavior.[53] Researchers were led to these conclusions through finding that inmates consumed considerably greater amounts of coffee, sugar, and processed foods than others.[54] It is unclear, however, whether inmates drink more coffee because of boredom or whether "excitable" personalities feel a need for the kind of stimulation available through coffee consumption. On the other hand, habitual coffee drinkers in nonprison populations have not been linked to crime, and other studies, like the one conducted by Mortimer Gross of the University of Illinois, show no link between the amount of sugar consumed by inmates and hyperactivity.[55] Nonetheless, some prison programs have been designed to limit intake of dietary stimulants through nutritional management and the substitution of artificial sweeteners for refined sugar. Vitamins have also been examined for their impact on delinquency. At least one researcher found that disruptive children consumed far less than optimal levels of vitamins B3 and B6 than did nonproblem youths.[56] Some researchers have suggested that the addition of these vitamins to the diets of children who are deficient in them could control unruly behavior and improve school performance.

Other nutrients have been studied to assess their possible behavioral impact. In 2003, for example, Ingrid Bergliot Helland reported that maternal diet during pregnancy can strongly affect IQ and early infant behavior and concluded that it might also determine the risk of delinquency and criminality in later life.[57] Helland and her colleagues supplemented the diets of pregnant and lactating women with either omega-3 (DHA) or omega-6 fatty acids and followed the development of their offspring for years after the supplementation program had ended. Helland found that children receiving dietary omega-3 supplementation had significantly higher IQ

Crime in the News

Lead Linked to Delinquent Behavior

Lead long has been known to lower intelligence and cause learning disabilities, but a new study shows the toxic metal also might contribute to juvenile delinquency.

In the study, delinquent children were found to have higher levels of lead in their body than non-delinquent children, Herbert Needleman, principal investigator and professor of child psychiatry and pediatrics at the University of Pittsburgh, told United Press International. The finding suggests children exposed to the metal could be at a higher risk of delinquency, he added.

"One of the most important facets about this work is it really shows that lead's effects on behavior can be even more important than its effect on cognition," Annette Kirshner of the National Institute of Environmental Health Sciences in Research Triangle Park, N.C., told UPI.

Needleman's group found that 200 youths convicted in the Juvenile Court of Allegheny County, Pa., had significantly higher levels of lead in their bones than non-delinquent youths from high schools in the Pittsburgh area. Bone lead levels in the delinquent kids came out to 11.0 parts per million, much higher than the 1.5 ppm in the non-delinquent group.

The study, which appears in the Jan. 6 issue of the journal *Neurotoxicology and Terotology,* agrees with other research begun in the late 1980s. Researchers have been following a group of teenagers since birth and have found "the higher the lead content the more the delinquency there is amongst the children," Kirshner said.

Previous research by Needleman also had suggested higher lead levels were associated with aggressive behavior. A 1996 study found boys with raised lead levels were prone to bullying and vandalism.

"Mothers of lead-poisoned children will tell you that their children's behavior changes after exposure," Needleman said. They become aggressive and inattentive.

"The most important thing that could be done is to remove lead from the environment before it gets in the children," he said. The biggest source of lead is paint in houses. "There are 30 million houses [in the United States] built before 1950 and almost all of them have lead-based paint in them," he said. About 4 million of those houses are deteriorating and those represent a serious danger to children because the paint is chipping, increasing the chance of exposure, he said. Most of those dilapidated houses

are in poor neighborhoods but some are also found in middle class areas.

Kirshner said lead fittings and pipes are another source of exposure and these plumbing components were still in use until the 1990s. In order to address the problem, "society really has to clean up deteriorating properties" and make them lead-safe, she said.

For the nearly 900,000 U.S. children estimated to be suffering from lead exposure, Kirshner said a program of nutritional supplementation and social enrichment could help reverse some of the damage. "It's not impossible but it's very hard to undo the effects of lead once a child is exposed," she said, adding that is why it is important to prevent exposure in the first place.

Discussion Questions

1. What does this article say is the likely link between childhood lead consumption and later criminality?

2. What steps can be taken to reduce childhood exposure to environmental lead? What steps have already been taken?

Leaky water pipes in an older home. Pipes like these sometimes contain lead, which can contaminate the water they carry. What role might childhood lead consumption play in the development of delinquency and antisocial behavior?
Source: AP Wide World Photos

For the latest crime and justice news, visit www.crimenews.info.

Source: Steve Mitchell, "Lead Linked to Delinquent Behavior," United Press International wire service, January 6, 2003, http://www.upi.com/print.cfm? StoryID=20030103−042001−1639r (accessed January 5, 2005).

levels by age four and performed better on problem-solving tests than those receiving omega-6 fatty acids.

A year later, a study of the relationship between omega-3 intake levels and chronic hostility among 3,600 urban young adults concluded that higher consumption of omega-3 fatty acids was related to significantly lower levels of hostility.[58] Researchers concluded that "high dietary intake of DHA and consumption of fish rich in omega-3 fatty acids may be related to lower likelihood of high hostility in young adulthood." Similarly, a 2007 study conducted in the United Kingdom found that antisocial behavior could be reduced in children through dietary supplementation with polyunsaturated fatty acids.[59]

In a study designed to test the hypothesis that dietary supplementation could reduce violence among prison populations, C. Bernard Gesch and colleagues supplemented the diets of 115 English young adult prisoners and compared their behavior with 116 inmates receiving placebos.[60] The experiment lasted 142 days, and supplements included vitamins, minerals, and essential fatty acids. Researchers found a 35.1% reduction in offense rates in the supplement group, with the greatest reduction "for the most serious incidents including violence." The Gesch study supports the findings of Stephen Schoenthaler and his colleagues, who previously found that nutritional supplementation could reduce antisocial acts by incarcerated offenders in California.[61] Schoenthaler reported a 30% decrease in the rate of serious rule violation for persons receiving dietary supplements similar to those used in the Gesch study. Read more about diet and its possible contribution to criminal behavior at Library Extra 5–1 at crimtoday.com.

LIBRARY
Extra
▪ ▪ ▪ ▪

In 1997, British researchers Roger D. Masters, Brian Hone, and Anil Doshi published a study purporting to show that industrial and other forms of environmental pollution cause people to commit violent crimes.[62] The study used statistics from the FBI's Uniform Crime Reporting Program and data from the U.S. Environmental Protection Agency's Toxic Release Inventory. A comparison between the two data sets showed a significant correlation between juvenile crime and high environmental levels of both lead and manganese. Masters and his colleagues suggested an explanation based on a neurotoxicity hypothesis. "According to this approach, toxic pollutants—specifically the toxic metals lead and manganese—cause learning disabilities, an increase in aggressive behavior, and—most importantly—loss of control over impulsive behavior. These traits combine with poverty, social stress, alcohol and drug abuse, individual character, and other social and psychological factors to produce individuals who commit violent crimes."[63]

According to Masters, the presence of excess manganese lowers levels of serotonin and dopamine in the brain. Both of these neurotransmitters are associated with impulse control and planning. Masters notes that low brain levels of serotonin are known to cause mood disturbances, poor impulse control, and increases in aggressive behavior.[64] Masters claims that children who are raised from birth on infant formula and who are not breast-fed will absorb five times as much manganese as breast-fed infants. Calcium deficiency is known to increase the absorption of manganese, and, says Masters, "a combination of manganese toxicity and calcium deficiency adds up to 'reverse' Prozac."[65]

In defense of his thesis, Masters cites other studies, the largest of which was an examination of 1,000 black children in Philadelphia that showed that the level of exposure to lead was a reliable predictor of the number of juvenile offenses among the exposed male population, the seriousness of juvenile offenses, and the number of adult offenses. Recent studies, including many of which Masters was unaware, seem to support his thesis.[66]

According to Masters, toxic metals affect individuals in complex ways. Because lead diminishes a person's normal ability to detoxify poisons, he says, it may heighten the effects of alcohol and drugs. Industrial pollution, automobile traffic, lead-based paints, and aging water-delivery systems are all possible sources of contamination. In a recent interview, Masters said, "The presence of pollution is as big a factor [in crime causation] as poverty. . . . It's the breakdown of the inhibition mechanism that's the key to violent behavior."[67] When brain chemistry is altered by exposure to heavy metals and other toxins, he said, people lose the natural restraint that holds their violent tendencies in check.

In 1999, researchers set out to test the hypothesis that enhancing brain levels of serotonin might reduce aggression and impulsivity in aggressive male criminals.[68] In the volunteer-only study, ten young male offenders were given daily injections of d, l-fenfluramine, a drug that makes serotonin more available to brain cells. Findings showed that "the drug produced a significant, dose-dependent decrease in aggressive responding . . . 2 to 4.5 hours after dosing." Moreover, "all ten subjects decreased their aggressive responding following the highest 0.8 mg/kg dose." Subjects exhibiting the highest rates of aggression showed the greatest decreases in aggression levels after being treated with d,l-fenfluramine. According to researchers, impulsivity similarly decreased.

In addition to chemical substances that are likely to be ingested and that may impact behavior, other environmental features have been linked to the likelihood of aggressive behavior. During the early 1980s, for example, Alexander G. Schauss and his followers were able to show that the use of a specific shade of pink could have a calming effect on people experiencing feelings of anger and agitation.[69] Findings indicated that exposure to pink produced an endocrine change, which caused a tranquilizing effect on the muscles. This involuntary effect, said researchers, was not subject to conscious control. As a result of such studies, jail cells in a number of locales—including Seattle, San Bernardino, San Mateo County (California), Southbridge (Massachusetts), New Orleans, and Charlotte (North Carolina)—were painted pink in hopes that aggressive tendencies among inmates might be reduced. Researchers supported such measures, saying that "the use of pink color in reducing aggression and causing muscular relaxation of inmates is humane and requires no medication or physical force."[70]

More recent studies have focused on prenatal exposure to substances like marijuana, tobacco smoke, and alcohol. In 2000, for example, L. Goldschmidt and colleagues reported the results of a ten-year study that monitored the development of the children of more than 600 low-income women. The study, which began during pregnancy, found that prenatal marijuana use was significantly related to increased hyperactivity, impulsivity, inattention symptoms, increased delinquency, and externalizing problems.[71] The findings remained significant even when researchers controlled for other lifestyle features.

Similarly, in 1998, David Fergusson and colleagues, in a study of 1,022 New Zealand children who had been followed for 18 years, found that "children whose mothers smoked one pack of cigarettes or more per day during their pregnancy had mean rates of conduct disorder symptoms that were twice as high as those found among children born to mothers who did not smoke during their pregnancy."[72] The observed relationship was twice as strong among male teens as among females. Similar relationships between prenatal smoking and aggression and hyperactivity in later life have been reported by Dutch researchers.[73] A similar 2006 meta-analysis by researchers at Washington State University found that smoking by pregnant mothers contributed slightly to their children's subsequent antisocial behavior.[74]

Prenatal alcohol exposure also seems to be linked to delinquency and psychiatric problems later in life. A 1999 study of 32 children by Tresa M. Roebuck and colleagues found that alcohol-exposed children exhibited greater delinquency and less intelligence than a control group of children who had not suffered from alcohol exposure while in the womb. The researchers concluded that their findings, which are consistent with the work of other researchers,[75] showed that "alcohol-exposed children, although less impaired intellectually, are more likely than children with mental retardation to exhibit antisocial behaviors, lack of consideration for the rights and feelings of others, and resistance to limits and requests of authority figures."[76] Learn more about the role of environmental contaminants, fetal alcohol exposure, and other such factors as they contribute to criminality at **Web Extra 5–5.** Read about pollution's possible link to crime, and toxic threats to child development at **Library Extras 5–2** and **5–3** at crimtoday.com.

WEB
Extra
■ ■ ■ ■

LIBRARY
Extra
■ ■ ■ ■

Hormones and Criminality

Hormones have also come under scrutiny as potential behavioral determinants. The male sex hormone **testosterone,** for example, has been linked to aggression. Most studies on the subject have consistently shown a relationship between high blood testosterone levels and increased aggressiveness in men. More focused studies have unveiled a direct relationship between the amount of the chemical present and the degree of violence used by sex offenders,[77] while other researchers have linked steroid abuse among bodybuilders to destructive urges and psychosis.[78] Contemporary investigations demonstrate a link between testosterone levels and aggression in teenagers,[79] while others show that adolescent problem behavior and teenage violence rise in proportion to the amount of testosterone in the blood of young men.[80] In 1987, for example, a Swedish researcher, Dan Olweus, reported that boys aged 15 to 17 showed levels of both verbal and physical aggression that correlated with the level of testosterone present in their blood.[81] Olweus also found that boys with higher levels of testosterone "tended to be habitually more impatient and irritable than boys with lower testosterone levels." He concluded that high levels of the hormone led to increased frustration and habitual impatience and irritability.

In what may be the definitive work to date on the subject, Alan Booth and D. Wayne Osgood conclude that there is a "moderately strong relationship between testosterone and adult deviance," but they suggest that the relationship "is largely mediated by the influence of testosterone on social integration and on prior involvement in juvenile delinquency."[82] In other words, measurably high levels of testosterone in the blood of young men may have some effect on behavior, but that effect is likely to be moderated by the social environment.

Similar conclusions were reached in 1998 by Swedish researchers who evaluated 61 men undergoing forensic psychiatric examinations for blood levels of free testosterone, total testosterone, and sex hormone–binding globulin (SHBG).[83] SHBG is known to determine the level of testosterone concentration in the blood and in body tissue. The Swedish researchers found that blood levels of total testosterone and SHBG were closely related to the extent of antisocial personality, alcoholism, and criminality exhibited by the subjects under study.

A 1997 study by Paul C. Bernhardt found that testosterone might not act alone in promoting aggression.[84] Bernhardt discovered that aggressive behavior in men may be influenced by high testosterone levels combined with low brain levels of the neurotransmitter serotonin. He postulates that testosterone's true role is to produce dominance-seeking behavior, but not necessarily overt aggression. When individuals are frustrated by their inability to achieve dominance, however, says Bernhardt, serotonin then acts to reduce the negative psychological impact of frustration, producing calmer responses. Men whose brains are lacking in serotonin, however, feel the effects of frustration more acutely and therefore tend to respond to frustrating circumstances more aggressively, especially when testosterone levels are high.

A 2007 study by University of Michigan researchers showed a relationship in humans between testosterone and vigilance to facial expressions of anger, which were considered to be signals of an impending dominance challenge. People with higher levels of testosterone were more prone to respond aggressively to displays of anger in others. According to the researchers, higher levels of testosterone "may generally decrease aversion to threatening stimuli, and/or may specifically facilitate approach towards signals of dominance challenge." It is conceivable, they said "that a signal of an impending dominance challenge could be rewarding to individuals that have a history of success in such encounters."[85] The researchers concluded that the "relationship between testosterone and dominance appears to be reciprocal: winners of dominance challenges show increases in [testosterone], and in turn, higher [testosterone] leads to a greater likelihood to aggress and/or to pursue further dominance challenges, in nonhuman animals and potentially also in humans."[86]

A few limited studies have attempted to measure the effects of testosterone on women. Women's bodies manufacture roughly one-tenth the amount of the hormone

testosterone

The primary male sex hormone. Produced in the testes, its function is to control secondary sex characteristics and sexual drive.

secreted by men. Even so, subtle changes in testosterone levels in women have been linked to changes in personality and sexual behavior.[87] One such study showed that relatively high blood levels of testosterone in female inmates were associated with "aggressively dominant behavior" in prison.[88]

Another study whose results were reported in 2003 attempted to measure the impact of high levels of androgens (male hormones, including testosterone) on both males and females.[89] The study examined the "externalizing behavior" of 87 14 year olds, 51 of whom were female and 36 of whom were male. Data on externalizing behavior, including aggression, were previously available from information gathered when the children were 8, 11, and 14 years old. Findings showed that boys with the highest blood plasma levels of androgens exhibited the most persistent aggression, while no association was found in females between aggression and androgen levels.

Fluctuations in the level of female hormones may also bear some relationship to law violation. In 1980, a British court exonerated Christine English of charges that she murdered her live-in lover after English admittedly ran him over with her car after an argument. English's defense rested on the fact that she was suffering from premenstrual syndrome (PMS) at the time of the homicide. An expert witness, Dr. Katharina Dalton, testified at the trial that PMS had caused English to be "irritable, aggressive, . . . and confused, with loss of self-control."[90]

Another case involving PMS was decided in 1991 by a Fairfax, Virginia, judge who dismissed drunk driving and other charges against Dr. Geraldine Richter, an orthopedic surgeon.[91] After being stopped for driving erratically, Richter allegedly kicked and cursed a Virginia state trooper and admitted to having consumed four glasses of wine. A Breathalyzer test showed her blood-alcohol level to be nearly 0.13%—above the 0.10% level Virginia law sets for drunk driving. Charges against Dr. Richter were dismissed after a gynecologist testified on her behalf, saying that the behavior she exhibited was likely to have been due primarily to PMS.

Although evidence linking PMS to violent or criminal behavior is far from clear, some researchers believe that a drop in serotonin levels in the female brain just before menstruation might explain the agitation and irritability sometimes associated with premenstrual syndrome. Serotonin has been called a "behavior-regulating chemical," and animal studies have demonstrated a link between low levels of the neurotransmitter present in the brain and aggressive behavior. For example, monkeys with low serotonin levels in their brains have been found to be more likely to bite, slap, and chase others of their kind. Studies at the National Institute on Alcohol Abuse and Alcoholism have linked low serotonin levels in humans to impulsive crimes. Men convicted of premeditated murder, for example, have been found to have normal serotonin levels, whereas those convicted of crimes of passion had lower levels.[92]

One 1998 study of 781 21-year-old men and women found a clear relationship between elevated *blood* levels of serotonin (which correspond to lower *brain* levels of the chemical) and violence in men.[93] The study controlled for a host of possible intervening factors, including gender, diet, psychiatric medications, illicit drug use, season of the year (during which the blood test was done), plasma levels of tryptophan (the dietary precursor of serotonin), alcohol and tobacco use, psychiatric diagnoses, platelet count, body mass, socioeconomic status, IQ, and history of suicide attempts. The relationship held true when both court records and self-reports of violence were assessed. No relationship between serotonin levels and aggression was seen in female subjects. According to the study's authors, "This is the first study to demonstrate that a possible index of serotonergic function is related to violence in the general population. . . . The epidemiological serotonin effect was not small, [but rather] indicated a moderate effect size in the population."

Similar research by Swedish neuropsychiatrists in 2003 found that a "dysregulation of serotonin" in the brain and central nervous system could lead to increased impulsivity, irresponsibility, aggression, and need for stimulation.[94] The researchers examined the cerebrospinal fluid (CSF) of 28 violent and sexual offenders and noted that an imbalance between levels of serotonin and dopamine was highly associated with psychopathic traits.

Other hormones, such as cortisol and the thyroid hormone T3, have also been implicated in delinquency and poor impulse control. In 2000, for example, Keith

McBurnett reported the results of a study that evaluated 38 boys between the ages of 7 and 12 who had been referred to a clinic for the management of behavioral problems.[95] The children were studied for four years, using various medical and psychological assessment tools. McBurnett and fellow researchers found that the "meanest" boys had the lowest levels of the hormone cortisol in their saliva. According to McBurnett, "Low cortisol levels were associated with persistence and early onset of aggression. . . . Boys with lower cortisol concentrations . . . exhibited triple the number of aggressive symptoms and were named as most aggressive by peers three times as often as boys who had higher cortisol concentrations." Although McBurnett did not explain why low cortisol levels might be linked to aggression, he suggested that "children with persistent conduct disorder may have genes that predispose them to produce certain hormones differently, or their hormone production may have been altered before or soon after birth."

A few years ago, two separate Swedish studies found evidence suggesting that elevated levels of the thyroid hormone T3 were related to alcoholism, psychopathy, and criminality.[96] Blood serum levels of the thyroid hormone FT4 (thyroxine), on the other hand, were negatively related to antisocial behavior. The researchers concluded that the results of their studies "indicate an intimate relationship between T3 and FT4, and abuse and antisocial behavior. . . . They emphasize the importance of further studies on T3 as a biological marker for abuse, social deviance, and repeated violent behavior."[97]

Finally, a few years ago a different kind of link between hormones and crime was identified when Swiss researchers published a study in the prestigous journal *Nature*, identifying what they called a trust hormone.[98] The presence in greater quantities of the hormone, a small protein called oxytocin, appears to make people more trusting, and the researchers showed that trust levels could be manipulated by having men inhale oxytocin. Oxytocin has also been called the "love hormone" because its levels in the brain spike during love making, and in women during breast-feeding. Those commenting on the research suggested that confidence schemes might one day be perpetrated by con men (or women) spraying oxytocin in the air.[99] Learn more about the possible role of hormones in criminality at **Web Extra 5–6.**

WEB
Extra

Wrestler Umaga, top, puts Bobby Lashley on the ropes during their match at Wrestlemania 23 at Ford Field in Detroit, Michigan, on April 1, 2007. The match featured a bet between Donald Trump and WWE Chairman Vince McMahon. Sex hormones, such as testosterone, have been linked to aggressive behavior. Testosterone also enhances secondary sexual characteristics like body hair and muscle mass in males. What kinds of crime might be hormonally influenced?

Source: AP Photo/Carlos Osorio

Crime in the News

Man Accused of Sexually Assaulting Child Undergoes Castration

A former YMCA employee accused of sexually assaulting a boy during a field trip underwent voluntary castration this week.

David Wayne Jones is only the second inmate to undergo the surgery in Texas, which is the only state where it is allowed by the prison system.

Jones, who acknowledged molesting more than 40 boys in the early 1990s, is accused of sexually assaulting a 5-year-old day camper in 1990 during a field trip to White Rock Lake in Dallas. The youth came forward after Jones' 1999 return to prison and prosecutors secured an indictment in 2001.

A trial date is set for June. If convicted, Jones could be sentenced to 99 years in prison. Jones pleaded guilty in 1991 to some felony charges of indecency with a child in exchange for a 15-year prison sentence. He also pleaded guilty at that time to aggravated sexual assault of a child not connected to the East Dallas YMCA.

Judy Johnson, who heads the Texas Department of Criminal Justice's sex-offender treatment program, said Tuesday that Jones has made progress since his 1991 incarceration and now seems ready to leave prison. She said that she thinks castration will help him control his urges and that he will now benefit more from continuing therapy.

But Johnson told *The Dallas Morning News* in Wednesday's edition that research data are lacking and "there is no 100 percent guarantee."

Jones' action came shortly before completion of the prison sentence and return home for further prosecution. He was expected to be jailed until a judge decides whether to grant him bail pending resolution of another sexual abuse charge which, like all previous cases against him, dates to his early 1990s job as a YMCA counselor.

David Wayne Jones, a one-time YMCA leader, was convicted of sexual abuse and later underwent voluntary surgical castration in a bid to lower his prison sentence. Might castration be an effective "treatment" for some sexual offenders?

Source: Texas Department of Criminal Justice

Discussion Questions

1. Should castration be available as a sentencing option to today's judges? Why or why not?

2. Should voluntary castration result in reduced sentences for violent sex offenders? Why or why not?

For the latest crime and justice news, visit www.crimenews.info.

Source: "Man Accused of Sexually Assaulting Child Undergoes Castration," Associated Press wire service, March 3, 2004, http://abclocal.go.com/ktrk/news/state/print_030304_APstate_castration.html (accessed January 13, 2006). Used with permission of The Associated Press Copyright © 2007. All rights reserved.

Weather and Crime

Weather may also have an influence on human behavior. Research on crime and meteorological variables has looked at everything from sunshine and humidity to wind speed, barometric pressure, and rainfall. After reviewing both published and unpublished research in this area, Ellen G. Cohn and James Rotton of Florida International University concluded that temperature is the only weather variable that is consistently and reliably related to criminal behavior (see Figure 5–2).[100] In general, field research has found a definite positive correlation between temperature and violent crime. As one might expect, more violent crime is reported to the police on warm days than on cold days. However, the relationship between temperature and criminal behavior is more complex than it first appears. Cohn and Rotton's research incorporates not only temperature but also a variety

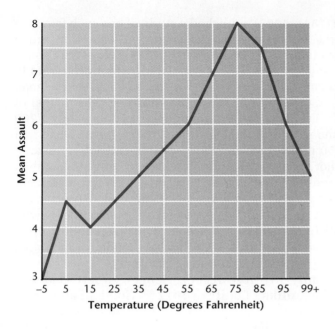

FIGURE 5–2

Assault as a Function of Temperature

Source: E. G. Cohn and J. Rotton, "Assault as a Function of Time and Temperature: A Moderator-Variable Time-Series Analysis," *Journal of Personality and Social Psychology,* Vol. 72 (1997), pp. 1322–1334. Data used with permission.

of time-based, or temporal, variables, such as the time of day and the day of the week. Their findings suggest that relationships between temperature and various types of criminal behavior are affected, or moderated, by the time of day, the day of the week, and the season of the year.

In a study of assaults in Minneapolis, Cohn and Rotton found that the relationships between temperature and assaults were strongest during evening and early hours of the night.[101] A replication conducted in Dallas also found that temperature's correlation with assaults was strongest during evening hours, which are usually the coolest time of day.[102] Other studies conducted in Minneapolis found that temperature was significantly correlated with certain property crimes (burglary, larceny, and robbery),[103] with domestic violence,[104] and with disorderly conduct.[105]

Cohn and Rotton's findings are consistent with predictions that might be derived from routine activities theory (discussed in Chapter 4). They suggest that uncomfortably hot and cold temperatures keep people apart, resulting in less opportunity for victims and motivated offenders to come into contact with one another. Temporal variables, such as time of day and day of week, moderate the relationship between temperature and crime by also affecting opportunity; offenders and victims are more likely to come into contact with each other during evening and weekend hours than during the day, when many people are busy at work or school or are engaged in other routine activities.

Other researchers have found an apparent link between barometric pressure and violent criminal offending. Using data on suicides and violent crimes during 1999 in the Louisville, Kentucky, area, Thomas J. Schory and colleagues discovered that "the total number of acts of violence and emergency psychiatry visits are significantly associated with low barometric pressure."[106] Low pressure, say the researchers, appears to be associated with changes in cerebral blood flow and may lead to increased impulsivity.

Genetics and Crime

Criminal Families

Some scholars have suggested that a penchant for crime may be inherited and that criminal tendencies are genetically based. Beginning in the late 1800s, researchers in the field of criminal anthropology focused on criminal families, or families that appeared to exhibit criminal tendencies through several generations.

Juke family

A well-known "criminal family" studied by Richard L. Dugdale.

Kallikak family

A well-known "criminal family" studied by Henry H. Goddard.

eugenics

The study of hereditary improvement by genetic control.

eugenic criminology

A perspective that holds that the root causes of criminality are passed from generation to generation in the form of "bad genes."

WEB
Extra
▪ ▪ ▪ ▪

In 1877, **Richard Louis Dugdale** (1841–1883) published a study of one such family—the **Juke family.**[107] Dugdale traced the Juke lineage back to a notorious character named Max, a Dutch immigrant who arrived in New York in the early 1700s. Two of Max's sons married into the notorious "Juke family of girls," six sisters, all of whom were said to be illegitimate. Max's male descendants were reputed to be vicious, and one woman named Ada had an especially bad reputation and came to be known as "the mother of criminals." By the time of the study, Dugdale was able to identify approximately 1,200 of Ada's descendants. Included among their numbers were 7 murderers, 60 habitual thieves, 90 or so other criminals, 50 prostitutes, and 280 paupers. Dugdale compared the crime-prone Jukes with another family, the pure-blooded progeny of Jonathan Edwards, a Puritan preacher and one-time president of Princeton University. Descendants of Edwards included American presidents and vice presidents and many successful bankers and businesspeople. No one was identified among the Edwards lineage who had had a run-in with the law. In 1916, **Arthur H. Estabrook** published a follow-up to Dugdale's work, in which he identified an additional 715 Juke descendants, including 378 more prostitutes, 170 additional paupers, and 118 other criminals.[108]

Following in the tradition of family tree researchers, **Henry Herbert Goddard** (1866–1957) published a study of the **Kallikak family** in 1912.[109] Goddard attempted to place the study of deviant families within an acceptable scientific framework via the provision of a kind of control group. For comparison purposes, he used two branches of the same family. One branch began as the result of a sexual liaison between Martin Kallikak, a Revolutionary War soldier, and a barmaid whose name is unknown. As a result of this union, an illegitimate son (Martin, Jr.) was born. After the war, Kallikak returned home and married a righteous Quaker girl, and a second line of descent began. Although the second, legitimate branch produced only a few minor deviants, the illegitimate line resulted in 262 "feebleminded" births and various other epileptic, alcoholic, and criminal descendants. (The term *feebleminded,* which was much in vogue at the time of Goddard's study, was later recast as "mentally retarded," and today people exhibiting similar characteristics might be referred to as "mentally handicapped" or "mentally challenged.") Because feeblemindedness appeared to occur with some predictability in Goddard's study, whereas criminal activity seemed to be only randomly represented among the descendants of both Kallikak lines, Goddard concluded that a tendency toward feeblemindedness was inherited but that criminality was not.

Studies like these, which focused on inherited mental degeneration, led to the **eugenics** movement of the 1920s and early 1930s and to the development of **eugenic criminology,**[110] which held that the root causes of criminality were largely passed from generation to generation in the form of "bad genes." Eugenic criminology replaced the idea of the "feebleminded criminal" with the "defective delinquent," and social policies developed during the eugenics movement called for the sterilization of mentally handicapped women to prevent their bearing additional offspring.[111] Those policies were supported by the federal Eugenics Record Office, which funded studies of "cacogenic" or "bad-gened" families, and were endorsed by the 1927 U.S. Supreme Court case of **Buck v. Bell.**[112] In *Buck,* Justice Oliver Wendell Holmes, Jr., writing in support of a Virginia statute permitting sterilization, said, "It is better for all the world, if instead of waiting to execute degenerate offspring for crime, or to let them starve for their imbecility, society can prevent those persons who are manifestly unfit from continuing their kind." Learn about the consequences of *Buck* v. *Bell* at **Web Extra 5–7.**

The eugenics movement continued in the United Kingdom into the 1960s, but was largely discredited in this country by intense condemnation of Nazi genetic research, mass sterilization, and eugenics programs, including those that led to the Holocaust. In 1962, Sir Julian Huxley, perhaps striving to rekindle positive interest in eugenics, gave the Galton Lecture to the English Eugenics Society, attesting to his belief that the general level of human abilities and performance could be improved by taking steps to improve on natural selection. Huxley argued that mankind could be improved "simply by encouraging the differential reproduction of human beings exhibiting generally desirable characteristics such as health, physical beauty, manual dexterity, longevity, athletic ability, intelligence, general mental ability, mathematical aesthetic and other special aptitudes, and capacity for leadership and for cooperative effort."[113]

The XYY "Supermale"

Recent developments in the field of human genetics have led to the study of the role of chromosomes, and sex-linked chromosomes in particular, in crime causation. The first well-known study of this type was undertaken by Patricia A. Jacobs,[114] a British researcher who in 1965 examined 197 Scottish prisoners for chromosomal abnormalities through a relatively simple blood test known as "karyotyping."[115] Twelve members of the group displayed chromosomes that were unusual, and seven were found to have an XYY chromosome. "Normal" male individuals possess an XY chromosome structure, and "normal" female individuals are XX. Some other unusual combinations might be XXX, wherein a woman's genetic makeup contains an extra X chromosome, and XXY, also called Klinefelter's syndrome, in which a man might carry an extra X, or female, chromosome. Klinefelter's men often have male genitalia but are frequently sterile and evidence breast enlargement and intellectual retardation. The XYY man, however, whose incidence in the prison population was placed at around 3.5% by Jacobs was quickly identified as potentially violent and was termed a **supermale.**

Following the introduction of the supermale notion into popular consciousness, a number of offenders attempted to offer a chromosome-based defense. In 1969, for example, Lawrence E. Hannell, who was adjudged a supermale, was acquitted of murder in Australia on the grounds of insanity.[116] Such a defense, however, did not work for Richard Speck, who also claimed to be an XYY man and was convicted of killing eight

supermale

A male individual displaying the XYY chromosome structure.

Mass murderer Richard Speck, hands cuffed and chained, looks down during an interview with the *Chicago Sun-Times* at Stateville Penitentiary in Illinois. Speck killed eight young nurses in 1966, and admitted during the interview that they would be alive today if one of the women had not spit in his face as he raped her. Speck's case helped popularize the notion of "supermales"—predators with a distinctive genetic makeup. Do contemporary understandings of biology support the idea of a "supermale"?
Source: AP Wide World Photos

Crime in the News

Scientific Study Concludes: Rape Is a Natural Product of Evolution

Rape is not, typically, the crime of male domination it has been portrayed as by sociologists and feminists in recent years, says a University of New Mexico biology professor.

Instead, UNM's Randy Thornhill and Colorado anthropologist Craig T. Palmer have developed a new theory that rape is a complex sexual crime with strong roots in human evolution.

Moreover, contend Thornhill and Palmer, rape "prevention efforts will founder until they are based on the understanding that rape evolved as a form of male reproductive behavior."

"We have to get real about rape," Thornhill said in a recent interview.

The two scientists co-authored an article titled "Why Men Rape" in the current issue of the journal *The Sciences.* The journal is published by the New York Academy of Sciences.

Thornhill and Palmer are to expound on their research in an upcoming book, *A Natural History of Rape: Biological Bases of Sexual Coercion,* by MIT Press.

In the article, Thornhill and Palmer take aim at the prevailing societal notion that rape isn't about sex but about male power and is "a symptom of an unhealthy society in which men fear and disrespect women."

Palmer and Thornhill say some sociologists advance a view that, they think, incorrectly assumes that rape is "unnatural behavior that has nothing to do with sex and one that has no corollary in the animal world."

They counter that rape is part of the male mental sexual psyche; was at least part of a successful male reproductive strategy in human evolutionary history; and is strong enough to survive today despite strong social sanctions and legal penalties.

But they do not equate "natural" with good and agree that their public mission is to make rape extinct as a trait in human beings.

In an interview, Palmer said the article aims to convince "those who accept evolution but don't see it as applying to the brain and behavior and particularly the behavior of rape."

"We have to convince them that behavior, including sexual, evolved, just like our morphology and anatomy," he said. "The brain evolved along with the rest of the body."

Palmer said they aren't arguing that men who rape are "genetically predisposed to rape" or that there is a rape gene. Rather, they say that all males appear to be genetically capable of rape, and it is an act which can be triggered by environmental conditions or interactions in life.

The two scientists contend that current thinking about what causes rape is so bankrupt that it ignores the reality that by definition rape requires sexual arousal of the rapist.

Thornhill cites his own study of insects called scorpionflies, in which males are equipped with an appendage used solely to grab a female's forewing and prevent her escape during involuntary mating. The "rape clamp" is used when a male scorpionfly fails to attract a female through the alternative reproduction strategy of offering nuptial gifts, such as a dead insect.

Palmer said the argument actually might get greater acceptance among lay people than in some scientific quarters because people instinctively know that men and women are not just biologically different but think differently, have different sexual agendas or goals and "respond to certain behaviors in different ways."

"These differences are what lie at the basis of rape and what made it a possibility in our evolutionary history," he said.

The scientists say this broke a long tradition of professional journals' sidestepping the issue of rape's evolutionary underpinnings as being politically incorrect.

Discussion Questions

1. Do you agree with the premise of this article, that human sexual behavior has biological roots that have been at least partially shaped by evolution? Why or why not?

2. If what this article says is true, what are the implications for society? For the justice system?

According to Jane Goodall's book The Chimpanzees of Gombe, mating behavior among chimpanzees often involves force. While behavioral scientists recognize the role of instinct in animal behavior, few are ready to extend a substantial role for genetic influences to human behavior that violates the law. Why does such a disparity exist?

Source: EyeWire Collection—Getty Images Photosdisc

Source: "Scientific Study Concludes: Rape Is a Natural Product of Evolution," Scripps Howard news service, January 11, 2000.

For the latest crime and justice news, visit www.crimenews.info.

Chicago nursing students in 1966. It was later learned that Speck did not carry the extra Y chromosome.

To date, there have been nearly 200 studies of XYY males. Although not all researchers agree, taken as a group these studies[117] tend to show that supermales:

- Are taller than the average male, often standing 6 foot 1″ or more
- Suffer from acne or skin disorders
- Have less than average intelligence
- Are overrepresented in prisons and mental hospitals
- Come from families with a lower than average history of crime or mental illness

The supermale phenomenon, also called the "XYY syndrome," may have been more sensationalism than fact. Little evidence suggests that XYY men actually commit crimes of greater violence than do other men, although they may commit somewhat more crimes overall. A 1976 Danish study of 4,000 men, which found precisely that, may have helped put the issue to rest.[118] The Danish survey, conducted of men born in Copenhagen between 1944 and 1947, also found that the incidence of XYY men was less than 1% in the general male population. Other recent researchers have similarly concluded that "studies done thus far are largely in agreement and demonstrate rather conclusively that males of the XYY type are not predictably aggressive."[119]

Chromosomes and Modern-Day Criminal Families

In 1993, Dutch criminologists caught worldwide attention with their claim that they had uncovered a specific gene with links to criminal behavior. Researcher H. Hilger Ropers, geneticist Han Brunner, and collaborators studied what media sources called "the Netherlands' most dysfunctional family."[120] Although the unnamed family displayed IQs in the near-normal range, they seemed unable to control their impulses and often ended up being arrested for violations of the criminal law. The arrests, however, were always of men. Tracing the family back five generations, Brunner found 14 men whom he classified as genetically given to criminality. None of the women in the family displayed criminal tendencies, although they were often victimized by their crime-prone male siblings. One brother raped a sister and later stabbed a mental hospital staffer in the chest with a pitchfork. Another tried to run over his supervisor with his car. Two brothers repeatedly started fires and were classified as arsonists. Another brother frequently crept into his sisters' rooms and forced them to undress at knifepoint.

According to Ropers and Brunner, because men have only one X chromosome, they are especially vulnerable to any defective gene. Women, with two X chromosomes, have a kind of backup system in which one defective gene may be compensated for by another wholesome and correctly functioning gene carried in the second X chromosome. After a decade of study, which involved the laboratory filtering of a huge quantity of genetic material in a search for the defective gene, Ropers and Brunner announced that they had isolated the specific mutation that caused the family's criminality. The gene, they said, is responsible for the production of an enzyme called monoamine oxidase A (MAOA). MAOA is crucially involved in the process by which signals are transmitted within the brain. Specifically, MAOA breaks down the chemicals serotonin and noradrenaline. Both are substances that have been linked to aggressive behavior in human beings. Because men with the mutated gene do not produce enough of the enzyme necessary to break down a lot of chemical transmitters, researchers surmise, their brains are overwhelmed with stimuli—a situation that results in uncontrollable urges and, ultimately, criminal behavior.

Behavioral Genetics

Sir Francis Galton (1822–1911) was the first Western scientist to systematically study heredity and its possible influence upon human behavior.[121] In 1907, Galton wrote that "the perpetuation of the criminal class by heredity is a question difficult to grapple with on many accounts. . . . It is, however, easy to show that the criminal nature tends to be inherited. . . . The true state of the case appears to be that the criminal population receives steady accessions from those who, without having strongly marked criminal natures, do nevertheless belong to a type of humanity that is exceedingly ill suited to play a respectable part in our modern civilization, though it is well suited to flourish under half-savage conditions, being naturally both healthy and prolific."[122] Galton's work contributed to the development of the field of **behavioral genetics,** which is the study of genetic and environmental contributions to individual variations in human behavior.

While Galton might have believed that heredity was in some way related to criminality, he had no opportunity to explore the relationship in depth. More recently, however, studies of the criminal tendencies of fraternal and identical twins have provided a methodologically sophisticated technique for ferreting out the role of heredity in crime causation. Fraternal twins, also called "dizygotic (DZ) twins," develop from different fertilized eggs and share only the genetic material common among siblings. Identical twins, also called **monozygotic (MZ) twins,** develop from the same egg and carry virtually the same genetic material. Hence, if human behavior has a substantial heritable component, twins should tend to display similar behavioral characteristics despite variations in their social environment. Similarly, any observed relationship might be expected to be stronger among monozygotic twins than among dizygotic twins.

One of the first studies to link MZ twins to criminality was published in the 1920s by German physician Johannes Lange.[123] Lange examined only 17 pairs of fraternal twins and 13 pairs of identical twins but found that in 10 of the 13 identical pairs both twins were criminal, whereas only 2 of the 17 fraternal pairs exhibited such similarity. Lange's findings drew considerable attention, even though his sample was small and he was unable to adequately separate environmental influences from genetic ones. The title of his book, *Verbrechen als Schicksal* (*Crime as Destiny*), indicates Lange's firm conviction that criminality has a strong genetic component.

A much larger twin study was begun in 1968 by European researchers Karl O. Christiansen and Sarnoff Mednick, who analyzed all twins (3,586 pairs) born on a selected group of Danish islands between 1881 and 1910.[124] Christiansen and Mednick found significant statistical support for the notion that criminal tendencies are inherited, and they concluded that 52% of identical twins and 22% of fraternal siblings displayed the same degree of criminality within the twin pair. Such similarities remained apparent even among twins who had been separated at birth and who were raised in substantially different environments.

The Minnesota Twin Family Study began in 1983.[125] The study's original goal was to establish a registry of all twins born in Minnesota from 1936 to 1955 for psychological research purposes. The Minnesota database has since expanded to include twins born between 1961 and 1964. The Minnesota registry conducts personality and interests tests with more than 8,000 twin pairs and family members using the mail. One of the study's most interesting findings seems to show that monozygotic twins reared apart are about as similar as are monozygotic twins reared together. The findings apply to multiple measures of personality and temperament, occupational and leisure-time interests, and social attitudes. Study authors warn, however, that "this evidence for the strong heritability of most psychological traits, sensibly construed, does not detract from the value or importance of parenting, education, and other propaedeutic interventions."[126]

In 1994, Dutch researchers reported finding substantial genetic influences on delinquent and aggressive behavior in a study that compared 221 pairs of biologically unrelated siblings in adoptive families with 111 pairs of biologically related siblings in similar settings.[127] Using a sophisticated study design, the researchers were able to conclude that "genetic influences accounted for 70% of the variance of aggressive behavior," while predicting only 39% of delinquency and 47% of attention-related problems.

---

behavioral genetics

The study of genetic and environmental contributions to individual variations in human behavior.

monozygotic (MZ) twins

Twins that develop from the same egg and that carry virtually the same genetic material.

In 1996, British researchers who studied 43 monozygotic and 38 dizygotic same-sex twins through the use of self-report questionnaires concluded that "common bad behaviors of the sort admitted to by the majority of adolescents have a substantially heritable component. Additive genetic effects account for most of the variation, with no evidence of a contribution from shared environment."[128] The researchers also determined that genetic effects on behavior appear to increase with age. The British research was supported by the findings of a joint United States–Australian examination of 2,682 adult twin pairs.[129] In that study, researchers found "a substantial genetic influence on risk for conduct disorder" (which was defined to include chronic stealing, lying, bullying, arson, property destruction, weapons use, cruelty to animals or people, fighting, aggression, truancy, and running away from home).

In 2003, researchers examined the behavior of 1,116 pairs of five-year-old twins participating in a longitudinal study and asked mothers, teachers, study-examiners, and the children themselves to evaluate the degree of the children's level of antisocial behavior.[130] Findings showed that antisocial children can be identified early in life, that their behavior can be nearly impossible to control by the time they reach kindergarten, and that heredity plays a far greater role in determining such behavior than does home life or parenting. The researchers concluded that genetic influences were extremely powerful determinants of antisocial behavior across diverse social settings. They wrote that "research and theory on the etiology of childhood antisocial behavior must look beyond the current focus on socioeconomic contexts and parenting processes, to incorporate genetic explanations and develop new theories of nature-nurture interplay."

Finally, in 2003, Florida State University researcher Jeanette Taylor studied two separate groups of teenaged male twins and concluded that antisocial traits among study subjects existed prior to adulthood and that they stemmed to a significant degree from genetic factors.[131] The study involved 142 monozygotic and 70 dizygotic twin pairs.

Twin studies appear to point to criminal genes that, once inherited, inevitably produce antisocial behavior. Such a conclusion, however, is not necessarily warranted. As we shall see later in this chapter, genes may simply influence the way in which people respond to their surroundings. Hence, so-called criminal genes may be nothing more than genetic predispositions to respond in certain ways to a crimogenic environment.

The Human Genome Project

Many of the questions criminologists have raised about the role of genetics in criminal behavior may soon be answered by the results of research undertaken by the Human Genome Project (HGP).[132] The HGP was an international research program designed to construct detailed maps of the human genome. It began in the United States in 1990 through a joint effort of the Department of Energy and the National Institutes of Health. Its purpose was to determine the complete nucleotide sequence of human DNA, to localize the nearly 100,000 genes within the human genome, and to determine the sequences of the 3 billion chemical base pairs that make up human DNA. According to the National Human Genome Research Institute, the scientific products of HGP comprise a resource of detailed information about the structure, organization and function of human DNA, information that constitutes the basic set of inherited "instructions" for the development and functioning of a human being. The HGP stores the information it develops in databases, with the goal of eventually transferring that information and associated technologies to the private sector. The transfer is meant to stimulate the multibillion-dollar U.S. biotechnology industry and to foster the development of new medical treatments and technologies. The HGP was officially declared completed on April 14, 2003[133]—almost exactly 50 years after James Watson and Francis Crick published their historic findings on the double helix three-dimensional structure of DNA.[134]

The acquisition and use of the genetic knowledge developed by the HGP are likely to have momentous implications for both individuals and society. In the area of crime control policy, HGP-developed information is expected to pose a number of choices for

Who's to Blame—The Individual or Society?

Hormones and Criminal Behavior

Lamont Ridgeway, 22, was arrested and charged with rape after 21-year-old Nicole Bachman called police to her Minneapolis home at 2:00 A.M. Ridgeway and Bachman had met in an evening art class at the local community college, and Bachman invited Ridgeway to her apartment for a glass of wine after the class was over. Officers couldn't help but notice that Bachman was an unusually attractive young woman whose clothes were in disarray. They also observed that she was visibly intoxicated and slurred her words as she spoke. Ridgeway was passed out on her couch, apparently after having had far too much to drink.

"He raped me!" Bachman told the two officers who responded to her call for help. "I told him to stop, and he wouldn't," she said.

Ridgeway was roused from sleep, arrested, searched, handcuffed, and taken to jail, where he was booked and charged with rape. After being advised of his rights not to speak and to have a lawyer represent him, he decided to tell the officers who were questioning him that it wasn't really rape. "She came on to me," he said. She took her blouse off, then her pants. And she gave me a lot to drink. Yeah, she said 'no,' but by then we were already there. I couldn't stop. Why would she want to, anyway?"

When Ridgeway's lawyer arrived he advised Ridgeway not to say anything more. The lawyer, hired by Ridgeway's wealthy parents, read the statement that he had given to the police and then hired a psychiatrist to help in building a defense that might stand up in court.

When the case went to trial two months later, the psychiatrist testified as an expert witness for the defense. He told the jury that blood tests showed that Ridgeway had abnormally large amounts of testosterone naturally occurring in his blood; that testosterone was the chemical messenger responsible for the male sex drive (which, he said, differed substantially from that of women); and that Ridgeway had consequently been unable to control his behavior on the night of the alleged rape. "The young man was simply doing what his hormones made him do," the psychiatrist testified. "It's my professional opinion," he concluded, "that with that amount of testosterone affecting his judgment, he really didn't have much choice in his behavioral responses once he was offered alcohol and was then visually stimulated by the young woman's removal of her clothes. If this was my patient," the psychiatrist added, "I'd treat him with the testosterone antagonist Depo-Provera, and we would see the strength of his sex drive substantially diminished. You could be sure that this kind of thing wouldn't happen again."

In response, the prosecution called their own expert, a noted biochemist who, citing various studies, said that there was no clearly established link between blood levels of testosterone and aggressive sexual behavior in human beings. "Even if there were," he said, "people are not mindless animals. We have free choice. We are not so driven by our blood chemistry that we cannot decide what we are going to do in any given situation."

Think about it:

1. With which expert witness do you most agree—the psychiatrist or the biochemist? Why?

2. Do you believe that blood chemistry can ever be an explanation for behavior? For crime?

3. If you answered "yes" to the previous question, then do you think that blood chemistry can ever be an effective excuse for criminality? If you answered "no," then why not?

4. How do our understandings of criminal motivation and crime causality influence our policies on the treatment, punishment, and reformation of those who violate the law?

---

public and professional deliberation. Hence, the analysis of the ethical, legal, and social implications of genetic knowledge and the development of policy options for public consideration are central components of the human genome research effort.

Some scientists are confident that future advances in the field of behavioral genetics brought about by the HGP will support the idea of behavioral **genetic determinism,** or the belief that genes are the major determining factor in human behavior. Others, however, warn that discoveries in behavioral genetics may need to be interpreted in terms of what is already known about social and psychological influences on behavior.

Early results associated with the HGP, however, are interesting. A few years ago, for example, researchers at the University of Texas Health Science Center in San Antonio announced the discovery of a pleasure-seeking gene that, they suspect, plays a role in deviant behavior, addictions, and maybe even murder and violence. The gene, called "DRD2 A1 allele," is normally involved in controlling the flow of dopamine. Dopamine, a powerful brain chemical, gives people a sense of well-being. When defective, however, the DRD2 A1 allele diminishes dopamine function, which may drive a person to take drugs, drink, or engage in activity that provides a dopamine-like experience. "We think they're seeking out ways of fixing the lack of pleasure," says Kenneth Blum, University of Texas Health Science Center, San Antonio. "You might

genetic determinism

The belief that genes are the major determining factor in human behavior.

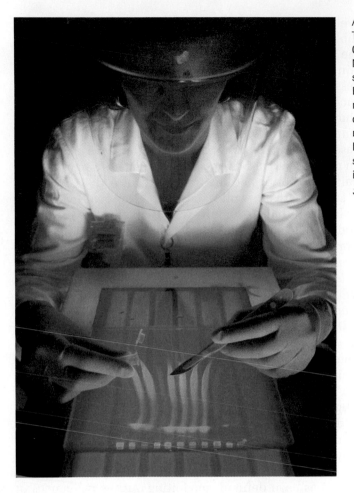

A genome researcher at work. The National Center for Human Genome Research at the National Institutes of Health supported the international Human Genome Project, a research program that determined the complete nucleotide sequence of human DNA. What ethical, legal, and social implications are inherent in such a project?

Source: Durand Trippett, SIPA Press

be a pleasure seeker for alcohol, drugs, sex or maybe you get it from violence or murder."[135]

More recent results, coming from the Dunedin Multidisciplinary Health and Development Study—a longitudinal study of 1,037 children born in the maternity hospital in Dunedin, New Zealand, between April 1, 1972, and March 31, 1973—point to what appears to be significant biosocial interaction between the enzyme monoamine oxidase A (MAOA) (mentioned earlier in this chapter) and early child abuse in leading to violence later in life.[136] Children who experience abuse—especially those exposed to erratic, coercive, and punitive parenting—frequently develop conduct disorders and display antisocial personality symptoms, and they are known to be at greater risk of becoming violent adult offenders than children who do not experience such maltreatment.[137] Moreover, previous research has demonstrated that the earlier children experience maltreatment, the more likely they are to display such problems in later life. Study authors, including Avshalom Caspi and Terrie E. Moffitt, recognized that childhood maltreatment appears to be a "universal risk factor for antisocial behavior" in adulthood, but they noted that not all maltreated children grow up to become criminal.[138] In an effort to identify vulnerability factors that might predispose some abused children to antisocial behavior, Caspi and Moffitt hypothesized that the development of antisocial behavior was mediated by an interaction between a gene responsible for the production of the enzyme MAOA and an environment variable (maltreatment). At the conclusion of the study, researchers determined that maltreatment "has lasting neurochemical correlates in human children" and found that deficient MAOA activity may cause "neural hyperreactivity" in children in response to threats. Hence, the authors said, "childhood maltreatment predisposes most strongly to adult violence among children whose MAOA is insufficient to constrain maltreatment-induced changes to neurotransmitter systems." Maltreated children with high MAOA activity did not develop antisocial behavior. The finding was supported by two separate Swedish studies published in 2007.[139]

Also in 2007, researchers at the University of Texas Southwestern Medical Center discovered that mice carrying certain mutations in what is called the Clock gene, exhibited manic behaviors, such as recklessness and hyperactivity, and also displayed a preference for addictive substances such as cocaine. Treatment with the antipsychotic medicine lithium caused them to behave normally. A month later, Francis McMahon of the National Institute of Mental Health in Bethesda, Maryland, reported finding a number of specific genes that might be associated with bipolar disorder. The genes apparently act by influencing how the brain responds to neurotransmitters such as dopamine.[140]

MRI studies of the human brain have confirmed the important role of MAOA activity in the brain. Andreas Meyer-Lindenberg and colleagues at the National Institute of Mental Health in Bethesda, Maryland, studied 142 adults with two unusual versions of the gene that triggers MAOA production.[141] One group had a gene variant that resulted in weak MAOA activity in the brain, leading to elevated concentrations of serotonin. The other group had a gene that resulted in excess MAOA production, resulting in serotonin concentrations at the low end of the normal range. Meyer-Lindenberg, a neuroscientist, found that brain scans of those with the weak-MAOA gene variant revealed unusually small inner-brain structures involved in the regulation of emotion. When presented with photos of faces displaying storng emotions, the same subjects showed intense neural activity in the amygdala and hippocampus—two areas of the brain associated with emotionality. They also exhibited relatively little activity in those parts of the brain that control impulses when asked to perform tasks requiring self-control. The observed effects were stronger in male than in female subjects. Lindenberg concluded that possession of the MAOA-light gene results in neurological characteristics that "weaken a person's ability to hold emotions and aggressive urges in check."[142]

The Human Genome Project and studies like those cited here notwithstanding, behavioral geneticists examining the crime problem face some daunting issues. Among them is the difficulty of coming up with a suitable definition of *crime,* determining how best to measure criminality once it has been defined, separating out the influences of the environment from what may be genetic influences on behavior, and distinguishing among the multiple and potentially interrelated influences of many genes. In the final analysis, the explanatory power of **heritability,** which is a statistical construct that estimates the amount of variation in a population that is attributable to genetic factors, appears to be limited by the fact that it may apply only to specific environments that existed at the time of a given study. As one noted geneticist says, "If the population or the environment changes, the heritability most likely will change as well. Most important, heritability statements provide no basis for predictions about the expression of the trait in question in any given individual."[143]

New understandings about how genes operate also seem to call into question previous notions that genes are strong determinants of human behavior. Researchers in the field of neurobiology, for example, have found 17 genes known as the CREB genes that are switched on and off in response to environmental influences. The CREB genes lay down neural pathways in the brain and form the basis of memory. The act of learning turns the CREB genes on and is made possible by them.[144] Hence, the CREB genes respond to human experience rather than determine it. As one writer says, "[T]hese genes are at the mercy of our behavior, not the other way around."[145] Similarly, the FOXP2 gene on chromosome 7 has been shown to allow the development of language skills in human beings. The CREB and FOXP2 genes have taught researchers that not only are genes not just carriers of heredity, but also they are active during life and respond to the environment. Seen this way, genes are both the cause and the consequence of our actions. They do not so much *cause* human action as *enable* it. Some writers suggest that such insights will soon allow us to fully appreciate the roles of both genetics and environment in eliciting specific forms of human behavior, and thereby leave the nature-nurture argument behind.[146]

Learn more about the Human Genome Project by visiting the National Human Genome Research Institute via **Web Extra 5–8.** You might also want to visit the U.S.

heritability

A statistical construct that estimates the amount of variation in a population that is attributable to genetic factors.

WEB
Extra

Department of Energy's Human Genome Program site at **Web Extra 5–9.** You can read about how DNA and genetics might influence human behavior at **Library Extras 5–4, 5–5,** and **5–6** at crimtoday.com.

WEB Extra

LIBRARY Extra

Male-Female Differences in Criminality

A number of contemporary writers propose that criminologists must recognize that "the male is much more criminalistic than the female."[147] As Chapter 2 describes, with the exception of crimes like prostitution and shoplifting, the number of crimes committed by men routinely far exceeds the number of crimes committed by women in almost all categories, and when women commit crimes, they are far more likely to assume the role of followers than leaders.[148] The data on the extent of male-female criminality show surprising regularity over time. The proportion of homicides committed by men versus women, for example, has remained more or less constant for decades (see Table 5–1). Similarly, the proportion of men murdered by men versus the proportion of women murdered by women has been consistent, showing a much greater propensity for men to murder one another.

If culture exercises the major role in determining criminality, as many social scientists today suggest, then we would expect to see recognizable increases in the degree and nature of female criminality over time, especially as changes in socialization practices, cultural roles, and other ethnographic patterns increase the opportunity for women to commit what had previously been regarded as traditionally male offenses. With the exception of a few crimes, such as embezzlement, drug abuse, and liquor law violations, however, such has not been the case. Although women comprise 51% of the population of the United States, they are arrested for only 18% of all violent crimes and 32% of property crimes[149]—a proportion that has remained surprisingly constant over the years since the FBI began gathering crime data more than half a century ago. Simply put, even with all the cultural changes that have created new possibilities for women in crime, few women have taken advantage of these newfound freedoms. Such apparent differences not only have existed over time but also can be seen in cross-cultural studies. Chapter 2 provides additional statistics of this sort.

Such findings are in contrast with the suggestions of authors like Freda Adler, who, in her 1975 book *Sisters in Crime,* proposed that as women entered "nontraditional occupations" and roles, there "would be a movement toward parity with men in the commission of crime in terms of both incidence and type."[150] Darrell J. Steffensmeier, who studied changes in women's criminality following publication of Adler's book, found almost no evidence to support the belief that a new female criminal is emerging or that female criminality is undergoing the kind of increase Adler might have expected.[151] The lack of contemporary validation for Adler's thesis suggests that something else is occurring; that is, some element other than cultural inhibition or equality of opportunity is preventing women from taking their place alongside men as equals in crime. Biological criminologists suggest that the organic correlates of gender provide the needed explanation.

In evaluating the criminality of women based on statistics alone, however, danger prevails of misidentifying causal factors operative in the behavior itself. Although men consistently commit more murders than women, for example, we should not jump to

TABLE 5–1   Male and Female Murder Perpetrators as a Percentage of All Arrests for Homicide, 1960–2000

1960		1975		1980		1990		2000	
Male	Female	Male	Female	Male	Female	Male	Female	Male	Female
82.5%	17.5%	84.7%	15.3%	87.2%	12.8%	89.6%	10.4%	87.5%	12.5%

Source: Adapted from Federal Bureau of Investigation, *Crime in the United States,* various years.

the conclusion that this bit of evidence shows a genetic predisposition toward interpersonal violence in men, which is absent in women. To do so would fail to recognize the role of other causal factors. Observable racial variation in crime rates has provided some writers with a basis for claiming that some racial groups are disproportionately violent, while attributing such violence to a genetic basis. A look at the statistics, for example, appears to show that in the United States, African Americans are more than six times as likely as whites to commit murder, three times as likely to commit rape, seven times as likely to rob, and twice as likely, on average, to commit any kind of crime.[152] Chapter 2 provides additional statistics of this sort.

Such statistics, however, can be inherently misleading because—unlike the undeniable and easily observable biological differences that exist between men and women—racial groupings are defined more by convention than by genetics. Some writers suggest that "pure" racial groups no longer exist and that even historical racial distinctions were based more on political considerations and social convention than on significant genetic differences.

The criminality of women (or relative lack thereof) may be culturally determined to a considerable degree. Nonetheless, the consistency of data that routinely show that women are far less likely than men to be involved in most property crimes, and less likely still to commit violent crimes, requires recognition. We have already evaluated the role that testosterone may play in increasing the propensity toward violence and aggression among men. A few authors suggest that testosterone is the agent primarily responsible for male criminality and that its relative lack in women leads them to commit fewer crimes. Some evidence supports just such a hypothesis. Studies have shown, for example, that female fetuses exposed to elevated testosterone levels during gestation develop masculine characteristics, including a muscular build and a demonstrably greater tendency toward aggression later in life.[153] Even so, genetically based behavioral differences between men and women are so moderated by aspects of the social environment, including socialization, the learning of culturally prescribed roles, and the expectations of others, that definitive conclusions are difficult to reach.

One recently proposed social-psychological explanation for homicidal behavior among women, for example, suggests that men who kill tend to do so out of a need to control a situation, whereas women who kill tend to do so because they have lost control over themselves.[154] The theory says "that women as a group are more 'controlled' than men, particularly with respect to their experience and expression of anger." Such control is said to emanate from the fact that "men are always the subjects and women the objects in [a]

Women's boxing, a relatively new sport, reflects women's changing social roles. Male-female differences in criminality, however, seem to display considerable regularity over time. Does this mean that men and women have inherently different behavioral tendencies?

Source: Agence France Presse/Getty Images

Criminal Profiles

Richard Benjamin Speck

In an appalling crime ranked number ten on *Time*'s list of the top 25 crimes of the twentieth century,[i] Richard Speck committed the mass murder of eight nurses from a community hospital in Chicago on the night of July 14, 1966.

Born the seventh of eight children, on December 6, 1941, Speck's early upbringing in Kirkwood, Illinois, included strict adherence to Baptist religious teachings. When Richard was just six years old, his father died, and his mother subsequently married a hard-fisted drinker with an arrest record. After the family relocated to Dallas, Texas, Speck performed poorly in school and began sinking into increasingly serious delinquent behavior. His drunken step-father's response was typically the administration of severe physical punishment for each of Speck's continuing transgressions.[ii] Speck himself became a heavy drinker, an affliction that would haunt him for the remainder of his life.

Interspersed with a series of incarcerations for various burglaries, thefts, check forgeries, and other low-level crimes, 18-year-old Speck married 15-year-old Shirley Malone in November 1962. Their brief marriage was marked by his repeated absence while imprisoned, punctuated by his physical abuse of both his wife and his mother-in-law whenever he was not in jail. The abuse of his wife included frequent instances of rape at knifepoint.[iii]

In January 1966, the couple divorced, and Speck left Texas to return by bus to Illinois, ending up in Monmouth, a small town near the Iowa border. Following the rape of a 65-year-old woman in early April and the murder of a barmaid 11 days later, Speck was interrogated. He was let loose when he became physically ill, after promising to return for further questioning. When he failed to show up as promised, investigators who went looking for him found that he had fled on a bus headed east, presumably to the Chicago area.

In May, Speck showed up at the Maritime Union Hall on Chicago's northwest side, where he managed to secure employment aboard an iron ore ship plying its trade in the Great Lakes. During his initial voyage, Speck was stricken with appendicitis, for which he was treated in a Michigan hospital. Returning to Chicago in mid-June, Speck was fired because of his continued drunkenness. He then spent the next three weeks doing odd jobs to finance his boozing and prostitutes.

A drunken Speck invaded a townhouse where nursing students from nearby South Chicago Community Hospital resided late on the evening of July 13, 1966. Within the first hour, he was able to capture and tie up nine women. One of the most baffling elements of this crime is the mystery of how Speck was able to control all nine women without any of them attempting to escape or making enough noise to attract the attention of someone from an adjacent building.

After securing all the victims, Speck spent the next three hours systematically taking each student to another room within the townhouse and killing her. Each was violently murdered by strangulation, multiple stab wounds, and/or a cut throat; one was also raped.

Evidently distracted by these activities, Speck lost count of the number of women he had captured. As a result, one of the women survived by rolling under a bed. Speck departed the townhouse at approximately 3:30 A.M. The survivor, Corazon Amurao, huddled in terror under the bed until almost 6:00 A.M. before she finally crawled out a window and began calling for help.[iv]

During the ensuing manhunt, Speck drank his way from bar to bar, ultimately retiring to a flophouse hotel with a prostitute. Afterward, he returned to his drinking binge, ending up in a rundown hotel where he took a room. In the room, he consumed an entire bottle of wine, then went to the communal bathroom at the end of the hall, broke the bottle, and used it to cut open his wrist and inner elbow.[v]

When Speck was found, he was placed under arrest, taken to Cook County Hospital to be treated for his injuries, then transferred to Cook County Jail. On a change of venue motion by the defense, the case was tried in Peoria. The jury returned a guilty verdict in just 49 minutes, and Speck was sentenced to death.[vi]

Speck achieved notoriety in the national press when, as this chapter points out, his lawyers offered the claim that he was an XYY supermale, apparently in the hopes that the claim could provide a defense to the charges against him. At the time the claim was made, the XYY theory was being debated in academic circles and had become popular with the public. Later tests showed, however, that Speck did not carry the extra Y chromosome.

Speck's death sentence was commuted to 50 to 100 years in prison when the U.S. Supreme Court voided the death penalty in 1972. He died of a heart attack on December 5, 1991.

An examination of Speck's brain after his death by a neuropathologist at the Chicago Institute of Neurosurgery, is reported to have found gross abnormalities. The boundary between two normally distinct areas of his brain—the hippocampus, which involves memory, and the amygdala, which deals with rage and other strong emotions—were found to be blurred, with cells from the areas encroaching unnaturally upon each other.[vii]

Three years after his death, Speck's story again sparked sensationalism when a popular television crime show aired footage of Speck's prison lifestyle. Wearing only blue panties and proudly displaying his medically enhanced breasts, Speck was shown to have engaged in anal intercourse with his cellmate/lover, snorted cocaine, and flashed wads of $100 bills in his Stateville (Illinois) prison cell.[viii] Speck also spoke in explicit terms about the murders. The show ignited a storm of public outrage over the "posh" living arrangements some prisoners enjoyed.

Notes:

i Howard Chua-Eoan, "The Top 25," *Crimes of the Century, Time,* http://www.time.com/time/2007/crimes/9.html (accessed May 22, 2007).

ii David Lohr, "Richard Speck," *Crime Magazine: An Encyclopedia of Crime,* August 2003, http://crimemagazine.com/03/richardspeck,0820.htm (accessed May 22, 2007).

iii Connie Fillippelli, "Richard Speck: Born to Raise Hell," Chapter 11, CourtTV Crime Library, 2007, http://www.crimelibrary.com/serial_killers/predators/speck/hell_11.html (accessed May 22, 2007).

iv Fillippelli, Chapter 16, http://www.crimelibrary.com/serial_killers/predators/speck/hell_16.html (accessed May 22, 2007).

v Troy Taylor, "Born to Raise Hell: The Life and Crimes of Richard Speck," *Weird & Haunted Chicago,* 2003, http://www.prairieghosts.com/speck.html (accessed March 14, 2007).

vi Fillippelli, Chapter 16.

vii Scott Fornek, "Was He Evil, Crazy—or Brain-damaged?" *Chicago Sun-Times,* July 11, 2006, http://findarticles.com/p/articles/mi_qn4155/is_20060711/ai_n16528144 (accessed May 20, 2007).

viii Denise Noe, "'Supermale' in Blue Panties: The Woman-Murderer Self-Womanized," *True Crime and Justice,* 1994, http://www.karisable.com/speck.htm (accessed May 22, 2007).

male-centric universe."[155] As a consequence of our culture's overemphasis on a woman's looks rather than on her performance, the theory says, women internalize a "self-image on the basis of appearance rather than substance of character," resulting in low self-esteem and low self-confidence. Low self-esteem, the argument goes, necessitates greater self-control and results in lower criminality among women. Such a perspective suggests that women tend to commit homicides only when driven "past the brink" of self-control, thus offering an explanation for why homicides committed by women are generally spontaneous rather than planned, why they usually involve the killing of intimates, and why they generally occur in the home. "Women generally view themselves as part of a collective of relationships around them," say some theorists, "and evaluate their self-worth based on the value and success of these relationships."[156] Hence, when relationships break down, a woman's self-worth may be negated, resulting in a lessening of control—and homicide may ensue.

Sociobiology

In the introduction to his insightful article summarizing sociobiology, Arthur Fisher writes, "Every so often, in the long course of scientific progress, a new set of ideas appears, illuminating and redefining what has gone before like a flare bursting over a darkened landscape."[157] To some, **sociobiology**—a theoretical synthesis of biology, behavior, and evolutionary ecology brought to the scientific community by **Edward O. Wilson** in his seminal 1975 work *Sociobiology: The New Synthesis*[158]—holds the promise of just such a new **paradigm.** In his book, Wilson defined *sociobiology* as "the systematic study of the biological basis of all social behavior" and as "a branch of evolutionary biology and particularly of modern population biology." Through his entomological study of social insects, especially ants, Wilson demonstrated that particular forms of behavior could contribute to the long-term survival of the social group. Wilson focused on altruism (selfless, helping behavior) and found that contrary to the beliefs of some evolutionary biologists, helping behavior facilitates the continuity of the gene pool among altruistic individuals. Wilson's major focus was to show that the primary determinant of behavior, including human behavior, was the need to ensure the survival and continuity of genetic material from one generation to the next.

Territoriality, another primary tenent of Wilson's writings, was said to explain much of the conflict seen between and among human beings, including homicide, warfare, and other forms of aggression. In Wilson's words, "Part of man's problem is that his intergroup responses are still crude and primitive, and inadequate for the extended extraterritorial relationships that civilization has thrust upon him." The "unhappy result," as Wilson terms it, may be "tribalism," expressed through the contemporary proliferation of street gangs, racial tension, and the hardened encampments of survivalist and separatist groups.

The sad results of territoriality, whatever its cause, can be seen in the deadly adventure of 15-year-old Michael Carter and his companions, who ended up in the wrong place at the wrong time. On June 18, 1997, Carter, from Highland Township, Michigan, and two of his friends hopped a CSX Transportation train headed for the town of Holly. The three were looking for a free ten-mile ride on their way to see friends. But they missed their jumping-off point, sailed past the town of Holly, and ended up in a run-down inner-city ghetto in the middle of Flint, Michigan, around midnight. Soon, the three were surrounded by gang members, led into a secluded area, and shot. Carter died at the scene, while friend Dustin Kaiser, also 15, survived a gunshot wound to the head. The 14-year-old girl who had accompanied the boys was raped and shot in the face but lived.[159]

As sociobiologists tell us, the violence and aggressiveness associated with territoriality is often reserved for strangers. The approach of sociobiology can explain intragroup aggression—or the violence that occurs within groups—as well as that which occurs between groups. Wilson writes that his theory suggests that within the group "a particularly severe form of aggressiveness should be reserved for actual or suspected adultery. In many human societies, where sexual bonding is close and personal knowledge of the behavior of others detailed, adulterers are harshly treated. The sin is regarded

---

sociobiology

The systematic study of the biological basis of all social behavior.

paradigm

An example, a model, or a theory.

to be even worse when offspring are produced."[160] Hence, territoriality and acquisitiveness extend, from a sociobiological perspective, to location, possessions, and even other people. Human laws, says Wilson, are designed to protect genetically based relationships that people have with one another, as well as their material possessions and their claimed locations in space. Violations of these intuitive relationships result in crime and in official reactions by the legal system.

Wilson's writing propelled researchers into a flurry of studies intended to test the validity of his assertions. One study, for example, found that Indian adult male Hanuman langurs (a type of monkey) routinely killed the young offspring of female langurs with whom they bonded when those offspring had been sired by other male langurs.[161] A Canadian study of violence in the homes of adoptive children found a human parallel to the langur study, showing that stepchildren run a 70 times greater risk of being killed by their adoptive parents than do children living with their natural parents.[162] Some writers concluded that "murderous behavior, warfare, and even genocide were unavoidable correlates of genetic evolution, controlled by the same genes for territorial behavior that had been selected in primate evolution."[163] Others suggested that biological predispositions developed during earlier stages of human evolution color contemporary criminal activity. Male criminals, for example, tend toward robbery and burglary—crimes in which they can continue to enact their "hunter instincts" developed long ago. The criminality of women, on the other hand, is more typical of "gatherers" when it involves shoplifting, simple theft, and so on.

Human behavioral predilections can be studied in a variety of ways. In the 1989 book *Evolutionary Jurisprudence,* John H. Beckstrom reported on his examination of over 400 legal documents that, he claimed, showed support for Wilson's contentions that humans tend to act so as to preserve territorial claims, the likelihood of successful reproduction, and the continuation of their own particular genetic material.[164] In his analysis, Beckstrom used legal claims and court decisions spanning over 300 years of judicial activity. Other theorists have gone so far as to imply that, among humans, there may be a gene-based tendency to experience guilt and to develop a conscience. Hence, notions of right and wrong, whether embodied in laws or in social convention, may flow from such a naturalistic origin. Learn more about sociobiology in general and the sociobiology of sociopathy at **Web Extras 5–10** and **5–11**.

As sociobiology began to receive expanded recognition from American investigators, some social scientists, believing the basic tenets of their profession to be challenged by

WEB
Extra
■ ■ ■ ■

Sociobiologists tell us that certain traits, such as territoriality, are common to both animals and humans. How might territoriality lead to crime?
Source: Paul Lally, Stock Boston

the movement, began to treat it as "criminology's anti-discipline."[165] Contemporary criminologist John Madison Memory writes, "By the early 1980s sociobiology presented such a significant threat to American criminology that it could no longer be ignored."[166] Criticisms were quick to come. Memory identifies many such critiques, including these charges:

- Sociobiology fails to convey the overwhelming significance of culture, social learning, and individual experiences in shaping the behavior of individuals and groups.
- Sociobiology is fundamentally wrong in its depiction of the basic nature of humans; there is no credible evidence of genetically based or determined tendencies to act in certain ways.
- Sociobiology is just another empirically unsupported rationale for the authoritative labeling and stigmatization of despised, threatening, powerless minorities.
- Humans are so thoroughly different from other animal species, even other primates, that there is no rational basis for the application to humans of findings from animal studies.

Many such criticisms were advanced by old-guard academics, some of whom still flourish, in an effort to prevent their own discipline's decline in influence in the face of otherwise convincing sociobiological claims. In the words of one observer, "Most criminologists, like most academicians, were wedded to a paradigm, and wedded even to the idea of paradigm, the idea that one great problem solution can permit the explanation of nearly all the unexplained variation in the field."[167] Today, many open-minded scholars are beginning to sense the growing need for a new synthesis—for a way in which to integrate the promise of biological theories like sociobiology with other long-accepted perspectives like sociology and psychology. As a result, the field of criminology appears ripe for a new multicausal approach.

Crime and Human Nature: A Contemporary Synthesis

During the mid-1980s, Arnold L. Lieber delivered an invited address at the annual meeting of the American Psychological Association in Denver, Colorado.[168] Lieber used the forum to describe his research on biology and crime, which linked phases of the moon to fluctuations in the incidence of violence among human beings. Nights around full moons, according to Lieber, show a significant rise in crime. Although critics found this type of research nonsensical, police officers, hospital personnel, ambulance drivers, and many late-night service providers who heard of Lieber's talk understood what he was describing. Many such individuals, in their own experience, had apparently seen validation of the "full moon thesis."

Shortly after Lieber's presentation, criminologist **James Q. Wilson** and psychologist **Richard J. Herrnstein** teamed up to write *Crime and Human Nature,* a book-length treatise that reiterates many of the arguments proposed by biological criminologists over the previous century.[169] Their purpose, at least in part, was to reopen discussion of biological causes of crime. "We want to show," Herrnstein said, "that the pendulum is beginning to swing away from a totally sociological explanation of crime."[170] Their avowed goal was "not to state a case just for genetic factors, but to state a comprehensive theory of crime that draws together all the different factors that cause criminal behavior."[171]

The constitutional factors that Wilson and Herrnstein cite as contributing to crime include the following:[172]

- **Gender.** "Crime," the authors say, "has been predominantly male behavior."
- **Age.** "In general, the tendency to break the law declines throughout life."

- **Body type.** "A disproportionate number of criminals have a mesomorphic build."
- **Intelligence.** Criminality is said to be clearly and consistently associated with low intelligence.
- **Personality.** Criminals are typically aggressive, impulsive, and cruel.

Although personality, behavioral problems, and intelligence may be related to environment, the authors say that "each involves some genetic inheritance." Wilson and Herrnstein do recognize social factors in the development of personality, but they suggest that constitutional factors predispose a person to specific types of behavior and that societal reactions to such predispositions may determine, to a large degree, the form of continued behavior.

Even more recently, some scientists have advanced the notion of *neuroplasticity* (sometimes called *brain plasticity* or *cortical plasticity*) to explain why some people experience significant changes in personality while undergoing new experiences. Neuroplasticity holds that the brain can alter its structure and function in response to experience. It is well-known, for example, that when portions of the brain are physically damaged through trauma, stroke, or other types of injury, adjacent parts of the brain can assume some of the psychological or motor functions that would have otherwise been lost. A few years ago, however, researchers found that the neural circuitry in the brains of practiced meditators had changed, apparently in response to thousands of hours spent meditating, as evidenced by the fact that the brain waves in the meditators were significantly different than those of nonmeditators.[173] Scientists who study neuroplasticity now believe that not only does the brain change in response to external stimuli or physical trauma, but that it is also malleable in response to internal stimuli—that is, thought. If true, simple self-improvement techniques that have long been the stuff of pop culture—like positive thinking and silently repeated self-affirmations—may actually foster positive alterations in personality and produce an increased likelihood of socially approved behaviors. A few years ago, for example, UCLA psychiatrist Jeffrey M. Schwartz demonstrated that patients suffering from obsessive compulsive disorder (OCD) are capable of consciously rechanneling compulsive urges into more socially acceptable activities, and that by doing so they can actually alter their brains' neuronal circuitry.[174] Hence, physical changes to the brain in response to experiences that were once thought possible only in the very young, also characterize adults in some situations. With these considerations in mind, some suggest that the interplay among heredity, biology, and the social environment may be much more complicated than once thought, and may provide the key nexus in any consideration of crime causation.

Former New Jersey Police Superintendent Carl Williams. Williams, a 35-year police veteran, was forced to resign when the "racial profiling" practices his officers used to target motorists became public. Possible links between race and crime, suggested by some researchers, are especially repugnant to many who criticize biological criminology. Why might varying rates of arrest and of criminal offending appear to be associated with race?

Source: AP Wide World Photos

Policy Implications of Biological Theories

In his recent book, *The Blank Slate: The Modern Denial of Human Nature*,[175] MIT cognitive scientist Steven Pinker tells readers that today's social scientists unjustly ignore the biological basis of human behavior, replacing it instead with three myths: (1) the myth of the blank slate, (2) the myth of the Noble Savage, and (3) the Ghost in the Machine myth. The blank slate myth holds that the human mind has no innate traits and that the human personality is fully malleable by society. The Noble Savage myth says that human nature is essentially good. The Ghost in the Machine myth holds that each person has an individual soul-like quality that can make choices that can be completely independent of any biological predispositions. These three myths, says Pinker, comprise the standard social science model of the modern era and have led to misguided social and political policies. It is only when the impact of biology on human behavior is fully recognized, says the author, that effective social policies—including those aimed at controlling crime—can be developed.

According to C. Ray Jeffery, a comprehensive biologically based program of crime prevention and crime control would include[176]

- "Pre- and postnatal care for pregnant women and their infants" to monitor and address potentially detrimental developmental conditions, which could lead to heightened aggression and crime later in life.
- Monitoring of children throughout the early stages of their development to identify "early symptoms of behavioral disorder."
- Monitoring of children in their early years to reduce the risk of exposure to violence-inducing experiences like child abuse and violence committed by other children.
- Neurological examinations, including CAT, PET, and MRI scans, "given when the need is evident."
- Biological research, conducted in our nation's prisons and treatment facilities, which might better identify the root causes of aggression and violence. Laws that prevent the experimental use of prison subjects, the analysis of the bodies of executed prisoners, and other similar types of biological investigations must change, says Jeffery.

Jeffery adds that the fundamental orientation of our legal system must also change to acknowledge contributions of biological criminologists. Such a change would replace or supplement our current "right to punishment" doctrine with a "right to treatment" philosophy. Jeffery concludes his analysis by saying, "If legal and political barriers prevent us from regarding antisocial behavior as a medical problem, and if we do not permit medical research on criminal behavior, how can we ever solve the crime problem?"[177]

The dangers of too great a dependence on biological approaches to crime, however, raise the specter of an Orwellian bogeyman in charge of every aspect of human social life, from conception to the grave—and include the possible abortion of defective fetuses, capital punishment in lieu of rehabilitation, and enforced sterilization. Precedent for such fears can be found in cases like *Buck* v. *Bell*,[178] discussed earlier in this chapter, in which the U.S. Supreme Court, influenced by the genetically based perspectives of the times, sanctioned state-enforced sterilization statutes.

Potential links between race and crime, suggested by some researchers, are especially repugnant to many who criticize biological criminology, seeing it as a reemergence of the eugenics movement of the early twentieth century. Ronald Walters, a political scientist at Howard University, for example, observes that "seeking the biological and genetic aspects of violence is dangerous to African-American youth. . . . When you consider the perception that black people have always been the violent people in this society, it is a short step from this stereotype to using this kind of research for social control."[179] According to University of Maryland criminologists Gary LaFree and Katheryn K. Russell, "[A] major reason for moving away from studies of differential crime rates by race, beginning in the 1960s, was to avoid negative associations between race and crime: blacks already were disadvantaged by the economy and the society. Thus, to imply that crime problems were more serious for blacks than for others seemed to be double victimization." However, the same authors add, "no group has suffered more than African-Americans by our failure to understand and control street crime."[180]

Although biological theories of crime may have problems, some criminologists believe that to ignore the potential contributions of biological theorists because of hypothetical policy consequences or because of the supposed danger of racial prejudice does a disservice to the science of criminology and denies the opportunity for compassionate and objective researchers to realistically assist in the process of crime reduction. In 1993, for example, the Youth Violence Initiative, begun under President George Bush to study problem behavior among American youth, was canceled by the Clinton administration because indications were that it might identify a disproportionate number of racial and ethnic minorities as delinquent.

In 1997, in an attempt to bring biological theorizing into the criminological mainstream, Lee Ellis and Anthony Walsh expanded on the theme of genetic predispositions, noting that "in the case of behavior, nearly all of the effects of genes are quite indirect because they are mediated through complex chains of events occurring in the brain. This means that there are almost certainly no genes for something as complex as criminal behavior. Nevertheless, many genes may affect brain functioning in ways that either increase or reduce the chances of individuals learning various complex behavior patterns, including behavior patterns that happen to be so offensive to others that criminal sanctions have been instituted to minimize their recurrence."[181]

Critiques of Biological Theories

In a recent critique of biological theories of crime, Nicole Hahn Rafter, a noted criminologist at Northeastern University, argued against the possible development of a contemporary eugenics movement based upon the findings of modern-day genetics. In *Creating Born Criminals,* Rafter attempted to demonstrate the need for contemporary researchers and policymakers to know how eugenic reasoning worked in the past so that they would be able to recognize the dangers posed by any theory that interprets social problems in biological terms and that sees what might be innate differences as evidence of biological inferiority.[182] While genetic solutions to human problems may seem to offer a near-future panacea, Rafter warns that policymakers must always be on their guard against the danger of oversimplifying social issues as complex as crime.

A focused critique of biological perspectives on crime causation is provided by Glenn D. Walters and Thomas W. White, who contend that "genetic research on crime has been poorly designed, ambiguously reported, and exceedingly inadequate in addressing the relevant issues."[183] Walters and White highlight the following specific shortcomings of studies in the area:

- Few biological studies adequately conceptualize criminality. "Several studies," they say, "have defined criminality on the basis of a single arrest."[184]

- Twin studies, in particular, have sometimes failed to properly establish whether a pair of twins is monozygotic or dizygotic. This is because some MZ twins are not identical in appearance, and only a few twin studies have depended on biological testing rather than on a simple evaluation of appearances.

- Problems in estimating the degree of criminality among sample populations are rife in biological (and in many other) studies of criminality. Interview data are open to interpretation, and existing statistical data on the past criminality of offenders are not always properly appreciated.

- Methodological problems abound in many studies that attempt to evaluate the role of genetics in crime. Walters and White mention, among other things, the lack of control or comparison groups, small sample sizes, the dropping out of subjects from study groups, biased sampling techniques, and the use of inappropriate forms of statistical analysis.
- Results obtained outside the United States may not be applicable within this country. Twin studies conducted in Sweden and Denmark provide an example of this potential lack of generalizability.

Walters and White nonetheless conclude that "genetic factors are undoubtedly correlated with various measures of criminality," but they add that "the large number of methodological flaws and limitations in the research should make one cautious in drawing any causal inferences at this point in time."[185]

SUMMARY

Contemporary criminology, stung in large part by social policy fiascoes engendered by the eugenics movement of 100 years ago, has shown considerable reluctance to adapt the contributions of biological theories to an understanding of criminality. An objective understanding of any social phenomenon, however, requires clear consideration of all available evidence. Modern proponents of biological perspectives on crime and crime causation point out that the link between the social environment and human behavior is continuously mediated by the brain. Human activity flows from the human mind, and the mind is biologically grounded in the brain. The brain itself is apparently subject to influences from other aspects of the body, such as genes, hormones, neurotransmitters, and the levels of various chemicals in the blood. Such realizations require only a small intellectual leap to the realization that biological aspects of the human organism may play similar contributory roles in criminal behavior.

Unfortunately for proponents of biological theories that seek to explain crime, sociological and psychological explanations for human behavior are well entrenched. In addition, studies purporting to have identified biological determinants of behavior have been energetically criticized on methodological and other grounds. As a consequence, many criminologists have concluded that while biology provides both a context for, and specific precursors to, human behavior, biological predispositions for behavior in most instances of human interaction are overshadowed by the role of volition, the mechanisms of human thought, and the undeniable influences of socialization and acculturation. Even so, any honest and comprehensive approach to human behavior must recognize the biological precursors of that behavior.

KEY TERMS

atavism, 171

behavioral genetics, 192

biological theory, 167

born criminal, 173

constitutional theory, 176

criminal anthropology, 170

criminaloids, 172

cycloid, 177

displastic, 177

ectomorph, 177

endomorph, 177

eugenic criminology, 188

eugenics, 188

genetic determinism, 194

heritability, 196

hypoglycemia, 178

Juke family, 188

Kallikak family, 188

masculinity hypothesis, 173

mesomorph, 177

monozygotic (MZ) twins, 192

paradigm, 200

phrenology, 170

schizoid, 177

sociobiology, 200

somatotyping, 176

supermale, 189

testosterone, 183

KEY NAMES AND CASES

QUESTIONS FOR REVIEW

1. What are the central assumptions of biological theories of crime? How do such theories differ from other perspectives that attempt to explain the same phenomena?

2. What biological factors does this chapter suggest might substantially influence human aggression?

3. What have research studies in the field of genetics had to say about possible causes of crime?

4. What is sociobiology? How do sociobiologists explain criminality?

5. What are some of the constitutional factors that this chapter identifies as linked to criminality?

6. What are the social policy implications of biological theories of crime? What U.S. Supreme Court case, discussed in this chapter, might presage a type of policy based on such theories?

7. Why have biological approaches to crime causation encountered stiff criticism? Do you agree or disagree with those who are critical of such perspectives? Why?

QUESTIONS FOR REFLECTION

1. This book emphasizes a social problems versus social responsibility theme. Which perspective is best supported by biological theories of crime causation? Why?

2. What does the author of this book mean when he writes, "Open inquiry . . . requires objective consideration of all points of view and an unbiased examination of each for its ability to shed light on the subject under study"? Do you agree or disagree with this assertion? Why?

WEB QUEST

Visit *Crime Times* on the World Wide Web at www.crimetimes. org. *Crime Times* offers one of the Web's best sources for reviews and information about research on biological causes of criminal, violent, and psychopathic behavior. Hard-copy versions of *Crime Times* in newsletter format are regularly mailed to selected members of Congress, medical schools, psychiatrists, criminologists, psychologists, researchers, foundations, justice system professionals, and media representatives. Both the newsletter and the Web versions of *Crime Times* focus on research concerning the link between aberrant behavior and neurochemical imbalances, physical injury, drugs, toxic environments, diet, food and chemical sensitivities, birth trauma, and genetic vulnerabilities to such factors.

If your instructor asks you to, review the archive of articles found at the *Crime Times* site, and pay special attention to those dealing with environmental contaminants and crime. Write a paper summarizing the research findings contained in these articles, being sure to provide a complete bibliography of the sources you used.

NOTES

[1] Nicole Rafter, "Earnest A. Hooton and the Biological Tradition in American Criminology," *Criminology*, Vol. 42, No. 3 (2004), p. 735.

[2] Quoted in Karen J. Winkler, "Criminals Are Born as Well as Made, Authors of Controversial Book Assert," *Chronicle of Higher Education*, January 16, 1986, p. 9.

[3] David P. Farrington, "Foreword," in David C. Rowe, *Biology and Crime* (Los Angeles: Roxbury, 2002), p. ix.

[4] Anastasia Toufexis, "Seeking the Roots of Violence," *Time*, April 19, 1993, p. 52.

[5] "Brain Tumour Causes Uncontrollable Paedophilia," *New Scientist*, October 21, 2002, http://www.newscientist.com/news/news.jsp?iD=NS99992943 (accessed September 12, 2007).

[6] Alwyn Barr, "Charles Joseph Whitman," *The Handbook of Texas Online* (The University of Texas at Austin), no date, http://www.tsha.utexas.edu/handbook/online/articles/view/WW/fwh42.html (accessed February 2, 2007).

[7] A. Raine, T. Lencz, K. Taylor, J. B. Hellige, S. Bihrle, L. Lacasse, M. Lee, S. Ishikawa, and P. Colletti, "Corpus Callosum Abnormalities in Psychopathic Antisocial Individuals," *Archives of General Psychiatry*, Vol. 60, No. 11 (November 2003), pp. 1134–1142.

[8] See, for example, Henrik Soderstrom et al., "Reduced Regional Cerebral Blood Flow in Non-psychotic Violent Offenders," *Psychiatry Research*, Vol. 98 (2000), pp. 29–41; and Antoine Bechara et al., "Insensitivity to Future Consequences Following Damage to Human Prefrontal Cortex," *Cognition*, Vol. 50, No. 7 (1994), pp. 7–15.

[9] Jose Leon-Carrion and Francisco Javier Chacartegui Ramos, "Blows to the Head during Development Can Predispose to Violent Criminal Behaviour: Rehabilitation of Consequences of Head Injury Is a Measure for Crime Prevention," *Brain Injury*, Vol. 17, No. 3 (March 2003), pp. 207–216.

[10] See, for example, Ann Pytkowicz Streissguth et al., "Fetal Alcohol Syndrome in Adolescents and Adults," *Journal of the American Medical Association*, Vol. 265, No. 15 (April 17, 1991).

[11] C. Ray Jeffery, "Biological Perspectives," *Journal of Criminal Justice Education*, Vol. 4, No. 2 (fall 1993), pp. 292–293.

[12] C. Ray Jeffery, "Genetics, Crime and the Canceled Conference," *Criminologist*, Vol. 18, No. 1 (January/February 1993), pp. 1–8.

[13] Toufexis, "Seeking the Roots of Violence," p. 53.

[14] C. Ray Jeffery, "The Genetics and Crime Conference Revisited," *Criminologist*, Vol. 21, No. 2 (March/April 1996), p. 3.

[15] Taken from "Hope for the 'Hopeless,'" *Crime Times*, Vol. 10, No. 2 (2004), p. 2.

[16] Jeffery, "Biological Perspectives," p. 298.

[17] Konrad Lorenz, *On Aggression* (New York: Harcourt, Brace and World, 1966).

[18] Ibid., p. 23.

[19] Ibid., p. 38.

[20] Ibid., p. 249.

[21] Ibid.

[22] "Physical Attractiveness and Criminal Behavior," *The Encyclopedia of Criminology*, http://www.fitzroydearborn.com/chicago/criminology/sample-physical.asp (accessed November 17, 2006).

[23] Cesare Lombroso, "Introduction," in Gina Lombroso-Ferrero, *Criminal Man According to the Classification of Cesare Lombroso* (1911; reprint, Montclair, NJ: Patterson Smith, 1972), p. xiv.

[24] Charles Darwin, *Descent of Man: And Selection in Relation to Sex*, rev. ed. (London: John Murray, 1874), p. 137.

[25] Auguste Comte, *A System of Positive Polity*, trans. John Henry Bridges (New York: Franklin, 1875). Originally published in four volumes, 1851–1854.

[26] See K. L. Henwood and N. F. Pidgeon, "Qualitative Research and Psychological Theorising," *British Journal of Psychology*, Vol. 83 (1992), pp. 97–111.

[27] Lombroso, "Introduction," in Lombroso-Ferrero, *Criminal Man According to the Classification of Cesare Lombroso*, p. xv.

[28] Della Fossetta, *Cerebellare Mediana in un Criminale* (Institute Lombardo di Scienze e Lettere, 1872), pp. 1058–1065, as cited and translated by Thorsten Sellin, "A New Phase of Criminal Anthropology in Italy," *The Annuals of the American Academy of Political and Social Science, Modern Crime*, No. 525 (May 1926), p. 234.

[29] The English-language version appeared in 1895 as Cesare Lombroso, *The Female Offender* (New York: D. Appleton, 1895).

[30] Marvin Wolfgang, "Cesare Lombroso," in Hermann Mannheim, *Pioneers in Criminology*, 2nd ed. (Montclair, NJ: Patterson Smith, 1972), p. 254.

[31] Charles Goring, *The English Convict: A Statistical Study* (London: His Majesty's Stationery Office, 1913; reprint, Montclair, NJ: Patterson Smith, 1972), p. 15.

[32] Ibid.

[33] Earnest A. Hooton, *Crime and the Man* (Cambridge, MA: Harvard University Press, 1939; reprint, Westport, CT: Greenwood Press, 1972).

[34] Ibid., pp. 57–58.

[35] Ibid., p. 72.

[36] Ibid., p. 75.

[37] Ibid., p. 388.

[38] Earnest A. Hooton, *The American Criminal: An Anthropological Study* (Cambridge, MA: Harvard University Press, 1939).

[39] Stephen Schafer, *Theories in Criminology: Past and Present Philosophies of the Crime Problem* (New York: Random House, 1969), p. 187.

[40] L. Arseneault et al., "Minor Physical Anomalies and Family Adversity as Risk Factors for Violent Delinquency in Adolescence," *American Journal of Psychiatry*, Vol. 157, No. 6 (June 2000), pp. 917–923.

[41] William H. Sheldon, *Varieties of Delinquent Youth* (New York: Harper & Brothers, 1949).

[42] Sheldon Glueck and Eleanor Glueck, *Unraveling Juvenile Delinquency* (Cambridge, MA: Harvard University Press, 1950).

[43] D. Hill and W. Sargent, "A Case of Matricide," *Lancet*, Vol. 244 (1943), pp. 526–527.

[44] William Dufty, *Sugar Blues* (Pandor, PA: Chilton, 1975).

[45] See, Court TV's Crime Library, "Twinkies as a Defense," Web posted at http://www.crimelibrary.com/criminal_mind/psychology/insanity/7.html. Accessed August 8, 2007.

[46] Nanci Hellmich, "Sweets May Not Be Culprit in Hyper Kids," *USA Today*, February 3, 1994, p. 1A, reporting on a study published in the *New England Journal of Medicine*.

[47] Ibid.

[48] See Adrian Raine et al., "Prefrontal Glucose Deficits in Murderers Lacking Psychosocial Deprivation," *Neuropsychiatry, Neuropsychology, and Behavioral Neurology*, Vol. 11, No. 1 (1998), pp. 1–7; and Adrian Raine et al., "Selective Reductions in Prefrontal Glucose Metabolism in Murderers," *Biological Psychiatry*, Vol. 36 (September 1, 1994), pp. 319–332.

[49] "PET Study: Looking Inside the Minds of Murderers," *Crime Times*, Vol. 1, No. 1–2 (1995), http://www.crime-times.org/95a/w95ap1.htm (accessed November 15, 2006).

[50] Raine et al., "Selective Reductions in Prefrontal Glucose Metabolism in Murderers."

[51] See, for example, A. R. Mawson and K. J. Jacobs, "Corn Consumption, Tryptophan, and Cross National Homicide Rates," *Journal of Orthomolecular Psychiatry*, Vol. 7 (1978), pp. 227–230;

and A. Hoffer, "The Relation of Crime to Nutrition," *Humanist in Canada,* Vol. 8 (1975), p. 8.

[52] See, for example, C. Hawley and R. E. Buckley, "Food Dyes and Hyperkinetic Children," *Academy Therapy,* Vol. 10 (1974), pp. 27–32; and Alexander Schauss, *Diet, Crime and Delinquency* (Berkeley, CA: Parker House, 1980).

[53] "Special Report: Measuring Your Life with Coffee Spoons," *Tufts University Diet and Nutrition Letter,* Vol. 2, No. 2 (April 1984), pp. 3–6.

[54] See, for example, "Special Report: Does What You Eat Affect Your Mood and Actions?" *Tufts University Diet and Nutrition Letter,* Vol. 2, No. 12 (February 1985), pp. 4–6.

[55] See *Tufts University Diet and Nutrition Newsletter,* Vol. 2, No. 11 (January 1985), p. 2; and "Special Report: Why Sugar Continues to Concern Nutritionists," *Tufts University Diet and Nutrition Letter,* Vol. 3, No. 3 (May 1985), pp. 3–6.

[56] A. Hoffer, "Children with Learning and Behavioral Disorders," *Journal of Orthomolecular Psychiatry,* Vol. 5 (1976), p. 229.

[57] I. B. Helland, L. Smith, K. Saarem, O. D. Saugstad, and C. A. Drevon, "Maternal Supplements with Very-long-chain Omega-3 Fatty Acids during Pregnancy and Lactation Augments Children's IQ at 4 Years of Age," *Pediatrics,* Vol. 111, No. 1 (January 2003), pp. 39–44.

[58] C. Iribarren, J. H. Markovitz, D. R. Jacobs, Jr., P. J. Schreiner, M. Daviglus, and J. R. Hibbeln, "Dietary Intake of Omega-3, Omega-6 Fatty Acids and Fish: Relationship with Hostility in Young Adults—The CARDIA Study," *European Journal of Clinical Nutrition,* Vol. 50, No. 1 (January 2004), pp. 24–31.

[59] David Benton, "The Impact of Diet on Anti-social, Violent and Criminal Behaviour," *Neuroscience and Biobehavioral Reviews,* Vol. 31 (2007), pp. 752–774.

[60] C. Bernard Gesch, Sean M. Hammond, Sarah E. Hampson, Anita Eves, and Martin J. Crowder, "Influence of Supplementary Vitamins, Minerals and Essential Fatty Acids on the Antisocial Behaviour of Young Adult Prisoners: Randomized, Placebo-controlled Trial," *British Journal of Psychiatry,* Vol. 181 (July 2002), pp. 22–28.

[61] S. Schoenthaler and I. D. Bier, "Addiction and Criminal Behaviour," in J. Brostoff and S. Challacombe, eds., *Food Allergy and Intolerance,* 2nd ed. (London: W. B. Saunders, 2002), pp. 985–1000.

[62] Roger D. Masters, Brian Hone, and Anil Doshi, "Environmental Pollution, Neurotoxicity, and Criminal Violence," in J. Rose, ed., *Environmental Toxicology* (London and New York: Gordon and Breach, 1997).

[63] Peter Montague, "Toxics and Violent Crime," *Rachel's Environment and Health Weekly,* No. 551 (June 19, 1997).

[64] See, for example, Jeffrey Halperin et al., "Serotonergic Function in Aggressive and Nonaggressive Boys with ADHD," *American Journal of Psychiatry,* Vol. 151, No. 2 (February 1994), pp. 243–248.

[65] Masters, Hone, and Doshi, "Environmental Pollution, Neurotoxicity, and Criminal Violence."

[66] See, for example, Rick Nevin, "How Lead Exposure Relates to Temporal Changes in IQ, Violent Crime, and Unwed Pregnancy," *Environmental Research,* Vol. 83, No.1 (May 2000), pp. 1–22.

[67] Quoted in Alison Motluck, "Pollution May Lead to a Life of Crime," *New Scientist,* Vol. 154, No. 2084 (May 31, 1997), p. 4.

[68] Don Cherek and Scott Lane, "Effects of d,1-fenfluramine on Aggressive and Impulsive Responding in Adult Males with a History of Conduct Disorder," *Psychopharmacology,* Vol. 146 (1999), pp. 473–481.

[69] See Alexander G. Schauss, "Tranquilizing Effect of Color Reduces Aggressive Behavior and Potential Violence," *Journal of Orthomolecular Psychiatry,* Vol. 8, No. 4 (1979), pp. 218–221; and David Johnston, "Is It Merely a Fad, or Do Pastel Walls Stop Jail House Brawls?" *Corrections Magazine,* Vol. 7, No. 3 (1981), pp. 28–32.

[70] Questions were raised, however, about the long-term effects of confinement in pink cells, and some researchers suggested that extended exposure to the color pink could generate suicidal impulses.

[71] L. Goldschmidt, N. L. Day, and G. A. Richardson, "Effects of Prenatal Marijuana Exposure on Child Behavior Problems at Age 10," *Neurotoxicology and Teratology,* Vol. 22, No. 3 (May/June 2000), pp. 325–336.

[72] David Fergusson, Lianne Woodward, and L. John Horwood, "Maternal Smoking during Pregnancy and Psychiatric Adjustment in Late Adolescence," *Archives of General Psychiatry,* Vol. 55 (August 1998), pp. 721–727.

[73] Jacob F. Orlebeke, Dirk L. Knol, and Frank C. Verhulst, "Increase in Child Behavior Problems Resulting from Maternal Smoking during Pregnancy," *Archives of Environmental Health,* Vol. 52, No. 4 (July/August 1997), pp. 317–321.

[74] Travis C. Pratt, Jean Marie McGloin, and Noelle E. Fearn, "Maternal Cigarette Smoking During Pregnancy and Criminal/Deviant Behavior: A Meta-Analysis," *International Journal of Offender Therapy and Comparative Criminology,* Vol. 50, No. 6 (2006), pp. 672–690.

[75] See, for example, Streissguth et al., "Fetal Alcohol Syndrome in Adolescents and Adults."

[76] Tresa M. Roebuck, Sarah N. Mattson, and Edward P. Riley, "Behavioral and Psychosocial Profiles of Alcohol-Exposed Children," *Alcoholism: Clinical and Experimental Research,* Vol. 23, No. 6 (June 1999), pp. 1070–1076.

[77] See, for example, R. T. Rada, D. R. Laws, and R. Kellner, "Plasma Testosterone Levels in the Rapist," *Psychosomatic Medicine,* Vol. 38 (1976), pp. 257–268.

[78] "The Insanity of Steroid Abuse," *Newsweek,* May 23, 1988, p. 75.

[79] Dan Olweus et al., "Testosterone, Aggression, Physical and Personality Dimensions in Normal Adolescent Males," *Psychosomatic Medicine,* Vol. 42 (1980), pp. 253–269.

[80] Richard Udry, "Biosocial Models of Adolescent Problem Behaviors," *Social Biology,* Vol. 37 (1990), pp. 1–10.

[81] Dan Olweus, "Testosterone and Adrenaline: Aggressive Antisocial Behavior in Normal Adolescent Males," in Sarnoff A. Mednick, Terrie E. Moffitt, and Susan A. Stack, eds., *The Causes of Crime: New Biological Approaches* (Cambridge: Cambridge University Press, 1987), pp. 263–282.

[82] Alan Booth and D. Wayne Osgood, "The Influence of Testosterone on Deviance in Adulthood: Assessing and Explaining the Relationship," *Criminology,* Vol. 31, No. 1 (1993), p. 93.

[83] E. G. Stalenheim et al., "Testosterone as a Biological Marker in Psychopathy and Alcoholism," *Psychiatry Research,* Vol. 77, No. 2 (February 1998), pp. 79–88.

[84] Paul C. Bernhardt, "Influences of Serotonin and Testosterone in Aggression and Dominance: Convergence with Social Psychology," *Current Directions in Psychological Science,* Vol. 6, No. 2 (April 1997), pp. 44–48.

[85] Michelle M. Wirth and Oliver C. Schultheiss, "Basal Testosterone Moderates Responses to Anger Faces in Humans," *Physiology and Behavior,* Vol. 90 (2007), pp. 496–505.

[86] Ibid., p. 502.

[87] Richard Udry, Luther Talbert, and Naomi Morris, "Biosocial Foundations for Adolescent Female Sexuality," *Demography,* Vol. 23 (1986), pp. 217–227.

[88] James M. Dabbs, Jr., and Marian F. Hargrove, "Age, Testosterone, and Behavior among Female Prison Inmates," *Psychosomatic Medicine,* Vol. 59 (1997), pp. 447–480.

[89] A. Maras, M. Laucht, D. Gerdes, C. Wilhelm, S. Lewicka, D. Haack, L. Malisova, and M. H. Schmidt, "Association of Testosterone and Dihydrotestosterone with Externalizing Behavior in Adolescent Boys and Girls, *Psychoneuroendocrinology,* Vol. 28, No. 7 (October 2003), pp. 932–940.

90 *Regina* v. *English*, unreported, Norwich Crown Court, November 10, 1981.

91 "Drunk Driving Charge Dismissed: PMS Cited," *Fayetteville* (NC) *Observer-Times*, June 7, 1991, p. 3A.

92 Toufexis, "Seeking the Roots of Violence," pp. 52–54.

93 Terrie E. Moffitt et al., "Whole Blood Serotonin Relates to Violence in an Epidemiological Study," *Biological Psychiatry*, Vol. 43, No. 6 (March 15, 1998), pp. 446–457.

94 H. Soderstrom, K. Blennow, A. K. Sjodin, and A. Forsman, "New Evidence for an Association between the CSF HVA:5–HIAA Ratio and Psychopathic Traits," *Journal of Neurology, Neurosurgery and Psychiatry*, Vol. 74 (2003), pp. 918–921.

95 Keith McBurnett et al., "Low Salivary Cortisol and Persistent Aggression in Boys Referred for Disruptive Behavior," *Archives of General Psychiatry*, Vol. 57, No. 1 (January 2000), pp. 38–43.

96 See E. G. Stalenheim, L. von Knorring, and L. Wide, "Serum Levels of Thyroid Hormones as Biological Markers in a Swedish Forensic Psychiatric Population," *Biological Psychiatry*, Vol. 43, No. 10 (May 15, 1998), pp. 755–761; and P. O. Alm et al., "Criminality and Psychopathy as Related to Thyroid Activity in Former Juvenile Delinquents," *Acta Psychiatrica Scandinavica*, Vol. 94, No. 2 (August 1996), pp. 112–117.

97 Stalenheim, von Knorring, and Wide, "Serum Levels of Thyroid Hormones as Biological Markers in a Swedish Forensic Psychiatric Population."

98 Michael Kosfeld, Markus Heinrichs, Paul J. Zak, Urs Fischbacher, and Ernst Fehr, "Oxytocin Increases Trust in Humans," *Nature*, Vol. 435 (June 2005), pp. 673–676.

99 "'Trust' Hormone Identified," *Red Herring*, June 2, 2005.

100 J. Rotton and E. G. Cohn, "Weather, Climate, and Crime," in R. Bechtel and E. Churchman, eds., *The 2002 Handbook of Environmental Psychology* (New York: Wiley, 2002), pp. 461–498.

101 E. G. Cohn and J. Rotton, "Assault as a Function of Time and Temperature: A Moderator-Variable Time-Series Analysis," *Journal of Personality and Social Psychology*, Vol. 72 (1997), pp. 1322–1334.

102 J. Rotton and E. G. Cohn, "Violence as a Curvilinear Function of Temperature in Dallas: A Replication," *Journal of Personality and Social Psychology*, Vol. 78 (2000), pp. 1074–1081.

103 E. G. Cohn and J. Rotton, "Weather, Seasonal Trends, and Property Crimes in Minneapolis, 1987–1988: A Moderator-Variable Time-Series Analysis of Routine Activities," *Journal of Environmental Psychology*, Vol. 20 (2000), pp. 257–272.

104 J. Rotton and E. G. Cohn, "Temperature, Routine Activities, and Domestic Violence: A Reanalysis," *Victims and Violence*, Vol. 16 (2001), pp. 203–215.

105 J. Rotton and E. G. Cohn, "Weather, Disorderly Conduct, and Assaults: From Social Contact to Social Avoidance," *Environment and Behavior*, Vol. 32 (2000), pp. 649–671.

106 Thomas J. Schory, Natasha Piecznski, Sunil Nair, and Rif S. EI-Mallakh, "Barometric Pressure, Emergency Psychiatric Visits, and Violent Acts," *Canadian Journal of Psychiatry*, Vol. 48 (October 2003), pp. 624–627.

107 Richard Louis Dugdale, *The Jukes: A Study in Crime, Pauperism, Disease, and Heredity*, 3rd ed. (New York: G. P. Putnam's Sons, 1895).

108 Arthur H. Estabrook, *The Jukes in 1915* (Washington, DC: Carnegie Institute of Washington, 1916).

109 Henry Herbert Goddard, *The Kallikak Family: A Study in the Heredity of Feeblemindedness* (New York: Macmillan, 1912).

110 See Nicole Hahn Rafter, *Creating Born Criminals* (Urbana: University of Illinois Press, 1997).

111 See Nicole Hahn Rafter, ed., *White Trash: The Eugenics Family Studies, 1877–1919* (Boston: Northeastern University Press, 1988).

112 *Buck* v. *Bell*, 274 U.S. 200, 207 (1927).

113 Sir Julian Huxley "How Can Man Improve Man?" *New Scientist*, June 15, 1962.

114 P. A. Jacobs, M. Brunton, and M. Melville, "Aggressive Behavior, Mental Subnormality, and the XYY Male," *Nature*, Vol. 208 (1965), p. 1351.

115 Biologists often define *karyotype* as "a photomicrograph of metaphase chromosomes in a standard array."

116 See David A. Jones, *History of Criminology: A Philosophical Perspective* (Westport, CT: Greenwood Press, 1986), p. 124.

117 Many of which have been summarized in J. Katz and W. Chambliss, "Biology and Crime," in J. F. Sheley, ed., *Criminology* (Belmont, CA: Wadsworth, 1991), pp. 245–272.

118 As reported by S. A. Mednick and J. Volavka, "Biology and Crime," in N. Morris and M. Tonry, *Crime and Justice: An Annual Review of Research*, Vol. 2 (Chicago: University of Chicago Press, 1980), pp. 85–158; and D. A. Andrews and James Bonta, *The Psychology of Criminal Conduct* (Cincinnati: Anderson, 1994), pp. 126–127.

119 T. Sarbin and J. Miller, "Demonism Revisited: The XYY Chromosomal Anomaly," *Issues in Criminology*, Vol. 5 (1970), p. 199.

120 Geoffrey Cowley and Carol Hallin, "The Genetics of Bad Behavior: A Study Links Violence to Heredity," *Newsweek*, November 1, 1993, p. 57.

121 See Joseph D. McInerney, "Genes and Behavior: A Complex Relationship," *Judicature*, Vol. 83, No. 3 (November–December 1999).

122 Sir Francis Galton, *Inquiry into Human Faculty and Its Development*, 2nd ed. (London: J. M. Dent and Sons, 1907).

123 Johannes Lange, *Verbrechen als Schicksal* (Leipzig: Georg Thieme, 1929).

124 Karl O. Christiansen, "A Preliminary Study of Criminality among Twins," in Sarnoff Mednick and Karl Christiansen, eds., *Biosocial Bases of Criminal Behavior* (New York: Gardner Press, 1977).

125 The Minnesota Twin Family Study, http://www.psych.umn.edu/psylabs/mtfs. Accessed August 10, 2007.

126 T. J. Bouchard et al., "Sources of Human Psychological Differences: The Minnesota Study of Twins Reared Apart," *Science*, Vol. 250, No. 4978 (1990), pp. 223–228.

127 Edwin J. C. G. van den Oord, Dorret I. Boomsma, and Frank C. Verhulst, "A Study of Problem Behaviors in 10- to 15-Year-Old Biologically Related and Unrelated International Adoptees," *Behavior Genetics*, Vol. 24, No. 3 (1994), pp. 193–205.

128 Peter McGuffin and Anita Thapar, "Genetic Basis of Bad Behaviour in Adolescents," *Lancet*, Vol. 350 (August 9, 1997), pp. 411–412.

129 Wendy Slutske et al., "Modeling Genetic and Environmental Influences in the Etiology of Conduct Disorder: A Study of 2,682 Adult Twin Pairs," *Journal of Abnormal Psychology*, Vol. 106, No. 2 (1997), pp. 266–279.

130 Louise Arseneault, Terrie E. Moffitt, Avshalom Caspi, Alan Taylor, Fruhling V. Rijsdijk, Sara R. Jaffee, Lennifer C. Ablow, and Jeffrey R. Measelle, "Strong Genetic Effects on Cross-situational Antisocial Behaviour among 5-Year-Old Children According to Mothers, Teachers, Examiner-Observers, and Twins' Self-Reports," *Journal of Child Psychology and Psychiatry*, Vol. 44, No. 6 (September 2003), pp. 832–848.

131 Jeanette Taylor, Bryan R. Loney, Leonardo Bobadilla, William G. Iacono, and Matt McGue, "Genetic and Environmental Influences on Psychopathy Trait Dimensions in a Community Sample of Male Twins," *Journal of Abnormal Child Psychology*, Vol. 31, No. 6 (December 2003), pp. 633–645.

132 Much of the information and some of the wording in this section come from the National Human Genome Research Institute's Web page at http://www.nhgri.nih.gov/HGP (accessed November 16, 2007).

133 Rick Weiss, "Genome Project Completed," *Washington Post*, April 15, 2003, p. A6.

[134] James Watson and Francis Crick, "Molecular Structure of Nucleic Acids: A Structure for Deoxyribose Nucleic Acid," *Nature*, Vol. 171 (April 1953), p. 737.

[135] Quoted in Tim Friend, "Violence Linked to Gene Defect: Pleasure Deficit May Be the Spark," *USA Today*, May 9, 1996. See the original research at Kenneth Blum et al., "Reward Deficiency Syndrome," *American Scientist*, Vol. 84 (March/April 1996), pp. 132–145, http://www.sigmaxi.org/amsci/Articles/96Articles/Blum-full.html (accessed January 5, 2005).

[136] For more information on the Dunedin Multidisciplinary Health and Development Study, see T. E. Moffitt, A. Caspi, M. Rutter, and P. A. Silva, *Sex Differences in Antisocial Behavior: Conduct Disorder, Delinquency and Violence in the Dunedin Longitudinal Study* (Cambridge: Cambridge University Press, 2001). Visit the Dunedin Multidisciplinary Health and Development Research Unit on the Web at http://healthsci.otago.ac.nz/dsm/dmhdru.

[137] See, for example, M. Rutter, H. Giller, and A. Hagell, *Antisocial Behavior by Young People* (Cambridge: Cambridge University Press, 1998).

[138] Avshalom Caspi, Joseph McClay, Terrie E. Moffitt, Jonathan Mill, Judy Martin, Ian W. Craig, Alan Taylor, and Richie Poulton, "Role of Genotype in the Cycle of Violence in Maltreated Children," *Science*, Vol. 298, No. 2 (August 2002), p. 851.

[139] Oreland, Nilsson et al., "Monoamine Oxidases: Activities, Genotypes and the Shaping of Behaviour," *Journal of Neural Transmission*, April 12, 2007; and Rickard L. Sjöberg, Kent W. Nilsson, et al., "Adolescent Girls and Criminal Activity: Role of MAOA-LPR Genotype and Psychosocial Factor," *American Journal of Medical Genetics Part B: Neuropsychiatric Genetics*, Volume 144B, Issue 2 (October, 2006), pp. 159–164.

[140] Baum, Akula, Cabanero, et al., "A Genome-wide Association Study Implicates Diacylglycerol Kinase Eta (DGKH) and Several Other Genes in the Etiology of Bipolar Disorder," *Molecular Psychiatry*, advance online publication, http://doi:10.1038/sj.mp.4002012 (accessed May 8, 2007).

[141] A. Meyer-Lindenberg et al., "Neural Mechanisms of Genetic Risk for Impulsivity and Violence in Humans," *Proceedings of the National Academy of Sciences*, Vol. 103, No. 16 (2006), pp. 6269–6274.

[142] Quoted in Bruce Bower, "Violent Developments: Disruptive Kids Grow into their Behavior," *Science News*, May 27, 2006, p. 328.

[143] McInerney, "Genes and Behavior."

[144] See, "The Genome Changes Everything: A Talk with Matt Ridley," http://www.edge.org/3rd_culture/ridley03/ridley_print.html (accessed February 10, 2007).

[145] Matt Ridley, "What Makes You Who You Are?" *Time*, June 2, 2003, pp. 55–63.

[146] "Genes Are So Liberating," *New Scientist*, May 17, 2003, http://www.newscientist.com/hottopics/humannature/article.jsp?id=2395520=The%20brain (accessed January 9, 2007).

[147] Jeffery, "Biological Perspectives," p. 300.

[148] Leanne Fiftal Alarid et al., "Women's Roles in Serious Offenses: A Study of Adult Felons," *Justice Quarterly*, Vol. 13, No. 3 (September 1996), pp. 432–454.

[149] Federal Bureau of Investigation, *Crime in the United States, 2006* (Washington, DC: US Department of Justice, 2007).

[150] Freda Adler, *Sisters in Crime: The Rise of the New Female Criminal* (New York: McGraw-Hill, 1975).

[151] Darrell J. Steffensmeir, "Sex Differences in Patterns of Adult Crime, 1965–1977: A Review and Assessment," *Social Forces*, Vol. 58 (1980), pp. 1098–1099.

[152] FBI, *Crime in the United States, 2000*, as computed by the author.

[153] See, for example, D. H. Fishbein, "The Psychobiology of Female Aggression," *Criminal Justice and Behavior*, Vol. 19 (1992), pp. 99–126.

[154] Robbin S. Ogle, Daniel Maier-Katin, and Thomas J. Bernard, "A Theory of Homicidal Behavior among Women," *Criminology*, Vol. 33, No. 2 (1995), pp. 173–193.

[155] Ibid., p. 177.

[156] Ibid., p. 179.

[157] Arthur Fisher, "A New Synthesis Comes of Age," *Mosaic*, Vol. 22, No. 1 (Spring 1991), pp. 2–9.

[158] The quotations attributed to Wilson in this section are from Edward O. Wilson, *Sociobiology: The New Synthesis* (Cambridge, MA: Belknap Press of Harvard University Press, 1975).

[159] Janet Zimmerman, "Six Held in Brutal Attack of Mich. Teens," *USA Today*, June 24, 1997, p. 3A.

[160] Wilson, *Sociobiology: The New Synthesis*, p. 327.

[161] Sarah Blaffer Hrdy, *The Langurs of Abu: Female and Male Strategies of Reproduction* (Cambridge, MA: Harvard University Press, 1977).

[162] Research by Martin Daly and Margo Wilson of McMaster University in Hamilton, Canada, as reported in Arthur Fisher, "A New Synthesis II: How Different Are Humans?" *Mosaic*, Vol. 22, No. 1 (Spring 1991), p. 14.

[163] Fisher, "A New Synthesis II," p. 11.

[164] John H. Beckstrom, *Evolutionary Jurisprudence: Prospects and Limitations on the Youth of Modern Darwinism throughout the Legal Process* (Urbana: University of Illinois Press, 1989).

[165] John Madison Memory, "Sociobiology and the Metamorphoses of Criminology: 1978–2000," unpublished manuscript.

[166] Ibid., p. 11.

[167] Ibid., p. 33.

[168] See also Arnold L. Lieber, *The Lunar Effect: Biological Tides and Human Emotions* (Garden City, NY: Anchor Press, 1978).

[169] James Q. Wilson and Richard J. Herrnstein, *Crime and Human Nature* (New York: Simon & Schuster, 1985).

[170] Quoted in Winkler, "Criminals Are Born as Well as Made," p. 5.

[171] Wilson and Herrnstein, *Crime and Human Nature*.

[172] Winkler, "Criminals Are Born as Well as Made," p. 8.

[173] Antoine Lutz, et al., Long-term Meditators Self-Induce High-Amplitude Gamma Synchrony During Mental Practice," *Proceedings of the National Academy of Sciences*, Vol. 101, No. 46 (November 16, 2004), pp. 16369–16373.

[174] Jeffrey M. Schwartz and Sharon Begley, *The Mind and the Brain: Neuroplasticity and the Power of Mental Force* (New York: Regan Books, 2002).

[175] Steven Pinker, *The Blank Slate: The Modern Denial of Human Nature* (New York: Viking Press, 2002).

[176] Jeffery, "Biological Perspectives," p. 303.

[177] Ibid.

[178] *Buck v. Bell*, 274 U.S. 200, 207 (1927).

[179] Toufexis, "Seeking the Roots of Violence," p. 53.

[180] Gary LaFree and Katheryn K. Russell, "The Argument for Studying Race and Crime," *Journal of Criminal Justice Education*, Vol. 4, No. 2 (fall 1993), p. 279.

[181] Ellis and Walsh, "Gene-Based Evolutionary Theories in Criminology," *Criminology*, Vol. 35, No. 2 (1997), pp. 229–230.

[182] Rafter, *Creating Born Criminals*.

[183] Glenn D. Walters and Thomas W. White, "Heredity and Crime: Bad Genes or Bad Research?" *Criminology*, Vol. 27, No. 3 (1989), pp. 455–485. See also P. A. Brennan and S. A. Mednick, "Reply to Walters and White: Heredity and Crime," *Criminology*, Vol. 28, No. 4 (November 1990), pp. 657–661.

[184] Ibid., p. 476.

[185] Ibid., p. 478.

Chapter 6

Psychological and Psychiatric Foundations of Criminal Behavior

Source: AP Wide World Photos

Outline

The antisocial child tends to become the antisocial teenager and then the antisocial adult, just as the antisocial adult then tends to produce another antisocial child.

—David Farrington[1]

We understand today that it is a cruel and ignorant practice to torture men and women whose mental disturbance expresses itself in the form of religious or other eccentricities, but we are still too deep in darkness to realize that the same is true of those whose quirks show themselves in criminality.

—Max G. Schlapp and Edward H. Smith[2]

Children will watch anything, and when a broadcaster uses crime and violence and other shoddy devices to monopolize a child's attention, it's worse than taking candy from a baby. It is taking precious time from the process of growing up.

—Newton N. Minow, Federal Communications Commission[3]

[The psychopath] lacks those normal human sentiments without which life in common is impossible.

—Gordon Allport[4]

Learning Outcomes

After reading this chapter, you should be able to

- Identify the major principles of psychological perspectives as they relate to criminal behavior
- List and describe some early psychological and psychiatric theories that purported to explain criminality
- Understand how criminality can be seen as a form of maladaptative behavior
- Understand how criminality can be seen as a form of adaptive behavior
- Describe the modeling theory of aggression and explain how aggressive patterns of behavior can be activated
- Describe behavior theory and explain the role of rewards and punishments in shaping behavior
- Explain attachment theory and describe the three forms of attachment
- Define *self-control* and describe how a lack of self-control can lead to crime
- Illustrate the legal concept of insanity and delineate the various legal standards for determining insanity
- Identify the types of crime control policies that might be based on psychological understandings of criminality
- Delineate the assumptions underlying the practice of criminal psychological profiling

Hear the author discuss this chapter at **crimtoday.com**

Introduction

Some crimes cry out for explanation. In November 2000, Perstephanie Elaine Muhammad (aka Perstephanie Elaine Simmons), a 30-year-old Cainhoy, South Carolina, resident, was arrested for the murder of her two young children. Muhammad had killed her three-year-old son, Yusan, by striking him in the head with an axe. She then stabbed her ten-year-old daughter, Ingrid, in the chest and slit her throat with a kitchen knife. An older daughter, Amber, escaped the mobile home where the killings took place and ran to a neighbor's house.[5] By the time police arrived, Muhammad, who was pregnant, had dumped the bodies of her dead children in a nearby field. After being taken into custody, Muhammad fought with officers and was charged with additional counts of assault on a police officer. Investigators soon discovered that Muhammad had been on medication for schizophrenia in the months before the killings but had stopped taking the drugs. She told psychiatrists that God spoke to her through the television and told her that the children had to be killed because they were evil robots. In 2001, Muhammad was allowed to plead not guilty by reason of insanity to two counts of murder and was ordered confined at a secure state hospital for the criminally insane in Columbia, South Carolina. Two years later, and fully medicated, she was moved to an ungated facility in preparation for possible release back into the community.

Ten years before the South Carolina killings, an infamous murderer captivated the nation's attention. Shortly after midnight on July 22, 1991, a handcuffed man flagged down a police car in suburban Milwaukee.[6] Officers soon learned that the man was Tracy Edwards, a 32-year-old city resident. The lurid story of homosexual abuse and physical attack that Edwards told led investigators to the apartment of a 31-year-old loner named Jeffrey Dahmer. Dahmer was quickly arrested, and a search of his apartment revealed the body parts of at least 11 people. In a confession to police, Dahmer told of how he had repeatedly lured men and boys to his apartment, murdered them, and then dismembered their bodies. Soon police investigations implicated Dahmer in a ten-year killing spree, which spanned several states and may have reached as far as Europe. Edwards, whom Dahmer had met in a shopping mall, explained that he went to Dahmer's apartment because Dahmer "seemed so normal."[7] One of Dahmer's victims, a 15-year-old boy, had earlier been discovered by police dazed and bleeding—and was returned to Dahmer's apartment after officers concluded that the situation involved nothing but a dispute between homosexual lovers.

Dahmer pleaded insane as a defense to charges of murder, but an expert witness at his trial, psychiatrist Park Dietz, testified that although Dahmer suffered from various psychological disorders, he could have chosen not to kill. Comparing Dahmer's sexual desires with someone who wants money but chooses not to rob, Dietz said, "The choice is exactly the same. . . . The freedom to make it is exactly the same."[8] In contrasting testimony, another expert witness claimed that Dahmer "had uncontrollable urges to kill and have sex with dead bodies."[9] Dahmer was sentenced to 15 consecutive life terms—1 each for the murders of his 15 victims[10]—but was himself murdered in prison by another inmate in late 1994.

Around the time that Dahmer died, another strange incident was making headlines around the world. In that case, housewife Lorena Bobbitt of Manassas, Virginia, was acquitted on charges of malicious wounding for admittedly severing her allegedly philandering husband's penis with one stroke from a sharp kitchen knife while he slept. Bobbitt drove away with the severed organ still clutched in her fist, and she threw it out of her car window onto a grassy field some distance from the couple's apartment. Rescue workers recovered the penis in a predawn search, and it was reattached during hours of microvascular surgery.[11] In defense of her actions, she accused her husband, John, of marital rape. At trial, the defense attorney, sounding very much like a pop psychologist, explained Mrs. Bobbitt's actions to the jury in these words: "Why did she cut his penis off? Something happened . . . that drove her over the edge. If this was sheer jealousy, she'd have cut his throat. But what did she attack? . . . The very thing that wounded her." Although John Bobbitt was later arrested and charged with raping his wife, a jury voted 12 to 0 to acquit him of all charges.[12]

Jeffrey Dahmer, perhaps the most infamous serial killer of the twentieth century. What explains the public's fascination with serial killers?

Source: Rosemary Jensen/Milwaukee Journal/SIPA Press

What motivates people to kill or maim or to commit other, less serious offenses? How can many killers seem so "normal" before exploding into criminality—giving no hints of the atrocities they are about to commit? How can a mother kill her own children and seemingly feel little or no remorse? For answers to questions like these, many people turn to psychological theories. Psychologists are the pundits of the modern age of behaviorism, offering explanations rooted in determinants that lie within individual actors. Psychological determinants of deviant or criminal behavior may be couched in terms of exploitative personality characteristics, poor impulse control, emotional arousal, an immature personality, and so on. Two contemporary commentators observe that "the major sources of theoretical development in criminology have been—and continue to be—psychological. A theory of criminal conduct is weak indeed if uninformed by a general psychology of human behavior."[13] Other writers go so far as to claim that any criminal behavior is only a symptom of a more fundamental psychiatric disorder.[14]

Before beginning a discussion of psychological theories, however, it is necessary to provide a brief overview of the terminology used to describe the psychological study of crime and criminality. **Forensic psychology,** one of the fastest-growing subfields of psychology, is the application of the science and profession of psychology to questions and issues relating to law and the legal system.[15] Forensic psychology is sometimes referred to as **criminal psychology,** and forensic psychologists are also called "criminal psychologists," "correctional psychologists," and "police psychologists." Unlike forensic psychologists (who generally hold Ph.D.s), forensic psychiatrists are medical doctors, and **forensic psychiatry** is a medical subspecialty that applies psychiatry to the needs of crime prevention and solution, criminal rehabilitation, and issues of the criminal law.[16]

What is the fundamental distinguishing feature of psychological approaches as opposed to other attempts to explain behavior? Criminologists Cathy Spatz Widom and Hans Toch offer the following insight: "Theories are psychological insofar as they focus on the individual as the unit of analysis. Thus any theory that is concerned with the behavior of individual offenders or which refers to forces or dynamics that motivate individuals to commit crimes would be considered to have a psychological component."[17] Another writer, Curt R. Bartol, defines *psychology* as "the science of behavior and mental processes."[18] Bartol goes on to say that "psychological criminology . . . is the science of the behavior and mental processes of the criminal. Psychological criminology," says Bartol, "focuses on individual criminal behavior—how it is acquired, evoked, maintained, and modified."

forensic psychology

The application of the science and profession of psychology to questions and issues relating to law and the legal system. Another term for **criminal psychology.**

criminal psychology

The application of the science and profession of psychology to questions and issues relating to law and the legal system. Another term for **forensic psychology.**

forensic psychiatry

A branch of psychiatry having to do with the study of crime and criminality.

Theory Versus Reality

What Is Forensic Psychology?

The American Academy of Forensic Psychology defines *forensic psychology* as "the application of the science and profession of psychology to questions and issues relating to law and the legal system." According to the academy, the practice of forensic psychology includes the following elements:

- Psychological evaluation and expert testimony regarding criminal forensic issues like trial competence, waiver of *Miranda* rights, criminal responsibility, death penalty mitigation, battered woman syndrome, domestic violence, drug dependence, and sexual disorders
- Testimony and evaluation regarding civil issues like personal injury, child custody, employment discrimination, mental disability, product liability, professional malpractice, civil commitment, and guardianship
- Assessment, treatment, and consultation regarding individuals with a high risk for aggressive behavior in the community, in the workplace, in treatment settings, and in correctional facilities
- Research, testimony, and consultation on psychological issues affecting the legal process, such as eyewitness testimony, jury selection, children's testimony, repressed memories, and pretrial publicity
- Specialized treatment service to individuals involved with the legal system
- Consultation to lawmakers about public policy issues with psychological implications

- Consultation and training for law enforcement, criminal justice, and correctional system personnel
- Consultation and training for mental health system practitioners on forensic issues
- Analysis of issues related to human performance, product liability, and safety
- Court-appointed monitoring of compliance with settlements in class-action suits affecting mental health or criminal justice settings
- Mediation and conflict resolution
- Policy and program development in the psychology-law arena
- Teaching, training, and supervision of graduate students, psychology, and psychiatry interns/residents and law students

Psychologists who already hold Ph.D.s and who are interested in the practice of forensic psychology may apply for certification by the American Board of Professional Psychology (ABPP), which awards a "Diplomate in Forensic Psychology" to those who function "at the highest level of excellence in his or her field of forensic competence." The ABPP diploma is awarded only to applicants who have received at least 100 hours of specialized training in forensic psychology and who have had 1,000 hours of experience in forensic psychology over a minimum of five years, although an LL.B. or a J.D. degree may substitute for two of those years. The diploma is generally recognized by the American judicial system as the definitive standard of professional competence in forensic psychology.

Source: Adapted with permission from the American Board of Forensic Psychology's Web page, http://www.abfp.com/brochure.asp (accessed August 5, 2007).

Major Principles of Psychological Theories

psychological theory

A theory derived from the behavioral sciences that focuses on the individual as the unit of analysis. Psychological theories place the locus of crime causation within the personality of the individual offender.

This brief section summarizes the central features of **psychological theories** of crime causation.[19] This cursory overview, however, is intended to provide more than a summary; it is meant to be a guide to the rest of this chapter.

Most psychological theories of crime causation make the following fundamental assumptions:

- The individual is the primary unit of analysis.
- Personality is the major motivational element within individuals because it is the seat of drives and the source of motives.
- Crimes result from abnormal, dysfunctional, or inappropriate mental processes within the personality.
- Criminal behavior, although condemned by the social group, may be purposeful for the individual insofar as it addresses certain felt needs. Behavior can be judged "inappropriate" only when measured against external criteria purporting to establish normality.

- *Normality* is generally defined by social consensus—that is, what the majority of people in any social group agree is "real," appropriate, or typical.
- Defective, or abnormal, mental processes may have a variety of causes, including a diseased mind, inappropriate learning or improper conditioning, the emulation of inappropriate role models, and adjustment to inner conflicts.

Early Psychological Theories

Twin threads ran through early psychological theories. One strand emphasized behavioral **conditioning;** the other focused mostly on personality disturbances and diseases of the mind. Together, these two foci constituted the early field of psychological criminology. The concept of conditioned behavior was popularized through the work of Russian physiologist Ivan Pavlov (1849–1936), whose work with dogs won the Nobel Prize in physiology and medicine in 1904. The dogs, which salivated when food was presented to them, were always fed in the presence of a ringing bell. Soon, Pavlov found, the dogs would salivate, as if in preparation for eating, when the bell alone was rung, even when no food was present. Hence, salivation, an automatic response to the presence of food, could be conditioned to occur in response to some other stimulus, demonstrating that animal behavior could be predictably altered via association with external changes arising from the environment surrounding the organism.

conditioning

A psychological principle that holds that the frequency of any behavior can be increased or decreased through reward, punishment, or association with other stimuli.

The Psychopath

The other thread winding its way through early psychological theories was that of mental disease, or **psychopathy.** It is important to note that psychologists and psychiatrists distinguish between the terms *psychopathy* and *psychopathology*. In the psychological literature, *psychopathology* "refers to any sort of psychological disorder that causes distress either for the individual or for those in the individual's life."[20] Hence, depression, schizophrenia, attention deficit hyperactivity disorder, alcoholism, bulimia, et cetera, can all be considered forms of psychopathology. *Psychopathy*, on the other hand, "refers to a very specific and distinctive type of psychopathology"[21]—and that is a personality disorder characterized by antisocial behavior and a lack of feelings—especially empathy or sensitivity toward others.

The concept of psychopathy has been called "one of the most durable, resilient and influential of all criminological ideas."[22] It may have evolved from the work of French physician Philippe Pinel (1745–1826), who described a form of "insanity without delirium." The concept is summarized in the words of Nolan D. C. Lewis, who wrote during his tenure as director of the New York State Psychiatric Institute and Hospital at Columbia University during World War II that "the criminal, like other people, has lived a life of instinctive drives, of desires, of wishes, of feelings, but one in which his intellect has apparently functioned less effectually as a brake upon certain trends. His constitutional makeup deviates toward the abnormal, leading him into conflicts with the laws of society and its cultural patterns."[23]

The term *psychopathy* comes from the Greek words *psyche* (meaning "soul" or "mind") and *pathos* ("suffering" or "illness"). The word, which appears to have been coined by German neurologist Richard von Krafft-Ebing (1840–1902),[24] made its way into English psychiatric literature through the writings of Polish-born American psychiatrist Bernard H. Glueck (1884–1972)[25] and British psychiatrist William Healy (1869–1963).[26] The **psychopath,** also called a **sociopath,** has been historically viewed as perversely cruel, often without thought or feeling for his or her victims.[27] By the Second World War, the role of the psychopathic personality in crime causation had become central to psychological theorizing. In 1944, for example, well-known psychiatrist David Abrahamsen wrote, "When we seek to explain the riddle of human conduct in general and of antisocial behavior in particular, the solution must be sought in the personality."[28]

psychopathy

A personality disorder characterized by antisocial behavior and lack of affect.

psychopath

An individual who has a personality disorder, especially one manifested in aggressively antisocial behavior, and who is lacking in empathy. Also called *sociopath*.

sociopath

Another term for a psychopath.

The concept of a psychopathic personality, which by its very definition is asocial, was fully developed by Georgian neuropsychiatrist **Hervey M. Cleckley** in his 1941 book *The Mask of Sanity* [29]—a work that was to have considerable impact on the field of psychology for many years to come. Cleckley described the psychopath as a "moral idiot," or as one who does not feel empathy with others, even though that person may be fully cognizant of what is objectively happening around him or her. The central defining characteristic of a psychopath came to be "poverty of affect," or the inability to accurately imagine how others think and feel. Hence, it becomes possible for a psychopath to inflict pain and engage in cruelty without appreciation for the victim's suffering. Charles Manson, for example, whom some regard as a psychopath, once told a television reporter, "I could take this book and beat you to death with it, and I wouldn't feel a thing. It'd be just like walking to the drugstore."

In *The Mask of Sanity,* Cleckley describes numerous characteristics of the psychopathic personality, some of which are listed here:

- Superficial charm and "good intelligence"
- Absence of delusions, hallucinations, or other signs of psychosis
- Absence of nervousness or psychoneurotic manifestations
- Inability to feel guilt or shame
- Unreliability
- Chronic lying
- Ongoing antisocial behavior
- Poor judgment and inability to learn from experience
- Self-centeredness and incapacity to love
- Unresponsiveness in general interpersonal relations
- An impersonal, trivial, and poorly integrated sex life
- Failure to follow any life plan

For Cleckley, "psychopathy was defined by a constellation of dysfunctional psychological processes as opposed to specific behavioral manifestations." [30] Cleckley noted that, in cases he had observed, the behavioral manifestations of psychopathy varied with the person's age, gender, and socioeconomic status.

Even though psychopaths have a seriously flawed personality, they can easily fool others into trusting them—hence the title of Cleckley's book. Cleckley described the good first impression made by a typical psychopath as follows: "More often than not, the typical psychopath will seem particularly agreeable and make a distinctly positive impression when he is first encountered. Alert and friendly in his attitude, he is easy to talk with and seems to have a good many genuine interests. There is nothing at all odd or queer about him, and in every respect he tends to embody the concept of a well-adjusted, happy person. Nor does he, on the other hand, seem to be artificially exerting himself like one who is covering up or who wants to sell you a bill of goods. He would seldom be confused with the professional backslapper or someone who is trying to ingratiate himself for a concealed purpose. Signs of affectation or excessive affability are not characteristic. He looks like the real thing."[31]

According to Cleckley, indicators of psychopathy appear early in life, often in the teenage years. They include lying, fighting, stealing, and vandalism. Even earlier signs may be found, according to some authors, in bed-wetting, cruelty to animals, sleep-walking, and fire setting.[32] Others have described psychopaths as "individuals who display impulsiveness, callousness, insincerity, pathological lying and deception, ego-centricity, poor judgment, an impersonal sex life, and an unstable life plan."[33]

The most definitive modern statement on psychopathy can be found in the Psychopathy Checklist (PCL), which was developed by Robert Hare.[34] The PCL consists of a series of ratings by qualified experts using information from subject interviews and official records. The PCL rates degree of psychopathy using two kinds of indicators: affective and interpersonal features (for example, glibness, emotional detachment, egocentricity, superficial charm, and shallow affect) and those traits associated with a chronic unstable and antisocial lifestyle (for example, irresponsibility, impulsivity, criminality, and proneness to boredom).[35] Hence, psychopathy, as understood today, has both emotional and behavior components.

A 2004 study of eight Canadian maximum security male prisoners classified as psychopaths according to the PCL found that the men were not only impaired emotionally, but also unable to efficiently process abstract words, perform abstract categorization tasks, understand metaphors, and process emotionally weighted words and speech.[36] The men participated in a test that compared their abilities to handle abstract concepts to those of normal men. During the test, the men's brains were scanned using functional magnetic resonance imaging (fMRI), and scans showed that a section of the brain in the psychopathic men did not activate as it should have. In pointing to what may be a physiological basis for psychopathy, the researchers concluded that their findings "support the hypothesis that there is an abnormality in the function of the right anterior superior temporal gyrus in psychopathy." Other studies in neurobiology have linked this part of the brain with abstract problem solving and insight.[37] Deficiencies in this part of the brain may also be associated with autism and the development of childhood schizophrenia.[38]

Some have questioned whether psychopaths merely lack empathy, or if they really don't know the difference between right and wrong. Recent research by Harvard University professor Marc Hauser seems to show that the ability to tell right from wrong, at least in everyday situations, is something that human beings are born with. Hauser, director of the Cognitive Evolution Labaratory at Harvard, says that we all enter this world with an innate moral faculty that allows us, once we have grown to adulthood, to quickly and without the need for conscious deliberation distinguish between good and evil, or right and wrong. Research that Hauser has conducted seems to show that our brains are hardwired to make moral distinctions—and that the same distinctions tend to be made across cultures, no matter how different those cultures might be. "The question," says Hauser, "is whether emotions are causally necessary for moral judgement. Take psychopaths: we know they have some kind of emotional deficit because they don't seem to feel remorse or empathy for their victims. Does this deficit corrupt their moral judgement because emotions are necessary to make the right decision? Or is their moral judgement actually intact, but their behavior is screwed up because their

WEB
Extra
■ ■ ■ ■

WEB
Extra
■ ■ ■ ■

LIBRARY
Extra
■ ■ ■ ■

emotions don't stop them from doing the wrong thing? My guess is the latter—that emotions flow from moral judgements and control behavior."[39] You can test your own sense of right and wrong by taking the Moral Sense Test (MST) online. The MST, which researchers are using to detail the nature of moral psychology, is accessible through Harvard University's Cognitive Evolution Laboratory online at **Web Extra 6–1** at crimtoday.com.

Traditionally, psychopathology has been regarded as difficult or impossible to treat. A 2006 study of adolescent psychopaths, however, found that "youth with psychopathic features who received intensive treatment had significantly lower rates of violent recidivism and a longer time to rearrest for violent behavior" than those who received treatment in a typical juvenile correctional facility.[40] Also, in 2007, the United Kingdom launched an unprecedented treatment and research program focused on what it termed "Dangerous People with Severe Personality Disorder" (DSPD).[41] To be eligible for the program, participants must be diagnosed with a severe personality disorder, and there must be a demonstrable link between that disorder and the risk of violent offending. Some say that the program, whose legal component allows detention of certain dangerous people on mental health grounds even if they haven't committed a crime, "holds the best chance yet of showing whether violent psychopaths can be reformed . . ." Learn more about the concept of the psychopath as a clinical construct by visiting the Society for Research in Psychopathology via **Web Extra 6–2**. Read about the issues involved in identifying criminal psychopaths via **Library Extras 6–1** and **6–2**.

Antisocial Personality Disorder

In recent years, the terms *sociopath* and *psychopath* have fallen into disfavor. In the attempt to identify sociopathic individuals, some psychologists have come to place greater emphasis on the type of *behavior* exhibited, rather than on identifiable personality traits. By 1968, the American Psychiatric Association's (APA's) *Diagnostic and Statistical Manual of Mental Disorders* had completely discontinued using the words *sociopath* and *psychopath,* replacing them with the terms *antisocial* and *asocial personality.*[42] In that year, the APA manual changed to a description of **antisocial (asocial) personality** types as "individuals who are basically unsocialized and whose behavior pattern brings them repeatedly into conflicts with society. They are incapable of significant loyalty to individuals, groups, or social values. They are grossly selfish, callous, irresponsible, impulsive, and unable to feel guilt or to learn from experience and punishment. Frustration tolerance is low. They tend to blame others or offer plausible rationalization for their behavior."[43] In most cases, individuals exhibiting, through their behavioral patterns, an antisocial personality are said to be suffering from **antisocial personality disorder** (sometimes referred to in clinical circles as "APD," "ASPD," or "ANPD").

The World Health Organization, in its *Classification of Mental and Behavioral Disorders,* describes antisocial personality disorder as a "personality disorder usually coming to attention because of a gross disparity between behavior and the prevailing social norms, [which is] characterized by at least three of the following: (a) callous unconcern for the feelings of others; (b) gross and persistent attitude of irresponsibility and disregard for social norms, rules and obligations; (c) incapacity to maintain enduring relationships, though having no difficulty in establishing them; (d) very low tolerance to frustration and a low threshold for discharge of aggression, including violence; (e) incapacity to experience guilt and to profit from experience, particularly punishment; [and] (f) marked proneness to blame others, or to offer plausible rationalizations, for the behavior that has brought the patient into conflict with society."[44] Other features of ASPD have been identified as lack of empathy, inflated and arrogant self-appraisal, and glib, superficial charm.[45]

Individuals manifesting the characteristics of an antisocial personality are, sooner or later, likely to run afoul of the law. As one writer says, "The impulsivity and aggression, the selfishness in achieving one's own immediate needs, and the disregard for society's

antisocial (asocial) personality

A term used to describe individuals who are basically unsocialized and whose behavior pattern brings them repeatedly into conflict with society.

antisocial personality disorder

A psychological condition exhibited by individuals who are basically unsocialized and whose behavior pattern brings them repeatedly into conflicts with society.

rules and laws bring these people to the attention of the criminal justice system."[46] Moreover, individuals who score high on psychological inventories designed to measure degree of psychopathy[47] have been found to exhibit high rates of both criminality and recidivism, and psychopaths who have also been diagnosed as schizophrenics display even higher levels of criminality.[48]

The causes of ASPD are unclear. Somatogenic causes, or those based on physiological features of the human organism, are said to include a malfunctioning of the central nervous system characterized by a low state of arousal that drives the sufferer to seek excitement and brain abnormalities that may have been present in most antisocial personalities since birth. Some studies show that **electroencephalograms (EEGs)** taken of individuals diagnosed as having antisocial personality disorder are frequently abnormal, reflecting "a malfunction of some . . . inhibitory mechanisms" that makes it unlikely that persons characterized by antisocial personality disorder will "learn to inhibit behavior that is likely to lead to punishment."[49] It is difficult, however, to diagnose antisocial personalities through physiological measurements because similar EEG patterns show up in patients with other types of disorders. Psychogenic causes, or those rooted in early interpersonal experiences, are said to include the inability to form attachments to parents or other caregivers early in life, sudden separation from the mother during the first six months of life, and other forms of insecurity during the first few years of life. In short, a lack of love or the sensed inability to unconditionally depend upon one central loving figure (typically the mother in most psychological literature) immediately following birth is often posited as a major psychogenic factor contributing to the development of antisocial personality disorder. Other psychogenic causes have been identified and include deficiencies in childhood role playing, the inability to identify with one's parents during childhood and adolescence, and severe rejection by others.

Most studies of antisocial personality types have involved male subjects. Only rarely have researchers focused on women with antisocial personalities, and it is believed that only a small proportion of those afflicted with ASPD are women.[50] What little research there is suggests that females with ASPD possess many of the same definitive characteristics as their male counterparts and that they assume their antisocial roles at similarly early ages.[51] The lifestyles of antisocial females, however, appear to emphasize sexual misconduct, including lifestyles involving abnormally high levels of sexual activity. Such research, however, can be misleading because the cultural expectations of female sexual behavior inherent in early studies may not always have been in keeping with reality. That is, early researchers may have had so little accurate information about female sexual activity that the behavior of women judged to possess antisocial personalities may have actually been far closer to the norm than originally believed.

Some recent studies that attempt to classify criminal offenders by type of mental disorder have determined that antisocial personality disorders characterize 46.6% of all inmates, while schizophrenics account for 6.3% of the inmate population, manic-depressives another 1.6%, drug-disordered persons 18.6%, depressed individuals 8.1%, and alcohol abuse–related sufferers another 33.1%.[52] A review of 20 such studies found great variation in the degree and type of disorders said to be prevalent among incarcerated offenders.[53] The studies categorized from 0.5% to 26% of all inmates as psychotic, 2.4% to 28% as mentally subnormal, 5.6% to 70% as antisocial personalities, 2% to 7.9% as neurotic, and 11% to 80% of inmates as suffering from mental disorders induced by alcoholism or excessive drinking. Generally, such studies conclude that few convicted felons are free from mental impairment of one sort or another.

Learn more about antisocial personality disorder at the National Library of Medicine via **Web Extra 6–3** at crimtoday.com. Possible forms of treatment for the disorder can be found at **Web Extra 6–4**.

Personality Types and Crime

In 1964, **Hans J. Eysenck,** a British psychiatrist, published *Crime and Personality,* a book-length treatise in which he explained crime as the result of fundamental personality characteristics.[54] Eysenck described three personality dimensions, each with links

electroencephalogram (EEG)

The electrical measurement of brain wave activity.

WEB
Extra
▪▪▪▪

Theory in Perspective

Types of Psychological and Psychiatric Theories

Psychological and Psychiatric Theories of criminology are derived from the behavioral sciences and focus on the individual as the unit of analysis.

- *Psychiatric Criminology,* also known as *Forensic Psychiatry.* An approach that envisions a complex set of drives and motives operating from recesses deep within the personality to determine behavior.

  Period: 1930s–present

  Theorists: Hervey M. Cleckley, many others

  Concepts: Psychopath, sociopath, antisocial and asocial personality

- *Psychoanalytic Criminology.* A psychiatric approach developed by Austrian psychiatrist Sigmund Freud which emphasizes the role of personality in human behavior and which sees deviant behavior as the result of dysfunctional personalities.

  Period: 1920s–present

  Theorists: Sigmund Freud, others

  Concepts: Id, ego, superego, sublimation, psychotherapy, Thanatos, neurosis, psychosis, schizophrenia

- *Frustration-Aggression Theory.* A perspective that holds that frustration is a natural consequence of living and a root cause of crime. Criminal behavior can be a form of adaptation when it results in stress reduction.

  Period: 1940s–present

  Theorists: J. Dollard, Albert Bandura, Richard H. Walters, S. M. Halleck

  Concepts: Frustration, aggression, displacement, catharsis, alloplastic and autoplastic adaptation

- *Modeling Theory.* A psychological perspective that says people learn how to behave by modeling themselves after others whom they have the opportunity to observe.

  Period: 1950s–present

  Theorists: Gabriel Tarde, Albert Bandura, others

  Concepts: Imitation, interpersonal aggression, modeling, disengagement

- *Behavior Theory.* A psychological perspective which posits that individual behavior that is rewarded will increase in frequency, while that which is punished will decrease.

  Period: 1940s–present

  Theorists: B. F. Skinner, others

  Concepts: Operant behavior, conditioning, stimulus-response, reward, punishment

- *Self-Control Theory.* A perspective that says the root cause of crime can be found in a person's inability to exercise socially appropriate controls over the self.

  Period: 1940s–present

  Theorists: Michael R. Gottfredson, Travis Hirschi, Harold Grasmick

  Concepts: Self-control, general theory, criminal opportunity

to criminality. Psychoticism, which Eysenck said "is believed to be correlated with criminality at all stages,"[55] is defined by such characteristics as a lack of empathy, creativeness, tough-mindedness, and antisociability. Psychoticism, said Eysenck, is also frequently characterized by hallucinations and delusions. Extroverts were described as carefree, dominant, and venturesome, operating with high levels of energy. "The typical extrovert," Eysenck wrote, "is sociable, likes parties, has many friends, needs to have people to talk to, and does not like reading or studying by himself."[56] Neuroticism, the third of the personality characteristics Eysenck described, was said to be typical of people who are irrational, shy, moody, and emotional.

According to Eysenck, psychotics are the most likely to be criminal because they combine high degrees of emotionalism with similarly high levels of extroversion. Individuals with such characteristics, claimed Eysenck, are especially difficult to socialize and to train. Eysenck cited many studies in which children and others who harbored characteristics of psychoticism, extroversion, and neuroticism performed poorly on conditioning tests designed to measure how quickly they would respond appropriately to external stimuli. Conscience, said Eysenck, is fundamentally a conditioned reflex. Therefore, an individual who does not take well to conditioning will not fully develop a conscience and will continue to exhibit the asocial behavioral traits of a very young child.

Eysenck's approach might be termed *biopsychology* because he claimed that personality traits were fundamentally dependent upon physiology, specifically upon the individual's autonomic nervous system, which Eysenck described as "underlying the behavioral trait of emotionality or neuroticism."[57] Some individuals were said to possess nervous systems that could not handle a great deal of stimulation. Such individuals, like the introvert, shun excitement and are easily trained. They rarely become criminal offenders. However, those who possess nervous systems that need stimulation, said Eysenck, seek excitement and are far more likely to turn to crime. As support for his thesis, Eysenck cited studies of twins showing that identical twins were much more likely than fraternal twins to perform similarly on simple behavioral tests. In particular, Eysenck quoted from the work of J. B. S. Haldane, who was reputed to be a "world-famous geneticist." Haldane, having studied the criminality of 13 sets of identical twins, concluded, "An analysis of the thirteen cases shows not the faintest evidence of freedom of the will in the ordinary sense of the word. A man of a certain constitution, put in a certain environment, will be a criminal. Taking the record of any criminal, we could predict the behavior of a monozygotic twin placed in the same environment. Crime is destiny."[58] Up to two-thirds of all behavioral variance, claimed Eysenck, could be attributed to "a strong genetic basis."

Early Psychiatric Theories

Psychological criminology, with its historical dual emphasis on (1) early forces that shape personality and (2) conditioned behavior, can be distinguished from **psychiatric criminology,** also known as "forensic psychiatry," which envisions a complex set of drives and motives operating from hidden recesses deep within the personality to determine behavior. Psychiatrist David Abrahamsen, writing in 1944, explained crime this way: "Antisocial behavior is a direct expression of an aggression or may be a direct or indirect manifestation of a distorted erotic drive. Crime," said Abrahamsen, "may . . . be considered a product of a person's tendencies and the situation of the moment interacting with his mental resistance."[59] The key questions to be answered by psychiatric criminology, according to Abrahamsen, are "What creates the criminal impulse?" and "What stimulates and gives it direction?" A later forensic psychiatrist answered the questions this way: "Every criminal is such by reason of unconscious forces within him."[60] Forensic psychiatry explains crime as being caused by biological and psychological urges mediated through consciousness. Little significance is placed upon the role of the environment external to the individual after the first few formative years of life. Psychiatric theories are derived from the medical sciences, including neurology, and, like other psychological theories, focus on the individual as the unit of analysis.

Criminal Behavior as Maladaptation

The Psychoanalytic Perspective

Perhaps the best-known psychiatrist of all time is **Sigmund Freud** (1856–1939). Freud coined the term **psychoanalysis** in 1896 and based an entire theory of human behavior on it. From the point of view of psychoanalysis, criminal behavior is maladaptive, or the product of inadequacies inherent in the offender's personality. Significant inadequacies may result in full-blown mental illness, which in itself can be a direct cause of crime. The psychoanalytic perspective encompasses diverse notions like personality, neurosis, and psychosis and more specific concepts like transference, sublimation, and repression. **Psychotherapy,** referred to in its early days as the "talking cure" because it highlighted patient-therapist communication, is the attempt to relieve patients of their mental disorders through the application of psychoanalytic principles and techniques.

According to Freud, the personality is made up of three components—the id, the ego, and the superego—as shown in Figure 6–1. The **id** is the fundamental aspect of

psychiatric criminology

Theories that are derived from the medical sciences, including neurology, and that, like other psychological theories, focus on the individual as the unit of analysis. Psychiatric theories form the basis of psychiatric criminology.

psychoanalysis

The theory of human psychology founded by Sigmund Freud on the concepts of the unconscious, resistance, repression, sexuality, and the Oedipus complex.

psychotherapy

A form of psychiatric treatment based on psychoanalytical principles and techniques.

FIGURE 6–1

**The Psychoanalytic
Structure of Personality**

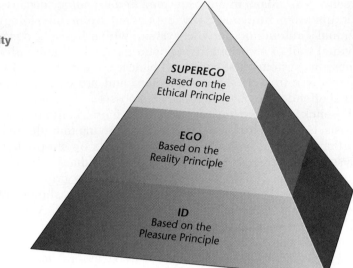

SUPEREGO
*Based on the
Ethical Principle*

EGO
*Based on the
Reality Principle*

ID
*Based on the
Pleasure Principle*

id

The aspect of the personality from which drives, wishes, urges, and desires emanate. More formally, the division of the psyche associated with instinctual impulses and demands for immediate satisfaction of primitive needs.

ego

The reality-testing part of the personality. Also called the *reality principle*. More formally, the personality component that is conscious, most immediately controls behavior, and is most in touch with external reality.

superego

The moral aspect of the personality; much like the conscience. More formally, the division of the psyche that develops by the incorporation of the perceived moral standards of the community, is mainly unconscious, and includes the conscience.

the personality from which drives, wishes, urges, and desires emanate. Freud focused primarily on love, aggression, and sex as fundamental drives in any personality. The id is direct and singular in purpose. It operates according to the pleasure principle, seeking full and immediate gratification of its needs. Individuals, however, were said to rarely be fully aware of the urges that percolate up (occasionally into awareness) from the id because it is a largely unconscious region of the mind. Nonetheless, from the Freudian perspective, each of us carries within our id the prerequisite motivation for criminal behavior. We are, each one of us, potential murderers, sexual aggressors, and thieves—our drives and urges kept in check only by other, controlling aspects of our personalities.

A second component of the personality, the **ego,** is primarily charged with reality testing. Freud's use of the word *ego* should not be confused with popular usage, whereby a person might talk about an "inflated ego" or an "egotistical person." For Freud, the ego was primarily concerned with how objectives might be best accomplished. The ego tends to effect strategies for the individual that maximize pleasure and minimize pain. It lays out the various paths of action that can lead to wish fulfillment. The ego inherently recognizes that it may be necessary to delay gratification to achieve a more fulfilling long-term goal.

The **superego,** the last component of the personality, is much like a moral guide to right and wrong. If properly developed, it assays the ego's plans, dismissing some as morally inappropriate while accepting others as ethically viable. The id of a potential rapist, for example, might be filled with lustful drives, and his ego may develop a variety of alternative plans whereby those drives might be fulfilled, some legal and some illegal. His superego will, if the individual's personality is relatively well integrated and the superego is properly developed, turn the individual away from law-violating behavior based on his sensual desires and guide the ego to select a path of action that is in keeping with social convention. When the dictates of the superego are not followed, feelings of guilt may result. The superego is one of the most misunderstood of Freudian concepts. In addition to elements of conscience, the superego also contains what Freud called the "ego-ideal," which is a symbolic representation of what society values. The ego-ideal differs from the conscience in that it is less forceful in controlling behavior in the absence of the likelihood of discovery.

Mirroring Freud's theory of personality is the dual ego theory of Italian criminologist Alfredo Niceforo (1876–1960). Niceforo, who taught criminology in Switzerland and Belgium, was influenced by the ideas of Cesare Lombroso, but proposed his own theory that every person has a "deep ego" of antisocial subconscious impulses that represent a

Sigmund Freud (1856–1939), examining a manuscript in the office of his Vienna home, circa 1930. How have Freud's theories influenced contemporary criminology?

Source: Corbis/Bettmann

throwback to precivilized times.[61] It is the struggle between this deep ego and a person's "superior ego," developed as a consequence of socialization, said Niceforo, that determines that person's actions. Crime and deviance, according to Niceforo, represent victories for the deep ego and result when it successfully avoids control by the superior ego.

Although Freud wrote little about crime per se, he did spend much of his time attempting to account for a variety of abnormal behaviors, many of which might lead to violations of the criminal law. One way in which a person might be led into crime, according to the perspective of psychoanalysis, is as the result of a poorly developed superego. In the individual without a fully functional superego, the mind is left to fall back on the ego's reality-testing ability. To put it simply, the ego, operating without a moral guide, may select a path of action that, although expedient at the time, violates the law. Individuals suffering from poor superego development are likely to seek immediate gratification without giving a great deal of thought to the long-term consequences of the choices they make.

From the Freudian point of view, inadequate sublimation can be another cause of crime. **Sublimation** is the psychological process whereby one item of consciousness comes to be symbolically substituted for another. Sublimation is often a healthy process. Freud held that many outstanding accomplishments of the human species were due to sublimation, through which powerful sexual and aggressive drives are channeled into socially constructive activity. However, crime can result from improper sublimation. According to Freud, for example, a man may hate his mother, his hatred being perhaps the faulty by-product of the striving for adult independence. He may, however, be unable to give voice to that hatred directly. Perhaps the mother is too powerful or the experience of confronting his mother would be too embarrassing. The man may act out his hatred for his mother by attacking other women whom he symbolically substitutes in his mind for the mother figure. Hence, from the Freudian perspective, men who beat their wives, become rapists, sexually harass coworkers, or otherwise abuse women may be enacting feelings derived from early life experiences that they would be unable to otherwise express.

Sublimation, like many other psychoanalytical concepts, is a slippery idea. Mother hatred, for example, although a plausible explanation for acts of violence by men against women, is difficult to demonstrate, and the link between such hidden feelings

sublimation

The psychological process whereby one aspect of consciousness comes to be symbolically substituted for another.

and adult action is impossible to prove. Even so, should an offender be so diagnosed, it would do little good for him to deny the psychoanalytical explanation assigned to him because doing so would only result in the professional reproach, "Yes, but you have hidden the knowledge of your true feelings from yourself. You are not aware of why you act the way you do!"

Freud also postulated the existence of a death instinct, which he called **Thanatos.** According to Freud, all living things, which he referred to as "animate matter," have a fundamental desire to relax back into an inanimate state, or death. Living, said Freud, takes energy and cunning. Hence, death, at least at some level, is an easier choice because it releases the organism from the need for continued expenditure of energy. Thanatos was seen as contributing to many of the advances made by the human species and as underlying a large proportion of individual accomplishments. Were it not for a wish to die, operative at some basic instinctual level, said Freud, few people would have the courage to take risks—and without the assumption of risk, precious little progress would be possible in any sphere of life. The notion of an innate death wish has been used to explain why some offenders seem to behave in ways that ensure their eventual capture. Serial killers who send taunting messages to the police, terrorists who tell the media of their planned activities or who take credit for public attacks, rapists who "accidentally" leave their wallets at the scene, and burglars who break into occupied dwellings may all, for the most part unconsciously, be seeking to be stopped, captured, punished, and even killed.

From the Freudian perspective, **neurosis,** a minor form of mental illness, may also lead to crime. Neurotic individuals are well in touch with reality but may find themselves anxious, fearful of certain situations, or unable to help themselves in others. Fear of heights, for example, may be a neurosis, as may be compulsive hand washing or eating disorders. A classic example of the compulsive neurotic can be found in the individual who uses paper towels to open doorknobs, refraining from touching the knob directly for fear of picking up germs. Although such behavior may be unreasonable from the point of view of others, it is reality based (there are germs on doorknobs) and, for the individual demonstrating it, probably unavoidable. Most neuroses do not lead to crime. Some, however, can. In 1991, for example, Stephen Blumberg of Des Moines, Iowa, was sentenced in federal court to nearly six years in prison and fined $200,000 for the theft of more than 21,000 rare books from hundreds of libraries.[62] Blumberg, whose compulsive interest in rare books began at yard sales and with searches in trash receptacles, may have seen himself as being involved in a messianic mission to preserve recorded history. Compulsive shoplifters may also be manifesting another form of neurosis—one in which a powerful need to steal can drive even well-heeled individuals to risk arrest and jail.

Freudian theory was very popular during the middle part of the twentieth century. By the 1980s, however, the notions of ego and id were considered antiquated by most psychiatrists. Attention shifted to the study of chemical imbalances in the brain, and psychopharmacology supplemented—if not replaced—the earlier ideas of Freud and his followers. In 2006, for example, Marti Olsen Laney, a neuroscience researcher in Portland, Oregon, found that the brains of introverted children functioned somewhat differently from those of extroverts.[63] According to Laney, brain scans of introverted kids found much more overall activty—especially in the brain's frontal lobes, which are areas associated with problem solving, introspection, complex thinking, and planning.

Recently, however, the field of psychiatry has seen a rekindling of interest in Freudian psychology. The reason, according to some contemporary thinkers, is that psychopharmacology, or the use of drugs to treat psychiatric symptoms and disorders, has been unable to provide an alternative grand theory of personality, emotion, and motivation.[64] Moreover, today's neuroscientists are busily creating a chemical map of the mind that seems to validate the general sketch that Freud provided decades ago. Soon a new and unified perspective that reconciles the work of neurologists and psychiatrists may emerge. The recognition of just such a possibility prompted Eric R. Kandel of Columbia University, the 2000 Nobel laureate in physiology or medicine, to say that psychoanalysis is "still the most coherent and intellectually satisfying view of the mind."[65] Read more about the life and work of Sigmund Freud at **Library Extra 6–3** at crimtoday.com.

Thanatos

A death wish.

neurosis

A functional disorder of the mind or of the emotions involving anxiety, phobia, or other abnormal behavior.

LIBRARY
Extra
∎∎∎∎

The Psychotic Offender

For many law-abiding citizens, extreme forms of criminal behavior are often difficult to understand, as the gruesome story of Gary Heidnik illustrates.[66] At his double-murder trial in 1988, Heidnik claimed insanity after he admittedly killed two women and tortured four others. All six women had been held captive in the basement of Heidnik's Philadelphia row house for four months, where they had been shackled with chains. One woman, who was chained to a wall and standing in a puddle of water, was electrocuted when Heidnik pushed a live electrical cord against her bare skin. He starved a second woman to death. Heidnik was arrested on March 24, 1987, after one of the captive women escaped and led police to the house. At the scene, police found evidence that Heidnik had mixed the ground flesh of at least one victim with dog food and fed it to the other captives.

A jury rejected Heidnik's claim of insanity and convicted him on two charges of first-degree murder. He was executed in July 1999. Assistant District Attorney Charles Gallagher, who prosecuted Heidnik, called the case one of the most complicated he has ever taken to court. "He's an evil man and he did evil things. That's what the death penalty is for," Gallagher said.

Some seemingly inexplicable forms of criminality may be the result of **psychosis.** Whereas neurotic individuals often face only relatively minor problems in living, psychotic people, according to psychiatric definitions, are out of touch with reality in some fundamental way. They may suffer from hallucinations, delusions, or other breaks with reality. The classic psychotic thinks he is Napoleon or sees spiders covering what others see only as a bare wall. Individuals suffering from a psychosis are said to be "psychotic." Psychoses may be either organic (that is, caused by physical damage to, or abnormalities in, the brain) or functional (that is, having no known physical cause). Canadian criminologist Gwynn Nettler says, "Thought disorder is the hallmark of psychosis. . . . People are called crazy when, at some extremity, they cannot 'think straight.'"[67] Nettler identifies three characteristics of psychotic individuals: "(1) a grossly distorted conception of reality, (2) moods, and swings of mood, that seem inappropriate to circumstance, and

psychosis

A form of mental illness in which sufferers are said to be out of touch with reality.

Gary Heidnik, executed by the Commonwealth of Pennsylvania in 1999. Heidnik *wanted* to die for his crimes. Should he have been executed? Was he psychotic?

Source: AP Wide World Photos

schizophrenic

A mentally ill individual who is out of touch with reality and who suffers from disjointed thinking.

paranoid schizophrenic

A schizophrenic individual who suffers from delusions and hallucinations.

(3) marked inefficiency in getting along with others and caring for oneself."[68] Psychotics have also been classified as schizophrenic or paranoid schizophrenic. **Schizophrenics** are said to be characterized by disordered or disjointed thinking, in which the types of logical associations they make are atypical of other people. **Paranoid schizophrenics** suffer from delusions and hallucinations.

Unfortunately, psychiatrists have not been able to agree on definitive criteria for schizophrenia that would allow for convenient application of the term. One prominent psychiatrist writes of "how varying. . . . schizophrenia may appear, ranging from no striking symptoms at all to conspicuous psychotic features. . . . Thus on the surface," he continues, "the schizophrenic may appear normal and, to some extent, lead a conventional life."[69] The same author later tells us, "Schizophrenia is not a clearly defined disease. . . . It is characterized rather by a . . . kind of alteration of thinking or feeling."[70] At the very least, then, we can safely say that schizophrenia is a disorganization of the personality. In its most extreme form, it may manifest itself by way of hallucinations, delusions, and seemingly irrational behavior.

With these caveats in mind, it is fair to say that psychoses may lead to crime in a number of ways. Following the Vietnam War, for example, a number of instances were reported in which former American soldiers suffering from a kind of battlefield psychosis killed friends and family members, thinking they were Vietcong soldiers—that is, the enemy. These men, who had been traumatized by battlefield experiences in Southeast Asia, relived their past on American streets. In other crimes committed by psychotics, thought disorders may be less obvious or may exist only temporarily.

The Link between Frustration and Aggression

In his early writings, Freud suggested that aggressive behavior is a response to frustration. Aggression toward others, Freud said, is a natural response to frustrating limitations imposed upon a person. The frustration-aggression thesis was later developed more fully in the writings of J. Dollard,[71] Albert Bandura, Richard H. Walters, and others. Dollard's frustration-aggression theory held that although frustration can lead to various forms of behavior—including regression, sublimation, and aggressive fantasy—direct aggression toward others is its most likely consequence. Because everyone suffers some form of frustration throughout life, beginning with weaning and toilet training, Dollard argued, aggression is a natural consequence of living. Dollard pointed out, however, that aggression could be manifested in socially acceptable ways (perhaps through contact sports, military or law enforcement careers, or simple verbal attacks) and that it could be engaged in vicariously by observing others who are acting violently (as in movies, on television, through popular fiction, and so on). Dollard applied the psychoanalytical term *displacement* to the type of violence that is vented on something or someone who is not the source of the original frustration and suggested that satisfying one's aggressive urges via observation was a form of "catharsis."

The story of Paul Calden, a former insurance company executive, provides us with an example of the frustration-aggression theory as it applies to real-life crime. In January 1993, the 33-year-old Calden, dressed in a business suit, opened fire with a 9 mm semiautomatic handgun on his former bosses in the Island Center Cafe, a Tampa, Florida, cafeteria—killing three people and injuring two others. Calden went up to the table where the five were eating, showed them the gun, shouted, "This is what you get for firing me!" and pulled the trigger.[72] He had been let go from his position as an underwriter with Fireman's Fund Insurance Company in March 1992. Calden then killed himself. He appears to have been acting out of frustrations born of his experience with having been fired.

Some psychologists have tried to identify what it is that causes some individuals to displace aggression or to experience it vicariously (through catharsis), while others respond violently and directly toward the immediate source of their frustrations. Andrew F. Henry and James F. Short, Jr., for example, writing in the 1950s, suggested that child-rearing practices are a major determining factor in such a causal nexus.[73] Restrictive parents who both punish and love their children, said Henry and Short, will engender in their children the ability to suppress outward expressions of aggression. When one parent punishes and the other loves, or when both punish but neither shows love, children can be expected to show anger directly and perhaps even immediately because they will not be threatened with the loss of love. Physical punishment, explained Henry and Short, rarely threatens the loss of love, and children so punished cannot be expected to refrain from direct displays of anger.

In 1960, Stewart Palmer studied murderers and their siblings to determine the degree of frustration to which they had been exposed as children.[74] He found that male murderers had experienced much more frustration than their brothers. More than twice as many frustrating experiences, ranging from difficult births to serious illnesses, childhood beatings, severe toilet training, and negative school experiences, were reported by the murderers than by their law-abiding siblings.

Crime as Adaptive Behavior

Some psychiatric perspectives have held that "crime is a compromise, representing for the individual the most satisfactory method of adjustment to inner conflicts which he cannot express otherwise. Thus, his acting out the crime fulfills a certain aim or purpose."[75] One pressing need of many criminals, according to some psychologists, is the need to be punished, which arises, according to psychiatric theory, from a sense of guilt. Psychiatrists who suggest that the need to be punished is a motivating factor in criminal behavior are quick to point out that this need may be a closely guarded secret, unknown even to the offender. Hence, from the psychiatric point of view, many drives, motives, and wishes are unconscious or even repressed by people who harbor them. The concept of repression holds that the human mind may choose to keep certain aspects of itself out of consciousness, possibly because of shame, self-loathing, or a simple lack of adequate introspection. The desire for punishment, however, sometimes

Westley Alan Dodd, hanged in 1993 in the state of Washington for murdering young boys whom he molested. "People need to know it's the only thing that will stop me," he said of his execution. Might there have been some other alternative?

Source: Benjamin Benschneider/ Seattle Times

comes to the fore. In 1993, for example, Westley Alan Dodd was hanged to death by authorities in Washington State for the kidnapping, rape, and murder of three little boys four years earlier. Dodd, who said he had molested dozens of children over the course of a decade, sought the death penalty after he was convicted, saying he deserved to die and vowing to sue the American Civil Liberties Union or anyone else who sought to save him.[76]

Crime can be adaptive in other ways as well. Some psychiatrists see it as an adaptation to life's stresses. According to Seymour L. Halleck, a psychiatrist and adjunct professor of law at the University of North Carolina at Chapel Hill, turning to crime can provide otherwise disenfranchised individuals with a sense of power and purpose.[77] In Halleck's words, "During the planning and execution of a criminal act the offender is a free man. . . . The value of this brief taste of freedom cannot be overestimated. Many of the criminal's apparently unreasonable actions are efforts to find a moment of autonomy."[78] Halleck says that crime can also provide "excellent rationalizations" for perceived inadequacies—especially for those whose lives have been failures when judged against the benchmarks of the wider society. "The criminal is able to say. . . , 'I could have been successful if I had not turned to crime. All my troubles have come to me because I have been bad.'" Hence, crime, according to Halleck, provides "a convenient resource for denying, forgetting or ignoring . . . other inadequacies."[79]

Insofar as the choice of crime reduces stresses that the individual faces by producing changes in the environment (empowerment), it is referred to as **alloplastic adaptation.** When crime leads to stress reduction as a result of internal changes in beliefs, value systems, and so forth, it is called **autoplastic adaptation.** The offender who is able to deny responsibility for other failures by turning to crime is said to be seeking autoplastic adaptation. Because other forms of behavior may also meet many of the same needs as does crime, Halleck points out, an individual may select crime over various other behavioral alternatives only when no reasonable alternatives are available or when criminal behavior has inherent advantages—as might be the case under instances of economic or social oppression. (That is, individuals who are actively discriminated against may find personal and political significance in violating the laws of the oppressing society.)

In any case, from Halleck's point of view, crime "has many advantages even when considered independently of the criminal's conscious or unconscious needs for gratification."[80] In other words, even though crime can be immediately rewarding or intensely pleasureful, says Halleck, such rewards are more "fringe benefits" than anything else. The central significance of criminal behavior for most offenders is that it "is an action which helps one survive with dignity."[81] Halleck tells us that "we cannot understand the criminal unless we appreciate that his actions are much more than an effort to find a specific gratification."[82] In the final analysis, criminal behavior is, from Halleck's point of view, a form of adjustment to stress and oppression.

In another approach to stress as a causative agent in crime commission, Arnold S. Linsky, Ronet Bachman, and Murray A. Straus suggest that stress may lead to aggression toward others and toward oneself (that is, self-destructive behavior like suicide, smoking, and abuse of alcohol).[83] Linsky and his colleagues attempt to measure stress at the societal level, arguing that although the relationship between stress and aggression has been studied at the individual level, "the neglect of social stress as an explanation for society-to-society differences in aggression may be partially due to a lack of an objective means of comparing the stressfulness of life in different societies."[84] Concluding that societal stress levels heighten levels of aggression, the authors suggest that social policies should be created to reduce the impact of such stressful events as having to stop work, foreclosing on a mortgage, and dropping out of school.

Finally, we should recognize that perceptions vary and that although criminal behavior may appear to be a valid choice for some individuals who are seeking viable responses to perceived stresses and oppression, their perceptions may not be wholly accurate. In other words, misperceived stress and oppression may still lead to crime, even when far simpler solutions may be found in a more realistic appraisal of the offender's situation.

alloplastic adaptation

A form of adjustment that results from changes in the environment surrounding an individual.

autoplastic adaptation

A form of adjustment that results from changes within an individual.

Modeling Theory

On December 1, 1997, 14-year-old Michael Carneal walked up to a student prayer group in his Kentucky high school and opened fire with a .22-caliber pistol. Like a trained marksman, he squeezed off eight shots, killing three students and wounding five others. Lieutenant Colonel Dave Grossman, a retired Army Ranger and former West Point assistant professor of psychology, was amazed at the accuracy of Carneal's shooting. "He . . . got eight hits on eight different targets, five of them head shots," says Grossman. It was, Grossman says, a "truly, truly stunning" feat of marksmanship.[85]

Where did Carneal learn to shoot like that? And what made him *want* to shoot? The local sheriff couldn't understand Carneal's motivation and fielded questions about a possible conspiracy or an anti-Christian terror campaign.[86] But no conspiracy ever came to light, and Carneal and his family were churchgoers themselves. Although not a criminologist, Grossman thinks he knows what caused the shootings. The colonel reviewed Carneal's psychiatric records and found that the teenager had spent hundreds of hours playing violent computer games—including *Quake*, *Redneck Rampage*, and *Resident Evil*—for months before the shooting. Grossman calls the games "hypnotic murder simulators" and says that they are surprisingly similar to military combat-training programs. "This boy was doing exactly what he was drilled to do," says Grossman. Some young men, like Carneal, says Grossman, "play these video games not twice a year, but hours every night, and they shoot every living creature in sight until they run out of bullets or run out of targets."

Do violent computer games lead to violent crime? While the jury is still out on that question, the importance of imitation and modeling in shaping behavior has long been studied. One of the earliest attempts to explain crime and deviance as learned behavior can be found in the work of Gabriel Tarde (1843–1904), a French social theorist of the late 1800s. Tarde discounted the biological theories of Lombroso and others, which were so prevalent in his day, and suggested that it was possible to infer certain regularities or laws that appeared to govern the social world. The basis of any society, Tarde believed, was imitation—or, more precisely, the tendency of people to pattern their behavior after the behavior of others. Tarde developed a theory of human behavior that built upon three laws of imitation and suggestion.[87] Tarde's first law held that individuals in close intimate contact with one another tend to imitate each other's behavior. His second law stated that imitation moves from the top down. This means that poor people tend to imitate wealthy people, youngsters tend to emulate those older than themselves, lower-class people tend to imitate members of the upper class, and so on. The third law of imitation is the law of insertion, which says that new acts and behaviors tend to either reinforce or replace old ones. Hence, the music of each generation replaces the music of the one that preceded it, the politics of young people eventually become the politics of the nation, fadish drugs are substituted for traditional ones, and new forms of crime tend to take the place of older ones (as when, for example, computer criminals become a more serious threat to financial institutions than bank robbers).

More recently, **Albert Bandura** developed a comprehensive **modeling theory** of aggression. Bandura tells us that "a complete theory of aggression must explain how aggressive patterns are developed, what provokes people to behave aggressively, and what sustains such actions after they have been initiated."[88] Although everyone is capable of aggression, he says, "people are not born with . . . repertories of aggressive behavior. They must learn them." He goes on to say, "The specific forms that aggressive behavior takes, the frequency with which it is expressed, the situation in which it is displayed, and the specific targets selected for attack are largely determined by social learning factors."

Modeling theory, a form of social learning theory, asserts that people learn how to act by observing others. In some of his early work, Bandura experimented with children who observed adult role models striking inflatable cartoon characters. When the children were observed following their encounter with adult behavior, they, too, exhibited similarly aggressive behavior. Bandura also studied violence on television and concluded

modeling theory

A form of social learning theory that asserts that people learn how to act by observing others.

Who's to Blame—The Individual or Society?

The Video Game Killer

In early 2008, 17-year-old Jason Sutter was pulled over in a small Midwestern town for various traffic offenses, which included speeding 70 mph in a 35 mph zone, running a red traffic light, failure to yield for a blue light and siren, and reckless driving. When officers discovered that he didn't have a driver's license, Sutter was handcuffed, briefly searched, placed in the back of a patrol car, and driven to the local police station for booking.

After he was photographed and fingerprinted, detective Joe Lockman sat down with him in a small interrogation room located behind the department's front desk. Lockman, a 25-year-veteran of the force, had been working late and was in the station at 2:00 A.M. when Sutter arrived. The building was nearly empty and Lockman decided to remove Sutter's handcuffs in preparation for what he hoped would be an informal chat with the young man who had agreed to talk. Sutter, who stood only 5 foot 4 inches tall and weighed 135 pounds, reminded Lockman of his son, and the detective hoped that he could teach the boy something about right and wrong.

As Lockman leaned forward to unshackle Sutter, a number of unfortunate details came together with deadly results. Unknown to Lockman, Sutter was a high-school dropout and video game fanatic who spent most of his waking hours playing violence-themed games—including three in which the "heroes" killed pursuing police officers. Moreover, Sutter had been improperly handcuffed with his hands in the front, giving him easy access to Lockman's service revolver, which Lockman wore on his right hip. It was an opportunity similar to ones Sutter had often taken in his video games. In a final deadly detail, Lockman—an old-timer on the force—carried an older model police special 38-caliber revolver instead of a 9 mm semiautomatic pistol, in the belief that the revolver was less likely to jam in an emergency. The revolver, however, which was loaded with deadly hollow-point ammunition, did not have a safety, and when Sutter grabbed the weapon he was able to immediately pull the trigger and fire two shots into Lockman's chest, killing him instantly.

After the shooting, Sutter fled out the front door of the police station past the surprised desk sergeant. The sergeant, realizing what had happened, pursued Sutter through the front door and the two exchanged shots. Sutter was wounded in the exchange and captured. He was taken to an area hospital where he underwent surgery and recovered. While in the hospital, he was charged with the murder of Detective Lockman, and the district attorney said that he would seek to have Sutter put away for the rest of his life.

Sutter's parents hired an attorney to defend their son. The lawyer held a press conference during which he announced his defense strategy claiming that Sutter had been brainwashed by video games, and that at the time of the shooting he had been unable to distinguish reality from fantasy. "Jason was confused by all that happened. He thought that he was playing a game," the attorney said. "He didn't realize that someone might really get hurt." He also announced that he was filing a lawsuit against the two media companies that had made the games Sutter played.

Think about it:

1. Who is primarily responsible for the murder of Detective Lockman, Sutter or the video game manufacturers? Do both bear at least some responsibility?

2. What role, if any, did society play in Detective Lockman's death? That is, should government regulations be in place to control the content of video games?

3. What role did free will and individual choice play in Sutter's quick decision to take Lockman's gun and shoot him? That is, how much control did Sutter have over his own behavior, and how much of his behavior was merely a response to experiences he had in the past?

---

that "television is an effective tutor. Both laboratory and controlled field studies in which young children and adolescents are repeatedly shown either violent or nonviolent fare, disclose that exposure to film violence shapes the form of aggression and typically increases interpersonal aggressiveness in everyday life."[89] A later study by other researchers showed that even after ten years, the level of violence engaged in by young adults was directly related to the degree of violent television they had been exposed to as children.[90]

Bandura explained modeling behavior by referring to the frequent hijacking of domestic airliners to Cuba, which occurred in the United States in the late 1960s and early 1970s. Such hijackings, Bandura found, followed immediately on the heels of similar incidents in Eastern European nations under Soviet domination. American hijackings, he said, were simply modeling those in Europe, and hijackers in this country were learning from news accounts of their foreign tutors.

Once aggressive patterns of behavior have been acquired, it becomes necessary to show how they can be activated. Aggression can be provoked, Bandura suggests, through physical assaults and verbal threats and insults, as well as by thwarting a person's hopes or obstructing his or her goal-seeking behavior. Deprivation and "adverse reductions in the conditions of life" (a lowered standard of living, the onset of disease, a spouse leaving or caught cheating, for example) are other potential triggers of aggression. Bandura adds, however, that a human being's ability to foresee the future consequences of present behavior infuses another dimension into the activation of learned patterns of aggression. That is, aggressive behavior can be perceived as holding future benefits for individuals exhibiting it. In short, it can be seen as a means to a desired end.

An example of aggression that resulted from thwarted goal seeking, and that may have been seen as holding future benefits for the boys involved, occurred on the evening of February 27, 1995. On that evening, teenage neo-Nazi skinhead brothers Bryan and David Freeman bludgeoned their parents and younger brother to death in the family's Allentown, Pennsylvania, home.[91] David was 15 years old at the time of the killings; Bryan was 17. The first to be killed was probably their 48-year-old mother, Brenda, who suffered massive head injuries and stab wounds. Investigators theorize that Brenda confronted the boys after their noisy late-night return home and was arguing with them when at least one son attacked her, smashing her skull with a club. She fell facedown in the carpeted hallway outside the bedroom her sons shared, trying to protect her head with her hands. One of the boys then jumped on his mother and stabbed her repeatedly in the back. After what may have been a brief conference, the brothers then made their way upstairs to their parents' bedroom, where their 54-year-old father, Dennis, was sleeping. There, they cut their father's throat and clubbed him to death before he could leave the bed. Next, they moved on to the bedroom of their younger brother, Eric, 11, crushing his skull with a hammer as he slept. Viewing the murder scene the next day, Lehigh County Coroner Wayne Snyder called the slayings "the most savage, brutal, cowardly acts of murder I've ever seen."[92]

By all accounts, the young Freeman brothers had normal childhoods. Then, about two years before the murders, they began to change. The changes were gradual at first but soon became more pronounced. The boys fell in with a rebellious crowd, took to drinking, and experimented with drugs.[93] Soon they stopped attending school regularly, shaved their heads, began bodybuilding, and paid for a series of garish tattoos to cover their arms and torsos. They began attending white supremacist meetings and collected fascist paraphernalia, including knives. Two weeks before killing their parents, the brothers paid to have their foreheads tattooed: Bryan with "Berserker" and David with "Seig Heil." Run-ins with the police had become routine, and, authorities believe, when their parents took away the boys' car and threatened to have them reinstitutionalized, the killings took place.

Bandura also says that individuals sometimes become aggressive because they are rewarded for doing so. The early-twentieth-century American concept of a "macho"—virile and masculine—male figure, for example, was often associated with the expectation of substantial reward. The macho male figure was the one who won the most respect from his fellows, inevitably came away with the greatest honors (on the playing field, in school, from the community, and so on), and eventually married the most desirable woman. Whether this perception was accurate, it was nonetheless subscribed to by a significant proportion of American men and, for many decades, served as a guide to daily behavior.

Another form of reward can flow from aggression. Bandura called it the "reduction of aversive treatment." By this he meant that simply standing up for oneself can improve the way one is treated by others. Oftentimes, for example, standing up to a bully is the most effective way of dealing with the harassment one might otherwise face. Similarly, there is an old saying that "the squeaky wheel gets the grease," and it means, quite simply, that people who are the most demanding will be recognized. Aggressive people often get what they go after.

Bandura recognized that everyone has self-regulatory mechanisms that can ameliorate the tendency toward aggression. People reward or punish themselves, Bandura said, according to internal standards they have for judging their own behavior. Hence, aggression may be inhibited in people who, for example, value religious, ethical, or moral standards of conduct like compassion, thoughtfulness, and courtesy. Nonetheless, Bandura concluded, people who devalue aggression may still engage in it via a process he called "disengagement," whereby rationalizations are constructed that overcome internal inhibitions. Disengagement may result from (1) "attributing blame to one's victims"; (2) dehumanization through bureaucratization, automation, urbanization, and high social mobility; (3) vindication of aggressive practices by legitimate authorities; and (4) desensitization resulting from repeated exposure to aggression in any of a variety of forms.

Modeling theory has been criticized for lacking comprehensive explanatory power. How, for example, can striking differences in sibling behavior, when early childhood experiences were likely much the same, be explained? Similarly, why do apparent differences exist between the sexes with regard to degree and type of criminality, irrespective of social background and early learning experiences? More recent versions of modeling theory, sometimes called "cognitive social learning theory,"[94] attempt to account for such differences by hypothesizing that reflection and cognition play a significant role in interpreting what one observes and in determining responses. Hence, few people are likely to behave precisely as others because they will have their own ideas about what observed behavior means and about the consequences of emulation.

Behavior Theory

behavior theory

A psychological perspective that posits that individual behavior that is rewarded will increase in frequency, while that which is punished will decrease.

operant behavior

Behavior that affects the environment in such a way as to produce responses or further behavioral cues.

reward

A desirable behavioral consequence likely to increase the frequency of occurrence of that behavior.

punishment

An undesirable behavioral consequence likely to decrease the frequency of occurrence of that behavior.

Behavior theory has sometimes been called the stimulus-response approach to human behavior. "At the heart of behavior theory is the notion that behavior is determined by environmental consequences which it produces for the individual concerned."[95] When an individual's behavior results in rewards, or in the receipt of feedback that the individual, for whatever reason, regards as pleasurable and desirable, then it is likely that the behavior will become more frequent. Under such circumstances, the behavior in question is reinforced. Conversely, when punishment follows behavior, chances are that the frequency of that type of behavior will decrease. The individual's responses are termed **operant behavior** because a person's behavioral choices effectively operate on the surrounding environment to produce consequences for the individual. Similarly, stimuli provided by the environment become behavioral cues that elicit conditioned responses from the individual. Responses are said to be conditioned according to the individual's past experiences, wherein behavioral consequences effectively defined some forms of behavior as desirable and others as undesirable. Behavior theory is often employed by parents seeking to control children through a series of **rewards** and **punishments.** Young children may be punished, for example, with spanking, the loss of a favored toy (at least for a period of time), a turned-off television, and so forth. Older children are often told what rules they are expected to obey and what rewards they can anticipate receiving if they adhere to those rules. They also know that punishments will follow if they do not obey the rules.

Rewards and punishments have been further divided into four conceptual categories: (1) positive rewards, which increase the frequency of approved behavior by adding something desirable to the situation—as when a "good" child is given a toy; (2) negative rewards, which increase the frequency of approved behavior by removing something distressful from the situation—as when a "good" child is permitted to skip the morning's chores; (3) positive punishments, which decrease the frequency of unwanted behavior by adding something undesirable to the situation—as when a "bad" child is spanked; and (4) negative punishments, which decrease the frequency of unwanted behavior by removing something desirable from the situation—as when a "bad" child's candy is taken away. According to behavior theory, it is through the application of rewards and punishments that behavior is shaped.

Behavior theory differs from other psychological theories in that the major determinants of behavior are envisioned as existing in the environment surrounding the individual rather than actually in the individual. Perhaps the best-known proponent of behavior theory is **B. F. Skinner** (1904–1990). Skinner, a former Harvard professor, rejected unobservable psychological constructs, focusing instead on patterns of responses to external rewards and stimuli. Skinner did extensive animal research involving behavioral concepts and created the notion of programmed instruction, which allows students to work at their own pace and provides immediate rewards for learning accomplishments.

Although behavior theory has much to say about the reformation of criminal offenders through the imposition of punishment, the approach is equally significant for its contributions to understanding the genesis of such behavior. As one writer states, "It is the balance of reinforcement and punishment in an individual's learning history which will dictate the presence or absence of criminal behavior."[96] According to the behavioral model, crime results when individuals "receive tangible rewards (positive reinforcement) for engaging in delinquent and criminal behavior, particularly when no other attractive alternative is available."[97]

A few years ago, for example, Sundahkeh "Ron" Bethune, 15, shot and killed a 26-year-old pizza deliveryman who gunned his car motor as Bethune attempted to rob him. Bethune, who had been dabbling in the drug trade and who could afford high-priced clothing, jewelry, and other accoutrements of apparent wealth, was esteemed by many other young people in his Morganton, North Carolina, community. When the deliveryman tried to run from Bethune in front of a group of his friends, Bethune saw no other choice but to kill him. "I just had to show them I wasn't some little punk," he said afterward in a prison interview.[98] Bethune did not think of the long-term consequences of his behavior on the night of the killing. All he wanted was to earn the approval of those who were watching him. The crowd's anticipated awestruck response to murder was all the reward Bethune needed to pull the trigger that night. He was sentenced to five years in prison for second-degree murder.

Behavior theory has been criticized for ignoring the role that cognition plays in human behavior. Martyrs, for example, persist in what may be defined by the wider society as undesirable behavior, even in the face of severe punishment—including the loss of their own lives. No degree of punishment is likely to deter a martyr who answers to some higher call. Similarly, criminals who are punished for official law violations may find that their immediate social group interprets criminal punishment as status enhancing. As an acquaintance of the author said, after being released from prison where he had served time for murder, "You woulda thought I had won a Grammy award or somethin'." Members of his community held him in awe. As he walked down the street, young people would say, "There goes John! You better not mess with John!" From the point of view of behavior theory, criminal punishments are in danger of losing sway over many forms of human behavior in today's diverse society. Our society's fragmented value system leads to various interpretations of criminal punishments, thereby changing the significance of experiences like arrest, conviction, and imprisonment. In times past, criminal offenders were often shunned and became social outcasts. Today, those who have been an adjudicated criminal may find that their new status holds many rewards.

Attachment Theory

Another psychological approach to explaining crime and delinquency is **attachment theory.** Attachment theory was first proposed in the 1950s by John Bowlby (1907–1990), an English child psychiatrist who observed children during his tenure at the London Child Guidance Clinic after World War II.[99] Bowlby was especially interested in the maladjusted behavior of children who lacked a solid relationship with a mother figure. After years of working with children, Bowlby concluded that for healthy personality development to occur, "the infant and young child should experience a warm, intimate, and continuous relationship with his mother (or permanent mother substitute) in which both find satisfaction and enjoyment."[100]

Bowlby identified three forms of attachment: secure attachment, anxious-avoidant attachment, and anxious-resistant attachment.[101] Only the first, he said, is a healthy form of attachment. It develops when a child is confident that the mother figure will be responsible and available when needed. The development of healthy attachment, then, is largely dependent upon the availability of a mother figure who is sensitive to signals from the child, who is accessible to the child, and who is lovingly responsive to the child's needs. The successful development of secure attachment between a child and his or her primary caregiver, Bowlby said, provides the basic foundation for all future

attachment theory

A social-psychological perspective on delinquent and criminal behavior that holds that the successful development of secure attachment between a child and his or her primary caregiver provides the basic foundation for all future psychological development.

psychological development. Bowlby believed that secure attachments form early in childhood as the developing infant experiences nurturing and protective care. Hence, children develop a secure psychological base if they are "nourished physically and emotionally, comforted if distressed [and] reassured if frightened."[102]

According to attachment theory, delinquent behavior arises whenever nonsecure attachments are created. Anxious-avoidant attachment, for example, develops when children feel rejection and develop a lack of confidence concerning parental support and care. Anxious-resistant attachment develops from similar experiences and results in feelings of uncertainty, which cause the child (and, later, the adult) to feel anxious, to become fearful of his or her environment, and to cling to potential caregivers or partners. Bowlby calls delinquents "affectionless," meaning that they have not formed intimate attachments as children and are thus unable to form such attachments later in life. Attachment theory predicts that the most problematic individuals will be those who were abandoned at an early age, who experienced multiple placements (in foster homes, and so on), who had to deal with the early absence of one or both parents, and who faced traumatic conditions in early childhood (physical, sexual, or other abuse).

Recent tests of attachment theory seem to confirm that difficulties in childhood (especially before the age of eight) produce adult criminality later in life.[103] Studies have shown that children who were raised in insecure environments are likely to engage in violent behavior as adults and that childhood insecurity leads to a relative lack of empathy.[104] Some attachment theorists believe that the development of empathy is the most important single factor leading to conformity. When children do not receive empathetic understanding from those around them while being socialized, they appear to become unable to see others around them as deserving of empathy, and they become more likely to inflict injury on those they encounter. Learn more about attachment theory by visiting the Attachment Research Center via **Web Extra 6–5**. Read about the development of attachment theory at **Library Extra 6–4** at crimtoday.com.

WEB
Extra
▪ ▪ ▪ ▪

LIBRARY
Extra
▪ ▪ ▪ ▪

Self-Control Theory

Many people, regardless of what they have learned and independently of flaws in their personality, are able to exercise self-control sufficient to keep them from getting into trouble with the law, even under the most challenging of circumstances. **Self-control** refers to a person's ability to alter his or her own states and responses.[105] Many psychologists suggest that "the capacity to override and alter the self's responses is a vital characteristic that sets human beings apart from other species."[106] Self-control is most obvious when exercised in the face of adversity, as when people override their own natural tendencies to act or when they act contrary to their preferences and impulses. Hence, self-control is both key to adaptive success and central to virtuous behavior, especially insofar as the latter requires conforming to socially desirable standards in place of the pursuit of selfish goals.

self-control

A person's ability to alter his or her own states and responses.

In the field of psychology, four types of self-control have been identified. The first type is impulse control, in which people resist temptations and refrain from acting on impulses that they consider to be socially or personally undesirable. Impulses subject to control include those to eat or drink, to take drugs, to act violently or aggressively, to engage in sexual activity, and so forth. A second type of self-control is exercised over the contents of the mind and includes suppression of unwanted thoughts, the focusing of thoughts or concentration, reasoning and analysis, and inference and guided intuition. A third type of self-control can be exercised over one's emotional and mood states, and a fourth type involves controlling performance—as when a person persists in the face of adversity or physical challenges. Since self-control permits the changing of the self, it is a premier adaptive skill. Self-control enables people who are able to exercise it to adjust themselves to a much wider range of circumstances than they otherwise could. Psychologists sometimes argue that the majority of today's personal and social problems (which include things like drug abuse, violence, school failure, alcoholism, unwanted pregnancy, venereal disease, irresponsible money management, underachievement, poor eating habits and obesity, lack of exercise, cigarette smoking, and delinquency and criminality) stem from deficiencies or failures in self-control.[107]

A somewhat different perspective on self-control is offered by criminologists Michael R. Gottfredson and Travis Hirschi as part of their *general theory of crime*, which is also discussed in Chapter 8. "Gottfredson and Hirschi's general theory of crime claims to be *general,* in part, due to its assertion that the operation of a single mechanism, low self-control, accounts for 'all crime, at all times'; acts ranging from vandalism to homicide, from rape to white-collar-crime."[108] Gottfredson and Hirschi define *self-control* as the degree to which a person is vulnerable to temptations of the moment.[109] They propose that self-control is acquired early in life and that low self-control is the premier individual-level cause of crime. Self-control, say Gottfredson and Hirschi, develops by the end of childhood and is fostered through parental emotional investment in the child, which includes monitoring the child's behavior, recognizing deviance when it occurs, and punishing the child. Some researchers have called the argument that self-control develops early in childhood and persists over time the *stability thesis*. In research reported in 2006, Florida State University criminologists Carter Hay and Walter Forrest conducted a test of the stability thesis, finding moderately strong support for it.[110] In other words, levels of self-control developed early in childhood tend to persist, say Hay and Forrest, but not as strongly as the general theory of crime would suggest. Sixteen percent of the study population showed changes in levels of self-control over time, and those individuals who demonstrated the greatest stability in levels of self-control were those who started at the highest levels.

Gottfredson and Hirschi recognize the sociological dimensions of criminality by noting that the link between self-control and crime depends substantially upon criminal opportunity, which in itself is a function of the structural or situational circumstances that an individual encounters. Hence, these theorists suggest that "the link between self-control and crime is not deterministic, but probabilistic, affected by opportunities and other constraints."[111]

Recent research appears to show that low self-control tends to lead to peer rejection and isolation—especially among juveniles.[112] Consequently, young people with low self-control tend to associate with their deviant peers, meaning that those with low levels of self-control are essentially self-selected into groups of people who share their characteristics. According to Constance L. Chapple at the University of Nebraska, one of the researchers working in this area, "the delinquent peer group may provide increased opportunities for crime or exert situational pushes towards delinquency" because of the lack of self-control that characterizes its members.[113]

Gottfredson and Hirschi reject the notion that some people have an enduring propensity to commit crime or that any such propensity compels people to do so.[114] Crimes, they say, require "no special capabilities, needs, or motivation; they are, in this sense, available to everyone."[115] Instead, Gottfredson and Hirschi suggest that some people have a lasting tendency to ignore the long-term consequences of their behavior, that such people tend to be impulsive, reckless, and self-centered, and that crime is often the end result of such tendencies.[116]

Building on the work of Gottfredson and Hirschi, Harold G. Grasmick identifies some of the characteristics of individuals with low levels of self-control.[117] According to Grasmick, such people are impulsive and seek immediate gratification. Those with higher levels of self-control are more inclined to defer gratification in favor of long-term gains. People with less self-control lack diligence, tenacity, and persistence, says Grasmick, and prefer simple tasks and want "money without work, sex without courtship, [and] revenge without court delays."[118] Grasmick also believes that risk seeking is an important determinant of self-control, and he says that people with little self-control are drawn to activities that are adventurous and exciting. Similarly, says Grasmick, these people prefer physical activity over contemplation or conversation and tend to be indifferent or insensitive to the needs of others. While those who lack self-control are not necessarily antisocial or malicious; they are predisposed to being self-centered. Finally, according to Grasmick, self-control is inversely associated with a low frustration tolerance and with an inclination to handle conflict through confrontation.

A meta-analysis (a summary analysis of other research) of 21 studies of self-control theory conducted by Travis Pratt and Francis Cullen in 2000 found considerable support for the thesis that lack of self-control plays a central role in crime and deviance.[119] Looking at various studies that explored self-control as a delinquency preventative—including those on self-reported juvenile delinquency, self-reported and projected crime and deviance among college students, adult criminal behavior, and official delinquency—Pratt and Cullen concluded that low self-control is "one of the strongest known correlates of crime."

More recently, Carter Hay of Washington State University studied the role that parenting plays in the development of self-control and concluded that effective parenting can contribute to the development of self-control in children.[120] Hay points out, however, that Gottfredson and Hirschi, while they recognized the importance of parenting in the development of self-control, failed to adequately consider the nature of effective parenting. For parenting to be effective, Hay found that it must involve fair and nonphysical forms of discipline. Harsh discipline and discipline that was imposed unfairly did not appear to contribute to the development of self-control in the children under study. According to Hay, "[T]he sort of discipline that teaches children to control their behavior is not simply that which consistently occurs in the wake of deviance; other factors may be consequential as well, including the extent to which discipline is perceived as fair and is not reliant on physical force."[121]

Finally, in 2002, Thomas J. Bernard and fellow researcher Karen L. Hayslett-McCall at Pennsylvania State University proposed a new theory of disproportionate male offending that combined elements of Gottfredson and Hirschi's theory of low self-control with ideas from attachment theory.[122] Bernard and Hayslett-McCall offered to explain the strong relationship between gender and criminality—specifically, the consistent finding that men are more likely than women to offend in almost all offense categories. They concluded that gender-based differences in offending are caused by disruptions in attachments to primary caregivers early in childhood and that such disruptions are more likely to occur in the lives of boys than they are in the lives of girls because of cultural differences in the way boys are treated. Boys, say the researchers, are held less, comforted less when they cry, and spoken to less than girls in their early years because of child-rearing patterns that are thoroughly ingrained in our culture. In their words, "boys disproportionately experience disruptions of early attachment and . . . these disruptions are causally related to elements of what is often described as the masculine gender role." Low self-control among males, conclude Hayslett-McCall and Bernard, is the final result of gendered differences in attachment disruptions.

Insanity and the Law

insanity (legal)

A legally established inability to understand right from wrong or to conform one's behavior to the requirements of the law.

insanity (psychological)

Persistent mental disorder or derangement.

Unfortunately for criminologists, psychological conceptions of mental illness, antisocial personality, and even psychopathy are not readily applicable to the criminal justice system, which relies instead on the legal concept of **insanity**.[123] Insanity, for purposes of the criminal law, is strictly a legal, not a clinical, determination. Seen this way, *insanity* is a term that refers to a type of defense allowable in criminal courts. While the legal concept of insanity is based upon claims of mental illness, it has no precise counterpart in the jargon of contemporary psychologists or psychiatrists, who speak instead in terms of mental status or, at most, psychosis and personality disorder. As a consequence, legal and psychiatric understandings of mental impairment rarely coincide.

In the 1992 case of ***Foucha* v. *Louisiana,*** the U.S. Supreme Court recognized the problem, saying, "It is by now well established that insanity as defined by the criminal law has no direct analog in medicine or science. The divergence between law and psychiatry is caused in part by the legal fiction represented by the words 'insanity' or 'insane,' which are a kind of lawyer's catchall and have no clinical meaning."[124]

Because insanity is a defense to criminal prosecution, a criminal defendant may be found "not guilty by reason of insanity" and avoid punitive sanctions, even when it is clear that he or she committed a legally circumscribed act. The burden of proving a claim of "not guilty by reason of insanity," however, falls upon the defendant.[125] Just as a person is assumed to be innocent at the start of any criminal trial, so, too, is the person assumed to be sane.

A defendant has a right to the opportunity to prove a claim of insanity in court and cannot be forced to take medications during trial that might control the condition. In 1992, for example, the U.S. Supreme Court, in the case of *Riggins* v. *Nevada*,[126] held that the "forced administration of antipsychotic medication" may have impaired the accused's ability to defend himself and violated due process guarantees.

In 2003, in the case of *Sell* v. *United States*,[127] the Court placed additional limits on the government's power to forcibly medicate some mentally ill defendants to make them competent to stand trial. The Court ruled that the use of antipsychotic drugs on a nonviolent offender who does not represent a danger while institutionalized must be in the defendant's best medical interest and be "substantially unlikely" to cause side effects that might compromise the fairness of the trial.

In 1984, the U.S. Congress enacted the Insanity Defense Reform Act (IDRA), part of the 1984 Crime Control and Prevention Act.[128] Congress had been spurred to action by John Hinckley's attempted assassination of then–President Ronald Reagan. At trial, Hinckley's lawyers claimed that their client's history of schizophrenia left him unable to control his behavior, and Hinckley was acquitted of the criminal charges that had been brought against him. Although Hinckley was institutionalized to prevent him from harming others, his release is mandated by federal law that existed at the time of his trial when (and if) he recovers.

Through the IDRA, Congress intended to prohibit the presentation, at trial, in federal court, of evidence of mental disease or defect, short of legal insanity, to excuse conduct.[129] Insanity under the act is defined as a condition in which the defendant can be shown to have been suffering under a "severe mental disease or defect" and, as a result, "was unable to appreciate the nature and quality or the wrongfulness of his acts."[130] The IDRA also placed the burden of proving insanity squarely on the defendant—a provision that has been unsuccessfully challenged a number of times since the act was passed.

The IDRA created a special verdict of "not guilty by reason of insanity" (NGRI).[131] Through a comprehensive civil commitment procedure, a defendant found NGRI can be held in custody pending a court hearing. The hearing must occur within 40 days of the verdict. At the conclusion of the hearing, the court determines whether the defendant should be hospitalized or released. In the words of the U.S. Supreme Court, "The Insanity Defense Reform Act of 1984 ensures that a federal criminal defendant found not guilty by reason of insanity will not be released onto the streets."[132]

The IDRA is especially significant because it contains a provision that permits mentally ill individuals to be held for trial in the hopes that they will recover sufficiently to permit their trial to proceed. The law allows for an initial hearing to determine the mental status of the defendant. If the defendant is found incompetent to stand trial, he or she will be committed to a hospital "for such a reasonable period of time, not to exceed four months, . . . to determine whether there is a substantial probability that in the foreseeable future he will attain the capacity to permit the trial to proceed; and . . . for an additional reasonable period of time until . . . his mental condition is so improved that trial may proceed." The law sets no maximum period of confinement, implying only that the defendant will undergo periodic review while institutionalized "if the court finds that there is a substantial probability that within such additional period of time he will attain the capacity to permit the trial to proceed."[133]

The *M'Naughten* Rule

One of the first instances within the Western legal tradition where insanity was accepted as a defense to criminal liability can be found in the case of Daniel M'Naughten (also spelled "McNaughton" and "M'Naghton"). M'Naughten was accused of the 1843 killing of Edward Drummond, the secretary of British Prime Minister Sir Robert Peel. By all accounts, M'Naughten had intended to kill Peel, but because he was suffering from mental disorganization, he shot Drummond instead, mistaking him for Peel. At his trial,

Crime in the News

Moms Who Killed Children Become Friends in Hospital

DALLAS—Two Texas women who killed their young children in cases that drew nationwide attention reportedly have formed a friendship at a state hospital.

Andrea Yates, who drowned her five children in the bathtub, and Dena Schlosser, whose baby died after she severed the girl's arms with a kitchen knife, became roommates at the Maple unit of the

The North Texas State Hospital in Vernon, Texas. The high security mental health institution is home to Andrea Yates, who drowned her five children in the bathtub, and Dena Schlosser, whose baby died after she severed the girl's arms with a kitchen knife. The two women were sent to the hospital after being found not guilty by reason of insanity in separate trials. They have reportedly become friends. Can they help each other? If so, how?

Source: Courtesy of Fred R. Hight. Used with permission of The Associated Press Copyright © 2007. All rights reserved.

M'Naughten rule

A standard for judging legal insanity that requires that offenders not know what they were doing, or if they did, that they not know it was wrong.

the defense presented information to show that M'Naughten was suffering from delusions, including the belief that Peel's political party was, in some vague way, persecuting him. The court accepted his lawyer's claims, and the defense of insanity was established in Western law. Other jurisdictions were quick to adopt the *M'Naughten* rule, as the judge's decision in the case came to be called. The ***M'Naughten* rule** holds that individuals cannot be held criminally responsible for their actions if at the time of the offense either (1) they did not know what they were doing or (2) they did not know that what they were doing was wrong.

Today the *M'Naughten* rule is still followed by many states when insanity is at issue in criminal cases. Critics of the *M'Naughten* rule say that although the notion of intent inherent within it appeals greatly to lawyers, "it is . . . so alien to current concepts of human behavior that it has been vigorously attacked by psychiatrists. An obvious difficulty with the *M'Naughten* rule is that practically everyone, regardless of the degree of his criminal disturbance, knows the nature and quality and rightness or wrongness of what he is doing."[134]

North Texas State Hospital after each was found not guilty by reason of insanity.

"We talk about our past, we talk about our memories, our fun memories, the things that our kids did," Schlosser told *The Dallas Morning News*.

Yates' ex-husband, Russell Yates, who regularly visits her at the hospital in Vernon, 174 miles northwest of Dallas, said Schlosser has become a friend.

"Hopefully, they can help each other through the long recovery process," he said.

The two women will likely be in the state's care for years, remaining at Vernon or another hospital until their doctors and judges agree they can be released.

Conversations between the women often revolve around their young daughters—Mary Yates was 6 months old and Maggie Schlosser was 10 months old when they died.

Schlosser's parents, Connie and Mick Macaulay of Canada, said their daughter once called in tears after talking with Yates.

"They'd talked a lot about Mary and Maggie," said Mick Macaulay, a mental health counselor. "They were feeling guilty, remorseful and sad."

Schlosser, 37, was already at the hospital when Yates, 42, arrived two months ago. Yates drowned her children at her family home in suburban Houston in 2001. Schlosser cut off her daughter's arms in her family home in suburban Dallas in 2004.

The women have much more in common. Both were married, stay-at-home moms who followed out-of-the-mainstream religious leaders. Both suffered from postpartum depression and psychosis after the birth of their daughters.

Yates, who had been a nurse, said she believed when she drowned her five children—Mary, Luke, 2, Paul, 3, John, 5, and Noah, 7—that she was protecting them from Satan. Schlosser,

who has a degree in psychology, said she wanted to offer her baby to God.

While Schlosser has no distinct memories of what she calls "the tragedy," she knows she killed Maggie. During her trial, psychiatrists said that in her delusional mind, she believed God wanted her to cut off the baby's arms.

"I had delusions that were going on that I didn't understand, but I believed them. I thought I was doing the right thing," she said.

Schlosser hopes to reconcile with her surviving daughters. The girls, 8 and 11, live with their father, who has filed for divorce.

She has written her daughters a letter a week since her arrest, telling them how much she loves and misses them. But she's waiting to mail them until the girls are ready to read them. She knows they aren't ready to see her yet.

"I'm willing to wait. I'll wait as long, I'll wait for the rest of my life," Schlosser said. "I love them dearly. My kids are my world, and they always will be."

Yates has no living children but will one day be buried with her children, a right she won in the divorce.

Discussion Questions

1. How do the perspectives discussed in this chapter help us understand the kinds of behaviors that led Schlosser and Yates to be institutionalized?

2. Do you believe that the women can help each other, as this article intimates?

3. Should either woman eventually be released back into society? If so, how would you know when they are ready for release?

Source: The Associated Press, "Moms Who Killed Children Become Friends in Hospital: Yates, Schlosser Share Room, Past," October 9, 2006, http://www.usatoday.com/printedition/news/20061009/a_yates09.art.htm.

For the latest crime and justice news, visit www.crimenews.info.

The Irresistible-Impulse Test

The *M'Naughten* ruling opened the floodgates for other types of insanity claims offered as defenses to charges of criminal activity. One interesting claim is that of irresistible impulse. The **irresistible-impulse test**—employed by 18 states, some of which also follow the dictates of *M'Naughten*—holds that a defendant is not guilty of a criminal offense if the person, by virtue of his or her mental state or psychological condition, was not able to resist committing the action in question. Some years ago, for example, a television advertisement claimed that a certain brand of potato chip was so good that, once you opened the container, you couldn't eat just one. Friends of the author would test themselves by purchasing the brand in question, opening the pack, and eating a chip. They would then try to resist the temptation to have another, thereby hoping to prove the commercial wrong. Although this may seem a silly exercise in self-assessment, it did prove a point. The commercial, in fact, was right most of the time. Additional chips were almost impossible to avoid for anyone who tried this experiment—especially if

irresistible-impulse test

A standard for judging legal insanity that holds that a defendant is not guilty of a criminal offense if the person, by virtue of his or her mental state or psychological condition, was not able to resist committing the crime.

Insanity can be used as a defense against criminal charges. Lorena Bobbitt sobs on the witness stand before acquittal on charges she severed her husband's penis with a kitchen knife. Bobbitt claimed a kind of irresistible impulse. Should she have been acquitted?

Source: Gary Hershorn, Corbis/ Bettmann

they kept the chips around for any length of time! Of course, eating potato chips is not a crime, even if the chips are irresistible.

Commercials aside, it is difficult for anyone to really know whether a given person in a particular situation was able to control his or her behavior. Kleptomania is a disorder in which an individual feels compelled to steal. Kleptomaniacs are often shoplifters but have also been known to be unable to resist the urge to steal while visiting the homes of friends or relatives.

In 1994, Lorena Bobbitt, whose case was described earlier in this chapter, was found not guilty by virtue of temporary insanity of charges of maliciously wounding her husband by cutting off his penis with a kitchen knife. Her attorneys successfully employed the irresistible-impulse defense, convincing the jury that Mrs. Bobbitt acted as a result of irresistible impulse after years of "physical abuse, verbal abuse and sexual abuse" at the hands of her husband. Her attorneys maintained that, while committing the crime, she had a brief psychotic breakdown and could not resist the impulse to maim her husband.

Scientific advances now on the horizon combine with the irresistible-impulse test to open a number of intriguing possibilities. One has to do with new colognes and perfumes that combine the usual scents with pheromones—chemical substances that, at least in insect form, have been shown to produce very predictable, and apparently uncontrollable, behavior. Pheromones, which stimulate the olfactory nerves to produce specific chemicals, which then target neuroreceptors in the brain, directly alter brain chemistry. Most uses of pheromones to date have been in the area of pest control, where sexual pheromones that attract specific types of male insects, for example, are released into the atmosphere to confuse the insect's mating behavior or to lure pests into a trap. Might these new toiletries lead to claims of uncontrollable sexual desire? Will toiletries containing human pheromones lead to instances of sexual attack? If so, will the attackers be held blameless on claims of irresistible impulse, and what will then be the civil liability of the product makers themselves?

The *Durham* Rule

In 1954, Judge David Bazelon of the U.S. Court of Appeals for the District of Columbia announced a new rule in the case of Monte Durham. In the words of the court, "The rule we now hold is simply that an accused is not criminally responsible if his unlawful act was the product of mental disease or mental defect." Judge Bazelon continued, defining the terms of the court's decision, "We use 'disease' in the sense of a condition which is considered capable of improving or deteriorating. We use 'defect' in the sense of a condition which is not considered capable of either improving or deteriorating and which may be congenital or the result of injury or the residual effect of a physical or mental disease."[135]

Although this new rule was intended to simplify the adjudication of mentally ill offenders, it has resulted in additional confusion. Many criminal defendants suffer from mental diseases or defects. Some show retarded mental development, others are dyslexic, a few are afflicted with Down's syndrome, others have cerebral palsy (which would perhaps meet Judge Bazelon's definition), and a vast number evidence some degree of neurosis or psychosis. The link between any of these conditions and criminal behavior in specific cases, however, is far from clear. Some people struggle with psychological disabilities or mental illnesses all their lives, never violating the criminal law. Others, with similar conditions, are frequent law violators. The **Durham rule** provides no way of separating one group from the other.

Finally, some observers have noted the "danger of circularity" in the *Durham* rule. If a person exhibits unusual behavior during the commission of a crime, the criminal behavior itself may be taken as a sign of mental disease, automatically exonerating the offender of criminal culpability.

Durham rule

A standard for judging legal insanity that holds that an accused is not criminally responsible if his or her unlawful act was the product of mental disease or mental defect.

The Substantial-Capacity Test

In the determination of insanity for purposes of criminal prosecution, 19 U.S. states adhere to the **substantial-capacity test,** a standard embodied in the Model Penal Code of the American Law Institute. The substantial-capacity test blends elements of the *M'Naughten* rule with the irresistible-impulse standard. Insanity is said to be present when a person lacks "the [substantial] mental capacity needed to understand the wrongfulness of his act, or to conform his behavior to the requirements of the law."[136] A lack of mental capacity does not require total mental incompetence, nor does it mandate that the behavior in question meet the standard of total irresistibility. The problem, however, of determining just what constitutes "substantial mental capacity," or its lack, has plagued this rule from its inception.

substantial-capacity test

A standard for judging legal insanity that requires that a person lack the mental capacity needed to understand the wrongfulness of his or her act or to conform his or her behavior to the requirements of the law.

The *Brawner* Rule

The **Brawner rule,** created in 1972 in the case of *United States* v. *Brawner,*[137] is unique among standards of its type. This rule, in effect, delegates responsibility to the jury to determine what constitutes insanity. The jury is asked to decide whether the defendant could be *justly* held responsible for the criminal act with which he or she stands charged, in the face of any claims of insanity or mental incapacity. Under the *Brawner* rule, which has not seen wide applicability, juries are left with few rules to guide them other than their own sense of fairness.

Brawner rule

A somewhat vague rule for determining insanity that was created in the 1972 federal court case of *United States* v. *Brawner* (471 F.2d 969), since superseded by statute, and asks the jury to decide whether the defendant could be *justly* held responsible for the criminal act with which he or she stands charged, in the face of any claims of insanity or mental incapacity.

Guilty but Mentally Ill

Frustrated by the seeming inability of criminal courts to effectively adjudicate mentally ill offenders and by the abuse of insanity claims by offenders seeking to avoid criminal punishments, several states have enacted legislation permitting findings of "guilty but insane" or **guilty but mentally ill (GBMI).** In 1997, for example, Pennsylvania multimillionaire John E. du Pont was found guilty but mentally ill in the shooting death of former Olympic gold medalist David Schultz during a delusional episode. Although defense attorneys were able to show that du Pont sometimes thought he saw Nazis in his trees, heard the walls talking, and had cut off pieces of his own skin in efforts to remove bugs from outer space, he was held criminally liable for Schultz's death and was sentenced to 13 to 30 years in confinement.

A GBMI verdict means that a person can be held responsible for a specific criminal act, even though a degree of mental incompetence may be present. In most GBMI jurisdictions, a jury must return a finding of "guilty but mentally ill" if (1) every statutory element necessary for a conviction has been proved beyond a reasonable doubt, (2) the

guilty but mentally ill (GBMI)

A finding that offenders are guilty of the criminal offense with which they are charged, but because of their prevailing mental condition, they are generally sent to psychiatric hospitals for treatment rather than to prison. Once they have been declared cured, however, such offenders can be transferred to correctional facilities to serve out their sentences.

Insanity became an issue at the 1997 murder trial of multimillionaire John E. du Pont. In 1996, du Pont shot and killed wrestler David Schultz during a delusional episode. Although defense attorneys were able to show that du Pont sometimes saw Nazis in his trees, heard the walls talking, and had cut off pieces of his skin to remove bugs from outer space, he was found guilty but mentally ill and was sentenced to serve 13 to 30 years in confinement. Should he have been absolved of criminal responsibility?

Source: Chris Gardner, AP Wide World Photos

defendant is found to have been *mentally ill* at the time the crime was committed, and (3) the defendant was not found to have been *legally insane* at the time the crime was committed. The difference between mental illness and legal insanity is crucial because a defendant can be mentally ill by standards of the medical profession but sane for purposes of the law.

Upon return of a GBMI verdict, a judge may impose any sentence possible under the law for the crime in question. Offenders adjudicated GBMI are, in effect, found guilty of the criminal offense with which they are charged but, because of their mental condition, are generally sent to psychiatric hospitals for treatment rather than to prison. Once they have been declared "cured," however, such offenders can be transferred to correctional facilities to serve out their sentences.

Federal Provisions for the Hospitalization of Individuals Found "NGRI"

Federal law provides for confinement in a "suitable facility" of criminal defendants found not guilty by reason of insanity (NGRI).[138] The law mandates a "psychiatric or psychological examination and report" and a hearing to be held within 40 days after the not guilty verdict. If the hearing court finds that the person's release would "create a substantial risk of bodily injury to another person or serious damage of property of another due to a present mental disease or defect," the statute says, "the court shall commit the person." To be released later, a person committed under the law "has the burden of proving by clear and convincing evidence that his release would not create a substantial risk of bodily injury to another person or serious damage of property of another due to a present mental disease or defect." The person can be discharged "when the director of the facility in which an acquitted person is hospitalized . . . determines that the person has recovered from his mental disease or defect to such an extent that his release, or his conditional release under a prescribed regimen of medical, psychiatric, or psychological care or treatment, would no longer create a substantial risk of bodily injury to another person or serious damage to property of another."

Criminal Profiles

Andrea Yates

Few crimes have shocked American society as deeply as the drowning of five young children by their mother, Andrea Pia (Kennedy) Yates, in a bathtub in their suburban Houston, Texas, home on January 20, 2001. Her subsequent trial, conviction, life sentence, successful appeal, and second trial brought the insanity defense based on a claim of postpartum psychosis under intense scrutiny. Ultimately, it is difficult to find a national consensus on the emotional issues involved in this horrifying event.

Yates's early life showed promise for future success. High school valedictorian and swim team captain, the middle class student from Houston went on to earn an undergraduate degree in nursing from the University of Texas. After obtaining a job as a registered nurse, she met Rusty Yates. Their shared deep Christian faith was a significant factor in their attraction to one another.

When Andrea and Rusty finally married after three years of dating, they planned on having as many children as God intended them to have. To family and friends, they confided that they thought there would ultimately be at least six children in their family.[i] The birth of their first child, Noah, a year after their marriage, however, brought unexpected difficulties.

Unaware of the extent of mental illness that had plagued her own family, the new mother was understandably tormented when she began to have violent visions of stabbings and came to believe that Satan was speaking directly to her. Yates hid these frightening experiences from everyone, including her husband. Instead, she publicly espoused their shared idealized notions of a strong, faith-based family, despite the mental and emotional upheavals that raged within her.

Events over the next few years led Andrea deeper into depression. The Yateses had two more children, after which Andrea

miscarried. She then had their fourth child, but the birth was followed by pronounced depressive manifestations—including chewed fingers, uncontrollable shaking, hallucinations, voices in her head, suicidal and homicidal thoughts, and two suicide attempts. Soon, she entered into a series of psychiatric counseling sessions with various doctors. A wide variety of drug therapies were tried, many of which Andrea rejected by flushing the prescriptions down the toilet.

Additionally, the Yateses came under the influence of a self-proclaimed "prophet," Michael Woroniecki, whose extreme views of a woman's family role included subservience to men and harsh judgment of "permissive" mothers who failed to keep their children on the spiritual straight and narrow. Mothers, he claimed, bore the sole responsibility for the spiritual health of their children.

Despite extensive hospitalizations and medication for her ongoing depression and emerging psychosis, and against the advice of her psychiatrist, Yates became pregnant again, delivering her fifth child, Mary, in November 2000. The pregnancy had resulted from the urging of her husband, who also ignored the strong medical opposition to the birth of another child.[ii]

When Yates's father died just $4\frac{1}{2}$ months after her fifth child was born, her mental health declined dramatically.[iii] Both a hospitalization at the end of March and her medication, however, were terminated by her psychiatrist, Dr. Mahommed Saeed, because, he claimed, she did not seem psychotic. Yates returned to the hospital again for ten days in May. Upon her release, she was advised to think positive thoughts and to see a psychologist.

Two days later, she systematically drowned each of her five children.

Following a sensational trial that was widely followed by the media, Yates was convicted and sentenced to life in prison. That conviction was subsequently overturned because of the false testimony of forensic psychologist Park Dietz.[iv] In July 2006, Yates was retried, but this time she was acquitted of capital murder charges and found not guilty by reason of insanity. She was immediately ordered to commitment in a mental hospital, where she will remain until she is no longer considered to be a threat to herself or others.[v]

Andrea Yates, center, who's admitted drowning her five children in a bathtub at the family home, leaves the Harris County Criminal Justice Center with her attorney George Parnham, after being found not guilty by reason of insanity in a second trial. Yates was sent to a maximum security mental hospital where she will be held until she is cured. What do you think should have been done with Yates?

Source: David J. Phillip, AP Wide World Photos

[i] Katherine Ramsland, "Andrea Yates: Ill or Evil?" Chapter 5, CourtTV Crime Library, 2007, http://www.crimelibrary.com/notorious_murders/women/andrea_yates/5.html (accessed June 16, 2007).

[ii] Charles Montaldo, "Profile of Andrea Yates," About: Crime/Punishment, 2007, http://crime.about.com/od/current/p/andreayates.htm (accessed June 16, 2007).

[iii] Ibid.

[iv] "Court Lets Stand Ruling that Tossed Andrea Yates' Murder Conviction," CourtTV News, November 9, 2005, http://www.courttv.com/trials/yates/110905_cnn.html (accessed June 16, 2007).

[v] "Jury: Yates Not Guilty by Reason of Insanity," July 26, 2006, MSNBC/Associated Press, http://www.msnbc.msn.com/id/14024728 (accessed June 16, 2007).

The federal statute has been used as a model by many of the states. A few laws that differ from the federal model have been held to be unconstitutional, especially when they permit the continued confinement of offenders who have been declared "well," even though they may still be dangerous. In 1992, for example, the U.S. Supreme Court, in the case of *Foucha* v. *Louisiana,* ordered the release of Terry Foucha, who had been adjudicated "not guilty by reason of insanity" in the state of Louisiana. Although a psychiatrist later found Foucha to have overcome a drug-induced psychosis that had been present at the time of the crime, a state court ordered Foucha returned to the mental institution in which he had been committed, ruling that he was dangerous on the basis of the same doctor's testimony. The psychiatrist found that although Foucha was "in good shape" mentally, he had "an antisocial personality." Foucha's antisocial personality was described as "a condition that is not a mental disease and is untreatable." The doctor, citing the fact that Foucha had been involved in several altercations at the institution, said that he would not "feel comfortable in certifying that [Foucha] would not be a danger to himself or to other people." In effect, the Supreme Court struck down a provision of the Louisiana law that made possible continued confinement of recovered persons who had once been deemed not guilty by reason of insanity when their continued confinement is predicated solely on the basis of the belief that they might represent a continuing danger to the community. Learn more about psychiatry and the law via Library Extras 6–5 and 6–6 at crimtoday.com.

LIBRARY Extra ▪ ▪ ▪ ▪

Social Policy and Forensic Psychology

Psychological theories continue to evolve. For example, recent research in the field has shown a stability of aggressiveness over time. That is, children who display early disruptive or aggressive behavior are, according to studies that follow the same individuals over time, likely to continue their involvement in such behavior as adults.[139] Some researchers have found that aggressiveness appears to stabilize over time.[140] Children who demonstrate aggressive traits early in life often evidence increasingly frequent episodes of such behavior until, finally, such behavior becomes a major component of the adolescent or adult personality. From such research, it is possible to conclude that problem children are likely to become problem adults.

Expanding research of this sort holds considerable significance for those who are attempting to assess dangerousness and to identify personal characteristics that would allow for the prediction of dangerousness in individual cases. The ability to accurately predict future dangerousness is of great concern to today's policymakers. In 1993, for example, Michael Blair, a convicted child molester paroled after serving 18 months of a ten-year prison sentence, was charged with the kidnap-slaying of young Ashley Estell, who disappeared from a soccer match in Plano, Texas. Ashley was found dead the next day.[141] Similarly, in November of that year, Anthony Cook was executed in Huntsville, Texas, for the slaying of law student Dirck VanTassel, Jr.[142] Cook killed VanTassel only 13 days after being paroled, robbing him of his wallet, watch, and wedding ring and shooting him four times in the head. Less than a month later, in what was to be a very sad case, Richard Allen Davis, a twice-convicted kidnapper, was arrested for the kidnap-murder of 12-year-old Polly Klaas.[143] Klaas was abducted from a slumber party in her Petaluma, California, home as her mother slept in the next room. Davis had been paroled only a few months earlier after serving an eight-year prison term for a similar offense.

Can past behavior predict future behavior? Do former instances of criminality presage additional ones? Are there other identifiable characteristics that violent offenders might manifest that could serve as warning signs to criminal justice decision makers faced with the dilemma of whether to release convicted felons? This, like many other areas, is one in which criminologists are still learning. One recent study found a strong relationship between childhood behavioral difficulties and later problem behavior.[144] According to the authors of the study, "Early antisocial behavior is the best predictor of later antisocial behavior. It appears that this rule holds even when the antisocial behavior is measured as early as the preschool period." Using children as young as three years old, researchers were able to predict later delinquency, leading them to conclude that "some antisocial behavioral characteristics may be components of temperament." A second study, which tracked a sample of male offenders for over 20 years, found that stable but as yet "unmeasured individual differences" account for the positive association that exists between past criminal behavior and the likelihood of future recurrence.[145] A 1996 analysis of recidivism studies by Canadians Paul Gendreau, Tracy Little, and Claire Goggin found that criminal history, a history of preadult antisocial behavior, and "criminogenic needs"—which were defined as measurable antisocial thoughts, values, and behavior—were all predictors of recidivism.[146]

Prediction, however, requires more than generalities. It is one thing to say, for example, that generally speaking 70% of children who evidence aggressive behavior will show violent tendencies later in life and quite another to be able to predict which specific individuals will engage in future violations of the criminal law. **Selective incapacitation** is a policy based on the notion of career criminality.[147] Career criminals, also called "habitual offenders," are people who repeatedly violate the criminal law. Research has shown that only a small percentage of all offenders account for most of the crimes reported to the police. Some studies have found that as few as 8% of all offenders commit as many as 60 serious crimes each per year.[148] A recent Wisconsin study found that imprisonment of individuals determined to be career offenders saved the state approximately $14,000 per year per offender when the cost of imprisonment was compared with the estimated cost of new crimes.[149] Researchers in the Wisconsin study concluded that "prison pays" and suggested that the state continue pursuing a policy of aggressive imprisonment of career offenders, even in the face of escalating costs and vastly overcrowded prisons. The strategy of selective incapacitation, however, which depends on accurately identifying potentially dangerous offenders in existing criminal populations, has been criticized by some authors for yielding a rate of "false positives" of over 60%.[150] Potentially violent offenders are not easy to identify, even on the basis of past criminal records, and sentencing individuals to long prison terms simply because they are thought likely to commit crimes in the future would no doubt be unconstitutional.

The federal 1984 Comprehensive Crime Control Act,[151] which established the U.S. Sentencing Commission, targeted career offenders. Guidelines created by the commission contain, as a central feature, a "criminal history" dimension, which substantially increases the amount of punishment an offender faces based on his or her history of law violations. The sentencing guidelines originally classified a defendant as a career offender if "(1) the defendant was at least 18 years old at the time of the . . . offense, (2) the . . . offense is a crime of violence or trafficking in a controlled substance, and (3) the defendant has at least two prior felony convictions of either a crime of violence or a controlled substance offense."[152] The definition, however, later came under fire for casting individuals with a history of minor drug trafficking into the same category as serial killers and the like.

Definitions of *dangerousness* are fraught with difficulty because, as some authors have pointed out, "dangerousness is not an objective quality like obesity or brown eyes, rather it is an ascribed quality like trustworthiness."[153] Dangerousness is not necessarily a personality trait that is stable or easily identifiable. Even if it were, some studies of criminal careers seem to show that involvement in crime decreases with age.[154] Hence, as one author states, if "criminality declines more or less uniformly with age, then many offenders will be 'over the hill' by the time they are old enough to be plausible candidates for preventive incarceration."[155]

No discussion of social policy as it relates to the insights of criminal psychology would be complete without mention of correctional psychology. **Correctional psychology**

selective incapacitation

A social policy that seeks to protect society by incarcerating the individuals deemed to be the most dangerous.

correctional psychology

The branch of forensic psychology concerned with the diagnosis and classification of offenders, the treatment of correctional populations, and the rehabilitation of inmates and other law violators.

is concerned with the diagnosis and classification of offenders, the treatment of correctional populations, and the rehabilitation of inmates and other law violators. Perhaps the most commonly used classification instrument in correctional facilities today is the Minnesota Multiphasic Personality Inventory, better known as the MMPI. Based on the results of an MMPI, an offender may be assigned to a security level, a correctional program, or a treatment program. Psychological treatment, when employed, typically takes the form of individual or group counseling. Psychotherapy, guided group interaction, cognitive therapy, behavioral modification, and various forms of interpersonal therapy are representative of the range of techniques used. Learn more about forensic psychology via **Library Extra 6–7,** and visit the American Association for Correctional and Forensic Psychology (AACFP) at **Web Extra 6–6** at crimtoday.com. AACFP is an organization of behavioral scientists and practitioners who are concerned with the delivery of high-quality mental health services to criminal offenders, and with promoting and disseminating research on the etiology, assessment, and treatment of criminal behavior.

LIBRARY
Extra
▪ ▪ ▪ ▪

WEB
Extra
▪ ▪ ▪ ▪

Social Policy and the Psychology of Criminal Conduct

A practical synthesis of psychological approaches to criminal behavior is offered by Donald A. Andrews and James Bonta in their 1994 book *The Psychology of Criminal Conduct.*[156] Andrews and Bonta prefer the term *psychology of criminal conduct,* or *PCC,* to distinguish their point of view from what they call "the weak psychology represented in mainstream sociological criminology and clinical/forensic sychology."[157] Any useful synthesis of contemporary criminal psychology, they claim, should be fundamentally objective and empirical. Clearly, they dislike many currently well-accepted perspectives, which they say have "placed higher value on social theory and political ideology than [on] rationality and/or respect for evidence."[158] Specifically, say Andrews and Bonta, "The majority of perspectives on criminal conduct that are most favored in mainstream criminology reduce people to hypothetical fictions whose only interesting characteristics are their location in the social system. Almost without exception, the causal significance of social location is presumed to reflect inequality in the distribution of social wealth and power." This kind of theorizing, the authors claim, "is a major preoccupation of mainstream textbook criminology, even though such a focus has failed to significantly advance understanding of criminal conduct."[159]

In *The Psychology of Criminal Conduct,* Andrews and Bonta do not attempt to develop a new behavior theory but, rather, ask for the objective application of what is now understood about the psychology of crime and criminal behavior. Their book is a call for practical coalescence of what is already known of the psychology of criminal offenders. Such coalescence is possible, they say, through the application of readily available, high-quality psychological findings. The authors claim, for example, that from the nearly 500 published reports on "controlled evaluations of community and correctional interventions," it is possible to conclude that treatment reduces recidivism "to at least a mild degree."[160] Further, a detailed consideration of published studies finds that, among other things, targeting higher-risk cases and using treatments outside of formal correctional settings, which extend to an offender's family and peers, are all elements of the most effective treatment strategies. Similarly, along with objective measures of the success of rehabilitation programs and strategies, Andrews and Bonta say, effective intervention and treatment services based on the use of psychological assessment instruments that have already demonstrated their validity, empirically established risk factors that can be accurately assessed, and accurately measured community crime rates are all ready and waiting to make a practical psychology of criminal conduct available to today's policymakers. In the words of Andrews and Bonta, "There exists now an empirically defensible general psychology of criminal conduct (PCC) that is of practical value. . . . It should speak to policy advisors, policy makers and legislators who must come to see that . . . human science is not just [a] relic of a positivistic past."[161] The major remaining issue "on which work is only beginning," say the authors, "is how to make use of what works."[162]

Criminal Psychological Profiling

During World War II, the War Department recruited psychologists and psychiatrists in an attempt to predict the future moves that the enemy forces might make. Psychological and psychoanalytic techniques were applied to the study of German leader Adolf Hitler, Italian leader Benito Mussolini, Japanese general and prime minister Hideki Tojo, and other Axis leaders. Such psychological profiling of enemy leaders may have given the Allies the edge in battlefield strategy. Hitler, probably because of his heightened sensitivity to symbols, his strong belief in fate, and his German ancestry (Freud was Austrian), became the central figure that profilers analyzed.

Today, criminal **psychological profiling** is used to assist police investigators seeking to better understand individuals wanted for serious offenses. Criminal psychological profiling is also called "criminal profiling" and "behavioral profiling." During a recent interview, famed profiler John Douglas, the retired FBI special agent who became the model for the Scott Glenn character in Thomas Harris's *Silence of the Lambs,* described criminal profiling this way: "It is a behavioral composite put together of the unknown subject after analyzing the crime scene materials, to include the autopsy protocol, autopsy and crime scene photographs, as well as the preliminary police reports. It is also a detailed analysis of the victim and putting that information together. To me, it's very much like an internist in medicine who now

psychological profiling

The attempt to categorize, understand, and predict the behavior of certain types of offenders based on behavioral clues they provide.

Scott Glenn, starring as Jack Crawford in the crime thriller *Silence of the Lambs*. The movie publicized the practice of criminal profiling. How can psychological profiling assist criminal investigations?

Source: Photo by Orion Pictures Corporation / ZUMA Press. © Copyright 1991 by Orion Pictures Corporation

attempts to put a diagnosis, say, on an illness; I'm trying to put a diagnosis on this particular case that's relative to motive, as well as the type of person(s) who would perpetrate that type of crime."[163]

Profilers develop a list of typical offender characteristics and other useful principles by analyzing crime scene and autopsy data in conjunction with interviews and other studies of past offenders. In general, the psychological profiling of criminal offenders is based on the belief that almost any form of conscious behavior, including each and every behavior engaged in by the offender during a criminal episode, is symptomatic of the individual's personality. Hence, the way in which a kidnapper approaches victims, for example; the manner of attack used by a killer; and the specific sexual activities of a rapist might all help paint a picture of the offender's motivations, personal characteristics, and likely future behavior. Sometimes psychological profiles can provide clues as to what an offender might do following an attack. Some offenders have been arrested, for example, after returning to the crime scene— a behavior typically predicted by specific behavioral clues left behind. Remorseful types can be expected to visit the victim's grave, permitting fruitful stakeouts of cemeteries.

While criminal profiling is not necessarily useful in every case, it can help narrow the search for an offender when used correctly in repetitive crimes involving an individual offender, such as serial rape or murder. Knowledge gleaned from profiling can also help in the interrogation of suspects and can be used to identify and protect possible victims before the offender has a chance to strike again.

Throughout the 1990s, the American public became enthralled with psychological profiling. A number of retired FBI profilers have written books and novels about their careers. One of the best known of these retired agents is John Douglas, who was mentioned earlier. Douglas's books, exposés of his profiling assignments, include *Mindhunter* (1996), *Journey into Darkness* (1997), and *Obsession* (1998). Another retired FBI profiler who helped popularize the field is Robert K. Ressler. Ressler's 1992 book *Whoever Fights Monsters,*[164] a tale of his years at the FBI fighting serial killers, is often credited with having created much of the public's contemporary fascination with psychological profiling.

Although psychological profiling is a contemporary favorite of the entertainment media, profilers have also contributed significantly to the scientific literature in criminology. For example, in a well-known study of lust murderers (men who kill and often mutilate victims during or following a forced sexual episode), FBI special agents Robert R. Hazelwood and John E. Douglas distinguished between the organized nonsocial and the disorganized asocial types.[165] The organized nonsocial lust murderer was described as exhibiting complete indifference to the interests of society and as being completely self-centered. He was also said to be "methodical and cunning," as well as "fully cognizant of the criminality of his act and its impact on society." His counterpart, the disorganized asocial lust murderer, was described this way: "The disorganized asocial lust murderer exhibits primary characteristics of societal aversion. This individual prefers his own company to that of others and would be typified as a loner. He experiences difficulty in negotiating interpersonal relationships and consequently feels rejected and lonely. He lacks the cunning of the nonsocial type and commits the crime in a more frenzied and less methodical manner. The crime is likely to be committed in close proximity to his residence or place of employment, where he feels secure and more at ease."[166]

During the 1980s, the FBI led the movement to develop psychological profiling techniques through its concentration on violent sex offenders and arsonists. Today, much of that work continues at the Behavioral Science Unit (BSU) at the FBI's Training Academy in Quantico, Virginia. The official mission of the BSU is to develop and provide programs of training, research, and consultation in the behavioral and social sciences for the FBI and the law enforcement community that will improve or enhance their administration, operational effectiveness, and understanding of crime. The BSU's research work focuses on developing new and innovative investigative approaches and techniques for the solution of crime by studying the offender and his or her behavior and motivation. The instructors offer courses on applied criminal psychology, clinical forensic psychology, community policing and problem-solving strategies, crime analysis, death investigation, gangs and gang behavior, interpersonal violence, research methodology, stress management in law enforcement, and violence in America. The BSU also coordinates with and supports other FBI units, such as the National Center for the Analysis of Violent Crime of the Critical Incident Response Group, which provides operational assistance to FBI field offices and law enforcement agencies. Visit the FBI's Behavioral Science Unit via **Web Extra 6–7.**

WEB
Extra
▪▪▪▪

SUMMARY

Psychological and psychiatric theories of criminal behavior emphasize individual propensities and characteristics in explanations of criminality. Whether the emphasis is on conditioned behavior, the development of parental attachment, or the psychoanalytic structure of the human personality, these approaches see the wellsprings of human motivation, desire, and behavioral choice as being firmly rooted in the personality.

Some theorists now consider the state of psychological criminology to be sufficiently advanced to allow for the development of a consistent and dependable social policy in the prediction of dangerousness and the rehabilitation of offenders. Similarly, the development of psychological profiling as a serious crime-fighting undertaking may change the nature of localized crime prevention strategies.

KEY TERMS

alloplastic adaptation, 230

antisocial (asocial) personality, 220

antisocial personality disorder, 220

attachment theory, 235

autoplastic adaptation, 230

behavior theory, 234

Brawner rule, 243

conditioning, 217

correctional psychology, 247

criminal psychology, 215

Durham rule, 243

ego, 224

electroencephalogram (EEG), 221

forensic psychiatry, 215

forensic psychology, 215

guilty but mentally ill (GBMI), 243

id, 223

insanity, 238

irresistible-impulse test, 241

M'Naughten rule, 240

modeling theory, 231

neurosis, 226

operant behavior, 234

paranoid schizophrenic, 228

psychiatric criminology, 223

psychoanalysis, 223

psychological profiling, 249

psychological theory, 216

psychopath, 217

psychopathy, 217

psychosis, 227

psychotherapy, 223

punishment, 234

reward, 234

schizophrenic, 228

selective incapacitation, 247

self-control, 236

sociopath, 217

sublimation, 225

substantial-capacity test, 243

superego, 224

Thanatos, 226

KEY NAMES AND CASES

Albert Bandura, 231

Hervey M. Cleckley, 218

Hans J. Eysenck, 221

Foucha v. *Louisiana,* 238

Sigmund Freud, 223

B. F. Skinner, 234

QUESTIONS FOR REVIEW

1. What are the major principles of psychological perspectives as they relate to criminal behavior?

2. Which of the early psychological and psychiatric theories that were offered explain criminality?

3. From a psychological perspective, how can criminal behavior be seen as a type of maladaptative behavior?

4. How can crime commission be a form of adaptive behavior?

5. How does modeling theory explain the occurence of criminality? How might aggressive patterns of behavior, once acquired, be activated?

6. What are the principles underlying behavior theory? How can rewards and punishments shape behavior?

7. What are the principles of attachment theory? What are the three forms of attachment discussed in this chapter?

8. How can a lack of self-control lead to crime? What can be done to enhance self-control?

9. What is insanity under the criminal law? What are the various legal standards for determining insanity?

10. What types of crime control policies might be based on psychological understandings of criminality?

11. What are the main assumptions underlying the practice of criminal psychological profiling?

QUESTIONS FOR REFLECTION

1. This book emphasizes a social problems versus social responsibility theme. Which perspective is best supported by psychological theories of crime causation? Why?

2. How do psychological theories of criminal behavior differ from the other types of theories presented in this book? How do the various psychological and psychiatric approaches presented in this chapter differ from one another?

3. How would the perspectives discussed in this chapter suggest that offenders might be prevented from committing additional offenses? How might they be rehabilitated?

4. How can crime be a form of adaptation to one's environment? Why would an individual choose such a form of adaptation over others that might be available?

5. Which of the various standards for judging legal insanity discussed in this chapter do you find the most useful? Why?

WEB QUEST

Visit *Psychiatric Times* on the World Wide Web at www.psychiatrictimes.com. Once there, locate the subject index by clicking on "Search by Topic." Review the articles to find those that might contribute to your understanding of criminality. If your instructor asks you to, create an annotated bibliography that lists those articles, along with a brief description of each.

Alternatively, you might wish to visit the Attachment Library provided by the Departments of Psychology and Child Psychiatry at the State University of New York at Stony Brook. The library contains a great deal of information on attachment research, along with a gallery of attachment artifacts. It is available at www.psychology.sunysb.edu/attachment. The site contains an important series of articles (click on "online articles") concerning attachment theory. Included are documents (click on "on line articles") entitled (1) "Mary Ainsworth Autobiographical Sketch," (2) "Learning to Love," (3) "Explaining Disorganized Attachment," (4) "Young Child in An Insecure Situation," (5) "Attachment and Socialization," (6) "Attachment and Dependency," (7) "Becoming Attached," (8) "Traits, Behavioral Systems, and Relationships," (9) "Origins of Attachment Theory," and (10) "Attachment and Psychopathology." If your instructor asks you to, review each of these articles, and write a brief summary of each.

NOTES

1. David Farrington, "Developmental Criminology and Risk-Focused Crime Prevention," in M. Maguire, R. Morgan, and R. Reiner, eds., *The Oxford Handbook of Criminology*, 3e (Oxford, England: Oxford University Press, 2002), p. 657.

2. Max G. Schlapp and Edward H. Smith, *The New Criminology* (New York: Boni and Liveright, 1928), p. 36.

3. "To U.S. Senate Subcommittee on Juvenile Delinquency," *New York Post,* June 19, 1961. Quotation number 8572 in

James B. Simpson, *Simpson's Contemporary Quotations* (Boston: Houghton Mifflin, 1988).

[4] Gordon W. Allport, in the foreword to W. McCord and J. McCord, *The Psychopath* (New York: D. Van Nostrand, 1964).

[5] Details for this story come from Herb Frazier, "Killer Could Leave Hospital: Schizophrenic Mother Killed 2 of Her Children," *Post and Courier* (Charleston), February 11, 2003; and "Woman Who Killed Children to Move to Ungated Facility," Associated Press, July 31, 2003.

[6] "Police Fear Killings Span 10 Years," *USA Today,* July 26, 1991, p. 3A.

[7] "Mutilator 'Seemed So Natural,'" *Fayetteville (NC) Observer-Times,* July 28, 1991, p. 7A.

[8] "Doctor: Dahmer Wanted to Freeze-Dry a Victim," *Fayetteville (NC) Observer-Times,* February 13, 1992, p. 7A.

[9] "Psychiatrist: Dahmer Lacked Will to Stop," *Fayetteville (NC) Observer-Times,* February 4, 1992, p. 5A.

[10] "Dahmer: 936 Years for 'Holocaust,'" *USA Today,* February 18, 1992, p. 1A.

[11] Carlos Sanchez and Marylou Tousignant, "Jury Acquits Bobbitt; Discrepancies, Lack of Evidence Cited," *Washington Post* wire service, November 11, 1993.

[12] Ibid.

[13] D. A. Andrews and James Bonta, *The Psychology of Criminal Conduct* (Cincinnati: Anderson, 1994), p. 69.

[14] See Adrian Raine, *The Psychopathology of Crime: Criminal Behavior as a Clinical Disorder* (Orlando, FL: Academic Press, 1993).

[15] American Board of Forensic Psychology, http://www.abfp.com/brochure.html (acccessed November 22, 2007).

[16] See the American Academy of Psychiatry and the Law, http://www.cc.emory.edu/AAPL (accessed December 20, 2007).

[17] Cathy Spatz Widom and Hans Toch, "The Contribution of Psychology to Criminal Justice Education," *Journal of Criminal Justice Education,* Vol. 4, No. 2 (fall 1993), p. 253.

[18] Curt R. Bartol, *Criminal Behavior: A Psychosocial Approach,* 3rd ed. (Upper Saddle River, NJ: Prentice Hall, 1991), p. 16.

[19] For additional information, see S. Giora Shoham and Mark C. Seis, *A Primer in the Psychology of Crime* (New York: Harrow and Heston, 1993); and Frederic L. Faust, "A Review of *A Primer in the Psychology of Crime,*" *Social Pathology,* Vol. 1, No. 1 (January 1995), pp. 48–61.

[20] Laurence Steinberg, "The Juvenile Psychopath: Fads, Fictions, and Facts," *National Institute of Justice Perspectives on Crime and Justice: 2001 Lecture Series,* Vol. V (Washington, DC: NIJ, 2002), pp. 35–64.

[21] Ibid.

[22] Nicole Hahn Rafter, "Psychopathy and the Evolution of Criminological Knowledge," *Theoretical Criminology,* Vol. 1, No. 2 (May 1997), p. 236.

[23] Nolan D. C. Lewis, "Foreword," in David Abrahamsen, *Crime and the Human Mind* (1944; reprint, Montclair, NJ: Patterson Smith, 1969), p. vii.

[24] As noted by Rafter, "Psychopathy and the Evolution of Criminological Knowledge." See Richard von Krafft-Ebing, *Psychopathia Sexualis* (1886; reprint, New York: Stein and Day, 1965); and Richard von Krafft-Ebing, *Textbook of Insanity* (Germany, 1879; reprint, Philadelphia: F. A. Davis, 1904).

[25] Bernard H. Glueck, *Studies in Forensic Psychiatry* (Boston: Little, Brown, 1916).

[26] William Healy, *The Individual Delinquent* (Boston: Little, Brown, 1915).

[27] Early writings about the psychopathic personality focused almost exclusively on men, and most psychiatrists appeared to believe that very few women (if any) possessed such traits.

[28] David Abrahamsen, *Crime and the Human Mind* (1944; reprint, Montclair, NJ: Patterson Smith, 1969), p. 23.

[29] Hervey M. Cleckley, *The Mask of Sanity,* 4th ed. (St. Louis, MO: C. V. Mosby, 1964).

[30] Quoted in Joseph P. Newman and Chad A. Brinkley, "Psychopathy: Rediscovering Cleckley's Construct," *Psychopathology Research,* Vol. 9, No. 1 (March 1998).

[31] Ibid.

[32] Gwynn Nettler, *Killing One Another* (Cincinnati: Anderson, 1982), p. 179.

[33] Ralph Serin, "Can Criminal Psychopaths Be Identified?" Correctional Service of Canada, October 22, 1999 http://www.csc-scc.gc.ca/text/pblct/forum/e012/e0121.shtml (accessed December 20, 2006).

[34] Robert D. Hare, "Checklist for the Assessment of Psychopathy in Criminal Populations," in M. H. Ben-Aron, S. J. Hucker, and C. D. Webster, eds., *Clinical Criminology* (Toronto: University of Toronto, Clarke Institute of Psychiatry, 1985), pp. 157–167.

[35] See Laurence Steinberg, "The Juvenile Psychopath: Fads, Fictions, and Facts," from which some of the wording in this paragraph is adapted.

[36] Kent A. Kiehl, Andra M. Smith, Adrianna Mendrek, Bruce B. Forster, Robert D. Hare, and Peter F. Liddle, "Temporal Lobe Abnormalities in Semantic Processing by Criminal Psychopaths as Revealed by Functional Magnetic Resonance Imaging," *Psychiatry Research: Neuroimaging,* Vol. 130 (2004), pp. 27–42.

[37] Julia C. Keller, "Aha! Study Finds Eureka Moments Light Up Brain," *Science and Theology News,* June 2004, http://www.stnews.org/feat_aha_0604.html (accessed December 12, 2006).

[38] Bertine Lahuis, Chantal Kemmer, and Herman Van Engeland, "Magnetic Resonance Imaging Studies on Autism and Childhood-Onset Schizophrenia in Children and Adolescents," *Acta Neuropsychiatrica,* Vol. 15, No. 3 (June 2003), p. 140.

[39] Ivan Semeniuk, "How We Tell Right from Wrong: An Interview with Marc Hauser," *New Scientist,* March 3, 2007, p. 44.

[40] Michael Caldwell, Jennifer Skeem, Randy Salekin, and Gregory Van Ryboek, "Treatment Response of Adolescent Offenders with Psychopathy Features: A 2-Year Follow-Up," *Criminal Justice and Behavior,* Vol. 33, No. 5 (2006), pp. 571–576.

[41] Peter Aldhous, "Violent, Antisocial, Past Redemption?" *New Scientist,* April 14, 2007, pp. 8–9.

[42] American Psychiatric Association, *Diagnostic and Statistical Manual of Mental Disorders,* 2nd ed. (Washington, DC: American Psychiatric Association, 1968).

[43] Ibid., p. 43.

[44] See Internet Mental Health, "Disorders: European Description," http://www.mentalhealth.com/icd (accessed January 5, 2007).

[45] Robert D. Hare, "Psychopathy and Antisocial Personality Disorder: A Case of Diagnostic Confusion," *Psychiatric Times,* Vol. 13, No. 2 (February 1996).

[46] Albert I. Rabin, "The Antisocial Personality—Psychopathy and Sociopathy," in Hans Toch, ed., *Psychology of Crime and Criminal Justice* (Prospect Heights, IL: Waveland, 1979), p. 330.

[47] Especially Hare's Revised Psychopathy Checklist, also called the Psychopathy Checklist–Revised (PCL–R). The PCL–R provides a numerical score reflecting the degree to which a person's symptoms match the traditional clinical conception of psychopathy. This score can be statistically analyzed into two factors, one covering attitudes and feelings, the other covering socially deviant behavior.

48 For recent research in this area, see A. Tengstrom et al., "Psychopathy (PCL–R) as a Predictor of Violent Recidivism among Criminal Offenders with Schizophrenia in Sweden," *Law and Behavior,* Vol. 24, No. 1 (2000), pp. 45–58. For additional information, see V. L. Quinsey et al., *Violent Offenders: Appraising and Managing Risk* (Washington, DC: American Psychological Association, 1998); and V. L. Quinsey, M. E. Rice, and G. T. Harris, "Actuarial Prediction of Sexual Recidivism," *Journal of Interpersonal Violence,* Vol. 10, No. 1 (1995), pp. 85–105.

49 R. D. Hare, *Psychopathy: Theory and Research* (New York: John Wiley and Sons, 1970).

50 L. N. Robins, *Deviant Children Grow Up* (Baltimore: Williams and Wilkins, 1966).

51 S. B. Guze, *Criminality and Psychiatric Disorders* (New York: Oxford University Press, 1976).

52 S. Hodgins and G. Cote, "The Prevalence of Mental Disorders among Penitentiary Inmates in Quebec," *Canada's Mental Health,* Vol. 38 (1990), pp. 1–4. Note: Categories are not mutually exclusive.

53 H. Prins, *Offenders, Deviants or Patients? An Introduction to the Study of Socio-Forensic Problems* (London: Tavistock, 1980).

54 Hans J. Eysenck, *Crime and Personality* (Boston: Houghton Mifflin, 1964).

55 Hans J. Eysenck, "Personality and Criminality: A Dispositional Analysis," in William S. Laufer and Freda Adler, eds., *Advances in Criminology Theory,* Vol. 1 (New Brunswick, NJ: Transaction, 1989), p. 90.

56 Eysenck, *Crime and Personality,* pp. 35–36.

57 Ibid., p. 92.

58 Ibid., p. 53, citing J. B. S. Haldane, "Foreword," in Johannes Lange, *Crime as Destiny: A Study of Criminal Twins* (London: G. Allen and Unwin, 1931), p. 53.

59 Abrahamsen, *Crime and the Human Mind,* p. vii.

60 P. Q. Roche, *The Criminal Mind: A Study of Communications between Criminal Law and Psychiatry* (New York: Grove Press, 1958), p. 52.

61 "Alfredo Niceforo," *Encyclopedia Britannica,* Encyclopedia Britannica Premium Service, http://www.britannica.com/eb/article?eu=57092 (accessed February 14, 2005).

62 "Nationline: Book Thief," *USA Today,* August 1, 1991, p. 3A.

63 Marti Olsen Laney, *The Hidden Gifts of the Introverted Child* (New York: Workman Publishing, 2006).

64 Mark Solms, "Freud Returns," *Scientific American,* Vol. 290, No. 5 (May 2004), pp. 82–90.

65 Eric R. Kandel, "Biology and the Future of Psychoanalysis: A New Intellectual Framework for Psychiatry Revisited," *American Journal of Psychiatry,* Vol. 156 (April 1999), pp. 505–524.

66 Anne Sciater, "Torturer-Killer Wants to Die Today, as Scheduled," *USA Today,* April 15, 1997, p. 2A.

67 Nettler, *Killing One Another,* p. 159.

68 Ibid., p. 155.

69 Abrahamsen, *Crime and the Human Mind,* p. 99.

70 Ibid., p. 100.

71 J. Dollard et al., *Frustration and Aggression* (New Haven, CT: Yale University Press, 1939).

72 Carl Weiser, "This Is What You Get for Firing Me!" *USA Today,* January 28, 1993, p. 3A.

73 Andrew F. Henry and James F. Short, Jr., *Suicide and Homicide: Economic, Sociological, and Psychological Aspects of Aggression* (Glencoe, IL: Free Press, 1954).

74 Stewart Palmer, *A Study of Murder* (New York: Crowell, 1960).

75 Abrahamsen, *Crime and the Human Mind,* p. 26.

76 Nancy Gibbs, "The Devil's Disciple," *Time,* January 11, 1993, p. 40.

77 Seymour L. Halleck, *Psychiatry and the Dilemmas of Crime: A Study of Causes, Punishment and Treatment* (Berkeley: University of California Press, 1971).

78 Ibid., p. 77.

79 Ibid., p. 78.

80 Ibid., p. 80.

81 Ibid.

82 Ibid.

83 Arnold S. Linsky, Ronet Bachman, and Murray A. Straus, *Stress, Culture, and Aggression* (New Haven, CT: Yale University Press, 1995).

84 Ibid., p. 7.

85 Adapted from Richard Danielson, "Programmed to Kill," *St. Petersburg Times,* March 22, 2000, http://www.sptimes.com/News/032200/Floridian/Programmed_to_kill.shtml (accessed December 5, 2005).

86 "Who Is Michael Carneal?" CNN Interactive, December 3, 1997, http://www.cnn.com/US/9712/03/school.shooting.pm (accessed December 5, 2003).

87 Gabriel Tarde, *The Laws of Imitation,* trans. E. C. Parsons (1890; reprint, Gloucester, MA: Peter Smith, 1962).

88 Albert Bandura, "The Social Learning Perspective: Mechanisms of Aggression," in Hans Toch, ed., *Psychology of Crime and Criminal Justice* (Prospect Heights, IL: Waveland, 1979), p. 198.

89 Ibid., p. 199.

90 M. M. Lefkowitz et al., "Television Violence and Child Aggression: A Follow-up Study," in G. A. Comstock and E. A. Rubinstein, eds., *Television and Social Behavior,* Vol. 3 (Washington, DC: U.S. Government Printing Office, 1972), pp. 35–135.

91 Aminah Franklin, "Brutal, Cowardly Murder: Police Say Threats Preceded Slaying of Salisbury Family," *Morning Call,* March 1, 1995, p. A1.

92 Ibid.

93 David Washburn, "Brothers Cultivated Defiant Attitude," *Morning Call,* March 1, 1995, p. A4.

94 Widom and Toch, "The Contribution of Psychology to Criminal Justice Education."

95 Ibid., p. 253.

96 C. R. Hollin, *Psychology and Crime: An Introduction to Criminological Psychology* (London: Routledge, 1989), p. 42.

97 Widom and Toch, "The Contribution of Psychology to Criminal Justice Education," p. 254.

98 "15-Year-Old Killer Feared Being Called a 'Little Punk,'" *Fayetteville (NC) Observer-Times,* December 26, 1993, p. 1A.

99 See Mary D. Salter Ainsworth, "John Bowlby, 1907–1990," *American Psychologist,* Vol. 47 (1992), p. 668.

100 John Bowlby, "The Nature of the Child's Tie to Its Mother," *International Journal of Psycho-Analysis,* Vol. 39 (1958), pp. 350–373.

101 See John Bowlby, *Maternal Care and Mental Health,* World Health Organization Monograph (1951); and John Bowlby, *A Secure Base* (New York: Basic Books, 1988).

102 Bowlby, *A Secure Base,* p. 11.

103 David P. Farrington and Donald J. West, "Effects of Marriage, Separation, and Children on Offending by Adult Males," *Current Perspectives on Aging and the Life Cycle,* Vol. 4 (1995), pp. 249–281.

104 Stephen A. Cernkovich and Peggy C. Giordano, "Family Relationships and Delinquency," *Criminology,* Vol. 25 (1987), pp. 295–313.

105 Roy F. Baumeister and Julie Juola Exline, "Self-Control, Morality, and Human Strength," *Journal of Social and Clinical Psychology,* Vol. 19, No. 1 (April 2000), pp. 29–42.

106 Ibid.

107 See R. F. Baumeister, T. F. Heatherton, and D. Tice, *Losing Control: How and Why People Fail at Self-Regulation* (San Diego: Academic Press, 1994).

108 Teresa C. LaGrange and Robert A. Silverman, "Low Self-Control and Opportunity: Testing the General Theory of Crime as an Explanation for Gender Differences in Delinquency," *Criminology,* Vol. 37, No. 1 (1999), p. 41.

109 M. R. Gottfredson and Travis Hirschi, *A General Theory of Crime* (Stanford, CA: Stanford University Press, 1990).

110 Carter Hay and Walter Forrest, "The Development of Self-Control: Examining Self-Control Theory's Stability Thesis," *Criminology,* Vol. 44, No. 4 (November 2006), pp. 739–772.

111 Ibid.

112 Constance L. Chapple, "Self-Control, Peer Relations, and Delinquency," *Justice Quarterly,* Vol. 22, No. 1 (March, 2005), pp. 89–106.

113 Ibid., p. 101.

114 Douglas Longshore, "Self-Control and Criminal Opportunity: A Prospective Test of the General Theory of Crime," *Social Problems,* Vol. 45, No. 1 (February 1998), pp. 102–114.

115 Gottfredson and Hirschi, *A General Theory of Crime,* p. 88.

116 Longshore, "Self-Control and Criminal Opportunity."

117 Harold G. Grasmick et al., "Testing the Core Empirical Implications of Gottfredson and Hirschi's General Theory of Crime," *Journal of Research in Crime and Delinquency,* Vol. 30 (1993), pp. 5–29.

118 Citing Gottfredson and Hirschi, *A General Theory of Crime,* p. 89.

119 Travis C. Pratt and Francis T. Cullen, "The Empirical Status of Gottfredson and Hirschi's General Theory of Crime: A Meta-analysis," *Criminology,* Vol. 38, No. 3 (2000), pp. 931–964.

120 Carter Hay, "Parenting, Self-Control, and Delinquency: A Test of Self-Control Theory, *Criminology,* Vol. 39, No. 3 (2001), pp. 707–736.

121 Ibid., p. 725.

122 Karen L. Hayslett-McCall and Thomas J. Bernard, "Attachment, Masculinity, and Self-Control: A Theory of Male Crime Rates," *Theoretical Criminology,* Vol. 6, No. 1 (February 2002), pp. 5–33.

123 In civil proceedings, however, the state may confine a mentally ill person if it shows "by clear and convincing evidence that the individual is mentally ill and dangerous." *Jones* v. *United States,* 463 U.S. 354 (1983).

124 *Foucha* v. *Louisiana,* 504 U.S. 71 (1992), Justices Kennedy and Rehnquist's dissenting opinion.

125 *Leland* v. *Oregon,* 343 U.S. 790 (1952).

126 *Riggins* v. *Nevada,* 504 U.S. 127 (1992).

127 *Sell* v. *United States,* 123 S. Ct. 2174 (2003).

128 18 U.S.C. § 17.

129 See, for example, *United States* v. *Pohlot,* 827 F.2d 889, 897 (3d Cir. 1987), *cert. denied,* 484 U.S. 1011 (1988).

130 18 U.S.C. § 401.

131 18 U.S.C. §§ 17 and 4242(b).

132 *Terrance Frank* v. *United States,* 113 S. Ct. 363 (1992).

133 October 12, 1984, P.L. 98–473, title II, § 403(a), 98 Stat. 2057.

134 Zalleck, *Psychiatry and the Dilemmas of Crime,* p. 213.

135 *Durham* v. *United States,* 214 F.2d 862 (D.C. Cir. 1954).

136 American Law Institute, *Model Penal Code: Official Draft and Explanatory Notes* (Philadelphia: The Institute, 1985).

137 *United States* v. *Brawner,* 471 F.2d 969 (D.C. Cir. 1972).

138 June 25, 1948, Ch. 645, 62 Stat. 855; October 12, 1984, P.L. 98–473, title II, § 403(a), 98 Stat. 2059; November 18, 1988, P.L. 100–690, title VII, § 7043, 102 Stat. 4400.

139 See, for example, D. P. Farrington, "Childhood Aggression and Adult Violence: Early Precursors and Later Life Outcomes," in D. J. Pepler and K. H. Rubin, eds., *The Development and Treatment of Childhood Aggression* (Hillsdale, NJ: Erlbaum, 1990), pp. 2–29; and R. E. Tremblay et al., "Early Disruptive Behavior: Poor School Achievement, Delinquent Behavior and Delinquent Personality: Longitudinal Analyses," *Journal of Consulting and Clinical Psychology,* Vol. 60, No. 1 (1992), pp. 64–72.

140 R. Loeber, "Questions and Advances in the Study of Developmental Pathways," in D. Cicchetti and S. Toth, eds., *Models and Integration: Rochester Symposium on Developmental Psychopathology* (Rochester, NY: University of Rochester Press, 1991), pp. 97–115.

141 "State Probing Release of Molester Now Charged with Murder," United Press International wire service, Southwestern edition, September 24, 1993.

142 "Texas Executes Convicted Killer Who Waived Appeals," Reuters, Western edition, November 10, 1993.

143 Christine Spolar, "California Town Cries as Polly Klaas Is Found; Twice-Convicted Suspect Faces Murder, Kidnapping Charges in Abduction of 12-Year-Old," *Washington Post* wire service, December 6, 1993.

144 Jennifer L. White et al., "How Early Can We Tell? Predictors of Childhood Conduct Disorder and Adolescent Delinquency," *Criminology,* Vol. 28, No. 4 (1990), pp. 507–528.

145 Daniel S. Nagin and David P. Farrington, "The Stability of Criminal Potential from Childhood to Adulthood," *Criminology,* Vol. 30, No. 2 (1992), pp. 235–260.

146 Paul Gendreau, Tracy Little, and Claire Goggin, "A Meta-analysis of the Predictors of Adult Offender Recidivism: What Works!" *Criminology,* Vol. 34, No. 4 (November 1996), pp. 575–607.

147 For one of the first and still definitive works in the area of selective incapacitation, see Peter Greenwood and Allan Abrahamsen, *Selective Incapacitation* (Santa Monica, CA: Rand, 1982).

148 M. A. Peterson, H. B. Braiker, and S. M. Polich, *Who Commits Crimes?* (Cambridge, MA: Oelgeschlager, Gunn and Hain, 1981).

149 Jeremy Travis, "But They All Come Back," papers from the Executive Session on Sentencing and Corrections, No. 7 (Washington, DC: National Institute of Justice, 2000).

150 J. Monahan, *Predicting Violent Behavior: An Assessment of Clinical Techniques* (Beverly Hills, CA: Sage, 1981).

151 The 1984 Amendment to § 200 of Title II (§ 200–2304) of P.L. 98–473 is popularly referred to as the "1984 Comprehensive Crime Control Act."

152 U.S. Sentencing Commission, *Federal Sentencing Guidelines Manual* (Washington, DC: U.S. Government Printing Office, 1987), p. 10.

153 Jill Peay, "Dangerousness—Ascription or Description," in M. P. Feldman, ed., *Developments in the Study of Criminal Behavior,* Vol. 2, *Violence* (New York: John Wiley and Sons, 1982), p. 211, citing N. Walker, "Dangerous People," *International Journal of Law and Psychiatry,* Vol. 1 (1978), pp. 37–50.

154 See, for example, Michael Gottfredson and Travis Hirschi, *A General Theory of Crime* (Stanford, CA: Stanford University Press, 1990); and Travis Hirschi and Michael Gottfredson, "Age and the Explanation of Crime," *American Journal of Sociology,* Vol. 89 (1983), pp. 552–584.

155 David F. Greenberg, "Modeling Criminal Careers," *Criminology,* Vol. 29, No. 1 (1991), p. 39.

156 Andrews and Bonta, *The Psychology of Criminal Conduct.*

157 Ibid., p. 1.

158 Ibid.

159 Ibid., pp. 20–21.

160 Ibid., p. 227.

161 Ibid.

162 Ibid., p. 236.

163 Interviewed by Amy Goldman, February 27, 1998, http://www. serialkillers.net/interviews/jdouglas2bak.html (accessed December 20, 2000).

164 Robert K. Ressler and Tom Shachtman, *Whoever Fights Monsters* (New York: St. Martin's, 1992).

165 Robert R. Hazelwood and John E. Douglas, "The Lust Murderer," *FBI Law Enforcement Bulletin* (Washington, DC: U.S. Department of Justice, April 1980).

166 Ibid.

PART 3

Crime Causation Revisited

> Crime is present not only in the majority of societies . . . but in all societies of all types. There is no society that is not confronted with the problem of criminality. Its form changes; the acts thus characterized are not the same everywhere; but, everywhere and always, there have been men who have behaved in such a way as to draw upon themselves penal repression. . . . There is, then, no phenomenon that represents more indisputably all the symptoms of normality, since it appears closely connected with the conditions of all collective life.
>
> —Emile Durkheim[i]

Crime is a social phenomenon, and central to any understanding of crime is the role that society, social institutions, and social processes play in its development and control. While some see crime as a conscious choice made by individual perpetrators seeking to maximize personal gratification, others give far less importance to the role of reason in criminal behavior—emphasizing, instead, the almost mechanistic workings of economic, social, and political conditions in producing violations of the law. Psychological theories see the criminal as a product of his or her environment, but sociological theories shift the emphasis to crime as a social product. Seen this way, it is criminality itself, rather than any individual criminal act, that needs explaining. Consequently, some sociological approaches to explaining crime have the power to allow us to see beyond the merely personal and extend our understanding to the structural underpinnings of criminality. In doing so, they suggest crime control policies that build upon features of our society that may be at least partially under our collective control.

In this part, we will examine a variety of sociological explanations for criminality, including perspectives that look for their explanatory power in the structure of society and in the complex relationships that exist between individuals and various social institutions (Chapter 7). The important—but more individually focused—role of social learning and interpersonal socialization, the various developmental pathways that different individuals take as they progress through the life course (Chapter 8), and the negative consequences of group conflicts and social inequality (Chapter 9) will all be explored.

---

iEmile Durkheim, *The Rules of the Sociological Method,* Tr. by W. D. Halls (New York: The Free Press, 1982), p. 67. Originally published in 1895.

Outline

If we would change the amount of crime in the community, we must change the community.

—Frank Tannenbaum[1]

I got a 14-shot Beretta, and I ain't worried about no police or anybody else.

—Broadway gangster Crip member "Antoine"[2]

Society prepares the crime; the criminal commits it.

—Chinese proverb

Learning Outcomes

After reading this chapter, you should be able to

- Explain the major principles of sociological theories and be able to identify three key sociological explanations for crime
- Show how the organization and structure of society may contribute to criminality, and explain what sociologists mean by the term *social structure*
- Identify three types of social structure theories and list the characteristics of each
- Identify modern-day crime control policies that reflect the social structure approach
- Assess the shortcomings of the social structure approach to understanding and preventing crime

Hear the author discuss this chapter at **crimtoday.com**

Introduction

There's an old saying something to the effect that you can take the criminal out of a bad environment, but you can't take the bad environment out of the criminal. While we don't necessarily believe this to be true, some people suggest that negative influences of the social environment—especially things like poverty, lack of education, episodes of discrimination, and other social disadvantageous experiences—predispose some people to lives of crime, and that such negative influences may remain active even when people's circumstances change.

In 2007, in what may be an illustrative example, 22-year-old Jesse Dee "Jay" Wise pleaded guilty to six counts of criminal homicide in the deaths of his grandmother, two aunts, two cousins, and an uncle.[3] The bodies of Wise's family members, the youngest of whom was 5-year-old Chance Wise, were found wrapped in sheets and blankets in the basement of the Lancaster County, Pennsylvania, home where Wise lived. Wise used clubs and knives in the killings, and the brutality of the deaths was revealed by investigators who described finding blood and bone fragments on walls and ceilings throughout the house. Wise, who has a history of drug abuse,[4] apparently killed the members of his family over the course of four days, and went on shopping sprees with their money after they died. Ironically, Wise's surviving grandfather, Jessie L. Wise, said the family had moved from New York City to the tranquil Pennsylvania Dutch countryside to get away from the bad influences of the city. Surviving family members asked prosecutors not to request the death penalty, and Wise was sentenced to life in prison without parole.

Although features of individual personality can always be identified as contributing factors in almost any crime, the motivation behind the Wise family killing may have arisen out of early experiences of social and economic deprivation that Jesse Wise lived through while growing up in New York City. Advocates of a social structure approach to explaining crime might well argue that relative poverty, academic failure, and subcultural values that focused on greed and excitement dictated the direction that the life of Jesse Wise would take—and that they established patterns of thought and behavior that proved impossible to break.

Major Principles of Sociological Theories

Theories that explain crime by reference to social structure are only one of three major sociological approaches to crime causation. (We will describe the other two in Chapters 8 and 9.) Before proceeding, however, it seems best to discuss some of the general features

Ecological theories suggest that crime shows an unequal geographic distribution. Why might certain geographic areas be associated with identifiable patterns of crime?

Source: Peter Turnley, Corbis

of the sociological viewpoint. Although sociological perspectives on crime causation are quite diverse, most build upon the following assumptions:

- Social groups, social institutions, the arrangements of society, and social roles all provide the proper focus for criminological study.
- Group dynamics, group organization, and subgroup relationships form the causal nexus out of which crime develops.
- The structure of society and its relative degree of organization or disorganization are important factors contributing to the prevalence of criminal behavior.
- Although it may be impossible to predict the specific behavior of a given individual, statistical estimates of group characteristics are possible. Hence, the probability that a member of a given group will engage in a specific type of crime can be estimated.

Sociological theories examine institutional arrangements within society (that is, **social structure**) and the interaction between and among social institutions, individuals, and groups (that is, **social processes**) as they affect socialization and have an impact on social behavior (that is, **social life**). Sociological theories are keenly interested in the nature of existing power relationships between social groups and in the influences that various social phenomena bring to bear on the types of behaviors that tend to characterize *groups* of people. In contrast to more individualized psychological theories, which have what is called a "micro" focus, sociological approaches utilize a "macro" perspective, stressing the type of behavior likely to be exhibited by group members rather than attempting to predict the behavior of specific individuals.

As noted in Chapter 1, sociological thought has influenced criminological theory construction more significantly than any other perspective during the past half century. This has probably been due, at least in part, to a widespread American concern with social problems, including civil rights, the women's movement, issues of poverty, and the decline in influence experienced by many traditional social institutions, such as the family, government, organized religion, and educational institutions.

Although all sociological perspectives on crime share the characteristics identified in this section, particular theories give greater or lesser weight to selected components of social life. Hence, we can identify three key sociological explanations for crime:

- Crime is the result of an individual's location within the structure of society. This approach focuses on the social and economic conditions of life, including poverty, alienation, social disorganization, weak social control, personal frustration, relative deprivation, differential opportunity, alternative means to success, and deviant subcultures and subcultural values that conflict with conventional values. (These are the primary features of *social structure theories*, which are discussed in this chapter.)
- Crime is the end product of various social processes, especially inappropriate socialization and social learning. This approach stresses the role of interpersonal relationships, the strength of the social bond, a lack of self-control, and the personal and group consequences of societal reactions to deviance as they contribute to crime. (These are the primary characteristics of *social process theories* and *social development theories*, which are discussed in Chapter 8.)
- Crime is the product of class struggle. This perspective emphasizes the nature of existing power relationships between social groups, the distribution of wealth within society, the ownership of the means of production, and the economic and social structure of society as it relates to social class and social control. (These are the primary features of *conflict theories*, which are discussed in Chapter 9.)

sociological theory

A perspective that focuses on the nature of the power relationships that exist between social groups and on the influences that various social phenomena bring to bear on the types of behaviors that tend to characterize groups of people.

social structure

The pattern of social organization and the interrelationships among institutions characteristic of a society.

social process

The interaction between and among social institutions, individuals, and groups.

social life

The ongoing and (typically) structured interaction that occurs between persons in a society, including socialization and social behavior in general.

Social Structure Theories Defined

social structure theory

A theory that explains crime by reference to some aspect of the social fabric. These theories emphasize relationships among social institutions and describe the types of behavior that tend to characterize groups of people rather than individuals.

The theories in this chapter are termed **social structure theories** because they explain crime by reference to the economic and social arrangements (or *structure*) of society. They see the various formal and informal arrangements between social groups (that is, the structures of society) as the root causes of crime and deviance. Structural theories predict that negative aspects of societal structures, such as disorganization within the family, poverty or income inequality within the economic arrangements of society, disadvantages brought about by a lack of success for some in the educational process, and so on, produce criminal behavior.

Although different kinds of social structure theories have been advanced to explain crime, they all have one thing in common: They highlight those arrangements within society that contribute to the low socioeconomic status of identifiable groups as significant causes of crime. Social structure theorists view members of socially and economically disadvantaged groups as being more likely to commit crime, and they see economic and social disenfranchisement as fundamental causes of crime. Poverty, lack of education, an absence of salable skills, and subcultural values conducive to crime are all thought to be predicated on the social conditions surrounding early life experiences, and they provide the causal underpinnings of social structure theories. Environmental influences, socialization, and traditional and accepted patterns of behavior are all used by social structuralists to portray the criminal as a product of his or her social environment—and the immediate social environment is itself viewed as a consequence of the structure of the society to which the offender belongs. Although criminality is recognized as a form of acquired behavior, it is depicted as the end result of social injustice, racism, and feelings of disenfranchisement to which existing societal arrangements give rise. Similarly, social structure, insofar as it is unfair and relatively unchangeable, is believed to perpetuate the fundamental conditions that cause crime. Consequently, viewed from a social structure perspective, crime is seen largely as a lower-class phenomenon, while the criminality of the middle and upper classes is generally discounted as less serious, less frequent, and less dangerous.

Types of Social Structure Theories

This chapter describes three major types of social structure theories: (1) social disorganization theory (also called "ecological approach"), (2) strain theory, and (3) culture conflict theory (also called "cultural deviance" theory). All have a number of elements in common, and the classification of a theory into one subcategory or another is often a matter of which aspects a writer chooses to emphasize rather than the result of any clear-cut definitional elements inherent in the perspectives themselves.

Social Disorganization Theory

social disorganization theory

A perspective on crime and deviance that sees society as a kind of organism and crime and deviance as a kind of disease or social pathology. Theories of social disorganization are often associated with the perspective of social ecology and with the Chicago School of criminology, which developed during the 1920s and 1930s.

The first type of social structure approach discussed in this chapter, **social disorganization theory,** is closely associated with the ecological school of criminology. Much early criminology in the United States is rooted in the study of urban settlements and communities[5] and in the human ecology movement of the early twentieth century. The idea of the community as a functional whole that directly determines the quality of life for its members was developed and explored around the beginning of the twentieth century by sociologists like Emile Durkheim (1858–1917),[6] Ferdinand Toennies (1855–1936),[7] and Georg Simmel (1858–1918).[8] Durkheim believed that crime was a normal part of all societies and that law was a symbol of social solidarity. Hence, for Durkheim, an act was "criminal when it offends strong and defined states of the collective conscience."[9]

Some of the earliest sociologists to study American communities were **W. I. Thomas** and **Florian Znaniecki.** In *The Polish Peasant in Europe and America,* Thomas and Znaniecki described the problems Polish immigrants faced in the early 1900s when

Theory in Perspective

Types of Social Structure Theories

Social structure approaches emphasize the role of poverty, lack of education, absence of marketable skills, and subcultural values as fundamental causes of crime. Social structure approaches portray crime as the result of an individual's location within the structure of society and focus on the social and economic conditions of life.

- *Social Disorganization.* Depicts social change, social conflict, and the lack of social consensus as the root causes of crime and deviance. An offshoot, social ecology, sees society as a kind of organism and crime and deviance as a kind of disease or social pathology.

  Period: 1920s–1930s

  Theorists: Robert Park, Ernest Burgess, W. I. Thomas, Florian Znaniecki, Clifford Shaw, Henry McKay

  Concepts: Social ecology, ecological theories, social pathology, social disorganization, Chicago School of criminology, Chicago Area Project, demographics, concentric zones, delinquency areas, cultural transmission (criminology of place, environmental criminology, defensible space, and the broken windows thesis represent, at least in part, a contemporary reinterpretation of early ecological notions)

- *Strain Theory.* Points to a lack of fit between socially approved success goals and the availability of socially approved means to achieve those goals. As a consequence, according to the perspective of strain theory, individuals who are unable to succeed through legitimate means turn to other avenues that promise economic and social recognition.

  Period: 1930s–present

  Theorists: Robert K. Merton, Steven F. Messner, Richard Rosenfeld, Peter Blau and Judith Blau, Robert Agnew

  Concepts: Anomie, goals, means, innovation, retreatism, ritualism, rebellion, differential opportunity, relative deprivation, distributive justice, general strain theory (GST)

- *Culture Conflict.* Sees the root cause of crime in a clash of values between variously socialized groups over what is acceptable or proper behavior.

  Period: 1920s–present

  Theorists: Thorsten Sellin, Frederic M. Thrasher, William F. Whyte, Walter Miller, Gresham Sykes, David Matza, Franco Ferracuti, Marvin Wolfgang, Richard A. Cloward, Lloyd E. Ohlin, Albert Cohen, many others

  Concepts: Subculture, violent subcultures, socialization, focal concerns, delinquency and drift, techniques of neutralization, illegitimate opportunity structures, reaction formation, conduct norms

---

they left their homeland and moved to American cities.[10] The authors noted how rates of crime rose among people who had been so displaced, and they hypothesized that the cause was the **social disorganization** that resulted from immigrants' inability to successfully transplant guiding norms and values from their home cultures into the new one. Learn more about early social disorganization perspectives via **Web Extra 7–1** at crimtoday.com. Read more about classical sociological theory at **Web Extra 7–2.**

The Chicago School

Some of the earliest sociological theories to receive widespread recognition can be found in the writings of **Robert Park** and **Ernest Burgess.**[11] In the 1920s and 1930s, Park and Burgess, through their work at the University of Chicago, developed what became known as **social ecology,** or the ecological school of criminology. The social ecology movement, which was influenced by the work of biologists on the interaction of organisms with their environments, concerned itself with how the structure of society adapts to the quality of natural resources and to the existence of other human groups.[12] As one writer puts it, social ecology is "the attempt to link the structure and organization of any human community to interactions with its localized environment."[13] Because ecological models build upon an organic analogy, it is easy to portray social disorganization as a disease or pathology.[14] Hence, social ecologists who studied crime developed a disease model built around the concept of **social pathology.** In its initial statement, social pathology was defined as "those human actions which run contrary to the ideals of residential stability, property ownership, sobriety, thrift, habituation to work, small business enterprise, sexual discretion, family solidarity, neighborliness, and discipline of

social disorganization

A condition said to exist when a group is faced with social change, uneven development of culture, maladaptiveness, disharmony, conflict, and lack of consensus.

WEB
Extra
····

FIGURE 7–1

Chicago's Concentric Zones

Source: Robert E. Park, Ernest W. Burgess, and R. D. McKenzie, *The City* (Chicago: University of Chicago Press, 1925), p. 55. Copyright © University of Chicago Press. Reprinted with permission.

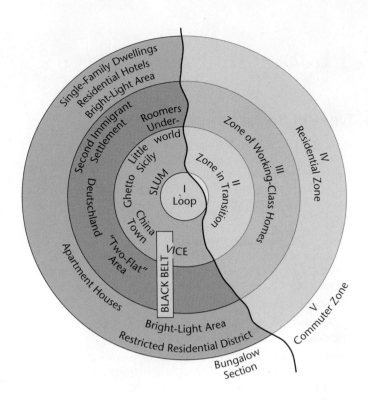

social ecology

An approach to criminological theorizing that attempts to link the structure and organization of a human community to interactions with its localized environment.

social pathology

A concept that compares society to a physical organism and that sees criminality as an illness.

will."[15] The term referred simply to behavior not in keeping with the prevalent norms and values of the social group. Over time, however, the concept of social pathology changed, and it came to represent the idea that aspects of society may be somehow pathological, or "sick," and may produce deviant behavior among individuals and groups who live under or are exposed to such social conditions.

Social disorganization and, therefore, social pathology may arise when a group is faced with "social change, uneven development of culture, maladaptiveness, disharmony, conflict, and lack of consensus."[16] Due to the rapid influx of immigrant populations at the beginning of the twentieth century, American cities were caught up in swift social change, and Park and Burgess saw in them an ideal focus for the study of social disorganization. Park and Burgess viewed cities in terms of concentric zones, which were envisioned much like the circles on a target (see Figure 7–1). Each zone had its unique characteristics wherein unique populations and typical forms of behavior could be found. Park and Burgess referred to the central business zone as Zone I, or the "loop," in which retail businesses and light manufacturing were typically located. Zone II, surrounding the city center, was home to recent immigrant groups and was characterized by deteriorated housing, factories, and abandoned buildings. It was portrayed as being in transition from residential to business uses. Zone III contained mostly working-class tenements, while Zone IV was occupied by middle-class citizens with single-family homes, each with its own yard and garage. Zone V, consisting largely of suburbs, was called the "commuter zone." Significantly, Park and Burgess noticed that residents of inner-city zones tended to migrate to outer zones as their economic positions improved.

Clifford Shaw and **Henry McKay,** other early advocates of the ecological approach, applied the concentric zone model to the study of juvenile delinquency. They conducted empirical studies of arrest rates for juveniles in Chicago during the years 1900–1906, 1917–1923, and 1927–1933. These years were associated with high rates of neighborhood transition, during which one immigrant group after another moved in rapid succession from the inner city toward the suburbs—a process that was repeated with the arrival of each new wave of immigrants. Shaw and McKay found that rates of offending remained relatively constant over time within zones of transition, and they concluded, therefore, that delinquency was caused by the nature of the environment in which immigrants lived rather than by some characteristic of the immigrant groups themselves.[17] Shaw and McKay saw social disorganization as the inability of local communities to solve common problems, and they believed that the degree of disorganization in a community was largely predicated upon the extent of residential mobility and racial heterogeneity present in that community. In effect, as a new immigrant group, like the Polish, replaced an old immigrant group, like the Irish, and became dominant in a particular location, the process of succession was complete. As a result of their studies, they developed the idea of **cultural transmission,** which held that traditions of delinquency were transmitted through successive generations of the same zone in the same way that language, roles, and attitudes were communicated.

Because early **ecological theories,** including those of Park and Burgess, were developed through a close focus on selected geographic locals, the methodology upon which they were predicated came to be known as "area studies"; and because 1920s Chicago served as the model for most such studies, they were soon collectively referred to as the **Chicago School of criminology.** Although the applicability of these early studies to other cities or to other time periods was questionable, it was generally accepted that the Chicago School had demonstrated the tendency for criminal activity to be associated with urban transition zones, which, because of the turmoil or social disorganization that characterized them, were typified by lower property values, impoverished lifestyles, and a general lack of privacy.

Even at the height of its popularity, the ecological school recognized that American crime patterns might be different from those found elsewhere in the world and that crime zones might exist in city areas other than those surrounding the core. Early comparisons of American, European, and Asian data, for instance, found higher crime rates at the so-called city gates (near-suburban areas providing access to downtown) in Europe and Asia.

The greatest contribution the ecological school made to criminological literature can be found in its claim that society, in the form of the community, wields a major influence on human behavior.[18] Similarly, ecological theorists of the Chicago School formalized the use of two sources of information: (1) official crime and population statistics and (2) ethnographic data. Population statistics, or demographic data, when combined with crime information, provided empirical material that gave scientific weight to ecological investigations. Ethnographic information, gathered in the form of life stories, or ethnographies, described the lives of city inhabitants. By comparing one set of data with the other—demographics with ethnographies—ecological investigators were able to show that life experience varied from one location to another and that personal involvement in crime had a strong tendency to be associated with place of residence. Learn more about the Chicago School of criminology at Web Extra 7–3.

The Criminology of Place

Ecological approaches to crime causation have found a modern rebirth in the **criminology of place.** The criminology of place, also called **environmental criminology,** is an emerging perspective within the contemporary body of criminological theory that builds upon the contributions of routine activities theory and situational crime prevention (both of which were discussed in Chapter 4), as well as ecological approaches. It emphasizes the importance of geographic location and architectural features as they are associated with the prevalence of victimization. Such "hot spots" of crime, including neighborhoods, specific streets, and even individual houses and businesses, have been identified by recent writers. Lawrence W. Sherman, for example, tells of a study that revealed that 3% of places (addresses and intersections) in Minneapolis produce 50% of all calls to the police.[19] Crime, noted Sherman, although relatively rare in Minneapolis and similar urban areas, is geographically concentrated.

Reflecting the questions first addressed by Shaw and McKay, another contemporary researcher, Rodney Stark, asks, "How is it that neighborhoods can remain the site of high crime and deviance rates despite a complete turnover in their populations? . . . There

cultural transmission

The transmission of delinquency through successive generations of people living in the same area through a process of social communication.

ecological theory

A type of sociological approach that emphasizes demographics (the characteristics of population groups) and geographics (the mapped location of such groups relative to one another) and that sees the social disorganization that characterizes delinquency areas as a major cause of criminality and victimization.

Chicago School of criminology

An ecological approach to explaining crime that examined how social disorganization contributes to social pathology.

WEB Extra

must be something about places as such that sustains crime."[20] Stark has developed a theory of deviant neighborhoods. It consists of 30 propositions, including the following:[21]

- To the extent that neighborhoods are dense and poor, homes will be crowded.
- Where homes are more crowded, there will be a greater tendency to congregate outside the home in places and circumstances that raise levels of temptation and offer opportunity to deviate.
- Where homes are more crowded, there will be lower levels of supervision of children.
- Reduced levels of child supervision will result in poor school achievement, with a consequent reduction in stakes in conformity and an increase in deviant behavior.
- Poor, dense neighborhoods tend to be mixed-use neighborhoods.
- Mixed use increases familiarity with and easy access to places offering the opportunity for deviance.

Central to the criminology of place is the **broken windows thesis,** which holds that physical deterioration and an increase in unrepaired buildings lead to increased concerns for personal safety among area residents.[22] Heightened concerns, in turn, lead to further decreases in maintenance and repair and to increased delinquency, vandalism, and crime among local residents, which spawn even further deterioration in both a sense of safety and the physical environment. Offenders from other neighborhoods are then increasingly attracted by the area's perceived vulnerability. In short, physical evidence of disorder, left unchecked, leads to crime by driving residents indoors and sending a message to would-be offenders that a neighborhood is out of control.[23]

The broken windows perspective was first advanced in a 1982 article by James Q. Wilson and George L. Kelling entitled "Broken Windows: The Police and Neighborhood Safety."[24]

The broken windows thesis led to an increase in the use of "order maintenance policing" and to a crackdown on quality-of-life offenses—such as panhandling, graffiti, littering, and prostitution—in some of our nation's cities. In 2000 in New York City, for example, then–Mayor Rudolph Giuliani announced a new police campaign using computer crime mapping to track and target offenses such as jaywalking, public urination, panhandling, graffiti, public drinking, and prostitution. "When we further the quality of life and advance New York City as a more civil society," said the mayor, "when we constantly reinforce the fact that our actions affect one another, we'll realize together that inconsiderate behavior yields disorder and, more importantly, we'll realize the meaning of truly considerate behavior, which lifts the City up and brings us together every day."[25]

Even within so-called high-crime neighborhoods and neighborhoods characterized by urban decay, however, crimes tend to be concentrated at specific locations, such as street blocks or multiple-family dwellings. This kind of microlevel analysis has also shown, for example, that some units within specific apartment buildings are much more likely to be the site of criminal occurrences than others. Apartments near complex or building entrances appear to be more criminally dangerous, especially if they are not facing other buildings or apartments. Likewise, pedestrian tunnels, unattended parking lots, and convenience stores with clerks stationed in less visible areas are often targeted by criminal offenders.

The criminology of place employs the concept of **defensible space,** a term that evolved out of a conference in 1964 at Washington University in St. Louis, Missouri.[26] *Defensible space* has been defined as "a surrogate term for the range of mechanisms— real and symbolic barriers, strongly defined areas of influence, and improved opportunities for surveillance—that combine to bring an environment under the control of its residents."[27] The St. Louis conference, which brought criminologists, police officers, and architects face to face, focused on crime problems characteristic of public housing areas. Findings demonstrated that specific architectural changes that enhanced barriers,

---

criminology of place

A perspective that emphasizes the importance of geographic location and architectural features as they are associated with the prevalence of criminal victimization.

environmental criminology

An emerging perspective that emphasizes the importance of geographic location and architectural features as they are associated with the prevalence of criminal victimization.

broken windows thesis

A perspective on crime causation that holds that physical deterioration in an area leads to increased concerns for personal safety among area residents and to higher crime rates in that area.

defensible space

The range of mechanisms that combine to bring an environment under the control of its residents.

defined boundaries, and removed criminal opportunity could do much to reduce the risk of crime—even in the midst of high-crime neighborhoods.

The criminology of place holds that location can be as predictive of criminal activity as the lifestyles of victimized individuals or the social features of victimized households. (*Place* has been defined by researchers as "a fixed physical environment that can be seen completely and simultaneously, at least on its surface, by one's naked eyes."[28]) Places can be criminogenic due to the routine activities associated with them. On the other hand, some places host crime because they provide the characteristics that facilitate its commission. In Sherman's study, for example, Minneapolis parks drew exhibitionists because they provided "opportunities for concealment" up until the moment when the "flasher" struck. Making changes to the parks, such as moving walkways some distance from trees and shrubbery, would reduce criminal opportunity.

Recognizing the importance of criminology of place, New York City police developed a program a few years ago designed to close businesses with repeated crime problems. Called Operation Padlock, the program appeared to be successful in reducing the incidence of certain kinds of crime. As Sherman points out, "neither capital punishment of places (as in arson of crack houses) nor incapacitation of the routine activities of criminal hot spots (as in revocation of liquor licenses) seems likely to eliminate crime. But since the routine activities of places may be regulated far more easily than the routine activities of persons, a criminology of place would seem to offer substantial promise for public policy as well as theory."[29]

Some crime prevention programs are combining ideas derived from the criminology of place with spatial mapping techniques to fight crime. The Theory versus Reality box in this chapter provides information about crime mapping techniques. Visit the National Institute of Justice's MAPS program via **Web Extra 7–4** to learn more about crime mapping, and read more about the broken windows thesis at **Library Extra 7–1** at crimtoday.com.

Recent studies of the broken windows concept have cast doubt upon the assertion, made by Wilson and Kelling, that police intervention into the process that links disorder and crime can be effective in reducing crime.[30] According to recent research, it may be that disorder and crime have common roots and that one is more associated with the other than produced by it.[31] Hence, efforts to target quality-of-life offenses in urban areas that are experiencing high levels of social disorganization may not have the desired effect of reducing crime. According to David Thacher, professor of public policy and urban planning at the University of Michigan, "[T]hese challenges to the broken windows

WEB
Extra
■ ■ ■ ■

LIBRARY
Extra
■ ■ ■ ■

Monitoring security cameras. Defensible space can be defined in terms of barriers to crime commission and preventative surveillance opportunities. How might such features be enhanced in high-crime areas?
Source: Remi Benali

theory have not yet discredited order maintenance policing with policymakers or the public. But among criminologists, order maintenance is clearly under siege."[32]

Strain Theory

The second type of social structure theory discussed in this chapter is strain theory. Strain can be thought of as the pressure that individuals feel to reach socially determined goals.[33] Strain theory depicts delinquency as a form of adaptive, problem-solving behavior, usually committed in response to problems involving frustrating and undesirable social environments. The classic statement of strain theory was offered in 1938 by **Robert K. Merton,** who developed the concept of anomie. *Anomie,* a French word meaning "normlessness," was popularized by Emile Durkheim in his 1897 book *Suicide.*[34] Durkheim used the term to explain how a breakdown of predictable social conditions can lead to feelings of personal loss and dissolution. In Durkheim's writings, *anomie* was a feeling of strain that resulted from not being personally embedded in society. It marked the loss of a sense of belonging.

Merton's use of the term *anomie* was somewhat different. In Merton's writings, **anomie** came to mean a disjunction between socially approved means to success and legitimate goals.[35] Merton maintained that legitimate goals, involving such things as wealth, status, and personal happiness, are generally portrayed as desirable for everyone. The widely acceptable means to these goals, however, including education, hard work, financial savings, and so on, are not equally available to all members of society. As a consequence, crime and deviance tend to arise as alternative means to success when individuals feel the strain of being pressed to succeed in socially approved ways but find that the tools necessary for such success are not available to them. Strain increases as the gulf between goals and the availability of the means necessary to achieve them widens. Merton's emphasis on the felt strain resulting from a lack of fit between goals and means led to his approach being called **strain theory.**

Complicating the picture further, Merton maintained, was the fact that not everyone accepts the legitimacy of socially approved goals. Merton diagrammed possible combinations of goals and means as shown in Table 7–1, referring to each combination as a mode of adaptation.

The initial row in Table 7–1 signifies acceptance of the goals that society holds as legitimate for everyone, with ready availability of the means approved for achieving those goals. The mode of adaptation associated with this combination of goals and means, *conformity,* typifies most middle- and upper-class individuals.

Innovation, the second form of adaptation, arises when an emphasis on approved goal achievement combines with a lack of opportunity to participate fully in socially acceptable means to success. This form of adaptation is experienced by many lower-class individuals who have been socialized to desire traditional success symbols, such as expensive cars, large homes, and big bank accounts, but who do not have ready access to approved means of acquiring them, such as educational opportunity. Innovative

anomie

A social condition in which norms are uncertain or lacking.

strain theory

A sociological approach that posits a disjunction between socially and subculturally sanctioned means and goals as the cause of criminal behavior.

TABLE 7–1   Goals and Means Disjuncture

	Goals	Means
Conformity	+	+
Innovation	+	−
Ritualism	−	+
Retreatism	−	−
Rebellion	±	±

Source: Adapted with the permission of The Free Press, a Division of Simon & Schuster Adult Publishing Group, from SOCIAL THEORY AND SOCIAL STRUCTURE, Revised & Enlarged Edition by Robert K. Merton. Copyright © 1967, 1968 by Robert K. Merton. All rights reserved.

Theory Versus Reality

The Criminology of Place, Routine Activities, and Crime Mapping

Today's law enforcement agencies are using routine activities theory (discussed in Chapter 4) along with the criminology of place to develop situational crime prevention techniques that combine technology with the spatial analysis of crime. One proponent of this approach is the Mapping and Analysis Program (MAPS) of the National Institute of Justice. Crime mapping, used in conjunction with geographic information systems (GIS), allows for the effective use of law enforcement resources by helping police administrators direct patrols to places where they are most needed. This box contains excerpts from a National Institute of Justice report on crime mapping.

In the routine activities interpretation, crimes are seen as needing three ingredients: a *likely offender,* a *suitable target,* and the *absence of a guardian* capable of preventing the criminal act. *Guardian* is broadly interpreted to mean anyone capable of discouraging, if only through his or her mere presence, or interceding in, criminal acts. The mention of guardians begs discussion of the *density paradox.* This refers to the idea that, on the one hand, high population densities create a high potential for crime because people and property are crowded in small spaces. There are many likely offenders and suitable targets. On the other hand, surveillance is plentiful, and criminal acts in public spaces are likely to be observed by others, who, however unwittingly, take on the role of guardians. Crime can be prevented or reduced by making people less likely to offend (by increasing guilt and fostering development of the "inner policeman" who tames criminal impulses), by making targets less available, and by making guardians more numerous or effective. The process of making targets less available in various ways has become known by the generic term *situational crime prevention.*

Putting the routine activities approach and its sibling, situational crime prevention, into a geographic context involves asking how each element is distributed in geographic space. Where are the likely offenders? (What is the geography of the youthful male population?) Where are the suitable targets? (What is the geography of convenience stores, malls, automated teller machines, poorly illuminated pedestrian areas?) Where are the guardians? (What is the potential for surveillance, both formal and informal, of targets or areas that may contain targets? Where are the public or quasipublic spaces that lack surveillance and are ripe for graffiti and other incivilities?)

The perspective that focuses on criminal spatial behavior develops a scenario in which the motivated (potential) criminal uses cues, or environmental signals, to assess victims or targets. Cues, or clusters of cues, and sequences of cues relating to the social and physical aspects of the environment are seen as a *template,* which the offender uses to evaluate victims or targets. Intimately tied to this process is the concept of *activity space,* the area in which the offender customarily moves about and that is familiar to him or her.

At the micro level of analysis, these concepts are useful in that it is known that activity spaces vary with demographics. For example, younger persons tend to have constricted activity spaces. They do not usually have the resources to travel far. Historically, women have had more geographically limited activity spaces than men due to the higher probability that men would work farther from home and that their jobs would be more likely to give them greater mobility. This is less true today but is still valid to some degree.

Analysts considering crime patterns from a theoretical perspective might think in terms of putting the crimes of interest through a series of "filter" questions. The most obvious is the question, How important is geography in explaining this pattern? (Is the pattern random, or not? If not, why not?) Can routine activity theory or criminal spatial behavior theory help explain this pattern? Is this pattern normal or unusual for this area? If the pattern is an anomaly, why is this? What resources can be brought to bear a better understanding of the social and other environmental dynamics of the area of interest? Analysts can take their intimate knowledge of the local environment and develop their own set of diagnostic questions, which could be the foundation of an analytic model.

For a list of Web sites displaying active crime maps, see **Web Extra 7–5.**

WEB
Extra

Discussion Questions

1. How does routine activities theory support the concepts involved in the spatial analysis of crime?

2. What is the density paradox? What implications does it have for crime prevention?

3. What "filter questions" are discussed in this box? Can you think of any other filter questions that might be asked?

Source: National Institute of Justice, "Mapping and Analysis for Public Safety (MAPS)," http://www.ojp.gov/nij/maps (accessed May 28, 2007); and Keith Harries, *Mapping Crime: Principles and Practice* (Washington, DC: National Institute of Justice, 1999), http://www.ojp.usdoj.gov/cmrc (accessed December 15, 2005).

behavioral responses, including crime, can be expected to develop when individuals find themselves so deprived. However, in Merton's words, "poverty as such, and consequent limitation of opportunity, are not sufficient to induce a conspicuously high rate of criminal behavior. Even the often mentioned 'poverty in the midst of plenty' will not necessarily lead to this result." It is only insofar as those who find themselves in poverty are pressured to achieve material success and the acquisition of other associated symbols of status that innovation results.

Third, *ritualism* describes the form of behavior that arises when members of society participate in socially desirable means but show little interest in goal achievement.

Crime in the News

Do Immigrants Make Us Safer?

In an age of Latino gangs and Chinese criminal networks, the notion that communities with growing immigrant populations tend to be unsafe is fairly well established, at least in the popular imagination. In a national survey conducted in 2000, 73 percent of Americans said they believe that immigrants are either "somewhat" or "very" likely to increase crime, higher than the 60 percent who fear they are "likely to cause Americans to lose jobs." Cities like Avon Park, Fla., have considered ordinances recently to dissuade businesses from hiring illegal immigrants, whose presence "destroys our neighborhoods." Even President Bush, whose perceived generosity to undocumented workers has earned him vilification on the right, commented in a speech (in May, 2006) that illegal immigration "strains state and local budgets and brings crime to our communities."

So goes the conventional wisdom. But is it true? In fact, according to evidence cropping up in various places, the opposite may be the case. Ramiro Martinez Jr., a professor of criminal justice at

U.S. Border Patrol agents help a girl over a ranch fence so she can be taken into custody in South Texas brush country north of Laredo, Texas, in 2006. For all the talk in Washington on immigration, illegal immigrants caught along the Mexican border have almost no reason to fear they will be prosecuted; and more than 97% are let go almost immediately after being caught. Should illegal immigration have more substantial criminal consequences associated with it?

Source: LM Otero/AP Wide World Photos

Florida International University, has sifted through homicide records in border cities like San Diego and El Paso, both heavily populated by Mexican immigrants, both places where violent crime has fallen significantly in recent years. "Almost without exception," he told me, "I've discovered that the homicide rate for Hispanics was lower than for other groups, even though their poverty rate was very high, if not the highest, in these metropolitan areas." He found the same thing in the Haitian neighborhoods of Miami. In his book "New York Murder Mystery," the criminologist Andrew Karmen examined the trend in New York City and likewise found that the "disproportionately youthful, male and poor immigrants" who arrived during the 1980s and 1990s "were surprisingly law-abiding" and that their settlement into once-decaying neighborhoods helped "put a brake on spiraling crime rates."

The most prominent advocate of the "more immigrants, less crime" theory is Robert J. Sampson, chairman of the sociology department at Harvard. A year ago, Sampson was an author of an article in *The American Journal of Public Health* that reported the findings of a detailed study of crime in Chicago. Based on information gathered on the perpetrators of more than 3,000 violent acts committed between 1995 and 2002, supplemented by police records and community surveys, it found that the rate of violence among Mexican-Americans was significantly lower than among both non-Hispanic whites and blacks.

In June, Sampson and I drove out to a neighborhood in Little Village, Chicago's largest Hispanic community. The area we visited is decidedly poor: in terms of per capita income, 84 percent of Chicago neighborhoods are better off and 99 percent have a greater proportion of residents with a high-school education. As we made our way down a side street, Sampson noted that many of the residents make their living as domestic workers and in other low-wage occupations, often paid off the books because they are undocumented. In places of such concentrated disadvantage, a certain level of violence and social disorder is assumed to be inevitable. As we strolled around, Sampson paused on occasion to make a mental note of potential trouble signs: an alley strewn with garbage nobody had bothered to pick up; a sign in Spanish in several windows, complaining about the lack of a park in the vicinity where children can play. Yet for all of this, the neighborhood was strikingly quiet. And, according to the data Sampson has collected, it is surprisingly safe. The burglary rate in the neighborhood is in the bottom fifth of the city. The overall crime rate is nearly in the bottom third.

Sampson's theory may be the most provocative yet. . . . Could illegal immigration be making the nation a more law-abiding place?

Sampson doesn't deny that crime may be underreported in immigrant neighborhoods. Nonetheless, he is quick to note that as the ranks of foreigners in the United States boomed during the 1990s—increasing by more than 50 percent to 31 million—America's cities became markedly less dangerous. That these two trends might be related has been overlooked, he says, in part because immigrants, like African-Americans, often trigger negative associations regardless of how they actually behave.

Not long ago, Sampson and Stephen W. Raudenbush, a sociologist who teaches at the University of Chicago, conducted an experiment to test this idea. The experiment drew on interviews with more than 3,500 Chicago residents, each of whom was asked how serious problems like loitering and public drinking were where they lived. The responses were compared with the actual level of chaos in the neighborhood, culled from police data and by having researchers drive along hundreds of blocks to document every sign of decay and disorder they could spot.

The social and ethnic composition of a neighborhood turned out to have a profound bearing on how residents of Chicago perceived it, irrespective of the actual conditions on the streets. "In particular," Sampson and Raudenbush found, "the proportion of blacks and the proportion of Latinos in a neighborhood were related positively and significantly to perceived disorder." Once you adjusted for the ethnic, racial and class composition of a community, "much of the variation in levels of disorder that appeared to be explained by what residents saw was spurious."

In other words, the fact that people think neighborhoods with large concentrations of brown-skinned immigrants are unsafe makes sense in light of popular stereotypes and subliminal associations. But that doesn't mean there is any rational basis for their fears. Such a message hasn't sat well with everyone. As the debate about immigration has grown more heated and polarized, Sampson has found himself barraged with hate mail. "Vicious stuff," he told me, "you know, thinly veiled threats, people saying, 'You should just come and look at the Mexican gangs here.'" But Sampson has also won some far-flung admirers. In Mexico, one of the nation's leading dailies, *La Reforma*, published a story hailing his findings, under the triumphal heading, "Son barrios de paisanos menos violentos que los blancos" ("Neighborhoods of our countrymen are less violent than white ones").

If immigrants really are making America safer, why is this so? "That," Sampson says, "is the $64,000 question." In discussing the persistence of poverty and the causes of crime, sociologists on the left often emphasize the importance of "structural" factors like unemployment and racism, while scholars on the right tend to focus on individual behavior like having an illegitimate child and using drugs. Sampson prefers to focus on the nature of the social interactions taking place in particular neighborhoods. At one point in Little Village, we strolled past a house where a couple of young girls were playing outside. It didn't seem that anybody was supervising them. Next door, however, an elderly woman was standing just inside the window. The window was open, and as Sampson and I passed by, her eyes did not leave us. "Did you notice that?" asked Sampson as we proceeded down the block. She was making sure the two strangers who had appeared weren't dangerous. It was an example of the kind of informal social control that Sampson says can prevent even the poorest neighborhoods from spiraling into chaos and that he suspects may distinguish many tight-knit immigrant communities.

But Sampson also notes the importance of another factor, one often stressed by conservatives: Mexicans in Chicago, his study found, are more likely to be married than either blacks or whites. "The family dynamic is very noticeable here," Sampson remarked as we passed a girl with long braided hair clutching her mother's hand. Her father followed a few steps behind. Sampson does not believe family structure explains everything: the data showed that in immigrant neighborhoods, even individuals who are not in married households

are 15 percent less likely to engage in crime. Yet neither did he discount its significance.

Before anyone rushes to conclude that crime would vanish from America's cities if only more foreigners moved here, it is worth considering something else Sampson's study uncovered. It is a finding as troubling as his basic thesis about immigrants is hopeful. Second-generation immigrants in Chicago were significantly more likely to commit crimes than their parents, it turns out, and those of the third generation more likely still.

Opponents of immigration frequently charge that Mexican immigrants threaten America's national identity because of their failure to assimilate. A more reasonable concern might be the opposite of this: not that foreigners in low-income neighborhoods refuse to adopt the norms of the native culture but that their children and grandchildren do.

The sociologists Alejandro Portes and Rubén G. Rumbaut conducted a multiyear longitudinal study of immigrant children in Miami and San Diego. The offspring of foreigners who grow up in impoverished ghettos, they have argued, particularly Mexican-Americans exposed to racial as well as economic discrimination, often lose the drive and optimism their parents had and come to share the widespread attitude among their inner-city peers that survival depends on brandishing an oppositional stance toward school authorities and, more broadly, a culture that looks down on them. "The learning of new cultural patterns and entry into American social circles does not lead in these cases to upward mobility but to exactly the opposite," Portes and Rumbaut contend, a process of "downward assimilation" that has created a new "rainbow underclass." Astoundingly, in a recent paper, Rumbaut and several doctoral students found that the incarceration rate among second-generation Mexicans was eight times higher than for the first generation; among Vietnamese, it was more than 10 times higher. Where the first-generation immigrants in their data were less likely to wind up in prison than native-born whites, the second (with the exception of Filipinos and Chinese) were more likely.

Such findings suggest the class and race divisions that cleave America's social landscape may prove decisive after all.

Recently, scholars have become increasingly interested in the historical origins of American violence. Richard Nisbett of the University of Michigan and others have traced our "culture of violence" back to the valorization of retribution and dueling among Scotch-Irish immigrants in the American South, suggesting that antique folkways have become encoded into the nation's DNA.

It is a dark view, perhaps, but Sampson is hopeful that the good news about crime in recent years can continue, albeit under certain conditions, among them less alarmism about the supposedly dangerous foreigners in our midst. Sampson shook his head when describing some of the correspondence he has received from people absolutely certain that immigrants are sowing mayhem in our streets. In the last few years, he noted, such people have had somewhat less cause for worry, since the numbers show the flow of newcomers has subsided a bit. Meanwhile, the crime rate in some cities has begun to creep back up. Sampson, for one, does not think this is a mere coincidence. Those clamoring for America to close its borders in order to prevent violence-prone strangers from flooding our shores may well get their way, he acknowledged, but they ought to be careful what they wish for.

(*continued*)

A ritualist may get a good education, work every day in an acceptable occupation, and appear outwardly to be leading a solid middle-class lifestyle, yet that person may care little for the symbols of success, choosing to live an otherwise independent lifestyle.

Retreatism describes the behavior of those who reject both the socially approved goals and means. They may become dropouts, drug abusers, or homeless persons or participate in alternative lifestyles, like communal living. Such individuals are often socially and psychologically quite separate from the larger society around them.

Merton's last category, *rebellion,* signifies a person, or rebel, who wishes to replace socially approved goals and means with some other system. Political radicals, revolutionaries, and antiestablishment agitators may fit into this category. Merton believed that conformity was the most common mode of adaptation prevalent in society, whereas retreatism was least common.

A 2006 study by sociologists Thomas M. Arvanites and Robert H. Defina at Villanova University tested a prediction based on Merton's theory: that negative economic conditions and declining business cycles can increase social strain, resulting in heightened rates for certain kinds of crimes, especially property crimes. By comparing economic conditions in American society over time with rates for such crimes, the researchers concluded that "an improving economy has a negative and statistically significant effect on all four index property crimes and robbery." Because financial gain is the primary purpose of robbery, they noted, "a finding that robbery is the only violent crime to be influenced by the business cycle was not surprising."[36]

Relative Deprivation

A contemporary version of Merton's anomie theory has been proposed by Steven F. Messner and Richard Rosenfeld, who suggest that inconsistencies in the American Dream are to be blamed for most criminal activity. Messner and Rosenfeld write, "Our thesis is that the American Dream itself exerts pressures toward crime by encouraging an anomic cultural environment, an environment in which people are encouraged to adopt an 'anything goes' mentality in the pursuit of personal goals."[37]

It is often said that Americans are the richest people on earth and that even the poorest Americans are far richer in terms of material possessions than the average citizen of many Third World nations. Even if such an assertion is true, however, it means little to someone who is poor when judged in terms of the relatively affluent standards of the United States. Hence, deprivation has an important psychological component, which means that it cannot be accurately assessed in absolute terms. **Relative deprivation** refers to the economic and social gap that exists between rich and poor who live in close proximity to one another.

According to sociologists Judith Blau and Peter Blau, two proponents of the relative deprivation concept, people assess their position in life by way of comparison with things and people they already know.[38] Hence, inner-city inhabitants develop an increasing sense of relative deprivation when growing up in impoverished communities

relative deprivation

A sense of social or economic inequality experienced by those who are unable, for whatever reason, to achieve legitimate success within the surrounding society.

with the opportunity to witness well-to-do lifestyles in nearby neighborhoods. According to the Blaus, relative deprivation creates feelings of anger, frustration, hostility, and social injustice on the part of those who experience it. Relative deprivation is also related to the notion of **distributive justice,** which refers to an individual's perception of his or her rightful place in the reward structure of society. Thus, according to the principle of distributive justice, even wealthy and socially privileged individuals may feel slighted or shortchanged if they feel they have been inadequately rewarded for their behavior or their accomplishments. The perception of what amounts to the rightful distribution of rewards, however, appears to be highly dependent upon cultural expectations. Hence, while even the most successful Americans may feel that they deserve more, studies show that Japanese society has been able to accommodate rapid socioeconomic growth without generating a felt sense of economic injustice, even among its least successful members, and without a substantial increase in crime.[39]

Recent surveys provide evidence for distinguishing between two types of relative deprivation: personal and group.[40] Personal relative deprivation is characteristic of individuals who feel deprived compared with other people. Group relative deprivation, on the other hand, is a communal sense of injustice that is shared by members of the same group. Hence, while people who experience personal deprivation are likely to feel socially isolated and personally stressed, those who believe the entire social group to which they belong is deprived relative to other groups are more prone to participate in social movements and may actively attempt to change the social system. Group relative deprivation can be a powerful force for social change. Some political analysts have suggested that the strain produced by relative deprivation compared to the West played an important role in the downfall of the Soviet Union and of communism in Eastern Europe.[41]

General Strain Theory

In 1992, strain theory was reformulated by **Robert Agnew** and others who molded it into a comprehensive perspective called **general strain theory (GST)**.[42] GST sees lawbreaking behavior as a coping mechanism that enables those who engage in it to deal with the socioemotional problems generated by negative social relations. According to GST, strain occurs when others do the following: (1) prevent or threaten to prevent an individual from achieving positively valued goals, like autonomy or financial success; (2) remove or threaten to remove positively valued stimuli that a person possesses, such as the loss of a romantic partner or the death of a loved one; or (3) present or threaten to present someone with noxious or negatively valued stimuli, like verbal insults or physical abuse. In 2006, Agnew restated the six central propositions of general strain theory as follows:[43]

1. Strains refer to events and conditions that are disliked by individuals. There are three major types of strain: Individuals may (a) lose something they value; (b) be treated in an aversive or negative manner by others, and (c) be unable to achieve their goals.

2. Strains increase the likelihood of *particular* crimes primarily through their impact on a range of negative emotional *states*. Certain kinds of strains, for example, might lead to revenge seeking, while others cause those who experience them to steal things of value, and so forth.

3. Those strains most likely to cause crime (a) are perceived as high in magnitude or (b) as unjust; (c) are associated with low self-control; and (d) create some pressure or incentive to engage in criminal coping.

4. The likelihood that individuals will react to strains with criminal behavior depends on a range of factors that influence the individual's (a) ability to engage in legal coping; (b) costs of crime, and (c) disposition of crime.

5. Patterns of offending over the life course, group differences in crime, and community and societal differences in crime can be partly explained in terms of differences in the exposure to strains conducive to crime (males, for example, are

distributive justice

The rightful, equitable, and just distribution of rewards within a society.

general strain theory (GST)

A perspective that suggests that lawbreaking behavior is a coping mechanism that enables those who engage in it to deal with the socioemotional problems generated by negative social relations.

more often exposed to strains conducive to crime, and are more likely than females to cope with strains through crime).

6. Crime can be reduced by reducing individuals' exposure to strains that are conducive to crime, and by reducing their likelihood of responding to strains with crime.

In Western societies, Agnew says, the strains most likely to cause crime include child abuse and neglect; negative secondary-school experiences; abusive peer relations; chronic unemployment; marital problems; parental rejection; erratic, excessive, and or/harsh supervision or discipline; criminal victimization; homelessness; racial, ethnic, or gender discrimination; and a failure to achieve selected goals.

Factors that increase the likelihood of criminal (as opposed to conformist) coping, include poor conventional coping skills and resources; the availability of criminal skills and resources; low levels of conventional social support; routine association with criminal others; personal beliefs and values that are favorable to crime; frequent exposure to situations where the costs of crime are low; low levels of social control, including weak bonds to conventional others, and a lack of investment in conventional institutions.

Strategies for reducing exposure to strains include eliminating strains conducive to crime, altering strains to make them less conducive to crime, removing individuals from exposure to strain, and equipping individuals with the traits and skills needed to avoid strains that are conducive to crime.

GST expands on traditional strain theory in several ways. First, it significantly widens the focus of strain theory to include all types of negative relations between an individual and others. Second, GST maintains that strain is likely to have a cumulative effect on delinquency after reaching a certain threshold. Third, general strain theory provides a more comprehensive account of the cognitive, behavioral, and emotional adaptations to strain than traditional strain approaches. Finally, GST more fully describes the wide variety of factors affecting the choice of delinquent adaptations to strain.

Agnew sees the crime-producing effects of strain as cumulative and concludes that whatever form it takes, "strain creates a predisposition for delinquency in those cases in which it is chronic or repetitive."[44] Predispositions may be manifested in the form of **negative affective states,** or emotions such as anger, fear, depression, and disappointment.

negative affective states

Adverse emotions that derive from the experience of strain, such as anger, fear, depression, and disappointment.

An analysis by Agnew of other strain theories found that all such theories share at least two central explanatory features.[45] Strain theories, Agnew said, (1) focus "explicitly on negative relationships with others, relationships in which the individual is not treated as he or she wants to be treated," and (2) argue that "adolescents are pressured into delinquency by the negative affective states—most notably anger and related emotions—that often result from negative relationships."[46]

In 1994, Raymond Paternoster and Paul Mazerolle tested some of the assumptions underlying GST through an analysis of data from the National Youth Survey.[47] They found partial support for GST and discovered that negative relations with adults, feelings of dissatisfaction with friends and school life, and the experience of stressful events (for example, family dissolution) were positively related to delinquency, as was living in an unpleasant neighborhood (one beset by social problems and physical deterioration). When conceived of more broadly as exposure to negative stimuli, general strain was found to be significantly related to delinquency.

Contrary to Agnew's hypothesis, however, Paternoster and Mazerolle found no evidence that the effects of strain were enhanced when they were experienced for longer periods of time or that they were diminished when adolescents classified the dimension of their life in which they experienced strain as "unimportant." Consistent with earlier findings,[48] Paternoster and Mazerolle found that feelings of general strain were positively related to later delinquency, regardless of the number of delinquent peers, moral beliefs, self-efficacy, and level of conventional social support. Some support was found for the belief that general strain leads to delinquency by weakening the conventional social bond and by strengthening the unconventional bond with delinquent peers.

In a recent test of general strain theory, Lisa M. Broidy of the University of New Mexico examined the intervening role of negative emotions and legitimate coping strategies as they impact the relationship between strain and crime.[49] Broidy found that strain can produce anger and other negative emotions but that different sources of strain tend to produce different emotions. "Hence," concluded Broidy, "although evidence of a relationship exists between strain and negative emotions, the nature of this relationship depends on the specific type of strain and negative emotions considered."[50] Broidy found that strain-induced anger—while particularly associated with an increased likelihood of criminal outcomes—was more likely to lead to criminal outcomes among men than among women, even though members of both genders experienced anger equally under certain specific types of strained circumstances. Broidy also discovered that "negative emotional responses to strain other than anger are associated with a significant increase in legitimate coping and significant decrease in illegitimate/criminal outcomes."

A 2002 study by Robert Agnew and associates further refined GST by explaining why some individuals are more likely than others to react to strain with delinquency.[51] The study employed the psychological concept of master personality traits and defined traits as "relatively stable ways of perceiving, thinking about, and behaving toward the environment and oneself." Study authors found that juveniles who measured high in negative emotionality and low in constraint were more likely to react to strain with delinquency. Drawing upon evidence that suggests traits may be both inherited and acquired, Agnew noted that the "incorporation of such traits into GST . . . represents an integration between strain theory and the rapidly growing research on behavioral genetics and crime."[52] Hence, it may be that certain biological factors make some individuals particularly susceptible to the effects of strain in their lives. Learn more about strain theory via **Web Extra 7–6.**

WEB
Extra

Culture Conflict Theory

The third type of social structure theory discussed in this chapter can be found in the culture conflict approach to explaining crime. **Culture conflict theory** (also called "cultural deviance theory") suggests that the root cause of criminality can be found in a clash of values between differently socialized groups over what is acceptable or proper behavior. The culture conflict concept is inherent in ecological criminology (which was discussed in the first part of this chapter) and its belief that zones of transition, because they tend to be in flux, harbor groups of people whose values are often at odds with those of the larger, surrounding society.

The culture conflict perspective found its clearest expression in the writings of **Thorsten Sellin** in his 1938 book *Culture Conflict and Crime.*[53] Sellin maintained that the root cause of crime could be found in different values about what is acceptable or proper behavior. According to Sellin, **conduct norms,** which provide the valuative basis for human behavior, are acquired early in life through childhood socialization. It is the clash of norms between variously socialized groups that results in crime. Because crime is a violation of laws established by legislative decree, the criminal event itself, from this point of view, is nothing other than a disagreement over what should be acceptable behavior. For some social groups, what we tend to call "crime" is simply part of the landscape—something that can be expected to happen to you unless you take steps to protect yourself. From this point of view, those to whom crime happens are not so much victimized as they are simply ill-prepared.

In 1997, Danish actress Annette Sorensen was arrested after leaving her toddler in a stroller outside of a Manhattan restaurant while she sat inside, drinking margaritas with the child's father. Sorensen was charged with endangering the welfare of a child. Her 14-month-old daughter, Liv, was placed in temporary foster care. Sorensen, who was in tears following her arrest, could not understand what had happened. "We do this in Denmark all the time," the Copenhagen resident told police.[54] Her daughter was soon ordered returned by a city judge, and Sorensen and the child flew home to Denmark, where children are routinely left in strollers outside of restaurants and other public places.[55]

culture conflict theory

A sociological perspective on crime that suggests that the root cause of criminality can be found in a clash of values between variously socialized groups over what is acceptable or proper behavior.

conduct norms

Shared expectations of a social group relative to personal conduct.

Sellin described two types of culture conflict. The first type, *primary conflict*, arises when a fundamental clash of cultures occurs. Sellin's classic example was that of an immigrant father who kills his daughter's lover following an old-world tradition that demands that a family's honor be kept intact. In Sellin's words, "A few years ago, a Sicilian father in New Jersey killed the sixteen-year-old seducer of his daughter, expressing surprise at his arrest since he had merely defended his family honor in a traditional way. In this case . . . [t]he conflict was external and occurred between cultural codes or norms. We may assume that where such conflicts occur . . . norms of one cultural group or area migrate to another and that such conflict will continue so long as the acculturation process has not been completed."[56]

The other type of conflict, *secondary conflict,* arose, according to Sellin, when smaller cultures within the primary one clashed. So it is that middle-class values, upon which most criminal laws are based, may find fault with inner-city or lower-class norms, resulting in the social phenomenon we call "crime."

In Sellin's day, prostitution and gambling provided plentiful examples of secondary conflict. Many lower-class inner-city groups accepted gambling and prostitution as a way of life—if not for individual members of those groups, then at least as forms of behavior that were rarely condemned for those choosing to participate in them. Today, drug use and abuse provide more readily understandable examples. For some segments of contemporary society, drug sales have become a source of substantial income, and the conduct norms that typify such groups support at least the relative legitimacy of lives built around the drug trade. In other words, in some parts of America, drug dealing is an acceptable form of business. To those who make the laws, however, it is not. It is from the clash of these two opposing viewpoints that conflict and crime emerge.

Subcultural Theory

Fundamental to the notion of culture conflict is the idea of subcultures. Like the larger culture of which it is a part, a **subculture** is a collection of values and preferences, which is communicated to subcultural participants through a process of socialization. Subcultures differ from the larger culture in that they claim the allegiance of smaller groups of people. Whereas the wider American culture, for example, may proclaim that hard work and individuality are valuable, a particular subculture may espouse the virtues of deer hunting, male bonding, and recreational alcohol consumption. Although it is fair to say that most subcultures are not at odds with the surrounding culture, some subcultures do not readily conform to the parameters of national culture. Countercultures, which tend to reject and invert the values of the surrounding culture, and criminal subcultures, which may actively espouse deviant activity, represent the other extreme. **Subcultural theory** is a sociological perspective that emphasizes the contribution made by variously socialized cultural groups to the phenomenon of crime.

Some of the earliest writings on subcultures can be found in **Frederic M. Thrasher**'s 1927 book *The Gang*.[57] Thrasher studied 1,313 gangs in Chicago. His work, primarily descriptive in nature, led to a typology in which he described different types of gangs. In 1943, **William F. Whyte,** drawing on Thrasher's work, published *Street Corner Society*.[58] Whyte, in describing his three-year study of the Italian slum he called "Cornerville," further developed the subcultural thesis, showing that lower-class residents of a typical slum could achieve success through the opportunities afforded by slum culture—including racketeering and bookmaking.

Focal Concerns

In 1958, **Walter Miller** attempted to detail the values that drive members of lower-class subcultures into delinquent pursuits. Miller described *lower-class culture* as "a long established, distinctively patterned tradition with an integrity of its own."[59] In Miller's words, "A large body of systematically interrelated attitudes, practices, behaviors, and values characteristic of lower-class culture are designed to support and maintain the basic features of the lower-class way of life. In areas where these differ from features of middle-class culture, action oriented to the achievement and maintenance of the

subculture

A collection of values and preferences that is communicated to subcultural participants through a process of socialization.

subcultural theory

A sociological perspective that emphasizes the contribution made by variously socialized cultural groups to the phenomenon of crime.

lower-class system may violate norms of the middle class and be perceived as deliberately nonconforming. . . . This does not mean, however, that violation of the middle-class norm is the dominant component of motivation; it is a byproduct of action primarily oriented to the lower-class system."

In the same article, entitled "Lower Class Culture as a Generating Milieu of Gang Delinquency," Miller outlined what he termed the **focal concerns** or key values, of delinquent subcultures. Such concerns included trouble, toughness, smartness, excitement, fate, and autonomy. Miller concluded that subcultural crime and deviance are not the direct consequences of poverty and lack of opportunity but emanate, rather, from specific values characteristic of such subcultures. Just as middle-class concerns with achievement, hard work, and delayed gratification lead to socially acceptable forms of success, said Miller, so, too, do lower-class concerns provide a path to subculturally recognized success for lower-class youth.

focal concerns

The key values of any culture, especially the key values of a delinquent subculture.

Miller found that trouble is a dominant feature of lower-class culture. Getting into trouble, staying out of trouble, and dealing with trouble when it arises become focal points in the lives of many members of lower-class culture. Miller recognized that getting into trouble is not necessarily valued in and of itself but is seen as an oftentimes necessary means to valued ends. In Miller's words, "[For] men, 'trouble' frequently involves fighting or sexual adventures while drinking; for women, sexual involvement with disadvantageous consequences."

Like many theorists of the time, Miller was primarily concerned with the criminality of men. The lower-class masculine concern with toughness that he identified, Miller admitted, may have been a product of the fact that many men in the groups he examined were raised in female-headed families. Miller's "toughness," then, may reflect an almost obsessive concern with masculinity as a reaction to the perceived threat of over identification with female role models. In words that sound as applicable today as when they were written, Miller tells us, "The genesis of the intense concern over 'toughness' in lower-class culture is probably related to the fact that a significant proportion of lower-class males are reared in a predominantly female household and lack a consistently present male figure with whom to identify and from whom to learn essential components of a 'male' role. Since women serve as a primary object of identification during the pre-adolescent years, the almost obsessive lower-class concern with 'masculinity' probably resembles a type of compulsive reaction-formation."

Miller described "smartness" as the "capacity to outsmart, outfox, outwit, dupe, take, [or] con another or others and the concomitant capacity to avoid being outwitted, taken or duped oneself. . . . In its essence," said Miller, "smartness involves the capacity to achieve a valued entity—material goods, personal status—through a maximum use of mental agility and a minimum of physical effort."

Excitement was seen as a search for thrills—often necessary to overcome the boredom inherent in lower-class lifestyles. Fighting, gambling, picking up women, and making the rounds were all described as derivative aspects of the lower-class concern with excitement. "The quest for excitement," said Miller, "find . . . its most vivid expression in the . . . recurrent 'night on the town' . . . a patterned set of activities in which alcohol, music, and sexual adventuring are major components."

Fate is related to the quest for excitement and to the concept of luck or of being lucky. As Miller stated, "Many lower-class persons feel that their lives are subject to a set of forces over which they have relatively little control. These are not . . . . supernatural forces or . . . organized religion . . . but relate more to a concept of 'destiny' or man as a pawn. . . . This often implicit world view is associated with a conception of the ultimate futility of directed effort toward a goal."

Autonomy, as a focal concern, manifests itself in statements like "I can take care of myself" and "No one's going to push me around." Autonomy produces behavioral problems from the perspective of middle-class expectations when it surfaces in work environments, public schools, or other social institutions built on expectations of conformity.

Miller's work is derived almost entirely from his study of black inner-city delinquents in the Boston area in the 1950s. As such, it may have less relevance to members of lower-class subcultures in other places or at other times

Delinquency and Drift

Members of delinquent subcultures are, to at least some degree, participants in the larger culture that surrounds them. How is it, then, that subcultural participants may choose behavioral alternatives that seemingly negate the norms and values of the larger society? In other words, how can a person give allegiance to two seemingly different sets of values—those of the larger culture and those of a subculture—at the same time?

Gresham Sykes and **David Matza** provided an answer to this question in their 1957 article "Techniques of Neutralization."[60] Sykes and Matza suggested that offenders and delinquents are aware of conventional values, understand that their offending is wrong, but engage in neutralizing self-talk before offending to mitigate the anticipated shame and guilt associated with violating societal norms.[61] Offenders, said Sykes and Matza, can overcome feelings of responsibility when involved in crime commission through the use of five types of justification:

- *Denying responsibility,* by pointing to one's background of poverty, abuse, lack of opportunity, and so on. Example: "The trouble I get into is not my fault."

- *Denying injury,* by explaining how insurance companies, for example, cover losses. Claims that "everyone does it" or that the specific victim could "afford it" fall into this category. Example: "They're so rich, they'll never miss it."

- *Denying the victim,* or justifying the harm done by claiming that the victim, for whatever reason, deserved the victimization. Example: "I only beat up drunks."

- *Condemning the condemners,* by asserting that authorities are corrupt or responsible for their own victimization. Offenders may also claim that society has made them into what they are and must now suffer the consequences. Example: "They're worse than we are. They're all on the take."

- *Appealing to higher loyalties*, as in defense of one's family honor, gang, girlfriend, or neighborhood. Example: "We have to protect ourselves."

In the words of Sykes and Matza, "It is our argument that much delinquency is based on what is essentially an unrecognized extension of defenses to crimes, in the form of justifications for deviance that are seen as valid by the delinquent but not by the legal system or society at large."[62]

techniques of neutralization

Culturally available justifications that can provide criminal offenders with the means to disavow responsibility for their behavior.

A few years later, Matza went on to suggest that delinquents tend to drift into crime when available **techniques of neutralization** combine with weak or ineffective values espoused by the controlling elements in society. In effect, said Matza, the delinquent "drifts between criminal and conventional action," choosing whichever is the more expedient at the time. By employing techniques of neutralization, delinquents need not be fully alienated from the larger society. When opportunities for crime present themselves, such techniques provide an effective way of overcoming feelings of guilt and of allowing for ease of action. Matza used the phrase "soft determinism" to describe drift, saying that delinquents are neither forced to make choices because of fateful experiences early in life, nor are they entirely free to make choices unencumbered by the realities of their situation.

More recent studies have found that whereas "only a small percentage of adolescents generally approve of violence or express indifference to violence . . . [a] large percentage of adolescents . . . accept neutralizations justifying the use of violence in particular situations."[63] The acceptance of such justifications by many young people today is seen as supporting high levels of adolescent violence. Studies have also found that young people who disapprove of violence but associate with delinquent peers often use neutralization techniques as justifications for violence in which they personally engage.[64]

Hard-core, active, noninstitutionalized drug dealers, street robbers, and carjackers have also been found to use neutralization techniques.[65] Similarly, sociologist Ken Levi found that professional contract killers, or hit-men, tend to begin their careers by adapting to the role of professional killer by learning to view killing as "just a job" or as "just business."[66] This allows them to deny responsibility for contracted killings, and to view themselves as "hired guns," and their victims as "targets" rather than people.

A 2003 study by sociologist Lois Presser of the University of Tennessee of remorse and neutralization among violent male offenders was based on interviews with 27 men who had committed serious violent crimes.[67] Presser found that the men excused or justified their violent actions through rationalizations including beliefs that (1) victims were to blame for harms that resulted from provoking the offender, (2) victims were themselves offenders or deserving of harm, (3) harm to a victim that was not premeditated or intended carried no blame, (4) the legal sanctioning of an offender negated any harm, and (5) harms to the offender and his family stemming from the crime negated any harms caused by the offender.

In innovative research published in 2008, Orly Turgeman-Goldschmidt of Israel's Bar-Ilan University conducted 54 unstructured, in-depth, face-to-face interviews with malicious Israeli computer vandals (crackers) in order to determine what kinds of neutralization techniques they might employ. Torgeman-Goldschmidt[68] found that the crackers used neutralization techniques common to other offenders, although the language in which these techniques were couched reflected the cyber-realm. Some hackers were found to be like political criminals, and assumed responsibility for their acts by means of internal justifications (that is, by attacking Al-Qaeda Web sites or bringing down the computers of the Arab news network Al-Jazeera, and seeing the activity as a positive contribution to their sociopolitical environment). These "hacktivists" as he called some of those in the study, defined themselves as hackers with political consciences.[69] Other hackers justified illegal hacking as simply being fun, rewarding, or self-fulfilling, and argued that anyone affected (that is, financial institutions) "can afford it." Turgeman-Goldschmidt also notes that hacking is the kind of crime in which a hacker might find it easy to deny responsibility because no physical harm seems to have occurred.

Violent Subcultures

Some subcultures are decidedly violent and are built around violent themes and around values supporting violent activities. In 1967, **Franco Ferracuti** and **Marvin Wolfgang** published their seminal work, *The Subculture of Violence: Toward an Integrated Theory of Criminology*,[70] which drew together many of the sociological perspectives previously advanced to explain delinquency and crime. According to some writers, the work of Ferracuti and Wolfgang "was substantively different from the other subculture theories, perhaps because it was developed almost a decade after delinquent-subculture theories and criminology had developed new concerns."[71] Ferracuti and Wolfgang's main thesis was that violence is a learned form of adaptation to certain problematic life circumstances and that learning to be violent takes place within the context of a subcultural milieu that emphasizes the advantages of violence over other forms of adaptation. Such subcultures are characterized by songs and stories that glorify violence, by gun ownership, and by rituals that tend to stress macho models. They are likely to teach that a quick and decisive response to insults is necessary to preserve one's prestige within the group. Subcultural group members have a proclivity for fighting as a means of settling disputes. Subcultures of violence both expect violence from their members and legitimize it when it occurs. In the words of Ferracuti and Wolfgang, "The use of violence . . . is not necessarily viewed as illicit conduct, and the users do not have to deal with feelings of guilt about their aggression."[72] In other words, for participants in violent subcultures, violence can be a way of life.

Ferracuti and Wolfgang based their conclusions on an analysis of data that showed substantial differences in the rates of homicides between racial groups in the Philadelphia area. At the time of their study, nonwhite men had a homicide rate of 41.7 per 100,000 versus a homicide rate of only 3.4 for white men. Statistics on nonwhite women showed a homicide rate of 9.3 versus 0.4 for white women. Explaining these findings, Ferracuti and Wolfgang tell us, "Homicide is most prevalent, or the highest rates of homicide occur, among a relatively homogeneous subcultural group in any large urban community. . . . The value system of this group, as we are contending, constitutes a subculture of violence. From a psychological viewpoint, we might hypothesize that the greater the degree of integration of the individual into this subculture, the higher the probability that his behavior will be violent in a variety of situations."[73]

Ferracuti and Wolfgang extend their theory of subcultural violence with the following "corollary propositions":[74]

- No subculture can be totally different from or totally in conflict with the society of which it is a part.

- To establish the existence of a subculture of violence does not require that the actors sharing in these basic value elements should express violence in all situations.

- The potential resort or willingness to resort to violence in a variety of situations emphasizes the penetrating and diffusive character of this culture theme.

- The subcultural ethos of violence may be shared by all ages in a subsociety, but this ethos is most prominent in a limited age group, ranging from late adolescence to middle age.

- The counternorm is nonviolence.

- The development of favorable attitudes toward violence and its use in a subculture usually involves learned behavior and a process of differential learning, association, or identification.

- The use of violence in a subculture is not necessarily viewed as illicit conduct, and the users therefore do not have to deal with feelings of guilt about their aggression.

Other writers have commented on geographic distinctions among violent subcultures in different parts of the United States. A body of criminological literature exists, for example, that claims that certain forms of criminal violence are more acceptable in the southern United States than in northern portions of the country.[75] Some writers have also referred to variability in the degree to which interpersonal violence has been accepted in the South over time, whereas others have suggested that violence in the South might be a traditional tool in the service of social order.[76] Without at least a modicum of expressive violence, such as lynchings, dueling, and outright fighting, these authors suggest, southern social solidarity following the Civil War might have been seriously threatened. In short, the notion of a "southern violence construct" holds that an "infernal trinity of Southerner, violence and weaponry"[77] may make crimes like homicide and assault more culturally acceptable in the South than in other parts of the country.

In 1998, James W. Clarke, a political science professor at the University of Arizona, advanced the notion that the high rate of black underclass homicide in the United States flows from a black subculture of violence created by generations of white-on-black violence that first emerged with the "generation of black males that came of age after emancipation."[78] According to Clarke, many black males learn from earlier generations to seek status through their ability to "harm, intimidate, and dominate others."[79]

Clarke traces the roots of white-on-black violence to the arrival of the first African slaves in America in the seventeenth century. He draws upon slave narratives, plantation documents, interviews with former slaves conducted by the Works Progress Administration, the Tuskegee Institute—NAACP files on lynching, historical state documents on convict labor, the testimony of victims of the Ku Klux Klan, and the Department of Justice's Peonage Files to document the black experience with violence in the United States. Clarke concludes that reforms built around social programs intent on alleviating joblessness and improving education cannot eliminate the violent subculture of the black underclass because the subculture shared by members of that group lacks the conventional values needed for such reforms to succeed. The culture of violence, Clarke argues, can be eliminated only through an emphasis on discipline and family structure.

In an interesting aside that further illustrates how violent subcultural norms are transmitted from generation to generation, Virginia Demery, 41, the mother of Larry Martin Demery, one of the men arrested and charged with killing Michael Jordan's father in North Carolina in the early 1990s, was convicted of using a shotgun in an assault on reporters who went to her mobile home following her son's arrest. Although no one was injured in the incident, reporters who brought criminal charges against her later said that members of the news media should be able to "expect a general amount of civility when they go to interview someone."[80] Ms. Demery gave reporters until the count of five to leave her property, but the gun discharged, accidentally she claimed, at the count of two.

The wider culture often recognizes, sometimes begrudgingly and sometimes matter-of-factly, a violent subculture's internal rules. Hence, when one member of such a subculture kills another, the wider society may take the killing less "seriously" than if someone outside the subculture had been killed. As a consequence of this realization, Franklin Zimring and his associates described what they called "wholesale" and "retail" costs for homicide, in which killings that are perceived to occur within a subculture of violence (when both the victim and the perpetrator are seen as members of a violent subculture) generally result in a less harsh punishment than do killings that occur outside of the subculture.[81] Punishments, said Zimring, relate to the perceived seriousness of the offense, and if members of the subculture within which a crime occurs accept the offense as part of the landscape, so, too, will members of the wider culture, which imposes official sanctions on the perpetrator.

Differential Opportunity Theory

In 1960, **Richard A. Cloward** and **Lloyd E. Ohlin** published *Delinquency and Opportunity*.[82] Their book, a report on the nature and activities of juvenile gangs, blended the subcultural thesis with ideas derived from strain theory. Cloward and Ohlin identified two types of socially structured opportunities for success: illegitimate and legitimate. They observed that whereas legitimate opportunities are generally available to individuals born into middle-class culture, participants in lower-class subcultures are often denied access to them. As a consequence, illegitimate opportunities for success are often seen as quite acceptable by participants in so-called illegitimate subcultures.

Cloward and Ohlin used the term **illegitimate opportunity structure** to describe pre-existing subcultural paths to success that are not approved of by the wider culture. Where illegitimate paths to success are not already in place, alienated individuals may undertake a process of ideational evolution through which "a collective delinquent solution" or a "delinquent means of achieving success" may be decided upon by members of a gang. Because the two paths to success, legitimate and illegitimate, differ in their availability to members of society, Cloward and Ohlin's perspective has been called "differential opportunity."

illegitimate opportunity structure

Subcultural pathways to success that the wider society disapproves of.

According to Cloward and Ohlin, delinquent behavior may result from the ready availability of illegitimate opportunities and the effective replacement of the norms of the wider culture with expedient subcultural rules. Hence, delinquency and criminality may become "all right," or legitimate, in the eyes of gang members and may even form the criteria used by other subcultural participants to judge successful accomplishments. In the words of Cloward and Ohlin, "A delinquent subculture is one in which certain forms of delinquent activity are essential requirements for the performance of the dominant roles supported by the subculture."[83] Its "most crucial elements" are the "prescriptions, norms, or rules of conduct that define the activities required of a full-fledged member."[84] "A person attributes legitimacy to a system of rules and corresponding models of behavior," wrote Cloward and Ohlin, "when he accepts them as binding on his conduct."[85] "Delinquents have withdrawn their support from established norms and invested officially forbidden forms of conduct with a claim to legitimacy."[86]

Cloward and Ohlin noted that a delinquent act can be "defined by two essential elements: it is behavior that violates basic norms of the society, and, when officially known, it evokes a judgment by agents of criminal justice that such norms have been violated."[87] For Cloward and Ohlin, however, crime and deviance are just as normal as any other form of behavior supported by group socialization. In their words, "Deviance and conformity generally result from the same kinds of social conditions," and "deviance ordinarily represents a search for solutions to problems of adjustment." In their view, deviance is just as much an effort to conform, albeit to subcultural norms and expectations, as is conformity to the norms of the wider society. They added, however, that "it has been our experience that most persons who participate in delinquent subcultures, if not lone offenders, are fully aware of the difference between right and wrong, between conventional behavior and rule-violating behavior. They may not care about the difference, or they may enjoy flouting the rules of the game, or they may have decided that illegitimate practices get them what they want more efficiently than legitimate practices."[88]

Cloward and Ohlin described three types of delinquent subcultures: (1) criminal subcultures, in which criminal role models are readily available for adoption by those being socialized into the subculture; (2) conflict subcultures, in which participants seek status through violence; and (3) retreatist subcultures, where drug use and withdrawal from the wider society predominate. Each subculture is thought to emerge from a larger, all-encompassing "parent" subculture of delinquent values. According to Cloward and Ohlin, delinquent subcultures have at least three identifiable features: (1) "acts of delinquency that reflect subcultural support are likely to recur with great frequency," (2) "access to a successful adult criminal career sometimes results from participation in a delinquent subculture," and (3) "the delinquent subculture imparts to the conduct of its members a high degree of stability and resistance to control or change."[89]

Cloward and Ohlin divided lower-class youth into four types, according to their degree of commitment to middle-class values and material achievement. Type I youths were said to desire entry to the middle class via improvement in their economic position. Type II youths were seen as desiring entry to the middle class but not improvement in their economic position. Type III youths were portrayed as desiring wealth without entry to the middle class. As a consequence, Type III youths were seen as the most crime-prone. Type IV youths were described as dropouts who retreated from the cultural mainstream through drug and alcohol use.

Cloward and Ohlin had substantial impact on American social policy through the sponsorship of David Hackett, President John F. Kennedy's head of the newly created Committee on Juvenile Delinquency and Youth Crime. Out of the relationship between the theorists and Hackett, the Mobilization for Youth program, established under the auspices of the 1961 Juvenile Delinquency Prevention and Control Act, was begun in 1962 with $12.5 million in initial funding.[90] Mobilization for Youth, a delinquency prevention program based on Cloward and Ohlin's opportunity theory, created employment and educational opportunities for deprived youths.

Reaction Formation

Another criminologist whose work is often associated with both strain theory and the subcultural perspective is **Albert Cohen.** Like Cloward and Ohlin, Cohen's work focused primarily on the gang behavior of delinquent youth. In Cohen's words, "When we speak of a delinquent subculture, we speak of a way of life that has somehow become traditional among certain groups in American society. These groups are the boys' gangs that flourish most conspicuously in the 'delinquency neighborhoods' of our larger American cities. The members of these gangs grow up, some to become law-abiding citizens and others to graduate to more professional and adult forms of criminality, but the delinquent tradition is kept alive by the age-groups that succeed them."[91]

Cohen argued that youngsters from all backgrounds are generally held accountable to the norms of the wider society through a "middle-class measuring rod" of expectations related to school performance, language proficiency, cleanliness, punctuality, neatness, nonviolent behavior, and allegiance to other similar standards. Like strain theorists, Cohen noted that unfortunately not everyone is prepared, by virtue of the circumstances surrounding his or her birth and subsequent socialization, for effectively meeting such expectations.

In an examination of vandalism, Cohen found that "nonutilitarian" delinquency, in which things of value are destroyed rather than stolen or otherwise used for financial gain, is the result of middle-class values turned upside down.[92] Delinquent youths, argued Cohen, who are often alienated from middle-class values and lifestyles through deprivation and limited opportunities, can achieve status among their subcultural peers via vandalism and other forms of delinquent behavior.

Children, especially those from deprived backgrounds, turn to delinquency, Cohen claimed, because they experience status frustration when judged by adults and others according to middle-class standards and goals, which they are unable to achieve. Because it is nearly impossible for nonmainstream children to succeed in middle-class terms, they may overcome anxiety through the process of reaction formation, in which hostility toward middle-class values develops. Cohen adapted **reaction formation** from psychiatric perspectives and used it to mean "the process in which a person openly rejects that which he wants, or aspires to, but cannot obtain or achieve."[93]

Cohen discovered the roots of delinquent subcultures in what he termed the "collective solution to the problem of status."[94] When youths who experience the same kind of alienation from middle-class ideals band together, they achieve a collective and independent solution and create a delinquent subculture. Cohen wrote, "The delinquent subculture, we suggest, is a way of dealing with the problems of adjustment. . . . These problems are chiefly status problems: certain children are denied status in the respectable society because they cannot meet the criteria of the respectable status system. The delinquent subculture deals with these problems by providing criteria of status which these children can meet."[95]

Cohen's approach is effectively summarized in a "theoretical scenario" offered by Donald J. Shoemaker, who says that lower-class youths undergo a working-class socialization that combines lower-class values and habits with middle-class success values.[96] Lower-class youth then experience failure in school because they cannot live up to the middle-class norms operative in American educational institutions. They suffer a consequent loss of self-esteem and increased feelings of rejection, leading to their dropping out of school and associating with delinquent peers. Hostility and resentment toward middle-class standards grow through reaction formation. Finally, such alienated youths achieve status and a sense of improved self-worth through participation in a gang of like-minded peers. Delinquency and crime are the result.

reaction formation

The process by which a person openly rejects that which he or she wants or aspires to but cannot obtain or achieve.

The Code of the Street

Recent work by Elijah Anderson, a University of Pennsylvania sociology professor, offers a contemporary subcultural ethnography that details the social mores that operate in some American inner cities today. Anderson studied African American neighborhoods along Philadelphia's Germantown Avenue and published the results of his findings in a 1990 book entitled *The Code of the Street*.[97] In *Code*, Anderson details aspects of contemporary street code that stress a hyperinflated notion of manhood that rests squarely on the idea of respect. "At the heart of the code is the issue of respect," says Anderson, "loosely defined as being treated 'right' or being granted one's 'props' (or proper due) or the deference one deserves." In street culture, a man's sense of worth is determined by the respect he commands when in public. The violent nature of street subculture, however, means that a man cannot back down from threats—no matter how serious they may be. Working-class African American families place high value on the man as head of the household, and he is expected to be a provider and strict disciplinarian. Economic and social circumstances, however, conspire to limit opportunities for legitimate success—driving many families to alternative means of making money. Men who are not able to live up to the role of provider tend to abandon their mates and their children and may then move through a series of unsuccessful relationships.

A crucial distinction between both families and individuals in inner-city neighborhoods like Germantown can be expressed as what Anderson calls the "decent family" and the "street family." "Decent" and "street" are labels that residents themselves use, says Anderson, and they mark people as either trying to uphold positive values or being oriented toward the street. Street life, he says, involves displays of physical strength and intellectual prowess meant to demonstrate that "I can take care of myself" and "I can take care of my own." Those who wholeheartedly embrace the street code are proud to live the "thug life" and identify with role models like Tupac Shakur and Snoop Doggy Dogg. A street orientation, says Anderson, means that people and situations

Who's to Blame—The Individual or Society?

Like Father, Like Son

Reginald Barfield, 22, was arrested for DUI (alcohol) and taken to jail. A judge set bail at $500, and his mother came to the jail to post bond for her son. She didn't have much money, so she used the services of a bondsman who charged her a $70 fee and arranged for Reginald's release. As she drove her son home, she began yelling at him, telling him that he had turned out just like his father, who had had a long-standing problem with alcohol.

"You're just like your father," she said. "And if you don't change, you'll end up just like him—dead."

Reginald became angry and blurted out that he drank because that was all he had known as a child.

"What do you mean?" his mother asked.

"Whenever dad had a problem, or when you two fought," Reginald said, "dad broke open a bottle and killed the pain. It worked for him. It works for me. So, you're right, I'm just like him. But it's not my fault. I learned it from him. You didn't stop him. And you didn't stop me."

Think about it:

1. Is Reginald right; did he learn his problem behavior from his father? What other factors might have contributed to his excessive use of alcohol?

2. Might the concept of reaction formation help explain Reginald's behavior? If so, how?

3. If you were Reginald's mother, to what degree would you hold your son responsible for his problem drinking behavior? To what degree would you hold him responsible if you were a judge hearing his case in court?

4. Are questions about responsibility merely exercises in blame-shifting? Is blame-shifting ever appropriate when assessing criminal responsibility?

become obstacles to be overcome or subdued. Hence, individuals who are street-wise learn to outsmart or "hustle" others while avoiding being hustled themselves.

Gangs Today

Gangs have become a major source of concern in contemporary American society. Although the writings of investigators like Cohen, Thrasher, and Cloward and Ohlin focused on the illicit activities of juvenile gangs in the nation's inner cities, most gang-related crimes of the period involved vandalism, petty theft, and battles over turf. The ethnic distinctions that gave rise to gang culture in the 1920s through the 1950s are today largely forgotten. Italian, Hungarian, Polish, and Jewish immigrants, whose children made up many of the early gangs, have been, for the most part, successfully integrated into the society that is modern America.

Today's gangs are quite different from the gangs of the first half of the twentieth century. In the 2004 National Youth Gang Center (NYGC) survey—a survey that is conducted annually by the Office of Juvenile Justice and Delinquency Prevention—2,296 law enforcement agencies responded to requests for information about gang activity in their communities.[98] Eighty percent of agencies serving a population of 50,000 or more reported gang-related problems in their areas, while only 12% of rural agencies reported such problems. Based on survey results, the NYGC estimates that approximately 760,000 gang members and 24,000 gangs were active in the United States in 2004.

In responding to the 2004 NYGC survey, 173 big city law enforcement agencies (that is, those serving populations of 100,000 or more) reported a gang problem along with gang homicide data. In two cities, Los Angeles and Chicago, more than half of all homicides were thought to be gang-related. Moreover, the number of gang homicides reported in those cities in 2004 was 11% higher than the previous eight-year average.

The 2004 NYGC survey confirmed previous findings that gang members are often involved in a variety of serious and violent crimes. Almost half of the law enforcement agencies reporting gang problems are involved in collaborative efforts with other law enforcement and criminal justice agencies to combat youth gangs and the serious and violent crimes they commit.

In addition to conducting the National Youth Gang Surveys, the NYGC provides a compilation of gang-related legislation, maintains a repository of gang-related literature,

Profiles in Crime

Sanyika Shakur, aka Monster Kody Scott

It is tempting to rely on Sanyika Shakur's compelling autobiography, *Monster: The Autobiography of an L.A. Gang Member,* as the primary reference for this box. But while much of the material is drawn from his memoir—as Shakur is undeniably the world's expert on his alter ego Monster Kody Scott—there is more to this story than can be gleaned from his own writings.

Shakur repeatedly justifies brutal assaults he has committed as being the only reasonable solution "[w]hen the police and other government agencies don't seem to care about what is going on in our communities, . . . [and] those of us who live in them must take responsibility for their protection and maintenance."[i] Yet he also chillingly recounts other assaults, and even murders, as being a form of self-administered therapy to relieve his tensions from such terrible pressures as his mother telling him she disapproved of his lawless lifestyle and use of drugs.

For example, he describes his need "to shoot somebody, eager to vent my anger," after being scolded by his mother for his criminality and marijuana use. This need, he relates, compelled the then 16-year-old Shakur to leave the house and go on the prowl on a bicycle, looking for a suitable victim or victims on whom to "vent." Upon encountering "three cats who looked about my age leaning against a van, talking and drinking beer," and coming to the conclusion that they were "enemies," he circled past them and opened fire with a .45-caliber pistol. After leaving one victim lying "motionless in the street," Shakur describes returning to his home, where he "put the bike in the garage . . . went to my room . . . [and] fell asleep. I slept very well."[ii]

Born in the tumultuous 1960s (1963), 11-year-old Kody Scott (he adopted the name Sanyika Shakur in prison some years later) earned initiation into the infamous Crips street gang—and into a life of persistently violent criminal conduct—with eight blasts from a shotgun at a group of the notorious Bloods, a rival gang. His teen years were an odyssey of violent crime, interspersed with repeated stays in various juvenile detention centers and, ultimately, the California State Penitentiary.

Sanyika Shakur (born Kody Scott), aka "Monster Kody," is photographed at Pelican Bay prison in June 1993 through Plexiglas. The gangster thug of the literary set was arrested again in 2007 on the porch of a south-central Los Angeles home while signing autographs for his fans. He is alleged to have beaten a man and stolen his car while out on parole. Is Shakur a villain or a hero?

Source: AP Wide World Photos/Susan Ragan

His "Monster" moniker came from one such crime. After robbing and beating a man, the victim had the audacity to strike Shakur in the face. In retaliation, Shakur further "beat him, and stomped him and disfigured him," leaving the young man in a coma.[iii] The severity of the damage caused one investigating police officer to opine that whoever had done the beating was a monster. Shakur decided to adopt the name later that night when he saw the looks on the faces of the people in his neighborhood. "[I]t was just power," he says, proudly. "And I felt it. And I just took that name."[iv]

Feared even by his fellow Crips, Shakur rose through the gang's leadership ranks until he eventually became one of its top leaders and achieved status as an Original Gangster (O.G.), the highest "honor" a gang member can receive. Throughout his autobiography, Shakur speaks with pride of committing his crimes out of an honor-bound "duty" to stand with his fellow Crips. To his way of thinking, adherence to the code of the gang justifiably trumps social prohibitions against killing and maiming—as long as one does so for the purpose of supporting the criminal activities of one's fellow lawbreakers.

Shakur also shrouds his behavior in a cloak of inevitability, asserting that there are no other options available to him and those like him by which they can achieve success within the legitimate American social system. He "portrays himself as the inevitable product of a hellish environment."[v] He speaks out against what he perceives as a contrived systematic mechanism for preventing minorities from advancement, and gives one the sense that he is attempting to create a Robin Hood-esque mystique about his criminality.

Shakur has been dubbed an "iconic figure" of the hip-hop culture by independent filmmaker Billy Wright, who further asserts that Shakur's "real life encapsulates what hip hop imagery is all about."[vi] Wright's current project, entitled *Can't Stop, Won't Stop,* tells the story of Shakur's life. Wright describes the film as a "tribute" to close friend Shakur.

In December 2006, already a fugitive for numerous parole violations (he was, at the time, out on parole from yet another term in the California State Penitentiary), Shakur allegedly broke into a man's home and beat him in order to steal the victim's car. Arrested for the offense on March 7, 2007, Shakur now faces a possible life sentence without the possibility of parole as a persistent felon, under California's "three strikes" law.[vii]

Notes:

[i] Sanyika Shakur, *Monster: The Autobiography of an L.A. Gang Member* (New York: Grove Press, 2004) reprint edition, p. 379.

[ii] Ibid, pp. 173–174.

[iii] Mandalit Del Barco, "Gang Member Turned Author Arrested in L.A.," *Morning Edition.* National Public Radio. March 9, 2007, http://www.npr.org/templates/story/story.php?storyId=7793148 (accessed July 14, 2007).

[iv] Ibid.

[v] Mark Horowitz, "In Search of a Monster," *Atlantic Monthly,* December 1993, http://www.theatlantic.com/doc/199312/monster (accessed July 14, 2007).

[vi] "America's O. G. Gangster—Monster Kody (aka Sanyika Shakur)." RapIndustry.com. 2007. Available at http://www.rapindustry.com/monster_cody.htm. Accessed September 14, 2007.

[vii] Del Barco.

Source: USA TODAY, October 23, 2006. Reprinted with permission.

WEB
Extra
■ ■ ■ ■

analyzes gang-related data and statistics, and coordinates the activities of the Youth Gang Consortium. You can visit the NYGC via **Web Extra 7–7.** Another group of special interest to anyone wanting to know more about gangs is the National Alliance of Gang Investigators Associations. Visit the Alliance via **Web Extra 7–8.**

Although its data are older than data available through the NYGC, the National Gang Crime Research Center's Project Gangfact provides a profile of gangs and gang members nationwide. The latest Gangfact report, based on data collected by 28 researchers in 17 states, found the following:[99]

- The average age for joining a gang, nationally, is 12.8 years of age.
- Over half who joined gangs have tried to quit.
- More than two-thirds of gangs have written rules for members to follow.
- Over half of all gangs hold regular weekly meetings.
- Nearly 30% of gangs require their members to pay dues.
- Approximately 55% of gang members were recruited by other gang members, while the remainder sought out gang membership.
- Most gang members (79%) said they would leave the gang if given a "second chance in life."
- Four-fifths of gang members reported that their gangs sold crack cocaine.
- Most gangs (70%) are not racially exclusive and consist of members drawn from a variety of ethnic groups.
- One-third of gang members report that they have been able to conceal their gang membership from their parents.
- Most gangs (83%) report having female members, but few allow female members to assume leadership roles.
- Many gang members (40%) report knowing male members of their gangs who had raped females.

Members of modern youth gangs generally identify with a name (such as the "Crips" and "Bloods," which are well-known Los Angeles–area gangs), a particular style of clothing, symbols, tattoos, jewelry, haircuts, and hand symbols.

Gangs can be big business. In addition to traditional criminal activities like burglary, extortion, vandalism, and protection rackets, drug dealing has become a mainstay of many inner-city gangs. Los Angeles police estimate that at least four city gangs earn over $1 million each per week through cocaine sales.[100] The potential for huge drug-based profits appears to have changed the nature of gangs themselves, making them more prone toward violence and cutthroat tactics. Gang killings, including the now-infamous drive-by shootings, have become commonplace in our nation's cities.

Rodney Dailey, a self-avowed former Boston-area drug dealer and gun-wielding gang member, says that in today's gang world, "shoot before you get shot is the rule." According to Dailey, "Things that normally people would have had fist-fights about can get you shot or stabbed" today.[101] Dailey is the founder of Gang Peace, an outreach group that tries to reduce gang-related violence.

Guns have become a way of life for many young gang members. As a young man named Jamaal, hanging around with friends outside Boston's Orchard Park housing project, recently put it, "We don't fight, we shoot." Police in the area describe how values among youth have changed over the past decade or two. Today they "think it's fun to pop someone," they say.[102]

Contemporary researchers, however, are drawing some new distinctions between gangs and violence. Some years ago, G. David Curry and Irving A. Spergel, in a study of Chicago communities, distinguished between juvenile delinquency and gang-related homicide.[103] They found that communities characterized by high rates of delinquency do not necessarily experience exceptionally high rates of crime or of gang-related homicides. They concluded that although gang activity may be associated with homicide, "gang homicide rates and delinquency rates are ecologically distinct community

> "I sit back and think, God left me here for a reason. He has something planned for me."
>
> Jahmol A. Norfleet
> December 5, 1985 - November 28, 2006

Teah Norfleet, flanked by Miniard Culpepper, right, and the Rev. Ray Hammond, attends an event announcing a fund to honor the memory of her brother Jahmol, shown on the poster. Jahmol Norfleet, a former gang leader, was shot in the head as he worked to preserve a gang truce in Boston's Roxbury neighborhood. Why do people join gangs?

Source: Republished with permission of Globe Newspaper Company, Inc., from the March 6th issue of The Boston Globe, © 2007.

problems." Gang-related homicide, they found, seems to be well explained by classical theories of social disorganization and is especially prevalent in areas of the city characterized by in-migration and by the "settlement of new immigrant groups." In their study, high rates of juvenile delinquency seemed to correlate more with poverty, which the researchers defined as "social adaptation to chronic deprivation." According to Curry and Spergel, "Social disorganization and poverty rather than criminal organization and conspiracy may better explain the recent growth and spread of youth gangs to many parts of the country. Moreover, community organization and social opportunity in conjunction with suppression, rather than simply suppression and incapacitation, may be more effective policies in dealing with the social problem."[104] In proposing a national gang strategy, Finn-Aage Esbensen reminds policymakers that many gang members are delinquent before they become associated with gangs.[105] Esbensen says that "concerns with gang suppression should not supplant efforts to implement effective delinquency intervention and prevention strategies."[106]

The concept of *co-offending* refers to the fact that youthful offenders tend to commit crimes in the company of their peers. Co-offending is especially prevalent in the lives of gang members. Research has shown that about 40 percent of juvenile offenders commit most of their crimes with others. Co-offenders are also more likely than solo offenders to be recidivists. When young co-offenders are compared with young solo offenders, only the co-offenders have high recidivism rates and only the co-offenders commit high numbers of violent crimes. In a 2005 study of co-offending, Temple University Professor Joan McCord found that violence appears to be learned in the company of others. McCord and fellow researchers, in a report produced with grant support from the National Institute of Justice, found that "Co-offending actually may increase the likelihood that offenders will commit violent crimes. When young offenders affiliate with offenders who have previously used violence, the result appears to be an increase in the likelihood that they will subsequently commit a violent crime." This suggests, they said "that young offenders pick up attitudes and values from their companions." Learn more about gangs from Professor Mike Carlie's online book, *Into the Abyss* via **Library Extra 7–2**, and read a report on co-offending at **Library Extra 7–3** at crimtoday.com.

LIBRARY
Extra
■ ■ ■ ■

Crime in the News

Gangs Taking Toll on Gem Sellers

FBI and local police are teaming up to combat a little noted but highly lucrative crime: robberies by gangs that target traveling jewelry and precious gem sales representatives.

Jewelry and gem salespersons reported 117 such robberies nationwide in the first nine months of this year, putting the industry on track for its lowest number of annual attacks since about 1990, according to a report by the industry group Jewelers' Security Alliance (JSA).

However, ripping off sales reps, who typically travel by car and carry hundreds of thousands of dollars worth of goods in small pieces of rolling luggage, remains a highly lucrative crime. The average theft this year has netted about $224,000. By contrast, the average bank robbery netted about $4,220 in 2004, the FBI estimated.

"It's a crime that's below the radar, and doesn't get nearly the attention of say, bank robbery," says John Kennedy, president of the JSA. "But in the past 10 years or so, it's become a fact of life for an industry where it had pretty much been unknown."

Interrogations of captured robbers have shown that most are illegal immigrants, usually Colombian or Ecuadorean, who have worked their way up in ethnic gangs by performing less serious robberies, says Daniel McCaffrey, an FBI agent in New York City who specializes in jewel theft.

After 1999, when sales reps endured a record 323 robberies and more than $76 million in losses, the FBI began to partner with local police task forces in New York City, Los Angeles, Houston, Miami and other jewel theft hot spots. Using stakeouts, stings and other methods, they've helped boost arrests and lower dollar losses each year since 2000. Figures kept by the Jewelers' Security Alliance show local, state and federal arrests increased 25%, from 456 in 2003 to 570 in 2004. Those included crimes against retailers as well as sales reps.

The targeting of traveling jewelry and gem salespeople has taken a toll on the trade.

Joseph Menzie, a former traveling salesman who is now a gem wholesaler in New York City, estimates that sales reps, who once

An armed robbery in progress. How might this victim have contributed to his own victimization?

Source: Brand X Pictures/Alamy Images

Policy Implications of Social Structure Theories

Theoretical approaches that fault social structure as the root cause of crime point in the direction of social action as a panacea. In the 1930s, for example, Clifford Shaw, in an effort to put his theories into practice, established the **Chicago Area Project.** Through the Chicago Area Project, Shaw sought to reduce delinquency in transitional neighborhoods. Shaw analyzed oral histories gathered from neighborhood citizens to determine that delinquents were essentially normal youngsters who entered into illegal activities at early ages, often through street play. Hence, he worked to increase opportunities for young people to embark on successful work careers.

The Chicago Area Project attempted to reduce social disorganization in slum neighborhoods through the creation of community committees. Shaw staffed these committees with local residents rather than professional social workers. The project had three broad objectives: (1) improving the physical appearance of poor neighborhoods, (2) providing recreational opportunities for youths, and (3) involving project members directly in the lives of troubled youths through school and courtroom mediation. The program also made use of "curbside counselors," street-wise workers who could serve as positive role models for inner-city youth. Although no effective assessment programs were

Chicago Area Project

A program focusing on urban ecology and originating at the University of Chicago during the 1930s, which attempted to reduce delinquency, crime, and social disorganization in transitional neighborhoods.

numbered in the thousands, now are down to about 600 to 800 full-time workers and declining each year. About 15% are women, he estimates.

"It used to be a great job for a young guy," Menzie says. "But now, forget it. Nobody young is coming in, and a lot of the old guys would get out if they could. . . . All of them have been hit (by robbers)."

When Menzie started in the mid-1970s, representing his grandfather's gem company out of New York City, going on the road to sell was a time-honored way of breaking into the jewelry business. The job featured travel, fellowship with other sales reps, and some prestige. Commissions of 4% to 15% afforded a decent living.

Because of the nature of their product, jewel and gem reps seemingly were impervious to changes that the Internet brought to the sales industry.

"The customer wants to hold the piece in her hand, so the retailer wants to see it and feel it, too," Menzie says. "That's where the salesman comes in."

Sales reps kept their product line of diamonds, watches, finished jewelry and gemstones such as emeralds and sapphires in small off-the-rack travel cases. They formed groups such as the Brotherhood of Traveling Salesmen, which collected annual dues and passed the hat when a sales rep died on the road to pay for return shipping of both the body and the product line.

Crime was an occasional problem. In more than 10 years on the road, Menzie remembers being followed once, on a freeway in Alabama. He eluded the chase car and found refuge at a small town police station.

For reasons that aren't clear, Ecuadorean and Colombian gangs began to target sales reps, FBI agent McCaffrey says.

They use Mapquest, Global Positioning System devices, cellphones, and telephone and property databases to identify and follow sales reps. It's not unusual for 20 or more crewmembers using several cars to follow prospective "scores" for days or weeks, McCaffrey says.

Some of the thieves' favorite methods, says McCaffrey, who has interviewed captured robbers, include:

- Cutting brake lines or spiking tires on a sales rep's car, then trailing him until he breaks down.
- Breaking into the parked car while the salesman is having coffee.
- Surprising the sales rep as he leaves his motel or home.

The robberies, which have netted nearly $600 million since 1995, according to the JSA, are forcing changes in the industry. Manufacturers and wholesalers, beset with rising insurance premiums, increasingly are using large trade shows to reach retailers. Reps who continue to travel carry more product, to compensate for higher gas and hotel costs.

In a sure sign of the times, the Brotherhood of Traveling Salesmen disbanded about a year ago, Menzie notes. The group, which dated from the 1930s, was down to about 100 members and had few new applicants. Those who remained, Menzie says, decided to cash out the group's account and get a check now rather than wait for each other to die off.

Discussion Questions

1. Why have gangs started targeting gem sales representatives?

2. What kinds of changes in the gem industry can be expected as a result of the kinds of crimes described in this article?

Source: Richard Willing, "Gangs Take Toll on Traveling Gem Sellers," *USA Today*, October 23, 2006. p. 3A, http://www.usatoday.com/printedition/news/20061023/a_insidejewels23.art.htm. Reprinted by permission.

For the latest crime and justice news, visit www.crimenews.info.

established to evaluate the Chicago Area Project during the program's tenure, in 1984 Rand Corporation reviewers published a 50-year review of the program, declaring it "effective in reducing rates of juvenile delinquency."[107]

Similarly, Mobilization for Youth, cited earlier in this chapter as an outgrowth of Cloward and Ohlin's theory of differential opportunity, provides a bold example of the treatment implications of social structure theories. Mobilization for Youth sought not only to provide new opportunities, but also through direct social action to change the fundamental arrangements of society and thereby address the root causes of crime and deviance. Leaders of Mobilization for Youth decided that "what was needed to overcome . . . formidable barriers to opportunity . . . was not community organization but community action" that attacked entrenched political interests. Accordingly, the program promoted "boycotts against schools, protests against welfare policies, rent strikes against 'slum landlords,' lawsuits to ensure poor people's rights, and voter registration."[108] A truly unusual government-sponsored program for its time, Mobilization for Youth was eventually disbanded amid protests that "the mandate of the President's Committee was to reduce delinquency, not to reform urban society or to try out sociological theories on American youths."[109]

The War on Poverty declared by the Kennedy and Johnson administrations during the 1960s and subsequent federal and state-run welfare programs that provide supplemental income assistance have been cited[110] as examples of programs that at least held the potential to reduce crime rates by redistributing wealth in American society.[111]

Such programs, however, have come under increasing fire recently, and the federal Welfare Reform Reconciliation Act of 1996[112] reduced or eliminated long-term benefits that had previously been available through avenues like the federal Aid to Families with Dependent Children (AFDC) program. The 1996 legislation also established stricter work requirements for welfare recipients through a new Welfare-to-Work program under the Personal Responsibility and Work Opportunity Reconciliation Act of 1996.[113]

Critique of Social Structure Theories

The fundamental assumption of social structure approaches is that social injustice, racism, and poverty are the root causes of crime. Hence, the social structure perspective is intimately associated with the first prong of this textbook's theme, the social problems approach, which was described in Chapter 1. If the assumptions that inform social structure theories are true, they largely negate the claims of those who advocate our theme's other prong, the social responsibility perspective.

Social structure explanations for criminality received an enormous boost during the 1960s with the report of President Lyndon B. Johnson's Commission on Law Enforcement and Administration of Justice, a widely disseminated and highly influential document that portrayed social inequality and stifled opportunity as fundamental causes of crime. Recently, however, a number of social commentators have begun to question the nature of the relationship among poverty, apparent social inequities, and crime.[114] Some now argue the inverse of the "root causes" argument, saying that poverty and what appear to be social injustices are produced by crime, rather than the other way around. Disorder, fear, and crime, they suggest, undermine positive social and economic institutions. Families, schools, churches, businesses, and other institutions cannot function properly in social settings where crime is a taken-for-granted part of the social landscape. If this proposed inverse relationship is even partially true, then addressing poverty and social inequality as the "root causes" of crime is not only an ineffective crime prevention strategy, but an unnecessarily costly one as well.

This chapter has identified three types of social structure theory, and each can be uniquely critiqued. Some authors have suggested, for example, that ecological theories give too much credence to the notion that spatial location determines crime and delinquency. The nature of any given location changes over time, they say, and evolutions in land-use patterns, such as a movement away from homeownership and toward rental or low-income housing, may seriously affect the nature of a neighborhood and the concomitant quality of social organization found there. Similarly, rates of neighborhood crime and delinquency may be "an artifact of police decision-making practices"[115] and may bear little objective relationship to the actual degree of law violation in an area. Such police bias (that is, enforcement efforts focused on low-income inner-city areas), should it exist, may seriously mislead researchers into categorizing certain areas as high in crime when enforcement decisions made by police administrators merely make them appear that way.

Another critique of the ecological school can be found in its seeming inability to differentiate between the condition of social disorganization and the things such a condition is said to cause. What, for example, is the difference between social disorganization and high rates of delinquency? Isn't delinquency a form of the very thing said to cause it? As Stephen J. Pfohl has observed, early ecological writers sometimes used the incidence of delinquency as "both an example of disorganization and something caused by disorganization,"[116] making it difficult to gauge the efficacy of their explanatory approach.

Similarly, those who criticize the ecological approach note that many crimes occur outside of geographic areas said to be characterized by social disorganization. Murder, rape, burglary, incidents of drug use, assault, and so on all occur in affluent, "well-established" neighborhoods as well as in other parts of a community. Likewise, white-collar, computer, environmental, and other types of crime may actually occur with a greater frequency in socially well-established neighborhoods than elsewhere. Hence, the ecological approach is clearly not an adequate explanation for all crime, nor for all types of crime.

From a social responsibility perspective, those who criticize strain theory note that Merton's original formulation of strain theory is probably less applicable to American society today than it was in the 1930s. That's because in the last few decades considerable effort has been made toward improving success opportunities for all Americans, regardless of ethnic heritage, race, or gender. Hence, it is less likely that individuals today will find themselves without the opportunity for choice, as was the case decades ago. Travis Hirschi criticizes contemporary strain theory for its inability "to locate people suffering from discrepancy" and notes that human beings are naturally optimistic—a fact, he says, that "overrides . . . aspiration-expectation disjunction." Hirschi concludes that "expectations appear to affect delinquency, but they do so regardless of aspirations, and strain notions are neither consistent with nor required by the data."[117] Similarly, recent studies have found that, contrary to what might be expected on the basis of strain theory, "delinquents do not report being more distressed than other youth."[118] Delinquent youths who are not afforded the opportunities for success that are available to others appear to be well shielded from sources of stress and despair through their participation in delinquency. Hence, "although strain theorists often have portrayed the lives of delinquents in grim terms . . . this depiction does not square well with the lived world of delinquency."[119]

Subcultural approaches, which constitute the last of the three types of social structure explanations for crime discussed in this chapter, have been questioned by some criminologists who see them as lacking in explanatory power. Canadian criminologist Gwynn Nettler, for example, criticizes the notion of violent subcultures by insisting that it is tautological, or circular. Nettler argues that saying that people fight because they are violent or that "they are murderous because they live violently" does little to explain their behavior. Attributing fighting to "other spheres of violence," he says, may be true, but it is fundamentally "uninformative."[120]

The subcultural approach has also been criticized for being racist because many so-called violent subcultures are said to be populated primarily by minorities. Margaret Anderson says that "the problem with this explanation is that it turns attention away from the relationship of black communities to the larger society and it recreates dominant stereotypes about blacks as violent, aggressive, and fearful. Although it may be true that rates of violence are higher in black communities, this observation does not explain the fact."[121] In sociological jargon, one might say that an observed correlation between race and violence does not necessarily provide a workable explanation for the relationship.

There are other problems with social structure theories that routinely link low levels of socioeconomic status (SES) to high levels of delinquency. A fundamental problem can be found in the fact that empirical studies have consistently found weak or nonexistent correlations between an individual's SES and his or her self-reported delinquency.[122] Moreover, such studies have shown that while low SES may promote delinquency by increasing social alienation and financial strain and by decreasing educational opportunity and occupational aspiration, high SES may also promote delinquency by increasing a person's willingness to take risks and by decreasing the influence of conventional values. Other studies have found parental monitoring (defined as knowing where the child is and what he or she is doing) and discipline to be far more effective predictors of the degree of delinquent involvement than low SES.[123]

Social structure theories suffer from another shortcoming that generally affects most other sociological perspectives on crime causation. In the words of Nettler, "The conceptual bias of social scientists emphasizes environments—cultures and structures—as the powerful causes of differential conduct. This bias places an intellectual taboo on looking elsewhere for possible causes as, for example, in physiologies. This taboo is . . . strongly applied against the possibility that ethnic groups may have genetically transmitted differential physiologies that have relevance for social behavior."[124] In this critique, Nettler is telling us that social scientists unnecessarily downplay the causative role of nonsociological factors. Many outside of sociology believe that such factors are important, but since sociological theorizing has captured the lion's share of academic attention over the past few decades, the role of other causative factors in the etiology of criminal behavior is in danger of being shortchanged.

Finally, some see the inability of social structure theories to predict which individuals—or at least what proportion of a given population—will turn to crime as a crucial failure of such perspectives. Although the large majority of people growing up in inner-city, poverty-ridden areas, for example, probably experience an inequitable opportunity

LIBRARY
Extra
····

structure firsthand, only a relatively small number of those people become criminal. It is true that substantially more people living under such conditions may become criminal than those living in other types of social environments. Nonetheless, a large proportion of people experiencing strain, as well as a large number of people raised in deviant subcultures, will still embrace noncriminal lifestyles—but social structure theories cannot tell us which ones. In his book *The Moral Sense,* James Q. Wilson suggests that most people—regardless of socialization experiences and the structural aspects of their social circumstances—may still carry within them an inherent sense of fairness and interpersonal morality.[125] If what Wilson suggests is even partially true, then the explanatory power of social structure theories will inevitably be limited by human nature itself. Read a PBS interview with Wilson at Library Extra 7–4.

SUMMARY

Sociological theories explore relationships among groups and institutions and envision crime as the result of social processes, as the natural consequence of aspects of social structure, or as the result of economic and class struggle. Social structure theories, with which this chapter has mostly been concerned, are only one of three types of sociological explanations for crime. Social structure theories emphasize poverty, lack of education, absence of marketable skills, and subcultural values as fundamental causes of crime.

Three subtypes of social structure theories can be identified: social disorganization theory, strain theory, and culture conflict theory. Social disorganization theory encompasses the notion of social pathology, which sees society as a kind of organism and crime and deviance as a kind of disease or social pathology. Theories of social disorganization are often associated with the perspective of social ecology and with the Chicago School of criminology, which developed during the

1920s and 1930s. Strain theory points to a lack of fit between socially approved success goals and the availability of socially approved means to achieve those goals. As a consequence, according to the perspective of strain theory, individuals unable to succeed through legitimate means turn to other avenues that promise economic and social recognition. Culture conflict theory suggests that the root cause of criminality can be found in a clash of values between differently socialized groups over what is acceptable or proper behavior.

Because theories of social structure look to the organization of society for their explanatory power, intervention strategies based on them typically seek to alleviate the social conditions that are thought to produce crime. Social programs based on social structure assumptions frequently seek to enhance socially acceptable opportunities for success and to increase the availability of meaningful employment.

KEY TERMS

anomie, 268

broken windows thesis, 266

Chicago Area Project, 288

Chicago School of criminology, 265

conduct norms, 275

criminology of place, 265

cultural transmission, 265

culture conflict theory, 275

defensible space, 266

distributive justice, 273

ecological theory, 265

environmental criminology, 265

focal concerns, 277

general strain theory (GST), 273

illegitimate opportunity structure, 281

negative affective states, 274

reaction formation, 283

relative deprivation, 272

social disorganization, 263

social disorganization theory, 262

social ecology, 263

social life, 261

social pathology, 263

social process, 261

social structure, 261

social structure theory, 262

sociological theory, 261

strain theory, 268

subcultural theory, 276

subculture, 276

techniques of neutralization, 278

KEY NAMES

Robert Agnew, 273

Ernest Burgess, 263

Richard A. Cloward, 281

Albert Cohen, 282

Franco Ferracuti, 279

David Matza, 278

Henry McKay, 264

Robert K. Merton, 268

QUESTIONS FOR REVIEW

1. What is the nature of sociological theorizing? What are the assumptions upon which sociological perspectives on crime causation rest? What three key sociological explanations for crime are discussed at the start of this chapter?

2. What do sociologists mean by the term *social structure?* How might the organization and structure of a society contribute to criminality?

3. What are the three types of social structure theories that this chapter describes? What are the major differences among them?

4. What are the policy implications of the theories discussed in this chapter? What kinds of changes in society and in government policy might be based on the theories discussed here? Would they be likely to bring about a reduction in crime?

5. What are the shortcomings of the social structure approach to understanding and preventing crime? Can these shortcomings be overcome?

QUESTIONS FOR REFLECTION

1. This book emphasizes a social problems versus social responsibility theme. Which of the theoretical perspectives discussed in this chapter best support the social problems approach? Which support the social responsibility approach? Why?

2. What do we mean by the term *ecological?* Do you believe that ecological approaches have a valid place in contemporary criminological thinking? Why?

3. How, if at all, does the notion of a "criminology of place" differ from more traditional ecological theories? Do you see the criminology-of-place approach as capable of offering anything new over traditional approaches? If so, what?

4. What is a violent subculture? Why do some subcultures seem to stress violence? How might participants in a subculture of violence be turned toward less aggressive ways?

WEB QUEST

A number of highly useful crime theory Web sites are maintained by professors who are actively engaged in scholarship in the criminology and criminal justice fields. Some of the best known of these sites include Cecil Greek's online links (www.criminology.fsu.edu/p/cjl-main.php) at Florida State University, Tom O'Connor's Megalinks in Criminal Justice (www.apsu.edu/oconnort) at Austin Peay State University, Matthew Robinson's Crime Theory Links (www. appstate.edu/~robinsnmb/theorylinks.htm) at Appalachian State University, and Bruce Hoffman's Crime Theory site (crimetheory.com) at Ohio University. Visit each of these sites and discover what they have to offer. If your instructor asks you to, write a summary of the materials describing social structure theories that you find at each site. Remember to check this textbook's site at crimtoday.com for updated URLs (look in the Web Quest section of each chapter).

NOTES

[1] Frank Tannenbaum, *Crime and the Community* (Boston: Ginn, 1938), p. 25.

[2] "L.A.: Waiting on a Razor's Edge," *Newsweek*, March 29, 1993, p. 28.

[3] Details for this story come from "Penn. Man Pleads Guilty to Killing 6 Relatives," MSNBC.com, June 15, 2007, http://www.msnbc.msn.com/id/19247451 (accessed July 1, 2007).

[4] "Man Who Killed 6 Relatives Pleads Guilty," *USA Today*, June 15, 2007, http://www.usatoday.com/news/nation/2007-06-15-bodies-in-basement_N.htm?csp=34 (accessed June 16, 2007).

[5] Charles R. Tittle, "Theoretical Developments in Criminology," *Criminal Justice 2000* (Washington, DC: National Institute of Justice, 2000), p. 70.

[6] Emile Durkheim, *The Division of Labor in Society*, trans. George Simpson (1893; reprint, New York: Free Press, 1947).

[7] Ferdinand Toennies, *Community and Society*, trans. Charles P. Loomis (1887; reprint, East Lansing: Michigan State University Press, 1957).

[8] Georg Simmel, "The Metropolis and Mental Life," in Donald N. Levine, ed., *On Individuality and Social Forms* (Chicago: University of Chicago Press, 1903).

[9] Durkheim, *The Division of Labor in Society*, p. 80.

[10] W. I. Thomas and Florian Znaniecki, *The Polish Peasant in Europe and America* (Boston: Gorham, 1920).

[11] Robert Park and Ernest Burgess, *The City* (Chicago: University of Chicago Press, 1925).

[12] "Human Ecology," *Encyclopaedia Britannica* online, http://britannica.com (accessed March 7, 2007).

[13] Peter Haggett, "Human Ecology," in Alan Bullock and Oliver Stallybrass, eds., *The Fontana Dictionary of Modern Social Thought* (London: Fontana, 1977), p. 187.

[14] For an excellent contemporary review of measuring the extent of social disorganization, see Barbara D. Warner and Glenn L. Pierce, "Reexamining Social Disorganization Theory Using Calls to the Police as a Measure of Crime," *Criminology*, Vol. 31, No. 4 (November 1993), pp. 493–513.

[15] Edwin M. Lemert, *Social Pathology* (New York: McGraw-Hill, 1951), p. 3.

[16] Ibid., p. 7.

[17] Clifford R. Shaw et al., *Delinquency Areas* (Chicago: University of Chicago Press, 1929).

[18] David Matza, *Becoming Deviant* (Upper Saddle River, NJ: Prentice Hall, 1969).

[19] Lawrence W. Sherman, Patrick R. Gartin, and Michael E. Buerger, "Hot Spots of Predatory Crime: Routine Activities and the Criminology of Place," *Criminology*, Vol. 27, No. 1 (1989), pp. 27–55.

[20] Rodney Stark, "Deviant Places: A Theory of the Ecology of Crime," *Criminology*, Vol. 25, No. 4 (1987), p. 893.

[21] Ibid., pp. 895–899.

[22] James Q. Wilson and George Kelling, "Broken Windows," *Atlantic Monthly*, March 1982, pp. 1–11.

[23] David Thacher, "Order Maintenance Reconsidered: Moving beyond Strong Causal Reasoning," *Journal of Criminal Law and Criminology*, Vol. 94, No. 2 (2004), pp. 381–414.

[24] James Q. Wilson and George L. Kelling, "Broken Windows: The Police and Neighborhood Safety," *Atlantic Monthly*, March 1982, http://www.theatlantic.com/politics/crime/windows.htm (accessed January 10, 2005).

[25] "The Next Phase of Quality of Life: Creating a More Civil City," Archives of Rudolph W. Giuliani, http://www.nyc.gov/html/rwg/html/98a/quality.html (accessed January 20, 2005).

[26] Oscar Newman, *Architectural Design for Crime Prevention* (Washington, DC: U.S. Department of Justice, 1973). See also Oscar Newman, *Creating Defensible Space* (Washington, DC: Office of Housing and Urban Development, 1996).

[27] Oscar Newman, *Defensible Space: Crime Prevention through Urban Design* (New York: Macmillan, 1972), p. 3. See also Ralph B. Taylor and Adele V. Harrell, *Physical Environment and Crime* (Washington, DC: National Institute of Justice, May 1996).

[28] Sherman, Gartin, and Buerger, "Hot Spots of Predatory Crime," p. 31.

[29] Ibid., p. 49.

[30] Bernard E. Harcourt, *Illusion of Order: The False Promise of Broken Windows Policing* (Cambridge, MA: Harvard University Press, 2001).

[31] Robert J. Sampson and Stephen W. Radenbush, "Systematic Social Observation of Public Spaces: A New Look at Disorder in Urban Neighborhoods," *American Journal of Sociology*, Vol. 105 (1999), p. 603.

[32] David Thacher, "Order Maintenance Reconsidered," p. 386.

[33] Thomas M. Arvanites and Robert H. Defina, "Business Cycles and Street Crime," *Criminology*, Vol. 44, No. 1 (2006), p. 141.

[34] Emile Durkheim, *Suicide: A Study in Sociology* (New York: Free Press, 1897).

[35] Robert K. Merton, "Social Structure and Anomie," *American Sociological Review*, Vol. 3 (October 1938), pp. 672–682; and Robert K. Merton, *Social Theory and Social Structure*, rev. ed. (New York: Free Press, 1957).

[36] Thomas M. Arvanites and Robert H. Defina, "Business Cycles and Street Crime," *Criminology*, Vol. 44, No. 1 (2006), pp. 139–164.

[37] Steven F. Messner and Richard Rosenfeld, *Crime and the American Dream* (Belmont, CA: Wadsworth, 1994), p. 68.

[38] J. Blau and P. Blau, "The Cost of Inequality: Metropolitan Structure and Violent Crime," *American Sociological Review*, Vol. 147 (1982), pp. 114–129.

[39] Masahiro Tsushima, "Economic Structure and Crime: The Case of Japan," *Journal of Socio-Economics*, Vol. 25, No. 4 (winter 1996), p. 497.

[40] Thomas F. Pettigrew, "Applying Social Psychology to International Social Issues," *Journal of Social Issues* (winter 1998), pp. 663–676.

[41] Fatos Tarifa, "The Quest for Legitimacy and the Withering Away of Utopia," *Social Forces*, Vol. 76, No. 2 (December 1997), p. 437.

[42] Robert Agnew, "Foundation for a General Strain Theory of Crime and Delinquency," *Criminology*, Vol. 30, No. 1 (February 1992), pp. 47–87.

[43] Adapted from Robert Agnew, *Pressured Into Crime: An Overview of General Strain Theory* (Los Angeles, CA: Roxbury, 2006), pp. 193–196.

[44] Ibid., p. 60.

[45] Agnew, "Foundation for a General Strain Theory of Crime and Delinquency."

[46] Ibid., p. 48.

[47] Raymond Paternoster and Paul Mazerolle, "General Strain Theory and Delinquency: A Replication and Extension," *Journal of Research in Crime and Delinquency*, Vol. 31, No. 3 (1994), pp. 235–263.

[48] Robert Agnew and Helene Raskin White, "An Empirical Test of General Strain Theory," *Criminology*, Vol. 30, No. 4 (1992), pp. 475–499.

[49] Lisa M. Broidy, "A Test of General Strain Theory," *Criminology*, Vol. 39, No. 1 (2002), pp. 9–35.

[50] Ibid., p. 29.

[51] Robert Agnew, Timothy Brezina, John Paul Wright, and Francis T. Cullen, "Strain, Personality Traits, and Delinquency: Extending General Strain Theory," *Criminology*, Vol. 40, No. 1 (2002), pp. 43–71.

[52] Ibid., p. 47.

[53] Thorsten Sellin, *Culture Conflict and Crime* (New York: Social Science Research Council, 1938).

[54] Rick Hampson, "Danish Mom Finds New York Doesn't Kid Around," *USA Today*, May 14, 1997, p. 3A.

[55] Although the practice may seem strange to Americans, the author, while teaching in Iceland, saw firsthand lines of unattended infants bundled into strollers awaiting their parents outside of restaurants and sports centers. The practice seems especially prevalent in Scandinavian countries, where the threat of child abduction is virtually unknown.

[56] Sellin, *Culture Conflict and Crime*, p. 68.

[57] Frederic M. Thrasher, *The Gang* (Chicago: University of Chicago Press, 1927).

[58] William F. Whyte, *Street Corner Society: The Social Structure of an Italian Slum* (Chicago: University of Chicago Press, 1943).

[59] The quotations attributed to Miller in this section are from Walter Miller, "Lower Class Culture as a Generating Milieu of Gang Delinquency," *Journal of Social Issues*, Vol. 14, No. 3 (1958), pp. 5–19.

[60] Gresham Sykes and David Matza, "Techniques of Neutralization: A Theory of Delinquency," *American Sociological Review*, Vol. 22 (December 1957), pp. 664–670.

[61] Volkan Topalli, "When Being Good Is Bad: An Expansion of Neutralization Theory," *Criminology* Vol. 43 (2005), p. 797.

[62] Ibid.

[63] Robert Agnew, "The Techniques of Neutralization and Violence," *Criminology*, Vol. 32, No. 4 (1994), p. 555.

[64] Ibid.

[65] Topalli, "When Being Good is Bad: An Expansion of Neutralization Theory," pp. 797–835.

[66] Ken Levi, "Becoming a Hit Man: Neutralization in a Very Deviant Career." *Urban Life*, Vol. 10 (1981), pp. 47–63.

[67] Lois Presser, "Remorse and Neutralization among Violent Male Offenders," *Justice Quarterly*, Vol. 20, No. 4 (2003), pp. 801–825.

[68] Orly Turgeman-Goldschmiidt, "The Rhetoric of Hackers' Neutralizations," in Frank Schmalleger and Michale pittaro, eds., *Crimes of the Internet* (Upper Saddle River, NJ: Prentice Hall, 2008).

[69] See, for example, Dorothy E. Denning, "Activism, Hacktivism, and Cyberterrorism: The Internet as a Tool for Influencing Foreign Policy." *Computer Security Journal,* Vol. 16 (2000), pp. 15–35; and Tim Jordan and Paul Taylor, *Hacktivism and Cyberwars: Rebels with a Cause?* (New York: Routledge, 2004).

[70] Franco Ferracuti and Marvin Wolfgang, *The Subculture of Violence: Toward an Integrated Theory of Criminology* (London: Tavistock, 1967).

[71] Frank P. Williams III and Marilyn D. McShane, *Criminological Theory* (Upper Saddle River, NJ: Prentice Hall, 1988), p. 79.

[72] Ferracuti and Wolfgang, *The Subculture of Violence.*

[73] Ferracuti and Wolfgang, *The Subculture of Violence*, p. 151.

[74] Ibid.

[75] For an excellent review of the literature, see F. Frederick Hawley, "The Southern Violence Construct: A Skeleton in the Criminological Closet" (paper presented at the annual meeting of the American Society of Criminology, 1988).

[76] Bertram Wyatt-Brown, *Southern Honor: Ethics and Behavior in the Old South* (Oxford: Oxford University Press, 1983).

[77] Hawley, "The Southern Violence Construct," p. 27.

[78] James W. Clarke, *The Lineaments of Wrath: Race, Violent Crime, and American Culture* (New Brunswick, NJ: Transaction, 1998), p. 4.

[79] Ibid.

[80] "Suspect's Mom Convicted of Shooting at Reporters," *Fayetteville (NC) Observer-Times*, September 29, 1993, p. 1A.

[81] Franklin Zimring et al., "Punishing Homicide in Philadelphia: Perspectives on the Death Penalty," *University of Chicago Law Review*, Vol. 43 (1976), pp. 227–252.

[82] Richard A. Cloward and Lloyd E. Ohlin, *Delinquency and Opportunity: A Theory of Delinquent Gangs* (Glencoe, IL: Free Press, 1960).

[83] Ibid., p. 7.

[84] Ibid., p. 13.

[85] Ibid., p. 16.

[86] Ibid., p. 19.

[87] Ibid., p. 3.

[88] Ibid., p. 37.

[89] Ibid., pp. 12–13.

[90] Stephen J. Pfohl, *Images of Deviance and Social Control*, 2nd ed. (New York: McGraw-Hill, 1994), pp. 224–225.

[91] Albert Cohen, *Delinquent Boys: The Culture of the Gang* (New York: Free Press, 1955), p. 13.

[92] Ibid.

[93] Donald J. Shoemaker, *Theories of Delinquency: An Examination of Explanations of Delinquent Behavior* (New York: Oxford University Press, 1984), p. 102, citing Cohen.

[94] Cohen, *Delinquent Boys*, p. 76.

[95] Ibid., p. 121.

[96] Shoemaker, *Theories of Delinquency*, p. 105.

[97] Elijah Anderson, *The Code of the Street: Decency, Violence, and the Moral Life of the Inner City* (New York: W. W. Norton, 1990).

[98] Arlen Egley, Jr., and Christina E. Ritz, *Highlights of the 2004 National Youth Gang Survey* (Washington, DC: Office of Juvenile Justice and Delinquency Prevention, 2006).

[99] National Gang Crime Research Center, *Achieving Justice and Reversing the Problem of Gang Crime and Gang Violence in America Today: Preliminary Results of the Project Gangfact Study* (Chicago: National Gang Crime Research Center, 1996).

[100] Carl Rogers, "Children in Gangs," *Criminal Justice, 1993–94* (Guilford, CT: Dushkin, 1993), pp. 197–199.

[101] "Youths Match Power, Fear, Guns," *Fayetteville (NC) Observer-Times*, September 6, 1993, p. 2A.

[102] Ibid.

[103] The quotations attributed to Curry and Spergel in this section are from G. David Curry and Irving A. Spergel, "Gang Homicide, Delinquency, and Community," *Criminology*, Vol. 26, No. 3 (1988), pp. 381–405.

[104] Ibid., p. 401.

[105] Finn-Aage Esbensen, "A National Gang Strategy," in J. Mitchell Miller and Jeffrey P. Rush, eds., *Gangs: A Criminal Justice Approach* (Cincinnati: Anderson, 1996).

[106] Cited in Mary H. Glazier, review of J. Mitchell Miller and Jeffrey P. Rush, eds., *Gangs: A Criminal Justice Approach*, in *Criminologist* (July/August 1996), p. 29.

[107] Steven Schlossman et al., *Delinquency Prevention in South Chicago: A Fifty-Year Assessment of the Chicago Area Project* (Santa Monica, CA: Rand, 1984).

[108] J. Robert Lilly, Francis T. Cullen, and Richard A. Ball, *Criminological Theory: Context and Consequences* (Newbury Park, CA: Sage, 1989), p. 80.

[109] Lamar T. Empey, *American Delinquency: Its Meaning and Construction* (Homewood, IL: Dorsey, 1982), p. 243.

[110] See James DeFronzo, "Welfare and Burglary," *Crime and Delinquency*, Vol. 42 (1996), pp. 223–230.

[111] Since overall rates of crime rose throughout much of the 1970s and 1980s, the effectiveness of such programs remains very much in doubt.

[112] Public Law 104–193 (August 22, 1996).

[113] Sec. 103 of the Welfare Reform Act of 1996.

[114] See, for example, George L. Kelling, "Crime Control, the Police, and Culture Wars: Broken Windows and Cultural Pluralism," in National Institute of Justice, *Perspectives on Crime and Justice: 1997–1998 Lecture Series* (Washington, DC: National Institute of Justice, 1998).

[115] Robert J. Bursik, "Social Disorganization and Theories of Crime and Delinquency: Problems and Prospects," *Criminology*, Vol. 26, No. 4 (1988), p. 519.

[116] Stephen J. Pfohl, *Images of Deviance and Social Control* (New York: McGraw-Hill, 1985), p. 167.

[117] Travis Hirschi, review of Delbert S. Elliott, David Huizinga, and Suzanne S. Ageton, *Explaining Delinquency and Drug Use*, in *Criminology*, Vol. 25, No. 1 (February 1987), p. 195.

[118] John Hagan, "Defiance and Despair: Subcultural and Structural Linkages between Delinquency and Despair in Life Course," *Social Forces*, Vol. 76, No. 1 (September 1997), p. 119.

[119] Ibid.

[120] Gwynn Nettler, *Killing One Another* (Cincinnati: Anderson, 1982), p. 67.

[121] Margaret Anderson, "Review Essay: Rape Theories, Myths, and Social Change," *Contemporary Crises*, Vol. 5 (1983), p. 237.

[122] Bradley R. Entner Wright et al., "Reconsidering the Relationship between SES and Delinquency: Causation but Not Correlation," *Criminology*, Vol. 37, No. 1 (February 1999), pp. 175–194.

[123] R. Larzelre and G. R. Patterson, "Parental Management: Mediator of the Effect of Socioeconomic Status on Early Delinquency," *Criminology*, Vol. 28 (1990), pp. 301–323.

[124] Nettler, *Killing One Another*, p. 54.

[125] James Q. Wilson, *The Moral Sense* (New York: Free Press, 1993).

Chapter

8

Theories of Social Process and Social Development

Source: Alistair Berg/Getty Images—Photonica Amana America, Inc.

Outline

Children learn to become delinquents by becoming members of groups in which delinquent conduct is already established.

—**Albert K. Cohen**[1]

It's like it ain't so much what a fellow does, but it's the way the majority of folks is looking at him when he does it.

—**William Faulkner**[2]

If the child who "steps off on the wrong foot" remains on an ill-starred path, subsequent stepping-stone experiences may culminate in life-course-persistent antisocial behavior.

—**Terrie E. Moffitt**[3]

I want to put the past behind me but it seems to pound me deeper in the ground with every corner I turn.

—**J.G. Toole, former D.C. prisoner**[4]

Learning Outcomes

After reading this chapter, you should be able to

- Recognize how the process of social interaction contributes to criminal behavior
- Identify and distinguish among a number of social process perspectives
- Identify current social policy initiatives that reflect the social process approach
- Critique social process theories of criminality
- Identify and distinguish among a number of social development perspectives
- Explain the central concepts of social development theories
- Identify the policy implications of social development theories
- Assess the shortcomings of social development perspectives

Hear the author discuss this chapter at crimtoday.com

Introduction

On a chilly February day in 2004, two huge rooms at the Jefferson County Fairgrounds near Golden, Colorado, were turned into a public showcase to hold the evidence that Jefferson County Sheriff's Department deputies had gathered from the Columbine High School in Littleton—scene of one of the nation's deadliest school shootings.[5] The 1999 rampage by 17-year-old Dylan Klebold and 18-year-old Eric Harris resulted in the deaths of 15 people—including the shooters, who took their own lives. More than 20 other people were wounded. The evidence display, five years in the making, included pipe bombs, guns used in the attack, bullet fragments, more than 700 spent shell casings, blood-stained furniture, knives carried by the attackers, and clothing worn by Klebold and Harris during their destructive rampage. Other, more mundane items were also available for viewing—like a computer display with a bullet hole in it; and a lost shoe, apparently abandoned by a student attempting to flee the carnage.

Also available to the public was a newly released videotape of the attackers that had been made in the hallways of Columbine High School five months before the killings. On the tape, Klebold and Harris are seen wearing trench coats and sunglasses, portraying hit men offering their services to students who had been victimized by bullies.[6]

Attendees at the display were provided with a document prepared by Colorado Attorney General Ken Salazar that looked into the two years leading up to the attacks. The report revealed that Jefferson County officers had had 15 contacts with Klebold and Harris, most of them based on complaints filed by neighbors. Investigators had once considered asking for a warrant to search Harris's home because of threats that he had placed on the Internet and because of a pipe bomb that was found along a bike path that Harris used. The warrant was never sought, however, after officers concluded that they lacked enough evidence to procure it.

"In the end," Salazar told reporters, "none of the many efforts to open up the Columbine records, including today's activity, will mean much beyond passing curiosity if we cannot learn from this tragedy."[7] What we might learn will be different depending on who we are. Criminologists continue to debate the influences in the lives of Harris and Klebold that led up to the Columbine shootings. One report, released three years after the shootings, indicated that Klebold and Harris were victims of bullying by other teenagers and might have been suffering from the depression, loneliness, and

Victims' family members look over evidence from the Columbine (Colorado) High School shootings that took place in 1999. The display was presented by the Jefferson County Sheriff's Office in 2004, prior to the evidence being archived. The evidence on display included the shotguns and pistols that Eric Harris and Dylan Klebold used to kill their schoolmates in the Columbine High School library and cafeteria. Might the killings have been prevented?

Source: Gary Caskey/Reuters– CORBIS NY

suicidal urges that victims of bullying can experience.[8] The killings, the report suggested, may have been the end result of those feelings.

We might also ask how others caught up in the Columbine tragedy found the courage to confront the shooters. Darrell Scott, for example, whose daughter Rachel was killed in the shootings and who was present at the fairgrounds, told CBS News, "[O]ne moment for me was when I saw the picture of Dave Sanders who was one of my heroes; who was the teacher that was killed at Columbine. There is a still shot of him as he's going up the stairs to confront the two boys and everyone else is running out of the cafeteria. And you can see in his stride, it's a purposeful stride toward his own death. He knew that he was going to possibly die when he confronted those boys. And he'll always be a hero of mine."[9]

A 2007 shooting spree at Virginia Tech University by a student suffering from mental problems resulted in the deaths of 33 people, and claimed the record for the nation's deadliest school shooting ever. That tragic event is discussed in Chapter 10. Learn more about school shooters and how they might be identified before they act from the FBI's National Center for the Analysis of Violent Crime by reading **Library Extra 8–1** at crimtoday.com, and read the federal *Report to the President on Issues Raised by the Virginia Tech Tragedy* at **Library Extra 8–2**.

LIBRARY
Extra
■ ■ ■ ■

The Social Process Perspective

The theories discussed in the first part of this chapter are called **social process theories,** or *interactionist perspectives*, because they depend on the process of interaction between individuals and society for their explanatory power. Social process theories of crime causation assume that everyone has the potential to violate the law and that criminality is not an innate human characteristic. According to social process theories, criminal behavior is learned in interaction with others, and the socialization process that occurs as the result of group membership is seen as the primary route through which learning occurs. Among the most important groups contributing to the process of socialization are the family, peers, work groups, and reference groups with which one identifies. Such groups instill values and norms in their members and communicate what are (for their members) acceptable world views and patterns of behavior.

Social process perspectives hold that the process through which criminality is acquired, deviant self-concepts are established, and criminal behavior results is active, open-ended, and ongoing throughout a person's life. They suggest that individuals who have weak stakes in conformity are more likely to be influenced by the social processes and contingent experiences that lead to crime, and they believe that criminal choices, once made, tend to persist because they are reinforced by the reaction of society to those whom it has identified as deviant.

social process theory

A theory that asserts that criminal behavior is learned in interaction with others and that socialization processes that occur as the result of group membership are the primary route through which learning occurs.

Types of Social Process Approaches

A number of theories can be classified under the social process umbrella. Among them are social learning theory, social control theory, labeling theory, reintegrative shaming, and dramaturgy. Learning theories place primary emphasis upon the role of communication and socialization in the acquisition of learned patterns of criminal behavior and the values that support that behavior. Control theories focus on the strength of the bond that people share with institutions and individuals around them, especially as those relationships shape their behavior. Labeling theory, also known as "societal reaction theory," points to the special significance of society's response to the criminal. It sees the process through which a person comes to be defined as a criminal, along with society's formal imposition of the label "criminal" upon that person, as a significant contributory factor in determining future criminality. Reintegrative shaming, a contemporary offshoot of labeling theory, emphasizes possible positive outcomes of the labeling process, while

Theory in Perspective

Types of Social Process Theories

Social Process Theories, also Known as Interactionist Perspectives

depend on the process of interaction between individuals and society for their explanatory power. Social process theories of crime causation assume that everyone has the potential to violate the law and that criminality is not an innate human characteristic. According to social process theories, criminal behavior is learned in interaction with others, and the socialization process that occurs as the result of group membership is seen as the primary route through which learning occurs.

- *Social Learning Theory (aka Learning Theory).* Says that all behavior is learned in much the same way and that crime, like other forms of behavior, is also learned. Places primary emphasis upon the role of communication and socialization in the acquisition of learned patterns of criminal behavior and the values that support that behavior.

  Period: 1930s–present

  Theorists: Edwin Sutherland, Robert Burgess, Ronald L. Akers, Daniel Glaser

  Concepts: Differential association, differential association–reinforcement (including operant conditioning), differential identification

- *Social Control Theory.* Focuses on the strength of the bond that people share with the institutions and individuals around them, especially as those relationships shape their behavior. Seeks to identify those features of the personality and of the environment that keep people from committing crimes.

  Period: 1950s–present

  Theorists: Walter C. Reckless, Howard B. Kaplan, Travis Hirschi, Michael Gottfredson, Charles R. Tittle, others

  Concepts: Inner and outer containment, self-derogation, social bond, control-balance

- *Labeling Theory (aka Societal Reaction Theory).* Points to the special significance of society's response to the criminal and sees continued crime as a consequence of limited opportunities for acceptable behavior that follow from the negative responses of society to those defined as offenders.

  Period: 1938–1940, 1960s–1980s, 1990s revival

  Theorists: Frank Tannenbaum, Edwin M. Lemert, Howard Becker, John Braithwaite, others

  Concepts: Tagging, labeling, outsiders, moral enterprise, primary and secondary deviance, reintegrative shaming, stigmatic shaming

- *Dramaturgy.* Depicts human behavior as centered around the purposeful management of impressions and seeks explanatory power in the analysis of social performances.

  Period: 1960s–present

  Theorists: Erving Goffman, others

  Concepts: Total institutions, impression management, back and front regions, performances, discrediting information, stigma, spoiled identity

dramaturgy demonstrates how people can effectively manage the impressions they make on others. It is to learning theories that we now turn our attention.

Learning Theory

Social **learning theory** says that all behavior is learned in much the same way and that crime, like other forms of behavior, is also learned. People learn to commit crime from others, and such learning includes the acquisition of norms, values, and patterns of behaviors conducive to crime. Hence, according to learning theory, criminal behavior is a product of the social environment and not an innate characteristic of particular people.

Differential Association

learning theory

A perspective that places primary emphasis upon the role of communication and socialization in the acquisition of learned patterns of criminal behavior and the values that support that behavior.

One of the earliest and most influential forms of learning theory was advanced by **Edwin Sutherland** in 1939. Sutherland's thesis was that criminality is learned through a process of **differential association** with others who communicate criminal values and who advocate the commission of crimes.[10] Sutherland emphasized the role of social learning as an explanation for crime because he believed that many of the concepts popular in the field of criminology at the time—including social pathology, genetic inheritance, biological characteristics, and personality flaws—were inadequate to explain the process by which an otherwise normal individual turns to crime. Sutherland was the first well-known criminologist to suggest that all significant human behavior is learned and that crime, therefore, is not substantively different from any other form of behavior.

Although Sutherland died in 1950, the tenth edition of his famous book, *Criminology*, was published in 1978 under the authorship of Donald R. Cressey, a professor at the University of California at Santa Barbara. The 1978 edition of *Criminology* contained the finalized principles of differential association (which, for all practical purposes, were complete as early as 1947). Nine in number, the principles read as follows:[11]

differential association

The sociological thesis that criminality, like any other form of behavior, is learned through a process of association with others who communicate criminal values.

1. Criminal behavior is learned.

2. Criminal behavior is learned in interaction with others in a process of communication.

3. The principal part of the learning of criminal behavior occurs within intimate personal groups.

4. When criminal behavior is learned, the learning includes (a) techniques of committing the crime, which are sometimes very complicated, sometimes very simple, and (b) the specific direction of motives, drives, rationalizations, and attitudes.

5. The specific direction of motives and drives is learned from definitions of the legal codes as favorable or unfavorable.

6. A person becomes delinquent because of an excess of definitions favorable to law violation over definitions unfavorable to law violation.

7. Differential associations may vary in frequency, duration, priority, and intensity.

8. The process of learning criminal behavior by association with criminal and anticriminal patterns involves all of the mechanisms that are involved in any other learning.

9. While criminal behavior is an expression of general needs and values, it is not explained by those general needs and values, since noncriminal behavior is an expression of the same needs and values.

Differential association found considerable acceptance among mid-twentieth-century theorists because it combined then-prevalent psychological and sociological principles into a coherent perspective on criminality. Crime as a form of learned behavior became the catchword of mid-twentieth-century criminology, and biological and other perspectives were largely abandoned by those involved in the process of theory testing.

Differential Association–Reinforcement Theory

In 1966, **Robert Burgess** and **Ronald L. Akers** published an article outlining what they called "a differential association–reinforcement theory of criminal behavior."[12] The perspective, which is often referred to as "differential reinforcement theory" or "sociological learning theory," expands on Sutherland's original idea of differential association by adding the idea of reinforcement. Reinforcement, a concept drawn from psychology, was discussed earlier in this textbook under the heading "Behavior Theory" in Chapter 6. In that chapter, we pointed out the power of punishments and rewards to shape behavior. In developing their perspective, Burgess and Akers integrated psychological principles of operant conditioning with sociological notions of differential association, and they reorganized Sutherland's nine principles into seven. The flavor of their approach is obvious in the first of these statements, which says, "Criminal behavior is learned according to the principles of operant conditioning."[13] Fundamental to this perspective is the belief that human beings learn to define behaviors that are rewarded as positive and that an individual's criminal behavior is rewarded at least sometimes by individuals and groups that value such activity.

Although the 1966 Burgess-Akers article only alluded to the term *social learning*, Akers began to apply that term to differential association–reinforcement theory with the 1973 publication of his book *Deviant Behavior: A Social Learning Approach*.[14] According to Akers, "The basic assumption in social learning theory is that the same learning process, operating in a context of social structure, interaction, and situation, produces both conforming and deviant behavior."[15] Akers identified two primary learning mechanisms. The first is differential reinforcement (also called "instrumental conditioning"), in which behavior is a function of the frequency, amount, and probability of experienced and perceived contingent rewards and punishments. The second is imitation, in which the behavior of others and its consequences are observed and modeled. These learning mechanisms, said Akers, operate in a process of differential association involving direct and indirect, verbal and nonverbal, communication, interaction, and identification with others. As with Sutherland's theory of differential association, the relative frequency, intensity, duration, and priority of associations remain important because they determine the amount, frequency, and probability of reinforcement of behavior that is either conforming or deviant. Interpersonal association also plays an important role because, as with Sutherland's theory, it can expose individuals to deviant or conforming norms and role models.

Akers has continued to develop learning theory, and in 1998, he published the book *Social Learning and Social Structure,* in which he explained crime rates as a function of social learning that occurs within a social structure.[16] He called this explanation the "social structure–social learning" (SSSL) theory of crime. Like Sutherland, Akers has summarized his approach in several concise propositions:[17]

1. Deviant behavior is learned according to the principles of operant conditioning.

2. Deviant behavior is learned both in nonsocial situations that are reinforcing or discriminating and through social interaction in which the behavior of others is reinforcing or discriminating for such behavior.

3. The principal part of the learning of deviant behavior occurs in those groups that comprise or control the individual's major source of reinforcements.

4. The learning of deviant behavior, including specific techniques, attitudes, and avoidance procedures, is a function of the effective and available reinforcers and the existing reinforcement contingencies.

5. The specific class of behavior learned and its frequency of occurrence are a function of the effective and available reinforcers and the deviant or nondeviant direction of the norms, rules, and definitions that in the past have accompanied the reinforcement.

6. The probability that a person will commit deviant behavior is increased in the presence of normative statements, definitions, and verbalizations that, in the process of differential reinforcement of such behavior over conforming behavior, have acquired discriminative value.

7. The strength of deviant behavior is a direct function of the amount, frequency, and probability of its reinforcement. The modalities of association with deviant patterns are important insofar as they affect the source, amount, and scheduling of reinforcement.

Akers's SSSL theory says that social learning is the social psychological mediating process through which social structural aspects of the environment work to cause crime. SSSL effectively integrates two levels of explanation—social structure and social learning—by specifying the links between the larger social context and the individual relationships that lead to criminal behavior.[18] Hence, a person's location in the social structure—as defined by age, gender, ethnicity, place of residence, and so on—is seen as a major determinate of how that person is socialized and what he or she will learn.

differential identification theory

An explanation for crime and deviance that holds that people pursue criminal or deviant behavior to the extent that they identify themselves with real or imaginary people from whose perspective their criminal or deviant behavior seems acceptable.

Differential Identification Theory

Like the approach of Ronald Akers, **Daniel Glaser**'s **differential identification theory** builds upon Sutherland's notion of differential association.[19] The central tenet of Glaser's differential identification theory is that "a person pursues criminal behavior to the extent that he identifies himself with real or imaginary persons from whose

A child watches his mother smoking a cigarette. Social learning theory says that social behavior is learned. Will this child grow up to be a smoker?

Source: James King-Holmes, Science Photo Library/Photo Researchers, Inc.

LIBRARY
Extra
▪▪▪▪

perspective his criminal behavior seems acceptable."[20] In effect, Glaser proposed that the process of differential association leads to an intimate personal identification with lawbreakers, resulting in criminal or delinquent acts. Glaser recognized that people will identify with various others and that some of these identifications will be relatively strong and others will be weak—hence the term *differential* identification. According to Glaser, however, it is not the frequency or the intensity of association that, as Sutherland believed, determines behavior, but the symbolic process of identification. Identification with a person, or with an abstract understanding of what that person might be like, can be more important than actual associations with real people. Hence, role models can consist of abstract ideas rather than actual people, and an individual might selectively identify with, say, a serial killer or a terrorist bomber, even though he or she has never met such a person. Glaser also recognized the role of economic conditions, frustrations with one's place in the social structure, learned moral creeds, and group participation in producing differential identifications. Alternatively, according to Glaser, identification with noncriminals offers the possibility of rehabilitation. Learn more about social learning and adolescent development via **Library Extras 8–3** and **8–4** at crimtoday.com.

Social Control Theory

According to Charles R. Tittle, a prominent sociologist at Washington State University with a specialty in crime and deviance, **social control theories** emphasize "the inhibiting effect of social and psychological integration with others whose potential negative response, surveillance, and expectations regulate or constrain criminal impulses."[21] In other words, social control theorists seek to identify those features of the personality and the environment that keep people from committing crimes. Controlling features of personality and the physical environment were identified earlier in Chapters 6 and 7, respectively. As Tittle observes, however, social control theorists take a step beyond static aspects of the personality and physical features of the environment in order to focus on the *process* through which social integration develops. It is the extent of a person's integration with positive social institutions and with significant others that determines that person's resistance to criminal temptations; social control theorists

social control theory

A perspective that predicts that when social constraints on antisocial behavior are weakened or absent, delinquent behavior emerges. Rather than stressing causative factors in criminal behavior, control theory asks why people actually obey rules instead of breaking them.

focus on the process through which such integration develops. Rather than stressing causative factors in criminal behavior, however, social control theories tend to ask why people actually obey rules instead of breaking them.[22]

Containment Theory

In the 1950s, a student of the Chicago School, **Walter C. Reckless,** wrote *The Crime Problem.*[23] Reckless tackled head-on the realization that most sociological theories, although conceptually enlightening, offered less than perfect predictability. That is, they lacked the ability to predict precisely which individuals, even those exposed to various "causes" of crime, would become criminal. Reckless thought that the sociological perspectives prevalent at the time offered only half of a comprehensive theoretical framework. Crime, Reckless wrote, was the consequence of social pressures to involve oneself in violations of the law, as well as of failure to resist such pressures. Reckless called his approach **containment theory,** and he compared it with a biological immune response, saying that only some people exposed to a disease actually come down with it. Sickness, like crime, Reckless avowed, results from the failure of control mechanisms—some internal to the person, and others external. In the case of sickness, external failures might include unsanitary conditions, the failure of the public health service, the unavailability of preventative medicine, or the lack of knowledge necessary to make such medicine effective. Still, disease will not result unless the individual's resistance to disease-causing organisms is low or unless the individual is in some other way weak or susceptible to the disease.

In the case of crime, Reckless wrote, *external containment* consists of "the holding power of the group."[24] Under most circumstances, Reckless said, "the society, the state, the tribe, the village, the family, and other nuclear groups are able to hold the individual within the bounds of the accepted norms and expectations."[25] In addition to setting limits, Reckless saw society as providing individuals with meaningful roles and activities. He saw such roles as an important factor of *external containment.*

Inner containment, said Reckless, "represents the ability of the person to follow the expected norms, to direct himself."[26] Such ability was said to be enhanced by a positive self-image, a focus on socially approved goals, personal aspirations that are in line with reality, a good tolerance for frustration, and a general adherence to the norms and values of society. A person with a positive self-image can avoid the temptations of crime simply by thinking, "I'm not that kind of person." A focus on socially approved goals helps keep people on the proverbial straight and narrow path. "Aspirations that are in line with reality" are simply realistic desires. In other words, if a person seriously desires to be the richest person in the world, disappointment will probably result. Even when aspirations are reasonable, however, disappointments will occur—hence the need for a good tolerance for frustration.

Reckless's containment theory is diagrammed in Figure 8–1. "Pushes toward Crime" represents those factors in an individual's background that might propel him or her into

containment theory

A form of control theory that suggests that a series of both internal and external factors contributes to law-abiding behavior.

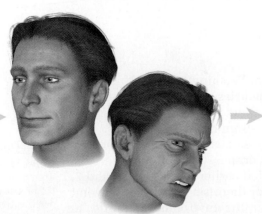
Pushes toward Crime

Pulls toward Crime

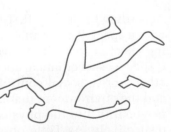
Containment   The Criminal Event

FIGURE 8–1

A Diagrammatic Representation of Containment Theory

criminal behavior. They include a criminogenic background or upbringing that involves participation in a delinquent subculture, deprivation, biological propensities toward deviant behavior, and psychological maladjustment. "Pulls toward Crime" signifies all the perceived rewards crime may offer, including financial gain, sexual satisfaction, and higher status. "**Containment**" is a stabilizing force and, if effective, blocks such pushes and pulls from leading the individual toward crime.

Reckless believed that inner containment was far more effective than external containment in preventing law violations. In his words, "As social relations become more impersonal, as society becomes more diverse and alienated, as people participate more and more for longer periods of time away from a home base, the self becomes more and more important as a controlling agent."[27]

containment

Aspects of the social bond that act to prevent individuals from committing crimes and that keep them from engaging in deviance.

Delinquency and Self-Esteem

As mentioned at the start of this section, social control theory predicts that when social constraints on antisocial behavior are weakened or absent, delinquent behavior will emerge. An innovative perspective on social control was offered by **Howard B. Kaplan** in the mid–1970s.[28] Kaplan proposed that people who are ridiculed by their peers suffer a loss of self-esteem, assess themselves poorly, and (thereby) abandon the motivation to conform. This approach has come to be known as the "self-derogation theory of delinquency."

A number of studies appear to support the idea that low self-esteem fosters delinquent behavior.[29] At the same time, however, it appears that delinquency can also enhance self-esteem, at least for some delinquents.[30] At least one study has found that delinquent behavior enhances self-esteem in adolescents whose self-esteem is already very low.[31]

Some researchers have examined ethnic identification as a factor in low self-esteem and as a precursor to delinquent behavior. In 1986, K. Leung and F. Drasgow tested Kaplan's self-derogation theory using white, African American, and Hispanic youth groups.[32] They concluded that while all three groups reported low self-esteem, only among white youngsters were low levels of self-esteem related to delinquent behavior. Other researchers, however, found no differences in self-esteem and delinquency between African American and white delinquents and nondelinquents.[33]

In 1990, in an effort to explain some of the contradictory findings of self-derogation research, Daphna Oyserman and Hazel Rose Markus proposed that "possible selves," rather than self-esteem, might be a major explanatory factor in delinquency.[34] According to the self-esteem approach of Oyserman and Markus, the degree of disjuncture between what people want to be and what they fear they might become is a good potential predictor of delinquency.[35] Hence, an adolescent who is confused about what he or she wants to be or fears becoming may resort to delinquency in order to resolve the conflict. Oyserman and Markus suggest that the highest levels of delinquency can be found among youths who lack balance between their expected selves ("Someday I'll be happily married and have a good job and a nice family") and their feared selves ("I could fail in school, be arrested, and end up in prison").

Social Bond Theory

An important form of control theory was popularized by **Travis Hirschi** in his 1969 book *Causes of Delinquency*.[36] Hirschi's approach was well received by criminologists and "epitomized social control theorizing for nearly three decades."[37] Hirschi argued that through successful socialization, a bond forms between individuals and the social group. When that bond is weakened or broken, deviance and crime may result. Hirschi described four components of the **social bond:**

social bond

The link, created through socialization, between individuals and the society of which they are a part.

- Attachment: a person's shared interests with others
- Commitment: the amount of energy and effort put into activities with others
- Involvement: the amount of time spent with others in shared activities
- Belief: a shared value and moral system

Crime in the News

Crime in an American Family

Rooster Bogle came up to the rich Willamette Valley in Washington State from Texas as a migrant worker in 1961, already having served hard time in prison and with a habit of beating his wife and teaching his children to steal.

Rooster, as Dale Vincent Bogle was known, taught them well. By the time the boys were 10 years old they were breaking into liquor stores for their dad or stealing tractor-trailer trucks, hundreds of them. The girls turned to petty crimes to support their drug addictions.

In time, everybody went to jail, or to state prison, as did many of Rooster's brothers and their families. By official count, 28 in the

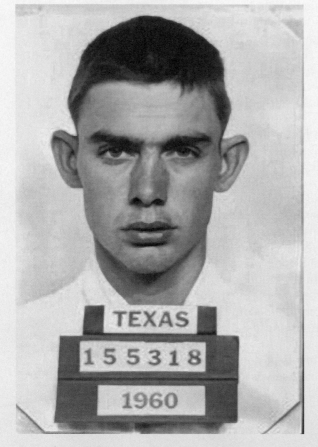

Rooster Bogle, patriarch of a clan with 28 current or former convicts. Can criminality be passed from one generation to the next? If so, how?

Source: New York Times Pictures

Bogle clan have been arrested and convicted, including several of Rooster's grandchildren. Rooster Bogle (rhymes with mogul) himself died in 1998, of natural causes.

"Rooster raised us to be outlaws," said Tracey Bogle, the youngest of Rooster's children by his wife, Kathryn, now 55. "There is a domino effect in a family like ours," Tracey said. "What you're raised with, you grow to become. You don't escape."

Tracey Bogle, who is 29, would know. He is serving a 15-year sentence for kidnapping, rape, assault, robbery and burglary at the Snake River Correctional Institution in the high desert of eastern Oregon near the Idaho border. He committed the crimes with one of his older brothers, Robert Zane Bogle. Their oldest brother, Tony, is serving a life term in Arizona for murder. Their mother was released from Klamath County jail only last month.

For all this criminal activity, the Bogle clan is merely an extreme example of a phenomenon that prison officials, the police and criminal justice experts have long observed, that crime often runs in families.

Justice Department figures show that 47 percent of inmates in state prisons have a parent or other close relative who has also been incarcerated, said Allen J. Beck of the Bureau of Justice Statistics. Similarly, the link between the generations is so powerful that half of all juveniles in custody have a father, mother or other close relative who has been in jail or prison, Mr. Beck said.

Despite this statistical evidence, until very recently states paid little attention to the family cycle of crime. But in the last year Oregon has introduced a pioneering program that tries to break the cycle by asking all newly admitted inmates whether they have a relative who has been incarcerated and whether they themselves have children.

The cost of ignoring this cycle of criminality is a burden to taxpayers, said Fay Gentle, the training and transition coordinator for the Oregon Department of Corrections. An analysis by her office found that the cost for incarcerating just five of the 28 convicted Bogle family members was almost $3 million. That is not counting the expense of their trials, or of probation or parole after their release, or the costs if they are arrested again.

A nephew of Rooster's, Louis Bogle, 42, will be a cost to Oregon for as long as he lives. In 1993, five days after his last release from prison, he went in search of methamphetamine. Louis had a total of 25 arrests, everything from drug possession and theft to endangering the welfare of a minor. He had always survived, but this time his luck ran out. He owed money to the Mexican drug dealers he went to buy methamphetamine from, so they shot him up with liquid Drano.

That put him in a coma. Louis recovered consciousness a month later but remains paralyzed from the neck down, a resident in a nursing home paid for by the state in the farm town of Lebanon.

In his writings, Hirschi cites the psychopath as an example of the kind of person whose attachment to society is nearly nonexistent.[38] Other relatively normal individuals may find their attachment to society loosened through "the process of becoming alienated from others [which] often involves or is based on active interpersonal conflict," says Hirschi. "Such conflict could easily supply a reservoir of socially derived hostility sufficient to account for the aggressiveness of those whose attachments to others have been weakened."[39]

"Too mean to die," Louis said, lying flat on his back on a hospital bed, his arms and chest festooned with prison tattoos.

There are a number of reasons that people with parents who have been incarcerated are more likely to be locked up themselves, Ms. Gentle said. Many grow up in families afflicted by poverty, abuse, neglect and drug use, all factors that can lead to criminality. But to Ms. Gentle, a critical reason is simply how the children in families like the Bogles learn to imitate their parents. "Instead of learning appropriate behavior, they are learning how to cheat, lie, steal and manipulate," Ms. Gentle said. "Kids are so eager to please, they imitate their parents."

For Tracey Bogle, now at the Snake River prison, some of his earliest memories are his mother's blood when Rooster got drunk and beat her. His father carried a knife and taught the boys to fight and steal. If they did not fight and steal, he beat them for being cowards. Rooster said he was a Gypsy, that his mother was a Gypsy from Germany, and so they would live by stealing.

So Tracey started with shoplifting food, toys and clothes, and then graduated rapidly to stealing semis, those big rigs running up and down Interstate 5 through Oregon. Semis were more desirable than cars because they carried much more gas and could go farther, and because they could survive a crash.

Once he and his brothers stole a semi in Salem and rammed it into the side of a gun store, right through the wall, making off with the guns. One semi he stole, loaded with $100,000 worth of sugar, landed him in the MacLaren Youth Correctional Facility in Salem when he was about 15. Altogether, he must have stolen 300 semis, Tracey figures.

That has netted him 12 years of incarceration since he quit school in eighth grade, most of his life since then, including jail time in Idaho, Nevada and California. But sitting in prison now, dressed in state-issue blue denim, he laughs loudly at his youthful memories. It was his childhood, the only one he knew, and so it was fun, even when it was painful.

For the girls in the extended Bogle family, most crime has involved drugs, but some have learned to be violent, too.

Florence Bogle Black, a niece of Rooster, remembers her father, Elvie, beating her mother when he was drunk and then when Florence was 11, sexually molesting her. "I don't hold it against him, he was drunk," Florence said. "But after that, I changed."

Soon she was doing drugs—methamphetamine, cocaine and heroin. "I would do whatever I could get, and if I didn't have the money, I'd lose all my morals," she said. She had her first baby at 15.

She was convicted of stabbing her husband and her best friend, who was also her husband's girlfriend. She was, she now recognizes, re-enacting the violence done to her.

Florence was saved by her sister, Tammie Bogle Stuckey, the recognized saint of the family, who has never been arrested or abused drugs but did go through two abusive marriages. Tammie now helps run five halfway houses for 45 newly released inmates as women's director of Stepping Out Ministry, a nonprofit religious agency started by her current husband, a former inmate himself.

"Working with these inmates, it seems perfectly normal," Tammie said. "They're just like my family."

Sometimes the residents in her transition houses are her family, including her brother Mark Bogle and a cousin, Jerrie Lynn Bogle Jones, convicted on prostitution charges related to her drug addiction.

One resident was her own son, Jason Bogle James, 27, who started drinking and taking acid at 13 and progressed to heroin and robbing a store, for which he was sentenced to five years in prison. When he was released, Tammie took him into her program, which has a strong Christian component, but found he was not serious about kicking his habit and was breaking her rules.

She kicked him out of the program and watched as his parole officer sent him back to jail when he failed a urine test. "I am actually relieved when he is in jail or prison," Tammie said, "'cause I know he's not out trying to get himself killed."

Being a Bogle in Oregon carries a reputation. Tammie and Ricky Bogle, 23, the son of one of her cousins, say they have been stopped repeatedly by the Salem police simply because their license plates were registered to a Bogle. Driving while Bogle is the local form of profiling.

But once Ricky was stopped in a stolen car. That got him 13 months in Oregon State Correctional Institution in Salem, where he is confined now, in solitary. "Man, when you are raised in this family," Ricky said, "it's hard to get away from it."

Discussion Questions

1. This article seems to say that crime runs in families. Is that assertion true? If so, why?

2. What kinds of social policies might be built upon the ideas expressed in this article?

The second component of the social bond—commitment—reflects a person's investment of time and energies into conforming behavior and the potential loss of the rewards that he or she has already gained from that behavior. In Hirschi's words, "The idea, then, is that the person invests time, energy, himself, in a certain line of activity—say, getting an education, building up a business, acquiring a reputation for virtue. Whenever he considers deviant behavior, he must consider the costs of this deviant behavior, the risk he runs of losing the investment he has made in conventional behavior."[40] For such a traditionally successful person, says Hirschi, "a ten-dollar-holdup is stupidity" because the potential for losing what has already been acquired through commitment to social norms far exceeds what stands to be gained. Recognizing that his approach applies primarily to individuals who have been successfully socialized into conventional society, Hirschi adds, "The concept of commitment assumes that the organization of society is such that the interests of most persons would be endangered if they were to engage in criminal acts."[41]

Involvement, for Hirschi, means "engrossment in conventional activities"[42] and is similar to Reckless's concept of meaningful roles. In explaining the importance of involvement in determining conformity, Hirschi cites the colloquial saying that "idle hands are the devil's workshop." Time and energy, he says, are limited, and if a person is busy at legitimate pursuits, he or she will have little opportunity for crime and deviance.

Belief, the last of Hirschi's four aspects of the social bond, sets his control theory apart from subcultural approaches. Hirschi says that unlike subcultural theory, "control theory assumes the existence of a common value system within the society or group whose norms are being violated. . . . We not only assume the deviant has believed the rules, we assume he believes the rules even as he violates them."[43] How can a person simultaneously believe it is wrong to commit a crime and still commit it? Hirschi's answer is that "many persons do not have an attitude of respect toward the rules of society."[44] That is, although they know the rules exist, they basically do not care. They invest little of their sense of self in moral standards.

In 1990, Hirschi, in collaboration with **Michael Gottfredson,** proposed a **general theory of crime** based on the concepts advanced earlier in control theory.[45] (Control theory and the general theory of crime are also discussed in Chapter 6.) Gottfredson and Hirschi began by asking, "What is crime?" Nearly all crimes, they concluded, are mundane, simple, trivial, easy acts aimed at satisfying desires of the moment. Hence, their general theory is built on a classical or rational choice perspective—that is, the belief that crime is a natural consequence of unrestrained human tendencies to seek pleasure and avoid pain. Crime, said Gottfredson and Hirschi, is little more than a subset of general deviant behavior. Hence, they concluded, crime bears little resemblance to the explanations offered in the media, by law enforcement officials, or by most academic thinkers on the subject.

According to Gottfredson and Hirschi, the offender is neither the diabolical genius of fiction nor the ambitious seeker of the American Dream often portrayed by other social scientists. On the contrary, offenders appear to have little control over their own desires. When personal desires conflict with long-term interests, those who lack self-control often opt for the desires of the moment, thus contravening legal restrictions and becoming involved in crime.[46] Central to Gottfredson and Hirschi's thesis is the belief

The social bond forms early in life. What might this child be learning?

Source: Steve Rubin, The Image Works

that a well-developed social bond will result in the creation of effective mechanisms of self-control. As others have noted, "For Gottfredson and Hirschi, self-control is the key concept in the explanation of all forms of crime as well as other types of behavior. Indeed, they believe that all current differences in rates of crime between groups and categories may be explained by differences in the management of self-control."[47]

Control–Balance Theory

Traditional control theories posit that deviance and crime result from either weak social bonds or low levels of self-control. A novel form of control theory can be found in **Charles R. Tittle**'s control-balance perspective.[48] Tittle's control-balance approach results from a blending of the social bond and containment perspectives. Tittle argues that too much control can be just as dangerous as too little. The crucial concept in Tittle's approach is what he calls the **control ratio.** The control ratio is the amount of control to which a person is subject versus the amount of control that person exerts over others. The control ratio is said to predict not only the probability that one will engage in deviance but also the specific form that deviance will take (Figure 8–2).

High levels of control, or overcontrol, are termed "control surplus," while low levels are called "control deficit." Individuals with *control surpluses* are able to exercise a great deal of control over others and will work to extend their degree of control even further. Their efforts lead to deviant actions involving exploitation, plunder, and decadence—frequently seen in cases of white-collar crime and political corruption.[49] Tittle says that control surpluses build upon "the fundamental drive toward autonomy." Such a drive, says Tittle, involves "a desire to extend control as far as possible" and results in forms of deviance that he terms "autonomous."[50]

A *control deficit* exists for people unable to exercise much control over others (and who are hence overly controlled). Control deficits result in deviance as an attempt to escape repressive controls. Deviance engendered by control deficit takes the form of predation (physical violence, theft, sexual assault, robbery, and so on), defiance (challenges to conventional norms, including vandalism, curfew violations, and sullenness), or submission (which Tittle describes as "passive, unthinking, slavish obedience to the expectations, commands, or anticipated desires of others"[51]). According to Tittle, however, control imbalance only sets the stage for deviance. Deviance ultimately occurs once a person realizes, at some level, that acts of deviance can reset the control ratio in a favorable way. Finally, opportunity also plays a significant role in Tittle's theory. "No matter how favorable the motivational and constraint configuration," says Tittle, "the actual likelihood of deviance occurring depends on there being an opportunity for it to happen."[52]

control ratio

The amount of control to which a person is subject versus the amount of control that person exerts over others.

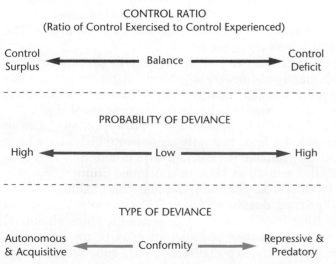

FIGURE 8–2

Control-Balance Theory

CONTROL RATIO
(Ratio of Control Exercised to Control Experienced)

Control Surplus ←——— Balance ———→ Control Deficit

- -

PROBABILITY OF DEVIANCE

High ←——— Low ———→ High

- -

TYPE OF DEVIANCE

Autonomous & Acquisitive ←——— Conformity ———→ Repressive & Predatory

Labeling Theory

A decade ago, James Hamm found himself at the center of a vicious controversy. Hamm, a convicted murderer, had served 18 years in prison for shooting a man in the head over a drug deal gone bad and was about to enter the Arizona State University School of Law. Hamm had been paroled less than a year earlier, after Arizona's parole board judged him "rehabilitated." While in prison, Hamm, a former divinity student, earned a bachelor's degree in sociology and had been active in Middle Ground Prison Reform, Inc., a prisoner rights group. While the 45-year-old Hamm worked on getting an education, students at the university were challenging his access to law school, saying that a convicted murderer did not deserve to be admitted. Mark Killian, then–Arizona Republican house speaker, said, "There are a lot of hard-working young people out there who could not get into law school because he did."[53] Members of the Arizona Board of Regents, which runs the state's public universities, called for a review of policies on admitting ex-convicts to the schools. Nonetheless, Hamm, who scored in the top 5% of all applicants taking the law school admissions test nationwide, was eventually admitted to law school and graduated in 1997. Following graduation, he passed the bar exam and applied to be allowed to practice law in Arizona. The state's parole board, however, refused to terminate Hamm's parole, leaving him ineligible to work as an attorney. James Hamm is presently employed as a paralegal working in the areas of criminal defense, civil rights, and appellate law.[54]

The case of James Hamm provides an example of how society's continued reaction to criminal behavior can change the course of an offender's life—often for the worse—even after he had paid his "dues." As a certain professor liked to say, while there are plenty of ex-cons, there is no such thing as an "ex-ex-con." Or "once a con, always a con." Society, it seems, never forgets.

Society's response to known or suspected offenders is important not only because it determines the individual futures of those who are labeled as criminals but also because it may contribute to a heightened incidence of criminality by reducing the behavioral options available to labeled offenders.

An early description of societal reaction to deviance can be found in the work of **Frank Tannenbaum.** Tannenbaum's book *Crime and the Community,* published in 1938, popularized the term **tagging** to explain what happens to offenders following arrest, conviction, and sentencing. Tannenbaum told his readers that crime was essentially the result of "two opposing definitions of the situation"—those of the delinquent and the community at large. "This conflict over the situation," he said, "is one that arises out of a divergence of values. As the problem develops, the situation gradually becomes redefined. The attitude of the community hardens definitely into a demand for suppression. There is a gradual shift from the definition of the specific acts as evil to a definition of the individual as evil, so that all his acts come to be looked upon with suspicion. . . . From the community's point of view, the individual who used to do bad and mischievous things has now become a bad and unredeemable human being. . . . The young delinquent becomes bad because he is defined as bad and because he is not believed if he is good. There is a persistent demand for consistency in character. The community cannot deal with people whom it cannot define."[55]

Tannenbaum used the phrase "dramatization of evil" to explain the process whereby an offender comes to be seen as ultimately and irrevocably "bad." After the process has been completed, Tannenbaum said, the offender "now lives in a different world. He has been tagged. . . The process of making the criminal, therefore, is a process of tagging."[56] Once a person has been defined as bad, few legitimate opportunities remain open to him or her. As a consequence, the offender finds that only other people who have been similarly defined by society as bad are available to associate with him or her. This continued association with negatively defined others leads to continued crime.

Using terminology developed by **Edwin M. Lemert,** it became fashionable to call an offender's initial acts of deviance "primary deviance" and the offender's continued acts of deviance, especially those resulting from forced association with other offenders, "secondary deviance." **Primary deviance,** Lemert pointed out, may be undertaken to solve some immediate problem or to meet the expectations of one's subcultural group.

tagging

The process whereby an individual is negatively defined by agencies of justice.

primary deviance

Initial deviance often undertaken to deal with transient problems in living.

Hence, the robbery of a convenience store by a college student temporarily desperate for tuition money, although not a wise undertaking, may be the first serious criminal offense ever committed by the student. The student may well intend for it to be the last, but if arrest ensues and the student is "tagged" with the status of a criminal, then secondary deviance may occur as a means of adjustment to the negative status. In Lemert's words, "When a person begins to employ his deviant behavior or a role based upon it as a means of defense, attack, or adjustment to the overt and covert problems created by the consequent societal reaction to him, his deviation is secondary."[57]

secondary deviance

Deviant behavior that results from official labeling and from association with others who have been so labeled.

Secondary deviance becomes especially important because of the forceful role it plays in causing tagged individuals to internalize the negative labels that have been applied to them. Through such a process, labeled individuals assume the role of the deviant. According to Lemert, "Objective evidences of this change will be found in the symbolic appurtenances of the new role, in clothes, speech, posture, and mannerisms, which in some cases heighten social visibility, and which in some cases serve as symbolic cues to professionalization."[58]

The name most often associated with labeling theory is that of **Howard Becker.** In 1963, Becker published *Outsiders: Studies in the Sociology of Deviance,*[59] the work in which the **labeling** perspective found its fullest development. In *Outsiders,* Becker described the deviant subculture of jazz musicians and the process by which an individual becomes a marijuana user, among other things. His primary focus, however, was to explain how a person becomes labeled as an outsider, as "a special kind of person, one who cannot be trusted to live by the rules agreed on by the group."[60] The central fact about deviance, says Becker, is that it is a social product, that "it is created by society." Society creates both deviance and the deviant person by responding to circumscribed behaviors. The person who engages in sanctioned behavior is, as part of the process, labeled a deviant. In Becker's words, "Social groups create deviance by making the rules whose infraction constitutes deviance, and by applying those rules to particular people and labeling them as outsiders. From this point of view, deviance is not a quality of the act the person commits, but rather a consequence of the application by others of rules and sanctions. . . . The deviant is one to whom that label has been successfully applied."[61] For Becker, as for other labeling theorists, no act is intrinsically deviant or criminal but must be defined as such by others. Becoming deviant, Becker noted, involves a sequence of steps that eventually lead to commitment to a deviant identity and participation in a deviant career.

labeling

An interactionist perspective that sees continued crime as a consequence of limited opportunities for acceptable behavior that follow from the negative responses of society to those defined as offenders.

In developing labeling theory, Becker attempted to explain how some rules come to carry the force of law, while others have less weight or apply only within the context of marginal subcultures. His explanation centered on the concept of **moral enterprise,** a term he used to encompass all the efforts a particular interest group makes to have its sense of propriety embodied in law. "Rules are the products of someone's initiative," said Becker, "and we can think of the people who exhibit such enterprise as moral entrepreneurs."[62]

moral enterprise

The efforts made by an interest group to have its sense of moral or ethical propriety enacted into law.

An early example of moral enterprise can be found in the Women's Christian Temperance Union (WCTU), a group devoted to the prohibition of alcohol. From 1881 to 1919, the WCTU was highly visible in its nationwide fight against alcohol—holding marches and demonstrations, closing drinking establishments, and lobbying legislators. Press coverage of the WCTU's activities swayed many politicians into believing that the lawful prohibition of alcoholic beverages was inevitable, and an amendment to the U.S. Constitution soon followed, ushering in the age of prohibition. Moral enterprise is similarly used, Becker claimed, by other groups seeking to support their own interests with the weight of law. Often the group that is successful at moral enterprise does not represent a popular point of view. The group is simply more effective than others at maneuvering through the formal bureaucracy that attends the creation of legislation.

Becker was especially interested in describing deviant careers—the processes by which individuals become members of deviant subcultures and take on the attributes associated with the deviant role. Becker argued that most deviance, when it first occurs, is likely to be transitory. That is, it is unlikely to occur again. However, transitory deviance can be effectively stabilized in a person's behavioral repertoire through the labeling process. Once a person is labeled "deviant," opportunities for conforming behavior are seriously reduced. Behavioral opportunities that remain open are primarily deviant ones. Hence, throughout the person's career, the budding deviant increasingly exhibits deviant behavior, not so much out of choice but, rather, because his or her choices are restricted by society. Additionally, successful deviants must acquire the techniques and resources necessary to undertake the deviant act (be it drug use or bank robbery) and must develop the mind-set characteristic of others like them. Near the completion of a deviant career, the person who has been labeled a deviant internalizes society's negative label, assumes a deviant self-concept, and is likely to become a member of a deviant subgroup. Becker says, "A drug addict once told me that the moment she felt she was really 'hooked' was when she realized she no longer had any friends who were not drug addicts."[63] In this way, says Becker, deviance finally becomes a "self-fulfilling prophecy." Labeling, then, is a cause of crime insofar as the actions of society in defining the rule breaker as deviant push the person further in the direction of continued deviance.

Labeling theory contributed a number of unique ideas to the criminological literature, including the following:

- Deviance is the result of social processes involving the imposition of definitions, rather than the consequence of any quality inherent in human activity itself.

- Deviant individuals achieve their status by virtue of social definition, rather than because of inborn traits.

- The reaction of society to deviant behavior and to those who engage in such behavior is the major element in determining the criminality of the person and of the behavior in question.

- Negative self-images follow from processing by the formal criminal justice system, rather than precede delinquency.

- Labeling by society and handling by the justice system tend to perpetuate crime and delinquency rather than reduce it.

Becker's typology of delinquents helped explain the labeling approach. It consisted of (1) the pure deviant, (2) the falsely accused deviant, and (3) the secret deviant. The pure deviant is one who commits norm-breaking behavior and whose behavior is accurately appraised as such by society. An example might be the burglar who is caught in the act of burglary and then tried and convicted. Such a person, we might say, has gotten what he or she deserves. The falsely accused individual is one who, in fact, is not guilty but is labeled "deviant" nonetheless. The falsely accused category in Becker's typology demonstrates the power of social definition. Innocent people sometimes end up in prison, and one can imagine that the impact of conviction and of the experiences that attend prison life can leave the falsely accused with a negative self-concept and with group associations practically indistinguishable from those of the true deviant. In effect, the life of the falsely accused is changed just as thoroughly as is the life of the pure deviant by the process of labeling. Finally, the secret deviant violates social norms, but his or her behavior is not noticed, and negative societal reactions do not follow. The secret deviant again demonstrates the power of societal reaction—in this case, by the very lack of consequences.

Although labeling theory fell into disregard during the late 1970s and early 1980s due to accusations that it was vague and ambiguous, criminologists have recently recast the approach as a developmental theory of structural disadvantage.[64] In other words, the theory is now seen as one that points out the cumulative effects over time of official intervention on future life chances and opportunities for approved success. Robert J. Sampson and John H. Laub have observed that labeling theory is "truly developmental in nature because of its explicit emphasis on processes over time."[65] Contemporary proponents of the labeling perspective, however, generally see labeling as only one factor contributing to cumulative disadvantages in life chances. In 2003, Jon Gunnar Bernburg and Marvin D. Krohn studied the impact of negative official intervention on young men in Rochester, New York. Data on the men were available from the time they were (on average) 13.5 years old until they reached the age of 22. In keeping with what labeling theory would predict, Bernburg and Krohn found that official intervention during adolescence led to increased criminality in early adulthood because it reduced life chances for educational achievement and successful employment. They also found that poor people were more negatively impacted by official processing, probably because they were already disadvantaged along other important social dimensions.[66]

Negative labels can carry significant visible liabilities, as well as hidden ones. A 2004 study by the Legal Action Center, a crime and justice policy group, for example, found that all 50 states have laws that hamper the ability of former offenders to reenter society.[67] Four states—Colorado, South Carolina, Georgia, and Virginia—were rated as places where ex-offenders have the least chance to become productive citizens.

According to the center, many states prohibit ex-offenders from obtaining professional licenses to work in businesses as diverse as real estate, medicine, and law. Twenty-seven states, in keeping with a requirement imposed by Congress on states seeking federal highway funds, revoke or refuse to issue drivers' licenses to former drug felons, effectively prohibiting access to many job sites. The federal requirement doesn't distinguish between those whose crimes involved the use of a vehicle and those whose crimes did not.

Recently, Mike S. Adams proposed a general sociological learning theory of crime and deviance that incorporates components of labeling theory and differential association.[68] Adams contends that "labeling effects are mediated by associations with delinquent peers." He concludes that labeling is not a direct cause of delinquency and crime but "appears to cause delinquency indirectly via the effects of associations with delinquent peer groups." In other words, "the causal chain linking primary to secondary deviance must incorporate links that account for the effects of associations with delinquent [peers]."[69] Learn more about labeling theory at **Web Extra 8–1**, and read about the post-prison consequences of a criminal label at Library Extra 8–5 at crimtoday.com.

WEB
Extra
■■■■

LIBRARY
Extra
■■■■

Reintegrative Shaming

In a contemporary offshoot of labeling theory, **John Braithwaite** and colleagues at the Australian National University (ANU) reported initial results of studies on reintegrative shaming in 1997.[70] In contrast to traditional labeling theory, which emphasizes stigmatization and the resulting amplification of deviance, reintegrative shaming describes processes by which a deviant is labeled and sanctioned but then brought back into a community of conformity through words, gestures, or rituals.

Braithwaite, along with Lawrence W. Sherman of the University of Maryland and Heather Strang at ANU, compared the effectiveness of traditional court processing of criminal offenders with a restorative justice approach operating in Canberra, Australia, known as "diversionary conferencing." The diversionary conferencing approach "consists of an emotionally intense meeting, led by a police officer, between admitted offenders and their supporters, usually family and friends, and the victim of the offense, together with their supporters. In the absence of a direct victim, a representative of the community in which the offense occurred expresses the victim perspective on the events. The group discusses the consequences of the offense for all the parties and then determines what restitution the offenders must comply with to repair the harm for which they are responsible and so avoid going to court."[71]

Called RISE, for Reintegrative Shaming Experiments, the project assessed the efficacy of each approach using criteria like these: (1) prevalence and frequency of repeat offending, (2) victim satisfaction with the process, (3) estimated cost savings within the justice process, (4) changes in drinking or drug use behavior among offenders, and (5) perceptions of procedural justice, fairness, and protection of rights.[72]

At the core of the study was Braithwaite's belief that two different kinds of shame exist. One is called "stigmatic shaming." **Stigmatic shaming** is thought to destroy the moral bond between the offender and the community. The other type of shame, **reintegrative shaming,** is thought to strengthen the moral bond between the offender and the community. According to Braithwaite, "Stigmatic shaming is what American judges employ when they make an offender post a sign on his property saying 'a violent felon lives here,' or a bumper sticker on his car saying 'I am a drunk driver.' Stigmatic shaming sets the offender apart as an outcast—often for the rest of the offender's life. By labeling him

stigmatic shaming

A form of shaming, imposed as a sanction by the criminal justice system, that is thought to destroy the moral bond between the offender and the community.

reintegrative shaming

A form of shaming, imposed as a sanction by the criminal justice system, that is thought to strengthen the moral bond between the offender and the community.

or her as someone who cannot be trusted to obey the law, stigmatic shaming says the offender is expected to commit more crimes."[73]

Braithwaite's alternative to stigmatic humiliation is "to condemn the crime, not the criminal."[74] Through carefully monitored diversionary conferences, Braithwaite hopes to give offenders the opportunity to rejoin the community as law-abiding citizens. To earn the right to a fresh start, says Braithwaite, offenders must express remorse for their past conduct, apologize to any victims, and repair the harm caused by the crime.

Preliminary results from the RISE studies support the claimed value of reintegrative shaming. To date, however, most such results have been measured through interviews with offenders following diversionary conferences and consist primarily of anecdotal evidence based on the reported feelings of respondents. Findings show that offenders are far more likely to feel ashamed of their crimes if handled through conferences rather than through formal court processing. Moreover, both offenders and victims report finding conferences fairer than official court proceedings. Learn more about the reintegrative shaming experiments at **Web Extra 8–2**.

Dramaturgy

WEB
Extra
▪ ▪ ▪ ▪

dramaturgical perspective

A theoretical point of view that depicts human behavior as centered around the purposeful management of interpersonal impressions.

Another social process approach to the study of criminology can be found in the work of **Erving Goffman.** Goffman's 1959 book *The Presentation of Self in Everyday Life* introduced students of criminology to the concept of dramaturgy.[75] The **dramaturgical perspective** says that individuals play a variety of nearly simultaneous social roles—such as mother, teacher, daughter, wife, and part-time real estate agent—and that such roles must be sustained in interaction with others. Shakespeare's famous claim that "all the world's a stage, and all the men and women merely players: They have their exits and their entrances; and one man in his time plays many parts"[76] provides a good summation of Goffman's dramaturgical approach.

Goffman argued that social actors present themselves more or less effectively when acting out a particular role and that role performances basically consist of managed impressions. Through communications, both verbal and nonverbal, social actors define the situations in which they are involved. A medical doctor, for example, may wear a lab coat and a name tag with her title emblazoned on it, carry a stethoscope and other medical accoutrements, and introduce herself as "Dr. Smith." Each choice the doctor makes, in what she wears or says or how she acts, is intended to convey, according to Goffman, medical authority—and to thereby establish certain rules of interpersonal interaction, that is, to demand a certain appropriate kind of subservience

Minor offenders perform court-ordered duties in public view. Some people believe that shaming can be an effective rehabilitative tool. What different kinds of shaming can you identify?

Source: L. Delevingne, Stock Boston

from specified others, including patients, nurses, and laboratory technicians. Medical doctors may, by way of their esoteric knowledge and the awe they inspire in patients and their families, mystify their audiences and thereby gain compliance with their wishes, which makes their jobs easier. Criminals, through a similar process of managed impressions and by way of the fear they engender in their victims, may likewise achieve cooperation.

Impression management, according to Goffman, is a complex process involving a never-ending give-and-take of information. Back regions (such as dressing rooms) in which actors prepare for their roles; front regions (such as offices) where furniture, degrees, and plaques are carefully placed; and personal displays of status or role occupancy all play a part in the management of impressions. When impression management has been successful, said Goffman, dramatic realization has occurred. "Together," he said, "the participants contribute to a single overall definition of the situation which involves not so much a real agreement as to what exists but rather a real agreement as to whose claims concerning what issues will be temporarily honored."[77]

Goffman also claimed that a performer can "be completely taken in by his own act," or on the other hand, "the performer may not be taken in at all by his own routine"[78] and may not be the person he represents himself as being. When the performer is not duped but others are, then the performance is a sham or a fraud. In such cases of misrepresentation, he said, "we may take a harsh view of performers such as confidence men who knowingly misrepresent every fact about their lives, [but] we may have some sympathy for those who have but one fatal flaw and who attempt to conceal the fact that they are, for example, ex-convicts."[79]

Deviant behavior finds its place in the dramaturgical perspective through the concept of discreditable disclosure. Some actors, said Goffman, may find themselves discredited by the introduction of new information, especially by information they have sought to hide. When such **discrediting information** is revealed, the flow of interaction is disrupted, and the nature of the performance may be altered substantially. In an example from real life, which was made into a play and the 1993 movie *M. Butterfly,* a French diplomat in China spent 20 years living with a Beijing opera singer, never knowing that "she" was really a he.[80] Such an interpersonal relationship must have required nothing less than heroic impression management, with the potential for discrediting information always close at hand.

Goffman would say that "to be a given kind of person" requires the dramatic realization of one's claimed status. What one is depends on how successful one is at acquiring the abilities necessary to convince others of one's claims. In his words, "A status, a position, a social place is not a material thing . . . It is a pattern of appropriate conduct, coherent, embellished, and well articulated . . . It is . . . something that must be enacted and portrayed, something that must be realized."[81]

Goffman's work takes on considerable relevance for criminology in his later writings, especially his book *Stigma: Notes on the Management of Spoiled Identity.*[82] In *Stigma,* Goffman advanced the notion that discredited, or stigmatized, individuals differ significantly from "normals" in the way that society responds to them. "By definition . . . ," he said, "we believe that a person with a stigma is not quite human. On this assumption we exercise varieties of discrimination, through which we effectively, if often unthinkingly, reduce his life chances. We construct a stigma-theory, an ideology to explain his inferiority and account for the danger he represents . . . We tend to impute a wide range of imperfections on the basis of the original one."[83] Stigmata (the plural of stigma) may be physical (such as birthmarks), behavioral (such as theft), or ideational (such as a low rank in the proverbial pecking order).

In *Stigma,* Goffman is primarily concerned with how "normals" and stigmatized individuals interact. At times, says Goffman, discredited individuals are known to others before they come into contact with them. When that happens, normal people approach the stigmatized with expectations of encountering further stigmatizing behavior. When discrediting information does not precede interpersonal encounters, the stigmatized individual may attempt to "pass" as normal using various techniques of concealment, including aliases and misrepresentation.

---

impression management

The intentional enactment of practiced behavior that is intended to convey to others one's desirable personal characteristics and social qualities.

discrediting information

Information that is inconsistent with the managed impressions being communicated in a given situation.

total institution

A facility from which individuals can rarely come and go and in which communal life is intense and circumscribed. Individuals in total institutions tend to eat, sleep, play, learn, and worship (if at all) together.

According to Goffman, societal reactions, although they may forcibly create social identities, are also instrumental in the formation of group identities. When similarly discredited individuals come together in like-minded groups, they may align themselves against the larger society. In so reacting, they may justify their own deviant or criminal behavior. At the conclusion of *Stigma,* Goffman reminded us, "The normal and the stigmatized are not persons, but rather perspectives. These are generated in social situations during mixed contacts by virtue of the unrealized norms that are likely to play upon the encounter."[84]

In another book, *Asylums,* Goffman described **total institutions**—facilities from which individuals can rarely come and go and in which communal life is intense and circumscribed.[85] Individuals in total institutions tend to eat, sleep, play, learn, and worship (if at all) together. Military camps, seminaries, convents, prisons, rest homes, and mental hospitals are all types of asylums, according to Goffman. Goffman believed that residents of total institutions bring "presenting cultures" with them to their respective facilities. In the case of prisons, for example, some inmates carry street culture into correctional facilities, whereas others, from different walks of life, bring a variety of other cultural baggage. However, said Goffman, residents undergo a period of "disculturation," during which they drop aspects of the presenting culture that are not consistent with existing institutional culture—a culture they must acquire. Read about jails as total institutions at Library Extra 8–6 at crimtoday.com.

LIBRARY
Extra
■ ■ ■ ■

Policy Implications of Social Process Theories

Social process theories suggest that crime prevention programs should work to enhance self-control and to build **prosocial bonds.** One program that seeks to build strong prosocial bonds while attempting to teach positive values to young people is the Juvenile Mentoring Program (JUMP) of the Office of Juvenile Justice and Delinquency Prevention (OJJDP). Fundamentally a social control initiative, JUMP was funded by Congress in 1992 under an amendment to the Juvenile Justice and Delinquency Prevention Act of 1974.[86] OJJDP-sponsored JUMP programs commenced operation in 1996. JUMP places at-risk youth in a one-on-one relationship with favorable adult role models. At-risk youths are defined as those who are at risk of delinquency, gang involvement, educational failure, or dropping out of school. General demographic information is used in conjunction with scores on a standardized risk-assessment instrument known as the Problem Oriented Screening Instrument for Teens in order to identify potential JUMP participants.

prosocial bonds

Bonds between the individual and the social group that strengthen the likelihood of conformity. Prosocial bonds are characterized by attachment to conventional social institutions, values, and beliefs.

Most recent data show 9,200 youths were enrolled in more than 200 JUMP programs nationwide (see Figure 8–3). The average age at the time of enrollment was just under 12 years. Although evaluation data are just beginning to come in on the project,[87] both youth and mentors were very positive when rating various aspects of their mentoring experiences. Learn more about JUMP at Library Extra 8–7.

LIBRARY
Extra
■ ■ ■ ■

FIGURE 8–3

Juvenile Mentoring Programs Nationwide

Source: Office of Juvenile Justice and Delinquency Prevention.

The Taming of the Shrew, performed in Tucson, Arizona. Some criminologists suggest that people, like actors on a stage, intentionally present themselves to others in ways calculated to produce predictable social responses. How might criminals manipulate impressions?

Source: First Image, The Image Works

Another social control–based program is Preparing for the Drug Free Years (PDFY).[88] PDFY is designed to increase effective parenting and is part of the Strengthening America's Families Project. OJJDP, which runs the program, says, "The PDFY curriculum is guided theoretically by the social development model, which emphasizes the role of bonding to family, school, and peers in healthy adolescent development. The model specifies that strong bonding to positive influences reduces the probability of delinquency and other problem behaviors."[89]

PDFY works with parents of children in grades four to eight in an effort to reduce drug abuse and behavioral problems in adolescents. It seeks to teach effective parenting skills as a way to decrease the risks that juveniles face. PDFY incorporates both behavioral skills training and communication-centered approaches into parent training. Through a series of 10 one-hour sessions, parents learn to (1) increase their children's opportunities for family involvement, (2) teach needed family-participation and social skills, and (3) provide reinforcement for positive behavior and appropriate consequences for misbehavior. Early studies show that program participation (session attendance) tends to be high and that the program is effective at improving general child-management skills among parents.[90] Learn more about PDFY at **Web Extra 8–3**.

A program that emphasizes the development of self-control is the Montreal Preventive Treatment Program.[91] It addresses early childhood risk factors for gang involvement by targeting boys from poor socioeconomic backgrounds who display disruptive behavior while in kindergarten. The program offers training sessions for parents that are designed to teach family crisis management, disciplining techniques, and other parenting skills. The boys participate in training sessions that emphasize the development of prosocial skills and self-control. At least one evaluation of the program showed that it was effective at keeping boys from joining gangs.[92]

WEB
Extra
■ ■ ■ ■

Critique of Social Process Theories

Criticisms of social process theories are many and varied. Perhaps the most potent criticism of association theory is the claim that Sutherland's initial formulation of differential association is not applicable at the individual level because even people who experience an excess of definitions favorable to law violation may still not become criminal. Likewise, those who rarely associate with recognized deviants may still turn to crime. In addition, the theory is untestable because most people experience a multitude of definitions—both favorable and unfavorable to law violation—and it is up to them to interpret just what those experiences mean. Hence, classifying experiences as either favorable or unfavorable to crime commission is difficult at best.

Other critics suggest that differential association alone is not a sufficient explanation for crime. If it were, then we might expect correctional officers, for example, to become criminals by virtue of their constant and continued association with prison inmates. Similarly, wrongly imprisoned people might be expected to turn to crime upon release from confinement. Little evidence suggests that either of these scenarios actually occurs. In effect, association theory does not seem to provide for free choice in individual circumstances, nor does it explain why some individuals, even when surrounded by associates who are committed to lives of crime, are still able to hold onto other, noncriminal values. Finally, association theory fails to account for the emergence of criminal values, addressing only the communication of those values.

Similarly, the labeling approach, although it successfully points to the labeling process as a reason for continued deviance and as a cause of stabilization in deviant identities, does little to explain the origin of crime and deviance. In addition, few, if any, studies seem to support the basic tenets of the theory. Critics of labeling have pointed to its "lack of firm empirical support for the notion of secondary deviance," and "many studies have not found that delinquents or criminals have a delinquent or criminal self-image."[93] There is also a lack of unequivocal empirical support for the claim that contact with the justice system is fundamentally detrimental to the personal lives of criminal perpetrators. Even if that supposition were true, however, one must ask whether it would ultimately be better if offenders were not caught and forced to undergo the rigors of processing by the justice system. Although labeling theory hints that official processing makes a significant contribution to continued criminality, it seems unreasonable to expect that offenders untouched by the system would forego the rewards of future criminality. Finally, labeling theory has little to say about *secret deviants,* or people who engage in criminality but are never caught. An important question about secret deviants, for example, is whether they can be expected to continue in lives of deviance if never caught.

Goffman's work has been criticized as providing a set of "linked concepts" rather than a consistent theoretical framework.[94] Other critics have faulted Goffman for failing to offer suggestions for institutional change or for not proposing treatment modalities based on his assumptions. Goffman's greatest failing may be in taking the analogy of the theater too far and convincing readers that real life is but a form of playacting. According to George Psathas, one of Goffman's critics, "Performing and being are not identical."[95]

Monks in a Buddhist monastery. People in total institutions share all aspects of their lives. How is a prison like a monastery?

Source: Woodfin Camp & Associates

The Social Development Perspective

Over the past 25 years, an emerging appreciation for the process of **human development** has played an increasingly important role in understanding criminality.[96] *Human development* refers to the relationship between the maturing individual and his or her changing environment and to the social processes that relationship entails. Students of human development recognize that the process of development occurs through reciprocal and dynamic interactions that take place between individuals and various aspects of their environment. The **social development perspective** understands that development, which begins at birth (and perhaps even earlier), occurs primarily within a social context. Unlike learning theory (discussed earlier in this chapter), however, social development theories see socialization as only one feature of that context. If socialization were the primary determinant of criminality, development theorists point out, then we might expect that all problem children would become criminals as adults. Since that doesn't happen, there must be other aspects to the development process that social learning theories don't fully appreciate.

According to the social development perspective, human development occurs on many levels simultaneously, including psychological, biological, familial, interpersonal, cultural, societal, and ecological. Hence, social development theories tend to be integrated theories, or theories that combine various points of view on the process of development. The rest of this chapter describes different kinds of social development theories. You can also learn more about such perspectives at Web Extra 8–4.

human development

The relationship between the maturing individual and his or her changing environment, as well as the social processes that the relationship entails.

social development perspective

An integrated view of human development that examines multiple levels of maturation simultaneously, including the psychological, biological, familial, interpersonal, cultural, societal, and ecological levels.

WEB
Extra
▪▪▪▪

Concepts in Social Development Theories

Most sociological explanations for crime involve the study of groups and the identification of differences among groups of offenders. In contrast, social development theories focus more on individual rates of offending and seek to understand both increases and decreases in rates of offending over the individual's lifetime. Social development theories generally employ longitudinal (over time) measurements of delinquency and offending, and they pay special attention to the transitions that people face as they move through the life cycle.

Most theories of social development recognize that a critical transitional period occurs as a person moves from childhood to adulthood. Life course theorists have identified at least seven developmental tasks that American adolescents must confront: (1) establishing identity, (2) cultivating symbiotic relationships, (3) defining physical attractiveness, (4) investing in a value system, (5) obtaining an education, (6) separating from family and achieving independence, and (7) obtaining and maintaining gainful employment.[97] It is generally recognized that youths are confronted with many obstacles, or risks, in their attempts to resolve these issues as they work to make a successful transition to adulthood. Figure 8–4 provides a conceptual model of the developmental processes that a maturing child experiences during adolescence. Learn more about the transitional process leading to adulthood at Web Extra 8–5 at crimtoday.com.

WEB
Extra
▪▪▪▪

The Life Course Perspective

Traditional explanations for crime and delinquency often lack a developmental perspective.[98] That is, they generally ignore developmental changes throughout the life course and frequently fail to distinguish between different phases of criminal careers. In contrast, developmental theories draw attention to the fact that criminal behavior tends to follow a distinct pattern across the life cycle. Criminality is relatively uncommon during childhood; it tends to begin as sporadic instances of delinquency during late adolescence and early adulthood and then diminishes and sometimes completely disappears from a person's behavioral repertoire by age 30 or 40. Of course, some people never commit crimes or do so only rarely, while others become career criminals and persist in lives of crime.

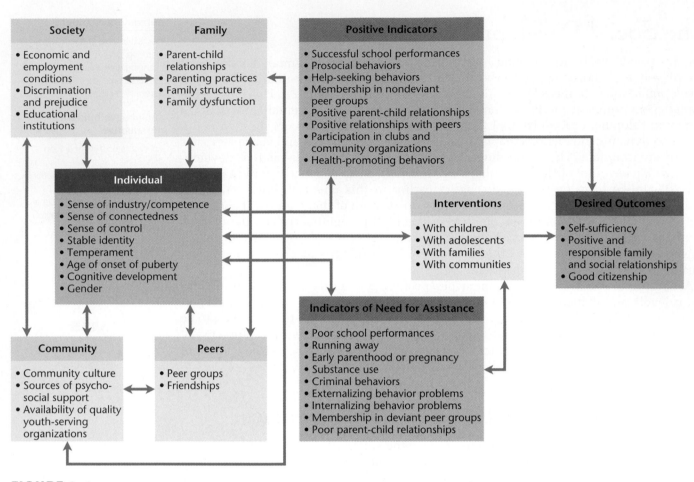

FIGURE 8–4

A Conceptual Model of Adolescent Development

Source: Family and Youth Services Bureau, *Understanding Youth Development: Promoting Positive Pathways of Growth* (Washington, DC: U.S. Department of Health and Human Services, 2000).

life course criminology

Draws attention to the fact that criminal behavior tends to follow a distinct pattern across the life cycle.

criminal career

The longitudinal sequence of crimes committed by an individual offender.

The life course perspective, which is quite popular among criminologists today, shifted the traditional focus away from asking why people begin offending, to questions about the dimensions of criminal offending over the entire life course.[99] Also known as **life course criminology,** the contemporary life course perspective has its roots in a 1986 National Academy of Sciences (NAS) panel report prepared by Alfred Blumstein, Jacqueline Cohen, Jeffrey Roth, and Christy Visher.[100] The NAS report emphasized the importance of the study of criminal careers and of crime over the life course. The NAS panel defined a **criminal career** as "the longitudinal sequence of crimes committed by an individual offender."[101] The report was especially important for its analysis of "offending development," a concept that underlies the life course perspective.

The panel noted that criminal careers could be described in terms of four dimensions: participation, frequency, duration, and seriousness. *Participation,* which refers to the fraction of a population that is criminally active, depends on the scope of criminal acts considered and the length of the observation period.[102] *Frequency* refers to the number of crimes committed by an individual offender per unit of time. Hence, a burglar who commits one burglary a year has a much lower frequency than one who is active monthly or weekly. Frequency is generally not constant and varies over the life course—even for habitual offenders. *Duration* refers to the length of the criminal career. A criminal career can be very short, consisting of only one offense, or it can be quite long, as in the case of habitual or chronic criminals. *Seriousness* is relatively self-explanatory, although it is worthwhile to note that some offenders with long criminal careers commit only petty crimes, while others are serious habitual offenders, and still others commit offenses with a mixed degree of seriousness.

Theory in Perspective

Social Development Theories

Social development theories are integrated theories of human development that examine many different levels simultaneously, including psychological, biological, familial, interpersonal, cultural, societal, and ecological aspects of development.

- *Life Course Theories.* Highlight the development of criminal careers, which are seen as the result of various criminogenic influences that affect individuals throughout the course of their lives.

Period: 1980s–present

Theorists: Alfred Blumstein, John H. Laub, Robert J. Sampson, Terrie E. Moffitt, David P. Farrington, Donald J. West, Lawrence E. Cohen, Richard Machalek

Concepts: Criminal career, life course, trajectory, turning points, age grading, social capital, developmental pathways, life course persisters, adolescence-limited offenders, persistence, desistance, cohort, cohort analysis, longitudinal research, evolutionary ecology

Life course criminology was given its name in a seminal book written by **Robert J. Sampson** and **John H. Laub** in 1993.[103] Earlier, the **life course** concept had already been defined as "pathways through the life span involving a sequence of culturally defined, age-graded roles and social transitions enacted over time."[104] Life course theories, which build on social learning and social control principles, recognize that criminal careers may develop as the result of various criminogenic influences, which affect individuals over the course of their lives.

Researchers who focus on the life course as it leads to delinquency, crime, and criminal identities are interested in evaluating the prevalence, frequency, and onset of offending, as well as identifying different developmental pathways to delinquency. Life course researchers ask a variety of questions: How do early childhood characteristics (for example, antisocial behavior) lead to adult behavioral processes and outcomes? How do life transitions (for example, shifts in relationships from parents to peers, transitions from same-sex peers to opposite-sex peers, transitions from attending school to beginning work, marriage, divorce, and so on) influence behavior and behavioral choices? How do offending and victimization interact over the life cycle?[105]

Life course researchers examine "trajectories and transitions through the age-differentiated life span."[106] A trajectory is a pathway or line of development through life, which is marked by a sequence of transitions in such areas as work, marriage, parenthood, and criminal behavior. "Trajectories refer to longer-term patterns and sequences of behavior, whereas transitions are marked by specific life events (for example, first job or the onset of crime) that are embedded in trajectories and evolve over shorter time spans."[107] The concept of age differentiation (or age grading) recognizes the fact that certain forms of behavior and some experiences are more appropriate (in terms of their social consequences) in certain parts of the life cycle than in others. Having a baby, for example, is more manageable when a woman is married, has a spouse with a dependable job and income, is covered by health insurance, and so on than during adolescence (when marital and employment transitions have yet to be successfully made). Life course theorists search for evidence of continuity between childhood or adolescent experiences and adult outcomes or lifestyles.

Three sets of dynamic concepts are important to the life course perspective: (1) activation, (2) aggravation, and (3) desistance.[108] *Activation* refers to the ways that delinquent behaviors, once initiated, are stimulated and the processes by which the continuity, frequency, and diversity of delinquency are shaped. Three types of activation are possible: (1) acceleration, or increased frequency of offending over time; (2) stabilization, or increased continuity over time; and (3) diversification, or the propensity of individuals to become involved in more diverse delinquent activities. *Aggravation,*

life course

Pathways through the age-differentiated life span; the course of a person's life over time.

the second dynamic process, refers to the existence of a developmental sequence of activities that escalate or increase in seriousness over time. *Desistance,* the third process, describes a slowing down in the frequency of offending (deceleration), a reduction in its variety (specialization), or a reduction in its seriousness (deescalation).[109] Desistance is discussed in greater detail later in this chapter.

Another central organizing principle of life course theories is linked lives. The concept of linked lives refers to the fact that human lives "are typically embedded in social relationships with kin and friends across the life span."[110] Family, friends, and coworkers exercise considerable influence on the life course of most people.

Glen H. Elder, Jr., has identified four important life course principles, which, taken together, provide a concise summary of life course theory.[111]

1. **The principle of historical time and place.** The life course of individuals is embedded in and shaped by the historical times and places they experience over their lifetime. Hence, children born in the United States during the Great Depression or in Nazi Germany during World War II were no doubt strongly influenced by the conditions around them. Similarly, surviving children whose parents were lost in the Holocaust experienced trajectories in their life course that would probably have been far different had they been born elsewhere or at a different time.

2. **The principle of timing in lives.** The developmental impact of a succession of life transitions or events is contingent on when they occur in a person's life. Early marriage, for example, or childbearing at an early age can significantly influence the course of people's lives through the long-term consequences of such events. People who start families early may find themselves excluded from further schooling by the demands of parenthood, and those who leave home and marry early may find that parental financial support is not as readily available to them as it might have been were they still living at home.

3. **The principle of linked lives.** Lives are lived interdependently and social and historical influences are expressed through this network of shared relationships. If a child or a spouse develops a serious illness, for example, the lives of other family members are likely to be affected. Caring for an ill family member is emotionally and financially costly, and it takes time. Because of such costs, opportunities that might have been otherwise available are likely to be lost.

4. **The principle of human agency. Human agency** refers to the fact that individuals construct their own life course through the choices they make and the actions they take within the opportunities and constraints of history and social circumstances. The example that Elder gives is of hard-pressed Depression-era parents who "moved their residence to cheaper quarters and sought alternative forms of income." In making such choices, they were involved in the process of building a new life course.

human agency

The active role that people take in their lives; the fact that people are not merely subject to social and structural constraints but actively make choices and decisions based on the alternatives that they see before them.

Life course theories are supported by research dating back well over half a century. During the 1930s, for example, **Sheldon Glueck** and **Eleanor Glueck** studied the life cycles of delinquent boys.[112] The Gluecks followed the careers of 500 nondelinquents and 500 known delinquents in an effort to identify the causes of delinquency. Study group participants were matched on age, intelligence, ethnicity, and neighborhood residence. Data were originally collected through psychiatric interviews with subjects, parent and teacher reports, and official records obtained from police, court, and correctional files. Surviving subjects were interviewed again between 1949 and 1965.

Significantly, the Gluecks investigated possible contributions to crime causation on four levels: sociocultural (socioeconomic), somatic (physical), intellectual, and emotional-temperamental. They concluded that family dynamics played an especially significant role in the development of criminality, and they observed that "the deeper the roots of childhood maladjustment, the smaller the chance of adult adjustment."[113] Delinquent careers, said the Gluecks, tend to carry over into adulthood and frequently lead to criminal careers. Read more about the life course perspective at Library Extra 8–8, and review

LIBRARY
Extra
▪ ▪ ▪ ▪

Profiles in Crime

Seung-Hui Cho

Seung-Hui Cho was born on January 18, 1984. He rarely talked and possessed a disassociated manner that has been described as an "empty face," as he displayed little reaction to what was occurring around him. Some people think that he may have had symptoms of autism. Cho came to America from the Republic of Korea when he was just eight years old, a sullen, withdrawn and brooding child. He is remembered today as the campus shooter who took the lives of 27 students and 5 professors at Virginia Tech University in 2007.

Interviewed after the tragic events at Virginia Tech, Cho's 84-year-old great-aunt Yang-Soon Kim said: "When I told his mother that he was a good boy, quiet but well behaved, she said she would rather have him respond to her when talked to than be good and meek."[i]

After coming to America and moving to the tight-knit Korean community in Centreville, Virginia, the family maintained an "uncommonly private"[ii] existence. Cho's progression through elementary school was unremarkable. At nearby Chantilly, Virginia's Westfield High School, where the slight, slender boy appeared to be too young to be there, the taciturn Cho was teased and bullied more than most, especially about his poor English and deep-throated voice, which didn't seem to fit his small body.[iii] Throughout his high school years, he remained a quiet and aloof loner who acted, a neighbor observed, "like he had a broken heart."[iv]

While others (including his own sister, Sun-Kyung) in the success-oriented community were heralded in the community newspaper for making the selection lists at some of the most elite Ivy League universities, Cho's good but less-than-stellar grades kept him off such lists. Instead, he matriculated to Virginia Tech in southwest Virginia's Blue Ridge Mountains.

Cho's freshman, sophomore, and junior years as an English major at Virginia Tech were noteworthy for the palpable anger of his writings. Although he never overtly threatened killing people or mentioned guns in particular, the disturbingly violent nature of his papers caused the chairwoman of the English Department to remove him from a creative writing class. She attempted to teach him one-on-one, then sought assistance from the university's counseling department and other university officials.[v]

The anger that seethed within Cho was also of concern to his fellow students, who openly discussed whether he could become a

Seung-Hui, Cho 23, of South Korea, identified by police as the shooter in a massacre that left 33 people dead at Virginia Tech in Blacksburg, Virginia, on April 16, 2007. The shooting is said to be the deadliest killing by a single gunman in modern U.S. history. How can crimes like Seung-Hui's be understood?

Source: AP Wide World Photos/Virginia State Police

school shooter.[vi] In a perceptive article after the shootings, *New York Times* columnist Benedict Carey eloquently explained that "the tragedy...illustrates how human social groups, whether in classrooms, boardrooms or dormitories, are in fact exquisitely sensitive to a threat in their midst."[vii]

The attacks on the Virginia Tech campus were planned and executed with near-military precision. Cho acquired two handguns in the weeks before the shootings, extra magazines, ammunition, and lengths of chain with which to secure the doors of classroom buildings so that potential victims would be unable to escape. Just days before the killings, he videotaped a raging manifesto-like diatribe/suicide note in which he blamed society for making him into what he'd become.[viii] In the video, Cho praised the Columbine High School shooters as martyrs, pronounced himself a Christ figure, and ranted against the hedonistic behavior, trust funds, and high-class living of the financially elite.[ix]

Shortly after 7:00 A.M. on April 16, 2007, Cho killed his first two victims, which police mistakenly believed to have been the result of a lovers' quarrel between one of the victims and her off-campus boyfriend. Their error gave Cho the time he needed to make his last preparations for another attack.[x]

Entering the campus's Norris Hall around 9:30 A.M., Cho secured the interior door handles with chains, then systematically set about slaughtering everyone he encountered. During the next 15 minutes, he fired more than 175 rounds of ammunition from two weapons, leaving 30 people dead within Norris Hall. When Cho heard police blast through the entrance doors to gain access to the building, Cho turned the gun on himself. His rampage is the worst event of its kind in U.S. history,[xi] leaving a total of 32 victims, plus his own tortured soul.

Notes:

[i] Kleinfield, N. R. "Before Deadly Rage, a Life Consumed by Troubling Silence," *New York Times*, April 22, 2007, http://www.nytimes.com/2007/04/22/us/22vatech.html?_r=1&n=Top%2fReference%2fTimes%20Topics%2fPeople%2fC%2fCho%2c%20Seung%2dHui&oref=slogin (accessed July 1, 2007).

[ii] Ibid.

[iii] "High School Classmates Say Gunman Was Bullied," MSNBC, April 19, 2007, http://www.msnbc.msn.com/id/18169776/ (accessed July 1, 2007).

[iv] Kleinfield.

[v] CNN.com, "Professor: Shooter's Writing Dripped With Anger," Cable News Network, April 18, 2007, http://www.cnn.com/2007/US/04/17/vtech.shooting/index.html (accessed July 1, 2007).

[vi] Kleinfield.

[vii] Benedict Carey, "When the Group Is Wise," *New York Times*, April 22, 2007, http://www.nytimes.com/2007/04/22/weekinreview/22carey.html?_r=1&ref=weekinreview&oref=slogin (accessed July 1, 2007).

[viii] Ned Potter, David Schoetz, Richard Esposito, Pierre Thomas, and the staff of ABC News, "Killer's Note: You Caused Me to Do This," ABC News, April 28, 2007, http://abcnews.go.com/US/Story?id=3048108&page=1 (accessed July 1, 2007).

[ix] Kleinfield.

[x] Ibid.

[xi] Aamer Madhani, E. A. Torriero, and Rex W. Huppke, "Danger Signs Festered Below Aloof Surface," *Chicago Tribune*, April 17, 2007, http://www.chicagotribune.com/news/nationworld/chi-070417vtech-shootings,0,1137509.story?page=1&coll=chi-homepagepromo440-fea (accessed July 1, 2007).

LIBRARY
Extra

a paper comparing the life course perspective to other theories discussed in this book at **Library Extra 8–9**.

Laub and Sampson's Age-Graded Theory

A few years ago, John H. Laub and Robert J. Sampson dusted off 60 cartons of nearly forgotten data that had been collected by the Gluecks and were stored in the basement of the Harvard Law School.[114] Upon reanalysis of the data, Laub and Sampson found that children who turned to delinquency were frequently those who had trouble at school and at home and who had friends who were already involved in delinquency. They also found that two events in the life course—marriage and job stability—seemed to be especially important in reducing the frequency of offending in later life.

Using a sophisticated computerized analysis of the Gluecks' original data, Laub and Sampson developed an "age-graded theory of informal social control."[115] Like Hirschi (discussed earlier), Laub and Sampson suggest that delinquency is more likely to occur when an individual's bond to society is weak or broken. Their theory, however, also recognizes "that social ties embedded in adult transitions (for example, marital attachment, job stability) explain variations in crime unaccounted for by childhood deviance."[116] Hence, although it incorporates elements of social bond theory, Laub and Sampson's perspective also emphasizes the significance of continuity and change over the life course.

Central to Laub and Sampson's approach is the idea of turning points in a criminal career. According to the age-graded theory, "the interlocking nature of trajectories and transitions may generate turning points or a change in the life course."[117] One highly significant turning point, for example, may occur when a person becomes a first-time parent and decides to settle down and abandon a carefree or even "fringe" lifestyle. The idea of turning points was first identified by G. B. Trasler in 1980. Trasler wrote, "As they grow older, most young men gain access to other sources of achievement and social satisfaction—a job, a girlfriend, a wife, a home and eventually children—and in doing so become gradually less dependent upon peer-group support."[118] Given the importance of turning points—which may turn a person either toward or away from criminality and delinquency—a clear-cut relationship between early delinquency and criminality later in life cannot be assumed. Turning points can occur at any time in the life course, although, like Trasler, Sampson and Laub identified two especially significant turning points: employment and marriage. Employers who are willing to give "troublemakers" a chance and marriage partners who insist on conventional lifestyles seem to be able to successfully redirect the course of a budding offender's life. Other important turning points can occur in association with leaving home, having children, getting divorced, graduating from school, receiving a financial windfall, and so on. According to Laub and Sampson, even chronic offenders can be reformed when they experience the requisite turning points, while individuals with histories of conventionality can begin offending in response to events and circumstances that undermine previously restraining social bonds.[119]

Because transitions in the life course are typically associated with age and because transitional events (like marriage) either enhance or weaken the social bond, Sampson and Laub contend that "age-graded changes in social bonds explain changes in crime." Since these events are not the result of "purposeful efforts to control," they are dubbed "informal social controls."[120]

In 2001, an examination of data from the Dunedin Study (referred to in Chapter 5) suggested the idea of life course interdependence, in which "the effects of social ties on crime vary as a function of criminal propensity."[121] In other words, prosocial ties that deter crime, such as education, marriage, and steady employment, are more likely to discourage criminality among those who are already predisposed to it than among those who are not. Hence, a good job means less (in terms of its crime prevention impact) to a conformist who is already committed to a law-abiding lifestyle than it does to a risk-taking individual living on the fringe of society. Researchers dubbed this the "social-protection effect." Conversely, they found that a "social-amplification effect" could be identified in antisocial ties that promote crime, such as delinquent friends, among individuals predisposed to criminality. The researchers concluded that certain features of the social environment, such as conventional social ties, could serve as positive turning points in the lives of antisocial individuals, while, at the same time, the social-amplification effect could produce negative turning points in the lives of the same people.

Another important concept in Laub and Sampson's theory is **social capital.** Laub and Sampson use the concept of social capital to refer to the degree of positive relationships, with other people and with social institutions, that individuals build up over the course of their lives.[122] Social capital can be enhanced by education, a consistent employment background, enriching personal connections, a "clean" record, a good marriage and family life, and so on. Social capital impacts directly on life course trajectories: The greater a person's social capital, the less the chance of criminal activity.[123]

A study of how two primary constituents of social capital—marriage and full-time employment—impact life course trajectories was reported by Matthew G. Yeager in 2003.[124] Yeager examined the lives of 773 adult male prisoners who were released from the Canadian federal prison system between 1983 and 1984 and followed them for a period of three years. He found that being married reduced the likelihood of return to prison. An even stronger indicator of postprison success, however, was full-time employment, which Yeager described as having "a strong suppression effect on general criminal recidivism." Because employment is something for which prisoners can be prepared and because it can be offered by the state or government, Yeager suggested that it provides a rare opportunity for successful intervention in the lives of released prisoners.

In 2006, Sampson and Laub reported on the application of sophisticated data-analysis techniques to subjects from the Glueck's original study group, who were reinterviewed at age 70. The 2006 study supported the conclusion that "being married is associated with an average reduction of approximately 35 percent in the odds of crime compared to nonmarried states for the same man."[125]

An interesting evaluation of social capital—in this case, commitment to a romantic partner, strong job attachment, and the nature of close friends among adult subjects—was reported by a group of criminologists in 2002.[126] They found that adolescent delinquency tended to result in involvement with an antisocial romantic partner for both males and females and that such a relationship, in turn, tended to influence the nature of adult relationships and to increase the likelihood of later criminality. Conventional romantic partners and friends, along with strong job attachment, were found to be especially likely to reduce the chance of criminality among young adult women, while only conventional adult friends had the same effect among males. Learn more about the concept of social capital via Library Extra 8–10 at crimtoday.com.

social capital

The degree of positive relationships with others and with social institutions that individuals build up over the course of their lives.

LIBRARY
Extra
▪▪▪▪

Moffitt's Dual Taxonomic Theory

Criminologists have long noted that although adult criminality is almost always preceded by antisocial behavior during adolescence, most antisocial children do not become adult criminals. In what has been called "the most innovative approach to age-crime relationships and lifecourse patterns,"[127] psychologist **Terrie E. Moffitt** developed a two-path (dual taxonomic) theory of criminality that helps to explain this observation.[128] Moffitt's two-path theory contends that, as a result of neuropsychological deficits (specifically, early brain damage or chemical imbalances) combined with poverty and family dysfunction, some people come to display more or less constant patterns of misbehavior throughout life.[129] These people are called "life course–persistent offenders" or "life course persisters." Life course persisters tend to fail in school and become involved in delinquency at an early age. As a consequence, their opportunities for legitimate success are increasingly limited with the passage of time.

Other teenagers, says Moffitt, go through limited periods where they exhibit high probabilities of offending. Probabilities of offending are generally highest for these people, says Moffitt, during the mid-teen years. This second group, called "adolescence-limited offenders," is led to offending primarily by structural disadvantages, according to two-path theory. The most significant of these disadvantages is the status anxiety of teenagers that stems from modern society's inadequacy at easing the transition from adolescence to adulthood for significant numbers of young people. Moffitt hypothesizes that a significant source of adolescent strain arises from the fact that biological maturity occurs at a relatively early age (perhaps as early as age 12) and brings with it the desire for sexual and emotional relationships, as well as personal autonomy.[130] Society, however, does not permit the assumption of autonomous adult roles until far later (around age 18). As adolescents begin to desire autonomy, says Moffitt, they are prevented from achieving it because of preexisting societal expectations and societally limited opportunities, resulting in what Moffitt calls a "maturity gap." They might be told, "You're too young for that," or "Wait until you grow up." Lacking the resources to achieve autonomy on their own, they are drawn into delinquent roles by lifelong deviants who have already achieved autonomy and who serve as role models for others seeking early independence. At least an appearance of autonomy is achievable for adolescence-limited offenders by engaging in actions that mimic those routinely undertaken by life course–persistent offenders. Once adolescence-limited offenders realize the substantial costs of continuing misbehavior, however, they abandon such social mimicry and the participation in delinquent acts that characterizes it. As they mature, they begin to aspire toward achieving legitimate autonomy. Those who fail to successfully make the transition add to the ranks of the life course–persistent population.

Moffitt notes that adolescence-limited offenders display inconsistencies in antisocial behavior, from one place to another. They might, for example, participate in illicit drug use with friends or shoplift in stores. They might also experiment sexually. Still, their school behavior is likely to remain within socially acceptable bounds, and they will probably act with respect toward teachers, employers, and adults. Life course–persistent offenders, on the other hand, consistently engage in antisocial behavior across a wide spectrum of social situations.

Research findings indicate that positive developmental pathways are fostered when adolescents are able to develop (1) a sense of industry and competency, (2) a feeling of connectedness to others and to society, (3) a belief in their ability to control their future, and (4) a stable identity.[131] Adolescents who develop these characteristics appear more likely than others to engage in prosocial behaviors, exhibit positive school performances, and be members of nondeviant peer groups. Competency, connectedness, control, and identity are outcomes of the developmental process. They develop through a person's interactions with his or her community, family, school, and peers. The following kinds of interactions appear to promote development of these characteristics:

- Interactions in which children engage in productive activities and win recognition for their productivity
- Interactions in which parents and other adults control and monitor adolescents' behaviors in a consistent and caring manner while allowing them a substantial degree of psychological and emotional independence
- Interactions in which parents and other adults provide emotional support, encouragement, and practical advice to adolescents
- Interactions in which adolescents are accepted as individuals with unique experiences based on their temperament, gender, biosocial development, and family, cultural, and societal factors

persistence

Continuity in crime, or continual involvement in offending.

desistance

The cessation of criminal activity or the termination of a period of involvement in offending behavior.

Farrington's Delinquent Development Theory

Life course theorists use the term **persistence** to describe continuity in crime, or continual involvement in offending. **Desistance,** on the other hand, refers to the cessation of criminal activity or to the termination of a period of involvement in offending behavior (that is, abandoning a criminal career). Desistance (which was mentioned briefly earlier in this chapter) can be unaided or aided. *Unaided desistance* refers to desistance that occurs without the formal intervention or assistance of criminal justice agencies like probation or parole agencies, the courts, or prison or jail. *Aided desistance*, which does involve agencies of the justice system, is generally referred to as "rehabilitation." As noted earlier in our discussion of adolescence-limited offenders, delinquents often mature successfully and grow out of offending. Even older persistent offenders, however, may tire of justice system interventions or lose the personal energy required for continued offending. Such offenders are said to have "burned out."

A number of early criminologists noted the desistance phenomenon, whereby offenders appear to undergo relatively intense periods of criminal involvement during the teenage years, with continued involvement extended into their twenties and even thirties. By age 35 or so, however, a kind of spontaneous desistance seems to occur. Marvin Wolfgang described the process as one of "spontaneous remission," although it was recognized far earlier. In 1833, Adolphe Quetelet argued that the penchant for crime diminished with age "due to the enfeeblement of physical vitality and the passions."[132] The Gluecks later developed the concept of maturational reform to explain the phenomenon and suggested that the "sheer passage of time" caused delinquents to "grow out" of this transitory phase and to "burn out" physiologically. "Ageing is the only factor," they concluded, "which emerges as significant in the reformative process."[133]

In 1985, Walter R. Grove proposed a maturational theory of biopsychosocial desistance that sees the desistance phenomenon as a natural or normal consequence of the aging process.[134] Grove wrote, "As persons . . . move through the life cycle, (1) they will shift from self-absorption to concern for others; (2) they will increasingly accept societal values and behave in socially appropriate ways; (3) they will become more comfortable with social relations; (4) their activities will increasingly reflect a concern for others in their community; and (5) they will become increasingly concerned with the issue of the meaning of life."[135]

Some criminologists argue, however, that the claim that aging causes desistance is meaningless because it doesn't explain the actual mechanisms involved in the desistance phenomenon. In other words, the claim that an offender "ages out" of crime offers no more explanatory power than the claim that turning 16 causes delinquency.

Longitudinal studies of crime in the life course conducted by **David P. Farrington** and **Donald J. West** have shown far greater diversity in the ages of desistance than in the ages of onset of criminal behavior.[136] In 1982, in an effort to explain the considerable heterogeneity of developmental pathways, Farrington and West began tracking a cohort of 411 boys born in London in 1953. The study, known as the **Cambridge Study in Delinquent Development,** is ongoing. It uses self-reports of delinquency as well as psychological tests and in-depth interviews. To date, participants have been interviewed eight times, with the earliest interviews being conducted at age eight.

Cambridge Study in Delinquent Development

A longitudinal (life course) study of crime and delinquency tracking a cohort of 411 boys born in London in 1953.

The Cambridge study reveals that life course patterns found in the United States are also characteristic of English delinquents. Farrington found that the study's persistent offenders suffered from "hyperactivity, poor concentration, low achievement, an antisocial father, large family size, low family income, a broken family, poor parental supervision, and parental disharmony."[137] Other risk factors for delinquency included harsh discipline, negative peer influences, and parents with offense histories of their own. Chronic offenders were found to have friends and peers who were also offenders, and offending was found to begin with early antisocial behavior, including aggressiveness, dishonesty, problems in school, truancy, hyperactivity, impulsiveness, and restlessness. Consistent with other desistance studies, Farrington found that offending tends to peak around the age of 17 or 18 and then declines. By age 35, many subjects were found to have assumed conforming lifestyles, although they were often separated or divorced with poor employment records and patterns of residential instability. Many former offenders were also substance abusers and consequently served as very poor role models for their children.

While studies of desistance are becoming increasingly common, one of the main methodological problems for researchers is determining when desistance has occurred. Some theorists conceptualize desistance as the complete or absolute stopping of criminal behavior of any kind, while others see it as the gradual cessation of criminal involvement.[138]

In 1990, Rolf Loeber and Marc LeBlanc identified four components of desistance.[139] Desistance, they said, can be conceptualized in terms of (1) *deceleration,* or a slowing down in the frequency of offending; (2) *specialization,* or a reduction in the variety of offenses; (3) *deescalation,* or a reduction in the seriousness of offending; and (4) *reaching a ceiling,* or remaining at a certain level of offending and not committing more serious offenses. Until desistance is better defined and conceptualized, it will remain difficult for researchers to investigate the topic.

Evolutionary Ecology

cohort analysis

A social scientific technique that studies over time a population with common characteristics. Cohort analysis usually begins at birth and traces the development of cohort members until they reach a certain age.

Because life course theory uses a developmental perspective in the study of criminal careers, life course researchers typically use longitudinal research designs involving cohort analysis. **Cohort analysis** usually begins at birth and traces the development of a population whose members share common characteristics, until they reach a certain age. One well-known analysis of a birth cohort, undertaken by **Marvin Wolfgang** during the 1960s, found that a small nucleus of chronic juvenile offenders accounted for a disproportionately large share of all juvenile arrests.[140] Wolfgang studied male individuals born in Philadelphia in 1945 until they reached age 18. He concluded that a small number of violent offenders were responsible for most of the crimes committed by the cohort. Six percent of cohort members accounted for 52% of all arrests. A follow-up study found that the seriousness of the offenses among the cohort increased in adulthood but that the actual number of offenses decreased as the cohort aged.[141] Wolfgang's analysis has since been criticized for its lack of a second cohort, or control group, against which the experiences of the cohort under study could be compared.[142] More recently, Wolfgang published a cohort analysis of 5,000 individuals born in the Wuchang district of the city of Wuhan in China. The study, from which preliminary results were published in 1996, used Chinese-supplied data to compare delinquents with nondelinquents. It found "striking differences in school deportment, achieved level of education, school dropout rate, type of employment, and unemployment rate" between the two groups.[143]

evolutionary ecology

An approach to understanding crime that draws attention to the ways people develop over the course of their lives.

The ecological perspective on crime control, pioneered by **Lawrence E. Cohen** and **Richard Machalek,** provides a contemporary example of a life course approach.[144] Like other life course theories, **evolutionary ecology** blends elements of previous perspectives—in this case, building upon the approach of social ecology—while emphasizing developmental pathways encountered early in life. According to University of Wyoming criminologist Bryan Vila, "the evolutionary ecological approach . . . draws attention to the ways people develop over the course of their lives. Experiences and environment early in life, especially those that affect child development and the transmission of biological traits and family management practices across generations, seem particularly important."[145] According to Vila, evolutionary ecology "attempts to explain how people acquire criminality—a predisposition that disproportionately favors criminal behavior—when and why they express it as crime, how individuals and groups respond to those crimes, and how all these phenomena interact as a dynamic self-reinforcing system that evolves over time."[146]

Thornberry's Interactional Theory

interactional theory

A theoretical approach to exploring crime and delinquency that blends social control and social learning perspectives.

Terence Thornberry has proposed what he calls an **interactional theory** of crime, which integrates social control and social learning explanations of delinquency.[147] In constructing his approach, Thornberry was attentive to the impact of social structure on behavior and noted how delinquency and crime seem to develop within the context of reciprocal social arrangements. Reciprocity was especially important to Thornberry because he believed that too many other theories were overly simplistic in their dependence on simple unidirectional causal relationships.

Theory Versus Reality

Social Influences on Developmental Pathways

A report by the Family and Youth Services Bureau (an agency of the U.S. Department of Health and Human Services) identified five "aspects of the social context" that can either promote or block the development of prosocial behavior among adolescents. These aspects include the following:

- *Biophysical aspects of the individual.* Biophysical characteristics that have been found to influence developmental pathways during adolescence include temperament, gender, cognitive development, and the age of onset of puberty. The influence of these factors on development depends to a large extent on how others in the social context react to them. Individuals bring these aspects of self to the interactions in which they are engaged, and the reaction of the social context to these aspects determines the quality and nature of the interactions.

- *Aspects of the society.* Society may be understood as the economic and institutional structures, values, and mores that constitute a national identity. Some of the aspects of society that influence the development of a sense of competency, connectedness, control, and identity are current economic and employment conditions, discrimination and prejudice, and educational institutions. Societal factors influence adolescent development directly and indirectly through their effects on communities and families. The societal factors of prejudice and discrimination often present barriers to positive developmental pathways for minority and economically disadvantaged youths. For these youths, community and family contexts are particularly important for moderating the potentially negative influences of societal factors.

- *Aspects of the community.* The community context (neighborhood or town) incorporates where individuals spend their time and with whom they spend it. The aspects of the community context that have been studied with respect to their effects on adolescent development include community culture, availability of sources of support to parents and youths, and availability of quality community institutional or organizational resources for children and youths. As with societal factors, community factors have both direct and indirect influences on developmental pathways during adolescence. Formal and informal broad-based community institutions and organizations, in particular, influence adolescent development directly by teaching and encouraging prosocial behaviors and indirectly by supporting parents in their parenting efforts.

- *Aspects of the family.* The following aspects of the family context have received considerable research attention with respect to their influences on developmental pathways: the quality of the parent-child relationship, parenting styles or practices, family structure, and family dysfunction. In general, family practices that serve to monitor and control adolescents' behaviors in a caring and consistent manner, provide support and encouragement to adolescents, and allow them psychological and emotional independence appear to be most effective in fostering the development of a sense of competency, connectedness, control over one's fate in life, and identity.

- *Aspects of peer relationships.* Research findings do not support the popular notion that adolescent problem behaviors are the result of peer pressure. In fact, current research suggests that peers do not direct adolescents to new behaviors as much as they reinforce existing dispositions that helped direct the adolescent to a particular peer group in the first place. Close friendships with peers during adolescence have been found to promote positive growth because they foster the development of conceptions of fairness, mutual respect, empathy, and intimacy. Through these conceptions, youths are able to develop a sense of connectedness to others and a stable sense of identity.

The information in the Family and Youth Services Bureau report suggests that interventions designed to assist youths in making successful transitions to adulthood will need to provide adolescents, either directly or through parents and community resources, with opportunities to engage in interactions that foster the development of a sense of competency, connectedness, control, and identity. The research also suggests that interventions must address children, families, and communities as a unit if they are to be effective for large numbers of children and their families.

Discussion Questions

1. How would you rank the five aspects of the social context identified in this box as impacting the development of prosocial behavior among adolescents in order of relative importance? Why would you choose such a ranking?

2. How might the five "aspects of the social context" interact?

3. Are there other important aspects of the social context that can be identified? If so, what might they be?

Source: Family and Youth Services Bureau, *Understanding Youth Development: Promoting Positive Pathways of Growth* (Washington, DC: U.S. Department of Health and Human Services, January 1997).

The fundamental cause of delinquency according to interactional theory is a weakening of a person's bond to conventional society.[148] Thornberry points out that adolescents who are strongly attached to their parents and family and who strive to achieve within the context of approved social arrangements, such as education, rarely turn to serious delinquency. It takes more than weak conventional bonds, however, for delinquency to develop. A further requirement, says Thornberry, is the presence of an environment in which delinquency can be learned and in which rule-violating behavior can be positively rewarded. Delinquent peers are especially important in providing the kind of environment necessary for criminal behavior to develop, and gang membership can play a highly significant role in the development and continuation of such behavior. Associating with delinquent peers, says Thornberry, leads to delinquent acts, but also involves a causal loop such that those who commit delinquent acts are likely to continue associating with others like themselves—creating a mechanism of social reinforcement and resulting in ever-escalating levels of criminal behavior. Thornberry also predicts that delinquents will seek out association with ever-more delinquent groups if their delinquency continues to be rewarded. Hence, delinquency, from the perspective of interactional theory, is seen as a process that unfolds over the life course.

In a test of interactional theory,[149] Thornberry used data drawn from the Rochester Youth Development Study, a multiwave panel study designed to examine drug use and delinquent behavior among adolescents in the Rochester, New York, area. Study findings, discussed in more detail in the next section, supported the loop-back aspects of interactional theory and showed that delinquency is part of a dynamic social process, and not merely the end result of static conditions. The study also found that the development of beliefs supportive of delinquent behavior tends to follow that behavior in time. In other words, commitment to delinquent values may be more a product of delinquent behavior that is rewarded than an initial cause of such behavior.

A further test of Thornberry's theory found that childhood maltreatment (as measured by official records) could be an important element of the developmental process leading to delinquency.[150] Researchers also found that the degree of maltreatment experienced in childhood bore at least some relationship to the extent of delinquent involvement later in life. While maltreatment appears to weaken the bond to conventionality, it also weakens the family bond. Suman Kaker of Florida International University, in an extension of interactional theory, notes that delinquency also puts stress on the family, resulting in a further weakening of the familial bond.[151]

Developmental Pathways

Researchers have found that manifestations of disruptive behaviors in childhood and adolescence are often age dependent, reflecting a developing capability to display different behaviors with age.[152] Budding behavioral problems can often be detected at an early age. In 1994, for example, Rolf Loeber and Dale F. Hay described the emergence of opposition to parents and aggression toward siblings and peers as a natural developmental occurrence during the first two years of life.[153] Loeber and Hay found, however, that as toddlers develop the ability to speak, they become increasingly likely to use words to resolve conflicts. As a consequence, oppositional behaviors decline between ages three and six, as children acquire greater verbal skills for expressing their needs and for dealing with conflict. Children who are unable, for whatever reason, to develop adequate verbal coping skills, however, distinguish themselves from the norm by committing acts of intense aggression, initiating hostile conflict, and being characterized by parents as having a difficult temperament.[154] Figure 8–5 shows the order in which disruptive and antisocial childhood behaviors tend to manifest between birth and late adolescence. Figure 8–6, in contrast, shows the order of development of skills and attitudes deemed necessary for successful prosocial development during childhood and adolescence.

One of the most comprehensive studies to date that has attempted to detail life pathways leading to criminality began in 1986. The study, called the Program of Research on the Causes and Correlates of Delinquency, is sponsored by the U.S. Department of Justice's Office of Juvenile Justice and Delinquency Prevention. The program, a longitudinal study that is producing ongoing results, intends to improve the understanding of serious delinquency, violence, and drug use by examining how youths develop within the context of family, school, peers, and community.[155] It has compiled data on

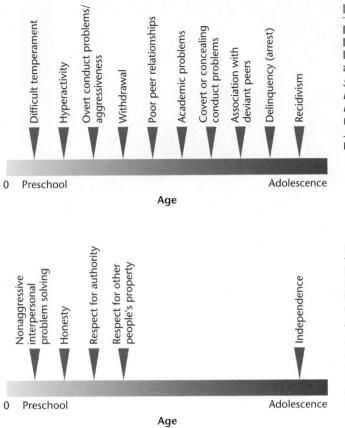

FIGURE 8-5

Manifestations of Disruptive and Antisocial Behaviors in Childhood and Adolescence

Source: Barbara Tatem Kelley et al., *Developmental Pathways in Boys' Disruptive and Delinquent Behavior* (Washington, DC: Office of Juvenile Justice and Delinquency Prevention, December 1997).

FIGURE 8-6

Developmental Tasks Necessary for Prosocial Development during Childhood and Adolescence

Source: Barbara Tatem Kelley et al., *Developmental Pathways in Boys' Disruptive and Delinquent Behavior* (Washington, DC: Office of Juvenile Justice and Delinquency Prevention, December 1997).

4,500 youths from three distinct but coordinated projects: the Denver Youth Survey, conducted by the University of Colorado; the Pittsburgh Youth Study, undertaken by University of Pittsburgh researchers; and the Rochester Youth Development Study, fielded by professors at the State University of New York at Albany.

The Causes and Correlates projects all use a similar research design. All of the projects are longitudinal investigations involving repeated contacts with youths during a substantial portion of their developmental years. In each project, researchers conduct individual, face-to-face interviews with inner-city youths considered to be at high risk for involvement in delinquency and drug abuse. Multiple perspectives on each child's development and behavior are obtained through interviews with the child's primary caretakers and in interviews with teachers. In addition to interview data, the studies collect extensive information from official agencies, including police, courts, schools, and social services.[156]

Program results show that (1) delinquency is related to individual risk factors like impulsivity; (2) the more seriously involved in drugs a youth is, the more seriously that juvenile will be involved in delinquency; (3) children who are more attached to and involved with their parents are less involved in delinquency; (4) greater risks exist for violent offending when a child is physically abused or neglected early in life; (5) students who are not highly committed to school have higher rates of delinquency, and delinquency involvement reduces commitment to school; (6) poor family life, and especially poor parental supervision, exacerbates delinquency and drug use; (7) affiliation with street gangs and illegal gun ownership are both predictive of delinquency; (8) living in a "bad" neighborhood doubles the risk for delinquency; and (9) family receipt of public assistance (welfare) is associated with the highest risk of delinquency (followed by low socioeconomic status).[157] Results also showed that "peers who were delinquent or used drugs had a great impact on [other] youth." In terms of desistance, program results show that "the best predictors of success were having conventional friends, having a stable family and good parental monitoring, having positive expectations for the future, and not having delinquent peers."[158]

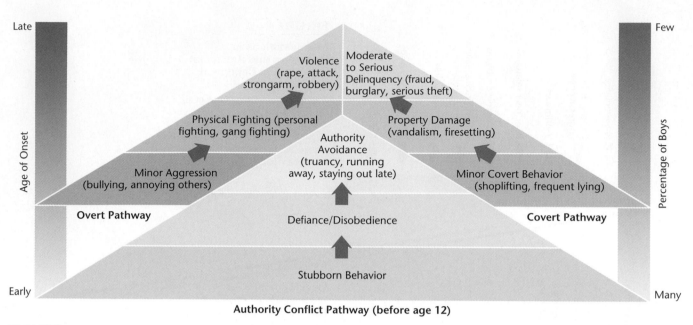

FIGURE 8–7

Three Pathways to Disruptive Behavior and Delinquency

Source: Barbara Tatem Kelley et al., *Developmental Pathways in Boys' Disruptive and Delinquent Behavior* (Washington, DC: Office of Juvenile Justice and Delinquency Prevention, December 1997).

Perhaps the most significant result of the Causes and Correlates study is the finding that three separate developmental pathways to delinquency exist. The pathways identified by the study are shown in Figure 8–7. They are[159]

- The *authority conflict pathway,* on which subjects appear to begin quite young (as early as three or four years of age). "The first step," said the study authors, "was stubborn behavior, followed by defiance around age 11, and authority avoidance—truancy, staying out late at night, or running away."

- The *covert pathway,* which begins with "minor covert acts such as frequent lying and shoplifting, usually around age 10." Delinquents following this path quickly progress "to acts of property damage, such as firestarting or vandalism, around age 11 or 12, followed by moderate and serious forms of delinquency."

- The *overt pathway,* in which the first step is marked by minor aggression such as "annoying others and bullying—around age 11 or 12." Bullying was found to escalate into "physical fighting and violence as the juvenile progressed along this pathway." The overt pathway eventually leads to violent crimes like rape, robbery, and assault.

WEB
Extra
■■■■

LIBRARY
Extra
■■■■

Researchers have found that these three different pathways are not necessarily mutually exclusive and can at times converge (see Figure 8–8). Self-report data show that simultaneous progression along two or more pathways leads to higher rates of delinquency than would otherwise occur.[160] Learn more about the Causes and Correlates study and view results from each study site at **Web Extra 8–6** at crimtoday.com. Read more about the Program of Research on the Causes and Correlates of Delinquency at **Library Extra 8–11**, and review literature on developmental pathways at **Library Extras 8–12** and **8–13**.

The Chicago Human Development Project

Another study that could produce substantially significant results began in 1990. The **Project on Human Development in Chicago Neighborhoods (PHDCN)** is jointly sponsored by the National Institute of Justice and the John D. and Catherine T. MacArthur

Overt Pathway

Covert Pathway

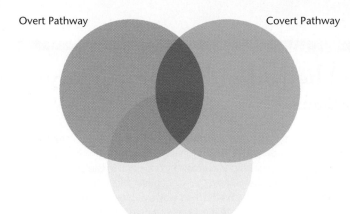

Authority Conflict Pathway

FIGURE 8–8

Single or Multiple Disruptive Pathways

Source: Barbara Tatem Kelley et al., *Developmental Pathways in Boys' Disruptive and Delinquent Behavior* (Washington, DC: Office of Juvenile Justice and Delinquency Prevention, December 1997).

The Project on Human Development in Chicago Neighborhoods uses this drawing as its masthead. The multidisciplinary project, which consists of a longitudinal analysis of how individuals, families, institutions, and communities evolve together, is jointly sponsored by the National Institute of Justice and the John D. and Catherine T. MacArthur Foundation. What results has the study produced?

Source: Hyde Park Bank Foundation

Foundation.[161] PHDCN is directed by physician Felton J. Earls, professor of human behavior and development at Harvard University's School of Public Health. Also involved in the project are Robert Sampson, professor of sociology at the University of Chicago, and Stephen Raudenbush, professor of education at Michigan State University. Earls and Albert J. Reiss describe the ongoing research as "the major criminologic investigation of this century."[162]

PHDCN, which consists of a longitudinal analysis of how individuals, families, institutions, and communities evolve together, is now "tracing how criminal behavior develops from birth to age 32."[163] It involves experts from a wide range of disciplines, including psychiatry, developmental and clinical psychology, sociology, criminology, public health and medicine, education, human behavior, and statistics.

The project is actually two studies combined into a single, comprehensive design. The first is an intensive study of Chicago's neighborhoods. This aspect of the project is evaluating the social, economic, organizational, political, and cultural components of each neighborhood. It seeks to identify changes that took place in the neighborhoods over the study's eight-year data-gathering period. The second project component consists of a series of coordinated longitudinal evaluations of 7,000 randomly selected

Project on Human Development in Chicago Neighborhoods (PHDCN)

An intensive study of Chicago neighborhoods employing longitudinal evaluations to examine the changing circumstances of people's lives in an effort to identify personal characteristics that may lead toward or away from antisocial behavior.

Who's to Blame—The Individual or Society?

Sexual Abuser Claims Victim Status

Mortimer Rataway was arrested after authorities received a report of a man struggling with a boy in a Short Stop food and beverage store. A police offer on nearby patrol arrived at the scene within minutes and observed Rataway forcing the boy, nine-year-old Justin, into an old sedan outside of the convenience store. When the officer asked Rataway what was going on, the boy blurted out that he had been kidnapped.

The officer had heard reports on his radio describing the kidnapping of a nine-year-old boy from a school bus stop in an adjacent city two days earlier, and quickly took Rataway into custody on suspicion of kidnapping.

Justin was taken to a special area reserved for juveniles in the local police station where he told detectives that he was the boy who had been kidnapped. Although he was physically okay, he told police that Rataway had forced him to engage in repeated masturbation, and that Rataway had taken many photographs of him naked.

A search of Rataway's apartment uncovered a number of digital cameras and a computer Web server hosting a child pornography site. The camera and computer contained photos of many other young boys. Some of the photos had probably been purchased over the Internet, but Rataway later admitted taking some of the others.

"I never hurt anybody," Rataway told investigators. "Most of the boys agreed to serve as models after I paid them. But I got carried away, and grabbed Justin because I thought he'd make one of my best models."

"Yeah, I'm gay," Rataway, told the police in a recorded statement. "And sure, I like boys. But it isn't my fault. When I was growing up as a young Catholic I was taught to enjoy my body and to like other men by the parish priest. Now I know that most priests are good men, and that the crisis in the Church has been way overblown by the media. But if that hadn't happened to me, I know I would have been straight, and I'm sure I would have gotten married and had kids of my own. Because of what happened to me when I was a kid, I'm as much a victim as anybody. It doesn't matter how much you punish me, I'm never going to change my sexual orientation."

Think about it:

1. Do you see Rataway as a criminal or a victim, as he claims he is? Might he be both?

2. Some people describe child molesters as "sick." Is Rataway "sick"? If so, how can he be cured?

3. Will sending Rataway to prison rehabilitate him? Why or why not? How can you ensure that he won't pose a future threat if he is one day released back into society?

4. Use this case to illustrate how our understandings of criminal motivation and crime causality influence our notions of fairness and justice in the treatment of offenders.

---

children, adolescents, and young adults. This aspect of the study is looking at the changing circumstances of people's lives and is attempting to identify personal characteristics that may lead toward or away from antisocial behavior. Researchers are exploring a wide range of variables—from prenatal drug exposure, lead poisoning, and nutrition to adolescent growth patterns, temperament, and self-image—as they try to identify which individuals might be most at risk for crime and delinquency. Additional features of the project include a study of children's exposure to violence and its consequences and an evaluation of child care and its impact on early childhood development. A variety of study methodologies is being used, including self-reports, individualized tests and examinations, direct observation, the examination of existing records, and reports by informants. The questions being explored can be described as follows:[164]

- **Communities.** Why do some communities experience high rates of antisocial behavior while other, apparently similar communities are relatively safe?
- **School.** Some children have achievement problems early in school. Others have behavioral or truancy problems. Some exhibit both kinds of problems, and others neither. Why do these differences exist? What are their causes and effects?
- **Peers.** Delinquent youths tend to associate with delinquent peers and usually act in groups. Does this association *lead* to delinquency, or is it simply a case of "like finding like"? Are the influences of peers equally important for girls and for boys, or are their developmental pathways entirely different?
- **Families.** Poor parenting practices are strongly associated with substance abuse and delinquency, but are they the cause of such behavior? If so, then social

programs in parenting skills could make a difference. But what if there are underlying factors, such as temperamental characteristics or social isolation, that cause problems in both parents and children?

- **Individual differences.** What health-related, cognitive, intellectual, and emotional factors in children promote positive social development? What factors put them at risk of developing antisocial behaviors?

PHDCN is already producing results and has led to targeted interventions intended to lower rates of offending. According to Sampson, "Instead of external actions (for example, a police crackdown), we stress in this study the effectiveness of 'informal' mechanisms by which residents themselves achieve public order. In particular, we believe that collective expectations for intervening on behalf of neighborhood children is a crucial dimension of the public life of neighborhoods."[165] Life course perspectives, like the perspective that informs PHDCN, often point to the need for early intervention with nurturant strategies that build self-control through positive socialization. As Bryan Vila points out, "There are two main types of nurturant strategies: those that improve early life experiences to forestall the development of strategic styles based on criminality, and those that channel child and adolescent development in an effort to improve the match between individuals and their environment."[166] Nurturant crime control strategies are discussed in more detail in Chapter 15. Learn more about the Project on Human Development in Chicago Neighborhoods at Web Extra 8–7.

WEB Extra ■ ■ ■ ■

Policy Implications of Social Development Theories

Social development strategies have been widely applied to juvenile justice and human services settings. The Office of Juvenile Justice and Delinquency Prevention has adopted the social development model as the foundation for its Comprehensive Strategy for Serious, Violent, and Chronic Juvenile Offenders program. The Comprehensive Strategy Program provides participating communities with a framework for preventing delinquency, intervening in early delinquent behavior, and responding to serious, violent, and chronic offending. It assists communities in establishing or modifying a juvenile justice "continuum of care" through risk-focused prevention, risk and needs assessment, structured decision making, and graduated sanctions training and technical assistance. OJJDP's Comprehensive Strategy Program centers around the following six components:

- Strengthening families in their role of providing guidance and discipline and instilling sound values as the first and primary teacher of children
- Supporting core social institutions, including schools, churches, and other community organizations, so that they can reduce risk factors and help children develop their full potential
- Promoting prevention strategies that enhance protective factors and reduce the impact of negative risk factors affecting the lives of young people at risk for high delinquency
- Intervening immediately and constructively when delinquent behavior first occurs
- Identifying and controlling a small segment of violent and chronic juvenile offenders
- Establishing a broad spectrum of *sanctions* that ensure accountability and a continuum of services

WEB Extra ■ ■ ■ ■

A few years ago the Office of Juvenile Justice and Delinquency Prevention began a national evaluation of the Comprehensive Strategy Program. Learn more about the program via Web Extra 8–8, where you can keep abreast of the ongoing evaluation.

Another contemporary example of social intervention efforts tied to a developmental model is Targeted Outreach, a program operated by Boys and Girls Clubs of America.[167] The program has its origins in the 1972 implementation of a youth development strategy based on studies undertaken at the University of Colorado, which showed that at-risk youths could be effectively diverted from the juvenile justice system through the provision of positive alternatives. Using a wide referral network made up of local schools, police departments, and various youth service agencies, club officials work to end what they call the "inappropriate detention of juveniles."[168]

The program's primary goal is to provide a positive, productive alternative to gangs for the youths who are most vulnerable to their influences or are already entrenched in gang activity. Currently, the program recruits at-risk youngsters—many as young as seven years old—and diverts them into activities that are intended to promote a sense of belonging, competence, usefulness, and self-control. A sense of belonging is fostered through clubs that provide familiar settings where each child is accepted. Competence and usefulness are developed through opportunities for meaningful activities, which young people in the club program can successfully undertake. Finally, Targeted Outreach provides its youthful participants with a chance to be heard and, consequently, with the opportunity to influence decisions affecting their future. To date, Targeted Outreach has served more than 10,000 at-risk youths. Organizers hope that Targeted Outreach will eventually involve more than 1.5 million youngsters between the ages of 7 and 17. Mobilization for Youth and Targeted Outreach both stand as examples of the kinds of programs that theorists who focus on the social structure typically seek to implement.

Critique of Social Development Theories

Social development theories have been criticized for, among other things, definitional issues. What, for example, do life course concepts like turning point, pathway, risk factor, persistence, desistance, and criminal career really mean? Precise definitions of such concepts are necessary if hypotheses derived from life course theories are to be tested. Some writers have identified "associated problems of how to develop risk/needs assessment devices and how to use these both in fundamental research (to maximize the yield of serious offenders while still making it possible to draw conclusions about the general population) and in applied research (to decide which populations should be targeted by interventions)."[169]

Like the social structural approaches discussed in Chapter 7, social development theories are intimately associated with the first prong of this textbook's theme—the social problems approach, which was described in Chapter 1. For policymakers, an important question is what role individual choice plays, if any, in human development. Do people actively select components of the life course? Do they influence their own trajectories? Since so many important life course determinants are set in motion in early childhood and during adolescence, should those who make wrong choices be held accountable?

SUMMARY

In this chapter, we discussed both social process and social development explanations for crime and criminality. Social process approaches include social learning theory, social control theory, labeling theory, reintegrative shaming, and dramaturgy. Social development theories, in contrast, focus on the life course and emphasize contingent events that affect the transitions that people make as they move through the life cycle.

While all of these perspectives assume that everyone has the potential to violate the law and while they all stress the important role of social interaction in crime causation, social development theories are the most comprehensive. They evaluate all aspects of the life experience, from birth through adolescence and into adulthood, for clues to the social conditions, individual circumstances, and life experiences that lead to crime and deviance. Crucial to the social development perspective is the idea that human development occurs simultaneously on many levels. Because they examine offending over the life course, theories of social development tend to make use of longitudinal studies, or the analysis of cohorts over time.

KEY TERMS

Cambridge Study in Delinquent Development, 327

cohort analysis, 328

containment, 305

containment theory, 304

control ratio, 309

criminal career, 320

desistance, 326

differential association, 300

differential identification theory, 302

discrediting information, 313

dramaturgical perspective, 314

evolutionary ecology, 328

general theory of crime, 308

human agency, 322

human development, 319

impression management, 315

interactional theory, 328

labeling, 311

learning theory, 300

life course, 321

life course criminology, 320

moral enterprise, 311

persistence, 326

primary deviance, 310

prosocial bonds, 316

Project on Human Development in Chicago Neighborhoods (PHDCN), 332

reintegrative shaming, 313

secondary deviance, 311

social bond, 305

social capital, 325

social control theory, 303

social development perspective, 319

social process theory, 299

stigmatic shaming, 313

tagging, 310

total institution, 316

KEY NAMES

Ronald L. Akers, 301

Howard Becker, 311

John Braithwaite, 313

Robert Burgess, 301

Lawrence E. Cohen, 328

David P. Farrington, 327

Daniel Glaser, 302

Eleanor Glueck, 322

Sheldon Glueck, 322

Erving Goffman, 314

Michael Gottfredson, 308

Travis Hirschi, 305

Howard B. Kaplan, 305

John H. Laub, 321

Edwin M. Lemert, 318

Richard Machalek, 328

Terrie E. Moffitt, 325

Walter C. Reckless, 304

Robert J. Sampson, 321

Edwin Sutherland, 300

Frank Tannenbaum, 310

Terence Thornberry, 328

Charles R. Tittle, 309

Donald J. West, 327

Marvin Wolfgang, 328

QUESTIONS FOR REVIEW

1. How does the process of social interaction contribute to criminal behavior?

2. What are the various social process perspectives discussed in this chapter? Describe each.

3. What kinds of social policy initiatives might be based on social process theories of crime causation?

4. What are the shortcomings of the social process perspective?

5. What are the various social development perspectives discussed in this chapter? Describe each.

6. What are the central concepts of social development theories? Explain each.

7. What kinds of social policy initiatives might be suggested by social development perspectives?

8. List and describe the various shortcomings of social development perspectives on criminality.

QUESTIONS FOR REFLECTION

1. This chapter describes both social process and social development perspectives. What are the significant differences between these two perspectives? What kinds of theories characterize each?

2. This textbook emphasizes a social problems versus social responsibility theme. Which of the perspectives discussed in this chapter (if any) best support the social problems approach? Which (if any) support the social responsibility approach? Why?

3. This chapter contains a discussion of the labeling process. Give a few examples of the everyday imposition of positive, rather than negative, labels. Why is it so difficult to impose positive labels on individuals who were previously labeled negatively?

4. Do you believe that Erving Goffman's dramaturgical approach, which sees the world as a stage and individuals as actors upon that stage, provides any valuable insights into crime and criminality? If so, what are they?

WEB QUEST

Visit the Office of Juvenile Justice and Delinquency Prevention on the World Wide Web at ojjdp.ncjrs.org. Browse the site to learn about the programs and initiatives supported by OJJDP. The programs listed, for example, include the Causes and Correlates of Delinquency Program, the Drug-Free Communities Support Program, the Juvenile Mentoring Program, the Safe Futures Program, and the Strengthening America's Families initiative. Select at least five of these programs or initiatives, and study the underlying philoso-phy associated with each. Which of these programs appear to be based on social process principles? On social development concepts? Are there any programs listed on the OJJDP site that seem to be built on assumptions drawn from social structural approaches? If so, which programs? After you have listed and described at least five programs or initiatives, classify each according to its theoretical underpinnings, and submit your findings to your instructor if asked to do so.

NOTES

[1] Albert K. Cohen, *Delinquent Boys: The Culture of the Gang* (Glencoe, IL: Free Press, 1955), p. 11.

[2] William Faulkner, *As I Lay Dying* (New York: Random House, 1964).

[3] Terrie E. Moffitt, "Adolescence-Limited and Life-Course-Persistent Antisocial Behavior: A Developmental Taxonomy," *Psychological Review*, Vol. 100, No. 4 (1993), pp. 674–701.

[4] Legal Action Center, *After Prison: Roadblocks to Reentry—A Report on State Legal Barriers Facing People with Criminal Records* (Washington, DC: Legal Action Center, 2004), www.lac. org/lac/upload/lacreport/LAC_PrintReport.pdf (accessed January 2, 2007).

[5] Details for this story come from Kirk Johnson, "Columbine Evidence Is Placed on Chilling Public Display," *New York Times*, February 27, 2004, http://www.carleton.ca/law/outlines/f03/ 3307bv-f03-ColumbineEvidence-mcnaught.html (accessed January 5, 2007); and Robert Weller, "Authorities Had Many Contacts with Killers before Columbine Massacre," *Denver Post*, February 27, 2004, http://www.denverpost.com/Stories/ 0,1413,36~53~1981294,00.html (accessed January 5, 2007).

[6] "Columbine Evidence Shown," *Richmond Times-Dispatch*, February 27, 2004, http://www.timesdispatch.com/servlet/ Satellite?pagename=RTD/MGArticle/RTD_BasicArticle& c=MGArticle&cid=1031773924178 (accessed January 5, 2007).

[7] "Columbine Report Stirs Anger," CBS News, February 26, 2004, http://www.cbsnews.com/stories/2003/10/22/national/ main579500.shtml (accessed January 5, 2007).

[8] Fight Crime, Invest in Kids, *Bullying Prevention Is Crime Prevention* (Washington, DC: Fight Crime, 2003).

[9] "Columbine: Were There Warnings?" CBS News, February 26, 2004, http://www.cbsnews.com/stories/2004/02/26/national/ main602460.shtml (accessed January 5, 2007).

[10] Edwin Sutherland, *Principles of Criminology*, 3rd ed. (New York: Lippincott, 1939).

[11] Edwin H. Sutherland and Donald R. Cressey, *Criminology* (New York: Lippincott, 1978).

[12] Robert Burgess and Ronald L. Akers, "A Differential Association–Reinforcement Theory of Criminal Behavior," *Social Problems*, Vol. 14 (1966), pp. 363–383.

[13] Ibid., p. 364.

[14] Ronald L. Akers, *Deviant Behavior: A Social Learning Approach* (Belmont, CA: Wadsworth, 1973).

[15] Ibid.

[16] Ronald L. Akers, *Social Learning and Social Structure: A General Theory of Crime and Deviance* (Boston: Northeastern University Press, 1998).

[17] Ronald L. Akers, *Deviant Behavior: A Social Learning Approach*, 3rd ed. (Belmont, CA: Wadsworth, 1985), pp. 40–41.

[18] Gang Lee, Ronald L. Akers, and Marian J. Borg, "Social Learning and Structural Factors in Adolescent Substance Use," *Western Criminology Review*, Vol. 5, No. 1 (2004), p. 17.

[19] Daniel Glaser, "Differential Association and Criminological Prediction," *Social Problems*, Vol. 8 (1960), pp. 6–14.

[20] Daniel Glaser, "Differential Identification," in Henry N. Pontel, ed., *Social Deviance: Readings in Theory and Research*, 3rd ed. (Upper Saddle River, NJ: Prentice Hall 1999), p. 146.

[21] Charles R. Tittle, "Theoretical Developments in Criminology," in National Institute of Justice, *Criminal Justice 2000*, Vol. 1, *The Nature of Crime: Continuity and Change* (Washington, DC: National Institute of Justice, 2000), p. 65.

[22] For a good overview of social control approaches, see George S. Bridges and Martha Myers, eds., *Inequality, Crime, and Social Control* (Boulder, CO: Westview Press, 1994).

[23] Walter C. Reckless, *The Crime Problem*, 4th ed. (New York: Appleton-Century-Crofts, 1967).

[24] Ibid., p. 470.

[25] Ibid.

[26] Ibid., p. 475.

[27] Ibid.

[28] Howard B. Kaplan, "Self-Derogation and Violence," paper presented at the first meeting of the International Society for Research on Aggression, Toronto, August 1974. See also Howard B. Kaplan and A. D. Pokorny, "Self-Derogation as an Antecedent of Suicidal Responses," paper presented at the Eighth International Congress on Suicide Prevention and Crisis Intervention, Jerusalem, October 19–22, 1975.

[29] Howard B. Kaplan, *Deviant Behavior in Defense of Self* (New York: Academic Press, 1980).

[30] M. Rosenberg, C. Schooler, and C. Schoenbach, "Self-Esteem and Adolescent Problems: Modeling Reciprocal Effects," *American Sociological Review*, Vol. 54 (1989), pp. 1004–1018.

[31] L. E. Wells, "Self-Enhancement through Delinquency: A Conditional Test of Self-Derogation Theory," *Journal of Research in Crime and Delinquency,* Vol. 26, No. 3 (1989), pp. 226–252.

[32] K. Leung and F. Drasgow, "Relation between Self-Esteem and Delinquent Behavior in Three Ethnic Groups: An Application of Item Response Theory," *Journal of Cross-Cultural Psychology,* Vol. 17, No. 2 (1986), pp. 151–167.

[33] G. Calhoun, Jr., S. Connley, and J. A. Bolton, "Comparison of Delinquents and Non-delinquents in Ethnicity, Ordinal Position and Self-Perception," *Journal of Clinical Psychology,* Vol. 40, No. 1 (1984), pp. 323–328.

[34] D. Oyserman and H. R. Markus, "Possible Selves in Balance: Implications for Delinquency," *Journal of Social Issues,* Vol. 46, No. 2 (1990), pp. 141–157.

[35] Daphna Oyserman and Hazel Markus, "The Sociocultural Self," in J. Suls, ed., *Psychological Perspectives on the Self,* Vol. 4 (Hillsdale, NJ: Erlbaum, 1993), pp. 187–220.

[36] Travis Hirschi, *Causes of Delinquency* (Berkeley: University of California Press, 1969).

[37] Tittle, "Theoretical Developments in Criminology," p. 65.

[38] Hirschi, *Causes of Delinquency.*

[39] Ibid.

[40] Ibid.

[41] Ibid.

[42] Ibid.

[43] Ibid.

[44] Ibid.

[45] Michael Gottfredson and Travis Hirschi, *A General Theory of Crime* (Stanford, CA: Stanford University Press, 1990).

[46] See also Michael R. Gottfredson and Travis Hirschi, "Criminality and Low Self-Control," in John E. Conklin, ed., *New Perspectives in Criminology* (Boston: Allyn & Bacon, 1996).

[47] Werner Einstadter and Stuart Henry, *Criminological Theory: An Analysis of Its Underlying Assumptions* (Fort Worth, TX: Harcourt Brace, 1995), p. 189.

[48] Charles R. Tittle, *Control Balance: Toward a General Theory of Deviance* (Boulder, CO: Westview Press, 1995).

[49] For an excellent summation of control-balance theory, see Alex R. Piquero and Matthew Hickman, "An Empirical Test of Tittle's Control Balance Theory," *Criminology,* Vol. 37, No. 2 (1999), pp. 319–341.

[50] Tittle, *Control Balance,* p. 181.

[51] Piquero and Hickman, "An Empirical Test of Tittle's Control Balance Theory," p. 327.

[52] Tittle, *Control Balance,* p. 95. For a good critique of control-balance theory, see Joachim J. Savelsberg, "Human Nature and Social Control in Complex Society: A Critique of Charles Tittle's Control Balance," *Theoretical Criminology,* Vol. 3, No. 3 (August 1999), pp. 331–338.

[53] "Killer's Admission to Law School Criticized," *Fayetteville (NC) Observer-Times,* September 12, 1993, p. 14A.

[54] See the biography of James Hamm at the Middle Ground Prison Reform, Inc., Web site, http://www.middlegroundprisonreform.org/hamm (accessed January 10, 2007).

[55] Frank Tannenbaum, *Crime and the Community* (New York: Atheneum Press, 1938), pp. 17–18.

[56] Ibid., p. 19.

[57] Edwin M. Lemert, *Social Pathology: A Systematic Approach to the Theory of Sociopathic Behavior* (New York: McGraw-Hill, 1951), p. 76.

[58] Ibid.

[59] Howard Becker, *Outsiders: Studies in the Sociology of Deviance* (New York: Free Press, 1963).

[60] Ibid., p. 1.

[61] Ibid., p. 9.

[62] Ibid., p. 147.

[63] Ibid., pp. 37–38.

[64] Jon Gunnar Bernburg and Marvin D. Krohn, "Labeling, Life Chances, and Adult Crime: The Direct and Indirect Effects of Official Intervention in Adolescence on Crime in Early Adulthood," *Criminology,* Vol. 41, No. 4 (2003), pp. 1287–1318.

[65] Robert J. Sampson and John H. Laub, "A Life-Course Theory of Cumulative Disadvantage and the Stability of Delinquency," in Terence P. Thornberry, ed., *Developmental Theories of Crime and Delinquency* (New Brunswick, NJ: Transaction, 1997).

[66] Jon Gunnar Bernburg and Marvin D. Krohn, "Labeling, Life Chances, and Adult Crime: The Direct and Indirect Effects of Official Intervention in Adolescence on Crime in Early Adulthood," *Criminology,* Vol. 41, No. 4 (2003), pp. 1287–1318.

[67] Legal Action Center, *After Prison: Roadblocks to Reentry.*

[68] Mike S. Adams, "Labeling and Differential Association: Towards a General Social Learning Theory of Crime and Deviance," *American Journal of Criminal Justice,* Vol. 20, No. 2 (1996), pp. 147–164.

[69] Ibid., p. 160.

[70] John Braithwaite and Heather Strang, "The Right Kind of Shame for Crime Prevention," *RISE Working Papers, Number 1* (Australian National University, 1997), http://www.aic.gov.au/rjustice/rise/working/risepap1.html (accessed March 11, 2005).

[71] *RISE Working Papers: Introduction* (Canberra: Australian National University, 1997).

[72] A number of papers have been released in the Reintegrative Shaming Experiments (RISE) series. They include Lawrence W. Sherman and Heather Strang, *The Right Kind of Shame for Crime Prevention* (Canberra: Australian National University, 1997); Heather Strang and Lawrence W. Sherman, *The Victim's Perspective* (Canberra: Australian National University, 1997); Lawrence W. Sherman and Geoffrey C. Barnes, *Restorative Justice and Offenders' Respect for the Law* (Canberra: Australian National University, 1997); and Lawrence W. Sherman and Heather Strang, *Restorative Justice and Deterring Crime* (Canberra: Australian National University, 1997).

[73] John Braithwaite and Heather Strang, "Restorative Justice and Offenders' Respect for the Law," *RISE Working Papers, Number 3* (Australian National University, 1997), http://www.aic.gov.au/rjustice/rise/working/risepap3.html (accessed March 11, 2005).

[74] Ibid.

[75] Erving Goffman, *The Presentation of Self in Everyday Life* (Garden City, NY: Doubleday, 1959), p. 135.

[76] William Shakespeare, *As You Like It* [1598–1600], Act II, Scene 7, line 139.

[77] Goffman, *The Presentation of Self in Everyday Life,* pp. 9–10.

[78] Ibid., p. 17.

[79] Ibid., p. 60.

[80] "People," *USA Today,* September 13, 1993, p. 2D.

[81] Goffman, *The Presentation of Self in Everyday Life,* p. 75.

[82] Erving Goffman, *Stigma: Notes on the Management of Spoiled Identity* (Upper Saddle River, NJ: Prentice Hall, 1963).

[83] Ibid., p. 5.

[84] Ibid., p. 138.

[85] Erving Goffman, *Asylums: Essays on the Social Situation of Mental Patients and Other Inmates* (Garden City, NY: Anchor, 1961).

[86] P.L. 93–415; 42 U.S.C. § 5667e.

[87] See, for example, Information Technology International's initial report data at http://www.itiincorporated.com/showpage.asp?sect=proj&pid=6 (accessed June 8, 2007).

[88] See Kevin Haggerty et al., *Preparing for the Drug Free Years* (Washington, DC: Office of Juvenile Justice and Delinquency Prevention, 1999), http://www.ncjrs.org/html/jjbulletin/9907/theo.html (accessed March 11, 2005).

[89] Ibid., at http://www.ncjrs.org/html/jjbulletin/9907/theo.html (accessed March 11, 2005).

[90] Haggerty et al., *Preparing for the Drug Free Years.*

91 Material in this paragraph is adapted from Finn-Aage Esbensen, "Preventing Adolescent Gang Involvement," *OJJDP Juvenile Justice Bulletin* (Washington, DC: Office of Juvenile Justice and Delinquency Prevention, September 2000).

92 See R. E. Tremblay et al., "From Childhood Physical Aggression to Adolescent Maladjustment: The Montreal Prevention Experiment," in R. D. Peters and R. J. McMahon, *Preventing Childhood Disorders, Substance Abuse, and Delinquency* (Thousand Oaks, CA: Sage, 1996), pp. 268–298.

93 Randy Martin, Robert J. Mutchnick, and W. Timothy Austin, *Criminological Thought: Pioneers Past and Present* (New York: Macmillan, 1990), p. 368.

94 Laurie Taylor, "Erving Goffman," *New Society,* December 1968, p. 836.

95 George Psathas, "Ethnomethods and Phenomenology," in Donald McQuarie, ed., *Readings in Contemporary Sociological Theory: From Modernity to Post-Modernity* (Toronto: Prentice Hall Canada, 1999).

96 For some influential writings of the period, see K. F. Riegel, "Toward a Dialectical Theory of Development," *Human Development,* Vol. 18 (1975), pp. 50–64; and U. Bronfenbrenner, *The Ecology of Human Development* (Cambridge: Harvard University Press, 1979).

97 R. M. Lerner, "Early Adolescence: Towards an Agenda for the Integration of Research, Policy and Intervention," in R. M. Lerner, ed., *Early Adolescence: Perspectives on Research, Policy, and Intervention* (Hillsdale, NJ: Erlbaum, 1993), pp. 1–13.

98 See T. P. Thornberry, *Developmental Theories of Crime and Delinquency* (Piscataway, NJ: Transaction, 1997).

99 Elaine Eggleston Doherty, "Self-Control, Social Bonds, and Desistance," *Criminology,* Vol. 44, No. 4 (November, 2006), pp. 807–808.

100 A. Blumstein et al., eds., *Criminal Careers and Career Criminals* (Washington, DC: National Academy Press, 1986).

101 See Alfred Blumstein et al., "Introduction: Studying Criminal Careers," in A. Blumstein et al., eds., *Criminal Careers and Career Criminals* (Washington, DC: National Academy Press), p. 12.

102 Blumstein et al., *Criminal Careers and Career Criminals,* pp. 12–30.

103 Robert J. Sampson and John H. Laub, *Crime in the Making: Pathways and Turning Points through the Life Course* (Cambridge, MA: Harvard University Press, 1993).

104 G. H. Elder, Jr., "Perspectives on the Life-Course," in G. H. Elder, Jr., ed., *Life-Course Dynamics* (Ithaca, NY: Cornell University Press, 1985).

105 Philip W. Harris, Wayne N. Welsh, and Frank Butler, "A Century of Juvenile Justice," *Criminal Justice 2000,* Vol. 1 (Washington, DC: National Institute of Justice, 2000).

106 G. H. Elder, Jr., ed., *Life-Course Dynamics* (Ithaca, NY: Cornell University Press, 1985).

107 Robert J. Sampson and John H. Laub, "Understanding Variability in Lives through Time: Contributions of Life-Course Criminology," in Alex Piquero and Paul Mazerolle, eds., *Life-Course Criminology: Contemporary and Classic Readings* (Belmont, CA: Wadsworth, 2001), p. 243.

108 Marc LeBlanc and Rolf Loeber, "Developmental Criminology Updated," in Michael Tonry, ed., *Crime and Justice: A Review of Research,* Vol. 23 (Chicago: University of Chicago Press, 1998).

109 Adapted from Harris, Welsh, and Butler, "A Century of Juvenile Justice," p. 379.

110 Glen H. Elder, Jr., "Time, Human Agency, and Social Change: Perspectives on the Life Course," *Social Psychology Quarterly,* Vol. 57, No. 1 (1994), pp. 4–15.

111 Glen H. Elder, Jr., "The Life Course as Developmental Theory," *Child Development,* Vol. 69, No. 1 (1998), pp. 1–12, from which some of the wording in this section is taken.

112 See, for example, the collected papers of Sheldon Glueck, 1916–1972, which are part of the David L. Bazelon collection at Harvard University Law School (Cambridge, MA). Results of the Gluecks' work were reported in S. Glueck and E. Glueck, *Unraveling Juvenile Delinquency* (New York: The Commonwealth Fund, 1950).

113 Sheldon Glueck and Eleanor Glueck, *Delinquents and Nondelinquents in Perspective* (Cambridge, MA: Harvard University Press, 1968).

114 John H. Laub and Robert J. Sampson, "Urban Poverty and the Family Context of Delinquency: A New Look at Structure and Process in a Classic Study," *Child Development,* Vol. 65 (1994), pp. 523–540. See also John H. Laub and Robert J. Sampson, "Turning Points in the Life Course: Why Change Matters to the Study of Crime," *Criminology,* Vol. 31, No. 3 (1993), pp. 301–325; and Robert J. Sampson and John H. Laub, "Crime and Deviance in the Life Course," *Annual Review of Sociology,* Vol. 18 (1992), pp. 63–84.

115 See John H. Laub and Leana C. Allen, "Life Course Criminology and Community Corrections," *Perspectives,* Vol. 24, No. 2 (Spring 2000), pp. 20–29.

116 Sampson and Laub, "Crime and Deviance in the Life Course," pp. 63–84.

117 John H. Laub, "The Life Course of Criminology in the United States: The American Society of Criminology 2003 Presidential Address," *Criminology,* Vol. 42, No. 1 (2004), pp. 1–26.

118 G. B. Trasler, "Aspects of Causality, Culture, and Crime," paper presented at the Fourth International Seminar at the International Centre of Sociological, Penal and Penitentiary Research and Studies, Messina, Italy, 1980.

119 Laub and Sampson, "Turning Points in the Life Course."

120 Ibid.

121 Bradley R. Entner Wright, Avshalom Caspi, Terrie E. Moffitt, and Phil A. Silva, "The Effects of Social Ties on Crime Vary by Criminal Propensity: A Life-Course Model of Interdependence," *Criminology,* Vol. 39, No. 2 (2001), pp. 321–348.

122 See Laub and Allen, "Life Course Criminology and Community Corrections," pp. 20–29.

123 Sampson and Laub, *Crime in the Making.*

124 Matthew G. Yeager, "Life-Course Study of Released Prisoners Suggests Importance of Employment for Offender Reintegration and Community Safety," *Offender Programs Report,* Vol. 7, No. 2 (July/August 2003), pp. 1, 28–32.

125 Robert J. Sampson, John H. Laub, and Christopher Wimer, "Does Marriage Reduce Crime? A Counterfactual Approach to Within-Individual Causal Effects," *Criminology,* Vol. 44, No. 3 (2006), pp. 465–508.

126 Ronald L. Simons, Eric Stewart, Leslie C. Gordon, Rand D. Conger, and Glen H. Elder, Jr., "A Test of Life-Course Explanations for Stability and Change in Antisocial Behavior from Adolescence to Young Adulthood," *Criminology,* Vol. 40, No. 2 (2002), pp. 401–434.

127 Tittle, "Theoretical Developments in Criminology," p. 68.

128 Moffitt, "Adolescence-Limited and Life-Course-Persistent Antisocial Behavior," pp. 674–701.

129 Adapted from Tittle, "Theoretical Developments in Criminology."

130 Moffitt, "Adolescence-Limited and Life-Course-Persistent Antisocial Behavior."

131 Family and Youth Services Bureau, *Understanding Youth Development: Promoting Positive Pathways of Growth* (Washington, DC: U.S. Department of Health and Human Services, 2000).

132 A. Quetelet, *A Treatise on Man and the Development of His Facilities* (Gainesville, FL: Scholars Facsimiles and Reprints, 1969).

133 Sheldon Glueck and Eleanor Glueck, *Later Criminal Careers* (New York: The Commonwealth Fund, 1937), p. 105.

[134] Walter R. Grove, "The Effect of Age and Gender on Deviant Behavior: A Biopsychosocial Perspective," in Alice S. Rossi, ed., *Gender and the Life Course* (New York: Aldine, 1985).

[135] Ibid., p. 128.

[136] David P. Farrington, "The Twelfth Jack Tizard Memorial Lecture: The Development of Offending and Antisocial Behavior from Childhood—Key Findings from the Cambridge Study in Delinquent Development," *Journal of Child Psychology and Psychiatry,* Vol. 360 (1995), pp. 929–964.

[137] David P. Farrington, "Explaining and Preventing Crime: The Globalization of Knowledge: The American Society of Criminology 1999 Presidential Address," *Criminology,* Vol. 38, No. 1 (February 2000), pp. 1–24.

[138] Piquero and Mazerolle, *Life-Course Criminology,* p. xv.

[139] Rolf Loeber and Marc LeBlanc, "Toward a Developmental Criminology," in M. Tonry and N. Morris, eds., *Crime and Justice: A Review of Research,* Vol. 12 (Chicago: University of Chicago Press, 1990).

[140] Marvin Wolfgang, Robert Figlio, and Thorsten Sellin, *Delinquency in a Birth Cohort* (Chicago: University of Chicago Press, 1972).

[141] Marvin Wolfgang, Terence Thornberry, and Robert Figlio, *From Boy to Man, from Delinquency to Crime* (Chicago: University of Chicago Press, 1987).

[142] Steven P. Lab, "Analyzing Change in Crime and Delinquency Rates: The Case for Cohort Analysis," *Criminal Justice Research Bulletin,* Vol. 3, No. 10 (Huntsville, TX: Sam Houston State University, 1988), p. 2.

[143] Marvin Wolfgang, "Delinquency in China: Study of a Birth Cohort," *National Institute of Justice Research Preview* (Washington, DC: 1996).

[144] Lawrence E. Cohen and Richard Machalek, "A General Theory of Expropriative Crime: An Evolutionary Ecological Approach," *American Journal of Sociology,* Vol. 94, No. 3 (1988), pp. 465–501; Lawrence E. Cohen and Richard Machalek, "The Normalcy of Crime: From Durkheim to Evolutionary Ecology," *Rationality and Society,* Vol. 6 (1994), pp. 286–308.

[145] Bryan Vila, "Human Nature and Crime Control: Improving the Feasibility of Nurturant Strategies," *Politics and the Life Sciences,* Vol. 16, No. 1 (March 1997), pp. 3–21.

[146] Ibid.

[147] Terence Thornberry, "Toward an Interactional Theory of Delinquency," *Criminology,* Vol. 25 (1987), pp. 863–891.

[148] See Terence P. Thornberry, Alan J. Lizotte, Marvin D. Krohn, Margaret Farnworth, and Sung Joon Jang, "Delinquent Peers, Beliefs, and Delinquent Behavior: A Longitudinal Test of Interactional Theory," *Criminology,* Vol. 32, No. 1 (1994), pp. 47–53.

[149] Terence P. Thornberry, Alan J. Lizotte, Marvin D. Krohn, Margaret Farnworth, and Sung Joon Jang, "Testing Interactional Theory: An Examination of Reciprocal Causal Relationships among Family, School and Delinquency," *Journal of Criminal Law and Criminology,* Vol. 82 (1991), pp. 3–35.

[150] Carolyn Smith and Terence P. Thornberry, "The Relationship between Childhood Maltreatment and Adolescent Involvement in Delinquency," *Criminology,* Vol. 33, No. 4 (1995), pp. 451–477.

[151] Suman Kakar, "Youth Gangs and Their Families: Effects of Gang Membership on their Families' Subjective Well-Being," *Journal of Crime and Justice,* Vol. 21 (1998), pp. 157–171.

[152] Barbara Tatem Kelley et al., *Developmental Pathways in Boys' Disruptive and Delinquent Behavior* (Washington, DC: Office of Juvenile Justice and Delinquency Prevention, December 1997).

[153] R. Loeber and D. F. Hay, "Developmental Approaches to Aggression and Conduct Problems," in M. Rutter and D. F. Hay, eds., *Development through Life: A Handbook for Clinicians* (Oxford, England: Blackwell Scientific, 1994).

[154] Ibid.

[155] The Causes and Correlates of Delinquency study is being conducted by Terence P. Thornberry of the Rochester Youth Development Study at the State University of New York at Albany, New York, Rolf Loeber of the Pittsburgh Youth Study at the University of Pittsburgh, and David Huizinga of the Denver Youth Survey at the University of Colorado.

[156] Adapted from Katharine Browning et al., "Causes and Correlates of Delinquency Program," *OJJDP Fact Sheet* (Washington, DC: U.S. Department of Justice, April 1999).

[157] Compiled from Katharine Browning and Rolf Loeber, "Highlights of Findings from the Pittsburgh Youth Study," *OJJDP Fact Sheet* (Washington, DC: U.S. Department of Justice, February 1999); Katharine Browning, Terence P. Thornberry, and Pamela K. Porter, "Highlights of Findings from the Rochester Youth Development Study," *OJJDP Fact Sheet* (Washington, DC: U.S. Department of Justice, April 1999); and Katharine Browning and David Huizinga, "Highlights of Findings from the Denver Youth Survey," *OJJDP Fact Sheet* (Washington, DC: U.S. Department of Justice, April 1999).

[158] Browning and Huizinga, "Highlights of Findings from the Denver Youth Survey."

[159] Kelley et al., *Developmental Pathways in Boys' Disruptive and Delinquent Behavior.*

[160] Ibid., p. 14.

[161] See Felton J. Earls and Albert J. Reiss, *Breaking the Cycle: Predicting and Preventing Crime* (Washington, DC: National Institute of Justice, 1994), http://www.ncjrs.org/txtfiles/break.txt (accessed March 12, 2006).

[162] Ibid.

[163] Ibid.

[164] Adapted from the MacArthur Foundation, "The Project on Human Development in Chicago Neighborhoods," http://www.macfound.org/research/hcd/hcd_5.htm (accessed January 5, 2006).

[165] Project on Human Development in Chicago Neighborhoods press release, "Study of Chicago Finds Neighborhood Efficacy Explains Reductions in Violence," no date, http://phdcn.harvard.edu/press/index.htm (accessed January 5, 2006).

[166] Vila, "Human Nature and Crime Control," p. 10.

[167] Robert W. Sweet, Jr., "Preserving Families to Prevent Delinquency," *Office of Juvenile Justice and Delinquency Prevention Model Programs, 1990* (Washington, DC: U.S. Department of Justice, April 1992).

[168] Ibid.

[169] Farrington, "The Twelfth Jack Tizard Memorial Lecture," p. 929.

Chapter 9

Social Conflict Theories

Outline

> Social stratification breeds envy. And that leads to crime.
>
> —Natalya Lemesheva, Russian schoolteacher[1]

> To move beyond criminal justice is to move beyond capitalism.
>
> —Richard Quinney[2]

> Gender differences in crime suggest that crime may not be so normal after all.
>
> —Kathleen Daly and Meda Chesney-Lind[3]

> [I] attribute the social and psychological problems of modern society to the fact that society requires people to live under conditions radically different from those under which the human race evolved.
>
> —The Unabomber[4]

Learning Outcomes

After reading this chapter, you should be able to

- Enumerate and describe three analytical perspectives on law and social order
- Describe the central tenants of radical criminology and critique that theory
- Identify and describe at least three emerging conflict theories that purport to explain crime
- Describe the crime control policy implications of social conflict theories

Hear the author discuss this chapter at **crimtoday.com**

Introduction

In April 1996, Harvard-educated Theodore Kaczynski, 52, a Lincoln, Montana, recluse, was arrested and charged with the infamous Unabomber terrorist bombings. Kaczynski admitted responsibility for the bombings in early 1998 and was sentenced to life in prison without parole. Today, he lives among some of the nation's most notorious criminals in the federal Supermax prison in Florence, Colorado, where he is known as prisoner number 04475-046.

The Unabomber's 18-year-long mail bomb campaign had targeted universities, airlines, and researchers. The attacks killed 3 people and injured 23 others in 16 separate bombing incidents. Prior to Kaczynski's arrest, a 56-page, 35,000-word "manifesto" was mailed to the offices of the *New York Times*, the *Washington Post*, and *Penthouse* magazine. Titled "Industrial Society and Its Future," the Unabomber manifesto was a rambling thesis condemning American social institutions and high technology—and calling for a new social order based on a return to simpler times. It blamed many of the world's existing problems on the Industrial Revolution and forecast an Orwellian future in which helpless humans would be controlled by computers. Excerpts from the manifesto were widely published and helped lead to Kaczynski's capture. The manifesto's introductory paragraphs (which use the word *we* in referring to the bomber) are reproduced in the Theory versus Reality box in this chapter. Read the Unabomber's entire manifesto online at **Web Extra 9–1**.

WEB
Extra
■ ■ ■ ■

Law and Social Order Perspectives

Kaczynski's idealism is reminiscent of the kind of thinking that characterized much of Europe during the mid- to late 1800s. Among the most important thinkers of that period, for the purposes of this chapter, were Karl Marx and Friedrich Engels. In 1848, in *The Communist Manifesto*, Marx and Engels advanced the idea that communism would inevitably replace capitalism as the result of a natural historical process or dialectic. The egalitarian ideals of these early writers fed the communist ideology that led to the Marxist-inspired Bolshevik Revolution of 1917, the fall of the Romanov dynasty in Russia, the coming to power of Vladimir Lenin and (later) Joseph Stalin in Russia, and the rise of the Soviet Union. Communism soon came to denote a totalitarian system in which a single political party controls the government, which in turn owns the means of production and distributes wealth with the professed aim of establishing a classless society.[5]

Ted Kaczynski, the self-confessed "Unabomber." Kaczynski admitted responsibility for 16 bombings over an 18-year period. The bombings resulted in 3 deaths and 29 injuries. In 1998, Kaczynski was sentenced to life in prison without the possibility of parole. What motivates criminals like the Unabomber?

Source: John Youngbear, AP Wide World Photos

Theory Versus Reality

The Unabomber and Domestic Terrorism

This box contains the introductory paragraphs of the Unabomber's rambling 56-page manifesto. The manifesto, entitled "Industrial Society and Its Future," was mailed to the *New York Times*, the *Washington Post*, and *Penthouse* magazine prior to Unabomber Ted Kaczynski's arrest. Kaczynski's misplaced idealism demonstrates how social conflict, and the ideologies borne of it, can lead to crime.

The Industrial Revolution and its consequences have been a disaster for the human race. They have greatly increased the life-expectancy of those of us who live in "advanced" countries, but they have destabilized society, have made life unfulfilling, have subjected human beings to indignities, have led to widespread psychological suffering (in the Third World to physical suffering as well) and have inflicted severe damage on the natural world. The continued development of technology will worsen the situation. It will certainly subject human beings to greater indignities and inflict greater damage on the natural world, it will probably lead to greater social disruption and psychological suffering, and it may lead to increased physical suffering even in "advanced" countries.

The industrial-technological system may survive or it may break down. If it survives, it MAY eventually achieve a low level of physical and psychological suffering, but only after passing through a long and very painful period of adjustment and only at the cost of permanently reducing human beings and many other living organisms to engineered products and mere cogs in the social machine. Furthermore, if the system survives, the consequences will be inevitable: There is no way of reforming or modifying the system so as to prevent it from depriving people of dignity and autonomy.

If the system breaks down the consequences will still be very painful. But the bigger the system grows the more disastrous the results of its breakdown will be, so if it is to break down it had best break down sooner rather than later.

We therefore advocate a revolution against the industrial system. This revolution may or may not make use of violence; it may be sudden or it may be a relatively gradual process spanning a few decades. We can't predict any of that. But we do outline in a very general way the measures that those who hate the industrial system should take in order to prepare the way for a revolution against that form of society.

Discussion Questions

1. What motivated the Unabomber? Why did he advocate "a revolution against the industrial system"?

2. Do you think that the Unabomber really believed his bombings would create a better world? If so, how did he think they would bring about such change?

The decline of European monarchies during the first half of the twentieth century, the rise of socialist ideals, and the advent of Marxist-inspired revolutions all conspired to change laws and create new kinds of criminal activity. Hence, an understanding of the interplay between law and social order is critical to any study of social change and of theories of criminology that emphasize the role of social conflict as it underlies criminality. Three analytical perspectives shed some light on this subject:

- The consensus perspective
- The pluralist perspective
- The conflict perspective

The Consensus Perspective

The **consensus model** of social organization (described briefly in Chapter 1) is built around the notion that most members of society agree on what is right and wrong and that the various elements of society—including institutions like churches, schools, government agencies, and businesses—work together toward a shared vision of the greater good. According to **Raymond J. Michalowski,** whose work is used to describe each of the three major approaches discussed in this section, the consensus perspective is characterized by four principles:[6]

- A belief in the existence of core values. The consensus perspective holds that shared notions of right and wrong characterize the majority of society's members.
- The notion that laws reflect the collective will of the people. Law is seen as the result of a consensus, achieved through legislative action, and represents a kind of social conscience.

consensus model

An analytical perspective on social organization that holds that most members of society agree about what is right and what is wrong and that the various elements of society work together in unison toward a common vision of the greater good.

- The assumption that the law serves all people equally. From the consensus point of view, the law not only embodies a shared view of justice, but also is itself perceived to be just in its application.
- The idea that those who violate the law represent a unique subgroup with some distinguishing features. The consensus approach holds that law violators must somehow be improperly socialized or psychologically defective or must suffer from some other lapse, which leaves them unable to participate in what is otherwise widespread agreement on values and behavior.

The consensus perspective was operative in American politics and characterized social scientific thought in this country throughout much of the early 1900s. It found its greatest champion in **Roscoe Pound,** former dean of the Harvard School of Law and one of the greatest legal scholars of modern times. Pound developed the notion that the law is a tool for engineering society. The law, Pound said, meets the needs of men and women living together in society and can be used to fashion society's characteristics and major features. Pound distilled his ideas into a set of jural postulates. Such postulates, Pound claimed, explain the existence and form of all laws insofar as laws reflect shared needs. Pound's postulates read as follows:[7]

- In civilized society men and women[8] must be able to assume that others will commit no intentional aggressions upon them.
- In civilized society men and women must be able to assume that they may control for beneficial purposes what they have discovered and appropriated to their own use, what they have created by their own labor, and what they have acquired under the existing social and economic order.
- In civilized society men and women must be able to assume that those with whom they deal in the general intercourse of society will act in good faith and hence
  1. Will make good reasonable expectations that their promises or other conduct will reasonably create.
  2. Will carry out their undertakings according to the expectations which the moral sentiment of the community attaches thereto.
  3. Will restore specifically or by equivalent what comes to them by mistake or [by an] unanticipated or not fully intended situation whereby they receive at another's expense what they could not reasonably have expected to receive under the circumstances.
- In civilized society men and women must be able to assume that those who are engaged in some course of conduct will act with due care not to cause an unreasonable risk of injury upon others.
- In civilized society men and women must be able to assume that those who maintain things likely to get out of hand or to escape and do damage will restrain them or keep them within their proper bounds.

The Pluralist Perspective

Contrary to the assumptions made by consensus thinkers, however, it has become quite plain to most observers of the contemporary social scene that not everyone agrees on what the law should say. Society today is rife with examples of conflicting values and ideals. Consensus is hard to find. Modern debates center on issues like abortion, euthanasia, the death penalty, the purpose of criminal justice agencies in a diverse society, social justice, the rights and responsibilities of minorities and other underrepresented groups, women's issues, the proper role of education, economic policy, social welfare, the function of the military in a changing world, environmental concerns, and appropriate uses of high technology. As many contemporary public forums indicate, there exists within America today a great diversity of social groups, each with its own point of view regarding what is right and what is wrong, and each with its own agenda. Add to that the plethora of self-proclaimed individual experts busily touting their own points of view, and anything but a consensus of values seems characteristic of society today.

Such a situation is described by some writers as "pluralist." A **pluralistic perspective** (described briefly in Chapter 1) mirrors the thought that a multiplicity of values and beliefs exists in any complex society and that each different social group will have its own set of beliefs, interests, and values. A crucial element of this perspective, however, is the assumption that although different viewpoints exist, most individuals agree on the usefulness of law as a formal means of dispute resolution. Hence, from a pluralist perspective, the law, rather than reflecting common values, exists as a peacekeeping tool that allows officials and agencies within the government to settle disputes effectively between individuals and among groups. It also assumes that whatever settlement is reached will be acceptable to all parties because of their agreement on the fundamental role of law in dispute settlement. The basic principles of the pluralist perspective include the following notions:[9]

	pluralist perspective
	An analytical approach to social organization that holds that a multiplicity of values and beliefs exists in any complex society but that most social actors agree on the usefulness of law as a formal means of dispute resolution.

- Society consists of many and diverse social groups. Differences in age, gender, sexual preference, ethnicity, and the like often provide the basis for much naturally occurring diversity.

- Each group has its own characteristic set of values, beliefs, and interests. Variety in gender, sexual orientation, economic status, ethnicity, and other forms of diversity produce interests that may unite like-minded individuals but that may also place them in natural opposition to other social groups.

- A general agreement exists on the usefulness of formalized laws as a mechanism for dispute resolution. People and groups accept the role of law in the settlement of disputes, and they accord decisions reached within the legal framework at least a modicum of respect.

- The legal system is value neutral. That is, the legal system is itself thought to be free of petty disputes and above the level of general contentiousness that may characterize relationships among groups.

- The legal system is concerned with the best interests of society. Legislators, judges, prosecutors, attorneys, police officers, and correctional officials are assumed to perform idealized functions that are beyond the reach of the everyday interests of self-serving groups. Hence, such official functionaries can be trusted to act in accordance with the greater good, to remain unbiased, and to maintain a value-free system for the enforcement of laws.

According to the pluralist perspective, conflict is essentially resolved through the peacekeeping activities of unbiased government officials exercising objective legal authority.

The Conflict Perspective

A third point of view, the **conflict perspective,** maintains that conflict is a fundamental aspect of social life itself that can never be fully resolved. At best, according to this perspective, formal agencies of social control merely coerce the unempowered or the disenfranchised to comply with the rules established by those in power. From the conflict point of view, laws become a tool of the powerful, useful in keeping others from wresting control over important social institutions. Social order, rather than being the result of any consensus or process of dispute resolution, rests upon the exercise of power through law. Those in power must work ceaselessly to remain there, although the structure that they impose on society—including patterns of wealth building that they define as acceptable and circumstances under which they authorize the exercise of legal power and military might—gives them all the advantages they are likely to need.

	conflict perspective
	An analytical perspective on social organization that holds that conflict is a fundamental aspect of social life itself and can never be fully resolved.

Profiles in Crime

Theodore John "Ted" Kaczynski (The Unabomber)

"The shutdowns," his family called them. A shy, introspective child and youth, Ted Kaczynski did not socialize easily or well, and he periodically underwent occasional episodes of intense and brooding withdrawal. As he grew older, the episodes were increasingly accompanied by a seething rage.[i]

There is no arguing his intellect. His academic abilities enabled him to skip both the sixth and eleventh grades, and he started undergraduate studies at Harvard at just 16 years of age. Kaczynski ultimately earned his doctoral degree at the young age of 25, but his intellectual development was not matched by his social and personal development. The promise of his remarkable early achievements foundered quickly.[ii] Consumed with obsessions and emotionally crippled, the reclusive Kaczynski resolved his contempt for society's technological advances by mounting a bombing campaign that ultimately killed 3 people and injured 29 others.

Born in Chicago on May 22, 1942, Kaczynski recalls his childhood as "uneventful." Interestingly, he claims to have been the victim of verbal and emotional abuse—but those claims never surfaced until he was in his twenties.

Upon completing his Ph.D., Kaczynski accepted an assistant professorship in mathematics at the University of California at Berkeley in 1967. However, in June of 1969, declaring that there was "no relevance" to what he was doing, he quit his teaching post. From then until his arrest on April 3, 1996, he worked only sporadically, including a brief time at the University of Michigan, and he usually worked only out of financial necessity. He finally ended up living off the land, assuming a hermit's existence of self-exile in a ramshackle cabin in the remote Montana wilderness that was to last almost 25 years.[iii]

Kaczynski also experienced lifelong difficulties with sexual relationships. While at the University of Michigan, he struggled with his own sexuality, coming to believe that he should undergo a sex change operation because fantasies of being a woman intensely excited him. Eventually, he initiated the process at the school's health care facility but, when finally seen by a doctor, he claimed to be there for a different reason entirely, then left in a rage. Subsequently, he described the experience as shameful and humiliating.[iv] In

ensuing years, he infrequently sought health system support as he attempted to establish meaningful relationships with women, but was never able to do so.

As he retreated deeper into his isolationist lifestyle, Kaczynski handwrote a lengthy manifesto that railed against contemporary life. The opening sentence of the manifesto's introduction clearly states Kaczynski's core complaint: "The Industrial Revolution and its consequences have been a disaster for the human race."[v]

Over an 18-year period that began on May 25, 1978, Kaczynski left or sent a total of 16 homemade pipe bombs to various targets, the last on April 24, 1995. He primarily targeted universities and airlines-related activities. (The FBI's designation of the investigation as the "Unabomb" case derives from these early university targets.) The first ten bombs resulted in serious injuries to numerous people. The eleventh, a bomb left in a paper bag near the rear entrance of a Sacramento, California, computer store on December 11, 1985, caused the first of three deaths that would result from Kaczynski's bombing campaign.[vi]

Kaczynski's intermittent attacks were shrouded in anonymity, a trait that was inexplicably broken when he began sending letters to a newspaper threatening to bomb an airplane. He also stated that he would stop the bombings if his 35,000-word manifesto was published in the *Washington Post*.[vii] Its publication was to eventually lead to his capture.

Upon reading the manifesto, David Kaczynski, Ted's younger brother, immediately realized that "the tone of the language, the approach, almost had the feeling for me of one of Ted's angry letters over the years....Some of those letters were addressed to the theme of technology just as the manifesto was."[viii] Although not wholly convinced that his brother was the long-sought Unabomber, the content and wording of the manifesto led David Kaczynski to contact the FBI.

That slim investigative thread led the FBI to Kaczynski's cabin in the isolated Montana wilderness, where they found overwhelming evidence that he was, in fact, the Unabomber. A live bomb, meticulous notes of past bombings, bomb-making materials, and the original copy of his infamous manifesto seemed to make the ensuing trial almost anticlimactic, and its results an almost foregone conclusion.

One of the best-known writers on social conflict was **Karl Marx.** Marx's writings on the conflicts inherent in capitalism led to the formulation of communist ideals and, many would say, to the rise of communist societies in the twentieth century.

According to Marx, two fundamental social classes exist within any capitalist society: the haves and the have-nots. Marx called these two groups the "bourgeoisie" and the "proletariat." The **proletariat** encompasses the large mass of people, those who are relatively uneducated and who are without power. In short, the proletariat comprises the workers. The **bourgeoisie** are the capitalists—the wealthy owners of the means of production (for example, the factories, businesses, land, and natural resources). Although Marx was German, the terms *proletariat* and *bourgeoisie* were taken from Marx's knowledge of the French language and are, in turn, derived from Latin. In ancient Rome, for example, members of that city's lowest class were propertyless and were individually referred to as *proletarius*.

proletariat

In Marxist theory, the working class.

On January 22, 1998, after reaching a plea agreement, Kaczynski pleaded guilty in the U.S. District Court in Sacramento to four bombings that occurred in 1985, 1993, and 1995. In accordance with the agreement, Kaczynski admitted to the three deaths his bombings had caused; all other charges pending against him as a result of his extended bombing campaign were resolved; and he was sentenced to a life term without parole.[ix] Kaczynski, inmate 04475-046, remains imprisoned at the maximum-security federal prison in Florence, Colorado. On January 22, 2007, he filed suit against the federal government and a group of his victims seeking to prevent the sale of more than 40,000 pages of his original writings and correspondence.[x]

[i] Paul Ferguson, "A Loner from Youth," CNN Interactive, http://www.cnn.com/SPECIALS/1997/unabomb/accused/early (accessed May 28, 2007).

[ii] Ted Ottley, "Ted Kaczynski: The Unabomber," CourtTV Crime Library, http://www.crimelibrary.com/terrorists_spies/terrorists/kaczynski/1.html (accessed May 28, 2007).

[iii] CNN and Time Interactive, "The Unabomb Case," Cable News Network, http://www.cnn.com/SPECIALS/1997/unabomb/index.html (accessed May 28, 2007).

[iv] Ottley.

[v] "The Unabomber's Manifesto: Industrial Society and Its Future," *Sacramento Bee*, http://www.unabombertrial.com/manifesto/index.html (accessed May 28, 2007).

[vi] CNN and Time Interactive.

[vii] Paul Ferguson, "Tracking the Unabomber: More Luck Than Computer Analysis," CNN Interactive, http://www.cnn.com/SPECIALS/1997/unabomb/investigation/puzzle/index.html (accessed May 28, 2007).

[viii] "When Your Brother Is the Unabomber," MSNBC, December 29, 2006, http://www.msnbc.msn.com/id/16304477 (accessed May 28, 2007).

[ix] "Kaczynski Admits He Is Unabomber, Sentenced to Life Without Parole," CNN Interactive, January 22, 1998, http://www.cnn.com/US/9801/22/unabomb.plea (accessed June 16, 2007).

[x] Serge F. Kovaleski, "Unabomber Wages Legal Battle to Halt Sale of Papers," *New York Times*, January 22, 2007, http://www.nytimes.com/2007/01/22/us/22unabomber.html?ex=1327122000&en=3fda08d949905a96&ei=5088&partner=rss nyt&emc=rss (accessed May 28, 2007).

Former University of California at Berkeley math professor Theodore John Kaczynski, aka the Unabomber, smiles and cups his hand to an ear during an interview in a visiting room at the Federal Administrative Maximum prison in Florence, Colorado, on August 30, 1999. What motivated Kaczynski?

Source: Stephen J. Dubner/Getty Images

According to Marx, the members of the proletariat, since they possess neither capital nor the means of production, must earn their living by selling their labor. Those belonging to the bourgeoisie, by the nature of their very position within society, stand opposed to the proletariat in ongoing class struggle. Marx saw such struggle between classes as inevitable in the evolution of any capitalist society, and he believed that the natural outcome of such struggle would be the overthrow of the capitalist social order and the birth of a truly classless, or communist, society. Learn more about the life and writings of Karl Marx at **Web Extras 9–2** and **9–3**.

Conflict theory in the social sciences has a long history. In 1905, the writings of **Willem Bonger** echoed Marxist principles by describing the ongoing struggle between the haves and the have-nots as a natural consequence of capitalist society.[10] Bonger advanced the notion that in such societies only those who lack power are routinely subject to the criminal law. Georg Simmel's 1908 text *Conflict and the Web of Group*

bourgeoisie

In Marxist theory, the class of people who own the means of production.

WEB
Extra
■ ■ ■ ■

Crime in the News

Author Faced Prison for Insulting Turkishness

ISTANBUL—One of Turkey's leading authors was acquitted on September 20, 2006 of "insulting Turkishness"—a crime Western-looking Turks view as an embarrassment and one of the biggest obstacles to joining the European Union.

The speedy court decision was seen as a step toward securing greater freedom of speech, but critics said until the law is abolished, Turkey will remain a place where authors are regularly put on trial.

A nationalist demonstrator gestures at a poster of Turkish writer Elif Shafak during a protest outside of a courthouse in Istanbul, Turkey, in 2006. A Turkish court acquitted Shafak, one of Turkey's leading authors, saying there was no evidence that she had "insulted Turkishness" in a novel she had written.

Source: AP Wide World Photos/Osman Orsal

"The fact remains that (Turkey's courts) established a restrictive interpretation of article 301 of the penal code which is not in line with the European Court of Human Rights and European standards of freedom of expression," EU spokeswoman Krisztina Nagy warned after the decision.

But the government is reluctant to change the law—which makes it a crime to insult Turkey, "Turkishness" or the government—because it has broad nationalist support.

EU officials counter the real damage to Turkey's image comes from putting writers like Elif Shafak on trial—a case brought by nationalist lawyers because of words spoken by the novelist's fictional characters.

The court ruled to acquit about an hour-and-a-half into the trial on the grounds there was "no evidence" Shafak had insulted Turkishness.

"I hope that the absurdity of this case—we're talking about fictional characters—will encourage people that it's time to act," said Joost Lagendijk, a senior European Parliament member who attended the trial and is a vocal supporter of Turkey's EU bid.

Lagendijk called on Turkey's pro-EU Prime Minister Recep Tayyip Erdogan, who has himself spent time in jail for reciting an Islamist poem in 1999, to intervene and change the law.

"Each court case that is started is a victory for those who don't want Turkey in the EU, and a defeat for me and those in the EU who are in favor of Turkey's accession," Lagendijk said.

But nationalist lawyers said they will continue to bring legal action against anyone who insults Turkey and vowed to appeal the Shafak decision.

Fiercely opposed to Turkey joining the EU and hostile to any foreign intervention, the lawyers spent most of the trial trying to eject non-Turkish observers—especially Lagendijk—from the packed Istanbul courtroom.

Affiliations highlighted the role of social conflict in two- and three-person groups, which Simmel called diads and triads.[11] Thorsten Sellin's notion of culture conflict, proposed in 1938 (and discussed in Chapter 7), also incorporated the notion of social conflict. Since Sellin's day, many other thinkers have contributed to the development of conflict theory. Before discussing specific ideas, however, it is important to understand the six key elements of the conflict perspective.[12]

- Society is made up of diverse social groups. As in the pluralist perspective, diversity is thought to be based on distinctions that people hold to be significant, such as gender, sexual orientation, and social class.
- Each group holds to differing definitions of right and wrong. Moralistic conceptions and behavioral standards vary from group to group.
- Conflict between groups is unavoidable. Conflict is based on differences held to be socially significant (such as ethnicity, gender, and social class) and is unavoidable because groups defined on the basis of these characteristics compete for power, wealth, and other forms of recognition.

"This is not a consulate court!" one of them yelled minutes after the case began.

"Let the foreigners go to hell! They can supervise their own country!" bellowed lawyer Fuat Turgut as he pushed his way through a crowd in the doorway.

The lawyers were repeatedly rebuffed and they eventually left the courtroom in protest, after which the judge moved quickly to acquit Shafak.

"The court concluded in a 1½-hour session that there was insufficient evidence to suggest that she committed a crime," Judge Irfan Adil Uncu said.

Erdogan said he was pleased with the acquittal and said Turkey was open to discussing article 301. But in implicit support of the intent behind the law, he added: "Criticism is one thing, insulting is another."

Justice Minister Cemil Cicek made similar remarks this week, asking a journalist for the *Turkish Daily News* whether he was willing to "let people curse at Turkey, insult Turkishness and get away with it."

Erdogan regularly files lawsuits over alleged personal insults, and on Wednesday was awarded $3,400 in a case against a journalist who suggested the prime minister might be mentally ill.

Shafak, 35, gave birth a few days earlier and was at a hospital in Istanbul and did not attend the trial. If convicted, she could have received a maximum three-year prison sentence.

Shafak's husband Eyup Can, editor-in-chief of the Turkish newspaper *Referans*, said he hoped the decision would be a model for future cases, and pushed for the abolition of article 301.

"For the judge to make this decision in the first hearing is an important step," Can said as he was congratulated by friends after the trial. "But the most painful thing is that Turkey has become famous as a country that tries writers."

In a sign public opinion may be turning in favor of change, nationalist protesters outside the courtroom—usually a rowdy, often violent group—were shouted down by other spectators.

Shafak's book, *The Bastard of Istanbul*, was released in Turkey on March 8 and has sold more than 50,000 copies. The court case was brought for words spoken by fictional Armenian characters regarding one of the most disputed episodes of Turkey's history, the mass killings of Armenians during the final years of the Ottoman Empire.

A Turkish court dropped charges last year against Orhan Pamuk, another leading novelist who also faced trial for writing about the killings of Armenians. The charges were dropped for technical reasons amid intense international pressure.

However, a high court recently confirmed a six-month prison sentence imposed on Armenian-Turkish journalist Hrant Dink for attempting to influence the judiciary after his newspaper ran articles criticizing the law.

Dink's sentence was suspended, meaning he will not go to jail unless he repeats the same offense.

Discussion Questions

1. Are there any laws in our society that might lead to charges similar to those of "insulting Turkishness"? If so, what might they be?

2. It seems as though some sections of the Turkish penal code criminalize ideas or beliefs. What fundamental principles in our own constitution would such laws contravene?

For the latest crime and justice news, visit www.crimenews.info.

- The fundamental nature of group conflict centers on the exercise of political power. Political power is the key to the accumulation of wealth and to other forms of power.

- Law is a tool of power and furthers the interests of those powerful enough to make it. Laws allow those in control to gain what they define (through the law) as legitimate access to scarce resources and to deny (through the law) such access to the politically disenfranchised.

- Those in power are inevitably interested in maintaining their power against those who would usurp it.

Central to the conflict perspective is the notion of social class. Some authors maintain that "class is nothing but an abbreviation to describe a way of living, thinking, and feeling."[13] For most sociologists, however, the concept of **social class** entails distinctions made between individuals on the basis of significant defining characteristics, such as race, religion, education, profession, income, wealth, family background, housing, artistic tastes, aspirations, cultural pursuits, child-rearing habits, speech, accent, and so forth. Individuals are assigned to classes by others and by themselves on the basis of

social class

Distinctions made between individuals on the basis of important defining social characteristics.

Theory in Perspective

Social Conflict Theories

Social conflict theories emphasize the power of conflict within society, which is thought to be based largely on inequities between social classes.

- *Radical Criminology.* Holds that the causes of crime are rooted in social conditions that empower the wealthy and the politically well organized but disenfranchise those who are less fortunate.

  Period: 1960s–present

  Theorists: Karl Marx, Ralf Dahrendorf, George B. Vold, Richard Quinney, William J. Chambliss, Raymond J. Michalowski, Austin Turk

  Concepts: Social class, bourgeoisie, proletariat

- *Left-Realist Criminology.* A branch of radical criminology that holds that crime is a "real" social problem experienced by the lower classes.

  Period: 1980s–present

  Theorists: Walter DeKeseredy, Jock Young

  Concepts: Radical realism, critical realism, street crime, social justice, crime control

- *Feminist Criminology.* A radical criminological approach to the explanation of crime that sees the conflict and inequality present in society as being based primarily on gender.

  Period: 1970s–present

  Theorists: Freda Adler, Rita J. Simon, Kathleen Daly, Meda Chesney-Lind, John Hagan

  Concepts: Power-control, gender socialization, empowerment

- *Peacemaking Criminology.* Holds that crime control agencies and citizens must work together to alleviate social problems, including crime.

  Period: 1980s–present

  Theorists: Harold E. Pepinsky, Richard Quinney

  Concepts: Compassionate criminology, restorative justice

- *Convict Criminology.* Consists of writings and musings on the subject matter of criminology by convicted felons and ex-inmates who have acquired academic credentials, or who are associated with credentialled others.

  Period: 2001–present

  Theorists: Ian Ross, Stephen Richards

  Concepts: Issues-based, personal experience as valid information, critical of system

characteristics that are both ascribed and achieved. Ascribed characteristics are those with which a person is born, such as race or gender, while achieved characteristics are acquired through personal effort or chance over the course of one's life and include such things as level of education, income, place of residence, and profession.

Although Marx concerned himself with only two social classes, most social scientists today talk in terms of at least three groups: the upper, middle, and lower classes. Some, such as Vance Packard, have distinguished among five hierarchically arranged classes (the real upper, semiupper, limited-success, working, and real lower classes), while further subdividing classes "horizontally" according to ascribed characteristics like race and religion.[14]

In his 1958 book *Theoretical Criminology*, **George B. Vold** described crime as the product of political conflict between groups, seeing it as a natural expression of the ongoing struggle for power, control, and material well-being.[15] According to Vold, conflict is "a universal form of interaction," and groups are naturally in conflict because their interests and purposes "overlap, encroach on one another and [tend to] be competitive."[16] Vold also addressed the issue of social cohesion, noting that as intergroup conflict intensifies, the loyalty of individual members to their groups increases. "It has long been realized that conflict between groups tends to develop and intensify the loyalty of group members to their respective groups," Vold wrote.[17] Vold's most succinct observation of the role conflict plays in contributing to crime was expressed in these words: "The whole political process of law making, law breaking, and law enforcement becomes a direct reflection of deep-seated and fundamental conflicts between interest groups. . . . Those who produce legislative majorities win control over the power and dominate the policies that decide who is likely to be involved in violation of the law."[18]

The tomb of Karl Marx, in Highgate Cemetery, London. Marxist thought underpins the writings of many radical criminologists. How did Marxism influence criminology?

Source: Rex Features USA Ltd.

From Vold's point of view, powerful groups make laws, and those laws express and protect their interests. Hence, the body of laws that characterize any society is a political statement, and crime is a political definition imposed largely upon those whose interests lie outside of those that the powerful, through the law, define as acceptable. In his writings about conflict, Vold went so far as to compare the criminal with a soldier, fighting, through crime commission, for the very survival of the group whose values he or she represents. In Vold's words, "The individual criminal is then viewed as essentially a soldier under conditions of warfare: his behavior may not be 'normal' or 'happy' or 'adjusted'—it is the behavior of the soldier doing what is to be done in wartime."[19] Vold's analogy, probably influenced by World War II, was meant to express the idea that crime is a manifestation of denied needs and values—that is, the cultural heritage of disenfranchised groups who are powerless to enact their interests in legitimate fashion. Hence, theft becomes necessary for many poor people, especially those left unemployed or unemployable by the socially acceptable forms of wealth distribution defined by law.

Conflict theorists of the early and mid-1900s saw in the concept of social class the rudimentary ingredients of other important concepts like authority, power, and conflict. **Ralf Dahrendorf,** for example, wrote that "classes are social conflict groups the determinant of which can be found in the participation in or exclusion from the exercise of authority."[20] For Dahrendorf, conflict was ubiquitous, a fundamental part of and coextensive with any society. "Not the presence but the absence of conflict is surprising and abnormal," he wrote, "and we have good reason to be suspicious if we find a society or social organization that displays no evidence of conflict. To be sure, we do not have to assume that conflict is always violent and uncontrolled. . . . We must never lose sight of the underlying assumption that conflict can be temporarily suppressed, regulated,

Deteriorating factories in Novokuznetsk, Siberia. Radical criminology has its origins in the writings of Karl Marx, whose thinking was strongly influenced by the social conditions of the industrial era. How did the downfall of the Soviet Union impact radical thought in criminology?

Source: Peter Turnley, Corbis/Bettmann

radical criminology

A perspective that holds that the causes of crime are rooted in social conditions that empower the wealthy and the politically well organized but disenfranchise the less fortunate.

Marxist criminology

A perspective on crime and crime causation based on the writings of Karl Marx.

channeled, and controlled but that neither a philosopher-king nor a modern dictator can abolish it once and for all."[21]

From Dahrendorf's perspective, it was power and authority that were most at issue between groups and over which class conflicts arose. Dahrendorf also recognized that situations characterized by conflict are rarely static and that it is out of conflict that change arises. For Dahrendorf, change could be either destructive or constructive. Destructive change brings about a lessening of social order, whereas constructive change increases cohesiveness within society. Dahrendorf's 1959 book *Class and Class Conflict in Industrial Society* set the stage for the radical writers of the 1960s and 1970s.

Another mid-twentieth-century conflict theorist, **Austin Turk,** said that in the search for an explanation of criminality, "one is led to investigate the tendency of laws to penalize persons whose behavior is more characteristic of the less powerful than of the more powerful and the extent to which some persons and groups can and do use legal processes and agencies to maintain and enhance their power position vis-à-vis other persons and groups."[22] In his 1969 seminal work, *Criminality and Legal Order,* Turk wrote that in any attempt to explain criminality, "it is more useful to view the social order as mainly a pattern of conflict" rather than to offer explanations for crime based on behavioral or psychological approaches.[23] Turk, like most other conflict criminologists, saw the law as a powerful tool in the service of prominent social groups seeking continued control over others. Crime was the natural consequence of such intergroup struggle because it resulted from the definitions imposed by the laws of the powerful upon the disapproved strivings of the unempowered.

Radical Criminology

The conflict perspective is today thoroughly entrenched in **radical criminology,** which is also diversely known as, or related to, schools of thought referred to as "new," "critical," or **Marxist criminology.** Radical criminology is the intellectual child of three important historical circumstances: (1) the ruminations of nineteenth-century social utopian thinkers, including Karl Marx, Friedrich Engels, Georg Wilhelm Friedrich Hegel, Georg Simmel, Willem Bonger, and Max Weber; (2) the rise of conflict theory in the social sciences; and (3) the dramatic radicalization of American academia in the 1960s and 1970s.

Radical criminologists of today are considerably more sophisticated than their Marxist forebears. Contemporary radical criminology holds that the causes of crime are rooted in social conditions that empower the wealthy and the politically well organized but disenfranchise those who are less fortunate. **William J. Chambliss,** a well-known spokesperson for radical thinkers, succinctly summarizes the modern perspective in these words: "What makes the behavior of some criminal is the coercive power of the state to enforce the will of the ruling class."[24]

In 1971, Chambliss, along with Robert T. Seidman, published a critically acclaimed volume entitled *Law, Order, and Power*. Their work represented something of a bridge between earlier conflict theorists and the more radical approach of the Marxists. Through its emphasis on social class, class interests, and class conflict, *Law, Order, and Power* presented a Marxist perspective stripped of any overt references to capitalism as the root cause of crime. "The more economically stratified a society becomes," Chambliss and Seidman wrote, "the more it becomes necessary for the dominant groups in the society to enforce through coercion the norms of conduct which guarantee their supremacy."[25] Chambliss and Seidman outlined their position in four propositions:[26]

- The conditions of one's life affect one's values and norms. Complex societies are composed of groups with widely different life conditions.

- Complex societies are therefore composed of highly disparate and conflicting sets of norms.

- The probability of a given group's having its particular normative system embodied in law is not distributed equally but is closely related to the political and economic position of that group.

- The higher a group's political or economic position, the greater the probability that its views will be reflected in laws.

Chambliss also believed that middle- and upper-class criminals are more apt to escape apprehension and punishment by the criminal justice system, not because they are any smarter or more capable of hiding their crimes than are lower-class offenders but because of a "very rational choice on the part of the legal system to pursue those violators that the community will reward them for pursuing and to ignore those violators who have the capability for causing trouble for the agencies."[27]

By the 1970s, Chambliss's writings assumed a much more Marxist flavor. In an article published in 1975, Chambliss once again recognized the huge power gap separating the haves from the have-nots.[28] Crime, he said, is created by actions of the ruling class that define as criminal such things as undertakings and activities that contravene the interests of the rulers. At the same time, he said, members of the ruling class will inevitably be able to continue to violate the criminal law with impunity because it is their own creation.

Soon the Marxist flavor of Chambliss's writing became undeniable. He began using Marxist terminology. "As capitalist societies industrialize and the gap between the bourgeoisie and the proletariat widens," he wrote, "penal law will expand in an effort to coerce the proletariat into submission."[29] For Chambliss, the economic consequences of crime within a capitalist society were partially what perpetuated it. "Crime reduces surplus labor," he wrote, "by creating employment not only for the criminals but for law enforcers, welfare workers, professors of criminology, and a horde of people who live off the fact that crime exists."[30] Socialist societies, claimed Chambliss, should reflect much lower crime rates than capitalist societies because a "less intense class struggle should reduce the forces leading to and the functions of crime."[31] Learn more about the writings of William J. Chambliss at Web Extra 9–4.

Although Chambliss provides much of the intellectual bedrock of contemporary radical criminology, that school of thought found its most eloquent expression in the writings of **Richard Quinney.** In 1974, Quinney, in an attempt to challenge and change

WEB
Extra
▪ ▪ ▪ ▪

American social life for the better, set forth his six Marxist propositions for an understanding of crime:[32]

- American society is based on an advanced capitalist economy.
- The state is organized to serve the interests of the dominant economic class—that is, the capitalist ruling class.
- Criminal law is an instrument of the state and ruling class used to maintain and perpetuate the existing social and economic order.
- Crime control in a capitalist society is accomplished through a variety of institutions and agencies established and administered by a governmental elite, representing ruling-class interests, for the purpose of establishing domestic order.
- The contradictions of advanced capitalism—the disjunction between existence and essence—require that the subordinate classes remain oppressed by whatever means necessary, especially through the coercion and violence of the legal system.
- Only with the collapse of the capitalist society and the creation of a new society, based on socialist principles, will there be a solution to the crime problem.

A few years later, Quinney published *Class, State, and Crime*, in which he argued that almost all crimes committed by members of the lower classes are necessary for the survival of individual members of those classes. Crimes, said Quinney—in fashion reminiscent of Vold's notion of the criminal as a soldier—are actually an attempt by the socially disenfranchised "to exist in a society where *survival* is not assured by other, collective means."[33] He concludes, "Crime is inevitable under capitalist conditions" because crime is "a response to the material conditions of life. Permanent unemployment—and the acceptance of that condition—can result in a form of life where criminality is an appropriate and consistent response."[34] The solution offered by Quinney to the problem of crime is the development of a socialist society. "The *ultimate meaning* of crime in the development of capitalism," he writes, "is the need for a socialist society."[35]

Contemporary radical criminology attributes much of the existing propensity toward criminality to differences in social class, and in particular to those arrangements within society that maintain class differences. As Quinney puts it, "Classes are an expression of the underlying forces of the capitalist mode of production."[36] "Within the class structure of advanced capitalism," he writes, "is the dialectic that increases class struggle and the movement for socialist revolution."[37] Table 9–1 depicts the class structure of the United States as Quinney portrayed it.

Today's radical criminologies can be divided into two schools: structuralist and instrumentalist. **Structural Marxism** sees capitalism as a self-maintaining system in which the law and the justice system work to perpetuate the existing system of power relationships. According to structural Marxism, even the rich are subject to certain laws designed to prevent them from engaging in forms of behavior that might undermine the system of which they are a part. Laws regulating trade practices and monopolies, for example, regulate the behavior of the powerful and serve to ensure survival of the capitalist system. **Instrumental Marxism,** on the other hand, sees the criminal law and the justice system as tools that the powerful use to control the poor and to keep them disenfranchised. According to instrumental Marxism, the legal system serves not only to perpetuate the power relationships that exist within society but also to keep control in the hands of those who are already powerful. A recently popular book by **Jeffrey H. Reiman** builds upon this premise. Entitled *The Rich Get Richer and the Poor Get Prison,* Reiman's work contends that the criminal justice system is biased against the poor from start to finish and that well-to-do members of society control the criminal justice system—from the definition of crime through the process of arrest, trial, and sentencing.[38] Reiman also claims that many of the actions undertaken by well-off people should be defined as criminal, but they aren't. Such actions include the refusal to make workplaces safe, the refusal to curtail deadly industrial pollution, the promotion of

structural Marxism

A perspective that holds that the structural institutions of society influence the behavior of individuals and groups by virtue of the type of relationships created.

instrumental Marxism

A perspective that holds that those in power intentionally create laws and social institutions that serve their own interests and that keep others from becoming powerful.

TABLE 9–1   Class Structure of the United States, with Estimated Percentages of the Adult Population

Capitalist class 1.5%	Those who own and control production and wield state power
Petty bourgeoisie 18.5%	Professionals, middle management, bureaucrats
Working class 80%	Technical and skilled working class
	Technical
	Teachers
	Nurses
	Medical technicians
	Skilled
	Craftsmen
	Clerical workers
	Salespeople
	Transportation workers
	Industrial workers
	Reserve army
	Unskilled working class
	Unskilled
	Industrial labor
	Service workers
	Office workers
	Salespeople
	Clerical workers
	Unemployed
	Pauperized poor

Source: Adapted from Richard Quinney, *Class, State, and Crime: On the Theory and Practice of Criminal Justice* (New York: David McKay, 1977), p. 77. Reprinted with permission.

---

unnecessary surgery, and the prescription of unnecessary drugs. This kind of self-serving behavior, says Reiman, creates occupational and environmental hazards for the poor and for those who are less well-off than the rule makers themselves. These conditions, claims Reiman, produce as much death, destruction, and financial loss as the so-called crimes of the poor. Learn more about radical criminology at **Web Extra 9–5.**

WEB Extra

Critical Criminology

Some writers distinguish between critical criminology and radical criminology, saying that the former is simply a way of critiquing social relationships that lead to crime, whereas the latter constitutes a proactive call for a radical change in the social conditions that lead to crime.

Gresham M. Sykes explains **critical criminology** this way: "It forces an inquiry into precisely how the normative content of the criminal law is internalized in different segments of society, and how norm-holding is actually related to behavior."[39] As David A. Jones states in his insightful *History of Criminology*, however, "Sometimes, it may be difficult to distinguish 'critical' from a truly Marxist criminology. One basis, advanced by Marvin Wolfgang, is that 'critical' criminology is 'more reactive than proactive,' meaning that 'critical' criminology does not aim to overthrow the 'ruling class' so much as it may criticize the way it believes such a group dominates society."[40]

A cogent example of the critical perspective in contemporary criminology can be had in the work of Elliott Currie. Currie claims that "'market societies'—those in which the pursuit of private gain becomes the dominant organizing principle of social and economic life—are especially likely to breed high levels of violent crime."[41] Market societies, says Currie, are characterized by more than free enterprise and a free market

critical criminology

A perspective that holds that crime is the natural product of a capitalist system.

Who's to Blame—The Individual or Society?

Human Trafficking, Illegal Aliens, and the American Dream

Jose Gonzales, a naturalized U.S. citizen who worked for a Houston-based trucking company, was driving a tractor trailer through a U.S. Customs checkpoint on the Mexican border near San Diego when his truck was searched and found to contain 45 illegal immigrants concealed in Brazilian-made caskets that were being shipped to Los Angeles. Each of the immigrants had been supplied with plastic bottles containing water, and a few even had portable radios to keep them entertained on what had been planned as an hours-long trip.

The illegal immigrants were interrogated and fingerprinted and then taken back across the border to the Mexican border town of Tijuana in a U.S. Customs and Border Protection van. They were released into the custody of a Mexican Federal Investigative Agency official at a local police station, with instructions not to attempt an illegal return into the United States.

Gonzales's fate was quite different. Arrested and charged under the federal Immigration and Nationalization Act with attempting to bring unauthorized aliens into the United States, he was held in a federal jail in southern California, where he met with his court-appointed lawyer. The lawyer, Felix Alverez, told Gonzales that agents had him cold, and that he might as well confess in return for a plea bargain that might get him only a brief stint in a federal correctional facility. "Why confess?" Gonzales replied. "I was only trying to help those

people have better lives. Many of them were my friends. I didn't even take money for what I was doing."

"Why you were doing what you were doing doesn't matter," Alverez said. "You broke the law, and they are going to punish you."

"No," Gonzales replied. "I am a citizen. I want a trial. You can show them that I was only trying to help unfortunate people live the American Dream. Most of the people who live here and are going to be on a jury have immigrant ancestors. A lot of them were illegal. They won't dare find me guilty."

Think about it:

1. Why did Gonzales attempt to smuggle illegal immigrants into the United States? Do you think it was primarily for money or for altruistic motives?

2. How likely would Gonzales have been to commit this offense if he had a different ancestry—say, African American or European?

3. What do you think of Gonzales's claim that a jury won't find him guilty? Should he be held responsible for violating the law? Why or why not?

---

economy. They are societies in which the striving after personal economic gain runs rampant and becomes the hallmark of social life. The conditions endemic to market societies lead to high crime rates because they undercut and overwhelm more traditional principles that "have historically sustained individuals, families, and communities." The United States is the world's premier market society, says Currie, and its culture provides "a particularly fertile breeding ground for serious violent crime." Similarly, the recent and dramatic rise in crime rates in former communist countries throughout Europe can be explained by the burgeoning development of new market societies in those nations. According to Currie, seven "profoundly criminogenic and closely intertwined mechanisms" operate in a market society to produce crime:

- "The progressive destruction of livelihood," which results from the long-term absence of opportunities for stable and rewarding work—a consequence of the fact that market societies view labor "simply as a cost to be reduced" rather than as an asset with intrinsic value.

- "The growth of extremes of economic inequality and material deprivation," which causes many children to spend their developmental years in poverty.

- "The withdrawal of public services and supports, especially for families and children," resulting from the fact that "it is a basic operating principle of market society to keep the public sector small."

- "The erosion of informal and communal networks of mutual support, supervision, and care," brought about by the high mobility of the workforce that is characteristic of market societies.

- "The spread of a materialistic, neglectful, and 'hard' culture," which exalts brutal forms of individualized competition.

- "The unregulated marketing of the technology of violence," including the ready availability of guns, an emphasis on advancing technologies of destruction (such as the military), and mass-marketed violence on television and in the other media.
- "The weakening of social and political alternatives," leaving people unable to cope effectively with the forces of the market society, which undermine their communities and destroy valuable interpersonal relationships.

Currie suggests that as more nations emulate the "market society" culture of the United States, crime rates throughout the world will rise. An increasing emphasis on punishment and the growth of huge prison systems, says Currie, will consequently characterize most of the world's nations in the twenty-first century.

Radical-Critical Criminology and Policy Issues

Some contemporary writers on radical criminology tell us that "Marxist criminology was once dismissed as a utopian perspective with no relevant policy implication except revolution. At best, revolution was considered an impractical approach to the problems at hand. Recently, however, many radicals have attempted to address the issues of what can be done under our current system."[42]

Most radical-critical criminologists of today have had to come to terms with the collapse of the Soviet Union, a society that represented utopian Marxism in practice. They have also had to recognize that a sudden and total reversal of existing political arrangements within the United States is highly unlikely. As a consequence, such theorists have begun to focus, instead, on promoting a gradual transition to socialism and to socialized forms of government activity. These middle-range policy alternatives include "equal justice in the bail system, the abolition of mandatory sentences, prosecution of corporate crimes, increased employment opportunities, and promoting community alternatives to imprisonment."[43] Likewise, programs to reduce prison overcrowding, efforts to highlight injustices within the current system, the elimination of racism and other forms of inequality in the handling of both victims and offenders, increased equality in criminal justice system employment, and the like are all frequently mentioned as midrange strategies for bringing about a justice system that is more fair and closer to the radical ideal.

Raymond J. Michalowski summarizes well the policy directions envisioned by today's radical-critical criminologists when he says, "We cannot be free from the crimes of the poor until there are no more poor; we cannot be free from domination of the powerful until we reduce the inequalities that make domination possible; and we cannot live in harmony with others until we begin to limit the competition for material advantage over others that alienates us from one another."[44]

Even so, few radical-critical criminologists seem to expect to see dramatic changes in the near future. As Michael J. Lynch and W. Byron Groves explain, "In the end, the criminal justice system has failed as an agent of social change because its efforts are directed at an individual as opposed to social remedies. . . . For these reasons, radicals suggest that we put our efforts into the creation of economic equality or employment opportunities to combat crime."[45]

Critique of Radical-Critical Criminology

Radical-critical criminology has been criticized for its nearly exclusive emphasis on methods of social change at the expense of well-developed theory. As William V. Pelfrey explains, "It is in the Radical School of Criminology that theory is almost totally disregarded, except as something to criticize, and radical methods are seen as optimum."[46]

Radical-critical criminology can also be criticized for failing to recognize what appears to be at least a fair degree of public consensus about the nature of crime—that is, that crime is undesirable and that criminal activity is to be controlled. Were criminal activity a true expression of the sentiments of the politically and economically disenfranchised, as some radical criminologists claim, then public opinion might be expected to offer support for at least certain forms of crime. Even the sale of illicit drugs, however—a type of crime that may provide an alternative path to riches for the otherwise disenfranchised—is frequently condemned by residents of working-class communities.[47]

An effective criticism of Marxist criminology, in particular, centers on the fact that Marxist thinkers appear to confuse issues of personal politics with social reality. As a consequence of allowing personal values and political leanings to enter the criminological arena, Marxist criminologists have frequently appeared to sacrifice their objectivity. Jackson Toby, for example, claims that Marxist and radical thinkers are simply building upon an "old tradition of sentimentality toward those who break social rules."[48] Such sentimentality can be easily discounted, he says, when we realize that "color television sets and automobiles are stolen more often than food and blankets."[49]

Marxist criminology has also been refuted by contemporary thinkers who find that it falls short in appreciating the multiplicity of problems that contribute to the problem of crime. Some years ago, for example, astute criminologist Hermann Mannheim critiqued Marxian assumptions by showing how "subsequent developments" have shown that "Marx was wrong in thinking" (1) "that there could be only two classes in a capitalist society," (2) that "class struggle was entirely concerned with the question of private property in the means of production," (3) "that the only way in which fundamental social changes could be effected was by violent social revolution," and (4) "that all conflicts were class conflicts and all social change could be explained in terms of class conflicts."[50]

Mannheim went on to point out that the development of a semiskilled workforce along with the advent of highly skilled and well-educated workers has led to the creation of a multiplicity of classes within contemporary capitalist societies. The growth of such classes, said Mannheim, effectively spreads the available wealth in those societies where such workers are employed and reduces the likelihood of revolution.

A now-classic critique of radical criminology was offered in 1979 by Carl Klockars.[51] Klockars charged that Marxists are unable to explain low crime rates in some capitalist countries, such as Japan, and that they seem equally unwilling to acknowledge or address the problems of communist countries, which often have terrible human rights records. Writing more than 20 years ago, Klockars claimed that Marxist criminologists behaved more like "true believers" in a "new religion" who were unwilling to objectively evaluate their beliefs.[52]

Marxist criminology has suffered a considerable loss of prestige among many would-be followers in the wake of the collapse of the former Soviet Union and its client states in Eastern Europe and other parts of the world. With the death of Marxist political organizations and their agendas, Marxist criminology seems to have lost some of its impetus. Many would argue that the work of writers like Quinney and Chambliss presaged the decline of Soviet influence and had already moved Marxist and radical criminology into new areas. The work of Elliott Currie (discussed earlier in this chapter) and others has since led in a post-Marxist direction, while retaining a critical emphasis on the principles out of which radical criminology was fashioned. Consequently, today's radical criminologists have largely rescinded calls for revolutionary change, while simultaneously escalating their demands for the eradication of gender, racial, and other inequalities in the criminal justice system; for the elimination of prisons; for the abolition of capital punishment; and for an end to police misconduct.

Emerging Conflict Theories

The radical ideas associated with mid-twentieth-century Marxist criminology contributed to the formation of a number of new and innovative approaches to crime and criminology. Among them are emerging conflict criminologies, such as left-realist criminology, feminist criminology, postmodern criminology, and peacemaking criminology. It is to these perspectives that we now turn our attention.

Left-Realist Criminology

Left-realist criminology, a recent addition to the criminological landscape, is a natural outgrowth of practical concerns with street crime, the fear of crime, and everyday victimization. Realist criminology faults radical-critical criminologists for romanticizing street crime and the criminals who commit it. Radical-critical criminologists, they charge, falsely imagine street criminals as political resisters in an oppressive capitalist society. While realist criminology does not reject the conflict perspective inherent in radical-critical criminology, it shifts the center of focus onto a pragmatic assessment of crime and the needs of crime victims. Realist criminology seeks to portray crime in terms understandable to those most often affected by it: victims and their families, offenders, and criminal justice personnel. The test insisted upon by realist criminology is not whether a particular perspective on crime control or an explanation of crime causation complies with rigorous academic criteria, but whether the perspective speaks meaningfully to those faced with crime on a routine basis. As one contemporary source states, "For realists crime is no less harmful to its victims because of its socially constructed origins."[53]

Realist criminology is generally considered synonymous with **left realism.** Left realism, also called "radical realism" or "critical realism," builds on many of the concepts inherent in radical and Marxist criminology, while simultaneously claiming greater relevance than either of its two parent perspectives. Left realism also tends to distance itself from some of the more visionary claims of early radical and Marxist theory.[54] Daniel J. Curran and Claire M. Renzetti portray left realism as a natural consequence of increasingly conservative attitudes toward crime and criminals in both Europe and North America. "Though not successful in converting many radicals to the right," they claim, "this new conservatism did lead a number of radical criminologists to temper their views a bit and to take what some might call a less romanticized look at street crime."[55]

Some authors credit **Walter DeKeseredy**[56] with popularizing left-realist notions in North America, and **Jock Young**[57] is identified as a major source of left-realist writings in England. Prior to the writings of DeKeseredy and Young, radical criminology, with its emphasis upon the crime-inducing consequences of existing power structures, tended to portray the ruling class as the "real criminals" and saw street criminals as social rebels who were acting out of felt deprivation. In contrast, DeKeseredy and Young were successful in refocusing leftist theories onto the serious consequences of street crime and upon the crimes of the lower classes. Left realists argue that victims of crime are often the poor and disenfranchised who fall prey to criminals with similar backgrounds. They see the criminal justice system and its agents not as pawns of the powerful but, rather, as institutions that could offer useful services if modifications were made to reduce their use of force and to increase their sensitivity toward the public.

A central tenet of left realism is that radical ideas must be translated into realistic social policies if contemporary criminology is to have any practical relevance. In a recent review of left realism in Australia and England, concrete suggestions with respect to community policing models, for example, are indicative of the direction left realists are headed. Instead of seeing the police as oppressors working on behalf of the state, left realists recommend that the police work with, and answer to, the communities they serve.[58] The major goal of left realism is therefore to achieve "a fair and orderly society" through a practical emphasis on social justice.[59] Hence, left realists are concerned with the reality of crime and the damage it does to the most vulnerable segments of the population.

left-realist criminology

An approach to the subject matter of criminology based on ideas inherent in the perspective of left realism.

left realism

A conflict perspective that insists on a pragmatic assessment of crime and its associated problems.

Critique of Left-Realist Criminology

Left-realist criminology has been convincingly criticized for representing more of an ideological emphasis than a theory. As Don C. Gibbons explains, "Left realism can best be described as a general perspective centered on injunctions to 'take crime seriously' and to 'take crime control seriously' rather than as a well-developed criminological perspective."[60] Realist criminologists appear to build upon preexisting theoretical frameworks but rarely offer new propositions or hypotheses that are testable. They do, however, frequently suggest crime control approaches that are in keeping with the needs of the victimized. Policies promulgated by left realists understandably include an emphasis on community policing, neighborhood justice centers, and dispute resolution mechanisms, whereas right realists are more punitive in their policy suggestions. Piers Beirne and James W. Messerschmidt summarize the situation this way: "What left realists have essentially accomplished is an attempt to theorize about conventional crime realistically while simultaneously developing a 'radical law and order' program for curbing such behavior."[61] Read some original writings in the area of critical criminology via **Library Extras 9–1** and **9–2** at crimtoday.com. Access an online version of the *Red Feather Dictionary of Critical Social Science* via **Library Extra 9–3.**

LIBRARY
Extra
■ ■ ■ ■

Feminist Criminology

As some have observed, "Women have been virtually invisible in criminological analysis until recently and much theorizing has proceeded as though criminality is restricted to men."[62] Others put it this way: "Criminological theory assumes a woman is like a man."[63] Beginning in the 1970s, however, advances in feminist theory were applied to criminology, resulting in what has been called a **feminist criminology.** Other strands of feminist thought inform feminist criminology, including liberal feminism, radical feminism, socialist feminism, and Marxist feminism. Each of these perspectives argues that conflict in society is based on inequalities due primarily to gender, although they may vary on the degree to which inequality exists.

Feminist criminology is a self-conscious corrective model intended to redirect the thinking of mainstream criminologists to include gender awareness. It points out the inequities inherent in patriarchal forms of thought. **Patriarchy** refers to male dominance. James W. Messerschmidt offers a definition of *patriarchy* that is in keeping with the traditions of Marxist criminology. Messerschmidt says that patriarchy is a "set of social relations of power in which the male gender appropriates the labor power of women and controls their sexuality."[64] Evidence of patriarchy can be found in many different places. The fact that crime is often seen as an act of aggression, for example, contributes to the perpetuation of a male-centered criminology in which men are biologically characterized as having an aggressive nature that needs to be channeled and controlled. Society's acceptance of the belief that men are predisposed to aggression, however, led to the socialization of women as passive actors, which has excluded them from criminological study and made them more susceptible to continued victimization by men. In other words, traditional criminology, like the society of which it has been a part, has been male-centered, and women have been largely ignored by criminologists, heightening their sense of powerlessness and dependence upon men.

feminist criminology

A self-conscious corrective model intended to redirect the thinking of mainstream criminologists to include gender awareness.

Early works in the field of feminist criminology include **Freda Adler**'s *Sisters in Crime*[65] and **Rita J. Simon**'s *Women and Crime*,[66] both published in 1975. In these books, the authors attempted to explain existing divergences in crime rates between men and women as being due primarily to socialization rather than biology. Women, claimed these authors, were taught to believe in personal limitations; they faced reduced socioeconomic opportunities and, as a result, suffered from lowered aspirations. As gender equality increased, they said, it could be expected that male and female criminality would take on similar characteristics. As Chapter 2 points out, however, such has not been the case to date, and the approach of Adler and Simon has not been validated by observations surrounding increased gender equality over the past few decades. Another early work, *Women, Crime and Criminology,* was published in 1977 by British sociologist Carol Smart.[67] Smart's book did much to sensitize criminologists to sexist traditions within the field and led to recognition of women's issues. Smart pointed out that men and women experience and perceive the world in different ways. She showed how important it is for women to have a voice in interpreting the behavior of other women, as opposed to having the behavior of women interpreted from a man's standpoint—a perspective that does not include women's experience.

patriarchy

The tradition of male dominance.

Early feminist theorizing may not have borne the fruit that some researchers anticipated, but it has led to a heightened awareness of gender issues within criminology.

Two of the most insightful contemporary proponents of the need to apply feminist thinking to criminological analysis are **Kathleen Daly** and **Meda Chesney-Lind.** Daly and Chesney-Lind are concerned about the existence of **androcentricity** in criminology, and they point out that "gender differences in crime suggest that crime may not be so normal after all."[68] In other words, traditional understandings of what is "typical" about crime are derived from a study of men only or, more precisely, from that relatively small group of men who commit most crimes. The relative lack of criminality exhibited by women, however, which is rarely acknowledged as having criminological significance, calls into question many traditional assumptions about crime—and especially the assumption that crime is somehow a "normal" part of social life. In general terms, Daly and Chesney-Lind have identified the following five elements of feminist thought that "distinguish it from other types of social and political thought":[69]

- Gender is not a natural fact but a complex social, historical, and cultural product; it is related to, but not simply derived from, biological sex difference and reproductive capacities.

- Gender and gender relations order social life and social institutions in fundamental ways.

- Gender relations and constructs of masculinity and femininity are not symmetrical but are based on an organizing principle of men's superiority and social, political, and economic dominance over women.

- Systems of knowledge reflect men's views of the natural and social world; the production of knowledge is gendered.

- Women should be at the center, not the periphery, of intellectual inquiry; they should not be invisible or treated as appendages to men.

androcentricity

A single-sex perspective, as in the case of criminologists who study only the criminality of males.

In a similar, but more recent, analysis of feminist criminology, Susan Caulfield and Nancy Wonders describe "five major contributions that have been made by feminist scholarship and practice" to criminological thinking: (1) a focus on gender as a central organizing principle of contemporary life; (2) an awareness of the importance of power in shaping social relationships; (3) a heightened sensitivity to the way in which social context helps shape human relationships; (4) the recognition that social reality must be understood as a process, and the development of research methods that take this into account; and (5) a commitment to social change as a crucial part of feminist scholarship and practice.[70] As is the case with most feminist writing in the area of criminology today, Caulfield and Wonders hold that these five contributions of feminist scholarship "can help to guide research and practice within criminology."[71]

Feminism is a way of seeing the world; it is not strictly a sexual orientation. To be a feminist is to "combine a female mental perspective with a sensitivity for those social issues that influence primarily women."[72] Central to understanding feminist thought in both its historical and its contemporary modes is the realization that feminism views gender in terms of power relationships. In other words, according to feminist approaches, men have traditionally held much more power in society than have women. Male dominance has long been reflected in the patriarchal structure of Western society, a structure that has excluded women from much decision making in socially significant areas. Sexist attitudes—deeply ingrained notions of male superiority—have perpetuated inequality between the sexes. The consequences of sexism and of the unequal gender-based distribution of power have been far reaching, affecting fundamental aspects of social roles and personal expectation at all levels.

Various schools of feminist thought exist, with liberal and radical feminism envisioning a power-based and traditional domination of women's bodies and minds by men throughout history. **Radical feminism** depicts men as fundamentally brutish, aggressive, and violent and sees men as controlling women through sexuality by taking advantage of women's biological dependence during childbearing years and their inherent lack of physical strength relative to men. Radical feminists believe, for example, that the sexual victimization of girls is a learned behavior, as young males are socialized

radical feminism

A perspective that holds that any significant change in the social status of women can be accomplished only through substantial changes in social institutions such as the family, law, and medicine.

to be aggressive, resulting in male domination over females. They view society as patriarchal and believe that because men control the law, women are defined as subjects. Those young women who are sexually and physically exploited may run away or abuse substances, thereby becoming criminalized. Hence, from the point of view of radical feminism, the exploitation of women by men triggers women's deviant behavior. The elimination of male domination should therefore reduce crime rates for women and "even precipitate a decrease in male violence against women."[73]

liberal feminism

A perspective that holds that the concerns of women can be incorporated within existing social institutions through conventional means and without the need to drastically restructure society.

Liberal feminists, although they want the same gender equality as other feminists, lay the blame for present inequalities on the development within culture and society of "separate and distinct spheres of influence and traditional attitudes about the appropriate role of men and women."[74] A book by Alida V. Merlo and Joycelyn M. Pollock, for example, points out that feminists are often blamed in today's political atmosphere for the recent upsurge in crime because many, by entering or creating innovative family structures, have lowered what might otherwise be the positive effect of traditional family values on crime control.[75] Liberal feminists call for elimination of traditional divisions of power and labor between the sexes as a way of eliminating inequality and promoting social harmony.

socialist feminism

A perspective that examines social roles and the gender-based division of labor within the family, seeing both as a significant source of women's subordination within society.

Socialist feminists, who provide a third perspective, see gender oppression as a consequence of the economic structure of society and as a natural outgrowth of capitalist forms of social organization. Egalitarian societies, from the socialist point of view, would be built around socialist or Marxist principles with the aim of creating a society that is free of gender and class divisions. The present, capitalist social structure sees men committing violent street crimes, with women more likely to commit property and vice crimes.[76]

A fourth and complementary feminist perspective has been identified by Sally S. Simpson, who refers to it as an alternative framework developed by women of color. In Simpson's words, "The alternative frameworks developed by women of color heighten feminism's sensitivity to the complex interplay of gender, class, and race oppression."[77]

power-control theory

A perspective that holds that the distribution of crime and delinquency within society is to some degree founded upon the consequences that power relationships within the wider society hold for domestic settings and for the everyday relationships among men, women, and children within the context of family life.

John Hagan built upon defining features of power relationships in his book *Structural Criminology,* in which he explained that power relationships existing in the wider society are effectively "brought home" to domestic settings and are reflected in everyday relationships among men, women, and children within the context of family life.[78] Hagan writes, "Work relations structure family relations, particularly relations between fathers and mothers and, in turn, relations between parents and their children, especially mothers and their daughters."[79] Hagan's approach, which has been termed **power-control theory,** suggests that "family class structure shapes the social reproduction of gender relations, and in turn the social distribution of delinquency."[80] In most middle- and upper-middle-class families, says Hagan, a paternalistic model, in which the father works and the mother supervises the children, is the norm. Under the paternalistic model, girls are controlled by both parents—through male domination and by female role modeling. Boys, however, are less closely controlled and are relatively free to deviate from social norms, resulting in higher levels of delinquency among males. In lower- and lower-middle-class families, however, the paternalistic model is frequently absent. Hence, in such families there is less "gender socialization and less maternal supervision of girls," resulting in higher levels of female delinquency.[81]

In a work supportive of Hagan's thesis, Evelyn K. Sommers conducted a series of four hour-long interviews with each of 14 female inmates in a Canadian medium-security prison.[82] Focusing on what led to violations of the criminal law, Sommers identified four common themes to explain the criminality of the women she interviewed: (1) financial need, (2) drug involvement, (3) personal anger rooted in sexual and physical abuse or a sense of loss, and (4) fear. Because "need" was identified as the cause of lawbreaking behavior by five women interviewed, Sommers concluded that women's criminality is based on two underlying issues: the effort to maintain connection within relationships (such as between mother and child) and a personal quest for empowerment (as single mothers are expected to be independent and capable of providing for themselves and their children).

In a cogent analysis, which encompasses much of contemporary feminist theory, Daly and Chesney-Lind suggest that feminist thought is more important for the way it informs and challenges existing criminology than for the new theories it offers. Much current feminist thought within criminology emphasizes the need for gender awareness. Theories of crime causation and prevention, it is suggested, must include women, and more research on gender-related issues in the field is badly needed. Additionally, say Daly and Chesney-Lind, "criminologists should begin to appreciate that their discipline and its questions are a product of white, economically privileged men's experiences"[83] and that rates of female criminality, which are lower than those of males, may highlight the fact that criminal behavior is not as "normal" as once thought. Because modern-day criminological perspectives were mostly developed by white middle-class men, the propositions and theories they advance fail to take into consideration women's "ways of knowing."[84] Hence, the fundamental challenge posed by feminist criminology is do existing theories of crime causation apply as well to women as they do to men? Or, as Daly and Chesney-Lind ask, given the current situation in theory development, "do theories of men's crime apply to women?"[85]

Other feminists have analyzed the process by which laws are created and legislation passed and have concluded that modern-day statutes frequently represent characteristically masculine modes of thought. Such analysts have concluded that existing criminal laws are overly rational and hierarchically structured, reflecting traditionally male ways of organizing the social world.[86]

Until recently, for example, many jurisdictions viewed assault victims differently based on the gendered relationships involved in the offense. Assault (or, more precisely, battery), for example, is defined as an attack by one person upon another. Until the last few decades of the twentieth century, however, domestic violence statutes tended to downplay the seriousness of the attacks involved, giving the impression that because they occurred within the home and the victims were typically women, they weren't as important to the justice system as other forms of assault. Hence, cases of domestic assault were often handled informally by responding officers, and offenders were rarely arrested or removed from the home.[87] Similarly, some would argue, legal definitions of prostitution, pornography, and rape are determined primarily by men's understanding of the behavior in question and not by the experiences of women. Hence, in traditional

Homewares icon Martha Stewart, 62, prior to her arrest and prosecution. In 2004, Stewart was sentenced to five months in prison for obstructing a federal investigation into her 2001 sale of shares of the biotechnology company ImClone Systems, Inc. Stewart was also ordered to spend two years on probation, including five months of monitored home detention, and was fined $30,000. She was released from prison in 2005, after spending five months at the federal prison for women in Alderson, West Virginia. Some say that the criminality of women is beginning to rival that of men. Might Stewart serve as an example of just such a trend? Why or why not?

Source: AP Wide World Photos

criminology, women receive special protection because they are considered vulnerable to crime, but the experiences of women do not define the nature of the law or of the justice system's response. Consequently, some analysts suggest, existing laws need to be replaced by, or complemented with, "a system of justice based upon . . . the specifically feminine principles of care, connection and community."[88]

In the area of social policy, feminist thinkers have pointed to the need for increased controls over men's violence toward women, the creation of alternatives (to supplement the home and traditional family structures) for women facing abuse, and the protection of children. They have also questioned the role of government, culture, and the mass media in promulgating pornography, prostitution, and rape and have generally portrayed ongoing crimes against women as characteristic of continuing traditions in which women are undervalued and controlled. Many radical feminists have suggested the replacement of men with women in positions of power, especially within justice system and government organizations, while others have noted that replacement still would not address needed changes in the structure of the system itself, which is gender biased due to years of male domination. Centrists, on the other hand, suggest a more balanced approach, believing that individuals of both genders have much to contribute to a workable justice system.[89] Learn more about feminist criminology at Web Extras 9–6 and 9–7.

WEB
Extra

Critique of Feminist Criminology

Some would argue that in the area of theoretical development, feminist criminology has yet to live up to its promise. Throughout the late 1970s and 1980s, few comprehensive feminist theories of crime were proposed; feminist criminology focused instead on descriptive studies of female involvement in crime.[90] Although such data gathering may have laid the groundwork for theory building, which is yet to come, few descriptive studies attempted to link their findings to existing feminist theory in any comprehensive way. Theory development suffered again in the late 1980s and early 1990s as an increased concern with women's victimization, especially the victimization of women at the hands of men, led to further descriptive studies with a somewhat different focus. Male violence against women was seen as adding support to the central tenet of feminist criminology that the relationship between the sexes is primarily characterized by the exercise of power (or lack thereof). Such singularity of focus, however, did not make for broad theory building. As one writer explains the current state of feminist criminology, "Feminist theory is a theory in formation."[91] To date, feminist researchers have continued to amass descriptive studies, while feminist analysis has hardly advanced beyond a framework for the "deconstruction" of existing theories—that is, for their reevaluation in light of feminist insights.[92] A fair assessment of the current situation would probably conclude that the greatest contributions of feminist thought to criminological theory building are yet to come.

Feminist criminology has faced criticism from many other directions. As mentioned previously, predicted increases in female crime rates have failed to materialize as social opportunities available to both genders have become more balanced. The **gender gap** in crime—with males accounting for much more law violation than females—continues to exist. As modern-day criminologist Karen Heimer notes, the gender gap is "virtually a truism in criminology." Says Heimer, "The relationship holds, regardless of whether the data analyzed are arrest rates, victimization incidence reports on characteristics of offenders, or self-reports of criminal behavior." And, Heimer notes, "as far as we can tell, males have always been more criminal than females, and gender differences emerge in every society that has been studied systematically."[93] Other critics have pointed to fundamental flaws in feminist thought, asking such questions as "If men have more power than women, then why are so many more men arrested?"[94] Gender disparities in arrest (unrelated to reported rates of crime) are rarely found,[95] however, and sentencing practices do not seem to favor women.[96] The chivalry hypothesis of many years ago, under which it was proposed that women are apt to be treated more leniently by the justice system because of their gender, does not appear to operate today.[97]

gender gap

The observed differences between male and female rates of criminal offending in a given society, such as the United States.

Some critics even argue that a feminist criminology is impossible. Daly and Chesney-Lind, for example, agree that although feminist thought may inform criminology, "a feminist criminology cannot exist because neither feminism nor criminology is a unified set of principles and practices."[98] In other words, according to these authors, a criminology built solely on feminist principles is unlikely because neither feminist thought nor criminology meets the strict requirements of formal theory building. Even with such a caveat in mind, however, it should still be possible to construct a gender-aware criminology—that is, one that is informed by issues of gender and that takes into consideration the concerns of feminist writers. A "feminist-oriented criminology," say Caulfield and Wonders, is one that will transgress traditional criminology. "This transgression, or 'going beyond boundaries,'" they write, "must occur at a number of levels across a number of areas covered within criminology" and will eventually move us toward a more just world.[99] Read more about feminist perspectives on crime and criminology at Library Extras 9–4, 9–5, and 9–6 at crimtoday.com.

LIBRARY
Extra
▪▪▪▪

Postmodern Criminology

Some significant, new approaches now emerging within criminology are largely the result of postmodernist social thought. Most such theories can be lumped together under the rubric "postmodern criminology." **Postmodern criminology** applies understandings of social change that are inherent in postmodern philosophy to criminological theorizing and to issues of crime control.

postmodern criminology

A brand of criminology that developed following World War II and that builds on the tenets inherent in postmodern social thought.

Postmodern thought, which developed primarily in Europe after World War II, represents "a rejection of the enlightenment belief in scientific rationality as the main vehicle to knowledge and progress."[100] One important aspect of postmodern social thought can be found in its efforts to demonstrate the systematic intrusion of sexist, racist, capitalist, colonialist, and professional interests into the very content of science. Contemporary feminist scholar Joycelyn M. Pollock puts it this way: "Post-modernism questions whether we can ever 'know' something objectively; so-called neutral science is considered a sham and criminology's search for causes is bankrupt because even the question is framed by androcentric, sexist, classist, and racist definitions of crime, criminals, and cause."[101]

Postmodern criminology is not so much a theory as it is a group of new and emerging criminological perspectives that are all informed by the tone of postmodernism. At the cutting edge of postmodern criminology can be found novel paradigms with such intriguing names as "chaos theory," "discourse analysis," "topology theory," "catastrophe theory," "Lacanian thought," "Godel's theorem," "constitutive theory," and "anarchic criminology."[102]

All postmodern criminologies build on the feeling that past criminological approaches have failed to realistically assess the true causes of crime and have therefore failed to offer workable solutions for crime control—or if they have, that such theories and solutions may have been appropriate at one time, but that they are no longer applicable to the postmodern era. Hence, much postmodern criminology is deconstructionist, and such theories are sometimes called "deconstructionist theories."

Deconstructionist theories are approaches that challenge—often quite effectively—existing criminological perspectives to debunk them and to work toward replacing them with approaches more relevant to the postmodern era. They intend to offer freedom from oppressive forms of thought by deconstructing and pulling apart the foundations of existing thought, knowledge, and belief in modern Western culture. Bruce DiCristina, for example, proposes one form of postmodern criminology that he calls "anarchic criminology."[103] Anarchic criminology is "a criminology which embraces alternative methods and epistemologies, encourages imaginative solutions to social and criminal problems, and in the process continually undermines encrusted hierarchies of certainty, truth, and power."[104]

deconstructionist theory

A postmodern perspective that challenges existing criminological theories in order to debunk them and that works toward replacing traditional ideas with concepts seen as more appropriate to the postmodern era.

Two especially notable authors in the field of postmodern criminology are **Stuart Henry** and **Dragan Milovanovic**,[105] whose constitutive criminology, which is rooted in phenomenology, claims that crime and crime control are not "object-like entities," but, rather, constructions produced through a social process in which offender, victim, and society are all involved.[106]

A central feature of constitutive criminology is its assertion that individuals shape their world, while also being shaped by it. Hence, the behaviors of those who offend and victimize others cannot be understood in isolation from the society of which they are a part. Individuals, however, tend to remain unaware of the role they play in the social construction of their subjective worlds, and they fail to realize that, at least to some degree, they are able to create new meanings while freeing themselves from old biases.

One area that demonstrates well constructionist notions is the sociology of law, which highlights the inherent interrelatedness between law and social structure. Milovanovic, for example, suggests the application of semiotics to the study of law.[107] *Semiotics* is a term akin to *semantics,* and both words derive from the Greek word *s[ebar]ma*, meaning "sign." Milovanovic sees semiotics as being especially useful in the study of law and criminology because everything we know, say, do, think, and feel is mediated through signs—a sign being anything that stands for something else. Hence, language, gestures, sensations, objects, and events are all interpreted by the human mind through the use of signs. A semiotic criminology is concerned, therefore, with identifying how language systems (for example, those of medicine, law, education, gangs, sports, prison communities, criminal justice practitioners, and criminologists) communicate uniquely encoded values. Such values are said to "oppress those who do not communicate meaning from within the particular language system in use" because they may prevent effective discourse with those in power.[108]

The application of semiotics to the study of law can be illustrated by the term *mental illness.* As a sign, this term is imbued with multiple—perhaps even contradictory—meanings. Possible interpretations for what this sign represents include a disease in need of treatment and a person needing psychiatric services. Moreover, *mental illness* means something different in the law (wherein the proper phrase is *legal insanity*) than it does in medicine or in the lay community. Different interpretations reflect different values, and these values can be traced to divergent interest groups. Moreover, as Milovanovic notes, the meaning of *mental illness* has changed over time—and continues to change.

Semiotics can also be applied directly to the notion of crime, as crime itself is a "socially constructed category," or sign. In the words of Henry and Milovanovic, crime "is a categorization of the diversity of human conflicts and transgressions into a single category 'crime,' as though these were somehow all the same. It is a melting of differences reflecting the multitude of variously motivated acts of personal injury into a single entity."[109] Such a statement, to the minds of constitutive criminologists, lays bare the true meaning of the word *crime,* effectively "deconstructing" it.

Crime should be understood, say Henry and Milovanovic, as an integral part of society—not as something separate and apart from it. From this perspective, a kind of false consciousness, or lack of awareness, gives rise to criminal activity. According to Werner Einstadter and Stuart Henry, crime is seen to be the culmination of certain processes that allow persons to believe that they are somehow not connected to other humans and society. These processes place others into categories or stereotypes and make them different or alien, denying them their humanity. These processes result in the denial of responsibility for other people and to other people.[110] Hence, from a constitutive point of view, crime is simply "the power to deny others," and crime is caused by "the structure, ideology and invocation of discursive practices that divide human relations into categories, that divide responsibility from others and to others into hierarchy and authority relations." Learn more about postmodern criminology at **Web Extra 9–8,** and read an interesting paper by Dragan Milovanovic at **Library Extra 9–7** at crimtoday.com.

WEB
Extra

LIBRARY
Extra

Critique of Postmodern Criminology

Ian Taylor, a British sociologist who lent focus to radical-critical criminology in the 1970s with the publication of two well-received books,[111] criticizes postmodern approaches to crime and deviance for their "increasing incoherence."[112] Not only do postmodern criminologists employ terminology that is only vaguely defined, but, Taylor seems to say, the "battle with orthodox criminology" has led postmodern approaches to increasingly obfuscate their most basic claims. A second result of the postmodern influence on criminology, says Taylor, "has been the development of a social account of crime that entirely lacks a value or ethical foundation."[113] Deconstructionism, for example, may challenge traditional theories, but unless it offers viable alternatives for crime control and prevention, it does little good. Taylor criticizes what he calls "privileged academic commentators working within the postmodern tradition" for being "nihilistic," and he says that "the idea of a critical criminology organized only around the libertarian idea of 'radical nonintervention' seem[s] entirely unhelpful as a point of departure."[114]

Peacemaking Criminology

Throughout much of history, formal agencies of social control, especially the police, officials of the courts, and correctional personnel, have been seen as pitted against criminal perpetrators and would-be wrongdoers. Crime control has been traditionally depicted in terms of a kind of epic struggle in which diametrically opposed antagonists continuously engage one another, but in which only one side can emerge as victorious. Recently, however, a new point of view known as **peacemaking criminology** has come to the fore. Criminology as peacemaking is a form of postmodern criminology that has its roots in Christian and Eastern philosophies. Peacemaking criminology advances the notion that social control agencies and the citizens they serve should work together to alleviate social problems and human suffering and thus reduce crime.[115] Peacemaking criminology, which includes the notion of service and which has also been called "compassionate criminology," suggests that "compassion, wisdom, and love are essential for understanding the suffering of which we are all a part and for practicing a criminology of nonviolence."[116]

peacemaking criminology

A perspective that holds that crime control agencies and the citizens they serve should work together to alleviate social problems and human suffering and thus reduce crime.

Peacemaking criminology is a relatively new undertaking, popularized by the works of **Harold E. Pepinsky**[117] and Richard Quinney,[118] beginning in 1986. Both Pepinsky and Quinney restate the problem of crime control from one of "how to stop crime" to one of "how to make peace" within society and between citizens and criminal justice agencies. Peacemaking criminology draws attention to many issues, among them (1) the perpetuation of violence through the continuation of social policies based on dominant forms of criminological theory, (2) the role of education in peacemaking, (3) "commonsense theories of crime," (4) crime control as human rights enforcement, and (5) conflict resolution within community settings.[119]

Commonsense theories of crime are derived from everyday experience and beliefs and are characteristic of the "person in the street." Unfortunately, say peacemaking criminologists, fanciful commonsense theories all too often provide the basis for criminological investigations, which in turn offer support for the naïve theories themselves. One commonsense theory criticized by peacemaking criminologists is the "black-male-as-savage theory,"[120] which holds that African American men are far more crime-prone than their white counterparts. Such a perspective, frequently given added credence by official interpretations of criminal incidence data, only increases the crime control problem by further distancing African Americans from government-sponsored crime control policies. A genuine concern for the problems facing all citizens, say peacemaking criminologists, would more effectively serve the ends of crime control.

Richard Quinney and John Wildeman summarize well the underpinnings of peacemaking criminology with these words: "(1) Thought of the Western rational mode is conditional, limiting knowledge primarily to what is already known; (2) each life is a spiritual journey into the unknown and the unknowable, beyond the ego-centered self; (3) human existence is characterized by suffering; crime is suffering; and the sources of suffering are within each of us; (4) through love and compassion, beyond the ego-centered self, we can end suffering and live in peace, personally and collectively; (5) crime can be ended only with the ending of suffering, only when there is peace and social justice; and (6) understanding, service, justice—all these flow naturally from love and compassion, from mindful attention to the reality of all that is, here and now. A criminology of peacemaking—a nonviolent criminology of compassion and service—seeks to end suffering and thereby eliminate crime."[121]

Elsewhere, Quinney writes, "A society of meanness, competition, greed, and injustice is created by minds that are greedy, selfish, fearful, hateful, and crave power over others. Suffering on the social level can be ended only with the ending of suffering on the personal level. Wisdom brings the awareness that divisions between people and groups are not between the bad and the good or between the criminal and the noncriminal. Wisdom teaches interbeing. We must become one with all who suffer from lives of crime and from the sources that produce crime. Public policy must then flow from this wisdom."[122]

Other contributors to the peacemaking movement include Bo Lozoff, Michael Braswell, and Clemens Bartollas. In *Inner Corrections,* Lozoff and Braswell claim that "we are fully aware by now that the criminal justice system in this country is founded on violence. It is a system which assumes that violence can be overcome by violence, evil by evil. Criminal justice at home and warfare abroad are of the same principle of violence. This principle sadly dominates much of our criminology."[123] *Inner Corrections,* which is primarily a compilation of previous works on compassion and prison experience, provides meditative techniques and prayers for those seeking to become more compassionate and includes a number of letters from convicts who demonstrate the book's philosophy.

In a work entitled "Correctional Treatment, Peacemaking, and the New Age Movement," Bartollas and Braswell apply New Age principles to correctional treatment.[124] "Most offenders suffered abusive and deprived childhoods," they write. "Treatment that focuses on the inner child and such qualities as forgiveness and self-esteem could benefit offenders. Some New Age teachings tempered by the ancient spiritual traditions may offer offenders the hope they can create a future that brings greater fulfillment than their past. This changed future may include growing out of the fear of victimization, becoming more positive and open to possibilities, viewing one's self with more confidence and humility, understanding the futility of violence, and attaining emotional and financial sufficiency."[125]

In a fundamental sense, peacemaking criminologists exhort their colleagues to transcend personal dichotomies to end the political and ideological divisiveness that separates people. "If we ourselves cannot know peace . . . how will our acts disarm hatred and violence?" they ask.[126] Lozoff and Braswell express the same sentiments this way: "Human transformation takes place as we change our social, economic and political structure. And the message is clear: without peace within us and in our actions, there can be no peace in our results. Peace is the way."[127]

Restorative Justice

peace model

An approach to crime control that focuses on effective ways for developing a shared consensus on critical issues that could seriously affect the quality of life.

Peacemaking criminology suggests that effective crime control can best be achieved by the adoption of a peace model based on cooperation rather than retribution. The **peace model** of crime control focuses on effective ways of developing a shared consensus on critical issues that could seriously affect the quality of life. These issues include major crimes like murder and rape but may also extend to property rights, rights to the use of new technologies, the ownership of information, and so on. Relatively minor issues, including sexual preference, nonviolent sexual deviance, gambling, drug use, noise, simple child custody claims, and publicly offensive behavior can be dealt with in ways that require few resources beyond those immediately available in the community.

participatory justice

A relatively informal type of criminal justice case processing that makes use of local community resources rather than requiring traditional forms of official intervention.

Alternative dispute resolution mechanisms play an important role in peacemaking perspectives.[128] Mediation programs, such as modern-day dispute resolution centers and neighborhood justice centers, are characterized by cooperative efforts to reach dispute resolution, rather than by the adversarial-like proceedings now characteristic of most American courts. Dispute resolution programs are based on the principle of **participatory justice,** in which all parties to a dispute accept a kind of binding arbitration by neutral parties. Now operating in over 200 areas throughout the country, dispute resolution centers often utilize administrative hearings and ombudsmen and are staffed by volunteers who work to resolve disputes without assigning blame.

The Community Dispute Settlement Program, which began in Philadelphia in the 1970s, was one of the earliest of modern-day community mediation programs in the country and has been well studied.[129] Mediation in America, however, has a long and varied history. For many years, Native American tribes have routinely employed dispute resolution mechanisms in dealing with behavioral problems and even crime. Perhaps the best-known dispute settlement mechanism among Native Americans today is the Navajo Peacemaker Court, which serves as an adjunct to the tribal court.[130]

Miami's "drug court," a local judicial initiative, provides an example of another kind of dispute resolution program. The drug court program, which began in 1989, diverts nonviolent drug users from the traditional path of streets to court to jail and is one of the first of its kind in the nation. Officially called the Dade County Diversion and Treatment Program, the drug court "channels almost all nonviolent defendants arrested on drug possession charges into an innovative court-operated rehabilitation program as an alternative to prosecution. . . . The program expands on the traditional concept of diversion to provide a year or more of treatment and case management services that include counseling, acupuncture, fellowship meetings, education courses, and vocational services along with strict monitoring through periodic urine tests and court appearances. Defendants who succeed in the program have their criminal cases dismissed."[131] Drug court processing appears to be successful at reducing the incidence of repeat offenses, does not result in a criminal record for those who complete the program, and offers drug-dependent offenders a second chance at gaining control over substance abuse problems.

Alternative dispute resolution strategies are not without their critics, who charge that such programs are often staffed by poorly qualified individuals who are ill-prepared to mediate disputes effectively. Nonetheless, as case-processing expenses continue to rise and as minor cases continue to flood justice system agencies, we can expect that an emphasis on alternative means of dispute resolution will continue.

Many alternative dispute resolution strategies are really a form of restorative justice. Postmodern writers describe **restorative justice** (also called "reparative justice," or RJ) as "a new system based on remedies and restoration rather than on prison, punishment and victim neglect."[132] They see it as "a system rooted in the concept of a caring community"[133] and hope that it will lead to social and economic justice and increased concern and respect for both victims and victimizers in the not-too-distant future. Restorative justice is more than a system, however; it is a modern social movement meant to reform the criminal justice system. The restorative justice movement, which stresses healing rather than retribution, is based upon three principles. The first is a view of crime "as more than simply law-breaking, an offense against governmental authority; [instead] crime is understood to cause multiple injuries to victims, the community and even the offender. Second, proponents argue that the criminal justice process should help repair those injuries. Third, they protest the government's apparent monopoly over society's response to crime,"[134] insisting that victims, offenders, and their communities must also be involved in a concerted effort to heal the harm caused by crime.

Restoration, or repairing the harm done by crime and rebuilding relationships in the community, is the primary goal of restorative justice. The effectiveness of restorative justice programs is measured by how much relationships were healed rather than by how much punishment was inflicted on the offender. Table 9–2 highlights some of the significant differences between traditional (or retributive) justice and restorative justice. Learn more about restorative justice at Web Extra 9–9, and read a paper on the topic of RJ at Library Extra 9–8 at crimtoday.com.

restorative justice

A postmodern perspective that stresses "remedies and restoration rather than prison, punishment and victim neglect."

WEB
Extra
■ ■ ■ ■

LIBRARY
Extra
■ ■ ■ ■

Critique of Peacemaking Criminology

Peacemaking criminology has been criticized as being naïve and utopian, as well as for failing to recognize the realities of crime control and law enforcement. Few victims, for example, would expect to gain much from attempting to make peace with their

TABLE 9-2	Differences between Retributive and Restorative Justice	
Retributive Justice		**Restorative Justice**
Crime is an act against the state, a violation of a law, an abstract idea.		Crime is an act against another person or the community.
The criminal justice system controls crime.		Crime control lies primarily with the community.
Offender accountability is defined as taking punishment.		Offender accountability is defined as assuming responsibility and taking action to repair harm.
Crime is an individual act with individual responsibility.		Crime has both individual and social dimensions of responsibility.
Victims are peripheral to the process of resolving a crime.		Victims are central to the process of resolving a crime.
The offender is defined by deficits.		The offender is defined by the capacity to make reparation.
The emphasis is on adversarial relationships.		The emphasis is on dialogue and negotiation.
Pain is imposed to punish, deter, and prevent.		Restitution is a means of restoring both parties; the goal is reconciliation.
The community is on the sidelines, represented abstractly.		The community is the facilitator in the restorative process by the state.
The response is focused on the offender's past behavior.		The response is focused on harmful consequences of the offender's behavior; the emphasis is on the future and on reparation.
There is dependence on proxy professionals.		There is direct involvement by both the offender and the victim.

Source: Adapted from Gordon Bazemore and Mark S. Umbreit, *Balanced and Restorative Justice: Program Summary* (Washington, DC: Office of Juvenile Justice and Delinquency Prevention, 1994), p. 7.

A homeless man in New York City. Peacemaking criminology holds that the alleviation of social problems and the reduction of human suffering will lead to a truly just world and will thus reduce crime. What do you think?

Source: Photo by Susan Rae/Susan Tannebaum

victimizers (although such strategies do occasionally work). Such criticisms, however, may be improperly directed at a level of analysis that peacemaking criminologists have not assumed. In other words, peacemaking criminology, while it involves work with individual offenders, envisions positive change on the societal and institutional level and does not suggest to victims that they attempt to effect personal changes in offenders.

Convict Criminology

The newest radical paradigm to emerge within the field of criminolgy is **convict criminology.** Formalzed in 2001 with the publication of the article "Introducing the New School of Convict Criminology" by Stephen C. Richards in the journal *Social Justice*,[135] convict criminology (also called *alternative criminology*) is not so much a school of thought as it is a body of writings and musings on the subject matter of criminology by convicted felons and ex-inmates who have acquired academic credentials, or who are associated with credentialled others. In 2002, with publication of the book, *Convict Criminology*, by Ian Ross and Stephen Richards, the writings of convict criminologists went mainstream and began garnering attention from within the discipline and from the media. Today's convict criminology, sometimes referred to as the New School of Convict Criminology, offers a blend of writings by credentialled ex-inmates and critical criminologists who have joined forces in distrust of mainstream criminology.[136] Convict criminology is largely issues-based and personal. As admitted to by its adherents, convict criminology is not without an agenda, and tends to assume a critical perspective with regard to the justice system—especially corrections. Similarly, the language of convict criminologists is different from that of academic criminologists who do not share their convict background. Convict criminologists tend to write about "convicts" instead of "offenders," and "inmates" instead of "prisoners." The distinction is an important one, because the terminology used by academic criminologists is "managerial" in the sense that it is consistent with the language of controlling agents in the justice system—police officers, correctional officers, probation and parole officers, court officials, and so on. By using the language of convict insiders, convict criminologists signify their allegiance to an insider's perspective, and refer to traditional criminology as *managerial criminology*.[137]

> **convict criminology**
>
> A new radical paradigm consisting of writings on the subject matter of criminology by convicted felons and ex-inmates who have acquired academic credentials, or who are associated with credentialled others.

The primary method used by convict criminologists is ethnographic. Ethnography is a branch of anthropology that involves studying other cultures, in this case, inmate society. Ethnographers, as discussed in Chapter 3 depend upon lived experiences and oral communicatons about them (for example, interviews, stories, and long hours spent listening to those whom they are studying). The advantage of convict criminologists is that they are their own subjects, and the long hours needed to gather experiences have already been spent—usually in prison, or in personal interaction with the justice system.

The prototype convict criminologist is John Irwin, who spent five years in California's Soledad Prison in the 1950s for armed robbery. While imprisoned, Irwin earned college credits and after release went on to attend San Francisco State College and then UCLA. Irwin says, "The point is, I made my transition from the life of a thief, drug addict, and convict to one of a 'respectable' professional. . . ." Irwin went on to write *The Felon*,[138] an academic work that shared the career criminal's point of view with interested readers.

Some of the most recent works in the area of convict criminology are the result of collaboration between traditional criminologists and ex-convicts. Among them are the books *Behind A Convict's Eyes*[139] and *Prison, Inc.: A Convict Exposes Life Inside a Prison Prison*[140]—both by the author team of K. C. Carceral (a convict serving life in prison who holds an associate's degree in paralegal studies), Thomas J. Bernard (a criminologist at Penn State University), and others.

Convict criminology is the source of a number of recommendations for improving the justice system. These recommendations stem primarily from the lived experiences of the convict criminologists themselves, and not from traditional forms of social scientific research. Nonetheless, the claim is sometimes made that experience is itself a kind of research, albeit a very personal one. Convict criminologists say that:[141]

1. Prisons hold far too many people, do not effectively reduce crime, and hold far too many people who have committed minor crimes.

2. Prison expansion has disproportionately and unfairly impacted the nation's poor—especially young men of color—who have made bad decisions in their lives and committed relatively harmless and bothersome crimes.

3. A substantial reduction in the number of federal and state prisoners is needed. Convict criminologists point out that many of today's prisoners are nonviolent drug offenders who committed property crimes in support of drug habits, or those who were caught with drugs in their possession either for personal use or resale. Diversion and treatment are recommended as viable alternatives to incarceration. Similarly, say convict criminologists, the nation's war on drugs—which they see as having a negative impact on all of society— should be terminated.

4. Corrections today can benefit significantly from the use of smaller prisons in place of the large institutions that now characterize many state facilities. Smaller prisons should become a model for American corrections, convict criminologists say, because they are less dangerous than large ones, and tend to result in heightened rates of rehabilitation.

5. Treatment should be given precedence over security because most inmates will eventually return to society, and it is treatment that offers the best hope for desistance from crime. Not only should institutional priorities be reversed, say convict criminologists, but treatment programs need to receive top-level funding.

LIBRARY Extra

Not everyone agrees that convict criminology offers an edge over traditional criminology. Critics say that having been in prison might actually distort a criminologist's view of his or her field rather than enhance it. Moreover, personal experience rarely gives anyone the entire picture needed to understand a phenomenon. Focusing on the injustices of prison life, for example, might keep one from appreciating the reformative effects of punishment. Read more about convict criminology at Library Extra 9–9 at crimtoday.com.

Policy Implications of Social Conflict Theories

The policy implications of social conflict theory are fairly clear: Bring about social change and redistribute the wealth in society, and crime rates will fall. At one extreme, radical-Marxist criminologists argue that the only effective way of reducing conflict is through a total dismantling of the existing capitalist system in the United States and its replacement by a socialist economic structure. At the other extreme are the calls of peacemaking criminologists for a practical application of the principles of conflict resolution. Between these two extremes lie left realism and feminist criminology, although the solutions they offer vary from the reduction of paternalism in all its forms to a practical recognition of the consequences of crime to victims.

SUMMARY

This chapter has described social conflict theories. Conflict theories hold that social conflict is the root cause of crime. For some conflict theorists, social order rests upon the exercise of coercive power rather than an agreed-upon consensus. Radical criminologists hold that the ongoing battle between the haves and the have-nots in capitalist societies leads to crime and to definitions of crime that unfairly criminalize the activities of the disenfranchised. They believe that criminal law is a tool of the powerful, who use it to perpetuate their control over the less fortunate.

Radical criminology and its contemporary offshoots, including feminist criminology, critical criminology, postmodernism, and peacemaking criminology, seek to redress injustices in society as a way of ending the marginalization of the politically and economically disentitled. Feminist criminology believes that the consequences of sexism and of the traditionally unequal gender-based distribution of power

within our patriarchal society have been far reaching, affecting fundamental aspects of social roles and personal expectation at all levels, including crime and the field of criminology. Postmodernists doubt that an objective study of crime is even possible; they believe that criminology's search for the causes of crime is implicitly doomed because the questions it raises are framed by sexist, class-specific, and racist assumptions. Hence, postmodernists attempt to deconstruct existing theories in hopes of revealing the fallacies inherent in traditional perspectives.

Convict criminology, the newest radical paradigm to emerge within the field of criminology, is a body of writings and musings on the subject matter of criminology by convicted felons and ex-inmates who have acquired academic credentials, or who are associated with credentialled others. Convict criminology is sometimes referred to as the New School of Convict Criminology. It is largely issues-based and consists of a blend of writings by credentialled ex-inmates and critical criminologists who have joined forces in distrust of mainstream criminology.

Unfortunately for most early social conflict theorists, not many of their predictions have come true. Conflict theorists, especially those of the more radical persuasion, have been criticized for being overly idealistic and for lacking an appreciation for the everyday problems of crime victims. The demise of the Soviet Union in the 1990s and the associated decline of world communism have further questioned the wisdom of some of the most fundamental concepts inherent in radical criminology and its intellectual descendants.

KEY TERMS

androcentricity, 363

bourgeoisie, 348

conflict perspective, 347

consensus model, 345

convict criminology, 373

critical criminology, 357

deconstructionist theory, 367

feminist criminology, 362

gender gap, 366

instrumental Marxism, 356

left realism, 361

left-realist criminology, 361

liberal feminism, 364

Marxist criminology, 354

participatory justice, 370

patriarchy, 362

peacemaking criminology, 369

peace model, 370

pluralistic perspective, 347

postmodern criminology, 367

power-control theory, 364

proletariat, 348

radical criminology, 354

radical feminism, 363

restorative justice, 371

social class, 351

socialist feminism, 364

structural Marxism, 356

KEY NAMES

Freda Adler, 362

Willem Bonger, 349

William J. Chambliss, 355

Meda Chesney-Lind, 363

Ralf Dahrendorf, 353

Kathleen Daly, 363

Walter DeKeseredy, 361

John Hagan, 364

Stuart Henry, 367

Karl Marx, 348

Raymond J. Michalowski, 345

Dragan Milovanovic, 367

Harold E. Pepinsky, 369

Roscoe Pound, 346

Richard Quinney, 355

Jeffrey H. Reiman, 356

Rita J. Simon, 362

Austin Turk, 354

George B. Vold, 352

Jock Young, 361

QUESTIONS FOR REVIEW

1. What three analytical perspectives on law and social order are described in this chapter?

2. What are the central tenants of radical criminology? What are its shortcomings?

3. What three emerging conflict perspectives discussed in this chapter purport to explain crime and criminality?

4. What are the crime control implicatons of social conflict theories?

QUESTIONS FOR REFLECTION

1. This book emphasizes a social problems versus social responsibility theme. Which of the theoretical perspectives discussed in this chapter (if any) support the social problems approach? Which (if any) support the social responsibility approach? Why?

2. Explain the differences among the consensus, pluralist, and conflict perspectives. Which comes closest to your way of understanding society? Why?

3. What is Marxist criminology? How, if at all, does it differ from radical criminology? From critical criminology?

4. Does the Marxist perspective hold any significance for contemporary American society? Why?

5. What are the fundamental propositions of feminist criminology? How would feminists change the study of crime?

6. What does it mean to say that traditional theories of crime need to be "deconstructed"? What role does deconstructionist thinking play in postmodern criminology?

WEB QUEST

This Web Quest requires you to visit two sites on the Web: (1) the Critical Criminology Division of the American Society of Criminology (ASC) at www.critcrim.org, and (2) recent selections from the *Critical Criminologist* (the newsletter of the ASC's Critical Criminology Division) at http://critcrim.org/the_critical_criminologist. First familiarize yourself with the availability of materials at each site, and get a general feel for

the materials available at both. Then read some of the electronic manuscripts and other postings at the *Critical Criminologist*. Which of those e-papers relate directly to the concepts discussed in this chapter? How do those materials expand upon the content of this chapter? Submit your answers to your instructor if asked to do so. Be sure to check the Web Quest section of crimtoday.com in case the URLs listed here change.

NOTES

[1] Natasha Alova, "Russia—Juvenile Crime," Associated Press, Northern edition, February 9, 1994.

[2] Richard Quinney, *Class, State, and Crime: On the Theory and Practice of Criminal Justice* (New York: David McKay, 1977), p. 145.

[3] Kathleen Daly and Meda Chesney-Lind, "Feminism and Criminology," *Justice Quarterly*, Vol. 5, No. 5 (December 1988), p. 527.

[4] The Unabomber, *Manifesto*, http://www.thecourier.com/manifest.htm (accessed March 16, 2006).

[5] "Communism," *Encyclopedia Britannica* online, http://britannica.com (accessed January 3, 2007).

[6] Raymond J. Michalowski, "Perspectives and Paradigm: Structuring Criminological Thought," in Robert F. Meier, ed., *Theory in Criminology* (Beverly Hills, CA: Sage, 1977), pp. 17–39.

[7] Roscoe Pound, *Social Control through the Law: The Powell Lectures* (Hamden, CT: Archon, 1968), pp. 113–114.

[8] Although Pound's postulates originally referred only to men, we have here used the now-conventional phrase "men and women" throughout the postulates to indicate that Pound was speaking of everyone within the social group. No other changes to the original postulates have been made.

[9] Adapted from Michalowski, "Perspectives and Paradigm."

[10] William Bonger, *Criminality and Economic Conditions* (Bloomington: Indiana University Press, 1969). Originally published in Amsterdam as *Criminalite et Conditions Economiques* (1905); translated into English in 1916.

[11] Georg Simmel, *Conflict and the Web of Group Affiliations* (New York: Free Press, 1964). Originally published in 1908.

[12] Adapted from Michalowski, "Perspectives and Paradigm."

[13] Quinney, *Class, State, and Crime.*

[14] Vance Packard, *The Status Seekers* (London: Harmondsworth, 1961).

[15] George B. Vold, *Theoretical Criminology* (New York: Oxford University Press, 1958).

[16] Ibid., p. 205.

[17] Ibid., p. 206.

[18] Ibid., pp. 208–209.

[19] Ibid., p. 309.

[20] Ralf Dahrendorf, *Class and Class Conflict in Industrial Society* (Stanford, CA: Stanford University Press, 1959).

[21] Ralf Dahrendorf, "Out of Utopia: Toward a Reorientation of Sociological Analysis," *American Journal of Sociology*, Vol. 64 (1958), pp. 115–127.

[22] Austin Turk, *Criminality and Legal Order* (Chicago: Rand McNally, 1969), p. vii.

[23] Ibid.

[24] William J. Chambliss, "Toward a Political Economy of Crime," in C. Reasons and R. Rich, eds., *The Sociology of Law* (Toronto: Butterworth, 1978), p. 193.

[25] William Chambliss and Robert T. Seidman, *Law, Order, and Power* (Reading, MA: Addison-Wesley, 1971), p. 33.

[26] Adapted from ibid., pp. 473–474.

[27] William J. Chambliss, *Crime and the Legal Process* (New York: McGraw-Hill, 1969), p. 88.

[28] Chambliss, "Toward a Political Economy of Crime."

[29] Ibid.

[30] Ibid., p. 152.

[31] Ibid.

[32] Richard Quinney, *Critique of the Legal Order: Crime Control in Capitalist Society* (Boston: Little, Brown, 1974), p. 16.

[33] Quinney, *Class, State, and Crime*, p. 58.

[34] Ibid.

[35] Ibid., p. 61.

[36] Ibid., p. 65.

[37] Quinney, *Class, State, and Crime*, p. 77.

[38] Jeffrey H. Reiman, *The Rich Get Richer and the Poor Get Prison: Ideology, Class and Criminal Justice*, 6th ed. (Boston: Allyn & Bacon, 2000).

[39] Gresham M. Sykes, "Critical Criminology," *Journal of Criminal Law and Criminology*, Vol. 65 (1974), pp. 206–213.

[40] David A. Jones, *History of Criminology: A Philosophical Perspective* (Westport, CT: Greenwood, 1986), p. 200.

[41] The quotations attributed to Currie in this section are from Elliott Currie, "Market, Crime, and Community," *Theoretical Criminology*, Vol. 1, No. 2 (May 1997), pp. 147–172.

[42] Michael J. Lynch and W. Byron Groves, *A Primer in Radical Criminology*, 2nd ed. (Albany, NY: Harrow & Heston, 1989), p. 126.

[43] Ibid., p. 128.

[44] Raymond J. Michalowski, *Order, Law, and Crime: An Introduction to Criminology* (New York: Random House, 1985), p. 410.

[45] Lynch and Groves, *A Primer in Radical Criminology*, p. 130.

[46] William V. Pelfrey, *The Evolution of Criminology* (Cincinnati: Anderson, 1980), p. 86.

[47] For a good overview of critiques of radical criminology, see J. F. Galliher, "Life and Death of Liberal Criminology," *Contemporary Crisis*, Vol. 2, No. 3 (July 1978), pp. 245–263.

[48] Jackson Toby, "The New Criminology Is the Old Sentimentality," *Criminology*, Vol. 16 (1979), pp. 516–526.

[49] Ibid.

[50] Hermann Mannheim, *Comparative Criminology* (Boston: Houghton Mifflin, 1965), p. 445.

[51] Carl Klockars, "The Contemporary Crisis of Marxist Criminology," *Criminology*, Vol. 16 (1979), pp. 477–515.

[52] Ibid.

[53] Werner Einstadter and Stuart Henry, *Criminological Theory: An Analysis of Its Underlying Assumptions* (Toronto: Harcourt, 1995), p. 233.

[54] For an excellent review of critical realism in a Canadian context, see John Lowman and Brian D. MacLean, eds., *Realist Criminology: Crime Control and Policing in the 1990s* (Toronto: University of Toronto Press, 1994).

[55] Daniel J. Curran and Claire M. Renzetti, *Theories of Crime* (Boston: Allyn & Bacon, 1994), p. 283.

[56] See M. D. Schwartz and W. S. DeKeseredy, "Left Realist Criminology: Strengths, Weaknesses, and the Feminist Critique," *Crime, Law, and Social Change*, Vol. 15, No. 1 (January 1991), pp. 51–72; W. S. DeKeseredy and B. D. MacLean, "Exploring the Gender, Race, and Class Dimensions of Victimization: A Left Realist Critique of the Canadian Urban Victimization Survey," *International Journal of Offender Therapy and Comparative Criminology*, Vol. 35, No. 2 (summer 1991), pp. 143–161; and W. S. DeKeseredy and M. D. Schwartz, "British and U.S. Left Realism: A Critical Comparison," *International Journal of Offender Therapy and Comparative Criminology*, Vol. 35, No. 3 (fall 1991), pp. 248–262.

[57] See Jock Young, "The Failure of Criminology: The Need for a Radical Realism," in R. Matthews and J. Young, eds., *Confronting Crime* (Beverly Hills, CA: Sage, 1986), pp. 4–30; Jock Young, "The Tasks of a Realist Criminology," *Contemporary Crisis*, Vol. 11, No. 4 (1987), pp. 337–356; and Jock Young, "Radical Criminology in Britain: The Emergence of a Competing Paradigm," *British Journal of Criminology*, Vol. 28 (1988), pp. 159–183.

[58] D. Brown and R. Hogg, "Essentialism, Racial Criminology, and Left Realism," *Australian and New Zealand Journal of Criminology*, Vol. 25 (1992), pp. 195–230.

[59] Roger Matthews and Jock Young, "Reflections on Realism," in Jock Young and Roger Matthews, eds., *Rethinking Criminology: The Realist Debate* (Newbury Park, CA: Sage, 1992).

[60] Don C. Gibbons, *Talking about Crime and Criminals: Problems and Issues in Theory Development in Criminology* (Upper Saddle River, NJ: Prentice Hall, 1994), p. 170.

[61] Piers Beirne and James W. Messerschmidt, *Criminology* (New York: Harcourt Brace Jovanovich, 1991), p. 501.

[62] Gibbons, *Talking about Crime and Criminals*, p. 165, citing Loraine Gelsthorpe and Alison Morris, "Feminism and Criminology in Britain," *British Journal of Criminology* (spring 1988), pp. 93–110.

[63] Sally S. Simpson, "Feminist Theory, Crime and Justice," *Criminology*, Vol. 27, No. 4 (1989), p. 605.

[64] James W. Messerschmidt, *Capitalism, Patriarchy and Crime: Toward a Socialist Feminist Criminology* (Totowa, NJ: Rowman and Littlefield, 1986).

[65] Freda Adler, *Sisters in Crime: The Rise of the New Female Criminal* (New York: McGraw-Hill, 1975).

[66] Rita J. Simon, *Women and Crime* (Lexington, MA: Lexington Books, 1975).

[67] Carol Smart, *Women, Crime and Criminology: A Feminist Critique* (London: Routledge, 1977).

[68] Daly and Chesney-Lind, "Feminism and Criminology," p. 527.

[69] Ibid., pp. 497–535.

[70] Daron Caulfield and Nancy Wonders, "Gender and Justice: Feminist Contributions to Criminology," in Gregg Barak, ed., *Varieties of Criminology: Readings from a Dynamic Discipline* (Westport, CT: Praeger, 1994), pp. 213–229.

[71] Ibid.

[72] Roslyn Muraskin and Ted Alleman, eds., *It's a Crime: Women and Justice* (Upper Saddle River, NJ: Prentice Hall, 1993), p. 1.

[73] F. P. Williams III and M. D. McShane, *Criminological Theory* (Upper Saddle River, NJ: Prentice Hall, 1994), p. 238.

[74] Carol Pateman, "Feminist Critiques of the Public/Private Dichotomy," in Anne Phillips, ed., *Feminism and Equality* (Oxford, England: Blackwell, 1987).

[75] Alida V. Merlo and Joycelyn M. Pollock, eds., *Women, Law and Social Control* (Needham Heights, MA: Allyn & Bacon, 1995).

[76] Williams and McShane, *Criminological Theory*, p. 238.

[77] Simpson, "Feminist Theory, Crime and Justice."

[78] John Hagan, *Structural Criminology* (New Brunswick, NJ: Rutgers University Press, 1989), p. 130.

[79] Ibid., p. 13.

[80] Ibid.

[81] Ibid.

[82] Evelyn K. Sommers, *Voices from Within: Women Who Have Broken the Law* (Toronto: University of Toronto Press, 1995).

[83] Daly and Chesney-Lind, "Feminism and Criminology," p. 506.

[84] Ibid.

[85] Ibid., p. 514.

[86] For an intriguing analysis of how existing laws tend to criminalize women and their reproductive activities, see Susan O. Reed, "The Criminalization of Pregnancy: Drugs, Alcohol, and AIDS," in Muraskin and Alleman, eds., *It's a Crime*, pp. 92–117; and Drew Humphries, "Mothers and Children, Drugs and Crack: Reactions to Maternal Drug Dependency," in Muraskin and Alleman, eds., *It's a Crime*, pp. 131–145.

[87] Ngaire Naffine, *Feminism and Criminology* (Philadelphia: Temple University Press, 1996).

[88] Dawn H. Currie, "Feminist Encounters with Postmodernism: Exploring the Impasse of the Debates on Patriarchy and Law," *Canadian Journal of Women and Law*, Vol. 5, No. 1 (1992), p. 10.

[89] For an excellent overview of feminist theory in criminology and for a comprehensive review of research regarding female offenders, see Joanne Belknap, *The Invisible Woman: Gender, Crime and Justice* (Belmont, CA: Wadsworth, 1996).

[90] Such studies are still ongoing and continue to add to the descriptive literature of feminist criminology. See, for example, Deborah R. Baskin and Ira Sommers, "Female Initiation into Violent Street Crime," *Justice Quarterly*, Vol. 10, No. 4 (December 1993), pp. 559–583; Scott Decker et al., "A Woman's Place Is in the Home: Females and Residential Burglary," *Justice Quarterly*, Vol. 10, No. 1 (March 1993), pp. 143–162; and Jill L. Rosenbaum, "The Female Delinquent: Another Look at the Role of the Family," in Muraskin and Alleman, eds., *It's a Crime*, pp. 399–420.

[91] Ronald L. Akers, *Criminological Theories: Introduction and Evaluation* (Los Angeles: Roxbury, 1994), p. 39.

[92] For additional insight into the notion of deconstruction as it applies to feminist thought within criminology, see Carol Smart, *Feminism and the Power of Law* (New York: Routledge, 1989).

[93] Karen Heimer, "Changes in the Gender Gap in Crime and Women's Economic Marginalization," in *The Nature of Crime: Continuity and Change—Criminal Justice 2000*, Vol. 1 (Washington, DC: National Institute of Justice, 2000), p. 428.

[94] Daly and Chesney-Lind, "Feminism and Criminology," p. 512.

[95] See, for example, Darrell J. Steffensmeier and Emile Andersen Allan, "Sex Disparities in Arrests by Residence, Race, and Age: An Assessment of the Gender Convergence/Crime Hypothesis," *Justice Quarterly*, Vol. 5, No. 1 (March 1988), pp. 53–80.

[96] Darrell Steffensmeier, John Kramer, and Cathy Streifel, "Gender and Imprisonment Decisions," *Criminology*, Vol. 31, No. 3 (August 1993), pp. 411–446. Gender-based differences, however, have been discovered in some instances of probation- and

parole-related decision making. See Edna Erez, "Gender, Rehabilitation, and Probation Decisions," *Criminology*, Vol. 27, No. 2 (1989), pp. 307–327; and Edna Erez, "Dangerous Men, Evil Women: Gender and Parole Decision-Making," *Justice Quarterly*, Vol. 9, No. 1 (March 1992), pp. 106–126.

[97] See, for example, Kathleen Daly, "Neither Conflict nor Labeling nor Paternalism Will Suffice: Intersections of Race, Ethnicity, Gender, and Family in Criminal Court Decisions," *Crime and Delinquency*, Vol. 35, No. 1 (January 1989), pp. 136–168.

[98] Citing Allison Morris, *Women, Crime and Criminal Justice* (New York: Blackwell, 1987).

[99] Caulfield and Wonders, "Gender and Justice," p. 229.

[100] Gregg Barak, "Introduction: Criminological Theory in the 'Postmodernist' Era," in Barak, ed., *Varieties of Criminology*, pp. 1–11.

[101] Joycelyn M. Pollock, *Criminal Women* (Cincinnati: Anderson, 1999), p. 146.

[102] For an excellent and detailed discussion of many of these approaches, see Dragan Milovanovic, *Postmodern Criminology* (Hamden, CT: Garland, 1997).

[103] Bruce DiCristina, *Methods in Criminology: A Philosophical Primer* (New York: Harrow and Heston, 1995).

[104] Jeff Ferrell, "Anarchy against the Discipline," review of Bruce DiCristina's *Methods in Criminology: A Philosophical Primer* (New York: Harrow and Heston, 1995), in *Journal of Criminal Justice and Popular Culture*, Vol. 3, No. 4 (August 15, 1995).

[105] See, for example, Stuart Henry and Dragan Milovanovic, *Constitutive Criminology: Beyond Postmodernism* (London: Sage, 1995); and Milovanovic, *Postmodern Criminology*.

[106] Milovanovic, *Postmodern Criminology*.

[107] Dragan Milovanovic, *Primer in the Sociology of Law*, 2nd ed. (New York: Harrow and Heston, 1994).

[108] Ibid.

[109] Henry and Milovanovic, *Constitutive Criminology*, p. 118.

[110] Werner Einstadter and Stuart Henry, *Criminological Theory: An Analysis of Its Underlying Assumptions* (Fort Worth, TX: Harcourt Brace, 1995), p. 291.

[111] Ian Taylor, Paul Walton, and Jock Young, *The New Criminology: For a Social Theory of Deviance* (London: Routledge, 1973); and Ian Taylor, Paul Walton, and Jock Young, *Critical Criminology* (London: Routledge, 1975).

[112] Ian Taylor, "Crime and Social Criticism," *Social Justice*, Vol. 26, No. 2 (1999), p. 150.

[113] Ibid.

[114] Ibid.

[115] For examples of how this might be accomplished, see F. H. Knopp, "Community Solutions to Sexual Violence: Feminist/Abolitionist Perspectives," in Harold E. Pepinsky and Richard Quinney, eds., *Criminology as Peacemaking* (Bloomington: Indiana University Press), pp. 181–193; and S. Caringella-MacDonald and D. Humphries, "Sexual Assault, Women, and the Community: Organizing to Prevent Sexual Violence," in Pepinsky and Quinney, eds., *Criminology as Peacemaking*, pp. 98–113.

[116] Richard Quinney, "Life of Crime: Criminology and Public Policy as Peacemaking," *Journal of Crime and Justice*, Vol. 16, No. 2 (1993), pp. 3–9.

[117] See, for example, Harold E. Pepinsky, "This Can't Be Peace: A Pessimist Looks at Punishment," in W. B. Groves and G. Newman, eds., *Punishment and Privilege* (Albany, NY: Harrow and Heston, 1986); Harold E. Pepinsky, "Violence as Unresponsiveness: Toward a New Conception of Crime," *Justice Quarterly*, Vol. 5 (1988), pp. 539–563; and Pepinsky and Quinney, eds., *Criminology as Peacemaking*.

[118] See, for example, Richard Quinney, "Crime, Suffering, Service: Toward a Criminology of Peacemaking," *Quest*, Vol. 1 (1988),

pp. 66–75; Richard Quinney, "The Theory and Practice of Peacemaking in the Development of Radical Criminology," *Critical Criminologist*, Vol. 1, No. 5 (1989), p. 5; and Richard Quinney and John Wildeman, *The Problem of Crime: A Peace and Social Justice Perspective*, 3rd ed. (Mayfield, CA: Mountain View Press, 1991)—originally published as *The Problem of Crime: A Critical Introduction to Criminology* (New York: Bantam, 1977).

[119] All of these themes are addressed, for example, in Pepinsky and Quinney, eds., *Criminology as Peacemaking*.

[120] For a good discussion of this "theory," see John F. Galliher, "Willie Horton: Fact, Faith, and Commonsense Theory of Crime," in ibid., pp. 245–250.

[121] Quinney and Wildeman, *The Problem of Crime*, pp. vii–viii.

[122] Quinney, "Life of Crime," abstract.

[123] Bo Lozoff and Michael Braswell, *Inner Corrections: Finding Peace and Peace Making* (Cincinnati: Anderson, 1989).

[124] Clemens Bartollas and Michael Braswell, "Correctional Treatment, Peacemaking, and the New Age Movement," *Journal of Crime and Justice*, Vol. 16, No. 2 (1993), pp. 43–58.

[125] Ibid.

[126] Ram Dass and Paul Gorman, *How Can I Help? Stories and Reflections on Service* (New York: Alfred A. Knopf, 1985), p. 165, as cited in Quinney and Wildeman, *The Problem of Crime*, p. 116.

[127] Lozoff and Braswell, *Inner Corrections*, p. vii.

[128] For a good overview of such programs, see Thomas E. Carbonneau, *Alternative Dispute Resolution: Melting the Lances and Dismounting the Steeds* (Chicago: University of Illinois Press, 1989).

[129] See, for example, J. E. Beer, *Peacemaking in Your Neighborhood: Reflections on an Experiment in Community Mediation* (Philadelphia: New Society, 1986); and J. Beer, E. Steif, and C. Walker, *Peacemaking in Your Neighborhood: Mediator's Handbook* (Philadelphia: Friends Mediation Service, 1987).

[130] For an excellent review of alternative dispute mechanisms among Native American groups, see D. LeResche, "Native American Perspectives on Peacemaking," *Mediation Quarterly*, Vol. 10, No. 4 (Summer 1993), complete issue.

[131] Peter Finn and Andrea K. Newlyn, *Miami's "Drug Court": A Different Approach* (Washington, DC: National Institute of Justice, June 1993), p. 2.

[132] Fay Honey Knopp, "Community Solutions to Sexual Violence: Feminist-Abolitionist Perspectives," in Pepinsky and Quinney, eds., *Criminology as Peacemaking*, p. 183.

[133] Ibid.

[134] Daniel Van Ness and Karen Heetderks Strong, *Restoring Justice* (Cincinnati: Anderson, 1997), p. 31.

[135] Stephen C. Richards, "Introducing the New School of Convict Criminology," *Social Justice*, Vol. 28, No. 1 (2001), p. 177.

[136] Stephen C. Richards and Jeffrey Ian Ross, "Convict Criminology," in Richard A. Wright and J. Mitchell Miller, eds., *Encyclopedia of Criminology*, Vol. 1 (New York: Routledge, 2005), pp. 232–236.

[137] Ibid., p. 233.

[138] John Irwin, *The Felon* (Upper Saddle River, NJ: Prentice Hall, 1970).

[139] K. C. Carceral, Thomas J. Bernard et al., *Behind a Convict's Eyes: Doing Time in a Modern Prison* (New York: Wadsworth, 2003).

[140] K. C. Carceral and Thomas J. Bernard, *Prison, Inc.: A Convict Exposes Life inside a Private Prison* (New York: New York University Press, 2006).

[141] Richards and Ross, "Convict Criminology"; op. cit., and Matthew B. Robinson, *Justice Blind: Ideals and Realities of American Criminal Justice*, 2nd ed. (Upper Saddle River, NJ: Prentice Hall, 2005).

PART 4

Crime in the Modern World

> Our war on terror begins with Al-Qaeda, but it does not end there. It will not end until every terrorist of global reach has been found, stopped, and defeated.
>
> —President George W. Bush[i]

> I wouldn't be in a legitimate business for all the . . . money in the world.
>
> —Gennaro Anguilo, Boston Organized Crime Boss[ii]

> You bring me a select group of hackers, and within 90 days I'll bring this country to its knees.
>
> —Jim Settle, retired director of the FBI's computer crime squad[iii]

CHAPTER 10 Crimes against Persons

CHAPTER 11 Crimes against Property

CHAPTER 12 White-Collar and Organized Crime

CHAPTER 13 Public Order and Drug Crimes

CHAPTER 14 Technology and Crime

CHAPTER 15 Globalization and Terrorism

In the first part of this book, specifically in Chapter 2, wo provided a brief overview of crime statistics and of the different kinds of crimes with which the American criminal justice system is typically concerned. In the six chapters that comprise this part, we will describe specific kinds of crimes and the offenders who commit them in considerably more detail.

Chapter 10 concerns itself with violent crimes, also known as "crimes against persons." Included here are brutal acts like murder, rape, and assault. Other predatory crimes, like stalking and sexual offenses against children, are also discussed, as are the situations and circumstances within contemporary American society that are thought to contribute to violence and predation. Chapter 11 looks at property crimes, including theft,

burglary, and arson. The activities of fences in buying and disposing of stolon goods are explored, and the relationship of property crimes to other forms of crime is examined. Chapter 12 describes white-collar and organized crime, while Chapter 13 looks at public order and drug crimes, and Chapter 14 analyzes the impact that high-technology crimes are having on our society and on efforts to enforce the law. Finally, in Chapter 15 we examine the powerful impact that globalization is having on our world to include human smuggling, the trafficking in persons, and other forms of transnational crime. Chapter 15 also includes a detailed investigation of terrorism—both domestic and international—and explores strategies for preventing future acts of terrorism both here and abroad.

---

[i] Address to Joint Session of Congress, September 20, 2001.

[ii] From a compilation of FBI tapes in "Anguilo's Republic," *New England Monthly*, July 1986.

[iii] Jim Settle, as quoted in Andrew Noel, "Unlocking the Door to Security," *Government Technology*, March 1999, http://www.govtech.net/ publications/gt/1999/mar/westby/westby.phtml (accessed March 01, 2001),

Source: Jochen Tack/Das Fotoarchiv/Peter Arnold, Inc.

In some 200 years of national sovereignty, Americans have been preoccupied repeatedly with trying to understand and control one form of violence or another.

—Albert J. Reiss, Jr. and Jeffrey A. Roth[1]

Although collective acts of violence and terrorist acts are more visible and receive greater media attention, most violence in this country lacks an ideological motivation and involves a dispute between a single victim and offender.

—Terance D. Miethe and Richard C. McCorkle[2]

Crime is committed by people who are tempted more and controlled less.

—Marcus Felson[3]

Can it really be that there is something unique about the genotype of the U.S. population which so dramatically predisposes it to violence?

—Steven Rose[4]

Learning Outcomes

After reading this chapter, you should be able to

- Explain the general nature of typologies and describe various typologies of violent crime
- Identify the key issues in explaining patterns of homicide
- Identify the key issues in explaining as well as preventing the crimes of rape and child sexual abuse

- List the different kinds of robbery and describe the criminal careers of robbers
- Identify various kinds of assault, and describe what is known about intimate partner violence
- Define *workplace violence* and tell what is known about the offense
- Explain the major patterns of stalking and identify the different types of stalkers

Hear the author discuss this chapter at **crimtoday.com**

Introduction

On April 17, 2007, a shooting spree at Virginia Tech University by Seung-Hui Cho, a student suffering from mental problems, resulted in the deaths of 33 people and claimed the record for the nation's deadliest school shooting ever.[5] The killings occurred in two shooting episodes separated by a couple of hours. Cho, a South Korean citizen whose family came to this country when he was eight years old, used the time between the shootings to stop at a campus post office and send a package of video clips, photos, and writings to NBC's New York City office. The package, which was misadressed and arrived late, included an 1,800-word manifesto that railed against rich students as "having everything" but still wanting more. "You had a hundred billion chances and ways to have avoided today," Cho said in one of the videos.[6]

Officials described Cho as a seriously disturbed young man who behaved oddly in class. He took pictures of other students and said "Kids write about murder and suicide all the time."[7] Virginia Tech English professor Nikiki Giovanni had been so frightened by Cho's poetry that she made him leave her class, and in 2005 a female student complained that Cho was stalking her. Relatives said that he often spoke in whispers, and that he often wore a hat and sunglasses to hide his face.

Fellow student Paul Kim, a senior English major, said Cho "Never spoke a word." Even when the professor asked questions, Kim said, "he never spoke. He constantly looked physically and emotionally down, like he was depressed."[8] A Criminal Profiles box in Chapter 8 tells the tale of Cho's upbringing and provides more details about the shooting. As you will learn in this chapter, shooting sprees are not typical homicides. Most homicides are individual events that are motivated by personal animosity. Unlike the people that Cho shot, most killers know their victims.

This chapter discusses violent criminal offending by focusing on homicide, rape, robbery, assault, workplace violence, and stalking. These offenses have long been classified as violent because they involve interpersonal harm or threat of harm. The range of possible harm varies from death, as in cases of homicide, to fear and loss of property, as is the case with robbery.

Abbey Schmidt, a freshman at Virginia Tech, gets an update on a friend who was seriously injured in a shooting rampage on campus earlier in the day on Monday, April 16, 2007, while in her dorm at Virginia Tech just across a parade field from Norris Hall where the shootings took place. Could the shootings have been prevented?

Source: News & Observer/Landov

Violent Crime Typologies

Criminologists use crime typologies to make sense of the patterns that characterize criminal offending. A **crime typology** categorizes offenses using a set of defined characteristics, such as legal categories, offender motivation, victim behavior, situational aspects of the criminal event, and offender peculiarities. Statutory definitions of crimes, for example, allow for the creation of a typology based on legal categories. Crime typologies "are designed primarily to simplify social reality by identifying homogeneous groups of crime behaviors that are different from other clusters of crime behaviors."[9] To be useful, the basis around which a typology is organized should serve a particular purpose. Some typologies in criminology use a single variable as the primary explanation for variation in criminal offending, while other typologies offer a number of variables that are thought to interact to produce certain patterns in violent offending. An example of a single-variable typology can be found in the general theory of crime advanced by Michael R. Gottfredson and Travis Hirschi (see Chapter 8), where the authors emphasize low self-control as the crucial determinant of variations in offending. Other theories, such as developmental and life course theories, focus on different explanatory variables or on a combination of factors. No one typology can perfectly capture all violent offending, and a given set of factors may better explain one type or facet of offending. For example, the individual-level factors that give rise to violent offending may not be the same factors that contribute to an increased frequency of offending, especially in terms of criminal careers.[10] While this chapter will rely on legal categories as the basis on which to distinguish among types of violent crimes, we will also discuss some of the motivational factors associated with violent offending.

crime typology

A classification of crimes along a particular dimension, such as legal categories, offender motivation, victim behavior, or the characteristics of individual offenders.

Homicide

State and federal statutes on criminal homicide distinguish among several different forms of this offense based on intent, circumstances, age, and the other considerations discussed in Chapter 2. As we noted in that chapter, homicide represents a small fraction of all violent crimes reported to the police in any given year—less than 0.1% in 2006.[11] Only about 23% of all homicides involve strangers, and the most frequent circumstance that precedes a homicide is an argument.[12] Approximately 16% of homicides occur during the commission of another felony, with robbery being the most common.[13]

Significant contributions to the understanding of the crime of homicide are being made today by the Homicide Research Working Group (HRWG). The Group was organized at the 1991 meeting of the American Society of Criminology (ASC), and now has hundreds of members representing many countries and academic and practice disciplines. Prior to the creation of the HRWG, work in lethal violence had been scattered among numerous disciplines and was largely uncoordinated. To address this lack of coordination, homicide experts from various disciplines, including criminology, public health, demography, medicine, sociology, criminal justice, and other fields, joined together to create the HRWG. Today, the HRWG publishes a periodic newsletter, maintains an active listserv for its members, and publishes the journal *Homicide Studies*. You can visit HRWG on the Internet at **Web Extra 10–1** and view the group's annual meetings proceedings at **Library Extra 10–1**.

While homicide offenders include men and women, young and old, rich and poor, homicide offending is very much patterned in terms of certain sociodemographics, with members of some groups being disproportionately involved as offenders. Distinctive patterns of homicide can be identified based on such factors as individual characteristics, cultural norms, community characteristics, geographic region, availability of weapons and weapons used, gang activity and affiliation, and the victim-offender relationship. All of these sociodemographic features have been used to further our understanding of homicide patterns and to create typologies surrounding homicide.

WEB
Extra

LIBRARY
Extra

The Subculture of Violence Thesis

Within the United States, there has been strong research interest in the subculture of violence thesis originally formulated by Marvin Wolfgang and Franco Ferracuti,[14] which was discussed in Chapter 7. These authors stressed the role of norms and values characteristic of certain groups in lifestyles of violence. Ethnic and racial differences in criminal activity reflect distinctive patterns of interaction with others, which are characterized by a shared sense of history, language, values, and beliefs. The existence of a subculture necessitates a sufficient number of people who share not only values and beliefs, but also a forum that expresses membership. Such a forum may be something as elusive as a street corner. It is primarily this subtlety associated with subcultural theory that makes it difficult to test empirically. The subculture of violence thesis has been the primary theoretical perspective used to explain the similarity between homicide victims and offenders. First, homicide statistics reveal that victims and offenders share similar sociodemographic characteristics, such as age, gender, and race. African Americans are disproportionately represented in the homicide statistics as both victims and offenders.[15] Second, victims and offenders who are intimately known to each other are disproportionately represented in homicide statistics. An analysis of supplemental homicide reports shows that approximately 60% of victims and offenders have some prior relationship.[16]

The subculture of violence thesis has also been explored at the community level, where the emphasis is on the importance of "critical masses" as support for the existence of subcultures.[17] Early research argued that the disproportionate rate at which African Americans commit homicide is associated with the presence of a large African American population, the "critical mass" necessary for the "transmission of violence-related models" and subcultural behavior patterns.[18] However, most of the research that found higher homicide rates to be associated with higher percentages of African Americans in the population did not take into consideration things like socioeconomic status, level of education, and so on.[19] Research by Robert Sampson using more sophisticated measures and stronger research designs revealed that the racial composition of an area alone did not have a significant effect on the homicide rates for either whites or blacks.[20]

Structural Explanations for Homicide

Other researchers have focused on regional variations in patterns of violent crimes, particularly in the South. The South has a long history of high homicide rates.[21] Subcultural theorists have proposed that the high rate of violent crime in the South reflects adherence to a set of violence-related norms that were generally accepted in earlier times but that have since become outdated in other regions.[22] While some researchers found that Southern origin had a significant effect on the production of high homicide rates in particular areas,[23] other researchers challenge subcultural theories for their inability to control for noncultural factors that might explain the findings.[24] Specifically, Colin Loftin and R. H. Hill conclude that the influences of structural variables, especially poverty, must be considered as alternative explanations for regional differences in homicide rates.[25] While no definitive answers exist on whether the high rates of violence in the South are attributable to a specific subculture of violence or to structural factors, there still remains evidence (that is, arrest statistics) that the South differs from other regions in terms of the frequency of homicides. Read more about serious violent crime and its characteristics via **Library Extras 10–2** and **10–3** at crimtoday.com.

LIBRARY
Extra
■ ■ ■ ■

The Victim-Offender Relationship

Several researchers have expanded upon Emile Durkheim's original insight that "while family life has a moderating effect upon suicide, it rather stimulates murder."[26] Wolfgang's 1958 study of homicides in Philadelphia revealed that approximately 25% of all homicides were between family members and that women were far more likely than men to be both offenders and victims within this category than within any other.[27] Males were more likely to be killed by friends and strangers than by their family members. However, when a male was killed by a female, the offender was most likely to be his spouse.[28] Other researchers have emphasized qualitative differences in the pattern of homicide within the victim-offender relationship. The work of Dwayne Smith and Robert Nash Parker represented the first systematic research that focused on differentiating homicide according to the victim-offender relationship.[29] Their work used two classifications of homicide: primary and nonprimary. **Primary homicides** are the most frequent and involve family members, friends, and acquaintances. These are usually characterized as **expressive crimes**[30] because they often result from interpersonal hostility, based on jealousy, revenge, romantic triangles, and minor disagreements. **Nonprimary homicides** involve victims and offenders who have no prior relationship and usually occur in the course of another crime, such as robbery. These crimes are referred to as **instrumental crimes** because they involve some degree of premeditation by the offender and are less likely to be precipitated by the victim. The difference between instrumental and expressive motives for homicide continues to be important in criminological research, and we will return to more research on this shortly.

Parker and Smith hypothesized that because of these qualitative distinctions in homicides, the effects of subcultural and structural measures could be very different once the type of homicide was taken into account.[31] Using state homicide rates, these researchers found that structural variables like poverty and the percentage of the population age 20 to 34 are important predictors of differences in primary homicide but are insignificant predictors for nonprimary homicide rates.[32]

Further attention to the heterogeneous nature of homicide is found within the work of K. R. Williams and R. L. Flewelling.[33] They disaggregated homicide rates according to two criteria: (1) the nature of the circumstances surrounding the homicide, which included whether there was some indicator of a fight or argument precipitating the homicide, and (2) the victim-offender relationship, distinguishing between victims and offenders who were family members, acquaintances, or strangers. By comparing how factors like poverty and population size have different effects on different types of

primary homicide

Murder involving family members, friends, and acquaintances.

expressive crime

A criminal offense that results from acts of interpersonal hostility, such as jealousy, revenge, romantic triangles, and quarrels.

nonprimary homicide

Murder that involves victims and offenders who have no prior relationship and that usually occurs during the course of another crime, such as robbery.

instrumental crime

A goal-directed offense that involves some degree of planning by the offender.

Armin Meiwes (right) stands next to his lawyer, Harald Ermel, in the district court in Kassel, Germany, on January 30, 2004. Meiwes confessed to killing, dismembering, and cannibalizing a 43-year-old computer specialist from Berlin whom he had met over the Internet. Meiwes was convicted of manslaughter and sentenced to eight years in prison. The case was complicated by a series of e-mail messages written by the mentally ill victim in which he repeatedly expressed a wish to be killed and eaten. How might the Internet contribute to violent victimization?

Source: AP Wide World Photos

homicide, Williams and Flewelling found that certain factors are more important in explaining one form of homicide over another. Poverty is a stronger predictor of family homicide, and population size is more important in explaining stranger homicide. Both the victim-offender relationship and the context of the homicide (for example, as the end result of a robbery) are crucial factors to take into account in explaining patterns of homicide.

Beginning in the 1980s, the intimate-partner homicide rate began to decline, a decline that has continued to the present day. Using homicide data from a sample of 29 large cities within the United States from 1976 to 1992, Laura Dugan, Daniel S. Nagin, and Richard Rosenfeld offer an **exposure-reduction theory** of intimate-partner homicide.[34] These researchers examined the ability of the "decline in domesticity, improved economic status of women, and growth in domestic violence resources" to explain decreases in intimate-partner homicide in urban areas.[35] These three factors, they argued, reduced intimate-partner homicides by reducing exposure to the ongoing violent dynamics that conventionally precede this form of homicide. Declining domesticity was measured by a decrease in marriage rates and by an increase in divorce rates, with divorces being one means by which individuals can peacefully exit a violent relationship. As women gain equality, more opportunities are available to them that may relieve their economic dependence on men. Finally, the greater the availability of domestic violence resources, such as advocacy, shelters, and other services, the lower the rate of intimate-partner homicide. These resources provide support and offer a way to relieve violence before it escalates to the point of homicide. Given the fact that intimate-partner homicide is often the final outcome of an ongoing violent relationship, "factors which facilitate exit from a violent relationship or inhibit the development of such relationships should reduce the rate of intimate partner homicide by a simple mechanism—the reduction of exposure to a violent partner."[36] Analysis of the data did support the major hypotheses offered by Dugan, Nagin, and Rosenfeld. Generally, as resources supporting dissolution or a nonviolent exit from a violent relationship increased, rates of intimate-partner homicide decreased. Read more about intimate partner violence at **Library Extra 10–4** at crimtoday.com.

exposure-reduction theory

A theory of intimate homicide that claims that a decline in domesticity, accompanied by an improvement in the economic status of women and a growth in domestic violence resources, explains observed decreases in intimate-partner homicide.

LIBRARY
Extra
■ ■ ■ ■

sibling offense

An offense or incident that culminates in homicide. The offense or incident may be a crime, such as robbery, or an incident that meets a less stringent criminal definition, such as a lover's quarrel involving assault or battery.

Instrumental and Expressive Homicide

Not all homicide offenders intend to kill their victims. This may be the case when the incident begins as a robbery motivated by instrumental ends, such as getting money. An argument may also precede a homicide, but this circumstance is expressive rather than instrumental because "the dominant motivation is the violence itself," even if lethal violence is not planned in advance.[37] The importance of instigating incidents is explored in research by Carolyn Rebecca Block and Richard Block, who use the instrumental-expressive continuum to formulate a discussion of homicide syndromes, or mechanisms that serve to "link lethal violence to nonlethal sibling offenses . . . [and that can] provide a mechanism by which the explanation and prevention of homicide can be organized."[38] The Blocks use the term **sibling offense** to refer to the incident that begins the homicide. A sibling offense may be a crime, such as robbery, or another incident, such as a lovers' quarrel. It is crucial to take these sibling offenses into account because they help explain why some robberies end in murder, while others do not. The Blocks developed a rather elaborate typology of homicide to illustrate how an understanding of the patterns of nonlethal violence can assist in the prevention of lethal violence. For example, there are a great many incidents of street gang violence, most of which do not end in death, and understanding those nonlethal incidents can assist in preventing homicides. An ongoing project in Chicago aimed at reducing street gang violence is an example of how homicide syndromes can be used to reduce the escalation of events that lead to death. As the Blocks state, the purpose behind the street gang violence project in Chicago "is to develop an early warning system for identifying potential street gang–related and competitive confrontational violence crisis areas."[39]

Victim Precipitation

When discussing homicide, the concept of **victim precipitation** focuses on the characteristics of victims that may have precipitated their victimization. Victim precipitation unfortunately seems to blame the victim, and the concept has been quite controversial at times. From a scholarly point of view, however, the thrust of the concept of victim precipitation is not to blame the victim for the event but to examine both individual and situational factors that may have contributed to and initiated the crime. This is especially important in studying patterns of homicide because quite often a homicide begins as a fight or an argument between people who know each other. The circumstances of the particular encounter determine whether the event will end as some type of assault or as a homicide. In his classic 1958 work on homicide, Marvin E. Wolfgang designated as many as 60% of cases where women had killed their husbands as victim precipitated, but only 9% of incidents where men had killed their wives as victim precipitated.[40] The gendered patterns of victim precipitation have not changed significantly since Wolfgang's investigation. Based on data on intimate-partner homicides in St. Louis, Missouri, Richard Rosenfeld analyzed data from 1980 to 1993 and designated slightly more than one-half of all homicides committed by women and only 12% of those committed by men as victim precipitated.[41]

Wolfgang also identified alcohol use as a factor in homicide cases where the "victim is a direct, positive precipitator in the crime."[42] He concluded that the positive and significant association between alcohol and victim-precipitated homicides may be explained by the fact that the victim was the "first to slap, punch, stab, or in some other manner commit an assault" and that if the victim had not been drinking, he or she would have been less violent.[43] Wolfgang's research on homicide revealed that most victims of spousal homicide had been drinking at the time of the incident, a situation that did not apply to homicide offenders.[44] Learn more about victim precipitation at the Howard League for Penal Reform via **Web Extra 10–2.**

victim precipitation

Contributions made by the victim to the criminal event, especially those that led to its initiation.

WEB
Extra
■■■■

A purse snatcher in action. Why do victimologists suggest that some people contribute to their own victimization?

Source: Martin Lee/Alamy Images

Criminal Profiles

Dennis Rader (The BTK Killer)

He "hid for more than 30 years in plain sight."[i] That's how a leading news service described Wichita, Kansas, serial killer Dennis Rader's evasion of capture for more than three decades. Rader, the so-called BTK (a nickname he gave himself to denote his propensity to "Bind, Torture, and Kill" his victims), lived a normal, rather mundane existence with his wife and two children. All the while, he concealed his second persona as a murderous predator. His "front" included his ordinance enforcement officer job in the Wichita suburb of Park City, service as a Cub Scout troop leader, and active participation in his Lutheran church.[ii]

Rader was born March 9, 1945, the eldest of four brothers. After high school, he did a four-year stint in the U.S. Air Force before returning to Park City, where he completed an undergraduate degree in administration of justice at Wichita State University in 1979. Beginning in 1974, Rader worked in a variety of positions at ADT Security Services over the next 14 years. Investigators believe that knowledge gained in this experience later enabled him to bypass home security systems so as to break into homes undetected.[iii] It was also in 1974 that Rader committed the first of what eventually became ten grisly murders.

His initial murderous foray occurred in mid-morning on January 15, 1974, when Rader killed four members of the Otero family: dad Joseph, mom Julie, 11-year-old Josephine, and 9-year-old Joseph II. Each victim was subjected to various acts of torture before ultimately being strangled. The bodies were discovered when 15-year-old Charlie Otero returned from school later that afternoon.[iv]

The shocking murders were only the start of a long criminal career. Kathryn Bright, 20, was stabbed to death just three months later, on April 4, 1974. Amazingly, her 19-year-old brother, Kevin, survived the attack despite being shot twice in the head.

Convicted BTK killer Dennis Rader listens during a court proceeding on October 12, 2005, at the El Dorado Correctional Facility in El Dorado, Kansas. A judge recommended that Rader receive treatment as a sexual offender and have restrictions placed on what he can receive or do in prison while he serves the rest of his life in prison. Rader, a 60-year-old former church congregation president and Boy Scout leader, pleaded guilty in 2005 to ten murders that haunted Wichita over three decades. Why wasn't he caught sooner?

Source: Travis Heying/AP Wide World Photos

Weapon Use

As previously noted, there are different perspectives on the role that weapons play in crime, with most of the discussion centering on the role of firearms in homicide. In examining the relationship between guns and homicide, Philip J. Cook and Mark H. Moore differentiate between instrumentality and availability. *Instrumentality* refers to the fact that the type of weapon used in a particular encounter has an effect on whether the encounter ends in death. For example, the involvement of a gun may mean the difference between a criminal event ending as an assault or as a homicide. When guns are used in robberies, the fatality rate is "three times as high as for robberies with knives and 10 times as high as for robberies with other weapons."[45] However, Cook and Moore warn, an examination of fatality rates in isolation does not necessarily support the idea that the involvement of a gun caused the fatality. Other factors must be considered, such as the intent of the offender. Offenders may select a weapon on the basis of their intent; those who take more lethal weapons to a crime may be more prepared to use deadly force.

Availability refers to issues surrounding how access to guns may increase their presence in all types of interactions, including criminal ones. As Cook and Moore argue,

Almost three years elapsed before BTK struck again on March 17, 1977, by strangling 26-year-old Shirley Vian. Uncharacteristically, BTK locked the three young Vian children in the closet and allowed them to survive. Just nine months later, on December 8, 1977, police found Nancy Jo Fox, 25, dead in her bedroom, strangled with a nylon stocking. BTK's final three killings occurred on April 27, 1985 (Marine Hedge), September 16, 1986 (Vicki Wegerle), and January 18, 1991 (Dolores Davis); all were strangled.[v]

A strange component of the BTK murders was the way the killer periodically wrote taunting letters to the local police and newspapers. His goal seemed to be to receive some kind of credit for the murders. In some writings, he expressed his indignation that other suspects were being accused of crimes he had committed, or that the story of his murderous activities were not receiving adequate press coverage. "How many do I have to kill before I get my name in the paper or some national attention?" he complained in the letter in which he also coined his BTK nickname.[vi]

The frequency of the BTK letters decreased by the end of the 1980s, as he apparently became dormant. In 1991, Rader became a Park City Compliance Officer,[vii] where he developed a reputation as a by-the-book "bureaucratic bully."[viii]

In March 2004, new BTK letters began surfacing. Over the course of the next year, a total of 11 communications were received. One, a computer floppy disk, was forensically identified as having been used by Rader's church, and had electronic residue that included the name "Dennis." That disk directly led to Rader's arrest on February 25, 2005. At his arraignment on May 3, Rader stood mute, and a trial date of June 27 was set.

Rader subsequently surprised everyone when, on June 27, he confessed in open court to the murders of ten people. In response to direct questioning from the judge, Rader recounted in chillingly graphic and dispassionate detail exactly how he had killed each of the ten victims.

At a sentencing hearing on August 17 and 18, 2005, Rader received the harshest possible sentence under Kansas law when Judge Gregory Waller gave him ten life sentences to be served consecutively. The consecutive service provision means that Rader must serve a minimum of 175 years before becoming eligible for parole consideration.[ix]

Notes:

i "Neighbors Paint Mixed Picture of BTK Suspect," MSNBC, February 27, 2005, http://www.msnbc.msn.com/id/7036219 (accessed June 16, 2007).

ii Ibid.

iii Ibid.

iv Marilyn Bardsley, Rachael Bell, and David Lohr, "BTK—Birth of a Serial Killer," CourtTV Crime Library, http://www.crimelibrary.com/serial_killers/unsolved/btk/index_1.html (accessed June 16, 2007).

v Ibid.

vi "Neighbors Paint Mixed Picture of BTK Suspect," MSNBC.

vii "Report: Daughter of BTK Suspect Alerted Police," Cable News Network, April 19, 2005.

viii Bardsley.

ix *State of Kansas* v. *Dennis Rader,* Office of the Sedgwick County, Kansas, District Attorney Web site, February 1, 2006, http://www.sedgwickcounty.org/da (accessed June 16, 2007).

"Availability can be thought of relative to time, expense, and other costs."[46] The ease of availability is important, given the relative spontaneity of some violent encounters. The availability of guns is important at the individual level as well as the community level because the greater the presence of guns in a particular neighborhood, the easier the access for individuals beyond their immediate households. Cook and Moore argue that gun availability is a much stronger factor in explaining lethal violence than gun instrumentality. Specifically, Cook and Moore recommend that "rather than a general effort to get guns off the streets, a more focused effort can be directed at prohibiting guns in particularly dangerous locations such as homes with histories of domestic violence, bars with histories of drunken brawls, parks in which gang fights tend to break out, and schools in which teachers and students have been assaulted."[47]

Alcohol and Drug Use

An important conceptual typology detailing the relationship between drugs and crime was developed by Paul J. Goldstein in an article first published in 1985.[48] According to Goldstein, the association of alcohol and illicit drugs with violent offending generally takes one of three forms. Drugs may be linked to violent offending through a *psychopharmacological* model, whereby either infrequent or chronic use of certain drugs produces violent behavior by lowering inhibitions or elevating aggressive tendencies. However, not all drugs produce such effects, and the relationship appears to hold only for people with certain types of personalities using certain substances in certain settings.

When crimes are committed to support a drug habit, Goldstein says that the concept of *economic compulsion* best describes the relationship between crime and drug use. Finally, he uses the idea of *systemic violence* to describe the connection between drugs and trafficking. Systemic violence can take several forms, ranging from rival drug wars to robberies of drug dealers.

Although distinct types of relationships between drugs and violence can be described, these relationships are not necessarily mutually exclusive. Thus, one or more of the kinds of relationships Goldstein describes may be present in a single criminal incident.

Goldstein and his colleagues attempted to apply this typology to a sample of 414 homicides in New York City during the 1980s. More than half of the homicide cases in the sample involved drugs, with the vast majority of these being classified as systemic. Most of these cases involved drugs other than alcohol, and all of the homicides where alcohol was present were classified as psychopharmacological.[49]

Researchers from the Drug Relationships in Murder Project (DREIM), which analyzed incarcerated homicide offenders in New York State, found that in the majority of homicide cases involving both alcohol and illicit drugs, the primary basis for the connection with the crime was psychopharmacological, which is not in line with Goldstein's research in New York.[50] Furthermore, there appears to be a bias in Goldstein's typology that favors the classification of incidents as systemic. Because the categories of the typology are not mutually exclusive, the same incident may fit in more than one category, and common incidents like robbing a drug dealer are often classified as systemic even though they clearly involve an economic motivation.[51]

One theoretical approach focused on explaining the role that alcohol plays in homicide is **selective disinhibition,** advanced by **Robert Nash Parker** and others.[52] According to this perspective, the "disinhibiting" effect of alcohol is social in nature rather than biochemical. In particular situations or interactions, the presence of alcohol may operate to suspend certain factors that could restrain the occurrence of violence and may operate to put into play certain factors that could increase the occurrence or lethal nature of violence. This perspective relies on the existence of norms that operate both to prohibit and to proscribe the use of violence in particular situations. According to Kathleen Auerhahn and Robert Nash Parker, "Norms that have the least institutional support are more likely to be disinhibited in a particular situation—that is, to lose their effectiveness in discouraging or inhibiting violence."[53] When violence is easily and readily recognized as being inappropriate in a particular situation, this is referred to as "passive constraint." In other violent encounters, "it takes active constraint—a proactive and conscious decision not to use violence to solve the dispute—to constrain or preclude violence."[54] Because alcohol can reduce both of these forms of constraint, "the selective nature of alcohol-related homicide is dependent on the interaction of an impaired rationality and the nature of the social situation."[55] Parker and his colleagues tested this model by analyzing data on homicides in several cities in 1980, in several cities between 1960 and 1980, and in several states from 1976 to 1983. One of the key findings from this research was the ability of alcohol as a variable to significantly predict primary homicide. In relationships between individuals who are known to each other, alcohol may operate to disinhibit restraints against violence, they found. The norms that operate to govern interactions between strangers are more rigid in terms of the type of conduct that is proscribed, whereas relationships between individuals who are known to each other exist on a broader continuum. Just as we can physically embrace our friends and loved ones in a way that is not deemed appropriate with a stranger, the use of violence against those who are known to us is treated with greater tolerance—a tolerance that can be increased even further in the presence of alcohol.[56]

selective disinhibition

A loss of self-control due to the characteristics of the social setting, drugs or alcohol, or a combination of both.

In his research using state-level data, Parker tested several hypotheses derived from competing theoretical perspectives about the effect of alcohol on homicide.[57] Five types of homicides were identified, based on the victim-offender relationship: "robbery, other felony, family intimate, family other, and primary nonintimate."[58] The theoretical perspectives that Parker compared were the economic deprivation, subcultural, social control, and routine activity theories. Concerning the power of variables derived from the economic deprivation approach, poverty had a stronger effect on both robbery and other felony homicides in states with "above average rates of alcohol consumption."[59] Alcohol consumption had direct effects on two of the three types of primary homicide.

Gangs

Gang membership may influence homicide in a number of ways. Analyzing data from Los Angeles, researchers found several differences between homicides involving gang members and those involving nongang members. They found that gang homicides were more likely to involve minority males, to make use of guns, to occur in public places, and to involve victims and offenders with no prior relationship.[60] Richard Rosenfeld and colleagues state that the association of gangs and homicide may be one of two general types: (1) gang-motivated violence, in which violent crime is the direct result of gang activity, and (2) gang-affiliated violence, in which individual gang members are involved in crime but not as a purposeful result of gang activity.[61] Using data from St. Louis, these researchers compared cases of gang-motivated homicide with gang-affiliated homicide and nongang youth homicide. Across all three homicide types, African American males were more likely to be participants, and there was very little difference in the neighborhood context. All three types of homicides clustered in disadvantaged communities—communities whose populations were predominantly African American. While gang-motivated homicides declined in the early 1990s, gang-affiliated homicides rose, leading the researchers to conclude that their continued increase "results from increased involvement of gang members—not gangs—in the drug trade."[62] This finding supports the work of other researchers who argue that youth gangs are primarily not organized enough to allow for a role in organized drug trade.

Los Angeles gang members show off their weapons. Scott Decker applies Colin Loftin's theory of violence as a contagion to the processes that are set into play as more gang members begin to carry guns. How does Loftin view assaultive violence as a contagious social process?

Source: Daniel Laine, Corbis/Bettmann

Serial Murder

Serial murder is a criminal homicide that "involves the killing of several victims in three or more separate events."[63] Serial killers are a source of both fascination and horror in our culture. Our fascination with serial killers is based on our disbelief that seemingly ordinary individuals could commit such atrocities. While seedy losers are found among serial killers, so, too, are charismatic, charming, and handsome college men like Ted Bundy. Across the continuum of types who are serial killers, "there is one trait that appears to separate serial killers from the norm: many are exceptionally skillful in their presentation of self so that they are beyond suspicion and thus are difficult to apprehend."[64] One factor that makes it difficult to identify serial killers, even with modern technology, is that these individuals often change the pattern of their offending, including their method of killing.[65]

James Alan Fox and Jack Levin have written extensively on both serial killing and **mass murder.** They offer ten myths of serial murder: (1) serial murder is at epidemic proportions, (2) serial killers have a distinct appearance, (3) all serial killers are insane, (4) all serial killers are sociopaths, (5) serial killers are primarily motivated by pornography, (6) traumatic childhoods are at the root of most serial killers' problems, (7) identification of serial killers prior to killing occurs is a straightforward task, (8) serial killers are primarily sexual sadists, (9) the victim's resemblance to a family member (usually the killer's mother) is the primary source of victim selection, and (10) serial killers want to be apprehended.[66] While annual figures as high as 5,000 victims of serial killers have been cited, this figure was based on the erroneous assumption that killings without a motive were attributable to serial killers, and it was also based on an accumulation of cases over time.[67] More reasonable estimates suggest that perhaps 100 murders each year are the result of serial killings.[68] While serial killers have been found among various age groups, among races, and between genders, the more typical serial killer is "a white male in his late twenties or thirties who targets strangers at or near his place of residence or work."[69] While acknowledging that the motivations for serial homicide are numerous, Fox and Levin contend that "murder is a form of expressive, rather than instrumental violence."[70] Unlike homicide generally, serial killing is more likely to involve strangers and rarely involves the use of guns.

The vast majority of serial killers are not legally insane or medically psychotic. "They are more cruel than crazy," according to Fox and Levin. "Their crimes may be sickening but their minds are not necessarily sick."[71] Many serial killers are diagnosed as sociopaths, a term for those with antisocial personalities. As discussed in Chapter 6, since they lack a conscience, sociopaths do not consider the needs or basic humanity of others in their decision making or their view of the world. They do not see themselves as being bound by conventional rules or by the expectations of others. Sociopaths view other people as "tools to be manipulated for the purpose of maximizing their personal pleasure."[72] However, many sociopaths neither are serial killers nor are involved in violent crime, even though "they may lie, cheat, or steal."[73]

Although not an exclusive characteristic of serial killers, sexual sadism is a strong pattern. In many of the typologies developed by researchers, this characteristic forms the basis for a type of serial killer. Typologies of serial killers are organized around different, but generally related, themes. Ronald Holmes and J. DeBurger developed a taxonomy based on an analysis of 400 cases. Their four different types of serial killers are differentiated by offender motivation, selection of victim, expected gain, and method of murder.[74] *Visionary serial killers* hear voices and have visions that are the basis for a compulsion to murder. *Comfort serial killers* are motivated by financial or material gain. *Hedonistic serial killers* murder because they find it enjoyable and derive psychological pleasure from killing. *Power seekers* operate from some position of authority over others, and their killings usually involve a period where the killer plays a kind of cat-and-mouse game with the victim. The nurse who poisons a patient, restores his or her health, and continues to repeat the cycle until the patient finally dies is an example of this kind of serial killer. Through the game, the killer gains attention or a boost in self-esteem.[75]

Gary L. Ridgway, 54, the self-confessed Green River strangler. Ridgway, reputed to be the nation's worst captured serial killer, admitted to killing 48 women over a 20-year period in the Pacific Northwest. He is now serving life in prison without possibility of parole. Why did it take so long to stop Ridgway?

Source: AP Wide World Photos

Refining the typology of Holmes and DeBurger, James Alan Fox and Jack Levin offer a three-part typology. They classify serial murderers as thrill motivated, mission oriented, or expedience directed. *Thrill-motivated killers,* the most common type of serial killer, may be of two types: the sexual sadist and the dominance killer. *Mission-oriented killers* are not as common and generally have either a reformist or a visionary orientation. Reformists want to rid the world of evil, and visionaries hear voices commanding them to do certain activities. Visionary killers are quite rare and tend to be genuinely psychotic. *Expedience-directed serial killers* are driven by either profit or protection. Profit-driven killers may kill for financial or material gain, and protection-oriented killers commit murder to mask other crimes, such as robbery.[76]

Although many studies of serial killers have highlighted the psychological characteristics of such offenders, James DeFronzo of the University of Connecticut, Storrs, and his coresearchers, point out that the incidence of male serial killers varies widely among the U.S. states—ranging from a high of 18.6 serial killers per 10 million residents in California, to a low of 3.4 per 10 million in Pennsylvania.[77] The interstate variation in the incidence of male serial killers, says DeFronzo, calls for a sociological examination of the factors that might help explain such differences. Among them, he says, might be factors representing the availability of vulnerable targets—such as the percentage of a state's population living in urban areas, the percentage of the state's divorced population, and the percentage of households with only one person. These kinds of sociological variables, says DeFronzo, show a positive relationship to the incidence and location of serial killings. Densely populated urban areas might provide a greater number of targets and a greater opportunity to escape apprehension, says DeFronzo. High percentages of divorced persons and one-person households might offer large pools of potentially vulnerable victims.

Female Serial Killers

Although the vast majority of serial killers are male, there have been female serial killers, and the patterns of their activities are sometimes distinct from those of male serialists.[78] The serial killer typology of Holmes and DeBurger, presented earlier, applies to women as well as men, except that women are rarely hedonistic serial killers.[79]

Serial killer Aileen Wuornos. Wuornos was executed by the state of Florida in 2002 after refusing further appeals. Although some women are moving into areas of traditional male criminality, the number of women committing violent crimes is still far smaller than the number of men. How does the criminality of women appear to differ from that of men?

Source: *Daytona Beach News Journal/Corbis/Sygma*

Female serial killers typically select their victims from among people who are known to them, unlike male serial killers, who tend to target strangers.[80] A type of serial killer found primarily among women is the *disciple killer,* who murders as the result of the influence of a charismatic personality. The women who killed at the behest of Charles Manson were of this type. The geographic area in which serial killers operate may be either stable or transient, with no clear preference among male serial killers. However, geographic stability characterizes almost all of the known female serial killers.[81]

Michael D. Kelleher and C. L. Kelleher researched female serial killers from a historical perspective and developed a typology based on motivation. Arguing that there are two broad categories of female serial killers—those who act alone and those who work in partnership with others—Kelleher and Kelleher present a typology based on distinct motivation, selection of victim, and method of killing.[82] The categories include the *black widow,* who generally kills spouses and usually for economic profit, and the *angel of death,* who generally kills "those in her care or who rely on her for some form of medical attention or similar support."[83] The typical career of a female serial killer is longer than that of her male counterpart. Other than women who commit their crimes with others, usually men, female serial killers tend to approach their crimes in a systematic fashion—a characteristic that may explain their longer careers.[84]

Apprehending Serial Killers

Fox and Levin contend that it is extremely difficult to identify and apprehend serial killers because of the cautiousness and skill with which they operate. Ironically, it is these very factors that allow them to operate long enough to be labeled serial killers. Individuals who are less skillful or cautious are generally apprehended because of physical evidence at the crime scene or the selection of a familiar victim. The Federal Bureau of Investigation (FBI) established the **Violent Criminal Apprehension Program (VICAP)** in 1985 to increase the efficiency and effectiveness of serial killer apprehension. Although Fox and Levin call VICAP an "excellent concept in theory," they note several practical problems with the program.[85] First, the complexity of the data and the associated record keeping have limited the degree of compliance by law enforcement officials, seriously affecting VICAP's potential usefulness. Second, the recognition of patterns among serial killers, even with the assistance of powerful computers, is not easily achieved. Finally, VICAP functions more as a detection tool than as an apprehension tool.

Violent Criminal Apprehension Program (VICAP)

The program of the Federal Bureau of Investigation focusing on serial murder investigation and the apprehension of serial killers.

In addition to VICAP, the FBI employs profilers who assist local law enforcement. According to Fox and Levin, "The FBI has done more to advance the art and science of offender profiling than any other organization."[86] Employing a primary classification system based on two prongs, FBI profiling theory distinguishes between *organized nonsocial killers* and *disorganized asocial killers.* Organized killers have a higher level of intelligence, better social skills, and a greater ability to function in all areas of life than do disorganized killers. These two types differ in the method of killing. Although variation certainly exists among them, the "organized/disorganized continuum is used as an overall guideline for drawing inferences from the crime scene to the behavioral characteristics of the killer."[87] Profiles typically do not yield high success rates in terms of actually leading law enforcement to apprehend a killer, but they are not intended to be the primary tool for apprehension. More recent attempts to identify serial killers rely on "geomapping" techniques to approximate the killer's probable location.[88] Most categorizations are based on the case histories and activities of known serial killers after apprehension. While we know a great deal about the patterns of serial murder, this does not necessarily translate into the ability to identify these killers easily before they have committed enough murders to come to the attention of the FBI—a rarity in itself, since only the "unsolvable" cases receive FBI attention. Learn more about serial killers from the FBI's Behavioral Analysis Unit via **Web Extra 10–3.**

WEB
Extra
▪ ▪ ▪ ▪

Mass Murder

M*ass murder* refers to the killing of more than three individuals at a single time.[89] Mass murder can follow the political motivations of the offenders, as was the case with the 1995 Oklahoma City bombing, in which 168 individuals, including children, were killed. Other mass murderers kill for more personal reasons. The mass killing at L'Ecole Polytechnique in Montreal, Canada, on December 6, 1989, by Marc Lepine was motivated by a hatred of women, feminists in particular. Lepine, who blamed feminists because he was denied admission to the engineering program at the school, shot and killed 14 female students. Lepine entered a classroom and ordered the male students and the professor to leave the room. Before he began firing, Lepine shouted, "I want the women! You're all a bunch of f-ing feminists! I hate feminists!"[90] He began firing, killing six of the nine women in the room. Lepine then went down the halls and into other parts of the university, killing women as he came across them, before finally turning the gun on himself. Mass murders are usually a shock because they often occur in everyday locales that are thought of as safe and because they erupt spontaneously. Although mass murders do not occur with great frequency, they cause great concern because they shatter the sense of safety that characterizes everyday life.

Jack Levin and James Alan Fox offer a four-part typology of mass murder that differentiates these crimes by motive and then further subdivides them by "victim-offender relationship, degree of planning, and randomness and state of mind of the perpetrator."[91] The four motive categories are revenge, love, profit, and terror. Mass murders that are motivated by *revenge* represent the largest category of such killings and may be against either particular individuals or groups of individuals, as was the case with Marc Lepine in Canada. Other revenge-motivated murderers may be less specific in the selection of a target, as in the case of George Hennard, who hated "all of the residents of the county in which he lived." In 1991, Hennard drove his truck through the front window of Luby's Cafeteria in Killeen, Texas, and then "indiscriminately opened fire on customers as they ate their lunch, killing 23."[92]

Some mass murders are motivated by *love,* Levin and Fox contend, though not in the way that most individuals would conventionally define actions that reflect love. Mass murders motivated by *profit* may result when the killer wants to eliminate witnesses to a crime. Mass murders motivated by *terror* include the killings by the Charles Manson family. Levin and Fox argue that mass murders motivated by anger or love are expressive in nature and that those motivated by profit and terror are more instrumental because there is some concrete goal to be achieved through the killings.[93]

Although most mass murders strike the public as senseless acts of a crazy person, Levin and Fox contend that "most massacrers are not madmen."[94] Yet why would someone like James Huberty, a former security guard, walk calmly into a fast-food restaurant in 1984 and fatally shoot 21 victims at random, most of whom were children? Why would Patrick Edward Purdy shoot and kill 5 children and wound 30 others at Cleveland Elementary School in Stockton, California, in 1989?[95] Levin and Fox argue that factors like frustration, isolation, blame, loss, and failure and other external and internal motivations and situational elements help make sense of these mass murders. They delineate three types of contributing factors: "*predisposers,* long-term and stable preconditions that become incorporated into the personality of the killer, which are nearly always present in his biography; *precipitants,* short-term and acute triggers, i.e., catalysts; and *facilitators,* conditions, usually situational, which increase the likelihood of a violent outburst but are not necessary to produce that response."[96] Using this typology to explain why, for example, most mass murderers are middle-aged, Levin and Fox contend that it takes a long time to accumulate the kind of rage and frustration that sets off some mass murderers. Mass murderers often select targets that have some significance for them, such as workers at a site of former employment. As Fox and Levin state, "A majority of mass killers target victims who are specially chosen, not just in the wrong place at the wrong time. The indiscriminate slaughter of strangers by a 'crazed' killer is the exception to the rule."[97] Unlike serial murderers, mass murderers are easy to apprehend because they rarely leave the scene of their crime, either because they commit suicide after the killings or because they stay long enough to be detected.

Rape

The violent crime of rape has generated much discussion and controversy over the years. To understand why, we must examine the changing legal definitions of *rape,* our societal understanding of rape, variations in the ways in which theoretical explanations of rape have evolved, and the development of rapist typologies. Concerns with improving the social, legal, medical, and social service response to rape were at the forefront of changes that have brought greater awareness of the extent and nature of violence against women. The significant evolution of this awareness is evidenced by federal legislation first enacted in 1994 and known as the **Violence Against Women Act (VAWA).** VAWA was reauthorized in 2000 and again in 2005. Additional information on VAWA is available in Chapter 15.

Attempts to measure the extent of rape have occupied a number of different researchers across various disciplines. The diversity of the scholars who have investigated the prevalence and incidence of rape partially explains why findings vary across research studies. There is no agreement on the number of women who are raped each year.[98] What is on the surface a simple matter is very difficult to pinpoint. The final number derived is determined by how rapes are counted and what data sources are used. According to the FBI's Uniform Crime Reporting Program, 92,455 completed or attempted rapes were reported to the police in 2006, and an estimated 63 of every 100,000 females in the country were reported victims of forcible rape.[99] However, the ability of official statistics to accurately assess the incidence of rape is hampered by victim reporting; most rapes are not reported to the police. Information reported from victims in the National Crime Victimization Survey (NCVS) reveals 198,850 rape incidents during 2006, or almost 2 attempted or completed rapes for every 1,000 residents age 12 or older.[100] Other problems with both measurement of rape and disclosure to researchers by victims also characterize the NCVS data and have led several researchers to question the accuracy of rape incidence based on these data.[101] The best current measure of the prevalence of rape comes from the **National Violence Against Women (NVAW) Survey.** According to estimates from the NVAW Survey, 17.6% of women reported either a completed or an attempted rape at some point during their lifetime. The prevalence rate for one year was 0.3% for attempted and completed rapes combined, which translates to slightly more than 300,000 rape victims and 876,064 rape incidents

Violence Against Women Act (VAWA)

A federal law enacted as a component of the 1994 Violent Crime Control and Law Enforcement Act and intended to address concerns about violence against women. The law focused on improving the interstate enforcement of protection orders, providing effective training for court personnel involved with women's issues, improving the training and collaboration of police and prosecutors with victim service providers, strengthening law enforcement efforts to reduce violence against women, and increasing services to victims of violence. VAWA was reauthorized by Congress in 2000 and 2005.

National Violence against Women (NVAW) Survey

A national survey of the extent and nature of violence against women conducted between November 1995 and May 1996 and funded through grants from the National Institute of Justice and the U.S. Department of Health and Human Services's National Center for Injury Prevention and Control.

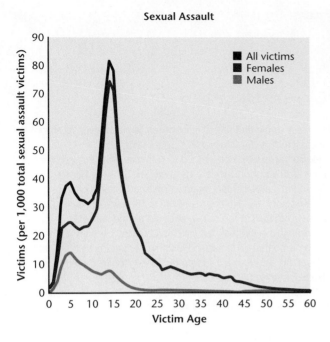

Sexual Assault

FIGURE 10–1

**Sexual Assault
Victimization Rates
by Age and Sex**

Source: Office of Juvenile Justice
and Delinquency Prevention,
*Juvenile Offenders and Victims: 2006
National Report* (Washington, DC:
OJJDP, 2006), p. 31.

annually in the population.[102] As Figure 10–1 shows, the risk of sexual assault victimization varies greatly by age as well as sex. The lifetime likelihood of being the victim of a violent crime or the victim of a particular violent crime is higher because risk accumulates over time.

Rape Myths

The ability to capture the extent of sexual violence against women remains hampered by sociocultural factors that contribute to underreporting. **Rape myths** are false assumptions about rape that continue to characterize much of the discourse surrounding sexual violence. Rape myths include notions that women bring false rape charges to "get even" with men, that women bring rape upon themselves by wearing provocative clothing, that women are "asking for it" by going to bars alone, and that women say no when they really mean yes. Since 1980, when Martha R. Burt first began researching rape myth ideology,[103] numerous other studies have supported widespread acceptance of these myths.[104] Rape myths serve to undermine the traumatic nature of this offense and to compartmentalize women into "good girls" and "bad girls," only one of whom is seen as a credible or sympathetic rape victim. Rape myths are culturally based and reflect attitudes toward women and their proper role and place in society. As feminists have long argued, rape myths serve to discount the experiences of women by placing stereotypical parameters around who can and who cannot be raped. Rape myths inhibit the reporting of rape and normalize rape as a crime of violence.[105] Largely as a result of such myths, women continue to report that agents of the criminal justice system do not respond with sensitivity and compassion toward their victimization. To argue that sexual violence is associated with rape myth ideology to the same extent that existed 20 years ago is just as naïve as to argue that rape myths do not continue to play a role in minimizing societal accountability for the level and acceptance of violence against women.

rape myth

A false assumption about rape such as "When a woman says no, she really means yes." Rape myths characterize much of the discourse surrounding sexual violence.

The Common Law Definition of Rape

Rape myths both fueled and supported the common law understanding of rape. Until the 1970s in the United States and the 1980s in Canada, rape was a common law offense. By this definition, rape was "carnal knowledge of a woman not one's wife by force or

Criminal Profiles

Karla Homolka

It was a case that kept the citizens of Canada enthralled in much the same way that the O.J. Simpson trial captivated the American public. It began with the rape of a young woman in May of 1987 and ultimately resulted in Karla Homolka being labeled "the most hated woman in Canada."[i]

On October 17, 1987, then-17-year-old Karla Homolka met then-23-year-old Paul Bernardo in an Ontario hotel restaurant. Their physical attraction was immediate and intense, and two hours later the couple had sex in one of the hotel's rooms. Thus began the convoluted relationship that would lead to three deaths, numerous rapes, and public outrage at the seeming leniency of the plea-bargained criminal sanctions Homolka was able to negotiate.[ii]

Unbeknownst to Homolka, handsome, boy-next-door Paul Bernardo had already embarked on a clandestine career as a serial rapist. In May of 1987, Bernardo raped a young woman in Scarborough, a small suburban town northeast of Toronto on the shores of Lake Ontario. Hers was to be the first of at least 14 rapes that the man dubbed the "Scarborough Rapist" would admit to committing during the next five years. Additionally, he was convicted of murdering two of his rape victims. However, it was the involvement of Karla Homolka in this sordid tale that ensures that this will never be your run-of-the-mill *boy-meets-girl, boy-rapes-girl, boy-kills-girl* kind of story.

As the relationship between Bernardo and Homolka evolved, Bernardo began to assert increasingly outrageous sexual demands with which Homolka willingly complied. Eventually, he expressed his annoyance that she had not been a virgin when he first met her. To resolve the problem, Homolka arranged to present Bernardo her own virgin younger sister, Tammy, as a Christmas gift. On December 23, 1990, then 15-year-old Tammy was fed alcohol laced with the sedative Halcion. When Tammy passed out, Bernardo raped and sodomized her while Homolka kept a drug-laced rag over Tammy's face to maintain her unconscious state. Both Bernardo and Homolka videotaped the rape as it was occurring. The tape also caught the extraordinarily tragic end of this episode, as Tammy threw up, then choked to death on her own vomit.[iii]

When Bernardo later complained to Homolka that she had cost him future sexual opportunities with Tammy by allowing her to die, Homolka found a replacement virgin whom she offered to Bernardo as a prewedding gift. Homolka invited a 15-year-old family acquaintance to dinner at the house she had rented with Bernardo. As with Tammy, the girl was fed Halcion until she became unconscious. Bernardo then videotaped Homolka performing sexual acts on the sleeping girl, then raped and brutally sodomized the girl as Homolka videotaped his acts.[iv]

On June 14, 1991, Bernardo abducted 14-year-old Leslie Mahaffy and brought her back to the house he shared with Homolka. After stripping and blindfolding the terrified girl, Bernardo woke his wife and proceeded to act as a movie director while videotaping Homolka performing lesbian sexual acts on Mahaffy. Homolka then took over the camera while Bernardo initiated a violent assault on the young girl, including brutal anal rape. Bernardo's violence continued to escalate until Mahaffy finally died. The two then dismembered her body and dumped the parts into Lake Ontario.[v]

Bernardo and Homolka married on June 29, 1991, and Bernardo continued his campaign of rape, often with Homolka's encouragement and assistance. At least one victim recalled seeing a woman videotaping her rape.

On April 16, 1992, the married rapists/killers abducted 16-year-old Kristen French from the parking lot outside of French's church. They then raped, tortured, and murdered the pretty young girl and left her nude body in a roadside ditch.

DNA evidence finally led to Bernardo's arrest on February 17, 1993. In short order, Homolka agreed to testify against him in exchange for a sentence of just 12 years for her role as an accomplice in the two manslaughters. (No charges have ever been brought for the death of Tammy Homolka.)

against her will." Although rape was clearly understood as a crime under the common law, it was a crime in which the legitimacy of the victim as a victim was challenged. Rape was construed quite narrowly, and the experience of many individuals regarding rape was not represented within this understanding because laws restricted the range of eligible rape victims. Specifically, the common law did not recognize men as victims, did not recognize rape within marriage, did not allow for acts of sexual penetration other than vaginal penetration by a penis, and did not allow for various means by which force could occur. Moreover, the rules of evidence required that the victim who brought forth a rape charge must demonstrate physical resistance to the attack and must have some form of corroboration that the rape occurred. The victim's previous sexual history could be admitted as relevant information. Furthermore, the sociocultural understanding of rape that predominated in the criminal justice system and in the wider society relied on gender stereotypes in which only certain kinds of women were deemed to be credible victims and only certain kinds of men were regarded as possible offenders. The sexual

In July 1993, Homolka pleaded guilty and her sentence, as agreed to in the plea bargain, was pronounced. Controversy exploded, however, when the numerous videotapes of the rapes and murders surfaced in September 1994, and the public became aware of the full extent of Homolka's willing participation in the atrocities.[vi]

Bernardo was convicted of the two murders on September 15, 1995, partly as a result of Homolka's testimony against him. He was sentenced to life in prison without possibility of parole for at least 25 years. Two months later he was declared a dangerous offender which, under Canadian law, virtually assures he will never receive parole release.

Public ire again boiled over following Homolka's release from prison on parole on July 4, 2005, when it became known that Homolka was complaining about the postrelease restrictions to which she was subjected. In February, 2007, the Canadian media reported that Homolka, with a new husband and a new name—Leanne Teale—had given birth to a baby boy.[vii]

A courtroom sketch of notorious Canadian sex criminal Karla Homolka, as she appeared in court in Joliette, Quebec, on June 3, 2005. She was set free after having served 12 years in prison for helping her former husband rape and murder three teenage girls, including her younger sister. Homolka remarried following release, and is the mother of a baby boy. She lives under the name Leanne Teale. Why are female sex killers so rare?

Source: Image © Reuters/Marianne Boucher/Landov LLC

Notes:

[i] Posted by Her Karma on *Vancouver Forum,* the Discover Vancouver Bulletin Board, July 3, 2005, http://www.discovervancouver.com/forum/topic.asp?TOPIC_ID=21791&whichpage=2 (accessed May 28, 2007).

[ii] Marilyn Bardsley, "Paul Bernardo and Karla Homolka." CourtTV Crime Library, http://www.crimelibrary.com/serial_killers/notorious/bernardo/index_1.html (accessed May 28, 2007).

[iii] Anne M. Griffy, "The Evil Within: The Twisted Minds of Paul Bernardo and Karla Homolka," Justice Junction, http://www.justicejunction.com/judicial_injustice_the_evil_within.htm (accessed May 27, 2007).

[iv] Ibid.

[v] Ibid.

[vi] Linda Diebel, "Professor Alan Young on Karla Homolka's Deal," *Toronto Star,* May 28, 2005, http://osgoode.yorku.ca/media2.nsf/83303ffe5af03ed585256ae6005379c9/47f95c9ce0cae54385257011007096ca!OpenDocument (accessed May 28, 2007).

[vii] "Victims' Families 'Distressed' Over Homolka Baby: Lawyer," CBC News, February 13, 2007, http://www.cbc.ca/canada/montreal/story/2007/02/13/homolka-baby.html (accessed May 28, 2007).

aspect of rape dominated both the legal construction of rape as a crime and the handling of rape cases by institutions.

Rape Law Reform

Rape law reform aimed to make the legal understanding of rape compatible with other violent crimes. Characterized as the second rape, rape investigations, especially at the trial stage, too often forced the victim through further trauma rather than focusing on assessing offender culpability.[106] Feminist groups, at the forefront of organized efforts to bring about rape law reform, were joined by law enforcement officials and prosecutors who supported efforts "to remove obstacles to the apprehension and conviction of offenders."[107] In 1975, Michigan became the first state to dramatically redefine *rape* to encompass a broader range of sexually assaultive behaviors, circumstances, and victims. Other states followed Michigan's lead, and by 1992, all states had made significant statutory changes to the common law offense definition of *rape*.[108] **Cassia Spohn** and **Julie Horney,** two of the most prolific researchers in the area of rape law reform, identify four common themes in all rape law reforms:[109]

- Redefining *rape* and replacing the single crime of rape with a series of graded offenses defined by the presence or absence of aggravating conditions
- Changing the consent standard by eliminating the requirement that the victim physically resist the attacker
- Eliminating the requirement that the victim's testimony be corroborated
- Placing restrictions on the introduction of evidence of the victim's prior sexual conduct

In some states, broad and sweeping changes were made to existing rape statutes.[110] This was certainly the case in Michigan, which for a time was considered the model for rape law reform. In other states, legal reform was more gradual, with slight changes being made to statutes in a step-by-step fashion. In Texas, for example, only very minor changes were made to existing rape statutes at any one time. Jurisdictions also varied in how the legal redefinition of *rape* occurred, with many states adopting a tiered approach, renaming the offense *sexual assault* of varying levels, similar to other crimes of assault. The change in terminology from *rape* to *sexual assault* was intended at a symbolic level to more fully capture the violent nature of the crime. Because of the history of sexism surrounding conventional rape laws and the processing of cases, it was argued, the term *rape* implied that the crime was fundamentally a sexual one. The more the sexual aspect of the crime was emphasized, the less the crime was seen as violent.

In one key way, individual rape law reform in states and at the federal level proceeded in different routes: the **rape shield laws.** These laws, first introduced in the 1970s as part of the legal reforms then under way, were intended to protect rape victims by ensuring that defendants did not introduce irrelevant facts about the victim's sexual past into evidence. Previously, no guidelines prevented the defense from bringing into evidence the victim's sexual history as a way to discredit her and to play to rape myth ideology. The rape shield laws varied in the amount of discretion left with the judge in terms of the type of evidence that could be introduced. However, these laws were quite necessary and sent the message that the courts would no longer be a party to a "second assault" on the victim.[111]

A number of expectations attached to rape law reform. Spohn and Horney identify four general changes that were anticipated in the wake of rape law reform. First, an increase in the reporting of rapes was expected because legal reforms would mean that victims would receive more sympathetic and effective treatment within the criminal justice system. Second, the reforms were expected to produce symbolic change that would emphasize the violent nature of rape. Third, legal reforms were expected to alter the decision-making structure of the criminal justice system by eliminating the consideration of extralegal evidence (for example, what the victim was wearing). Finally, reform was expected to remove the barriers preventing more effective prosecution and higher conviction rates for rape.[112] Learn more about rape law reform at **Web Extra 10–4.**

The Effects of Rape Law Reform

What have been the effects of rape law reform? Have the reforms changed the way rape cases are handled by the criminal justice system? Have legal changes altered the social landscape enough to affect the reporting behavior of rape victims? Questions like these, which highlight some of the goals of rape law reform, have been addressed in research by Spohn and Horney in the most thorough empirical assessment of rape law reform to date.[113] The researchers selected six urban jurisdictions in which to evaluate rape law reforms. Three jurisdictions represented areas of strong legal reform, and three represented areas of weaker reform. This distinction was important because Spohn and Horney expected that the effects of rape law reform would be the most dramatic in areas where

rape shield law

A statute providing for the protection of rape victims by ensuring that defendants do not introduce irrelevant facts about the victim's sexual history into evidence.

WEB
Extra
■ ■ ■ ■

reforms had been comprehensive and strong. Strong reforms were represented by jurisdictions where the entire rape statute had been revised and where elements of reform, such as the rape shield laws, offered little discretion to judges. Spohn and Horney analyzed data from court records of all processed rape cases in the six jurisdictions from 1970 through 1984. They also collected all police reports of rape during this period. To assess the impact of legal reform, the researchers looked at several outcome measures, such as whether there was a change in the reporting of rapes to the police, in the indictment of rape cases by prosecutors, and in the conviction rates for offenders. In addition to statistical analysis of cases and reports, the researchers conducted interviews with a sample of more than 150 judges, prosecutors, and defense attorneys.[114]

As previously noted, Spohn and Horney hypothesized that the impact of rape law reform would be the most pronounced in jurisdictions characterized by strong reforms. While their findings supported this hypothesis in some ways, there was far from uniform support. Detroit, Michigan, was one of the three jurisdictions they included with strong reforms. The reforms in Michigan did accomplish some of the expected ends, such as an increase in reports, indictments, and convictions. However, other expected outcomes of reform, such as a greater percentage of convicted rape offenders being sentenced to incarceration, did not materialize. In jurisdictions like Illinois, where reform efforts were less comprehensive, the effects of reform were weak to nonexistent on all of the outcome measures used. Jurisdictions with weak reforms, like Houston, saw significant increases in reports of rape following reform implementation—an effect not seen in Philadelphia, a jurisdiction implementing stronger reforms.[115]

One of the common findings of studies of this type is that new legislation has only a limited effect on changing the behavior of courtroom work groups unless they embrace the reforms or unless the reforms actually force instrumental changes. Spohn and Horney used interviews with criminal justice officials to place their statistical analysis within the context of the legal environment in which rape cases are processed. One of the explicit goals of legal reform was to change the way in which agents of the criminal justice system respond both to the crime of rape and to the victim. Similar to other legal changes that emerge from grassroots activism, the reforms had to be "interpreted and applied by decision makers who may not share the goals of those who championed their enactment and who therefore may not be committed to their implementation."[116] The officials that Spohn and Horney interviewed expressed strong support for the legal changes in their jurisdictions and claimed that the treatment of rape victims had improved significantly. While the statistical analysis revealed no dramatic changes in how officials handled rape cases as the result of legal reforms, the interviews helped interpret this. Some changes, such as more serious attention being given to simple rape cases (that is, cases without aggravating characteristics like the presence of a weapon), were already occurring in jurisdictions prior to rape law reforms. Case law in several jurisdictions had already produced changes such that "a scintilla of corroboration" to a rape charge was sufficient in many rape cases.[117] The researchers stated that "reformers should find encouragement in some evidence for the effectiveness of rape shield laws. Officials in all jurisdictions rated evidence relating to a complainant's sexual history low in importance."[118] Spohn and Horney conclude with the key observation that legal reforms take time to produce large-scale change and that rape law reforms must be continually evaluated for more evidence of how change is occurring.

The Social Context of Rape

Although rape can occur in almost any social context, certain social situations are characterized by a higher prevalence of rape and by a difference in the offender's motivation. A number of contexts within which the crime of rape occurs are described in this section.

Acquaintance Rape

The vast majority of rapes occur when the victim and the offender have some prior relationship—though not necessarily an intimate or a familial one. Some researchers

Crime in the News

Rapist Preys on Men

BAYTOWN, Texas—A rapist who has struck at least five times since April in and around Baytown has not only spread fear in this working-class community but also piqued the interest of those who study the criminal mind. The reason: He preys on other men.

That makes him something of a rarity in the world of crime.

"It's the least prevalent kind of serial rape, and largely underreported," said Jack Levin, a leading criminologist and director of the Brudnick Center on Violence at Northeastern University in Boston.

Levin and other experts say male-on-male rape sometimes stems from sexual encounters gone bad. But that does not appear to be the case with the rapist in this oil-refining town of 70,000 people about 30 miles east of Houston.

Instead, he methodically identifies and stalks young men and attacks them at gunpoint or knifepoint in or near their homes, according to police Capt. Roger Clifford. Sometimes he robs his victims, too, but rape appears to be the primary motivation, police said.

"This is certainly of interest, an interesting case," Levin said.

The U.S. Justice Department says one in 33 men in the United States has been a victim of a rape or attempted rape, compared with one in six women. Experts say men are far less likely to report a rape to authorities, because they fear being perceived as weak or see the attack as an assault on their masculinity.

In fact, investigators in Baytown fear there may be other victims of the rapist who are too ashamed to come forward.

"There's a lot of emotional damage that goes with being raped, especially when the victims are men," said Lynn Parrish, a spokeswoman for the National Rape, Abuse & Incest National Network. But she added: "The best way to get this rapist off the street is for more people to come forward."

Three of the attacks have occurred in the city, the other two on the outskirts of town. The most recent attack was Nov. 30. Clifford would not give details of the rapes but said at least one victim managed to thwart the attack.

No one has been seriously hurt.

"But it's only going to take one victim who resists enough or in the wrong way until the gun is going to go off, the knife is going to be used, and we're going to have a victim with serious injuries or who's dead," Clifford said.

Criminologists have seen cases of serial killers who raped or otherwise had sex with their male victims among them, John Wayne Gacy and Jeffrey Dahmer. But psychologically, this is a different phenomenon.

Levin said it is rare for a serial rapist to become a serial killer.

"I think the reason has to do with the absence or presence of a conscience," he said. "A serial rapist is more likely to have a conscience. Otherwise they'd take the life and silence the victim."

Victims have described the Baytown attacker as a clean-shaven black man, 18 to 21 years old, 5-foot-10 to 6 feet tall and about 200 pounds, with a shaved head. Police have released a sketch and are working with the FBI's behavioral sciences unit to develop a psychological profile. DNA testing also is under way.

Fliers with the sketch have been circulated around schools and Baytown's Lee College, with an enrollment of about 6,000.

Jay Ali, an 18-year-old who works at the local mall, said he has been spreading the word among friends. "There's a loose psycho running around raping men," he said.

The local paper, *The Baytown Sun,* has run the sketch and details of the crimes at the top of its front page nearly every day since the most recent attack, and an electronic bulletin board on its Web site is filled with discussion about the rapes.

"I have selfish reasons for wanting this guy caught," Marie W. wrote in a posting Dec. 12. "I have a son who fits this guy's target group. . . . I want him off the streets and locked up like yesterday."

Downtown Houston, Texas. The Houston–Sugar Land–Baytown area is the sixth largest metropolitan area in the United States with a population of 5.5 million people. In 2006, the Baytown area was rocked by news that a rapist was preying on fellow men. Why are criminologists especially interested in finding the perpetrator?

Source: © Walter Bibikow/JAI/CORBIS All Rights Reserved

Discussion Questions

1. Why is the kind of rape described here likely to go unreported?

2. How might the emotional impact of the crime of rape differ for male and female victims?

3. If you were a psychological profiler working on this case, what kind of personal characteristics might you expect the offender to exhibit?

For the latest crime and justice news, visit www.crimenews.info.

and activists who work with rape victims have stated that **acquaintance rape** is the most common scenario for rapes. Acquaintance rape has been referred to as a "hidden crime" because it represents a type of sexual assault that is not reported to the police and that is quite susceptible to rape myth ideology. Among adults, acquaintance rape usually occurs within the context of a dating relationship. For this reason, a great deal of the empirical research on acquaintance rape has focused on the college setting, where dating is a salient characteristic of the social life of undergraduate students.

Researchers have identified college campuses as places that typically have a high incidence of rape. Although E. J. Kanin reported in a 1957 *American Journal of Sociology* article that as many as 20% of college women had experienced either a completed or an attempted rape,[119] societal awareness and concern for rape on college campuses did not emerge until the 1980s. Helping to publicize the problem have been a number of high-profile rape cases on college campuses in which the victims not only went public with their experiences but also grabbed headlines and the covers of major publications like *Time, Newsweek,* and *People.*[120] Some of these cases include the rape of Katie Koestner at the College of William and Mary, the rape of Kristen Buxton at Colgate University, and the rape of Christy Brzonkala at the Virginia Polytechnic Institute and State University. In the last case, the victim filed for civil relief under the Violence against Women Act. The case ultimately went before the U.S. Supreme Court, which affirmed the rulings of lower courts that invalidated a VAWA provision that provided a federal civil remedy for the victims of gender-motivated violence. The Court held that the clause could not withstand constitutional scrutiny.[121] Not only has media publicity emphasized the reality of the college setting as a site of rape, but also in 1992 the Campus Sexual Assault Victims' Bill of Rights Act became law.[122] It requires campus authorities to "conduct appropriate disciplinary hearings, treat sexual assault victims and defendants with respect, making their rights and legal options clear, and cooperate with them in fully exercising those rights."[123]

One of the most prolific researchers on rape, especially of rape among college students, is **Mary P. Koss.** Koss found that approximately 28% of women reported having experienced an attempted or a completed rape since the age of 14.[124] Based on incidents occurring in the last 12 months, Koss calculated an incidence rate of 76 per 1,000 women. Based on comparable estimates from the National Crime Survey (NCS), Koss's estimate was 10 to 15 times the rate obtained with NCS data.[125] Approximately 57% of the rapes involved dating partners, and 73% of the rape victims reported that the offender was drinking. Other studies on college campuses have found similarly high levels of rape and sexual assault.[126]

A great deal of the research on rape in college settings has focused on identifying the unique factors of campus life that may be conducive to rape. Some researchers contend that college fraternities "create a sociocultural context in which the use of coercion in sexual relations with women is normative and in which the mechanisms to keep this pattern of behavior in check are minimal at best and absent at worst."[127] Rather than focusing on the pathological nature of individual males in fraternities, these researchers have identified characteristics of the social organization of fraternities that contribute to the formation of attitudes and behaviors that objectify women and normalize sexual coercion. These characteristics include "a preoccupation with loyalty, group protection and security, use of alcohol as a weapon, involvement in violence and physical force, and an emphasis on competition and superiority."[128] Learn more about campus rape at **Web Extra 10–5**.

While social organizations like fraternities may reinforce rape myth ideology, other social organizations exist on college campuses around the country that challenge this ideology. The increased awareness of campus rape has led to the development of services and programs that assist victims of sexual violence and that present information that challenges rape myths. State and federal funding has produced a variety of programs that aim to alter the atmosphere surrounding sexual violence on college campuses. Initially, most of these programs either were aimed at women or focused on rape as primarily a women's issue, but newer programs treat rape as an issue for men. Groups like Men against Rape at Tulane University and Men Overcoming Violence (MOVE), which is active throughout New England, were organized to develop programs and initiatives that

acquaintance rape

Rape characterized by a prior social, though not necessarily intimate or familial, relationship between the victim and the perpetrator.

WEB
Extra
■ ■ ■ ■

WEB
Extra
■■■■

involve men in the effort to stop rape. Programs range from anger-management groups to male mentoring. For more information about some of these groups, you can visit the National Coalition against Violent Athletes via **Web Extra 10–6** and Mentors in Violence Prevention via **Web Extra 10–7**.

Marital Rape

spousal rape

The rape of one spouse by the other. The term usually refers to the rape of a woman by her husband.

As previously mentioned, under common law there was no such crime as **spousal rape.** One of the most challenging aspects of rape law reform was the elimination of the marital exemption for rape. In 1978, one year after Oregon removed the marital exemption from its rape statutes, John Rideout became the first American husband indicted for raping his wife.[129] The Rideout case captured media attention not only because it was the first case of its kind, but also because of the sensational nature of the back-and-forth relationship between the Rideouts. A made-for-television movie of this case was even produced in 1980. In her analysis of rape cases that received enormous media attention, Lisa M. Cuklanz examined the Rideout case and argued that the central issue in this case was the credibility of the new law.[130] The first case that goes to court under any new law should be as strong as possible, but the Rideout case did not fit this scenario because "the preponderance of damaging personal information about Greta Rideout suggested a verdict of 'not guilty' for John even at the very beginning of the trial."[131] At the time of the Rideout case, evidence of the victim's sexual history was allowed. Such evidence damaged Greta Rideout's credibility as a rape victim and illustrated that "she was on trial as much as her husband." Cuklanz notes that in this case, the victim was tried first, "the law second, and the defendant third."[132] At the trial's conclusion, John Rideout was acquitted, and the Rideouts briefly reconciled before finally divorcing.

As Cuklanz notes in her analysis, the media coverage of the Rideout case did not include commentary about the nature of marital rape that could have helped the audience understand the interactional dynamics of the case. In the absence of such information, "character evidence underscored the validity of the traditional interpretation that posited confusion, manipulation, and personal gain as motives."[133] In research on judicial treatment of battered women, James Ptacek highlights the crucial role that such information can play in how criminal justice personnel understand the motivations and situations of both the victims and the offenders who come before them in the courtroom. Judges whom Ptacek interviewed in his research commented that an understanding of the dynamics of battering greatly assisted them in responding to victims because this understanding "challenged the prevailing 'commonsense' understandings embodied in both written law and judicial practice that dismiss woman battering as 'trivial' and enforce the barrier of 'family privacy' on behalf of violent men."[134]

In an article published in 1982, David Finkelhor and Kersti Yllo said that "the marriage license is a raping license."[135] The first research to systematically examine spousal rape was **Diana E. H. Russell**'s random sample of 930 women in San Francisco in 1990.[136] Approximately 14% of women who had ever been married reported at least one attempted or completed rape by their husbands. Based on an analysis of the interview data, Russell developed a four-part typology of men who rape their wives:[137]

- Husbands who prefer raping their wives to having consensual sex with them
- Husbands who are able to enjoy both rape and consensual sex with their wives or who are indifferent to which it is
- Husbands who would prefer consensual sex with their wives but are willing to rape them when their sexual advances are refused
- Husbands who might like to rape their wives but do not act out these desires

Thus, rather than being one-dimensional, rape within marriage has several forms that reflect the various nuances of motivation on the part of offenders.

Rape in Prison

Correctional institutions provide a setting in which same-sex rape can be common. Charles Crawford, professor of sociology at Western Michigan University, refers to males who are sexually assaulted in prison as the "forgotten victims."[138] While the high prevalence of rape within prisons has been documented by prison researchers for some time, the victimization of prisoners does not raise the type of societal outrage that is reserved for crimes against "law-abiding" victims. Rape has been documented in both men's and women's prisons, but the patterns differ. Based on published research, rape within women's prisons primarily takes the form of male staff attacking female inmates, whereas in men's prisons, the assaults involve only inmates. While precise estimates of the extent of rape in prison are difficult to develop because of a lack of data, researchers who studied three prisons in Nebraska found that 22% of respondents reported to have been sexually assaulted.[139]

Theoretical Perspectives on Rape

Several theoretical perspectives have been offered to explain individual motivations for rape, why rape is more prevalent in particular contexts, and how certain cultural values may reinforce rape. Many of these perspectives attempt to explain how rape is patterned according to the context, the victim-offender relationship, and the motivations of the rapist.

Feminist Perspectives

There is no one feminist perspective on rape, but for the sake of simplicity we will discuss the common elements that run through the various feminist perspectives. As discussed in Chapter 9, feminists view gender as a social construct rather than as a biological given, and they regard as problematic the way in which gender is used to structure social relations and institutions. The patriarchal relations and structures within our society that contribute to the privileged status of men are inseparable from rape itself because rape serves as a social control mechanism, some feminists argue. Rape is viewed as an act of power or domination in which the "tool" used to subordinate is sexual. Rape is a crime of violence that is sexual in nature, but this aspect is considered to be secondary to the power dynamics that occur in rapes.[140]

Socialization patterns, cultural practices, structural arrangements, media images, norms surrounding sexuality, and women's status in society all combine to create a rape culture in which both men and women come to view male aggression as normal, even in sexual relations.[141] Within this culture, women are blamed for their own rape by virtue of the fact that males are naturally incapable of controlling their sexual desire. For feminists like **Catherine MacKinnon**[142] and **Andrea Dworkin**,[143] rape and sex are not easily distinguishable under patriarchy because the male dominance that characterizes patriarchy is inherent in both the act of rape and the social construction of sex. Who women are and what women choose for themselves become problematic in the perspectives of these feminists because heterosexuality is "compulsory" under patriarchy. The views of feminists like MacKinnon and Dworkin are often met with resistance by others and are misunderstood as "male bashing." MacKinnon and Dworkin do not focus on individual males as somehow being either "good" or "bad." Rather, they focus on the construction of gender and all that flows from it under patriarchy. Patriarchal relations construct male and female to be opposite poles of social existence and being, with *male* defined by dominance and *female* defined by that which is not male—and is generally inferior and subordinate. Under such constructions, MacKinnon and Dworkin ask, how can anyone ever freely choose any kinds of relationships, sexual or otherwise?

The work of Dworkin, MacKinnon, and others also stresses the existence of a rape culture that has the effect of equating sex with violence and objectifying women to the point that they lack an identity separate from that which is defined by men. Pornography is often thought to contribute to the manner in which women are objectified. In pornography, violence and sex are combined in a manner that makes the association normative. In an essay first published in 1974, Robin Morgan asserted that "pornography is the theory, and rape the practice."[144] Susan Brownmiller also discussed both pornography and prostitution as institutions that encourage and support social patterns and responses to rape.[145] While not everyone shares the same view of the role of pornography in supporting the inequality of women and in justifying violence against women, pornography is frequently associated with rape in the writings and research of many prominent feminists.

James W. Messerschmidt acknowledges the positive contributions of feminist thought but critiques these perspectives for their often one-dimensional view of masculinity.[146] Ngaire Naffine also shares Messerschmidt's positive evaluation of this body of work and says that "Dworkin is trying to shatter our complacency about everyday life for women, to get us to see the daily criminal violence and injustice done to women that has been rendered utterly ordinary and so invisible."[147] In his critique of feminist perspectives, Messerschmidt analyzes the various expressions of masculinity that are constructed within particular situations and as a response to particular social conditions. He says, "Middle-class, working-class, and lower-working class young men exhibit unique types of public masculinities that are situationally accomplished by drawing on different forms of youth crime."[148] Just as there is no one single strain of femininity, so, too, with masculinity. Messerschmidt also contends that the response of the state to violence against women is not monolithic. While there are limits to how the state will respond in behalf of women, the state is viable as a site for positive change in terms of women and feminist ideals. The emergence of rape crisis centers, changes in institutional protocol regarding rape victims, and other similar strategies illustrate that a state that is basically patriarchal in nature can be pushed to respond to women in ways that are positive and that increase women's autonomy. **Neil Websdale** echoes these sentiments in his research on rural woman battering by stating that "organizations set up by the state to further women's interests have played a significant role in improving the status of women."[149] Websdale maintains that some settings, such as those within rural areas, display stronger adherence to patriarchal relations than others; this distinction is crucial to understand that any setting contains many individuals and groups that do not use violence against women and that do not view rape as normative.

The Psychopathological Perspective

The psychopathological perspective on rape is based on two assumptions: (1) Rape is the "result of idiosyncratic mental disease," and (2) "it often includes an uncontrollable sexual impulse."[150] While acknowledging that rape is connected to issues like power and anger, the frequently cited work of **Nicholas Groth**[151] contains elements of this psychopathological perspective.[152] Groth's work was based on an analysis of 348 imprisoned convicted rapists. Approximately half of the rapists had attacked young or middle-aged women, while the other half had attacked children, elderly women, or other men. For rapists who had attacked women, 55% reported that the rape was committed to exert control over the women—a type of crime Groth labeled *power rape.* Power rapists, unlike anger rapists, did not purposefully set out to harm the victim. Power rapes are generally planned, Groth said, "although the actual assault may be opportunistic in origin."[153] In the attacks that Groth labeled *anger rapes,* which totaled about 40% of the sample, the men attacked their victims in anger; usually the attack was impulsive and involved no prior planning on the part of the offender. These assaults were often quite brutal, and following the rape, the offender felt relief because he was able to relieve his anger. The remaining 5% Groth called *sadistic rapes;* these involved a combination of power and anger motives.[154] According to Groth, in sadistic rape, "aggression itself is eroticized," and these rapes frequently involve torture.[155] While not denying that these types of rapists exist, some researchers claim that Groth's model does not appear to successfully characterize the majority of men who rape, and yet this model has been applied as if that were the case.[156] However, Diana E. H. Russell did find elements of Groth's model to be useful in developing her own typology for men who rape within marriage.[157] Several of the factors that Groth identifies as important to understanding the motivation and pattern of rapes are found in other typologies of rapists.

An Integrated Theory of Rape

Larry Baron and **Murray A. Straus** offer what they term "an integrated theory of rape."[158] They combine elements from other theoretical explanations of rape into one model that argues that higher levels of gender inequality, social disorganization, and support for legitimate violence combine to produce higher rape rates at the state level.

Support for legitimate violence refers to norms and institutional arrangements that serve to justify the expression of violence in certain contexts as normative. The norms need not directly relate to a particular crime. As Baron and Straus note, there is a "cultural spillover" effect in which "cultural support for rape may not be limited to beliefs and attitudes that directly condone rape and other criminal violence."[159] Rather, when a community legitimizes the use of violence to resolve any kind of situation, this creates a type of spillover effect in which other types of interactions and dynamics come to be governed by similar norms and understandings. Thus, one would expect to see high rates of rape associated with high rates of other violent crime.

Gender inequality is related to rates of rape because as women's status in society improves, rape is challenged as a mechanism of social control over women. This occurs as socialization patterns change and as women attain positions of power within society. The connection between gender inequality and rape is supported in cross-cultural and anthropological research.[160] *Social disorganization* refers to the inability of communities to sustain viable social institutions—institutions that serve as a buffer to all sorts of social ills, including criminal activity. Poverty alone is not enough to directly produce crime. However, in the absence of other factors that strengthen institutional structures within communities, poverty is linked to crime by virtue of its association with other factors.

In a test of their theory at the state level, Baron and Straus found support for the direct effect of gender inequality on rape rates. The higher the level of gender inequality—a combination of several measures relating to economic indicators—the higher a state's rape rate. They also examined the direct effect of pornography and found that higher rates of pornography, as measured by things like circulation rates for certain magazines, were associated with higher rates of rape within the state. High levels of social disorganization, measured by such things as residential mobility, percentage of female-headed households, and divorce rates, were also tied to increased rates of rape. While Baron and Straus found no direct support for the relationship between legitimate violence and rape, they argue that there is an indirect effect in which states with higher rates of gender inequality have higher rates of legitimate violence. This association between legitimate violence and gender inequality also has the effect of increasing rape rates such that in states with greater economic inequality the status of women is lower; where the status of women is lower, the rate of rape tends to be higher.[161]

Evolutionary/Biological Perspectives

Within the evolutionary perspective, "humanity is a product of evolution in which both physical and social traits conducive to survival are selected and survive through a process of natural selection. Propagation is the key to survival of a trait, as a genetic predisposition can be passed on only through offspring."[162] Natural selection favors those traits that are most adaptive, and over several generations it is these traits that survive. An evolutionary perspective does not identify rape per se as an adaptation but, rather, focuses on certain motives and ends that are conducive to rape. The environment is also thought to play a role because "genes cannot make traits without environmental causes acting in concert."[163] According to **Randy Thornhill** and **Craig T. Palmer,** "[s]election favored different traits in females and males, especially when the traits were directly related to mating. Although some of these differences could have arisen from what Darwin called natural selection, most of them are now believed to have evolved through sexual selection."[164] *Sexual selection* refers to the observation that some traits appear to

Who's to Blame—The Individual or Society?

Exotic Dancer Claims Rape

Twenty-one-year-old Carla Maybe-Love called 911 from her cell phone at 3:00 A.M. on a Sunday morning, telling the 911 operator who answered that she had just been raped.

"Ma'am, are you injured? Are you in need of immediate medical assistance?" the operator asked.

"No, no, I'm okay," Carla told her.

"Are you safe, is anyone threatening you? Is anyone there with you?" the operator continued.

"I'm okay. I'm back home. Alone," Carla said.

Carla gave her address and the operator dispatched a patrol car to the location.

The female officer who arrived encouraged Carla to go with her to the hospital for an examination and for evidence collection. Once Carla had been signed in at the emergency room, the officer took a report of the incident.

Carla described herself as an exotic dancer and for-hire personal companion, who spent her evenings entertaining men of all ages. "I show them a good time," she said," "and there's nothing illegal about that. But that don't give them the right to rape me," she told the officer.

Carla then went on to tell the officer how she had been hired by two men who were attending a local convention to come to their hotel room with a friend and put on a show. "Dancing, that's all we were supposed to do," she said. The men, she said, called a number of their friends in to their room to watch the show. At some point, Carla told the officer, she had to go to the bathroom. That's when, she said, a man followed her and pushed her into the small room, locking the door behind them. "That's when it happened," she said. "He put his hand around my throat, and he raped me."

Think about it:

1. Assuming that Carla is telling the truth about what happened, how would you explain this crime? That is, why did it happen, and how might it have been prevented?

2. In your opinion, does Carla bear any responsibility for her own victimization? Why or why not?

---

survive not because they are related to survival, but because they further the attainment of mates or defense against competition over mates. This is said to apply primarily to males because "male fitness is limited by access to the opposite sex much more directly than is female fitness, with the result that females compete for mates much less than do males."[165] The specialized jargon and knowledge that informs evolutionary perspectives make it difficult to understand how they apply to social behaviors like rape, and these perspectives have been severely criticized for justifying rape as "natural." Proponents of the usefulness of evolutionary perspectives on rape contend that evolutionary perspectives can explain why rape is so prevalent and why it takes the forms that it does, and they argue that "biology provides understanding, not justification, of human behavior."[166] The conceptualization of rape as sex is not meant to carry only negative connotations because "the view that rape is always motivated at least in part by sexual desire and that sexual desire may be sufficient motivation to produce rape behavior in some situations implies nothing about what people should do. Also, the view that differences in sexual desire between males and females are evolved and biological implies nothing about the ease or difficulty with which these differences can be changed."[167] Evolutionary perspectives contend that the feminist position on rape that equates it primarily with expressions of violence diminishes the fact that there is a biologically based sexual motivation and that ignoring this eliminates one avenue by which rape may be understood and prevented. Rather than being counter to the agenda of feminists, evolutionary psychologists offer their perspective as another avenue through which rape can be approached, understood, and thereby prevented.

Typologies of Rapists

Several researchers have attempted to develop typologies of rapists. Nicholas Groth's work represents one of the first systematic attempts to do this based on empirical evidence, which he gathered in his capacity as a prison psychologist. **Robert R. Hazelwood and Ann Burgess** developed a four-part typology of rapists based on the motivation of the offender.[168] Like Groth's, their typology revolves around the themes of power, anger, and sadism. The four types of rapists they identified are power-assertive, power-reassurance, anger-retaliatory, and anger-excitation rapists. *Power-assertive rapists* plan their crimes and use a great deal of force to subdue the victim. This type of rapist acts out of a hypermasculinity in which the rapist is "simply exercising his prerogative as a male to commit rape."[169] These rapists often employ a type of seduction to subdue their victims initially, and they generally attack their victims several times during the same incident. *Power-reassurance rapists,* the most common type among rapists who attack strangers, generally act out of a sense of social and sexual inadequacy. Robert Hazelwood contends that these are the rapists who are referred to in popular jargon as the "gentleman rapists." They select their victims in advance through stalking and may even attempt to contact the victim after the rape. These rapists generally do not set out to consciously degrade their victims, and they generally target victims of their own age. *Anger-retaliatory rapists* are clearly motivated by anger, and rape becomes the means by which the anger is expressed. These rapists may attack either the actual source of their anger or a representative. Hazelwood contends that this type of rapist "uses the *blitz approach,* subduing the victim with the immediate application of direct and physical force, thereby denying her any opportunity to defend herself."[170] *Anger-excitation rapists* are "sexually stimulated and/or gratified by the victim's response to the infliction of physical and emotional pain."[171] These are generally the rapists whose crimes involve the most planning and the most careful execution, even though the victim selected is generally a stranger. These rapists are "most likely to record activities with the victim," and the nature of the rape is definitely intended to "create pain, humiliation, and degradation for the victim."[172]

Based on interviews with 61 serial rapists, Dennis J. Stevens offers a typology of his own based on motivations. At the time of the interview, the rapists were all incarcerated in a South Carolina maximum-security prison for the crime of rape. Using Nicholas Groth's "Protocol for the Clinical Assessment of the Offender's Sexual Behaviors" to structure the interview, Stevens explored the areas of premeditation, victim selection, style of attack, degree of violence associated with the rape, accompanying fantasies, role of aggression, and other topics. One of the major findings that emerged from Stevens's research was the role of lust as a primary motive among a large proportion of the rapists (42%). While acknowledging that "lust is not a new idea concerning predatory rape,"[173] Stevens believes it to be a primary rather than a secondary motive for rapists. With those Stevens identified as *lust rapists,* a minimal amount of force accompanied the rape. These men selected victims based on the most available target. *Righteous rape* motives formed the primary element for 15% of the rapists. This group viewed their victims as responsible for the attack because these offenders believed that in some "silent deal" the "sex" had already been negotiated and consented to by the victim. Stevens contends that these men saw themselves as "not guilty by reason of circumstance," and they spent a great deal of energy justifying the rape. Like the lust rapists, they "characterized sexual intimacy as their primary objective."[174] *Peer rape* motives, present in 3% of the rapists, took the form of holding friendship responsible for the rape. The rapists claimed, "I had no choice, I ran with bad company."[175] *Control and anger rapes* were committed by 6% of the rapists. These cases included more "violence than necessary to accomplish rape," and the rape itself was described by the rapists as "secondary to the violence powered by their anger."[176] *Supremacy rape* motives were held by 13% of rapists, and these rapes were characterized by more violence than necessary to subdue the victim during all stages of the attack. Stevens stated that with these rapists, sexual contact was insignificant compared with the punishment given to the victim during and after the attack. *Fantasy rape* motives, primary among 16% of the serial rapists, were characterized by individuals "trying to regain some imaginary goal that had been part of their past."[177] The sex act involved in the rape was less important to these men than the ideas in their heads—ideas that were sometimes quite violent in nature. Stevens classified the motives of 3% of the rapists he interviewed as unclear.[178] A constant theme that emerged throughout Stevens's interviews with the rapists was that for most of them, the amount of force that accompanied the rape was just enough to accomplish the victim's submission. In cases in which extreme violence accompanied all stages of the rape, the violence would have been present regardless of the level of victim resistance. Therefore, one of the conclusions made by Stevens is that advocating the idea that women should not resist their attackers is ill-advised.

Another way to approach a typology of men who rape is represented in the work of **Diana Scully,** a professor at Virginia Commonwealth University.[179] Scully's research involved intensive interviews with 114 convicted rapists in seven prisons, all of whom volunteered to be interviewed. Scully rejects the psychopathological perspective on rape and instead employs a feminist sociocultural perspective premised on several assumptions. First, rape is "socially learned behavior," involving "not only behavioral techniques, but also a host of values and beliefs, like rape myths, that are compatible with sexual aggression against women."[180] This premise is based on the assumption that both positive and negative forms of social behavior are learned "socially through direct association with others as well as indirectly through cultural context."[181] Second, Scully views rape not as a reflection of pathology, but as a reflection of a continuum of normality in which it is important to understand "how sexual violence is made possible in a society" and "what men who rape gain from their sexually violent behavior."[182] Scully thus approached these interviews with convicted rapists from the feminist perspective of wanting to understand the explanations given by the rapists and their sociocultural beliefs about women and sexual violence.

Scully identified several patterns to the rationalizations used by men who rape, and she organized these according to two broad types of rapists: admitters and deniers. *Admitters,* the largest category of rapists, included those men who acknowledged that their offense constituted a rape and who provided information that largely corresponded to official records. Even though acknowledging their offense as a rape, admitters purposefully downplayed the amount of force used or other key facts about their offense. Scully uses as an example a rapist who appeared to be quite traumatized during the interview as he discussed his offense but who also failed to mention that the 70-year-old woman he had raped was his grandmother. *Deniers* contended that the sexual relations with their victims were consensual and that the rape offense for which they had been convicted was erroneous. With this group, there were more obvious discrepancies between the information they provided and the official records than with the group of admitters. Several of those whom Scully designated as deniers had, in fact, used weapons in their offense yet still believed that the sexual relations did not involve force or coercion.

In the interviews, Scully explored how these two groups could operate from an understanding of reality that justified their behavior and tended to normalize it, as well as what they gained from such behavior. While some of the rapists in the admitter group relied on rape myth ideology, this was a more prevalent pattern among the deniers. The rape myths' definition of a very narrow group of individuals as legitimate rape victims was a common theme in the interviews given by these rapists. While variations existed, the majority of rapists in both groups expressed little guilt or empathy for their victims. Scully states, "Sexually violent men identify with traditional images of masculinity and male gender role privilege; they believe very strongly in rape stereotypes, and for them, being male carries the right to discipline and punish women."[183] While men who rape may not all operate from the same level of adherence to definitions of *masculinity,* they all benefit by the societal assignment of such characteristics as power, force, and the sexual double standard implicit in such definitions. As Scully states, "Hierarchical gender relations and the corresponding values that devalue women and diminish them to exploitable objects or property are the factors that render feeling rules inoperative and empower men to rape."[184] When the status of women in our society, both economically and socially, is considered along with cultural depictions of women found in everything from seemingly benign advertisements to more shocking pornography, women emerge as a group that can in some ways still be victimized with relative impunity. In a society where sex and violence are equated and where gender is socially constructed as a hierarchy of difference, we send messages that provide justifications for rape and sexual coercion. The strength of these messages does not require that all men be rapists; it is enough that the potential for rape is established, as well as the ideology that excuses the violence of those who do rape. Read more about the violent criminal victimization of women in America via **Library Extra 10–5** at crimtoday.com.

Child Sexual Abuse

In what can only be described as a very sad case, Dr. William Ayres, 75, a child psychiatrist who once headed the American Academy of Child and Adolescent Psychiatry was arrested in 2007 and charged with molesting three male children who were his patients in the 1960s.[185] Prosecutors said that they would present evidence showing that Ayers had molested young boys in his care for decades.

Child sexual abuse (CSA) is a term encompassing a variety of criminal and civil offenses in which an adult engages in sexual activity with a minor, exploits a minor for purposes of sexual gratification, or exploits a minor sexually for purposes of profit. The term encompasses a variety of activities and motivations, including child molestation, child sexual exploitation (CSE), and the commercial sexual exploitation of children (CSEC).

The National Institute of Justice observes that "few criminal offenses are more despised than the sexual abuse of children, and few are so little understood in terms of incidence (the number of offenses committed), prevalence (the proportion of the population who commit offenses), and reoffense risk."[186] Moreover, says NIJ, studies on the psychology, behavior, treatment, and recidivism rates of child molesters have often yielded inconsistent findings.

NIJ also notes that the assumption that sexual crimes against children and teenagers are underreported is now commonly accepted. Sexual offenses, says the agency, are apparently more likely than other types of criminal conduct to elude the attention of the criminal justice system. Self-reports from both sex offenders and sexually abused children reveal far more abuse than officially reported.[187] The Child Molestation Research and Prevention Institute, based in Atlanta, Georgia, estimates that at least two out of every ten girls, and one out of every ten boys, are sexually abused by the time they turn 14.[188]

child sexual abuse (CSA)

A term encompassing a variety of criminal and civil offenses in which an adult engages in sexual activity with a minor, exploits a minor for purposes of sexual gratification, or exploits a minor sexually for purposes of profit.

One of the most informative offender self-report studies on the adult sexual victimization of children comes from research conducted slightly more than two decades ago.[189] In that study, investigators recruited 561 adult subjects who engaged in what the researchers described as "child-focused sexual behavior." The subjects, who were guaranteed anonymity, were recruited through health care workers, media advertising, presentations at meetings, and in other ways. All were free from confinement at the time of the interviews. The 561 adults interviewed reported a total of 291,737 "paraphiliac acts" over the course of their adult lives committed against 195,407 victims under the age of 18. The five most commonly reported acts involved criminal conduct, and were as follows:

- Nonincestuous child molestation with a female victim (224 of the 561 subjects reported 5,197 acts against 4,435 victims).

- Nonincestuous child molestation with a male victim (153 of the 561 subjects reported 43,100 acts against 22,981 victims).

- Incest with a female victim (159 of the 561 subjects reported 12,927 acts against 286 victims).

- Incest with a male victim (44 of the 561 subjects reported 2,741 acts against 75 victims).

- Rape (126 of the 561 subjects reported 907 acts against 882 victims).

These five categories included a total of 64,872 self-reported acts, although the total number of individual victims could not be determined since many subjects reported multiple kinds of acts across different categories. Nonetheless, the results of this study make it clear that, in cases of child sexual abuse, a relatively small number of offenders can commit a large number of crimes.

Crime in the News

Serial Child Sex Abuser Sentenced to 150 Years

SAN JOSE, Calif. (AP)—A man prosecutors said was one of the nation's most prolific child molesters was sentenced Monday to 150 years in prison for abusing two 12-year-old boys.

Dean Arthur Schwartzmiller, 64, who also had been convicted of sexual assaults in several states over three decades, was sentenced to the maximum term on 11 felony counts of child molestation and one misdemeanor charge of child pornography possession.

Schwartzmiller represented himself during his trial last year but asked for an attorney to represent him during the sentencing phase.

Dean Arthur Schwartzmiller smiles with his attorney, Melinda Hall, left, in a San Jose, California, courtroom, on January 29, 2007, as he is sentenced to 150 years to life for sexually abusing two 12-year-old boys. Schwartzmiller, 64, a child molester with convictions in several states over three decades and a knack for avoiding prison, was sentenced on 11 felony counts of child molestation and one misdemeanor charge of child pornography possession. How did Schwartzmiller manage to stay out of prison for so long?

Source: AP Wide World Photos Paul Sakuma

During the nearly three-week trial, prosecutor Steve Fein showed jurors a map of the "places and decades where the defendant has molested young boys." It included an estimated 100 accusers dating to 1969 in eight U.S. states, Mexico and Brazil.

When Schwartzmiller was arrested in June 2005, investigators found a memoir describing abuse, binders full of child pornography and 1,500 notebook pages with headings including "blond boys," "no, but yes boys," and "best of the best, 13 and under."

Schwartzmiller, who acted as his own attorney during his October trial, told jurors that he was innocent and maligned by a society that doesn't accept men who love boys.

During his testimony, Schwartzmiller said the memoir and notebook entries were fiction.

He blamed roommate Frederick Everts—also a convicted child molester—for the child porn. Schwartzmiller also said he could not have molested the two San Jose boys, who are cousins, because he was either at a construction job or bedridden with a bad back at the time.

Although police say Schwartzmiller appears to have spent much of the past three decades in California, he has also been arrested on child molestation charges in New York, Idaho, Oregon, Arkansas and Washington. He has lived in Nevada, Texas and Washington.

Schwartzmiller has used aliases including Dean Harmon and Dean Miller, authorities said. He apparently gained the trust of victims and parents by working as a home renovation contractor. He didn't register as a sex offender so he did not appear in the "Megan's Law" databases in California or other states, police said.

Police said Schwartzmiller befriended the two San Jose boys with gifts, invited them to his house for video games and movies, and molested them.

Judge Edward Lee said that despite Schwartzmiller's legal savvy in getting some previous charges dismissed, he will spend the rest of his days filing appeals from a prison cell.

"For all that above-average intelligence and charm, I have a couple of faults (with you)—an English teacher might call them tragic faults," Lee said. "You have no empathy for your victims; that's not particularly unusual. And you cannot see yourself as others see you."

Discussion Questions

1. How could an offender like Schwartzmiller, convicted of sexual assaults over three decades in several states, be free from confinement?

2. Why would Schwartzmiller tell jurors that he was maligned by a society that doesn't accept men who love boys? How would jurors likely react to such an argument?

3. Why did the judge tell Schwartzmiller that "you cannot see yourself as others see you?" Do you think the judge is right?

Typology

Almost all pedophiles are male, with one study of more than 4,400 offenders finding fewer than 0.5% of convicted child sex offenses committed by females.[190] Other than that, little can be said about similarities among child sexual abusers. As individuals, they tend to be highly dissimilar from one another in terms of personal characteristics, life experiences, and criminal histories. No single "molester profile" exists.[191] Child molesters appear to arrive at deviancy via multiple pathways and engage in many different sexual and nonsexual "acting-out" behaviors. Figure 10–2 shows the number of registered predatory child sex offenders by state.

Typologies of child sex offenders are many and varied. One typology, developed at the Massachusetts Treatment Center (MTC) for Sexually Dangerous Persons classifies offenders along a number of dimensions, including (1) the amount of contact with children, (2) the kinds of sexual acts engaged in, (3) the relationship of the offender to the victim, (4) the amount of physical injury to the victim, and (5) the amount of planning in offenses.[192] The MTC model produces six offender types, as shown in Table 10–1.

In 1983 Nicholas Groth and his associates proposed a different kind of typology—a simple, two-part distinction whereby offenders were classified as either "regressed" or "fixated."[193] Regressed offenders, said Groth, are attracted sexually primarily to their own age groups but are passively aroused by minors. Generally speaking, the use of

Registered Sex Offenders, state-by-state

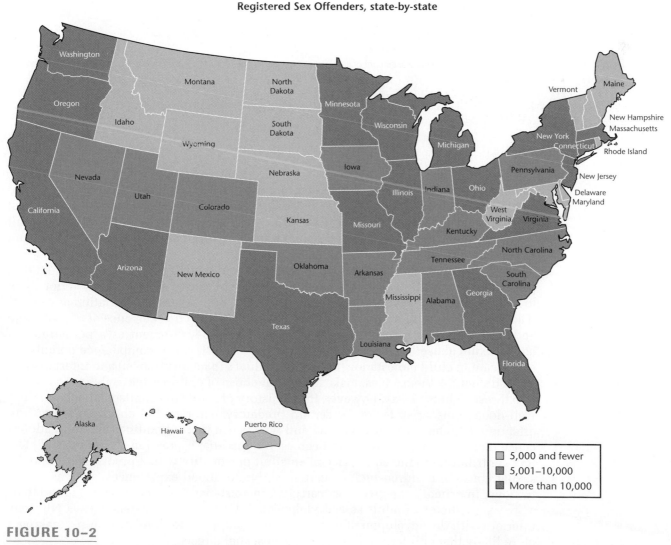

Legend:
- 5,000 and fewer
- 5,001–10,000
- More than 10,000

FIGURE 10–2

Registered Sex Offenders by State

Source: USA TODAY, June 16, 2006. Reprinted with permission.

TABLE 10–1 **Hypothetical Profiles of Child Sex Predators**

	Interpersonal	Narcissistic	Exploitative	Muted Sadistic	Nonsadistic Aggressive	Sadistic
Amount of Contact with Children	High	High	Low	Low	Low	Low
Sexual Acts	Fondling, Caressing, Frottage, (Nonphallic Sex)	Phallic Nonsadistic Sex	Phallic Nonsadistic Sex	Sodomy "Sham" Sadism[a]	Phallic Non Sadistic Sex	Sadism
Relationship of Offender to Victim	Known	Known or Stranger	Stranger	Stranger	Stranger	Stranger
Amount of Physical Injury to Victim	Low	Low	Instrumental[b]	Instrumental[b]	High	High
Amount of Planning in Offenses	High[c]	Moderate	Low	Moderate	Low	High

[a] "Sham" sadism implies behaviors or reported fantasies that reflect sadism without the high victim injury present in the Sadistic type.

[b] Instrumental aggression implies only enough force to gain victim compliance.

[c] Interpersonal types know their victims and may spend a considerable amount of time "grooming" them (setting them up), but the offenses often appear to be unplanned or spontaneous.

Source: Adapted from Robert A. Prentky, Raymond A. Knight, and Austin F. S. Lee, *Child Sexual Molestation: Research Issues* (Washington, DC: National Institute of Justice, 1997).

alcohol, drugs, or other inhibition-lowering substances, combined with social circumstances providing opportunity, can cause the regressed offender to act out his interest in having sexual encounters with children. Fixated offenders, said Groth, are adult pedophiles who engage in planned sexual acts with children, and whose behavior is not necessarily influenced by drugs or alcohol.

A U.S. Department of Justice publication, representing a compilation of studies produced by the NIJ, shows that most victims of childhood sexual abuse do not go on to become child molesters.[194] However, NIJ points out, sexual victimization as a child, if accompanied by other intervening factors—such as the co-occurrence of physical and verbal abuse—may contribute to the child-victim's development as a perpetrator of child sexual abuse later in life. Similarly, says the NIJ, social competence deficits are significant in child molestation, but an individual's inadequate social and interpersonal skills do not, by themselves, make his sexual abuse of children inevitable.

NIJ researchers do say, however, that a history of impulsive, antisocial behavior is a well-documented risk factor for certain predatory, extrafamilial child molesters; and offenders who have this background and who began their offending careers in adolescence tend to demonstrate higher degrees of nonsexual aggression. Other possible factors contributing to the emergence of an adult personality with a predisposition to the sexual abuse of children include certain early childhood experiences, such as a high turnover in primary caregivers or "caregiver inconstancy," (which has been found to be a strong predictor of adult sexual violence).[195] Caregiver inconstancy, says NIJ, may interfere with the development of viable, age-appropriate adult relationships, making it more likely that children will be selected as sexual targets.

One concept often discussed in relationship to child sexual abusers is *sexual focus.* Sexual focus in child molesters can be described in terms of two separate dimensions.

The first is intensity of pedophilic interest, or the degree to which offenders are focused or "fixated" on children as sexual objects. The second dimension involves the exclusivity of preference for children as sexual objects.

Some evidence exists to suggest that child molestation may be related to an offender's restaging of his own childhood sexual victimization.[196] Tests of the restaging theory on a sample of 131 rapists and child molesters revealed that child molesters who committed their first assault when they were 14 or younger were sexually victimized at a younger age than offenders who committed their first assault in adulthood; they also experienced more severe sexual abuse than offenders with adult onset of sexual aggression.[197]

Nonetheless, sexual victimization alone appears to be unable to fully explain child molestation. Studies show that most victims of childhood sexual abuse do not go on to become perpetrators.[198] As is true for other kinds of maltreatment, childhood sexual victimization may be one critical element in the presence or absence of a variety of other factors (for example, co-occurrence of other types of abuse, availability of supportive caregivers, ego strength of child-victim at the time of abuse, availability of treatment, and so forth), all of which appear to moderate the likelihood of becoming a child molester.

Not all adults involved in the sexual abuse of children pursue personal sexual gratification. Some have a profit motive, as is the case in instances of *commercial sexual exploitation of children,* or CSEC. CSEC refers to all offenses in which an adult victimizes a child sexually for profit, including the prostituting of a child, and creating or trafficking in child pornography. According to the United Nation's Children's Fund (UNICEF), lives of tens of thousands of children in the United States, and tens of millions of children worldwide are involved in CSEC.[199] UNICEF says the number of sexually exploited children worldwide may exceed 100 million, not all of whom are located in "poor" or "developing" countries. Richard J. Estes of the University of Pennsylvania School of Social Work believes that "some portion of these children are in the 'employment' of well organized networks of traffickers in child and adult sex, at least some of which also engage in the sale of illegal drugs, money laundering activities and other criminal activities."[200] CSEC offenses include child pornography, juvenile prostitution, trafficking in children for sexual purposes, and child sex tourism (trafficking in persons is discussed in more detail in Chapter 15).

A screen capture of the sexoffender.com home page. Sexoffender.com is a commercial site that combines sex offender information from many states. The U.S. Department of Justice's National Sex Offender Public Registry can be accessed at www.nsopr.gov. Community notification laws frequently result in the posting of online offender databases. How do such databases help victims?

Source: © Copyright 1973–2004 Sexoffender.com & Childmolester. com - All Rights Reserved

In a comprehensive review of the literature[201] on CSEC, Estes notes that child sexual exploitation appears to be "fueled" by: (1) the use of "survival sex" by runaway and thrown-away children to provide for their subsistence needs; (2) the presence of preexisting adult prostitution markets in communities where large numbers of street youth are concentrated; (3) prior history of child sexual abuse and child sexual assault; (4) poverty; (5) the presence of large numbers of unattached and transient males in local communities—including military personnel, truckers, and conventioneers; (6) for some girls, membership in gangs; (7) the promotion of child prostitution by parents, older siblings and boyfriends; (8) the recruitment of children as "sex workers" by organized crime units; and, increasingly (9) illegal trafficking of children for sexual purposes both within and to the United States from developing countries located in Asia, Africa, Central and South America, and Central and Eastern Europe. "Other young people" says Estes, "are recruited into 'sex work' through forced abduction, by pressure from their parents, [and] through deceptive agreements between parents and traffickers in the CSEC, including unrecognized representatives of crime rings." Read a comprehensive report on the commercial sexual exploitation of children in the United States, Canada, and Mexico via **Library Extra 10–6** at crimtoday.com.

LIBRARY
Extra
■■■■

Robbery

In June 2006, a home-invasion robbery in Indianapolis resulted in the deaths of seven people, including three children under the age of 12.[202] Prosecutors said that the two men arrested and charged with the killings, James Stewart, 30, and Desmond Turner, 28, attacked the home after hearing that it contained a safe holding money and drugs. Anecdotal evidence seems to say that home invasion–type robberies, officially referred to as residential robberies, are increasing in number throughout the United States. In response to the growing threat from such crimes, the Hidalgo County, Texas, sheriff's office created a special unit to curtail such robberies—regularly committed by criminals in the Rio Grande Valley area who dress like SWAT officers and stage assaults on homes. Hidalgo County Sheriff Guadalupe Trevino says that many of the men are current or former Mexican police officers targeting "stash houses" filled with illegal immigrants who are unlikely to go to authorities.[203]

Robbery is classified as a violent crime because it involves the threat or use of force. It is, however, also a property crime in that the express purpose of robbery is to take the property of another.[204] Robberies can occur in different locations and are quite often categorized in this manner by both law enforcement agencies and social science researchers. Robberies that occur on the highway or street are often referred to as highway robberies or "muggings." Muggings and robberies that occur in residences are types of **personal robbery.** While residential robberies are most certainly deterred by the presence of security precautions, the effectiveness of deterrents depends on the type of neighborhood in which the residence is located. Terance D. Miethe and David McDowall found that security precautions that tend to be effective in neighborhoods characterized by a viable social control structure are ineffective in socially disorganized neighborhoods.[205] Security precautions, such as not leaving the home unoccupied, are not enough in socially disorganized neighborhoods to compensate for the strong effect that neighborhood context has on increasing the likelihood of robbery. Simply put, homes and persons do not exist as potential targets for motivated offenders in a vacuum; they appear as more or less attractive targets based on their perceived vulnerability and the social context of the surrounding neighborhood in which they are found.

Robberies that occur in commercial settings, such as convenience stores, gas stations, and banks, are **institutional robberies.**[206] Several research studies have found that institutional robberies may be prevented through environmental and policy changes. Scott A. Hendricks and his colleagues found in a study of convenience store robberies that "the robber chooses a target based on various situational crime prevention factors."[207] These factors include staffing, hours of operation, cash-handling policy, and characteristics of the surrounding neighborhood. For example, the researchers found

personal robbery

Robbery that occurs on the highway or street or in a public place (and that is often referred to as "mugging") and robbery that occurs in residences.

institutional robbery

Robbery that occurs in commercial settings, such as convenience stores, gas stations, and banks.

that "the odds of convenience store robbery were twice as high for older neighborhoods than newer neighborhoods."[208] Many of the precautions that lower the risk of robbery are costly, however, and not all businesses can afford them. As Richard T. Wright and Scott H. Decker note, "This puts businesses located in high-crime neighborhoods in a no-win situation because their clientele frequently are too poor to bear increased prices to support crime prevention measures."[209] Additionally, if the business fails as a result of robberies, the community loses again because the exodus of businesses that are forced to relocate makes the community less viable. Most of the robbers interviewed by Wright and Decker in their ethnographic study of robbers who selected commercial targets generally selected liquor stores, taverns, and pawnshops because of the large amount of cash available. They also targeted businesses with low levels of customer activity because they viewed customers as an unpredictable risk factor. The robbers interviewed as part of Floyd Feeney's research in California during the 1970s reported very little planning overall, but those who engaged in commercial robbery were much more likely to report planning than those who engaged in personal robberies (60% compared with 30%).[210]

The Lethal Potential of Robbery

Robbery carries the threat of injury for the victim—and too often lethal injury. Reported injuries were found among one in every three robbery victims whose data were entered into the National Incident Based Reporting System.[211] Robbery provides the context for 7% of all homicides annually. In 2006, approximately 16% of all homicides occurred during the commission of another felony. Among these cases, robbery was the most likely felony to result in homicide, accounting for almost one-half (43%) of all felony murders.[212] The weapon most often used in robbery homicides is a firearm, accounting for 42% of all cases; the type of firearm used in the vast majority of these cases (85%) is a handgun.[213]

Criminal Careers of Robbers

Are robbers specialists or generalists? This distinction refers to whether individuals who engage in robbery specialize in only this crime or whether they vary the types of crimes they commit. The majority of robbery offenders are generalists who have a fairly lengthy but varied criminal career.[214] Research on a sample of inmates in California prisons found that less than 10% of convicted robbers could be labeled specialists who engaged solely in robbery to the exclusion of other offenses.[215] In a survey of inmates sponsored by Rand Corporation, approximately 18% of offenders were primarily involved in only one type of offense.[216] James Q. Wilson and Allan Abrahamse used data from a Rand survey of inmates in 1978 to explore the type of monetary returns offenders earned from their crimes.[217] For the purposes of this analysis, Wilson and Abrahamse decided to group offenders according to offense type—a task that proved problematic because specialization among offenders was not the norm. Diversity in offense type appears to be the norm for the vast majority of offenders, based on both ethnographic and survey data.

Robbery and Public Transportation

One setting in which crime prevention strategies may be quite effective is public transportation. According to Martha J. Smith and Ronald V. Clarke, "Robbery on mass transit is a rare event, even in systems with relatively high numbers of incidents such as New York City."[218] Viewing the prevalence of robbery on public transportation as reflecting a "lack of supervision," Smith and Clarke contend that the majority of these robberies follow one of three scenarios. First, offenders will purposefully select their victims from among passengers in isolated areas of large subway stations, especially when the station is not crowded. Security measures, such as using closed-circuit television monitoring and closing off unused parts of the station, may serve to effectively deter these offenders.[219] Second, offenders will select their victims outside the station at particular locales and times that are relatively isolated. Finally, offenders will act on opportunity, and often "lie in wait" for passengers leaving public transportation.[220] Prevention strategies to deter these types of robberies include a variety of surveillance techniques. In addition to targeting public transportation customers, robbers also target the staff in order to steal the fare money. Smith and Clarke state that policies such as exact fare collection and other similar changes "led to a dramatic fall in the number of bus robberies in New York City."[221]

According to Smith and Clarke, "Transit workers with perhaps the greatest risk of robbery are taxicab drivers, who carry cash, travel by themselves around cities with strangers, and do not choose their destinations."[222] Derek Cornish offers several strategies that taxicab drivers can use to prevent robberies.[223] These tactics range from having a weapon to screening passengers for potential threats. While "drivers can use informal passenger screen practices such as refusing to pick up fares at certain locations," such screening practices "can discriminate against those who live in poorer areas or are from certain racial or age groups, making it difficult for them to use the service."[224] These very practices have recently been the subject of debate because of claims of discrimination.

Other strategies, such as the installation of protection partitions between the driver and passenger, can be quite effective in deterring crime. In New York City, such partitions are "required on all yellow cabs and livery cars operated by more than one driver, but individual drivers who own their cars say the partitions are too expensive."[225] In response to the high number of killings of cab drivers in robbery incidents, then–New York City Mayor Rudolph Guiliani created a $5 million grant program to assist livery cab companies with the cost of installing the protective partitions. A pilot program begun in August 1999 installed digital surveillance cameras in cabs.[226] Under the New York City Police Department's special Taxi-Livery Task Force, created in 1992, police in unmarked cars stop taxis in particular neighborhoods, often according to some strategy, such as every fifth taxi. A similar strategy was also adopted in Boston, again as a response to the substantial number of violent crimes, especially robberies, experienced by cab drivers. While the Boston statute withstood court review, the New York Court of Appeals ruled in December 1999 that the policy of the police department "gave officers too much discretion to stop taxis carrying passengers when they had no reason to suspect any crime was afoot."[227] The U.S. Supreme Court was asked to review both rulings and declined, allowing the rulings of the lower courts to stand.

Policies like those in Boston and New York clearly illustrate the tension involved in policing a democratic society; measures that might prevent certain forms of crime must be weighed against the potential violation of individual liberties. This issue becomes even more complex when a high risk of victimization is experienced by members of a particular occupational group who must function within criminogenic settings or who must interact frequently with strangers.

The Motivation of Robbers

Research tends to support the idea that most robberies, of both people and places, involve very little planning on the part of the offender. Floyd Feeney's research in California during the early 1970s found little evidence that the majority of bank robbers had even been in the bank before the robbery.[228] Most of the robbers Feeney studied did very little planning, no matter what the target, and the planning that did occur was minor and "generally took place the same day as the robbery and frequently within a few hours of it."[229] The motivation and decision making of street robbers have recently been evaluated in a series of research studies conducted by Bruce A. Jacobs, Richard Wright, and others at the University of Missouri at St. Louis. We will examine several of the most important pieces of this large, qualitative study involving 86 currently active robbers in St. Louis. To be considered an active robber for the purpose of the

A bank photo shows Ashley Nicole Miller (top photo, left) and Heather Lyn Johnston, both 19, as they robbed a bank located in a grocery store in Acworth, Georgia, in 2007. Cameras caught the fashionably dressed unarmed teenagers smiling and giggling as they produced a hold-up note and were handed money. Some news outlets were quick to christen the pair the "Barbie Bandits." Mug shot photos show the two following their arrest after it was discovered that the robbery was an inside job aided by Benny Herman Allen, a 22-year-old bank employee. Why are female bank robbers the exception rather than the rule?

Source: Courtesy Cobb County Sheriff's Office

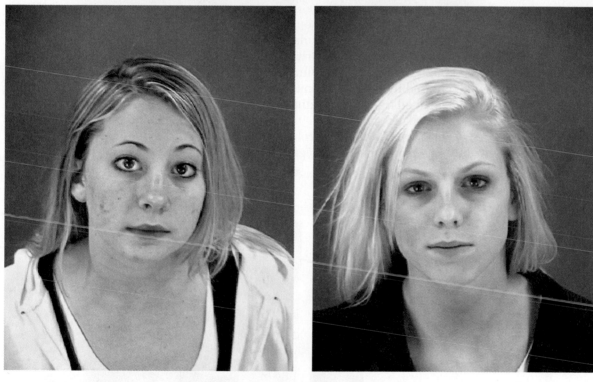

research study, "the individual had committed a robbery in the recent past, defined him- or herself as currently active, and was regarded as active by other offenders."[230] Jacobs and Wright found that the decision to offend, like other decisions, occurs as part of ongoing social action that is "mediated by prevailing situations and subcultural conditions."[231] "Fast cash" was the direct need that robbery satisfied, but this need can be properly understood only against the backdrop of street culture. Jacobs and Wright hypothesized that street culture was the intervening force that connected background factors (such as low self-esteem, deviant peer relations, and weak social bonds) to the motivation to offend. They found that the majority of robbers gave little thought to planning robberies until they found themselves needing money. For less than half of the robbers, the financial need was for basic necessities; mostly, it was connected to a fairly hedonistic lifestyle. The daily activity of most street robbers was characterized as a "quest for excitement and sensory stimulation" with a "general lack of social stability" in terms of residence or ties to conventional activities or institutions.[232]

Jacobs and Wright considered three alternatives that these individuals could have employed for money: (1) performing legitimate work, (2) borrowing, and (3) committing other crimes. Legitimate employment was not a viable option for these individuals for several reasons. Most of the robbers had neither the skills nor the education to obtain decent-wage jobs, and even if they did have such resources, their perceived need for cash was too immediate for legitimate work to satisfy. Additionally, legitimate work was viewed as an impediment to their "every night is a Saturday night" lifestyle. Borrowing money was not a viable route because many had no one to turn to for a loan, and for those who did, borrowing was not part of the self-sufficient code of the streets. Robbery was preferable to other crimes because it was perceived to be safer than crimes like burglary and quicker than other crimes requiring the translation of stolen goods into cash. Other research has found that some robberies do, in fact, begin as another crime, such as burglary, and become robberies more by accident than design.[233] Jacobs and Wright conclude that the economic motivation behind robbery should not be interpreted as "genuine financial hardship" but, rather, as a constant, ongoing crisis situation experienced as a result of the logic of the street context of robbers' daily lives.[234] For the individuals whom Jacobs and Wright interviewed, "being a street robber . . . is a way of behaving, a way of thinking, an approach to life."[235] Such individuals are unlikely to be easily deterred by legal sanctions, and the rationality of their decision making is unlikely to be adequately explained outside the context of street culture participation.

In 2006, Trevor Bennett and Fiona Brookman interviewed 120 English robbery offenders in a study funded by Britain's Economic and Social Research Council (ESRC).[236] Bennett and Brookman found that financial gain was only one of the many motivations reported by robbers themselves. Others included a "sheer desire to fight," to set right a perceived injustice, to enhance one's street credibility, and "just for kicks." Some offenders participating in the study had been arrested as many as 50 times, and reported that they were addicted to robbery. One told the researchers, "I was more addicted to robbing than I was to drugs." Drug connections were mentioned in 60% of all robberies studied.

Some robbers seem to give little thought to planning their crimes until they need "fast cash." Might this person be an attractive target for such robbers?

Source: Ed Bailey—AP Wide World Photos

Drug Robberies

In their ethnographic research on armed robbers, Richard T. Wright and Scott H. Decker found that "six out of every ten offenders who specialized in street robbery—forty-three of seventy-three—said that they usually preyed on individuals who themselves were involved in lawbreaking."[237] These are generally the cases that are not reflected in official statistics on crime because the victims do not report their victimization to the police. Due to their involvement in illegal behavior, these individuals can be victimized with relative impunity. Because an overriding motivation behind the robberies for many of the offenders in Wright and Decker's research was to get high, it follows that drug dealers would be an obvious target. Among offenders who stated that they selected victims involved in crime, the vast majority targeted drug dealers, though rarely major drug dealers. According to Wright and Decker, "Almost all of these offenders targeted young, street-level dealers who sold quantities of crack cocaine directly to consumers."[238] According to one robber, the attraction of robbing drug dealers was twofold because drug dealers carry drugs as well as cash: "It satisfies two things for me; my thirst for drugs and the financial aspect."[239] The neighborhoods in which these robbers lived and conducted their routine activities were generally characterized by an abundance of drug dealers, which increased their suitability as targets. Because they were also unlikely to report their victimization to the police, drug customers were also perceived as ideal targets. Wright and Decker further state that within the neighborhoods where these offenders operate, "an ability to mind one's own business is regarded as a crucial survival skill."[240] Thus, "from the offenders' perspective, this made such settings ideal for stickups; bystanders are disinclined to get involved and witnesses are reluctant to make a police report."[241] Additionally, the offenders were well aware that the police did not take drug robberies seriously. However, these factors do not consider the one element that makes robbery of drug dealers very risky: "There always is a possibility of violent retaliation" by the drug dealer.[242]

Further analysis of the ethnographic research on the armed robbers in St. Louis by Bruce A. Jacobs, Volkan Topalli, and Richard Wright explored the issue of retaliation by asking "Why should offenders elect to reduce their chances of getting arrested at the cost of increasing their odds of being killed?"[243] To answer this, the researchers looked at the findings from 25 in-depth interviews with active drug robbers, which were conducted as part of the larger study of robbers in St. Louis. The researchers conceptualized retaliation as an informal sanction "capable of deterrence in its own right; to be sure, it may be the sole sanction offenders face."[244] Drug dealers who are victimized are cut off from one avenue of redress, the formal sanctions provided by police, and hence they "have a strong incentive to retaliate."[245]

The drug robbers interviewed in the St. Louis study were completely aware of the risk involved in targeting drug dealers. They sought to minimize this risk by selecting one of three strategies: intimidation, anonymity maintenance, and hypervigilance. As a general guideline, drug robbers primarily targeted dealers "whose retributive potential was weak."[246] These targets were street corner dealers who were fairly inexperienced, sold drugs in small quantities, and held very little if any status in the organized drug trade. Additionally, the drug robbers used "verbal and physical tactics" in their encounters with these dealers that were purposefully designed to intimidate the dealer to the point that the thought of retaliation was almost eliminated. One offender claimed that he approached drug dealers in a way that left no doubt that "I'm gonna retaliate first."[247] Some of the offenders stated that "some street corner dealers simply dismissed robberies as an occupational hazard and accepted their losses with equanimity."[248] The second strategy used by robbers who targeted drug dealers, anonymity maintenance, involved robbing only those dealers with whom they were totally unfamiliar. In this way, "retaliation becomes moot" because the victim does not know the robber.[249] Hypervigilance, the third strategy, refers to how offenders consciously "devoted a significant portion of their day-to-day cognitive resources to minimizing the prospect of postoffense victim contact."[250] For offenders engaged in a substantial volume of robberies, the chances of running into a victim were increased, even if the victim was initially unknown to them.

Offenders avoided the sites of previous robberies until they could be fairly sure that the threat of recognition or retaliation had subsided. The nomadic lifestyle of the drug robbers, involving movement from place to place, allowed them to easily avoid such places.

Even so, the street lifestyle was "an encapsulated social world" and the "streets enmesh participation in an expansive web of relations."[251] To a large extent, circumstances and situations bring offenders and victims together in unexpected ways, such that "the more members of a network there are, and the denser that network is, the more likely run-ins become. Bus stops, mini-malls, grocery stores, bars, theaters, and fast-food restaurants emerge as contexts fraught with potential risk."[252] These features of the environment not only hinder the offender's ability to manage the risk of retaliation, but also increase the potential for violence within the entire community itself, based on the extent of drug robberies. As Jacobs and his colleagues conclude, this community effect represents the "contagion-like processes through which violence is contracted and contained,"[253] and if "street justice" is stronger than the formal justice represented by law enforcement, the community becomes increasingly unstable. "The more entrenched informal justice becomes, and the more likely formal authorities will 'look the other way,'"[254] the more the community becomes disorganized and violence spreads beyond robbers and their victims. This becomes one set of dynamics that creates and sustains the "tangled web of violence we see in so many high-crime urban locales across the country."[255]

The Gendered Nature of Robbery

According to **Jody Miller,** "[w]ith the exception of forcible rape, robbery is perhaps the most gender differentiated serious crime in the United States."[256] Women represent robbery offenders in approximately 11% of all incidents.[257] James W. Messerschmidt contends that the "robbery setting provides the ideal opportunity to construct an 'essential' toughness and 'maleness'. . . . Within the social context that ghetto and barrio boys find themselves, then, robbery is a rational practice for 'doing gender' and for getting money."[258]

Miller's research goal was to assess the extent to which gender organizes robbery offending. To accomplish this, she analyzed a subset of the interviews with active robbers from the research data used by Jacobs and Wright. The sample that Miller used consisted of 37 robbers, 14 of whom were women and 23 of whom were men. The two groups were matched on the characteristics of current age and age at first robbery. In her examination of motivations for robbery, Miller found that economic incentives were the primary motivation among both men and women. There were, however, significant differences in the way in which men and women carried out street robberies. Men exhibited a fairly uniform pattern. Their robberies were characterized by "using physical violence and/or a gun placed on or at close proximity to the victim in a confrontational manner."[259] The presence of a gun was almost a constant in robberies conducted by men. While perceiving women to be easier targets, male robbers tended to rob other men rather than women because of another perception, that men tended to carry more money. The majority of the males targeted as victims were those involved in "street life."

Female robbers, on the other hand, did not exhibit one clear style but instead tended to fall into one of three patterns. The robbery of other women in a "physically confrontational manner" was the most prevalent way in which female robbers worked, but also present were the strategies of using their sexuality to attract male victims and acting as accomplices to male robbers in offenses against other men.[260] Except when robbing men, female robbers as a general rule did not use guns. Miller concludes that, rather than reflecting different motivations, the different strategies for robbery selected by men and women "reflect practical choices made in the context of a gender-stratified environment—one in which, on the whole, men are perceived as strong and women are perceived as weak."[261] While similar cultural and structural forces can drive the offending of men and women in the same way, gender continues to exert an influence on shaping the nature of these interactions in robbery incidents. Learn more about the crime of robbery at **Web Extra 10–8.**

WEB
Extra
▪ ▪ ▪ ▪

Assault

Assault is the "prototype of violent crime."[262] Not only is assault the most common violent crime, but also it is the starting point for more serious incidents of interpersonal violence. While there is a tremendous legal difference between assault and homicide, James Garbarino states that this legal difference has "very limited psychological significance" in that many assaults represent "potentially lethal violence." It is important to understand, he says, that assaults can kill, "even if they don't actually end a human life."[263] Garbarino supports his point by stating that social scientists have a difficult time predicting which person will end up taking a life, and thus it is "more practical to identify [those] who are at greatest risk for engaging in potentially lethal violence."[264]

The profile of a typical offender in aggravated assault mirrors that of homicide, with disproportionate involvement of males, African Americans, 15- to 34-year-olds, those of lower socioeconomic status, those with prior arrest records, and offenders demonstrating little evidence of offense specialization.[265] Also consistent with most homicides, aggravated assaults are "spontaneous, triggered by a trivial altercation or argument that quickly escalates in the heat of passion."[266]

Based on statistics from the NCVS, the overall decline in the crime rate between 1993 and 2006 is primarily due to decreases in the rate of simple assault. In 2006, victims reported 3,505,620 victimizations, a rate of 14.6 per 1,000 residents age 12 or older. The majority of assaults reported by victims are simple rather than aggravated assault. The definition of *aggravated assault* used by the NCVS is "attack or attempted attack with a weapon, regardless of whether or not an injury occurred and attack without a weapon when serious injury results."[267] Aggravated assaults are detailed according to those involving injury and those without injury. The victims and offenders in aggravated assault are for the most part equally likely to be strangers or nonstrangers to each other. When you look at the gender of the victim, a pattern emerges. A slight majority of male victims are assaulted by a stranger, whereas slightly more than one-third (39%) of female victims are assaulted by a stranger in aggravated assaults. Simple assaults, by contrast, are more likely in general to involve nonstrangers (58%). Almost one-half (47%) of male victims are assaulted by nonstrangers, whereas 71% of female victims are assaulted by nonstrangers in these cases. Whether it is an aggravated or a simple assault, the largest category of nonstranger offenders of female victims is represented by friends and acquaintances, followed by intimate partners. Weapons are present in less than one-fourth (23%) of all assaults, and when a weapon is present, it is most likely to be something other than a gun or a knife.[268]

Stranger Assault

The possibility of stranger violence elicits a great deal of fear and concern among most members of the population. Based on research using victimization data in both the United States and Great Britain, "the probability of suffering a serious personal crime by strangers is very low,"[269] with this likelihood varying by demographic characteristics like gender, age, marital status, and lifestyle. For example, individuals who have an active social life away from home and in the evening are far more likely to be victimized by strangers, but this effect depends very much on the community context in which the individuals engage in their leisure pursuits.

Marc Riedel and Roger K. Przybylski propose that stranger violence consists of two primary types of stranger relationships.[270] One type of violence between strangers results from the "exploitation of a setting," as is often the case in robberies in which the offenders case the store in advance.[271] Some encounters between strangers, however, are less calculated, and violence can "emerge from more spontaneous encounters between strangers in routine settings such as bars or sporting events."[272] Generally, this is the situation of the typical assault, where something as benign as an offensive remark escalates into violence. Because "confrontational stranger violence occurs in [certain types of] public settings," there is a strong likelihood that assault victims and offenders will be about the same age. Settings in which assaults frequently occur, such as bars, are generally restricted on the basis of age, and they "acquire local reputations that attract a clientele that is usually homogeneous in age."[273] Thus, compared with assaults within the family, stranger assaults are more likely to involve victims and offenders of similar ages.

Assault within Families

As the statistics from several sources reveal, the majority of assaults involve victims and offenders who are known to each other, quite often in a familial or an intimate relationship. In the sections that follow, the familial context of assault is examined, with a special emphasis on how key variables like weapons, alcohol, and other factors help us understand the patterns of these crimes.

Invading the Castle

The current societal awareness of issues surrounding violence among family members did not arise primarily from within criminology. While the statistics on homicide have long supported the violent potential of families, criminologists were not the pioneers in studies centered on the violent aspects of our society's most basic institution. Richard J. Gelles, a leading family-violence researcher, correctly asserted in the 1970s that violence within the family concerned criminologists only when someone was killed.[274] Criminology as a discipline began to give more attention to violent behavior within the family just as societal attention turned to viewing the halo of privacy that has long surrounded the family with a bit more scrutiny. Empirical research concerning the phenomenon of family violence encounters several problems due to the nature of the issue itself. The family as a social institution is intensely private. The discussion of physical, emotional, and sexual violence among family members violates this privacy. These types of abuse also represent extremely sensitive parts of a person's experience, which individuals may be reluctant to discuss. The very terrain of family violence invades the "image of the castle [which] implies freedom from interference from outsiders."[275] This image was corroborated in the late 1970s when Michael Hindelang conducted research on crime-reporting behavior. Two of the most common reasons for not reporting crimes to the police were that it was a "private matter" and that there might be reprisal from the offender. Current research shows that such rationales supporting nonreporting continue to characterize incidents involving violence among family members.[276]

Early Studies of Family Violence

The initial research on violence within the family came from official records and small clinical studies. Official records consistently revealed that women were more likely than men to become victims of domestic violence. Based on an examination of emergency room victims in the late 1970s, Evan Stark and colleagues found that approximately 25% of all women who had been injured had been the victim of a spousal attack.[277] Murray Straus and colleagues at the University of New Hampshire were the first to develop a survey methodology for the study of family violence nationally. They conducted the first National Survey on Family Violence (NSFV) in 1975 with a representative sample of 2,146 families. The second NSFV was conducted in 1985 with a sample of 4,032 households.[278] In both surveys, the key tool developed for measuring family violence was the Conflict Tactics Scale. This scale contains a series of 18 items that range from calm discussion to the use of a potentially lethal weapon. The questions using this measure are presented in the context of disagreements with family members and how such disagreements are resolved. The questions initially ask about positive techniques, such as calmly discussing an issue, and gradually proceed to more coercive tactics, such as using a knife on a family member. The sequence in which questions are asked serves to facilitate responses. The questions begin with parent-child relationships, where the use of physical force, such as spanking, is widely viewed as legitimate, and then proceeds to husband-wife relationships. By the time respondents reach the questions concerning spousal behavior, Straus reasoned that familiarity with the questions would diminish the respondent's uneasiness about answering whether he or she had ever hit a spouse.[279] The rate of violence between spouses in the 1985 National Survey on Family Violence was 161 per 1,000 couples.[280] While this rate was lower than that reported in 1975, it still remained higher than estimates produced from other studies not specifically directed at family violence, such as the NCVS.

Current Survey Information on Family Violence

In the years since survey research was first used to estimate violence against family members, other surveys have emerged to assess this phenomenon, and existing data sources have been improved to better measure family violence. The FBI has begun releasing specialized reports based on available National Incident-Based Reporting System (NIBRS) data. As explained in Chapter 2, NIBRS provides the data gathering methodology that will one day replace older data formats used by the FBI's Uniform Crime Reporting Program. As originally constituted, the UCR Program did not include information on victims and offenders for offenses other than homicide, so data from the program did not lend itself to an analysis of nonlethal criminal behavior within the family. NIBRS data will provide for such a possibility, and will allow for more specialized data analysis. Nineteen states submitted data in NIBRS format for 2006, and the FBI compiled a special report on these data based on an analysis of family incidents. Using a measure of violent crime that includes murder, rape, robbery, and assault, recent NIBRS data revealed that 51% of violent crimes involved victims and offenders who were related. Among all offenses involving family members that came to the attention of the police, the overwhelming majority (94%) were assaults, a percentage that is "4 points higher than the frequency of assault offenses in overall crimes of violence."[281] Thus, while assault is the most frequently occurring violent crime both among the general population and within the family, the percentage is even higher within the family. While aggravated assault accounted for 18% of all violent offenses, the percentage of all family violence offenses involving aggravated assaults is slightly smaller at 15%.[282]

Compared with aggravated assaults generally, firearms are less likely to be used within the family, where fists, hands, and knives are more common. A slight majority of aggravated assault offenses involve some type of injury both in the general population (57.5%) and within the family (60.8%). Women are more likely to be the victims of both aggravated assaults and simple assaults within the family than in the general population (60% versus 41% and 72% versus 60%, respectively).[283] Learn more about family violence and the crimes it entails via Web Extra 10–9.

WEB
Extra
▪ ▪ ▪ ▪

Intimate-Partner Assault

Intimate-partner assault is one of several terms used to characterize assaultive behavior that takes place between individuals involved in an intimate relationship. Several researchers have noted that terms like *spouse assault* are inappropriate because they give the misleading impression that male and female spouses are equally likely to be victims.[284] Based on research using various data sources, the overwhelming majority of victims of marital violence within heterosexual relationships are women. This empirical reality does not deny that men can be the victims of violence at the hands of their wives; it merely states that based on official records, self-reports, hospital emergency room records, and small clinical samples, it is women who emerge as victims. It is in line with this empirical reality that Neil Websdale entitles his ethnographic exploration of violence in rural areas of Kentucky *Rural Woman Battering and the Justice System*.[285] However, the terms *woman battering* and *wife assault* are biased in terms of heterosexual relationships, and hence some researchers now use the term *intimate-partner assault* because it avoids this bias. We will use this term in our discussion because it now frequently appears in the literature on assault among intimates and because it reflects the changing nature of most sexual assault laws and mandatory arrest laws,

intimate-partner assault

A gender-neutral term used to characterize assaultive behavior that takes place between individuals involved in an intimate relationship.

which are both becoming gender neutral and moving away from the legal relationship as the criterion that defines an intimate relationship.

For many individuals, the notion of assault between intimate partners gives rise to the response "If I was hit, I would leave." This type of response places the burden on the victim to justify why she stayed and takes the burden off the offending behavior of her partner. More crucially, this type of response ignores the reality that most women do leave violent relationships, a behavior that may trigger a particularly violent response by the male partner, labeled **separation assault** by Martha R. Mahoney.[286] Separation assault clearly illustrates what feminists like Liz Kelly mean when they state that "the use of explicit force/violence is in fact a response to the failure of, or resistance to, other forms of control."[287] A woman who attempts to leave a violent relationship is seen as violating the right of her husband to control her, and even if she does manage to leave, many times the husband will follow her and attempt to take her back. Neil Websdale offers a dramatic example of separation assault from the ethnographic research that he conducted in the early 1990s. Glenda Greer worked as a secretary in a local elementary school in Waynesburg, Kentucky, for 11 years. She was a respected member of the community and had come to have an important place in the lives of many children at her school. Glenda had filed for divorce from her husband, Shannon Greer, based on a pattern of abuse within the marriage. On May 11, 1990, Shannon Greer walked into his soon-to-be-former wife's place of employment and shot her with a 12-gauge shotgun, killing her. He then left the school, drove down a back road, and killed himself. When the police found Shannon Greer's body, the divorce papers were in the car, and scribbled on the papers was a note written by Shannon Greer that said, "There was not a divorce."[288] While not all assaults upon women by their male partners end in homicide, the reality is that some most certainly have,[289] and the dynamics that leaving often sets into motion should be remembered. According to a judge interviewed by James Ptacek in a study on judicial treatment of women applying for restraining orders, the increased awareness of the judiciary concerning the seriousness of assaults among intimate partners means that "no judge wants to be the one who didn't grant a restraining order to the woman found face down in the morning."[290]

Violent relationships between intimate partners are characterized by a cycle of violence in which numerous forms of social control may be used. Neil Websdale maintains that in rural communities, the relative geographic isolation of most families makes it easy for men who batter their wives to also control their movement and everyday activities. Men in Websdale's research disconnected telephone lines, disabled cars, and threatened women at their place of work. These actions narrowed the abused partner's options to leave, especially in the case of women in rural settings where powerful notions of family loyalty and gender roles work against leaving as an option. As Websdale notes in his research, many women who are battered by their husbands must face the fact that if they leave their husbands, they will, in effect, be leaving their communities. Physical assaults often involve other tactics of abuse, such as emotional abuse and attacks or threats against children. This is especially salient in that most women who have reported abuse by intimate partners also had dependent children.[291]

In analyzing the cases of women in two counties in Massachusetts who applied for restraining orders during 1992 and 1993, as well as observations in the courtroom, **James Ptacek** developed a typology of the type of strategies that men used to control women in violent relationships.[292] Ptacek analyzed both the types of abuse that women reported in their petitions for restraining orders and the rationales that the women provided in their affidavits that "gave some indication of the objectives behind the men's violence and abuse."[293] In 18% of the cases, the woman reported that her male partner had used violence to prevent her from leaving, and in 22% of the cases, the woman reported that violence was used to get back at her for leaving. Ptacek argues that women are assaulted in the process of leaving their abusers, and some of the incidents of separation assault had occurred more than a year following legal separation or divorce. Another tactic used by men was "punishment, coercion, and retaliation against women's actions concerning children,"[294] which could take several forms. Some men

---

separation assault

Violence inflicted by partners on significant others who attempt to leave an intimate relationship.

attacked their wives during pregnancy, other men attacked women who challenged their parental authority over the children, and still other men attacked partners who had requested child support through the courts. In about 12% of the cases, the affidavits of women revealed that men used violence in response to other types of legal action. Ptacek labeled this "retaliation or coercion against women's pursuit of court or police remedies," in which the men responded with violence to actions that women were thought to have taken, whether those actions were real or imaginary. The final motivation for the violence of males was "retaliation for other perceived challenges to authority." These challenges included comments that the woman made concerning her male partner's behavior, ranging from drinking behavior to financial matters. As with the other motivational categories, the challenge to male authority was viewed as actionable, and violence was considered a justified course of action.[295] Ethnographic research like that of Neil Websdale and James Ptacek is an important avenue for increasing our knowledge of intimate-partner violence. Another source of recent information is survey research, specifically the NVAW Survey, which was mentioned earlier in this chapter.

One goal of the NVAW Survey was to estimate both the extent and the nature of physical abuse among intimate partners. At some point during their lifetime, 22% of women and slightly more than 7% of men report having been physically assaulted by an intimate partner. During the study year, slightly more than 1% of women and less than 1% of men reported physical assault by an intimate partner. The vast majority of the specific behaviors considered to be physical assault were acts like grabbing and shoving rather than more serious acts involving a gun or knife. Among both same-sex and opposite-sex relationships, males most often perpetrate intimate-partner violence. "Same-sex cohabiting women were nearly three times more likely to report being victimized by a male partner [in the past] than by a female partner."[296] The increased risk of assault for both men and women who are separated from intimate partners was also confirmed in the NVAW Survey. Both men and women who were separated from their partners were more likely to report physical assault than those currently living with their partners. This supports Ptacek's findings, as well as other research that establishes that leaving an abusive partner is common, as is the violence that follows.[297]

On the extent of injury in intimate-partner assaults, the NVAW Survey reveals that women are more likely than men to report injuries and that most of the injuries received are minor in nature. More findings from the NVAW Survey are presented in the section of this chapter that examines stalking. Learn more about intimate-partner violence via Web Extra 10–10.

WEB
Extra
∎ ∎ ∎ ∎

Workplace Violence

On January 30, 2006, former postal worker Jennifer San Marco, 44, committed the United States' deadliest workplace shooting by a woman when she shot and killed eight people and herself.[298] San Marco's shooting spree began at the home of a former neighbor in Goleta, California, and ended when she shot six workers at a Santa Barbara County mail processing facility a short time later. San Marco, who had once worked at the mail facility, had been removed from the processing center by sheriff's deputies in 2001 and sent for a psychiatric examination after coworkers said she had been acting irrationally. In June 2003, the U.S. Postal Service placed San Marco on retirement, citing psychological problems.

Workplace violence is a significant problem in America today, and incidents of workplace violence are more common than generally believed. According to the FBI, "workplace violence is now recognized as a specific category of violent crime that calls for distinct responses from employers, law enforcement, and the community."[299] Workplace violence includes murder, rape, robbery, and assault committed against persons who are at work or on duty. On average, 1.7 million nonfatal, violent workplace victimizations are committed every year. Assaults, both simple and aggravated, account for the largest number of workplace violence incidents, affecting approximately 11.7 out of every 1,000 persons in the workforce annually. Another 900 or so work-related homicides

workplace violence

The crimes of murder, rape, robbery, and assault committed against persons who are at work or on duty.

FIGURE 10–3

Annual Rate of Violent Workplace Victimization by Occupation

Source: Detis T. Duhart, *Violence in the Workplace, 1993–99* (Washington, DC: Bureau of Justice Statistics, 2001), p. 4.

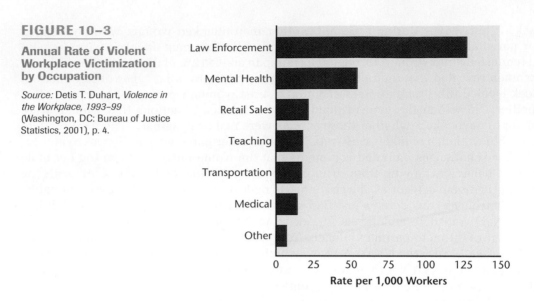

occur annually. Workplace violence accounts for approximately 18% of all violent crime that occurs in the United States. As might be expected, police officers experience workplace violence at rates higher than persons employed in any other occupation, while college or university professors are among persons least likely to be victimized (Figure 10–3).

All workplace violence falls into four broad categories, as follows:

Type 1: Violent acts by criminals who have no other connection with the workplace, but enter to commit robbery, acts of terrorism, or another crime.

Type 2: Violence directed at employees by customers, clients, patients, students, inmates, or any others for whom an organization provides services.

Type 3: Violence against coworkers, supervisors, or managers by a present or former employee.

Type 4: Violence committed in the workplace by someone who doesn't work there, but has a personal relationship with an employee, such as an abusive spouse or domestic partner.

Type 1 violence, or violence committed by criminals otherwise unconnected to the workplace, accounts for nearly 80 percent of all workplace homicides.[300] In such incidents the motive is usually theft, and in a great many cases the criminal is carrying a gun or other weapon, increasing the likelihood that the victim will be killed or seriously wounded. This type of violence falls heavily on particular occupational groups whose jobs make them vulnerable: for example, taxi drivers, late-night retail or gas station clerks, and others who are on duty at night, who work in isolated locations or dangerous neighborhoods, and who carry or have access to cash.

Type 2 workplace violence typically involves assaults on an employee by a customer, patient, or someone else receiving a service.[301] In general, the violent acts occur as workers are performing their daily tasks. In some occupations, dealing with dangerous people is a part of the job, as in the case of police officers, correctional officers, security guards, or some mental health workers. For those in other occupations, violent reactions by a customer or client are unpredictable, and may be triggered by an argument, anger at the quality of service or denial of service, delays, or some other precipitating event.

Employees experiencing the largest number of Type 2 assaults are those in health-care occupations—nurses in particular, as well as doctors, and aides who deal with psychiatric patients; members of emergency medical response teams; and hospital employees working in admissions, emergency rooms, and crisis or acute care units. Type 3 and Type 4 violence—incidents involving violence by past or present employees and acts committed by domestic abusers or arising from other personal relationships that

Workplace shooter Michael "Mucko" McDermott. On December 26, 2000, the 43-year-old software consultant killed seven people with an AK-47 automatic rifle at the offices of his former employer, Edgewater Technologies, in Wakefield, Massachusetts. In 2002, McDermott was convicted of seven counts of first-degree murder and sentenced to seven consecutive life terms. Defense attorneys had maintained that McDermott was mentally ill at the time of the killings, but prosecutors said that he was angry over company plans to garnish his wages to pay back taxes. Can anything be done to reduce the number of incidents of workplace violence?

Source: AP Wide World Photos

follow an employee into the workplace—is often the kind of workplace violence reported in the media. Violence in these categories is no less damaging than any other violent act, but when the violence comes from an employee or someone close to an employee, there is a much greater chance that some warning sign will have reached the employer prior to the violent act.

A recent Bureau of Justice Statistics study reveals the following facts about workplace violence.[302]

- Private-sector and federal government employees are victimized at similar rates.
- More than 80% of all workplace homicides are committed with a firearm.
- Rape and sexual assault, robbery, and homicide account for a small percentage (6%) of all workplace violent crime. The majority of workplace violent incidents (almost 19 of every 20) are aggravated or simple assaults.
- Except for rape and sexual assault, males experience more workplace violence than do females. About two-thirds of all robberies, aggravated assaults, and simple assaults in the workplace are committed against males.
- Persons aged 20–34 experience workplace violence at a rate higher than any other age group.
- The workplace violent crime rate for whites (13 per 1,000 in the workforce) is 25% higher than the black rate (10 per 1,000) and 59% higher than the rate for other races (8 per 1,000). Whites experience more than four-fifths of all rapes and sexual assaults (88%), robberies (81%), aggravated assaults (86%), and simple assaults (89%) occurring in the workplace. This contrasts with overall violent crime (including both workplace and nonworkplace violence), for which blacks have the highest rates.
- Most workplace victimizations are intraracial. About 6 in 10 white and black victims of workplace crime perceived their assailant to be of the same race.

- Almost 4 of every 10 robberies occurring while the victim was at work or on duty are committed against persons in retail sales or transportation.
- Twelve percent of all workplace violence victims sustain injuries from the incident. Of those injuries sustained from workplace violence incidents, about 10 out of 11 are minor injuries.

The National Institute for Occupational Safety and Health (NIOSH)[303] recommends a number of prevention strategies that may lower the incidence of workplace violence, including environmental design factors that physically separate workers from customers: bullet-resistant barriers or enclosures, high counters to prevent customer access to workers and goods, and limited avenues of access and egress.[304] Also recommended are enhanced administrative controls such as staffing plans and work practices that include the prescreening of patients or customers and the training and education of employees in conflict resolution strategies.

Visit NIOSH's occupational violence center to learn more about workplace violence and techniques to prevent it at **Web Extra 10–11** at crimtoday.com. Read a Bureau of Justice Assistance survey of workplace violence at **Library Extra 10–7**, and learn about recommendations for curtailing workplace violence from the FBI at **Library Extra 10–8**. A Canadian perspective on workplace violence is available at **Library Extra 10–9**.

WEB
Extra
■ ■ ■ ■

LIBRARY
Extra
■ ■ ■ ■

Stalking

stalking

A course of conduct directed at a specific person that involves repeated visual or physical proximity; nonconsensual communication; verbal, written, or implied threats; or a combination thereof that would cause a reasonable person fear.

While **stalking** behavior is not new, the labeling of this behavior as one worthy of societal concern, and undesirable enough to be criminalized, is relatively new. Several high-profile cases have illustrated the dangerous potential of stalking behavior. John Hinkley was obsessed with actress Jodie Foster and thought to capture her attention and admiration by shooting then–President Ronald Reagan in 1981. Mark David Chapman, the man who shot John Lennon in 1980, considered himself to be "one of Lennon's biggest fans." Talk-show host David Letterman was stalked from 1988 to 1993 by a woman who professed her love for him by breaking into his house repeatedly, trespassing on his property, and stealing his car. While the high-profile cases may capture media attention because they involve celebrities, stalking often involves average individuals as they go about their lives.

The first antistalking statute was passed in 1990 in California.[305] At present, all states and the federal government have antistalking laws. Rather than being an offense that occurs once, stalking is conceptualized as a pattern of behavior that causes victims to fear for their personal safety. The definition used in the Model Antistalking Code for States, developed by the National Institute of Justice, is "a course of conduct directed at a specific person that involves repeated visual or physical proximity, nonconsensual communication, or verbal, written or implied threats, or a combination thereof, that would cause a reasonable person fear."[306] *Repeated* is defined to mean at least two occasions. Individual antistalking laws vary in terms of the type of definition given to the term *repeated* and in terms of the requirements connected to threats by the perpetrator and fear by the victim. While the majority of states require that the perpetrator make a "credible threat," some states include threats against family members. Other states demand that the conduct of the perpetrator constitute an implied threat, and they evaluate this in relation to the level of fear expressed by the victim.[307]

Statutory definitions of *stalking* encompass a number of diverse but interrelated behaviors, such as making phone calls, following the victim, sending letters, making threats in some manner, vandalizing property, and watching the victim. Rather than viewing these behaviors in isolation from one another, antistalking laws take into account the totality of the circumstances, so that seemingly benign behaviors are seen in light of how they are connected to other behaviors. This acknowledges that while sending unwanted letters might be seen as innocuous behavior, when this activity is combined with following the victim and standing outside his or her place of work or residence, the behavior takes on a more threatening tone and may be the precursor for more serious offenses like assault, rape, and murder.[308]

The Extent of Stalking

The only national-level data on the nature and extent of stalking come from the NVAW Survey. The survey data are used in several of the sections that follow to identify and characterize a number of the key issues concerning stalking. The definition of *stalking* used in the NVAW Survey closely follows that in the Model Antistalking Code for States.[309] For the behaviors in their totality to satisfy the definition of *stalking* used in the NVAW Survey, the respondents had to have reported victimization on more than one occasion and to have reported they were "very frightened or feared bodily harm."[310]

The same definition of *stalking* was used to ask individuals to report the relevant experiences both over their lifetime and during the past 12 months. In the late 1990s, approximately 8% of women and 2% of men reported being stalked at some point during their life. Using the survey data to generate estimates for the general population, this means that about 1 in every 12 women (8.2 million) and 1 in every 45 men (2 million) are stalked at some point in their life. The annual prevalence rate was 1% of all women surveyed and 0.4% of all men, translating to roughly 1,006,970 women and 370,990 men every year. An overwhelming majority (90%) of individuals surveyed reported being stalked by only one individual during their life.[311] These estimates were based on the strictest definition of *stalking,* which required that in addition to repeated behaviors that fall within the scope of stalking, the survey respondent had to report a high level of fear. When a lower threshold of fear is used to construct the measure, the estimates are even higher: 12% of women and 4% of men reported being stalked at some point in their life, and 6% of women and 1.5% of men reported being stalked annually.[312]

Upon examination of the type of behaviors that stalkers engaged in, Patricia Tjaden and Nancy Thoennes, the principal investigators for the NVAW Survey, concluded that antistalking laws that require that an overt threat be made against the victim before action can be taken against the stalker are ill-advised. While victims reported high levels of fear, stalkers in less than half of the cases made overt threats. In the case of both male and female victims, the vast majority reported being followed or spied on in some way; many received unwanted telephone calls, and many reported receiving unwanted items through the mail and being victims of vandalism.[313]

Types of Stalkers

A 1999 psychiatric study of 145 Canadian stalkers who had been referred to a forensic psychiatry center for treatment found that most were men (79%), and that many were unemployed (39%).[314] Perhaps not surprisingly, most (52%) had never had an intimate relationship. Five types of stalkers were identified as follows:

- **rejected stalkers** who pursue their victims in order to reverse, correct, or avenge a felt rejection (for example, divorce, separation, termination).
- **intimacy seeking stalkers** who want to establish an intimate, loving relationship with their victims. They may see the victim as a soul mate with whom they are fated to be.
- **incompetent suitors** who have a romantic or sexual interest in their victims despite having poor social or courting skills.
- **resentful vendetta-motivated stalkers** who act out of a sense of wrong or a grievance against their victims. Their intent is generally to frighten and distress the victim.
- **predatory stalkers** who spy on their victims in preparation for attacks, which are usually sexual in nature.

LIBRARY
Extra
■ ■ ■ ■

Delusional disorders were found to be common among the stalkers treated, and 30% were determined to suffer consistently from delusions about those they stalked. Stalking behavior among those studied lasted anywhere from 4 weeks to 20 years, with an average of 12 months. Rejected and intimacy-seeking stalkers tended to persist the longest in stalking behavior. Sixty-three percent of the stalkers made threats toward their victims, and 36% were assaultive. The researchers concluded that "Stalkers have a range of motivations, from reasserting power over a partner who rejected them to the quest for a loving relationship." Read more about the types of stalkers identified in the social scientific literature and their motivations at **Library Extra 10–10** at crimtoday.com.

Victim–Offender Relationships in Stalking

The majority of stalking victims identified in the NVAW Survey are women (78%, or four out of every five victims). The majority of individuals who stalk are men; 94% of women and 60% of men identify a male as the stalker. The majority of stalking victims are young, with 52% between the ages of 18 and 29 and 22% between the ages of 30 and 39. Results from the NVAW Survey confirmed previous research that showed that the majority of victims know their stalker. A stranger was identified as the stalker in only 23% of the cases where a woman was stalked and 36% of the cases where a man was stalked. For women who are stalked, the majority (59%) are more likely to be stalked by an intimate partner than by a stranger, an acquaintance, or a relative other than the spouse. On the other hand, the majority of men are stalked by strangers or acquaintances (70%), usually a male in both cases (90%). Tjaden and Thoennes state that while there is no clear explanation for this finding, it may be related to a greater risk of stalking among homosexual as opposed to heterosexual men. The survey found that stalking was more likely to be experienced by male respondents who indicated that they had lived as a couple with another male. According to Tjaden and Thoennes, "In some stalking cases involving male victims and stranger or acquaintance perpetrators, the perpetrator may be motivated by hatred toward homosexuals, while in others the perpetrator may be motivated by sexual attraction."[315] The belief that stalkers suffer from mental illness or personality disorder was not confirmed by the survey findings, as only 7% of the victims stated that they were stalked by offenders who were "mentally ill or abusing drugs or alcohol."[316]

Stalking in Intimate–Partner Relationships

Almost one-fourth (21%) of female respondents in the NVAW Survey who had been stalked by an intimate partner stated that they were stalked before the end of the relationship, 43% indicated that the stalking occurred after the relationship had ended, and slightly over one-third (36%) reported that they were stalked both before and after the end of the relationship with their partner.[317] The survey found that other forms of violence often accompany stalking. For women stalked by an intimate partner, 81% were also physically assaulted and almost one-third were sexually assaulted by their stalker. The percentage of women experiencing assault of either kind by a current or former intimate partner who stalked them was higher than the percentage experiencing some form of assault but no stalking (20% of women who had ever married or lived with a male partner had experienced physical assault by that partner and 5% had experienced sexual assault).[318] Men who stalked their former wives were "significantly more likely than ex-husbands who did not stalk to engage in emotionally abusive and controlling behavior toward their wife."[319]

Consequences of Stalking

Respondents in the NVAW Survey reported a number of diverse consequences of stalking that affected their life negatively. Women who had been stalked reported a significantly higher level of concern for their personal safety than those who had not been stalked. Almost one-third reported seeking counseling, and slightly more than one-fourth lost time from work due to the stalking incidents. Women took a variety of extra self-protective measures as a response to the stalking, with 17% stating they had bought a gun, 11% stating they had changed residences, and 11% stating they had moved out of state. The women who had been stalked were more likely than the men to have obtained a protective order against their stalker (23% versus 10%, respectively).[320]

Since the definition used in the NVAW Survey to assess stalking required high levels of fear on the part of victims, it is worthwhile to explore the data on whether the victims reported these activities to the police. A higher percentage of women than men reported the stalking to police (55% versus 48%, respectively). When asked reasons for not reporting to the police, the responses of stalking victims were consistent with the more general reasons often given for not reporting crimes to the police: 20% defined it as not a police matter, 17% did not believe the police could do anything, 16% were afraid of reprisal from the stalker, 12% resolved it on their own, and smaller percentages reported that the police would not believe them or that it was a private matter.[321] Responses to questions on satisfaction with law enforcement's handling of the case indicated that about half of respondents approved of police procedure. In cases where an arrest was made in the stalking, three-fourths of the victims in those cases were satisfied with the police handling of the case.[322]

Cyberstalking

Another type of stalking, **cyberstalking,** has received attention as efforts progress to better understand the consequences of our increased reliance on electronic communication and the Internet.[323] While no standard definition of *cyberstalking* exists, this term refers to the use of electronic communication like e-mail or the Internet to harass individuals. A 1999 report from then–Attorney General Janet Reno made the following recommendations to help control cyberstalking:[324]

cyberstalking

An array of high-technology related activities in which an offender may engage to harass or "follow" individuals, including e-mail and the Internet.

- A review of all stalking laws at the state level is needed to ensure that provisions for cyberstalking are included.
- An amendment to federal law is needed to make transmission of communication in specified forms of commerce actionable if the intent involves threatening behavior or causes the recipient fear.
- Training on cyberstalking should be offered at all levels of law enforcement.
- A Web site with information on cyberstalking should be created and made available to the public.

WEB
Extra
■ ■ ■ ■

LIBRARY
Extra
■ ■ ■ ■

Learn more about the crime of stalking from the Stalking Resource Center run by the National Center for Victims of Crime at **Web Extra 10–12**, and read an article describing the growing use of technology and other menacing stalking behaviors at **Library Extra 10–11**. Find out more about the activities of cyberstalkers and how to combat the crime of cyberstalking at **Library Extra 10–12** at crimtoday.com.

SUMMARY

Violent offending is a very diverse activity that ranges from cold-blooded, calculated murder to simple assaults that result in little to no injury. Biosocial factors, weapon availability, developmental factors, and the victim-offender relationship have all influenced the violent crime typologies developed by different researchers. Homicide represents the rarest form of violent crime and can take many forms, ranging from the terror caused by serial killing and mass murder to the shock and confusion associated with murder in intimate settings. Patterns of murder have been found to vary along subcultural dimensions and along social structural dimensions, such as economic inequality and community social disorganization. The unique motivational context of homicide has been the subject of extensive research for some time.

This chapter points out that workplace violence is a significant problem in America today, and incidents of workplace violence are more common than generally believed. Workplace violence includes murder, rape, robbery, and assault committed against persons who are at work or on duty.

KEY TERMS

acquaintance rape, 403

child sexual abuse (CSA), 411

crime typology, 383

cyberstalking, 433

exposure-reduction theory, 386

expressive crime, 385

institutional robbery, 416

instrumental crime, 385

intimate-partner assault, 425

mass murder, 392

National Violence against Women
  (NVAW) Survey, 396

nonprimary homicide, 385

personal robbery, 416

primary homicide, 385

rape myth, 397

rape shield law, 400

selective disinhibition, 390

separation assault, 426

serial murder, 392

sibling offense, 386

spousal rape, 404

stalking, 430

victim precipitation, 387

Violence Against Women Act (VAWA), 396

Violent Criminal Apprehension
  Program (VICAP), 394

workplace violence, 427

KEY NAMES

Larry Baron, 407

Ann Burgess, 408

Andrea Dworkin, 405

James Alan Fox, 392

Nicholas Groth, 406

Robert R. Hazelwood, 408

Julie Horney, 400

Mary P. Koss, 403

Jack Levin, 392

Catherine MacKinnon, 405

Jody Miller, 422

Craig T. Palmer, 407

Robert Nash Parker, 390

James Ptacek, 426

Diana E. H. Russell, 404

Diana Scully, 410

Cassia Spohn, 400

Murray A. Straus, 407

Randy Thornhill, 407

Neil Websdale, 406

QUESTIONS FOR REVIEW

1. What is a typology? What are some of the typologies of violent crime that this chapter discusses?

2. What are the key issues to be considered in explaining patterns of homicide?

3. What are the key issues to be considered in explaining as well as preventing the crimes of rape and child sexual abuse?

4. What are the different kinds of robbery that this chapter discusses? Describe the criminal careers of robbers.

5. What different kinds of assault can be identified? Describe what is known about intimate partner violence.

6. Provide a useful definition of *workplace violence*. What do we know about the offense?

7. Explain the major patterns of stalking.

QUESTIONS FOR REFLECTION

1. Why are crime typologies useful for understanding patterns of violent crime?

2. Are violent crimes primarily rational activities?

3. Why was rape law reform necessary? What have been the beneficial aspects of reform for rape victims?

4. Is robbery primarily a rational activity? Why or why not?

WEB QUEST

Visit the FBI's National Center for the Analysis of Violent Crime (NCAVC) on the Web at www.fbi.gov/hq/isd/cirg/ncavc.htm. NCAVC, part of the FBI's Critical Incident Response Group, investigates and researches unusual and repetitive violent crimes in this country and abroad.

Describe in your own words the three major organizational components of NCAVC and explain the mission of each. Submit your completed assignment to your instructor if asked to do so.

NOTES

1 Albert J. Reiss, Jr., and Jeffrey A. Roth, eds., *Understanding and Preventing Violence* (Washington, DC: National Academy Press, 1993), p. xi.

2 Terance D. Miethe and Richard C. McCorkle, *Crime Profiles: The Anatomy of Dangerous Persons, Places, and Situations* (Los Angeles: Roxbury, 1998), p. 19.

3 Marcus Felson, *Crime and Everyday Life* (Thousand Oaks, CA: Pine Forge, 1998), p. 34.

4 Steven Rose, *Times Higher Education Supplement,* Vol. 10 (1995), p. ii.

5 Details for this story come from Elaine Cassel, "The Tragedy at Virginia Tech: Cho Seung Hui and the Psychology of School Shooters," http://writ.news.findlaw.com/cassel/20070420.html, from which some of the wording in this paragraph is taken.

6 "Killer's Manifesto: 'You Forced Me into a Corner,'" CNN.com, April 18, 2007, http://www.cnn.com/2007/US/04/18/vtech. shooting (accessed June 17, 2007).

7 Ian Shapria and Michael E. Ruane, "Student Who Wrote About Death and Spoke in Whispers, But No One Imagined What Cho Seung Hui Would Do," *Washington Post,* April 18, 2007, p. A1.

8 Ibid. Includes only homicides in which the offender is known.

9 Miethe and McCorkle, *Crime Profiles,* p. 2.

10 Neil Alan Weiner and Marvin E. Wolfgang, eds., *Violent Crime, Violent Criminals* (Thousand Oaks, CA: Sage, 1989).

11 Federal Bureau of Investigation, *Crime in the United States, 2006.*

12 Ibid. Includes only homicides in which the offender is known.

13 Ibid.

14 Marvin Wolfgang and Franco Ferracuti, *The Subculture of Violence: Towards an Integrated Theory in Criminology* (1967; reprint, Beverly Hills, CA: Sage, 1982).

15 Marc Reidel and Margaret A. Zahn, *The Nature and Patterns of American Homicide* (Washington, DC: U.S. Government Printing Office, 1985). See also Margaret A. Zahn and P. C. Sagi, "Stranger Homicide in Nine American Cities," *Journal of Criminal Law and Criminology,* Vol. 78, No. 2 (1987), pp. 377–397.

16 Kirk R. Williams and Robert L. Flewelling, "The Social Production of Criminal Homicide: A Comparative Study of Disaggregated Rates in American Cities," *American Sociological Review,* Vol. 53, No. 3 (1988), pp. 421–431.

17 Lynne A. Curtis, *American Violence and Public Policy* (New Haven, CT: Yale University Press, 1985); and Lynne A. Curtis, *Violence, Race and Culture* (Lexington, MA: Lexington Books, 1975).

18 Claude S. Fisher, "Toward a Subcultural Theory of Urbanism," *American Journal of Sociology,* Vol. 80 (1975), p. 1335.

19 Steven Messner, "Poverty, Inequality and Urban Homicide Rate," *Criminology,* Vol. 20 (1982), pp. 103–114; and Steven Messner, "Regional and Racial Effects on the Urban Homicide Rate," *American Journal of Sociology,* Vol. 88 (1983), pp. 997–1007.

20 Robert Sampson, "Neighborhood Family Structure and the Risk of Personal Victimization," in James Byrne and Robert J. Sampson, eds., *The Social Ecology of Crime* (New York: Springer-Verlag, 1985); and Robert J. Sampson, "Structural Sources in Variation in Race-Age Specific Rates of Offending across Major U.S. Cities," *Criminology,* Vol. 23, No. 4 (1985), pp. 647–673.

21 S. Hackney, "Southern Violence," in H. D. Graham and T. R. Gurr, eds., *History of Violence in America: Report of the Task Force on Historical and Comparative Perspectives to the National Commission on the Causes and Prevention of Violence* (New York: Bantam, 1960), pp. 505–528; and L. W. Shannon, "The Spatial Distribution of Criminal Offenses by States," *Journal of Criminal Law, Criminology, and Police Science,* Vol. 45 (1954), pp. 264–273.

22 Hackney, "Southern Violence"; Wolfgang and Ferracuti, *The Subculture of Violence.*

23 R. D. Gastil, "Homicides and a Regional Culture of Violence," *American Sociological Review,* Vol. 36 (1971), pp. 412–427; Hackney, "Southern Violence."

24 Colin Loftin and R. H. Hill, "Regional Subculture and Homicide: A Comparison of the Gastil-Hackney Thesis," *American Sociological Review,* Vol. 39 (1974), pp. 714–724.

25 Ibid.

26 Emile Durkheim, *Suicide: A Study in Sociology* (1951; reprint, Glencoe, IL: Free Press, 1967), p. 354.

27 Marvin E. Wolfgang, *Patterns in Criminal Homicide* (New York: Wiley, 1958).

28 Ibid.

29 Rosert Nash Parker and Dwayne M. Smith, "Deterrence, Poverty and Type of Homicide" *American Journal of Sociology,* Vol. 85 (1979), pp. 614–624; and M. Dwayne Smith and Robert Nash Parker, "Types of Homicide and Variation in Regional Rates," *Social Forces,* Vol. 59 (1980), pp. 136–147.

30 The distinction between expressive and instrumental crimes has been incorporated into much research on different crimes. This approach originated in the work of Richard Block and Franklin Zimring, "Homicide in Chicago, 1965–1970," *Journal of Research in Crime and Delinquency,* Vol. 10 (1973), pp. 1–12.

31 Parker and Smith, "Deterrence, Poverty and Type of Homicide."

32 Ibid.

33 Williams and Flewelling, "The Social Production of Criminal Homicide."

34 Laura Dugan, Daniel S. Nagin, and Richard Rosenfeld, "Explaining the Decline in Intimate Partner Homicide," *Homicide Studies,* Vol. 3, No. 3 (1999), p. 189.

35 Ibid., p. 208.

36 Ibid., p. 190.

37 Terance D. Miethe and Kriss A. Drass, "Exploring the Social Context of Instrumental and Expressive Homicides: An Application of Qualitative Comparative Analysis," *Journal of Quantitative Criminology,* Vol. 15, No. 1 (1999), p. 3.

38 Carolyn Rebecca Block and Richard Block, "Beginning with Wolfgang: An Agenda for Homicide Research," *Journal of Crime and Justice,* Vol. 24, No. 2 (1991), p. 42.

39 Ibid., p. 54.

40 Wolfgang, *Patterns in Criminal Homicide.*

41 Richard Rosenfeld, "Changing Relationships between Men and Women: A Note on the Decline in Intimate Partner Homicide," *Homicide Studies,* Vol. 1, No. 1 (1997), pp. 72–83.

42 Wolfgang, *Patterns in Criminal Homicide,* p. 2.

43 Ibid., p. 9.

44 Ibid.

45 Philip J. Cook and Mark H. Moore, "Guns, Gun Control, and Homicide," in M. Dwayne Smith and Margaret A. Zahn, eds., *Studying and Preventing Homicide: Issues and Challenges* (Thousand Oaks, CA: Sage, 1999), p. 252.

46 Ibid., p. 254.

47 Ibid., p. 266.

48 Reprinted as Paul J. Goldstein, "The Drugs/Violence Nexus: A Tripartite Conceptual Framework," in James A. Inciardi and Karen McElrath, eds., *The American Drug Scene* (Los Angeles: Roxbury, 1995).

49 Paul Goldstein et al., "Crack and Homicide in New York City, 1988: A Conceptually Based Event Analysis," *Contemporary Drug Problems,* Vol. 16, cited in Kathleen Auerhahn and Robert Nash Parker, "Drugs, Alcohol, and Homicide," in Smith and Zahn, eds., *Studying and Preventing Homicide.*

50 Auerhahn and Parker, "Drugs, Alcohol, and Homicide."

51 Ibid.

52 Ibid.

53 Ibid., p. 107.

54 Ibid., pp. 107–108.

55 Ibid., p. 108.

56 Ibid.

57 Robert Nash Parker, "Bringing 'Booze' Back In: The Relationship between Alcohol and Homicide," *Journal of Research in Crime and Delinquency,* Vol. 32, No. 1 (1995), pp. 3–38.

58 Ibid., p. 4.

59 Ibid., p. 25.

60 Cheryl L. Maxsong, M. A. Gordon, and Malcolm W. Klein, "Differences between Gang and Nongang Homicides," *Criminology,* Vol. 23, No. 2 (1985), pp. 209–222.

61 Richard Rosenfeld, Timothy M. Bray, and Arlen Egley, "Facilitating Violence: A Comparison of Gang-Motivated, Gang-Affiliated, and Nongang Youth Homicides," *Journal of Quantitative Criminology,* Vol. 15, No. 4 (1999), pp. 495–516.

62 Ibid., p. 513.

63 Bureau of Justice Statistics, *Report to the Nation on Crime and Justice,* 2nd ed. (Washington, DC: U.S. Government Printing Office, 1988), p. 4.

64 James Alan Fox and Jack Levin, "Multiple Homicide: Patterns of Serial and Mass Murder," in Michael Tonry, ed., *Crime and Justice: A Review of Research,* Vol. 23 (1998), p. 413.

65 Ibid.

66 James Alan Fox and Jack Levin, "Serial Murder: Myths and Realities," in Smith and Zahn, eds., *Studying and Preventing Homicide,* pp. 79–96.

67 Ibid.

68 Fox and Levin, "Multiple Homicide," p. 412.

69 Ibid., p. 413.

70 Ibid., p. 415.

71 Fox and Levin, "Serial Murder," p. 84.

72 Ibid.

73 Ibid.

74 Ronald Holmes and J. DeBurger, "Profiles in Terror: The Serial Murderer," *Federal Probation,* Vol. 49, No. 3 (1985), pp. 29–34.

75 Ibid.

76 Fox and Levin, "Serial Murder."

77 James DeFronzo, Ashley Ditta, Lance Hannon, and Jane Prochnow, "Male Serial Homicide: The Influence of Cultural and Structural Variables," *Homicide Studies,* Vol. 11, No. 3 (2007).

78 Stephen T. Holmes, Eric Hickey, and Ronald M. Holmes, "Female Serial Murderesses: Constructing Different Typologies," *Journal of Contemporary Criminal Justice,* Vol. 7, No. 4 (1991), pp. 245–256.

79 Ibid.

80 Ibid.

81 Ibid.

82 Michael D. Kelleher and C. L. Kelleher, *Murder Most Rare: The Female Serial Killer* (Westport, CT: Praeger, 1998).

83 Ibid., p. 11.

84 Ibid., p. 7.

85 Fox and Levin, "Multiple Homicide," p. 427.

86 Ibid.

87 Ibid., p. 428.

88 Ibid., p. 429.

89 Thomas O'Reilly-Fleming, "The Evolution of Multiple Murder in Historical Perspective," in Thomas O'Reilly-Fleming, ed., *Serial and Mass Murder: Theory, Research, and Policy* (Toronto: Canadian Scholars' Press, 1996).

90 Cited in James Alan Fox and Jack Levin, *Overkill: Mass Murder and Serial Killing Exposed* (New York: Plenum, 1994), p. 202.

91 Jack Levin and James Alan Fox, "A Psycho-social Analysis of Mass Murder," in O'Reilly-Fleming, ed., *Serial and Mass Murder,* p. 65.

92 Ibid., p. 66.

93 Ibid.

94 Ibid., p. 69.

95 Ibid., p. 71.

96 Ibid., p. 69.

97 Fox and Levin, *Overkill,* p. 149.

98 For an overview of the measurement of rape in national surveys, see Debra S. Kelley, "The Measurement of Rape," in James F. Hodgson and Debra S. Kelley, eds., *Sexual Violence: Policies, Practices, and Challenges in the United States and Canada* (New York: Praeger, 2001). For a more detailed exploration of this topic, see Bonnie S. Fisher and Francis T. Cullen, "Measuring the Sexual Victimization of Women: Evolution, Current Controversies, and Future Research," in *Criminal Justice 2000: Measurement and Analysis of Crime and Justice* (Washington, DC: U.S. Department of Justice, Office of Justice Programs, 2000).

99 FBI, *Crime in the United States, 2006.*

100 Bureau of Justice Statistics, *Criminal Victimization, 2006* (Washington, DC: U.S. Department of Justice, Office of Justice Programs, 2007).

101 Diana E. H. Russell and Rebecca M. Bolen, *The Epidemic of Rape and Child Sexual Abuse in the United States* (Thousand Oaks, CA: Sage, 2000). See also Mary P. Koss, "The Underdetection of Rape: Methodological Choices Influence Incidence Estimates," *Journal of Social Issues,* Vol. 48, No. 1 (1992), pp. 61–75; and Mary P. Koss, "The Measurement of Rape Victimization in Crime Surveys," *Criminal Justice and Behavior,* Vol. 23 (1996), pp. 55–69.

102 Patricia Tjaden and Nancy Thoennes, *Prevalence, Incidence, and Consequences of Violence against Women: Findings from the National Violence against Women Survey* (Washington, DC: National Institute of Justice and Centers for Disease Control and Prevention, 1991).

103 Martha R. Burt, "Cultural Myths and Supports for Rape," *Journal of Personality and Social Psychology,* Vol. 38 (1980), pp. 217–230.

104 For example, see Mary P. Koss et al., "Nonstranger Sexual Aggression: A Discriminant Analysis of the Psychological Characteristics of Undetected Offenders," *Sex Roles,* Vol. 12 (1985), pp. 981–992.

105 Martha R. Burt, "Rape Myths," in Andrea Parrot and Laurie Bechhofer, eds., *Acquaintance Rape: The Hidden Crime* (New York: John Wiley & Sons, 1991).

106 Gary LaFree, *Rape and Criminal Justice: The Social Construction of Sexual Assault* (Belmont, CA: Wadsworth, 1989). See also Jeanne C. Marsh, Alison Geist, and Nathan Caplan, *Rape and the Limits of Law Reform* (Boston: Auburn, 1982).

107 Harriet R. Galvin, "Shielding Rape Victims in the State and Federal Courts: A Proposal for the Second Decade," *Minnesota Law Review,* Vol. 70 (1986), pp. 763–916.

108 Cassia Spohn and Julie Horney, *Rape Law Reform: A Grassroots Revolution and Its Impact* (New York: Plenum, 1992).

109 Ibid., p. 21.

110 Ibid., p. 129.

111 Ibid.

112 Ibid., pp. 21–22.

113 Ibid.

114 Julie Horney and Cassia Spohn, "Rape Law Reform and Instrumental Change in Six Urban Jurisdictions," *Law and Society Review,* Vol. 25, No. 1 (1991), pp. 117–153.

115 Spohn and Horney, *Rape Law Reform.*

116 Ibid., p. 167.

117 Ibid., p. 162.

118 Ibid., p. 129.

119 E. J. Kanin, "Male Aggression in Dating-Courtship Relations," *American Journal of Sociology,* Vol. 63 (1957), cited in Martin D. Schwartz and Molly S. Leggett, "Bad Dates or Emotional Trauma? The Aftermath of Campus Sexual Assault," *Violence against Women,* Vol. 5, No. 3 (1999), pp. 197–204.

120 See Frances P. Bernat, "Rape Law Reform," in James F. Hodgson and Debra S. Kelley, eds., *Sexual Violence: Policies, Practices, and Challenges in the United States and Canada* (New Brunswick, CT: Praeger, 2001).

121 *U.S. v. Morrison,* 120 S. Ct. 1740 (2000).

122 Public Law 102–325, section 486(c).

123 Carol Bohmer and Andrea Parrot, *Sexual Assault on Campus: The Problem and the Solution* (New York: Lexington Books, 1993), pp. 15–16.

124 Mary P. Koss, C. J. Gidycz, and N. Wisniewski, "The Scope of Rape: Sexual Aggression and Victimization in a National Sample of Students in Higher Education," *Journal of Consulting and Clinical Psychology*, Vol. 55 (1987), pp. 162–170.

125 Mary P. Koss, "Hidden Rape: Sexual Aggression and Victimization in a National Sample of Students in Higher Education," in Patricia Searles and Ronald J. Berger, eds., *Rape and Society: Readings on the Problem of Sexual Assault* (Boulder, CO: Westview Press, 1995).

126 B. L. Yegidis, "Date Rape and Other Forced Sexual Encounters among College Students," *Journal of Sex Education and Therapy*, Vol. 12 (1986), pp. 51–54.

127 Patricia Yancey Martin and Robert A. Hummer, "Fraternities and Rape on Campus," *Gender and Society*, Vol. 3, No. 4 (1989), p. 462.

128 Ibid.

129 Diana E. H. Russell, *Rape in Marriage* (Bloomington: Indiana University Press, 1990), p. 18.

130 Lisa M. Cuklanz, *Rape on Trial: How the Mass Media Construct Legal Reform and Social Change* (Philadelphia: University of Pennsylvania Press, 1996).

131 Ibid., p. 49.

132 Ibid., p. 53.

133 Ibid., p. 62.

134 James Ptacek, *Battered Women in the Courtroom: The Power of Judicial Responses* (Boston: Northeastern University Press, 1999), p. 119.

135 David Finkelhor and Kersti Yllo, "Forced Sex in Marriage," *Crime and Delinquency*, Vol. 28, No. 3 (1982), pp. 459–478.

136 Russell, *Rape in Marriage.*

137 Ibid., p. 133.

138 Charles Crawford, "Sexual Assault behind Bars: The Forgotten Victims," in Hodgson and Kelley, eds., *Sexual Assault.*

139 Cindy Struckman-Johnson et al., "Sexual Coercion Reported by Men and Women in Prison," *Journal of Sex Research*, Vol. 33, No. 1 (1996), pp. 67–76.

140 Susan Brownmiller, *Against Our Will: Men, Women, and Rape* (New York: Simon & Schuster, 1975).

141 Dianne Herman, "The Rape Culture," in Jo Freeman, ed., *Women: A Feminist Perspective* (Palo Alto, CA: Mayfield, 1984).

142 Catherine MacKinnon, *Toward a Feminist Theory of the State* (Cambridge, MA: Harvard University Press, 1989); and Catherine MacKinnon, *Only Words* (Cambridge, MA: Harvard University Press, 1993).

143 See Andrea Dworkin, *Pornography: Men Possessing Women* (New York: Plenum, 1981); Andrea Dworkin, "Questions and Answers," in Diana E. H. Russell, ed., *Making Violence Sexy: Feminist Views on Pornography* (New York: Teachers College Press, 1993); and Andrea Dworkin, "Against the Male Flood: Censorship, Pornography, and Equality," in Patricia Smith, ed., *Feminist Jurisprudence* (New York: Oxford University Press, 1993).

144 Robin Morgan, *The Word of a Woman: Feminist Dispatches, 1968–1992* (New York: W. W. Norton, 1992), p. 88.

145 Brownmiller, *Against Our Will.*

146 James W. Messerschmidt, *Masculinities and Crime: Critique and Reconceptualization of Theory* (Lanham, MD: Rowman and Littlefield, 1993).

147 Ngaire Naffine, *Feminism and Criminology* (Philadelphia: Temple University Press, 1996), p. 101.

148 Messerschmidt, *Masculinities and Crime*, p. 119.

149 Neil Websdale, *Rural Woman Battering and the Justice System: An Ethnography* (Thousand Oaks, CA: Sage, 1998), p. 208.

150 Diana Scully and Joseph Marolla, "Riding the Bull at Gilley's: Convicted Rapists Describe the Rewards of Rape," *Social Problems*, Vol. 32, No. 2 (1985), p. 252.

151 Nicholas Groth, *Men Who Rape: The Psychology of the Offender* (New York: Plenum, 1979).

152 Scully and Marolla, "Riding the Bull at Gilley's."

153 Nicholas Groth, "Rape and Sexual Offenses," in Neil Alan Weiner, Margaret A. Zahn, and Rita J. Sagi, eds., *Violence: Patterns, Causes, Public Policy* (New York: Harcourt Brace Jovanovich, 1990), p. 76.

154 Groth, *Men Who Rape.*

155 Groth, "Rape and Sexual Offenses," p. 76.

156 Scully and Marolla, "Riding the Bull at Gilley's."

157 Russell, *Rape in Marriage.*

158 Larry Baron and Murray A. Straus, *Four Theories of Rape in American Society: A State-Level Analysis* (New Haven, CT: Yale University Press, 1989).

159 Ibid., p. 147.

160 For examples, see Peggy Reeves Sanday, "The Socio-cultural Context of Rape: A Cross-cultural Study," *Journal of Social Issues*, Vol. 37 (1981), pp. 5–27.

161 Baron and Straus, *Four Theories of Rape in American Society*, p. 184.

162 Robert T. Sigler, Ida M. Johnson, and Etta F. Morgan, "Forced Sexual Intercourse: Contemporary Views," in Roslyn Muraskin, ed., *It's a Crime: Women and Justice* (Upper Saddle River, NJ: Prentice Hall, 2000), p. 352.

163 Randy Thornhill, "The Biology of Human Rape," *Jurimetrics*, Vol. 39, No. 2 (1999), p. 138.

164 Randy Thornhill and Craig T. Palmer, *A Natural History of Rape* (Cambridge, MA: MIT Press, 2000), p. 53.

165 Martin Daly and Margo Wilson, *Homicide* (New York: Aldine De Gruyter, 1988), p. 140.

166 Thornhill and Palmer, *A Natural History of Rape*, p. 199. See also Katharine K. Baker, "What Rape Is and What It Ought Not to Be," *Jurimetrics*, Vol. 30, No. 3 (1999), p. 233.

167 Craig T. Palmer, David N. DiBari, and Scott A. Wright, "Is It Sex Yet? Theoretical and Practical Implications of the Debate over Rapists' Motives," *Jurimetrics*, Vol. 39, No. 3 (1999), pp. 281–282.

168 R. R. Hazelwood and A. N. Burgess, eds., *Practical Aspects of Rape Investigation: A Multidisciplinary Approach* (New York: CRC Press, 1995).

169 Robert R. Hazelwood, "Analyzing the Rape and Profiling the Offender," in Hazelwood and Burgess, eds., *Practical Aspects of Rape Investigation*, p. 162.

170 Ibid., p. 163.

171 Ibid., p. 164.

172 Ibid., p. 165.

173 Dennis J. Stevens, *Inside the Mind of a Serial Rapist* (San Francisco: Austin and Winfield, 1999), p. 39.

174 Ibid., p. 42.

175 Ibid., p. 41.

176 Ibid., p. 47.

177 Ibid., p. 50.

178 Ibid., p. 51.

179 Diana Scully, *Understanding Sexual Violence: A Study of Convicted Rapists* (New York: Routledge, 1990).

180 Ibid., p. 59.

181 Ibid.

182 Ibid.

183 Ibid., p. 165.

184 Ibid., p. 166.

185 Kim Curtis, "Child Psychiatrist Accused of Molesting," *USA Today*, April 6, 2007.

186 Robert A. Prentky, Raymond A. Knight, and Austin F. S. Lee, *Child Sexual Molestation: Research Issues* (Washington, D.C.: National Institute of Justice, 1997), p. 1.

187 G. G. Abel, J. V. Becker, M. S. Mittelman, J. Cunningham-Rathner, J. L. Rouleau, and W. D. Murphy, "Self-Reported Sex Crimes of Nonincarcerated Paraphiliacs," *Journal of Interpersonal Violence*, Vol. 2 (1987), pp. 3–25.

188 Child Molestation Research and Prevention Institute, "Some Facts," http://www.childmolestationprevention.org (accessed June 5, 2007).

189 Abel et al, "Self-Reported Sex Crimes of Nonincarcerated Paraphilics,"

190 B. M. Maletzky, "Factors Associated with Success and Failure in the Behavioral and Cognitive Treatment of Sexual Offenders," *Annals of Sex Research,* Vol. 6 (1993), pp. 241–258.

191 Robert A. Prentky, Raymond A. Knight, and Austin F. S. Lee, *Child Sexual Molestation: Research Issues* (Washington, DC: National Institute of Justice, 1997), from which much of the information and some of the wording in this section is taken.

192 Robert A. Prentky, Raymond A. Knight, and Austin F. S. Lee, *Child Sexual Molestation: Research Issues* (Washington, DC: National Institute of Justice, 1997), p. 7

193 A. Nicholas Groth, W. F. Hobson, and T. S. Gary, "The Child Molester: Clinical Observations," *Journal of Social Work and Child Sexual Abuse,* Vol. 1, No. 2 (1982), pp. 129–144.

194 *Child Sexual Molestation: Research Issues,* op. cit.

195 Ibid.

196 Ibid., p. 3.

197 R. A. Prentky and R. A. Knight, "Age of Onset of Sexual Assault: Criminal and Life History Correlates," in G. C. N. Hall, R. Hirschman, J. R. Graham, and M. S. Zaragoza, eds., *Sexual Aggression: Issues in Etiology, Assessment, and Treatment,* (Washington, DC: Taylor & Francis, 1993), pp. 43–62.

198 *Child Sexual Molestation: Research Issues,* op. cit.

199 Charlotte Bunch, "The Intolerable Status Quo: Violence Against Women and Children," in UNICEF, *The Progress of Nations* (1997).

200 Richard J. Estes, "The Sexual Exploitation of Children: A Working Guide to the Empirical Literature," August 2001, http://www.sp2.upenn.edu/~restes/CSEC_Files/CSEC_Bib_August_2001.pdf (accessed July 7, 2007); and Richard J. Estes and Neil Alan Weiner, "The Commercial Sexual Exploitation of Children in the U.S., Canada, and Mexico," http://www.sp2.upenn.edu/~restes/CSEC_Files/Exec_Sum_020220.pdf (accessed July 5, 2007).

201 "The Sexual Exploitation of Children: A Working Guide to the Empirical Literature," p. 1.

202 Larry Copeland and Nick Martin, "Police in Some Areas See Increase in Home Invasions," *USA Today,* June 8, 2006, p. 5A.

203 Ibid.

204 Note that while purse snatching and pocket picking involve the express goal of taking someone's property, they are classified as property crimes because they do not involve the same type of direct contact with the victim as does robbery.

205 Terance D. Miethe and David McDowall, "Contextual Effects in Models of Criminal Victimization," *Social Forces,* Vol. 71, No. 3 (1993), pp. 741–760.

206 Miethe and McCorkle, *Crime Profiles,* p. 87.

207 Scott A. Hendricks et al., "A Matched Case-Control Study of Convenience Store Robbery Risk Factors," *Journal of Occupational and Environmental Medicine,* Vol. 41, No. 11 (1999), p. 995.

208 Ibid., p. 1003.

209 Richard T. Wright and Scott H. Decker, *Armed Robbers in Action: Stickups and Street Culture* (Boston: Northeastern University Press, 1997), p. 88.

210 Floyd Feeney, "Robbers as Decision Makers," in Derek B. Cornish and Ronald V. Clarke, eds., *The Reasoning Criminal* (New York: Springer-Verlag, 1986).

211 Brian A. Reaves, *Using NIBRS Data to Analyze Violent Crime* (Washington, DC: U.S. Department of Justice, Office of Justice Programs, Bureau of Justice Statistics, 1993).

212 FBI, *Crime in the United States, 2006.*

213 Ibid.

214 Thomas Gabor et al., *Armed Robbery: Cops, Robbers, and Victims* (Springfield, IL: Charles C. Thomas, 1987).

215 Mark A. Peterson and Harriet B. Braiker, *Doing Crime: A Survey of California Prison Inmates* (Santa Monica, CA: Rand Corporation, 1980).

216 Mark A. Peterson and Harriet B. Braiker, *Who Commits Crimes: A Survey of Prison Inmates* (Boston, MA: Oelgeschlager, Gunn, and Hain, 1981).

217 James Q. Wilson and Allan Abrahamse, "Does Crime Pay?" *Justice Quarterly,* Vol. 9 (1992), pp. 359–377.

218 Martha J. Smith and Ronald V. Clarke, "Crime and Public Transport," in Michael Tonry, ed., *Crime and Justice: A Review of Research,* Vol. 27 (Chicago: University of Chicago Press, 2000), pp. 169–234.

219 Ibid., p. 179.

220 Ibid., p. 180.

221 Ibid., p. 181.

222 Ibid., p. 182.

223 Derek Cornish, "The Procedural Analysis of Offending and Its Relevance for Situational Prevention," in Ronald V. Clarke, ed., *Crime Prevention Studies,* Vol. 3 (Monsey, NY: Criminal Justice Press, 1994), cited in Smith and Clarke, "Crime and Public Transport," in Tonry, ed., *Crime and Justice,* p. 181.

224 Smith and Clarke, "Crime and Public Transport," p. 181.

225 "Another NYC Cabbie Slain: Seventh Livery Driver Killed This Year," APBnews.com, April 15, 2000, http://www.apbnews.com/newscenter/breakingnews/2000/04/15/cabs0415_01.html (accessed January 14, 2005).

226 Amy Worden, "NYC Taxis Get Anti-Crime Cabby Cams," APBnews.com, November 17, 1999, http://www.apbnews.com/safetycenter/transport/1999/11/17/cabcam117_01.html (accessed January 14, 2001).

227 "Supreme Court Lets Taxi-Stop Rulings Stand: NYC Searchers Too Intrusive, but Boston Sweeps Legal," APBnews.com, December 4, 2000, http://www.apbnews.com/newscenter/breakingnews/2000/12/04/taxi1204_01.html (accessed January 14, 2001).

228 Feeney, "Robbers as Decision Makers."

229 Ibid., p. 59.

230 Jody Miller, "Up It Up: Gender and the Accomplishment of Street Robbery," *Criminology,* Vol. 36, No. 1 (1998), p. 43.

231 Bruce A. Jacobs and Richard Wright, "Stick-Up, Street Culture, and Offender Motivation," *Criminology,* Vol. 37, No. 1 (1999), p. 150.

232 Ibid., p. 155.

233 S. Morrison and I. O'Donnell, "An Analysis of the Decision Making Processes of Armed Robbers," in R. Homel, ed., *Crime Prevention Studies,* Vol. 5. *The Politics and Practice of Situational Crime Prevention* (Monsey, NY: Criminal Justice Press, 1996). See also Gabor et al., *Armed Robbery.*

234 Jacobs and Wright, "Stick-Up, Street Culture, and Offender Motivation," p. 163.

235 Ibid., pp. 167–168.

236 Trevor Bennett and Fiona Brookman, "A Qualtative Study of the Role of Violence in Street Crime," reported in Annika Howard, "Street Robbery Is Not Just About Money," *Medical News Today,* http://www.medicalnewstoday.com/printerfriendlynews.php?newsid=57730, December 1, 2006. Accessed August 24, 2007.

237 Richard T. Wright and Scott H. Decker, *Armed Robbers in Action: Stickups and Street Culture* (Boston: Northeastern University Press, 1997), p. 62.

238 Ibid., p. 63.

239 Ibid.

240 Ibid., p. 65.

241 Ibid.

242 Ibid., p. 66.

243 Bruce A. Jacobs, Volkan Topalli, and Richard Wright, "Managing Retaliation: Drug Robbery and Informal Sanction Threats," *Criminology,* Vol. 38, No. 1 (2000), p. 173.

244 Ibid.

245 Ibid., p. 177.

246 Ibid.

247 Ibid., p. 179.

[248] Wright and Decker, *Armed Robbers in Action,* p. 67.

[249] Jacobs, Topalli, and Wright, "Managing Retaliation," p. 180.

[250] Ibid., p. 185.

[251] Ibid., p. 188.

[252] Ibid.

[253] Ibid., p. 172.

[254] Ibid., p. 194.

[255] Ibid.

[256] Miller, "Up It Up," p. 37.

[257] FBI, *Crime in the United States, 2006,* based on arrests.

[258] Messerschmidt, *Masculinities and Crime,* p. 107. Also cited in Miller, "Up It Up," p. 38.

[259] Miller, "Up It Up," p. 47.

[260] Ibid., p. 51.

[261] Ibid., p. 61.

[262] Reiss and Roth, eds., *Understanding and Preventing Violence,* p. 3.

[263] James Garbarino, *Lost Boys: Why Our Sons Turn Violent and How We Can Save Them* (New York: Free Press, 1999), p. 25.

[264] Ibid.

[265] Miethe and McCorkle, *Crime Profiles,* p. 25.

[266] Ibid., p. 27.

[267] Bureau of Justice Statistics, *Criminal Victimization 2006* (Washington, DC: U.S. Department of Justice, Office of Justice Programs, 2007), p. 172.

[268] Callie Marie Rennison, *Criminal Victimization, 1999: Changes 1998–1999 with Trends 1993–1999* (Washington, DC: U.S. Department of Justice, Office of Justice Programs, 2000).

[269] Robert J. Sampson, "Personal Violence by Strangers: An Extension and Test of Predatory Victimization," *Journal of Criminal Law and Criminology,* Vol. 78, No. 2 (1987), p. 342.

[270] Marc Riedel and Roger K. Przybylski, "Stranger Murders and Assault: A Study of a Neglected Form of Stranger Violence," in Anna Victoria Wilson, ed., *Homicide: The Victim/Offender Connection* (Cincinnati: Anderson, 1993).

[271] Ibid., p. 376.

[272] Ibid.

[273] Ibid.

[274] Richard J. Gelles, *The Violent Home: A Study of Physical Aggression between Husbands and Wives* (Beverly Hills, CA: Sage, 1974).

[275] Murray A. Straus, Richard J. Gelles, and S. K. Steinmetz, *Behind Closed Doors: Violence in the American Family* (New York: Anchor Books, 1980), p. 31.

[276] Michael Hindelang, *Criminal Victimization in Eight American Cities* (Cambridge, MA: Ballinger, 1976).

[277] Evan Stark, A. Flitcraft, and W. Frazier, "Medicine and Patriarchical Violence: The Social Construction of a Private Event," *International Journal of Health Service,* Vol. 9, No. 3 (1979), pp. 461–493.

[278] Murray A. Straus, "The National Family Violence Surveys," in Murray A. Straus and Richard J. Gelles, eds., *Physical Violence in American Families: Risk Factors and Adaptations to Violence in 8,145 Families* (New Brunswick, NJ: Transaction, 1990).

[279] Murray A. Straus, "The Conflict Tactics Scales and Its Critics: An Evaluation and New Data on Validity and Reliability," in Straus and Gelles, eds., *Physical Violence in American Families.*

[280] Murray A. Straus and Richard J. Gelles, "How Violent Are American Families? Estimates from the National Family Violence Research and Other Studies," in G. Hotaling, ed., *New Directions in Family Violence Research* (Newbury Park, CA: Sage, 1988).

[281] Federal Bureau of Investigation, *Crime in the United States, 2006.*

[282] Ibid.

[283] Ibid.

[284] For representative examples of this, see R. E. Dobash et al., "The Myth of Sexual Symmetry in Marital Violence," *Social Problems,* Vol. 39, No. 1 (1992), pp. 71–91; and R. E. Dobash and R. Dobash, *Women, Violence, and Social Change* (New York: Routledge, 1992).

[285] Websdale, *Rural Woman Battering and the Justice System.*

[286] Martha R. Mahoney, "Legal Issues of Battered Women: Redefining the Issue of Separation," *Michigan Law Review,* Vol. 90, No. 1 (1991), p. 6.

[287] Liz Kelly, *Surviving Sexual Violence* (Minneapolis: University of Minnesota Press, 1988), p. 23.

[288] Websdale, *Rural Woman Battering and the Justice System,* p. 32.

[289] See M. W. Zawit, *Violence between Intimates* (Washington, DC: U.S. Department of Justice, Bureau of Justice Statistics, 1994).

[290] Ptacek, *Battered Women in the Courtroom,* p. 6.

[291] Websdale, *Rural Woman Battering and the Justice System.*

[292] Ptacek, *Battered Women in the Courtroom.*

[293] Ibid., p. 29.

[294] Ibid. p. 82.

[295] Ibid., pp. 86–87.

[296] Patricia Tjaden and Nancy Thoennes, *Extent, Nature, and Consequences of Intimate Partner Violence* (Washington, DC: National Institute of Justice, 2000), p. 30.

[297] M. L. Bernard and J. L. Bernard, "Violent Intimacy: The Family as a Model for Love Relationships," *Family Relations,* Vol. 32 (1983), pp. 283–286.

[298] Martin Kasindorf, "Ex-postal Worker's Behavior Called Increasingly Bizzare," *USA Today,* February 2, 2006, p. 3A.

[299] FBI, *Workplace Violence: Issues in Response* (Quantico, VA: FBI, 2004), from which the information in this section is taken.

[300] Ibid., p. 13, from which some of the wording in this paragraph is adapted.

[301] Ibid., p. 14, from which some of the wording in this paragraph is adapted.

[302] Detis T. Duhart, *Violence in the Workplace, 1993–99* (Washington, DC: Bureau of Justice Statistics, 2001).

[303] National Institute for Occupational Safety and Health, *Violence in the Workplace: Risk Factors and Prevention Strategies,* July 1996, http://www.cdc.gov/niosh/violcont.html (accessed July 21, 2006).

[304] Ibid.

[305] Violence against Women Grants Office, *Stalking and Domestic Violence: The Third Annual Report to Congress under the Violence against Women Act* (Washington, DC: Violence against Women Grants Office, 1998).

[306] Ibid., p. 6.

[307] Ibid.

[308] Ibid.

[309] Patricia Tjaden and Nancy Thoennes, *Stalking in America: Findings from the National Violence against Women Survey* (Washington, DC: National Institute of Justice, 1998), p. 7.

[310] Ibid.

[311] Ibid.

[312] Ibid.

[313] Ibid.

[314] Paul E. Mullen et al., "Assessing and Managing the Risks in the Stalking Situation," *Journal of the American Academy of Psychiatry and Law,* Vol. 34 (2006), pp. 439–450; and Paul E. Mullen et al., "Study of Stalkers," *American Journal of Psychiatry,* Vol. 156 (August 1999), pp. 1244–1249.

[315] Ibid., p. 6.

[316] Ibid., p. 8.

[317] Ibid. See also Tjaden and Thoennes, *Extent, Nature, and Consequences of Intimate Partner Violence.*

[318] Tjaden and Thoennes, *Stalking in America.*

[319] Ibid., p. 8.

[320] Ibid., p. 10.

[321] Ibid.

[322] Ibid.

[323] T. Gregorie, *Cyberstalking: Dangers on the Information Highway* (Arlington, VA: National Center for Victims of Crime, 2000).

[324] Janet Reno, *Cyberstalking: A New Challenge for Law Enforcement and Industry—A Report from the U.S. Attorney General to the Vice President* (Washington, DC: U.S. Department of Justice, 1999).

Crimes against Property

Outline

The professional thief does not regard society in general as an enemy or perpetrate crimes against society because of hatred toward society. Rather than hate society, the professional thief rejoices in the welfare of the public. He would like to see society enjoy continuous prosperity, for then his own touches will naturally be greater.

—Edwin Sutherland[1]

We are all waiting to become victims of a burglar whose intuition about time coincides with our routine.

—George Rengert and John Wasilchick[3]

Although few people have the talent to become professional fences and fewer still actually do so, anybody can buy stolen property and an unknown, but probably quite large, number of people in the United States do.

—Carl B. Klockars[2]

Like physics and physiology, criminogenesis derives from a movement of physically bounded and identifiable entities about the physical world—movements that can be tracked according to map, clock, and calendar.

—Marcus Felson[4]

Learning Outcomes

After reading this chapter, you should be able to

- Identify the major forms of property crime and explain the distinction between professional criminals and other kinds of property offenders
- Describe the prevalence of and list the types of larceny-theft
- Describe the prevalence of burglary and list the types of burglars and their motivations
- Explain the activities of stolen property receivers and describe how stolen goods are distributed
- Define *arson* and describe the activities of fire setters

Hear the author discuss this chapter at **crimtoday.com**

Introduction

On the evening of December 5, 1980, Dr. Michael Halberstam, a prominent cardiologist and brother of famed author David Halberstam, was returning home with his wife. The Halberstams lived in Great Falls, Virginia, an affluent suburb of Washington, DC. When Dr. Halberstam entered his residence, he confronted a burglar, who shot him and then fled. Though seriously wounded, Halberstam pursued the burglar and ran him down with his car. Although Halberstam died, the burglar, Bernard Welch, lived. Welch was found to have been a very active thief and a fugitive from another state. Since escaping from a New York prison several years before the Halberstam burglary, Welch had been pursuing a lucrative career as a burglar—so profitable that he had driven a new Mercedes to the crime scene. A search of Welch's residence revealed millions of dollars in stolen goods. Details of Welch's career as a burglar, along with photos of the merchandise found in his home, soon filled the front pages of local newspapers.[5] Welch's criminal career was unique. As a professional thief, Welch was far from typical, and his success and skill level placed him in a category shared by few.

Professional criminals are rare in the world of theft, whether the target selected is someone's residence or the "high-brow" world of art museums. The March 18, 1990, theft of several valuable paintings worth more than $300 million from the Stewart Gardner Museum in Boston remains "the unsolved art crime of the century."[6] Two people disguised as Boston police officers entered the museum, incapacitated security guards, and made off with the paintings as well as surveillance tapes. The Boston art theft was atypical for several reasons. According to Lynne Chafinch, an expert in art crime theft with the Federal Bureau of Investigation (FBI), the vast majority of "stolen art is lower value" and hence represents works that will not be easily recognized.[7] Even though the FBI maintains a listing of stolen art and cultural property in its National Stolen Art File, the bureau investigates such thefts only if they occur in a "museum as defined by federal statute, [and then] a stolen artwork has to be either more than 100 years old and worth more than $5,000 or less than 100 years old and worth more than $100,000."[8] According to Don Hrycyk, who leads the art theft unit of the Los Angeles Police Department, one of the few of its kind nationally, many of the people involved in art theft are common burglars who steal art along with any other goods available. Other art thieves do not fit a conventional criminal profile and instead come from the ranks of college professors, gallery owners, and individuals involved in insurance fraud.[9] In more than a decade of such investigation, Hrycyk noted that about the only type of crook that he hasn't come across is the sophisticated, debonair thief portrayed in movies like *Entrapment* and *The Thomas Crown Affair*.[10] Learn more about art theft at **Web Extra 11–1**.

WEB
Extra

Persistent and Professional Thieves

While legal distinctions separate the offenses of larceny and burglary, both are basically property crimes of theft, and hence in some way all such offenders are thieves. Before discussing the legal classifications of property crimes, some basic differences between persistent thieves and professional thieves should be noted. While many thieves are persistent, this does not make them professionals. Willie Sutton, a famous bank robber, saw himself as a professional and defined a professional thief quite simply as "a man who wakes up every morning thinking about committing a crime, the same way another man gets up and goes to his job."[11] In a classic study of the professional thief, Edwin H. Sutherland defines this offender as one who "makes a regular business of stealing," plans carefully, possesses "technical skills and methods which are different from those of other professional criminals," and moves from locale to locale in offending pursuits.[12] **Neil Shover** defines **professional criminals** as those "who commit crime with some degree of skill, earn reasonably well from their crimes, and despite stealing over long periods of time, spend rather little time incarcerated."[13] This is certainly not the

professional criminal

A criminal offender who makes a living from criminal pursuits, is recognized by other offenders as professional, and engages in offending that is planned and calculated.

profile of most offenders, who continue to commit crimes but never exhibit signs of a professional approach to crime. Rather than being viewed as professional, they are best understood as persistent.

Persistent thieves are those who continue in "common-law property crimes despite their, at best, ordinary level of success."[14] Rather than specializing to any significant degree, the vast majority of persistent thieves alternate between a variety of crimes like burglary, robbery, car theft, and confidence games. Even though they exhibit a generalist approach to offending, persistent thieves may have "crime preferences" that take the form of characteristics like "whether to avoid or to confront their victim(s)."[15]

Similarly, **offense specialization,** a preference for a certain type of offense, is quite limited among property offenders and does not allow for the classification of most offenders as professionals or specialists. A significant number of property offenders are fully immersed in a street culture and lifestyle characterized by a hedonistic approach to life and a disregard for conventional pursuits. Their everyday lives are usually filled with a wide array of petty crimes, including confidence games gambling, and minor thefts.[16]

Malcolm W. Klein used the term *cafeteria-style offending* in his research to refer to the heterogeneous and unplanned nature of offending among gang members.[17] In analyzing offending among gang members for possible patterns, Klein was "reminded of a cafeteria display with [several] choices of food. Imagine the gang member walking along the display, choosing to try a little petty theft, then a group assault, then some truancy, then two varieties of malicious mischief, and so on."[18] Other researchers have used Klein's term to refer to the style of offending found among both violent offenders and property offenders. Research using data sources ranging from official crime statistics to self-reports of offenders to ethnographies confirms that a minimal level of specialization exists among property offenders.[19] Shover, who has studied burglary and professional thieves over the last two decades, suggests that designations like "burglar" have little utility if conceived of in a strict sense of exclusive offending within that crime type.

persistent thief

One who continues in common-law property crimes despite no better than an ordinary level of success.

offense specialization

A preference for engaging in a certain type of offense to the exclusion of others.

A burglary in progress. Burglary is a property crime that can turn violent if victims encounter the perpetrator. What are the characteristics of a professional burglar?

Source: David Simson, Stock Boston

Many offenders engaged in burglary prefer this type of offending to offenses like robbery because burglary does not involve direct contact with victims, among other reasons. These individuals may engage in other types of offenses, even occasional robbery, but for the most part, their offending is characterized primarily by burglaries of the same type.[20]

occasional offender

A criminal offender whose offending patterns are guided primarily by opportunity.

Because of the short-term and sporadic nature of their offending, property offenders are also known as **occasional offenders.**[21] The label "occasional" refers not to the frequency of offending but to the nature and character of offending. **John R. Hepburn** defines occasional property offenders as those whose crimes "occur on those occasions in which there is an opportunity or situational inducement to commit the crime."[22] This observation, which fits well with rational choice theory discussed in Chapter 4, has been confirmed in subsequent research, most recently in the work of Richard T. Wright and Scott H. Decker, who state that the burglars they interviewed are not a "continually motivated group of criminals; the motivation for them to offend is closely tied to their assessment of current circumstances and prospects."[23] This does not mean that offenders plan their crimes carefully; it means only that they are seeking to achieve some personal benefit through criminal activity. An offenders' assessment of the situation at hand may not even be accurate, and some offenders don't succeed in obtaining the benefits they desire. This is because they rarely have all the information they need, they do not devote enough time to planning their actions, they take risks, and they make mistakes. This is how we all behave in everyday decision making and it is what theorists call *limited* or *bounded rationality.*[24] So, while some degree of rationality characterizes the criminal activity of most property offenders, it is only a limited or bounded rationality.

Criminal Careers of Property Offenders

Criminologists have long studied the criminal careers of offenders, both violent offenders and property offenders. Neil Alan Weiner defines a criminal career as "criminal behavior is an integrated, dynamic structure of sequential unlawful acts that advances within a wider context of causal and correlative influences, including among others, those of biological, psychological, and informal social and formal criminal justice origins."[25] As this definition illustrates, the concept of a career implies a rational progression through defined stages, with some type of planning or formalized logic to the progression.

According to Alfred Blumstein and colleagues, a criminal career in property offending consists of three distinct phases.[26] The first phase is the "break-in" period, which characterizes the early years of an offender's career. It is a time when young offenders become increasingly committed to criminal careers and explore various kinds of criminality. During this period, residual career length (the expected time still remaining in a career) increases. The initial phase generally lasts for the first 10 to 12 years for a property offender's career. The second, or "stable" period, which begins around age 30 for those who first embark on criminal careers when they are around 18, is the time of highest commitment. It is the period in an offender's career when he or she identifies most closely with a criminal lifestyle; it is probably also the period when rehabilitation efforts are most likely to fail. The final, or "burnout," phase of a criminal career begins around age 40, says Blumstein. It is characterized by increasing dropout rates and by a lowered commitment to criminal lifestyles.

As noted, Blumstein was describing the careers of property offenders. In a study of violent offending, however, D. S. Elliott and his colleagues examined data from the National Youth Survey and found that the careers of violent offenders were typically quite short—averaging just 1.58 years.[27] Only about 4% of subjects studied by Elliott had a violent criminal career of five years or more. Unlike other researchers, however, Elliott defined career length as the maximum number of consecutive years the individual was classified as a serious violent offender during the study period

An assumption long attached to criminal careers was the idea that offending becomes more serious and more frequent over time, an assumption strongly challenged by

Michael R. Gottfredson and Travis Hirschi.[28] While the idea of deviance and crime as an orderly process similar to the rationality of conventional activities may be appealing for social policy purposes, evidence on offense specialization and the trajectories associated with chronic offending offers more support for crime as a fragmented pursuit than as a "career." Some researchers have found that while there exists a certain logic to the lifestyle of most offenders, it is not one that easily complies with "a concept appropriate in a distinctly different culture (lawful society)."[29]

Based on ethnographic research on street criminals in urban settings, **Mark S. Fleisher** argues that the "social maturation" of the street life cycle "allows hustlers at any age to speak and act like adolescents and never acquire responsibilities similar to those marking social maturation in lawful society. In the sociocultural world of hustlers, youth is marked by gang membership, 'kids crimes,' the onset of drug and alcohol addictions, and juvenile detention."[30] From the cradle to the grave, the lifestyle of street criminals is "created less by design than by default."[31] This finding, repeatedly confirmed in ethnographic research, does not lessen the responsibility of offenders for their offenses, but calls into question the usefulness of concepts borrowed from conventional society. Fleisher argues that street criminals do not have careers, and thinking of their offenses or the pattern of their lives as following from a series of life events similar to those outside this sociocultural environment will do little to increase understanding of the patterns of property offending. There is too little planning in how the street criminal approaches life and crime to constitute a career. As will be explored throughout this chapter, the type of offense specialization existing among property offenders is a loosely based preference for certain types of offending but not necessarily for a particular offense.

Property Offenders and Rational Choice

Research on property crimes is often investigated from the perspective of rational choice theories, discussed in Chapter 4. One definition of *rationality* is offered by Dermot Walsh: "activities identified by their impersonal, methodical, efficient, and logical components."[32] While the decision making, motivation, and target selection of property offenders will be explored throughout this chapter, it is crucial to understand now that the rationality of the typical criminal offender is not the same as "the rationality used by the civil engineer."[33] In line with the research of Thomas Bennett and Richard Wright on the rationality surrounding decision making by burglars,[34] Walsh's research concludes that offenders employ a "limited, temporal rationality." Walsh says, "Not all these men are highly intelligent, and few are equipped to calculate Bentham-style, even supposing the information were available. Yet it is very common for rationality to be used. Of course it is partial and limited rather than total, but at the time, the actor feels he has planned enough and weighed enough data."[35] This is in many ways no different from the limited type of rationality that many conventional individuals employ in their daily activities. While some offenders, certainly those closer to the end of the continuum marked professional, will use a higher degree of rationality and still others will at times exhibit behavior that is totally senseless, most expressions of rationality are not as dramatically clear. As Neil Shover and David Honaker state, "Rationality is not a dichotomous variable," and given the extent to which it is shaped by the social context of offenders' lives, researchers must "learn more about the daily worlds that comprise the immediate contexts of criminal decision making behavior."[36]

The extent to which property crimes are rational pursuits for either expressive or instrumental gains is a question that will be addressed by examining a wide variety of research on typologies of property crime offending. The property crimes discussed in this chapter include larceny-theft, motor vehicle theft, burglary, and arson. These offenses were introduced in Chapter 2, which provided offense definitions from several sources, along with statistical information on prevalence. Although some of the earlier material is referenced in this chapter, you should refer back to Chapter 2 for more detail. Learn more about trends in property crimes from **Library Extra 11–1** at crimtoday.com.

LIBRARY
Extra
■ ■ ■ ■

Criminal Profiles

Frank W. Abagnale, Jr. ("Catch Me If You Can")

High school dropout Frank Abagnale never met a credential he couldn't cheerfully ignore. He simply assumed any role that needed a credential and let you assume that he had it—or helped you assume he had it by showing you convincing forgeries of qualifying documents. Airline pilot? Not a problem for a guy wearing the right uniform and carrying a fake ID card. Lawyer? Simply forge a Harvard Law diploma, pass the bar, and hire on as a staff attorney in a state attorney general's office. Pediatrician? College professor at Brigham Young University? Stockbroker? FBI Agent? (Yes, FBI Agent!) These are but a few of the personas this bright and charming phony assumed during a five-year con spree in the 1960s.[i]

How did he do it? *Chutzpah,* mostly.

Born April 17, 1948, Abagnale started by conning his father out of $2,500 just after the younger Abagnale's sixteenth birthday. Allowed to use his father's gas credit card, Abagnale schemed for spending money by using the card to buy tires from a gas station, then sell them back to the station owner at half price for cash.[ii] The scam was discovered at the same time that Abagnale's parents were divorcing, which gave him an excuse to run off to New York.

He was a 16-year-old runaway when he made his first big score—$40,000—by printing up a bunch of bank deposit slips with his own account number (obtained, of course, under a false name) printed on them in magnetic ink. He then placed them at the service desk in the bank's lobby in place of the generic deposit slips provided by the bank for customer use. Other customers used the slips to make deposits, thinking that the deposit would be credited to their own accounts. In reality, the automated processing equipment would read Abagnale's account number magnetically encoded on the slip and credit his account for the amount of the deposit. When the account balance reached $40,000, he simply withdrew the funds and closed the account.

Abagnale impersonated a Pan Am pilot for more than two years, but he wisely never attempted to fly a plane. He simply used the role as a means to obtain free air travel all over the world by invoking an employment perk that is common throughout the industry: being able to fly free in a "jump" or vacant seat.

After five years of tricking people around the world, it was this very scam that finally got the then-21-year-old arrested in 1969, when an Air France flight attendant recognized him from a wanted poster on the bulletin board in the employee's lounge. Abagnale subsequently served time in prisons in France (six months) and Sweden (six months) before he was finally extradited to the United States. Convicted of federal forgery charges, he received a 12-year sentence to federal prison.[iii]

Abagnale's exploits during that infamous five-year period of nonstop cons were the subject of Steven Spielberg's highly successful film *Catch Me If You Can,* released in 2002.

After Abagnale had served four years of his sentence, his tale significantly diverged from that of the ordinary felon. Because he had been so incredibly good at what he had done—he did, after all, confound the best investigators in the world for more than five years—Abagnale received an offer from the U. S. government that changed his life.

Larceny-Theft

As noted in Chapter 2, the Uniform Crime Reporting System defines *larceny-theft* as "the unlawful taking, carrying, leading, or riding away of property from the possession, or constructive possession, of another."[37] As a form of theft, larceny (as opposed to burglary) does not involve the use of force or other means of illegal entry. For this reason as well as others, larceny is a crime "less frightening than burglary because to a large, perhaps even to a preponderant extent, it is a crime of opportunity, a matter of making off with whatever happens to be lying around loose: Christmas presents in an unlocked car, merchandise on a store counter, a bicycle in a front yard."[38] Just about anything can be stolen. In California during November 2000, for example, thieves stole "more than 1,200 young orange trees during nightly raids at the San Joaquin Valley, heartland of the state's citrus crop."[39] The volume and specialized focus of crimes like this are clearly the province of professional thieves; orange trees are not the kind of item easily bartered on the street corner or the local pawn shop.

Prevalence and Profile of Larceny-Theft

Larceny is the most frequently occurring property offense, according to both official data compiled by the FBI and data from the National Crime Victimization Survey (NCVS). Within the offenses subsumed under the category of larceny in UCR/NIBRS data, the largest category is theft from motor vehicles, followed by shoplifting and theft

Frank Abagnale, Jr. poses for a photo at the Four Seasons Hotel in Beverly Hills, California. Abagnale, portrayed by actor Leonardo DiCaprio in the film Catch Me If You Can, is the real-life subject of a book he wrote about his time as a successful con artist. How does Abagnale differ from most other property offenders?

Source: AP Wide World Photos/Lucy Nicholson

Seeking to learn how to prevent future Abagnale-like scams, the U.S. government asked Abagnale to teach them how he did the things he did and how to prevent them in the future. Specifically, they wanted to tap his innate ability to manipulate official documents in such a way as to virtually eliminate any chance of detection. In exchange, the government offered to immediately release him from prison.[iv]

And that is how Frank Abagnale, the most successful con man of the twentieth century, morphed into a world-renowned expert on forgery, embezzlement, and document security. Today, he heads Abagnale and Associates, a highly respected secure document consultancy. Abagnale has become an extraordinarily successful author and lecturer whose speeches, according to multiple-Oscar-winner Tom Hanks, "may be the best one-man show you will ever see."[v]

Notes:

[i] Bernie Alexander, "Frank Abagnale: From Fraud to FBI," AskMen.com, http://www.askmen.com/toys/special_feature/36_special_feature.html (accessed July 10, 2007).

[ii] Norman Swan, "Frank Abagnale–New Life," *Life Matters,* March 17, 2000, http://www.abc.net.au/rn/talks/lm/stories/s111098.htm (accessed July 10, 2007).

[iii] Rachael Bell, "Skywayman: The Story of Frank W. Abagnale Jr.," CourtTV Crime Library, http://www.crimelibrary.com/criminal_mind/scams/frank_abagnale/index.html (accessed July 10, 2007).

[iv] Ibid.

[v] Keppler Speakers home page, http://www.kepplerspeakers.com/speakers/speakers.asp?1+EV+1175 (accessed May 21, 2007).

from buildings.[40] Offenses like pocket picking and purse snatching constitute a small percentage of all larcenies, less than 1% each. Just as rates of different offenses within the category of larceny differ, so, too, do estimated losses to victims. As discussed in Chapter 2, data from both the UCR/NIBRS and the NCVS provide some basis to estimate the value of loss due to property crimes. Generally, thefts from large structures like buildings generate greater losses than do petty-level personal thefts. While the aggregate economic loss is quite high, slightly more than one-third of all losses individually are under $50. Personal items like jewelry and camera equipment, the largest category of stolen items, constitute almost one-fourth of all stolen goods. The NCVS category of theft covers items taken from motor vehicles, and these account for almost 13% of all items stolen. Firearms and cash constitute smaller percentages, ranging from less than 1% for firearms and 7% for cash.[41]

Theft on College Campuses

Any locale can be the setting for theft. As Marcus Felson notes, "A college campus is a giant delivery system. It funnels students, faculty, staff, and various products into one general location and moves them from building to building to deliver education. It also delivers crime opportunities."[42] Felson, who developed the routine activities perspective, states that "crime feeds off the physical form of local life," a form "organized by how people and things move about in everyday life. In the ways that they move around, people often prevent crime, whether they are aware of it or not, and both people and things sometimes contribute to crime in their presences or their absences."[43]

Larceny is not only the most common index offense, but also the most frequent on college campuses. While the Crime Awareness and Campus Security Act of 1990 (described in Chapter 2) mandates that institutions of higher learning compile and make public data on certain index offenses, crimes of theft are exempt from the requirement. **Magnus Seng,** a researcher who has investigated theft on college campuses, notes that "to omit theft is to present a misleading picture of crime on campus."[44]

Some researchers have conducted independent investigations of theft on college campuses. Seng, for example, gathered data from incident reports at two campuses of Loyola University in Chicago during 1993. The two campuses had different characteristics; for example, one was located in an area with higher theft rates. Seng wanted to investigate whether the nature and prevalence of crime in the areas surrounding the campuses affected the nature of crime on campus. He found that reported thefts were lower on campus than in the surrounding areas. There was some diversity in the type of stolen items, with purses and wallets being the largest category (22%), followed by cash (14%), bicycles (10%), and about equal percentages of audiovisual and lab/office equipment. Consistent with the value of stolen property in the surrounding area, "over three quarters (77%) of these thefts were classified as involving items worth $300 or less."[45] Members of the university staff had the highest victimization rates for thefts, followed by members of the faculty. Students had the lowest rates. Seng investigated exactly where the thefts occurred and focused on the type of buildings, as this was another factor that distinguished the two campuses. Seng classified all buildings by type, such as classroom, office, multipurpose use, student residence, and so forth. He found that the difference in the design of the campuses was a major determinant of differences in theft rates—a factor more important than the theft rates in surrounding areas. Thefts were more frequent on the campus with the largest number of buildings and the largest population of students, faculty, and staff. Approaching theft as primarily a crime of opportunity, Seng found that the larger campus afforded "more targets of opportunity" for theft.[46]

Elizabeth Ehrhardt Mustaine and Richard Tewksbury, using a probability sample of college students in eight states, examined the importance of both individual lifestyle and community characteristics as they impact the likelihood of being the victim of a larceny.[47] Similar to other, more sophisticated tests of routine activities theory, their research revealed that both (1) measures of individual lifestyle (such as the way in which an individual spends leisure time), and (2) characteristics of the community where the individual resides, are predictors of victimization. Mustaine and Tewksbury emphasized that an individual's lifestyle need not be "unhealthy" to reflect increased risk of victimization. College students, for example, who spend a significant amount of time studying away from their residence, or who are involved in numerous organizations on campus, have an increased risk of major theft victimization. Self-protective measures, such as installing additional door locks and owning a dog, appear to be quite effective deterrents to victimization and result in a lower likelihood of suffering either a minor or a major theft. Mustaine and Tewksbury conclude that, as in the general population, the "specifics of where you are, what your behaviors are, and what you are doing to protect yourself are the more important aspects of lifestyle influencing victimization risk."[48] Learn more about theft on college campuses at **Web Extra 11–2.**

WEB
Extra

Motor Vehicle Theft

As noted in Chapter 2, the UCR Program defines *motor vehicle theft* as "the theft or attempted theft of a motor vehicle," where the term *motor vehicle* refers to various means of transportation, including automobiles, buses, motorcycles, and snowmobiles.[49] Automobiles are the type of vehicle most often stolen. The frequency with which thefts of motor vehicles occur and the cultural association of automobiles with status warrant special focus. Cars represent more than merely a possession; for many Americans, they are an extension of their identity. The type of car one drives reflects social status. It is well-known that a Lexus is more expensive than a Volkswagen, and a minivan is not a car that any self-respecting teenager would take for a joyride.

Similar to home-invasion robbery or residential burglary, the theft of a car violates the victim in a way that goes beyond financial loss. Besides representing an invasion of the victim's possessions and personal space, auto theft creates a significant inconvenience. The theft of a car makes it difficult for many people to get to work and sometimes requires them to take time away from work to take care of the incident. Motor vehicle theft is the offense for which the highest percentage of victims report that the incident required them to miss some time at work. In 22% of all motor vehicle thefts, the victim reports losing time at work, compared with about 7% for household burglary and 12% for violent crimes like robbery. As with other offenses, approximately one-third of the victims of motor vehicle theft miss work for less than one day and about one-half for anywhere from one to five days.[50]

Prevalence and Profile of Motor Vehicle Theft

As noted in Chapter 2, approximately 1.2 million vehicles were reported stolen in 2006, with an estimated total value in excess of $7.9 billion. The largest percentage of stolen vehicles were in a parking lot or garage at the time of the theft.[51] A significant percentage of motor vehicle thefts take place either at or quite near the victim's residence, with approximately 17% taking place on a street near the home.[52] If a broader definition of *near* is used, the percentage of auto thefts taking place near the victim's residence increases. Depending on the neighborhood in which the victim resides, *near home* can mean different things, and the same distance from the residence in urban communities may be more of a risk for motor vehicle theft than in other communities. Marcus Felson contends that the risks posed by where one parks are related to population density. "In low-density areas, one finds more personal garages and opportunities to park right near the home or office. Those living or working in high-density areas are more likely to have street parking and higher risk of auto theft."[53] According to one study, the most common activity that victims were engaged in at the time of the motor vehicle theft was sleeping (41%), followed by leisure activities away from the home (15%), activities at home (14%), and employment (10%).[54]

Based on data from NCVS for 2006, on average 81% of all motor vehicle thefts, both attempted and completed, are reported to the police. As is seen with other offenses, the reporting percentage is higher (90%) for completed motor vehicle thefts than for attempted incidents (54%).[55] While the rate of motor vehicle victimization is the same for the lowest-income households (under $7,500) as for the highest-income households ($75,000 or more), the rate of reporting increases with the income level of the household.[56] Based on available data, approximately 62% of stolen cars are recovered.[57] Both law enforcement agencies and insurance companies keep records of recovered vehicles, but each employs its own definition of *recovery*. No matter what the condition of the vehicle, law enforcement agencies will consider any found vehicle to be recovered. Insurance companies use definitions that are based on how much damage was done to the vehicle relative to its market value. Even if the 62% recovery rate is a conservative estimate, it must be kept in mind that recovery of a stolen vehicle does not guarantee that the auto is in its original state. Almost "one-third of the recovered stolen vehicles are completely stripped at 'chop shops' and another third are stripped of easy-to-sell accessories like radios, air bags, and seats."[58] Stripping cars for parts has increased since the 1970s, as has the variety of venues for such activities—an issue to which we will return shortly.

Cars are stolen for a variety of reasons, including joyriding, temporary transportation needs, use in a crime, and stripping. As we will discuss later, each of these rationales is representative of a fairly distinctive offender profile, with teenagers, for example, most likely to take cars for joyriding. Given the wide variety of rationales supporting automobile theft, almost any type of car is potentially a target. However, thieves tend to prefer certain cars. For the past several years, Honda Accords and Toyota Camrys have been two of the models preferred by thieves.[59] According to Robert Bryant, chief executive officer of the National Insurance Crime Bureau, "Vehicle thieves follow market trends and target the most popular vehicles because they provide the best market for stolen vehicle parts and illegal export to other countries."[60]

Theft of Car Parts

The theft of car parts is variously motivated. Some car parts are worth a significant sum on the illegal market and can be sold easily by even the most inexperienced thieves. Novice thieves usually do not have access to the type of network required to sell "hot cars." Also, stolen car parts are more difficult to identify than are entire cars.[61]

In the United States, the Motor Vehicle Theft Law Enforcement Act,[62] passed by Congress in 1984, "called for the marking of the major sheet metal parts of high-theft automobiles with Vehicle Identification Numbers (VINs). The point of the law was to enable detection of persons engaged in the presumably widespread sale of stolen parts to the auto body repair industry."[63] While previous legislation had required the marking of the transmission, engine, and frame, the requirement to mark additional parts reflected a presumption "that chopping accounts for the theft of a very high proportion of automobiles, particularly those lines which exhibit high theft rates."[64] While data on how many car thefts are carried out for stripping are scarce, some research has been conducted in this regard both in the United States and elsewhere.

Some researchers report that while theft of vehicle parts constitutes most automobile crime, the exact nature of what is taken from the car has not been the subject of extensive research.[65] Conventional wisdom held that stereo equipment was the primary target. Using data from the 1998 British Crime Survey, Joanna Sallybanks and Nerys Thomas found that "the most frequently stolen items were external parts of the vehicle, such as body panels, windshield wipers, mirrors, luggage racks, antennas, and tires and wheels, followed by stereo equipment and 'other' items (bags, briefcases, cameras, clothing, etc.)."[66] Over the past few years, the theft of stereo equipment has held constant, but the theft of external parts has increased significantly. When vehicle parts are the objects of theft, these incidents are even less likely to be reported to the police than other types of thefts. In 1997, for example, 20% of thefts involving car parts and 72% of thefts of stereo equipment were reported to the police. Sallybanks and Thomas offer four reasons that car parts are stolen: "expense of replacing car parts," "lack of availability of car parts for older models," "the demand for license plates," and "youth crazes, e.g. the fashion for wearing VW badges."[67] Further analysis of data on the type

A Philadelphia police officer carries parts of stolen cars out of a chop shop during a raid. A chop shop is a place where stolen cars are disassembled and their parts sold. Why is the sale of parts often more profitable for criminals than the sale of stolen vehicles?

Source: George Widman, AP Wide World Photos

of cars stolen supports the first two of these explanations. Concerning fashion trend crazes that drive theft of external parts, VW "redesigned their car badges in order to halt" this theft, "but this proved only a temporary palliative—in the 1980s the Beastie Boys, a rap-rock group, re-introduced the fashion."[68]

Joyriders: Car Theft for Fun

A certain percentage of car thefts are opportunistic in nature, committed by teenagers, usually in groups, for the purpose of fun or thrills. These offenses are referred to as **joyriding.** Because such thefts generally involve the temporary appropriation of a vehicle primarily to satisfy needs ranging from excitement to personal autonomy, joyriding is often characterized as an "expressive act with little or no extrinsic value."[69] This motivation for auto theft is not characterized by planning and quite often resembles the following scenario provided by Michael Gottfredson and Travis Hirschi: "The typical auto theft [involves] a car left unlocked on a public street or in a public parking lot with the keys in the ignition or in plain view [that] is entered by a 16-year-old male or group of males and is driven until it runs out of gas or until the offenders must attend to other obligations."[70]

joyriding

An opportunistic car theft, often committed by a teenager seeking fun or thrills.

Most vehicles stolen for purposes of joyriding are recovered, usually found abandoned and often after they have been crashed. The types of vehicles stolen for joyriding are distinct from those stolen for other purposes. Joyriders favor sports cars, particularly American-made cars.[71] While the majority of auto thefts involve victims and offenders who are unknown to each other, cars stolen for joyriding are one of the exceptions to this pattern. While adolescents may select a vehicle for joyriding that belongs to strangers, they are more likely to select the car of a known owner.[72]

Available research offers no definite answer as to whether there is a distinctive social class profile of the joyriding offender. Following the early work of William W. Wattenberg and James Balliestri,[73] the "favored-group hypothesis" associates higher social class with greater involvement in auto theft because of greater access to cars and an earlier association of cars as status symbols. On the other hand, the "disadvantaged-group hypothesis" contends that youths from lower socioeconomic classes are more likely to be involved in car thefts because conventional means of acquiring status symbols like cars are blocked, and they are left with only the avenue of illegitimate acquisition.[74] Although some support has been found for each of these perspectives, other research has failed to find a link between social class and involvement in auto theft among adolescents.[75]

Jockeys: Car Theft for Profit

Jockey is a slang term for car thieves who are regularly involved in "steal-to-order jobs."[76] In horse racing, the value of a jockey lies in how quickly he or she can ride a horse to the finish line; for professional car thieves, "the quicker the ride, the more productive the race, and the more races are made, the more productive the jockey."[77] This type of car theft was characterized in American movies like *Gone in 60 Seconds,* in which the lead character, a former jockey, must once again take the reins and successfully steal 50 designated cars in a 24-hour period to save his brother from death by unscrupulous characters.

jockey

A professional car thief involved regularly in calculated, steal-to-order car thefts.

While representing the most costly and most serious form of auto theft, professional thefts are not as common as thefts for other uses, such as joyriding. Like joyriders, professional auto thieves operate in groups, but their groups are characterized by a great deal more planning and calculation in target selection. The cars targeted by professional thieves are luxury cars that may be driven across national borders or shipped overseas. Professional thefts have the lowest recovery rates. Still, professionals are only a small part of the vehicle theft problem. Hence, Ronald V. Clark and Patricia M. Harris contend that "successful action against professional theft [would] have less effect on the scale of the overall problem than against thefts for temporary use and much less than against thefts from the vehicle."[78] Learn more about motor vehicle theft at **Web Extra 11–3.**

WEB
Extra
■ ■ ■ ■

Shoplifting and Employee Theft

According to the National Retail Security Survey (NRSS), an annual survey by the University of Florida, "Theft cost U.S. retailers a staggering $33.6 billion" in 2002.[79] Each incident of shoplifting was estimated to cost the retailer on average $265.40, and thefts by employees averaged $1,762.00 per incident. The largest category of loss is employee theft; 47% of loss results from employee theft, compared with 32% from shoplifting. While the survey shows that both employee theft and shoplifting have increased over time, employee theft has grown at a faster rate. "The theft of merchandise by employees can range from the simple act of walking out the door with stolen goods to complex schemes requiring the manipulation of documents and/or involving several employees."[80] Most of the employees engaging in theft of either cash or merchandise are short-term workers. They are typically found in retail establishments with higher-than-average sales and a significant degree of turnover in management. Many retailers perceive the issue of internal theft to be much more serious than the economic loss caused by customer shoplifting.

Retailers must consider that efforts to combat shoplifting might impact sales. This concern was reflected by a marketing director who commented, "You don't want to hinder sales by intimidating the shopper. We used to think just about stopping shoplifting. We didn't think enough about selling more merchandise."[81]

Technology represents one of the best ways to address both shoplifting and employee theft. The use of computerized inventory counts to track merchandise is quite useful in quickly identifying thefts by employees. As will be discussed shortly, the widespread prevalence of shoplifting among youths means that increased security personnel in stores are less successful at detection than are electronic and other devices. Personnel must know whom to target to be successful, while security systems make shoplifting more difficult for everyone.[82] The NRSS found that "retailers' loss prevention budget averaged only 0.57 percent of annual retail sales."[83] The very technological developments that make managing inventory lists easier are the same techniques that most effectively manage the greatest loss to retailers—employee theft—without seriously undermining the attractiveness of the store to shoppers. Most of us are so familiar with antitheft devices attached to goods that we do not interpret this as an unusual part of the shopping experience. The effectiveness of these technological marvels is touted by Don Taylor, director of market planning for Sensormatic, a leading electronic security provider, who says that "when you're in a retail store environment, antitheft tags are worth their weight in gold."[84] While the majority of shoppers are not thieves, all shoppers are exposed to the same techniques used to safeguard against the actions of a few, and hence these particular strategies may adversely affect the attractiveness of the environment for honest shoppers.

The theft of merchandise from commercial establishments represents as common and prevalent a crime today as in the past. Historically, shoplifting "was most likely a concern that plagued the first merchants who placed their goods out in a public market place."[85] In cities like New York during the late 1800s and early 1900s, shoplifting was pervasive among middle-class women. While previous periods had seen the involvement of the disadvantaged, especially youths, in shoplifting, the involvement of the middle class was viewed as especially troubling. One explanation for middle-class involvement cites a change in the production, distribution, and marketing of goods. Women who once created goods for their families now went shopping for those goods in a new venue, the department store. Among other things, "department stores were designed to heighten sensory stimulation and create a desire for the merchandise."[86] Some authors of the early twentieth century suggested that "this new level of temptation and the assignment of shopping to weak-willed and sexually disordered females inevitably led to more shoplifting."[87] Another explanation offered for shoplifting among middle-class women was kleptomania. Because public officials of the early 1900s had no strong inclination to bring members of the middle class into court, kleptomania became a way to minimize the offenses of this group, "thus legitimatizing the actions of the stores and the courts to dismiss or acquit those afflicted with this women's sickness."[88]

Today, shoplifting continues to be an offense that crosses class lines, although it is not an offense committed primarily by women. The dominant motivation used today to explain shoplifting does not rely on medical labels. Even though "respectable" people continue to be found among those who commit this offense, there is no evidence that these individuals constitute a significant segment of offenders.

Who Shoplifts?

On December 6, 2002, actress Winona Ryder was sentenced to three years of probation and required to perform 480 hours of community service for shoplifting more than $5,500 in merchandise from a Beverly Hills, Calfornia, Saks Fifth Avenue store a year earlier. At sentencing, Superior Court Judge Elden Fox warned the 31-year-old Ryder that "If you steal again, you will go to jail."[89] The judge also ordered the two-time Academy Award nominee to participate in a court-approved drug-counseling program.

Although Ryder's case was widely covered by the news media, she is not a typical shoplifter. In self-reports of offending, official arrest data, and store records, juveniles are overrepresented as shoplifters. While variation exists in the frequency of offending among adolescents, most offending patterns are fairly sporadic and characterized by a greater prevalence among younger adolescents. The sporadic nature of shoplifting among adolescents is typical across all social classes, even though the most serious and chronic forms are found among the economically disadvantaged. While females represent the majority of offenders in some shoplifting data sources, this finding has been seriously challenged in research since the 1970s.[90]

Lloyd W. Klemke's research, which used self-report techniques to assess juvenile shoplifting, revealed that almost two-thirds of the sample had shoplifted at some point in their lifetime.[91] Klemke's sample consisted of high school students from four different schools in the Pacific Northwest. A significantly higher percentage of males compared with females reported shoplifting during the year considered. Although previous research by **Mary Owen Cameron** using department store records had revealed that females were more likely than males to be apprehended for shoplifting,[92] Klemke found the reverse to be true. The difference in these findings may be attributed to the fact that Klemke's research included only adolescents, whereas Cameron's research also included adults.

Two-time Academy Award nominee Winona Ryder reacts as a guilty verdict is read in her 2002 trial. Ryder was sentenced to three years of probation and required to perform 480 hours of community service for shoplifting more than $5,500 in merchandise from a Beverly Hills, California, Saks Fifth Avenue store a year earlier. The actress was also ordered to participate in a court-approved drug-counseling program. Is Ryder a typical shoplifter?

Source: Steve Grayson/Reuters/ Landov LLC

In line with Cameron's findings, Klemke "found petty theft to be the dominant pattern for shoplifting" and described such theft as infrequent enough to correspond to the "sporadic pilfering" Cameron reported.[93] Klemke found the frequency of shoplifting to vary by the social class of the offender.

Youths from lower-income households are more likely to shoplift than their higher-income counterparts. However, this relationship is a moderate one at best, and the fact remains that shoplifting is reported by a solid majority of youths in several self-report studies. The relationship between social class and likelihood of shoplifting is stronger among adults. While research in this area is sparse, JoAnn Ray's study of shoppers in Spokane, Washington, revealed that out of a random sample, those in lower-income groups were three times more likely to shoplift as those in higher-income brackets.[94]

Among Klemke's other findings was a "maturing out" pattern, whereby "shoplifting activity peaked in the under ten age category" and decreased considerably as the youths entered adolescence.[95] These findings are contrary to other research that supports escalation during late adolescence.

An Adolescent Phase?

No one type of youth is most likely to shoplift. That a majority of youths report such activity makes shoplifting one of the largest categories of unofficial delinquency—that is, delinquency that is not detected by authorities. This finding has been observed in research outside the United States. Shoplifting was so prevalent in Janne Kivivuori's research on Finnish adolescents, for example, that she concluded that it was "culturally paradigmatic" and that the adolescents themselves viewed it as a normal phase of adolescence.[96] This observation is in line with other research purporting that given its prevalence across a wide variety of individuals, juvenile delinquency is almost by definition a period in a person's life when shoplifting will occur.[97] Shoplifting that assumes the form of "adolescence-limited phasic behavior can be seen as normal for at least three reasons: because of its relatively high prevalence, because adolescents are expected to loosen their ties to social control, and because our culture is full of descriptions under which periodical crises and phases make sense."[98] Adolescence-limited offenders, discussed in Chapter 8, are the largest group of those engaged in delinquency for whom the onset and desistance from deviance can be fairly well predicted.[99] Using a large and randomly selected sample of Finnish adolescents, Kivivuori estimated the extent to which shoplifting could be characterized as episodic in nature and looked for identifiable periods of intense activity. The typical phase of shoplifting for the Finnish adolescents began around age 13 and ended by age 14. As in other research, 26% of the adolescents reported a lack of money as the primary rationale for shoplifting, with an equal percentage reporting excitement as the primary reason. Equally revealing were the findings on why the adolescents ceased to shoplift. Almost one-third of the sample reported boredom as the reason, followed by 21% who were apprehended and 11% who cited wisdom as their primary rationale for desistance. While Kivivuori concludes that juveniles who engage in phases of intense shoplifting may steal more than juveniles whose shoplifting is not characterized by such phases, there is still no evidence that intense shoplifting reflects significant psychological problems. Shoplifting appears to be one of several forms of deviant behavior during adolescence, and "a shoplifting phase is one of the many cafeteria items selected by juveniles whose ties to sources of social control have been weakened."[100]

Shoplifting as a Gateway Offense

gateway offense

An offense, usually fairly minor in nature, that leads to more serious offenses. Shoplifting, for example, may be a gateway offense to more serious property crimes.

Evidence has long supported the notion that shoplifting is part of the early offense history of a certain segment of property offenders. Hence, shoplifting may be a kind of **gateway offense**—an offense that represents a starting point leading to more serious and chronic types of offending. Frederick M. Thrasher's classic study of gangs in Chicago, published in 1927, detailed how various forms of property crime were found among boys in gangs.[101] Although shoplifting was quite prevalent, there was no indication that

Crime in the News

Thieving Divas Hit Big Easy Boutiques

NEW ORLEANS—Along a funky stretch of Magazine Street, shopkeepers are on the alert for criminals dressed to steal.

A gang of cross-dressing shoplifters, tall, slender men in brassy blonde wigs, stiletto heels and skintight tank tops, have been terrorizing clothing stores for months. They've hit at least a half-dozen times since shops reopened after Katrina hit on Aug. 29.

"This is the way they get the stuff they want to wear," says Noel Barras, owner of Winky's clothing and gift shop, one of the fixtures on this hip street of antique stores and clothing boutiques.

The designer-purse toting bandits are yet another blow for a community struggling to stay alive after Katrina. Magazine Street did not flood and these shops were some of the first in the city to reopen last fall, giving the city one of its first economic boosts.

A shop called Turncoats, which sells slinky tank tops and T-shirts, recently got looted for about $2,000, says owner Wes Davis. The female impersonators don't seem to be carrying weapons and instead use distracting props like fake babies or real toddlers.

Kendra Bonga, the manager of Winky's on Magazine Street in New Orleans, brings her dog, Dr. Phibes, to work for protection against gang theft. What other types of remedies might be available to store owners?

Source: Cheryl Gerber for USA Today

"It was all the loudest, the brightest of our inventory," Davis says of the stolen goods. "Neon green zip-ups, hot pink tank tops. Loud, fun, go-out clothing. . . . They use the fact that you don't want to stare at them, and that gives them time to rip you off."

The shoplifters strike an intimidating pose, towering well over 6 feet in their high heels, Davis says. When they're not wearing wigs, they sport dreadlocks with a blond streak down the middle. Once their arms are full of merchandise, they flee in a white Toyota driven by what appears to be a woman, Barras says.

Police response has been tepid, store owners say. The department is so overwhelmed by a recent spike in violent crime that the National Guard has been called in to help patrol city streets. So officers don't have much time for Magazine Street's woes.

"That's way down the priority list right now," Capt. John Bryson says.

Store owners have devised their own protection system, notifying one another by phone if the thieves are seen on the street. "If one person sees them then they tell everyone else and we lock our doors," Barras says.

Cross-dressing crooks are not new here: Davis remembers a different group hitting the upscale shops of Canal Place Mall six years ago. Nor are they strictly a New Orleans thing. In the early 1990s, a large, loose-knit group of "transvestite fashion robbers" pilfered designer clothes in shops from Miami to Manhattan. In 2004, cross-dressers were arrested in Alabama for stealing cars that police said they used to drive to transvestite beauty pageants. And in April, a cross-dressing shoplifter in Omaha died in a high-speed car chase with police.

"It's sad that we were the first here to get the economy going and now we have no protection," Barras says.

Discussion Questions

1. How does shoplifting differ from other kinds of larceny?

2. Why have the police been slow in responding to shopkeepers' needs?

3. What kind of impact might this kind of crime, if it continues, have on New Orleans?

Source: Anne Rochell Konigsmark, "Thieving Divas Hit Big Easy Boutiques," *USA Today,* July 9, 2006. Reprinted with permission.

For the latest crime and justice news, visit www.crimenews.info.

it served as a starting point for more serious offending, at least in any formal sense. Shoplifting is not an offense limited in any systematic way by the age of the offender; in its simplest form, it requires little skill or training and is accomplished within several different venues. It is less likely that shoplifting forms an impetus for increasing levels of involvement in more serious forms of property crime than it is likely that shoplifting satisfies material and sensational needs among a group of individuals who are fairly nonspecialized in their offending.

Other research has offered more support for shoplifting as a gateway to more serious offending. In interviews with 60 repeat property offenders in a Tennessee prison, **Kenneth D. Tunnell** found that some offenders had begun with shoplifting and that late offenses reflected a calculated move to more serious property crimes. Tunnell found that among the majority of persistent property offenders, their careers "consisted of progressive steps, with each step representing a different crime type of specialty."[102] Tunnell offers no direct research, however, that supports the idea that offenders move systematically from lesser to more serious forms of property offending. Additionally, offenders often fall back on lesser offenses like shoplifting if the occasion presents itself or if such offenses appear to be attractive and profitable. Thus, offenders do not clearly move in a linear fashion from one type of property offense to another; the process is more like a feedback loop that is sporadic and fragmented in its progression forward.

Meaningful Typologies for Shoplifting

Several researchers have attempted to use research findings to formulate shoplifting typologies that focus on the motivation and frequency of offending as the primary means of distinguishing among the quite heterogeneous group that shoplifts. Mary Owen Cameron distinguished between those who engaged professionally in shoplifting and those who were novices. The former group, the **boosters,** were a small percentage of all those apprehended for shoplifting. Boosters usually sold the items that they stole rather than engaging in shoplifting primarily for their own personal consumption. The large group of novice shoplifters, the **snitches,** was characterized by a tendency to steal for their own personal gratification, quite often stealing items of small monetary value.[103]

Richard H. Moore's typology of shoplifters goes beyond the preliminary categorization offered by Cameron and further builds upon motivational variation among these offenders. *Impulsive shoplifters* were inexperienced, rarely planned the offense in advance, and were quite remorseful upon apprehension. *Occasional shoplifters* made up about 15% of Moore's sample, a representation similar to that of the impulsive group. The offending of the occasional group was more frequent than that of the impulsive group and was motivated primarily by peer pressure. The smallest group was the *episodic shoplifters,* who generally had psychological problems. *Amateur shoplifters* were the largest type, making up slightly more than one-half of the sample. Shoplifting was a fairly regular activity for this group, and their offending incidents were calculated to maximize profit and minimize risk. *Semiprofessional shoplifters,* making up almost 12% of the sample, were the group for whom shoplifting was an integral part of their everyday lives. Members of this group possessed the greatest degree of skill and expertise in their offending and showed a clear preference for more expensive items. Moore found that it was only the semiprofessional shoplifters who, like the boosters in Cameron's research, stole merchandise for resale to others.[104] Because Moore's sample consisted entirely of convicted shoplifters, the extent to which the typology he developed is applicable to the majority of shoplifters, those who are never apprehended, is unclear.

In another attempt to develop a meaningful typology of shoplifters, **Frank J. McShane** and **Barrie A. Noonan** used a sophisticated statistical technique called "cluster analysis" to sort shoplifters into groups, taking into account relevant demographic characteristics, prior offending history, psychological factors, and measures of life purpose.[105] Using data on 75 subjects who had been apprehended for shoplifting in a variety of retail stores, McShane and Noonan identified four clusters of shoplifter types. *Rebels,* accounting for almost 19% of the sample, were primarily composed of younger females with a significant prior history of offending. *Reactionaries* were slightly more than 27% of the sample and were similar to the rebels in that they often had the economic wherewithal to pay for the stolen merchandise. Members of this group were older, had higher levels of education, and were more likely to be married and to be male, compared with members of other groups. A "distinguishing characteristic of these shoplifters was that occupational pressure was found to be the exclusively reported psychosocial stressor."[106] *Enigmas* were almost one-half of the sample (41.43%), and these offenders, like reactionaries, were older and slightly more likely to be male than most other groups, with a low likelihood of prior criminal offending. Members of this group "were characterized by a notable lack of apparent psychosocial stressors preceding

booster

A frequent shoplifter.

snitch

An amateur shoplifter.

apprehension."[107] The final group, the *infirm,* was more likely to be female than male, and this category was most likely to contain the elderly. Perhaps this latter finding explains another defining characteristic of this group, their tendency to have "experienced more previous episodes of chronic illness."[108]

The Thrill of It All

Many shoplifters have the economic means to afford the items they steal; many have significant amounts of money on them at the time of their offenses. Hence, there must be some motivation that drives shoplifters other than financial need. Is shoplifting a thrill-seeking activity? Jack Katz, whose work was discussed in Chapter 4, argues that many property crimes, including shoplifting, represent "sneaky thrills"—in other words, it is not a desire for the object that leads to the crime but the crime that makes the object desirable.[109] Referring to adolescents in particular, Katz states that "quite apart from what is taken, they may regard 'getting away with it' as a thrilling demonstration of personal competence, especially if it is accomplished under the eyes of adults."[110] Using self-report data from college students in his classes over a three-year period, Katz concludes that many individuals, once they are apprehended for shoplifting, report feelings of profound degradation, reflecting their basic awareness that shoplifting is wrong. The sense of thrill does not last, as further evidenced by the Finnish adolescents in Kivivuori's research who cited boredom as a reason for desistance from shoplifting. Learn more about the crime of shoplifting at **Web Extra 11–4.**

WEB
Extra
▪▪▪▪

Burglary

In 1967, the President's Commission on Law Enforcement and Administration of Justice noted that the high prevalence of burglaries and the numerous costs incurred by burglary victims make this offense one of the "major reasons for America's alarm about crime."[111] Burglary continues to be a highly prevalent crime. Based on a recent examination of victimization data, 72% of households within the United States are burglarized at least once over the average lifetime.[112] In contrast to lifetime risk, the risk of burglary within any given year is much lower. Even so, burglary is feared because the offense invades the sanctity and privacy of the home and threatens the existence of businesses. Who are the offenders? Are they primarily professionals who plan their offenses with great care and carry out their tasks with precision and finesse? While the image of the professional burglar is part of our popular culture, it is far removed from the reality of how most burglars operate. The overwhelming majority of burglars are not charismatic figures who silently steal into a dwelling and make off with the contents of a safe.

As discussed in Chapter 2, burglary involves unlawful entry into a structure for the purpose of felony commission, generally a theft. The structure may be a business, a residence, or some other type of building. Force is not a necessary ingredient of burglary, but burglaries are differentiated by whether force is used. In its collection of crime data, the FBI distinguishes among burglaries involving forcible entry, unlawful entry, and attempted forcible entry.[113] According to UCR/NIBRS data for 2006, the majority of burglaries involve forcible entry, followed in prevalence by unlawful entry and then by attempted forcible entry. In 2006, as in previous years, a slight majority of all burglaries occurred during the day; however, residential burglaries are more likely to occur during the evening.[114] In contrast to robbery, burglary is generally "a victim-avoiding crime."[115] Most residential burglars commit their offenses at a time when residents are unlikely to be home, and the knowledge of such information is important in target selection.

The consequences of both residential and commercial burglary can be quite profound for the victim. Residential burglaries, by definition, do not involve direct confrontation between the victim and the offender; however, the fear left in the aftermath of the offense can have lasting effects on the victim. The invasion of one's home produces a level of fear and apprehension beyond the dollar loss of the property taken. In cases of commercial burglary, because the targets are likely to be smaller, more economically precarious businesses, the loss from burglaries can seriously affect the business's continued viability.[116]

The Social Ecology of Burglary

Just as the propensity for property crime offending varies among individuals, so do rates of property crime across large aggregate units like states, cities, and communities. Burglary rates are higher in large metropolitan areas and in particular regions of the country, such as the South. Most research on variations in property crime at the aggregate level has examined how economics influences rates of crime. Lifestyle theory[117] and routine activities theory[118] (described in Chapter 4) have had a significant impact on explanations of how the nature and level of property crime offending have changed in response to alterations in the routine activities and structures of daily living. Both of these theoretical perspectives emphasize how criminal opportunity is affected by the everyday activities and environments experienced by victims and offenders. For a criminal act to occur, three ingredients are necessary: (1) someone who wants something (a *motivated offender*) coming into direct contact with (2) someone who has that thing (a *suitable target*) and (3) the lack of anything or anyone to inhibit the crime (a *capable guardian*). Individuals, families, and communities all respond to changes in technology, changes in the production and distribution of services and goods, and changes in the structure of the population. Advances in technology, for example, have made televisions, radios, stereos, and other electronic devices lighter and smaller over time, and more portable. Hence, they've become more suitable targets because they are easier to steal.[119] Consequently, some of the observed changes in crime rates since say, the 1970s when downsizing of electronics began in earnest, are not solely related to an increased supply of motivated offenders, but to changes in the patterns of routine activities. The basic contention of both lifestyle theory and routine activities theory is that what people do, where they do it, how often they do it, and with whom they do it all influence the risk of criminal victimization. The idea is to explore not why people commit crimes but, rather, "how the structure of social life makes it easy or difficult for people to carry out these inclinations," which are taken as a given.[120] The structure of everyday life in one's city, neighborhood, home, workplace, and so forth not only constrains the opportunity for individuals to act on inclinations to commit crimes, but also limits the ability of people to avoid victimization. As Marcus Felson says, "To attack other people or their property, you usually need to gain direct access to them. You have to find or stumble upon them, or they may stumble upon you. . . . The criminal event is a systematic result of the convergence of people and things over space and time. Routine activities provide choices to individuals, including criminals, and set the stage for subsequent events determining the success of the offender in carrying out the crime, or of the potential victim in avoiding victimization."[121]

In a study of residential burglary, Lawrence E. Cohen and David Cantor set out to test Michael Hindelang's hypothesis that household wealth was a more important factor in selection of burglary targets than was ease of access to the household.[122] Cohen and Cantor wanted to resolve often contradictory findings of previous research on the relationship between the impact of income and race on burglary victimization. Research by P. H. Ennis in the late 1960s, for example, had found that while burglary rates were higher for blacks than for whites, there was an interaction between race and income.[123] The lowest white income groups and the highest black income groups had the highest victimization risk. Cohen and Cantor found that, independent of race, the highest income households and the lowest income households in areas both within and outside the central city had the highest victimization risk. Their findings appear to show that high income and low income households are both targeted—one because it is thought to have items of special value, and the other because it provides ease of access.

Using data from the British Crime Survey, Robert J. Sampson and John D. Wooldredge estimated the risk for crimes like burglary and personal theft.[124] Given the specific implications of two components of opportunity theory for victimization risk—the proximity of suitable targets and motivated offenders and the spatial structure of community organization—these researchers were concerned with the impact of community context on lifestyle. For example, opportunity theory hypothesizes that single-adult households are associated with a decrease in guardianship and a correspondingly greater risk of victimization than are two-adult households. The proportion of such households may vary between communities; "regardless of one's household composition and even proximity to offenders, living in a community with low guardianship and surveillance may increase victimization risk."[125] The ability of an individual's living arrangement to predict victimization risk may not be a significant factor in victimization risk once relevant structural factors are considered. Hence, the determining factor may be more where the household is located and the nature of the surrounding households than the nature of a particular household. The findings from Sampson and Wooldredge's research revealed that the highest victimization risk for burglary was found within single-adult households compared with households with at least two adults. Also, younger heads of households and those households left unguarded had the highest victimization risk. Of the seven community-level variables included in the analysis, all but one had moderate to strong effects. The highest victimization risks were for residents in areas characterized by high unemployment, high building density, primary individual households, and single-parent households with children. Thus, even controlling for the individual-level factor of single-person households, the community measure of percentage of single-adult households continues to have a significant effect on increasing the risk of burglary victimization.

In looking at personal theft, Sampson and Wooldredge found that victimization risk for this offense was less for those who are married, older, and male.[126] Victimization risk was higher for individuals with more education and for women. Sampson and Wooldredge explain that these findings are consistent with the predictions of opportunity theory because of the facts that people of higher socioeconomic status are attractive targets and that the association of purse snatching with personal theft helps to explain the greater victimization risk for women. The community factors of the percentage of single adults with children, social cohesion, and street activity were significantly related to victimization risk. Areas characterized by a high degree of family disruption, low social cohesion, and a large amount of street activity had higher victimization risks for personal theft. Sampson and Wooldredge conclude that an overemphasis on individual patterns and lifestyle masks the more substantial effect that neighborhood context has on victimization risks for property crimes like burglary and personal theft. You can learn more about burglary trends by visiting the Bureau of Justice Statistics via **Web Extra 11–5**. Read about the most common targets of burglars at **Library Extra 11–2**.

WEB
Extra
■ ■ ■ ■

LIBRARY
Extra
■ ■ ■ ■

Types of Burglars

Building on **Mike Maguire**'s three-part typology of burglary types, Neil Shover analyzes how the social organization of burglary may vary. Maguire offered three basic categories of burglars; low-level, middle-range, and high-level.[127] *Low-level burglars,* primarily found among juveniles, often do their crimes "on the spur of the moment," usually work with others, and are easily dissuaded from a particular target by sound locks, alarms, and/or other such security devices. The rewards gained from offending for this group are generally not significant, and many desist from burglary as they get older and as they feel "the pull of conventional relationships and fear of more severe adult sanctions."[128] Members of this group do not develop connections that allow them to move large volumes of stolen goods.

Middle-range burglars are generally a bit older, though they may have begun their offending in burglary as juveniles. These offenders quite often go back and forth between legitimate pursuits and involvement in crime. The use of alcohol and other drugs is more common among middle-range offenders than among the other two groups of burglars.

Theory Versus Reality

Ethnographic Research on Active Burglars

Ethnographic research purports to understand the nature of burglary by getting as close as possible to the everyday social world of burglars. Rather than focusing on a very large group of burglars, such as those represented by arrest statistics, ethnographic research (discussed in Chapter 9) attempts to understand a burglar's way of life and hence offers a depth of insight rarely achieved in survey research or research using official data. However, the information solicited in ethnographic research is taken from a small group of research subjects—as small as one if a case study approach is used. Ethnographic research is often dangerous, costly, and time-consuming. The question arises, then, of whether it is worthwhile. Commenting on his own use of this approach in early work on burglars, Neil Shover acknowledged, "A great deal of time and leg work was required to set up and conduct these free-world interviews, and on balance I am not certain they were worth it. I elicited virtually nothing in them which had not been obtained in the earlier stages of the study when I was concentrating upon prison inmates and reading autobiographies."[i]

Do criminologists learn anything special about burglars by focusing on active burglars who are not currently incarcerated? This question is especially important because imprisoned burglars may be quite different from those still on the streets. Incarcerated offenders represent failure, while those who are free are relatively successful burglars who have avoided apprehension. This distinction, however, may be more myth than reality for the vast majority of burglars. The professionalized nature of burglary is quite minimal at best and hence not really the primary rationale for the usefulness of ethnographic data. The true benefit that comes from studying active burglars is related to an essential methodological issue common to all research endeavors; it is the classic issue of how individuals behave when they know they are being studied. In the case of studying burglars who are active versus those who are incarcerated, Richard T. Wright and Scott H. Decker note that individuals behave differently "in the wild" than in the jailhouse. The researchers rely on statements made by two of the pioneers in criminology, Edwin Sutherland and Donald Cressey, more than 30 years ago: "Those who have had intimate contacts with criminals in the open know that criminals are not 'natural' in police stations, courts, and prisons, and that they must be studied in their everyday life outside of institutions if they are to be understood."[ii] It is this concern for getting as close as possible to the social world one is studying that marks the tradition of ethnography. A further benefit in studying offenders outside institutional settings is the elimination of any bias or distortions that the setting may have on the subject's ability or willingness to be open with the interviewer. Offenders who are currently incarcerated may feel that even in the face of assurances of confidentiality, they can affect their chances of being released by what they say or do not say to the researchers. As Wright and Decker state, "Assurances of confidentiality notwithstanding, many prisoners remain convinced that what they say will affect their chances of being released and, therefore, they portray themselves in the best possible light."[iii]

Ethnographic research has already been described in Chapter 10, where research by Richard Wright and Scott Decker on armed robbers was discussed. This chapter presents further ethnographic research by Wright and Decker, this time on residential burglars. During 1989, the researchers located and interviewed 105 active residential burglars in St. Louis, Missouri. To qualify for inclusion in Wright and Decker's research, the offenders had to meet one of three criteria: they had to (1) have committed a residential burglary within two weeks prior to contact, (2) define themselves as residential burglars, or (3) be labeled as residential burglars by other offenders so identified. Research subjects were identified by the field workers whom Wright and Decker employed, most of whom were ex-offenders. The interviews with the subjects were all conducted in the field. Building on previous research on active offenders not currently incarcerated, Wright and Decker provide insight into various facets of the offending of burglars, including an examination of their motivation, target selection, entry method, search for valuable goods, and disposal of goods. In addition to answering questions, the offenders were asked to reconstruct their most recent residential burglary offense.

Defining the eligibility of subjects for research and using field workers are common practices in ethnographic research. Similar strategies were followed in the other ethnographic research projects discussed in this chapter. They include research on 30 active burglars in an urban Texas setting by Paul F. Cromwell and his colleagues[iv] and research on the professional fence by Darrell J. Steffensmeier.[v] As you read through the discussion of research in this chapter, keep in mind the strengths of ethnographic research and the insights to be gained by studying criminal offenders within their social and cultural contexts.

Discussion Questions

1. What is ethnographic research? How does it differ from other types of research in the field of criminology?

2. Can criminologists learn anything special about burglary by focusing on active burglars who are not currently incarcerated—rather than on burglars who are imprisoned?

3. What does the ethnographic research on residential burglars that has been conducted by Richard Wright and Scott Decker add to our knowledge about burglary?

Notes:

i Neil Shover, "Structures and Careers in Burglary," *Journal of Criminal Law, Criminology, and Police Science,* Vol. 63, No. 4 (1972), p. 541.

ii Edwin Sutherland and Donald Cressey, *Criminology,* 8th ed. (Philadelphia: Lippincott, 1970), p. 68, cited in Richard T. Wright and Scott H. Decker, *Burglars on the Job: Streetlife and Residential Break-Ins* (Boston: Northeastern University Press, 1994), p. 5.

iii Wright and Decker, *Burglars on the Job,* p. 5.

iv Paul F. Cromwell, James N. Olson, and D'Aunn Wester Avary, *Breaking and Entering: An Ethnographic Analysis of Burglary* (Newbury Park, CA: Sage, 1991).

v Darrell J. Steffensmeier, *The Fence: In the Shadow of Two Worlds* (Savage, MD: Rowman and Littlefield, 1986).

These offenders select targets that take into account both the potential payoff and the risk involved; however, this group is not as easily dissuaded by security devices as are the low-level burglars. While their take from their crimes may be substantial at times, they lack the type of connections that would permit dealing in stolen goods on a large scale.

High-level burglars are professionals. Burglary is an offense characterized by a large prevalence of co-offending, and high-level burglars work in organized crews and "are connected with reliable sources of information about targets."[129] Members of this group earn a good living from the proceeds of their crimes, which are carefully planned, including target selection, generally with the assistance of outside sources. Shover characterizes members of this group as "misfits in a world that values precise schedules, punctuality, and disciplined subordination to authority. High-level thieves value the autonomy to structure life and work as they wish."[130] Professional burglars may be known to the police, but due to their "task-force approach to organization," their activities remain largely concealed from detection.[131] It is only high-level burglars who would attempt such large-scale thefts as the art theft described at the beginning of this chapter.

Burglary Locales

Burglars at any level may target both residences and commercial buildings. Although most research has been devoted to residential burglary, many of the findings on patterns of offenders apply to both types. Police reports generally detail the time of the burglary; nighttime residential burglary and daytime commercial burglary are considered the most serious. Evening hours are considered the time burglars are most likely to face homeowners, and daytime hours are the time considered to present the greatest risk of confrontation between offenders and customers or workers.[132] According to NCVS data, a slightly larger percentage of residential burglaries takes place during the daytime than during the evening hours. One-third of burglary reports do not contain information on when the burglary occurred, so those incidents could significantly change the temporal pattern of occurrence.[133]

Burglary is known as a "cold" crime because there is usually very little physical evidence to link the offender to the offense, and by the time that the victims realize that they have been burglarized and have called the police, the burglar is usually long gone. This is more true of residential than commercial burglaries, as the latter are more likely to involve alarms or other security devices. Data from the NCVS also reveal that approximately 44% of victims were working or engaged in leisure activities away from home when their residence was burglarized. Approximately 13% of victims reported being asleep during the burglary.[134]

The Motivation of Burglars

Rational choice perspectives have guided a great deal of research on decision making among property offenders. As discussed in Chapter 4, rational choice perspectives do not necessarily contend that the decision-making process that individuals use is defined by only one objective or shared view of rationality. Instead, decision making is thought to be guided by the peculiar logic of the offender's perspective. The way in which offenders work out the logic of their decisions may not make sense objectively, but their decisions have their own internal logic from the standpoint of the offenders' social world and reflect the fact that many decision makers are "limited information processors with various simplifying strategies for resolving decisions."[135] These limitations and assumptions must be kept in mind when considering why some individuals commit residential burglary.

The most prevalent rationale behind the offense of residential burglary is economic in nature: a need for fast cash.[136] However, this need for cash is not necessarily characterized by the demand to satisfy the basic necessities of life or to maintain a conventional lifestyle. Based on ethnographic research conducted in Texas[137] and in St. Louis,[138] it is safe to say that active burglars do not, as a whole, have a conventional lifestyle; most of their everyday concerns revolve around maintaining their street status and supporting a lifestyle of self-indulgence and often gratuitous consumption of drugs. Wright and Decker contend that the need to maintain a party lifestyle, to "keep up appearances," and to provide basic necessities for themselves and their families are all key factors that drive offenders' decisions to commit a burglary.[139]

As in the ethnographic research on the lifestyle of armed robbers, discussed in Chapter 10, Wright and Decker found that the vast majority of the residential burglars they interviewed were committed to an "every night is a Saturday night" lifestyle. Thus, when offenders discussed their offending as a means of survival, it had to be interpreted against the backdrop of this lifestyle, for it was only within this context that an understanding of what they meant by "survival" emerged. The vast majority of offenders were committed to street culture, and almost three-fourths of the money they obtained from burglary pursuits went to support their party lifestyle—a lifestyle that included illicit drugs, alcohol, and sexual pursuits. Keeping up appearances, another crucial part of street culture, resulted in the "need" to buy things that assisted in maintaining street status, such as the right clothes and the right car. While some of the offenders interviewed by Wright and Decker did use the proceeds from their burglaries to pay their bills, the researchers also note that "the bills were badly delinquent because the offenders avoided paying them for as long as possible—even when they had the cash—in favor of buying, most typically, drugs."[140] The lifestyle of these offenders all but guaranteed that "the crimes they commit will be economically motivated," but it is not an economic motivation that results from a desire to satisfy needs as opposed to wants.[141]

Burglaries of commercial establishments are generally thought to be associated even more with instrumental ends, usually economic gain, than are residential burglaries. The same is true of professional burglars who invest more planning and strategy into their offenses. Far from operating from a standpoint of limited rationality, these offenders are calculating and carefully weigh risks and benefits. As Shover details in his work on burglars, professionals use quite sophisticated planning techniques because they are motivated to find targets with high payoffs.[142]

What causes offenders to focus on burglary as their crime of choice? Some offenders selected burglary quite simply because "they regarded burglary as their 'main line.'"[143] Because most of the offenders interviewed by Wright and Decker regarded themselves as hustlers, "people who were always looking to get over by making some fast cash," they would commit offenses other than burglary if a chance opportunity presented itself.[144] Otherwise, they stayed with the familiar, which was burglary. For many, burglary was not as risky as selling drugs, which has increasingly carried stiffer penalties, which offenders fear. Robbery was perceived as too risky because it involves direct confrontation with the victim and hence a higher likelihood of being injured. Some offenders stated that they did not own the necessary equipment for robberies—namely, guns. Because guns can be easily translated into cash in the street economy, "offenders who are in need of immediate cash often are tempted to sell their weapon instead of resorting to a difficult or risky crime."[145]

A small number of offenders in Wright and Decker's research in St. Louis indicated that "they did not typically commit burglaries as much for the money as for the psychic rewards."[146] This is consistent with Jack Katz's concept of sneaky thrills. As Katz contends, "If we looked more closely at how [offenders] define material needs, we might get a different image of these 'serious thieves.'"[147] Based on his ethnographic research with property offenders, Kenneth D. Tunnell concluded that "excitement was present but only as a latent benefit—a by-product of the criminal act."[148]

Target Selection

The sites for commercial burglaries are usually selected on the basis of the suitability of the target. Retail establishments are four times as likely to be burglarized as are other types of establishments, such as wholesale or service businesses. Based on a study of commercial burglaries in Philadelphia, Simon Hakim and Yochanan Shachmurove offer three reasons for the dominance of retail stores as burglary targets: "The merchandise is exposed so that the burglar knows precisely what his expected loot is, the merchandise is new and enjoys a high resale value to a fence, and burglars do not need to spend intrusion time searching for the loot."[149] Because burglars can "survey the facility while legitimately shopping or browsing through the store," retail establishments, especially those located away from major thoroughfares in places where police response time will be slower, are prime targets.[150]

How do residential burglars select their targets? According to Wright and Decker, most residential burglars already have potential targets in mind before committing their offenses. This does not mean that the targets have been extensively observed or the burglaries carefully planned. Generally, burglars select a target through their knowledge of the occupants, "through receiving a tip," or "through observing a potential target."[151]

While a prior relationship between victims and offenders has long characterized many violent crimes, property crimes are generally not thought of as involving known victims. Certainly, the pattern of the victim-offender relationship in property crimes does not mirror that found within violent crimes, but there are some interesting dynamics in the case of residential burglaries. While the residential burglars interviewed by Wright and Decker rarely selected residences of close friends or relatives as targets, they did quite often purposefully select as targets residences of individuals otherwise known to them.[152] This finding supported earlier research by Neil Shover showing that close to one-half of all burglary offenders targeted a residence of someone known to them.[153] Offenders may target known drug offenders because they know they can be victimized with relative impunity. The context of a job also provided offenders the opportunity to get to know the occupants of the household and the daily routine as well as to determine target suitability. The use of this strategy was common among offenders who discussed repeatedly victimizing the same household. While offenders did occasionally target residences of friends and loved ones, it was generally only in two scenarios. The first scenario occurred when an argument or some type of wrongdoing on the victim's part had occurred; in this case, the burglary was as much for revenge as for economic gain. The other scenario involved the offender having such a desperate need for money that anyone was fair game. While many offenders expressed remorse over having burglarized the homes of close family members, this was not universally the case, and burglars' expressions of remorse must be interpreted with the knowledge that "their allegiances seemed forever to be shifting to suit their own ends."[154]

Burglars may also select a target based on information from "tipsters," those who "regularly pass on intelligence about good burglary opportunities for a fee or a cut of the take."[155] This is not a very common method for most burglars, who generally lack such connections. Those who are able to use tipsters may do so in a variety of ways. Some offenders use individuals who work in service capacities within households and businesses, while others act in collusion with insurance agents or other middle-class people who feed the offender information in exchange for money or for some of the stolen merchandise.

The ethnographic research that Wright and Decker conducted in St. Louis made clear that only very rarely was a burglary target chosen on the "spur of the moment," but the type of observation that went into the selection was quite fragmented. However, fragmented observation may sometimes be all that is required. Given the lackadaisical nature of much household security and the fact that approximately one-fourth of burglaries do not involve any type of forced entry, "the world affords abundant poorly protected opportunities for burglars."[156] However, this does not mean that burglars are primarily opportunistic; such a designation runs counter to the primary concerns of most residential burglars. An open door or window is viewed less as an opportunity to commit burglary and more as a sign that the residence is occupied and hence an undesirable target. Opportunistic burglaries do occur, but they do not fit the scenario of an open window inviting access. More commonly, by chance alone, the offender happens to be in a place to observe the resident of a household departing. Because of the uncertain nature of these kinds of opportunities presenting themselves, motivated offenders "usually relied on a more proactive strategy to locate potential burglary sites."[157] While offenders do not go out actively searching for potential targets as a general rule, they are "continually 'half looking' for targets."[158]

Target selection is also influenced by other key elements. One of the most important is signs of occupancy because "most offenders are reluctant to burglarize occupied dwellings." This finding, according to Wright and Decker, is "beyond dispute."[159] Burglars have reported that they avoid occupied homes because they want to avoid injury to their victims and to themselves. For some offenders, the fear of their own injury was greater than the fear of apprehension. As one offender claimed in Wright and Decker's research, "I'd rather for the police to catch me versus a person catching me breaking in their house because the person will kill you."[160] To ensure that a residence was unoccupied, offenders would knock on the door, offering some excuse if someone actually answered, phone the residence, or even phone the householder at work.

Most residential burglars also avoid residences with complex security devices because they generally lack the expertise to bypass the system. Even the offenders who engaged targets with alarms would only do so with certain alarms, again because of their lack of expertise. Only a small fraction of the offenders had anything like a sophisticated understanding of alarm security systems. Dogs also will deter an offender from a potential target. Dogs could injure the offender, and even small dogs make noise. Generally, a particular target was selected after the area, and generally offenders tended to stay within the same areas, sometimes within walking distance, because of a lack of access to cars. As one offender in Wright and Decker's research noted, "It's hard as hell getting on a bus carrying a big picture or a vase."[161]

Costs of Burglary

While the economic loss caused by burglary is difficult to estimate with any degree of accuracy, burglary is associated with several types of losses for the individual and the community. According to the NCVS, well over three-fourths (86%) of all household burglaries involve some type of economic loss. Approximately 20% of household burglaries involve losses exceeding $1,000, with 21% involving loss amounts between $250 and $1,000, 24% involving loss amounts between $50 and $249, and slightly more than 14% involving losses under $50.[162] Remaining categories, not described here, total another 21%. What do offenders steal from homes? According to self-reports of victims of household burglary, 29% of items stolen from homes are personal in nature, with the largest category being jewelry or clothing. Household furnishings represent 11% of all stolen items, and tools and cash represent the items most likely to be stolen in about 12% (6% each) of incidents. Another type of crime cost can be gauged by looking at whether victims lose time from work as a result of their victimization. Among all victims of household burglaries, approximately 7% lose some time from work. Of this group, one-third lose less than one day, and slightly over one-half lose anywhere from one to five days, with the remaining 7% losing six days or more.[163]

Using NCVS data to test the relationship between criminal victimization and a household's decision to move, **Laura Dugan**'s research reveals that property crimes like burglary have a greater effect on the decision to move than do violent crimes.[164] Dugan had hypothesized that experiencing a violent crime rather than a property crime would have the greater effect on the decision to move—a hypothesis that was not supported by the data she analyzed. Instead, she found that a household's likelihood of moving increases after experiencing a criminal victimization near the home, an effect that was significant and strong for property crime but not for violent crime. Why might this be? Dugan states, "With property crimes like burglary, the anonymity of the offender makes it more likely that the victim blames the entire neighborhood [and] once the neighborhood is a focus for blame, a move is deemed the most effective prevention."[165] Victims generally move not after one victimization but after several such victimizations, suggesting that it is repeated property victimization near the home that makes people move. The association of property crime victimization and a household's decision to move is a "particularly costly form of precautionary behavior"[166] in that individuals incur costs associated with unplanned relocation. Communities are also affected because the more affluent households are the ones that are the most likely to relocate after experiencing victimization.

The Burglary-Drug Connection

During the 1980s, the once parallel rates of robbery and burglary began to diverge, with robbery increasing and burglary decreasing. Using city-level data from 1984 to 1992, research by Eric Baumer and colleagues linked these changes to the effects that an increased demand for crack cocaine had in altering structures of offending.[167] As a stimulant, crack use is characterized by short highs that are then "followed by an intense desire for more crack."[168] If users are funding their drug habit through criminal pursuits, they need to rely on offenses that complement the demands of their drug of choice. This means that offenses like robbery, which can net cash quickly, directly, and at any time, are better suited to the habits and needs of crack users than is burglary, which is more likely to net stolen goods than cash. As crack use spread throughout inner-city communities, it had the effect over time of "flooding the informal economy with guns, jewelry, and consumer electronic goods" to such an extent that "there is little money to be made through burglary in these neighborhoods."[169] As the illicit market for crack drove down the street value of stolen property, "dramatically enhancing the attractiveness of cash,"[170] burglary became an offense with diminishing rewards. Ethnographic research on active burglars supported the claim that in areas characterized by a strong crack cocaine trade, there was also a "preference for cash-intensive crimes like robbery and a corresponding reduced preference for burglary."[171] The decision making of offenders basically changed as a response to the illicit drug market, but the change was not necessarily associated with a motivational change in the commission of the offense. Certain users of crack are continuing to commit crime as a means of supporting their habit, and this individual-level need may change the nature of the informal economy in certain communities. When stolen goods lose their street value, offenders must modify their behavior in response. They shift to another offense that gets them what they need. This is consistent with research previously discussed that emphasizes that rather than being strictly committed to one type of property offense, most property offenders are generalists.

The Sexualized Context of Burglary

Although economic gain is the primary motive for the vast majority of burglaries, some criminologists say that there exists a category of burglaries with "hidden sexual forces lying at their root."[172] According to Louis B. Schlesinger and Eugene Revitch, the sexual dynamics associated with burglaries may be of two general and interrelated types. One is expressed as fetishes in which the offender steals particular items, not for their material value but because they provide an outlet for sexual gratification. Another type, voyeuristic burglaries, have a more subtle sexual dynamic in which the goal may be only to "look around, to inspect the drawers,"[173] but not to actually take anything. Schlesinger and Revitch analyzed the clinical records of 52 sexual murderers and found that the majority of these offenders had a history of burglaries. Burglary may serve as a precursor to more serious offenses and may constitute part of a pattern of sexual offending. The possible underlying sexual dynamics of burglary may be overlooked in routine investigations of burglary in the absence of a conscious mandate to look for such signs. Apparently, a certain number of sexually motivated homicides begin as other offenses, such as burglary, and the ability to link the two early in the investigation can be important for effective forensic assessment. Hence, details of burglary should be more purposefully evaluated, as they could be related to a progression of events that could culminate in homicide.

Mark Warr has investigated the connection of sexual offenses with property crimes from a different perspective.[174] Not only can sexual motives underlie property crimes, Warr argues, but also the theoretical perspective of opportunity theory, discussed in Chapter 7, can explain patterns of rape and burglary. In Warr's conceptualization, "residential rape and burglary can be viewed as crimes of stealth that involve the unlawful entry of a structure" and hence "have very similar opportunity structures."[175] Using city-level arrest data, Warr finds support for his contention that both the type of residence and the type of people victimized are similar enough in certain rape and burglary incidents to call into question the idea that rape shares a criminal etiology exclusively with violent offending. Warr does not question the violent nature of rape but instead pursues another aspect of the heterogeneity of criminal etiology. Just as the label of violent crime encompasses a great number of diverse criminal behaviors more or less similar to each other, many of these incidents share attributes of nonviolent or property crimes. For a certain category of rape termed *home-intrusion rape,* "the traditional distinction between violent crime and property crime may not apply," and such incidents represent a "hybrid offense"; they are "a violent crime with the opportunity structure of a property crime."[176] According to Warr, the correspondence in the opportunity structures of rape and burglary warrants consideration if research and investigative procedures are to identify the "proximate causes of rape."[177]

Stolen Property

According to **Darrell J. Steffensmeier,** "[T]he 1827 English statute— 'a person receiving stolen property knowing the same to be stolen is deemed guilty of a felony'—is the prototype of subsequent American law. The exact wording may vary from one state to another, but the basic elements of the crime— 'buying and receiving,' 'stolen property,' and 'knowing it to be stolen'—have remained essentially intact."[178] As previously discussed, a small number of thieves steal for their own consumption and steal mostly cash. In these cases, there is no need to translate the goods into cash. But in other cases, it is necessary to consider how stolen goods are translated into cash. There are several answers to this question because "there are many paths that stolen property may take from thieves to eventual customers."[179] Receiving stolen property is engaged in for various levels of profit by individuals and groups with varying skill levels. Some burglars commit their offenses specifically to get something they know someone wants. In this case, the burglar sells the merchandise directly to a waiting customer.[180] Burglars also may sell to people who are known to them or may take stolen goods to places like flea markets or auctions. Other paths to disposing of stolen goods "involve the thief and dabbling 'middlemen' who buy and sell stolen property under the cover of a bar, a luncheonette, or an auto service station with the encouragement, if not the active participation, of the proprietor."[181] Some burglars also sell their merchandise to merchants and represent it as legal goods. The most complicated path from the thief to customers is through a **fence.** The use of a professional fence is the least common method of disposing of stolen goods for the majority of thieves, but it is the most common method used by professional burglars.

fence

An individual or a group involved in the buying, selling, and distribution of stolen goods.

Steffensmeier links the rise of the fence to the availability of mass-produced goods made possible by industrialization.[182] Although there were certainly individuals who dealt in stolen goods before industrialization, it was only with mass-production techniques that it actually became profitable enough for significant numbers of people to serve as fences. Steffensmeier used the case study method to research the fence, just as **Carl Klockars** did in his classic work.[183] Klockars detailed the career of Vincent Swaggi, who had been a successful fence for more than 20 years. Steffensmeier profiled Sam Goodman, a white male almost 60 years old, whom he began interviewing in early 1980.[184] Building on Klockars's definition, Steffensmeier defines a *fence* as one who "purchases stolen goods both on a regular basis, and for resale."[185] The most crucial defining characteristics of the professional fence are that he or she has "direct contact with thieves," "buys and resells stolen goods regularly and persistently," and thus is a "public dealer—recognized as a fence by thieves, the police, and others acquainted with the criminal community."[186] Steffensmeier and other researchers have recognized variations among fences. Some fences are "occasional" in that their receipt of stolen goods is infrequent. Still other variations and distinguishing characteristics exist among the wide variety of those who in some way are part of the puzzle of how stolen goods move from original owner to the open market.

The Role of Criminal Receivers

In their ethnographic research on residential burglars, **Paul F. Cromwell** and his colleagues offer a three-part typology of criminal receivers: professional receivers, avocational receivers, and amateur receivers.[187] *Professional receivers* are those who fit the definition provided by Steffensmeier. The use of a professional fence to dispose of stolen goods is uncommon among the majority of residential burglars, who lack "sophisticated underworld connections."[188] Such connections often distinguish "high-level burglars" from the more typical and prevalent residential burglars.[189] Burglars and other thieves who develop access to fences cite a number of advantages in disposing of stolen goods in this way. The professional fence offers a safe and quick means of disposing of goods. This is especially the case with burglars who have committed a high-visibility crime, stealing goods that are easily recognizable. In Wright and Decker's ethnographic research on residential burglars, one burglar who had stolen from a local celebrity's house stated, "We couldn't just sell [the jewelry] on the street, it was like too hot to handle."[190] Fences are also the best outlet for a large volume of stolen goods, as this is one factor that distinguishes professional fences from other types. Some professional fences are "generalists" who deal in a wide variety of stolen goods, and others are "specialists" who deal only in certain types of goods. Goodman, the professional fence described in Steffensmeier's research, started as a specialist but evolved into a generalist as a "function of greater capital and a growing knowledge of varied merchandise."[191] The vast majority of professional fences are involved in a legitimate business that serves as a cover for their criminal activity and facilitates it. Goodman operated a secondhand store whose inventory partially matched the stolen goods he received, a characteristic that makes him a "partly covered fence." Fences who are "fully covered" do not deal in stolen goods that are outside their inventory in the legitimate business. "Noncovered" fences are those whose "illicit lines of goods are distinct from the legitimate commerce."[192] The more a fence is able to cover illicit activities by incorporating them into legitimate enterprises, the safer the fence is from criminal detection and prosecution.

There is a great deal of variety in the businesses that fences use as a front for their criminal activity. They generally range from those viewed by the "community-at-large as strictly clean," like restaurants, to businesses that "are perceived as clean but somewhat suspect," like auto parts shops and antique shops, to businesses that are viewed as "quasi-legitimate or marginal," like pawnshops.[193] Goodman's business, a secondhand store, was quasi-legitimate.

Some of the residential burglars interviewed by Wright and Decker stated that they avoided marginal businesses like pawnshops when disposing of stolen goods because, given the increasingly strict regulations of pawnshops, owners must often demand identification and take photos of those selling to them, and they have "hot sheets" of recently stolen goods. In addition, pawnshops generally do not provide the greatest return on the merchandise. Given the fact that many residential burglars commit their offenses for fast cash, "pawnshops almost always [have] the upper hand in negotiations."[194] The residential burglars who did regularly use pawnshops reported having an established relationship with the owner that enabled them "to pawn stolen property 'off camera'" because they had made transactions with the owner previously that had not resulted in "bringing additional police pressure to bear on his business."[195]

A second type of fence found in the ethnographic research is the *avocational receiver*. For this group, the buying of stolen property is a part-time endeavor "secondary to, but usually associated with, their primary business activity."[196] This is a fairly diverse

A Las Vegas pawn shop. Could this shop serve as a front for a fencing operation?
Source: Buddy Mays, Corbis

group that can include individuals involved in respectable occupations, such as the lawyers or bail bondsmen who "provide legitimate professional services to property offenders who cannot pay for these services with anything but stolen property."[197] Others involved in illegitimate occupations, such as drug dealers, may also accept stolen goods. As opposed to the professional fence, the avocational receiver is distinguished by the "frequency of purchase, volume of activity, and level of commitment to the criminal enterprise."[198] Wright and Decker stated that "many of the tough inner-city neighborhoods of St. Louis have an informal economy that operates in part on the sale of stolen property" and that "drug dealers often play a prominent role in this economy, both as buyers and sellers."[199]

Amateur receivers are those "otherwise honest citizens who buy stolen property on a relatively small scale, primarily, but not exclusively, for personal consumption. Crime is peripheral rather than central to their lives."[200] These individuals are quite sporadic in their involvement in activities that generate stolen goods. Cromwell and colleagues cite as an example a "public-school teacher who began her part-time fencing when she was approached by a student who offered her a 'really good deal' on certain items."[201] While these individuals do not engage in receiving stolen property at the same level as professional or avocational fences, "they represent a large market for stolen goods" because they "compensate for lack of volume with their sheer numbers."[202] Stuart Henry's study of property crime among ordinary people, which he termed "hidden-economy crime," described the involvement of ordinary citizens in a wide variety of property offenses, including receiving stolen property.[203] Learn more about how fences operate at **Web Extra 11–6**.

WEB
Extra
■ ■ ■ ■

Arson

As noted in Chapter 2, the FBI defines *arson* as "any willful or malicious burning or attempt to burn, with or without intent to defraud, a dwelling house, public building, motor vehicle or aircraft, personal property of another, etc."[204] It is only after a fire has been investigated and officially classified as arson by the proper investigative authorities that the FBI records the incident as an arson. Fires that are suspicious or of unknown

Who's to Blame—The Individual or Society?

Body Parts for Sale

On March 20, 2008, Dr. Paul Sutter, a Palm Beach, Florida, plastic surgeon, was arrested and charged with a federal crime after he allegedly purchased facial bones that he knew had been illegally removed from a cadaver, and implanted them into a wealthy female patient undergoing elective facial reconstructive surgery following a car accident. The doctor and a mortician, who sold him the bones, were both charged with violating the National Organ Transplant Act of 1984, which expressly prohibits interstate trafficking in human tissue for profit.

In an interview the doctor gave after posting bail, Sutter told reporters "I understand that there's a law against what I did. But it's not my fault that the materials I need to work with are frequently so hard to acquire. There needs to be a better system in place for the distribution of bones and other tissues that are so desperately needed by patients like the woman whose face I reconstructed in this case."

Think about it:

1. Why did Sutter violate the law? What do you think was his primary motivation for what he did?

2. Do you think it would have mattered to Sutter's patient, had she known that the bones used in her surgery had been acquired illegally?

3. Can body parts be considered items of property, like a person's other possessions? If so, should he or she have the right to sell them—perhaps to the highest bidder?

---

origins are not included in the FBI's arson statistics.[205] Several diverse motives may underlie arson, from profit to thrill seeking.

On August 1, 2003, a 206-unit San Diego condominium complex burned down while under construction. A 12-foot banner found at the scene declared, "If you build it, we will burn it." The banner was signed with the letters *ELF,* which stand for the Earth Liberation Front. Less than a month later, ELF arsonists attacked a number of car dealerships in Los Angeles, targeting those that sold gas-guzzling SUVs such as Hummers. Although one person was arrested, he was soon released.

The ELF, described as an ecoterrorist group by law enforcement officials, may have begun in California as the Environmental Life Force in 1977. Although the original ELF disbanded after only a year, some of its members became affiliated with the Earth First movement. The present-day ELF appears to be a destructive offshoot of that movement.[206] The organization targets what it deems to be threats to the environment—including residential and commercial construction in environmentally sensitive areas, bioengineered crops, certain types of animal research facilities, lumber mills, mink farms, military recruiting offices, and even Starbucks restaurants.

Arson appears to be the ELF's favorite protest method. A statement on the North American ELF Web site—which is reminiscent of the Marxist rhetoric described in Chapter 9—proclaims, "The ELF realizes the profit motive caused and reinforced by the capitalist society is destroying all life on this planet. The only way, at this point in time, to stop that continued destruction of life is to by any means necessary take the profit motive out of killing."[207]

Although ELF activities have resulted in few arson arrests, three self-identified members of the ELF pled guilty in 2004 to federal charges of conspiracy to destroy by fire vehicles and property used in interstate commerce. The guilty pleas followed an FBI investigation into arson fires in and around Richmond, Virginia, that had occurred in 2002.[208]

The ELF appears to be supported by a number of subgroups, which it calls revolutionary cells. Among them are the Animal Liberation Brigade, the Direct Action Front, the Frogs, and the Vegan Dumpster Militia. The ELF, which by its own count was responsible for 75 "illegal direct actions" in North America in 2003,[209] maintains a Web site, which can be seen at **Web Extra 11–7.**

Between 1989 and 1996, a wave of arsons at predominantly African American churches throughout the United States caused enormous concern that these arsons were hate crimes. Some people even contended that the fires were part of an organized effort by "members of various hate groups to start an all-out war between the races."[210]

WEB
Extra

Crime in the News

Urban Ecoterrorism

A sabotage campaign by the nation's most radical environmental group has moved from the countryside to the doorstep of the nation's biggest cities.

The Earth Liberation Front (ELF), a movement that originated in the forests of the Pacific Northwest, has claimed responsibility for a string of arsons in the suburbs of Los Angeles, Detroit, San Diego and Philadelphia in the past 12 months. No one has been charged in any of the attacks.

The attacks, which included the costliest act of environmental sabotage in U.S. history, have targeted luxury homes and SUVs, the suburban status symbols that some environmentalists regard as despoilers of the Earth.

"Their actions used to be aimed at 'out in the country' industries," said Ron Arnold of the Bellevue, Washington–based Center for the Defense of Free Enterprise, who has written several books criticizing the environmental movement's radical wing. "Now they're moving from a save-the-wilderness focus to an anti-capitalist focus."

This summer, environmentalists in Southern California turned six-figure luxury homes under construction into charred sticks of wood, destroyed an unfinished 206-unit apartment complex and firebombed brand-new Hummers, the mammoth sport-utility vehicles that start at $50,000.

Rod Coronado, a legendary figure in the underground movement who is serving as an ELF spokesman and has drawn scrutiny from the FBI, said the group is being transformed by a new generation of activists.

"When I got involved in the mid-80s, tree-spiking"—pounding spikes into trees to prevent loggers with chainsaws from cutting them down—"was a big deal," said Coronado, 37, who played a part in sinking two whaling ships in Iceland and served time in prison for an arson attack at a Michigan State University animal-research lab. "What that's morphed into is a more urban environmental movement, whereby people are fighting for the last wild places in urban areas."

He said the young activists are "doing the only thing they know to do and that is strike a match and draw a whole lot of attention to their dissatisfaction with protecting the environment."

The ELF is the FBI's No. 1 domestic terrorism priority. The organization has done more than $100 million damage, but caused no

Imprisoned Earth Liberation Front member Craig Marshall. What motivates people like Marshall? How are they like other property offenders? How do they differ?

Source: Robbie McClaran, mcclaran-c.marshal

deaths, since it split off from the radical environmental group Earth First! and surfaced in the United States five years ago.

The ELF first took aim at urban sprawl in 2000, when it burned luxury homes and condos under construction on New York's Long Island. But Phil Celestini, the agent in charge of the FBI's domestic terrorism operations unit in Washington, noted that the San Diego fires "are taking place in more densely populated areas than in the past."

The level of concern about church arsons resulted in President Clinton's signing of the Church Arson Prevention Act of 1996,[211] legislation designed to increase penalties for church arsons and to accomplish other objectives, such as the rebuilding of destroyed churches. The National Church Arson Task Force arrested 199 suspects in 150 of the 429 arsons under investigation and concluded that most of the arsons were the result of individuals acting alone rather than as part of an organized conspiracy.[212] While members of hate groups were certainly among the suspects arrested, so, too, were religious zealots, Satanists, and those motivated by revenge and greed. In November 1999, a minister and his accomplices were arrested for setting fire to their church; the suspected motive was a $270,000 insurance policy.[213] Another high-profile case of church arson involved Jay Scott Ballinger, who pleaded guilty in July 2000 to federal charges of setting fire to 26 churches across eight states over a five-year period. Federal prosecutors

On August 1, 2003, a fire destroyed a five-story, 206-unit apartment complex under construction in San Diego's University City neighborhood.

The damage estimate of $50 million made it "the single largest act of property destruction ever committed by one of these groups in the history of the country," Celestini said. "It's sheer dumb luck and providence that someone has not been killed. You set a fire that big, there's no way of predicting what the ultimate consequences will be."

In the wake of the attacks, other San Diego developers have installed security cameras and hired guards to keep an eye on properties around the clock, said Russ Valone, of the California Building Industry Association, which has offered a $25,000 reward for information leading to an arrest in the apartment complex arson.

"Let me tell you who the other victims of this are: You and me," Valone said. "Our insurance pays a price. The more claims an insurance company pays out, the more they have to raise their premiums. So, everybody in the city, everybody in the county, everybody in the country pays in some small way for the damage created by these maniacs."

Guidelines posted on the ELF's Web site stress the need to take "all necessary precautions against harming life." But the group's message has been mixed.

In a communique issued after a U.S. Forest Service research center in Pennsylvania was attacked last year, the ELF said: "While innocent life will never be harmed in any action we undertake, where it is necessary, we will no longer hesitate to pick up the gun to implement justice."

The ELF operates in a series of anonymous cells and uses the Internet to communicate and broadcast its message. But it has little organization, no fees and no membership list, frustrating FBI efforts to penetrate the group.

The recent case of an Oregon college student serving time in prison for a firebombing in 2001 opened a window into the ELF.

Jacob Sherman, a student at Portland State University, said he fell under the spell of Michael J. Scarpitti, known as Tre Arrow, a forest activist who is now the FBI's most-wanted "eco-terrorist."

According to court documents, Arrow "groomed" Sherman and slowly introduced him to radical protesting. Sherman stopped bathing, refused to wear shoes and began eating a strict vegan diet to imitate Arrow.

Sherman was no James Bond of the forest: His father called the FBI after his son drove home reeking of gasoline the night three logging company trucks were attacked. Sherman, 19 at the time, also blabbed to his girlfriend, who in turn told her father, a deputy state fire marshal, said Sherman's attorney, Andy Bates.

Authorities say Scarpitti, 29, has ties to California, Pennsylvania, Florida, Colorado, Ohio and Oregon. He is a suspect in at least one arson outside Oregon—the fire at the Forest Service research center in Pennsylvania.

In the San Diego attacks, the FBI has focused on Coronado, the ELF's self-described spokesman. Search warrants obtained by The Associated Press show FBI agents raided the homes of two local activists in a search for videotaped copies of a speech Coronado delivered in San Diego on August 1, 2003—the same day of the $50 million apartment arson.

Coronado has said he had nothing to do with the fire.

Mainstream environmental groups have taken pains to distance themselves from the ELF.

"The ELF are not environmentalists. They are arsonists," said Carl Pope, head of the Sierra Club.

However, People for the Ethical Treatment of Animals, whose members stormed a Victoria's Secret runway show last year, donated $1,500 to the ELF in 2001, according to the group's tax returns.

PETA said the money was used to send two people to Washington to testify at a congressional hearing on behalf of an ELF spokesman. PETA said the spokesman was being harassed by the FBI for speaking his mind.

Discussion Questions

1. What characteristics do ecoterrorists share in common with other criminals? With other terrorists? How do they differ?

2. What alternative strategies might groups like the ELF use to achieve their goals?

Source: Seth Hettena and Laura Wides, "Urban Eco-Terrorism," Associated Press, October 2, 2003.

For the latest crime and justice news, visit www.crimenews.info.

say that Ballinger is the "most prolific church arsonist" apprehended since the work of the National Church Arson Task Force began. Ballinger was not a white supremacist but instead someone who considered himself to be a "missionary of Lucifer"; he attempted to make converts by signing people to contracts with the devil.[214] Ballinger was originally facing the death penalty because of the death of a firefighter during one of the fires, but plea negotiations mean that he will spend 42 years in prison.

Fire Setters

The scenario that comes to mind when most people think of arson is of "some crooked businessman torching his establishment in order to collect the insurance money." This is also the image that comes to the minds of property claims adjusters, argues Ken Brownlee in a recent article in *Claims* magazine.[215] While representing one part of the reality of arson, he says, arson for profit "has been only a minor part of the loss due to arson for more than a decade."[216] The crooked businessperson may represent one type of arsonist but is atypical of arsonists in general.

Whatever the motive, the vast majority of those involved in arson are juveniles. This pattern has been the case for some time. According to UCR/NIBRS data, juveniles represent the offenders in arson incidents at a much higher rate than is found in any other index offense; 49% of all arsons that are cleared are found to have involved a juvenile offender. Juveniles are a bit more likely to be involved in arsons in cities than in suburbs or rural areas. Overall, among the arson types, "juveniles account for 21 percent of the clearances for arsons of mobile property, 40 percent of structural arson clearances and 41 percent of clearances for arsons of all other property."[217] Juveniles are quite often the culprits in both residential and commercial fires. According to Jay K. Bradish, editor of *Firehouse* magazine, "Arson is the third leading cause of residential fires and the second-leading cause of residential fire deaths nationwide. Arson is the leading cause of deaths and injuries and accounts for the highest dollar loss in commercial fires."[218] In both residential and commercial arson, juveniles are involved more often than adults.

Eileen M. Garry says that there are three general groups of juvenile fire setters.[219] The first consists of children younger than 7 who generally start fires either accidentally or out of curiosity. The second group is children between the ages of 8 and 12 who may start fires out of curiosity, but "a greater proportion of their fire setting represents underlying psychosocial conflicts."[220] The final group, youths between the ages of 13 and 18, has had a history of fire setting, usually undetected. It is believed that many of the fires started by juveniles may go undetected by law enforcement officials because they are started on school property, perhaps even accidentally, and are discovered early by janitors or other school staff who do not report the incidents. In response to a growing awareness of the problem created by juvenile fire setters, several agencies and organizations, including the U.S. Fire Administration, have developed model programs to mobilize community agencies across the nation to deal more effectively with juvenile fire setters. For more information on the problem of fire setting among juveniles, as well as the prevalence of and issues surrounding arson in the United States, visit the National Fire Data Center online via **Web Extra 11–8**. Learn more about the crime of arson from **Library Extra 11–3** at crimtoday.com.

WEB
Extra
■ ■ ■ ■

LIBRARY
Extra
■ ■ ■ ■

SUMMARY

Property crimes vary along a continuum from crimes that are so petty in nature that they are not even noticed by the victim to crimes on a scale so large that the associated economic loss can be vast. The property crimes of professional thieves are characterized by greater planning and financial reward than are those of the vast majority of thieves, who are referred to as "persistent" or "occasional." Strict specialization is rarely found among property offenders, who typically move back and forth between similar types of property crimes, with infrequent involvement in personal crimes like robbery. While a certain degree of rationality characterizes the crimes and actions of the majority of thieves, it is only a limited or bounded rationality that must be interpreted and understood within the social and cultural context of the everyday lives, situations, and needs of offenders.

The prototypical property crime is a larceny, usually petty in nature. The legal boundaries of larceny are determined by

the value of the merchandise taken. One of the most frequent larcenies is shoplifting, a crime that is quite prevalent, especially among adolescents. As with all property crimes, shoplifting may be carried out by professionals, but generally this is not the case.

One of the most serious forms of property crime is burglary, categories of which are distinguished legally by the amount of force used to gain entry into the structure. Both residences and commercial establishments are victimized by burglars. Other factors, such as the time of day, characterize the offense of burglary. As property criminals, burglars can often cross the line to more serious violent crimes like homicide, rape, and robbery. Even in the absence of violent crime, the social costs of burglary to the victim and to society are numerous.

Property crimes usually involve stolen goods that need to be translated into cash. The movement of stolen goods, a criminal offense, has been studied from several perspectives. Those who move stolen goods range from the professional fence, whose business is buying and selling stolen goods in volume, to the amateur receiver, who quite often resembles an ordinary citizen.

Arson, like the other property crimes examined in this chapter, has the potential to result in both great economic loss and loss of life. Although arson for profit and for protest certainly occurs, the majority of arsons involve adolescents who bring a variety of personal motives to fire setting.

KEY TERMS

booster, 456

fence, 466

gateway offense, 454

jockey, 451

joyriding, 451

occasional offender, 444

offense specialization, 443

persistent thief, 443

professional criminal, 442

snitch, 456

KEY NAMES

Mary Owen Cameron, 453

Paul F. Cromwell, 467

Laura Dugan, 464

Mark S. Fleisher, 445

John R. Hepburn, 444

Malcolm W. Klein, 443

Lloyd W. Klemke, 453

Carl Klockars, 466

Mike Maguire, 459

Frank J. McShane, 456

Richard H. Moore, 456

Barrie A. Noonan, 456

Magnus Seng, 448

Neil Shover, 442

Darrell J. Steffensmeier, 466

Kenneth D. Tunnell, 455

QUESTIONS FOR REVIEW

1. What are the major forms of property crime that this chapter discusses? Explain the differences between professional property offenders and persistent property offenders.

2. What are the different kinds of larceny-theft discussed in this chapter, and how common is each?

3. How frequently does burglary occur? What are the types of burglars discussed in this chapter? How do the motivations of the various types of burlgars differ? In what ways are they the same?

4. What kinds of illegal activities are receivers of stolen property generally involved in? How do stolen goods get resold?

5. What is arson, and what different kinds of arson can be identified? What motivates arsonists?

QUESTIONS FOR REFLECTION

1. To what extent is "thrill seeking" a motivation behind certain types of property offenses? How might it contribute to the crime of shoplifting?

2. Why is so much attention given to shoplifting among adolescents? Should it be? Why or why not?

3. How are "honest" citizens and professional criminal receivers connected?

4. To what extent are property offenders rational actors? Use examples from larceny, burglary, and receipt of stolen property to illustrate your answer.

5. What does the "sexualized context" of burglary mean? How can burglary have a sexual component or motivation?

6. How are drugs involved in the offending patterns of some burglars? Might effective drug-treatment programs reduce the number of burglaries committed? Why?

WEB QUEST

Visit the Art Theft Recovery Project on the Web at www.saztv. com. Gather information on the types of resources available at the site, the personnel associated with the art theft recovery program, and the site's "major cases."

What does the site list as the "world's most wanted art" for the current year? Submit this information to your instructor if asked to do so.

NOTES

[1] Edwin Sutherland, *The Professional Thief* (Chicago, IL: University of Chicago Press, 1937), p. 172.

[2] Carl B. Klockars, *The Professional Fence* (New York: Free Press, 1974).

[3] George Rengert and John Wasilchick, *Suburban Burglary: A Time and a Place for Everything* (Springfield, IL: Charles C. Thomas, 1985), p. 52.

[4] Marcus Felson, "Linking Criminal Choices, Routine Activities, Informal Control, and Criminal Outcomes," in Derek B. Cornish and Ronald V. Clarke, eds., *The Reasoning Criminal: Rational Choice Perspectives on Offending* (New York: Springer-Verlag, 1986), p. 127.

[5] Neil Shover, *Great Pretenders: Pursuits and Careers of Persistent Thieves* (Boulder, CO: Westview Press, 1996).

[6] William Spain, "Art Crime of the Century Still Frustrates: Empty Frames Still Hang in Boston Museum," APB News, June 16, 2000, http://apbnews.com/newscenter/breakingnews/2000/06/16/artcrime_gardner0161_01.html (accessed December 1, 2000).

[7] William Spain, "Inside the World of Art Theft: Trade Ranks Third after Drugs, Arms Sales," APB News, June 16, 2000, http://apbnews.com/newscenter/breakingnews/2000/06/16/artcrime0616_01.html (accessed September 3, 2004).

[8] Ibid.

[9] Ibid.

[10] Ibid.

[11] Cited in Thomas Gabor, *Everybody Does It! Crime by the Public* (Toronto: University of Toronto Press, 1994), p. 11.

[12] Sutherland, *The Professional Thief,* p. 3.

[13] Shover, *Great Pretenders,* p. xiii.

[14] Ibid., pp. xii–xiii.

[15] Ibid., p. 63.

[16] Mark S. Fleisher, *Beggars and Thieves: Lives of Urban Street Criminals* (Madison: University of Wisconsin Press, 1995), p. 29.

[17] Malcolm W. Klein, "Offense Specialization and Versatility among Juveniles," *British Journal of Criminology,* Vol. 24 (1984), pp. 185–194.

[18] Ibid., p. 186.

[19] Neil Shover, "Burglary," in Michael Tonry, ed., *Crime and Justice: A Review of Research* (Chicago: University of Chicago Press, 1991).

[20] See Shover, *Great Pretenders;* and Shover, "Burglary."

[21] John R. Hepburn, "Occasional Property Crime," in Robert F. Meier, ed., *Major Forms of Crime* (Beverly Hills, CA: Sage, 1984).

[22] Ibid., p. 76.

[23] Richard T. Wright and Scott H. Decker, *Burglars on the Job: Streetlife and Residential Break-Ins* (Boston: Northeastern University Press, 1994), p. 35.

[24] See Center for Problem-Oriented Policing, "Crime Analysis for Problem Solvers in 60 Small Steps," from which the wording for this definition is taken, http://www.popcenter.org/learning/60steps/index.cfm?stepNum=10 (accessed May 31, 2007).

[25] Neil Alan Weiner, "Violent Criminal Careers and 'Violent Career Criminals': An Overview of the Research Literature," in Neil Alan Weiner and Marvin E. Wolfgang, eds., *Violent Crime, Violent Criminals* (Newbury Park, CA: Sage, 1989), p. 39.

[26] A. Blumstein, J. Cohen, J. A. Roth, and C. A. Visher, eds., *Criminal Careers and "Career Criminals,"* 2 vols. (Washington, DC: National Academy Press, 1986).

[27] D. S. Elliott, "Serious Violent Offenders: Onset, Developmental Course, and Termination: 1993 Presidential Address," *Criminology,* Vol. 32, No. 1 (1994), pp. 1–22. See also D. S. Elliott, D. Huizinga, and B. Morse, "Self-Reported Violent Offending: A Descriptive Analysis of Juvenile Violent Offenders and Their Offending Careers," *Journal of Interpersonal Violence,* Vol. 1, No. 4 (1987), pp. 472–514.

[28] Michael R. Gottfredson and Travis Hirschi, "Science, Public Policy, and the Career Paradigm," *Criminology,* Vol. 26 (1988), pp. 37–55.

[29] Fleisher, *Beggars and Thieves,* p. 11.

[30] Ibid., p. 10.

[31] Ibid., p. 11.

[32] Dermot Walsh, "Victim Selection Procedures among Economic Criminals: The Rational Choice Perspective," in Cornish and Clarke, eds., *The Reasoning Criminal,* p. 40.

[33] Ibid., p. 50.

[34] Thomas Bennett and Richard Wright, *Burglars on Burglary* (Aldershot, Hants, England: Gower, 1984).

[35] Walsh, "Victim Selection Procedures among Economic Criminals," p. 50.

[36] Neil Shover and David Honaker, "The Socially Bounded Decision Making of Persistent Property Offenders," *Howard Journal,* Vol. 31, No. 4 (1992), p. 290.

[37] Ramona R. Rantala and Thomas J. Edwards, *Effects of NIBRS on Crime Statistics* (Washington, DC: Office of Justice Programs, 2000), p. 12.

[38] President's Commission on Law Enforcement and Administration of Justice, *The Challenge of Crime in a Free Society* (New York: Avon, 1968), p. 64.

[39] David Barry, "Thieves Peel Off with 1,200 Orange Trees: Culprits Strike California Groves at Night," APB News, November 27, 2000, http://www.apbnews.com/newscenter/breakingnews/2000/11/27/trees1127_01.html (accessed December 1, 2000).

[40] Federal Bureau of Investigation. *Crime in the United States, 2006.*

[41] BJS, *Criminal Victimization, 1999* (Washington, DC: Bureau of Justice Statistics, 2000), Table 84.

[42] Marcus Felson, *Crime and Everyday Life* (Thousand Oaks, CA: Pine Forge, 1998), p. 75.

[43] Ibid.

[44] Magnus Seng, "Theft on Campus: An Analysis of Larceny-Theft at an Urban University," *Journal of Crime and Justice,* Vol. 19, No. 1 (1996), p. 34.

[45] Ibid., p. 36.

[46] Ibid., 40.

47 Elizabeth Ehrhardt Mustaine and Richard Tewksbury, "Predicting Risks of Larceny Theft Victimization: A Routine Activity Analysis Using Refined Lifestyle Measures," *Criminology*, Vol. 36, No. 4 (1998), pp. 829–858.

48 Ibid., p. 852.

49 FBI, *Crime in the United States, 2006.*

50 BJS, *Criminal Victimization, 1999*, Tables 87 and 89.

51 Ibid., Table 61.

52 Ibid.

53 Felson, *Crime and Everyday Life*, p. 32.

54 BJS, *Criminal Victimization, 1999*, Table 64.

55 BJS, *Criminal Victimization, 2006* (Washington, DC: Bureau of Justice Statistics, 2007).

56 Ibid.

57 Caroline Wolf Harlow, *Motor Vehicle Theft* (Washington, DC: Bureau of Justice Statistics, 1988).

58 Kevin Blake, "What You Should Know about Car Theft," *Consumer's Research*, October 1995, cited in Terance D. Miethe and Richard McCorkle, *Crime Profiles: The Anatomy of Dangerous Persons, Places, and Situations* (Los Angeles: Roxbury, 1998), p. 156.

59 "Japanese Cars Top Thieves' Wish Lists," APB News, November 14, 2000, http://www.apbnews.com/newscenter/ breakingnews/2000/11/14/cartheft/1114_01.htm (accessed December 1, 2000).

60 Ibid.

61 Miethe and McCorkle, *Crime Profiles.*

62 Public Law No. 98–547, 98 Stat. 2754 (1984).

63 Patricia M. Harris and Ronald V. Clarke, "Car Chopping, Parts Marking and the Motor Vehicle Theft Law Enforcement Act of 1984," *Sociology and Social Research*, Vol. 75 (1991).

64 Ibid., p. 228.

65 Joanna Sallybanks and Nerys Thomas, "Thefts of External Vehicle Parts: An Emerging Problem," *Crime Prevention and Community Safety: An International Journal*, Vol. 2 (2000), pp. 17–22.

66 Ibid., p. 18.

67 Ibid., p. 19.

68 Ibid., p. 20.

69 Miethe and McCorkle, *Crime Profiles*, p. 156.

70 Michael Gottfredson and Travis Hirschi, *A General Theory of Crime* (Stanford, CA: Stanford University Press, 1990), p. 35.

71 Ronald V. Clarke and Patricia M. Harris, "Auto Theft and Its Prevention," in Tonry, ed., *Crime and Justice.*

72 Miethe and McCorkle, *Crime Profiles*; and Clarke and Harris, "Auto Theft and Its Prevention."

73 William W. Wattenberg and James Balliestri, "Automobile Theft: A Favored Group Delinquency," *American Journal of Sociology*, Vol. 57 (1952).

74 Miethe and McCorkle, *Crime Profiles.*

75 For research reporting no effect of social class, see Charles H. McCaghy, Peggy C. Giordano, and Trudy Knicely Henson, "Auto Theft: Offender and Offense Characteristics," *Criminology*, Vol. 15 (1977), pp. 367–385.

76 Pierre Trembley, Yvan Clermont, and Maurice Cusson, "Jockeys and Joyriders: Changing Patterns in Car Theft Opportunity Structures," *British Journal of Criminology*, Vol. 34, No. 3 (1994), p. 314.

77 Ibid.

78 Clarke and Harris, "Auto Theft and Its Prevention," p. 23.

79 Richard C. Hollinger and Lynn Langton, *2003 National Retail Security Survey: Final Report* (Tallahassee, FL: University of Florida, 2004).

80 Gabor, *Everybody Does It!*, p. 80.

81 Silverman, "Crime and Punishment."

82 Klemke, *The Sociology of Shoplifting*, p. 16.

83 Silverman, "Crime and Punishment."

84 Ibid.

85 Klemke, *The Sociology of Shoplifting*, p. 16.

86 Ibid., p. 20.

87 Ibid.

88 Ibid., p. 19.

89 "Ryder Sentenced, No Prison Time," *USA Today*, December 9, 2002, http://www.usatoday.com/life/2002_12_06_ winona_sentenced_x.htm (accessed January 5, 2006).

90 Klemke, *The Sociology of Shoplifting.*

91 Lloyd W. Klemke, "Exploring Juvenile Shoplifting," *Sociology and Social Research*, Vol. 67, No. 1 (1982), pp. 59–75.

92 Mary Owen Cameron, *The Booster and the Snitch: Department Store Shoplifting* (New York: Free Press of Glencoe, 1964).

93 Klemke, "Exploring Juvenile Shoplifting," p. 62.

94 JoAnn Ray, "Every Twelfth Shopper: Who Shoplifts and Why?" *Social Casework*, Vol. 68 (1987).

95 Klemke, "Exploring Juvenile Shoplifting," p. 71.

96 Janne Kivivuori, "The Case of Temporally Intensified Shoplifting," *British Journal of Criminology*, Vol. 38, No. 4 (1998), p. 663.

97 Ibid. For support for this point, see also Robert Sampson and John Laub, "Crime and Deviance over the Life Course: The Salience of Adult Social Bonds," *American Sociological Review*, Vol. 55, No. 5 (1990), pp. 609–627; and David Farrington, "Age and Crime," in Michael Tonry and Norval Morris, eds., *Crime and Justice: An Annual Review of Research*, Vol. 7 (Chicago: University of Chicago Press, 1986).

98 Kivivuori, "The Case of Temporally Intensified Shoplifting," p. 678.

99 Terrie Moffitt, "Adolescence-Limited and Life-Course Persistent Antisocial Behavior: A Developmental Taxonomy," *Psychological Review*, Vol. 100, No. 4 (1993), pp. 674–701.

100 Kivivuori, "The Case of Temporally Intensified Shoplifting."

101 Frederick M. Thrasher, *The Gang: A Study of 1,313 Gangs in Chicago* (Chicago: University of Chicago Press, 1927).

102 Kenneth D. Tunnell, *Choosing Crime: The Criminal Calculus of Property Offenders* (Chicago: Nelson-Hall, 1992), p. 122.

103 Cameron, *The Booster and the Snitch.*

104 Richard H. Moore, "Shoplifting in Middle America: Patterns and Motivational Correlates," *International Journal of Offender Therapy and Comparative Criminology*, Vol. 23, No. 1 (1984), pp. 55–64.

105 Frank J. McShane and Barrie A. Noonan, "Classification of Shoplifters by Cluster Analysis," *International Journal of Offender Therapy and Comparative Criminology*, Vol. 37, No. 1 (1993), pp. 29–40.

106 Ibid., p. 35.

107 Ibid., p. 36.

108 Ibid.

109 Jack Katz, *Seductions of Crime: Moral and Sensual Attractions in Doing Evil* (New York: Basic Books, 1988).

110 Ibid., p. 9.

111 President's Commission, *The Challenge of Crime in a Free Society*, p. 64.

112 Herbert Koppel, *Lifetime Likelihood of Victimization* (Washington, DC: Bureau of Justice Statistics, 1987).

113 FBI, *Crime in the United States, 2006.*

114 Ibid.

115 Shover, *Great Pretenders*, p. 64.

116 Shover, "Burglary."

117 For representative examples of this perspective, see Michael J. Hindelang, *Criminal Victimization in Eight American Cities* (Cambridge, MA: Ballinger, 1978); and Michael J. Hindelang, Michael R. Gottfredson, and James Garolfalo, *Victims of Personal Crime: An Empirical Foundation for a*

Theory of Personal Victimization (Cambridge, MA: Ballinger, 1978).

[118] For representative discussions of this perspective, see Lawrence E. Cohen and Marcus Felson, "Social Change and Crime Rate Trends: A Routine Activity Approach," *American Sociological Review,* Vol. 44 (1979), pp. 588–607; and Marcus Felson and Lawrence E. Cohen, "Human Ecology and Crime: A Routine Activity Approach," *Human Ecology,* Vol. 8 (1980), pp. 398–405.

[119] Felson and Cohen, "Human Ecology and Crime."

[120] Felson, "Linking Criminal Choices."

[121] Ibid., p. 120.

[122] Lawrence E. Cohen and David Cantor, "Residential Burglary in the United States: Life-Style and Demographic Factors Associated with the Probability of Victimization," *Journal of Research in Crime and Delinquency,* Vol. 18, No. 1 (1981), pp. 113–127.

[123] P. H. Ennis, *Criminal Victimization in the United States: A Report of the National Survey, Field Surveys II: President's Commission on Law Enforcement and Administration of Justice* (Washington, DC: U.S. Government Printing Office, 1967).

[124] Robert J. Sampson and John D. Wooldredge, "Linking the Micro- and Macro-Level Dimensions of Lifestyle-Routine Activity and Opportunity Models of Predatory Victimization," *Journal of Quantitative Criminology,* Vol. 3 (1987), pp. 371–393.

[125] Ibid., p. 373.

[126] Ibid.

[127] Mike Maguire, *Burglary in a Dwelling* (London: Heinemann, 1982), cited in Shover, "Burglary," p. 89.

[128] Shover, "Burglary," p. 90.

[129] Ibid., p. 91.

[130] Ibid., p. 92.

[131] Ibid.

[132] Miethe and McCorkle, *Crime Profiles.*

[133] Bureau of Justice Statistics, *Criminal Victimization, 1999,* Table 59.

[134] Ibid., Table 64.

[135] Tunnell, *Choosing Crime,* p. 5.

[136] See Paul F. Cromwell, James N. Olson, and D'Aunn Wester Avary, *Breaking and Entering: An Ethnographic Analysis of Burglary* (Newbury Park, CA: Sage, 1991); and Wright and Decker, *Burglars on the Job.*

[137] Cromwell, Olson, and Avary, *Breaking and Entering.*

[138] Wright and Decker, *Burglars on the Job.*

[139] Ibid., p. 38.

[140] Ibid., pp. 45–46.

[141] Ibid., p. 47.

[142] See Shover, *Great Pretenders.*

[143] Wright and Decker, *Burglars on the Job,* p. 51.

[144] Ibid., p. 52.

[145] Ibid., p. 56.

[146] Ibid.

[147] Katz, *Seductions of Crime,* p. 79.

[148] Tunnell, *Choosing Crime,* p. 41.

[149] Simon Hakim and Yochanan Shachmurove, "Spatial and Temporal Patterns of Commercial Burglaries: The Evidence Examined," *American Journal of Economics and Sociology,* Vol. 55, No. 4 (1996), p. 445.

[150] Ibid., p. 452.

[151] Wright and Decker, *Burglars on the Job,* p. 63.

[152] Ibid.

[153] Shover, "Burglary."

[154] Wright and Decker, *Burglars on the Job,* p. 72.

[155] Ibid., p. 73.

[156] Shover, "Burglary," p. 83.

[157] Wright and Decker, *Burglars on the Job,* p. 100.

[158] Ibid., p. 80.

[159] Ibid., p. 110.

[160] Ibid., p. 113.

[161] Ibid., p. 86.

[162] BJS, *Criminal Victimization, 1999,* Tables 81 and 83.

[163] Ibid., Tables 87 and 89.

[164] Laura Dugan, "The Effect of Criminal Victimization on a Household's Moving Decision," *Criminology,* Vol. 37, No. 4 (1999), pp. 903–930.

[165] Ibid., p. 924.

[166] Ibid., p. 905.

[167] Eric Baumer et al., "The Influence of Crack Cocaine on Robbery, Burglary, and Homicide Rates: A Cross-City, Longitudinal Analysis," *Journal of Research in Crime and Delinquency,* Vol. 35, No. 3 (1998), pp. 316–340.

[168] Ibid., p. 317.

[169] Ibid.

[170] Ibid.

[171] Ibid., p. 319.

[172] Louis B. Schlesinger and Eugene Revitch, "Sexual Burglaries and Sexual Homicide: Clinical, Forensic, and Investigative Considerations," *Journal of the American Academy of Psychiatry and the Law,* Vol. 27, No. 2 (1999), p. 228.

[173] Ibid., p. 232.

[174] Mark Warr, "Rape, Burglary, and Opportunity," *Journal of Quantitative Criminology,* Vol. 4, No. 3 (1988), pp. 275–288.

[175] Ibid., pp. 217–218.

[176] Ibid., p. 287.

[177] Ibid., p. 286.

[178] Darrell J. Steffensmeier, *The Fence: In the Shadow of Two Worlds* (Savage, MD: Rowman and Littlefield, 1986), p. 10.

[179] Ibid., p. 9.

[180] Ibid. See also Wright and Decker, *Burglars on the Job.*

[181] Steffensmeier, *The Fence,* p. 9.

[182] Ibid.

[183] Klockars, *The Professional Fence.*

[184] Steffensmeier, *The Fence.*

[185] Ibid., p. 13.

[186] Ibid.

[187] Cromwell, Olson, and Avary, *Breaking and Entering.*

[188] Wright and Decker, *Burglars on the Job,* p. 167.

[189] Shover, "Burglary," p. 103.

[190] Wright and Decker, *Burglars on the Job,* p. 169.

[191] Steffensmeier, *The Fence,* p. 25.

[192] Ibid., p. 23.

[193] Ibid., p. 21.

[194] Wright and Decker, *Burglars on the Job,* p. 179.

[195] Ibid., pp. 175–176.

[196] Cromwell, Olson, and Avary, *Breaking and Entering,* p. 74.

[197] Ibid., p. 75.

[198] Ibid., p. 76.

[199] Wright and Decker, *Burglars on the Job,* p. 181.

[200] Cromwell, Olson, and Avary, *Breaking and Entering,* p. 76.

[201] Ibid., p. 77.

[202] Ibid.

[203] Stuart Henry, *The Hidden Economy: The Context and Control of Borderline Crime* (Oxford: Martin Robertson, 1978).

[204] FBI, *Crime in the United States, 2006.*

[205] Ibid.

[206] See "Earth Liberation Front," *The Free Dictionary,* http://encyclopedia.thefreedictionary.com/Earth%20Liberation%20Front (accessed July 20, 2004).

[207] North American Earth Liberation Front Press Office (NAELFPO), "Frequently Asked Questions," http://www.earthliberationfront.com/library/elf_faq.pdf (accessed August 3, 2007).

[208] Earth Liberation Front, "Three Plead Guilty to Earth Liberation Actions," http://www.earthliberationfront.com/news/2004/011304.shtml (accessed August 1, 2006).

209 Earth Liberation Front, "Underground Direct Action Totals for 2003," January 13, 2004, http://www. earthliberationfront.com/news/2004/011304r.shtml (accessed July 18, 2006).

210 Sarah A. Soule and Nella Van Dyke, "Black Church Arson in the United States, 1989–1996," *Ethnic and Racial Studies,* Vol. 22, No. 4 (1999), p. 725.

211 Public Law 104–155.

212 "Report Issued on Church Burnings," *Christian Century,* Vol. 114, No. 19 (June 18, 1997).

213 Angie Cannon and Chitra Ragavan, "Another Look at the Church Fire Epidemic," *U.S. News and World Report,* November 22, 1999, p. 26.

214 Ibid.

215 Ken Brownlee, "Ignoring Juvenile Arson Is Like Playing with Fire," *Claims,* Vol. 48, No. 3 (March 2000), p. 106.

216 Ibid.

217 FBI, *Crime in the United States, 2004.*

218 Brownlee, "Ignoring Juvenile Arson Is Like Playing with Fire," p. 106.

219 Eileen M. Garry, *Juvenile Firesetting and Arson,* Office of Juvenile Justice and Delinquency Prevention Fact Sheet 51 (Washington, DC: Office of Juvenile Justice and Delinquency Prevention, 1997).

220 Ibid., p. 1.

Outline

More money has been stolen at the point of a pen than at the point of a gun.

—Woody Guthrie[1]

Two men can keep a secret, as long as one of them is dead.

—Organized crime proverb

Corrupt corporate executives are no better than common thieves when they betray employees and steal from investors.

—Former U.S. Attorney General John Ashcroft[2]

"Do you know what the Mafia is?"
"The what?"
"The Mafia? M-a-f-i-a?"
"I'm sorry. I don't know what you're talking about."

—Crime boss Salvatore Moretti[3]

Learning Outcomes

After reading this chapter, you should be able to

- Meaningfully discuss white-collar crime and its conceputalization
- Describe the nature of organized crime and be able to list some significant organized criminal groups operating today
- Recommend some policies for the control of organized crime

Introduction

Corporate and white-collar crime took center stage in 2002, as financial scandals exploded across America's economic landscape, leading President George W. Bush to call upon Congress to stiffen penalties for unscrupulous business executives. The president's call came amid declining stock market values, shaken investor confidence, and threats to the viability of employees' pension plans in the wake of what appeared to have been a corporate crime wave involving illegal activities that had been planned and undertaken by executives at a number of large corporations. Among the firms ensnared by scandal were former energy broker Enron Corporation; telecommunications giant WorldCom, Inc.; cable services provider Adelphia Communications Corporation; accounting firm Arthur Andersen, LLP; business and consumer services provider Cendant; former telecommunications company Global Crossing; drug maker Johnson & Johnson; and bankrupt retailer Kmart. Read the president's spoken address on corporate responsibility via **Library Extra 12–1** at crimtoday.com.

LIBRARY
Extra

The collapse of energy trading giant Enron Corporation, which had used complex off-balance-sheet partnerships to hide losses and inflate revenues, set the stage for massive reforms in the business and financial world, as well as for federal and state investigations into the accounting practices and business dealings of all publicly traded companies in the United States. Enron Corporation, whose corporate banner once declared that it was "the world's leading company," was formed by the merger of Houston Natural Gas and Omaha, Nebraska–based InterNorth Corporation in 1985— a combination that created the first nationwide natural gas pipeline system. In 2000, Enron's annual revenues reached $100 billion, reflecting the growing significance of energy trading among the company's activities. Share prices for Enron's stock grew quickly during 2000 as the company positioned itself as a major player in what appeared to be a lucrative energy trading business. The business, which did not require that Enron own or produce any of the energy that it traded, began to unravel in 2001, when bankrupt California utility Pacific Gas and Electric Co. was unable to pay $570 million for energy that it had purchased, and Enron was subsequently unsuccessful in bids to extend its credit lines. In November 2001, Enron executives surprised stockholders when they revised the company's financial statements for the prior five years in order to account for hundreds of millions of dollars in losses that they had previously hidden. A month later, Enron filed for Chapter 11 bankruptcy protection and laid off

President George W. Bush signs the Sarbanes-Oxley corporate reform bill on July 30, 2002, as (L–R) Attorney General John Ashcroft, Representative Michael Oxley (R–OH), Secretary of Commerce Donald Evans, and Senators Paul Sarbanes (D–MD), Trent Lott (R–MS), and Tom Daschle (D–SD) look on. The law substantially changed business accounting practices and imposed tough penalties on violators. What social forces gave rise to the Sarbanes-Oxley Act?

Source: Alex Wong, Getty Images, Inc.–Liaison

more than 4,000 workers. The bankruptcy wiped out at least $24 billion of value in retirement plans, stock accounts, and mutual funds as the company's stock plummeted.

Enron's bankruptcy was followed by congressional hearings into the collapse of the company and by a U.S. Department of Justice investigation. Investigators wanted to know how five of the company's former officers made over $300 million in profits from sales of company stock prior to bankruptcy, while ordinary investors lost everything. Allegations emerged that Enron had conspired with other energy trading companies to illegally manipulate power and natural gas prices in western states—leading to huge gains, including a record $485 million windfall profit in a single day.[4] Most of the charges against the company and its officials, however, centered on allegations that the company had artificially inflated its profits and concealed debts through the fraudulent use of special purpose corporate entities that it had created. Those entities were used, according to investigators, to remove debt from the company's balance sheet and to buy assets from Enron in order to allow the company to show profits far greater than any it was actually earning.

The rise and fall of Enron, which had become the seventh largest corporation in America prior to bankruptcy, were depicted in a made-for-television movie, *The Crooked E: The Unshredded Truth about Enron*, which aired on CBS on January 5, 2003.[5] For an in-depth look at some of the problems Enron faced in its final days, see a letter written in August 2001 by Enron senior executive Sherron Watkins to the company's chairman, Kenneth Lay, at **Web Extra 12–1**. As the letter shows, Watkins warned Lay that the company could soon "implode in a wave of financial scandals."

On August 28, 2002—less than a year after the collapse of Enron—a federal grand jury indicted former WorldCom, Inc., top executives Scott Sullivan, 40, and Buford Yates, 46, on charges of conspiring to commit securities fraud, committing **securities fraud,** and making false filings with the Securities and Exchange Commission (SEC).[6] Sullivan, the company's former chief financial officer, allegedly tried to disguise increasing losses at WorldCom by instructing Yates and other executives to improperly shift $3.8 billion in operating costs to other accounts in 2001 and 2002 in order to hide them from auditors and to falsely inflate profits by $5 billion.[7] Yates was the company's director of general accounting. Also named in the seven-count indictment were two other WorldCom accounting executives, Betty Vinson and Troy Normand. David Myers, WorldCom's former controller, had been charged in an earlier criminal complaint filed by federal prosecutors. On July 21, 2002, WorldCom, Inc., filed for the largest-ever U.S. bankruptcy, claiming assets of $107 billion and debt of $41 billion. Two weeks later, the company announced that it had uncovered another $3.3 billion in additional accounting irregularities going back to 1999 and that it would further reduce reported assets by more than $50 billion.[8] WorldCom continued to operate under federal bankruptcy protection before merging with MCI, Inc., in 2003. In 2006, the merged companies were purchased by Verizon Communications and now operate under the Verizon name.

Financial scandals have a long and ubiquitous history in the United States, sometimes involving government regulators themselves. In 1929, for example, the Teapot Dome scandal embroiled the administration of President Warren Harding. The scandal began in 1921, when Secretary of the Interior Albert B. Fall secretly leased naval oil reserves at Teapot Dome, Wyoming, and Elk Hills, California, to developers without asking for competitive bids. A Senate investigation later revealed that large sums of federal money had been loaned to developers without interest. Fall was eventually fined and sent to prison, and a 1927 U.S. Supreme Court decision ordered the fields restored to the U.S. government.

White-Collar Crime

In 1939, famed criminologist **Edwin H. Sutherland** defined *white-collar crime* during his presidential address to the American Sociological Society. **White-collar crime,** said Sutherland, consists of violations of the criminal law "committed by a person of

---

WEB
Extra
▪ ▪ ▪ ▪

securities fraud

The theft of money resulting from intentional manipulation of the value of equities, including stocks and bonds. Securities fraud also includes theft from securities accounts and wire fraud.

white-collar crime

Violations of the criminal law committed by persons of respectability and high social status in the course of their occupation.

Crime in the News

Courts Get Tough on White Collar Criminals

There was a time in the not-too-distant past when white-collar criminal prosecutions were delicate affairs, where prosecutors worked hard not to treat wealthy and powerful defendants as anything as distasteful as, well, criminals.

No more.

The tactics and strategies used in the successful prosecution of the former Enron chief executives, Jeffrey K. Skilling and Kenneth L. Lay, highlight the transformation that has occurred in recent years in the investigation and prosecution of white-collar crime, a change that has brought many of the techniques applied to drug cases and mob prosecutions into the once-genteel legal world of corporate wrongdoers.

No longer are defendants allowed to surrender themselves quietly, outside the view of the press. Now, as Mr. Skilling and Mr. Lay learned firsthand, there are "perp walks" where the handcuffed defendant is brought in by law enforcement for booking. Cases are not resolved with a fine or a short stay in a "country club" prison; now defendants face decades of real jail time, sentences that can preclude them from being considered for minimum-security prisons.

Witnesses are squeezed, with threats against family members and stints in solitary confinement. Those who fail to cooperate are

U.S. Justice Department Enron Task Force members, from left, John C. Hueston, Kathryn H. Ruemmler, Cliff Striclin, and Sean M. Berkowitz, are pictured in front of the Bob Casey Federal Court House in Houston, Texas, on Friday, May 12, 2006. The task force argued the case against former Enron executives in federal court for 60 days. It was disbanded after Jeffrey Skilling, former Enron CEO was convicted and given a lengthy prison sentence. What did the Enron scandal involve?

Source: Carlos Javier Sanchez/Bloomberg News/Landov

indicted, or deemed unindicted co-conspirators, a designation that places potential witnesses in a state of indefinite legal limbo. And companies that want to settle a criminal case can often do so only by taking the once unusual step of waiving their right to protect the confidentiality of their communications with their lawyers.

"Our prosecutors will use the tools legally available to us to solve these crimes and bring the perpetrators to justice," said Bryan Sierra, a Justice Department spokesman.

Legal experts heralded such aggressive approaches as crucial to the government's securing convictions of Mr. Lay and Mr. Skilling. "Prosecutors in white-collar cases are looking at the range of legal tactics that are available to them that they have used for years in other kinds of cases, and they are not just ruling out those tactics because it is a white-collar case," said Christopher Wray, the former head of the Justice Department's criminal division and now head of the government investigations practice at the law firm of King & Spalding.

The expressions of approval, however, were accompanied by concern about whether such tactics can go too far.

"It is hard to take issue with the means they have used to achieve their success, in light of the outcome yesterday," said Robert A. Mintz, a former federal prosecutor who is now a white-collar criminal defense attorney with McCarter & English. "But there are people that feel that the government has built many of these cases with a sledgehammer, pounding potential defendants into cooperating as a means to achieve their ends—in this case the conviction of Lay and Skilling."

But if a sledgehammer is used in the investigation and preparation for trial, prosecutors now wield a scalpel in discerning whether a corporate executive can be deemed to have violated the law.

As the case against Mr. Lay and Mr. Skilling showed, the laws for corporate conduct are being interpreted strictly, requiring honesty in all actions and statements to avoid prosecution. Failure to be forthright, even in subtle ways, can result in a criminal trial. The convictions could set a precedent that haunts other executives. In the past, some of the charges, particularly those against Mr. Lay, might not have survived in a civil trial. Today, subtle dishonesties can be part of a broader effort to construct a huge—and successful—criminal case.

In the Enron case, defense lawyers tried to portray the use of the government's hardball tactics as reason to disbelieve witnesses that pleaded guilty and agreed to testify against their bosses, Mr. Skilling and Mr. Lay.

When the former chief financial officer of Enron, Andrew S. Fastow, balked at cutting a deal with the government, prosecutors started putting pressure on his wife, Lea. She eventually pleaded guilty to income tax evasion for not reporting tens of thousands of dollars in kickback checks from one of Mr. Fastow's off-the-books schemes. Ms. Fastow went to prison for a year.

respectability and high social status in the course of his occupation."[11] Many criminologists do not properly understand crime, Sutherland claimed, because they fail to recognize that the secretive violations of public and corporate trust by those in positions of authority are just as criminal as predatory acts committed by people of lower social standing.

Defense lawyers also elicited testimony that the government may have "hot boxed" Ben F. Glisan Jr., the former treasurer of Enron, after he pleaded guilty to fraud and agreed to a five-year prison sentence. Mr. Glisan was put in solitary confinement for the first 11 days of his sentence and was later moved into a low-security facility for about six months, where he shared a cell with two other inmates. He said he feared for his physical safety.

Later, Mr. Glisan agreed to testify before the grand jury and was granted a series of furloughs, or time away from prison, by the government. Then, in February 2004, he was brought into the federal courthouse in shackles. He was led onto an elevator. There was Mr. Skilling, in handcuffs; he had been arrested and was entering a plea of not guilty to 35 criminal charges.

A prosecutor, Kathryn H. Ruemmler, later tried to portray Mr. Glisan's treatment in the prison system as out of her hands, suggesting that the Bureau of Prisons made decisions completely independently of the Justice Department.

Mr. Glisan said he did not necessarily buy that, especially when it came to his remarkably coincidental run-in with Mr. Skilling on the elevator.

"Did you believe for one second, sir, that that was a coincidence?" Daniel Petrocelli, Mr. Skilling's lead lawyer, asked Mr. Glisan on the stand.

"I didn't believe that, no" Mr. Glisan said.

Other, more subtle tactics were used that some outside defense lawyers were surprised to see applied. For example, the government agreed to cut some deals with cooperating witnesses that left them with substantial sums of money. Mark Koenig, the former director of investor relations, for example, said he was left with $5 million, which acted almost like an upfront bonus for his continued cooperation, legal experts said.

Federal prosecutors have been accused of trying to gain cooperation from companies by suggesting that the government would allow a company to stay in business if it sacrifices certain executives or pushes them to fire certain lawyers.

The tactic is an issue in the prosecution of accounting firm KPMG, where the government told the firm that, if it continued to pay for outside lawyers for its executives, the government would look on that as an "act of treason or noncooperation," said Joel Androphy, a criminal defense lawyer in Houston. "This has been an effective but controversial tool."

The waiver of so-called attorney-client privilege was one of the government's conditions for deferment of criminal charges it was planning to bring against the class-action law firm Milberg Weiss. When the firm refused to go along this month, an indictment was issued.

The neutralizing of certain crucial witnesses by the government's use of a threat of prosecution has prevented defense lawyers from pursuing more corroboration for accused top executives. It was an issue in both the WorldCom case involving the chief executive Bernard J. Ebbers and in the Enron case, where several executives said they would plead the Fifth Amendment if called to the stand.

Prosecutors have even begun using hidden microphones—a tactic more common in political corruption cases—to try to gather evidence against corporate executives. In the case of Richard M. Scrushy, the former chief executive of HealthSouth, investigators wired a former chief financial officer's necktie to covertly record conversations with his boss. It did not ultimately work: in 2005, Scrushy was acquitted of 36 fraud and conspiracy charges by a federal jury.[9] In 2007, however, Scrushy's luck ran out when he was sentenced to seven years in prison and fined $150,000 plus ordered to pay restitution of $267,000 to the United Way as the result of a bribery conviction in a federal government corruption case involving former Alabama governor Don Siegelman.[10]

Some criminal lawyers bristle at the new tactics. "They're despicable," said Jamie Wareham, the chairman of the global litigation practice at Paul, Hastings, Janofsky & Walker. "The government doesn't need to do many of these things. In most cases, they are over-egging on a victory they are going to get anyway."

However the tactics are viewed, they are working much of the time. In the Enron case, jurors said they rejected strident defense arguments that the government had coerced witnesses into pleading guilty to crimes they did not commit and had coached them to accuse Mr. Skilling and Mr. Lay of crimes. "I didn't think they seemed rehearsed," a juror, Donald Martin, an electrical designer, said in an interview. The government "had the documentation to back up what they were saying."

Discussion Questions

1. Why were white collar criminals treated lieniently during much of the twentieth century?

2. What led to the recent change in public and official attitudes toward white collar criminals?

3. In your opinion, should white collar offenders receive special treatment from the justice system? Why or why not?

Source: Kurt Eichenwald and Alexei Barrionuevo, "Tough Justice for Executives in Enron Era," *New York Times*, May 27, 2006. Copyright © 2006 by the New York Times Co. Reprinted with permission.

For the latest crime and justice news, visit www.crimenews.info.

Sutherland told those gathered for the address: "My thesis is that the traditional/conception(s) and explanations of crime [are] misleading and incorrect; that crime is in fact not closely correlated with poverty or with the psychopathic and sociopathic conditions associated with poverty, and that an adequate explanation of criminal behavior must proceed along quite different lines. The conventional explanations are invalid principally because they are derived from biased samples. The samples are biased in that they have not included vast areas of criminal behavior of persons not in the lower class."[12]

The criminality of upper-class persons "has been demonstrated again and again in the investigations of land offices, railways, insurance, munitions, banking, public utilities, stock exchanges, the oil industry, real estate, reorganization committees, receiverships, bankruptcies and politics," said Sutherland.[13] For still other examples, Sutherland pointed to those he called "the robber barons" of the nineteenth century, citing Cornelius Vanderbilt's famous response to inquiries about his sometimes flagrantly illegal activities. "You don't suppose you can run a railroad in accordance with the statutes, do you?" the wealthy Vanderbilt reportedly quipped.

In a later study that is still widely cited by criminologists, Sutherland reported on the frequency with which the nation's 70 largest corporations violated the law.[14] He found that each of the corporations he studied had been sanctioned by courts or by administrative commissions and that the typical corporation had an average of 14 decisions against it. Ninety-eight percent of corporations were recidivists, or commit crime after crime, Sutherland said, while 90% could be called "habitual criminals" under the habitual offender statutes that existed at the time of his study. "Sixty of the corporations [had] decisions against them for restraint of trade, fifty-four for infringements (generally, of patents), forty-four for unfair labor practices, twenty-seven for misrepresentation in advertising, twenty-six for [illegal] rebates, and forty-three for miscellaneous offenses," wrote Sutherland.[15] He also found that of the 70 largest corporations studied, "thirty were either illegal in their origin or began illegal activities immediately after their origin."[16] Such businesses may have been built upon price-fixing or unregulated commodities offerings or via unlawful and clandestine negotiations with government regulators.

The only real difference between modern-day white-collar criminals and those of the past, Sutherland claimed, is that today's criminals are more sophisticated. Although no hard-and-fast figures were available to Sutherland, he estimated that the "financial cost of white-collar crime is probably several times as great as the financial cost of all the crimes which are customarily regarded as the 'crime problem.'"[17]

Sutherland also noted that white-collar criminals are far less likely to be investigated, arrested, or prosecuted than are other types of offenders. When they are—on rare occasions—convicted, white-collar criminals are far less likely to receive active prison terms than are "common criminals." If they are sent to prison, the amount of time they are ordered to serve is far less than one would expect, given the amount of damage their crimes inflict on society. The deference shown to white-collar criminals, according to Sutherland, is due primarily to their social standing. Many white-collar criminals are well respected in their communities, and many take part in national affairs. Few are perceived as mean-spirited or even ill-intentioned. Private citizens who do not fully understand business affairs sometimes assume that those charged with white-collar crimes were unwittingly caught up in obscure government regulations or that government agencies chose to make examples of a few unfortunate, but typical, businesspeople.

Given these kinds of sentiments, criminologists felt compelled for years to address the question "Is white-collar crime crime?" As recently as 1987, writers on the subject were still asking, "Do persons of high standing commit crimes?"[18] Although most criminologists today would answer the question with a resounding *yes*, members of the public have been far slower to accept the notion that violations of the criminal law by businesspeople share conceptual similarities with street crime. Attitudes, however, are changing as more headline-making charges are being filed against corporations and their representatives for illegal activities.

The bankruptcy of WorldCom, Inc., in 2002 and the collapse of Enron Corporation in 2001 led to a widening scandal as class action lawsuits were filed against what remained of both companies. Nearly a dozen investment banks and law firms were accused of collusion with former WorldCom and Enron executives with intent to defraud investors. One of the most widely publicized lawsuits was brought by the University of California's board of regents, which sought to recover $145 million that had been lost by the university through Enron-related investments.[19] Among the defendants named in the civil suit were England's Barclays Capital, Germany-based Deutsche Bank, JPMorgan, Citigroup, Merrill Lynch, CSFB, Lehman Brothers, Bank of America, and Canadian Imperial Bank. Other groups that were reported to be planning to sue were the Florida State Board of Administration, a pension fund for state employees, which lost more than $100 million in the WorldCom bankruptcy and $328 million on its Enron investments; the California Public Employees' Retirement System (known as Calpers), which lost $565 million on WorldCom investments; the New York State Common Retirement Fund, which reported losing $300 million; and the New York City pension fund, which lost $100 million in retirement monies contributed by the city's teachers, police, and firefighters.[20]

Allegations of criminal wrongdoing soon spread to other companies. In 2002, officials at cable television provider Adelphia Communications were charged with failing to adequately disclose loans and loan guarantees of $3.1 billion to the company's founder, John J. Rigas, and members of his family. About the same time, executives at a number of corporations were accused by the SEC, stockholders, and independent prosecutors of intentionally misstating revenues or hiding losses. Among them were Computer Associates International; CMS Energy; Dynegy; Global Crossing; Halliburton; Lucent Technologies; Network Associates; Qwest Communications International, Inc.; Reliant Resources; Trump Hotels and Casinos; Waste Management; Xerox; and Kmart (which filed for bankruptcy in 2002, and emerged from the process a year later after closing more than 600 stores). Executives at CMS Energy, Dynegy, and Reliant Resources admitted overstating revenues by falsifying numbers on energy trades in which their companies were involved; Lucent Technologies, without admitting to any serious wrongdoing, reduced reported revenues for 2000 by $679 million; Trump Hotels and Casino agreed to change the way it reported earnings, also without admitting any wrongdoing; and Xerox paid a $10 million fine for misstating revenues that it said it had earned between 1997 and 2000 by improperly including future payments on existing contracts.

Also in 2002, ImClone founder Dr. Sam Waksal pled guilty to six federal charges of bank fraud and conspiracy in an **insider trading** scandal that threatened the home decorating empire of Martha Stewart. Prosecutors alleged that Waksal had tipped off family members and friends, including Stewart and her stock broker, that the Food and Drug Administration would not approve his company's experimental cancer drug, Erbitux.[21] Waksal, 55, who admitted to **bank fraud** for forging the name of ImClone's chief attorney to a document securing a line of credit, was sentenced to seven years in prison, while Martha Stewart was ordered to spend five months behind bars.

The crisis in the country's equity markets worsened as collusion between accounting giant Arthur Andersen and embattled Enron Corporation executives was revealed after Andersen officials were caught shredding documents related to the government's investigation of the energy company. Soon, other accounting firms came under scrutiny, although the improprieties in which they were alleged to have been involved didn't immediately bring criminal charges. Deloitte & Touche, the auditing firm that kept Adelphia Communications's books, was accused of having helped guarantee loans to the Rigases. Ernst & Young was sued by the SEC, which accused the firm of violating federal rules requiring a separation of interests. The SEC claimed that Ernst & Young had maintained an improper business relationship with PeopleSoft Corporation at the time that it was generating the company's financial statements. KPMG, which audited Xerox, was alleged to have had a similar relationship with its client; PricewaterhouseCoopers, the accounting firm that served as auditors for MicroStrategy, settled a similar case against it without admitting fault.[22]

Securities firms were pulled into the fray when Salomon Smith Barney (the investment arm of Citigroup, Inc.); Goldman Sachs Group, Inc.; Merrill Lynch & Co.; Deutsche Bank AG; and U.S. Bancorp's Piper Jaffray unit came under investigation by federal regulators on suspicion that they had created conflicts of interests in handing out shares in initial public offerings of companies that they supported financially to select stock-research analysts.[23] Regulators also charged the firms with providing biased research to mislead investors into buying stock in companies in which the firms had vested inter-

insider trading

Equity trading based on confidential information about important events that may affect the price of the issue being traded.

bank fraud

Fraud or embezzlement that occurs within or against financial institutions that are insured or regulated by the U.S. government. Financial institution fraud includes commercial loan fraud, check fraud, counterfeit negotiable instruments, mortgage fraud, check kiting, and false credit applications.

ests. Although some felt that criminal charges of securities fraud would be brought, an agreement between the SEC and the Wall Street firms reached in December of 2002 ended the possibility of criminal prosecution and required the companies to pay $1.4 billion in fines.[24] The firms also agreed to insulate their research analysts from investment banking activities, to ban the setting aside of shares in initial public offerings for certain corporate executives, to provide independent investment research to their customers, and to make public what had previously been proprietary information about their stock ratings and investment price targets. Allegations against the securities firms were settled without requiring them to admit any wrongdoing.

Some individual investment advisors, however, were made to face criminal charges. On June 10, 2002, for example, Alan B. Bond, a New York money manager and president of Albriond Capital Management Company, was convicted in a three-week trial of six counts of defrauding pension funds of millions of dollars and was sent straight to jail.[25] He received a 12 1/2 year prison sentence. Table 12–1 describes the terminology of white-collar crime, and Table 12–2 details the cases involving some of the nation's leading companies and their former executives at the start of 2008.

The insider trading scam of stock market tycoon Ivan Boesky and the securities fraud conviction of junk bond king Michael Milken in the 1980s show how fortunes can be amassed through white-collar law violations. Boesky was estimated to have netted a profit of $250 million for himself and a few close friends, while Milken paid a $600 million fine—far less than the amount he is estimated to have reaped from illegal trading.

The nationwide savings and loan (S&L) disaster of the 1980s, which some have called the "biggest white-collar crime in history," serves as another example of white-collar crime. The savings and loan fiasco was the result of years of intentional mismanagement and personal appropriation of funds by institutional executives. Although the actual amount of money lost or stolen during the scandal may never be known, it is estimated to run into the hundreds of billions of dollars. The collapse of just one such institution, Charles Keating's California-based Lincoln Savings and Loan Association, cost taxpayers—who were left to redeem the insolvent institution—approximately $2.5 billion, while the collapse of Neil Bush's Silverado Banking S&L in Denver cost nearly $1 billion. Some experts say that the "bailout" of S&Ls nationwide cost American taxpayers $500 billion[26]—much more than has ever been stolen in all bank robberies throughout the history of our country.

WEB
Extra
▪▪▪▪

Another type of white-collar crime sprang from the low interest rates characteristic of the early and mid-1990s. Sham banking operations, often with high-sounding names and seemingly prestigious addresses, flourished—offering high interest rates and double-digit rates of return on investments held by the bank. Unfortunately, such "phantom banks," as they were dubbed by the federal comptroller of the currency, evaporated as quickly as they were formed, leaving investors stunned and sometimes penniless. Some of the schemes involved the sale of certificates of deposit in offshore banks, like those in the Caribbean; others bilked investors by convincing them to buy millions of dollars of what was supposed to be newly privatized Russian stock; and still more offered the seemingly irresistible chance to earn exorbitant returns through sophisticated overseas investments. Recently, the Federal Deposit Insurance Corporation (FDIC) issued a list of 60 unregulated business entities illegally conducting banking businesses within the United States. Canadian officials added another 200 suspects to the list. As one expert on illegal banking operations explained, "It's difficult to prosecute the criminals who run phantom banks because many times the victims are unwilling to press charges or the schemes take months to unravel."[27] Learn more about white-collar crime and law enforcement's response from the National White Collar Crime Center via **Web Extra 12–2.**

Definitional Evolution of White-Collar Crime

One early writer on white-collar crime explained, "The chief criterion for a crime to be 'white-collar' is that it occurs as a part of, or a deviation from, the violator's occupational role."[28] This focus on the violator, rather than on the offense, in deciding whether

TABLE 12–1 The Terminology of White-Collar Crime

Antitrust violation: Any activity that illegally inhibits competition between companies and within an industry, such as price fixing and monopolies in restraint of trade. Antitrust violations are infractions of the Sherman Act (15 U.S.C. §§ 1–7) and the Clayton Act (15 U.S.C. §§ 12–27).

Bank fraud (also financial fraud or financial institution fraud): Fraud or embezzlement that occurs within or against financial institutions that are insured or regulated by the U.S. government. Financial institution fraud includes commercial loan fraud, check fraud, counterfeit negotiable instruments, mortgage fraud, and false credit applications.

Bankruptcy fraud: The misleading of creditors through the concealment and misstatement of assets. Bankruptcy fraud also involves illegal pressure on bankruptcy petitioners.

Economic espionage/trade secret theft: The theft or misappropriation of proprietary economic information (that is, trade secrets) from an individual, a business, or an industry.

Embezzlement: The unlawful misappropriation for personal use of money, property, or other thing of value entrusted to the offender's care, custody, or control.

Environmental law violation: Any business activity in violation of federal and state environmental laws, including the discharge of toxic substances into the air, water, or soil, especially when those substances pose a significant threat of harm to people, property, or the environment.

Government fraud: Fraud against the government, especially in connection with federal government contracting and fraud in connection with federal and/or federally funded programs. Such programs include public housing, agricultural programs, defense procurement, and government-funded educational programs. Fraudulent activities involving government contracting include bribery in contracts or procurement, collusion among contractors, false or double billing, false certification of the quality of parts or of test results, and substitution of bogus or otherwise inferior parts.

Health-care fraud: Fraudulent billing practices by health-care providers, including hospitals, home health care, ambulance services, doctors, chiropractors, psychiatric hospitals, laboratories, pharmacies, and nursing homes that affect health-care consumers, insurance providers, and government-funded payment providers, such as Medicare and Medicaid. Fraudulent activities include receiving kickbacks, billing for services not rendered, billing for unnecessary equipment, and billing for services performed by a lesser qualified person.

Insider trading: Equity trading based on confidential information about important events that may affect the price of the issue being traded. Because confidential information confers advantages on those who possess it, federal law prohibits them from using that knowledge to reap profits or to avoid losses in the stock market.

Insurance fraud: Fraudulent activity committed by insurance applicants, policyholders, third-party claimants, or professionals who provide insurance services to claimants. Such fraudulent activities include inflating, or "padding," actual claims and fraudulent inducements to issue policies and/or establish a lower premium rate.

Kickbacks: The return of a certain amount of money from seller to buyer as a result of a collusive agreement.

Mail fraud: The use of the U.S. mail in furtherance of criminal activity.

Money laundering: The process of converting illegally earned assets, originating as cash, to one or more alternative forms to conceal such incriminating factors as illegal origin and true ownership.

Securities fraud: The theft of money resulting from intentional manipulation of the value of equities, including stocks and bonds. Securities fraud also includes theft from securities accounts and wire fraud.

Tax evasion: Fraud committed by filing false tax returns or not filing tax returns at all.

Wire fraud: The use of an electric or electronic communications facility to intentionally transmit a false and/or deceptive message in furtherance of a fraudulent activity.

Sources: Cynthia Barnett, *The Measurement of White-Collar Crime Using Uniform Crime Reporting Data,* FBI, Criminal Justice Information Services Division, http://www.fbi.gov/ucr/whitecollarforweb.pdf (accessed June 18, 2007); Clifford Karchmer and Douglas Ruch, "State and Local Money Laundering Control Strategies," *NIJ Research in Brief* (Washington, DC: National Institute of Justice, 1992); and Legal Information Institute, *White-Collar Crime: An Overview,* http://www.law.cornell.edu/topics/white_collar.html (accessed July 1, 2007).

to classify a crime as "white-collar" was accepted by the 1967 Presidential Commission on Law Enforcement and Administration of Justice. In its classic report, *The Challenge of Crime in a Free Society*, members of the commission wrote, "The 'white-collar' criminal is the broker who distributes fraudulent securities, the builder who deliberately uses defective material, the corporation executive who conspires to fix prices, the legislator who peddles his influence and votes for private gain, or the banker who misappropriates funds in his keeping."[29]

TABLE 12–2 American Corporations Suspected of Wrongdoing, Investigations in Progress, and Court Sentences as of the Start of 2008

	Allegations
Adelphia Communications Corporation	The company's founder and his family were accused of improperly appropriating $3.2 billion of the firm's monies for their personal use. Prosecutors said that the founder and his family used their influence with the company to (1) illegally pay for their apartments in New York, (2) build a golf course on land they owned, and (3) help purchase
Arthur Andersen, LLP	The company was charged with obstructing an SEC investigation into Enron Corp.'s collapse. Employees in the company's Houston office destroyed thousands of documents related to its work with Enron Corp. that might have proved useful in the Enron investigation.
Bristol-Myers Squibb	The company was charged by 32 state attorney generals in a civil lawsuit filed in U.S. District Court in Washington, D.C., with conspiring with California-based American Bioscience, Inc., to unlawfully maintain a monopoly over the anticancer drug Taxol by fraudulently securing patents in violation of
Citigroup, Inc.	The company's securities arm, Salomon Smith Barney, through a former telecom analyst, is accused of providing unfounded stock recommendations in order to acquire additional investment-banking business.
Enron Corp.	Accused of using aggressive accounting practices to hide massive debt and to artificially create the appearance of profits when none existed.
Global Crossing, Ltd.	May have artificially inflated revenues through a capacity-swapping scheme with Qwest Communications.
Qwest Communications International, Inc.	May have artificially inflated revenues through a capacity-swapping scheme with Global Crossing, Ltd.
Sotheby's and Christie's Auction Houses	A six-year price fixing conspiracy that swindled customers out of more than $100 million.
Tenet Healthcare	Doctors at one of the company's hospitals may have performed unnecessary heart surgeries; the company may have routinely engaged in billing practices that overcharged Medicare; and the company may have recruited physicians to refer patients to its hospitals in ways unacceptable under federal guidelines.
ImClone Systems, Inc.	The company's former CEO was arrested on charges of bank fraud and conspiracy in June 2002. He is also accused of insider trading and of giving advance notice to family and friends that applications concerning the drug maker's cancer drug were about to be rejected—allowing them to sell shares ahead of a significant price decline.
Merrill Lynch & Co.	Accused of overly optimistic investment assessments concerning companies in dealings with the firm's underwriters. Former executives charged with fraudulent financial deals involving Enron Corp.
Rite Aid Corp.	Securities and accounting fraud leading to a reduction in reported earnings of $1.6 billion in 2000. Three former executives were indicted on criminal charges of conspiracy, securities fraud, mail fraud, and wire fraud.
Tyco International, Ltd.	Theft of more than $170 million through unauthorized compensation, improper loans, bonuses, and compensation of its CEO and CFO; $430 million in illegal stock sales.
MCI/WorldCom, Inc.	Massive accounting fraud to hide costs and inflate profits by around $7 billion over three years. Investors were wiped out, and 20,000 employees lost their jobs.

the Buffalos Sabres hockey team, (4) create a family-run investment firm, and (5) subsidize a documentary film in which they had a personal interest.

both federal and state laws in order to keep generic forms of the drug off the market.

The People												
John J. Rigas, founder and CEO	Joseph Berardino, former CEO	Jack Grubman, former telecom analyst	Kenneth Lay, former CEO	Gary Winnick, Global Crossing chairman	Richard Notebaert, Qwest chairman and CEO	A. Alfred Taubman, former Sotheby's Chairman	Jeffrey C. Barbakow, CEO	Dr. Samuel Waksal, former CEO	Henry Blodget, former Internet analyst	Martin L. Grass, former chairman and CEO	L. Dennis Kozlowski, former CEO	Bernard Ebbers, former CEO
Timothy Rigas, former CEO	David Duncan, partner		Jeffrey Skilling, former CEO		Joseph Nacchio, former Qwest chairman and CEO	Sir Anthony Tennant, Christie's	Thomas B. Mackey, COO	Martha Stewart, decorating maven and friend of Waksal	David Komansky, CEO	Franklin Brown, former chief counsel and vice chairman	Mark Swartz, former CFO	Scott Sullivan, former CFO
Michael Rigas, former executive VP			Andrew S. Fastow, former CFO			Diana "DeDe" Brooks, former Sotheby's CEO		Peter Bacanovic, stock broker for Waksal, Stewart	Robert Furst, Daniel Bayly, and James A. Brown, former managing directors	Franklyn Bergonzi, former CFO	Mark Belnick, former general counsel	David Myers, former controller
James R. Brown, former vice president			Michael J. Kopper, former managing director					Douglas Faneuil, brokerage assistant at Merrill Lynch				Buford Yates, former accounting director
Michael C. Mulcahey, former vice president and assistant treasurer			Ben Glisan, former treasurer									Betty Vinson and Troy Normand, executives under Myers
			Hunter Shively, former vice president									

(continued)

489

TABLE 12–2 (continued)

	Adelphia Communications Corporation	Arthur Andersen LLP	Bristol-Myers Squibb	Citigroup, Inc.	Enron Corp.	Global Crossing, Ltd.	Qwest Communications International, Inc.	Sotheby's and Christie's Auction Houses	Tenet Healthcare	ImClone Systems, Inc.	Merrill Lynch & Co.	Rite Aid Corp.	Tyco International, Ltd.	MCI/WorldCom, Inc.
What happened	The Rigas family members resigned from the company and gave up their seats on the company's board of directors. John and Timothy Rigas were found guilty of conspiracy and bank and securities fraud. Jurors were unable to agree on charges against	The company was convicted of obstruction and received a sentence of five years' probation and a $500,000 fine. It also lost its licenses to conduct business in the U.S. and Berardino resigned in March 2002; Duncan pleaded guilty to obstruction		Grubman resigned and the firm paid $5 million to settle charges that it issued misleading research about equities in which it had a vested interest. The company agreed to pay $240 million to settle predatory lending charges.	Fastow was sentenced in 2006 to six years in prison after pleading guilty to charges of conspiracy to commit wire fraud and securities fraud and agreeing to cooperate with prosecutors. Kopper pleaded guilty to money laundering and conspiracy to commit wire fraud.	Global Crossing filed for bankruptcy protection in January 2002.	The company restated $2.2 billion in revenues because of bad accounting. Nacchio resigned as chairman and CEO and agreed in October 2003 to pay $400,000 to settle charges that he unjustly profited from initial public stock offerings.	Taubman was sentenced to serve one year in federal prison and fined $7.5 million. He completed his sentence in June 2003. Brooks received a three-year probationary sentence and was ordered to serve six months of home detention and fined $350,000. She was	FBI agents raided offices in one of the company's hospitals in late 2002 looking for evidence of wrongdoing.	Waksal pleaded guilty to bank fraud and conspiracy charges and was sent to prison for 7 years. Bacanovic and Faneuil lost their jobs at Merrill Lynch, and Faneuil pleaded guilty to accepting a bribe to cover up the incident. In 2004, Stewart	The firm agreed to pay $100 million to settle a probe by the New York attorney general's office and to separate investment analysts' activities from the firm's investment-banking business.	Former president Timothy J. Noonan pleaded guilty to failing to report a felony and is reported to be cooperating with prosecutors. Brown was found guilty of conspiracy and obstruction of justice. Five other executives, including Grass, pleaded guilty to wrongdoing.	Kozlowski and Swartz indicted on charges of stealing company funds. Kozlowski, who resigned, was also indicted on New York state charges of tax evasion and evidence tampering stemming from $13 million in art sales. Belnick charged with falsifying	Jack Grubman, telecom analyst at Salomon Smith Barney Vinson and Normand pleaded guilty to fraud on October 11, 2002. Sullivan pleaded guilty to federal fraud charges in 2004. Ebbers was indited in 2004 of fraud and conspiracy charges.

Michael Rigas. Mulcahey was acquitted of all charges. John Rigas entered federal prison in August 2007.

The records and covering up $14 million in improper company loans.

The company reached a settlement with the Securities and Exchange Commission and neither admitted nor denied any wrongdoing.

was convicted of charges that she traded stock illegally based on inside information.

also ordered to perform 1,000 hours of community service.

charges and testified against the firm.

Glisan pleaded guilty to conspiracy in 2003 and was sentenced to 5 years in prison. Fastow was sentenced to 10 years in prison in a plea deal and cooperated with prosecutors.

The ongoing saga

The case has yet to be resolved.

The company has surrendered all its state licenses and has closed its U.S. operations.

Prosecutors and civil claimants are seeking forfeiture of $2.5 billion from the Rigases in what they say are illegal proceeds.

Investigations are ongoing at the Securities and Exchange Commission and the U.S. Department of Justice.

Skilling was convicted in 2006 of lying to investigators about the company's financial condition, and was sentenced to 24 years and 4 months in prison. In 2006, Lay was found guilty on 10 of 11 counts of criminal conspiracy

Four former managers have been indicted and investigations are ongoing at the SEC and the U.S. Department of Justice.

Although criminal charges have not been brought, Barbakow had accepted responsibility for some problems and planned to discuss his future compensation with the company's board of directors.

Tennant, who lives in England, refuses to recognize the jurisdiction of American courts.

The company is facing the potential for civil suits by disgruntled investors and may face further action by regulatory agencies. It has agreed to cooperate in the investigations.

Bergonzi pleaded guilty to one count of conspiracy in a deal with prosecutors that called for him to testify against the others. Grass was convicted in 2004 and sentenced against Bayly, Furst, and Brown. Also in

Kozlowski and Swartz's first trial ended in a mistrial. Kozlowski was retried and convicted, and is currently serving an 8 and 1/2 to 25 year sentence in a New York prison. An internal audit by the company, conducted at the end

Vinson and Normand cooperated with investigators as prosecutions against the others proceed. Sullivan agreed to testify against Ebbers and received a five-year prison sentence. Ebbers was vindicated of securities fraud. He is

(continued)

TABLE 12–2 (continued)

Adelphia Communications Corporation	Arthur Andersen LLP	Bristol-Myers Squibb	Citigroup, Inc.	Enron Corp.	Global Crossing, Ltd.	Qwest Communications International, Inc.	Sotheby's and Christie's Auction Houses	Tenet Healthcare	ImClone Systems, Inc.	Merrill Lynch & Co.	Rite Aid Corp.	Tyco International, Ltd.	MCI/WorldCom, Inc.
				and fraud. He died of a heart attack before sentencing.							2004, Brown was sentenced to 10 years in federal prison.	of 2002, concluded that aggressive accounting had inflated the company's 2002 profits by $400 million, but that the practice did not amount to intentional fraud.	serving a 25-year prison sentence.

Source: This table was developed using information from many sources, including: Stephanie Armour, "Till White-Collar Crimes Do Us Part," *USA Today*, May 24, 2007, p. 3B, Leslie Cauley, "Rigas Tells His Side of the Adelphia Story," *USA Today*, August 6, 2007, p. 1B; Edward Iwata, "Enron's Key Lay: Cuffed but Confident," *USA Today*, July 9, 2004, p. 1B; David Lieberman and Michael McCarthy, "Adelphia Founder, Son are Convicted," *USA Today*, July 9, 2004, p. 1B; Paul Davidson et. al., "Former WorldCom CEO Ebbers Indicted," *USA Today*, March 3, 2004, p. 1B; Thor Valdmanis, "Former WorldCom CEO Enters Not Guilty Pleas," *USA Today*, March 4, 2004, p. 1B; Constance L. Hayes, "She Asserts a 'Small, Personal Matter' Became a Fatal Circus," *New York Times*, July 16, 2004; Andrew Backover, "Final WorldCom Report: Many to Blame," *USA Today*, January 27, 2004, p. 1B; Edward Iwata, "First Enron Executive Goes to Prison," *USA Today*, September 10, 2003; Edward Iwata, "Merrill Bows to Hard-Line Reforms," *USA Today*, September 18, 2003, p. 1B; Andrew Backover and Kevin Maney, "MCI Hit with 1st Criminal Charges," *USA Today*, August 28, 2003, p. 1B; Andrew Backover, "Due Try to do Right by Qwest," *USA Today*, March 13, 2003, p. 3B; Kevin McCoy, "Tyco Acknowledges More Accounting Tricks," *USA Today*, December 31, 2002, p. 3B; "A Question of Accountability," *New York Times*, June 16, 2002, p. BU12; Devlin Barrett, "Waksal Pleads Guilty to Six Charges, "Associated Press, October 15, 2003; David Leonhardt, "Options Payday: Raking it in, Even as Stocks Sag," *New York Times*, December 29, 2002, http://www.nytimes.com/2002/12/29/business/yourmoney/29CASH.html?ex=1041742800&en=8f0e 4b7dd00ac985&ei=5035&partner=MARKETWATCH (Accessed December 29, 2002); Sherri Day, "Ex-Chief of Sotheby's Sentenced to Probation for Price-Fixing," *New York Times*, April 29, 2002; and Kurt Eichenwald, "Ex-Enron Official Admits Payments to Finance Chief," *New York Times*, August 22, 2002.

Criminal Profiles

Bernard John Ebbers (WorldCom)

An article published on the *Forbes* magazine Web site in 2002 almost gleefully reported the resignation of Bernard "Bernie" Ebbers as chief executive officer (CEO) of WorldCom, the once high-flying telecommunications giant. It cited the stunning drop in the value of the corporation's stock, from more than $60 per share in 1999 to less than $5 per share in early 2002, and called Ebbers's departure "one of the two major events marking the formal end of the telecom frenzy" of the 1990s.[i] The Web page on which the article appeared also provided links to earlier *Forbes* articles that describe Ebbers's futile, failing efforts to prevent the catastrophic collapse of the telecommunications empire that the former owner of a chain of Mississippi motels "stitched . . . together like Frankenstein's monster" from the numerous firms he had snapped up during the "go-go 1990s."[ii]

As shocking as the events reported in the article are, they pale in comparison to the rumors, reports, and, ultimately, the nine-count indictment[iii] that on March 2, 2004, named Ebbers as the major player in a criminal conspiracy to defraud stockholders. The indictment painstakingly documented the manner in which Ebbers and others "scheme[d] to inflate artificially the price of WorldCom common stock by hiding from investors the truth about WorldCom's declining operating performance and financial results."[iv]

Given the extraordinary detail of the damning financial evidence in the indictment, Ebbers' conviction at the end of the ensuing trial came as little surprise. Somewhat more attention-getting, however, was the stiff 25-year sentence handed down by U.S. District Judge Barbara Jones on July 13, 2005, a stiff punishment that she justified by stating "I find that a sentence of anything less would not reflect the seriousness of this crime."[v]

Just how serious were Ebbers's crimes? Perhaps *New York Times* journalist Floyd Norris said it best with the headline of his article the day following Ebbers's sentencing: "A Crime So Large It Changed the Law."[vi]

Canadian-born Ebbers, a native of Edmonton, Alberta, was born on August 27, 1941. The second oldest of five children, Ebbers lived in both California and New Mexico while growing up as the son of a traveling salesman. The family ended up back in Edmonton, where Ebbers finished high school, then took courses at both the University of Alberta and Calvin College. [vii]

Ebbers returned to the United States when he attended Mississippi College, a Southern Baptist institution, on a basketball scholarship. After completing an undergraduate degree in physical education in 1967, Ebbers remained in Mississippi, where he operated a chain of motels. In the early 1980s, he became an early investor in the rapidly expanding telecommunications industry, eventually becoming CEO of Long Distance Discount Services, Inc., (LDDS) in 1985. Under his aggressive leadership, the company acquired an average of six independent telecommunications companies per year over the next ten years.

In 1995, LDDS renamed itself WorldCom, and continued its voracious pursuit of more and bigger acquisitions. Ebbers became a financial world celebrity in October 1997 when WorldCom made an unsolicited $40 billion bid to acquire MCI Communications, and received numerous business awards when the deal closed in September 1998.[viii]

Ebbers has always been somewhat unorthodox, often wearing boots and jeans in the staid world of suits as the uniform of business. He also espoused a deep commitment to Southern Baptist principles and was active in his church. The cushion of his $1.4 billion personal net worth served to shield him for a time from the consequences of his criminal conduct, which had such a devastating effect on so many WorldCom investors. Although his high-priced lawyers may have successfully delayed the day of reckoning for Ebbers, he is now serving his 25-year sentence in the low-security section of the dormitory-style Oakdale Federal Correction Complex in Louisiana.[ix] He will not be eligible for his first parole consideration until 2027, when he will be almost 86 years old.

Notes:

i Mark Lewis, "The Rise and Fall of Bernie Ebbers," *Forbes*, April 30, 2002, http://www.forbes.com/2002/04/30/0430wcom.html (accessed June 1, 2007).

ii Ibid.

iii Indictment, *United States of America* v. *Bernard J. Ebbers*, S3 02 Cr. 1144 (BSJ), U.S. District Court, Southern District of New York, Multiple dates, http://fl1.findlaw.com/news.findlaw.com/cnn/docs/worldcom/usebbers504ind3s.pdf (accessed June 1, 2007).

iv "U.S. Charges Ex-WorldCom CEO Bernard Ebbers; Former WorldCom CFO Scott Sullivan Pleads Guilty," U.S. Department of Justice press release, March 24, 2004, http://www.fbi.gov/dojpressrel/pressrel04/world030204.htm (accessed June 1, 2007).

v "Ebbers Sentenced to 25 Years in Prison," MSNBC, July 13, 2005, http://www.msnbc.msn.com/id/8474930 (accessed June 1, 2007).

vi Floyd Norris, "A Crime So Large It Changed the Law," *New York Times*, July 14, 2005, http://select.nytimes.com/gst/abstract.html?res=F50E10F639540C778DDDAE0894DD404482&n=Top%2fReference%2fTimes%20Topics%2fPeople%2fE%2fEbbers%2c%20Bernard%20J%2e (accessed June 1, 2007).

vii "Biography Information About Bernie Ebbers," Answers.com, http://www.answers.com/topic/bernie-ebbers (accessed June 1, 2007).

viii Ibid.

ix Denise Pappalardo, "For Ebbers, Oakdale Is No Place Like Home," *Network World*, September 27, 2006, http://www.networkworld.com/news/2006/092706-ebbers-prison.html (accessed June 1, 2007).

Over the past few decades, however, the concept of white-collar crime has undergone considerable refinement.[30] The reason, according to the U.S. Department of Justice, is that "the focus [in cases of white-collar crime] . . . has shifted to the nature of the crime instead of the persons or occupations involved."[31] The methods used to

Former WorldCom CEO Bernard Ebbers exits Manhattan federal court in 2006. Ebbers was out on appeal after being convicted in 2005 of orchestrating an $11 billion accounting scandal that bankrupted the once-giant telecommunications company. He is currently serving 25 years at the medium-security Federal Correctional Institution in Oakdale, Louisiana. Was his sentence too harsh? Too lenient?

Source: AP Wide World Photos/Louis Lanzano

commit white-collar crime, such as the use of a computer, and the special skills and knowledge necessary for attempted law violation have resulted in a contemporary understanding of white-collar crime that emphasizes the type of offense being committed, rather than the social standing or occupational role of the person committing it. Some reasons for this shift are changes in the work environment and in the business world itself. Others are pragmatic. In the words of the Justice Department, "The categorization of 'white-collar crime' as crime having a particular modus operandi [committed in a manner that utilizes deception and special knowledge of business practices and committed in a particular kind of economic environment] is of use in coordinating the resources of the appropriate agencies for purposes of investigation and prosecution."[32]

Between the early definitions of *white-collar crime* and those that came later, many other investigators refined the conceptual boundaries surrounding the term. **Herbert Edelhertz,** for example, defined *white-collar crime* as any "illegal act or series of illegal acts committed by nonphysical means and by concealment or guile, to obtain money or property, to avoid the payment or loss of money or property, or to obtain business or personal advantages."[33] **Gilbert Geis,** another early writer on the subject, grappled with the notion of "upperworld crime," which he called "a label designed to call attention to the violation of a variety of criminal statutes by persons who at the moment are generally not considered, in connection with such violations, to be the 'usual' kind of underworld and/or psychologically aberrant offenders."[34] Many writers, however, were quick to realize that upperworld, or white-collar, crime might have its counterpart in certain forms of blue-collar crime committed by members of less prestigious occupational groups. Hence, the term *blue-collar crime* emerged as a way of classifying the law-violating behavior of people involved in appliance and automobile repair, yard maintenance, house cleaning, and general installation services.

Finally, in an effort to bring closure to the concept of work-related crime, the term *occupational crime* emerged as a kind of catchall category. **Occupational crime** can be defined as "any act punishable by law that is committed through opportunity created in the course of an occupation which is legal."[35] Occupational crimes include the job-related law violations of both white- and blue-collar workers. One of the best typologies of occupational crime to emerge in recent years is that offered by **Gary S. Green** in his book *Occupational Crime*. Green identifies four categories of occupational crime:[36]

- **Organizational occupational crime:** crimes committed for the benefit of an employing organization. In such instances, only the organization or the employer benefits, not individual employees.
- **State authority occupational crime:** crimes by officials through the exercise of their state-based authority. Such crime is occupation specific and can be committed only by officials in public office or by those working for them.

occupational crime

Any act punishable by law that is committed through opportunity created in the course of an occupation that is legal.

WEB
Extra
▪ ▪ ▪ ▪

LIBRARY
Extra
▪ ▪ ▪ ▪

Theory Versus Reality

White-Collar Crime: The Initial Statement

At least one eminent criminologist has called the concept of white-collar crime "the most significant . . . development in criminology, especially since World War II."[i] The roots of the concept go back to 1939, when Edwin Sutherland first coined the term *white-collar crime* in his presidential address to the American Sociological Society. Details of that address are discussed elsewhere in this chapter. His speech concluded with the following five points:

1. White-collar criminality is real criminality, being in all cases in violation of the criminal law.

2. White-collar criminality differs from lower-class criminality principally in an implementation of the criminal law, which segregates white-collar criminals administratively from other criminals.

3. The theories of the criminologists that crime is due to poverty or to psychopathic and sociopathic conditions statistically associated with poverty are invalid because, first, they are derived from samples which are grossly biased with respect to socioeconomic status; second, they do not apply to the white-collar criminals; and third, they do not even explain the criminality of the lower class, since the factors are not related to a general process characteristic of all criminality.

4. A theory of criminal behavior which will explain both white-collar criminality and lower-class criminality is needed.

5. A hypothesis of this nature is suggested in terms of differential association and social disorganization.

Discussion Questions

1. Why is white-collar crime possibly the most significant development in criminology since World War II?

2. Why did Sutherland have to remind people that "white-collar criminality is real criminality"? Why might some have thought otherwise?

[i] Donald J. Newman, "White-Collar Crime: An Overview and Analysis," *Law and Contemporary Problems*, Vol. 23, No. 4 (autumn 1958).

Source: Edwin Sutherland, "White-Collar Criminality," *American Sociological Review*, Vol. 5 (February 1940), pp. 1–12.

- **Professional occupational crime:** crimes by professionals in their capacity as professionals. The crimes of physicians, attorneys, psychologists, and the like are included here.

- **Individual occupational crime:** crimes by individuals as individuals. This is a kind of catchall category that includes personal income tax evasion, the theft of goods and services by employees, the filing of false expense reports, and the like.

For an interesting presentation of white-collar and occupational crime typologies, visit the National Check Fraud Center and Cornell Law School's white-collar crime page via **Web Extras 12–3** and **12–4**. Learn more about white-collar crime and its measurement from **Library Extra 12–2** at crimtoday.com.

Corporate Crime

Corporate malfeasance, another form of white-collar crime, has been dubbed "corporate crime." **Corporate crime** can be defined as "a violation of a criminal statute either by a corporate entity or by its executives, employees, or agents acting on behalf of and for the benefit of the corporation, partnership, or other form of business entity."[37] Corporate crimes come in many forms, ranging from prior knowledge about exploding gas tanks on Pinto automobiles and GM pickup trucks to price-fixing and insider securities trading. Culpability, which often results in civil suits against the corporation along with possible criminal prosecutions, is greatest where company officials can be shown to have had advance knowledge about product defects, dangerous conditions, or illegal behavior on the part of employees.

In 2002, in an example of how corporations can be held criminally responsible for the acts of their officials, the accounting firm of Arthur Andersen was convicted of

corporate crime

A violation of a criminal statute either by a corporate entity or by its executives, employees, or agents acting on behalf of and for the benefit of the corporation, partnership, or other form of business entity.

Kansas City pharmacist Robert R. Courtney, 48, who pleaded guilty in 2002 to 20 felony counts charging him with the fraudulent distribution of diluted intravenous chemotherapy drugs to at least 34 patients. Other charges included tampering with consumer products, adulteration of drugs, and misbranding of drugs. Courtney, who is estimated to have made hundreds of thousands of dollars in the scheme, was caught when a drug salesman noticed that he was billing doctors for more medication than he was buying. His ten-year prison sentence was upheld in 2004 by the U.S. Court of Appeals for the Eighth Circuit. How does Sutherland's definition of *white-collar crime* apply in a case like this?

Source: AP Wide World Photos

obstruction of justice after its employees destroyed documents related to Enron Corporation audits. Arthur Andersen, which had served as Enron's auditor, was forced to relinquish its U.S. licenses and closed its American offices. The company had also paid more than $130 million to settle issues relating to questionable accounting practices in its work with another company, Waste Management, in the late 1990s. The company had provided accounting services for WorldCom, Inc., prior to the arrest of that company's chief financial officer and other executives.[38] In 2005, however, the firm was at least partially vindicated when its conviction was overturned by the U.S. Supreme Court, which found that the instructions given to the jury in the 2002 trial had been flawed.[39]

In a somewhat similar but earlier case, aircraft maintenance company SabreTech was convicted in 1999 in federal court in Miami of eight counts of causing the air transportation of hazardous materials and of one count of failing to provide training in the handling of hazardous materials. The charges resulted from the actions of company employees in improperly packaging oxygen canisters, blamed for the 1996 crash of a ValuJet airplane in the Florida Everglades. In that disaster, 110 people died. The case marked the first time that a maintenance company faced criminal charges in connection with an air disaster in the United States. The company, which went out of business, was also charged in state court with numerous counts of murder and manslaughter in the crash. "This is the first criminal homicide prosecution involving a passenger aircraft tragedy in the United States," said Florida State Attorney Katherine Fernandez-Rundle.[40]

Two of the most massive corporate liability issues in U.S. history were settled in September 1994. In one case, U.S. District Court Judge Sam Pointer gave final approval to a class action suit against makers and sellers of silicon gel breast implants.[41] The decision, which had taken years to reach, cleared the way for implant recipients to be paid $4.25 billion over 30 years. Of the 2 million American women who had breast implants, approximately 90,000 filed claims under the action. Women whose claims were approved were eligible to receive between $105,000 and $1.4 million each, depending on age, health, and medical condition. Claimants had argued that many of the parties involved in the manufacture and surgical implantation of the implants were aware of the dangers represented by their products but had opted to market them anyway.

In an interesting aside, which many claimed was a continuing effort to cover up critical issues in the case, Mayo Clinic researchers reported in the prestigious *New England Journal of Medicine* at the time of the implant settlement that no link could be found between implants and the autoimmune and other disorders reportedly suffered by women claiming to be negatively affected by the implants. It was later revealed that financial support for the study had come from precisely those groups with the most to lose in the financial settlement. Among the contributors were the American Society of Plastic and Reconstructive Surgeons ($500,000), Plastic Surgery Education Foundation ($300,000), American Society of Aesthetic Plastic Surgeons ($210,000), Dow Corning ($500,000), and Bristol-Myers Squibb ($100,000).[42] Even so, on November 17, 2006, the U.S. Food and Drug Administration (FDA) reapproved the use of silicone gel-filled breast implants for use in women ages 22 and older after reviewing an extensive amount of data from clinical trials and determining the products to be "safe and effective."[43] The FDA approved silicone gel-filled breast implants with a number of conditions, including requiring each company that manufactures them to: (1) conduct a large postapproval study; (2) continue its core study through ten years; (3) conduct a focus group study of the patient labeling; (4) continue laboratory studies to further characterize types of device failure; and (5) track each implant in the event, for example, that health professionals and patients need to be notified of updated product information.

The second corporate liability case settled in 1994 involved Union Carbide Corporation, which agreed to sell its remaining holdings in Union Carbide India Limited to Indian company McLeod Russel India.[44] McLeod Russel was the highest bidder in a closed-door auction ordered by India's Supreme Court as part of the American company's punishment for a chemical leak at its storage facilities in Bhopal, India, on December 3, 1984. The tragedy in Bhopal, which many claim was due to criminal negligence, caused more than 3,000 deaths and disabled thousands of residents. Union Carbide had originally been ordered by Indian state courts to pay $81 million to the government as compensation for disaster victims. The country's Supreme Court later ordered the company to pay $470 million as final compensation. Another court then required the seizure of Union Carbide's remaining Indian assets and ordered that they be sold to the highest bidder. Union Carbide officials, who were threatened with murder charges, left the country.

In November 1999, the largest product liability settlement in history was reached between state attorneys general and representatives of the tobacco industry.[45] According to the terms of the agreement, tobacco companies agreed to pay $206 billion to 46 states over 25 years in compensation for the harmful health effects of tobacco and to reimburse the states and the federal government for monies spent on medical problems associated with tobacco use. Under the terms of the agreement, tobacco companies will spend another $1.7 billion to study youth smoking and to finance antismoking advertising. The four other states had reached their own settlements for an additional $40 billion before the federally endorsed settlement was reached.

In 2004, officials at the Justice Department in Washington, D.C. announced plans to sue the tobacco industry for $280 billion—claiming that the industry had illegally engaged in racketeering to mislead the public about the dangers of smoking for more than 50 years.[46] In 2005, however, a U.S. appeals court judge ruled that the Justice Department could not proceed with its suit, and agreed with lawyers for tobacco companies that the case should have come under criminal RICO laws, which require a higher burden of proof than civil proceedings.[47]

Finally, in 2006, tobacco firms gained relief in what had been the largest punitive-damages award ever granted by a U.S. jury when the Florida Supreme Court tossed out a $145 billion judgment against the companies. The court found that "the punitive damages award is excessive as a matter of law."[48] The suit had its origins in a 1994 court action brought by Florida pediatrician Howard Engle and five other plaintiffs on behalf of smokers throughout the country. The court's ruling also decertified the class of plaintiffs, meaning that the suit is unlikely to be reinstated.

Product liability cases, such as that involving the tobacco companies, are generally not based on claimed violations of the criminal law. A relatively new area of corporate and white-collar criminality, which is defined solely in terms of violations of the

Cleanup workers monitor toxic waste at an illegal dump site. Crimes against the environment have recently become an area of special concern to criminologists. Why have such offenses only recently been recognized as crimes?

Source: Gabe Palmer, CORBIS, NY

environmental crime

A violation of the criminal law that, although typically committed by businesses or by business officials, may also be committed by other people or by organizational entities and that damages some protected or otherwise significant aspect of the natural environment.

criminal law, is that of crimes against the environment.[49] **Environmental crimes** are violations of the criminal law, which, although typically committed by businesses or by business officials, may also be committed by other individuals or organizational entities, and which damage some protected or otherwise significant aspect of the natural environment.

Whaling in violation of international conventions, for example, constitutes a form of environmental crime. So, too, does intentional pollution, especially when state or federal law contravenes the practice. Sometimes negligence contributes to environmental criminality, as in the case of the 1,000-foot *Valdez* supertanker owned by Exxon Corporation, which ran aground off the coast of Alaska in 1989, spilling 11 million gallons of crude oil over 1,700 miles of pristine coastline. In September 1994, an Alaskan jury ordered Exxon to pay $5 billion in punitive damages to 14,000 people affected by the 1989 spill and another $287 million in actual damages to commercial fishermen in the region. Exxon also agreed to pay $100 million in criminal fines.

Other acts against the environment violate more conventional statutes, although their environmental impact may be obvious. The devastating fires set in oil fields throughout Kuwait by retreating Iraqi Army troops during the Gulf War in 1991 provide an example of arson that resulted in global pollution while negatively affecting fossil fuel reserves throughout much of the Middle East. These intentional fires, while properly classified as environmental criminality, also serve as an example of ecological terrorism because they were set for the purpose of political intimidation.

Learn more about environmental crimes from the Duke Environmental Law and Policy Forum and the Federal Bureau of Investigation (FBI) at **Web Extras 12–5** and **12–6**. Read about the conviction and sentencing of some defendants in environmental crime prosecutions at **Library Extra 12–3**.

WEB
Extra
▪ ▪ ▪ ▪

LIBRARY
Extra
▪ ▪ ▪ ▪

Causes of White-Collar Crime

When Edwin H. Sutherland first coined the term *white-collar crime*, he wrote, "A hypothesis is needed that will explain both white-collar criminality and lower-class criminality."[50] The answer Sutherland gave to his own challenge was that "white-collar criminality, just as other systematic criminality, is learned."[51] He went on to apply elements of his famous theory of differential association (discussed in Chapter 8) to white-collar crime, saying that "it is learned in direct or indirect association with those who already practice the behavior."[52]

Other authors have since offered similar integrative perspectives. **Travis Hirschi** and **Michael Gottfredson** (whose work was discussed in Chapters 6 and 8), for example, in an issue of the journal *Criminology* published half a century after Sutherland's initial work, write, "In this paper we outline a general theory of crime capable of organizing the facts about white-collar crime at the same time it is capable of organizing the facts about all forms of crime."[53] Their analysis of white-collar crime focuses squarely on the development of the concept itself. Hirschi and Gottfredson suggest that if we were not aware of the fact that the concept of white-collar crime arose "as a reaction to the idea that crime is concentrated in the lower class, there would be nothing to distinguish it from other" forms of crime.[54] "It may be, then," they write, "that the discovery of white-collar criminals is important only in a context in which their existence is denied by theory or policy."[55] In other words, nothing is unusual about the idea of white-collar crime other than the fact that many people are loath to admit that high-status individuals commit crimes just as do those of lower status.

In fact, say Hirschi and Gottfredson, white-collar criminals are motivated by the same forces that drive other criminals: self-interest, the pursuit of pleasure, and the avoidance of pain. White-collar crimes certainly have special characteristics. They are not as dangerous as other "common" forms of crime; they provide relatively large rewards; the rewards they produce may follow quickly from their commission; sanctions associated with them may be vague or only rarely imposed; and they may require only minimal effort from those with the requisite skills to engage in them.

Hirschi and Gottfredson conclude, however, that criminologists err in assuming that white-collar criminality is common or that it is as common as the forms of criminality found among the lower classes. They reason that the personal characteristics of most white-collar workers are precisely those that we would expect to produce conformity in behavior. High educational levels, a commitment to the status quo, personal motivation to succeed, deference to others, attention to conventional appearance, and other inherent aspects of social conformity—all of which tend to characterize those who operate at the white-collar level—are not the kinds of personal characteristics associated with crime commission. "In other words," say Hirschi and Gottfredson, "selection processes inherent to the high end of the occupational structure tend to recruit people with relatively low propensity to crime."[56]

One other reason most criminologists are mistaken about the assumed high rate of white-collar criminality, Hirschi and Gottfredson tell us, is because "white-collar researchers often take organizations as the unit of analysis" and confuse the crimes committed by organizational entities with those of individuals within those organizations.[57] Similarly, rates of white-collar offending tend to lump together the crimes of corporations with crimes committed by individual representatives of those organizations when making comparisons with the rate of criminal activity among blue-collar and other groups.

A complementary perspective by Australian criminologist **John Braithwaite** says that white-collar criminals are frequently motivated by a disparity between corporate goals and the limited opportunities available to businesspeople through conventional business practices.[58] When pressured to achieve goals that may be unattainable within the existing framework of laws and regulations surrounding their business's area of endeavor, innovative corporate officers may turn to crime to meet organizational demands.[59]

Braithwaite believes that a general theory covering both white-collar and other forms of crime can be developed by focusing on inequality as the central explanatory variable in all criminal activity.[60] Although alienation from legitimate paths to success may lead lower-class offenders to criminal activity in an effort to acquire the material possessions necessary for survival, greed can similarly motivate relatively successful individuals to violate the law in order to acquire even more power and more wealth.[61] New types of criminal opportunities and new paths to immunity from accountability arise from inequitable concentrations of wealth and power. Inequality thus worsens both crimes of poverty motivated by the need to survive and crimes of wealth motivated by greed.

Braithwaite also suggests that corporate culture socializes budding executives into clandestine and frequently illegal behavioral modalities, making it easier for them to violate the law when pressures to perform mount. The hostile relationship that frequently exists between businesses and the government agencies that regulate them may further spur corporate officers to evade the law. Braithwaite emphasizes his belief that the potential for shame associated with discovery—whether by enforcement agencies, the public, or internal corporate regulators—can have a powerful deterrent effect on most corporate executives because they are fundamentally conservative individuals who are otherwise seeking success through legitimate means.[62]

Braithwaite also recommends implementation of an "accountability model," which would hold all those responsible for corporate crimes accountable.[63] Rather than merely punishing corporations through fines, personal punishment meted out to corporate lawbreakers, says Braithwaite, should have the potential to substantially reduce white-collar offending.[64]

In sum, Braithwaite contends that an integrated theory of organizational crime would include insights garnered from (1) strain theories, as to the distribution of legitimate and illegitimate opportunities; (2) subcultural theory, as applied to business subcultures; (3) labeling theory, or the way stigmatization can foster criminal subculture formation; and (4) control theory, as to how potential white-collar offenders can be made accountable.[65]

Curtailing White-Collar and Corporate Crime

It is generally agreed that it is far easier to convict street criminals than white-collar criminals. It may even be difficult for prosecutors to show that a crime has occurred. "When someone breaks into a house and takes the TV and VCR," says Harvard University criminal law professor William Stuntz, "it's a matter of proving who did it. With white-collar crime," says Stuntz, "it's usually not even clear what happened."[66] Stuntz used Enron Corporation as an example where, he said, "we know the broad outlines of what might have happened . . . but not exactly what can be charged."[67]

White-collar crimes are difficult to investigate and prosecute for a number of other reasons. For one thing, white-collar criminals are generally better educated than other offenders and are therefore better able to conceal their activities.[68] Similarly, cases against white-collar offenders must often be built on evidence of a continuing series of offenses, not a single crime, such as a bank robbery. Often, the evidence involved is only understandable to financial or legal experts and can be difficult to explain to jurors. Finally, business executives, because they often have the financial resources of an entire corporation at their disposal, and because they sometimes earn salaries and bonuses in the millions of dollars, are able to hire excellent defense attorneys and can tie up the courts with motions and appeals that might not be as readily available to defendants with lesser resources.

Events such as the collapse of Enron Corporation left investors around the world leery of American stock markets and forced federal legislators to enact sweeping financial reform. At the same time, the SEC renewed efforts to enforce existing regulations and mandated new rules for investment bankers. By the start of 2001, the atmosphere of distrust that had been created by corporate criminals had become so severe that President George W. Bush felt it necessary to make significant efforts to help restore investor confidence and to bring order to American financial markets. Consequently, the president created a federal Corporate Fraud Task Force within the U.S. Department of Justice and on July 30, 2002, signed the Sarbanes-Oxley Act (officially known as the Public Company Accounting Reform and Investor Protection Act), which set stiff penalties for corporate wrongdoers. Members of the Corporate Fraud Task Force include the Secretary of the Treasury, the Chairman of the SEC, the Chairman of the Commodities Futures Trading Commission, the Chairman of the Federal Energy Regulatory Commission, and the Chairman of the Federal Communications Commission.[69] The official goals of the task force were (1) to provide direction for the investigation and prosecution of cases of securities fraud, accounting fraud, mail and wire fraud, money laundering, tax fraud, and other related financial crimes committed by commercial entities and their directors and officers; (2) to provide recommendations to the attorney general for the allocation of the resources of the Department of Justice for investigation and prosecution of significant financial crimes; (3) to facilitate cooperation among federal departments and agencies in the investigation and prosecution of significant financial crimes; (4) to develop methods to enhance cooperation among the federal, state, and local authorities responsible for the investigation and prosecution of significant financial crimes; and (5) to recommend changes in rules, regulations, or policies that can improve the effective investigation and prosecution of such crimes.

The Corporate Fraud Task Force has remained active since its creation, although it is expected to be disbanded with the change in administrations. In 2007 the U.S. Department of Justice announced that activities of the task force had resulted in 1,236 fraud convictions, including those of 214 chief executive officers and 53 chief financial officers since 2002.[70] In announcing the convictions, then-attorney general Alberto Gonzales noted that "perhaps the most important accomplishment is the criminal conduct that never occurred because of the widespread deterrent effect" of the task force.[71]

The Sarbanes-Oxley Act has been called the most far-reaching reform of American business practices since the time of Franklin Delano Roosevelt. The law authorizes new funding for investigators and for the development of new technologies at the SEC targeted at uncovering corporate wrongdoing. Under the Sarbanes-Oxley Act, the SEC has the authority to bar dishonest corporate directors and officers from ever again serving in positions of corporate responsibility. Similarly, penalties for obstructing justice and for shredding documents are greatly increased, corporate officers who profit illegally can be forced to return their gains to investors, and the maximum federal prison term for common types of corporate fraud was increased from 5 to 20 years.

The Sarbanes-Oxley Act also requires chief executive officers and chief financial officers to personally vouch for the truth and fairness of their companies' financial disclosures and establishes an independent oversight board to regulate the accounting profession. The board is required to set clear standards to uphold the integrity of public audits and has the authority to investigate abuses and to discipline offenders. Similarly, the Sarbanes-Oxley Act prohibits auditing firms from providing consulting services that create conflicts of interest. Finally, under the law, officials in public corporations are barred from buying or selling stock during periods when employees are prevented from making stock transactions in their retirement or 401(k) accounts.

The Sarbanes-Oxley Act is comprised of 11 sections, or titles. Of special interest are Title VIII (the Corporate and Criminal Fraud Accountability Act of 2002), Title IX (the White Collar Crime Penalty Enhancement Act of 2002), and Title XI (the Corporate Fraud Accountability Act of 2002). View the Sarbanes-Oxley Act in its entirety at **Web Extra 12–7.**

WEB
Extra
■ ■ ■ ■

The Sarbanes-Oxley Act is the latest in a long line of federal legislation relating to the conduct of American business that extends back more than 100 years. Some of the earliest such legislation can be found in the federal Sherman Act,[72] which became law in 1890. The Sherman Act was passed to eliminate restraints on trade and competition and, specifically, to prevent the development of trusts and monopolies in restraint of trade. The Clayton Act,[73] passed in 1914, prohibits mergers and acquisitions in which the effect "may be substantially to lessen competition, or to tend to create a monopoly."

The Securities Act of 1933[74] and the Securities Exchange Act of 1934[75] were enacted by federal legislators reeling from the effects of the Great Depression, which began with the stock market crash of 1929. Often referred to as the "truth in securities" law, the Securities Act of 1933 has two basic objectives: (1) to require that investors receive financial and other significant information concerning securities being offered for public sale and (2) to prohibit deceit, misrepresentations, and other fraud in the sale of securities.

The Securities Exchange Act of 1934 gave birth to the SEC and conferred upon the SEC broad authority over all aspects of the securities industry. This includes the power to register, regulate, and oversee brokerage firms, transfer agents, and clearing agencies as well as the nation's stock exchanges. The act also identified and prohibited certain types of conduct in the markets and provides the SEC with disciplinary powers over regulated entities and persons associated with them. Finally, the act empowered the SEC to require periodic reporting of information by companies with publicly traded securities.

Certain forms of occupational crime may be easier to address than others. Individual occupational crimes especially may be reduced by concerted enforcement and protective efforts, including enhanced Internal Revenue Service (IRS) auditing programs, theft-deterrent systems, and good internal financial procedures. Consumer information services can help eliminate fraudulent business practices, and increases in both victim awareness and reporting can help target both businesses and individuals responsible for various forms of white-collar or occupational crime.

However, as Donald J. Newman has observed, "if white-collar crime is intrinsic to and normative within the value structure of our society, then no punishment or treatment program will effectively eradicate it."[76] Similarly, Gary S. Green points out that "professional occupational criminals will probably continue to enjoy immunity from prosecution. Hence, they are unlikely to be deterred by sanction or threat and are unlikely to be formally disqualified by their professional organizations. They will therefore feel free and be free to continue or begin their criminal activities."[77]

In the book *The Criminal Elite: The Sociology of White-Collar Crime*, **James William Coleman** suggests four areas of reform through which white-collar crime might be effectively addressed:[78]

- **Ethical.** Ethical reforms include such things as working to establish stronger and more persuasive codes of business ethics. Courses on ethical business might be offered in universities, and corporations could school their employees in right livelihood, or ethical ways of conducting business.

- **Enforcement.** Enforcement reforms center on the belief that white-collar criminals must be more severely punished, but they also include such things as better funding for enforcement agencies dealing with white-collar crime, larger research budgets for regulatory investigators, and the insulation of enforcement personnel from undue political influence.

- **Structural.** Structural reforms "involve basic changes in corporate structure" to make white-collar crime more difficult to commit. Coleman suggests adding members of the public to corporate boards of directors; changing the process whereby corporations are chartered to include control over white-collar crime; enhancing the flow of information among businesses, the public, and administrative bodies; and implementing the "selective nationalization of firms that have long records of criminal violations."[79]

- **Political.** Political reforms, according to Coleman, center on eliminating campaign contributions from corporations and businesses but also include increasing the level of fairness in determining government grants, government purchases, and government contracts. The government, says Coleman, must also police itself. Although this includes enforcing current laws that are intended to regulate the activities of elected officials and administrative personnel, Coleman concludes that "there is some question about how effectively the government can ever police itself."[80]

Like Coleman, a number of corporate leaders are calling for companies and business executives to develop an enhanced set of ethical standards for corporate responsibility that could be applied from within the business world as a means of self-control. The Center for Innovation in Corporate Responsibility (CICR), for example, suggests that companies replace the old notion of improving their bottom line, or profits, with the concept of a triple bottom line. CICR defines the *triple bottom line* as "an innovative business approach which integrates financial, environmental, and social considerations into performance measurement and assessment."[81] In other words, says CICR, a company's success should be judged in terms of what it contributes to society and how it protects the environment—as well as how much money it makes.

Learn more about corporate responsibility and ethical business practices from the Interfaith Center on Corporate Responsibility and the Center for Business Ethics and Social Responsibility at **Web Extras 12–8** and **12–9**. Similar resources, including many government links, the American Institute of Certified Public Accountants's Antifraud and Corporate Responsibility Center, and the Carnegie Mellon Center for International Corporate Responsibility, can be found at **Web Extras 12–10** and **12–11**. Links to various corporate codes of ethics can be found online at **Web Extra 12–12**.

WEB
Extra

Organized Crime

Organized criminal groups have always existed. An early written account of **organized crime** describes the activities of Jonathan Wild, a notorious brigand of the early 1700s.[82] Wild was born in Wolverhampton, Staffordshire, England, in 1682 to "persons of decent character and station." He received a formal education, which was unusual for the times, and at age 15 was apprenticed to a buckle maker. Married at 22, Wild left his wife and new son a year later for the excitement of nearby London. Not long after his arrival in the city, Wild was arrested for nonpayment of debts and thrown into Wood-street Compter, a prison that held debtors and other prisoners, both male and female. During the four years he spent in prison, Wild became intimate with a female inmate by the name of Mary Milliner, who was described as "one of the most abandoned prostitutes and pickpockets on the town." Wild later said that he also used his time in prison to "learn the secrets of the criminals there under confinement." Upon release, he shared a home with Milliner, calling her his wife.

Milliner ran a bar on what was then known as Cock Alley in Cripplegate, one of the most notorious parts of London. Soon, the bar became a hangout for thieves and other criminals. Wild capitalized on the situation and began purchasing all types of stolen goods and fencing them to merchants and the general public. As one writer of the times observed, "He was at first at little trouble to dispose of the articles brought to him by thieves at something less than their real value, no law existing for the punishment of the receivers of stolen goods." However, the authorities, hearing of Wild's organized criminal activity, soon passed a law forbidding the receipt and sale of stolen items. As a consequence, the value of stolen goods plummeted. Soon, however, Wild discovered a way around the new law. One commentator described his solution this way: "[Wild called a meeting of thieves in the city and proposed] that when they made prize of anything, they should deliver it to him . . . saying that he would restore the goods to the owners by which means greater sums might be raised, while the thieves would remain perfectly secure from detection." Soon Wild was running the largest criminal organization in England and evading the law by returning stolen goods to their rightful owners in exchange for handsome rewards.

As he rose in both power and wealth, Wild displayed ruthless organizational skills. If a thief or burglar in Wild's gang demanded too much money or threatened to unmask the operation, Wild would have him apprehended and hung—collecting whatever official reward had been offered for the felon's capture. As Wild's organization grew, he hired ships to transport excess inventory to France, the Netherlands, and Belgium. Soon he was trading internationally in stolen goods and living in grand style. Because of his ability to gather intelligence throughout the criminal underworld as well as in the ghettos of London, Wild gained the confidence of advisors to George I—a relationship that kept him out of harm's way for many years. With the death of George I, however, and increasing British hostility to criminal activity, Wild was finally arrested and charged with running a criminal organization. Sentenced to hang, Wild was executed at Tyburn Prison on May 24, 1725.

organized crime

The unlawful activities of the members of a highly organized, disciplined association engaged in supplying illegal goods and services, including gambling, prostitution, loan-sharking, narcotics, and labor racketeering.

History of Organized Crime in the United States

Much of what most Americans traditionally think of today as organized crime—the **Mafia** or **La Cosa Nostra**—has roots that predate the establishment of the United States as a sovereign power. For hundreds of years, secret societies—the products of extreme

Mafia

Another name for Sicilian organized crime, or ***Cosa Nostra.***

La Cosa Nostra

Literally, "our thing." A criminal organization of Sicilian origin. Also call *the Mafia, the Outfit, the Mob, the syndicate,* or simply *the organization.*

poverty, feudalism, a traditional disregard for the law, and (some would say) national temperament—have flourished in Italy.[83] During the nineteenth century, the Italian Camorra, based in Naples, became infamous for extortion and murder. The Camorrian code demanded total silence, and the organization issued to its members printed licenses to kill. Italian criminal organizations that came to the United States with the wave of European immigrants during the late nineteenth and early twentieth centuries included the Mafia and the Black Hand. The Black Hand (in Italian, *La Mano Negro*) "specialized in the intimidation of Italian immigrants,"[84] typically extorting protection money and valuables. The Black Hand became especially powerful in Detroit, St. Louis, Kansas City, and New Orleans.

The Mafia, with roots in Sicily, worked to become a quasi-police organization in the Italian ghetto areas of the burgeoning American cities of the industrial era—often enforcing its own set of laws or codes when official intervention was lacking. One of the first well-documented conflicts between the Mafia and American law enforcement came on March 13, 1909, when New York City police officials learned that NYPD Lieutenant Joseph Petrosino had been assassinated upon his arrival in Palermo, Italy. Petrosino had gone to Palermo to investigate allegations that Mafia bosses in New York City were importing Black Hand assassins from the "old country" to do their dirty work. As Petrosino visited the Palermo Court of Justice, he was killed by a single bullet allegedly fired by Mafia boss Vito Cascio Ferro. Although Ferro was arrested and charged with the crime, local deputies provided him with an alibi, and he was never convicted.

Secret societies in Italy were all but expunged during the 1930s and early 1940s under Fascist dictator Benito Mussolini. Surviving Mafia members became vehemently anti-Fascist, sentiments that endeared them to American and allied intelligence services during World War II. Following the war, mafioso leaders resumed their traditional positions of power within Italian society, and links grew between American criminal organizations and those in Italy.

In his comprehensive book *Organized Crime*, Howard Abadinsky, a professor of criminal justice at St. John's University in Jamaica, New York, reports that the first mention of the Mafia in New York can be found in a *New York Times* article dated October 21, 1888.[85] The article quotes police inspector Thomas Byrnes as saying that a murder victim named Antonio Flaccomio was "an Italian fruit dealer and a member of a secret society." The society, said Byrnes, was called the Mafia; its members were fugitives from Sicily, an island in the south of Italy.

A Rose by Any Other Name—La Cosa Nostra

ethnic succession

The continuing process whereby one immigrant or ethnic group succeeds another by assuming its position in society.

Other organized criminal groups, including Jewish and Irish gangs, flourished in New York City prior to the arrival of large numbers of Italian immigrants in the late 1800s. Ethnic succession has been as much a reality in organized crime as in most other aspects of American life. **Ethnic succession** refers to the continuing process whereby one immigrant or ethnic group succeeds another through assumption of a particular position in society.

Throughout the late nineteenth and early twentieth centuries, for example, Jewish gangsters like Meyer Lansky, Benjamin "Bugsy" Siegel, "Dutch" Schultz, and Lepke Buchalter ran many of the "rackets" in New York City, only to have their places taken by Italian immigrants who arrived a few years later. Almost forgotten today is Arnold Rothstein, a famous Jewish gangster who was able to translate many ill-gotten gains into real estate holdings and other legitimate commercial ventures. Among those who remember, Rothstein has been called the "most important organizer and innovator"[86] among Jewish criminal operatives in turn-of-the-century New York and the "Godfather" of organized crime in the city. Italian American organized criminals are themselves not immune to ethnic succession, which has continued into the present day, with gangs of African Americans, Hispanics, and Asian Americans now running significant aspects of the drug trade and controlling other illicit activities in many parts of the country.

Even so, organized criminal activity in the United States throughout the past half century has largely been the domain of Italian American immigrants and their descendants, especially those of Sicilian descent. As one observer notes, "To beat rival organizations, criminals of Sicilian descent reproduced the kind of illegal groups they had belonged to in the old country and employed the same rules to make them invincible."[87] Hence, it was not long before American Mafia leaders had taken over from their criminal predecessors, many of whom were either killed or forced to turn to more legitimate forms of enterprise.

As a consequence of historical events that are well documented, it is both realistic and useful to discuss American organized crime primarily in terms of Sicilian American involvement. A few caveats must be stated, however. For one thing, although many Sicilians who emigrated to this country had either ties to, or experience with, Mafia organizations in the old country, most did not. Many Sicilian Americans emigrated to America to escape Mafia despotism at home, and most became productive members of their adopted society. Relatively few involved themselves in organized crime. Those who did created an organization known variously as the Mafia, the Outfit, the Mob, La Cosa Nostra ("our thing"), the syndicate, or simply the organization. Other terms applied to Sicilian American organized crime include *crime cartel* and the *confederation*.

Joseph Valachi is generally credited with popularizing the term *Cosa Nostra*. In 1963, Valachi, a member of the Genovese crime family, used the term while testifying before the McClellan Committee, which was holding hearings on organized crime. Following the hearings, the name Cosa Nostra became increasingly popular with both the American press and the public and has at least partially replaced the term *Mafia* as the *nom du jour* of Italian American criminal organizations.

The term *Mafia*, however, is still in widespread use. Hence, in the paragraphs that follow, Sicilian American organized criminal groups are referred to as both the Mafia and La Cosa Nostra—terms that have been used interchangeably by police investigators, the press, the public, and government commissions over the years.

Actor James Gandolfini, who played Tony Soprano in the HBO hit series *The Sopranos*. The popularity of shows like *The Sopranos* demonstrate America's fascination with organized crime and with the lives of organized crime figures. How does American culture view the "gangster"? How do classic gangster images support idealized notions of the "thug life" among some young people today?

Source: HBO, Picture Desk Inc./Kobal Collection

Prohibition and Official Corruption

By the 1920s, Mafia influence extended to most American cities. But it was the advent of Prohibition that gave organized crime its vital financial wherewithal. In 1919, the U.S. Congress passed the Eighteenth Amendment to the U.S. Constitution, ushering in an age of prohibition on the manufacture, transportation, and sale of alcoholic beverages. The Eighteenth Amendment reads as follows:

> Section 1. After one year from the ratification of this article the manufacture, sale, or transportation of intoxicating liquors within, the importation thereof into, or the exportation thereof from the United States and all territory subject to the jurisdiction thereof for beverage purposes is hereby prohibited.

> —**U.S. Constitution,** *Eighteenth Amendment, 1919*

In many ways, the advent of Prohibition was a godsend for Mafia leaders. Prior to Prohibition, Mafia operations in American cities were "small-time," concerned mostly with gambling, protection rackets, and loan-sharking. Many mafiosi, however, also belonged to a brotherhood called Unione Siciliana, whose members were well versed in the manufacture of low-cost, high-proof, untaxed alcohol,[88] an expertise that had been brought from their native country. In addition, the existing infrastructure of organized crime permitted easy and efficient entry into the running and sale of contraband liquor. As one writer explained, "By its nature, bootlegging required national (even international) organization. The liquor came from Canada or Europe, necessitating an extra-national arrangement. It rode at anchor outside the territorial limits in bottoms belonging to the underworld. It had to be picked up by small craft to be smuggled ashore. The contraband had to get by the Coast Guard, Customs, and cops. The cargo had to be loaded on trucks, carried across bridges and highways, protected against hijackers, delivered to warehouses, [and] redistributed to retailers. And somewhere, somehow, there had to be collectors, bookkeepers, accountants, enforcers, personnel men, and masterminds to make the rum-running pay."[89]

Prohibition gave existing Mafia families the opportunity to accumulate unheralded wealth. As Abadinsky puts it, "Prohibition enabled men who had been street thugs to become crime overlords."[90] Others describe it this way: "Prohibition proved to be the catalyst that established the wealth and power of modern organized crime syndicates."[91]

The huge profits to be had from bootlegging led to the wholesale bribery of government officials and to the quick corruption of many law enforcement officers throughout the country. Nowhere was corruption more complete than in Chicago, where runners working for organized crime distributed illegal alcohol under police protection[92] and corrupt city government officials received regular payoffs from criminal cartels.

In 1929, President Herbert Hoover appointed the National Commission on Law Observance and Enforcement, better known as the Wickersham Commission after its chairman, George Wickersham. The commission produced a series of 14 reports. Three of them, *Observance and Enforcement of Prohibition, Lawlessness in Law Enforcement,* and *The Police,* either mentioned or decried the corrupting influence Prohibition was having on professional law enforcement in America. Fourteen years after it had been passed, the Eighteenth Amendment was repealed, and with it Prohibition ended.

> Section 1. The eighteenth article of amendment to the Constitution of the United States is hereby repealed.

> —**U.S. Constitution,** *Twenty-first Amendment, 1933*

Unfortunately, the heritage of Prohibition-associated corruption is still with us. Official corruption has become an institutionalized part of American life in some parts of the country. As one writer explains, "American cities have a long history of corrupt relations between some illegal enterprises and local police or politicians. For criminal entrepreneurs, payments to politicians or police can be viewed either as normal business expenses in return for services to the enterprise or as extortionate demands that eat into the profits of the enterprise. For police and politicians, levying regular assessments on illegal entrepreneurs has provided a source of extra income as well as a way to oversee neighborhood enterprises that could not be legally controlled. Historically, oversight by local political organizations (or the police) has been the most important source of coordination for illegal enterprises in American cities."[93]

In 1967, the Task Force on Organized Crime, part of President Johnson's Commission on Law Enforcement and Administration of Justice, concluded that "all available data indicate that organized crime flourishes only where it has corrupted local officials."[94] Sometimes the roots of corruption reach far deeper. As one writer notes, "The line between organized crime and corrupt officials is often unclear, at times nonexistent. . . . In both Chicago and New York those who ran organized criminal activities, gambling and prostitution, were political figures and often elected officials."[95]

The Centralization of Organized Crime

The Prohibition era was a tumultuous time for American organized crime. While its leaders grappled for the huge profits to be reaped from the sale of illegal alcohol, they simultaneously worked to consolidate their power. Gang warfare—not unlike the drive-by shootings and execution-style slayings that now characterize inner-city youth gangs—was the order of the day.

One of the most infamous gangland wars of all time erupted in Chicago in the mid-1920s, when Alphonse "Al" Capone, an up-and-coming thug, decided to make a city-wide grab for power. Following a number of spectacular killings (dubbed "massacres" by the press), Capone was successful in forging a crime syndicate, and he declared himself the leader of all of Chicago's organized crime families. For a time, his claim remained disputed, primarily by George "Bugs" Moran, who had inherited the leadership of a local gang. In a bid to end competition, Capone lured Moran's men to a garage on Chicago's East Side on the ruse that a truckload of bootleg liquor was soon to arrive. Once inside the garage, Moran's men were surprised by five of Capone's executioners. Three were dressed as police officers, while the other two wore plainclothes. The uniformed men ordered the Moran gang against the garage wall, where the plainclothes killers machine-gunned them to death. The killings, which became known as the Saint Valentine's Day massacre, established Capone as undisputed ruler of organized crime in Chicago.

Similar efforts at consolidation were being made nationwide. On April 15, 1931, influential New York City crime figure Giuseppe "Joe the Boss" Masseria was gunned down in a restaurant in the Coney Island section of Brooklyn. His killing, part of what has been called the Castellammarese War, appears to have been ordered by another of the city's bosses, Salvatore Maranzano. Following Masseria's death, Maranzano declared himself the "boss of bosses" over all of New York's crime families. Maranzano, however, soon lost favor with more "Americanized" Mafia figures and was himself killed in September 1931 by armed men who entered his office disguised as immigration officials.

During the next two days, 30 Mafia leaders died in similar gang-ordered executions across the country. By the close of 1931, when the smoke settled and the killings stopped, the Mafia had become an integrated, coordinated criminal organization able to settle most disputes internally and capable of shielding its activities from the prying eyes of investigators. A 1939 exposé written by J. Richard Davis, former attorney for one of New York's crime families, credited the centralization of control to the rise of Charles "Charlie Lucky" Luciano, also known as "Lucky Luciano," who "became leader of the *Unione Siciliani* in 1931. . . . The 'greasers' in the *Unione*," wrote Davis, "were killed off, and the organization was no longer a loose, fraternal order of Sicilian blackhanders and alcohol cookers, but rather the framework for a system of alliances which were to govern the underworld."[96] Another author described it this way: "In 1931 organized crime units across the United States formed into monopolistic corporations, and those corporations, in turn, linked themselves together in a monopolistic cartel."[97]

Following 1931, Mafia activity went underground. The Mafia's success at hiding its operations was so great that one expert was able to write, "There is a considerable body of police opinion in the United States which holds that the Mafia in America died in September 1931, on 'Purge Day.'"[98]

As the 1967 President's Commission on Law Enforcement and Administration of Justice observed, Mafia activity remained nearly invisible and investigations of Mafia operations lay dormant until the 1950s. In the words of the commission: "After World War II there was little national interest in the problem [of organized crime] until 1950, when the U.S. Attorney General convened a national conference on organized crime."[99]

Organized crime reemerged into the national spotlight in 1951 when the federal Special Committee to Investigate Organized Crime in Interstate Commerce[100] (better known as the **Kefauver Committee** after its chairman, Estes Kefauver) reported that "a nation-wide crime syndicate known as the Mafia operate[s] in many large [American] cities, and the leaders of the Mafia usually control the most lucrative rackets in their cities."[101] Although the Kefauver Committee, which interviewed hundreds of witnesses, noted that it had "found it difficult to obtain reliable data concerning the extent of Mafia operation, the nature of Mafia organization, and the way it presently operates,"[102] it was able to reach the following conclusions:

Kefauver Committee

The popular name for the federal Special Committee to Investigate Organized Crime in Interstate Commerce, formed in 1951.

- A nationwide crime syndicate exists, known as the Mafia, whose tentacles are found in many large cities.
- The American Mafia has international linkages that appear most clearly in connection with narcotics traffic.
- Mafia leaders are usually found in control of the most lucrative rackets in their cities.
- Indications suggest centralized direction and control in these rackets, but leadership appears to be in a group rather than in a single individual.

Public interest in organized crime was again roused when authorities learned of a national meeting of at least 75 leaders of criminal cartels scheduled for November 1957. The purpose of the meeting, held at the home of Joseph Barbara in the small New York town of Apalachin, was never uncovered. Some speculate that syndicate leaders may have met to split up the empire of the recently murdered Albert Anastasia, who was himself reputed to have been a ruthless killer. Barbara, born in Castellammarese del Golfo, Italy, was boss of a northeastern Pennsylvania crime family and died two years after the meeting.

The 1957 meeting resulted in raids on Barbara's house and the arrest of many well-known organized crime figures. In 1959, Joseph Bonanno and 26 others were convicted of obstruction of justice for their refusal to reveal the meeting's purpose. Their convictions, however, were overturned in 1960 by the U.S. Second Circuit Court of Appeals, which reasoned in *United States* v. *Bufalino*[103] that the suspects had been arrested without probable cause.

The picture that eventually emerged from years of federal investigations into Italian American organized criminal groups was of 24 crime families operating in the United States under the direction of a "commission," whose membership consisted of the bosses of the nation's most powerful families. The following, taken directly from the 1967 President's Commission report, summarizes what was believed to be true of organized crime at the time of the report: "Today the core of organized crime in the United States consists of 24 groups operating as criminal cartels in large cities across the nation. Their membership is exclusively Italian, they are in frequent communication with each other, and their smooth functioning is insured by a national body of overseers. . . . The wealthiest and most influential core groups," the report concluded, "operate in States including New York, New Jersey, Illinois, Florida, Louisiana, Nevada, Michigan, and Rhode Island."[104] The report placed membership in organized crime at 5,000 nationwide and said that "each of the 24 groups is known as a 'family' with membership varying from as many as 700 men to as few as 20."

Family organization was said to consist of (1) a boss, whose primary functions were described as "maintaining order and maximizing profits," (2) an underboss, who was said to collect information for the boss and to relay messages to and from him, (3) the counselor, or consigliere, who serves as an advisor, (4) numerous lieutenants, or *caporegime*, some of whom "serve as chiefs of operating units," and (5) soldiers, or *soldati*, representing the lowest level of family membership, who "operate a particular illicit enterprise," such as a loan-sharking operation, a lottery, or a smuggling operation. "Beneath the soldiers," the commission found, "are large numbers of employees and . . . agents who are not members of the family and not necessarily of Italian descent. These are people who do most of the actual work in the various enterprises." Unlike the family members who give them orders, "they have no buffers or other insulation from law enforcement." The structure of a typical Sicilian American organized crime family is shown in Figure 12–1.

The President's Commission also found that organized crime members swear allegiance to a code of conduct, which "stipulates that underlings should not interfere with the leaders' interests and should not seek protection from the police. They should be 'standup guys' who go to prison in order that the bosses may amass fortunes. The code gives leaders exploitative authoritarian power over everyone in the organization. Loyalty, honor, respect, absolute obedience—these are inculcated in family members through ritualistic initiation and customs within the organization, through material rewards, and through violence."

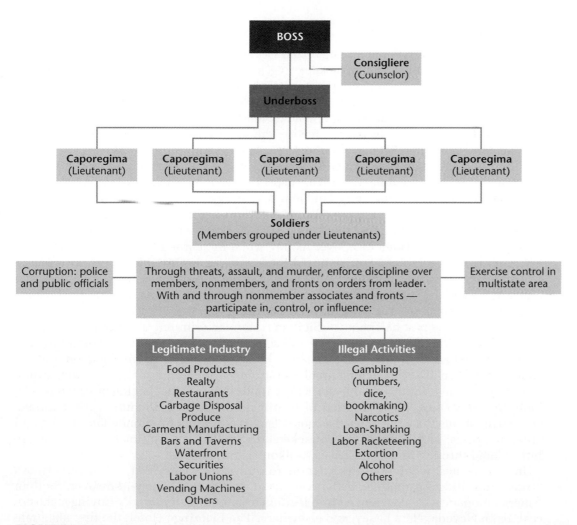

FIGURE 12–1

A Typical Organized Crime Family

Source: President's Commission on Law Enforcement and Administration of Justice, *The Challenge of Crime in a Free Society* (Washington, DC: U.S. Government Printing Office, 1967), p. 47.

La Cosa Nostra Today

Some writers maintain that at least 24 organized crime families of Sicilian American heritage continue to operate throughout the United States today. Of these, five operate out of New York:[105]

Luciano/Genovese family (300–400 core members)

Mineo/Gambino family (400–500 core members)

Reina/Lucchese family (125 core members)

Profaci/Colombo family (100 core members)

Bonanno family (75 core members)

WEB
Extra
■ ■ ■ ■

Chicago is home to other influential Cosa Nostra families, including the Carlisi family (sometimes called the "Outfit"). The Scarfo organization (run by Nicodemo "Little Nicky" Scarfo) and the Stanfa organization operate in Philadelphia. New Orleans serves as headquarters for the Marcello gang (headed by Carlos Marcello); organized crime in New England is controlled by Ray Patriarca, Jr., and his henchmen; and the Civella mob runs racketeering activities in Kansas City, Missouri. Learn more about Cosa Nostra families now operating in the United States at **Web Extra 12–13.**

Activities of Organized Crime

The 1976 federal Task Force on Organized Crime identified five types of activity that may qualify as organized crime: racketeering, vice operations, theft/fence rings, gangs, and terrorism. Whatever its source, however, money is the centerpiece of, and primary motivation for, all organized criminal activity. Near the start of the Great Depression, notorious Chicago gangster Al Capone achieved the distinction of being listed in the *Guinness Book of World Records* as having the highest income of any individual in a single year—more than $105 million in 1927.[106]

Things haven't changed much since Capone's day. As one expert on organized crime explains, "It is cash that dominates every aspect of the mob machines.... The mobsters' working days are spent worrying about and scheming over money, and finally, quarreling and killing for money, almost all of it derived illegitimately."[107] The same expert gives the example of Philadelphia crime boss Nicky Scarfo, who "even considered killing his own wife, Domenica, over money when he learned that 'little by little, she had robbed him of around four hundred thousand' for her gambling sprees at Trump Plaza in Atlantic City."[108] No amount of money seems too small for concern, and—as in much of the wider society—money often becomes a way of keeping score as to who have been the most successful at what they have done.

Throughout the past half century, Sicilian American criminal cartels have continued to be involved in (1) the establishment and control of both legalized and illicit forms of gambling, including lotteries, bookmaking, horse-race wagering, and bets on athletic contests; (2) loan-sharking, which involves the lending of money at rates far higher than legally prescribed limits; (3) large-scale drug trafficking; (4) the fencing of stolen goods, including securities; (5) infiltration of legitimate businesses, including labor unions and corporations that can be used as quasi-legitimate fronts for money laundering and other activities; and (6) labor union racketeering via which legitimate businesses are intimidated through threats of strikes, walkouts, and sabotage.

In some states, where lotteries are now run by state government, organized crime's "take" from illegal gambling has been reduced. Not to be outdone, however, Sicilian American operatives have moved into legitimate gambling, reportedly buying stakes in casinos in Nevada, New Jersey, and elsewhere. The Flamingo Hotel, the first elaborate hotel-casino in Las Vegas, was said to have been built by crime boss "Bugsy" Siegel and funded by organized crime leaders throughout the country.[109] Cleveland syndicate leader Moe Dalitz is reputed to have financed the Stardust Hotel, and federal officials claim that at least $14 million was illegally skimmed from the hotel's operations

Mob informant Joseph Valachi testifying before Senate investigators in 1963. How has organized crime changed since Valachi's time?

Source: Locs Mags (UPI), Corbis/ Bettmann

between 1973 and 1983.[110] Although New Jersey has made Herculean efforts to keep organized crime from influencing casino operations in Atlantic City, some writers point out that "Local 54 of the Hotel Employees and Restaurant Employees Union . . . which represents 22,000 casino hotel employees, has long been dominated by the Bruno family of Philadelphia."[111]

Organized crime is involved in many other kinds of rackets besides gambling. Some evidence suggests, for example, that organized crime today is becoming increasingly active in the illegal copying and distribution of copyrighted software, music, and other forms of recorded media, including videotapes, compact discs, and cassette tapes. The provision of elaborately staged videotaped pornographic productions, including "snuff movies" (in which a sex "star" is actually killed on screen), and elements of child pornography can also be traced to organized criminal activity.

Some sense of the profit derived from the activities of organized crime can be gained from official estimates of the money being collected by Scarfo's gang at the time of his indictment in 1986 on charges of first-degree murder. Scarfo operated illegitimate businesses throughout Philadelphia and southern New Jersey. When he was arrested, his gang was estimated to be taking in "$25,000,000 to $30,000,000 annually from illegal gambling (numbers, video poker, sports betting), and millions more from loansharking, shakedowns of drug dealers and labor union racketeering. Even bigger deals were in the making: Scarfo was preparing to control more than $200,000,000 in Philadelphia waterfront-development projects, as well as to infiltrate the union benefits plans of Atlantic City's bartenders and waitresses."[112]

Code of Conduct

A strict code of conduct governs behavior among members of organized Sicilian American criminal groups. This code, sometimes called *omertà* (or "manliness"), is unwritten. Members are formally introduced to the code through an initiation ritual, which has changed little since it was brought to American shores by Sicilian immigrants well over a hundred years ago. The code of **omertà** functions to concentrate power in the hands of crime bosses, while ensuring their protection. As officials with one federal task force stated, "Those aspects of the code which prohibit appealing to outside authorities for justice while at the same time advocating great loyalty, respect and honor are probably

omertà

The informal, unwritten code of organized crime, which demands silence and loyalty, among other things, of family members.

most essential to the concentration of power in the hands of a few, and hence to exploitation of lower-status men by their leaders."[113]

A few years ago, the FBI electronically eavesdropped on a house in Medford, Massachusetts, in which Joseph Russo, a New England Cosa Nostra consigliere, conducted an initiation ritual for four new family members. Twenty-one men attended the candlelight ceremony. This was the first time authorities had ever captured a Cosa Nostra induction on tape. As each young man swore to uphold omertà and took a vow of silence never to betray the organization or tell its secrets, he held a burning picture of a Catholic saint and prayed: *Come si brucia questa santa, cosi si brucera la mia anima* ("As burns this saint, so will burn my soul"), a reference to the death awaiting anyone who violates the code.[114]

Another initiate described his induction into Philadelphia's Scarfo gang this way: "I was driven to this million-dollar house in Philadelphia, with a big swimming pool and a big table laid out with food—shrimp, steaks, meatballs, peppers, olives, spaghetti—and about forty chairs. I was on cloud nine. Scarfo is at the head of this long table and says, 'Nick, do you know why you're here?' I said, 'No.' You're supposed to say no. . . . So next, he says, 'We want you to be one of us. Now, look around this table and tell me if there is anyone you have bad feelings with.' I look around and say 'no.' . . . So he makes a speech about how much I've done for the family and then says that I have the freedom to leave now and that I'll always be their friend. There would be no hard feelings if I didn't want to join. I said, 'No, I want to be one of you.' . . . Scarfo points to a gun and a knife on a table and asks if I'd use these for any of these friends around the table. Then he lights a small piece of tissue paper in my hand while I say, 'May I burn like the saints in hell if I ever betray any of my friends.' He also pricks my trigger finger. Then you go around the table and kiss everyone. Then we have a feast and then you're told the rules. In the days that follow, you go around and meet the guys who weren't at the ceremony. Then word just seems to spread everywhere you go. And everywhere you go, the respect that you receive from nonmembers is enormous."[115]

The rules of the Scarfo family, said this inductee, included the following: "The family doesn't fool with kidnapping, counterfeit money or bonds. You can shake down or rob drug dealers, but you can't protect them, lend them money or deal drugs yourself. No fooling with a member's wife. You can't even look at another guy's wife. That's automatic death. Even hitting another member is automatic death. He can ask for your life. You're supposed to report once a week to your capo, unless there's a good excuse. You can't go out of town without telling him. You always have to touch base. You're also told that silence is the code and this thing comes first. It comes before your mother, your father, your sister, your brother."[116]

Federal investigators and others studying organized crime have identified seven general features characteristic of the code that family members everywhere swear to:[117]

- Do not be an informer. Do not "rat" on others, and do not sell out.
- Be a member of the team. Be loyal to members of the organization.
- Do not interfere with the interests of others. Do not rock the boat.
- Be rational. Do not engage in battle if you cannot win.
- Be a man of honor. Have class. Be independent.
- Respect women and your elders.
- Be a "stand-up" guy (stand-up guys take the "rap," shielding others). Keep your eyes and ears open and your mouth shut.

Like any informal unwritten code, omertà has many other implicit rules and is fraught with nuances fully understood only by those raised within its traditions. The code, however, imposes two clear and indisputable requirements on all family members: (1) Obey your superiors and (2) keep silent. Failure to adhere closely to either rule means death. The 1967 President's Commission report stated it this way: "The basic principle of justice in the Sicilian Mafia, as in American organized crime, is deterrence from deviation by means of the threat of certain, swift, uniform and severe punishment."[118]

An example is provided by the FBI investigation focusing on New York City crime boss John Gotti (then head of the Gambino family), which yielded a wealth of secretly

WEB
Extra
■ ■ ■ ■

recorded conversations between Gotti and other organized crime figures. This is what Gotti told his underboss, Frank "Frankie Loc" LoCascio, about why a subordinate had to die: "Anytime you got a partner who don't agree with us, we kill him," Gotti explained. "He didn't rob nothin'. Know why he's dying?" Gotti continued. "He's gonna die because he refused to come in when I called. He didn't do nothing else wrong."[119]

The code of omertà is similar to the values found among career criminals everywhere. As one federal report stated, "There is a striking similarity between both the code of conduct and the enforcement machinery used in the confederation of organized criminals and the code of conduct and enforcement machinery which governs the behavior of prisoners."[120] Learn more about La Cosa Nostra at **Web Extra 12–14**.

Other Organized Criminal Groups

According to Howard Abadinsky, a hallmark of true criminal organizations is that they function independently of any of their members, including their leaders, and have a continuity over time as personnel within them change.[121] Abadinsky describes the James Gang, which dissolved with the death of its leader, Jesse James. In contrast, says Abadinsky, "when Al Capone was imprisoned fifty years later, the 'Capone Organization' continued, and in its more modern form (the 'Outfit') it continues to operate in Chicago."[122]

Although, until now, we have restricted our discussion of organized crime to Sicilian American criminal enterprise, it is both useful and realistic to mention the existence of other organized criminal groups in the United States—each characterized by some degree of organizational continuity that is independent of its membership. Among such criminal associations are groups that have been diversely referred to as the Black Mafia, the Cuban Mafia, the Haitian Mafia, the Colombian cartels, the Russian Mafia, Asian criminals (Chinese Tongs and street gangs, Japanese Yakuza, Vietnamese gangs, and Taiwan's Triads), and others. Included here, as well, might be inner-city gangs (the most well known of which are probably the Los Angeles Crips and Bloods and the Chicago Vice Lords), international drug rings, outlaw motorcycle gangs (such as the Hell's Angels and the Pagans), and other looser associations of small-time thugs, prison gangs, and drug dealers.

Noteworthy among these groups are the Latino organized bands, including Dominican, Colombian, Mexican, and Cuban importers of cocaine and other drugs. Although it is not known precisely how much cocaine has entered this country illegally, much of it has been handled by the Medellín and Cali Cartels, headquartered in Colombia, South America. The Medellín and Cali Cartels consist of approximately 35 organized groups that often cooperate with one another and that have financed their own small armies for protection of both their operations and their personnel. Although recent arrests and some deaths have cut into the cartels' influence, it is believed that they are still responsible for the majority of cocaine entering the United States.

Even though it is difficult to categorize such a diversity of groups with any consistency, it is impossible to discuss each of them in a volume of this size. Whether the principle of ethnic succession (discussed earlier) will continue to apply to organized criminal activity is open to debate—although in some American cities, Cosa Nostra operatives have already begun to be replaced by Puerto Rican, Salvadoran, African American, and even Russian gangs. In part, such replacement is due to federal and state law enforcement efforts, which have seriously affected activities of the mob in some areas of the United States.

Where Sicilian American organized criminal activity continues to flourish, connections with the "old country" sometimes still remain. In late 1994, for example, New York City police, in conjunction with federal authorities, announced the arrest of 79 suspects in New York and Italy, all charged with drug conspiracy. Drug-running activities were said to have centered on New York City's Famous Original Ray's Pizza Restaurant on Third Avenue near Forty-third Street. Authorities alleged that the pizza parlor was used as a halfway point in an international drug ring whose ultimate aim was to provide cocaine to "three long-standing organized crime groups in Italy, where cocaine sells for three times what it costs in New York."[123] Among those arrested were Aniello, Francesco, and Roberto Ambrosio—brothers of Italian American descent who ran the pizzeria. Learn

Anthony Accetturo (center), an alleged leader of the Lucchese crime family, celebrating after his acquittal on federal racketeering charges. The trial lasted nearly two years. How does the "code" of organized crime protect its members?

Source: Peter Cannata, AP Wide World Photos

LIBRARY
Extra
■■■■

about how organized crime in the United States is changing via **Library Extra 12–4** and view an online dictionary of organized crime via **Library Extra 12–5** at crimtoday.com.

Transnational Organized Crime

transnational organized crime

Unlawful activity undertaken and supported by organized criminal groups operating across national boundaries.

While the focus of most organized crime scholars in this country has been on big-city crime families, transnational organized crime is emerging as one of the most pressing challenges of the early twenty-first century. **Transnational organized crime** (which is also discussed in Chapter 15) refers to unlawful activity undertaken and supported by organized criminal groups operating across national boundaries.

In a conference in Seoul, Korea, former Assistant U.S. Attorney General Laurie Robinson discussed transnational organized crime, saying, "The United States recognizes that we cannot confront crime in isolation. With criminals' ability to cross international borders in a few hours, and the advances of our modern age, such as the Internet and telecommunications, crime can no longer be viewed as just a national issue. It is clear crime does not respect international boundaries. It is clear crime is global. As recent economic trends demonstrate, what happens in one part of the world impacts all the rest. And crime problems and trends are no different."[124]

As early as 1995, delegates to the Ninth United Nations Congress on the Prevention of Crime and the Treatment of Offenders in Cairo, Egypt, agreed that transnational organized crime is now a "major force in world finance, able to alter the destinies of countries at critical stages of their economic development." Participants in the conference identified the world's major crime clans as the (1) Hong Kong–based Triads, (2) South American cocaine cartels, (3) Italian Mafia, (4) Japanese Yakuza, (5) Russian *Mafiya*, and (6) West African crime groups—each of which extends its reach well beyond its home country.

Russian organized crime is of special interest, both because it has grown quickly following the collapse of the Soviet Union and because it has taken root in the United States and in other countries outside of the former Soviet sphere of influence. Within Russia itself, "rampant, unchecked organized crime has laid waste to noteworthy democratic reforms and contributed to an economic and moral meltdown within the 15 newly independent republics. Intelligence reports emanating out of Russia peg the numerical size of the Russian

Mafia (*Mafiya*) at 100,000 members owing allegiance to 8,000 stratified crime groups who control 70–80% of all private business and 40% of the nation's wealth."[125] The 5,000-member drug-running organization *Solntsevskaya*, based in the Moscow suburb of Solntsevo, may be the largest organized crime faction currently operating in Russia. Mafia leaders, or "made guys," are referred to as *vory y zakone*, which can be translated as "thieves in law," the Russian word for godfather is *krestnii otets*, and soldiers are known as *boyevik*.

With the dissolution of Soviet-style controls between 1992 and 1994, the Russian mafia quickly seized control of the country's banking system through the investment of ill-gotten gains, money laundering, intimidation, fraud, murder, and the outright purchase of financial institutions. Ninety-five Russian bankers were murdered by *Mafiya* operatives between 1995 and 2000, and hundreds of reform-minded business leaders and investigative journalists have been assassinated or kidnapped.[126] In September, 2006, Russian Central Bank Deputy Chairman Andrei Kozlov was fatally shot as he left a soccer stadium in Moscow. Kozlov had been a crusader against money laundering and had suspended or withdrawn the licenses of dozens of banks. After Kozlov's death, President Vladimir Putin created a task force to combat financial crime.

The Analytical Center for Social and Economic Policies, a Russian think tank, estimates that four out of every five Russian businesses pay protection money to the mob.[127] In response to the wave of organized crime that Russia is currently experiencing, more than 25,000 private security firms have sprung up throughout the country. Analysts say, however, that few of these firms are legitimate, with many being fronts for Russian gangsters.[128]

Russian organized criminals differ from their counterparts in the United States because their ranks consist largely of ex-KGB officers, veterans of the 1979–1989 war in Afghanistan, underpaid military officers, and former Communist Party operatives who formed powerful economic alliances with traditional gangsters and black marketeers years ago. As some observers note, Russian organized crime seems to be a natural outgrowth of the corrupt practices of officials who operated in the days of strict Soviet control, combined with a huge underground criminal black market that had already developed a complex organizational structure long before the Soviet Union fell apart.[129]

While Russian organized crime profits from American-style activities like narcotics, prostitution, racketeering, and illicit gambling, it is also heavily involved in human trafficking, product diversion and counterfeiting of popular Western goods (including software, video, and music duplication), and illicit arms sales and smuggling on a massive scale.

Over the past decade or two, hundreds of thousands of Russian citizens have emigrated to the United States. As U.S. officials have now discovered, many of these people were former black market profiteers and hard-core offenders who had been released by the KGB from the Soviet gulag.[130] Among them was Marat Balagula, a black market criminal from Odessa who quickly formed alliances between the Russian *Mafiya* and the American Cosa Nostra. Balagula was responsible for the creation of a large-scale East Coast gasoline-tax scam that earned him millions of dollars in a short period of time.

Russian organized criminal groups today operate out of 17 American cities in 14 states. According to one source, "The FBI believes there are 15 separate organized crime groups and 4,000 hard-core Mafia criminals from the former Soviet Union at work in the U.S. They are engaged in money laundering, automobile theft, smuggling, contract murder, loan-sharking, medical insurance fraud, narcotics, and credit card and telecommunications fraud. The theft of electronic serial numbers from cellular phones and the duplication (cloning) of these PIN numbers have grown into a multimillion-dollar industry."[131]

The globalization of crime has necessitated the enhanced coordination of law enforcement efforts in different parts of the world and the expansion of American law enforcement activities beyond national borders. U.S. police agencies routinely send agents to assist law enforcement officers in other countries who are involved in transnational investigations. For additional information on transnational organized crime, see **Web Extra 12–15**. You can read more about transnational criminal organizations at **Library Extra 12–6**, and learn more about organized crime in Russia via **Library Extra 12–7**. **Web Extra 12–16** provides a link to Radio Free Europe's Web site on high-profile killings in the post-Soviet period in Russia.

LIBRARY
Extra
▪▪▪▪

WEB
Extra
▪▪▪▪

Organized Crime and the Law

For many years, American law enforcement agencies had few special weapons in the fight against organized crime. Instead, they prosecuted organized criminal operatives under statutes directed at solitary offenders, using laws like those against theft, robbery, assault, gambling, prostitution, drug abuse, and murder. Innovative prosecutors at times drew upon other statutory resources in the drive to indict leaders of organized crime. On October 17, 1931, for example, Al Capone was convicted on various charges of income tax evasion after federal investigators were able to show that he had paid no taxes on an income in excess of $1 million. Laws regulating the sale of alcohol and drugs and statutes circumscribing acts of prostitution have also been used against organized criminals, although with varying degrees of success.

The first federal legislation aimed specifically at curtailing the activities of organized crime is known as the Hobbs Act, a term that encompasses a series of statutes that were passed beginning in 1946. In essence, the Hobbs Act made it a violation of federal law to engage in any form of criminal behavior that interferes with interstate commerce. It also criminalized interstate or foreign travel in furtherance of criminal activity and made it a crime to use the highways, telephone, or mail in support of activities like gambling, drug trafficking, loan-sharking, and other forms of racketeering.

Racketeer Influenced and Corrupt Organizations (RICO)

A statute that was part of the federal Organized Crime Control Act of 1970 and that is intended to combat criminal conspiracies.

The single most important piece of federal legislation ever passed that specifically targets the activities of organized crime is the **Racketeer Influenced and Corrupt Organizations (RICO)** statute, which was part of the federal Organized Crime Control Act of 1970. The Organized Crime Control Act defines *organized crime* as "the unlawful activities of the members of a highly organized, disciplined association engaged in supplying illegal goods and services, including but not limited to gambling, prostitution, loansharking, narcotics, labor racketeering, and other unlawful activities of members of such organizations." The RICO portion of the act brought together under one single piece of legislation the many and diverse activities of American organized crime and made each punishable in a variety of new ways. RICO did not make racketeering itself illegal but, rather, focused on the ill-gotten gains derived from such activity, specifying that it shall be unlawful for anyone involved in a pattern of racketeering to derive any income or proceeds from that activity. RICO's definition of *racketeering activity* includes

Georgiy Gleyzer being escorted from the federal building in New York City. Gleyzer was arrested in connection with Russian mob activities and charged with terrorizing citizens of Russian communities in New York. What is the future of Russian organized crime in the United States?

Source: Suzanne Plunkett, AP Wide World Photos

a. any act or threat involving murder, kidnapping, gambling, arson, robbery, bribery, extortion, dealing in obscene matter, or dealing in narcotic or other dangerous drugs, which is chargeable under State law and punishable by imprisonment for more than one year,

b. any act that is indictable under any of the following provisions of title 18, United States Code: section 201 (relating to bribery), section 224 (relating to sports bribery), sections 471, 472, and 473 (relating to counterfeiting), section 659 (relating to theft from interstate shipment) . . . section 664 (relating to embezzlement from pension and welfare funds), sections 891–894 (relating to extortionate credit transactions), section 1029 (relating to fraud and related activity in connection with access devices), section 1084 (relating to the transmission of gambling information), section 1341 (relating to mail fraud), section 1343 (relating to wire fraud), section 1344 (relating to financial institution fraud), sections 1461–1465 (relating to obscene matter), section 1503 (relating to obstruction of justice), section 1510 (relating to obstruction of criminal investigations), section 1511 (relating to the obstruction of State or local law enforcement), section 1512 (relating to tampering with a witness, victim, or an informant), section 1513 (relating to retaliating against a witness, victim, or an informant), section 1951 (relating to interference with commerce, robbery, or extortion), section 1952 (relating to racketeering), section 1953 (relating to interstate transportation of wagering paraphernalia), section 1954 (relating to unlawful welfare fund payments), section 1955 (relating to the prohibition of illegal gambling businesses), section 1956 (relating to the laundering of monetary instruments), section 1957 (relating to engaging in monetary transactions in property derived from specified unlawful activity), section 1958 (relating to use of interstate commerce facilities in the commission of murder-for-hire), sections 2251–2252 (relating to sexual exploitation of children), sections 2312 and 2313 (relating to interstate transportation of stolen motor vehicles), sections 2314 and 2315 (relating to interstate transportation of stolen property), section 2321 (relating to trafficking in certain motor vehicles or motor vehicle parts), sections 2341–2346 (relating to trafficking in contraband cigarettes), sections 2421–2424 (relating to white slave traffic),

c. any act that is indictable under title 29, United States Code, section 186 (dealing with restrictions on payments and loans to labor organizations) or section 501(c) (relating to embezzlement from union funds),

d. any offense involving fraud connected with a case under title 11, fraud in the sale of securities, or the felonious manufacture, importation, receiving, concealment, buying, selling, or otherwise dealing in narcotics or other dangerous drugs, punishable under any law of the United States, or

e. any act that is indictable under the Currency and Foreign Transactions Reporting Act.

Punishments provided for under RICO include **asset forfeiture,** which makes it possible for federal officials to seize the proceeds of those involved in racketeering. In the words of the statute, "Whoever violates any provision of . . . this chapter shall be fined . . . or imprisoned not more than 20 years (or for life if the violation is based on a racketeering activity for which the maximum penalty includes life imprisonment), or both, and shall forfeit to the United States, irrespective of any provision of State law . . . any property . . . derived from any proceeds that the person obtained, directly or indirectly, from racketeering activity or unlawful debt collection." Hence, as a result of RICO, federal agents are empowered to seize the financial and other tangible fruits of organized criminal activity, including businesses; real estate; money; equities; gold and other commodities; vehicles, including airplanes and boats; and just about anything else that can be shown to have been acquired through a pattern of racketeering activity.

asset forfeiture

The authorized seizure of money, negotiable instruments, securities, or other things of value. In federal antidrug laws, the authorization of judicial representatives to seize all monies, negotiable instruments, securities, or other things of value furnished or intended to be furnished by any person in exchange for a controlled substance, and all proceeds traceable to such an exchange.

Money Laundering

Money laundering refers to the process by which illegal gains are disguised as legal income. A more formal definition is offered by the National Institute of Justice, which says that money laundering is "the process of converting illegally earned assets, originating as cash, to one or more alternative forms to conceal such incriminating factors as illegal origin and true ownership."[132]

Title 18, Section 1956 of the U.S. Criminal Code specifically prohibits what it calls the "laundering of monetary instruments" and defines *money laundering* as efforts "to conceal or disguise the nature, the location, the source, the ownership, or the control of the proceeds of specified unlawful activity." To assist in the identification of money

money laundering

The process of converting illegally earned assets, originating as cash, to one or more alternative forms to conceal such incriminating factors as illegal origin and true ownership.

launderers, a provision of the 1986 federal Money Laundering Control Act requires that banks report to the government all currency transactions in excess of $10,000. Similarly, the Bank Secrecy Act (BSA), formally known as the Currency and Foreign Transactions Reporting Act, requires financial institutions in the United States to assist government agencies in detecting and preventing activities related to money laundering. The law requires that financial institutions report cash transactions exceeding an aggregate amount of $10,000 daily per account, and to report suspicious financial activity to authorities. These requirements are well-known to high-end money launderers, who routinely evade them by dealing in commodities like gold, by using foreign banks, or by making a series of smaller deposits and transfers, often involving numerous financial institutions.

Reliable official estimates of the amount of money laundered in the United States are hard to establish. In 1984, however, the President's Commission on Organized Crime estimated that approximately $15 billion of illicit U.S. drug proceeds move illegally every year into international financial channels.[133] Of that amount, $5 billion was thought to be taken out of the country as currency. In 2007, the Drug Enforcement Administration reported that estimates provided to it by the International Monetary Fund pegged worldwide money laundering activities at between 2% and 5% of the world's gross domestic product, or about $600 billion annually.[134]

A few years ago, the most notorious of foreign banks set up to serve the needs of money launderers, drug dealers, terrorists, and other assorted ne'er-do-wells was closed when banking regulators in the United States, England, and several other countries seized branch assets and arrested many of the bank's officers. The Bank of Credit and Commerce International (BCCI) was chartered in Luxembourg and opened branches throughout the world, including at least one in the Bahamas—islands already known for their role in providing infamous "offshore" banking services, which, while trading in currencies internationally, offer customers considerable secrecy and very limited reporting requirements.

BCCI soon grew into one of the largest banks in the world and opened offices in 72 countries. Its friends in America included former President Jimmy Carter, Washington lawyer Clifford Clark, and Orrin Hatch, a powerful senator.[135] Although evidence suggests that BCCI may have provided assistance to U.S. Central Intelligence Agency (CIA) operatives, it also "served to smuggle arms to Syria, Iran, and Libya, and to launder money for the Medellín cartel and Golden Triangle drug warlord Khun Sa."[136] After repeated indictments of top officials, BCCI closed its doors in 1991. During the decade or so that it was in existence, however, it is estimated that many billions of dollars flowed through its

Attorney General Robert Kennedy describing a link between the Teamsters and organized crime. How influential is organized crime in American society today?

Source: UPI, Corbis/Bettmann

numerous branch offices, the majority of it from drug cartels and terrorist organizations seeking to hide the source of their revenues.

If anything, the money laundering problem appears to be getting worse. A report by the Senate Permanent Subcommittee on Investigations found, for example, that "billions of dollars are now leaving our country every year to be put into the flow of commerce and returned to this country as laundered capital."[137]

In 1994, however, in what many experts saw as contrary to the trend in enforcement activities needed to curb organized crime and drug trafficking, the U.S. Supreme Court made money laundering convictions harder to obtain. The case involved Waldemar and Loretta Ratzlaf, high-stakes gamblers from Oregon with lines of credit at 15 casinos in New Jersey and Nevada.[138] In 1988, in an apparent attempt to hide $160,000 in gambling losses from the IRS, the Ratzlafs went to several banks in Nevada and California and bought cashier's checks of less than $10,000 each to pay the debt. Their check purchases came under IRS scrutiny as a result of an investigation into the couple's 1986 tax return. In that year, casino records showed that the couple had engaged in large cash transactions with a number of casinos, but they had reported no gambling income on their tax return.

Authorities accused the Ratzlafs of "organizing financial transactions" to evade the currency-reporting requirement of the 1986 federal Money Laundering Control Act. Both Ratzlafs were convicted in federal court in Nevada on charges of conspiracy and interstate travel in aid of racketeering. Waldemar Ratzlaf was sentenced to 15 years in prison and fined $26,300, while Loretta Ratzlaf was sentenced to 10 months of home detention and fined $7,900.

The couple's lawyers appealed through the Ninth U.S. Circuit Court of Appeals and finally to the U.S. Supreme Court. The Court, in a 5-to-4 decision, found in favor of the Ratzlafs, saying that federal authorities had failed to prove that the couple knew they were violating the law.[139] The words of Justice Ruth Bader Ginsburg summarize the opinion of the majority: "Not all currency structuring serves an illegal goal. . . . Under the government's construction an individual would commit a felony against the United States by making cash deposits in small doses, fearful that the bank's reports would increase the likelihood of burglary, or in an endeavor to keep a former spouse unaware of his wealth."

In a separate dissenting opinion, however, Justice Harry A. Blackmun criticized the Court's majority, writing, "Waldemar Ratzlaf—to use an old phrase—will be laughing all the way to the bank." Ratzlaf, said Blackmun, "was anything but uncomprehending as he traveled from bank to bank converting his bag of cash to cashier's checks in $9,500 bundles" to pay the debt.

Policy Issues: The Control of Organized Crime

In a cogent analysis of organized crime, Gary W. Potter tells us that "the question of what we [should] do about organized crime is largely predicated on how we conceptualize organized crime."[140] Potter criticizes current policies for focusing "almost exclusively on *criminal* aspects of organized crime." It is, says Potter, "the *organized* aspects of organized crime which offer the most useful data for formulating future policy."[141]

To understand organized crime and to deal effectively with it, according to Potter, we must study the social context within which it occurs. Such study reveals "that organized crime is simply an integral part of the social, political, and economic system,"[142] says Potter. Any effective attack on organized crime, therefore, would involve meeting the demands of the consumers of organized crime's products and services. Potter suggests this can be accomplished either by punishing the consumers more effectively or by educating them about the perils of their own behavior.

Fighting corruption in politics and among law enforcement personnel and administrators is another track Potter suggests in the battle against organized crime. If organized crime has been successful at least partially because it has been able to corrupt local politicians and enforcement agents, then, Potter asks, why not work to reduce corruption at the local level?

Who's to Blame—The Individual or Society?

Gangs, Teenagers, and Peer Pressure

Fourteen-year-old Lakisha Jackson found herself in trouble with the law at her junior high school prom when her 18-year-old boyfriend, Jamal Carter, was caught smoking pot behind the curtain covering the school's stage. Jamal told off-duty police officers working the dance that the marijuana wasn't his, but that Lakisha had given it to him.

Jamal was known to the officers as a member of the Top 6 gang, and bore a number of tattoos indicating his gang affiliation. Officers from the police department's juvenile division were called to the school, and both Lakisha and Jamal were taken to the police station for questioning. No additional drugs were found on either youth.

What bothered officers, however, was Lakisha's hostile attitude. While they expected that Jamal would refuse to say more than he already had about the source of the marijuana, they had hoped that Lakisha would either refute Jamal's story or tell them where she had gotten the substance. Lakisha, however, refused to say anything about the incident, calling the officers "pigs," and telling them to mind their own business. "I don't rat on nobody," was all she would volunteer.

A police psychologist who was present during the interviews later explained the youth's behavior in terms of gang and subcultural loyalties. "Even if this case involved a serious crime like a murder—maybe even especially then—you wouldn't get any cooperation from these kids," he said. "You can be sure that if they knew who committed a crime they wouldn't talk. It's not only part and parcel of their gang loyalties, but pretty much a value inherent in the subculture in which they've been raised. Maybe in another neighborhood things would be different—but not here."

Think about it:

1. Do you agree with the police psychologist? Is his explanation for why these youngsters won't talk to the police a plausible one, or is there likely to be some other explanation?

2. If the psychologist is correct in his assessment of the situation, then do you think that Lakisha and Jamal should "know better" than to let subcultural values influence them? Why or why not?

3. Are the police likely to get any more information from Lakisha or her boyfriend? Why or why not?

Howard Abadinsky recommends four approaches to the control of organized crime, each involving changes at the policy-making level:[143]

- Increasing the risk of involvement in organized crime by increasing the resources available to law enforcement agencies that are useful in fighting organized crime. A greater proportion of tax revenues, for example, might be moved into the fight against organized crime. The 1994 Violent Crime Control and Enforcement Act, which puts more law enforcement officers on the streets, should be helpful in freeing up others to investigate organized crime.

- Increasing law enforcement authority so as to increase the risks of involvement in organized crime. Money laundering statutes that expand the scope of law enforcement authority, racketeering laws, and forfeiture statutes all may be helpful in this regard. Abadinsky also suggests providing a special "good faith" exception "to the exclusionary rule in prosecutions involving RICO violations."[144]

- Reducing the economic lure of involvement in organized crime by making legitimate opportunities more readily available. Educational programs, scholarships, job-training initiatives, and so on might all play a role in such a strategy.

- Decreasing organized criminal opportunity through decriminalization or legalization. This last strategy is perhaps the most controversial. It would decriminalize or legalize many of the activities from which organized crime now draws income. State-run gambling and the ready and legitimate availability of narcotics and other substances, provide examples of the kinds of policy changes necessary to achieve this goal.

Strict enforcement of existing laws is another option. It is a strategy that has been used with considerable success by a number of federal and state law enforcement operations that have targeted organized crime. In 1987, for example, Nicholas "The Crow" Caramandi agreed to testify in 11 criminal trials against organized crime figures, resulting in more than 52 convictions, mostly in the Pennsylvania and New Jersey areas. Caramandi had bargained for lessened sentences in his own convictions on murder, racketeering, and extortion charges. A few years ago, Caramandi was released from prison and now lives far from Philadelphia under the federal witness relocation program with a new identity and a mob-ordered sentence of death hanging over him.

One of the most spectacular mob trials was that of John "Dapper Don" Gotti, who took over control of New York's Gambino crime family after orchestrating the murder of "Big Paul" Castellano in 1985. Over the years, Gotti had been arrested on many occasions and had been prosecuted at least five times for various offenses. His ability to escape conviction earned him the title "The Teflon Don." That changed on April 2, 1992, when Gotti was convicted on 13 federal charges, including murder and racketeering. Following the trial, Gotti was sentenced to life in prison without possibility of parole. Gotti's major mistake appears to have been to participate personally in several executions, including that of Castellano. Gotti died of cancer at a federal prison hospital in 2002 at the age of 61. After Gotti went to prison, his son, John, Jr., took over control of the family. In 1999, however, the younger Gotti pleaded guilty to charges of bribery, extortion, gambling, fraud, tax evasion, and loan-sharking and was sentenced to six and a half years in prison.[145] Recently released from prison, John Jr., was tried on a number of racketeering charges, resulting in three hung juries. Following his last trial, he vowed to leave New York and has said that he might move his family to the Midwest or to Florida.

The senior Gotti's downfall came at the hands of Salvatore "Sammy the Bull" Gravano, a former underboss in the Gambino crime family. Gravano, who admitted to 19 murders, shared family secrets with federal investigators in return for leniency and succor through the federal witness protection program. Gravano also spent days on the witness stand testifying against his former boss. Federal prosecutor Zachary Carter later called Gravano "the most significant witness in the history of organized crime."[146] In 1997, Gravano again assumed center stage when he testified in federal district court in Brooklyn as the star prosecution witness in the murder and racketeering trial of Vincent Gigante, reputed head of the powerful Genovese crime family. Gravano was assailed by defense lawyers for being a notorious liar and for leading "a life of lies," facts he largely admitted in his best-selling book, *Underboss*.[147] Although Gravano was sent to Phoenix, Arizona, under the witness protection program, he found it hard to lead a straight life, and in 2000, he was arrested on three separate occasions on drug-running and money laundering charges. He has also been indicted by a New York federal grand jury and charged with financing and running a major ecstasy drug ring in conjunction with an Israeli organized crime syndicate.[148]

Some say that in the face of increased law enforcement pressure, La Cosa Nostra is doomed. According to the FBI, most major crime families have now been decimated by enhanced investigation efforts, often supplemented by wiretaps and informant testimony.

Salvatore "Sammy the Bull" Gravano, who admitted to 19 murders, has been called the "most significant witness in the history of organized crime." How has La Cosa Nostra been impacted by witnesses like Gravano?

Source: J. Markowitz, Corbis/Sygma

WEB
Extra
▪▪▪▪

The FBI claims that a total of 1,173 Cosa Nostra bosses, soldiers, and associates throughout the country have been convicted during the last six years alone. Imprisoned bosses now include not only New York's John Gotti, Jr., but also Los Angeles's Peter Milano and the leaders of Kansas City's Civella family. Also, a few years ago, 13 members of New England's Patriarca family were convicted of murdering Billy Grasso, one of their under-bosses, and were sent to prison. In 1999, federal authorities issued indictments charging 39 reputed members of five different New York City–area Mafia families with racketeering, murder, extortion, robbery, mail fraud, loan-sharking, illegal gambling, and trafficking in stolen property and counterfeit goods. Among those targeted was 54-year-old Vincent "Vinny Ocean" Palermo, reputed to be the acting head of the New Jersey–based DeCavalcante family. Palermo testified for the prosecution and received a reduced term. Read the indictments in the case at **Web Extra 12–17**.

Can La Cosa Nostra survive such pressure? Nicholas Caramandi says yes. "It's such a bureaucracy . . . this thing of ours," says Caramandi. "You can't kill it. . . . It's the second government. . . . We serve needs. People come to us when they can't get justice, or to borrow money that they can't get from the bank. . . . It never dies. It's as powerful today as it ever was. It's just more glorified and more out in the open."[149] The Mob, says Caramandi, reaches all the way to the highest levels of political power. Survival is ensured through well-placed friends in America's highest elected offices. Just before going to prison, John Gotti, Sr., told his underbosses, "This is gonna be Cosa Nostra till I die. . . . Be it an hour from now or be it tonight or a hundred years from now, it's gonna be Cosa Nostra."[150]

SUMMARY

This chapter discusses white-collar and organized crime, as well as the crimes of corporations. While such crimes have a long and varied history in the United States, white-collar and corporate crime assumed new importance at the start of the twenty-first century as a number of American corporations and numerous corporate officers came under investigation for a variety of alleged misdeeds. As equity markets tumbled, government regulators moved to bring about compliance with existing standards, and legislators were quick to enact strict criminal punishments for those continuing to offend. Unfortunately, comprehensive theoretical understandings of white-collar offending are, at best, still in a formative state. Consequently, it is impossible at this point to describe a theory of white-collar crime, or a theory of organized crime, except insofar as those concepts can be contained within other theoretical perspectives—as was the case with Sutherland's attempt to explain white-collar crime in terms of differential association. John Braithwaite's attempt to integrate a variety of theoretical approaches into a general theory that explains all forms of crime, including white-collar crime, may be the most comprehensive theory of organizational crime to date.

Although both white-collar and organized crime appear to be prevalent in the United States today, and organized and white-collar criminals often share similar goals, such as acquiring wealth and social position, there seems to be considerable variation in commitment between the two types of offenders. Many organized criminals evidence a long tradition of criminal involvement, often in the form of racketeering, which is largely unknown to most white-collar offenders. Similarly, organized crime wraps its members in a kind of deviant subculture with a detailed code of conduct, which affects them throughout their lives. White-collar criminals, on the other hand, have typically achieved positions of power and social respectability through conformity and approved forms of achievement. They often come from cultural backgrounds that support adherence to the law. Hence, most white-collar offenders are probably drawn to criminal activity for the immediate financial rewards it offers, whereas organized criminals are more apt to see crime as a way of life and to condemn the conformist activities of others.

If such differences are true, then white-collar crime may be effectively prevented by strict enforcement efforts, which, by their very example, serve as a strong general deterrent to other would-be offenders. Organized criminal groups, on the other hand, given their long-standing commitment to criminal activities, are unlikely to be affected by such threats.

KEY TERMS

asset forfeiture, 517

bank fraud, 485

corporate crime, 495

La Cosa Nostra, 503

environmental crime, 498

ethnic succession, 504

insider trading, 485

Kefauver Committee, 508

Mafia, 503

money laundering, 517

occupational crime, 494

omertà, 511

organized crime, 503

Racketeer Influenced and Corrupt Organizations (RICO), 516

securities fraud, 481

transnational organized crime, 514

white-collar crime, 481

KEY NAMES

John Braithwaite, 499

James William Coleman, 502

Herbert Edelhertz, 494

Gilbert Geis, 494

Michael Gottfredson, 499

Gary S. Green, 494

Travis Hirschi, 499

Edwin H. Sutherland, 481

QUESTIONS FOR REVIEW

1. What is white-collar crime? How did the idea of white-collar crime develop in the criminological literature?

2. What is organized crime? How does it differ from white-collar crime?

3. What strategies does this chapter discuss for combating the activities of organized crime? Which seem best to you? Why? Can you think of any other strategies that might be effective? If so, what are they?

QUESTIONS FOR REFLECTION

1. What linkages, if any, might exist between white-collar and organized crime?

2. What types of white-collar crime has this chapter identified? Is corporate crime a form of white-collar crime? Is occupational crime a form of white-collar crime?

3. Describe a typical organized crime family, as outlined in this chapter. Why does a crime family contain so many different "levels"?

4. What is money laundering? How might money laundering be reduced or prevented? Can you think of any strategies this chapter does not discuss for the reduction of money laundering activities in the United States? If so, what are they?

WEB QUEST

Visit the National White Collar Crime Center (NW3C) at www.nw3c.org. Explore the center's Web site to learn what NW3C does and to see which agencies are members of the center. Be sure to click on the "What's New," "Careers," and "Initiatives" options on the NW3C home page. Describe what you learn in a brief document, and submit it to your instructor if asked to do so.

NOTES

1. As cited on the Woody Guthrie Web page, http://asms.k12.ar.us/classes/humanities/amstud/96–97/wguthrie/influence.htm (accessed April 2, 2007).

2. Quoted in Andrew Backover, "Two Former WorldCom Executives Charged in Scandal," *USA Today*, August 2, 2002, p. 1A.

3. U.S. Senate, testimony before the Kefauver Committee on organized crime, 1951.

4. David Barboza, "Millions Made, Lost in Just Days," *New York Times*, December 11, 2002.

5. Bill Murphy, "CBS Flick Shows Difficulty of Making Drama out of Enron," *Houston Chronicle*, December 23, 2002, http://www.chron.com/cs/CDA/story.hts/special/enron/1712675 (accessed January 5, 2006).

6. Deborah Solomon, Jerry Markson, and Susan Pulliam, "WorldCom's Sullivan, Yates Are Indicted by Grand Jury," *Wall Street Journal*, August 28, 2002.

7. Jim Hopkins, "Former WorldCom Executives Indicted," *USA Today*, August 29, 2002, p. 1A.

8. Barnaby J. Feder and Seth Schiesel, "WorldCom Finds $3.3 Billion More in Irregularities," *New York Times*, August 9, 2002, p. 1A.

9. Greg Farrell, "Scrushy Acquitted of all 36 Charges," *USA Today*, June 28, 2005, http://www.usatoday.com/money/industries/health/2005-06-28-scrushy_x.htm (accessed September 1, 2007).

10. Bob Johnson, "Scrushy Gets Nearly 7 Years in Prison," *USA Today*, June 29, 2007, p. 2B.

11. Edwin H. Sutherland, "White-Collar Criminality," *American Sociological Review*, Vol. 5, No. 1 (February 1940), pp. 2–10.

12. Ibid.

13. Ibid.

14. Edwin H. Sutherland, "Crime of Corporations," in Albert Cohen, Alfred Lindesmith, and Karl Schuessler, eds., *The Sutherland Papers* (Bloomington: Indiana University Press, 1956), pp. 78–96.

15. Ibid.

16. Ibid.

17. Sutherland, "White-Collar Criminality."

18. Travis Hirschi and Michael Gottfredson, "Causes of White-Collar Crime," *Criminology*, Vol. 25, No. 4 (1987), p. 952.

19. "Enron Suit Implicates Nine U.S. Banks," BBC News, April 8, 2002, http://uspolitics.about.com/gi/dynamic/offsite.htm?site= http://news.bbc.co.uk/1/hi/in%5Fdepth/business/2002/enron (accessed January 3, 2007).

20. Leslie Wayne, "Irate at Scandals and Big Losses, Pension Funds Are Going to Court," *New York Times*, June 28, 2002, p. 1C.

[21] Devlin Barrett, "Waksal Pleads Guilty to Six Charges," Associated Press, October 15, 2002.

[22] Much of the information in this paragraph and the next comes from "A Question of Accountability," *New York Times*, June 16, 2002, p. BU12.

[23] "Analyzing the Analysts: More Trouble for Street," *Wall Street Journal*, August 2, 2002, http://online.wsj.com/page/0,,2_0807,00.html (accessed January 23, 2006).

[24] Thor Valdmanis, "Some Investors Balk at $1.4 Billion Wall Street Deal," *USA Today*, December 23, 2002, http://www.usatoday.com/money/companies/regulation/2002-12-23-settle_x.htm (accessed February 28, 2007).

[25] Patrick McGeehan, "Investment Manager Found Guilty of Fraud," *New York Times*, June 11, 2002, p. C6.

[26] *USA Today*, April 2, 1991, pp. B1-B2.

[27] Karen Gullo, " 'Phantom' Banks across the Country Bilking Investors," Associated Press, September 11, 1994.

[28] Donald J. Newman, "White-Collar Crime: An Overview and Analysis," *Law and Contemporary Problems*, Vol. 23, No. 4 (autumn 1958).

[29] President's Commission on Law Enforcement and Administration of Justice, *The Challenge of Crime in a Free Society* (Washington, DC: U.S. Government Printing Office, 1967), p. 47.

[30] For excellent reviews of the evolution of the concept of white-collar crime, see K. Schlegel and D. Weisburd, "White-Collar Crime: The Parallax View," in Kip Schlegel and David Weisburd, eds., *White-Collar Crime Reconsidered* (Boston: Northeastern University Press, 1992), pp. 3–27; and K. Schlegel and D. Weisburd, "Returning to the Mainstream: Reflections on Past and Future White-Collar Crime Study," in Schlegel and Weisburd, eds., *White-Collar Crime Reconsidered*, pp. 352–365.

[31] Task Force on Organized Crime, *Organized Crime* (Washington, DC: U.S. Government Printing Office, 1976).

[32] Ibid.

[33] Herbert Edelhertz, *The Nature, Impact and Prosecution of White-Collar Crime* (Washington, DC: National Institute of Law Enforcement and Criminal Justice, 1970).

[34] Gilbert Geis, "Upperworld Crime," in Abraham S. Blumberg, ed., *Current Perspectives on Criminal Behavior: Original Essays on Criminology* (New York: Alfred A. Knopf, 1974).

[35] Gary S. Green, *Occupational Crime* (Chicago: Nelson-Hall, 1990), p. 12.

[36] Ibid., p. 16.

[37] Michael L. Benson, Francis T. Cullen, and William J. Maakestad, *Local Prosecutors and Corporate Crime* (Washington, DC: National Institute of Justice, 1993).

[38] Jonathan D. Glater and Kurt Eichenwald, "Audit Lapse at WorldCom Puzzles Some," *New York Times*, June 28, 2002, p. 1C.

[39] *Arthur Andersen LLP* v. *United States*, 544 U.S. 696 (2005).

[40] "SabreTech Charged with Murder in ValuJet Crash," CNN, July 13, 1999, http://fyi.cnn.com/US/9907/13/valujet.indictments.03 (accessed March 28, 2007).

[41] Michael Clements, "Breast Implant Pact OK'd: $4.25 Billion Is Available to Claimants," *USA Today*, September 2, 1994, p. 1A.

[42] "Plastic Surgeons, Manufacturers Helped Finance Breast-Implant Study," *USA Today*, September 2, 1994, p. 10A.

[43] "FDA Approves Silicone Gel-Filled Breast Implants After In-Depth Evaluation," U.S. Food and Drug Administration press release, November 17, 2006, http://www.fda.gov/bbs/topics/NEWS/2006/NEW01512.html (accessed July 1, 2007).

[44] Rahul Sharma, "Union Carbide Quits India a Decade after Bhopal," Reuters, September 9, 1994.

[45] Details of the Attorneys General Master Settlement Agreement (MSA) and associated court filings can be accessed at http://www.tobaccoresolution.com.

[46] Ron Scherer, "In the Largest Suit Yet, U.S. Sues the Tobacco Industry," *The Christian Science Monitor*, September 20, 2004. Web posted at http://www.csmonitor.com/2004/0920/p03s01-usju.html (accessed August 31, 2007).

[47] See CBS News Online, "Tobacco Timeline," Web posted at http://www.cbsnews.com/htdocs/tobacco/timeline.html (accessed August 31, 2007).

[48] Vanessa O'Connell, "Tobacco Industry Wins Big at Florida High Court," *The Wall Street Journal* Online" July 7, 2006, http://online.wsj.com/article/SB115219854214999611.html?mod=djemTEW (accessed September 1, 2007).

[49] Of course, environmental damage inflicted by corporations can result in civil liability as well as violate criminal statutes.

[50] Edwin H. Sutherland, "White-Collar Criminality."

[51] Ibid.

[52] Ibid.

[53] Hirschi and Gottfredson, "Causes of White-Collar Crime," p. 949.

[54] Ibid., p. 951.

[55] Ibid., p. 956.

[56] Ibid., p. 960.

[57] Ibid.

[58] Braithwaite began many of his studies of white-collar crime with investigations into the criminal activities of pharmaceutical company executives. See, for example, John Braithwaite, *Corporate Crime in the Pharmaceutical Industry* (London: Routledge and Kegan Paul, 1984).

[59] For a test of this thesis, see Anne Jenkins and John Braithwaite, "Profits, Pressure and Corporate Lawbreaking," *Crime, Law, and Social Change*, Vol. 20, No. 3 (1993), pp. 221–232.

[60] John Braithwaite, "Poverty, Power, White-Collar Crime and the Paradoxes of Criminological Theory," *Australian and New Zealand Journal of Criminology*, Vol. 24, No. 1 (1991), pp. 40–48.

[61] Toni Makkai and John Braithwaite, "Criminological Theories and Regulatory Compliance," *Criminology*, Vol. 29, No. 2 (1991), pp. 191–217.

[62] John Braithwaite and Gilbert Geis, "On Theory and Action for Corporate Crime Control," *Crime and Delinquency*, Vol. 28, No. 2 (1982), pp. 292–314. See also Brent Fisse and John Braithwaite, *The Impact of Publicity on Corporate Offenders* (Albany: State University of New York Press, 1983).

[63] Brent Fisse and John Braithwaite, "Accountability and the Control of Corporate Crime: Making the Buck Stop," in Mark Findlay and Russell Hogg, eds., *Understanding Crime and Criminal Justice* (North Ryde, Australia: Law, 1988), pp. 93–127.

[64] Brent Fisse and John Braithwaite, *Corporations, Crime and Accountability* (New York: Cambridge University Press, 1994).

[65] John Braithwaite, "Criminological Theory and Organizational Crime," *Justice Quarterly*, Vol. 6, No. 3 (1989), pp. 333–358.

[66] Joan Biskupic, "Why It's Tough to Indict CEOs," *USA Today*, July 24, 2002, p. 1A.

[67] Ibid.

[68] Ibid.

[69] See "Executive Order Establishment of the Corporate Fraud Task Force," July 9, 2002, http://www.whitehouse.gov/news/releases/2002/07/20020709-2.html (accessed January 2, 2005).

[70] John R. Wilke, *The Wall Street Journal Online*, July 17, 2007, http://online.wsj.com/article/SB118469845609569168.html (accessed September 1, 2007).

[71] Ibid.

[72] 15 U.S.C. Section 1.

[73] 15 U.S.C. Sections 12–27.

[74] 15 U.S.C. Section 77.

[75] 15 U.S.C. Section 78.

[76] Newman, "White-Collar Crime."

[77] Green, *Occupational Crime*, p. 256.

[78] James William Coleman, *The Criminal Elite: The Sociology of White-Collar Crime*, 3rd ed. (New York: St. Martin's Press, 1994).

[79] Ibid., p. 250.

[80] Ibid., p. 252.

[81] Web posting on the Center for Innovation in Corporate Responsibility's home page, http://www.cicr.net (accessed January 2, 2007).

[82] The details of this account are taken from Camden Pelham, *The Chronicles of Crime: The Newgate Calendar—A Series of Memoirs and Anecdotes of Notorious Characters* (London: T. Miles, 1887), pp. 57–65.

[83] Much of the information in this section comes from Julian Symons, *A Pictorial History of Crime* (New York: Bonanza, 1966).

[84] Ibid.

[85] Howard Abadinsky, *Organized Crime*, 4th ed. (Chicago: Nelson-Hall, 1994).

[86] Ibid., p. 112.

[87] Luigi Barzini, *The Italians* (New York: Atheneum, 1965).

[88] Abadinsky, *Organized Crime*, p. 132.

[89] Gus Tyler, "The Crime Corporation," in Abraham S. Blumberg, ed., *Current Perspectives on Criminal Behavior: Original Essays on Criminology* (New York: Alfred A. Knopf, 1974), p. 197, citing Hank Messick, *The Silent Syndicate* (New York: Macmillan, 1966), pp. vii–xii.

[90] Abadinsky, *Organized Crime*, p. 173.

[91] Ibid.

[92] John Kilber, *Capone: The Life and World of Al Capone* (Greenwich, CT: Fawcett, 1971).

[93] Mark H. Haller, "Illegal Enterprise: A Theoretical and Historical Interpretation," *Criminology*, Vol. 28, No. 2 (May 1990), p. 209.

[94] President's Commission on Law Enforcement and Administration of Justice, *Task Force Report: Organized Crime* (Washington, DC: U.S. Government Printing Office, 1967).

[95] Anthony E. Simpson, *The Literature of Police Corruption* (New York: John Jay Press, 1977).

[96] J. Richard Davis, "Things I Couldn't Tell till Now," *Collier's*, August 19, 1939, p. 35.

[97] Robert W. Ferguson, *The Nature of Vice Control in the Administration of Justice* (St. Paul, MN: West, 1974), p. 379.

[98] Symons, *A Pictorial History of Crime*, p. 226.

[99] President's Commission, *The Challenge of Crime in a Free Society*, p. 196.

[100] Special Committee to Investigate Organized Crime in Interstate Commerce, U.S. Senate, 82nd Congress, 1951.

[101] President's Commission, *The Challenge of Crime in a Free Society*, p. 192, citing the Kefauver Committee report.

[102] Ibid.

[103] *United States* v. *Bufalino*, 285 F.2d. 408 (2d. Cir. 1960).

[104] The quotations attributed to the 1967 President's Commission report in this section are from President's Commission, *The Challenge of Crime in a Free Society*, p. 195.

[105] As identified by Abadinsky in *Organized Crime*.

[106] As cited in ibid., pp. 186–187.

[107] William Sherman, "Kingpins of the Underworld," *Cosmopolitan*, Vol. 212, No. 3 (March 1992), pp. 158–162.

[108] Ibid.

[109] Abadinsky, *Organized Crime*, pp. 311–312.

[110] Ibid., p. 313.

[111] Ibid.

[112] Richard Behar, "In the Grip of Treachery," *Playboy*, November 1991, p. 92.

[113] President's Commission on Law Enforcement and Administration of Justice, *Task Force Report: Organized Crime* (Washington, DC: U.S. Government Printing Office, 1967).

[114] Sherman, "Kingpins of the Underworld."

[115] Behar, "In the Grip of Treachery."

[116] Ibid.

[117] See, for example, "Corleone Family Rules," http://www.webmaze.com/memberpages/doncorleone/rules.html (accessed April 2, 2007). See also "Santino's Mafia Code," http://organizedcrime.about.com/newsissues/organizedcrime/blsantino_1.htm (accessed April 2, 2007).

[118] President's Commission, *The Challenge of Crime in a Free Society*.

[119] Secretly tape-recorded conversations played at the 1992 racketeering trial of John Gotti, http://ganglandnews.com/locascio.htm (accessed April 2, 2007).

[120] President's Commission, *Task Force Report: Organized Crime*, p. 41.

[121] Abadinsky, *Organized Crime*.

[122] Ibid., p. 5.

[123] Joseph B. Treaster, "In Pizza Connection II, 79 Seized in Raids in New York and Italy," *New York Times*, September 16, 1994, p. 1A.

[124] Laurie Robinson, address given at the Twelfth International Congress on Criminology, Seoul, South Korea, August 28, 1998.

[125] Richard Lindberg and Vesna Markovic, *Organized Crime Outlook in the New Russia: Russia Is Paying the Price of a Market Economy in Blood*, Search International, http://www.search-international.com/Articles/crime/russiacrime.htm (accessed January 4, 2007).

[126] Ibid.

[127] Gary T. Dempsey, "Is Russia Controlled by Organized Crime?" *USA Today* magazine, May 1999.

[128] Lindberg and Markovic, *Organized Crime Outlook in the New Russia*.

[129] Dempsey, "Is Russia Controlled by Organized Crime?"

[130] Lindberg and Markovic, *Organized Crime Outlook in the New Russia*.

[131] Ibid.

[132] Clifford Karchmer and Douglas Ruch, "State and Local Money Laundering Control Strategies," *NIJ Research in Brief* (Washington, DC: National Institute of Justice, 1992), p. 1.

[133] President's Commission on Organized Crime, *The Cash Connection: Organized Crime, Financial Institutions, and Money Laundering* (Washington, DC: U.S. Government Printing Office, 1984).

[134] U.S. Drug Enforcement Administration, "Money Laundering," http://www.usdoj.gov/dea/programs/money.htm (accessed June 18, 2007).

[135] According to Abadinsky, *Organized Crime*, p. 427.

[136] Ibid.

[137] Carolyn Skorneck, "Money Laundering," Associated Press, Northern edition, April 7, 1994.

[138] Laurie Asseo, "Scotus-Money Reporting," Associated Press, Northern edition, January 11, 1994.

[139] *Ratzlaf* v. *United Sates*, 114 S. Ct. 655 (1994).

[140] Gary W. Potter, *Criminal Organizations: Vice, Racketeering, and Politics in an American City* (Prospect Heights, IL: Waveland, 1994), p. 183.

[141] Ibid.

[142] Ibid.

[143] Abadinsky, *Organized Crime*, p. 507.

[144] Ibid., p. 508.

[145] "'Junior' Gotti Gets Nearly 6 1/2 Years," Associated Press, September 3, 1999.

[146] "5-Year Prison Term for Mafia Turncoat," *USA Today*, September 27, 1994, p. 3A.

[147] Peter Maas, *Underboss: Sammy the Bull Gravano's Story of Life in the Mafia* (New York: HarperCollins, 1997). According to Ronald Kuby, an attorney suing Gravano to reclaim book royalties under New York's "Son of Sam" law, a roundabout method had been used to pay Gravano in order to avoid the provisions of the law. Kuby claimed that documents would show that author Peter Maas, Gravano, HarperCollins, and International Creative Management, the agent for the book, had conspired to hide payments made to Gravano. To learn more about the case, visit http://www.crimelibrary.com/gangsters2/gravano/24.htm.

[148] "'Sammy the Bull' Faces More Drug Charges," Associated Press, December 21, 2000.

[149] Behar, "In the Grip of Treachery."

[150] Bonnie Angelo, "Wanted: A New Godfather," *Time*, April 13, 1992, p. 30.

13

Public Order and Drug Crimes

Outline

As the Republican governor of New Mexico, I'm neither soft on crime nor pro-drugs in any sense. I believe a person who harms another person should be punished. But as a successful businessman, I also believe that locking up more and more people who are nonviolent drug offenders, people whose real problem is that they are addicted to drugs, is simply a waste of money and human resources.

—Former Governor Gary E. Johnson[1]

For the sake of our children, I implore each of you to be unyielding and inflexible in your opposition to drugs.

—Nancy Reagan[3]

The myth that anti-drug efforts do not work is refuted by the tireless, everyday efforts of our partners in this struggle: parents, teachers, coaches, and community leaders throughout the nation. They are a tribute to what works and what has kept these levels from skyrocketing.

—"Drug Czar" John P. Walters[2]

I am an escort in America, and [prostitution] absolutely should be legalized. It hurts nobody. It's not the government's job to police the bedroom. If a man wants to buy [sex], who cares?

—A Georgia Escort[4]

Learning Outcomes

After reading this chapter, you should be able to

- Provide an overview of the history of drugs, drug abuse, and drug control legislation in the United States
- Define *dangerous drugs*, identify the types of psychoactive substances that are controlled by law, and describe their characteristics and effects
- Describe drug trafficking and government efforts to curtail it
- Explain the relationship between drug trafficking, drug use, and other forms of crime
- Identify the pros and cons of various drug-control strategies
- Define *prostitution* and describe various kinds of prostitutes and their clients

Hear the author discuss this chapter at **crimtoday.com**

Introduction

In early July 1997, the childhood home of Mexico's top drug lord, Amado Carrillo Fuentes, was prepared for his funeral.[5] Dirty blankets lay over an open crypt, and candles burned in the home's small chapel, which was adorned with figures of Jesus, the Virgin of Guadalupe, and Jesus Malverde—claimed by drug dealers as their patron saint. Five-foot rose wreaths lined the pathway to the house, where hundreds of wooden chairs stood stacked against walls.

Although mourners gathered to pay respects to Carrillo's mother and sisters, there could be no funeral. Carrillo's body was in the possession of Mexican authorities, who were busy studying and cataloging the corpse. Carrillo, the authorities said, had died two days earlier in a botched attempt by plastic surgeons to change his appearance.

Before his death, Carrillo, the 42-year-old son of Mexican peasants, had replaced the Medellín Cartel's Pablo Escobar as the biggest shipper of cocaine to U.S. cities, earning an estimated $100 million a month in the illicit drug trade. Much of the money was used to pay off thousands of local, state, and federal officials (both in Mexico and in the United States). Carrillo earned the nickname "Lord of the Skies" after arranging to ferry Colombian cocaine into the United States. At one time, he was said to have brought jumbo jet loads of cocaine from Colombia to Mexico, smuggling it across the Mexico–Texas border. At the time of his death, Carrillo's organization had nearly displaced Colombian drug merchants in New York and other American cities, and Carrillo's net worth was estimated to have reached an astounding $25 billion![6]

Carrillo had been very open in his drug dealing until the arrest in February 1997 of General Jesus Gutierrez Rebollo, former head of Mexico's federal antidrug agency. It was reputed that Carrillo would even stroll around the plazas in Juarez, Mexico, to show that he was above the law. On the run from the Mexican national police (the *Federales*) since the general's arrest, Carrillo died in a desperate attempt to escape a closing dragnet of law enforcement officials. U.S. drug agents were told that Carrillo succumbed to heart failure at a Mexico City hospital following ten hours of extensive plastic surgery. Doctors who had performed the operation—for which Carrillo had rented an entire floor of the hospital, cordoning it off with heavily armed guards—fled after his death. Prior to surgery, Carrillo had just returned from Russia, where he had been trying to arrange a safe haven for his family and his money. In an interesting footnote to this story, rumors started circulating throughout Mexico following Carrillo's death that he had been secretly assassinated by Drug Enforcement Administration (DEA) agents who had slipped lethal drugs into the medications used during the drug lord's plastic surgery. Many Mexicans believed the rumors because Carrillo died on the Fourth of July—American Independence Day. His death on that date, said the rumor mill, was a silent message to other drug runners, putting them on notice that they might be next.[7]

History of Drug Abuse in the United States

Carrillo's death illustrates the desperation that today often characterizes the lives of those involved with illegal drugs—from the highest-level "dealers" to the saddest and most addicted of users. The widespread use of illegal drugs affects all segments of society. Even more problematic still is the fact that almost all forms of illicit drug use in America are associated with other forms of criminality. Drugs, and their relationship to crime, provide one of the most significant policy issues of our time. Famed *Washington Monthly* columnist Paul Savoy once reported polls showing that Americans "are so fearful about the drug-driven crime epidemic that more than half of those polled . . . expressed an opinion [which] favored cutting back the constitutional rights of criminal defendants and overruling Supreme Court decisions that limit police conduct in gathering evidence."[8]

The rampant and widespread use and abuse of mind- and mood-altering drugs, so commonplace in the United States today, is of relatively recent origin. Throughout the 1800s and early 1900s, the use of illegal drugs in America was mostly associated with artistic individuals and fringe groups. One hundred years ago, drug abuse, as we understand it today, was almost exclusively confined to a small group of musicians, painters, poets, and other highly imaginative individuals seeking to enhance their creativity. Although it is true that medicinal elixirs of the period contained a variety of potent substances, including cocaine, alcohol, and opium, the lives of relatively few Americans were seriously affected at the time by any drug other than alcohol. One significant exception existed in the form of "opium dens," which flourished in West Coast cities and eventually made their way across the country as a result of increased Asian immigration. Some Chinese immigrants brought opium products with them and introduced other segments of the American population to opium smoking.

Psychoactive substances gained widespread acceptance during the hippie movement, a period of newfound freedoms embraced by a large number of American youths during the late 1960s and early 1970s. The movement, which was characterized by slogans like "If it feels good, do it" and "Tune in, turn on, drop out," promoted free love, personal freedom, experimentation with subjective states of consciousness, and "mind expansion." Cheech and Chong movies, "flower power," paisley clothes, bell-bottom jeans, long hair on men, and Eastern religions all flourished within the context of a drug-fed countercultural movement.

One influential figure in the drug-inspired movement of the times was Harvard professor Timothy Leary. Leary formed the League of Spiritual Discovery in the mid-1960s, describing it as "an orthodox, psychedelic religion that permits the use of LSD and marijuana as sacraments by League members."[9] With the advent of the hippie era, marijuana, LSD, hashish, psilocybin, and peyote burst upon the national scene as an ever-growing number of individuals began to view drugs as recreational substances and as more and more young people identified with the tenor of the period.

psychoactive substance

A substance that affects the mind, mental processes, or emotions.

Extent of Abuse

Current data on drug abuse in the United States are available through a variety of sources, such as the Monitoring the Future (MTF) study, conducted by the University of Michigan's Institute for Social Research with funding from the National Institute on

Smoker in an opium den in Chinatown, San Francisco, circa 1925. How have American attitudes toward drugs changed over time?

Source: UPI, Corbis/Bettmann

National Survey on Drug Use and Health (NSDUH)

A national survey of illicit drug use among people 12 years of age and older that is conducted annually by the Substance Abuse and Mental Health Services Administration.

Office of National Drug Control Policy (ONDCP)

A national office charged by Congress with establishing policies, priorities, and objectives for the nation's drug-control program. ONDCP is responsible for annually developing and disseminating the *National Drug-Control Strategy.*

Drug Abuse at the National Institutes of Health; the **National Survey on Drug Use and Health (NSDUH),** conducted annually by the Substance Abuse and Mental Health Services Administration (SAMHSA); the National Narcotics Intelligence Consumers Committee's *NNICC Report*, published in conjunction with the DEA; the National Institute of Justice's quarterly Arrestee Drug Abuse Monitoring Program report; the **Office of National Drug Control Policy's (ONDCP)** *Pulse Check: National Trends in Drug Abuse*, which reports at least once a year on drug-use trends; and annual reports published by SAMHSA's Drug Abuse Warning Network.

According to NSDUH survey data that were released in 2007, an estimated 20.4 million Americans aged 12 and older were current users of illicit drugs in 2006, meaning that they used an illicit drug at least once during the 30 days prior to being interviewed.[10] In 2006, as in prior years, men had higher rates of current illicit drug use than women (10.5% versus 6.2%). However, rates of nonmedical psychotherapeutic drug use were similar for males (3.2%) and females (2.5%).

Marijuana, the most commonly used illicit drug in 2006, was used by 73% of those reporting drug use. Approximately 53% of illicit drug users consumed only marijuana, 20% used marijuana and another illicit drug, and the remaining 27% used an illicit drug but not marijuana in the past month. Hence, overall, about 47% of current illicit drug users in 2006 (an estimated 10 million Americans) were users of illicit drugs other than marijuana and hashish, with or without the use of marijuana (see Figure 13–1).[11]

Of the 10 million users of illicit drugs other than marijuana, 7 million were using psychotherapeutics nonmedically. This represents 2.8% of the population aged 12 and older. Psychotherapeutics include pain relievers (5.2 million users), tranquilizers (1.8 million users), stimulants (1.2 million users), and sedatives (0.4 million users).

In 2006, an estimated 2.4 million Americans (0.8% of the population aged 12 and older) were current cocaine users. The estimated number of current crack users was 702,000 in 2006, and an estimated 1.0 million Americans (or 0.4% of the population) were current hallucinogen users. Included among the hallucinogen users were 582,000 Ecstasy users (0.2% of the population). Survey results also showed that an estimated 136,000 Americans (or 0.1% of the population) were current heroin users.

Ten percent of youths (aged 12 to 17) reported current use of illicit drugs in 2006, with marijuana reported as the most common illicit drug. Around 7% of youths were current users of marijuana in 2006. The percentage using illicit drugs in the 30 days prior to being interviewed was slightly higher for boys (9.8%) than for girls (9.7%). In this age group, boys had a slightly higher rate of marijuana use than girls (6.8% versus 6.4%), but girls were somewhat more likely to use psychotherapeutics nonmedically

FIGURE 13–1

Types of Drugs Used in the Past Month by Illicit Drug Users, Age 12 and Older, 2006

Source: Substance Abuse and Mental Health Services Administration, *2006 National Survey on Drug Use and Health* (Washington, DC: U.S. Government Printing Office, 2007).

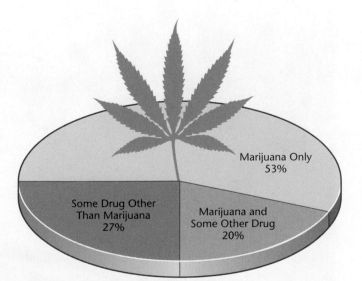

20.4 Million Illicit Drug Users

than boys (3.5% versus 3.1%). The use of illicit substances by young people aged 12 to 17 is shown graphically in Figure 13–2.

The highest rate of illicit drug use was found among people aged 18 to 25, with rates of current use around 20%. For these older youths, use is dominated by marijuana, with 16.3% reporting current marijuana use in 2006. As Figure 13–3 shows, rates of use generally decline in each successively older age group, with only 2.4% of people aged 55 to 59 and 0.7% of those aged 65 and older reporting current illicit use.

The NSDUH reported that rates of illicit drug use for major racial and ethnic groups in 2006 were 8.5% for whites, 8.9% for Hispanics, and 9.8% for blacks. The rate was highest among the American Indian/Alaska Native population (13.7%) and among people reporting multiple race (11.8%). Asians had the lowest rate (3.6%).

The rate of illicit drug use in metropolitan areas was higher than the rate in nonmetropolitan areas: 8.7% in large metropolitan areas, 8.3% in small metropolitan

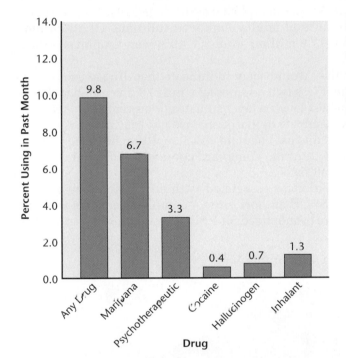

FIGURE 13–2

Past Month Illicit Drug Use among Youths Aged 12 to 17, 2006

Source: Substance Abuse and Mental Health Services Administration, *2006 National Survey on Drug Use and Health* (Washington, DC: U.S. Government Printing Office, 2007).

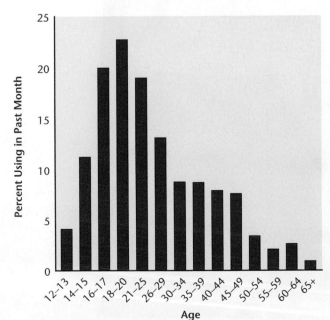

FIGURE 13–3

Past Month Illicit Drug Use by Age, 2006

Source: Substance Abuse and Mental Health Services Administration, *2006 National Survey on Drug Use and Health* (Washington, DC: U.S. Government Printing Office, 2007).

areas, and 6.8% in nonmetropolitan areas. Rural counties had a 7.8% rate of illicit drug use.

The National Survey and the MTF study show a leveling or declining national trend in illicit drug use, marijuana use, and cigarette use among adolescents since 1997, following a period of significant increases in the early 1990s.

As in previous National NSDUH surveys, the 2006 survey found that substance-abuse rates remain highly correlated with educational status. Among young adults 18 years and older, those who have not completed high school have the highest rate of abuse (9.2%), whereas college graduates have the lowest rate of abuse (5.9%). This is despite the fact that adults who had completed four years of college were more likely to have tried illicit drugs in their lifetime than adults who had not completed high school (50.1% versus 37.2%). Hence, it appears that the more education a person receives, the more likely that person is to discontinue using drugs with age.

Current employment status was also found to be highly correlated with rates of illicit drug use. The NSDUH found that 18.5% of unemployed adults (aged 18 and older) were illicit drug users, compared with 8.8% of adults employed full-time. Of all current illicit drug users aged 18 and older (17.9 million adults), 74.9% were employed either full-time or part-time.

If NSDUH results are accurate, they would seem to indicate that drug abuse is now substantially less of a problem than it was two decades ago. In 1979, the number of current illicit drug users was at its highest level, when estimates of current users reached 25 million. The largest ever annual estimate of marijuana use put routine users at 22.5 million in 1979, while the largest cocaine use estimate was 5.3 million in 1985—figures far greater than those of today. Growth of the American population in the meantime gives the estimated decline even greater weight.

There are some methodological problems associated with any nationwide survey. In recognition of these problems, NSDUH authors write, "Sample size, coverage, and validity problems are likely to be more pronounced for NSDUH estimates of heavy users

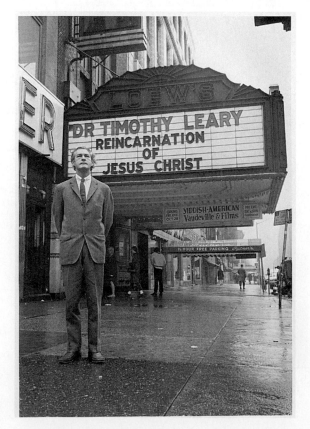

Dr. Timothy Leary, guru of the 1960s new consciousness movement, shown here in New York in 1966. Leary died in 1996, and his ashes were shot into space a year later. What was Leary's message?

Source: UPI, Corbis/Bettmann

than for other measures generated by the survey. Therefore, estimates of heavy use are considered conservative, and changes over time are generally not statistically significant. For example, the [NSDUH] has produced estimates of about 600,000 frequent cocaine users with no significant changes in the size of this population since 1985. By using various other data sources and making a number of assumptions (many of which are of uncertain validity), researchers have estimated that there are over 2 million frequent cocaine users in the U.S. . . . Clearly there is considerable uncertainty about the size of the heavy drug-using population."[12] Read the latest NSDUH report at Library Extra 13–1.

Whereas the use of illicit drugs provides one measure of the drug problem facing our country, the ready availability of such drugs provides another. Data from the National Crime Victimization Survey show that two of three students aged 12 to 19 report ready availability of illegal drugs at their school.[13] Students in public schools report a wider availability of drugs than do those in private schools, and students in higher grades (9 through 12) report more drugs available to them than do those in the lower grades. Similar rates of availability were reported by white students (69% of whom said drugs were available to them at school), black students (67%), and students living in cities (66%), suburban areas (67%), and rural areas (71%).

LIBRARY
Extra
▪ ▪ ▪ ▪

Young People and Drugs

While NSDUH data provide a picture of drug abuse among all those 12 years of age and older, the National Institute on Drug Abuse's MTF study provides data on drug abuse among junior high school and high school students. It has tracked 12th graders' illicit drug use, the perceived availability of drugs, and attitudes toward drugs since 1975. In 1991, 8th and 10th graders were added to the survey. The year 2006 survey gathered responses from over 50,000 students in more than 400 schools across the nation about lifetime use, past-year use, past-month use, and daily use of drugs, alcohol, and cigarettes and smokeless tobacco. Our overview of MTF data provides information about overall levels of illicit drug use among high school students, with some detailed data about marijuana use and availability in 2006. For access to the full 2006 MTF survey, which describes the use of many other drugs, including inhalants, view Library Extra 13–2 at crimtoday.com.

LIBRARY
Extra
▪ ▪ ▪ ▪

MTF researchers note that in the late twentieth century, illicit drug use among young Americans had reached extraordinarily high levels. By 1975, when the MTF survey began, the majority of young people (55%) reported having used an illicit drug by the time they left high school. This figure rose to two-thirds (66%) by 1981 before a long and gradual decline to 41% by 1992—when a low point was reached. After 1992 the proportion rose again, reaching a high of 55% in 1999. It stood at 48% in 2006.[14]

Because marijuana use is much more common than the use of any other illicit drug, trends in marijuana use significantly influence the index of "any illicit drug use" reported by the survey. In 1975, however, over one-third (36%) of 12th graders had tried some illicit drug other than marijuana. This figure rose to 43% by 1981, then declined for a long period to a low of 25% in 1992. Some increase followed in the 1990s as the use of a number of drugs rose steadily, and it reached 30% by 1997. Since then, the rate has fallen to 27% in 2006.

Marijuana has been the most widely used illicit drug throughout the 32 years of this study. Annual marijuana use (that is, use within the past year) peaked at 51% among 12th graders in 1979, following a rise that began during the 1960s. Use then steadily declined for the next 13 years, bottoming out at 22% in 1992—a decline of more than half. The 1990s, however, saw a resurgence in marijuana use. After a considerable increase, annual prevalence rates peaked in 1996 at the 8th grade level, and in 1997 at 10th and 12th grade levels. Following the peak, there was a gradual decline among 8th graders, but the decline appeared to halt in 2005, with an annual prevalence rate in 2006 about equal to that of 2004. In the upper grades, only a very modest decline occurred between 1997 and 2002, followed by a continuing gradual decline since.

Anna Nicole Smith, right, leaves the U.S. Supreme Court in Washington, DC, with her son Daniel in 2006. Daniel died on September 10, 2006, while visiting his mother in a Bahamian hospital where she had just given birth. Anna Nicole died unexpectedly in a Florida hotel room five months later. Both deaths appear to have been the result of pharmaceutical drug interaction. Could the deaths have been prevented?

Source: Manuel Balce Ceneta/PA Photos/Landov LLC

FIGURE 13-4

Annual Amount Spent on Illegal Drugs in the United States

Source: Office of National Drug Control Policy, *Drug Data Summary* (Washington, DC: ONDCP, 2003).

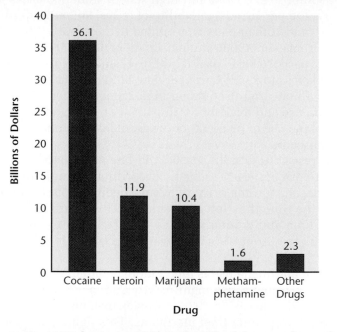

Since the MTF survey began in 1975, between 83% and 90% of the members of every senior class have said that they could get marijuana "fairly easily" or "very easily" if they wanted some. It seems, therefore, that marijuana has remained a highly accessible drug. Since 1991, when data were also available for 8th and 10th graders, marijuana has become considerably less accessible to younger adolescents. Still, in 2006 two-fifths of 8th graders (40%) and almost three-quarters of all 10th graders (71%) reported it as being accessible, as compared to 85% of seniors.

Costs of Abuse

ONDCP estimates that in 2000, Americans spent $64.8 billion to purchase illegal drugs (see Figure 13–4).[15] The true costs of drug abuse, however, are difficult to measure. Included among them would be measurable expenditures such as those for law enforcement

Theory Versus Reality

The Harvard Alcohol Study

In 1993, the Harvard School of Public Health conducted its first College Alcohol Study (CAS). The study surveyed a random sample of students at 140 colleges in 39 states and the District of Columbia. The study was the first national examination of the drinking patterns of college students.

The original CAS identified a style of drinking that study authors called "binge drinking." *Binge drinking* was defined as the consumption of five or more drinks in a row for men and four or more for women at least once in the two weeks preceding the survey. The CAS, with its emphasis on binge drinking, focused media attention on alcohol-related college deaths, including deaths from acute alcohol poisoning, falls, drownings, automobile accidents, fires, and hypothermia resulting from exposure to the elements. The study also led to passage of a congressional resolution to address binge drinking as a national problem and to the appointment of a National Institute on Alcoholism and Alcohol Abuse special task force on college drinking.

The CAS was repeated in 1997, 1999 and 2001, and plans are for it to be continued in the future. The study reports on the drinking behavior of four categories of students: (1) frequent binge drinkers—defined as those students who had binged three or more times in the past two weeks; (2) occasional binge drinkers—those students who had binged one or two times in the same period; (3) nonbinge drinkers—those students who had consumed alcohol in the past year but who had not binged in the previous two weeks; and (4) abstainers—those students who had not consumed alcohol in the past year.

The 2001 CAS surveyed students at 119 four-year colleges that also participated in the 1993, 1997, and 1999 studies. Responses in the four survey years were compared to determine trends in heavy alcohol use, alcohol-related problems, and encounters with college and community prevention efforts. In 2001, approximately two in five college students reported binge drinking, a rate almost identical to rates in the previous three surveys. Very little change in overall college binge drinking was observed in the surveys over time, although a sharp rise in frequent binge drinking was noted among students attending all-women's colleges. The most significant finding, however, was an observed 18% increase in the college student population that reported driving under the influence of alcohol in the previous year.

The study also found that about 19% of surveyed students were abstainers and 23% were frequent binge drinkers. As in the earlier studies, binge drinkers, and particularly frequent binge drinkers, were more likely than other students to experience alcohol-related problems. At colleges with high binge-drinking rates, students who did not binge drink were at high risk of experiencing the secondhand effects of others' heavy drinking. These secondhand effects included having study patterns interrupted, being kept awake at night, being insulted or humiliated, being subjected to unwanted sexual advances, and having to take care of drunken fellow students.

Survey data continue to be analyzed and the relationship between college drinking and other social issues is being explored by researchers at the Harvard School of Public Health. Recent publications based on CAS data cover topics such as the prevalence of rape in heavy-drinking college environments, drinking patterns and mental health among college-age women, and the drinking patterns among students at colleges that ban the use of alcohol. For the latest research reports based on CAS data, visit the Harvard School of Public Health's College Alcohol Study information page at www.hsph.harvard.edu/cas/AlcoholIndex.html.

Discussion Questions

1. Do you know students who consume alcohol on or off campus? If so, do you think that the College Alcohol Study categories provide a useful way of classifying the different kinds of drinking patterns among members of the student body?

2. What percentage of the student body at your school would you assign to each of the CAS categories?

3. Why might such categories be useful to policymakers?

Sources: Henry *Weschler* et. al., "Trends in College Binge Drinking During a Period of Increased Prevention Efforts: Findings From 4 Harvard School of Public Health College Alcohol Study Surveys: 1993–2001," http://www.hsph.harvard.edu/cas/Documents/trends/Trends.pdf (accessed July 10, 2007); Ralph Hingson et. al., "Magnitude of Alcohol-Related Mortality and Morbidity Among U.S. College Students Ages 18–24: Changes from 1998 to 2001," *Annual Review of Public Health,* Vol. 26 (2005), pp. 259–279; and Henry Weschler et al., "College Binge Drinking in the 1990s: A Continuing Problem: Results of the Harvard School of Public Health 1999 College Alcohol Study," http://www.hsph.harvard.edu/cas/rpt2000/CAS2000rpt.shtml (accessed January 15, 2006).

activities intended to prevent drug growing, importation, and use; criminal justice case processing; drug-treatment programs; steps to prevent money laundering; and time lost from work as a result of drug involvement. More difficult to quantify, but equally real, are other costs related to drug abuse, such as death and sickness resulting from exposure to controlled substances, drug-related crime, the fragmentation of families and other relationships caused by illegal drug use, changes in attitudes and worldview among the American population due to drug-crime fear, lost human potential, and the image of the United States on the world stage. In 2000, for example, the latest year for which the Centers for Disease Control and Prevention (CDC) analysis of death certificate data is available,

TABLE 13–1   Direct Costs of Illegal Drug Use

Type of Cost	Millions
Federal drug expenditures	$12,630
Law enforcement[a]	3,200
Interdiction	2,600
International	1,150
Drug prevention	1,960
Drug treatment	3,720
State and local drug-crime expenditures	5,239
Enforcement of drug laws	2,007
Adjudication of drug-law violators	123
Correction of drug-law violators	3,071
State prisons	1,158
Local jails	890
Juveniles	224
Probation, pardon, and parole	677
Other corrections	122
Other criminal justice–related expenditures	38
Health-care costs for illegal drug users	2,272
Short-stay hospitals	1,242
Specialty institutions	570
Office-based physicians	52
Support services	201
Other professional services	17
Medical care for drug-related AIDS cases	126
Support services for drug-related AIDS cases	64
Total	$20,141

Sources: Figures are the author's estimates from a variety of sources, including Office of National Drug Control Policy, *The National Drug Control Strategy 2007* (Washington, DC: ONDCP, 2007); and Office of National Drug Control Policy, *National Drug Control Strategy: FY 2008 Budget Summary* (Washington, DC: ONDCP, 2007).

[a]Not all law enforcement categories are shown.

there were 19,698 drug-induced deaths (that is, deaths resulting directly from drug consumption, primarily overdose) in America.[16]

Similarly, acquired immunodeficiency syndrome (AIDS), many cases of which can be traced to intravenous drug use, has proved to be a costly disease in social terms. Researchers at the CDC say that AIDS is already the leading cause of death of black and Hispanic men aged 25 to 44. And AIDS, says the CDC, "has become the second leading cause of death among black women aged 25 to 44."[17] Homicide is the second leading cause of death for black and Hispanic men in that age group. The CDC finds 73 AIDS cases for every 100,000 black women, but only 5 per 100,000 white women. Of AIDS cases among minority women, 47% are traceable to intravenous drug use, while 37% appear to be due to heterosexual intercourse.

Other costs, such as lost productivity due to drug abuse, are estimated to total $77.6 billion annually.[18] More than half of the total, or $43.8 billion, is estimated lost earnings due to drug-related crime victimization, while the remainder of the total is estimated to be suffered by drug abusers themselves.

Tables 13–1 and 13–2 show the estimated financial and social costs of illegal drug use in the United States per year. Table 13–1 includes dollar amounts spent on systemwide efforts at drug control, and Table 13–2 lists types of costs that are much more difficult to quantify.

TABLE 13–2 Indirect Costs of Illegal Drug Use

Criminal Justice Expenditures on Drug-Related Crime

- Costs to prosecute drug offenders
- Investigating robberies, burglaries, and thefts for drug money and adjudicating and punishing the offenders
- Investigating assaults and homicides in the drug business (or by a drug user who has lost control) and adjudicating and punishing the offenders

Health-Care Costs

- Injuries resulting from drug-related child abuse or neglect
- Injuries from drug-related accidents
- Injuries from drug-related crime
- Premature death
- Other medical care for illegal drug users, including volunteer services and outpatient services, such as emergency room visits
- Resources used in nonhospital settings

Lost Productivity Costs

- Of drug-related accident victims
- Of drug-related crime victims
- Time away from work and homemaking to care for drug users and their dependents
- Drug-related educational problems and school dropouts
- Offenders incarcerated for drug-related or drug-defined crimes

Other Costs to Society

- Loss of property values due to drug-related neighborhood crime
- Property damaged or destroyed in fires and in workplace and vehicular accidents
- Agricultural resources devoted to illegal drug cultivation or production
- Toxins introduced into public air and water supplies by drug production
- Workplace prevention programs, such as drug-testing and employee-assistance programs
- Averting behavior by potential victims of drug-related crime
- Pain and suffering costs to illegal drug users and their families and friends
- Private legal costs

Sources: National Institute on Drug Abuse and National Institute on Alcohol Abuse and Alcoholism, *The Economic Costs of Alcohol and Drug Abuse in the United States, 1992* (Washington, DC: U.S. Government Printing Office, 1998); Bureau of Justice Statistics, *Drugs, Crime and the Justice System: A National Report from the Bureau of Justice Statistics* (Washington, DC: U.S. Government Printing Office, December 1992); and *The Real Cost of the Drug War,* http://briancbennet.com (accessed, October 1, 2004).

Types of Illegal Drugs

By convention, controlled substances are generally grouped according to both pharmacological and legal criteria into the following seven categories: narcotics, depressants, stimulants, hallucinogens, cannabis, anabolic steroids, inhalants. A separate eighth category, that of dangerous drugs, provides a kind of legal and definitional catchall. The DEA uses the term **dangerous drugs** to refer to "broad categories or classes of controlled substances other than cocaine, opiates, and cannabis products."[19] The seven major categories, and some of the drugs each contains, are described in the following paragraphs.[20] Table 13–3, which comes directly from the DEA, summarizes the differences among the drug categories and shows the uses and effects of various types of controlled substances. Learn more about each type of drug at Web Extra 13–1. Read the federal statute describing the various categories of controlled substances at Library Extra 13–3 at crimtoday.com.

dangerous drug

A term used by the DEA to refer to "broad categories or classes of controlled substances other than cocaine, opiates, and cannabis products." Amphetamines, methamphetamines, PCP (phencyclidine), LSD, methcathinone, and "designer drugs" are all considered to be dangerous drugs.

WEB
Extra
∎∎∎∎

LIBRARY
Extra
∎∎∎∎

Who's to Blame—The Individual or Society?

His Brother's Keeper

In March 2008, Nicole Smithfield received a letter from her former boyfriend, Derek Little. The letter came from the state's maximum security prison where Derek was serving life without possibility of parole for the murder of his older brother, Hamilton. The brothers had grown up together and attended school in the same small town where Nicole lived. Derek began dealing drugs at age 13, bringing in a few dollars selling marijuana to some friends at school. By the time he was 24, Derek was operating one of the largest drug distribution networks in the county, and bringing in thousands of dollars a week. He drove an expensive car, had the best clothes and high-tech gadgets, and carried a lot of cash with him wherever he went. People who knew him said that he also carried a 9-shot semiautomatic pistol strapped to his waist.

Hamilton took a different path and joined the army. He went to Afghanistan and then to Iraq for two tours of duty. One night, when he was home on leave, Hamilton stopped by his brother's house and an argument ensued. Hamilton wanted Derek to get out of the drug business and to turn his life around. "It's only a matter of time before you get arrested," Hamilton told his brother. "Do you want to spend the rest of your life in prison?"

"I'm too smart for that," Derek responded. "I've got too many layers (of dealers) protecting me. They'll never get anything on me."

"Yeah—but what about all the lives you're affecting? What about all the kids from our neighborhood who are getting strung out on drugs because of you? You're preying on society," Hamilton said, angry now. "And if you don't quit, I'll make you."

"What do you mean by that?" Derek asked, jumping out of his chair.

"I just think you need to stop, and if I have to, then I'll find a way to make you," Hamilton said, and left, beginning the walk home to his mother's mobile home less than a mile away.

According to evidence presented at his trial, that's when Derek got into his pickup truck and started down the road, accelerating to 80 mph before swerving onto the shoulder and hitting his brother. Hamilton's body flew 40 feet through the air before hitting the ground and then tumbled another 30 feet through the brush.

Prosecutors tried to present additional evidence showing that Derek was likely responsible for the deaths of three other people who had threatened him during the past two years, or who had said that they would turn him in to authorities—but the judge would not allow the jury to hear those claims. When the trial concluded, Derek was found guilty of killing his brother, and sentenced to life in prison without the possibility of parole.

Think about it:

1. How is it that two brothers raised in the same environment might choose such different paths? What might explain their choices?

2. How would you explain the attraction that the drug trade seems to have for so many people in this country?

3. If you were able to set crime control policies for the nation, how would you address the drug problem? Would you consider the decriminalization of any substances? If so, which ones and why?

Stimulants

Stimulants include cocaine and crack cocaine, amphetamines like Dexedrine and Benzedrine, and methamphetamine. Stimulants act as their name implies: They stimulate the central nervous system and result in higher heart rate, elevated blood pressure, and increased mental activity. Legitimate uses of stimulants include increased alertness, reduced fatigue, weight control, and topical analgesic (pain-killing) action. Such drugs are used illegally, however, by those seeking to produce states of excitability and feelings of competence and power.

Cocaine, the use of which has spread rapidly through American population centers, is available in powdered form or as small "rocks" of crack. Crack cocaine, which is much less expensive than powdered cocaine, is made by mixing cocaine powder with water and baking soda or ammonia. It is usually smoked in a "crack pipe" and is named for the fact that it makes crackling sounds when burned.

Powdered cocaine is inhaled or snorted, but it may also be mixed with volatile chemicals and "freebased" or smoked or injected. Cocaine produces effects similar to other stimulants—euphoria, a sense of intense stimulation, psychic and physical well-being, and what may seem like boundless energy—although cocaine "highs" are generally both more intense and more immediate than those produced by other drugs. Prolonged cocaine use can cause delusions, hallucinations, weight loss, and overall physical deterioration.

Cocaine sells in Colombia for $1,350 to $3,900 per pound and in the United States for $6,600 to $11,350 per pound (80% pure) at the wholesale level. Once cut and diluted

TABLE 13-3 Drugs of Abuse—Uses and Effects

Drugs	CSA Schedules	Trade or Other Names	Medical Uses	Dependence Physical	Dependence Psycho-logical	Tolerance	Duration (Hours)	Usual Method	Possible Effects	Effects of Overdose	Withdrawal Syndrome
Narcotics											
Heroin	Substance I	Diamorphine, Horse, Smack, Black tar, *Chiva, Negra (black tar)*	None in U.S., analgesic, antitussive	High	High	Yes	3–4	Injected, snorted, smoked	Euphoria, drowsiness, respiratory depression, constricted pupils, nausea	Slow and shallow breathing, clammy skin, convulsions, coma, possible death	Watery eyes, runny nose, yawning, loss of appetite, irritability, tremors, panic, cramps, nausea, chills and sweating
Morphine	Substance II	MS-Contin, Roxanol, Oramorph SR, MSIR	Analgesic	High	High	Yes	3–12	Oral, injected			
Hydrocodone	Substance II, Product III, V	Hydrocodone w/ Acetaminophen, Vicodin, Vicoprofen, Tussionex, Lortab	Analgesic, antitussive	High	High	Yes	3–6	Oral			
Hydro-morphone	Substance II	Dilaudid	Analgesic	High	High	Yes	3–4	Oral, injected			
Oxycodone	Substance II	Roxicet, Oxycodone w/ Acetaminophen, OxyContin, Endocet, Percocet, Percodan	Analgesic	High	High	Yes	3–12	Oral			
Codeine	Substance II, Products III, V	Acetaminophen, Guaifenesin or Promethazine w/Codeine, Fiorinal, Fioricet or Tylenol w/Codeine	Analgesic, antitussive	Moderate	Moderate	Yes	3–4	Oral, injected			
Other Narcotics	Substance II, III, IV	Fentanyl, Demerol, Methadone, Darvon, Stadol, Talwin, Paregoric, Buprenex	Analgesic, antidiarrheal, antitussive	High–Low	High–Low	Yes	Variable	Oral, injected, snorted, smoked			

(continued)

TABLE 13-3 (Continued)

Drugs	CSA Schedules	Trade or Other Names	Medical Uses	Dependence Physical	Dependence Psychological	Tolerance	Duration (Hours)	Usual Method	Possible Effects	Effects of Overdose	Withdrawal Syndrome
Depressants											
Gamma-Hydroxybutyric Acid	Substance I, Product III	GHB, Liquid Ecstasy, Liquid X, Sodium Oxybate, Xyrem_	None in U.S., anesthetic	Moderate	Moderate	Yes	3–6	Oral	Slurred speech, disorientation, drunken behavior without odor of alcohol, impaired memory of events, interacts with alcohol	Shallow respiration, clammy skin, dilated pupils, weak and rapid pulse, coma, possible death	Anxiety, insomnia, tremors, delirium, convulsions, possible death
Benzodiazepines	Substance IV	Valium, Xanax, Halcion, Ativan, Restoril, Rohypnol (Roofies, R-2), Klonopin	Antianxiety, sedative, anticonvulsant, hypnotic, muscle relaxant	Moderate	Moderate	Yes	1–8	Oral, injected			
Other Depressants	Substance I, II, III, IV	Ambien, Sonata, Meprobamate, Chloral Hydrate, Barbiturates, Methaqualone (Quaalude)	Antianxiety, sedative, hypnotic	Moderate	Moderate	Yes	2–6	Oral			
Stimulants											
Cocaine	Substance II	Coke, Flake, Snow, Crack, *Coca, Blanca, Perico, Nieve,* Soda	Local anesthetic	Possible	High	Yes	1–2	Snorted, smoked, injected	Increased alertness, excitation, euphoria, increased pulse rate & blood pressure, insomnia, loss of appetite	Agitation, increased body temperature, hallucinations, convulsions, possible death	Apathy, long periods of sleep, irritability, depression, disorientation
Amphetamine/ Methamphetamine	Substance II	Crank, Ice, Cristal, Krystal Meth, Speed, Adderall, Dexedrine, Desoxyn	Attention deficit/ hyperactivity disorder, narcolepsy, weight control	Possible	High	Yes	2–4	Oral, injected, smoked			

Drug	CSA Schedules	Trade or Other Names	Medical Uses	Physical Dependence	Psychological Dependence	Tolerance	Duration (hours)	Usual Method	Possible Effects	Effects of Overdose	Withdrawal Syndrome
Methylphenidate	Substance II	Ritalin (Illy's), Concerta, Focalin, Metadate	Attention deficit/hyperactivity disorder	Possible	High	Yes	2–4	Oral, injected, snorted, smoked			
Other Stimulants	Substance III, IV	Adipex P, Ionamin, Prelu-2, Didrex, Provigil	Vaso-constriction	Possible	Moderate	Yes	2–4	Oral			
Hallucinogens											
MDMA and Analogs	Substance I	(Ecstasy, XTC, Adam), MDA (Love Drug), MDEA (Eve), MBDB	None	None	Moderate	Yes	4–6	Oral, snorted, smoked	Heightened senses, teeth grinding and dehydration	Increased body temperature, electrolyte imbalance, cardiac arrest	Muscle aches, drowsiness, depression, acne
LSD	Substance I	Acid, Microdot, Sunshine, Boomers	None	None	Unknown	Yes	8–12	Oral	Illusions and hallucinations, altered perception of time and distance	(LSD) Longer, more intense "trip" episodes	None
Phencyclidine and Analogs	Substance I, II, III	PCP, Angel Dust, Hog, Loveboat, Ketamine (Special K), PCE, PCPy, TCP	Anesthetic (Ketamine)	Possible	High	Yes	1–12	Smoked, oral, injected, snorted	Unable to direct movement, feel pain, or remember		Drug-seeking behavior *Not regulated
Other Hallucinogens	Substance I	Psilocybe mushrooms, Mescaline, Peyote Cactus, Ayahausca, DMT, Dextromethorphan* (DXM)	None	None	None	Possible	4–8	Oral			
Cannabis											
Marijuana	Substance I	Pot, Grass, Sinsemilla, Blunts, *Mota, Yerba, Grifa*	None	Unknown	Moderate	Yes	2–4	Smoked, oral	Euphoria, relaxed inhibitions, increased appetite, disorientation	Fatigue, paranoia, possible psychosis	Occasional reports of insomnia, hyperactivity, decreased appetite
Tetrahydrocannabinol	Substance I, Product III	THC, Marinol	Antinauseant, appetite stimulant	Yes	Moderate	Yes	2–4	Smoked, oral			

(continued)

TABLE 13–3 (Continued)

Drugs	CSA Schedules	Trade or Other Names	Medical Uses	Dependence		Tolerance	Duration (Hours)	Usual Method	Possible Effects	Effects of Overdose	Withdrawal Syndrome
				Physical	Psycho-logical						
Narcotics											
Hashish and Hashish Oil	Substance I	Hash, Hash oil	None	Unknown	Moderate	Yes	2–4	Smoked, oral			
Anabolic Steroids											
Testosterone	Substance III	Depo Testosterone, Sustanon, Sten, Cypt	Hypogonadism	Unknown	Unknown	Unknown	14–28 days	Injected	Virilization, edema, testicular atrophy, gyneco-mastia, acne, aggressive behavior	Unknown	Possible depression
Other Anabolic Steroids	Substance III	Parabolan, Winstrol, Equipose, Anadrol, Dianabol, Primabolin-Depo, D–Ball	Anemia, breast cancer	Unknown	Yes	Unknown	Variable	Oral, injected			
Inhalants											
Amyl and Butyl Nitrite		Pearls, Poppers, Rush, Locker Room	Angina (Amyl)	Unknown	Unknown	No	1	Inhaled	Flushing, hypotension, headache	Methemo-globinemia	Agitation
Nitrous Oxide		Laughing gas, Balloons, Whippets	Anesthetic	Unknown	Low	No	0.5	Inhaled	Impaired memory, slurred speech, drunken behavior, slow onset vitamin deficiency, organ damage	Vomiting, respiratory depression, loss of consciousness, possible death	Trembling, anxiety, insomnia, vitamin deficiency, confusion, hallucinations, convulsions
Other Inhalants		Adhesives, Spray Paint, Hair Spray, Dry Cleaning Fluid, Spot Remover, Lighter Fluid	None	Unknown	High	No	0.5–2	Inhaled			

Source: U.S. Department of Justice, Drug Enforcement Administration.

(cocaine is often mixed with sugar and other substances), the American retail price of powdered cocaine skyrockets to between $36,300 and $136,000 per pound. Crack cocaine sells for $3 to $40 per vial, each of which contains several small "rocks." The Office of National Drug Control Policy estimates that the total annual amount spent on illegal cocaine in the United States is $36.1 billion.

Other stimulants include amphetamines with street names like "bennies," "speed," and "uppers." Amphetamines produce mental alertness and increase the ability to concentrate. They are used medically to treat narcolepsy, obesity, and some forms of brain dysfunction. They also cause talkativeness, reduce fatigue, and result in wakefulness. Abuse produces irritability, overexhaustion, and—in cases of prolonged abuse—psychosis and death from cardiac arrest.

One drug now catching the attention of many is methamphetamine, a stimulant chemically related to other amphetamines but with stronger effects on the central nervous system. Street names for the drug include "speed," "meth," and "crank." Methamphetamine is used in pill form or in powdered form for snorting or injecting.[21] Crystallized methamphetamine, known as "ice," "crystal," or "glass," is a smokable and still more powerful form of the drug. The effects of methamphetamine use include increased heart rate and blood pressure, increased wakefulness, insomnia, increased physical activity, decreased appetite, and anxiety, paranoia, or violent behavior. The drug is easily made in simple home "laboratories" from readily available chemicals, and recipes describing how to produce the substance circulate on the Internet. Methamphetamine appeals to the abuser because it increases the body's metabolism, produces euphoria and alertness, and gives the user a sense of increased energy. Methamphetamine, an increasingly popular drug at "raves" (all-night dancing parties), is not physically addictive but can be psychologically addictive. High doses or chronic use of the drug increases nervousness, irritability, and paranoia.

In 1996, the growing popularity of methamphetamine led to passage of the federal Comprehensive Methamphetamine Control Act. The act is discussed in more detail later in this chapter.

Depressants

The depressant family includes barbiturates, sedatives, and tranquilizers like Nembutal, Seconal, Phenobarbital, Quaalude, Sopor, Valium, Librium, Thorazine, and Equanil. Depressants are used legitimately to obtain release from anxiety, for the treatment of psychological problems, and as mood elevators. Illegitimate users employ these substances to produce intoxication, to counter the effects of other drugs, or to treat themselves for drug withdrawal.

Depressants are often prescribed by physicians seeking to control patients' stress-related symptoms and to induce relaxed states and even sleep. Individuals who have experienced recent traumatic events, for example, may find that the temporary use of prescribed depressants helps to alleviate the psychic distress that they would otherwise feel. If abused, however, depressants may lead to psychological dependence and to addiction.

Cannabis

The cannabis category includes marijuana, hashish, cannabis plants, sinsemilla, and hashish oil—all of which are collectively referred to as "marijuana." Marijuana is a relatively mild, nonaddictive drug with limited hallucinogenic properties. The primary active chemical in marijuana is tetrahydrocannabinol. Although legitimate uses for cannabis have not been fully recognized, some research suggests that the substance can be used in the treatment of pain and glaucoma and as a supplement to cancer treatments (cannabis appears to control the nausea associated with chemotherapy). Marijuana is used illegitimately to induce states of euphoria, gaiety, detachment, relaxation, intoxication, and focused awareness. Time distortion, increased sex drive, enhanced appetite, uncontrollable giddiness, and short-term memory loss tend to accompany its use.

Fans in Seattle mourn the death of Kurt Cobain, after Nirvana's lead singer committed suicide in 1994. Drugs were once called "the love of Cobain's brief life." How could drugs be so attractive?

Source: Grant M. Haller

Street names for marijuana include "pot," "grass," and "weed." Most marijuana is smoked in the form of dried leaves, stems, and flowers of the marijuana plant (or, more accurately, the Indian hemp plant), although processed marijuana "oil" and the cake form of hashish are also widely available. Hashish is made from resins found on the surface of the female marijuana plant and is considerably more potent than other forms of cannabis.

Most of the marijuana consumed in the United States either is grown within the country or comes from Mexico. Although one marijuana plant produces between one and two pounds of dried leaves and stems, marijuana is generally sold to consumers in one-ounce bags. One pound of dried marijuana costs dealers $450 to $2,700, while users pay $25 to $1,000 per one-ounce bag, depending on the reputed potency of the particular variety they are purchasing. Single marijuana cigarettes, sometimes called "joints" or "reefers," sell for $1 to $5. Overall, the Office of National Drug Control Policy estimates that the total amount spent on illegal marijuana in the United States is $10.4 billion annually.

Narcotics

Narcotics, including such drugs as opium, morphine, heroin, methadone, codeine, and Dilaudid, have a number of legitimate uses, including pain relief, antidiarrheal action, and cough suppression. Street use of these drugs is intended to induce pleasure, euphoria, a lack of concern, and general feelings of well-being. The use of narcotics produces drowsiness and relaxation, accompanied by a dreamlike state of reverie. Narcotics are thought to mimic or enhance the activity of endorphins, which are proteins produced by the brain that control pain and influence other subjective experiences.

Heroin and morphine, which are generally sold as a white powder, are derived from opium and are usually injected into the body, although they may also be smoked or eaten. Sometimes users inject these drugs under the skin, a practice called "skin-popping," but most addicts prefer direct intravenous injection for the strong and immediate effects it produces.

One pound of 70% to 90% pure heroin sells in Southeast Asia for $2,700 to $5,000. At the wholesale level in the United States, the same substance brings $40,000 to $110,000 per pound, while mid-level dealers pay up to $270,000 for that amount. Dealers "cut" the drug, effectively diluting it with a variety of other substances. One writer describes it this way: "Once in the United States, heroin may be stepped on (diluted) as many as seven to ten times. What started out in some remote Asian laboratory as 99 percent pure heroin is cut with lactose (milk sugar, a by-product of milk processing), quinine, cornstarch, or almost any other powdery substance that will dissolve when heated. . . . Ultimately, the heroin sold on the street is less than 10 percent pure and sometimes as little as 1 percent to 4 percent pure."[22] Street-level dealers sell diluted heroin in 0.1-gram single-dose bags for as much as $46 each, which translates into an effective retail price of more than $2 million per pound for imported heroin. ONDCP estimates that the total amount spent on heroin in the United States is $11.9 billion annually.

Although narcotics, including heroin, tend to be highly toxic when taken in large doses, frequent users build up tolerances and require ever larger doses for the desired effects to be induced. Physical addiction may result in drug dependence, and symptoms of withdrawal may appear if the drug is not available. Withdrawal symptoms include nervousness, restlessness, severe abdominal cramps, watery eyes, nasal discharge, and—in later stages—vomiting, diarrhea, weight loss, and pain in the large muscles of the body, especially the back and legs.

Hallucinogens

Hallucinogens, which include drugs like LSD (lysergic acid diethylamide), PCP, peyote, mescaline, psilocybin, MDA, MDMA, belladonna, and mandrake, have no official legitimate use. Street use of these drugs is intended to produce "mind expansion," hallucinations, creative mental states, and perceptual distortions—all of which have been popularly called "psychedelic experiences" or "trips."

The exact process by which hallucinogens act upon the mind is not known, and the effects of these drugs are unpredictable. LSD "trips," for example, may produce pleasurable hallucinations and sensations or may result in frightening experiences for the user. During such episodes, uncontrollable nightmarish phantasms may appear to users who are no longer able to distinguish external reality from their own subjective states.

Anabolic Steroids

Anabolic steroids include the substances nandrolene, oxandrolene, oxymetholone, and stanozolol. Steroids are used legitimately for weight gain; for the treatment of arthritis, anemia, and connective tissue disorder; and in the battle against certain forms of cancer. Some bodybuilders, professional athletes, and others seeking to build body bulk and to increase strength have created a secondary market in steroids that has resulted in their ready availability through illegal channels of distribution.

Inhalants

Inhalants include a wide variety of psychotropic substances like nitrous oxide, carbon tetrachloride, amyl nitrite, butyl nitrite, chloroform, Freon, acetate, and toluene. They are highly volatile substances, which generally act as central nervous system depressants. Inhalants are found in fast-drying glues, nail polish remover, room and car deodorizers, lighter fluid, paint thinner, kerosene, cleaning fluids, household sealants, and gasoline. Although some of these substances, such as ether, nitrous oxide, amyl nitrate, and chloroform, have legitimate medical uses, others are employed only to produce a sense of light-headedness often described in colloquial terms as a "rush." The use of inhalants "can disturb vision, impair judgment, and reduce muscle and reflex control."[23]

Inhalants have been called "gateway drugs," or substances that initiate young people into illicit drug use. Easy access to these chemicals is ensured by the fact that few inhalants are subject to legislative control beyond simple administrative regulations. Most inhalants are easily available, being found on household shelves, in hardware stores, and on the shelves of general merchandisers.

WEB
Extra

Based on self-reports from members of surveyed households who are 12 years of age or older, an estimated 22.9 million Americans have used inhalants at some point in their lives, and more than 2.0 million have used these drugs within the past year.[24] In 2001, first-time inhalant users had a mean age of just 15.7 years—the youngest mean inhalant initiation age since 1963 and the youngest mean initiation age of any substance in the MTF survey.[25] Almost 12% of high school seniors report having experimented with some form of inhalant. Learn more about inhalants at the National Inhalant Prevention Coalition's Web site via **Web Extra 13–2.**

Pharmaceutical Diversion and Designer Drugs

pharmaceutical diversion

The process by which legitimately manufactured controlled substances are diverted for illicit use.

The pharmaceutical diversion and subsequent abuse of legitimately manufactured controlled substances are a major source of drug-related addiction or dependence, medical emergencies, and death. **Pharmaceutical diversion** occurs through illegal prescribing by physicians and illegal dispensing by pharmacists and their assistants. "Doctor shopping," the process of finding a physician who is overly liberal in the type and amount of drug prescribed, and visits to numerous physicians for the purpose of collecting large quantities of prescribed medicines are practices that exacerbate the problem. Depressants, including sedatives, tranquilizers, and antianxiety drugs (especially Xanax and Valium), along with stimulants and anabolic steroids, constitute the types of drugs most often diverted.

designer drugs

New substances designed by slightly altering the chemical makeup of other illegal or tightly controlled drugs.

A number of drugs, especially those that fall into the "designer" category, are manufactured in clandestine drug facilities, which are sometimes called "basement laboratories" because they are operated by individuals out of their homes. As the National Institute of Justice (NIJ) notes, "Clandestine laboratories range from small crude operations in sheds, bathtubs, mobile homes, boats, and motel rooms to highly sophisticated operations with professional quality laboratory glassware and equipment."[26] **Designer drugs** are so named because "they are new substances designed by slightly altering the chemical makeup of other illegal or tightly controlled drugs."[27] Designer drugs like Nexus, a new reputed aphrodisiac, usually fall under the rubric "synthetic narcotic" or "synthetic hallucinogen."

Designer drugs require the use of a number of specifically identifiable chemicals in their production. Similarly, opium, cocaine, and other naturally occurring psychoactive substances require the use of chemicals in step-by-step processes to make them ready for street-level distribution and consumption. The Chemical Diversion and Trafficking Act (CDTA) of 1988 placed the distribution of 8 essential chemicals used in the production of illicit drugs, as well as 12 "precursor chemicals" (from which drugs could be made), under federal control. The CDTA also regulates the distribution of machines that can produce pharmaceutical capsules and tablets. In 1994, the Domestic Chemical Diversion Control Act[28] added 32 other chemicals to the list, bringing the total number of drug-related chemical substances under federal control to 52.

Drug Trafficking

drug trafficking

Manufacturing, distributing, dispensing, importing, and exporting (or possession with intent to do the same) a controlled substance or a counterfeit substance.

In everyday usage, the phrase *drug trafficking* can have a variety of meanings. On one hand, it can refer to smuggling—that is, the illegal shipment of controlled substances across state and national boundaries. On the other hand, it can mean the sale of controlled substances. Hence, in colloquial usage, a person who "traffics" in drugs may simply sell them. Technically speaking, **drug trafficking** includes manufacturing, distributing, dispensing, importing, and exporting (or possessing with intent to do the same) a controlled substance or a counterfeit substance.[29] Federal law enforcement agencies, in their effort to reduce trafficking, focus largely on the prevention of smuggling and on the apprehension of smugglers.

Drugs like cocaine, heroin, and LSD are especially easy to smuggle because relatively small quantities of these drugs can be adulterated with other substances to provide large amounts of illicit commodities for sale on the street. Figures 13–5 and 13–6 provide maps of major cocaine and heroin trafficking routes (sometimes called "pipelines") worldwide. Most cocaine that enters the United States originates in the Western Hemisphere, especially in the South American nations of Colombia, Peru, and Bolivia. Transportation routes into the United States include (1) shipment overland from South America through Central America, (2) direct shipments to U.S. ports concealed in containers or packed with legitimate products, (3) flights into the United States via commercial airplanes or in private aircraft, and (4) airdrops to vessels waiting offshore for smuggling into the United States.

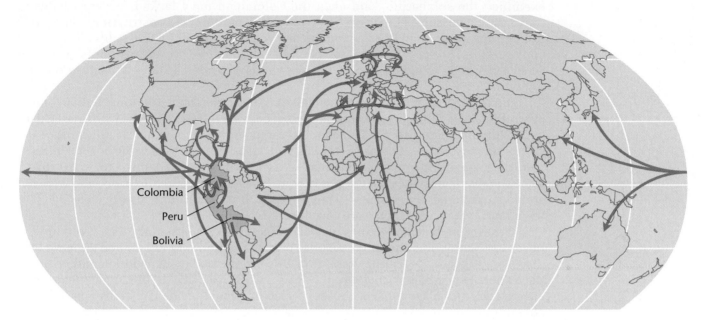

FIGURE 13–5

Global Cocaine Trafficking: Major Countries of Origin and Routes of Transportation

Source: Adapted from the Office of National Drug Control Policy, *The National Drug Control Strategy: 2000 Annual Report* (Washington, DC: U.S. Government Printing Office, 2000), p. 78.

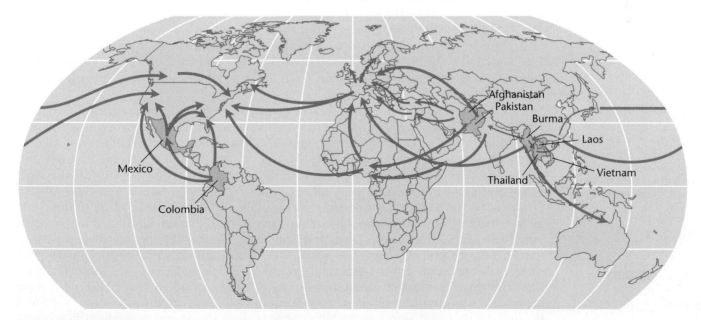

FIGURE 13–6

Global Heroin Trafficking: Major Countries of Origin and Routes of Transportation

Source: Adapted from Office of National Drug Control Policy, *The National Drug Control Strategy: 2000 Annual Report* (Washington, DC: U.S. Government Printing Office, 2000), p. 81.

Most cocaine entering the United States is smuggled aboard maritime vessels. Fishing vessels with hidden compartments, cargo ships plying international waters, and even private submersibles have all been used in smuggling operations. In 2000, for example, Colombian authorities, with help from the DEA, seized a sophisticated 90-foot-long submarine that was under construction by drug traffickers in a warehouse in Bogotá. With a pressurized double hull and a high-tech navigation system, the submarine was designed for deep-sea use and would have been very difficult to detect. Colombian navy captain Fidel Azula, a former submarine captain who examined the submarine, said even the Colombian navy lacked the knowledge to build such a vessel. "This is unmistakably of superb naval construction," he said.[30] Indications were that Russian engineers were involved in the sub's design and construction. Police were led to the find by suspicious area residents who had seen Americans hanging around the warehouse, located in a cow pasture off of a highway.

Annual seizures of cocaine in the United States total about 140 tons. In 2007, however, officials were surprised at the amount of cocaine seized when the U.S. Coast Guard cutter *Sherman* stopped the Panamanian cargo ship *Gatun* about 20 miles off of the California coast.[31] Twenty tons of cocaine, with an estimated street value of $600 million, were discovered and transported to the Coast Guard facility in Alameda to be destroyed. The 14 crew members aboard the *Gatun* were Panamanians and Mexicans who were not armed and offered no resistance when stopped. It was not immediately clear if any of them knew what cargo they were carrying.

Other especially large seizures of cocaine include 2.7 metric tons discovered hidden in canvas bags amid a shipment of coffee beans imported into Miami and 7 metric tons discovered aboard the fishing vessel *Don Celso* and seized by Ecuadorian authorities at the Port of Esmeraldes.[32] In 1998, U.S. Customs Service agents in Laredo, Texas, discovered more than 2 tons of cocaine concealed in a double-walled cooking grease tanker attempting to enter the United States. Based on a street value for cocaine of up to $45,000 per pound, the seizure had an estimated street value of $196 million. Agents were alerted when a narcotic detector dog alerted positively to the rear wheel area of the tanker truck.[33] The most cocaine ever seized at one time, 47,554 pounds, was found in Sylmar, California, on September 29, 1989.[34]

Some trafficking methods are highly creative. As a DEA report states, "Unusual methods of concealment [include] cocaine concealed in a shipment of beach towels, inside spools of industrial thread, inside cans of lard, sealed within quartz crystals, in drums of fruit pulp, in fish meal, and in avocado paste. In addition, U.S. Customs Service and U.S. Fish and Wildlife officers seized several kilograms of cocaine from within a shipment of boa constrictors. The cocaine, wrapped in condoms, had been inserted into the snakes' intestines."[35]

heroin signature program (HSP)

A DEA program that identifies the geographic source of a heroin sample through the detection of specific chemical characteristics in the sample peculiar to the source area.

WEB
Extra
▪ ▪ ▪ ▪

LIBRARY
Extra
▪ ▪ ▪ ▪

The DEA follows heroin trafficking through its **heroin signature program (HSP),** which identifies the geographic source area of a heroin sample through the laboratory detection of specific chemical characteristics in the sample that are peculiar to that area. The signature program employs special chemical analyses to identify and measure chemical constituents of a sample of seized heroin. Results of the HSP show that 62% of heroin in the United States originates in South America, 17% in Southeast Asia, 16% in Southwest Asia, and 5% in Mexico. According to the DEA, most heroin originating in Southeast Asia is produced in the Golden Triangle area, which encompasses Burma, Laos, and Thailand. Shipments are "controlled by ethnic Chinese criminal groups . . . while U.S.-based ethnic Chinese traffickers with links to these international criminal groups [are] the most prolific importers and distributors of Southeast Asian heroin" within the United States.[36] HSP data were based on examination of over 800 random samples, including some obtained through undercover purchases, domestic seizures, and seizures made at U.S. ports of entry. Learn more about the DEA and the heroin signature program at **Web Extra 13–3.** Learn more about the different kinds of controlled substances at **Library Extra 13–4** at crimtoday.com.

Drugs and Crime

While the manufacture, sale, transportation, and use of controlled substances are themselves criminal, drugs and crime are also linked in other ways. The addict who is so habituated to the use of illegal drugs that he or she steals to support a "habit," the drug importer who kills a rival dealer, and the offender who commits a criminal act due to the stimulation provided by drugs all provide examples of how drug abuse may be linked to other forms of criminal activity.

Recognizing these differences, the Bureau of Justice Statistics (BJS) distinguishes between drug-defined and drug-related crimes. **Drug-defined crimes** are "violations of laws prohibiting or regulating the possession, use, or distribution of illegal drugs."[37] The costs of all drug-defined crime, says BJS, are directly attributable to illegal drug use. **Drug-related crimes,** on the other hand, "are not violations of drug laws but are crimes in which drugs contribute to the offense."[38] Illegal drug use, says BJS, "is related to offenses against people and property in three major ways: (1) pharmacologically drugs can induce violent behavior, (2) the cost of drugs induces some users to commit crimes to support their drug habits, [and] (3) violence often characterizes relations among participants in the drug distribution system."[39]

According to the U.S. Department of Justice, "There is extensive evidence of the strong relationship between drug use and crime." This relationship can be summarized in the following three points, each of which, the department says, is supported "by a review of the evidence."[40]

- Drug users report greater involvement in crime and are more likely than nonusers to have criminal records.
- People with criminal records are much more likely than others to report being drug users.
- Crimes rise in number as drug use increases.

One national initiative that attempts to measure the degree to which criminal offenders use controlled substances is the **Arrestee Drug Abuse Monitoring (ADAM) Program,** begun by the NIJ in 2000. The ADAM program gathers data on drug use, drug and alcohol dependency and treatment, and drug market participation among booked male arrestees within 48 hours of arrest. ADAM data consist of urinalysis results and information reported to interviewers by arrestees regarding their drug use. Urine specimens collected from arrestees are sent to a central laboratory, where they are analyzed for the presence of ten drugs: cocaine, opiates, marijuana, PCP, methadone, benzodiazepines (for example, Valium), methaqualone, propoxyphene (that is, Darvonlike substances), barbiturates, and amphetamines. Tests can detect the use of most drugs within the past two to three days, and marijuana and PCP can be detected as long as three weeks after use.

ADAM funding was cut in federal fiscal year 2004 and 2005 budgets, and the program was temporarily suspended. A revised ADAM program, known as ADAM II, is just now getting off the ground.[41] ADAM II intends to track trends in the prevalence and types of drug use among booked arrestees in ten sites and will survey 250 arrestees every two weeks.[42] The new program will be smaller in scope than the original ADAM initiative, but will continue to gather the same kinds of data.[43] ADAM data are useful because they make it possible to identify levels of drug use among arrestees, track changes in patterns of drug use, identify specific drugs that are abused in each jurisdiction, alert officials to trends in drug use and the availability of new drugs, provide data to help understand the drug-crime connection, and evaluate law enforcement and jail-based programs and their effects.

ADAM's 2000 annual report, published in 2003, was its last official document before program funding was suspended. The report showed that 64% of the adult male arrestees in 35 reporting American cities tested positive for drug use.[44] ADAM researchers uncovered significant differences in the patterns of arrestee drug use by city. For example, the percentage of male arrestees who tested positive for any drug ranged

drug-defined crime

A violation of the laws prohibiting or regulating the possession, use, or distribution of illegal drugs.

drug-related crime

A crime in which drugs contribute to the offense (excluding violations of drug laws).

Arrestee Drug Abuse Monitoring (ADAM) Program

National Institute of Justice program, that tracks trends in the prevalence and types of drug use among booked arrestees in urban areas.

from 50% in San Antonio to 77% in Atlanta. The range among female arrestees was even more pronounced, from a low of 22% in Laredo to 81% in New York City.[45]

Marijuana was the drug most commonly used by arrestees, followed by cocaine. At least 31% of adult male arrestees in a majority of sites tested positive for cocaine. Cocaine-positive rates for women ranged from 7.8% in San Jose to 59.2% in Chicago, and cocaine-positive rates for men ranged from 11% in Laredo to 49% in Atlanta.

The study also found that the proportion of adult male arrestees testing positive for marijuana was greater than the rate for female adult arrestees in all sites. Adult male marijuana-positive rates ranged from 28.5% in Des Moines to 57% in Oklahoma City. Adult female marijuana-positive rates ranged from 17.2% in Laredo to 44.7% in Oklahoma City.

Among juvenile detainees, marijuana was the most commonly used drug—more than six times higher than cocaine use for juvenile males and females alike. Among the sites that collect juvenile data, male detainees were more likely to test positive for the use of any drug than were female detainees. At every site, more than 40% of juvenile males and 20% of juvenile females tested positive for marijuana.

The use of opiates, such as heroin and opium, remained relatively low, compared with the prevalence of cocaine and marijuana among adult arrestees. Only eight sites had adult opiate-positive rates of 10% or higher. The proportion of women testing positive for opiates was greater than that for men in many sites. In only three sites—Chicago, New Orleans, and New York City—did more than 15% of adult male arrestees test positive for opiates. In five sites—Chicago, Detroit, New York City, Portland, Tucson and Seattle—more than 15% of female adult arrestees tested positive for opiates.

Consistently high percentages of overall use among arrestees, however, may mask differences in trends for specific drugs and in specific segments of the arrestee population. Methamphetamine use among ADAM arrestees, for example, appears to be concentrated mainly in the western part of the United States, particularly in Portland, Sacramento, Salt Lake City, San Diego, San Jose, and Spokane, where more than 20% of both the men and the women tested positive for the drug. The survey found that methamphetamine use among juvenile arrestees followed a pattern similar to that of adult arrestees in that methamphetamine was more commonly used by females and was most often detected at sites in the West and Southwest. Learn more about ADAM at **Web Extra 13-4.** Read an ADAM publication online at **Library Extra 13-5** at crimtoday.com.

WEB
Extra

LIBRARY
Extra

Other information on drug use by offenders at the time of the offense comes from the National Crime Victimization Survey (NCVS), which gathers data from victims of violent crime who are asked to report their impressions about offenders. In a recent year, for example, 33% of all victims of violent crime included in the survey reported that they believed their assailants were under the influence of drugs or alcohol at the time the crime occurred. Another 46% of victims stated that they did not know whether the offender was under the influence of drugs.

Offender self-reports collected by BJS researchers show that among jail inmates[46]

- Forty-four percent used illegal drugs in the month before the offense for which they were arrested.
- Thirty percent used illegal drugs daily in the month before the offense.
- Twenty-seven percent used illegal drugs at the time of the offense.
- Cocaine and crack cocaine were the drugs most commonly abused by jail inmates.

Surveys of state prison inmates reveal much the same pattern. Of inmates in state prisons, 61% say that they or their victims were under the influence of drugs or alcohol at the time of the offense, 50% report having been under the influence of alcohol or drugs, and 30% say their victims were under the influence of alcohol or drugs.[47] Nearly 40% of youths incarcerated in long-term state-operated facilities report having been under the influence of illegal drugs at the time of their offense.[48] When self-reports of jail and state prison inmates are evaluated to determine the proportion reporting having ever used drugs, nearly 80% of adult inmates report such use, while 83% of incarcerated juveniles say they have used drugs at some point in their lives.[49]

Surveys of drug-related crime have also been conducted in recent years. Interviews with adult prison inmates, for example, revealed that 24% of female and 16% of male inmates committed their offenses to get money to buy drugs. The same surveys show that approximately 30% of all robberies, burglaries, and thefts are committed to obtain drug money, while 5% of murders result from such criminal activities.[50]

Illegal Drugs and Official Corruption

Sometimes the corrupting influence of drugs and drug money extends beyond street crime and street criminals. Lucrative drug profits have the potential to corrupt official agents of control, as the Mollen Commission study of police corruption in New York City found. The Mollen Commission, headed by former Judge Milton Mollen, made its report on July 6, 1994, and found that the severity of police corruption in New York City had worsened drastically since previous investigations into the subject. According to the report, "Police have crossed the line into actively engaging in criminal activity including robbery, drug dealing and even a killing."[51] It called today's corrupt police "criminals in blue uniforms," contrasting the severity of their illegal activity with prior forms of corruption that simply involved turning a "blind eye" to crime.

Much illegal police activity was found to be drug-related, with drug monies providing powerful incentives toward corruption. The report found that police officers in certain precincts banded together and regularly robbed drug dealers, sold drugs, and conducted illegal raids to confiscate additional drugs for personal gain. The commission found that "some precincts were much more prone to corruption, particularly in minority communities because of high levels of drug activity within their borders. . . . Unlike 20 years ago, when an officer took bribes it was to turn his head away from crime. This time these [bad] cops are the criminals," Judge Mollen said, commenting on the commission's report.[52]

It is not only police officers who face the threat of corruption from the lucrative monetary rewards to be reaped from dealing drugs. In the mid-1990s, for example, 20 District of Columbia corrections officers and employees were given stiff prison sentences after being convicted of drug-smuggling activities. Even with those convictions, however, few believed that corruption in the District's prisons had been ended. U.S. District Judge Royce Lamberth, who sentenced the former officers, observed that "even as the latest prison guard drug ring was being shut down . . . corruption continues today as I sit in this courtroom."[53]

Social Policy and Drug Abuse

The history of drug-control policy in the United States is as interesting as it is diverse. Prior to 1907, any and all drugs could be bought and sold in the United States without restriction. Manufacturers and distributors were not regulated and were not even required to disclose the contents of their products. Patent medicines of the time were trade secrets whose names were patented although their ingredients were known only to the manufacturers. The era of patent medicines came to an end with enactment of the federal Pure Food and Drug Act of 1906. The law required manufacturers to list their ingredients and specifically targeted mood-changing chemicals. "For purposes of this Act," the law read, "an article shall . . . be deemed misbranded . . . if the package fails to bear a statement on the label of the quantity or proportion of any alcohol, morphine, opium, cocaine, heroin, alpha or beta eucaine, chloroform, cannabis, chloral hydrate, or acetanilide." Although the law required disclosure of the chemical composition of marketed substances, it did not outlaw them

The Harrison Act, passed by Congress in 1914, was the first major piece of federal antidrug legislation. The Harrison Act required anyone dealing in opium, morphine, heroin, cocaine, or their derivatives to register with the federal government and to pay a tax of $1.00 per year. The act, however, only authorized the registration of physicians, pharmacists, and other medical professionals, effectively outlawing street use of these drugs. However, by 1920, court rulings severely curtailed the use of heroin for medical purposes, saying its prescribed use only prolonged addiction. Hence, the beginning of complete federal prohibition over at least one major drug can be traced to that time.

In 1919, the Eighteenth Amendment to the U.S. Constitution, which prohibited the manufacture, sale, and transportation of alcoholic beverages, was ratified. The Volsted Act, passed by Congress in 1919 over President Wilson's veto, mandated Prohibition and defined "intoxicating liquors" as those containing more than 0.5% alcohol. Support for Prohibition began to wane not long after the amendment was enacted. Objections to Prohibition included the claims that it gave the government too much power over people's personal lives, that it was impossible to enforce, that it corrupted agents of enforcement, and that it made many bootleggers wealthy. The coming of the Great Depression, which began in 1929, magnified the effect of lost alcohol tax revenues on the federal government, and in 1933 Congress proposed and the states ratified the Twenty-first Amendment, which repealed Prohibition.

In 1937, passage of the Marijuana Tax Act effectively outlawed marijuana, a federal stance that was reinforced by the Boggs Act of 1951. The Boggs Act also mandated deletion of heroin from the list of medically useful substances and required its complete removal from all medicines. The 1956 Narcotic Control Act increased penalties for drug traffickers and made the sale of heroin to anyone under age 18 a capital offense.

The most comprehensive federal legislation to address controlled substances to date is the 1970 Comprehensive Drug Abuse Prevention and Control Act. Title 2 of that act is referred to as the Controlled Substances Act (CSA). It established five schedules that classify psychoactive drugs according to their medical use, degree of psychoactivity, and adjudged potential for abuse. Table 13–3, which appears earlier in this chapter, outlines the various drug schedules under federal law. Penalties under federal law are generally more severe for possession of higher-category substances (Schedule I being the highest), but they vary by amount possessed, the purpose of possession (for sale or personal use), and the offender's criminal history.

The vast amounts of money associated with the illegal drug trade have the potential to corrupt public officials and agents of control. How can that potential be reduced?

Source: Steve Starr, Saba Press Photos, Inc./Corbis

Theory Versus Reality

Drug Courts and Public Policy

Since the 1980s, the drug epidemic in the United States and the adoption of tougher drug policies by lawmakers and officials have contributed to an abundance of drug cases on judicial dockets in many U.S. jurisdictions. About 20 years ago, in response to the ever-growing number of drug cases and the cycle of recidivism common among drug offenders, some state and local jurisdictions began experimenting with a new type of judicial proceeding known as "drug courts." Drug courts, which are generally used for nonviolent drug offenders, seek to identify eligible participants early in case processing. They offer an alternative to incarceration, which has not been effective in breaking the cycle of drugs and crime.

Drug court programs, which may divert offenders from further handling by other official agencies, feature supervised treatment and periodic drug testing. Their purpose is to use the authority of the court to reduce crime by changing defendants' drug-using behavior. Defendants are typically diverted to drug court programs in exchange for the possibility of dismissed charges or reduced sentences.

Judges who preside over drug court proceedings monitor the progress of defendants through treatment programs through frequent status hearings—and they prescribe sanctions and rewards in collaboration with prosecutors, defense attorneys, treatment providers, and others. Treatment options are determined by the judge, who holds the offender personally and publicly accountable for treatment progress.

In exchange for the defendant's successfully completing treatment, the court may dismiss the original charge, reduce or set aside a previously imposed sentence, impose a lesser penalty, or dispense any combination of these options. Although some basic elements are common to many drug court programs, the programs vary in terms of their approaches, participant eligibility, program requirements, type of treatment provided, sanctions and rewards, and other practices.

Treatment has been shown to work—if substance abusers stay involved. However, between 80% and 90% of conventional drug treatment clients drop out before 12 months. By providing a structure that links supervision and treatment, drug courts work to exert legal pressure on defendants to enter and remain in treatment long enough to realize benefits. According to the NIJ, more than two-thirds of participants who begin treatment through a drug court complete it in a year or more—a six-fold increase in retention compared with programs outside the justice system.

Title V of the Violent Crime Control and Law Enforcement Act of 1994 (Public Law 103–322) specifically authorizes the awarding of federal grants for drug court programs that include court-supervised drug treatment. In 1995, the federal Drug Courts Program Office was established to implement and support provisions of the act and has since funded the development and establishment of drug courts across the country.

A 2006 NIJ review of drug courts, which synthesized findings from five NIJ-funded studies, found that drug courts can substantially reduce recidivism and promote other positive outcomes. The review determined that the average investment per drug court program participant was $5,928, while cost savings included $2,329 in avoided criminal justice system costs, and $1,301 in reduced victimization costs over a 30-month period. The same review showed that overall, drug court participants were rearrested (for any charge) less often than their counterparts in the comparison group (randomly selected from all felony drug cases that did not enter drug court): 53% versus 65%, respectively.

Discussion Questions

1. What is the purpose of drug courts? What do you think will be their future?

2. Do you think drug courts are a good idea? Why or why not?

Sources: National Institute of Justice, *Drug Courts: The Second Decade* (Washington, DC: National Institute of Justice, 2006); Richard S. Gebelein, *Rebirth of Rehabilitation: Promise and Perils of Drug Courts* (Washington, DC: Department of Justice, 2000); Ken Wallentine, "Drug Courts: A Change in Tactics," *Police*, Vol. 24, No. 4 (April 2000), pp. 54–56; and U.S. General Accounting Office, *Drug Courts: Overview of Growth, Characteristics, and Results* (Washington, DC: GAO, 1997).

Another federal initiative, the 1988 Anti-Drug Abuse Act, proclaimed the goal of a "drug-free America by 1995." Although many of the act's provisions, like the preamble that contained the "drug-free" phrase, were more rhetoric than substance, the act substantially increased penalties for recreational drug users and made weapons purchases by suspected drug dealers more difficult. The law also denied federal benefits—ranging from loans (such as federal student loans) to contracts and licenses—to federal drug convicts.

In 1991, steroids were added to the list of Schedule III controlled substances by congressional action, and in 1996, the Drug-Induced Rape Prevention Act[54] increased penalties for trafficking in the drug Rohypnol, which is known as the "date rape drug" because of its growing use by "young men [who] put doses of the drug in women's drinks without their consent in order to lower their inhibitions."[55] Rohypnol (whose generic name is flunitrazepam) is a powerful sedative manufactured by Hoffmann LaRoche

Pharmaceuticals. A member of the benzodiazepine family of depressants, it is legally prescribed in 64 countries for insomnia and as a preoperative anesthetic. Seven to ten times more powerful than Valium, Rohypnol is readily available on the black market. It dissolves easily in drinks and can leave anyone who unknowingly consumes it unconscious for hours, making the person vulnerable to sexual assault. The drug is variously known as "roples," "roche," "ruffles," "roofies," and "rophies" on the street.

Another date rape drug, gammahydroxybutyrate (GHB), has effects similar to those of Rohypnol. GHB, a central nervous system depressant, was once sold in health food stores as a performance enhancer for use by bodybuilders. Rumors that GHB stimulates muscle growth were never proved. The intoxicating effects of GHB, however, soon became obvious. In 1990, FDA banned the use of GHB except under the supervision of a physician. Learn more about abused drugs from the DEA via Library Extra 13–6 at crimtoday.com.

Recent Legislation

Recent drug-control legislation of note includes the Comprehensive Methamphetamine Control Act (CMCA) of 1996 and relevant portions of the Violent Crime Control and Law Enforcement Act of 1994. The CMCA (1) contains provisions for the forfeiture and seizure of chemicals used in the manufacture of methamphetamine, (2) added iodine to the list of chemicals controlled under the Chemical Diversion and Trafficking Act of 1988 and the Domestic Chemical Diversion Control Act of 1993, (3) created new reporting requirements for distributors of combination products containing ephedrine, pseudoephedrine, and phenylpropanolamine, and (4) increased penalties for the manufacture and possession of equipment used to make controlled substances.

The far-reaching Violent Crime Control and Law Enforcement Act of 1994 included a number of drug-related provisions. Specifically, the act

- Authorized $1 billion in Edward Byrne Memorial Formula Grant Program monies to reduce or prevent juvenile drug- and gang-related activity in federally assisted, low-income housing areas.
- Authorized $1.6 billion for direct funding to localities around the country for anticrime efforts, such as drug treatment, education, and jobs, through a legislative subsection known as the Local Partnership Act.
- Allocated other drug-treatment monies for the creation of state and federal programs to treat drug-addicted prisoners. The act also created a treatment schedule for all drug-addicted federal prisoners and requires drug testing of federal prisoners upon release.
- Provided $1 billion for drug court programs for nonviolent offenders with substance-abuse problems. Participants are intensively supervised, given drug treatment, and subjected to graduated sanctions—ultimately including prison terms—for failing random drug tests.
- Provided stiff new penalties for drug crimes committed by gang members and tripled penalties for using children to deal drugs near schools and playgrounds.
- Established "drug-free zones" by increasing penalties for drug dealing in areas near playgrounds, school yards, video arcades, and youth centers.
- Increased penalties for drug dealing near public housing projects.
- Expanded the federal death penalty to include large-scale drug trafficking and mandated life imprisonment for criminals convicted of three drug-related felonies.
- Created special penalties for drug use and drug trafficking in prison.

Drug-Control Strategies

Throughout the years, major policy initiatives in the battle against illicit drugs have included (1) antidrug legislation and strict enforcement, (2) interdiction, (3) crop control, (4) forfeiture, and (5) antidrug education and drug treatment.[56] Current policy is in keeping with calls for the strict enforcement of antidrug-abuse laws, although much enforcement emphasis in recent years has shifted from targeting users to the arrest, prosecution, and incarceration of the distributors of controlled substances. Similar shifts have occurred among employers, some of whom no longer wait for drug-influenced behavioral problems to arise but instead require routine drug testing as a condition of employment and retention.

In 2006, nearly 1.9 million people were arrested for drug-law violations throughout the United States.[57] The 2006 arrest total was 1% lower than in 1998, 11% higher than the 1995 level, and 40% higher than in 1992.[58] Enforcement activities within the United States also include the seizure and destruction of illegal drugs and clandestine drug laboratories. In 2006, for example, DEA agents destroyed 6,435 methamphetamine laboratories across the nation.[59]

Interdiction is an international drug-control policy that aims to stop drugs from entering the country illegally. To avoid duplication of seizure reports, the Federal-wide Drug Seizure System (FDSS) consolidates seizure reports from the FBI, DEA, U.S. Customs Service, U.S. Border Patrol, and U.S. Coast Guard. In 2006, federal agents seized 322,438 kilograms of marijuana, 69,826 kilograms of cocaine, and 805 kilograms of heroin.[60] More than half of all cocaine and much of the heroin, marijuana, and methamphetamine in the United States is thought to enter the country from Mexico. In one year, U.S. Border Patrol personnel, Customs agents, and Coast Guard officials oversee the legal entry of more than 300 million people, 90 million cars, 5 million trucks, and 600,000 railroad cars into the United States from Mexico. Difficult terrain and oceans make southwestern borders especially hard to police. Drugs cross the desert in armed pack trains as well as on the backs of human "mules." They are tossed over border fences and whisked away on foot or by vehicle.[61] Operators of ships find gaps in U.S./Mexican interdiction coverage and position drugs close to the border for eventual transfer to the United States. Small boats in the Gulf of Mexico and eastern Pacific deliver drugs directly into the United States, and instances of corruption in U.S. border agencies contribute to the difficulty in interdiction enforcement.

A third strategy, crop control, has both international and domestic aspects. During 2005, for example, the DEA's Domestic Cannabis Eradication and Suppression Program was responsible for the eradication of 3,938,151 cultivated outdoor marijuana plants and 270,935 indoor marijuana plants in the United States. In addition, the same program was responsible for 11,922 arrests, and agents seized 3,707 weapons and $26,911,262 in assets.[62] In 2000, two DEA operations code-named Conquistador and Columbus resulted in the eradication of coca plants in Panama, Colombia, Venezuela, Bolivia, Ecuador, and other Latin American countries with a production potential of 25,790 kilograms.[63] Learn more about specific DEA domestic and overseas operations and task forces at Web Extra 13–5.

Forfeiture, or asset forfeiture, is another strategy in the battle against illegal drugs. Forfeiture is a legal procedure that authorizes judicial representatives to seize "all moneys, negotiable instruments, securities, or other things of value furnished or intended to be furnished by any person in exchange for a controlled substance . . . [and] all proceeds traceable to such an exchange."[64] Unfortunately, asset forfeiture laws have at times been abused by enforcement agencies. As one writer explains, "There have, in the past, been cases where innocent parties have had property seized and had to spend a considerable amount on lawyers' fees to get it back. Parents have had homes confiscated because children sold drugs there. Farms have been taken even though the owners were acquitted of growing marijuana on an isolated part of the property."[65] Recent U.S. Supreme Court decisions, however, now require that property owners be given notice of any pending seizures and be allowed the opportunity to respond to government charges.[66]

interdiction

An international drug control policy that aims to stop drugs from entering the country illegally.

WEB
Extra
■ ■ ■ ■

The Court has also acted to restrain seizures of property far more valuable than the proceeds of the underlying crime with which the property owner has been charged.[67]

Antidrug education and drug treatment have gained significant popularity over the past decade. Those favoring educational attacks on the problem of drug abuse are quick to claim that other measures have not been effective in reducing the incidence of abuse. Antidrug education programs often reach targeted individuals through schools, corporations, and media campaigns. A short TV commercial of a few years ago, for example, recited the lines "This is your brain. This is your brain on drugs," while showing an egg, followed by an egg sizzling in a frying pan. School-based programs are numerous, with many being built on the principles developed by Project D.A.R.E. (Drug Abuse Resistance Education), which began as a joint effort of the Los Angeles Police Department and the Los Angeles Unified School District in 1983. D.A.R.E. uses uniformed police officers and other "experts" to explain issues of drug abuse to school-aged children and attempts to build resistance to what might otherwise be perceived by youths as attractive drug-related activities. D.A.R.E. focuses on developing competent decision-making skills, combating negative forms of peer pressure, and providing meaningful alternatives to drug use. Unfortunately for advocates of such programs, however, a number of recent studies have questioned the effectiveness of D.A.R.E.-type interventions, finding—after repeated evaluations—that their "effects on drug use, except for tobacco use, are nonsignificant."[68]

The Office of National Drug Control Policy

In 1988, with passage of the Anti-Drug Abuse Act, Congress established the Office of National Drug Control Policy (ONDCP) and endorsed as a national policy goal the creation of a drug-free America. The director of ONDCP is a member of the president's cabinet and is the principal national spokesperson on illicit drug use and related issues.

The ONDCP mission is to establish policies, priorities, and objectives for the nation's drug-control program. The stated goals of that program are to reduce illicit drug use, manufacturing, and trafficking; to reduce drug-related crime and violence; and to ameliorate drug-related health consequences. To achieve these goals, the director of ONDCP is charged with producing and publishing a national drug-control strategy. That strategy directs the nation's antidrug efforts and establishes a program, a budget, and guidelines for cooperation among federal, state, and local entities. Prior to 2000, Congress required the president to submit a national drug-control strategy each year. Public Law 105–277 now requires the president to submit to Congress only an annual report on the progress in implementing the strategy.

The national drug-control strategy currently takes a long-term view of the nation's drug problem and focuses on prevention, treatment, research, law enforcement, protection of U.S. borders, drug-supply reduction, and international cooperation.

The strategy focuses on young people, seeking to educate them about the dangers of illegal drugs, alcohol, and tobacco. It also stresses the need to protect borders from drug incursion and to cut the drug supply more effectively in domestic communities. It emphasizes initiatives to share intelligence and make use of the latest technology in these efforts. As a major gateway for the entry of illegal drugs into the United States, the Southwest border receives considerable attention within the strategy. Resources have also been allocated to close other avenues of drug entry into the United States, including the Virgin Islands, Puerto Rico, the Canadian border, and all airports and seaports. The strategy also seeks to curtail illegal drug trafficking in the transit zone between source countries, and U.S.-led multinational efforts in the Caribbean, Central America, Europe, and the Far East are coordinated under the strategy in an effort to exert maximum pressure on drug traffickers. The strategy's stated goals, called "national priorities," are reprinted here along with excerpts of official narrative:[69]

> **Priority 1: Stopping use before it starts—education and community action.** The *National Strategy* points to the Miami-Dade Juvenile Assessment Center as an exemplary program of early intervention that targets first-time drug users, or juveniles who are at risk of beginning

Crime in the News

States List Meth Offenders on the Web

States frustrated with the growth of toxic methamphetamine labs are creating Internet registries to publicize the names of people convicted of making or selling meth, the cheap and highly addictive stimulant plaguing communities across the nation.

The registries—similar to the sex-offender registries operated by every state—have been approved within the past 18 months in Tennessee, Minnesota and Illinois. Montana has listed those convicted of running illegal drug labs on its Internet registry of sexual and violent offenders since 2003. Meth-offender registries are being considered in Georgia, Maine, Oklahoma, Oregon, Washington state and West Virginia.

The new registries represent the latest effort by governments against meth, which can be made from household ingredients such as cold medicines that contain pseudoephedrine. As meth labs have spread east from California during the past decade, most states have increased penalties for meth manufacturing and restricted the sale of medicines used to make the drug. Those laws have contributed to a decline in meth labs, according to the DEA, which reported that authorities found more than 17,000 labs in 2003 and more than 12,000 last year.

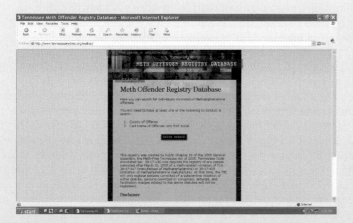

The state-run Tennessee Methamphetamine Offender Registry Database online. Available at www.tennesseeanytime.org/methor, the registry allows users to search online for individuals convicted of a methamphetamine offense. What's the purpose of such databases? Do you think they are a good idea?

Source: © 2004 - 2007 Tennessee Anytime

Source: Donna Leinwand, "States List Meth Offenders on Web," *USA Today*, August 23, 2006, http://www.usatoday.com/news/nation/2006-08-22-meth-registries_x.htm, accessed August 28, 2007. Reprinted with permission

For the latest crime and justice news, visit www.crimenews.info.

Tennessee has more than 400 people in its meth-offender database, which was created partly in response to complaints from landlords and other property owners about the toxic waste created after chemicals are "cooked" to make meth.

Illinois lawmakers approved a meth-offender registry in June, and last month Minnesota Gov. Tim Pawlenty used his executive powers to create a registry that is to be online by Dec. 31.

The registries generally include the names, birthdates and offenses of convicted meth manufacturers, dealers and traffickers. The dates of their convictions and the locations of their crimes also are included. The listings are not as specific as those in sex-offender registries, which include offenders' addresses and photos.

Officials in Minnesota and elsewhere say residents and landlords will be able to use the registries to check for meth offenders in their communities. "We want to arm citizens with information, so they can protect themselves and their communities," says Brian McClung, a spokesman for Pawlenty.

The meth-offender registries have not been challenged in court, but the American Civil Liberties Union (ACLU) and other critics say there are legal and practical drawbacks to them.

Graham Boyd, director of the ACLU's Drug Policy Litigation Project, says the prospect of being listed on a meth-offender registry for at least several years after a conviction amounts to an extra punishment "that's not allowed under our Constitution."

However, three years ago the U.S. Supreme Court rejected a similar double-jeopardy argument when it upheld state registries for sex offenders, who the court said posed a unique threat to communities.

If meth registries are challenged in court, a key question would be whether meth offenders are as much of a threat to public safety as sex offenders.

Studies consistently have shown that offenders who abuse drugs have high re-arrest rates. Recidivism rates among sex offenders can vary widely.

Boyd also says drug users could use meth-offender registries to locate dealers. "One group for whom this registry is going to be an incredibly good resource is people looking to buy methamphetamine," he says.

Discussion Questions

1. What's the purpose of state-run meth offender databases?

2. How might such databases backfire?

a drug-using career. In Miami-Dade, all juvenile arrestees are sent to a central facility called the Juvenile Assessment Center (JAC). The JAC brings together specialists from law enforcement and social services in an effort to provide coordinated services to youth as they enter the juvenile justice system. All arrestees are thoroughly assessed, and those who run the program have found a drug problem lies at the root of many behavioral problems. "Unfortunately," says center director Wansley Walters, "a lot of kids move through the

Sergeant Jeff Yurkiewicz of the Pennsylvania State Police K-9 unit leads his dog, Jake, through a search for drugs and contraband at the Allegheny County Jail in Pittsburgh. More than 20 dogs were brought in to sweep through the entire jail for drugs. How do controlled substances enter correctional facilities?

Source: AP Wide World Photos

system without having their drug use connected to their behavior problems." Through careful screening, the JAC staff tailor interventions for each child. One may require lengthy residential treatment, another might need no more than counseling and participation in realistic discussions about the risks of drug use. "Frankly," says Walters, "some children just need some attention—and that may be all [it takes] to modify their behavior."

Following up with brief interventions for young people who do try illegal drugs or alcohol appears to be critical. Hence, the *National Strategy* highlights the importance of student drug testing, calling it "a prevention approach that accomplishes both goals: deterring drug use while guiding users to needed treatment or counseling." Student drug testing programs advance the strategy's goal of intervening early in a young person's drug career. They employ research-based prevention approaches to guide users into counseling or drug treatment, and to deter others from experimenting with drugs. The purpose of random testing, according to the *National Strategy*, is not to catch, punish, or expose students who use drugs, but to prevent the development of drug dependence and to help drug-dependent students become self-confident and drug-free. Effective testing programs, say *National Strategy* authors, include clear-cut consequences for students who use illegal drugs, such as suspension from an athletic activity, until the student has completed counseling.

The psychology behind student drug testing programs is straightforward, says Lisa Brady, principal of Hunterdon Central Regional High School in Flemington, New Jersey. "They give kids an 'out,'" Brady says. "Kids will tell you that the program gives them a reason to say no. They're just kids, after all; they need a crutch. Being able to say, 'I'm a cheerleader,' 'I'm in the band,' 'I'm a football player,' and 'My school drug tests'—it really gives them some tools [they need] to be able to say no."

Priority 2: Healing America's drug users—getting treatment resources where they are needed. The *National Strategy* uses the public health model as a way to understand the epidemiology of drug use and control its spread. The public health model, say strategy authors, is the only understanding of addiction that can explain why people continue to use drugs when the consequences are "a devastating disease of the brain and a terrible loss of human potential." Conventional wisdom on the topic, the authors say, suggests that young adults use drugs because they think they are invincible. Adults, presumably wiser but also self-destructive or simply optimistic, are thought to recognize the dangers but use drugs anyway. They watch an addict, say strategy authors, and tell themselves that things will be different for them. But the conventional wisdom only explains so much. "Why," ask the authors, "do people initiate the use of methamphetamine—a drug that can cause a complete unraveling of home life, work, and social connections in a matter of months?"

The public health model suggests a deeper explanation, they say, and that is that many people use drugs because they know someone who is using and not suffering any apparent consequences. Drug dependence spreads, say *National Strategy* authors, "because the vectors of contagion are 'asymptomatic' users who do not yet show the consequences of their drug habit, and who do not have the slightest awareness of their need to seek help." Hence, says the strategy, it is especially important to intervene with users during this "honeymoon" phase. One new approach suggests using the existing medical infrastructure—which already has extensive experience in identifying problem drinkers—to screen for drug use and offer appropriate and even brief interventions. The Department of Health and Human Services has recently awarded seven grants to advance the understanding of screening and brief intervention in treatment. In Chicago, for example, Cook County Hospital emergency room staff as well as doctors and nurses in other areas of the hospital are currently being trained to detect the signs of developing drug use and direct users into treatment.

Priority 3: Disrupting the markets—attacking the economic basis of the drug trade.
Authors of the *National Strategy* point out that the drug trade is a profit-making business, one whose necessary balance of costs and rewards can be disrupted, damaged, and destroyed. The main reason supply reduction matters to drug policy, they say, is that it makes drugs more expensive, less potent, and less available; and price, potency, and availability are thought to significantly influence both addicted use and casual use.

The drug trade is a worldwide market, embodying the strengths of a flexible, multinational enterprise and the weaknesses of a complex, far-flung illegal network that has to launder proceeds, pay bribes, and deal with the risks of betrayal by coconspirators and violence from competitors. Hence, since 2002, the strategy has focused on such sectors as the drug trade's agricultural sources, its processing and transportation systems, its organizational hierarchy, and its financing mechanisms. According to strategy authors, "We are now attacking the drug trade in all of its component parts, and we have made progress on all fronts. The U.S. Government's master list of targeted trafficking organizations is shorter this year [2004], thanks to the elimination of eight major trafficking organizations during the past fiscal year. Another seven organizations were weakened enough to be classified as "significantly disrupted."

The United States continues to focus international drug control efforts on source countries. International drug-trafficking organizations and their production and trafficking infrastructures are most concentrated, detectable, and vulnerable to effective law enforcement action in source countries. In addition, the cultivation of coca and opium poppies and the production of cocaine and heroin are labor intensive. For these reasons, cultivation and processing are relatively easier to disrupt than other aspects of the trade. The international drug-control strategy seeks to bolster source-country resources, capabilities, and political will to reduce cultivation, attack production, interdict drug shipments, and disrupt and dismantle trafficking organizations, including their command and control structure and financial underpinnings.

Visit the Office of National Drug Control Policy via **Web Extra 13–6**. Read the most recent *National Drug Control Strategy* in its entirety at **Library Extra 13–7** at crimtoday.com.

WEB
Extra
■ ■ ■ ■

LIBRARY
Extra
■ ■ ■ ■

Policy Consequences

There can be little doubt that the "war on drugs" has been a costly one. The federal government's fiscal year 2008 drug-control budget is $12.961 billion,[70] which represents an increase of $167 million, or 1.3%, over the fiscal year 2007 budget. Broken down by priorities within ONDCP's national drug-control strategy, Priority 1 funding (Stopping use before it starts—education and community action) totals $1.6 billion; Priority 2 funding (Healing America's drug users—getting treatment resources where they are needed) totals $3 billion; and Priority 3 funding (Disrupting the markets—attacking the economic basis of the drug trade) totals $8.3 billion. Budget allocations for specific functions include $1.863 billion for prevention, $2.941 billion for treatment, $1.435 billion for international crop control programs, $3.286 billion for interdiction, and $3.475 billion for domestic law enforcement.

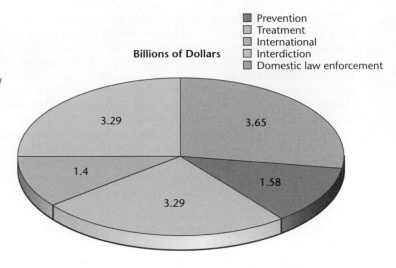

FIGURE 13–7

Federal Drug-Control Spending, 2008

Source: Office of National Drug Control Policy, *National Drug Control Strategy: FY 2008 Budget Summary* (Washington, DC: ONDCP, March 2007), p. 9.

Billions of Dollars

■ Prevention
□ Treatment
■ International
□ Interdiction
■ Domestic law enforcement

3.29   3.65
1.4
3.29   1.58

Seen another way, domestic law enforcement activities (the Priority 3 strategy, including all federal law enforcement programs within the nation's borders) accounted for the lion's share of federal antidrug expenditures, while demand-reduction programs (that is, educational activities) absorbed the smallest part of the antidrug budget. Figure 13–7 depicts actual and projected federal drug-control spending by functional area for fiscal year 2008. When state monies spent on the control of illegal drugs and the enforcement of drug laws are added to funds spent on antidrug-abuse education, and when the personal and social costs of drug abuse, identified earlier, are added in, the total cost of the war on drugs has been enormous.

The drug war has been costly in other ways as well. University of Delaware Professor James A. Inciardi describes the current situation this way: "As an outgrowth of the U.S. 'war on drugs' during the 1980s and early 1990s, all phases of the criminal justice process have become 'drug driven.'"[71] The same could be said of the nation's system of civil justice. "Although at first blush it may seem unrelated," says writer J. Michael McWilliams, "the 'war on drugs' has had a major impact on the civil justice system at both the state and federal levels. Our courts, like all of government and commerce, are institutions of limited resources. To the extent that court resources must be diverted to deal with the enormous influx of drug prosecutions, these resources are not available to resolve civil matters. . . . In some jurisdictions, drug cases account for as much as two-thirds of the criminal case filings. America's major cities have been especially affected."[72] In Los Angeles, for example, three-quarters of all criminal prosecutions are for drug charges or drug-related crimes.[73]

Strict enforcement has combined with a lock-'em-up philosophy to produce astonishingly high rates of imprisonment for drug offenders. The proportion of federal prisoners who are sentenced drug offenders rose from 38% in 1986 to 53% in 1990 and, according to the Bureau of Prisons, is 55% today.[74] Part of the increase is due to congressional action that, beginning in 1986, required high mandatory minimum sentences in drug cases, so that even first-time offenders were sentenced to long prison terms instead of probation. Approximately 70% of all first-time offenders in federal prisons are serving drug sentences. This is also true of 85% of illegal immigrants who are federal prisoners and 66% of female federal prisoners.[75]

Alternative Drug Policies

A number of alternative drug-control policies have been tried at both state and local levels. Primary among them have been decriminalization and legalization. Both strategies are "based on the assumption that drug abuse will never be eliminated."[76] Whereas **decriminalization** typically reduces criminal penalties associated with the personal possession of a controlled substance, **legalization** eliminates "the laws and associated

decriminalization

The redefinition of certain previously criminal behaviors into regulated activities that become "ticketable" rather than "arrestable."

legalization

Elimination of the laws and criminal penalties associated with certain behaviors—usually the production, sale, distribution, and possession of a controlled substance.

criminal penalties that prohibit its production, sale, distribution, and possession."[77] Decriminalization enhances personal freedoms in the face of state control, whereas legalization "is aimed," in part, "at reducing the control that criminals have over the drug trade."[78] Other arguments in favor of legalization include the following notions:

- In a free society, people should be permitted to do what they want, as long as they don't harm others. Drug use is considered by many to be a "victimless crime" that harms no one other than the user. Existing drug laws, say advocates of legalization, make criminals out of otherwise law-abiding individuals.

- Keeping drugs illegal means that they will continue to be high-priced. Legalizing them could greatly lower the price. The expense of illicit drugs, kept artificially high by their illegal status, encourages the commission of many drug-related crimes, such as robbery and burglary, by users seeking to feed their habits. Legalize drugs, some argue, and many other forms of crime will decline.

- Legalizing drugs would also reduce other forms of "vice," such as prostitution, pornography, and gambling, because many such offenses are also committed in an effort to obtain money to purchase high-priced drugs.

- Legalizing drugs would reduce the influence of criminal cartels now closely involved in the production, transportation, and sale of controlled substances.

- The illegal status and associated high cost of drugs indirectly victimize others, such as the family members of drug abusers, property owners in drug-infested areas, and taxpayers who must foot the enforcement bill. Legalization would end these forms of victimization.

- Drug legalization would dramatically reduce the opportunity for official corruption, which is now frequently associated with the illicit drug trade. Enforcement agents, politicians, correctional officers, and representatives of the judiciary would cease to be subject to corrupting influences dependent upon the vast financial resources available to drug-trafficking cartels.

- The legalization of drugs would result in increased tax revenues because drugs could be taxed just as alcohol and cigarettes are today.

- The legalization of drugs would allow for better control over public health issues related to drug use. The spread of AIDS, for example, caused in large part by the use of dirty needles in heroin injection, could be better controlled if sterilized needles were made legally available. Similarly, drug quality and potency could be monitored and ensured, resulting in fewer overdoses and emergency room visits by drug users, who are now uncertain of the chemical composition of the substances they consume.

Were controlled substances to be legalized, they might still be dispensed under controlled conditions (as in liquor stores), and penalties might still accrue to those who used them injudiciously (as while driving a car).

In 1996, California and Arizona voters passed resolutions legalizing the medical use of marijuana under certain circumstances. The thrust of California's Proposition 215, which the voters approved, is contained in the following language taken from the proposition: "(A) To ensure that seriously ill Californians have the right to obtain and use marijuana for medical purposes where that medical use is deemed appropriate and has been recommended by a physician who has determined that the person's health would benefit from the use of marijuana in the treatment of cancer, anorexia, AIDS, chronic pain, spasticity, glaucoma, arthritis, migraine, or any other illness for which marijuana provides relief. (B) To ensure that patients and their primary caregivers who obtain and use marijuana for medical purposes upon the recommendation of a physician are not subject to criminal prosecution or sanction."

Although the California law permits possession of marijuana for valid medicinal purposes, buying and selling the drug remain illegal, meaning that legitimate users may have to grow their own supply or buy it on the black market. Arizona law requires

Visitors to a cannabis festival in Amsterdam sample marijuana from a "bong." What are the advantages and disadvantages of drug legalization in the United States?

Source: Sjoerd Van Delden, AP Wide World Photos

prescribing physicians to write a scientific opinion explaining why the drug is appropriate for a specific patient, and a supportive second opinion is required before the drug can be legally used.

In 1999, Maine voters passed a referendum permitting some sick people to use small amounts of marijuana, and 26 other states and the District of Columbia have passed various laws and resolutions allowing therapeutic research programs involving the use of marijuana or asking the federal government to lift its ban on medical use of the drug.[79] Federal law enforcement agencies, however, have pointedly announced that they will continue to enforce federal antidrug laws prohibiting marijuana possession by citizens of *all* states. The agencies' stance spotlights an emerging policy issue—that is, who controls America's drug policy, the states or the federal government? In May 2001, the U.S. Supreme Court prohibited California marijuana-growing clubs from distributing the drug to those who are ill or in pain.[80] The ruling effectively prohibits the use of medical marijuana in virtually all situations.

Opponents of drug legalization argue that

WEB
Extra

- Reducing official control over psychoactive substances is immoral and socially irresponsible and would result in heightened costs to society from drug abuse.

- Drug legalization would simply increase the types of problems now associated with alcohol abuse, such as lost time from work, drug-induced criminality (especially violence), the loss of personal self-control, and the severing of important social relationships.

- Drug laws are enforceable; we are winning the "war on drugs"; and the fact that laws are not *easily* enforceable is no reason to eliminate them. (Laws against murder and rape, for example, have not entirely eliminated such crimes, and there is no conclusive evidence that laws seriously reduce the numbers of crimes committed in any category in which intense needs or emotions are involved as motivating factors.)

Learn more about drug abuse and social policy at **Web Extra 13–7.**

Prostitution

Prostitution can be defined as the offering of one's self for hire for the purpose of engaging in sexual relations, or the act or practice of engaging in sexual activity for money or its equivalent. As the second part of this definition indicates, in heterosexual prostitution involving men as clients (or "johns"), and women as sexual "service providers," the man can also be charged with and found guilty of the offense of prostitution. Except for parts of Nevada, prostitution is a criminal act throughout the United States, where it is generally classified as a misdemeanor.

The activities of prostitutes have not always been illegal. In early Greece, for example, some prostitutes even held exalted positions as temple maidens with whom sexual intercourse served as a form of deity worship. The Grecian *hetaerae*, or common prostitutes, were generally accorded high social status and their trade as sex workers was seen as a respectable occupation.[81]

In the United States, over 92,000 men, women, and juveniles are arrested yearly for the crime of prostitution.[82] The number of juveniles engaging in prostitution is estimated to be between 100,000 and 300,000 annually.

prostitution

The offering of one's self for hire for the purpose of engaging in sexual relations, or the act or practice of engaging in sexual activity for money or its equivalent.

Morals Legislation

Laws against prostitution have a long and varied history in the United States. Underlying the statutes, however, are fundamental questions about whether or not to legislate morality. The question of whether and to what extent the criminal law should reflect and enforce the morality of the society it represents is one of the classic debates in criminal law literature. Most people agree that actions that harm others should be controlled, but not everyone sees sex work, especially when willingly undertaken, as harmful.

Some people argue that every organized society is permitted, and perhaps even obligated, to enforce morality by means of criminal or other legal sanctions. In a classic work on the "conservative thesis," legal philosopher H. L. A. Hart notes that the majority in society often believe that they have the right to follow their own moral convictions, as well as the right to preserve their "moral environment" as a thing of value.[83] Preserving one's moral environment, says Hart, implies the power to insist that all members of society abide by certain moral convictions. Hart went on to identify a "disintegration thesis" under which it could be maintained that public morality is the "cement of society," which must be kept in place in order to prevent social disintegration. Arguments in favor of criminalizing street prostitution can be seen in Table 13–4.

Hart was himself a legal positivist, meaning that he held the personal view that laws are rules made by human beings, and that, as such, they have no necessary or fundamental connection to morality. Hart would have likely agreed with British Jurist Patrick Devlin, who argued the need for "toleration of the maximum individual freedom that is consistent with the integrity of society" and with the rights of others. The classic statement that the law should not unnecessarily criminalize what are personal moral decisions that harm no one (other than, perhaps the person making them) was offered by the nineteenth-century English philosopher John Stuart Mill. Mill argued that society should interfere with an individual's freedom of action only "to prevent harm to others. His own good, either physical or moral, is not a sufficient warrant" for interference.

A Typology of Prostitutes

There are many different venues within which sexual services are sold.[84] They include so-called red-light districts, commercial houses of prostitution, massage parlors, nude photography or studios, strip clubs, stag parties, and erotic dance theaters. Using location as the basis for a typology of prostitutes produces the following categories: streetwalkers, bar/hotel prostitutes, call girls, hotel/brothel prostitutes, and others who don't clearly fit any of these categories.

> **TABLE 13–4 Harms Caused by Street Prostitution**
>
> ***Moral and Nuisance Concerns***
> - Prostitution offends some citizens' moral standards.
> - Prostitution is a nuisance to passersby and to nearby residents and businesses.
> - Prostitutes and clients offend uninvolved people in the area when they solicit them.
> - Juveniles, less capable of making informed choices, may become prostitutes.
>
> ***Public Health Concerns***
> - Prostitutes and clients may spread sexually transmitted diseases such as syphilis, herpes, and AIDS.
> - Used condoms, syringes, and other paraphernalia left on the ground are unsightly and potentially hazardous.
> - Prostitutes who do not have access to proper facilities may relieve themselves or bathe in public.
>
> ***Personal Safety Concerns***
> - Clients may harm prostitutes.
> - Clients or prostitutes may be defrauded, robbed, or assaulted.
> - Pimps may financially and physically exploit prostitutes and clients.
>
> ***Spillover-Effect Concerns***
> - Street prostitution and street drug markets are often linked.
> - Prostitution may provide a seedbed for organized crime.
> - Prostitutes create parking and traffic problems where they congregate.
> - Prostitution attracts strangers and criminals to a neighborhood.
>
> ***Economic Concerns***
> - Legitimate businesses may lose customers who avoid the area because of prostitution.
> - Prostitutes' presence may negatively affect the area economy, reducing property values and limiting property use.
>
> ***Civil Rights Concerns***
> - Prostitutes, as citizens, have rights that need to be protected.
>
> ***Police Integrity Concerns***
> - Policing prostitution creates special opportunities for police officers to engage in unethical conduct, such as taking payments in exchange for nonenforcement, because prostitutes, pimps, and clients are in weak positions to complain about police misconduct.
>
> *Source*: Adapted from Michael S. Scott and Kelly Dedel, *Street Prostitution*, 2nd ed. (Washington, DC: Office of Community Oriented Policing Services, U.S. Department of Justice, 2006).

Streetwalkers are generally seen as the lowest class of prostitute because they solicit customers in public—often from curbsides and on foot. They tend to be highly visible, and their dress is revealing, which tends to both advertise their services and entice customers. Streetwalkers perform their services in customers' cars, in alleyways, in nearby hotels, darkened doorways, and so on. Streetwalkers command the lowest prices and have little bargaining power over things like condom use and choice of sexual practices. They also face the highest risk of harm from customers and others. They also run the highest risk of arrest.

Bar/hotel prostitutes, as the name implies, work in bars, clubs, and hotels. They may have a standing relationship with managers, bartenders, and security personnel—with whom they share their profits or for whom they provide "free" services. They tend to "work" conventions, sporting events, and business meetings. Desk clerks, valets, and even discreet concierge employees sometimes refer clients to prostitutes. Services are typically provided in the establishment, perhaps in a dark corner or back room, or in a hotel room rented by the customer or prostitute. The prices charged by bar/hotel prostitutes varies considerably according to the prestige of the

Crime in the News

Centerfold Accused in Call-Girl Ring

DULUTH, Ga.—For years, Lisa Ann Taylor's neighbors suspected something was going on behind the doors of her white-columned, million-dollar mansion in one of suburban Atlanta's most exclusive neighborhoods.

Scantily clad women were seen posing for photos in the driveway. Cars and trucks came and went at all hours. And there were loud parties.

Despite repeated calls to police about the suspicious goings-on, there was no evidence of a crime. That is, until six weeks ago, when authorities were tipped off to a website showing Taylor—a former Penthouse Pet of the Month—sprawled topless on an ottoman and brazenly advertising services ranging from $300 one-hour photo shoots to "dream dates" that included a one-hour "show."

Police raided the red-brick mansion Wednesday and found what they described as a high-class brothel and the headquarters of a call-girl ring whose customers received favors limited only by their imaginations and their ability to pay.

Among the services offered was sex with the centerfold and other women for an entire weekend for $10,000, District Attorney Danny Porter said.

"Whatever was asked for had a price," Porter said.

Taylor, 42, and her alleged business partner and fellow call girl, 30-year-old Nicole Probert, were arrested on charges of prostitution, racketeering and conspiracy to possess cocaine. They were released from jail Thursday on $27,000 bail each.

The brothel's customers included doctors, lawyers and businessmen, and they, too, could face charges, the district attorney said, in a warning that could make men jittery across Atlanta and beyond. Taylor and her friends are accused of using their website to offer their services during visits to Boston, New York, Chicago and suburban Milwaukee.

Probert's attorney David Fuller denied she was involved in prostitution. He said she is a successful real estate developer and a single mother who recently came into an inheritance and did not need money.

"This is just not her. This is a nightmare for her. She can't believe this is happening," Fuller said.

It was not immediately known if Taylor had an attorney.

The mansion is near the ninth hole at Sugarloaf Country Club, home of the PGA's BellSouth Classic each May. It is in a gated neighborhood, about 20 miles from Atlanta, whose current or former residents include rapper Bow Wow, Atlanta Falcons wide receiver Brian Finneran and Washington Redskins tight end Brian Kozlowski.

Porter could not say for sure how long the illegal activity was going on, but neighbors have been complaining for at least three years.

Among other things, neighbors thought it was odd that all the basement windows were blacked out. Also, they saw lots of modest-looking cars and trucks that appeared out of place in the well-to-do neighborhood. In addition, scantily clad women were seen in the windows of Probert's house in nearby Lawrenceville.

Taylor—a 1985 Penthouse centerfold who used the name Melissa Wolf professionally—also held lavish Halloween parties, which were advertised in fliers passed out through the neighborhood and included fireworks, costumed characters, professional decorations and a haunted house for children. But some parents declared the house off-limits for trick-or-treating.

"The neighbors told us they wouldn't let their kids go to the house because they were afraid of who might answer the door," the district attorney said.

The prosecutor's office said it was tipped off to the website by *The Gwinnett Daily Post*, after an editor got an anonymous call from someone who pointed out websites where Taylor's alleged customers could rate her services.

Carol Northcutt, 49, who lives a block away, said many neighbors knew Taylor was in the adult entertainment industry. Northcutt said she once saw a photo shoot in Taylor's driveway with scantily clad women posing in a convertible.

"I knew she was in adult films and that there were cars in and out," she said. But prostitution? "Did I think for a minute it was that? No."

Lisa Ann Taylor, a 1985 Penthouse Pet who modeled under the name Melissa Wolf, speaks during a news conference in Norcross, Georgia, in 2007. Taylor, 42, was accused of running a high-class brothel from her million-dollar home in the Sugarloaf Country Club community in Duluth, Georgia. She was also charged with racketeering and conspiracy to possess cocaine. Why is prostitution illegal in most parts of the United States?

Source: AP Wide World Photos/John Bazemore

Discussion Questions

1. Prostitution is sometimes called a victimless crime. What does that mean?

2. Is there such a thing as a truly victimless crime? Why or why not?

3. Do you think that prostitution is a true victimless crime? Explain your answer.

For the latest crime and justice news, visit www.crimenews.info.

Criminal Profiles

Heidi Lynne Fleiss

"Alexander the Great conquered the world at 32. I conquered it at 22."[i] What more could the media want? Hollywood; young, good-looking women selling sex; a mysterious list of rich celebrity clients that kept (and keeps) threatening to crop up; and a young, attractive, articulate, and outspoken advocate of a woman's right to sell her body for sex sensationally outed as the "madam to the stars."[ii] Wow!

Fleiss's cachet in the sex trade was the stable of exceptionally beautiful young women she kept available for clients willing to pay top dollar. And top dollar it was, with some of the prostitutes making from $1,500 to as much as $1 million per customer. Their services even included travel to Paris, London, and other overseas locations to meet the demands of the rich and desiring.[iii]

But Fleiss did not recruit members for her workforce—they found *her*. Some were drawn by the potential for high earnings, as Fleiss paid her girls 40% of the profit from each "booking," including tips. For others, the lure was the chance to frolic in the environment of the rich and famous. The lifestyle the women enjoyed was beyond the dreams of most and included the opportunity to party with some of the richest and most powerful men in the world. Through mid-1993, Fleiss pocketed several million dollars per year from her role in the enterprise.

Heidi Fleiss's notorious high-priced prostitution ring was the stuff of Hollywood lore, but no more so than her arrest, trial, incarceration, and post-release emergence as an unrepentant sex entrepreneur. Fleiss was initially arrested in June 1993 on state charges that included five counts of pandering and one count of narcotics possession. On July 28, 1994, during her state trial, she was indicted by a federal grand jury on charges of income tax evasion, money laundering, and 14 counts of conspiracy.

Fleiss was convicted in federal court of income tax evasion, money laundering, and eight counts of conspiracy in August 1995. She also pled guilty in state court to the pandering charges. The combined sentences resulted in her serving three years in prison.

Renowned Hollywood Madame Heidi Fleiss at the Melbourne, Australia, Stock Exchange for the start of trading of "The Daily Planet" bordello—the first brothel in the world to be listed on a national stock exchange. For years, Fleiss's prostitution business had catered to the rich and famous in Hollywood and Los Angeles. She spent 20 months in prison after being convicted in 1995 on federal charges of conspiracy, tax evasion, and money laundering. Should Fleiss have received a longer sentence?

Source: Regis Martin/Getty Images

Even her father, millionaire Dr. Paul Fleiss, became ensnared in Fleiss's legal woes when he was indicted on federal charges for allegedly signing a $1 million bank loan under false pretenses. Dr. Fleiss was ultimately convicted of money laundering related to his daughter's prostitution ring. His sentence included one day in jail, three years of probation, and 625 hours of community service.[iv]

establishment with which they are associated. The woman's risk of harm and arrest are low to moderate as long as the collaborative relation with the establishment is maintained.

Call girls work for escort services on an "outcall" basis. Escort services frequently advertise the availability of girls with flyers, in newspapers, or even in the yellow pages, on TV, and via the Internet (where it is sometimes referred to as "cyberprostitution"). Consequently, call girls are not restricted to specific locales. Most call girls see relatively well-to-do clients who prefer the anonymity of a referral service, and many of the service's customers are regulars who maintain a standing relationship with the service. Prostitutes are typically assigned by the agency to customers who may select them from pictures posted on the Internet or printed in brochures. Fees are often charged to credit cards by the customer before the girl is dispatched. Once on site, however, prostitutes may negotiate with the customer for specific services. Through this arrangement the escort service tends to insulate itself from legal action—claiming that it simply arranged for companionship. Call girls depend on the agency to screen customers, and screening can be done by referrals from other agencies or by established clients who have established relationships with the agency. Prices in this market segment reach the highest

Born in Los Angeles on December 30, 1965, Heidi Fleiss showed a precocious flair for business as early as age 12. A popular and responsible babysitter, she soon found herself with more job offers than she could handle herself, so she established a babysitting service by hiring her friends from school to handle some of the jobs. She, of course, got a cut of all the fees.

Her school performance, however, did not keep pace with her business enterprise. Low grades in junior high and high school ultimately led to her dropping out in the tenth grade. For the next few years, she held a variety of low-wage jobs from which she took little pleasure. Fleiss's aspirations never wavered, however, and she was constantly on the lookout for the right opportunity.

That opportunity came about when she and a friend attended a party at 61-year-old millionaire financier Bernie Cornfeld's estate. Impressed with Fleiss, Cornfeld hired her as his personal secretary, an arrangement that, in short order, evolved into a personal relationship. Fleiss sought to deepen the relationship to a live-in level, which she hoped would result in her enjoying a financially secure life of privilege and hedonistic pursuits. Cornfeld, however, had a well-known appetite for classical beauties, which he enthusiastically indulged. His continued dalliances signaled an unwillingness to remain in a monogamous relationship, and the couple eventually broke up.

Still, Fleiss walked away with newly acquired business skills learned from associating with Cornfeld and his friends. A chance meeting with the reigning queen madam of the Los Angeles area, Madam Alex, gave Fleiss entrée to the sex industry.

Madam Alex was, at that time, looking for a replacement to take over her business operations so that she could live a privileged retirement. Fleiss's business acumen fit the bill so well that she increased Madam Alex's profits by more than 400%. But when Madam Alex proved to be less than generous in sharing her largess, Fleiss went off on her own.

And the rest is sex industry history. Ultimately, Fleiss's client base included top producers, directors, and movie stars from the Hollywood scene, as well as some of the world's most famous (and wealthiest) men. Business tycoons, Middle Eastern sheiks, members of royalty, and various heads of state are counted among those to whom she provided women for sexual services.[v]

Since her release from prison, Fleiss has parlayed her notoriety into a series of successful business ventures, including a men's apparel store in Los Angeles called "Heidi's Wear." A book (*Pandering*), a DVD (*Sex Tips*), a Web site, and repeated appearances on late-night talk shows have kept her in the public eye. Ever the sensationalist, Fleiss's current project, which she describes as a "stud farm,"[vi] involves converting a brothel in southern Nevada into a resort staffed by male prostitutes to service Fleiss's hoped-for female customers.[vii]

Recently, Fleiss was hired by Australia's first-ever publicly traded brothel. The Daily Planet, as the brothel is called, hired Fleiss to spice up its stock listing and tout itself as a recession-proof, five-star hotel with the best available amenities in all of Australia.[viii]

Notes:

[i] "Then & Now: Heidi Fleiss," CNN, June 19, 2005, http://www.cnn.com/2005/US/02/28/cnn25.tan.fleiss (accessed June 1, 2007).

[ii] Rachael Bell, "Heidi Fleiss: The Million Dollar Madam," CourtTV Crime Library, http://www.crimelibrary.com/notorious_murders/celebrity/heidi_fleiss/index.html (accessed June 1, 2007).

[iii] Ibid.

[iv] Ibid.

[v] Ibid.

[vi] "Fleiss Plans Makeover for Nevada Brothel," *USA Today*, November 16, 2005, http://www.usatoday.com/life/people/2005-11-16-fleiss_x.htm (accessed June 1, 2007).

[vii] Steve Friess, "Betting on the Studs," *Newsweek*, December 12, 2005, http://www.msnbc.msn.com/id/10313009/site/newsweek (accessed June 1, 2007).

[viii] "News Around the World," Associated Press, Melbourne, June 2, 2003, http://heidifleiss.com/news-press.htm (accessed May 21, 2007).

levels, and escorts have considerable bargaining power over such things as the use of condoms and the kinds of sexual services provided. Call girls face the lowest risk of harm or arrest.

House or brothel prostitutes ply their trade in legal environments—but are limited to only a few venues in the United States. Legalized prostitution, however, is common in a number of other countries, including Australia (where laws vary by state), New Zealand, the Netherlands (which outlaws pimping and trafficking of human beings), and Germany (where advertising sex services remains illegal). In countries where prostitution is legal, it is still subject to health and locality controls, as well as age and other restrictions. In such locales, prostitutes are generally licensed sex workers who pay taxes, belong to unions, and are eligible for government benefits such as unemployment wages, medical services, and so on. Some countries tolerate prostitution, but restrict activities associated with it, such as pimping, the operation of brothels, advertising services, etc. Others technically permit prostitution but have other kinds of restrictions which can make its practice difficult. In this category are countries like Brazil, Canada, Costa Rica, Scotland, and Denmark (where prostitution is legal, but profiting from it is not). Some countries, like Sweden, allow the selling of sexual services, but criminalize pimping and the purchasing of sex services (on the theory that such activity demeans women). In Japan, vaginal prostitution is illegal, but fellatio for money is not considered prostitution.

In the United States, brothel prostitution is an option available to the governments of rural counties in Nevada. Nevada's house prostitutes operate with posted fees, and generally earn 40% to 60% of the revenue they generate. State law requires that they be fingerprinted, undergo regular health examinations, and keep financial records for tax purposes. Rhode Island is the only other state in the United States in which the selling of sexual services is not specifically outlawed, although operating a brothel and engaging in solicitation for the purpose of prostitution are.

Clients of Prostitutes

About ten years ago, the NIJ undertook sponsorship of an extensive look at prostitutes' clients—commonly known as "johns."[85] The NIJ-funded study, conducted by Martin A. Monto of the University of Portland, explored the sex-related behavior characteristic of men who solicited prostitutes. The study, whose results were published in 2000,[86] examined the effects of the First Offender Prostitution Program (FOPP) in San Francisco, California, and similar programs in other cities. These programs offered johns an opportunity to pay a fine and attend a daylong seminar rather than go to jail. Participants were advised that no further legal action would be taken against them if they successfully avoided rearrest for a year. If there was a subsequent offense, however, the individual was prosecuted for the new offense and the original charge was reinstated.

Monto surveyed 1,291 men arrested for soliciting street prostitutes before they participated in FOPP, and in other "johns programs" in Las Vegas, Nevada; Portland, Oregon; and Santa Clara, California. He collected data on why men visit prostitutes, their attitudes regarding violence against women, and the consequences of seeing sex as a commodity.

Monto found that 72% of the men surveyed had attended some college. They ranged in age from 18 to 84 years, with a median age of 37, and were less likely to be married than other men. Although their motives for seeking sex with a prostitute differed, there were similarities among certain groups. Married clients and college graduates were more likely to want a different kind of sex than they had with their regular partners. Unmarried clients and noncollege graduates reportedly felt shy and awkward when trying to meet women but did not feel intimidated by prostitutes.

Monto also explored the men's attitudes toward the rape myths discussed in Chapter 10. Less than one-half of 1% of the men surveyed indicated acceptance of the majority of rape myths identified there. Twenty percent, however, demonstrated acceptance of four or more such myths. Although the evidence wasn't clear, researchers believed that it is this latter group that may be responsible for perpetrating violent acts against women for hire.

Monto also measured the degree to which clients regarded sexuality as a commercial commodity and found that the greater a client's belief that women and sex were commercial products, the more frequently he would visit prostitutes. This mind-set was also a strong predictor of the acceptance of rape myths, less frequent condom use with prostitutes, and a disinclination to view prostitution as a demeaning profession for women.

Finally, Monto and his colleagues studied the recidivism of those clients who participated in the San Francisco and Portland programs. Although both programs had a recidivism rate of about 2%, researchers acknowledge that conclusions about the programs' efficacy in reducing recidivism were hampered by a lack of available baseline data for comparative purposes. Read Monto's entire 80-page report on street prostitution at **Library Extra 13–8** at crimtoday.com.

LIBRARY
Extra
▪ ▪ ▪ ▪

Feminist Perspectives on Prostitution

Prostitution represents a significant issue in today's feminist thought. Some feminist thinkers argue that prostitution exploits and demeans women, while also subjecting them to the dangers of violence and disease. In the 1980s Andrea Dworkin, an ex-prostitute and antipornography crusader, wrote in her writings that commercial sex is a form of rape perpetrated by poverty and frequent overt violence (often by pimps).[87]

Others take quite a different approach, saying that selling sex need not be inherently exploitative and might actually be liberating because it fulfills a woman's rights to control her body and her sexuality. Those in this camp are likely to see prostitution as legitimate sex work, and to argue for the legalization of prostitution with added protections for those who choose sex work as a trade. The recent redefinition of prostitution as sex work has been accompanied by the development of a sex worker activism movement, comprising organizations such Call off Your Old Tired Ethics (COYOTE) in the United States, and the Australian Prostitutes Collective in that country. COYOTE was founded in 1973 and advocates for the repeal of prostitution laws and an end to the stigma associated with sex work. The Australian Prostitutes Collective was created in 1983 in Melborune, and changed its name to the Victorian Prostitutes Collective (VPC) in 1988. VPC operates safe houses for the protection of women victims of violence, and is the only pro-prostitution organization in the world with government funding.[88]

Feminists who believe that prostitution is inherently exploitative reject the idea that prostitution can be reformed. These feminists believe that the assumptions that women exist for men's sexual enjoyment, that all men "need" sex, or that the bodily integrity and sexual pleasure of women is irrelevant underlie the whole idea of prostitution, and make it an inherently exploitative, sexist practice. One feminist argument against Dworkin's position is that prostitution, insofar as it colludes with the perception of an inherent "need" on the part of men for sexual release, is exploiting men more than it exploits women.

In an interesting critique of what he calls "extreme radical feminist theory," as represented by the writings of Dworkin and others, sociologist Ronald Weitzer of George Washington University says that four core claims characterize this body of literature.[89] They are:

1. Prostitution involves male domination and exploitation of women regardless of historical time period, societal context, or legal status.

2. Violence is omnipresent in prostitution.

3. Female prostitutes lack agency (that is, they cannot actively make choices about whether or not to stay in prostitution).

4. Legalization or decriminalization would only make the situation worse.

Weitzer sees such claims as counterproductive in that they tend to stifle debate over prostitution, and effectively divert research programs through what he calls "considerable ideological contamination of our understanding of prostitution." Extreme feminists, Weitzer says, have contributed to a growing moral panic over prostitution by tying it to sex trafficking and, in particular, the trafficking of children for sex. Many of the radicals' claims, says Weitzer, are simply false. Violence is not inevitably associated with prostitution, some prostitutes (especially those engaged in legal prostitution) see themselves positively, and prostitution can be lawfully organized in ways that protect the prostitutes' health, rights, and freedoms.

Legalization and Decriminalization

A number of arguments have been made in favor of legalizing or decriminalizing prostitution. Under outright legalization, women beyond a specified age would be able to offer paid sexual services with few restrictions, as is currently the case in parts of Nevada. Decriminalization, on the other hand, would significantly reduce the criminal penalties associated with prostitution, but would still regulate the practice and might require counseling and alternative employment programs for women in that line of work in an effort to curtail the practice.

Those who argue in favor of legalization say that current practices by the justice system tend to force prostitution out of areas where it might naturally be found (that is, certain hotels, massage parlors, etc.), and onto the streets and into other parts of the community. Similarly, they say, keeping prostitution illegal means that prostitutes will continue to be viewed as easy targets for pimps, sex offenders, and violent predators.

Finally legalization frees law enforcement resources to be used in the prevention and investigation of more serious types of crime.

Those who argue against legalization[90] say that legalization promotes other crimes like sex trafficking, and that it will expand the sex industry rather than eliminate it. The Coalition Against Trafficking in Women-International (CATW) conducted two studies on sex trafficking and prostitution in which it interviewed almost 200 victims of commercial sexual exploitation. CATW found that "women in prostitution indicated that prostitution establishments did little to protect them, regardless of whether they were in legal or illegal establishments." Citing one respondent to the surveys, CATW relayed the observation that "The only time they protect anyone is to protect the customers."

SUMMARY

The focus of this chapter is public order crimes, specifically drug offenses and prostitution. Drug abuse has a long and varied history in American society. Policy responses to abuse have been equally diverse. Controlled substances are generally grouped according to both pharmacological and legal criteria into the following seven categories: stimulants, depressants, cannabis, narcotics, hallucinogens, anabolic steroids, and inhalants. A separate eighth category, that of dangerous drugs, provides a kind of legal and definitional catchall.

Drugs are linked to other kinds of offenses as drug users commit both property and personal crimes to acquire the money necessary to continue uninterrupted use, and drug traffickers use violence and intimidation to gain access to profitable markets. Although recent statistics on drug use show some decline, a hard-core population of illicit drug users remains. Strategies to reduce the flow of illegal drugs into this country, while meeting with some success, are being increasingly supplemented with programs of education and treatment intended to reduce the demand for controlled substances. In the meantime, the potential for official corruption in the face of a lucrative drug trade remains high. Drug traffickers are now in control of vast amounts of money, leading some to suggest that only legalization can solve the secondary problems of drug-related crime, official corruption, and drug-related public health concerns.

Prostitution, the second main focus of this chapter, is a morals offense with a long and varied history in the United States. Various kinds of prostitutes, ranging from streetwalkers to call girls, were discussed, and the clients of prostitutes, or *johns*, were described. Finally, feminist perspectives on prostitution were explored, and critiques of some of these perspectives were offered. As this chapter points out, the fundamental question underlying morals offenses like prostitution and drug use is whether and to what extent the criminal law should reflect and enforce the morality of the society it represents.

KEY TERMS

Arrestee Drug Abuse Monitoring (ADAM) Program, 549

dangerous drug, 537

decriminalization, 560

designer drugs, 546

drug-defined crime, 549

drug-related crime, 549

drug trafficking, 546

heroin signature program (HSP), 548

interdiction, 555

legalization, 560

National Survey on Drug Use and Health (NSDUH), 530

Office of National Drug Control Policy (ONDCP), 530

pharmaceutical diversion 546

prostitution, 563

psychoactive substance, 529

QUESTIONS FOR REVIEW

1. What are some of the laws that criminalize and restrict the use of drugs in the United States, and what drugs do they control? How did those laws come into being, and why?

2. What is a *dangerous drug*? What are the various controlled substance categories described by federal

   law? How do the types of illegal drugs discussed in this chapter fit into those categories?

3. How do controlled substances reach the drug-consuming portion of the American public? How might drug trafficking be curtailed?

4. What is the relationship between drug trafficking, drug abuse, and other forms of crime?

5. What government efforts have been made to reduce the incidence of drug use in America? What are the pros and cons of each?

6. What is prostitution? What are the various types of prostitutes identified in this chapter?

QUESTIONS FOR REFLECTION

1. This book emphasizes a social problems versus social responsibility theme. Which of the social policy approaches to controlling drug abuse discussed in this chapter (if any) appear to be predicated upon a social problems approach? Which (if any) are predicated upon a social responsibility approach? Explain the nature of the relationship.

2. What are some of the costs of illicit drug use in the United States today? Which costs can be more easily reduced than others? How would you reduce the costs of illegal drug use?

3. What is the difference between decriminalization and legalization? Should drug use remain illegal? What do you think of the arguments in favor of legalization? Those against?

4. What is asset forfeiture? How has asset forfeiture been used in the fight against illegal drugs? How have recent U.S. Supreme Court decisions limited federal asset seizures? Do you agree that such limitations were necessary? Why?

5. How is prostitution like other crimes? How does it differ?

6. Do you think that prostitution should be legalized? Why or why not?

WEB QUEST

Visit the federal Office of National Drug Control Policy at www.whitehousedrugpolicy.gov, and read the *National Drug Control Strategy* posted there. What topics are covered in the document? Who wrote the foreword? What message was that person trying to communicate? Summarize the information that the document provides about each major drug category, and briefly describe the main points of the drug-control program that it outlines. Which of the strategy's stated goals do you think deserves the most attention? Why? Submit your work to your instructor if asked to do so.

NOTES

1 Gary E. Johnson, "Bad Investment," A Mother Jones.com Special Report, July 10, 2001, http://www.motherjones.com/prisons/investment.html (accessed July 30, 2006).

2 "New Drug Czar Targets 'Unacceptably High' Rates of Drug Use Among Students," ONDCP press release, December 19, 2001, http://www.whitehousedrugpolicy.gov/news/press01/121901.html (accessed February 3, 2007).

3 Address to the nation with President Ronald Reagan, September 14, 1986.

4 The Netscape "Politics" discussion list, May 4, 2007, http://politics.netscape.com/story/2007/02/27/should-we-legalize-prostitution-and-other-tales-from-germany (accessed July 10, 2007).

5 The information in this section comes from Niko Price, "Drug Lord's Body Hangs in Limbo," Associated Press, July 6, 1997; and Michael J. Sniffen, "DEA Eyes Drug Death Aftermath," Associated Press, July 7, 1997.

6 "Did U.S. Anti-Narcotics Agents Kill the Lord of the Skies?" *Independent* (London), via Simon & Schuster NewsLink, July 12, 1997.

7 Ibid.

8 Paul Savoy, "When Criminal Rights Go Wrong: Forget Liberal. Forget Conservative. Think Common Sense," *Washington Monthly*, Vol. 21, No. 11 (December 1989), p. 36.

9 http://librearts.com/wsn8439.html (accessed September 21, 2007).

10 Data in this section are derived from Substance Abuse and Mental Health Services Administration, *2006 National Survey on Drug Use and Health* (Rockville, MD: SAMHSA, 2007).

11 Numbers total more than 100% because of rounding.

12 Drug Enforcement Administration, *Overview of Drug Use in the United States*, www.dea.gov/stats/overview.htm (accessed April 8, 2007).

13 Bureau of Justice Statistics, *Drug and Crime Facts, 1993* (Washington, DC: U.S. Department of Justice, August 1994), p. 25.

14 Information in this section comes from Loyd D. Johnston, Patrick M. O'Malley, Jerald G. Bachman, and John E. Schulenberg, *Monitoring the Future National Results on Adolescent Drug Use: Overview of Key Findings, 2006* (Bethesda, MD: National Institute on Drug Abuse, 2006).

15 Office of National Drug Control Policy, *Drug Data Summary Fact Sheet* (Washington, DC: ONDCP, March 2003), p. 1, http://www.whitehousedrugpolicy.gov/pdf/drug_datasum.pdf (accessed May 18, 2007).

16 Ibid., p. 2.

17 Mike Cooper, "CDC Charts Impact of AIDS among Blacks, Hispanics," Reuters, September 8, 1994.

18 National Institute on Drug Abuse and National Institute on Alcohol Abuse and Alcoholism, *The Economic Costs of Alcohol*

and *Drug Abuse in the United States, 1992* (Washington, DC: U.S. Government Printing Office, 1998).

[19] National Narcotics Intelligence Consumers Committee, *The NNICC Report, 1996: The Supply of Illicit Drugs to the United States* (Arlington, VA: Drug Enforcement Administration, 1997), p. 69.

[20] Most of the information in the paragraphs that follow is taken from ibid. and from the Office of National Drug Control Policy, *Pulse Check: Trends in Drug Abuse, January–June 1998* (Washington, DC: ONDCP, 1998).

[21] Much of the information in this section comes from the National Institute on Drug Abuse's Web site, http://www.nida.nih.gov, (accessed January 6, 2007); and from the Office of National Drug Control Policy, *Pulse Check: Special Report; Methamphetamine Trends in Five Western States and Hawaii* (Washington, DC: ONDCP, 1997).

[22] James A. Inciardi, *The War on Drugs II* (Mountain View, CA: Mayfield, 1992), p. 69.

[23] Michael D. Lyman and Gary W. Potter, *Drugs in Society: Causes, Concepts and Control* (Cincinnati: Anderson, 1991), p. 45.

[24] National Inhalant Prevention Coalition Web site, http://www.inhalants.org (accessed January 6, 2007).

[25] Ibid.

[26] Sherry Green, *Preventing Illegal Diversion of Chemicals: A Model Statute* (Washington, DC: National Institute of Justice, November 1993), p. 2.

[27] Ibid., p. 79.

[28] The provisions of the Domestic Chemical Diversion Control Act of 1993 became effective April 16, 1994.

[29] As defined by federal law and precedent.

[30] "Colombian Drug Smugglers' Submarine an Evolutionary Step," Associated Press, September 8, 2000.

[31] National Briefing: "Largest Drug Seizure at Sea," *New York Times*, April 24, 2007, http://query.nytimes.com/gst/fullpage.html?res=9801EEDD143EF937A15757C0A9619C8B63 (accessed May 10, 2007).

[32] National Narcotics Intelligence Consumers Committee, *The NNICC Report, 1996.*

[33] "Not So Slick: Customs Fishes Two Tons of Cocaine out of Cooking Grease Tanker in Laredo," *U.S. Customs Service News*, May 14, 1998.

[34] DEA, "Record Drug Seizures," http://www.dea.gov/major/seizures.htm (accessed January 8, 2007).

[35] National Narcotics Intelligence Consumers Committee, *The NNICC Report, 1993* (Washington, DC: U.S. Government Printing Office, 1994).

[36] Ibid., p. 35.

[37] Bureau of Justice Statistics, *Drugs, Crime and the Justice System* (Washington, DC: U.S. Government Printing Office, 1992), p. 2.

[38] Ibid.

[39] Ibid., p. 126.

[40] Ibid., p. 2.

[41] See Federal Register, Vol. 71. No. 218 (November 13, 2006), http://a257.g.akamaitech.net/7/257/2422/01jan20061800/edocket.access.gpo.gov/2006/pdf/E6-19103.pdf (accessed July 27, 2007).

[42] See, Office of National Drug Control Policy, "Improving Federal Drug-Related Data Systems," http://www.whitehousedrugpolicy.gov/publications/policy/ndcs06_data_supl/ds_improv_fed_drg.pdf (accessed July 27, 2007).

[43] Abt Associates, Inc., "Arrestee Drug Abuse Monitoring Program (ADAM) II," March 14, 2007. Prepared for Robert L. Cohen, Executive Office of the President, Office of National Drug Control Policy, Washington, DC.

[44] National Institute of Justice, *Arrestee Drug Abuse Monitoring (ADAM) Program: 2000 Annual Report* (Washington, DC: NIJ, 2003).

[45] Much of the material in this section is adapted from NIJ, Office of Justice Programs, "Study Shows Substantial Levels of Drug Use among Arrestees across the Nation," *OJP News*, July 20, 2000.

[46] BJS, *Drug and Crime Facts, 1993*, pp. 4–5.

[47] Ibid., p. 6.

[48] Ibid.

[49] Ibid., p. 7.

[50] Ibid., p. 8.

[51] "Study: Bad NYC Cops 'Criminals in Blue,'" United Press International wire service, Northeastern edition, July 7, 1994.

[52] Ibid.

[53] "Judgment on Corrections," *Washington Post* wire service, July 5, 1994.

[54] Public Law 104–305.

[55] "'Rophies' Reported Spreading Quickly throughout the South," *Drug Enforcement Report*, June 23, 1995, pp. 1–5.

[56] For an excellent overview of policy initiatives in the area of drug control, see Doris Layton MacKenzie and Craig D. Uchida, *Drugs and Crime: Evaluating Public Policy Initiatives* (Thousand Oaks, CA: Sage, 1994).

[57] FBI, *Crime in the United States, 2006* (Washington, DC: U.S. Dept. of Justice, 2007).

[58] Ibid., p. 239.

[59] DEA, "Maps of Methamphetamine Lab Incidents," http://www.usdoj.gov/dea/concern/map_lab_seizures.html (accessed July 7, 2007).

[60] DEA, "Stats & Facts," http://www.usdoj.gov/dea/statistics.html#seizures (accessed May 18, 2007).

[61] Office of National Drug Control Policy, *National Drug Control Strategy: 2007 Annual Report*, p. 89.

[62] DEA, *National Drug Threat Assessment, 2007* http://www.usdoj.gov/dea/concern/18862/marijuana.htm (accessed January 5, 2007).

[63] DEA, "Operations Conquistador and Columbus," http://www.dea.gov/major/conquistador.htm (accessed January 8, 2007).

[64] 21 U.S.C. Section 881(a)(6).

[65] "Notice, Hearing and Seizure," *Washington Post* online, December 16, 1994.

[66] *United States* v. *James Daniel Good Real Property*, 510 U.S. 43, 81–82 (1993).

[67] *Austin* v. *United States*, 113 S. Ct. 2801, 15 L. Ed. 2d 448 (1993).

[68] Fox Butterfield, no headline, *New York Times* news service, http://www.nytimes.com (accessed April 16, 1997), citing Office of Justice Programs, *Preventing Crime: What Works, What Doesn't, What's Promising* (Washington, DC: U.S. Department of Justice, 1997).

[69] Office of National Drug Control Policy, *National Drug Control Strategy: 2004* (Washington, DC: The White House, 2004).

[70] Much of the information in this section comes from Office of National Drug Control Policy, *National Drug Control Strategy: FY 2008 Budget Summary* (Washington, DC: ONDCP, 2007).

[71] James A. Inciardi, *Criminal Justice* (Orlando, FL: Harcourt Brace Jovanovich, 1993), p. v.

[72] J. Michael McWilliams, "Setting the Record Straight: Facts about Litigation Costs and Delay," *Business Economics*, Vol. 27, No. 4 (October 1992), p. 19.

[73] Ibid.

[74] Paige M. Marrison and Allen J. Beck, *Prisoners in 2005* (Washington, DC: U.S. Bureau of Justice Statistics, November 2006).

[75] "Who Is in Federal Prison?" *Washington Post*, October 3, 1994.

[76] Lyman and Potter, *Drugs in Society*, p. 316.

[77] Inciardi, *The War on Drugs II*, p. 239, noted.

[78] Lyman and Potter, *Drugs in Society*, p. 316.

[79] *Newsweek*, February 3, 1997, pp. 20–23.

[80] *United States* v. *Oakland Cannabis Buyers, Cooperative*, 532 U.S. 483 (2001).

[81] "Prostitution," *The Columbia Encyclopedia* (New York: Columbia University Press), http://www.answers.com/topic/prostitution#Columbia_Encyclopedia (accessed July 6, 2007).

[82] FBI, *Crime in the United States, 2006.*

[83] H. L. A. Hart, *The Concept of Law* (Oxford, England: Oxford University Press, 1997).

[84] Much of the information in this section is derived from The Law Library: American Law and Legal Information, "Typology of Prostitution," *Crime and Justice*, Vol. 3, http://law.jrank.org/pages/1879/Prostitution-Typology-prostitution.html (accessed July 10, 2007).

[85] Marilyn C. Moses, "Understanding and Applying Research on Prostitution," *NIJ Journal*, No. 255 (November 2006), http://www.ojp.usdoj.gov/nij/journals/255/prostitution_research.html (accessed July 25, 2007).

[86] Martin A. Monto, *Focusing on the Clients of Street Prostitutes: A Creative Approach to Reducing Violence Against Women*, final report submitted to the National Institute of Justice, Washington, DC: June 9, 2000, http://www.ncjrs.gov/pdffiles1/nij/grants/182860.pdf (accessed July 25, 2007).

[87] Andrea Dworkin, *Intercourse* (New York: The Free Press, 1987).

[88] "Sex Workers' Rights Organizations," Everything.com, July 12, 2001, http://everything2.com/index.pl?node_id=1106423 (accessed July 25, 2007).

[89] Ronald Weitzer, "The Growing Moral Panic over Prostitution and Sex Trafficking," *The Criminologist*, Vol. 30, No. 5 (September/October, 2005), pp. 1 and 3.

[90] Janice G. Raymond, "10 Reasons for Not Legalizing Prostitution," Coalition Against Trafficking in Women International, March 25, 2003, http://www.rapereliefshelter.bc.ca/issues/prostitution_legalizing.html (accessed July 25, 2007).

Chapter

14

Technology and Crime

Outline

Disaffected states, terrorists, proliferators, narcotraffickers, and organized criminals will take advantage of the new high-speed information technology environment and other advances in technology to integrate their illegal activities and compound their threat to stability and security around the world.

—National Intelligence Council (CIA)[1]

The world isn't run by weapons anymore, or energy, or money. It's run by ones and zeros—little bits of data—it's all electrons.... There's a war out there, a world war. It's not about who has the most bullets. It's about who controls the information—what we see and hear, how we work, what we think. It's all about information.

—Sneakers[3]

We need to take the fight against computer crime to the next level. Federal law enforcement agencies need new tools, and we need to make state and local law enforcement agencies more a part of this team effort. We also need to authorize investigative techniques to uncover the culprits behind these crimes, even when the culprits are overseas.

—Senator Patrick Leahy[2]

Crime is not static. Existing patterns get displaced by new ones.

—Georgette Bennett[4]

Learning Outcomes

After reading this chapter, you should be able to

- Describe the link between technological advances and crime, and explain how technology can be used by both criminals and crime fighters
- Describe how technology can provide criminal opportunity; and use computer crime as an illustration
- Provide a profile of computer criminals, including a history of hacking and a description of cyberspace
- Define *identity theft*, describe how identities can be stolen, and explain what can be done to reduce the crime's negative impact on its victims

- Describe some of today's technologies that are being used to fight crime
- Explain what is being done today to combat computer crime and to secure the Internet
- Identify some of the personal freedoms that are threatened by today's need for advanced security, and explain the nature of that threat

Hear the author discuss this chapter at **crimtoday.com**

Introduction

On March 22, 2007, a federal judge in Philadelphia struck down the 1998 federal Child Online Protection Act (COPA), holding that the law—which was intended to ban commercial Web sites from making sexually explicit material available to children under the age of 17—was overly broad and inconsistent with free speech guarantees inherent in the U.S. Constitution. The judge's ruling was a second legal setback for COPA, because the U.S. Supreme Court had already barred enforcement of important sections of the law in 2004.[5]

As originally formulated, COPA required that Web site operators use credit cards or adult access codes and personal identification numbers to keep minors from seeing pornography deemed "harmful."[6] Violators faced up to six months in prison and fines of as much as $50,000 a day. The Justices, however, felt that COPA would unduly burden constitutionally protected speech and concluded that less restrictive measures could be used to effectively protect minors. In the Court's majority opinion, Justice Anthony Kennedy wrote that "content-based prohibitions, enforced by severe criminal penalties, have the constant potential to be a repressive force in the lives of a free people." At the time, the Court did not actually declare COPA unconstitutional. Instead, the Justices sent the case back to a lower court with instructions to make sure that the penalties the law imposes on pornographers are the "least restrictive" way to protect children without violating the First Amendment rights of adults.[7]

It was the restrictive nature of the law that Federal District Court Judge Lowell Reed, Jr., found unacceptable in 2007. Reed determined that far less restrictive methods, such as software filters, were available to parents to control their children's use of the Internet. "Despite my personal regret at having to set aside yet another attempt to protect our children from harmful material," Judge Reed said, he was blocking the law out of concern that "perhaps we do the minors of this country harm if First Amendment protections, which they will with age inherit fully, are chipped away in the name of their protection."[8]

Some years earlier, in 2002, the U.S. Supreme Court had invalidated portions of the 1996 Child Pornography Prevention Act (CPPA),[9] a federal law that had attempted to expand a ban on child pornography to include images that *appear* to be of children under 18 engaged in sexually explicit acts.[10]

Pornographers have not won every court battle, however. In 2003, the Justices upheld the Children's Internet Protection Act,[11] which requires public and school libraries that receive government Internet discounts to install software filters on their computers that can be used to block pornography.[12]

These and other Court decisions highlight the highly profitable business of online pornography—a business that some say is the most profitable on the Internet. According to CBS News, adult Web sites were the only ones to turn a profit in the early days of the Internet. Such sites, says CBS, "have pioneered and helped to develop numerous technological breakthroughs from online payment methods to streaming video."[13]

The Advance of Technology

Technology and criminology have always been closely linked. The con artist who uses telephones in a financial scam, the robber who uses a firearm and drives a getaway car, even the murderer who wields a knife—all employ at least rudimentary forms of technology in the crimes they commit.

Technology can be employed by both crime fighters and lawbreakers. Early forms of technology, including the telegraph, the telephone, and the automobile, were embraced by agents of law enforcement as soon as they became available. Evidence derived from fingerprint and ballistics analysis is routinely employed by prosecutors, and emerging technologies promise to keep criminologists and law enforcement agents in step with high-tech offenders.

Technology that is taken for granted today was at one time almost unthinkable. Telephones, for example, were invented just over a century ago, and mass-produced automobiles are newer still. Even firearms are of relatively recent origin if one considers the entire history of humankind, and the manufacture of contemporary cutting instruments would be impossible were it not for an accumulation of technological expertise beginning with the progress in metallurgy during the Iron Age.

As technology advances, it facilitates new forms of behavior. Just as we can be sure that everyday life in the future will be substantially different from life today, so, too, can we be certain that tomorrow's crimes will differ from those of today. In the future, personal crimes of violence and traditional property crimes will undoubtedly continue to occur, but advancing technology will create new and as yet unimaginable opportunities for criminals positioned to take advantage of it and of the power such technology will afford.

A frightening preview of such possibilities can be had in events surrounding the collapse of the Soviet Union more than a decade ago. The resulting social disorganization in that part of the world made the acquisition of fissionable materials, stolen from former Soviet stockpiles, simple for even relatively small outlaw organizations. In what has since become a nightmare for authorities throughout the world, Middle Eastern terrorist groups are known to be making forceful efforts to acquire former Soviet nuclear weapons and the raw materials necessary to manufacture their own bombs. Some evidence also suggests that nuclear weapons parts may have already been sold to wealthy international drug cartels and organized criminal groups, who may now be hoarding them to use as bargaining chips against possible government prosecution. Speaking before the House of Representatives Foreign Affairs Committee in the mid-1990s, then–CIA Director James Woolsey warned of the possibility "that Russian organized crime groups will be able to obtain and sell nuclear weapons or weapons-grade materials as a target of opportunity. We should not rule out the prospect that organized crime could be used as an avenue for terrorists to acquire weapons of mass destruction."[14] Russian Defense Minister Igor Rodionov issued a similar warning. Rodionov said his country's cash-starved armed forces were in such a perilous state that nuclear missiles and weapons systems might not be controllable.[15]

Bret and Sammy of the Sammy4U show adult Web site, which broadcasts the daily activities of nudists on the Internet. Bret and Sammy, a former stripper, work out of their home in Florida using video streaming technology. Should the federal government regulate such productions?

Source: Preston C. Mack

Crime in the News

Net War on Child Porn

As pedophiles swarm the Internet, an unprecedented war against child pornography is intensifying.

Internet service providers (ISPs) such as AOL are using sophisticated technology to identify porn sites. Credit card companies are tracking purchases. More police detectives are posing as minors online.

"We have hit the tipping point," says Michelle Collins, director of the child exploitation unit at the National Center for Missing & Exploited Children. She says high-profile cases such as that of John Mark Karr, the former suspect in the JonBenét Ramsey slaying, have made the public realize that pornographic pictures of children are crime-scene photos. Karr was freed from a California jail this month after 5-year-old charges of possessing child porn were thrown out when police said that evidence had disappeared.

"There is a lot of unprecedented activity. It's just meeting the escalating problem," says Drew Oosterbaan, chief of the Justice Department's child exploitation section. In the past four months:

- President Bush signed a bill to increase the number of prosecutors, computer forensic examiners and federal-state task forces assigned to child porn. It tripled to $150,000 the maximum penalty for downloading child porn and allows adults photographed when they were kids to sue those who buy, sell or distribute the photos.

- The National Center for Missing & Exploited Children launched a victim identification lab to share pornographic photos—with graphic details obscured—with police agencies nationwide. The goal: Find victims by identifying background elements in a picture that will lead to the location of abuse.

- Five ISPs, criticized by such lawmakers as Democratic Rep. Bart Stupak of Michigan for not doing enough, announced they will build a database. The companies—AOL, Yahoo, Microsoft, Earthlink and United Online—will give each picture a signature and then scan their sites for matches.

- The national center has begun giving daily notices of every reported porn site to ISPs registered with its CyberTipline. If police are not investigating the site, a company can close it or block subscriber access.

- Credit card firms representing 87% of the U.S. market have formed a coalition to let police and the national center know about porn sites their customers use. The aim: End the profit by 2008 by making arrests and closing pornographers' accounts.

- Public service ads that teach kids and parents how to recognize a pedophile's online lures are being funded by, among others, the Justice Department and MySpace.com, a website popular with teens.

- A study by the University of New Hampshire found that 34% of kids 10–17 saw unwanted sexual material online in the past year, up from 25% five years ago.

Despite all the activity, those on the front lines say they are losing the war against child pornography.

"The images are propagating faster than we can police. It's far worse than people realize," says Wyoming police investigator Flint Waters. He co-chairs the technology committee of the Internet Crimes Against Children program, a network of 46 regional task forces.

In the past 24 months, Waters says, the task forces have identified 6.5 million pornographic pictures of children online, up from 3,600 three years ago. Forty percent originated in the USA.

"We're constantly playing catch-up," says Waters, who has developed software that identifies the location of porn distributors. "The funding hasn't kept up with the problem. If you quadruple my funding, I still couldn't keep up."

A key reason is that much child porn isn't about money but pedophilia, the sexual attraction to kids. Many images are traded free like baseball cards.

"It's an extension of child molestation—another sick feature," says inspector Jane Wilcox of the Toronto Sex Crimes Unit, which worked with the U.S. Justice Department to bust a porn ring in March that included a Sunday school teacher, a soccer referee, a mailman and a computer software engineer. In a chat room they used, a man broadcast a live video of himself molesting an 11-month-old baby.

Few victims report the abuse. Of more than 800 online child-porn victims identified by the national center, Collins says only about 30 blew the whistle. She says some are too young to describe what happened. Others are afraid. More than a third, 36%, were abused by a parent, 10% to 15% by another relative and 30% by other people they know. About 10% are enticed by strangers to post photos; 5% do it unasked.

Pedophiles can be treated but not cured, says Fred Berlin of the Johns Hopkins Sexual Disorders Clinic. He says many want treatment, but few get it in prison or after their release. Berlin says some child porn users don't realize they may be committing a federal offense that could send them to prison and require them to register as a sex offender. "The Internet blurs the distinction between reality and fantasy," he says.

The Internet's seeming anonymity lures otherwise law-abiding men to child porn, says Patrick Carnes, author of *In the Shadows of the Net: Breaking Free of Compulsive Online Sexual Behavior.* He calls the Internet the "crack cocaine" of sex addiction: "It moves people into areas they would not otherwise go."

Carnes says users may be emotionally immature. "At heart, they're still 14," he says. Online, he says, they find others who share their interests and, feeling validated, soon become heavy viewers.

More than 99% of those arrested for possessing child porn are men, according to a 2005 study funded by the Justice Department. Most, 83%, had images of prepubescent kids; 80% had pictures of sexual penetration.

Another reason online child porn is difficult to stop is that predators are adept at avoiding detection.

Police are "right to feel outgunned. It's not only a matter of resources but of skill," says Philip Jenkins, author of *Beyond*

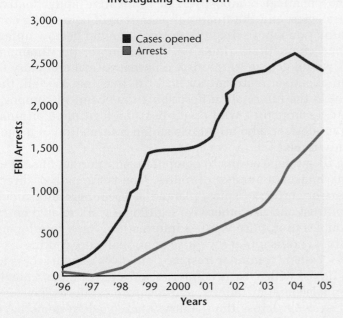

FIGURE 14–1

Investigating Child Pornography

Source: FBI Innocent Images National Initiative Unit and Julie Snider, *USA Today*. Reprinted with permission.

Tolerance: Child Pornography on the Internet. He says child pornographers started using the Internet in the early 1980s, a 20-year head start on police, and they know how to cover their cybertracks.

Some pedophiles use private Internet radio stations and chat groups to trade ideas on evading detection. If credit card companies close their accounts, some move to alternate online payment services.

They set up "modeling" sites featuring scantily clad young girls in seductive poses and contend that such sites are legal because they do not show genitalia, but people operating such sites have been prosecuted. Sheila Sellinger of Indiana pleaded guilty this year to selling pornographic images of a 10-year-old girl. She got an 11-year prison sentence.

Predators entice kids with gifts and compliments to post provocative pictures of themselves online.

"The seduction was slow. Each request only went a bit further than the last," Justin Berry, 19, told a congressional panel in April. When he was 13, he testified, men he met online asked him to film himself with his shirt off. He did so with his webcam, and they sent him money and gifts in the mail.

For five years, he ran a porn site viewed by more than a thousand men who paid him to strip naked, masturbate and have sex with female prostitutes on camera. At least two men have been charged, including Gregory Mitchell, who was sentenced in July to 150 years in prison.

Prosecution can be challenging. Sometimes evidence is lacking, because few Internet companies keep information on users' e-mail and website visits for long. Attorney General Alberto Gonzales has asked companies to retain such data, but some have balked over questions of cost and customers' privacy.

Some pornographers use web-hosting or domain registry companies to set up sites. Unlike ISPs, they are not required to report porn to police. Some pornographers are based overseas. Most countries don't consider possessing child porn a crime, and 122 have no laws against distributing it online, according to the International Centre for Missing & Exploited Children in Alexandria, Va.

Organized crime is involved in some of those global operations, says Carlos Ortiz, a former assistant U.S. attorney in Newark who tracked down a Florida company called Connections USA that was processing $1 million a month in credit card purchases of child porn and sending the money to a company in Belarus. The investigation led to more than 1,200 arrests.

"I'm really worried. It's tough to find a technical fix," says investigator Waters, who is trying to refine his software so it can track an image's distribution.

Hours spent looking at disturbing images are "brutal," he says. To cheer him, his wife hung a photo in his office of a man dressed as Santa Claus holding their two kids. Shortly after the picture was taken, Waters discovered the man trying to lure teen girls online.

"We're always faced with problems that are bigger than we can address," says Justice Department's Drew Oosterbaan. He says the department is trying to use existing resources more effectively. "Is it enough? Probably not."

Still, a growth in arrests provides hope, says David Finkelhor, director of the Crimes Against Children Research Center at the University of New Hampshire. "As more people get caught, others may get very nervous, and we may see a slowdown in traffic."

Discussion Questions

1. Why do some officials involved in the battle against online child pornography feel as though they are losing the war?

2. What role does organized crime play in the ongoing availability of online child pornography? What makes organized criminal activity in this area so lucrative?

Source: Wendy Koch, "In Shadows of Net, War on Child Porn Rages," *USA Today*, October 17, 2006, p. 13A. Reprinted with permission.
For the latest crime and justice news, visit www.crimenews.info.

High Technology and Criminal Opportunity

The twenty-first century has been described by some as the epitome of the postindustrial information age. Information, as many now recognize, is vital to the success of any endeavor, and certain forms of information hold nearly incalculable value. Patents on new products, the chemical composition of innovative and effective drugs, corporate marketing strategies, and the financial resources of competing corporations are all forms of information whose illegitimate access might bestow unfair advantages upon unscrupulous competitors. Imagine, for example, the financial wealth and market share that would accrue to the first pharmaceutical company to patent a true AIDS cure, or an effective treatment for bird flu. Imagine, as well, the potential profitability inherent in the information describing the chemical composition of that drug—especially to a competitor who might beat the legitimate originator of the substance to the patent desk or who might use stolen information in a later bid to challenge patents already issued.

High-tech criminals seeking illegitimate access to computerized information and to the databases that contain it have taken a number of routes. One is the path of direct access, by which office workers or corporate spies, planted as seemingly innocuous employees, violate positions of trust and use otherwise legitimate work-related entry to a company's computer resources to acquire wanted information. Such interlopers typically steal data during business hours under the guise of normal work routines.

Another path of illegal access, called "computer trespass," involves remote access to targeted machines. Anyone equipped with a home computer and a modicum of knowledge about computer modems, telecommunications, and log-on procedures has easy access to numerous computer systems across the country. Many such systems have few, if any, security procedures in place to thwart would-be invaders. In one case, for example, a Silicon Valley software company learned that a fired software developer had been using a telephone connection to enter the company's computers.[16] By the time she was caught, she had copied several million dollars' worth of the company's programs. It was later learned that the stolen software had been slated for illicit transmission to collaborators in Taiwan. Had the scheme succeeded, many thousands of "pirated" copies of the software would have been distributed at great financial loss to the legitimate copyright owners. In a similar scenario, a Florida television news editor was arrested after moving to a new job with a different station for allegedly entering his former employer's computer via the Internet and copying researched stories.[17]

More exotic techniques used to steal data stored in computers extend to reading the electromagnetic radiation produced by such machines. Electromagnetic field (EMF) decoders, originally developed for military purposes, can scan radio frequency emanations generated by all types of computers. Keystroke activity, internal chip-processed computations, disk reads, and the like can all be detected and interpreted at a distance by such sophisticated devices under favorable conditions. Computers secured against such passively invasive practices are rarely found in the commercial marketplace. Those available to commercial organizations generally conform to a security standard developed by the U.S. military called **TEMPEST.** TEMPEST standards were created under a U.S. Department of Defense program that seeks to develop methods of reducing or eliminating unintended electronic emissions from computers and other electromagnetic devices. Recently, wireless networking has rekindled fears of data theft.

Some criminal perpetrators intend simply to destroy or to alter data without otherwise accessing or copying the information. Disgruntled employees, mischievous computer **hackers,** business competitors, and others may all have varied degrees of interest in destroying a company's records or computer capabilities.

In 1988, in the first criminal prosecution of a person accused of creating a **computer virus,** Texas programmer Donald Gene Burleson was arrested for allegedly infecting a former employer's computer with a program designed to destroy the information it contained. Since Burleson's arrest, many imitators have taken similar paths of revenge. According to Richard Baker, author of the respected *Computer Security Handbook,*

TEMPEST

A standard developed by the U.S. government that requires that electromagnetic emanations from computers designated as "secure" be below levels that would allow radio receiving equipment to "read" the data being computed.

hacker

A person who uses computers for exploration and exploitation.

computer virus

A set of computer instructions that propagates copies or versions of itself into computer programs or data when it is executed.

"The greatest threat to your computers and data comes from inside your company, not outside. The person most likely to invade your computer is not a gawky youngster in some other part of the country but an employee who is currently on your payroll."[18]

Technically speaking, **computer crime,** which involves a wide variety of potential activities, is any violation of a federal or state computer crime statute. Many argue that only those crimes that employ computer technology as central to their commission and that could not be committed without it may properly be called "computer crimes." However, David L. Carter, a professor in the School of Criminal Justice at Michigan State University, has developed a broader classification scheme that includes four general types of computer crimes:[19] (1) crimes in which computers serve as targets—for example, crimes involving theft of intellectual property stored on a computer or techno-vandalism, (2) crimes in which computers serve as the instrumentality of the crime—for example, use of a computer to obtain account information stored in another computer, (3) crimes in which the computer is incidental to other crimes—use of computers to store illegal gambling information or a database of drug buyers, and (4) crimes associated with the prevalence of computers—those that take advantage of the needs that computers create, such as the need for software. An FBI typology distinguishes among five types of computer crimes: (1) internal computer crimes, such as viruses; (2) Internet and telecommunications crimes, including illegal hacking; (3) support of criminal enterprises, such as databases supporting drug distribution; (4) computer-manipulation crimes, such as embezzlement; and (5) hardware, software, and information theft.[20] Table 14–1 lists these five categories, with additional examples of each. Learn more about computer crime typologies by reading **Library Extra 14–1** at crimtoday.com.

A recent estimate by the U.S. Secret Service in conjunction with the CERT Cybersecurity Center at Carnegie Mellon University puts the annual cost of computer crime in the United States at around $666 million.[21] Another industry group, the Computer Security Institute (CSI), recently surveyed 313 business organizations and found that computer crime cost companies an average of $168,000 each in 2006.[22]

Global estimates of lost revenues due to pirated software (known as "Warez" in the computer underground) dwarf even that amount. **Software piracy,** or the unauthorized and illegal copying of software programs, is rampant. The Software and Information Industry Association (SIIA) distinguishes among various forms of software piracy:[23]

- **Softlifting:** purchasing a single licensed copy of software and loading the same copy onto several computers
- **Internet piracy:** making unauthorized copies of copyrighted software available to others electronically via the Internet
- **Software counterfeiting:** illegally duplicating and distributing copyrighted software in a form designed to make it appear to be legitimate
- **Original equipment manufacturer (OEM) unbundling:** selling as stand-alone software programs that were intended to be bundled with specific accompanying hardware
- **Hard disk loading:** installing unauthorized copies of software onto the hard disks of personal computers, often as an incentive for the end user to buy the hardware from that particular hardware vendor
- **Renting:** unauthorized renting of software for temporary installation, use, or copying

According to the Business Software Alliance, global losses from software piracy totaled nearly $40 billion in 2006.[24] North America (at $8.1 billion), Asia ($11.6 billion), and Western Europe ($10.6 billion) accounted for the vast majority of worldwide revenue losses. Some countries have especially high rates of illegal use. Of all the computer software in use in China, for example, it is estimated that 82% has been illegally copied. Learn more about software piracy from the Business Software Alliance via **Web Extra 14–1.**

According to some experts, losses like these may be just the beginning. As one technological visionary observes, "Our society is about to feel the impact of the first generation

computer crime

Any violation of a federal or state computer crime statute.

LIBRARY
Extra
■ ■ ■ ■

software piracy

The unauthorized and illegal copying of software programs.

WEB
Extra
■ ■ ■ ■

TABLE 14–1 Categories of Computer Crime

Internal Computer Crimes (Malware)
Trojan horses
Logic bombs
Trapdoors
Viruses

Internet and Telecommunications Crimes
Phone phreaking
Hacking
Denial of service attacks
Illegal Web sites
Dissemination of illegal material (that is, child pornography)
Misuse of telephone systems
Theft of telecommunications services
Illegal eavesdropping
Illegal Internet-based gambling

Support of Criminal Enterprises
Databases to support drug distribution
Databases to support loan-sharking
Databases to support illegal gambling
Databases to keep records of illegal client transactions
Electronic money laundering
Communications in furtherance of criminal conspiracies

Computer-Manipulation Crimes
Embezzlement
Electronic fund transfer fraud
Other fraud/phishing
Extortion threats/electronic terrorism

Hardware, Software, and Information Theft
Software piracy (Warez)
Thefts of computers
Thefts of microprocessor chips
Thefts of trade secrets and proprietary information
Identity theft

---

of children who have grown up using computers. The increasing sophistication of hackers suggests that computer crime will soon soar, as members of this new generation are tempted to commit more serious offenses."[25]

While the theft or damage of information represents one area of illegitimate criminal activity, the use of technology in direct furtherance of criminal enterprise constitutes another. Illegal activity based on advanced technologies is as varied as the technologies themselves. Nuclear blackmail may represent the extreme technologically based criminal threat, whereas telephone fraud and phone "phreaking" are examples of low-end crimes that depend on modern technology for their commission. Some authors prefer the term **cybercrime** to distinguish crimes that involve the use of computers or the manipulation of digital data from other technologically sophisticated crimes.

One of the earliest forms of cybercrime was phone phreaking. **Phone phreaks** use special dial-up access codes and other restricted technical information to avoid long-distance charges. Some are able to place calls from pay phones, while others fool telephone equipment into billing other callers. As a top telecommunications security

cybercrime

Crime committed with the use of computers or via the manipulation of digital forms of data.

phone phreak

A person who uses switched, dialed-access telephone services for exploration and exploitation.

expert explains, "Many organizations discover they have been victims of telephone fraud only after their telephone bill arrives in a carton instead of an envelope."[26]

As some companies have been surprised to learn, the responsibility for payment of stolen telephone time may rest with them. A few years ago, for example, a U.S. district court ordered Jiffy Lube International, Inc., to pay AT&T $55,727 for long-distance calls made by computer hackers who had stolen the company's access codes. Judge Frank Kaufman said the law "squarely places responsibility upon a customer, such as Jiffy Lube, for all calls whether or not authorized."[27] In effect, Judge Kaufman sent a message to corporations nationwide that they can be held responsible for ensuring the security of their own telephone services.

A new form of phone phreaking emerged about ten years ago. It involves the electronic theft of cellular telephone numbers and access codes. Thieves armed with simple mail-order scanners and low-end computers can "literally grab a caller's phone number and identification number out of the air."[28] Say experts, "Those numbers are [then] used to program computer chips, which are placed inside other cellular phones—or 'clones'—so the long-distance calls appear on the victim's bill."[29] Such high-profile figures as former New York Mayor Rudolph Giuliani and his police commissioner have been among the victims of cellular phone piracy.

Recent developments in voice-over Internet protocol (VoIP) technology have made the theft of telecommunications services less lucrative, but VoIP technology has opened the door to new kinds of crimes. The U.S. Department of Justice (DOJ) has gone on record as being concerned about the fast growth of VoIP communications services because they make surveillance and wiretapping difficult and can facilitate "drug trafficking, organized crime and terrorism."[30] Laura Parsky, a deputy assistant attorney general in the DOJ, told investigators at a recent Senate hearing that "[i]f legal loopholes allow criminals to use new technologies to avoid law enforcement detection, they would use these technologies to coordinate terrorist attacks, to sell drugs throughout the United States and to pass along national security secrets to our enemies." The hearing was held to consider changes to the proposed VoIP Regulatory Freedom Act, which, if passed, might require telecommunications providers to build "back doors" into VoIP networks that would allow for court-ordered wiretaps to be successfully enforced.

phishing

Pronounced "fishing." An Internet-based scam to steal valuable information such as credit card numbers, social security numbers, user IDs, and passwords.

A relatively new form of high-technology fraud is phishing. **Phishing** (pronounced "fishing") is a scam that uses official-looking e-mail messages to steal valuable information such as credit card numbers, social security numbers, user IDs, and passwords from victims. The e-mail messages appear to come from a user's bank, credit card company, retail store, or ISP and generally inform the recipients that some vital information in their account urgently needs to be updated. Those who respond are provided with an official-looking Web form on which they can enter their private financial information. Once the information is submitted, it enters the phisher's database.

The Anti-Phishing Working Group—a coalition of banks and ISPs—recently estimated that a typical phishing scheme reaches up to 1 million e-mail inboxes. The watchdog group had identified more than 55,600 different phishing Web sites by June 2007.[31] Some observers have noted that in addition to losses suffered by individuals and institutions, phishing has the potential to threaten the viability of e-commerce and to call into question the safety of all Web-based financial transactions.[32]

The federal Violent Crime Control and Law Enforcement Act of 1994 made it illegal to use interstate telephone lines in furtherance of telemarketing fraud and expanded federal jurisdiction to cover cases of insurance fraud and frauds committed against the elderly, even when such crimes do not involve use of the mail or telephone. Learn more about telemarketing fraud and Internet-based fraud at the National Fraud Information Center via **Web Extra 14–2**. Read an important criminological discourse on cybercrime via **Library Extra 14–2** at crimtoday.com.

WEB
Extra
■■■■

LIBRARY
Extra
■■■■

Technology and Criminal Mischief

Not all computer crime is committed for financial gain. Some types of computer crime, including the creation and transmission of destructive computer viruses, "worms," spyware, and other malicious forms of programming code (often called *malware*), might better be classified as "criminal mischief." Perhaps not surprisingly, these types of activities are typically associated with young, technologically sophisticated male miscreants seeking a kind of clandestine recognition from their computer-savvy peers. Computer crimes committed by youthful and idealistic offenders may represent a new form of juvenile delinquency—one aimed at expressing dissatisfaction with the status quo.

Dr. Ali-Reza Ghasemi and his wife, Shahla Ghasemi, of Tampa, Florida, lost $400,000 to an advance-fee scheme on the Internet. Advance-fee schemes, often called Nigerian e-mail fraud because so many of the messages appear to come from Nigeria, promise victims a lot of money in return for advancing fees to cover legal services and transfer the funds. How can you tell when an e-mail message is likely to be a fraud?

Source: William S. Speer/Bloomberg News/Landov

1	ILOVEYOU, AKA Loveletter and The Love Bug (2000) *Caused $10 to $15 billion dollars in estimated damages.*
2	Sobig.F (2003) *Caused $5 to $10 billion dollars in estimated damages; over 1 million PCs infected*
3	Blaster (2003) *Caused $5 to $10 billion dollars in estimated damages; over 1 million PCs infected*
4	Code Red (2001) *Caused $2.6 billion in estimated damages*
5	Melissa (1999) *Caused $300 to $600 million dollars in estimated damages*
6	CIH, AKA the Chernobyl virus (1998) *Caused $20 to $80 million dollars in estimated damages; huge amounts of data destroyed*
7	Bagle (2004) *Tens of millions of dollars in estimated damages*
8	Sasser (2004) *Tens of millions of dollars in estimated damages*
9	SQL Slammer (2003) *Affected half-a-million servers worldwide*
10	MyDoom (2004) *Slowed global Internet performance by 10 percent and Web load times by up to 50 percent*

FIGURE 14–2

The Ten Most Damaging Computer Viruses and Worms of All Time, by Amount of Damage

Source: Adapted from George Jones, "The 10 Most Destructive PC Viruses Of All Time," *Tech Web*, July 05, 2006, http://www.techweb.com/tech/160200005.

Viruses have shown signs of becoming effective terrorist-like tools in the hands of young, disaffected "technonerds" intent on attacking or destroying existing social institutions. A computer virus is simply a computer program that is designed to secretly invade computer systems and either to modify the way in which they operate or to alter the information they store.[33] Other types of destructive programs are logic bombs, worms, and Trojan horse routines. Distinctions among these programs are based on either the way in which they infect targeted machines or on the way in which they behave once they have managed to find their way into a computer. Figure 14–2 provides an overview of some of the most damaging computer viruses of all times.

Viruses may spread from one machine to another via modem or high-speed cable and DSL connections (when files are downloaded), through networks or direct links (such as those provided by popular programs like LapLink Pro and the Windows "Direct Connection" option), and through the exchange of floppy disks, CD-ROMs, or magnetic backup media. Most viruses hide inside executable computer software, or in the so-called boot sectors of floppy or hard disks. Recently, however, rogue codes known as "Macro viruses" have been secreted into text documents. The most famous of these, the Concept virus, affects users of Microsoft's Word software. Similarly, HTML files, which form the backbone of the World Wide Web, may be infected with viruses lurking inside Java script or Macromedia Shockwave–generated code. Some users also worry that "cookies," or small programs sent to users' machines by servers on the Web, may spread viruses.

Viruses don't infect only desktop and laptop machines. Some viruses have been written that can interfere with the operation of popular handheld devices, including personal digital assistants (PDAs) and mobile phones. In 2000, for example, a Swedish software developer accidentally released Liberty Crack—a disabling software code that enters handheld devices like the Palm and Handspring products.[34]

Perhaps the most insidious forms of destructive programming making the rounds of the computer world today are polymorphic viruses. A polymorphic virus is one that uses advanced encryption techniques to assemble varied (yet entirely operational) clones of itself. Hence, polymorphic viruses have the ability to alter themselves once they have infected a computer. This strategy is effective in circumventing most security devices that depend on scanning techniques to recognize viral signatures. Simply put, when viruses change, they can no longer be recognized. In typical leapfrog fashion, as

Crime in the News

Good Cybercitizens Help ID-Theft Victims

SAN FRANCISCO—For a few hours a day, Steven Peisner calls strangers across the USA—sometimes at night—and reads to them their Social Security numbers and credit card data.

Though many recipients immediately suspect he is an ID thief, Peisner's intent is just the opposite: He is a digital whistle-blower.

"My motivation is to be a good citizen and put a dent in (fraudulent e-mail) phishing scams," says Peisner, president of SellitSafe.com, which provides anti-phishing services for online merchants. He works closely with law enforcement and computer-security experts. Peisner, 43, is one of several avenging angels nationwide looking out for the well-being of ID-theft victims. They share a fervent desire to publicize the widespread availability of stolen personal data on the Internet.

- Betty "BJ" Ostergren, a former insurance-claims supervisor in Virginia, occasionally warns consumers that their Social Security numbers are posted on public government websites. For the past four years, she has spent several hours a day digging through sites for Social Security numbers. So far, she's uncovered 18,000 records.

- Janice Forster, 50, a paralegal in North Carolina, this year started FindMyId.com, a website devoted to educating consumers about ID theft. In the past week, she mailed more than 100 letters to North Carolina residents informing them that their personal information is available on the Internet.

"I just want to make a difference," says Forster, who had never before been involved in a grass-roots movement. "In good conscience, I can't watch this happen to people."

That's why Peisner called Christopher Buckley, a high school teacher in Los Angeles, late at night during Labor Day weekend to inform Buckley that his credit card number was on the ccpower forum, a black-market website where criminals deal in stolen personal data. "I was shocked he called but glad he did," says Buckley, 31, who mistakenly forked over information via e-mail to someone claiming to be from PayPal.

There is a method to Peisner's madness. As phishing continues to escalate, the safest course for consumers may be to warn them over the phone. There is little in the way of software to warn consumers they have been phished.

"We need to take control of the situation," says Peisner, who does not profit from his advice to consumers but sells his company's services to businesses. "The police have their hands full with these types of cases. It's up to consumers like me to take action."

Since May, good Samaritan Peisner has scoured the Internet forums of cybercrooks, looking for the names of ID-theft victims whose personal information is for sale online. The same day, he informs victims that their names—not to mention Social Security numbers, credit card information and phone numbers—are floating in cyberspace. Peisner calmly tells them he has come across their filched profiles and they should immediately close their credit card and/or bank accounts. To make his point resonate, he reads to victims their stolen information as it appears in the forums.

Symantec detected 157,477 unique phishing messages during the first half of 2006, up 81% from the last six months of 2005. Home PCs were targets of 86% of security threats in the first six months of 2006, according to a Symantec report released Monday.

The incidents have soared as attacks become more sophisticated. Tried-and-true scams aimed at customers of AOL, eBay, PayPal, Citibank, Bank of America and other high-profile companies continue. But the deceptive e-mail messages and websites have gotten much craftier. Customer names and addresses now routinely appear in phishing e-mail. Previously, scams were addressed to "Dear valued (company name) member," say security experts.

Good cybercitizen Steven Peisner tracks cybercrime transactions in chat rooms and hacker forums, then contacts victims to warn them. Is Peisner providing a valuable service, or is he intruding on others' privacy?

Source: Photo by Robert Hanashiro. (c) 2006 USA TODAY. Reprinted with Permission.

when crime-fighting techniques are overtaken and surpassed by new technologies favoring lawbreakers and then later regain ascendancy, polymorphic viruses have—over the last few years—largely rendered signature-based antivirus scanning technologies obsolete. Unfortunately, although many hardware devices and software products now on the market offer some degree of virus protection to individual and commercial users, new viruses are constantly being created, which may soon have the ability to circumvent all security procedures now in place. The only fully effective technique for avoiding viral contamination is the complete and total isolation of computer equipment—a strategy as unlikely to be maintained as it is to be implemented.

"This is slick stuff," says Ron O'Brien, senior security analyst at Sophos. He says recent phishing attempts actually warn customers about phishing and ask them to update their information for security reasons. To assure wary users, the 800 phone number of a targeted company is included in the e-mail. The scam often works, he says.

The scam is just the latest iteration in an evolving cycle of phishing attempts that surface every few months, says Dennis Maicon, executive vice president of financial-services solutions at computer-security firm Digital Resolve. Late last year, phishers typically preyed on customers of large financial institutions, warning them in e-mails to update their accounts or risk losing them. Early this year, phishers used the same scam but on customers of regional banks and credit unions.

Phishers also are ensnaring corporate customers with bogus phone trees that ask consumers to enter personal information. How the scam works: An e-mail advises victims to call a number to verify basic data. But the number is actually recording data with the intent to steal it, according to law enforcement officials. The stolen information often winds up on cybercrime forums, websites that function as digital marketplaces.

The speed of transactions on those forums can be quick, victims say.

Scott London, an attorney in Santa Barbara, Calif., can vouch for that. Soon after he surrendered personal data to a PayPal-targeted phishing scam on Aug. 18, it was posted on the CardersMarket forum.

In less than one minute, $100 was pulled from his bank account. An e-mail receipt from the real PayPal confirmed the withdrawal seconds later. Another 15 minutes later, more than $1,200 in airline tickets, electronic equipment and two other items were charged to London's Chase-issued MasterCard.

By the time Peisner called to warn London, the charges had been made. But London took Peisner's advice and notified his bank and credit card issuer. "It could have been worse if not for Steven," London says.

Peisner admits it can be a thankless job, rousting strangers at night and telling them their innermost financial secrets. "One guy in Florida wants to kill me," he says.

But those are the occupational hazards of being a do-gooder.

For many victims, Peisner is the first line of defense. Most software doesn't notify the consumer until after an illegal purchase. Peisner tells them as soon as he spots their information in carding forums.

On a typical day, he contacts more than a dozen victims. To gain their trust, he explains who he is and what he has found online—usually the victim's name, address, Social Security number and credit card number. He advises them to contact their credit card issuer and bank and to monitor their credit reports for two to three years. Victims range in age from 19 to 88, and they are universally shocked when he calls, Peisner says.

"Steven scared me to death, but he saved me a lot of grief," says Stephen Sanders, 55, a retiree from Carmel, Calif., who was the victim of phishing scam targeting eBay/PayPal users last month. Sanders closed his bank account and discontinued his credit card the next day. He also flagged credit reports.

Absent consumer advocates, there is little that tech vendors can do to immediately alert phishing victims.

AOL, Yahoo, Microsoft and other providers of Internet service continue to refine their anti-phishing filters. Yahoo this month rolled out a service that better protects consumers from phishing sites. Future versions of Microsoft Internet Explorer and other browsers such as Opera and Firefox will include built-in phishing filters.

Still, newer phishing attacks can slip through.

AOL offers free features that inform users whenever a financial transaction is made over their AOL account. Customers can set up e-mail spending alerts for themselves, based on the amount of a transaction and when it occurs, says Michael Jones, technical director of AOL's anti-spam operations.

But until phishing is eviscerated, and short of directly warning intended victims, consumers will continue to be hooked by phishing attempts. Even though Buckley was quickly tipped off by Peisner, cybercrooks rang up $1,000 in charges to his credit card before he could cancel it. "Just think of the damage they could have done if Steven didn't call me," Buckley says. "For that, I'll always be grateful to him."

Discussion Questions

1. What is phishing? What role does it play in identity theft?

2. How can you protect yourself from identity theft?

3. Does protecting yourself require that you forego such common contemporary activities as online shopping or online banking? Why or why not?

Source: Jon Swartz, "Good Cybercitizens Keep Watch over ID-theft Victims," *USA Today*, September 28, 2006, p. 6B. Reprinted with permission. For the latest crime and justice news, visit www.crimenews.info.

Once certain forms of malicious software code have successfully invaded a computer, they can take over the machine and use it to send out additional copies of themselves, or use the machine to send spam or other information (including the legitimate user's personal information) to various places on the Internet. Learn more about computer viruses at **Web Extra 14–3.**

WEB
Extra
■ ■ ■ ■

Computer Crime and the Law

In late 2000, the Justice Department of the Philippines dismissed criminal charges against Onel de Guzman.[35] De Guzman, a former student at the Philippines AMA Computer

College, admitted that he had unleashed the ILOVEYOU (or Love Bug) virus on the Internet on May 4, 2000, but refused to say whether he had authored it. The virus replicated rapidly throughout the world, gathering passwords from infected computers and sending them to several e-mail accounts in the Philippines. By the time the virus had run its course, official estimates were that it had caused over $10 billion in damages.[36] Because the Philippines had no law against computer crime, however, de Guzman was originally charged with theft and violation of an access device. Those laws, prosecutors finally decided, were not applicable to de Guzman's activities, and the charges were dropped. Although President Joseph Estrada signed a new law covering electronic commerce and computer hacking in June 2000, it could not be applied retroactively to the Love Bug case.

In the early years of computer-based information systems, most U.S. jurisdictions, like the Philippines, often tried to prosecute unauthorized computer access under preexisting property crime statutes, including burglary and larceny laws. Unfortunately, because the actual carrying off of a computer is quite different from simply copying or altering some of the information it contains, juries frequently could not understand the applicability of such laws to high-tech crimes, and computer criminals were often exonerated. As a result, all states and the federal government developed computer-crime statutes specifically applicable to invasive activities aimed at illegally accessing stored information. Federal statutes of relevance to crimes committed with or against computer equipment and software include (1) the Cyber Security Enhancement Act of 2002;[37] (2) The Digital Theft Deterrence and Copyright Damages Improvement Act of 1999;[38] (3) the No Electronic Theft Act of 1997;[39] (4) the Communications Decency Act as amended; (5) the Computer Fraud and Abuse Act of 1984[40] and its amendments—especially Section 290001 of Title 29 of the Violent Crime Control and Law Enforcement Act of 1994, which is known as the Computer Abuse Amendments Act of 1994; (6) the Electronic Communications Privacy Act of 1986; (7) the National Stolen Property Act;[41] and (8) the Federal Wiretap Act of 1968.

For the most part, federal laws protect equipment owned by the federal government or a financial institution or computers that are accessed across state lines without prior authorization.[42] The U.S. Criminal Code, Title 18, Section 1030(a), defines as criminal the intentional unauthorized access to a computer used exclusively by the federal government or any other computer used by the government when such conduct affects the government's use. The same statute also defines as criminal the intentional and unauthorized access to two or more computers in different states and conduct that alters or destroys information and causes loss to one or more parties in excess of $1,000.[43] Punishment specified under federal law is a maximum sentence of five years and a fine of up to $250,000 upon conviction. The Computer Abuse Amendments Act of 1994, however, adds the provision that "any person who suffers damage or loss by reason of a violation of [this] section . . . may maintain a civil action against the violator to obtain compensatory damages and injunctive relief or other equitable relief." The 1994 provision is intended to support civil actions in federal court against computer criminals by those suffering monetary losses as a result of computer crimes.

The **Cyber Security Enhancement Act** of 2002 (CSEA),[44] which is part of the Homeland Security Act of 2002, directed the U.S. Sentencing Commission to take several factors into account in creating new sentencing guidelines for computer criminals. The law told the commission to consider not only the financial loss caused by computer crime, but also the level of planning involved in the offense, whether the crime was committed for commercial or private advantage, and whether malicious intent existed on the part of the perpetrator. Under the law, computer criminals can face life in prison if they put human lives in jeopardy. The law is intended to help deter cybercrime by subjecting computer criminals to substantial criminal penalties. The law also makes it easier for law enforcement agencies to obtain investigative information from ISPs and shields from lawsuits ISPs who hand over user information to law enforcement officers without a warrant. The information in question, however, should be that which poses an immediate risk of injury or death.

The **Digital Theft Deterrence and Copyright Damages Improvement Act** of 1999 amended Section 504(c) of the Copyright Act and increased the amount of damages that could be awarded in cases of copyright infringement—a crime that is intimately associated with software piracy. Enacted in 1997, the **No Electronic Theft Act** (NETA, or NETAct)

Cyber Security Enhancement Act

Part of the Homeland Security Act of 2002, this federal law directed the U.S. sentencing commission to take several specific factors into account in creating new sentencing guidelines for computer criminals.

Digital Theft Deterrence and Copyright Damages Improvement Act

Passed in 1999, this federal law (Public Law 106–160) attempted to combat software piracy and other forms of digital theft by amending Section 504(c) of the Copyright Act, thereby increasing the amount of damages that could potentially be awarded in cases of copyright infringement.

No Electronic Theft Act

A 1997 federal law (Public Law 105–147) that criminalizes the willful infringement of copyrighted works, including by electronic means, even when the infringing party derives no direct financial benefit from the infringement (such as when pirated software is freely distributed online). In keeping with requirements of the NETA, the U.S. Sentencing Commission enacted amendments to its guidelines on April 6, 2000, to increase penalties associated with electronic theft.

criminalizes the willful infringement of copyrighted works, including by electronic means, even when the infringing party derives no direct financial benefit from the infringement (such as when pirated software is freely distributed online). In keeping with requirements of the NETA, the U.S. Sentencing Commission enacted amendments to its guidelines on April 6, 2000, to increase penalties associated with electronic theft.

In 1996, President Bill Clinton signed the **Communications Decency Act (CDA)** into law. The CDA, which is Title 5 of the Telecommunications Act of 1996,[45] sought to protect minors from harmful material on the Internet. A portion of the CDA criminalized the knowing transmission of obscene or indecent messages to any recipient under 18 years of age. Another section prohibited the knowing sending or displaying to a person under 18 any message "that, in context, depicts or describes, in terms patently offensive as measured by contemporary community standards, sexual or excretory activities or organs." The law provided acceptable defenses for those who took "good faith . . . effective . . . actions" to restrict access by minors to prohibited communications, and to those who restricted such access by requiring certain designated forms of age proof, such as a verified credit card or an adult identification number.

Shortly after the law was passed, however, the American Civil Liberties Union (ACLU) and a number of other plaintiffs filed suit against the federal government, challenging the constitutionality of the law's two provisions relating to the transmission of obscene materials to minors. In 1996, a three-judge federal district court entered a preliminary injunction against enforcement of both challenged provisions, ruling that they contravened First Amendment guarantees of free speech. The government then appealed to the U.S. Supreme Court. The Court's 1997 decision **Reno v. ACLU**[46] upheld the lower court's ruling and found that the CDA's "indecent transmission" and "patently offensive display" provisions abridge "the freedom of speech" protected by the First Amendment. Justice John Paul Stevens wrote for the majority, "It is true that we have repeatedly recognized the governmental interest in protecting children from harmful materials. But that interest does not justify an unnecessarily broad suppression of speech addressed to adults."

As noted in the story that begins this chapter, most other federal legislation aimed at keeping online pornography away from the eyes of children has not fared any better when reviewed by the Court. It remains to be seen whether the 1998 Child Online Protection Act (COPA) can be modified to meet Court muster. And although the Children's Internet Protection Act (CIPA), which requires public and school libraries receiving certain kinds of federal funding to install pornography filters on their Internet-linked computers, was approved, most observers acknowledge that the Court has placed the Internet in the same category as newspapers and other print media, where almost no regulation is permitted.

The computer-crime laws of individual states are rarely modeled after federal legislation. As a result, they contain great variation. Texas law, for example, criminalizes "breach of computer security." A breach of security occurs when an individual "knowingly accesses a computer, computer network, or computer system without the effective consent of the owner" or when someone "intentionally or knowingly gives a password, identifying code, personal identification number, debit card number, bank account number, or other confidential information about a computer security system to another person without the effective consent of the person employing the computer security system to restrict access to a computer, computer network, computer system, or data."[47]

In contrast to Texas, the state of Virginia specifically defines *computer crime* according to the following categories: "theft of computer services, computer invasion of privacy, computer trespass, computer fraud, [and] personal trespass by computer" (via which physical injury accrues to someone by virtue of unauthorized access to a computer, as may happen in the case of disruption of utility services).[48]

Ambiguities in existing computer-crime laws, complicated by rapid changes in technology, can make it difficult even to tell when a crime has occurred. In 1995, for example, 20-year-old University of Michigan student Jacob Alkhabaz (aka Jake A. Baker) became the first person ever indicted for writing something on the Internet when he was arrested by the FBI and charged with five counts of interstate transmission of threats.[49] Alkhabaz had posted a series of stories on the Internet about his fantasy of torturing, raping, and murdering a female classmate. One of his messages contained the phrase

Communications Decency Act

A federal statute signed into law in 1996, the CDA is Title 5 of the federal Telecommunications Act of 1996 (Public Law 104–104, 110 Stat. 56). The law sought to protect minors from harmful material on the Internet, and a portion of the CDA criminalized the knowing transmission of obscene or indecent messages to any recipient under 18 years of age. In 1997, however, in the case of *Reno* v. *ACLU* (521 U.S. 844), the U.S. Supreme Court found the bulk of the CDA to be unconstitutional, ruling that it contravenes First Amendment free speech guarantees.

"Just thinking about it anymore doesn't do the trick. I need to do it." Another note read "Torture is foreplay, rape is romance, snuff (killing) is climax."[50]

Although Alkhabaz might have been punished by a sentence of up to five years in prison, Detroit U.S. District Judge Avern Cohn threw out the charges after Alkhabaz had spent 29 days in jail.[51] Cohn ruled that Alkhabaz's violent-sounding Internet writings were protected under the free speech clause of the U.S. Constitution. Notably, Alkhabaz had been charged with communicating threats rather than computer crime because his activities were not specifically covered under federal computer-crime laws. Had they been, a different verdict might have resulted.

Such cases illustrate how certain, as of yet unimaginable, future illegitimate activities employing computer equipment may not be adequately covered by existing law. On the other hand, some crimes committed with the use of a computer may be more appropriately prosecuted under "traditional" laws. For that reason, some experts distinguish among computer crime (defined earlier), computer-related crime, and computer abuse. **Computer-related crime** is "any illegal act for which knowledge of computer technology is involved for its investigation, perpetration, or prosecution," whereas **computer abuse** is said to be "any incident without color of right associated with computer technology in which a victim suffered or could have suffered loss and/or a perpetrator by intention made or could have made gain."[52] Learn more about digital crime of all kinds from the Computer Crime and Intellectual Property Section (CCIPS) of the Criminal Division of the DOJ via **Web Extra 14–4**.

A Profile of Computer Criminals

In 1997, FBI agents arrested Adam Quinn Pletcher, 21, and charged him with trying to extort $5.25 million from Microsoft founder and chairman Bill Gates.[53] Pletcher, a loner from Illinois who spent hour after hour in front of his computer, allegedly sent several letters to Gates, demanding the money and threatening to kill him or his wife, Melinda, if Gates did not respond to an America Online service known as "NetGirl." The service, an online dating forum, was to serve as a secure medium for the exchange of messages between Gates and the extortionist. FBI agents nabbed Pletcher after he sent a disk to Gates that held erased files containing the names of Pletcher's parents. Some months earlier, Pletcher had made headlines in Chicago when he was accused of running scams on his Internet Web page, including offering fake driver's licenses for sale, telling people he could get them cars at bargain prices and then pocketing their money, running an illegal raffle that offered $10 chances to win an expensive automobile, and offering "free" pagers that cost more than $50 in service charges. By all accounts, Pletcher was a hacker—a technologically sophisticated loner.

It is from hacker subculture that computer criminals tend to come. Hackers and hacker identities are a product of **cyberspace,** that etheric realm where computer technology and human psychology meet. Cyberspace exists only within electronic networks and is the place where computers and human beings interact with one another. For many hackers, cyberspace provides the opportunity for impersonal interpersonal contact, technological challenges, and game playing. Fantasy role-playing games are popular among hackers and may engross many "wave riders," who appear to prefer what in technological parlance is called "virtual reality" to the external physical and social worlds that surround them. As one writer states, "Cyberspace is hacker heaven."[54]

Literature that glorifies cyberspace and the people who inhabit it is called "cyberpunk," and hackers are sometimes called "cyberpunks." An understanding of cyberpunk literature is crucial for those wanting to gain an appreciation for how hackers think. According to Paul Saffo of the Institute for the Future in Menlo Park, California, "Anyone trying to make sense of [contemporary] computing . . . should add some cyberpunk books to their reading lists." Says Saffo, "Cyberpunk may become the counterculture movement" of the future. He adds that "the cyberpunk trend is likely to be matched by an increase in the number of cyber-outlaws penetrating networks for criminal ends."[55] Young, idealistic, and immature, hackers of this genre typically take on pseudonyms

---

computer-related crime

Any illegal act for which knowledge of computer technology is involved in its perpetration, investigation, or prosecution.

computer abuse

Any unlawful incident associated with computer technology in which a victim suffered or could have suffered loss or in which a perpetrator by intention made or could have made gain.

WEB
Extra
■ ■ ■ ■

cyberspace

The computer-created matrix of virtual possibilities, including online services, wherein human beings interact with one another and with the technology itself.

Simon Vallor, the 22-year-old Welsh Web site designer who was sentenced to two years in prison in 2002 for creating mass-mailer computer viruses. His viruses, named Gokar, Redesi, and Admirer, infected more than 27,000 computers and spread to 42 different countries. Should those who write malicious computer code be sent to prison?

Source: Stefan Rousseau/PA Photos

that other hackers can identify but that also provide at least the illusion of anonymity. Phiber Optik, Acid Phreak, Knight Lightning, Time Lord, Nightcrawler, and Dark Angel are only a few of the many pseudonyms that are either now in use or have been used by hackers in recent years.

No one knows the actual identity of many of these people, but computer-security experts have come up with a rough profile of the average hacker.[56] He is a male between the ages of 16 and 25 and lives in the United States. He is a computer user, but not a programmer, who hacks with software written by others. His primary motivation is to gain access to Web sites and computer networks, not to profit financially.

Some of the most infamous computer hackers of recent years, those composing the Atlanta-based Legion of Doom, fit the hacker profile well. Some years ago, three Legion members were sentenced to prison terms of 14 to 21 months and were ordered to pay $233,000 each in restitution to BellSouth Corporation for breaking into its computer systems and stealing confidential data. After serving their jail time, some Legion members found themselves sought after by high-tech employers who wanted to exploit their skills in the development of proprietary computer-security systems. Other "legionnaires" formed a company called Comsec Data Security to help provide private businesses with the expertise necessary to fend off electronic intrusions.

The History and Nature of Hacking

Some authors have suggested that computer hacking began with the creation of the interstate phone system and direct distance dialing, implemented by AT&T in the late 1950s.[57] Early switching devices used audible tones that were easily duplicated by electronics hobbyists, and "blue boxes" capable of emulating such tones quickly entered the illicit marketplace.

Although phone phreaking has been practiced for more than 40 years, a form of illegal telephone access that has recently come to the fore is voice-mail hacking. Private voice-mail boxes used for storing verbal messages have become the targets of corporate

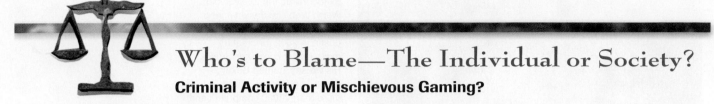

Who's to Blame—The Individual or Society?

Criminal Activity or Mischievous Gaming?

Late last year, Kelvin Mutchnak was arrested and charged under federal law with interfering with the operation of computers owned by the federal government. The computers, mostly Apple Mac Pros and G5's, ran Apple's latest operating system, popularly referred to as Mac OS X Leopard, and were located in Veteran's Administration (VA) hospitals across the country.

Mutchnak was especially taken with the long-standing popular impression that Apple's operating system was secure and impenetrable—a myth that computer hackers had long known was untrue, but which Apple corporate officials had done little to dispel. The feeling of those who worked for Apple, Mutchnak concluded, was that the popular myth could help sell computers. Nonetheless, most hackers continued to focus their efforts on Microsoft's Windows operating system because of its greater popularity, and because it was easier to hack. Since the advent of Windows Vista in 2006, however, and with the introduction of Macintosh computers able to dual boot both Vista and Leopard, and able to run both simultaneously, attention in the hacker community had increasingly turned to identifying backdoors into the Macintosh operating system.

Soon Mutchnak was devoting all of his spare time to dispelling Apple's myth of invincibility, and to writing malware—malicious software code—that could successfully invade almost any of Apple's higher-end computers that were connected to the Internet.

After writing a malicious script that he could insert into a tiny QuickTime video, Mutchnak sent the video as an e-mail attachment to VA hospital computers, making the e-mail look as though it contained administrative data that would be of significance to people in charge of the facilities. Although the e-mail had to be opened and the video file clicked on, and although the person reading the mail had to be logged in under an administrative account (most, he found, were), Mutchnak's plan was very successful, and soon most Macintosh computers in federally run hospitals across the country were infected. Unfortunately for Mutchnak, however, federal anticyberterrorism officials had been running a drill responding to a mock cyberterrorism attack when his e-mail made its way onto the Net. Within minutes of its release, Mutchnak's malicious e-mail had been traced to the IP address assigned to his home by his ISP.

A warrant for his arrest was drawn up, and Mutchnak was arrested by federal agents who charged him with violating various federal computer crime laws, including one meant to deter terrorists.

Think about it:

1. Do you believe that Mutchnak saw his activity as criminal? As terrorist activity? If not, how did he perceive it?

2. Was Mutchnak, as he claimed, doing a service by showing weaknesses in the parts of the nation's computer infrastructure?

3. Might there have been other ways for Mutchnak to make his point? Would those ways have been as effective as the computer mischief in which he engaged? Why or why not?

---

raiders and young vandals alike. In a recent case, two teenage New York City brothers caused an estimated $2.4 million in lost business by gaining illegal access to the New Hampshire–based International Data Group's voice-mail system. The brothers were angry at not having received a poster promised with their magazine subscription. Security experts at the company, who first thought that the mailboxes were malfunctioning, were alerted to the intentional disruptions by obscene outgoing messages planted by the brothers that greeted unsuspecting callers.[58]

Voice-mail fraud, another form of telephone crime, involves schemes in which mailbox access codes are shared in such a way that callers to toll-free numbers can leave messages for one another in voice-mail boxes, thereby avoiding personal long-distance charges.[59] Companies that provide access to voice-mail systems through toll-free numbers often learn of the need for access code security only after they have been victimized by such schemes.

Although the hacker lifestyle may have begun with phone phreaking, phone phreaks represent only one type of hacker. Hackers can be distinguished both by their purpose and by their method of operation. Such categorization, however, is merely descriptive. Other, more useful distinctions can be made on the basis of personality and lifestyle. Some experts have suggested that hackers can be classified according to psychological characteristics into the following groups:[60]

- **Pioneers:** individuals who are fascinated by the evolving technology of telecommunications and explore it without knowing exactly what they are going to find. Few hard-core criminals are found among this group.

- **Scamps:** hackers with a sense of fun. They intend no overt harm.

- **Explorers:** hackers who are motivated by their delight in the discoveries associated with breaking into new computer systems. The farther away such systems are geographically from the hacker's physical location, or the more secure such systems are, the greater the excitement associated with breaking into them.

- **Game players:** those who enjoy defeating software or system copy protection and who may seek to illegally access computer systems with games to play. Hacking itself becomes a game for this sort of hacker.

- **Vandals:** malicious hackers who deliberately cause damage with no apparent gain for themselves. The original 414 Gang in Milwaukee, for example, which broke into the Sloan-Kettering Cancer Institute's computers and wiped out patient records, provides an example of this type of hacker.

- **Addicts:** classic computer "nerds" who are addicted to hacking and to computer technology. They may also be addicted to illicit drugs, as some hacker bulletin board systems post information on drugs as well as on modems, passwords, and vulnerable systems.

Psychologist Percy Black argues for the existence of an underlying theme in all cases of hacking. It is, he says, "the search for a feeling of power, possibly stemming from a deep-seated sense of powerlessness."[61] Hence, hacking may serve as compensation for feelings of personal inferiority. By challenging the machine and by winning against machine culture, hackers go through a kind of rite of passage into adulthood, whereby they prove themselves capable of success.

Because most hackers are young adolescent males, however, it may be important to realize that, as one expert on hackers says, "their other favorite risky business is the time-honored adolescent sport of trespassing. They insist on going where they don't belong. But then teen-age boys have been proceeding uninvited since the dawn of human puberty. It seems hard-wired. The only innovation is in the new form of the forbidden zone and the means of getting in it."[62]

Unfortunately, however, not all computer hackers are simply kids trying their hand at beating technological challenges. As Garry M. Jenkins, assistant director of the U.S. Secret Service, put it around the time of Operation Sun Devil (a joint two-year undercover operation of the Secret Service, local and state law enforcement officers, and private telephone security personnel), "Recently, we have witnessed an alarming number of young people who, for a variety of sociological and psychological reasons, have become attached to their computers and are exploiting their potential in a criminal manner. Often, a progression of criminal activity occurs that involves telecommunications fraud (free long-distance phone calls), unauthorized access to other computers (whether for profit, fascination, ego, or the intellectual challenge), credit card fraud (cash advances and unauthorized purchases of goods), and then moves on to other destructive activities like computer viruses. . . . Our experience shows that many computer hacker suspects are no longer misguided teenagers mischievously playing games with their computers in their bedrooms. Some are now high-tech computer operators using computers to engage in unlawful conduct."[63] Learn more about hackers and information security at the CERT Coordination Center, one of the best security sites on the Internet. Located at the Software Engineering Institute, a federally funded research and development center operated by Carnegie Mellon University, CERT can be reached via **Web Extra 14–5**.

Not all high-tech crimes are committed using computer technology. Many technologically sophisticated professional criminals are operating today, some of whom use the diverse fruits of high technology in the furtherance of serious criminal activity. The theft of money is a major goal of such activity. Some years ago, for example, technologically sophisticated thieves in New York City rolled a fake automated teller machine (ATM) into the local Buckland Hills shopping mall. Although the machine did not dispense money, it did record the information contained on the

WEB
Extra
■ ■ ■ ■

magnetic strips of legitimate banking cards inserted by would-be customers. The personal information numbers that the customers entered were also recorded. Armed with the necessary codes for legitimate accounts, the thieves then fabricated their own cards and used them to withdraw thousands of dollars from real ATM machines across the city.

Although most people probably think of money as dollar bills, money today is really only information—information stored in a computer network, possibly located within the physical confines of a bank, but more likely existing as bits and bytes of data on service providers' machines. Typical financial customers give little thought to the fact that very little "real" money is held by their bank, brokerage house, mutual fund, or commodities dealer. Nor do they often consider the threats to their financial well-being by activities like electronic theft or the sabotage of existing accounts. Unfortunately, however, the threat is very real. Computer criminals equipped with enough information, or able to ferret out the data they need, can quickly and easily send vast amounts of money anywhere in the world.

Although billions of dollars' worth of electronic transactions occur every day, no reliable estimates exist as to the losses suffered in such transactions due to the activities of technologically adept criminal perpetrators. Accurate estimates are lacking largely because sophisticated high-tech thieves are so effective at eluding apprehension and even detection that reliable loss figures are impossible to ascertain.

Web sites can also facilitate criminal activity. A few years ago, for example, U.S. Customs Service agents involved in Operation Longarm carried out raids on child pornographers and suspected pedophiles in 18 states using names taken from a pedophile site. According to the Customs Service, the computerized transmission of illegal pornography among pedophiles is rapidly becoming more popular than smutty magazines.[64] On June 18, 2007, for example, British police, aided by U.S. investigators arrested 200 suspects in an Internet pornography ring that streamed live video of children being sexually abused. The ring involved more than 700 suspects worldwide, and authorities in 35 countries participated in the investigation. Thirty-one children were rescued as a result of the operation. Some of them were only a few months old.[65]

Computer Crime as a Form of White-Collar Crime

White-collar crime is discussed in detail in Chapter 12. It is important here, however, to recognize that a number of contemporary analysts believe that computer crime may be nothing other than a new form of white-collar crime. Some suggest that it is the ultimate expression of white-collar crime.

In what may be the definitive work to date on high-tech professional crime, Donn B. Parker, author of the National Institute of Justice's *Computer Crime: Criminal Justice Research Manual*, compares white-collar criminals with computer criminals. Both share what Parker calls "common criminal behavior-related issues," such as the following:[66]

- Both types of acts are often committed through nonviolent means, although certain industrial, consumer, and environment-related crimes have life-threatening consequences.

- Access to computers or computer storage media, through employment-related knowledge or technical skills, is often needed.

- These acts generally involve information manipulations that either directly or indirectly create profits or losses.

- These crimes can be committed by an individual, by several individuals working in collusion, or by organizations, with the victims in the last case ranging from individual clients, customers, or employees to other organizations.

Criminal Profiles

Kevin Mitnick

At the time of his arrest in February 1995, Kevin Mitnick was the most wanted computer criminal in United States history. There's little wonder as to why: His crimes included wire fraud, computer fraud, and wire communication interception, and the cost to his victims included millions of dollars in lost licensing fees, marketing delays, lost research and development, and the costs of repairing compromised computer systems.[i]

Cloned cellular telephones, hacker software programs, "sniffer" devices and so-called "social engineering" were the tools Mitnick used to conduct the computer crime spree that launched a lengthy investigation beginning in 1992. The evidence amassed by the FBI during its three-year probe was sufficient to force Mitnick to accept a plea bargain rather than risk more severe penalties by going to trial.[ii] His corporate victims included Motorola, Novell, Fujitsu, Sun Microsystems, and Nokia Mobile Phones, Ltd., among others; and he used University of Southern California computer systems to hide software code and obscure his identity.

Born August 6, 1963, and a product of a blue-collar upbringing in California's San Fernando Valley, Mitnick's 1981 juvenile arrest for stealing computer manuals from Pacific Bell led to his being placed on probation. The experience had little deterrent effect, however, as evidenced by his subsequent arrests in 1989 (for computer fraud and possession of unauthorized access devices related to hacking into MCI and Digital Equipment computers) and in 1992 (for computer fraud and possession of unauthorized access devices for allegedly hacking into California Department of Motor Vehicles computers).[iii]

It is said that Mitnick served as the inspiration for the 1983 film *War Games* by hacking into the U.S. Department of Defense's North American Defense Command (NORAD) computers in 1982.[iv] To this day, Mitnick denies that allegation and claims that simple curiosity and thrill-seeking motivated his misadventures. His

grandmother lays the blame for his actions on Mitnick's overwhelming curiosity.

An intriguing element of Mitnick's case was the manner in which he was finally caught. Computer expert Tsutomu Shimomura, infuriated after Mitnick hacked into and stole information from his home computer, employed a dramatic cybersleuthing effort to track Mitnick down, resulting in Mitnick's arrest by the FBI in a Raleigh, North Carolina, apartment complex. Shimomura and *New York Times* reporter John Markoff subsequently published *Takedown*, an account of Shimomura's experience in chasing down the elusive Mitnick.

Mitnick remains somewhat disgruntled by what he believes was excessive media hype that led to his being unfairly characterized as "Osama bin Mitnick."[v] His actual transgressions, he contends, were far less serious than those depicted in sensationalistic press reports.

As a result of his 1995 arrest, Mitnick spent more than five years in prison, with more than eight months of it in solitary confinement. Now in his early forties, a significantly matured Mitnick has done a 180-degree turnaround in his approach to computer security. On March 1, 2000, he testified before the U.S. Senate's Governmental Affairs Committee, during which he suggested that the millions of dollars corporations spend on firewalls and secure access devices are negated by the "the weakest link in the security chain: the people who use, administer and operate computer systems."[vi] Mitnick regaled the committee with tales of his use of "social engineering" (what he defines as "using manipulation, influence and deception to get a . . . trusted insider to . . . release information and to perform some sort of action item") that enables a hacker to successfully attack the insider's own computer system.

Mitnick now heads up a highly successful computer consulting firm which specializes—not too surprisingly—in advising on computer security issues. Disturbingly, he suggests that it is easier to hack today than it was years ago, citing social engineering as still an extraordinarily effective technique for computer exploit. Mitnick's message is clear: Notwithstanding tremendous advances in both hardware and software security measures, the weak link is still the human element.[vii]

Computer hacker turned author Kevin Mitnick poses for a portrait in 2002, in Las Vegas. Barred by the terms of his probation from using computers, ex-convict hacker Kevin Mitnick turned to writing about them, baring the tricks of his former trade in a book titled The Art of Deception. Mitnick was granted an exemption to use a computer to write his book. What is he doing today?

Source: Joe Cavaretta/AP Wide World Photos

Notes:

i Kevin Mitnick Sentenced to Nearly Four Years in Prison, U.S. Department of Justice Press Release, August 9, 1999; and "Computer Hacker Ordered to Pay Restitution to Victim Companies Whose Systems were Compromised," United States Attorney's Office, Central District of California, August 9, 1999, http://www.cybercrime.gov/mitnick.htm (accessed June 2, 2007).

ii Ibid.

iii John Christensen, "The Trials of Kevin Mitnick" CNN, March 18, 1999, http://www.cnn.com/SPECIALS/1999/mitnick.background (accessed June 2, 2007).

iv Ibid.

v "A Convicted Hacker Debunks Some Myths," CNN, October 13, 2005, http://www.cnn.com/2005/TECH/internet/10/07/kevin.mitnick.cnna (accessed June 2, 2007).

vi Elizabeth Wasserman, "Mitnick Schools Feds on Hacking 101," CNN, March 3, 2000, http://archives.cnn.com/2000/TECH/computing/03/03/mitnick.the.prof/mitnick.the.prof.html (accessed June 2, 2007).

vii "A Convicted Hacker Debunks Some Myths."

According to Parker, computer crime and white-collar crime also share the following similarities:

- These crimes are often difficult to detect, with discovery quite often started by accident or by customer complaint rather than as the result of direct investigation.
- The general public views many of these acts as less serious than crimes involving physical violence.
- These crimes cost individuals, organizations, and society large amounts of money and other resources.
- Prevention of these crimes requires a combination of legal, technical, managerial, security, and audit-monitoring controls.

Identity Theft

identity theft

The unauthorized use of another individual's personal identity to fraudulently obtain money, goods, or services; to avoid the payment of debt; or to avoid criminal prosecution.

Identify theft—the misuse of another individual's personal information to commit fraud[67]—is a crime that often makes headlines, and which appears to be rapidly growing in both scope and frequency. Identity theft, which involves obtaining credit, merchandise, or services by fraudulent personal representation, is a special kind of larceny. As such we might have placed discussion of it in Chapter 11, where property crimes (and larceny-theft) are discussed. At the same time, however, identity theft has the "feel" of a personal crime (even though it doesn't involve violence) because few things are more personal than one's identity. So, it could have found a place in Chapter 10, where violent personal crimes are detailed. We decided to place it in this chapter on technology crimes, however, because even though it is not always a computer crime, (and may not even be a high-technology crime) many identity thieves make use of computers, and the sale of identities often occurs through illicit Internet brokerage sites run by professional criminals who make their living as identity traders. As the DOJ notes, "the advent of information technology and computer literacy has joined with the accessibility of personal information to produce a rapid increase in identity theft as the method of choice for criminals."[68] The DOJ also says that the lack of severe consequences, and inconsistencies in investigation and prosecution, have all added to the value of identity theft for offenders. Usually, individuals learn that they have become identity theft victims only after being denied credit or employment, or when a debt collector seeking payment for a debt the victim did not incur contacts them. It should be noted that one of the most threatening aspects of identity theft is its potential relationship to international terrorism. Even where terrorism is not involved, identity theft could be used broadly by transnational crime rings.

Generally speaking, the misuse of stolen personal information can be classified into two broad categories. The first is *existing account fraud*, and it occurs when thieves obtain account information involving credit, brokerage, banking, or utility accounts that are already open. Existing account fraud is typically a less costly, but more prevalent, form of identity theft. A stolen credit card may lead to thousands of dollars in fraudulent charges, for example, but the card generally will not provide a thief with enough information to establish a false identity. Moreover, most credit card companies, as a matter of policy, do not hold consumers liable for fraudulent charges, and federal law caps liability of victims of credit card theft at $50.

The second, and more serious, category is *new account fraud*. In new account fraud, identity thieves use personal information, such as Social Security numbers, birth dates, and home addresses, to open new accounts in the victim's name, make charges indiscriminately, and then disappear. While this type of identity theft is less likely to occur, it imposes much greater costs and hardships on victims. In addition, identity thieves sometimes use stolen personal information to obtain government, medical, or other benefits to which the criminal is not legally entitled.

A recent Federal Trade Commission (FTC) survey conducted estimated the annual number of victims of some form of identity theft at 9.91 million adults or about 4.6% of the United States population.[69] Approximately 27.3 million adults were estimated to have become victims during the previous five years. Actual dollar losses for businesses and victims in the United States are estimated roughly at $53 billion for 2004.[70] Out-of-pocket losses can reach thousands of dollars for individual victims of new account identity theft, and the cost to repair one's identity can be enormous in terms of both time and money. Victims of new account identity theft, for example, must correct fraudulent information in their credit reports and monitor their reports for future inaccuracies, close existing bank accounts and open new ones, and dispute charges with individual creditors.

In addition to the losses that result when identity thieves fraudulently open accounts or misuse existing accounts, monetary costs of identity theft include indirect costs to businesses for fraud prevention and mitigation of the harm once it has occurred (for example, for mailing notices to consumers and upgrading systems). Similarly, individual victims often suffer indirect financial costs, including the costs incurred in both civil litigation initiated by creditors and in overcoming the many obstacles they face in obtaining or retaining credit. Victims of nonfinancial identity theft, for example, health-related or criminal record fraud, face other types of harm and frustration.

Consumers' fears of becoming identity theft victims can also harm the digital economy. In a 2006 online survey conducted by the Business Software Alliance and Harris Interactive, nearly 30% of adults interviewed said that security fears caused them to shop online less or not at all during the 2005–2006 holiday season.[71] Similarly, a 2005 Cyber Security Industry Alliance survey found that 48% of consumers avoided making purchases on the Internet because they feared that their financial information might be stolen.[72]

Identity theft became a federal crime in 1998 with the passage of the Identity Theft and Assumption Deterrence Act.[73] The law makes it a crime whenever anyone "knowingly transfers or uses, without lawful authority, a means of identification of another person with the intent to commit, or to aid or abet, any unlawful activity that constitutes a violation of federal law, or that constitutes a felony under any applicable state or local law."

The 2004 Identity Theft Penalty Enhancement Act[74] added two years to federal prison sentences for criminals convicted of using stolen credit card numbers and other personal data to commit crimes. It also prescribed prison sentences for those who use identity theft to commit other crimes, including terrorism, and it increased penalties for defendants who exceed or abuse the authority of their position in unlawfully obtaining or misusing means of personal identification.

Anyone can fall prey to identity theft—even celebrities. In 2000, for example, golfer Tiger Woods learned that his identity had been stolen and that credit cards taken out in his name had been used to steal $17,000 worth of merchandise, including a 70-inch TV, stereos, and a used luxury car. In 2001, the thief, 30-year-old Anthony Lemar Taylor, who looks nothing like Woods, was convicted of falsely obtaining a driver's license using the name of Eldrick T. Woods (Tiger's given name), Woods's Social Security number, and his birth date. Because Taylor already had 20 previous convictions of all kinds on his record, he was sentenced to 200 years in prison under California's three-strikes law.[75] Like Woods, most victims of identity theft do not even know that their identities have been stolen until they receive bills for merchandise they haven't purchased.

Identity Theft Incidence

In 2006, the Bureau of Justice Statistics (BJS) reported its first statistical overview of identity theft in information derived from the National Crime Victimization Survey (NCVS).[76] For statistical reporting purposes, BJS defined identity theft to include the following three behaviors, (1) the unauthorized use or attempted use of existing credit cards; (2) the unauthorized use or attempted use of other existing accounts such as checking accounts; and (3) the misuse of personal information to obtain new accounts or loans, or to commit other crimes.

BJS surveyors found that at least one member of 3% of all households in the United States had been the victim of identity theft during the previous 6 months. Extrapolating to a 12-month period, the data appear to show that 6% of all U.S. households are victimized by some form of identity theft annually. The most common type of identity theft uncovered by BJS was the unauthorized use of credit cards, experienced by 1.7 million households in the 6-month period covered by the survey. About 900,000 households reported being victimized by the theft of an existing account other than a credit card account— including the use or attempted use of a wireless telephone account, bank account, or debit/check card account without the account holder's permission. Approximately 500,000 households were victimized by the use of personal information to obtain new credit cards or loans, run up debts, open other accounts, or otherwise commit theft, fraud, or some other crime. The identity theft experienced by more than 400,000 households encompassed two or more types of thefts that occurred during the 6-month period covered by the survey.

The BJS survey also revealed that about 1 in 6 victimized households had to pay higher interest rates as the result of identity theft, and 1 in 9 households were denied phone or utility service as a consequence of being victimized. Seven percent of the victimized households were turned down for insurance or had to pay higher rates; 5% became subject to a civil suit or judgment; and 4% became the subject of a criminal investigation. About one-fifth of victimized households reported that they also experienced other kinds of problems.

BJS estimated total dollar losses to surveyed households as a result of identity theft during the 6-month period at about $3.2 billion. Among households actually sustaining a loss and for which the amount of the loss was known, about 1 in 20 reported losing more than $5,000, but 55% reported losing less than $500. The average amount of money involved in any type of identity theft in which there was a loss was put at $1,290. For households experiencing misuse of personal information, the average loss was $2,360, and it was $2,630 for households experiencing multiple types of theft at the same time.

The Identity Theft Life Cycle

In 2007, the President's Identity Theft Task Force, a group that is described later in this chapter, concluded that identity theft has at least three stages in its "life cycle," and said that it must be attacked at each of those stages. The first stage, the Task Force said, is when the identity thief attempts to acquire a victim's personal information. According to the National White Collar Crime Center, identity thieves use several common techniques to acquire personal information. Some engage in "Dumpster diving," going through trash bags, cans, or Dumpsters to get copies of checks, credit card and bank statements, credit card applications, or other records that typically bear identifying information. Others use a technique called "shoulder surfing." It involves simply looking over the victim's shoulder as he or she enters personal information into a computer or on a written form. Eavesdropping is another simple, yet effective, technique that identity thieves often use. Eavesdropping can occur when the victim is using an ATM machine, giving credit card or other personal information over the phone, or dialing the number for their telephone calling card. Criminals can also obtain personal identifying information from potential victims through the Internet. Some Internet users, for example, reply to "spam" (unsolicited e-mail) that promises them all sorts of attractive benefits while requesting identifying data, such as checking account or credit card numbers and expiration dates, along with the victim's name and address.[77] Identity theft perpetrated through the use of high technology depends on the fact that a person's legal and economic identity in contemporary society is largely "virtual" and supported by technology.

The second stage in the theft of an identity is when the thief attempts to misuse the personal information that he or she has acquired. In this stage, the Task Force says, criminals either make an effort to sell the information that they've collected or try to use it themselves.

The third stage, according to the Task Force occurs when an identity thief has completed his or her crime and is enjoying the benefits, while the victim is realizing the harm. At this point in the life cycle of identity theft, victims are first learning of the crime, often after being denied credit or employment, or being contacted by a debt collector seeking payment for a debt the victim did not incur.

Identity Thieves: Who They Are

Unlike some groups of criminals, identity thieves cannot be readily classified.[78] For the most part, victims are not in a good position to know who stole their information or who misused it. According to the FTC's survey of identity theft, about 14% of victims claim to know the perpetrator, who may be a family member, friend, or in-home employee. Identity thieves can act alone or as part of a criminal enterprise. Each poses unique threats to the public.

According to law enforcement agencies, identity thieves often have no prior criminal background and sometimes have preexisting relationships with the victims. Identity thieves have been known to prey on people they know, including coworkers, senior citizens for whom they are serving as caretakers, and even family members. Some identity thieves rely on techniques of minimal sophistication, such as stealing mail from homeowners' mailboxes or trash containing financial documents. In some jurisdictions, identity theft by illegal immigrants has resulted in passport, employment, and Social Security fraud. Occasionally, small clusters of individuals with no significant criminal records work together in a loosely knit fashion to obtain personal information and even to create false or fraudulent documents.[79]

Law enforcement agencies around the country have observed a steady increase in the involvement of groups and organizations of repeat offenders or career criminals in identity theft. Some of these groups—including national gangs such as the Hell's Angels and MS-13—are formally organized, have a hierarchical structure, and are well-known to law enforcement because of their longstanding involvement in other major crimes such as drug trafficking. Other groups are more loosely-organized and, in some cases, have taken advantage of the Internet to organize, contact each other, and coordinate their identity theft activities more efficiently. Members of these groups often are located in different countries and communicate primarily via the Internet. Other groups have a real-world connection with one another and share a nationality or ethnic group.

Law enforcement agencies also have seen increased involvement of foreign organized criminal groups in computer- or Internet-related identity theft schemes. In Asia and Eastern Europe, for example, organized groups are increasingly sophisticated both in the techniques they use to deceive Internet users into disclosing personal data, and in the complexity of tools they use, such as keyloggers (programs that record every keystroke as an Internet user logs onto his computer or a banking Web site), spyware (software that covertly gathers user information through the user's Internet connection, without the user's knowledge), and botnets (networks of computers that criminals have compromised and taken control of for some other purpose, ranging from distribution of spam and malicious computer code to attacks on other computers). According to law enforcement agencies, such groups also are demonstrating increasing levels of sophistication and specialization in their online crime, even selling goods and services—such as software templates for making counterfeit identification cards and payment card magnetic strip encoders—that make the stolen data even more valuable to those who have it.

What Can Be Done?

In 2006, the federal Office of Community Oriented Policing Services (the COPS Office), in conjunction with the Major Cities Chiefs Association (MCCA), released a report entitled *A National Strategy to Combat Identity Theft*. The *Strategy*, which is available as Library Extra 14–3 at crimtoday.com, recognized identity theft as a pervasive crime that requires cooperation among law enforcement agencies, the federal and state governments, and citizens in order to develop a comprehensive and effective response. The report

LIBRARY
Extra
■ ■ ■ ■

suggested six components of an effective national strategy for preventing and responding to the crime of identity theft as follows:

- **Public awareness campaigns:** Public education has proven highly successful in the past to curtail national levels of alcohol and cigarette use.
- **Victim assistance:** Frequently, victimization focuses on dollar loss and dismisses the emotional trauma or time needed to restore records and identity.
- **Partnership and collaboration:** A staple for police departments, private industry, and others following the September 11 terrorist attacks. Many permutations and combinations are available when one considers the many functions within a jurisdiction—for example, a single function across jurisdictions, such as a statewide or regional collaboration, or multiple functions across several jurisdictions.
- **Legislation:** Legislative action is needed for several reasons: private industry may not be willing to enact certain protections without a federal government mandate, or local police agencies may overlook the significance of taking identity theft reports, no matter how minor, to feed into a larger data bank for analysis.
- **Information protection:** A critical variable and those combating identity theft should be as imaginative as needed.
- **Training:** There was no doubt throughout the project that training is paramount, especially for police officers, investigators, and prosecutors.

On May 10, 2006, President George W. Bush established The President's Task Force on Identity Theft via Executive Order number 13402. In forming the task force, the president called for a coordinated approach among government agencies to combat identity theft and to craft a strategic plan to make the federal government's efforts more effective and efficient in the areas of identity theft awareness, prevention, detection, and prosecution. The Task Force was chaired by then-Attorney General Alberto R. Gonzales and co-chaired by FTC Chairman Deborah Platt Majoras. Its report, released in mid-2007, said that "Identity theft depends on access to consumer data. Reducing the opportunities for thieves to get the data is critical to fighting the crime. Government, the business community, and consumers have roles to play in protecting data."[80] The Task Force made a number of recommendations to combat identity theft, including the following:

- Decrease the unnecessary use of social security numbers in the public sector by developing alternative strategies for identity management.
- Establish national standards to require private sector entities to safeguard the personal data they compile and maintain and to provide notice to consumers when a breach occurs that poses a significant risk of identity theft.
- Have federal agencies implement a broad, sustained awareness campaign to educate consumers, the private sector, and the public sector on deterring, detecting, and defending against identity theft.
- Create a National Identity Theft Law Enforcement Center to allow law enforcement agencies to coordinate their efforts and information more efficiently, and investigate and prosecute identity thieves more effectively.
- Ensure that government agencies work together to provide victims with the knowledge, tools, and assistance needed to minimize the damage and begin the recovery process.
- Provide specialized training about victim recovery to first responders and others offering direct assistance to identity theft victims by (1) training law enforcement officers, (2) providing educational materials for first responders that can be used as a reference guide for identity theft victims, and (3) designing nationwide training for victim assistance counselors.

- Create and distribute an ID Theft Victim Statement of Rights.
- Amend criminal restitution statutes to ensure that victims recover the value of time spent in trying to remediate the harms suffered.
- Assess whether to implement a national system that allows victims to obtain an identification document for authentication purposes.

Learn more about identity thieves and how they operate via the Identity Theft Resource Center at **Web Extra 14–6**. Read about how to prevent your own victimization and what to do if your identity is stolen via **Library Extras 14–4** and **14–5** at crimtoday.com.

WEB
Extra
■ ■ ■ ■

LIBRARY
Extra
■ ■ ■ ■

Technology in the Fight against Crime

Technology is a double-edged sword. On one hand, it arms evildoers with potent new weapons of crime commission, while on the other, it provides police agencies and criminal justice personnel with powerful tools useful in the battle against crime. Law enforcement capabilities and criminally useful or evasive technologies commonly leapfrog one another. Consider, for example, the relatively simple case of traffic radar, which has gone through an elaborate technological evolution from early "always-on" units through trigger-operated radar devices to today's sophisticated laser speed-measuring apparatus. Each change was an attempt by enforcement agencies to keep a step ahead of increasingly sophisticated radar-detection devices marketed to drivers everywhere. Although cutting-edge laser speed units are invisible to most radar detectors, laser radar detectors *do* exist. Their usefulness, however, is open to debate because they generally alert the speeding driver too late. On the other hand, radar-jamming devices are now increasingly used by people who are apparently intent on breaking speed limit laws, and laser jammers are also available. Not to be outdone, suppliers to law enforcement agencies have created radar-detector detectors, which are used by authorities in states where radar detectors have been outlawed.[81]

Other than traffic radar, the most potent technology in law enforcement service today includes computer databases of known offenders (including public access to sex offender databases), machine-based expert systems, cellular communications, video surveillance (often combined with face-recognition technology), electronic eavesdropping, DNA analysis, and less-lethal weapons. For example, transponder-based automated vehicle location (AVL) systems now use patrol car–based transmitters in tandem with orbiting global positioning satellites to pinpoint police vehicle locations to within 50 feet. Dispatchers making use of such information can better allocate the resources available on a given shift and are able to substantially reduce police response times in crisis situations. Similarly, chip-based transponders are now being installed in private vehicles to deter thieves and to help trace stolen automobiles.

Computer-aided dispatch (CAD) systems, representing yet another area of advanced crime-fighting technology, are becoming increasingly sophisticated. In jurisdictions where CAD systems function, police dispatchers are prompted by computers for important information that allows them to distinguish one place from another (such as the location of a particular McDonald's restaurant) within a city. CAD systems can also quickly provide information about how often officers have been called to a given site and can tell responding officers what they might expect to find based on past calls from that location. As one writer enticingly states, "Imagine this response from a 911 call-taker: 'Yes, Ms. Smith, we are aware that beer-drinking youths at the corner of Hollywood and Vine have been a problem over the past six weeks, and in fact, we've responded seven times to requests to disperse them. As soon as one of our patrol cars frees up on a robbery call, I'll be sure that it goes over to disperse the group. And by the way, we are unaware of any serious crimes that can be attributed to these youths. But please feel free to call us immediately if you observe any criminal activities.'"[82] The same software that facilitates such a response will routinely inform responding officers about police experience with the suspects, provide background checks as a matter of course, tell whether they are likely to find registered guns at the address, and relay information about outstanding warrants on anyone who lives there. It can also inform dispatchers when responding officers do not call back after a statistically determined period of time for that type of call—alerting dispatchers to potential threats to officer safety.

Other, even more innovative crime-fighting technologies are on the horizon. The "Spiderman snare," for example, now being tested for its usefulness in incapacitating fleeing suspects, is a fine net 16 feet in diameter. Compressed into a small, shotgun-like shell, the net has small weights at its circumference and is designed to wrap itself around a target when fired. The snare's impact is harmless, and test subjects report being able to watch with open eyes as the net wraps around them. Similarly, a discolike strobe light, which quickly disorients human targets, is on the drawing board. The special frequency light emitted by the strobe rapidly causes intense dizziness, leaving subjects unable to resist cuffing and arrest. Operators wear special glasses designed to counter the influence of the light. Finally, a form of electronic warfare may be on the verge of being launched against speeders driving today's high-tech, computer-equipped cars. Because high-speed chases pose a substantial danger to the public, scientists have developed an aimed electromagnetic pulsing device that can be used to temporarily disable a vehicle's electrical system, causing the engine to stall. The prototype is said to be safe enough to use on vehicles driven by pacemaker-equipped drivers.

As new technologies are developed, their potential usefulness in law enforcement activities is evaluated by the FBI, the National Institute of Justice (NIJ), and other agencies. NIJ's Technology Assessment Program (TAP) focuses on four areas of advancing technology: protective equipment, such as "bulletproof" vests and other body armor; forensic sciences, including the applicability of advances in DNA technology; transportation and weapons, such as electronic "stun guns" and other new less-than-lethal weapons; and communications and electronics, including computer security, electronic eavesdropping, and so on. Other groups, such as the National Computer Security Association, the American Cryptography Association, and the American Society for Industrial Security, bring more specialized high-tech expertise to the private security and public law enforcement professions.

DNA Technology

On January 16, 2001, Christopher Ochoa, 34, was released from a Texas prison after serving 13 years for a murder he did not commit.[83] Ochoa had confessed to the rape and murder of 20-year-old Nancy DePriest at a Pizza Hut in Austin in 1988. Although Ochoa later said he had been coerced by homicide detectives into confessing, no one believed him. A decade after he began serving a life sentence, however, law students at the Wisconsin Innocence Project at the University of Wisconsin–Madison took an interest in his case. They studied surviving information and concluded that DNA evidence conclusively proved that someone else had killed DePriest. The students, led by their law professor, took the evidence to state District Judge Bob Perkins, who called the case "a fundamental miscarriage of justice" and ordered Ochoa set free. According to authorities, evidence of DePriest's murder now points to Texas inmate Achim Joseph Marino, who confessed to her murder in 1996 following a religious conversion. Marino, who is currently serving three life sentences for other crimes, has provided investigators with the gun and handcuffs used to commit the crime. The law students involved in the case matched DNA samples taken from mouth swabs of Marino with the DNA found in semen taken from the victim's body. Without the technology known as **DNA profiling,** Ochoa would still be in prison—and DePriest's real killer would be unknown.

A person's genetic code is contained in his or her deoxyribonucleic acid (DNA), whose composition is unique to each individual, except in the case of identical twins. DNA samples can be taken from blood, hair, semen, saliva, or even small flakes of skin left at the scene of a crime. In cases of rape, for example, semen or pubic hairs left behind by the perpetrator and removed from the victim or gathered at the scene can provide the DNA evidence necessary for identifying a suspect. In cases of murder, victims

DNA profiling

The use of biological residue found at the scene of a crime for genetic comparisons in aiding the identification of criminal suspects.

sometimes fight with their attackers, retaining small bits of the killer's skin under their fingernails—thereby providing a tissue sample useful in DNA analysis.

After processing, DNA profiles appear like bar codes on film negatives. These codes can exonerate a suspect in the eyes of expert analysts—or provide nearly irrefutable evidence of guilt.

DNA evidence is long lasting; fossilized DNA is now being used to reconstruct genetic maps of long-extinct plant and animal species. Although DNA analysis is theoretically possible using only a single cell, most reputable DNA laboratories require a considerably greater quantity of material to conduct an effective analysis. That, however, may soon change. Using a technique called "polymerase chain-reaction technology," a Nobel Prize–winning technique, minute strands of DNA can be effectively amplified so that even the identity of a person taking a single puff from a cigarette can be accurately established. Although the cost and complexity of such enhancements are still prohibitive, technological advances are expected to bring the technique within the range of forensic analysts within a decade.

The National Research Council calls DNA profiling "a highly reliable forensic tool"[84] but admits that it is not infallible. Although obvious differences in scrutinized DNA samples can easily eliminate a suspect, testing provides less certainty with positive identification. Human error in conducting the tests is perhaps the greatest threat to reliable results. As of this writing, at least 20 states and the federal government generally accept DNA evidence in criminal trials. Other jurisdictions, including California, are less clear in their recognition of DNA testing, and trial judges in those states may offhandedly exclude the use of such evidence when experts disagree as to its validity.

In 1993, the U.S. Supreme Court, in the civil case of *Daubert* **v.** *Merrell Dow Pharmaceuticals, Inc.*,[85] revised the criteria for the admissibility of scientific evidence by rejecting a previous admissibility standard established in the 1923 case of *Frye* **v.** *United States.*[86] The *Daubert* Court ruled that the older *Frye* standard, requiring "general acceptance" of a test or procedure by the relevant scientific community, "is not a necessary precondition to the admissibility of scientific evidence." The baseline rule for the admissibility of scientific evidence, said the Court, is established by Rule 402 of the *Federal Rules of Evidence*, which was published after *Frye* and supersedes it. Rule 402 says that in a trial, "all relevant evidence is admissible, except as otherwise provided by the Constitution of the United States, by Act of Congress, by these Rules, or by other rules prescribed by the Supreme Court pursuant to statutory authority." The Court went on to say that although "the *Frye* test was displaced by the Rules of Evidence [that] does not mean . . . that the Rules themselves place no limits on the admissibility of purportedly scientific evidence. Nor is the trial judge disabled from screening such evidence. To the contrary, under the Rules the trial judge must ensure that any and all scientific testimony or evidence admitted is not only relevant, but reliable." The real test for the admissibility of scientific expert testimony, said the Court, is for the trial judge to decide "at the outset . . . whether the expert is proposing to testify to (1) scientific knowledge that (2) will assist the trier of fact to understand or determine a fact in issue." The Court concluded that the task of the trial judge is one of "ensuring that an expert's testimony both rests on a reliable foundation and is relevant to the task at hand. Pertinent evidence based on scientifically valid principles," said the Court, "will satisfy those demands."

The plaintiffs in *Daubert* did not argue the merits of DNA testing but claimed instead that the drug Bendectin caused birth defects. Nonetheless, the ***Daubert*** **standard** eased the criteria for the introduction of scientific evidence at both civil and criminal trials—and effectively cleared the way for the use of DNA evidence in the courtroom.[87] Specifically, the *Daubert* Court found that the following factors may be used to determine whether any form of scientific evidence is reliable:

- Whether it has been subjected to testing
- Whether it has been subjected to peer review
- Known or potential rates of error
- The existence of standards controlling application of the techniques involved

***Daubert* standard**
_____

A test of scientific acceptability applicable to the gathering of evidence in criminal cases.

One observer, discussing the general quality of DNA identification methods, notes, "The challenges today are no longer technical; instead they lie in taking the technology and building a meaningful legal infrastructure around it."[88] In other words, it appears to be only a matter of time until DNA evidence will be accepted throughout jurisdictions nationwide (and, probably, worldwide). Once that occurs, it is likely that DNA databases, similar in purpose to today's widely used fingerprint archives, will be established in individual states and at the national level. Today, a number of states and the federal government (through the FBI laboratory) have begun building digitized forensic DNA databases, and in 1998 the FBI announced that its National DNA Index System (NDIS) had begun operation.[89] NDIS enables public forensic laboratories throughout the United States to exchange and compare DNA profiles electronically, thereby linking unsolved serial violent crimes to each other and to known offenders. By June 1998, all 50 states had passed legislation requiring convicted offenders to provide samples for DNA databasing, and all states have been invited to participate in NDIS. The federal DNA Identification Act of 1994[90] authorizes the FBI to establish DNA indexes for (1) offenders convicted of crimes, (2) samples recovered from crime scenes, and (3) samples recovered from unidentified human remains. Although at this point there has been no coordination between the federally funded multibillion-dollar Human Genome Project and forensic DNA programs, future collaboration between the two could lead to explosive growth in the use of human DNA in criminal case processing.

In 1995, British police, operating under the aegis of a new nationwide crime bill, became the first national police force in the world to begin routine collection of DNA samples from anyone involved in a "recordable" offense (a serious crime).[91] As scientific techniques continue to be refined, it appears likely that genetic profiling will become one of the most significant crime-fighting technologies of the twenty-first century. In the words of one forensics expert, "Genetic profiling—the use of biotechnology to identify the unique characteristics of an individual's DNA—is about to become as prevalent as the Breathalyzer and more important than the fingerprint."[92]

In 1996, the NIJ released a comprehensive report on the applicability of DNA testing to criminal case processing. The report, entitled *Convicted by Juries, Exonerated by Science*, called DNA testing "the most important technological breakthrough of twentieth-century forensic science" and provided a detailed review of 28 cases in which post-conviction DNA evidence exonerated defendants who had been sentenced to lengthy prison terms.[93] The 28 cases were selected on the basis of a detailed examination of records that indicated the convicted defendants might have actually been innocent. The men in the study had served, on average, seven years in prison, and most had been tried and sentenced prior to the widespread availability of reliable DNA testing.

LIBRARY
Extra
■ ■ ■ ■

LIBRARY
Extra
■ ■ ■ ■

The report concluded, "Momentum is growing, spurred in part by the public's education from the Simpson trial, for DNA testing in criminal cases. Juries may begin to question cases where the prosecutor does not offer 'conclusive' DNA test results if the evidence is available for testing. More defense attorneys in court-appointed cases may file motions for DNA testing and request the State to pay for the tests."[94] Learn more about the science behind forensic DNA testing and how it has been used to convict as well as exonerate criminal defendants at Library Extra 14–6. An assessment of its likely future is available as Library Extra 14–7 at crimtoday.com.

Computers as Crime-Fighting Tools

The widespread use of computers and computer applications in a diversity of professions has been one of the most far-reaching social phenomena of recent years. Computers are now used to keep records of every imaginable sort, from point-of-sale contacts to inventory maintenance and production schedules. Even organized criminal groups have been known to use computers to record criminal transactions. Computers assist in the design of new technologies and aid in the assignment of resources to problem areas. Police departments, prisons, and courts now commonly employ computer software to schedule facilities and personnel; to keep track of defendants, witnesses, and cases; and to keep account of budgetary matters.

Computers also connect people. The Internet contains a large number of law- and law enforcement–oriented newsgroups and provides access to United Nations and worldwide crime data through its link to the United Nations Criminal Justice Information Network. Other computer services provide access to security information and to software useful in law enforcement administration. Specialized World Wide Web sites, such as the Society of Police Futurists International's home page, the International Association of Chiefs of Police site, and the SEARCH Group's file server, link law enforcement professionals and criminologists throughout the country.

Other innovative computer technologies facilitate the work of enforcement agents. Among them are automated fingerprint identification systems, or AFISs (often with interstate and even international links); computerized crime scene simulations and reenactments; expert systems; and online clearinghouses containing data on criminal activity and on offenders. AFIS, a technology developed some years ago by Hewlett-Packard and Cogent Systems, allows investigators to complete in a matter of minutes what would otherwise consume weeks or months of work manually matching a suspect's fingerprints against stored records. AFIS computers are able to compare and eliminate from consideration many thousands of fingerprints per second, sometimes leading to the identification of a suspect in a short time. "Live-Scan" technology, developed jointly by IBM and Identix, allows for the easy inkless digitizing of fingerprints from live suspects. In like manner, the Bureau of Alcohol, Tobacco, and Firearms' new Bulletproof software takes a 360-degree picture of a bullet's ballistic characteristics and then compares it with others stored in a database to isolate a small universe of potential matches.

Once crime-related information or profiles of criminal offenders have been generated, they are typically stored in a database and often made accessible to law enforcement agencies at other sites. Some of today's most widely used online criminal information services are the FBI's National Crime Information Center, the Violent Criminal Apprehension Program, and METAPOL—an information-sharing network run by the Police Executive Research Forum. Other specialized database programs now track inner-city gang activity and gang membership, contain information on known sexual predators, and describe missing children.

PC radios provide another high-tech weapon in the war on crime. These devices—which are essentially combinations of laptop computers and police radios—were initially tested by the Baltimore, Maryland, police department. Mobile data terminals placed in police cars are proving useful in the apprehension of both traffic violators and other, more serious offenders. Officers use PC radios to (1) obtain motor vehicle information, (2) get detailed information when answering a call, and (3) report incidents either by saving data on disk or by transmitting it to other locations, such as police headquarters. PC radios have also helped befuddle drug dealers who themselves routinely use police scanners to keep abreast of enforcement activities. The digitized transmissions of such devices consist of machine code that cannot be easily read by drug dealers or other criminals trying to outguess the police.

Forensic expert systems, representing yet another computerized law enforcement technology, deploy machine-based artificial intelligence to draw conclusions and to make recommendations to investigators and others interested in solving problems related to crime and its commission. **Expert systems,** developed by professional "knowledge engineers" who work with "knowledge bases" and computer software called "inference engines," attempt to duplicate the decision-making processes used by skilled investigators in the analysis of evidence and in the recognition of patterns that such evidence might represent. One such system is currently being perfected by the FBI's National Center for the Analysis of Violent Crime (NCAVC). The NCAVC expert system attempts to profile serial killers by matching clues left at a crime scene with individual personality characteristics. While the NCAVC system is becoming increasingly sophisticated, it has not yet replaced human investigators. As one FBI developer puts it, "There is certainly no possibility that the system we are devising will ever replace skilled human profilers. Rather, the system will function as a profiler's assistant or consultant."[95]

expert systems

Computer hardware and software that attempt to duplicate the decision-making processes used by skilled investigators in the analysis of evidence and in the recognition of patterns that such evidence might represent.

Finally, a number of specialized computer software programs, such as ImAger, which is produced by Face Software, Inc., and Compusketch, a product of Visatex Corporation, assist police artists in rendering composite images of suspects and missing victims.

Combating Computer Crime

In 1982, sales of information security software products to private companies and government agencies totaled only $51 million. By 1997, expenditures exceeded $425 million, and by 2003, they had grown astronomically to $1.17 billion.[96] Research conducted by Infonetics Research, an international market research and consulting firm specializing in data networking and telecommunications, indicates that worldwide network security appliance and software sales reached more than $4.5 billion in 2006, and were expected to surpass $5 billion in 2007.[97] Among the products in use are **data encryption,** keylog detectors, and Web servers supporting major security protocols. Data encryption is the process by which information is encoded, making it unreadable to all but its intended recipients.

Software alone, however, is not enough. Any effective program intended to secure a company or business operation against the threat of high-tech crime must be built on a realistic threat analysis. **Threat analysis,** sometimes called "risk analysis," involves a complete and thorough assessment of the kinds of perils facing an organization. Some risks, such as floods, tornadoes, hurricanes, and earthquakes, arise from natural events and are often unpredictable. Others, including fire, electrical outages, and disruptions in public services, may be of human origin—but equally difficult to presage. Theft, employee sabotage, and terrorist attacks constitute yet another category of risk—those brought about by intentional human intervention. Responses to unpredictable threats can nonetheless be planned, and strategies for dealing with almost any kind of risk can be implemented. Unless and until an organization adequately assesses the threats to its continuing operation, however, it will be unable to formulate a plan to deal effectively with such risks. Hence, threat analysis is a must for businesses and other organizations preparing to meet the many diverse challenges of today's world.

Once specific threats are identified, strategies tailored to dealing with them can be introduced. For example, one powerful tool useful in identifying instances of computer crime when they occur is the audit trail. Properly defined, an **audit trail** is "a sequential record of system activities that enables auditors to reconstruct, review, and examine the sequence of states and activities surrounding each event in one or more related transactions from inception to output of final results back to inception."[98] In other words, audit trails, which (once implemented) are recorded in some form of computer memory, trace and record the activities of computer operators and facilitate the apprehension of computer criminals.

Unfortunately, although most large companies and financial institutions have fairly extensive computer-security programs, few small businesses, schools, hospitals, and individuals have any real understanding of the need for security in the use of their computers. "What is surprising about computer crime," says computer-security expert Kenneth Rosenblatt, "is how little is being done to deter it: industry will not beef up security, the police are not equipped to catch electronic thieves, and judges do not hand down the kind of sentences that will impress would-be computer criminals. New strategies are urgently needed."[99]

Police Investigation of Computer Crime

Unfortunately, even with new laws for backup, few police departments are prepared with either the time or the qualified personnel to effectively investigate crimes committed by computer criminals. When it comes to computer-crime investigations, one technology expert concludes, "Police departments are simply unsuited to the task."[100] Although specialized computer-crime units have been created in some jurisdictions, they are often poorly funded and seriously understaffed.

---

data encryption

The process by which information is encoded, making it unreadable to all but its intended recipients.

threat analysis

A complete and thorough assessment of the kinds of perils facing an organization.

audit trail

A sequential record of computer system activities that enables auditors to reconstruct, review, and examine the sequence of states and activities surrounding each event in one or more related transactions from inception to output of final results back to inception.

Most state and local police departments do not have personnel skilled in the investigation of such crimes. Most officers know little about tracing the activities of computer criminals, and some police investigators find it difficult to understand how a crime can actually have occurred when nothing at the scene appears to be missing or damaged. Horror stories of botched police investigations are plentiful. They include tales of officers standing by while high-tech offenders perform seemingly innocuous activities that destroy evidence, of seized magnetic or optical media allowed to bake in the sun on the dashboards of police vehicles, and of the loss of evidence stored on magnetic media due to exposure to police clipboards and evidence lockers containing magnets.

Police departments also sometimes intentionally avoid computer-crime investigations because they may be complex and demanding. The amount of time and money spent on computer-crime investigations, it is often felt, could better be spent elsewhere. It is not unusual for these investigations to cross state lines and to involve a number of telecommunications companies and other services. Additionally, investigators who spend a lot of time on crimes involving computers tend to not be promoted as readily as their more glamorous counterparts in the homicide and property crime divisions, and personnel who are truly skilled in computer applications are apt to take jobs with private industries where pay scales are far higher than in police work. As a consequence of these considerations and others, many police departments and the investigators who staff them frequently accord computer crime a low priority, focusing instead on highly visible offenses, such as murder and rape, and seeing computer-crime victims as too wealthy to be seriously affected by the crimes they experience.

The situation is changing, however, thanks to federal intervention. In 1992, the FBI formed a National Computer Crime Squad (NCCS)[101] to investigate violations of the federal Computer Fraud and Abuse Act of 1984[102] and other federal computer-crime laws. Later, most of the FBI's larger offices established their own computer-crime squads to conduct high-tech investigations in the areas they serve. Prior to the creation of the Department of Homeland Security, the FBI's Washington Field Office housed the agency's Infrastructure Protection and Computer Intrusion Squad (IPCIS). IPCIS was responsible for investigating unauthorized intrusions into major computer networks belonging to telecommunications providers, private corporations, U.S. government agencies, and public and private educational facilities.[103] The squad, whose duties have been transferred to DHS, also investigated the illegal interception of signals (especially cable and satellite signal theft) and the infringement of copyright laws related to software.

WEB
Extra
▪ ▪ ▪ ▪

A similar agency, the Computer Crime and Intellectual Property Section within the Criminal Division of the DOJ, began in 1991 as the DOJ's Computer Crime Unit. The CCIPS staff consists of about two dozen lawyers who focus exclusively on the issues raised by computer and intellectual property crime. CCIPS staffers work closely on computer-crime cases with assistant U.S. attorneys known as "computer and telecommunications coordinators" in U.S. attorney's offices around the country.[104] CCIPS attorneys take a leading role in litigating some computer crime and intellectual property investigations and a coordinating role in some national investigations. Section attorneys advise federal prosecutors and law enforcement agents, comment upon and propose legislation, coordinate international efforts to combat computer crime, litigate cases, and train federal law enforcement groups. Visit CCIPS via **Web Extra 14–7**.

One of the first large-scale federal computer-crime operations took place in 1997, when FBI agents raided the homes and offices of about a dozen Webmasters suspected of pirating software in eight cities across the country. The operation, code-named Cyber Strike, resulted from NCCS monitoring of Internet Relay Chat channels and file transfers over the Internet.[105]

Automated monitoring of network traffic is an area of considerable interest to law enforcement officials. One network "sniffer" created by the FBI called **DCS–1000** (previously known as "Carnivore") was a diagnostic tool intended to assist in criminal investigations by monitoring and capturing large amounts of Internet traffic. DCS–1000 was to be installed by FBI agents in ISP data centers as the need arose to monitor the electronic communications of individuals suspected of federal crimes like terrorism. The DCS–1000 sniffer could snoop essentially all data flowing through a network and

DCS–1000

An FBI-developed network diagnostic tool that is capable of assisting in criminal investigations by monitoring and capturing large amounts of Internet traffic. Previously called *Carnivore*.

save the bits that fit a specific profile—e-mail sent to or received from a particular user name, for example, or all data sent to Web sites from a particular address. DCS–1000 could scan millions of e-mail messages per second, processing as much as 6 gigabytes (6,000 megabytes) of data every hour.[106] The Carnivore/DCS–1000 initiative was abandoned by the FBI in 2005, however, when the agency concluded that readily available commercial eavesdropping software was available that could perform the same tasks.[107] Learn more about the challenges facing American law enforcement agencies when it comes to computer- and Internet-related crime by reading **Library Extra 14–8** at crimtoday.com.

LIBRARY
Extra
■ ■ ■ ■

Dealing with Computer Criminals

While any effective policy for dealing with computer and high-tech crime must recognize the issues associated with personal freedoms and individual rights in the information age, a second aspect of effective policy necessarily relates to crime control. How can high-tech criminals be deterred? If they succeed in committing criminal acts, how can they be reformed? Kenneth Rosenblatt, who focused on computer crimes during his work as a California district attorney, suggests three sanctions that he feels would be especially effective in deterring high-tech offenders:[108]

- Confiscating equipment used to commit a computer crime
- Limiting the offender's use of computers
- Restricting the offender's freedom to accept jobs involving computers

Such penalties, says Rosenblatt, could be supplemented by a few days or weeks in a county jail, with longer periods of incarceration applicable in serious cases. "In my experience," Rosenblatt adds, "one of the best ways to hurt computer offenders, especially young hackers, is to take away their toys."[109]

Securing the Internet

America is quickly moving toward becoming a service-oriented, information-rich society. John Naisbitt, author of *Megatrends,* explained it this way: "The transition from an industrial to an information society does not mean manufacturing will cease to exist or become unimportant. Did farming end with the industrial era? Ninety percent of us produced 100 percent of the food in the agricultural era; now 3 percent of us produce 100 percent. . . . In the information age, the focus of manufacturing will shift from the physical to more intellectual functions on which the physical depends."[110]

Although goods and materials will always need to be created, transported, and distributed, it is information that forms the lifeblood of the new world order. Information, many pundits believe, is now the most valuable resource of our age, comparable to—and even exceeding—the value that natural resources like oil, gas, coal, and gold held over the past few centuries. As Naisbitt states, "Information is an economic entity because it costs something to produce and because people are willing to pay for it."[111] Nations that are able to effectively manage valuable information and that can make it accessible to their citizens will receive enhanced productivity and greater wealth as a reward. Moving information safely and securely is also important, and today a large part of that responsibility falls to the Internet. The Internet is a way of moving data quickly and of making information accessible to masses of citizens who can use it productively. The **Internet,** the world's largest computer network, had its beginnings a couple of decades ago with the linkage of military and scientific computer facilities already existing on the Arpnet and Milnet. Today, the Internet consists of a vast resource of tens of thousands of computers around the world that are all linked together.

The Internet provides some amazing and constantly growing capabilities—not the least of which are access to Web sites, e-mail, mailing lists, newsgroups, and file transfer

Internet

The world's largest computer network.

capability. Although in its early days Internet access was originally restricted to commercial users, researchers, and university personnel, access to the Internet is routine today. A large number of direct ISPs furnish Internet access to anyone able to pay the monthly fee. Web browsers combine with search engines like Google to make it easy to search the tremendous amount of information on the Web and to interact with other Internet users.

Unfortunately, as the Internet has grown, it has been targeted by hackers and computer criminals, some of whom have introduced rogue computer programs into the network's machines. In 1988, for example, the infamous Internet "worm" written by Cornell University graduate student Robert T. Morris, Jr., circulated through computers connected to the Internet, effectively disabling many of them. Morris was later arrested and sentenced in 1990 to 400 hours of community service and three years of probation. He was also fined $10,000. Since Morris's day, many other hackers have exploited loopholes in the software and hardware supporting the Internet.

In 1996, in response to the growing threat to the nation's information systems, President Clinton created the Commission on Critical Infrastructure Protection.[112] The commission was charged with assessing threats to the nation's computer networks and recommending policies to protect them. Security issues related to information systems that control the nation's telecommunications, electric power, oil and gas, banking and finance, transportation, water supply, emergency services, and government operations were studied by the commission, which issued its report in October 1997. Among its recommendations, the commission proposed (1) establishing an Information Analysis and Warning Center to collect information on computer security breaches in industry and government; (2) creating legislation to permit private companies to conduct special background checks when hiring computer experts for sensitive positions; (3) creating a White House office to coordinate the information security roles of government, including the departments of Commerce, Defense, Energy, Justice, Treasury, and Transportation; and (4) quadrupling research on cyberspace security to $1 billion by the year 2004.[113]

The National Infrastructure Protection Center (NIPC) was created in 1998 and was located at the FBI's headquarters in Washington, D.C. NIPC's mission was to serve as the federal government's center for threat assessment, warnings, investigation, and response for threats or attacks against the nation's critical infrastructures. Its successor, the Information Analysis and Infrastructure Protection (IAIP) Directorate, operates today within the Department of Homeland Security. Visit IAIP via Web Extra 14–8.

WEB
Extra
▪ ▪ ▪ ▪

In February 2000, the President's Working Group on Unlawful Conduct on the Internet released a report entitled *The Electronic Frontier: The Challenge of Unlawful Conduct Involving the Use of the Internet.*[114] The group reported that "similar to the technologies that have preceded it, the Internet provides a new tool for wrongdoers to commit crimes, such as fraud, the sale or distribution of child pornography, the sale of guns or drugs or other regulated substances without regulatory protections, or the unlawful distribution of computer software or other creative material protected by intellectual property rights. In the most extreme circumstances, cyberstalking and other criminal conduct involving the Internet can lead to physical violence, abductions, and molestation." Some criminal activities, the group observed, "employ both the product delivery and communications features of the Internet." Pedophiles, for example, "may use the Internet's file transfer utilities to distribute and receive child pornography, and use its communications features to make contact with children."

The group said that "although the precise extent of unlawful conduct involving the use of computers is unclear, the rapid growth of the Internet and e-commerce has made such unlawful conduct a critical priority for legislators, policymakers, industry, and law enforcement agencies." One reason is the Internet's potential to reach vast audiences easily, meaning that the potential scale of unlawful conduct is often much wider in cyberspace than in the real world.

Significantly, said the report's authors, cybercriminals are no longer hampered by the existence of national or international boundaries because information and property can be easily transmitted through communications and data networks. As a result, a criminal no longer needs to be at the actual scene of the crime (or anywhere nearby) to prey on his or her victims. A computer server running a Web page designed to defraud senior citizens, for example, might be located in Thailand, and victims of the scam could be scattered throughout the world. A child pornographer might distribute photographs or videos via e-mail making its way through the communications networks of several countries before reaching the intended recipients. Likewise, evidence of a crime can be stored at a remote location, either for the purpose of concealing the crime from law enforcement and others or simply because of the design of the network. To clarify its point about jurisdictional issues, the working group gave this example: "A cyberstalker in Brooklyn, New York, may send a threatening e-mail to a person in Manhattan. If the stalker routes his communication through Argentina, France, and Norway before reaching his victim, the New York Police Department may have to get assistance from the Office of International Affairs at the Department of Justice in Washington, D.C., which, in turn, may have to get assistance from law enforcement in (say) Buenos Aires, Paris, and Oslo just to learn that the suspect is in New York." In this example, the working group points out, the perpetrator needs no passport and passes through no checkpoints as he commits his crime, while law enforcement agencies are burdened with cumbersome mechanisms for international cooperation—mechanisms that often derail or slow investigations. Because the gathering of information in other jurisdictions and internationally will be crucial to investigating and prosecuting cybercrimes, the President's Working Group concluded that "all levels of government will need to develop concrete and reliable mechanisms for cooperating with each other." Read the entire text of *The Electronic Frontier* via **Web Extra 14–9**.

WEB
Extra

Finally, in September 2003, the U.S. government established the United States Computer Emergency Readiness Team (US–CERT). US–CERT is a partnership between the Department of Homeland Security and the public and private sectors. It was created to protect the nation's Internet infrastructure and to coordinate defenses against cyberattacks across the nation. US–CERT is in charge of the National Cyber Alert System, which it describes as "America's first cohesive national cyber security system for identifying, analyzing, and prioritizing emerging vulnerabilities and threats."[115] The Cyber Alert System relays computer security update and warning information to anyone who subscribes to its bulletins, and it provides all citizens—from computer security professionals to home computer users with basic skills—with free, timely, actionable information to better secure their computer systems. Visit US–CERT at **Web Extra 14–10**.

WEB
Extra

Policy Issues: Personal Freedoms in the Information Age

The continued development of telecommunications resources has led not only to concerns about security and data integrity, but also to an expanding interest in privacy, free speech, and personal freedoms. While the First and Fourth Amendments of the Constitution guarantee each of us freedom of speech and security in our "persons, houses, papers, and effects, against unreasonable searches and seizures," it is understandably silent on the subject of electronic documents and advanced forms of communication facilitated by technologies that did not exist at the time of the Constitutional Convention.

Within the context of contemporary society, we are left to ask, "What is speech? What are papers?" Do electronic communications qualify for protection under the First Amendment, as does the spoken word? In an era when most houses are wired for telephones and many support data links that extend well beyond voice capabilities, it becomes necessary to ask what constitutes one's "speech" or one's "home." What, exactly, is speech? Does e-mail qualify as speech? Where does the concept of a home begin and end for purposes of constitutional guarantees? Do activities within the home that can be accessed from without (as when a computer Web site is run out of a home) fall under the same constitutional guarantees as a private conversation held within the physical confines of a house?

These and questions like them will be debated for years to come. In 1990, however, concerned individuals banded together to form the Electronic Frontier Foundation, a

Theory Versus Reality

Press Release Announcing the Formation of the Electronic Frontier Foundation

In 1990, the Electronic Frontier Foundation (EFF) came into being. What follows are excerpts from the original press release announcing formation of the EFF.

FOR IMMEDIATE RELEASE

NEW FOUNDATION ESTABLISHED TO ENCOURAGE COMPUTER-BASED COMMUNICATIONS POLICIES

Washington, D.C., July 10, 1990—Mitchell D. Kapor, founder of Lotus Development Corporation and ON Technology, today announced that he, along with colleague John Perry Barlow, has established a foundation to address social and legal issues arising from the impact on society of the increasingly pervasive use of computers as a means of communication and information distribution. The Electronic Frontier Foundation (EFF) will support and engage in public education on current and future developments in computer-based and telecommunications media. In addition, it will support litigation in the public interest to preserve, protect and extend First Amendment rights within the realm of computing and telecommunications technology.

Initial funding for the Foundation comes from private contributions by Kapor and Steve Wozniak, co-founder of Apple Computer, Inc. The Foundation expects to actively raise contributions from a wide constituency.

Source: The Electronic Frontier Foundation.

citizens' group funded by private contributions that set for itself the task of actively assisting in refining notions of privacy and legality as they relate to telecommunications and other computer-based media. In the foundation's own words, "The Electronic Frontier Foundation (EFF) was founded in July of 1990 to ensure that the principles embodied in the Constitution and the Bill of Rights are protected as new communications technologies emerge. From the beginning, EFF has worked to shape our nation's communications infrastructure and the policies that govern it in order to maintain and enhance First Amendment, privacy and other democratic values. We believe that our overriding public goal must be the creation of Electronic Democracy."[116] As Mitch Kapor, EFF cofounder and former president of Lotus Development Corporation, explained, "It is becoming increasingly obvious that the rate of technology advancement in communications is far outpacing the establishment of appropriate cultural, legal and political frameworks to handle the issues that are arising."[117]

EFF, which also supports litigation in the public interest, has been an active supporter of the public advocacy group Computer Professionals for Social Responsibility (CPSR), based in Palo Alto, California. CPSR maintains a Computing and Civil Liberties Project much in keeping with EFF's purpose. Initial EFF litigation focused on a request for full federal government disclosure of information regarding the seizure of Jackson Games's computer equipment. Jackson Games, an Austin-based game manufacturer, was a target in the U.S. Secret Service's Operation Sun Devil. In a second action, the foundation sought *amicus curiae* (friend of the court) status in a federal case against Craig Neidorf, a 20-year-old University of Missouri student who had been editor of the electronic newsletter *Phrack World News.* EFF also supported challenges to the Communications Decency Act that resulted in the 1997 Supreme Court ruling in *Reno* v. *ACLU,* which found key provisions of the act to be unconstitutional. Visit the EFF on the Web via **Web Extra 14–11.**

WEB
Extra

SUMMARY

High-technology offenses could dramatically change our understanding of crime. Illegal wire transfers of huge asset stores, bioterrorism, nuclear subterfuge, and computer crime are emerging as novel forms of criminal enterprise. Some forms of high-tech crime, committed without regard for national borders or even the need for physical travel, hold dangers never before imagined. A destructive high-technology incursion into computers of the nation's financial centers, for example, could throw the economy into chaos. A single incident of nuclear terrorism could destroy more property and claim more human lives than decades of traditional criminal activity.

The very nature of contemporary society dictates that crimes exploiting high technology will always be with us. It can only be hoped that enforcement technologies continue to keep abreast of technologies that serve criminal purposes. Unfortunately, however, no one is able to realistically assess the current extent of high-tech crime, let alone accurately imagine all the forms that future high-tech crimes will take.

Efforts to control high-tech crime open a Pandora's box of issues related to individual rights in the face of criminal investigation and prosecution. Such issues extend from free speech considerations to guarantees of technological privacy in the midst of digital interconnectedness. As we move through the early decades of the twenty-first century, it will be necessary for our society to strike an acceptable balance between constitutional guarantees of continued freedom of access to legitimate activities based on high technology and enforcement initiatives that can deal effectively with the massive threat high-tech crimes represent.

KEY TERMS

audit trail, 606

Communications Decency Act, 589

computer abuse, 590

computer crime, 581

computer-related crime, 590

computer virus, 580

Cyber Security Enhancement
    Act, 588

cybercrime, 582

cyberspace, 590

data encryption, 606

Daubert standard, 603

DCS–1000, 607

Digital Theft Deterrence
    and Copyright Damages Improvement
    Act, 588

DNA profiling, 602

expert systems, 605

hacker, 580

identity theft, 596

Internet, 608

No Electronic Theft Act, 588

phishing, 584

phone phreak, 582

software piracy, 581

TEMPEST, 580

threat analysis, 606

KEY CASES

Daubert v. *Merrell Dow*
    Pharmaceuticals, Inc., 603

Frye v. *United States,* 603

Reno v. *ACLU,* 589

QUESTIONS FOR REVIEW

1. How does advancing technology produce new forms of crime? How does it affect crime fighting?

2. How does technology provide criminal opportunity? Why does advancing technology sometimes necessitate new criminal laws?

3. What different types of computer criminals does this chapter describe? Why do some hackers commit criminal mischief?

4. What is identity theft? How can identities be stolen? What can be done to reduce the impact of identity theft on victims?

5. What new technologies are being used in today's fight against crime?

6. What is being done to combat computer crime and to secure the Internet today?

7. What are some of the personal freedoms that are threatened by today's need for advanced security?

QUESTIONS FOR REFLECTION

1. This book emphasizes a social problems versus a social responsibility theme. Which perspective best explains the involvement of capable individuals in criminal activity necessitating high-tech skills? What is the best way to deal with such criminals?

2. What is the difference between high-tech crime and traditional forms of criminal activity? Will the high-tech crimes of today continue to be the high-tech crimes of tomorrow? Why?

3. What forms of high-tech crime can you imagine that this chapter has not discussed? Describe each briefly.

4. Do you believe that high-tech crimes will eventually surpass the abilities of enforcement agents to prevent or solve them? Why?

5. What different kinds of high-tech offenders can you imagine? What is the best way to deal with each type of offender? Give reasons for your answers.

WEB QUEST

On November 23, 2001, the 41-nation Council of Europe (www.coe.int) finalized its Convention on Cybercrime—an international treaty to standardize cybercrime laws throughout Europe. The council's efforts focused closely on laws against online pornography, hacking, fraud, viruses, and other Internet criminal activity. The treaty requires each member country to assume responsibility for developing legislation to ensure that individual offenders can be held liable for crimes outlined in the treaty. The treaty also standardizes methods of securing cyberevidence and tracking and prosecuting cybercriminals—who routinely operate without regard for national borders.

Work to ratify the treaty took four years and met stiff opposition from many powerful groups who objected to a number of the treaty's provisions because of concerns over individual privacy. The need to balance individual privacy with the needs of law enforcement agencies continues to be a source of concern for council members. Some interest groups are especially concerned that giving European police agencies the power to monitor communications on the Internet, as provided for in the treaty, will allow for the identification of political dissidents and lead to the persecution of minorities.

Access the council's Cybercrime Convention and related information on the Internet at http://conventions.coe.int/Treaty/Commun/QueVoulezVous.asp?NT=185&CM=8&DF=6/2/2007&CL=ENG.

Review the treaty and develop a personal statement encompassing your views on the treaty's provisions. What do you like about the treaty? What do you find problematic? Why? Submit your conclusions to your instructor if requested to do so.

NOTES

[1] National Intelligence Council, *Global Trends 2015: A Dialogue about the Future with Nongovernment Experts* (Washington, DC: Central Intelligence Agency, December 2000), p. 10.

[2] David Noack, "'Love Bug' Damage Worldwide: $10 Billion," APB News, May 8, 2000, www.apbnews.com/newscenter/internetcrime/2000/05/08/lovebug_impact0508_01.html (accessed January 22, 2006).

[3] MCA/Universal Pictures, 1992.

[4] Georgette Bennett, *Crimewarps: The Future of Crime in America* (New York: Anchor, 1987), p. xiii.

[5] *Ashcroft* v. *ACLU*, 535 U.S. 564 (2002).

[6] James Vincini, "Supreme Court Bars Enforcement of Internet Porn Law," ABC News online, June 29, 2004, http://abcnews.go.com/wire/US/reuters20040629_330.html (accessed July 29, 2007).

[7] Michael McGough, "Supreme Court Blocks Law to Protect Kids from Internet Porn," Post-Gazette.com, June 30, 2004, http://www.post-gazette.com/pg/04182/339554.stm (accessed July 29, 2007).

[8] Ian Urbina, "Federal Judge Blocks Online Pornography Law," *New York Times*, March 22, 2007, http://www.nytimes.com/2007/03/22/us/22cnd-porn.html?ex=1182225600&en=d7ec9a5a5472681a&ei=5070 (accessed June 17, 2007).

[9] 18 U.S.C. Section 2256(8).

[10] *Ashcroft* v. *The Free Speech Coalition*, 535 U.S. 234 (2002).

[11] Public Law 106–554.

[12] *United States* v. *American Library Association, Inc.*, 593 U.S. 194 (2003).

[13] "Porn in the U.S.A.," CBS News.com, May 21, 2003, http://www.cbsnews.com/stories/2003/11/21/60minutes/main585049.shtml (accessed July 29, 2006).

[14] Robert Green, "CIA Warns of Nuclear Threat from Russian Gangs," Reuters, June 27, 1994.

[15] "Fears Grow over Russia's Nuclear Arsenal," Reuters, February 7, 1997.

[16] Kenneth Rosenblatt, "Deterring Computer Crime," *Technology Review*, Vol. 93, No. 2 (February/March 1990), pp. 34–41.

[17] Ibid.

[18] Richard H. Baker, *The Computer Security Handbook* (Blue Ridge Summit, PA: TAB Books, 1985).

[19] David L. Carter, "Computer Crime Categories: How Technocriminals Operate," *FBI Law Enforcement Bulletin*, http://nsi.org/Library/Compsec/crimecom.html (accessed January 11, 2007).

[20] Catherine H. Conly and J. Thomas McEwen, "Computer Crime," *NIJ Reports,* January/February 1990, p. 3.

[21] David McGuire, "Study: Online Crime Costs Rising," *Washington Post*, May 24, 2004, http://www.washingtonpost.com/wp-dyn/articles/A53042-2004May24.html (accessed July 30, 2005).

[22] Dan Briody, "Keep Out," *Inc.*, March 2007, http://www.inc.com/magazine/20070301/technology-security.html (accessed June 17, 2007).

[23] Software and Information Industry Association, *Report on Global Software Piracy 2000*, p. 7, http://www.siia.net/piracy/pubs/piracy2000.pdf.

[24] Business Software Alliance, http://www.bsa.org/globalstudy/upload/2007-Losses-Global.pdf (accessed July 24, 2007).

[25] Gary H. Anthes, "Software Pirates' Booty Topped $13B, Study Finds," *Computerworld,* January 6, 1997, p. 24.

[26] Stephen R. Purdy, "Protecting Your Telephone Systems against Dial-Tone Thieves," *Infosecurity News*, July/August 1993, p. 43.

[27] "Out Slicked," *Infosecurity News*, July/August 1993, p. 11.

[28] Paul Keegan, "High Tech Pirates Collecting Phone Calls," *USA Today*, September 23, 1994, p. 4A.

[29] Ibid.

30 Fraser Lovatt, "U.S. Department of Justice: VoIP Fosters Crime, Drugs and Terrorism," Digital-Lifestyles.info, June 18, 2004, http://digital-lifestyles.info/display_page.asp?section=business&id=1318 (accessed August 1, 2006).

31 The Anti-Phishing Working Group, "Phishing Activity Trends," http://www.antiphishing.org/reports/apwg_report_april_2007.pdf (accessed June 17, 2007).

32 Gregg Keizer, "Gartner: Phishing Attacks Threaten E-Commerce," Security Pipeline.com, www.securitypipeline.com/news/20000036 (accessed July 30, 2007).

33 This and most other definitions related to computer crime in this chapter are taken from Donn B. Parker, *Computer Crime: Criminal Justice Resource Manual* (Washington, DC: National Institute of Justice, 1989).

34 "Palm, Other Handheld Devices to Face Virus Threats," Reuters, August 31, 2000, http://www.bostonherald.com/business/technology/palm08312000.htm (accessed January 11, 2006).

35 "New 'Love Bug' Charges Sought," Associated Press, September 5, 2000, www.msnbc.com/news/455702.asp (accessed January 12, 2006).

36 Noack, "'Love Bug' Damage Worldwide: $10 Billion."

37 Section 225 of the Homeland Security Act, Public Law 107–296.

38 Public Law 106–160.

39 Public Law 105–147.

40 Title 18 U.S.C. Section 1030.

41 And as amended by the National Information Infrastructure Protection Act of 1996; Public Law 104–294.

42 18 U.S.C. Section 1029.

43 As described in M. Gemignani, "Viruses and Computer Law," *Communications of the ACM,* Vol. 32 (June 1989), p. 669.

44 Enacted as Section 225 of the Homeland Security Act of 2002, H.R. 5710.

45 Public Law 104–104, 110 Stat. 56.

46 *Reno* v. *ACLU,* 521 U.S. 844 (1997).

47 Texas Penal Code, Section 33.01.

48 Virginia Criminal Code, Sections 18.2–152.2 through 18.2–152.7.

49 Brian S. Akre, "Internet-Torture," Associated Press, February 10, 1995.

50 Ibid.

51 Jim Schaefer and Maryanne George, "Internet User's Charges Dismissed—U.S. Criticized for Pursuing U-M Case," *Detroit Free Press,* June 22, 1995.

52 Parker, *Computer Crime.*

53 Steve Miletich, no title, *Seattle Post-Intelligencer,* via Simon & Schuster NewsLink online, May 21, 1997.

54 Paul Saffo, "Desperately Seeking Cyberspace," *Personal Computing,* May 1989, p. 247.

55 Ibid.

56 John Markoff, "Cyberpunks," *New York Times Upfront,* Vol. 132, No. 15 (March 27, 2000), pp. 10–14.

57 J. Bloombecker, "A Security Manager's Guide to Hacking," *DATAPRO Reports on Information Security,* Report IS35–450–101, 1986.

58 Marc Robins, "Case of the Ticked-Off Teens," *Infosecurity News,* July/August 1993, p. 48.

59 For more information, see Ronald R. Thrasher, "Voice-Mail Fraud," *FBI Law Enforcement Bulletin,* July 1994, pp. 1–4.

60 J. Maxfield, "Computer Bulletin Boards and the Hacker Problem," *EDPACS, the Electric Data Processing Audit, Control and Security Newsletter* (Arlington, VA: Automation Training Center, October 1985).

61 Percy Black, personal communication, 1991. As cited in M. E. Kabay, "Computer Crime: Hackers" (undated electronic manuscript).

62 John Perry Barlow, "Crime and Puzzlement: In Advance of the Law on the Electronic Frontier," *Whole Earth Review* (fall 1990), p. 44.

63 As cited in ibid.

64 "Computer Porn," *Time,* March 15, 1993, p. 22.

65 Details for this story come from "Britain, U.S. Break Up Online Pedophile Ring," http://www.msnbc.msn.com/id/19288057 (accessed June 18, 2007).

66 Parker, *Computer Crime.*

67 The President's Identity Theft Task Force, *Combating Identity Theft: A Strategic Plan* (Washington, DC: U.S. Department of Justice, 2007), from which much of the information comes, and from which some of the wording is taken or adapted.

68 Office of Community Oriented Policing Services, *A National Strategy to Combat Identity Theft* (Washington, DC: COPS Office, 2006), for which some of the materials in this section are taken.

69 Federal Trade Commission, *Identity Theft Survey Report,* Prepared by Synovate, September 2003.

70 Ibid.

71 See Business Software Alliance, *Consumer Confidence in Online Shopping Buoyed by Security Software Protection, BSA Survey Suggests,* January 12, 2006, http://www.bsacybersafety.com/news/2005-Online-Shopping-Confidence.cfm.

72 See Cyber Security Industry Alliance, *Internet Security Voter Survey,* June 2005, https://www.csialliance.org/publications/surveys_and_polls/CSIA_Internet_Security_Survey_June_2005.pdf.

73 U.S. Code, Title 18, Section 1028.

74 H.R. 1731 (2004).

75 "Three Strikes, He's Out: Woods' Identity Thief Gets 200 Years-to-Life," Associated Press, April 28, 2001.

76 Katrina Baum, *Identity Theft, 2004* (Washington, DC: Bureau of Justice Statistics, 2006).

77 Much of the information in this paragraph is adapted from National White Collar Crime Center, "WCC Issue: Identity Theft," http://www.nw3c.org/papers/Identity_Theft.pdf (accessed May 18, 2007).

78 The information, and some of the wording, in this section is taken from *Combating Identity Theft: A Strategic Plan,* op. cit.

79 *See* U.S. Attorney's Office, Southern District of Florida, press release, July 19, 2006, http://www.usdoj.gov/usao/fls/PressReleases/060719-01.html.

80 Ibid., pp. 22–51.

81 For insight into how security techniques often lag behind the abilities of criminal perpetrators in the high-technology arena, see James A. Fagin, "Computer Crime: A Technology Gap," *International Journal of Comparative and Applied Criminal Justice,* Vol. 15, Nos. 1 and 2 (spring/fall 1991), pp. 285–297.

82 Richard Larson, "The New Crime Stoppers: State-of-the-Art Computer Technology Promises a Return to Neighborhood-Oriented Policing," *Technology Review,* Vol. 92, No. 8 (November/December 1989), p. 26.

83 "DNA Frees Man Sentenced to Life," Associated Press, January 16, 2001, www.msnbc.com/news/517172.asp (accessed January 17, 2005).

84 Michael Schrage, "Today, It Takes a Scientist to Catch a Thief," *Washington Post,* March 18, 1994.

85 *Daubert* v. *Merrell Dow Pharmaceuticals, Inc.,* 509 U.S. 579 (1993).

86 *Frye* v. *United States,* 54 App. D.C. 46, 47, 293 F. 1013, 1014 (1923).

87 For the application of *Daubert* to DNA technology, see Barry Sheck, "DNA and Daubert," *Cardozo Law Review,* Vol. 15 (1994), p. 1959.

88 Schrage, "Today, It Takes a Scientist to Catch a Thief."

89 See FBI press release, October 13, 1998, http://www.fbi.gov/pressrm/pressrel/pressrel98/dna.htm (accessed January 22, 2003).

90 42 U.S.C. § 14132.

91 "British Police to Use DNA to Catch Burglars," Reuters, June 16, 1994.

92 Schrage, "Today, It Takes a Scientist to Catch a Thief."

93 Edward Connors et al., *Convicted by Juries, Exonerated by Science: Case Studies in the Use of DNA Evidence to Establish Innocence after Trial* (Washington, DC: National Institute of Justice, 1996).

94 Ibid.

95 Roland Reboussin, "An Expert System Designed to Profile Murderers," in Frank Schmalleger, ed., *Computers in Criminal Justice: Issues and Applications* (Bristol, IN: Wyndham Hall Press, 1990), p. 239.

96 Japan Electronics Industry Association, *Industry Monitor: High-Tech Sector*, "Security Software Demand to Show Strong Growth—Week Ended June 27, 2004," http://www.irstreet.com/top/im/im20040627.pdf (accessed July 30, 2006).

97 Kate Dostart, "Network Security, Content Security Markets to Grow in 2007," Networking.com, March 29, 2007, http://searchnetworking.techtarget.com/originalContent/0,289142,sid7_gci1249441,00.html (accessed June 27, 2007).

98 Parker, *Computer Crime*, p. xiii.

99 Kenneth Rosenblatt, "Deterring Computer Crime," *Technology Review*, Vol. 93, No. 2 (February/March 1990), pp. 34–41.

100 Ibid.

101 The NCCS can be found at http://www.fbi.gov/programs/nccs/comcrim.htm.

102 As modified in 1986, 1988, and later years.

103 Adapted from the FBI's Washington Field Office Infrastructure Protection and Computer Intrusion Squad home page at http://www.fbi.gov/programs/ipcis/ipcis.htm.

104 Adapted from the Computer Crime and Intellectual Property Section of the Criminal Division of the U.S. Department of Justice home page at http://www.cybercrime.gov.

105 Wylie Wong, "FBI Targets BBS Operators, Seizes Hardware in Software Piracy Sting," *Computerworld*, February 3, 1997, p. 24.

106 "How Powerful Is Carnivore?" Associated Press, November 17, 2000, http://www.msnbc.com/news/491454.asp (accessed January 12, 2004).

107 The Liberty Coalition, "Carnivore/DCS–1000," http://www.libertycoalition.net/backgrounders/carnivore-dcs-1000 (accessed June 17, 2007).

108 Rosenblatt, "Deterring Computer Crime."

109 Ibid.

110 John Naisbitt, *Megatrends: Ten New Directions Transforming Our Lives* (New York: Warner, 1982), p. 36.

111 Ibid.

112 Gary H. Anthes, "White House Launches Cybershield," *Computerworld*, July 22, 1996, p. 29.

113 M. J. Zuckerman, "Clinton to Get Cyberterror Plan," *USA Today*, October 9, 1997, p. 1A.

114 The quotations attributed to the President's Working Group in this section are from President's Working Group on Unlawful Conduct on the Internet, *The Electronic Frontier: The Challenge of Unlawful Conduct Involving the Use of the Internet* (Washington, DC: White House, 2000), http://www.usdoj.gov/criminal/cybercrime/unlawful.htm (accessed April 16, 2007).

115 United States Computer Emergency Readiness Team, "About Us," http://www.us-cert.gov/aboutus.html (accessed August 1, 2007).

116 Original EFF Statement of Purpose, from the EFF Web site, http://eff.org/abouteff.html (accessed April 20, 2001). For the EFF's most recent statement of purpose see http://www.eff.org/about (accessed June 2, 2007).

117 S. Mace, "Kapor and Wozniak Establish Electronic Policy Foundation," *InfoWorld*, Vol. 12, No. 29 (July 16, 1990), p. 6.

Chapter 15

Globalization and Terrorism

Outline

... international implications for America's criminal justice system have never been greater. As the country's social, economic, and technological climate continue to undergo major changes, globalization is also producing new challenges for criminal justice practitioners and researchers. Among the more significant aspects of this change ... are the international dimensions of crime, the impact of legal and illegal immigration, transnational organized crime, technological influences on global criminality, and the influence of a more diversified American culture.

—Richard H. Ward, Associate Vice President, Sam Houston State University[1]

Criminal behavior cannot ultimately be understood apart from the cultural context in which it occurs.

—Piers Beirne, Professor of Criminology and Legal Studies, University of Southern Maine[2]

Those who employ terrorism....strive to subvert the rule of law and effect change through violence and fear.

—National Stratgey for Combating Terrorism

Learning Outcomes

After reading this chapter, you should be able to

- Define *globalization* and tell how it impacts contemporary criminal and terrorist activity
- Explain comparative criminology and describe the advantages of a comparative approach to the study of crime and criminals
- Define *terrorism*, and identify various types of terrorism and possible methods for the control of terrorism

Hear the author discuss this chapter at **crimtoday.com**

Introduction

In 2007, officials of Cincinnati-based Chiquita Brands International admitted in federal court that executives with the company had paid protection money to Colombian terrorists to help secure their most profitable banana-growing operations.[3] Under a plea arraignment, the company pleaded guilty to one count of doing business with a terrorist organization—a crime under federal law—and will pay a $25 million fine. The deal, however, allowed the identities of several senior executives involved in the illegal protection payments to remain anonymous. Attorneys for Chiquita said that the company was forced to make the payments and was acting only to ensure the safety of its workers.

Globalization

The payment of protection monies to a South American terrorist organization by an Ohio-based banana importer illustrates the complexity of contemporary international business operations—which often occur in the midst of intricate political situations and which can be impacted by the interests of a wide variety of groups. On a global scale, society is experiencing a period of unprecedented change. Both the substance and the pace of change are fundamentally different from what has occurred in past decades and centuries. Sequences of events are no longer occurring in relative isolation, and are happening ever more quickly. No longer are discrete groups of people affected by each change; rather, there is greater simultaneity of occurrence, swifter interpenetration, and increased feedback of one set of changes upon another.[4]

The increasing integration of previously isolated events in all spheres of endeavor, and their overlapping impact on people far and wide, is an important aspect of **globalization.** The economist Thomas L. Friedman says that globalization will likely be the most pervasive influence affecting the entire world in the first part of the twenty-first century.[5]

Globalization can be defined as a process of social homogenization by which the experiences of everyday life, marked by the diffusion of commodities and ideas, can foster a standardization of cultural expressions around the world.[6] Globalization, which today is occuring in many spheres, including communications, economics, science, education, and business, involves the progressive erosion of the influence of nation-states and the rise in influence of global decision makers at both public and private levels.

Not long before the Chiquita Brands story broke, South Korean stem cell scientist Hwang Woo Suk provided another example of how globalization is expanding criminal possibilities when he admitted that he had falsified research data, and that he had not been successful in obtaining stem cells from cloned human embryos.[7] What astonished authorities, however, was a statement by the Seoul National University medical researcher that he wanted his research to appear to be successful so that he could receive additional funding to carry out research on frozen tissue samples from now-extinct Russian mammoths. The tissue, Suk said, had been provided by the Russian Mafia who had been paid off using money that had been slated for human stem cell research. His real goal, Suk told prosecutors at his trial over misappropriated funds, had been to clone a mammoth from the last Ice Age.

Globalization is making it impossible for policymakers to ignore criminal activity in other parts of the world, especially where that crime is perpetrated by transnational criminal and terrorist organizations. *Transnational crime,* or **transnational organized crime**, refers to unlawful activity undertaken and supported by organized criminal groups operating across national boundaries. Transnational crime and the internationally organized criminal groups that support it have emerged as one of the most pressing challenges of the early twenty-first century. The growing globalization of crime has necessitated the enhanced coordination of law enforcement efforts in different parts of the world and the expansion of American law enforcement activities beyond national borders.

globalization

A process of social homogenization by which the experiences of everyday life, marked by the diffusion of commodities and ideas, can foster a standardization of cultural expressions around the world.

transnational organized crime

Unlawful activity undertaken and supported by organized criminal groups operating across national boundaries.

Afghans collect resin from a poppy field in Lashkar Gah, south of Kabul, Afghanistan, in 2007. Afghanistan is one of the top producers of opium in the world, where its growth is largely controlled by Taliban militia who either befriend or intimidate local poppy growers. Much of the heroin manufactured from opium produced in Afghanistan is sold in the United States, completing an international cycle that forms one aspect of globalization and serves as a source of funds for the ongoing Taliban resistance in Afghanistan. How can the cycle be broken?

Source: AP Wide World Photos/ Abdul Khaliq

Transnational Crimes

According to the National Institute of Justice (NIJ), transnational crime groups have profited more from globalization than legitimate businesses, which are subject to domestic and host country laws and regulations. NIJ points out that transnational criminal syndicates and networks, abetted by official corruption, blackmail, and intimidation, can use open markets and open societies to their full advantage.[8]

The list of transnational crimes is long, and ranges from relatively simple fraudulent e-mail and phishing schemes that are globally perpetrated, to the much more dangerous and threatening illegal trafficking in human beings, human organs, and illicit drugs. It includes the activities of multinational drug cartels, the support of terrorist groups by criminal organizations seeking armed protection, and sometimes well-funded and politically sophisticated efforts by organized criminal groups seeking to supplant the ruling regime in countries or regions with others sympathetic to their operations.

No one is immune from the economic effects of transnational crime, and some of the threats hit especially close to home. Recently, for example, the entire 32-member police force of Villa Madero, in Mexico's Michoacán state, resigned or failed to show up for work after being threatened by drug traffickers.[9] Members of the town's police force complained about a lack of weapons and communications equipment needed to protect themselves and the town's citizens. Worse yet, in some parts of Mexico, the local police have had to be disarmed because of fears that they are taking bribes and are working with drug traffickers.

Larry Birns, director of the Council on Hemispheric Affairs and an expert on Mexican affairs, says that in recent years Mexican drug cartels have wrested control of what the United Nations estimates[10] is an annual $142 billion Central American drug trafficking operation from Colombians. Birns claims that Mexican "President Felipe Calderon may be the constitutionally elected leader of the nation, but in reality, drug cartels and warlords exercise *de facto* authority over much of the [country]."[11]

Armed incursions into the United States by Mexican drug traffickers wearing what appear to be Mexican military uniforms,[12] the not-so-infrequent beheadings of reporters and others who speak out against drug-related corruption,[13] and the assassinations or attempted assassinations of Mexican political leaders opposed to the drug trade have raised alarms about the future of the Mexican political system. In a World Press analysis of the current situation titled "The Government and the Drug Lords: Who Rules Mexico?" Birns points out that "in the past several months there have been a growing number of assassinations, which most likely can be attributed to the drug cartels 'punishing' the government." The son of Vidal Barraza, commander of the Special Prosecutor's Office, was gunned-down in the Mexican state of Chihuahua. Similarly, state law enforcement commander and SWAT leader, Abraham Eduardo Farias Martinez was shot several times in the head in 2007, as he drove to an antidrug meeting. His murder was the eighth homicide of a Mexican antidrug agent in the first three months of 2007, and the 17th registered killing in the town of Nuevo Leon in the first 100 days of that year. Even Mexican President Calderon has admitted that he and his family have received death threats due to his highly publicized antidrug-trafficking stance.

Human Smuggling and Trafficking

In February 2007, 34-year-old Juan Balderas-Orosco pleaded guilty in federal court in Austin, Texas, to smuggling women into the United States to work as prostitutes.[14] According to court documents, Balderas-Orosco and 11 associates illegally brought hundreds of women into the country from Latin American countries and forced each of them to have sex with as many as 40 men a day. The women were moved between more than a dozen brothels in Texas and Oklahoma to keep them disoriented and to prevent them from making friends in the community who might help them.

According to the United Nations,[15] trafficking in persons and human smuggling are some of the fastest growing areas of international criminal activity today. There are important distinctions that must be made between these two forms of crime. Following federal law, the U.S. State Department defines **human smuggling** as "the facilitation, transportation, attempted transportation or illegal entry of a person(s) across an international border, in violation of one or more country's laws, either clandestinely or through deception, such as the use of fraudulent documents." In other words, human smuggling refers to illegal immigration in which an agent is involved for payment to help a person cross a border clandestinely.[16] Human smuggling may be conducted to obtain financial or other benefits for the smuggler, although sometimes people engage in smuggling for other motives, such as to reunite their families. Human smuggling generally occurs with the consent of the persons being smuggled, and those people often pay a smuggler for his services. Once in the country they've paid to enter, they will usually no longer be in contact with the smuggler. The State Department notes that the vast majority of people who are assisted in illegally entering the United States annually are smuggled, rather than trafficked.

Although smuggling might not involve active coercion, it can be deadly. In January 2007, for example, truck driver Tyrone Williams, 36, a Jamaican citizen living in Schenectady, New York, was sentenced to life in prison for causing the deaths of 19 illegal immigrants in the nation's deadliest known human smuggling attempt.[17] Williams locked more than 70 immigrants in a container truck during a 2003 trip from South Texas to Houston, but abandoned the truck about 100 miles from its destination. The victims died from dehydration, overheating, and suffocation in the Texas heat before the truck was discovered and its doors opened.

In contrast to smuggling, **trafficking in persons (TIP)** can be compared to a modern-day form of slavery, prompting Secretary of State Condoleezza Rice to say that "defeating human trafficking is a great moral calling of our day."[18] Trafficking involves the exploitation of unwilling or unwitting people through force, coercion, threat, or deception, and includes human rights abuses such as debt bondage, deprivation of liberty, or lack of control over freedom and labor. Trafficking is often undertaken for purposes of sexual exploitation or labor exploitation.

U.S. government officials estimate that 800,000 to 900,000 victims are trafficked globally each year and that 17,500 to 18,500 are trafficked into the United States.[19] Women and children comprise the largest group of victims, and they are often physically

human smuggling

Illegal immigration in which an agent is involved for payment to help a person cross a border clandestinely.

trafficking in persons (TIP)

The exploitation of unwilling or unwitting people through force, coercion, threat, or deception.

Miss Brazil 2002, Taiza Thomsen, is pictured arriving at Nnamdi Azikiwe International Airport, in Abuja, Nigeria, on November 11, 2002. Thomsen vanished in 2006—a suspected victim of human traffickers. Months later, however, she was found in London working as a nude dancer. What different forms does human trafficking take?

Source: Pius Otomi Ekpei/AFP/Getty Images

and emotionally abused. Although TIP is often an international crime that involves the crossing of borders, it is important to note that TIP victims can be trafficked within their own countries and communities. Traffickers can move victims between locations within the same country and often sell them to other trafficking organizations.

The International Labor Organization (ILO), the United Nations agency charged with addressing labor standards, employment, and social protection issues, estimates that there are 12.3 million people in forced labor, bonded labor, forced child labor, and sexual servitude throughout the world today.[20] Other estimates range as high as 27 million.[21]

It is sometimes difficult to distinguish between a smuggling and a trafficking case because trafficking often includes an element of smuggling (that is, the illegal crossing of a national border). Moreover, some trafficking victims may believe they are being smuggled when they are really being trafficked, but are unaware of their eventual fate. This happens, for example, where women trafficked for sexual exploitation may have thought they were agreeing to work in legitimate industries for decent wages—part of which they may have agreed to pay to the trafficker who smuggled them. They didn't know that upon arrival the traffickers would keep them in bondage, subject them to physical force or sexual violence, force them to work in the sex trade, and take most or all of their income. United Nations literature notes that Chinese syndicates are notorious for continuing to control the lives of migrants at their destination, that they discipline them by force, and extract heavy payment for smuggling services—holding "their clients as virtual hostages until the fees have been paid."[22]

The U.S. Department of State's 2007 *Trafficking in Persons* report, says that "human trafficking is a multi-dimensional threat. It deprives people of their human rights and freedoms, it increases global health risks, and it fuels the growth of organized crime."[23] At the individual level, the report notes, "human trafficking has a devastating impact on individual victims, who often suffer physical and emotional abuse, rape, threats against self and family, document theft, and even death."

TABLE 15–1 **Distinguishing between Human Trafficking and Smuggling**

Trafficking	Smuggling
Must contain an element of force, fraud, or coercion (actual, perceived, or implied), unless under 18 years of age involved in commercial sex acts.	The person being smuggled is generally cooperating.
Forced labor and/or exploitation.	No forced labor or other exploitation.
Persons trafficked are victims.	Persons smuggled are violating the law. They are not victims.
Enslaved, subjected to limited movement or isolation, or had documents confiscated.	Persons are free to leave, change jobs, etc.
Need not involve the actual movement of the victim.	Facilitates the illegal entry of person(s) from one country into another.
No requirement to cross an international border.	Smuggling always crosses an international border.
Person must be involved in labor/services or commercial sex acts (that is, must be "working").	Person must only be in country or attempting entry illegally.

Source: Adapted from U.S. Department of State, Bureau for International Narcotics and Law Enforcement Affairs, Human Smuggling and Trafficking Center, *Distinctions Between Human Smuggling and Human Trafficking* (Washington, DC: January 1, 2005).

Note: This chart is meant to be conceptual and is not intended to provide precise legal distinctions between smuggling and trafficking.

The distinction between smuggling and trafficking are sometimes very subtle, but key components that generally distinguish trafficking from smuggling are the elements of fraud, force, or coercion. However, under U.S. law, if the person is under 18 and induced to perform a commercial sex act, then it is considered trafficking, regardless of whether or not fraud, force, or coercion is involved. Table 15–1 provides a guide to distinguishing criminal trafficking from smuggling.

According to the United Nations, human smuggling and trafficking have become a worldwide industry that "employs" millions of people and leads to the annual turnover of billions of dollars.[24] The United Nations also says that many of the routes used by smugglers have become well established and are widely known. Routes from Mexico and Central America to the United States, for example; from West Asia through Greece and Turkey to Western Europe; and within East and Southeast Asia are well-worn and regularly traveled. More often than not, the United Nations says, the ongoing existence of flourishing smuggling routes is facilitated by weak legislation, lax border controls, corrupt officials, and the power and influence of organized crime.

While there are significant differences between TIP and human smuggling, the underlying conditions that give rise to both of these illegal activities are often similar. Extreme poverty, lack of economic opportunity, civil unrest, and political uncertainty are all factors that contribute to social environments in which human smuggling and trafficking in persons occurs.

Federal Immigration and Trafficking Legislation

The United States had what were essentially open national borders until the 1880s, when limited federal controls on immigration began. One of the nation's first immigration laws sought to end a huge influx of mostly male workers coming from China. Called the Chinese Exclusion Act, it became law in 1882 and was enforced for ten years.

The law was enacted in response to the large numbers of Chinese laborers who had emigrated to the western United States in the mid-1800s looking for work—and who often took jobs on railroads and in the mining industry.

One of the first comprehensive pieces of federal immigration legislation was the 1924 Immigration Act. It limited the number of immigrants who could be admitted from any one country to 2% of the number of people from that country who were already living here. Quotas were calculated using the Census of 1890. The law also barred immigration from specific parts of the Asia-Pacific Triangle, which included Japan, China, the Philippines, Laos, Thailand, Cambodia, Korea, and other countries.

The Immigration and Nationality Act (INA) of 1952[25] established the Immigration and Naturalization Service (INS), while continuing numerical quotas. The INA provided criminal penalties for anyone bringing or attempting to bring unauthorized aliens into the United States. Thirteen years later, the Immigration and Nationality Act amendments of 1965[26] abolished national-origin quotas.

In recognition of human smuggling and TIP as serious social issues, Congress passed the Trafficking Victims Protection Act of 2000 (TVPA) on October 28, 2000.[27] The TVPA is a comprehensive statute that addresses the significant problem of trafficking of persons for the purpose of committing commercial sex acts, or for the purpose of subjecting them to involuntary servitude, peonage, debt bondage, or slavery. The legislation also increases the protections afforded to victims of trafficking.

The TVPA defines "severe forms of trafficking as: "a.) **sex trafficking** in which a commercial sex act is induced by force, fraud, or coercion, or in which the person induced to perform such an act has not attained 18 years of age; or b.) the recruitment, harboring, transportation, provision, or obtaining of a person for labor or services, through the use of force, fraud, or coercion for the purpose of subjection to involuntary servitude, peonage, debt bondage, or slavery."[28]

> **sex trafficking**
>
> The recruitment, harboring, transportation, provision, or obtaining of a person for the purpose of a commercial sex act.

Under the TVPA, human trafficking does not require the crossing of an international border, nor does it even require the transportation of victims from one locale to another. That's because victims of severe forms of trafficking are not always illegal aliens; they may be U.S. citizens, legal residents, or visitors. Victims do not have to be women or children—they may also be adult males.

The Homeland Security Act of 2002 (HSA) dissolved the INS and transferred most of its functions to the Department of Homeland Security. Three DHS branches exist today in place of the INS. They are: (1) Citizenship and Immigration Services (CIS), (2) Customs and Border Protection (CBP), and (3) Immigration and Customs Enforcement (ICE).

The Trafficking Victims Protection Reauthorization Act (TVPRA) of 2003 added a new initiative to the original law to collect foreign data on trafficking investigations, prosecutions, convictions and sentences. The most recent data (for 2006) show that reporting jurisdictions prosecuted 5,808 persons for trafficking-related offenses, and secured 3,160 convictions.[29] The number of reported foreign prosecutions is the lowest since reporting began in 2003.

Finally, section 7202 of the Intelligence Reform and Terrorism Prevention Act of 2004 established the Human Smuggling and Trafficking Center within the U.S. State Department. The Secretary of State, the Secretary of Homeland Security, the Attorney General and members of the national Intelligence Community oversee the Center. The Center was created to achieve greater integration and overall effectiveness in the U.S. government's enforcement of issues related to human smuggling, trafficking in persons, and criminal support of clandestine terrorist travel. Visit the Human Smuggling and Trafficking Center at Web Extra 15–1, and read the U.S. Department of State's 240-page 2007 *Trafficking in Persons Report* at Library Extra 15–1 at crimtoday.com.

> **WEB**
> Extra
> ....
>
> **LIBRARY**
> Extra
> ....

Comparative Criminology

The globalization of crime has led to a resurgence in interest in **comparative criminology,** or the study of crime on a cross-national level. By comparing crime patterns in one country with those in another, theories and policies that have been taken for granted in

> **comparative criminology**
>
> The cross-national study of crime.

Life Sentence for Beslan Bomber

VLADIKAVKAZ, Russia (AP)—The only suspect known to have survived the Beslan school siege was convicted in the deaths of more than 300 people—many of them children—and sentenced to life in prison Friday, touching off an emotional scene in which the mothers of some victims tried to attack the defendant in court.

The verdict returned by the court in southern Russia ended a year-long trial in the September 2004 hostage-taking that survivors and relatives of those who died say has left essential questions unanswered.

The attack killed 331 people, more than half of them children, as well as 31 suspected militants and 11 elite special forces soldiers. Most of the victims died when explosions tore through the school and security forces stormed the building.

Prosecutors had demanded the death penalty for Nur-Pashi Kulayev, but Russia imposed a moratorium on capital punishment when it joined the Council of Europe a decade ago.

"Kulayev deserves the death penalty, but is sentenced to life in prison because a moratorium is in place," Judge Tamerlan Aguzarov said.

Asked whether he understood the verdict, Kulayev, a Chechen, nodded his freshly shaved head up and down. His lawyer said later Kulayev plans to appeal.

As the judge read the verdict, some victims' mothers threw themselves shrieking on the glass-metal cage where Kulayev has stood throughout the trial. Police struggled to restrain them.

Militants attacked the school Sept. 1, 2004, taking more than 1,100 children, parents and staff hostage and herding them into a gymnasium, which they rigged with explosives.

Survivors and victims' relatives claim many deaths occurred because troops fired at the school from tanks and flame-throwers, setting off a fire that caused the roof to collapse over many wounded.

The judge said Kulayev detonated a bomb that harmed hostages and government troops. He said 16 male hostages whom the

militants executed on the first day of the assault had died in part due to Kulayev's actions.

Kulayev was also found guilty of shooting children and other hostages who tried to escape the school on the chaotic third day of the crisis. He had claimed in court that while he participated in the raid, he did not kill anyone.

Deputy Prosecutor General Nikolai Shepel, who led the government's case, said he was satisfied with the verdict.

"Kulayev has been pronounced guilty on all counts," Shepel told reporters.

But victims' relatives were deeply critical of the trial, and the Mothers of Beslan activist group accused prosecutors of carrying out a "superficial and one-sided investigation."

The group said investigators had not probed who was responsible for a chain of alleged errors including failure to take security measures in spite of a heightened terrorism danger, refusal to negotiate with the hostage-takers, lack of preparation for storming the school, and "uncontrolled use of tanks, flame-throwers, grenade-launchers and other weapons."

Many victims' relatives have accused the government of a cover-up, saying the militants had help from corrupt officials to allow them to cross heavily policed territory to reach Beslan. They say many victims died needlessly in a botched rescue.

"I did not go to court to become convinced of Kulayev's guilt, but to reconstruct all the circumstances of the terrorist attack and find the truth," said Aneta Gadiyeva, whose daughter was killed. "But I did not learn anything new and did not get any answers."

Kulayev, during a visit by his lawyer after the verdict, looked tired and depressed, said the lawyer, Albert Pliyev.

"My client does not agree with the verdict. We will prepare an appeal and file it with a higher court," he told The Associated Press.

The lawyer said Kulayev maintained he had unwillingly joined the hostage-taking and had been made a scapegoat.

On the street outside the court, pandemonium broke out after the court session as relatives shouted and tussled with one another and with reporters.

"I expected the death penalty and it is not right he was sentenced to life in prison," said Rita Sidakova, a leader of the Mothers of Beslan activist group.

But Ella Kesayeva, of the rival Voice of Beslan organization, said Kulayev remained too valuable a witness and that he should not be killed.

"Preserving Kulayev's life gives us hope that all circumstances of the terrorist act in Beslan sooner or later will be investigated," Kesayeva said. "Alive, Kulayev can give evidence on the main part of the case. We hope to learn the truth about Beslan."

Discussion Questions

1. What motivated the terrorists who carried out the Beslan school bombing? Were their goals met?

2. Do you agree with the judge who in this case said that Nur-Pashi Kulayev deserves the death penalty? Why or why not?

3. What happened to the other perpetrators?

A woman cries as she looks at the pictures of children killed at their school in Beslan, Russia, by Chechen separatist rebels in 2004. Three hundred and thirty-one people died in Beslan when terrorists took children and their teachers hostage in the school. How does the United States define terrorism? Would the U.S. definition include the Beslan attack? What kinds of incidents might be excluded?

Source: © Yuri Kochetkov / epa / CORBIS All Rights Reserved

For the latest crime and justice news, visit www.crimenews.info.

one place can be reevaluated in the light of world experience. As some noted **comparative criminologists** have observed, "The challenge for comparative criminologists is to develop theories with increased specificity while managing to construct them in such a way that they can be applied across more than one culture or nation-state. This eventually must demand that theories be developed to conceptualize societies as totalities and that theories that manage to provide a world context in which total societies behave be further constructed.[30]

Some have used the term *globalization of knowledge* to describe the increase in understanding that results from a sharing of information between cultures. The globalization of knowledge is beginning to play a significant role in both the process of theory formation within criminology and the development of American crime control policies. According to some, "Globalization will make it increasingly difficult for nation-states to ignore the criminal justice information of other countries. Politicians and influential bureaucrats increasingly will be forced to answer as to why their country displays crime rates, prosecution rates, incarceration rates, or rates of violence or gun ownership that are strikingly different from similar countries."[31]

Two years ago, as recipient of the prestigious Vollmer Award in Criminology, Franklin E. Zimring, of the University of California, Berkeley, addressed the American Society of Criminology telling the assembly that "over the past decade I have become convinced that transnational comparisons are a necessary part of virtually all serious work in criminal justice and the study of criminal behavior."[32] Zimring went on to bemoan the fact that American criminology had been self-obsessed and "particularly inattentive to the value and necessity ot transnational comparisons." Zimring sees comparative efforts as providing a context for evaluating knowledge and reviewing observations. Using such a contextual perspective, Zimring demonstrated that the crime decline in the United States during the 1990s was not unique to America—and that the same decline occurred in Canada at exactly the same time. "Whatever was driving the decline in the United States was also operating in Canada," Zimring concluded.

comparative criminologist

A criminologist involved in the cross-national study of crime.

Ethnocentrism

One important issue facing comparative criminologists is **ethnocentrism.** Ethnocentrism, or culture-centeredness, can interfere with the work of comparative criminologists in a number of ways, including the ways in which crime statistics are gathered, analyzed, and presented. Researchers can begin to avoid being ethnocentric by realizing that it is quite common for people to regard that with which they are familiar as somehow superior or more desirable than that with which they are less familiar. Using a fork while eating, for example, is usually more comfortable for most Americans than using chopsticks.

Because people are socialized from birth into a particular culture, they tend to prefer their own culture's way of doing things over that of any other. Native patterns of behavior are seen as somehow "natural" and therefore better than foreign ones. The same is true for values, beliefs, and customs. People tend to think that their religion holds a spiritual edge over other religions, that their values and ethical sense are superior to those of others, and that the fashions they wear, the language they speak, and the rituals of daily life in which they participate are somehow better than comparable practices elsewhere. Ethnocentric individuals rarely stop to think that people in other parts of the world frequently cling to their own values, beliefs, and standards of behavior with just as much fervor as they do. Hence, ethnocentrism is not a uniquely American phenomenon.

Only in recent years have American students of criminology begun to closely examine crime in other cultures. Unfortunately, not all societies are equally open, and it is not always easy to explore them. In some societies, even the *study* of crime is taboo. As a result, data-gathering strategies taken for granted in Western culture may not be well received elsewhere. One author, for example, has observed that in China, "the seeking of criminal justice information through face-to-face questioning takes on a different meaning in Chinese officialdom than it does generally in the Western world. While we

ethnocentrism

The phenomenon of "culture-centeredness" by which one uses one's own culture as a benchmark against which to judge all other patterns of behavior.

accept this method of inquiry because we prize thinking on our feet and quick answers, it is rather offensive in China because it shows lack of respect and appreciation for the information given through the preferred means of prepared questions and formal briefings."[33] Hence, most of the information available about Chinese crime rates comes by way of officialdom, and routine Western social science practices like door-to-door interviews, participant observation, and random surveys might produce substantial problems for researchers who attempt to use such techniques in China.

Similar difficulties arise in the comparison of crime rates from one country to another. The crime rates of different nations are difficult to compare because of (1) differences in the way a given crime is defined, (2) diverse crime-reporting practices, and (3) political, social, economic, and other influences on the reporting of statistics to international agencies.[34]

Issues in Reporting

Definitional differences create what may be the biggest problem. For cross-national comparisons of crime data to be meaningful, it is essential that the reported data share conceptual similarities. Unfortunately, that is often not the case. Nations report offenses according to the legal criteria by which arrests are made and under which prosecution can occur. Switzerland, for example, includes bicycle thefts in its reported data on what we call "auto theft" because Swiss data gathering focuses more on the concept of personal transportation than it does on the type of vehicle stolen. The Netherlands has no crime category for robberies, counting them as thefts. Japan classifies an assault that results in death as an assault or an aggravated assault, not as a homicide. Greek rape statistics include crimes of sodomy, "lewdness," seduction of a child, incest, and prostitution. Communist China reports only robberies and thefts that involve the property of citizens; crimes against state-owned property fall into a separate category.

Reporting practices vary substantially between nations. The International Criminal Police Organization (INTERPOL) and the United Nations are the only international organizations that regularly collect crime statistics from a large number of countries. Both agencies can only request data and have no way of checking on the accuracy of the data reported to them. Many countries do not disclose the requested information, and those that do sometimes make only partial reports. In general, small countries are more likely to report than are large ones, and nonsocialist countries are more likely to report than are socialist nations.

International reports of crime are sometimes delayed, making comparisons even more difficult. Complete, up-to-date data are difficult to acquire, since the information made available to agencies like the United Nations and INTERPOL is reported at different times and according to schedules that vary from nation to nation. In addition, official United Nations world crime surveys are conducted infrequently. To date, only nine such surveys have been undertaken.[35]

Economic differences among countries compound these difficulties. Auto theft statistics, for example, when compared between countries like the United States and China, need to be placed in an economic as well as a demographic context. While the United States has two automobiles for every 3 people, China has only one car for every 100 of its citizens. For the Chinese auto theft rate to equal that of the United States, every automobile in the country would have to be stolen nearly twice each year!

Crime statistics also reflect social and political contexts. Some nations do not accurately admit to the frequency of certain kinds of culturally reprehensible crimes. Communist countries, for example, appear loathe to report crimes like theft, burglary, and robbery because the very existence of such offenses might appear to demonstrate felt inequities within the Communist system. Likewise, the social norms in some societies may make it almost impossible for women to report cases of rape or sexual abuse, while in others, women are encouraged to come forward. Figure 15–1 was developed by the United Nations Office on Drugs and Crime to graphically represent some of the difficulties inherent in compiling international crime statistics.

With all these caveats in mind, it may still be instructive to look at rates of crime in other countries and to attempt comparisons with rates of crime in the United States.

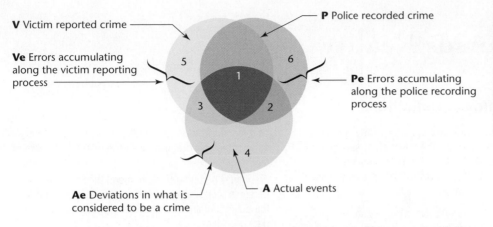

FIGURE 15–1

Sources of Error in International Crime Data

Source: United Nations Office on Drugs and Crime, "Compiling and Comparing International Crime Statistics,"http://www.unodc.org/unodc/en/crime_cicp_surveys_3.html. Reprinted with permission.

A	Actual events
Ae	Deviations in whether an event is considered a crime or not, e.g.: different definitions used in different jurisdictions.
P	Police recorded crime
Pe	Errors that accumulate along the police recording process, e.g.: data entry errors at the source and at intermediated stages of the recording process, aggregation errors, interpretation errors, missing regions or double count, transmission errors (e.g. lost mail), etc.
V	Victim reported crime
Ve	Errors that accumulate along the victim reporting process e.g.: victimless crimes, data entry at the source and at intermediate stages of the reporting process, interpretation errors, sampling errors, statistical errors, transmission errors, etc.
1	Crime is recorded by the police and reported by the victim
2	Crime is recorded by the police but not reported by victim
3	Crime is reported by victim but not recorded by the police
4	A crime happens but is neither recorded by the police nor reported by the victim
5	Victim reports a crime that never happened (e.g. for purposes of insurance fraud)—*in reality this area is much smaller than depicted in the schematic*
6	Police record a crime that never happened (e.g. to attract a higher budget)—*in reality this area is much smaller than depicted in the schematic*

As mentioned earlier, one of the most useful tools for international crime rate comparisons is *The Ninth United Nations Survey on Crime Trends and the Operations of Criminal Justice System,* which covers the years 2003–2004.

As noted in Chapter 2, U.S. violent crime rates seem high when compared with violent crime rates of other developed countries. American crime rates, however, are far from being the highest in the world (Figure 15–2), and United Nations surveys typically place crime rates in the United States well below world highs. While lawless areas without strong central governments and countries experiencing strong social upheaval might be expected to have high violent crime rates, some other parts of the world do, too. Murder rates in Colombia and South Africa, for example, are more than 12 times that of the United States. Russia has a murder rate that is almost four times the U.S. rate, and homicide rates in Mexico are more than three times as great as those in the United States. Similarly, the rate of reported rape in South Africa is four times as great as that of the United States, while Canada and Australia have rape rates more than double the U.S. figure. Spain has a robbery rate many times higher than that of the United States, and at least a few countries have rates of assault that are greater than that reported in the United States.

See more international crime statistics at **Web Extra 15–2**, and visit the National Institute of Justice's International Center at **Web Extra 15–3**. The comprehensive Global Criminology Website run by Professor Robert W. Winslow at San Diego State University

WEB
Extra
▪▪▪▪

WEB
Extra
▪▪▪▪

Theory Versus Reality

United Nations Offense Definitions

The United Nations Office on Drugs and Crime regularly conducts a survey of international crime trends. The latest such survey, the ninth, covers the years 2003–2004. In an effort to standardize reporting practices, the United Nations provides the following crime definitions to guide survey participants.

Intentional homicide may be understood to mean death deliberately inflicted on a person by another person, including infanticide.

Non-intentional homicide may be understood to mean death not deliberately inflicted on a person by another person. That includes the crime of manslaughter but excludes traffic accidents that result in the death of persons.

Assault may be understood to mean physical attack against the body of another person, including battery but excluding indecent assault. Some criminal or penal codes distinguish between aggravated assault and simple assault, depending on the degree of resulting injury. If such a distinction is made in your country, please provide the relevant data for aggravated assault under the category "Major assault." Under the category "Total assault" should be included data on both aggravated assault (i.e., major assault) and simple assault. Please provide the main criterion for distinguishing between aggravated assault and simple assault if such a distinction is made in your country.

Rape may be understood to mean sexual intercourse without valid consent. Please indicate whether statutory rape is included in the data provided. If, in your country, a distinction is made between sexual assault and actual penetration, please provide relevant information.

Robbery may be understood to mean the theft of property from a person, overcoming resistance by force or threat of force.

Theft may be understood to mean the removal of property without the property owner's consent. "Theft" excludes burglary and housebreaking as well as theft of a motor vehicle. Some criminal and penal codes distinguish between grand and petty theft, depending on the value of the goods and property taken from their rightful owner. If such a distinction is made in your country, please provide the relevant data for grand theft under the category "Major theft." The category "Total theft" should include data on both grand theft (i.e., major theft) and petty theft. Please provide the main criterion for distinguishing between grand theft and petty theft if such a distinction is made in your country.

Automobile theft may be understood to mean the removal of a motor vehicle without the consent of the owner of the vehicle.

Burglary may be understood to mean unlawful entry into someone else's premises with the intention to commit a crime.

Fraud may be understood to mean the acquisition of another person's property by deception. Please indicate whether the fraudulent obtaining of financial property is included in the data provided.

Embezzlement may be understood to mean the wrongful appropriation of another person's property that is already in the possession of the person doing the appropriating.

Drug-related crimes may be understood to mean intentional acts that involve the cultivation, production, manufacture, extraction, preparation, offering for sale, distribution, purchase, sale, delivery on any terms whatsoever, brokerage, dispatch, dispatch in transit, transport, importation, exportation and possession of internationally controlled drugs. . . .

Bribery and/or corruption may be understood to mean requesting and/or accepting material or personal benefits, or the promise thereof, in connection with the performance of a public function for an action that may or may not be a violation of law and/or promising as well as giving material or personal benefits to a public officer in exchange for a requested favor.

Kidnapping may be understood to mean unlawfully detaining a person or persons against their will (or national equivalent, e.g., using force, threat, fraud or enticement) for the purpose of demanding for their liberation an illicit gain or any other economic gain or other material benefit, or in order to oblige someone to do or not to do something.

Recorded crimes may be understood to mean the number of penal code offences or their equivalent (i.e., various special law offences), but excluding minor road traffic offences and other petty offences, brought to the attention of the police or other law enforcement agencies and recorded by one of those agencies.

If the categories . . . above are not fully compatible with the legal code in your country, please try to adjust the data as far as possible. Alternatively, you may indicate . . . what kinds of crime are included in your statistics that might be comparable to the categories suggested or how the comparable types of crime are defined in your country.

View the entire *United Nations Survey on Crime Trends* questionnaire online at www.justicestudies.com/pubs/unsurvey.pdf. The United Nations' *Criminal Justice Assessment Toolkit* (2006) is available at http://justicestudies.com/pubs/untoolkit.pdf.

Source: United Nations Office on Drugs and Crime, *Questionnaire for the Ninth United Nations Survey on Crime Trends and the Operations of Criminal Justice Systems* (New York: United Nations, 2005).

Country	Crime Rate
Dominica	112.79 per 1,000 people
New Zealand	108.12 per 1,000 people
Finland	102.15 per 1,000 people
Denmark	93.64 per 1,000 people
Chile	90.00 per 1,000 people
United Kingdom	86.04 per 1,000 people
Montserrat	83.49 per 1,000 people
United States	**81.55 per 1,000 people**
Netherlands	80.84 per 1,000 people
South Africa	80.02 per 1,000 people
Canada	76.89 per 1,000 people
Germany	76.02 per 1,000 people
Norway	72.60 per 1,000 people
France	62.67 per 1,000 people
Seychelles	53.39 per 1,000 people
Hungary	44.80 per 1,000 people
Estonia	41.03 per 1,000 people
Czech Republic	38.19 per 1,000 people
Italy	38.03 per 1,000 people
Switzerland	37.02 per 1,000 people
Portugal	35.96 per 1,000 people
Slovenia	34.93 per 1,000 people
Poland	32.80 per 1,000 people
Korea, South	31.95 per 1,000 people
Mauritius	29.69 per 1,000 people

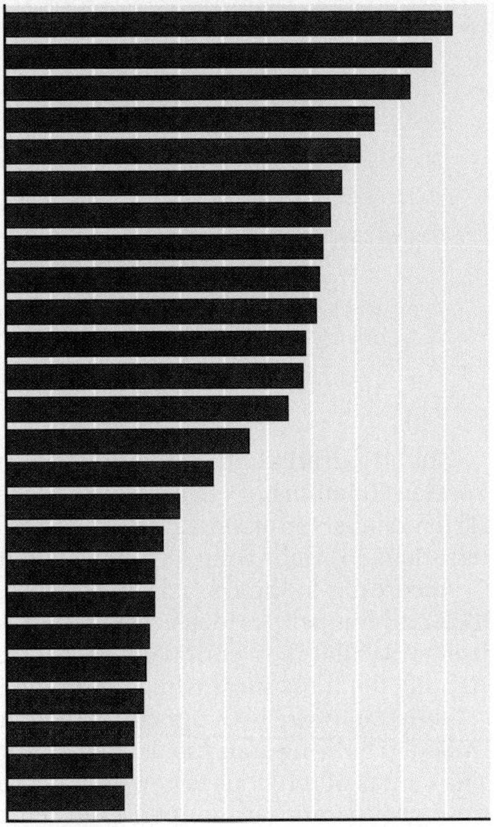

FIGURE 15–2

The United States in World Context: Total Crimes per Capita, by Country

Source: Compiled from *The Seventh United Nations Survey on Crime Trends and the Operations of Criminal Justice Systems* (New York: United Nations Office on Drugs and Crime, Center for International Crime Prevention, 2004). Reprinted with permission.

WEB Extra ▪▪▪▪

LIBRARY Extra ▪▪▪▪

can be reached at Web Extra 15–4. Read an intriguing paper on comparative criminology at Library Extra 15–2 at crimtoday.com. The *Ninth United Nations Survey on Crime Trends*, which covers 64 countries, is available at Library Extra 15–3, and the *European Sourcebook of Crime and Criminal Justice Statistics* can be accessed via Library Extra 15–4.

Terrorism

The most infamous attack of international terrorism to date took place on September 11, 2001, when members of Osama Bin Laden's al-Qaeda Islamic terrorist organization attacked New York City's World Trade Center and the Pentagon using commandeered jetliners. Following the attacks, which left more than 3,000 people dead[36] and resulted in billions of dollars' worth of property damage, the United States declared a worldwide war on international terrorism.

The U.S. Department of State defines **terrorism** as "premeditated, politically motivated violence perpetrated against noncombatant targets by subnational groups or clandestine agents, usually intended to influence an audience."[37] Paul Pillar, former deputy chief of the CIA's Counterterrorist Center, has identified four key features of terrorism that distinguish it from other forms of violence.[38] Those features are shown in Table 15–2.

Terrorist acts are inherently criminal because they violate the criminal law (that is, many jurisdictions have laws against terrorism); because they involve criminal activity, such as hijacking, kidnapping, and arson; and because they produce criminal results, such as homicide and property destruction. The primary distinction between violent criminal acts and acts of terrorism, however, has to do with the political motivation or social ideology of the offender.[39] Hence, bombings, hostage taking, and other similar terrorist-like acts that are undertaken for mere individual or pecuniary gain, when no political or social objectives are sought by the perpetrators, do not qualify as "terrorism."

terrorism

Premeditated, politically motivated violence perpetrated against noncombatant targets by subnational groups or clandestine agents, usually intended to influence an audience.

TABLE 15–2 **Characteristics of Terrorism**

Terrorism Usually Is	Terrorism Usually Is Not
Premeditated or planned	Impulsive, or an act of rage
Politically motivated (that is, intended to change the existing political order)	Perpetrated for criminal gain (that is, illicit personal or, financial benefit)
Aimed at civilians	Aimed at military targets or combat-ready troops
Carried out by subnational groups	Perpetrated by the army of a country

---

domestic terrorism

The unlawful use of force or violence by a group or an individual who is based and operates entirely within the United States and its territories without foreign direction and whose acts are directed at elements of the U.S. government or population.

international terrorism

The unlawful use of force or violence by a group or an individual who has a connection to a foreign power or whose activities transcend national boundaries against people or property to intimidate or coerce a government, the civilian population, or any segment thereof in furtherance of political or social objectives.

Not all terrorists share the same motivation. The Washington, DC–based Council on Foreign Relations offers a typology of terrorism, consisting of six types of terrorism:[40] (1) nationalist terrorism, (2) religious terrorism, (3) state-sponsored terrorism, (4) left-wing terrorism, (5) right-wing terrorism, and (6) anarchist terrorism.

According to the council, nationalist terrorists seek to form a separate state of their own and frequently depict their activities as a fight for liberation—usually from a political entity that they portray as unfair and repressive. Such groups, says the council, are "among the most successful at winning international sympathy and concessions."

Religious terrorists pursue their own vision of the divine will and use violence intended to bring about social and cultural changes that are in keeping with that vision. The claims of religious terrorists are hard to counter in the minds of their followers, and such groups are rarely open to accommodation or compromise. As Bruce Hoffman, director of the Washington office of RAND (formerly the RAND Corporation) notes, the most extreme religious terrorists can sanction "almost limitless violence against a virtually open-ended category of targets: that is, anyone who is not a member of the terrorists' religion or religious sect."[41]

State-sponsored terrorist groups are deliberately used by radical states as foreign policy tools—or, as Hoffman puts it, as "a cost-effective way of waging war covertly, through the use of surrogate warriors or 'guns for hire.'" State-sponsored terrorist organizations are discussed in greater detail later in this chapter.

Left-wing terrorists seek to destroy economies based on free enterprise and to replace them with socialist or communist economic systems. Right-wing terrorists are motivated by fascist ideals and work toward the dissolution of democratic governments. Right-wing terrorist leaders seek personal political power and often envision themselves as likely candidates for the role of beneficent dictator. Anarchist terrorists are revolutionaries who seek to overthrow all established forms of government. Table 15–3 shows groups that are representative of each kind of terrorism. A glance at the table shows that some groups, such as Hezbollah (a religiously motivated terrorist organization that has received financial support from Iran), may fit into more than one category.

Other kinds of terrorist typologies can also be described. The United States, for example, is faced today with having to deal with two main types of terrorism: domestic and international. **Domestic terrorism** refers to the unlawful use of force or violence by a group or an individual who is based and operates entirely within the United States and its territories without foreign direction and whose acts are directed at elements of the U.S. government or population.[42] **International terrorism,** in contrast, is the unlawful use of force or violence by a group or an individual who has a connection to a foreign power or whose activities transcend national boundaries against persons or property to intimidate or coerce a government, the civilian population, or any segment thereof, in furtherance of political or social objectives.[43] International terrorism is sometimes incorrectly called *foreign terrorism,* a term that, strictly speaking, refers only to acts of terrorism that occur outside of the United States.

TABLE 15–3 **Types of Terrorist Groups**

Nationalist	Religious	State-Sponsored	Left-Wing	Right-Wing	Anarchist
Irish Republican Army, Basque Fatherland and Liberty, Kurdistan Workers' Party	Al-Qaeda, HAMAS, Hezbollah, Aum Shinrikyo (Japan)	Hezbollah (backed by Iran), Abu Nidal Organization (Syria, Libya), Japanese Red Army (Libya)	Red Brigades (Italy), Baader-Meinhof Gang (Germany), Japanese Red Army	Neo-Nazis, skinheads, white supremacists	Some contemporary antiglobalization groups

Source: Derived from information provided by the Council on Foreign Relations and the Markle Foundation, *Types of Terrorism,* http://www.terrorismanswers.com/terrorism/types.html, and http://www.cfr.org/issue/135/terrorism.html (accessed January 10, 2006, and July 10, 2007).

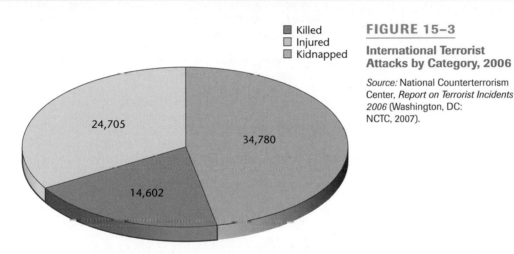

■ Killed
□ Injured
■ Kidnapped

24,705

34,780

14,602

FIGURE 15–3

International Terrorist Attacks by Category, 2006

Source: National Counterterrorism Center, *Report on Terrorist Incidents 2006* (Washington, DC: NCTC, 2007).

International Terrorism

According to the National Counterterrorism Center (NCTC), approximately 14,000 terrorist attacks occurred around the world during 2006, resulting in almost 15,000 deaths (Figure 15–3).[44] In 2006, attacks rose by 3,000, a 25% increase over 2005; while deaths rose by 5,800, a 40% increase over the previous year. The largest number of terrorist incidents and deaths reported in 2006 occurred in the Middle East and South Asia. These two locales accounted for 90% of the nearly 300 high-casualty attacks in 2006 that killed ten or more people. Of the 14,000 reported attacks, 45% (about 6,600) of them occurred in Iraq, where approximately 13,000 fatalities—65% of the worldwide total—were reported.

Violence against noncombatants in eastern and sub-Saharan Africa, particularly related to attacks associated with turmoil in or near Sudan and Nigeria, rose 64% in 2006, climbing to 422 from the approximately 256 attacks reported for 2005. The number of reported incidents in 2006 fell for Europe and Eurasia by 15%; for South Asia by 10%; and for the Western Hemisphere by 5%. No high-casualty attacks occurred in Western Europe, and only one occurred in Southeast Asia, in the southern Philippines. In Indonesia, there were no high-casualty attacks and 95% fewer victims of terror than in 2005. The approximately 750 attacks in Afghanistan during 2006 were 50% more than the nearly 500 attacks reported for 2005.

The worldwide total of people injured in terrorist incidents rose substantially in 2006—by 54%—with most of the rise stemming from a doubling of the reported number of injuries in Iraq since 2005. Although kidnappings in Iraq during 2006 rose sharply by

Who's to Blame—The Individual or Society?

The Making of a Suicide Bomber

Khaled Al-Rasheed was born in New York City to Egyptian parents and repeatedly visited the Middle East with his father. His last trip was in 2008 when Khaled spent part of the summer with his grandparents near the world-famous Aswan dam. Although his American passport didn't show it, Khaled, a Muslim, had traveled extensively throughout the Arab world while he was growing up, sometimes in the company of his father, and sometimes with his grandfather.

He had seen firsthand the damage done by the first Gulf War in 1991, much of which hadn't been repaired by the time he first visited the region. He had also experienced the resentment festering among the huge non-Arab populations in Saudi Arabia and Kuwait, where oil money paid for the extravagant lifestyles of the royal families but didn't find its way into the hands of the working class.

By the time he was 15, he had befriended a group of radical young Islamists living in Jordan, who blamed the problems in the Middle East on the Great Satan—their name for America. "Americans are stealing our region's wealth," he was told, "and polluting the holy land with their vice and nonbelief."

Returning to the United States in the fall of 2008, Khaled had become radicalized and was ready to strike a blow in what he saw as a worldwide holy war against nonbelievers. As a U.S. citizen, he could travel easily in and out of the country, and on one of his trips he was able to smuggle in the equipment necessary to manufacture a new kind of explosive—one that could be packed into condoms and swallowed like the heroin and cocaine that often crossed the country's southern borders. Equipped with a small blasting-cap whose thin wire ran up the esophagus and into his mouth, the last charge to be swallowed could be set off by simply biting down on a tiny switch clenched between Khaled's molars. The device, which used very little metal, was virtually undetectable.

One day, Khaled swallowed six explosive-filled condoms, passed through security, and boarded a plane at New York's John F. Kennedy airport. Once the plane, bound for Los Angeles, was airborne, Khaled bit down on the detonator. To his surprise, nothing happened. An hour into the flight, however, one of the swallowed condoms ruptured, and Khaled became violently ill as its contents entered his digestive system. Taken off the plane when it landed in Los Angeles, he was taken to a hospital where the explosives were discovered. An operation saved his life and he recovered in the medical wing of the Los Angeles County Men's Central Jail.

Think about it:

1. What does it mean to say, as this scenario does, that "Khaled had become radicalized"? Might the term be applied to other kinds of offenders? If so, which ones?

2. How could someone like Khaled, born in America, be so taken with a foreign ideology?

3. If you were in charge of policy making for America's "war on terror," what would you want to see happen to Khaled?

4. If you were a judge in charge of sentencing Khaled for his attempted terrorist attack, what kind of sentence would you give him? Is there any chance that he might be rehabilitated? What does "rehabilitation" mean in this context?

300%, kidnappings worldwide declined by more than 50% in 2006 because of a steep drop of approximately 22,000 kidnappings in Nepal.

Of the terrorist incidents for which the attackers were known or for which claims of responsibility were made, nearly 300 various subnational groups—many of them well-known foreign terrorist organizations such as al-Qaēda in Iraq (AQI)—or clandestine agents were connected to attacks in various ways. Of these groups Sunni terrorists, more than any other group, claimed that they conducted the largest number of incidents with the highest casualty totals.

In 2006, most attacks were perpetrated by terrorists using conventional fighting methods, such as mortars, bombs, and small arms. Bombing incidents increased by 30% from 2005, and death tolls in these incidents during 2006 rose by 39% and injuries by 45%. The use of suicide bombing attacks overall fell 12%, most notably in the use of suicide car bombers.

Approximately 39,000 individuals worldwide were either killed or injured by terrorist attacks in 2006. Well over 50% of those victimized by terrorism were Muslims. Most were victims of attacks in Iraq, and approximately 70% of those killed or injured were civilians. View the latest edition of the National Counterterrorism Center's *Report on Terrorist Incidents* via **Library Extra 15–5** at crimtoday.com.

LIBRARY
Extra

Experts warn that the United States may soon suffer from more incidents of international terrorism. As one terrorism expert explains, "As long as the United States remains actively engaged in the world, as it clearly must, there will be governments and groups committed to the use of violence to attack U.S. interests and further their own political goals."[45]

In this surveillance photo released by the Brooklyn U.S. Attorney's Office, an unidentified police informant, right, is shown with alleged bomb plotter Shahawar Matin Siraj, center, and his alleged coconspirator James Elshafay in New York City on August 21, 2004. Siraj, 23, was arrested on the eve of the 2004 Republican National Convention on charges that he wanted to attack a subway station in Herald Square, a dense shopping district in the city that includes Macy's department store. What is the nature of the threat represented by "home grown" terrorists like Siraj, and how does it differ from that represented by international terrorist organizations like Al-Qaeda?

Source: Brooklyn US Attorney's Office, HO/AP Wide World Photos

Domestic Terrorism

The 1995 terrorist bombing of the Alfred P. Murrah federal building in downtown Oklahoma City, Oklahoma, in which 168 people died and hundreds more were wounded, demonstrated just how vulnerable the United States is to terrorist attacks from domestic sources. The nine-story building—which included offices of the Social Security Administration, the Drug Enforcement Administration, the Secret Service, and the Bureau of Alcohol, Tobacco, and Firearms and a daycare center called America's Kids—was devastated by the homemade bomb. The fertilizer and diesel fuel device used in the attack was estimated to have weighed approximately 1,200 pounds. It was left in a parked rental truck on the 5th Street side of the building. The blast left a crater 30 feet wide and 8 feet deep and spread debris over a ten-block area.

In June 1997, a federal jury found 29-year-old Timothy McVeigh guilty of 11 counts ranging from conspiracy to first-degree murder in the bombing. Jurors concluded that McVeigh had conspired with Terry Nichols, a friend he had met while both were in the army, and with unknown others to use a truck bomb to destroy the Murrah Building. Prosecutors argued that the attack was intended to avenge the 1993 assault on David Koresh's Branch Davidian complex in Waco, Texas, which left 78 cult members dead. The Waco incident happened two years to the day before the Oklahoma City attack. Following the guilty verdicts, McVeigh was sentenced to die.[46] His coconspirator, Terry Nichols, was convicted of eight counts of involuntary manslaughter but escaped the death penalty. In late 1999, McVeigh requested that all appeals on his behalf be dropped and that an execution date be set. He was executed at the Terre Haute, Indiana, federal correctional facility on June 11, 2001.

A less lethal, but still frightening series of terrorist incidents in late 2001 and early 2002 involved the mailing of letters laced with "weapons-grade" (highly dispersible) anthrax. The mailings, which were sent to members of Congress and to the news media, caused the deaths of 5 people and sickened at least 17 others—resulting in the shutdown of contaminated mail facilities and government buildings.[47] From the initial reports of anthrax illnesses in New York and Florida in early September and October 2001 to the discovery of

Criminal Profiles

Mohammed Atta

The "Criminal Profiles" boxes found in preceding chapters have been presented in a way that seeks to describe the influences that led the subjects of the profiles to commit what many regard as sensational crimes. The intent of those profiles is to provide some insight into the evolution of markedly antisocial behavior. We were able to develop those profiles by researching the wealth of reliable and detailed information that is available on the personal backgrounds and offenses of each of the people profiled.

This profile box is somewhat different. Background information regarding Mohammed Atta, the subject of this box, is sparse, unreliable, and rife with conflicting claims. Given that Atta trained as a terrorist, came from the Middle East, and likely made efforts to live a life "under the radar," it is unsurprising that extensive research into Atta's pre-9/11 life yields little information about which one can feel confident. Although some facts about Atta's life are verifiable, many of the available sources appear to be speculative or outright rumor.

We know, for example, that Atta was born in Kafr El Sheikh in Egypt's Nile Delta, grew up in Cairo, and received an undergraduate degree in architecture from Cairo University. He is known to have resided in Germany from 1993 to 1999, where he pursued an urban planning degree at the University of Harburg-Hamburg, in Germany. Reliable records also show that he was a licensed pilot who moved to Venice, Florida, in 2000 to pursue additional flight training at Huffman Aviation International. Records and witness information also show that he was a committed fundamentalist Muslim.[i] We can conclude that he was intensely motivated by personal ideals, zealous and spiritual beliefs, most of which were acquired through his life experiences.

Other claims, however, cannot be as readily confirmed. For example, England's *Telegraph* online daily newspaper reported on December 13, 2003, that documents it had obtained showed that during the summer of 2001 Atta underwent an intensive three-day "work programme" in Baghdad under the tutelage of notorious Palestinian terrorist Abu Nidal. The handwritten, top secret memo the *Telegraph* had acquired was, ostensibly, prepared by the former head of Iraq's Intelligence Service and submitted to then–President Saddam Hussein. The memo purportedly lauds Atta's "extraordinary

effort" in preparing to lead the team that would be "responsible for attacking the targets that we have agreed to destroy."[ii] Unfortunately, numerous subsequent investigations—including the U.S. government's own National Commission on Terrorist Attacks on the United States (the so-called 9/11 Commission)—have failed to confirm a direct link between Hussein's Iraqi government and the al Qaeda terrorist group of which Atta was a member and which later claimed responsibility for the World Trade Center attacks.[iii]

Likewise, there are persistent reports that Atta had been in Israeli custody following his arrest for blowing up a bus in Israel in 1986. Urban legend contends that Atta was subsequently released at the insistence of President Bill Clinton and Secretary of State Warren Christopher, to prevent Palestinian withdrawal from the Oslo peace accords unless the Israelis released Atta and others. (Other reports claim that the U.S. interventionists were actually President Ronald Reagan and Secretary of State George Schultz, which is absurd in view of the fact that the Oslo Agreement occurred during Clinton's presidency.) This tale has been debunked by reports from the *Jewish News* Weekly[iv] and the Anti-Defamation League.[v] Both agencies deny that Atta was ever held by the Israelis, and claim that the man the Israelis imprisoned for the 1986 attack was, in fact, Mahmoud Abed Atta, a Palestinian (the Anti-Defamation League identifies him as a Jordanian and a naturalized U.S. citizen) associate of Abu Nidal's terror organization.[vi]

These and hundreds of other examples illustrate the difficulty of pinning down reliable information on Atta. Frustratingly, the more one digs, the more one encounters conflicting information that reduces effect research to the perusal of countless "did not, did too" reports. It is exasperating in the extreme—and an intentionally contrived morass designed by the terrorists themselves to aid in their evasion of detection and apprehension.

Thus, the predictable outcome of all but the most tenacious, obstinate, and creative investigative efforts focused on the secretive members of known terrorist organizations is exponentially increasing confusion. The more one comes to know, the less one is able to understand. Researchers inquiring into the intentionally obscured background of a man whose life was dedicated to the perpetration

anthrax spores in a letter mailed to the United States Senate on October 15, a series of escalating safety concerns about opening, handling, and even being in the proximity of mail, especially in government offices in Washington, DC, led to disruptions in, and then total curtailments of, mail delivery service at many federal agencies. No agency was hit harder than the Department of Justice, where anthrax was found in a central mail facility.[48] The attacks turned mail delivery into a potentially lethal experience. What followed was widespread testing of exposed locations and the irradiation treatment of all undelivered mail. It was months before full mail service was restored to all government offices.

cyberterrorism

A form of terrorism that makes use of high technology, especially computer technology and the Internet, in the planning and carrying out of terrorist attacks.

Cyberterrorism

A new kind of terrorism, called **cyberterrorism,** is lurking on the horizon. Cyberterrorism is a form of terrorism that makes use of high technology—especially computers, the Internet, and the World Wide Web—in the planning and carrying out of terrorist

September 11 hijacker Mohammed Atta. Why do we know so little about him?

Source: Portland Police Department/AP Wide World Photos

of illegal acts in the misguided pursuit of religious dogma—as defined by zealous adherence to radical Islamic fundamentalism—can hardly expect to find open records and free access to information. This is the predictable outcome of any investigative effort focused on a secretive member of a known terrorist organization.

In Atta's case, extensive scrutiny of existing information sources reveals a confusing and often conflicting profile of a man whose movements and activities during the period immediately preceding the World Trade Center attacks cannot be reliably confirmed. Available news reports starkly conflict with official documents. Some government agency documents conflict with the documentary evidence provided by other government agencies. "Highly reliable" information reported by reputable news sources in the period immediately following the attacks has subsequently proven to be almost completely inaccurate.

It is the nature of the terrorists' nether world. Secrecy, disinformation, obfuscation and orchestrated confusion are tools of the trade in such an environment. The creation of uncertainty serves a primary goal of all terrorist agents: to delay official responses to terrorist activity by bogging official agencies down in the pursuit of false leads. These manufactured delays are tactical measures that serve to protect such agents from rapid official responses to their attacks, thus, enhancing their ability to evade capture and sometimes facilitating their availability for use in future terrorist operations.

The life experiences and complex motivations of terrorists do not fit the motivational patterns of the (for lack of a better word) *ordinary* criminals described in previous chapters. Those seeking to understand terrorist behavior would probably be best served by examining the cultural, educational, ideological, and religious influences that shape the terrorists' world views, as those same views also serve to justify in the terrorist's mind even the most horrendous behavior in their pursuit of "correcting" perceived wrongs.

Notes:

i John Hooper, "The Shy, Caring, Deadly Fanatic," *The Observer (Hamburg)*, September 23, 2001, http://observer.guardian.co.uk/waronterrorism/story/0,,556630,00.html (accessed June 3, 2007).

ii Con Coughlin, "Terrorist Behind September 11 Strike Was Trained by Saddam," *Telegraph (United Kingdom),* December 13, 2003, http://www.telegraph.co.uk/news/main.jhtml?xml=/news/2003/12/14/wterr14.xml&sSheet=/portal/2003/12/14/ixportaltop.html (accessed June 3, 2007).

iii Walter Pincus and Dana Milbank, "Al-Qaeda-Hussein Link Is Dismissed," *Washington Post,* June 17, 2004, http://www.washingtonpost.com/wp-dyn/articles/A47812-2004Jun16.html (accessed June 3, 2007).

iv "Internet Rumors Aside, Atta Held by Israel not Hijacker," *The Jewish News Weekly,* November 16, 2001, http://www.jewishsf.com/content/2-0-/module/displaystory/story_id/17214/edition_id/340/format/html/displaystory.html (accessed June 3, 2007).

v "A Case of Mistaken Identity: Mohammad Atta Not Linked to Bus Bombing," Anti-Defamation League, 2001, http://urbanlegends.about.com/gi/dynamic/offsite.htm?site=http://www.adl.org/rumors/atta%5Frumors.asp (accessed June 3, 2007).

vi Netlore Archive, "Muhammad Atta," About.com: Urban Legends and Folklore, http://urbanlegends.about.com/library/blatta.htm (accessed June 3, 2007).

attacks. Whereas the most common forms of terrorism target people and things— in short, the physical world—cyberterrorism targets software, information, and communications—that is, the virtual world. The term *cyberterrorism* was coined in the 1980s by Barry Collin, a senior research fellow at the Institute for Security and Intelligence in California, who used it to refer to the convergence of cyberspace and terrorism.[49] It was later popularized by a 1996 RAND report that warned of an emerging "new terrorism," which is being implemented by the way in which terrorist groups organize and use technology. The report warned of a coming "netwar," or "infowar," consisting of coordinated cyberattacks on our nation's economic, business, and military infrastructure.[50] A country's **infrastructure** consists of the basic facilities, services, and installations needed for its functioning—such as transportation and communications systems, water and power lines, and institutions that serve the public, including banks, schools, post offices, and prisons.[51]

infrastructure

The basic facilities, services, and installations needed for the functioning of a community or society, such as transportation and communications systems, water and power lines, and public institutions, including schools, post offices, and prisons.

Following the RAND report, then–President Bill Clinton announced the formation of the President's Commission on Critical Infrastructure Protection (PCCIP) to study the critical components of the life support systems of the nation, determine their vulnerabilities to a wide range of threats, and propose a strategy for protecting them in the future.[52] Eight critical infrastructure components were identified: telecommunications, banking and finance, electrical power, oil and gas distribution and storage, water supply, transportation, emergency services, and government services.[53] PCCIP was the first national effort to address the vulnerabilities created by the information age.[54]

In 1998, the federal National Infrastructure Protection Center (NIPC) was created to serve as a focal point within the U.S. government for threat assessment, warning, investigation, and response to threats or attacks against the nation's critical infrastructure. NIPC functions have since been assumed by various groups within the Department of Homeland Security's (DHS) Information Analysis and Infrastructure Protection (IAIP) Directorate.

The Critical Infrastructure Assurance Office (CIAO) was created by a Presidential Decision Directive in May 1998 to coordinate the federal government's initiatives on critical infrastructure protection. Its responsibilities expanded in 2001, when President George W. Bush signed an executive order establishing the President's Critical Infrastructure Protection Board (PCIPB).[55] In September 2002, the board released a study called *The National Strategy to Secure Cyberspace.* The study found that "for the United States, the Information Technology Revolution quietly changed the way business and government operate. Without a great deal of thought about security, the nation shifted the control of essential processes in manufacturing, utilities, banking, and communications to networked computers. As a result, the cost of doing business dropped and productivity skyrocketed."[56] Consequently, the board found, "our economy and national security are fully dependent upon information technology and the information infrastructure. A network of networks directly supports the operation of all sectors of our economy—energy (electric power, oil and gas), transportation (rail, air, merchant marine), finance and banking, information and telecommunications, public health, emergency services, water, chemical, defense industrial base, food, agriculture, and postal and shipping. The reach of these computer networks exceeds the bounds of cyberspace. They also control physical objects such as electrical transformers, trains, pipeline pumps, chemical vats, radars, and stock markets."[57]

In 2003 the functions of the Critical Infrastructure Assurance Office were transferred to the National Cyber Security Division (NCSD) of the newly created Department of Homeland Security (DHS). According to DHS, the creation of NCSD both improved protection of critical cyberassets by "maximizing and leveraging the resources" of previously separate offices.[58]

Scenarios describing cyberterrorism possibilities are imaginative and diverse. Some have suggested that a successful cyberterrorist attack on the nation's air traffic control system might cause multiple airplanes to collide in midair or that an attack on food and cereal processing plants that drastically alters the levels of certain nutritional supplements might sicken or kill a large proportion of our nation's young children. Other such attacks might cause the country's power grid to collapse or muddle the records and transactions of banks and stock exchanges. The possible targets of such attacks are almost endless.

In an effort to protect vital interests from future acts of terrorism, the U.S. government is building a whole new Internet of its own. Dubbed "GovNet," the service is planned to be a private voice and data network based on the Internet Protocol (IP), but with no connectivity with commercial or public networks. The service would provide secure voice and data communication by remaining physically and electronically separate from existing Internet routers and gateways. A key feature of this network is that it must be able to perform its functions with no risk of penetration or disruption from users on other networks.[59] The idea for GovNet was first offered by Richard Clarke, President Bush's cybersecurity advisor, in late 2001. "We'll be working . . . to secure our cyberspace from a range of possible threats, from hackers to criminals to terrorist groups, to foreign nations, which might use cyber war against us," Clarke said in an interview on the topic.[60]

Terrorism and Technology

The technological sophistication of state-sponsored terrorist organizations is rapidly increasing. Handguns and even larger weapons are now being manufactured out of plastic polymers and ceramics. Capable of firing Teflon-coated armor-piercing hardened ceramic bullets, such weapons are extremely powerful and impossible to uncover with metal detectors. Evidence points to the black market availability of other sinister items, including liquid metal embrittlement (LME). LME is a chemical that slowly weakens any metal it contacts. Some experts say that it could easily be applied with a felt-tipped marker to fuselage components in domestic aircraft, causing delayed structural failure.[61] Similarly, backpack-type electromagnetic pulse generators may soon be available to terrorists. Such devices could be carried into major cities, set up next to important computer installations, and activated to wipe out billions of items of financial, military, or other information now stored on magnetic media. International terrorists, along with the general public, have easy access to maps and other information that could be used to cripple the nation. The approximately 500 extremely high-voltage (EHV) transformers on which the nation's electric grid depends, for example, are largely undefended but in the recent past were specified with extreme accuracy on easily available Web-based power network maps.

It is now clear that at least some terrorist organizations are seeking to obtain weapons of mass destruction (WMDs), involving possible chemical, biological, radiological, and nuclear threats. A Central Intelligence Agency (CIA) report made public in 2003 warned that al-Qaeda's "end goal" is to use WMDs. The CIA noted that the group had "openly expressed its desire to produce nuclear weapons" and that sketches and documents recovered from an al-Qaeda facility in Afghanistan contained plans for a crude nuclear device.[62]

A 2003 study by Harvard University researchers found that the United States and other countries were moving too slowly in efforts to help Russia and other former Soviet-bloc nations destroy poorly protected nuclear material and warheads left over from the cold war.[63] The study also warned that most civilian nuclear reactors in Eastern Europe are "dangerously insecure." Experts say the amount of plutonium needed to make one bomb can be smuggled out of a supposedly secure area in a briefcase or even in the pocket of an overcoat.

Biological weapons were banned by the 1975 international Biological Weapons Convention (BWC),[64] but biological terrorism (or bioterrorism), which seeks to disperse destructive or disease-producing biologically active agents among civilian or military populations, is of considerable concern today. *Bioterrorism*, one form of biocrime, is defined by the Centers for Disease Control and Prevention (CDC) as the "intentional or threatened use of viruses, bacteria, fungi, or toxins from living organisms to produce death or disease in humans, animals, or plants."[65] The infamous anthrax letters mailed to at least four people in the United States in 2001 (discussed earlier) provide an example of a bioterrorism incident intended to create widespread fear among Americans. Five people, including mail handlers, died, and 23 others were infected.[66] Other possible bioterror agents include botulism toxin, brucellosis, cholera, glanders, plague, ricin, smallpox, tularemia Q fever, and a number of viral agents like viral hemorrhagic fevers and severe acute respiratory syndrome (SARS). Experts fear that technologically savvy terrorists could create their own novel bioweapons through bioengineering, a process that uses snippets of made-to-order DNA, the molecular code on which life is based.[67] Learn more about biological agents via the CDC Web site at Web Extra 15–5, and visit the Center for the Study of Bioterrorism via Web Extra 15–6. An intriguing paper on the topic of bioterrorism from the CDC is available as Library Extra 15–6 at crimtoday.com.

WEB
Extra

WEB
Extra

LIBRARY
Extra

The War on Terrorism

During the first years of the Bush presidency, terrorist attacks and corporate scandals demanded the attention of federal legislators and the Oval Office. Three important legislative initiatives resulted. The first, the USA PATRIOT Act,[68] was rushed through Congress in response to the September 11, 2001, attacks on the World Trade Center and

Pentagon ("USA PATRIOT" stands for "Uniting and Strengthening America by Providing Appropriate Tools Required to Intercept and Obstruct Terrorism"). It became law on October 26, 2001. The second, the Sarbanes-Oxley Act, was signed into law on July 30, 2002, as a response to a series of corporate bankruptcies and a declining stock market brought on by the misdeeds of executives at a number of the nation's large corporations. The Sarbanes-Oxley Act, which established new requirements for corporate governance and set stiff criminal punishments for violators, is discussed in Chapter 12. The third, the Homeland Security Act of 2002, became law on November 25, 2002, and established a new cabinet-level department charged with helping to prevent, protect against, and respond to acts of terrorism on American soil. In establishing the new Department of Homeland Security, the act restructured the executive branch of the federal government.

The USA PATRIOT Act

Like the Homeland Security Act, the USA PATRIOT Act was designed to fight terrorism. However, it contains provisions that apply to other forms of criminal activity as well. The act permits longer jail terms for certain suspects arrested without a warrant, broadens "sneak and peak" search authority (searches conducted without notice), and enhances the power of prosecutors. The law also increases the ability of federal authorities to tap phones (including wireless devices), share intelligence information, track Internet usage, crack down on money laundering, and protect the country's borders.

The USA PATRIOT Act is not a stand-alone law. It amends more than 15 federal statutes and rules, including the federal Wiretap Statute,[69] the Bank Secrecy Act of 1970,[70] the federal Pen Register and Trap and Trace Statute,[71] the Electronic Communications Privacy Act (ECPA),[72] the Foreign Intelligence Surveillance Act of 1978 (FISA),[73] the Federal Rules of Criminal Procedure,[74] immigration laws, and the Family Education Rights and Privacy Act (FERPA).[75]

The USA PATRIOT Act led some to question whether the government unfairly expanded police powers at the expense of individual rights and civil liberties. Prior to passage, the legislation had been questioned by the American Civil Liberties Union (ACLU), which feared that it would substantially reduce the constitutional rights of individuals facing justice system processing. After the bill became law, the ACLU pledged to work with the president and law enforcement agencies across the country "to ensure that civil liberties in America are not eroded. . . ."[76] Some of the law's strictest provisions were slated to "sunset" at the end of 2005, but most were renewed by congressional action before they could expire.

The Department of Homeland Security

The Homeland Security Act of 2002,[77] enacted to protect America against terrorism, established the federal Department of Homeland Security (DHS), which is also charged with protecting the nation's critical infrastructure against terrorist attack. The new department began operations on March 1, 2003, with former Pennsylvania governor Tom Ridge as its director. The director is a member of the President's Cabinet.

Experts say that the creation of DHS is the most significant transformation of the U.S. government since 1947, when President Harry S. Truman merged the various branches of the armed forces into the Department of Defense in an effort to better coordinate the nation's defense against military threats.[78] DHS coordinates the activities of 22 disparate domestic agencies by placing administration of those agencies under five "directorates," or departmental divisions:

1. **Border and Transportation Security (BTS).** BTS is responsible for maintaining security of the nation's borders and transportation systems. The largest of the directorates, it is home to the Transportation Security Administration, the U.S. Customs Service, the border security functions of the former Immigration and Naturalization Service,[79] the Animal and Plant Health Inspection Service, and the Federal Law Enforcement Training Center.

2. **Emergency Preparedness and Response (EPR).** EPR works to ensure that the nation is prepared for, and able to recover from, terrorist attacks and natural disasters.

3. **Science and Technology (S&T).** This directorate coordinates the department's efforts in research and development, including preparing for and responding to the full range of terrorist threats involving weapons of mass destruction.

4. **Information Analysis and Infrastructure Protection (IAIP).** IAIP merges under one roof the functions of identifying and assessing a broad range of intelligence information concerning threats to the homeland, issuing timely warnings, and taking appropriate preventive and protective action.

5. **Management.** The Management Directorate is responsible for budgetary, managerial, and personnel issues within DHS.

Besides the five directorates, several other critical agencies have been folded into the new department or were created.[80]

United States Coast Guard (USCG).   The commandant of the Coast Guard reports directly to the secretary of DHS. However, the USCG also works closely with the undersecretary of BTS and maintains its existing identity as an independent military service. Upon declaration of war or when the president so directs, the Coast Guard will operate as an element of the Department of Defense, consistent with existing law.

United States Secret Service.   The primary mission of the Secret Service is the protection of the president and other government leaders, as well as security for designated national events. The Secret Service is also the primary agency responsible for protecting U.S. currency from counterfeiters and safeguarding Americans from credit card fraud.

Bureau of Citizenship and Immigration Services.   While BTS is responsible for enforcing our nation's immigration laws, the Bureau of Citizenship and Immigration Services, a new agency, dedicates its energies to providing efficient immigration services and easing the transition to American citizenship.

Office of State and Local Government Coordination.   This office ensures close coordination between local, state, and federal governments to ensure an effective terrorism-prevention effort and to provide quick responses to terrorist incidents.

Office of Private Sector Liaison.   The Office of Private Sector Liaison provides the business community with a direct line of communication to DHS. The office works directly with individual businesses and through trade associations and other nongovernmental organizations to foster dialogue between the private sector and DHS on the full range of issues and challenges that America's businesses face today.

Office of Inspector General.   The Office of Inspector General serves as an independent and objective inspection, audit, and investigative body to promote effectiveness, efficiency, and economy in DHS's programs and operations and to prevent and detect fraud, abuse, mismanagement, and waste.

Figure 15–4 shows the organizational chart for the DHS. You can reach DHS on the Web via **Web Extra 15–7**.

WEB Extra

Terrorism Commissions and Reports

In recent years, a number of government and private groups have issued reports on terrorism and America's preparedness to deal with threats of terrorism. One of the most important was the Gilmore Commission, officially known as the Advisory Panel to Assess Domestic Response Capabilities for Terrorism Involving Weapons of Mass Destruction. The Gilmore Commission was established by Section 1405 of the National Defense Authorization Act for Fiscal Year 1999.[81] That act directed that a federally

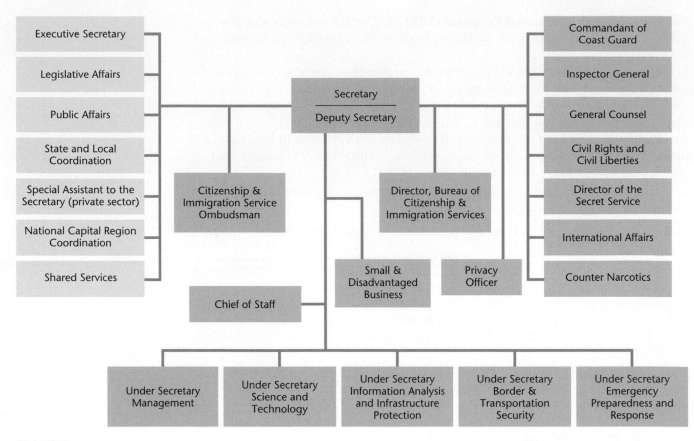

FIGURE 15–4

Department of Homeland Security

Source: Department of Homeland Security.

funded research and development center provide research, analytical, and other support to the advisory panel during the course of its activities and deliberations. Under contract with the Department of Defense, RAND has been providing that support and is the corporate author of the three annual Gilmore Commission reports to the president and Congress that have been issued to date.

The first of these reports, which was published on December 15, 1999, provides an in-depth overview of terrorist threats facing the United States. The second report, which was published on December 14, 2000, focuses on the need for a national antiterrorism strategy to encompass the full spectrum of deterrence, prevention, preparedness, and response. It calls for coordination among state and local officials and addresses intelligence, law enforcement, fire services, public health, and emergency medical and emergency management issues involved in the fight against terrorism.

The third Gilmore Commission report was published on December 15, 2001, and was the first major antiterrorism report to be released in the United States after the events of September 11, 2001. It emphasizes the need for improvements in state and local response capabilities, enhanced immigration standards and better border control, improved security against cyberattacks, and an expanded role for the military in fighting terrorism. The three Gilmore Commission reports are available in their entirety as Library Extras 15–7, 15–8, and 15–9 at crimtoday.com.

Another important group, the U.S. Commission on National Security in the 21st Century, also known as the Hart-Rudman Commission, has reported in three phases as follows:

LIBRARY
Extra
■■■■

- **Phase I report: New World Coming: American Security in the 21st Century (September 15, 1999).** The Phase I report discusses relevant economic,

Members of the National Commission on Terrorist Attacks upon the United States (aka the 9/11 Commission) (from left): Thomas H. Kean, Lee H. Hamilton, Fred F. Fielding, Bob Kerrey, John F. Lehman, and Richard Ben-Veniste. The commission's report, released on July 22, 2004, called for a major overhaul of U.S. intelligence agencies and for a realignment of federal expenditures on homeland security. Acts of terrorism generally involve a multitude of criminal law violations. What crimes were committed by the terrorists who attacked the World Trade Center and the Pentagon?

Source: Doug Mills/The New York Times

technological, and intellectual influences throughout the global community and underscores the powerful forces of social and political fragmentation now occurring in many places in the world. This new world order, the report concludes, requires a new and comprehensive U.S. international strategy.

- **Phase II report: Seeking a National Strategy: A Concert for Preserving Security and Promoting Freedom (April 15, 2000).** The Phase II report suggests U.S. antiterrorism priorities for the future, including defending the homeland; maintaining America's internal social cohesion, economic competitiveness, technological ingenuity, and military strength; assisting with the macroeconomic and political integration of key major powers, such as China, Russia, and India; promoting growth of the global economy; establishing needed international laws and agreements; adapting existing alliances to meet new challenges; and helping sustain international stability.

- **Phase III report: Roadmap for National Security (January 31, 2001).** The Phase III report examines multiple potential threats to homeland security. The document emphasizes the need to capitalize on America's strengths in the sciences and education and suggests that the human requirements needed for adequate national security are not being met.

LIBRARY
Extra

All three reports are available in their entirety as **Library Extras 15–10, 15–11,** and **15–12** at crimtoday.com.

After leaving Congress, former Senators Gary Hart and Warren Rudman collaborated on a follow-up antiterrorism report sponsored by the Washington, DC–based Council on Foreign Relations. That report, entitled *America Still Unprepared—America Still in Danger,*[82] was released on October 25, 2002. It concluded that the United States remains "dangerously unprepared" to prevent or respond to attacks by well-organized terrorist groups. "America's own ill-prepared response," said the report, "could hurt its people to a much greater extent than any single attack by a terrorist."

A third group, the National Commission on Terrorism (also known as the Bremmer Commission), was established under the federal Omnibus Consolidated and Emergency Supplemental Appropriations Act of 1999[83] to review and assess the laws, regulations, policies, directives, and practices relating to combating international terrorism directed against the United States, as well as to recommend changes needed to improve U.S. counterterrorism performance. The commission's report, which was transmitted to the president on June 7, 2000, is entitled *Countering the Changing Threat of International*

LIBRARY
Extra
▪ ▪ ▪ ▪

Terrorism. It outlines the changing face of international terrorism and offers diplomatic, intelligence, and law enforcement options for addressing that threat, and is available in its entirety as Library Extra 15–13 at crimtoday.com.

Finally, on July 22, 2004, the National Commission on Terrorist Attacks upon the United States (better known as the 9/11 Commission), released a highly anticipated 567-page report. The report said that the September 11, 2001, attacks should have come as no surprise because the U.S. government had received clear warnings that Islamic terrorists were planning to strike at targets within the United States. The report, which was nearly two years in the making, said that the United States is still not properly prepared to adequately deal with terrorist threats and called for the creation of a new federal intelligence-gathering center to unify the more than a dozen federal agencies currently gathering terrorism-related intelligence at home and abroad. The report also said that the United States, along with the world's other economically advanced nations, must create a global strategy of diplomacy and public relations to counter Islamic terror networks and to defeat their ideology. "To Muslim parents," the report said, "terrorists like bin Laden have nothing to offer their children but visions of violence and death. America and its friends have the advantage—our vision can offer a better future."

The commission was created by the president and Congress on November 27, 2002,[84] and charged with investigating the "facts and circumstances relating to the terrorist attacks on September 11, 2001, including those relating to intelligence agencies, law enforcement agencies, diplomacy, immigration issues and border control, the flow of assets to terrorist organizations, commercial aviation, the role of congressional oversight and resource allocation, and other areas determined relevant by the Commission."[85] Commission members reviewed more than 2.5 million pages of documents and interviewed more than 1,200 individuals in ten countries. The entire 567-page report is available as Library Extra 15–14 at crimtoday.com.

LIBRARY
Extra
▪ ▪ ▪ ▪

Countering the Terrorist Threat

Although the Bremmer Commission report was issued prior to the events of September 11, 2001, many of its findings and recommendations still ring true today. Among them are the following:[86]

- International terrorism poses an increasingly dangerous and difficult threat to America.
- Countering the growing danger of the terrorist threat requires significantly stepping up U.S. efforts.
- Priority one is to prevent terrorist attacks. The U.S. intelligence and law enforcement communities must use the full scope of their authority to collect intelligence regarding terrorist plans and methods.
- U.S. policies must firmly target all states that support terrorists.
- Private sources of financial and logistical support for terrorists must be subjected to the full force and sweep of U.S. and international laws.
- A terrorist attack involving a biological agent, deadly chemicals, or nuclear or radiological material, even if it succeeds only partially, could profoundly affect the entire nation. The government must do more to prepare for such an event.
- The president and Congress should reform the system for reviewing and funding government counterterrorism programs to ensure that the activities and programs of various agencies are part of a comprehensive plan.

The U.S. Department of State, in its publication *Patterns of Global Terrorism,*[87] makes a number of policy recommendations for use in the fight against international terrorism. "Money," says the report, "is like oxygen to terrorists, and it must be choked-off." In September 2001, President George W. Bush issued an executive order imposing stiff penalties on anyone who provides financial support to terrorists or their organizations.[88] The order blocks the assets of designated individuals and organizations linked to global terrorism and prohibits financial transactions with the terrorist groups, leaders, and corporate and charitable fronts listed in the order. It also establishes America's ability to block the U.S. assets of, and deny access to U.S. markets to, the foreign banks that refuse to freeze terrorists' assets.

In 2003, the White House released its official *National Strategy for Combating Terrorism*.[89] The strategy includes a multipronged initiative aimed at reducing both the threat severity and international reach of international terrorist organizations. The goals of the *National Strategy* are as follows:

- Defeat terrorists and their organizations by identifying, locating, and destroying them.

- Deny sponsorship, support, and sanctuary to terrorists by helping other nations fulfill their responsibilities and obligations to combat terrorism.

- Diminish the underlying conditions that terrorists seek to exploit by resolving regional disputes; by fostering economic, social, and political development; by encouraging market-based economies; by supporting good governance and the rule of law; and by "winning the war of ideas" to ensure that ideologies that promote terrorism do not find fertile ground in any nation.

- Defend U.S. citizens and interests at home and abroad by implementing strong and effective security measures and by enhancing measures intended to ensure the integrity, reliability, and availability of critical physical and information-based infrastructures (including transportation and information systems).

The July 2004 report of the National Commission on Terrorist Attacks Upon the United States proposed sweeping changes within the U.S. intelligence community, including the creation of the position of National Intelligence Director (NID). Soon afterward, the Intelligence Reform and Terrorism Prevention Act of 2004 (IRTPA) facilitated the creation of the National Counterterrorism Center (NCTC) under the newly-created position of NID.[90] The NID acts as the principal advisor to the president, the National Security Council, and the Homeland Security Council for intelligence matters related to national security. The NCTC serves as the primary organization in the U.S. government for integrating and analyzing all intelligence pertaining to terrorism and counterterrorism, and to conduct strategic counterterrorism operational planning. Today, intelligence analysts at the NCTC have access to dozens of networks and information systems from across the intelligence, law enforcement, military, and homeland security communities. These systems contain foreign and domestic information pertaining to international terrorism and sensitive law enforcement activities.[91] Located at the Liberty Crossing Building in McLean, Virginia, the NCTC is a multiagency organization dedicated to eliminating the terrorist threat to U.S. interests at home and abroad. Learn more about countering terrorist threats at Library Extra 15–15 at crimtoday.com. The *National Strategy* is available in its entirety at Library Extra 15–16. Visit the National Counterterrorism Center at Web Extra 15–8.

LIBRARY
Extra

LIBRARY
Extra

WEB
Extra

Foreign Terrorist Organizations

From the late 1970s to the mid-1990s, U.S. antiterrorism policy focused largely on deterring and punishing state sponsors of terrorism as opposed to terrorist groups themselves.[92] In 1996, passage of the federal Anti-Terrorism and Effective Death Penalty Act[93] signaled an important shift in policy. That legislation recognized the transnationalism of many of today's terrorist organizations, and created a legal category of **foreign terrorist organizations (FTOs).** It banned funding, granting of visas, and other material support to such organizations and their members. The USA PATRIOT Act[94] extended and strengthened the provisions of that legislation.

foreign terrorist organization (FTO)

A foreign organization that engages in terrorist activity that threatens the security of U.S. nationals or the national security of the United States and that is so designated by the U.S. secretary of state.

Palestinian boys, wearing green ribbons on their heads symbolizing support of HAMAS, brandish plastic rifles as they march through the streets of the West Bank town of Nablus in a protest rally against Israeli aggression. Some argue that terrorists already control the hearts and minds of young people in many parts of the world. What can be done to change that?

Source: AP Wide World Photos/ Nasser Ishtayeh

Federal law requires that any organization considered for FTO designation must (1) be *foreign*, (2) engage in terrorist activity as defined in Section 212(a)(3)(B) of the Immigration and Nationality Act,[95] and (3) threaten the security of U.S. nationals *or* the national security (national defense, foreign relations, *or* economic interests) of the United States.

The U.S. Department of State holds the authority to designate any group external to the United States as an FTO. The designation process involves an exhaustive interagency review, in which all evidence of a group's activity, from both classified and open sources, is scrutinized. The State Department, working closely with the Justice and Treasury Departments and the intelligence community, prepares a detailed "administrative record," which documents the terrorist activity of the designated FTO.

Under federal law, FTO designations are subject to judicial review. In the event of a challenge to a group's FTO designation in federal court, the U.S. government relies upon the administrative record to defend the designation decision. These administrative records contain intelligence information and are therefore classified. FTO designations expire in two years unless renewed.

Once an organization has been designated as an FTO, a number of legal consequences ensue. Following a designation, it becomes unlawful for a person in the United States or subject to the jurisdiction of the United States to provide funds or other material support to a designated FTO. Similarly, representatives and certain members of a designated FTO, if they are aliens, can be denied visas or kept from entering the United States. Finally, U.S. financial institutions must block funds of designated FTOs and their agents and report the blockage to the Office of Foreign Assets Control within the U.S. Department of the Treasury. Designated FTOs can be found in Table 15–4.

The State Department also has the authority to designate selected foreign governments as *state sponsors* of international terrorism. There are six countries currently designated state sponsors of terrorism: Cuba, Iran, Libya, North Korea, Sudan, and Syria. According to the State Department, Iran remains the most active state

TABLE 15–4 Designated Foreign Terrorist Organizations

Abu Nidal Organization (ANO)

Abu Sayyaf Group (ASG)

Al-Aqsa Martyrs Brigade

Ansar al-Islam (AI)

Armed Islamic Group (GIA)

Asbat al-Ansar

Aum Supreme Truth (Aum) Aum Shinrikyo, Aleph

Basque Fatherland and Liberty (ETA)

Communist Party of Philippines/New People's Army (CPP/NPA)

Al-Gama's al-Islamiyya (Islamic Group, IG)

HAMAS (Islamic Resistance Movement)

Harakat ul Mujahidin (HUM)

Hezbollah (Party of God)

Islamic Movement of Uzbekistan (IMU)

Jaish-e-Mohammed (JEM)

Jemaah Islamiya (JI)

Al-Jihad (Egyptian Islamic Jihad, EIJ)

Kahane Chai (Kach)

Kongra-Gel (KGK, formerly Kurdistan Workers' Party, PKK, KADEK)

Lashkar-e-Tayyiba (LT)

Lashkar I Jhangvi (LJ)

Liberation Tigers of Tamil Eelam (LTTE)

Mujahedin-e Khalq Organization (MEK or MKO)

National Liberation Army (ELN)—Columbia

Palestine Islamic Jihad (PIJ)

Palestine Liberation Front (PLF)

Popular Front for the Liberation of Palestine (PFLP)

Popular Front for the Liberation of Palestine—General Command (PFLP-GC)

Al-Qaeda

Real IRA (RIRA)

Revolutionary Armed Forces of Colombia (FARC)

Revolutionary Nuclei (RN)

Revolutionary Organization 17 November (17 November)

Revolutionary People's Liberation Party/Front (DHKP/C)

Salafist Group for Call and Combat (GSPC)

Sendero Luminoso (Shining Path or SL)

United Self-Defense Forces/Group of Colombia (AUC)

Note: For more detailed descriptions of these organizations, see the U.S. Department of State publication *Patterns of Global Terrorism*, http://www.state.gov/s/ct/rls/pgtrpt; and National Counterterrorism Center, *Report on Terrorist Incidents, 2006*, http://www.terrorisminfo.mipt.org/pdf/Country-Reports-Terrorism-2006-NCTC-Annex.pdf.

sponsor of terrorism in the world today. Iran's Islamic Revolutionary Guard Corps (IRGC) and the Ministry of Intelligence and Security (MOIS) continue to be involved in the planning and support of terrorist acts and support a variety of groups that use terrorism to pursue their goals. The State Department points out that the Iranian government continues to provide support to numerous terrorist groups, including the Lebanese Hezbollah, HAMAS, and the Palestine Islamic Jihad (PIJ), all of which seek to undermine Middle East peace negotiations through the use of terrorism. Iraq continued to provide safe haven and support to a variety of Palestinian terrorist groups, as well as bases, weapons, and protection to the Mujahedin-e Khalq (MEK), an Iranian terrorist group that opposes the current Iranian regime. Syria continued to provide safe haven and support to several terrorist groups, some of which oppose the Middle East peace negotiations. At the time of the State Department report, Libya was attempting to mend its international image following its surrender in 1999 of two Libyan suspects for trial in the Pan Am 103 bombing. In early 2001, one of those suspects was convicted of murder, and judges in the case found that he had acted "in furtherance of the purposes of . . . Libyan Intelligence Services." Cuba continued to provide a safe haven to several terrorists and U.S. fugitives and maintained ties to state sponsors and Latin American insurgents. North Korea harbored several hijackers of a Japanese Airlines flight to North Korea in the 1970s and maintained links to other terrorist groups. At the start of 2007, Sudan continued to provide a safe haven for members of al-Qaeda, the Lebanese Hezbollah, al-Gama'a al-Islamiyya, Egyptian Islamic Jihad, the PIJ, and HAMAS, although it has been engaged in a counterterrorism dialogue with the United States since mid-2000. Learn more about terrorist activities in individual countries from the Department of State's Country Reports on Terrorism via **Library Extra 15–17** at crimtoday.com.

LIBRARY
Extra
■ ■ ■ ■

The 2001 USA PATRIOT Act[96] created a Terrorist Exclusion List (TEL) with immigration consequences for groups that it names. The federal government may deport aliens living in the United States who provide material assistance to organizations listed on the TEL and may refuse entry to the country to anyone who assists or solicits assistance for those organizations.

At the individual level, the U.S. government's Terrorist Identities Datamart Environment (TIDE) serves as a central repository of information on international terrorist identities.[97] TIDE supports the federal government's various terrorist screening systems or "watchlists" and the U.S. Intelligence Community's overall counterterrorism efforts. The Terrorist Identities Group (TIG) is located in NCTC's Information Sharing & Knowledge Development Directorate (ISKD), and is responsible for building and maintaining TIDE. The TIDE database includes, to the extent permitted by law, all information the U.S. government has related to the identities of individuals known or lawfully suspected to be or have been involved in terrorism-related activities. Federal agencies nominate individuals for inclusion in TIDE based on evaluations of available intelligence and law enforcement antiterrorism information. Federal data analysts then create and enhance TIDE records based on their review of nominations received. Every day, TIDE analysts transmit a sensitive data set containing terrorist identifiers to the Terrorist Screening Center (TSC) for use in the federal government's consolidated watchlist. The consolidated watchlist supports screening processes to detect and interdict known and suspected terrorists at home and abroad and is used to create and maintain the Transportation Security Administration's "no-fly list," the Department of State's visa database, and other similar databases.

In 2006, the United States and Russia joined together to initiate the Global Initiative to Combat Nuclear Terrorism. The two countries called upon "like-minded nations to expand and accelerate efforts that develop partnership capacity to combat nuclear terrorism on a determined and systematic basis."[98] The initiative has grown and today includes approximatley two dozen other partner nations.

Today U.S. policy focuses largely on terrorist organizations like al-Qaeda and its affiliated networks, and state supporters.[99] In the future, however, it may be that new brands of terrorists will emerge: individuals who are not affiliated with any established terrorist organization and who are apparently not agents of any state sponsor. The terrorist Ramzi Ahmed Yousef, who is believed to have masterminded the 1993 World Trade Center bombing, apparently did not belong to any larger, established, and previously identified group, although he may have had some ties to al-Qaeda operatives. Also, the worldwide threat of individual or "boutique" terrorism, or that of "spontaneous" terrorist activity, such as the bombing of bookstores in the United

States after Ayatollah Khomeini's death edict against British author Salman Rushdie, appears to be on the increase. Thus, one likely profile for the terrorist of the twenty-first century may well be a private individual not affiliated with any established group, but drawing on other similarly minded individuals for support. Because the U.S. international counterterrorism policy framework has been sanctions-oriented, and has traditionally sought to pin responsibility on state sponsors, changes in policy are being considered and implemented.

Another problem surfacing in the wake of the number of incidents associated with Islamic fundamentalist groups is how to condemn and combat such terrorist activity, and the extreme and violent ideology of specific radical groups, without appearing to be anti-Islamic in general. A desire to punish a state for supporting international terrorism may also conflict with other foreign policy objectives involving that nation. Learn more about terrorism from the Terrorism Research Center via **Web Extra 15–9**. You can visit the National Counterterrorism Center via **Web Extra 15–10**.

WEB Extra

The Future of Terrorism

The Congressional Research Service recently identified three trends in modern terrorism.[100] The first trend, one that makes terrorism especially difficult to combat, is toward loosely organized, self-financed, international terrorist networks. A second recent trend is toward terrorism that is religiously or ideologically motivated. Groups using religion as a pretext, such as radical Islamic fundamentalist groups, pose serious terrorist threats of varying kinds to U.S. interests and call upon other like-minded people throughout the world to join their causes. A third trend is the recent growth of cross-national links among different terrorist organizations, which may involve combinations of military training, funding, technology transfer, or political advice. The Congressional Research cites intelligence reports showing, for example, that Chechen rebels have been trained in al-Qaeda terrorist camps in Afghanistan and even in Chechnya itself. Al-Qaeda funding reputedly helped establish the Islamic separatist group Abu Sayyaf in the Philippines. Similarly, some intelligence reports suggest the possibility of mid- and low-level cooperation between al-Qaeda and the Lebanese Hezballah in such areas as weapons smuggling, money laundering and training for terrorist operations.

Looming over the entire issue of international terrorism is a trend toward proliferation of WMDs. For instance Iran, seen as the most active state sponsor of terrorism, has been aggressively seeking a nuclear arms capability. Iraq is thought to be stockpiling chemical and biological agents, and to be rebuilding its nuclear weapons program. North Korea recently admitted to having a clandestine program for uranium enrichment. Also, indications have surfaced that al-Qaeda has attempted to acquire chemical, biological, radiological and nuclear weapons. As a result, stakes in the war against international terrorism are increasing and margins for error in selecting appropriate policy instruments or combinations of them to prevent terrorist attacks are diminishing.

SUMMARY

This chapter focuses on two topics: (1) globalization and its impact on crime and criminal activity and (2) terrorism, both domestic and international. Globalization refers to the increasing integration of previously isolated events in all areas of life, and the effects of that integration on people throughout the world. Globalization has made it impossible for U.S. policymakers to ignore criminal activity in other parts of the world, especially where that crime is perpetrated by transnational criminal and terrorist organizations. Transnational crime, an especially important consequence of globalization, refers to unlawful activity undertaken and supported by organized criminal groups operating across national boundaries. Transnational crime and the internationally organized criminal groups that support it have emerged as one of the most pressing challenges for criminologists in the twenty-first century. Transnational criminal activities include crimes like fraudulent e-mail and phishing schemes, drug running, international trade in weapons of mass destruction, sex tourism, and illegal trafficking in human beings and human organs.

Trafficking in persons and human smuggling are two of the fastest growing areas of international criminal activity today. Human smuggling refers to illegal immigration in which a criminal agent is involved for payment to help a person cross a border clandestinely. Human trafficking, in contrast, involves the exploitation of unwilling or unwitting people through force, coercion, threat, or deception, and includes human rights abuses such as debt bondage, deprivation of liberty, or lack of control over freedom and labor. Trafficking is often undertaken for purposes of sexual exploitation or labor exploitation.

As the second part of this chapter discusses, criminologists have increasingly focused on understanding and preventing terrorism since the 2001 attacks on the World Trade Center and Pentagon by Muslim extremists. Terrorism, however, differs from most other forms of criminal offending in that its goal is political—meaning that acts of terrorism are undertaken by those seeking to bring about change in the existing social order. This chapter defines *terrorism* as premeditated, politically motivated violence perpetrated against noncombatant targets by subnational groups or clandestine agents, usually intended to influence an audience. Terrorism brings with it the threat of massive destruction and large numbers of casualties. Domestic and international terrorism are the two main forms of terrorism with which this chapter deals. Specific forms of terrorist activity, such as cyberterrorism and attacks on information-management segments of our nation's critical infrastructure, could theoretically shut down or disable important infrastructure services like electricity, food processing, military activity, and even state and federal governments. The vigilance required to prevent terrorism, both domestic and international, has resulted in new laws that restrict a number of freedoms that many Americans have previously taken for granted.

KEY TERMS

comparative criminologist, 625

comparative criminology, 623

cyberterrorism, 634

domestic terrorism, 630

ethnocentrism, 625

foreign terrorist organization (FTO), 643

globalization, 618

human smuggling, 620

infrastructure, 635

international terrorism, 630

sex trafficking, 623

terrorism, 629

trafficking in persons (TIP), 620

transnational organized crime, 618

QUESTIONS FOR REVIEW

1. What is globalization? How does it impact criminal activity in today's world? In the United States? How does it affect terrorism?

2. What is comparative criminology? What are the advantages of a comparative approach in the study of criminology?

3. What is terrorism? What types of terrorism does this chapter discuss?

QUESTIONS FOR REFLECTION

1. What are the advantages of a comparative perspective in criminology? Are there any disadvantages? If so, what are they?

2. What types of terrorism has this chapter identified? Are there any that it might have missed? If so, what are they?

3. Has the "war against terrorism" affected you personally? If so, how?

4. Has the average American had to sacrifice any rights or freedoms in the fight against terrorism? If so, what rights or freedoms have been sacrificed?

5. Some people say that the only way to secure freedom is to curtail it during times of national crisis. Can this be true? Why?

WEB QUEST

Visit the National Counterterrorism Center (NCTC) at www. nctc.gov, and familiarize yourself with the site's features. What is the NCTC's mission? When was it established? What information does the Worldwide Incidents Tracking System provide? The Counterterrorism Calendar? What other kinds of information are available through the NCTC? Submit your findings to your instructor if asked to do so.

NOTES

[1] Richard H. Ward, "The Internationalization of Criminal Justice," in Charles M. Friel, ed., *Boundary Changes in Criminal Justice Organizations* (Washington, DC: National Institute of Justice, July, 2000).

[2] Piers Beirne, "Cultural Relativism and Comparative Criminology," *Contemporary Crisis*, Vol. 7 (1983), pp. 371–391.

[3] "Chiquita Pleads Guilty to Paying Terrorists to Protect Workers," Associated Press, March 19, 2007, http://www.usatoday.com/money/industries/food/2007-03-19-chiquita-terrorism_N.htm.

[4] Adapted from John McHale, "Futures Critical: A Review," in *Human Futures: Needs, Societies, Technologies* (Guildford, Surrey, UK: IPC Business Press Limited, 1974), p. 13.

[5] Thomas L. Friedman, *The Lexus and the Olive Tree* (New York: Anchor Books, 2000).

[6] Adapted from "Globalization," *Encyclopedia Britannica, 2007,* Encyclopedia Britannica Premium Service, http://www.britannica.com/eb/article?eu5369857 (accessed July 23, 2007).

[7] Michelle Healy, "Disgraced Scientist Points to Mafia Link," *USA Today*, October 25, 2006, p. 7D.

[8] National Institute of Justice, *Asian Transnational Organized Crime and Its Impact on the United States* (Washington, DC: NIJ, 2007), p. 1.

[9] "Mexico: Drug Cartels a Growing Threat," World Press, November 2, 2006, http://www.worldpress.org/Americas/2549.cfm (accessed July 9, 2007).

[10] Ibid., citing United Nations sources.

[11] Larry Birns and Alex Sánchez, "The Government and the Drug Lords: Who Rules Mexico?," World Press, April 23, 2007, http:// www.worldpress.org/Americas/2763.cfm (accessed June 4, 2007).

[12] Kevin Mooney, "Mexican Soldiers Freelancing for Drug Cartels on U.S. Soil," Cybercast News Service, December 21, 2006, http://www.cnsnews.com/ViewNation.asp?Page=/Nation/archive/200612/NAT20061221a.html (accessed July 7, 2007).

[13] "Severed Head of Mexican Politician Dumped Outside Newspaper's Office," Associated Press, http://www.foxnews.com/story/0,2933,275713,00.html (accessed July 7, 2007).

[14] "Man Pleads Guilty to Smuggling Women for Prostitution in Brothel Ring," Associated Press, February 10, 2007, http://www.usatoday.com/news/nation/2007-02-10-immigrant-brothel_x.htm, from which details for this story are taken.

[15] Bureau for International Narcotics and Law Enforcement Affairs, Human Smuggling and Trafficking Center, *Distinctions Between Human Smuggling and Human Trafficking* (Washington, DC: January 1, 2005).

[16] Raimo Väyrynen, "Illegal Immigration, Human Trafficking, and Organized Crime," United Nations University/World Institute for Development Economics Research, Discussion Paper No. 2003/72 (October, 2003), p. 16.

[17] Details for this story come from "Immigrant Smuggler Faulted in 19 Deaths Sentenced to Life in Prison," Associated Press, January 18, 2007, http://www.usatoday.com/news/nation/2007-01-18-smuggler_x.htm.

[18] Office of the Under Secretary for Democracy and Global Affairs, *Trafficking in Persons Report* (U.S. Department of State: Washington, DC, June 2007).

[19] Ibid., p. 8.

[20] Ibid.

[21] Ibid.

[22] *Distinctions Between Human Smuggling and Human Trafficking*, p. 16.

[23] *Trafficking in Persons Report*, p. 5.

[24] Ibid.

[25] Title 8, United States Code, Section 1324.

[26] Public Law 89–236.

[27] Trafficking Victims Protection Act of 2000, Div. A of Public Law 106–386, § 108, as amended.

[28] *Trafficking in Persons Report*, p. 7.

[29] Ibid., p. 36.

[30] Gregory J. Howard, Graeme Newman, and William Alex Pridemore, "Theory, Method, and Data in Comparative Criminology," in David Duffee, ed., *Criminal Justice 2000: Volume IV Measurement and Analysis of Criminal Justice* (Washington, DC: NIJ, 2000), p. 189.

[31] Ibid.

[32] Franklin E. Zimring, "The Necessity and Value of Transnational Comparative Study: Some Preaching from a Recent Convert," *Criminology and Public Policy*, Vol. 5, No. 4 (2006), pp. 615–622.

[33] Robert Lilly, "Forks and Chopsticks: Understanding Criminal Justice in the PRC," *Criminal Justice International* (March/April 1986), p. 15.

[34] See United Nations Office on Drugs and Crime, "Compiling and Comparing International Crime Statistics," http://www.unodc.org/en/crime_cicp_surveys_3.html (accessed June 5, 2007).

[35] For information about the latest survey, see *The Ninth United Nations Survey on Crime Trends and the Operations of Criminal Justice Systems* (New York: United Nations, 2006), http://www.unodc.org/unodc/en/crime_clip_surveys.html (accessed July 10, 2006).

[36] As of January 1, 2003, the New York City Office of Emergency Management said that 2,795 people died in the attacks on the World Trade Center. Another 184 people died in the attack on the Pentagon (including those aboard the crashed airliner), and 44 people died aboard hijacked United Airlines Flight 93, which crashed in a Pennsylvania field.

[37] U.S. Department of State, *Patterns of Global Terrorism, 2001* (Washington, DC: U.S. Government Printing Office, 2002), http://www.state.gov/s/ct/rls/pgtrpt/2001/ (accessed January 2, 2003).

Note: Until 2004, *Patterns of Global Terrorism* was made available to the public annually by the U.S. Department of State. As of 2004, however, the report became unavailable after its methodology was challenged by the Bush administration.

[38] Paul R. Pillar, *Terrorism and U.S. Foreign Policy* (Washington, DC: The Brookings Institution, 2001).

[39] See Michael J. Lynch and W. Byron Groves, *A Primer in Radical Criminology* (Monsey, NY: Willow Tree Press, 1990), p. 39; and Michael J. Lynch et al., *The New Primer in Radical Criminology: Critical Perspectives on Crime, Power and Identity* (Monsey, NY: Willow Tree Press, 2000).

[40] Council on Foreign Relations and the Markle Foundation, *Types of Terrorism*, http://www.terrorismanswers.com/terrorism/types.html (accessed January 10, 2007).

[41] Bruce Hoffman, *Inside Terrorism* (New York: Columbia University Press, 1998), p. 91.

[42] Adapted from *FBI Policy and Guidelines: Counterterrorism*, http://www.fbi.gov/contact/fo/jackson/cntrterr.htm (accessed March 4, 2006).

[43] Adapted from *FBI Policy and Guidelines: Counterterrorism*, op. cit.

[44] National Counterterrorism Center, *Report on Terrorist Incidents, 2006* (Washington, DC: National Counterterrorism Center, 2007).

[45] Peter Flory, "Terrorism Must Continue to Be a Top Priority," *Insight on the News*, Vol. 10, No. 21 (May 23, 1994), pp. 37–38.

[46] The death penalty was imposed for the first-degree murders of eight federal law enforcement agents who were at work in the Murrah Building at the time of the bombing. While the killings violated Oklahoma law, only the killings of the federal agents fell under federal law, which makes such murders capital offenses.

[47] Scott Shane, "A Year Later, Clues on Anthrax Still Few," SunSpot.Net, October 9, 2002, http://www.sunspot.net/news/printedition/balte.anthrax09oct09001612,0,6275426.story?coll=bal%2Dpe%2Dasection (accessed January 21, 2003).

[48] U.S. Department of Justice, Office of Information and Privacy, FOIA Post, "Anthrax Mail Emergency Delays FOIA Correspondence," http://www.usdoj.gov/oip/foiapost/2001foiapost21.htm (accessed January 31, 2003).

[49] See Barry Collin, "The Future of Cyberterrorism," *Crime and Justice International* (March, 1997), pp. 15–18.

[50] John Arquilla and David Ronfeldt, *The Advent of Netwar* (Santa Monica, CA: Rand, 1996).

[51] Adapted from Dictionary.com, http://dictionary.reference.com/search?q=infrastructure (accessed January 10, 2007).

[52] The PCCIP was established by Executive Order 13010.

[53] As described in Dorothy E. Denning, "Activism, Hactivism, and Cyberterrorism: The Internet as a Tool for Influencing Foreign Policy," paper presented at the Internet and International Systems: Information Technology and American Foreign Policy Decisionmaking Workshop, San Francisco, CA, December 10, 2001.

[54] Critical Infrastructure Assurance Office, "Resource Library," http://www.ciao.gov/resource/index.html (accessed January 10, 2002).

[55] Executive Order 13231 *(Critical Infrastructure Protection in the Information Age)*, October 16, 2001.

[56] President's Critical Infrastructure Protection Board, *The National Strategy to Secure Cyberspace* (Washington, DC: U.S. Government Printing Office, September 18, 2002), p. 3.

[57] Ibid.

[58] "Ridge Creates New Division to Combat Cyber Threats," Department of Homeland Security press release, June 6, 2003, http://www.dhs.gov/dhspublic/display?content=916 (accessed September 20, 2006).

[59] U.S. General Services Administration, "GovNet Planned to Protect Critical Government IT Functions from Cyber Attacks," GSA News Release Number 9890, October 10, 2001, http://w3.gsa.gov/web/x/publicaffairs.nsf/dea168abbe828fe9852565c600519794/1c10e9ac670553b885256ae100668beb?OpenDocument (accessed January 21, 2005).

[60] "U.S. Plans New Secure Government Internet," Associated Press, October 11, 2001.

[61] Technological devices described in this section are discussed in G. Gordon Liddy, "Rules of the Game," *Omni*, January 1989, pp. 43–47, 78–80.

[62] CIA Directorate of Intelligence, *Terrorist CBRN: Materials and Effects* (Washington, DC: CIA, 2003).

[63] Matthew Bunn, Anthony Wier, and John P. Holden, *Controlling Nuclear Warheads and Materials: A Report Card and Action Plan* (Cambridge, MA: Nuclear Threat Initiative and Harvard University, 2003).

[64] "Fact Sheet: The Biological Weapons Convention" (Washington, DC: Bureau of Arms Control, 2002), http://www.state.gov/t/ac/rls/fs/10401.htm (accessed August 8, 2006).

[65] Ali S. Kahn et al., *Biological and Chemical Terrorism: Strategic Plan for Preparedness and Response* (Atlanta, GA: Centers for Disease Control, April 21, 2000), http://www.cdc.gov/mmwr/preview/mmwrhtml/rr4904a1.htm (accessed August 2, 2007).

[66] Council on Foreign Relations, "Terrorism: Questions and Answers—The Anthrax Letters," http://www.terrorismanswers.com/weapons/anthraxletters.html (accessed August 3, 2006).

[67] See Rick Weiss, "DNA by Mail: A Terror Risk," *Washington Post*, July 18, 2002.

[68] Public Law 107–56.

[69] 18 U.S.C. Sections 2510–2522.

[70] Public Law 91–508, Title I.

[71] 18 U.S.C. Sections 3121–3127.

[72] 18 U.S.C. Sections 2701–2712.

[73] 50 U.S.C. Sections 1801–1811.

[74] See, especially, Rules 41 and 41a (Search Warrants).

[75] 20 U.S.C. Section 1232g; 34 C.F.R. Part 99.

[76] Stefanie Olsen. "PATRIOT Act Draws Privacy Concerns," CNET News.com, October 26, 2001, http://news.cnet.com/news/0-1005-200-7671240.htm?tag=rltdnws (accessed November 3, 2002).

[77] Public Law 107–296.

[78] U.S. Department of Homeland Security, "DHS Organization: Building a Secure Homeland," http://www.dhs.gov/dhspublic/theme_home1.jsp (accessed August 2, 2004).

[79] On March 1, 2003, the Immigration and Naturalization Service became part of the U.S. Department of Homeland Security, and its functions were divided into various bureaus within that department.

[80] The information in this section comes from: U.S. Department of Homeland Security, "DHS Organization: Department Components," http://www.dhs.gov/dhspublic/display?theme=9&content=858 (accessed August 2, 2006).

[81] Public Law 105–261.

[82] Gary Hart, Warren B. Rudman, and Stephen E. Flynn, *America Still Unprepared—America Still in Danger* (Washington, DC: Council on Foreign Relations, 2002).

[83] Public Law 105–277.

[84] Public Law 107–306, November 27, 2002.

[85] National Commission on Terrorist Attacks upon the United States, "Preface," in *The 9/11 Commission Report*.

[86] National Commission on Terrorism, "Executive Summary," in *Countering the Changing Threat of International Terrorism* (Washington, DC: The Commission, June 7, 2000), http://w3.access.gpo.gov/nct/nct2.pdf (accessed January 10, 2007).

[87] U.S. Department of State, *Patterns of Global Terrorism 2001* (Washington, DC: U.S. Government Printing Office, 2002), http://www.state.gov/s/ct/rls/pgtrpt/2001 (accessed January 2, 2003). Previously available annually, *Patterns of Global Terrorism* has been superseded by the National Counterterrorism Center's yearly *Report on Terrorist Incidents*, http://www.terrorisminfo.mipt.org/pdf/Country-Reports-Terrorism-2006-NCTC-Annex.pdf.

[88] Executive Order 13224.

[89] *National Strategy for Combating Terrorism.*

[90] The NCTC was established by Executive Order in 2004, although Congress codified the NCTC in the Intelligence Reform and Terrorism Prevention Act of 2004 (IRTPA) and placed the NCTC within the Office of the Director of National Intelligence.

[91] National Counterterrorism Center, *NCTC and Information Sharing* (Washington, DC: NCTC, 2006), p. I, from which some of the wording in this paragraph is taken.

[92] *Terrorism, the Future, and U.S. Foreign Policy*, p. 5.

[93] Public Law 104–132.

[94] Public Law 107–56.

[95] 8 U.S.C. § 1-1599.

[96] Public Law 107–56.

[97] Information in this paragraph is taken from National Counterterrorism Center, "Terrorist Identities Datamart Environment (TIDE)," May 20, 2007, http://www.nctc.gov/docs/Tide_Fact_Sheet.pdf (accessed June 11, 2007).

[98] The White House, "Announcing the Global Initiative to Combat Nuclear Terrorism: Joint Statement by U.S. President George Bush and Russian Federation President V.V. Putin," St. Petersburg, Russia, July 15, 2006, http://www.state.gov/p/eur/rls/or/69021.htm (accessed July 21, 2007).

[99] Information in this paragraph comes from *Terrorism, the Future, and U.S. Foreign Policy*, p. 6.

[100] Congressional Research Service, *Terrorism, the Future, and U.S. Foreign Policy* (Washington, DC: Library of Congress, April 11, 2003), from which the material in this section is derived.

Epilogue

Outline

Introduction

Techniques of Futures Research

Future Crimes

The New Criminologies

Policies of the Future

Can We Solve the Problem of Crime?

- Symbolism and Public Policy

FUTURE DIRECTIONS

As surely as the future will bring new forms of technology, it will bring new forms of crime.

—Cynthia Manson and Charles Ardai[1]

He who controls the past, controls the future. He who controls the future, controls the past.

—George Orwell[3]

The rise of a new kind of economy, never before known, threatening to many, demanding rapid changes in work, life style, and habits, hurls large populations—terrified of the future—into spasms of diehard reaction. It opens cleavages that fanatics rush to fill. It arms all those dangerous minorities who live for crisis in the hopes of catapulting themselves onto the national or global stage and transporting us all into a new Dark Age.

—Alvin Toffler[2]

Learning Outcomes

After reading this epilogue, you should be able to

- Describe futures research and explain some of the techniques used for assessing the future
- Identify some possible future crimes and explain how criminal activity in the future may differ from criminal activity today
- List and describe some specific predictions about the future of criminological theorizing
- Outline some possible crime control policies of the future and explain why new strategies may be necessary
- Provide an informed opinion as to whether the crime problem can ultimately be solved

Hear the author discuss this epilogue at **crimtoday.com**

Introduction

Canadian criminologist Gwynn Nettler once told a story of two people passing on a street in New York City.[4] One carried a pint of whiskey; the other had $100 in gold coins. In March 1933, near the end of the Prohibition era, the person with the alcohol would have been committing a crime, but the person carrying the gold would have been regarded as law-abiding. A year later, however, the same two people passing on the street would have occupied exactly the opposite legal positions. The repeal of Prohibition legalized carrying whiskey in most places, but gold hoarding became a federal crime in 1934, and it remained so until 1974.

It is easy to look back in time and assess the legal standing of people like those in Nettler's story, but predicting what crimes the future will bring is far more difficult. Those who study the future are called **futurists.** Futurist criminologists try to imagine how crime will appear in both the near and the distant future. **Future criminology** is the study of likely futures as they relate to crime and its control.

The future is an abstract concept through which human beings bring symbolic order to the present and meaning to past endeavors.[5] From our present point of view, multiple futures exist, each of which is more or less probable, and each of which may or may not come to pass. In other words, the future contains an almost limitless number of possibilities, any of which might unfold but only a few of which actually will. The task of the futurist is to effectively distinguish among these impending possibilities, assessing the likelihood of each and making more or less realistic forecasts based on such assessments.

Some assumptions about the future, such as estimates of future world populations, can be based on existing and highly credible public or private statistics and mathematical analyses of trends. Others, however, are more intuitive and result from the integration of a wide range of diverse materials derived from many different sources. As one futurist explains, "Before we can plan the future, we must make some assumptions about what that future will be like. . . . Assumptions about the future are not like assumptions in a geometry exercise. They are not abstract statements from which consequences can be derived with mathematical precision. But we need to make some assumptions about the future in order to plan it, prepare for it, and prevent undesired events from happening."[6]

Best known among groups that study the future is the World Future Society, which publishes *The Futurist,* a journal of well-considered essays about probable futures. Individual futurists who have become well known to the general public include Alvin Toffler, author of the trilogy of futurist titles *Future Shock,*[7] *Powershift,* and *The Third Wave;*[8] John Naisbitt, author of *Megatrends: Ten New Directions Transforming Our Lives;*[9] Peter F. Drucker, who has written many books with futuristic themes, among them *Management Challenges for the 21st Century*[10] and *Post-Capitalist Society;*[11] and Francis Fukuyama, who has authored *Our Posthuman Future*[12] and *The End of History and the Last Man.*[13] Within criminology, the Society of Police Futurists International (PFI) represents the cutting edge of research into future crime-control policy. PFI evolved from a conference of approximately 250 educators and practitioners representing most states and 20 different nations that was held at the FBI National Academy in Quantico, Virginia, in 1991. The society's Millennium Conference was held at the National Academy in July 2000. PFI members apply the principles of futures research to gain an understanding of the world as it is likely to be in the future.[14]

In 2002, PFI joined with the FBI to create the Futures Working Group (FWG). The FWG's aim is to "develop and encourage others to develop forecasts and strategies to ethically maximize the effectiveness of local, state, federal, and international law enforcement bodies as they strive to maintain peace and security in the 21st century."[15] A recent report by the FWG forsees a future in which the increasing effects of globalization will lead to a world of new crimes, like energy smuggling, and produce conditions whereby what is good economically for oneself or one's company may not be good for

futurist

One who studies the future.

future criminology

The study of likely futures as they impinge on crime and its control.

one's country.[16] The FWG sees the Internet as highly influential in shaping the future of the social world. "The biggest change that the Information Age may bring about," says the report, "is the redefinition of boundaries. The boundaries between criminal syndicates, terrorist groups, and gangs will continue to disappear. . . . Physical boundaries will be replaced by electronic and philosophical ones as individuals discover new virtual communities."[17] Learn more about the PFI at the Society's Web site via **Web Extra EP–W1**. Read the FWG's recent publication, *Policing 2020: Exploring the Future of Crime, Communities, and Policing* at **Library Extra EP-L1**.

Another group actively attempting to discern the future is the United Kingdom's government-led Foresight program, which "brings people, knowledge and ideas together to look ahead and prepare for the future."[18] Foresight's Crime Prevention Panel released a report in 2001 entitled *Just around the Corner,* focusing on the year 2020.[19] The report provides a summation of the views of 60 experts given three tasks: to describe crimes of the near future, to identify methods to reduce and detect those crimes, and to decide what role science and technology will play in future criminality and crime prevention. According to Foresight's Crime Prevention Panel, a number of social characteristics will affect future crimes in Great Britain and throughout the world. One of these is what the panel calls "individuality and independence." The panel believes that greater individuality and personal independence will arise as traditional family forms decline over the next decade or two. Once traditional families no longer provide the "foundation" of society and more people find themselves living in single-person households, says the panel, "there will be more self-centered, self-indulgent and hedonistic psychologies." Traditional limits on antisocial behavior will erode, the panel predicts, as individuals gravitate toward membership in like-minded groups, many of which "may reinforce rather than challenge anti-social views."

A second social characteristic that will affect crime in the future, says the panel, is what it terms "Information Communication Technology (ICT) usage." The panel predicts that crimes like electronic theft and fraud will occur with increasing rapidity, reducing the likelihood that offenders can be caught. Web sites are predicted to become highly targeted properties, and sites written in English will be the hardest hit. Such attacks will raise the need for increased acceptability of digital evidence in courts and will require jurors, judges, and attorneys to be educated in relevant technologies.

Technology is also leading to the growth of an impersonal society, says the panel, in which people meet and interact in virtual space rather than in physical society. As a consequence, the panel fears, physical space may become an increasingly hostile and dangerous place— "a dehumanized environment" in which "people may become less 'real' to one another leading to more extreme reactions, interactions and the reluctance to intervene in conflicts."

A third social characteristic relevant to understanding and predicting future forms of criminality, according to the panel, is globalization. Globalization, which refers to the increasingly international character of social life, is having an impact on much of society, including technology, commerce, communication, and crime. "Already," says the panel, "crimes on the internet, drug dealing, and smuggling show the power of global crime and the difficulties it poses for local level law enforcement." Local crimes and small-time perpetrators will be replaced or supplemented by crimes and criminal groups with global scope, the panel predicts.

The panel notes that criminal organizations, like organizations everywhere, "are adapting to the opportunities offered by the flexibility of the internet." However, says the panel, modern technology offers individuals new opportunities to commit crimes that may be virtually unsolvable: "The clear danger is being at the mercy of a small technologically knowledgeable elite." At the same time, the panel warns, large numbers of people either won't have the opportunity to acquire advanced technological skills or will be unable to learn them. The consequence will be a technologically disenfranchised underclass whose existence will "further fuel crime and reduce the opportunities for access to mainstream society."

WEB
Extra
■ ■ ■ ■

LIBRARY
Extra
■ ■ ■ ■

William L. Tafoya, founder of the Society of Police Futurists International (PFI). Regarded by many in the field as a visionary, Dr. Tafoya is a retired FBI special agent, teaching at the University of New Haven. What are the goals of PFI?

Source: Dr. William Tafoya. Reprinted with permission

WEB
Extra

For more details about Foresight and for access to the complete report of Foresight's Crime Prevention Panel, visit **Web Extra EP–W2.**

Techniques of Futures Research

Futures research has been described as "a multidisciplinary branch of operations research" whose principal aim "is to facilitate long-range planning based on (1) forecasting from the past supported by mathematical models, (2) cross-disciplinary treatment of its subject matter, (3) systematic use of expert judgment, and (4) a systems-analytical approach to its problems."[20] In the words of PFI founder **William L. Tafoya**, "Futures research offers both the philosophy and the methodological tools to analyze, forecast, and plan in ways rarely seen" in crime control planning. "Guided by insight, imagination, and innovation, a new perspective awaits criminal justice professionals willing to attempt creative new approaches to dealing with crime and criminals."[21]

Central to futures research is a futurist perspective, which some authors say is built around five principles:[22]

futures research

"A multidisciplinary branch of operations research" whose principal aim "is to facilitate long-range planning based on (1) forecasting from the past supported by mathematical models, (2) cross-disciplinary treatment of its subject matter, (3) systematic use of expert judgment, and (4) a systems-analytical approach to its problems."

- The future is determined by a combination of factors, not the least of which is human choice. In other words, what we decide today will have a significant effect tomorrow.
- There are alternative futures. Hence, a range of decision and planning choices is always available in the present.
- We operate within an interdependent, interrelated system. Hence, any major decision, development, or force that affects any part of the system is likely to affect the entire system.

- Tomorrow's problems are developing today. Minor problems ignored today may have catastrophic consequences even a few years from now. Hence, distinct trends and developments and even gradual changes cannot be ignored.
- We should regularly develop possible responses to potential changes. We should monitor trends and developments and not hesitate to use our collective creativity and judgment to develop forecasts, projections, and predictions—or to take action.

The techniques of futures research include trend extrapolation, cross-impact analysis, the **Delphi Method,** simulations and models, environmental scanning, **scenario writing,** and strategic assessment. **Trend extrapolation,** perhaps the simplest of the techniques listed here, makes future predictions based on the projection of existing trends. **Cross-impact analysis** attempts to analyze one trend or event in light of the occurrence or nonoccurrence of a series of related events.[23] The social consequences of the aging of the baby-boomer population, for example, will be intimately affected by the future economic health of the U.S. economy, along with the availability of medical and social programs to care for geriatric segments of the population.

The Delphi Method, developed at RAND by Olaf Helmer and Norman Dalkey, involves a number of steps designed to elicit expert opinion until a general consensus is reached. The steps involved include (1) problem identification, (2) development of an expert panel, (3) questions directed at the panel, and (4) the collection and synthesis of responses. The Delphi Method does not stop with one iteration of this sequence, however, but provides feedback to the experts and allows them to refine their responses.

Simulations and models attempt to replicate the system under study by reproducing its conditions in a form that can be readily manipulated to assess possible outcomes. A wind tunnel, for example, provides an environment in which models of airplanes can be tested. Many of today's simulations are based upon mathematical models and make use of computer technology in an effort to create simulated environments, and this is true of demographic and economic models, which are sometimes used to predict future criminality.

Environmental scanning is a targeted effort to collect as much information as possible in "a systematic effort to identify in an elemental way future developments (trends or events) that could plausibly occur over the time horizon of interest"[24] and that might affect one's area of concern. In other words, it is impossible to predict the future without having an informed sense of what is happening now, especially where important trends are concerned. Scenario writing builds upon environmental scanning by attempting to assess the likelihood of a variety of possible outcomes once important trends have been identified. Scenario writing develops a list of possible futures and assigns each a degree of probability or likelihood. While not necessarily predicting a specific future, scenario writers tend to highlight a range of possible outcomes. **Strategic assessment** provides an appreciation of the risks and opportunities facing those who plan for the future.

A comprehensive futures research approach, for example, might identify an important trend that shows affluent middle- and upper-class citizens fleeing cities and suburbs for the safety of enclosed residential enclaves surrounded by secure perimeters and patrolled by paid private security personnel. Many likely scenarios could then be envisioned, including a further decline in America's cities as the moneyed classes abandon them, continued growth of street and property crimes in metropolitan areas, and rampant victimization of the urban working poor. Although crime control strategies might be developed to counter the imagined threat to cities, many risks must be considered in any planning. A serious decline in the value of the dollar, for example, as recently experienced, could cause gated communities to unravel and could create a shortfall of the tax dollars that would be needed to pay for enhanced policing in cities. The influx of new and large immigrant populations, likely to add to the burgeoning number of inner-city dwellers, could add another new dimension to overall crime control planning.

Delphi Method

A technique of futures research that uses repetitive questioning of experts to refine predictions.

scenario writing

A technique intended to predict future outcomes, that builds upon environmental scanning by attempting to assess the likelihood of a variety of possible outcomes once important trends have been identified.

trend extrapolation

A technique of futures research that makes future predictions based on the projection of existing trends.

cross-impact analysis

A technique of futures research that attempts to analyze one trend or event in light of the occurrence or nonoccurrence of a series of related events.

environmental scanning

"A systematic effort to identify in an elemental way future developments (trends or events) that could plausibly occur over the time horizon of interest" and that might affect one's area of concern.

strategic assessment

A technique that assesses the risks and opportunities facing those who plan for the future.

Whatever techniques a futurist employs, however, it is important to remember that these techniques are no better than the data they use. Futurists who have made their mark on criminology include Georgette Bennett, **Bernard Levin**, Richter H. Moore, Jr., Allen Sapp, Gene Stephens, and William Tafoya. Their work, other emerging theoretical explanations for crime, and new suggestions for crime-control policy are discussed in this chapter. Learn more via **Web Extra EP–W3**.

WEB
Extra

Future Crimes

Murder, rape, robbery, and the other types of "everyday" crime that have become mainstays of contemporary criminological analysis will continue to occur in the future, to be sure, but other new and emergent forms of criminality will grow in frequency and number. Recently, for example, Joseph F. Coates, president of the future-oriented think tank of Coates & Jarratt, predicted that by the year 2025, "socially significant crime—that is, the crimes that have the widest negative effects—in the advanced nations will be increasingly economic and computer based. Examples include disruption of business, theft, introduction of maliciously false information, and tampering with medical records, air traffic control, or national-security systems."[25] Another futurist predicts that "the top guns of twenty-first-century criminal organizations will be educated, highly sophisticated, computer-literate individuals who can wield state-of-the-art information technology to the best advantage—for themselves and for their organizations."[26]

In a wide-ranging overview of future crimes, **Richter H. Moore, Jr.,** painted a picture of future criminality that includes many dimensions. Already present are elements of what Moore predicted: "Computer hackers are changing bank records, credit accounts and reports, criminal-history files, and educational, medical, and even military records."[27] Identity manipulation, said Moore, will be a nexus of future criminality. "By the twenty-first century," he wrote, "genetic-based records will include a birth-to-death dossier of a person and will be the method of criminal identification." Already, the U.S. military is using genetic testing to assign unique identification codes to each of its soldiers. In the event of war, such codes will allow for the identification of human remains from as little as a single cell. DNA coding, unique to each of us, may soon form the basis for nearly foolproof identification technologies, which will take the science of personal identification far beyond fingerprinting, blood-type matching, or photography. The science of bioengineering, however, which is now undergoing clinical trials in the treatment of various forms of disease, may soon be clandestinely employed for the illegal modification of human DNA, with the goal of effectively altering a person's identity. It is but one more step by which the theft of computer-based genetic identification records could make it possible for one person to effectively imitate another in our future society.

Moore describes many other crimes of the future. Within a few decades, he says, "criminal organizations will be able to afford their own satellites." Drug trafficking and money laundering operations could be coordinated via satellite communications, couriers and shipments could be tracked, and satellite surveillance could provide alerts of enforcement activity. Likewise, says Moore, "prostitution rings will use modern technology to coordinate global activities," and children and fetuses may "become subject to unlawful trafficking." The illegal disposal of toxic materials, an activity that organized crime has already explored, may become even more profitable for criminal entrepreneurs as many more hazardous substances are produced in the face of ever-tighter controls. The supply of nuclear materials and military-quality armaments to "private armies . . . terrorists, hate groups, questionable regimes, independent crime groups, and individual criminals" will be a fact of life in the twenty-first century, as will the infiltration of governments and financial institutions by sophisticated criminals whose activities are supported by large, illegally acquired fortunes.

Another writer, **Georgette Bennett**, whose seminal book *Crimewarps* was published in 1987 and helped establish the study of criminal futures as a purposeful endeavor, says that American society will experience major changes in both what society considers criminal and who future offenders will be. Some areas of coming change that Bennett predicts (many of which have already happened) are[28]

- A decline in street crime, such as robbery and assault
- An increase in white-collar crimes, especially high-technology crimes
- An increase in the involvement of women in crime
- An increase in crime commission among the elderly
- A shift in high crime rates from the Frost Belt to the Sun Belt
- Safer cities, with increasing criminal activity in small towns and rural areas

For an even more futuristic look at the possibilities for criminal behavior inherent in emerging technologies, and the need for new laws that would define that behavior as criminal, read the "Crime in the News" box in this chapter. It describes the possibilities inherent in the blending of animal and human DNA to create chimeras—or human-animal blends. Questions about whether such technology should be regulated, or some aspects of it criminalized, may soon have to be answered. Learn more about the changing nature of crime in America via **Library Extra EP–L2** and **Web Extra EP–W4** at crimtoday.com.

LIBRARY
Extra
■ ■ ■ ■

WEB
Extra
■ ■ ■ ■

The New Criminologies

Along with futures research, new and emerging criminological theories provide a picture of what criminology will be like in the years and decades to come. In an intriguing article entitled "Explaining Crime in the Year 2010," L. Edward Wells suggests that "when it comes to explaining crime, we seem to have an embarrassment of riches but a poverty of results."[29] In other words, although many explanations for criminal behavior have come and gone, "none has proven noticeably more effective in explaining, predicting, or controlling crime."[30] That may be about to change, says Wells. Contemporary criminological theorizing is interdisciplinary and conservative in its approach to crime causation, and major changes in the premises upon which criminological theories are built are unlikely without significant ideological shifts or changes in basic components of the social structure, such as the economy, the political system, or the family. Significant social change, however, can bring about the need for new theoretical formulations, says Wells. "Legal events in the 1960s and 1970s," for example, "changed abortion from a criminal act to a routine medical procedure."[31] Similarly, an aversion to even minor forms of physical force may now be leading to a redefinition of crimes like child abuse, spousal abuse, elder abuse, and sexual aggression. Hence, our basic understanding of criminal violence may be undergoing a fundamental modification that will require a concomitant change in our attempts to theorize about its causes.

Wells sees similar possibilities for theoretical change about to be introduced by advances in scientific knowledge. Should research on the human genome, for example, yield definitive evidence that some forms of aggression and violence are biologically grounded, it will provide the basis for an entirely new and emergent group of biological explanations for at least certain forms of criminal activity.

Wells makes a number of specific predictions about the future of criminological theorizing. He predicts that future explanations of crime will be[32]

- More eclectic than past theories and less tied to a single theoretical tradition or discipline
- More comparative and less confined to a single society or single dominant group within society
- Predominantly *individualistic* rather than collective and *voluntaristic* rather than deterministic
- More applied and pragmatic in orientation

A surrealistic image of bar-coded babies points to the highly controversial subject of human cloning. Should human cloning be legal?

Source: Ron Lowery, Corbis-NY

- More oriented toward explaining white-collar crime
- Reflective of a renewed appreciation for the biological foundations of human behavior, assigning more theoretical substance to biological and medical factors

Unfortunately, from approximately 1960 until 1985, criminology suffered through a few "black decades," in which theory building fell by the wayside as a generation of criminologists trained in quantitative analysis repeatedly tested existing ideas at the expense of developing new ones. In the mid-1980s, however, a new and dynamic era of theory building was unleashed. Frank P. Williams III and Marilyn D. McShane explain, "As if the restraints on theory building had created a pent-up demand, criminologists began exploring new theoretical constructs during the 1980s. Slowly at first, and then with great rapidity, theoretical efforts began to emerge."[33]

A number of these new approaches, including postmodernism, feminist criminology, and peacemaking criminology, were discussed in previous chapters. One perspective that deserves special attention, however, is what David P. Farrington terms the "risk factor prevention paradigm."[34] Farrington identified the paradigm during his 1999 presidential address to the American Society of Criminology. As Farrington explained, "The basic idea of the paradigm is very simple: Identify the key risk factors for offending and implement prevention methods designed to counteract them." Farrington said that the risk factor prevention paradigm experienced "an enormous increase in influence in criminology" during the 1990s. The paradigm is especially important because of the potential it holds for guiding criminological research, crime-control policy, and theoretical development well into the twenty-first century. The main challenges for the paradigm, Farrington said, "are to determine which risk factors are causes, to establish what are protective factors, to identify the active ingredients of multiple component interventions, to evaluate the effectiveness of area-based intervention programs, and to assess the monetary costs and benefits of interventions."

Policies of the Future

Gene Stephens, one of the best-known futurists of the past decade or two to focus on crime, observes that "crime is increasing worldwide, and there is every reason to believe the trend will continue."[35] In particular, observes Stephens, street crimes are escalating in formerly Communist countries throughout Eastern Europe and in other European nations, such as those in Scandinavia and the United Kingdom. According to Stephens, although a number of official measures show that crime is currently on the decline in the United States, America was one of the first nations to experience a rapid rise in criminality because it was the most advanced nation on the globe. The United States is a highly diverse, multicultural, industrialized, and democratic society, which strongly supports individual freedoms and has fostered a strong sense of personal independence among its citizens.

Multiculturalism and heterogeneity, says Stephens, increase anomie, and previously isolated and homogeneous societies like Japan, Denmark, China, and Greece are now facing a growing cultural diversity due to international migration, the expansion of new social ideals, and an increase in foreign commerce. "Heterogeneity in societies will be the rule in the twenty-first century," says Stephens, "and failure to recognize and plan for such diversity can lead to serious crime problems, especially in emerging multicultural societies." Stephens's thesis is best summarized in this passage from his work: "The connection between crime and culture cannot be overemphasized: There are high-crime and low-crime cultures around the world. In the years ahead, many low-crime cultures may become high-crime cultures because of changing world demographics and politicoeconomic systems. In general, heterogeneous populations in which people have lots of political freedom (democracy) and lots of economic choice (capitalism) are prime candidates for crime unless a good socialization system is created and maintained."

Homogeneous nations—in which citizens share backgrounds, life experiences, and values—produce citizens who are generally capable of complying with the wishes of the majority and who can legislate controls over behavior, that are not difficult for most citizens to respect. In such societies, a tradition of discipline, a belief in the laws, and an acceptance of personal responsibility are typically the norm.

Diverse societies, on the other hand, suffer from constant internal conflict, with much of that conflict focused on acceptable ways of living and working. Heterogeneous societies tend to place a strong emphasis on individualism, and disagreement about the law and social norms is rife. Characteristic of such cultures is the fact that lawbreakers tend to deny responsibility and go to great lengths to avoid capture and conviction. To highlight the difference between homogeneous and heterogeneous societies, Stephens points out that in some highly homogeneous cultures, such as Japan, those who break norms will often punish themselves, even if their transgressions are not publicly discovered. Such self-punishing behavior would be almost unthinkable in an advanced heterogeneous society like the United States. As Stephens explains, "Some nations, such as the United States, face pervasive *anomie* due to their lack of restraints on human desires."

Heterogeneity can arise in numerous ways, even within a society that had previously been relatively homogeneous. One source of increasing and important differences in American society today, for example, has been the growth of a technological culture, which has produced two separate and distinct groups: the technologically capable and those who are incapable of utilizing modern technology. To these two groups we might add a third: the technologically aware, or those who realize the importance of technology but who, for whatever reason—be it age, lack of education, poverty, or other life circumstances—have not yet acquired the skills necessary to participate fully in what our highly technological society has to offer. In Stephens's words: "More people are turning to street crime and violence because they find themselves unprepared, educationally or emotionally, to cope with the requirements for success in the new era."

Another reason that crime rates are high—and growing—in increasingly heterogeneous societies, according to Stephens, is that such societies often display a lack of consistent child-care philosophies and child-rearing methods. "In some societies," says Stephens, "parents are seen as primarily responsible for their children, but all citizens share in that responsibility, since everyone's welfare is affected by the proper socialization of each child." In others, children are viewed as the parents' property, and little is expected of parents other than that they be biologically capable of reproducing. No requirements are set in such societies for parental knowledge, skills, income, education, and so on. Stephens describes child-rearing practices in such societies as "helter-skelter, catch-as-catch-can child care." Lacking child-rearing standards in which the majority of members of society can meaningfully participate, heterogeneous societies tend to produce adults who are irresponsible and who do not adhere to legal or other standards of behavior.

According to Stephens, future crimes will be plentiful, with countries around the world experiencing explosive growth in their crime rates. "The United States," he says, "was the first industrialized, democratic, heterogeneous nation and thus the first to face the crime problems associated with *anomie*." Now, however, other nations are undergoing increased modernization, with many entering the postmodern era previously occupied solely by the United States. "We can theorize," says Stephens, "that crime will be a growth industry in many countries as they find themselves gripped by the same social forces that have long affected the United States."

Other authors have similarly attempted to describe crime control issues that may face future policymakers.[36] Richter H. Moore, Jr., for example, identifies the following seven issues that are likely to concern crime control planners in the near future:[37]

- **New criminal groups.** According to Moore, "Groups such as Colombian drug cartels, Jamaican posses, Vietnamese gangs, various Chinese groups, and Los Angeles black street gangs are now a much bigger concern than the Mafia," and the criminal activity and influence of these new groups are growing rapidly. Traditional law enforcement responses, such as those developed to deal with Italian American Mafia organizations, may be inappropriate in the face of the new challenges these groups represent.

- **Language barriers.** According to Moore, "U.S. law-enforcement officials now find themselves hampered by a lack of understanding about the language and culture of some of the new criminal groups" operating in America. Cuban, Mexican, Colombian, Japanese, and Chinese criminals and criminal organizations are becoming commonplace, and such groups are increasingly involved in international communications and travel.

- **Distrust by ethnic communities.** Recent immigrant groups have been slow to assimilate into American culture and society. As a consequence, many of these groups hold strongly to native identities, distancing themselves from formal agencies of social control, such as the police. As Moore points out, "In many of their countries of origin, new immigrants see police as corrupt, self-serving individuals, a viewpoint often not without foundation." A distrust of police and government representatives is nearly instinctual for members of such groups, making the work of law enforcement within the context of immigrant communities challenging and often difficult.

- **Greater reliance on community involvement.** Moore observes that "due to the increasing costs of electronic surveillance, informant programs, undercover operations, and witness-protection programs, police are now encouraging community members to become more involved in their own security." The involvement of private citizens in the battle against crime may be the only realistic solution to the problem. Neighborhood watch groups, the use of community volunteers within criminal justice organizations, and other neighborhood self-help programs, such as school- and church-based education, all suggest the future of neighborhood-based crime-control policy.

- **Regulating the marketplace.** Moore advises that decriminalization and legalization will become of increasingly greater concern to future legislators who will focus on "regulating the marketplace" for criminal activities like gambling, drug trafficking, and prostitution.

- **Reducing public demand.** Similarly, according to Moore, future crime-control policies will aim to reduce involvement in criminal activity "through better education" and other policies that will, over the long term, lower the demand for drugs and other illegal services.

- **Increased treatment.** Although in contrast with many of today's get-tough policies, Moore sees a greater emphasis in the future on the treatment of all forms of criminality, including drug abuse, gambling, rape, and other lawbreaking behaviors.

Learn more about possible crime control policies of the future from Library Extra EP–L3 at crimtoday.com.

LIBRARY
Extra
■ ■ ■ ■

Can We Solve the Problem of Crime?

In 1956, European writer Hermanus Bianchi[38] emphasized what he saw as the difference between criminology and what he termed *Kriminalpolitik.* Criminology, said Bianchi, should be considered a "metascience" or "a science of wider scope [than that of criminal law, jurisprudence, criminal justice, or corrections] whose terminology can be used to clarify the conceptions of its subdisciplines. Far from being a mere auxiliary to the criminal law," said Bianchi, "it is therefore superior to it."[39]

For Bianchi and other writers of the time, the concept of **Kriminalpolitik** referred to the political handling of crime, or—as we might say today—a criminology-based social policy. Bianchi believed that if criminology were to remain pure, it could not afford to sully its hands, so to speak, with political concerns. Today, however, the image esteemed by criminologists and the expectations they hold for their discipline are quite different than they were in Bianchi's time. Many criminologists expect to work hand in hand with politicians and policymakers, forging crime control agendas based on scientific knowledge and criminological theorizing. Some would say that this change in attitude represents a maturation of the discipline of criminology.

Whether effective crime control policies can ever be implemented, however, is another question. A number of critics argue that only drastic policy-level changes can address the real issues that underlie high rates of crime and criminal activity. Drug legalization, the elimination of guns throughout America, nightly curfews, and close control of media violence, say such reformers, may be necessary before crime can be curbed. "Reforms that substantially will lower the crime rate are unlikely because of cultural taboos," says Lawrence Friedman, a Stanford University law professor and author of the book *Crime and Punishment in American History.* According to Friedman, "If you add up all the taboos we have—against legalization of drugs, real gun control, paying taxes for social programs we might at least try—it's hard not to come to the conclusion that there isn't much we can do about crime." Many existing taboos, say such thinkers, are rooted in citizens' demands for individual freedoms. "At one time in South Korea," says Friedman, "they had an absolute curfew between midnight and 5 A.M. The police kept everyone off the streets. It was as hard on burglars as other citizens and very effective at squelching crime. But most Americans would consider that an unacceptable inroad on their personal lives."[40]

Complicating the picture further is the fact that numerous interest groups, each with its own agenda, are clamoring to be heard by policymakers. As Robert D. Pursley, a professor of criminal justice at Buffalo State College, states, "Our nation's efforts to deal with crime remind us that crime, among other things, is a highly political issue that has been transformed into a racially volatile subject. This issue provides an excellent window into political policymaking. Opposing ideological lines have divided our efforts to develop comprehensive anticrime programs. Deep fissures in our social fabric have contributed to conflicting attitudes about crime and its control."[41]

Racial divisiveness has created one of those fissures. Pursley writes, "Our anticrime programs and studies of traditional street crimes, especially those involving violence, show that such crimes are disproportionately the acts of young African-American males. So long as black men commit violent crimes at a rate that is six to eight times

Kriminalpolitik

The political handling of crime. Also, a criminology-based social policy.

higher than that found among whites and three to four times higher than that among Latino males, race and crime will be threads of the same cloth. These facts have become unpopular and certainly not politically correct to discuss in certain circles, but they remain facts. No attempt to silence those who raise such issues by denouncing them as 'racists' can conceal these statistics."[42]

Pursley is telling us, in effect, that for some groups in some locales, violations of the criminal law are simply part of the landscape. Among certain segments of the American population, crime may be an accepted way of doing business, and criminal activity, even when discovered, might not necessarily be stigmatizing. Moreover, those who commit crimes may hold positions of prestige or highly visible public offices when their constituencies fail to condemn illicit behavior. Ultimately, they may even serve as role models to youngsters—albeit dubious role models. Although such a perspective is undoubtedly a minority point of view, it seriously impacts the ability of policymakers to establish consistent policies in the battle against crime.

Symbolism and Public Policy

When all the political crime-fighting rhetoric has ended and all the dollars have been spent, some expect that crime will still be with us. Many analysts of the contemporary scene see all crime control policies, especially those at the federal level, as largely symbolic. As Nancy E. Marion, a professor of political science at the University of Akron, explained a few years ago, "[M]any of the policies supported by the federal government may in actuality be symbolic gestures to appease the public rather than attempts to reduce crime. One reason for the presence of symbolic policies . . . is simply that the federal government cannot reduce crime—it is not within the government's capacity to do so."[43] Marion says that congressional power is fragmented through the influence of special interest groups, and as a result, the potential of crime control initiatives is effectively dispersed by the time any legislation is enacted. In addition, says Marion, the American political system is decidedly shortsighted, focusing only on issues that are likely to win elections. Similarly, due to changes in incumbents (often every two to four years), it is impossible to establish consistent crime control policies. Whereas a Democratic president may hold office for four years, for example, it is likely that a Republican president will take office with the next election—and in the meantime, a nearly continuous shuffling of cabinet members, senators, representatives, U.S. Supreme Court justices, agency heads, federal judges, and so on is occurring. Similar changes at the state level ensure constant modification of laws, enforcement practices, and criminal sanctions. Without a consistent, long-term, national and interstate approach to crime fighting, Marion suggests, crime rates can never be substantially impacted by federal policies.

Even consistent policies may be inaccurately targeted. As Marion explains, "One reason we cannot stop crime in the United States is because many elements of the crime problem we believe to be true simply are not. Because of the way crime is presented in the media, crime events 'become distorted and are given unprecedented social consideration.' These myths help to sustain our views of crime, criminals, and the system as a whole."[44] Part of the mythology of crime, some claim, is belief in criminological theories of limited usefulness. Another problem flows from our inability to effectively conceptualize crime itself. Laws may merely reflect moral conceptions of the political majority. Both morality and law are subject to change, making it difficult to accurately define crime. Hence, as critics of contemporary crime-fighting policies indicate, if we do not fully understand what crime is or what causes it, how can we create an effective policy for controlling it?

Some people, like Alfred Blumstein of Carnegie Mellon University, say the answer is possibly found in increased expenditures on criminological research. According to Blumstein, "That we are in this confused state is not surprising when we recognize that the nation spends less than $25 million per year for research at the National Institute of Justice on the problem that seems to be the nation's greatest concern. Contrast this with $11 billion for health research at the National Institutes of Health, $600 million on mental health, and $165 million for dental research. With so small a research effort, it is not surprising that we reach out for programs with little ability to assess the impact that they might have on the intended objective, and that we operate in a pre-Galilean mode when we debate crime policy."[45] Or, as Carl J. Jensen and Bernard H. Levin write in the Futures Working Group's report, *Policing 2020*, "In a rapidly changing world, those who play catch-up . . . will never catch up."[46]

KEY TERMS

cross-impact analysis, 657

Delphi Method, 657

environmental scanning, 657

future criminology, 654

futures research, 656

futurist, 654

Kriminalpolitik, 663

scenario writing, 657

strategic assessment, 657

trend extrapolation, 657

KEY NAMES

Georgette Bennett, 658

Bernard Levin, 658

Richter H. Moore, Jr., 658

Gene Stephens, 660

William L. Tafoya, 656

QUESTIONS FOR REVIEW

1. What is futures research? Explain some of the techniques used by futurists for assessing the future.

2. List and describe some possible future crimes and tell how they might differ from the kinds of criminal activity that we are familiar with today.

3. What are some of the specific predictions about the future of criminological theorizing that this chapter offers?

4. Why might new crime fighting strategies be necessary in the future? What kinds of innovative crime control strategies might the future bring?

5. Can the problem of crime be solved? If so, how? If not, why not?

QUESTIONS FOR REFLECTION

1. This book emphasizes a social problems versus social responsibility theme. Which perspective do you think will be dominant in twenty-first-century crime control planning? Why?

2. Do you believe it is possible to know the future? What techniques are identified in this chapter for assessing

possible futures? Which of these do you think holds the most promise? Why?

3. What kinds of crime control policies do you think the future will bring? Will they be consistent with present understandings of civil liberties? Why or why not?

WEB QUEST

Visit the World Future Society on the Web at www.wfs.org. The society's Web site (under the "Ideas" menu item) offers several moderated forums that permit you to share your thoughts with futurists around the world. Forums include

- The Social Innovation Forum, which presents ideas outlining ideas for urban development, social reform, and other proposals for improving life in the future
- The Wisdom of the World Forum, in which British scholar Bruce Lloyd has collected quotes containing wisdom essential for humanity in the new

millennium. You can submit your own quotes for possible posting.

- Global Strategies Forum offers ideas and proposals resolving the complex issues facing the world today and in the near-term future
- The Methodologies Forum, in which professional futurists, planners, and forecasters share tips and useful tools for futuring
- Cyber Society Forum, which explores how life may look in the future as information technology changes the world

- Education Forum, which offers ideas and innovations for improving education, including strategies for K–12, higher education, vocational or professional training, and lifelong learning and life enhancement

This Web Quest requires you to search through the forums to identify topics, posted papers, or contributed comments dealing with criminology, crime, and criminal justice. Identify such materials, summarize each, and submit them to your instructor if asked to do so.

NOTES

[1] Cynthia Manson and Charles Ardai, eds., *Future Crime: An Anthology of the Shape of Crime to Come* (New York: Donald I. Fine, 1992), p. ix.

[2] Alvin Toffler, *Powershift: Knowledge, Wealth, and Violence at the Edge of the Twenty-first Century* (New York: Bantam, 1990), p. 255.

[3] George Orwell, *1984* (New York: New American Library Classics, 1990).

[4] This story is adapted from Gary LaFree et al., "The Changing Nature of Crime in America," in Gary LaFree, ed., *Criminal Justice 2000: Volume III—The Nature of Crime—Continuity and Change* (Washington, DC: National Institute of Justice, 2000).

[5] Darlene E. Weingand, "Futures Research Methodologies: Linking Today's Decisions with Tomorrow's Possibilities," paper presented at the Sixty-First International Federation of Library Associations and Institutions annual conference, August 20, 1995, http://www.ifla.org/IV/ifla61/61-weid.htm (accessed June 16, 1998, and July 10, 2007).

[6] Joseph F. Coates, "The Highly Probable Future: 83 Assumptions about the Year 2025," *Futurist*, Vol. 28, No. 4 (July/August 1994), p. 51.

[7] Alvin Toffler, *Future Shock* (New York: Random House, 1970).

[8] Alvin Toffler, *The Third Wave* (New York: Bantam, 1981).

[9] John Naisbitt, *Megatrends: Ten New Directions Transforming Our Lives* (New York: Warner, 1982).

[10] Peter F. Drucker, *Management Challenges for the 21st Century* (New York: Harper, 1999).

[11] Peter F. Drucker, *Post-Capitalist Society* (New York: Harper, 1994).

[12] Francis Fukuyama, *Our Posthuman Future: Consequences of the Biotechnology Revolution* (New York: Farrar, Straus and Giroux, 2002).

[13] Francis Fukuyama, *The End of History and The Last Man* (New York: Avon Books, 1992).

[14] Although this chapter cannot cover all future aspects of the criminal justice system, readers are referred to C. J. Swank, "Police in the Twenty-First Century: Hypotheses for the Future," *International Journal of Comparative and Applied Criminal Justice*, Vol. 17, Nos. 1 and 2 (spring/fall 1993), pp. 107–120, for an excellent analysis of policing in the future.

[15] Joseph A. Schafer, ed., *Policing 2020: Exploring the Future of Crime, Communities, and Policing* (Quantico, VA: The Futures Working Group, 2007).

[16] Ibid., p. 32.

[17] Ibid.

[18] The Foresight Web site, http://www.foresight.gov.uk (accessed March 22, 2007).

[19] The quotations attributed to the panel in this section are from Foresight Crime Prevention Panel, *Just around the Corner: A Consultation Document*, http://www.foresight.gov.uk/servlet/DocViewer/docnoredirect=883 (accessed January 22, 2007).

[20] Society of Police Futurists International, *PFI: The Future of Policing* (brochure), no date.

[21] William L. Tafoya, "Futures Research: Implications for Criminal Investigations," in James N. Gilbert, ed., *Criminal Investigation: Essays and Cases* (Columbus, OH: Charles E. Merrill, 1990), p. 214.

[22] Frederick R. Brodzinski, "The Futurist Perspective and the Managerial Process," *Utilizing Futures Research*, No. 6 (1979), pp. 8–19.

[23] Weingand, "Futures Research Methodologies."

[24] George F. Cole, "Criminal Justice in the Twenty-First Century: The Role of Futures Research," in John Klofas and Stan Stojkovic, eds., *Crime and Justice in the Year 2010* (Belmont, CA: Wadsworth, 1995).

[25] Joseph F. Coates et al., *2025: Scenarios of U.S. and Global Society Reshaped by Science and Technology* (Winchester, VA: Oakhill Press, 1997).

[26] Richter H. Moore, Jr., "Wiseguys: Smarter Criminals and Smarter Crime in the Twenty-First Century," *Futurist*, Vol. 28, No. 5 (September/October 1994), p. 33.

[27] The quotations attributed to Moore in this section are from ibid., pp. 33–37.

[28] Georgette Bennett, *Crimewarps: The Future of Crime in America* (Garden City, NY: Anchor/Doubleday, 1987).

[29] L. Edward Wells, "Explaining Crime in the Year 2010," in Klofas and Stojkovic, eds., *Crime and Justice in the Year 2010*, pp. 36–61.

[30] Ibid.

[31] Ibid., pp. 48–49.

[32] Ibid., pp. 54–57.

[33] Frank P. Williams III and Marilyn D. McShane, *Criminological Theory*, 2nd ed. (Upper Saddle River, NJ: Prentice Hall, 1994), p. 257.

[34] The quotations attributed to Farrington in this section are from David P. Farrington, "Explaining and Preventing Crime: The Globalization of Knowledge," *Criminology*, Vol. 38, No. 1 (February 2000), pp. 1–24.

[35] The quotations attributed to Stephens in this section are from Gene Stephens, "The Global Crime Wave," *Futurist*, Vol. 28, No. 4 (July/August 1994), pp. 22–29.

[36] For an interesting and alternative view of the future—one that evaluates what might happen if the insight provided by feminist perspectives on crime were implemented—see M. Kay Harris, "Moving into the New Millennium: Toward a Feminist Vision of Justice," in Barry W. Hancock and Paul M. Sharp, eds., *Public Policy, Crime, and Criminal Justice*, 2nd ed. (Upper Saddle River, NJ: Prentice Hall, 2000), pp. 407–419.

[37] Moore, "Wiseguys," p. 33.

[38] Hermanus Bianchi, *Position and Subject-Matter of Criminology* (Amsterdam: North-Holland, 1956).

[39] Hermann Mannheim, *Comparative Criminology* (New York: Houghton Mifflin, 1965), p. 18.

[40] "Can Anything Really Be Done?" *USA Today* magazine, Vol. 122, No. 2587 (April 1994), p. 6.

[41] Robert D. Pursley, *Introduction to Criminal Justice*, 6th ed. (New York: Macmillan, 1991), p. 677.

[42] Ibid.

[43] Marion, *A History of Federal Crime Control Initiatives, 1960–1993*, p. 244.

[44] Ibid., p. 249.

[45] Blumstein, "Seeking the Connection between Crime and Punishment."

[46] Carl J. Jensen and Bernard H. Levin, "The World of 2020: Demographic Shifts, Cultural Change, and Social Challenge," in Joseph A. Schafer, ed., *Policing 2020: Exploring the Future of Crime, Communities, and Policing* (Quantico, VA: The Futures Working Group, 2007), p. 33.

Glossary

Numbers appearing in parentheses after each term and its associated definition refer to the chapter in which that term appears.

acquaintance rape Rape characterized by a prior social, though not necessarily intimate or familial, relationship between the victim and the perpetrator. (10)

administrative law Law that regulates many daily business activities. Violations of these regulations generally result in warnings or fines, depending on their adjudged severity.

Age of Reason See **Enlightenment.**

aggravated assault (UCR) An unlawful attack by one person upon another for the purpose of inflicting severe or aggravated bodily injury. See also **simple assault.** (2)

alloplastic adaptation A form of adjustment that results from changes in the environment surrounding an individual. (6)

androcentricity A single-sex perspective, as in the case of criminologists who study only the criminality of males. (9)

anomie A social condition in which norms are uncertain or lacking. (7)

anomie theory See **strain theory.**

Anti-Drug Abuse Act A federal law (Public Law 99–570) enacted in 1986 that established new federal mandatory minimum sentences for drug offenses.

antisocial (asocial) personality A term used to describe individuals who are basically unsocialized and whose behavior pattern brings them repeatedly into conflict with society. (6)

antisocial personality disorder A psychological condition exhibited by individuals who are basically unsocialized and whose behavior pattern brings them repeatedly into conflicts with society.[1] (6)

applied research Scientific inquiry that is designed and carried out with practical applications in mind. (3)

Arrestee Drug Abuse Monitoring (ADAM) Program A National Institute of Justice program, that tracks trends in the prevalence and types of drug use among booked arrestees in urban areas. (13)

arson The willful or malicious burning or attempt to burn, with or without intent to defraud, of a dwelling house, public building, motor vehicle or aircraft, personal property of another, and so on. (2)

asocial personality See **antisocial personality.**

assault See **aggravated assault; simple assault.**

asset forfeiture The authorized seizure of money, negotiable instruments, securities, or other things of value. In federal antidrug laws, the authorization of judicial representatives to seize all monies, negotiable instruments, securities, or other things of value furnished or intended to be furnished by any person in exchange for a controlled substance, and all proceeds traceable to such an exchange. (12)

atavism A term used by Cesare Lombroso to suggest that criminals are physiological throwbacks to earlier stages of human evolution. The term is derived from the Latin term *atavus,* which means "ancestor." (5)

attachment theory A social-psychological perspective on delinquent and criminal behavior that holds that the successful development of secure attachment between a child and his or her primary caregiver provides the basic foundation for all future psychological development. (6)

audit trail A sequential record of computer system activities that enables auditors to reconstruct, review, and examine the sequence of states and activities surrounding each event in one or more related transactions from inception to output of final results back to inception. (14)

autoplastic adaptation A form of adjustment that results from changes within an individual. (6)

bank fraud   Fraud or embezzlement that occurs within or against financial institutions that are insured or regulated by the U.S. government. Financial institution fraud includes commercial loan fraud, check fraud, counterfeit negotiable instruments, mortgage fraud, check kiting, and false credit applications. (12)

behavior theory   A psychological perspective that posits that individual behavior that is rewarded will increase in frequency, while that which is punished will decrease. (6)

behavioral genetics   The study of genetic and environmental contributions to individual variations in human behavior. (5)

bias crime   See **hate crime.**

biological theory   A theory that maintains that the basic determinants of human behavior, including criminality, are constitutionally or physiologically based and often inherited. (5)

booster   A frequent shoplifter. (11)

born criminal   An individual who is born with a genetic predilection toward criminality. (5)

bourgeoisie   In Marxist theory, the class of people who own the means of production. (9)

Brady Handgun Violence Prevention Act   A federal law (Public Law 103–159) enacted in 1993 that initiated a national background checking system for all potential gun purchasers.

***Brawner* rule**   A somewhat vague rule for determining insanity that was created in the 1972 federal court case of *United States* v. *Brawner* (471 F.2d 969), since superseded by statute, and asks the jury to decide whether the defendant could be *justly* held responsible for the criminal act with which he or she stands charged, in the face of any claims of insanity or mental incapacity. (6)

broken windows thesis   A perspective on crime causation that holds that physical deterioration in an area leads to increased concerns for personal safety among area residents and to higher crime rates in that area. (7)

bulletin board system (BBS)   A computer accessible by telephone and used like a bulletin board to leave messages

and files for other users. Also called *computer bulletin board.*

burglary   By the narrowest and oldest definition, the trespassory breaking and entering of the dwelling house of another in the nighttime with the intent to commit a felony. Also, the unlawful entry of a structure to commit a felony or a theft. (2)

burglary (UCR)   The unlawful entry of any fixed structure, vehicle, or vessel used for regular residence, industry, or business, with or without force, with intent to commit a felony or a larceny.

Cambridge Study in Delinquent Development   A longitudinal (life-course) study of crime and delinquency tracking a cohort of 411 boys born in London in 1953. (8)

capable guardian   One who effectively discourages crime. (4)

capital punishment   The legal imposition of a sentence of death upon a convicted offender. Also called *death penalty.* (4)

carjacking   The stealing of a car while it is occupied. (2)

Chicago Area Project   A program focusing on urban ecology and originating at the University of Chicago during the 1930s, which attempted to reduce delinquency, crime, and social disorganization in transitional neighborhoods. (7)

Chicago School of criminology   See **ecological theory.**

child sexual abuse (CSA)   A term encompassing a variety of criminal and civil offenses in which an adult engages in sexual activity with a minor, exploits a minor for purposes of sexual gratification, or exploits a minor sexually for purposes of profit. (10)

civil law   The body of law that regulates arrangements between individuals, such as contracts and claims to property.

Classical School   A criminological perspective of the late 1700s and early 1800s that had its roots in the Enlightenment and that held that humans are rational beings, that crime is the result of the exercise of free will, and that punishment can be effective in reducing the incidence of crime, as it negates

the pleasure to be derived from crime commission. (4)

clearance rate   The proportion of reported or discovered crimes within a given offense category that are solved. (2)

Code of Hammurabi   An early set of laws established by the Babylonian king Hammurabi, who ruled the ancient city from 1792 to 1750 B.C. (4)

cohort   A group of individuals having certain significant social characteristics in common, such as gender and date and place of birth. (2)

cohort analysis   A social scientific technique that studies over time a population with common characteristics. Cohort analysis usually begins at birth and traces the development of cohort members until they reach a certain age. (8)

Commission on Law Observance and Enforcement   See **Wickersham Commission.**

common law   Law originating from usage and custom rather than from written statutes. The term refers to nonstatutory customs, traditions, and precedents that help guide judicial decision making. (4)

Communications Decency Act   A federal statute signed into law in 1996, the CDA is Title 5 of the federal Telecommunications Act of 1996 (Public Law 104–104, 110 Stat. 56). The law sought to protect minors from harmful material on the Internet, and a portion of the CDA criminalized the knowing transmission of obscene or indecent messages to any recipient under 18 years of age. In 1997, however, in the case of *Reno* v. *ACLU* (521 U.S. 844), the U.S. Supreme Court found the bulk of the CDA to be unconstitutional, ruling that it contravenes First Amendment free speech guarantees. (14)

comparative criminologist   A criminologist involved in the cross-national study of crime. (15)

comparative criminology   The cross-national study of crime. (15)

Comprehensive Crime Control Act   A far-reaching federal law (Public Law 98–473) enacted in 1984 that mandated new federal sentencing guidelines, eliminated parole at the federal level, limited the use of the insanity defense in federal criminal courts, and increased federal penalties associated with drug dealing.

computer abuse Any unlawful incident associated with computer technology in which a victim suffered or could have suffered loss or in which a perpetrator by intention made or could have made gain.[2] (14)

computer bulletin board See **bulletin board system (BBS).**

computer crime Any violation of a federal or state computer crime statute. See also **cybercrime.** (14)

computer-related crime Any illegal act for which knowledge of computer technology is involved in its perpetration, investigation, or prosecution. (14)

computer virus A set of computer instructions that propagates copies or versions of itself into computer programs or data when it is executed. (14)

conditioning A psychological principle that holds that the frequency of any behavior can be increased or decreased through reward, punishment, or association with other stimuli. (6)

conduct norms Shared expectations of a social group relative to personal conduct. (7)

confidentiality See **data confidentiality.**

conflict perspective An analytical perspective on social organization that holds that conflict is a fundamental aspect of social life itself and can never be fully resolved. (9)

confounding effects A rival explanation, or competing hypothesis, that is a threat to the internal or external validity of a research design. (3)

consensus model An analytical perspective on social organization that holds that most members of society agree about what is right and what is wrong and that the various elements of society work together in unison toward a common vision of the greater good. (9)

constitutional theory A theory that explains criminality by reference to offenders' body types, inheritance, genetics, or external observable physical characteristics. (5)

constitutive criminology The study of the process by which human beings create an ideology of crime that sustains the notion of crime as a concrete reality.

containment Aspects of the social bond that act to prevent individuals from committing crimes and that keep them from engaging in deviance. (8)

containment theory A form of control theory that suggests that a series of both internal and external factors contributes to law-abiding behavior. (8)

control group A group of experimental subjects that, although the subject of measurement and observation, is not exposed to the experimental intervention. (3)

control ratio The amount of control to which a person is subject versus the amount of control that person exerts over others. (8)

controlled experiment An experiment that attempts to hold conditions (other than the intentionally introduced experimental intervention) constant. (3)

control theory See **social control theory.**

convict criminology A new analytical paradigm consisting of writings on the subject matter of criminology by convicted felons and ex-inmates who have acquired academic credentials, or who are associated with credentialled others. (9)

corporate crime A violation of a criminal statute either by a corporate entity or by its executives, employees, or agents acting on behalf of and for the benefit of the corporation, partnership, or other form of business entity.[3] (12)

correctional psychology The branch of forensic psychology concerned with the diagnosis and classification of offenders, the treatment of correctional populations, and the rehabilitation of inmates and other law violators. (6)

correlation A causal, complementary, or reciprocal relationship between two measurable variables. See also **statistical correlation.** (2)

Cosa Nostra Literally, "our thing." A criminal organization of Sicilian origin. Also called *the Mafia, the Outfit, the Mob, the syndicate,* or simply *the organization.* (12)

crime Human conduct in violation of the criminal laws of a state, the federal government, or a local jurisdiction that has the power to make such laws. (1)

crime typology A classification of crimes along a particular dimension, such as legal categories, offender motivation, victim behavior, or the characteristics of individual offenders. (10)

Crime Victims' Rights Act A 2004 federal law that establishes statutory rights for victims of federal crimes, and gives victims the necessary legal authority to assert those rights in federal courts.

criminal anthropology The scientific study of the relationship between human physical characteristics and criminality. (5)

criminal career The longitudinal sequence of crimes committed by an individual offender. (8)

criminal homicide The illegal killing of one human being by another. (2)

criminal homicide (UCR) The UCR category that includes and is limited to all offenses of causing the death of another person without justification or excuse. (2)

criminal justice The scientific study of crime, the criminal law, and components of the criminal justice system, including the police, courts, and corrections. (1)

criminal justice system The various agencies of justice, especially the police, courts, and corrections, whose goal it is to apprehend, convict, punish, and rehabilitate law violators. (1)

criminal law The body of law that regulates actions that have the potential to harm the interests of the state or the federal government.

criminal psychology See **forensic psychology.** (6)

criminal receiver See **fence.**

criminalist A specialist in the collection and examination of the physical evidence of crime. (1)

criminality A behavioral predisposition that disproportionately favors criminal activity. (1)

criminality index The actual extent of the crime problem in a society. The criminality index is computed by adding the actual crime rate and the latent crime rate. (2)

criminalize To make illegal. (1)

criminaloids A term used by Cesare Lombroso to describe occasional criminals who were pulled into criminality primarily by environmental influences. (5)

criminologist One who is trained in the field of criminology. Also, one who studies crime, criminals, and criminal behavior. (1)

criminology An interdisciplinary profession built around the scientific study of crime and criminal behavior, including their forms, causes, legal aspects, and control. (1)

criminology of place See **environmental criminology.** (7)

critical criminology See **radical criminology.** (9)

cross-impact analysis A technique of futures research that attempts to analyze one trend or event in light of the occurrence or nonoccurrence of a series of related events. (Epilogue)

cultural transmission The transmission of delinquency through successive generations of people living in the same area through a process of social communication. (7)

culture conflict theory A sociological perspective on crime that suggests that the root cause of criminality can be found in a clash of values between variously socialized groups over what is acceptable or proper behavior. (7)

Cyber Security Enhancement Act Part of the Homeland Security Act of 2002, this federal law directed the U.S. sentencing commission to take several specific factors into account in creating new sentencing guidelines for computer criminals. (14)

cybercrime Crime committed with the use of computers or via the manipulation of digital forms of data. See also **computer crime.** (14)

cyberspace The computer-created matrix of virtual possibilities, including online services, wherein human beings interact with one another and with the technology itself. (14)

cyberstalking An array of high-technology related activities in which

an offender may engage to harass or "follow" individuals, including e-mail and the Internet. (10)

cyberterrorism A form of terrorism that makes use of high technology, especially computer technology and the Internet, in the planning and carrying out of terrorist attacks. (15)

cycloid A term developed by Ernst Kretschmer to describe a particular relationship between body build and personality type. The cycloid personality, which was associated with a heavyset, soft type of body, was said to vacillate between normality and abnormality. (5)

dangerous drug A term used by the Drug Enforcement Administration to refer to "broad categories or classes of controlled substances other than cocaine, opiates, and cannabis products." Amphetamines, methamphetamines, PCP (phencyclidine), LSD, methcathinone, and "designer drugs" are all considered to be dangerous drugs. (13)

dangerousness The likelihood that a given individual will later harm society or others. Dangerousness is often measured in terms of recidivism, or the likelihood of new crime commission or rearrest for a new crime within a five-year period following arrest or release from confinement. (4)

dark figure of crime The numerical total of unreported crimes that are not reflected in official crime statistics. (2)

data confidentiality The ethical requirement of social scientific research to protect the confidentiality of individual research participants, while simultaneously preserving justified research access to the information participants provide. (3)

data encryption The process by which information is encoded, making it unreadable to all but its intended recipients. (14)

date rape Unlawful forced sexual intercourse with a woman against her will that occurs within the context of a dating relationship. (2)

Daubert standard A test of scientific acceptability applicable to the gathering of evidence in criminal cases. (14)

DCS–1000 A network diagnostic tool that is capable of assisting in criminal investigations by monitoring and

capturing large amounts of Internet traffic. Previously called *Carnivore.* (14)

death penalty See **capital punishment.**

deconstructionist theory A postmodern perspective that challenges existing criminological theories in order to debunk them and that works toward replacing traditional ideas with concepts seen as more appropriate to the postmodern era. (9)

decriminalization The redefinition of certain previously criminal behaviors into regulated activities that become "ticketable" rather than "arrestable." (13)

defensible space The range of mechanisms that combine to bring an environment under the control of its residents. (7)

Delphi Method A technique of futures research that uses repetitive questioning of experts to refine predictions. (Epilogue)

demographics The characteristics of population groups, usually expressed in statistical fashion. (2)

demography The study of the characteristics of population groups.

descriptive statistics Statistics that describe, summarize, or highlight the relationships within data that have been gathered. (3)

designer drugs "New substances designed by slightly altering the chemical makeup of other illegal or tightly controlled drugs."[4] (13)

desistance The cessation of criminal activity or the termination of a period of involvement in offending behavior. (8)

desistance phenomenon The observable decrease in crime rates that is invariably associated with age. (2)

determinate sentencing A criminal punishment strategy that mandates a specified and fixed amount of time to be served for every offense category. Under the strategy, for example, all offenders convicted of the same degree of burglary would be sentenced to the same length of time behind bars. Also called *fixed sentencing.* (4)

deterrence The prevention of crime. See also **general deterrence; specific deterrence.** (4)

deterrence strategy A crime-control strategy that attempts "to diminish motivation for crime by increasing the perceived certainty, severity, or celerity of penalties."[5]

deviant behavior Human activity that violates social norms. (1)

differential association The sociological thesis that criminality, like any other form of behavior, is learned through a process of association with others who communicate criminal values. (8)

differential identification theory An explanation for crime and deviance that holds that people pursue criminal or deviant behavior to the extent that they identify themselves with real or imaginary people from whose perspective their criminal or deviant behavior seems acceptable. (8)

Digital Theft Deterrence and Copyright Damages Improvement Act Passed in 1999, this federal law (Public Law 106–160) attempted to combat software piracy and other forms of digital theft by amending Section 504(c) of the Copyright Act, thereby increasing the amount of damages that could potentially be awarded in cases of copyright infringement. (14)

disclosure (of research methods) The provision of information to potential subjects informing them of the nature of the research methods to be used by the social scientific study in which their involvement is planned.

discrediting information Information that is inconsistent with the managed impressions being communicated in a given situation. (8)

displacement A shift of criminal activity from one location to another. (4)

displastic A mixed group of offenders described by constitutional theorist Ernst Kretschmer as highly emotional and often unable to control themselves. They were thought to commit mostly sexual offenses and other crimes of passion. The term is largely of historical interest. (5)

distributive justice The rightful, equitable, and just distribution of rewards within a society. (7)

dizygotic (DZ) twins Twins that develop from separate ova, and that carry the genetic material shared by siblings. (5)

DNA fingerprinting See **DNA profiling.**

DNA profiling The use of biological residue found at the scene of a crime for genetic comparisons in aiding the identification of criminal suspects. (14)

domestic terrorism The unlawful use of force or violence by a group or an individual who is based and operates entirely within the United States and its territories without foreign direction and whose acts are directed at elements of the U.S. government or population.[6] (15)

dramaturgical perspective A theoretical point of view that depicts human behavior as centered around the purposeful management of interpersonal impressions. Also called *dramaturgy*. (8)

dramaturgy See **dramaturgical perspective.**

drug-defined crime A violation of the laws prohibiting or regulating the possession, use, or distribution of illegal drugs. (13)

drug-related crime A crime in which drugs contribute to the offense (excluding violations of drug laws). (13)

drug trafficking Manufacturing, distributing, dispensing, importing, and exporting (or possession with intent to do the same) a controlled substance or a counterfeit substance.[7] (13)

Durham rule A standard for judging legal insanity that holds that an accused is not criminally responsible if his or her unlawful act was the product of mental disease or mental defect. (6)

ecological theory A type of sociological approach that emphasizes demographics (the characteristics of population groups) and geographics (the mapped location of such groups relative to one another) and that sees the social disorganization that characterizes delinquency areas as a major cause of criminality and victimization. Also called *Chicago School of criminology*. (7)

ectomorph A body type originally described as thin and fragile, with long, slender, poorly muscled extremities and delicate bones. (5)

ego The reality-testing part of the personality. Also called the *reality principle*. More formally, the personality component that is conscious, most immediately controls behavior, and is most in touch with external reality.[8] (6)

electroencephalogram (EEG) The electrical measurement of brain wave activity. (6)

encryption See **data encryption.**

endomorph A body type originally described as soft and round or overweight. (5)

Enlightenment A social movement that arose during the eighteenth century and that built upon ideas like empiricism, rationality, free will, humanism, and natural law. Also called *Age of Reason*. (4)

environmental crime A violation of the criminal law that, although typically committed by businesses or by business officials, may also be committed by other people or by organizational entities and that damages some protected or otherwise significant aspect of the natural environment. (12)

environmental criminology An emerging perspective that emphasizes the importance of geographic location and architectural features as they are associated with the prevalence of criminal victimization. (*Note:* As the term has been understood to date, environmental criminology is not the study of environmental crime but, rather, a perspective that stresses how crime varies from place to place.) Also called *criminology of place*. (7)

environmental scanning "A systematic effort to identify in an elemental way future developments (trends or events) that could plausibly occur over the time horizon of interest"[9] and that might affect one's area of concern. (Epilogue)

ethnic succession The continuing process whereby one immigrant or ethnic group succeeds another by assuming its position in society. (12)

ethnocentrism The phenomenon of "culture-centeredness" by which one uses one's own culture as a benchmark against which to judge all other patterns of behavior. (15)

eugenic criminology A perspective that holds that the root causes of criminality are passed from generation to generation in the form of "bad genes." (5)

eugenics The study of hereditary improvement by genetic control. (5)

evidence-based That which is built on scientific findings; and especially practices and policies founded upon the results of randomized controlled experiments. (3)

evolutionary ecology An approach to understanding crime that draws attention to the ways people develop over the course of their lives. (8)

experiment See **controlled experiment; quasi-experimental design**.

experimental criminology A form of contemporary criminology that makes use of rigorous social scientific techniques, especially randomized controlled experiments and the systematic review of research results. (3)

expert systems Computer hardware and software that attempt to duplicate the decision-making processes used by skilled investigators in the analysis of evidence and in the recognition of patterns that such evidence might represent. (14)

exposure-reduction theory A theory of intimate homicide that claims that a decline in domesticity, accompanied by an improvement in the economic status of women and a growth in domestic violence resources, explains observed decreases in intimate-partner homicide. (10)

expressive crime A criminal offense that results from acts of interpersonal hostility, such as jealousy, revenge, romantic triangles, and quarrels. (10)

external validity The ability to generalize research findings to other settings. (3)

felony A serious criminal offense, specifically one punishable by death or by incarceration in a prison facility for a year or more.

felony murder A special class of criminal homicide in which an offender may be charged with first-degree murder when that person's criminal activity results in another person's death. (2)

feminist criminology A self-conscious corrective model intended to redirect the thinking of mainstream criminologists to include gender awareness. (9)

fence An individual or a group involved in the buying, selling, and distribution of stolen goods. Also called *criminal receiver*. (11)

first-degree murder Criminal homicide that is planned or involves premeditation. (2)

focal concerns Key values of any culture, especially the key values of a delinquent subculture. (7)

folkways Time-honored customs. Although folkways carry the force of tradition, their violation is unlikely to threaten the survival of the group. See also **mores**. (4)

forcible rape (UCR) The carnal knowledge of a female forcibly and against her will. Assaults or attempts to commit rape by force or threat of force are also included in the UCR definition; however, statutory rape (without force) and other sex offenses are excluded. (2)

foreign terrorist organization (FTO) A foreign organization that engages in terrorist activity that threatens the security of U.S. nationals or the national security of the United States and that is so designated by the U.S. secretary of state. (15)

forensic psychiatry A branch of psychiatry having to do with the study of crime and criminality. (6)

forensic psychology The application of the science and profession of psychology to questions and issues relating to law and the legal system. (6)

forfeiture See **asset forfeiture.**

frustration-aggression theory A theory that holds that frustration, which is a natural consequence of living, is a root cause of crime. Criminal behavior can be a form of adaptation when it results in stress reduction.

future criminology The study of likely futures as they impinge on crime and its control. (Epilogue)

futures research "A multidisciplinary branch of operations research" whose principal aim "is to facilitate long-range planning based on (1) forecasting from the past supported by mathematical models, (2) cross-disciplinary treatment of its subject matter, (3) systematic use of expert judgment, and (4) a systems-analytical approach to its problems."[10] (Epilogue)

futurist One who studies the future. (Epilogue)

gateway offense An offense, usually fairly minor in nature, that leads to more serious offenses. Shoplifting, for example, may be a gateway offense to more serious property crimes. (11)

gender gap The observed differences between male and female rates of criminal offending in a given society, such as the United States. (9)

general deterrence A goal of criminal sentencing that seeks to prevent others from committing crimes similar to the one for which a particular offender is being sentenced. (4)

general strain theory (GST) A perspective that suggests that lawbreaking behavior is a coping mechanism that enables those who engage in it to deal with the socioemotional problems generated by negative social relations. (7)

general theory A theory that attempts to explain all (or at least most) forms of criminal conduct through a single, overarching approach. (1)

general theory of crime a perspective on crime, developed by Travis Hirschi and Michael Gottfredson, that asserts "that the operation of a single mechanism, low self-control, accounts for 'all crime, at all times'; [including] acts ranging from vandalism to homicide, from rape to white-collar-crime."[11] (8)

genetic determinism The belief that genes are the major determining factor in human behavior. (5)

globalization A process of social homogenization by which the experiences of everyday life, marked by the diffusion of commodities and ideas, can foster a standardization of cultural expressions around the world.[12] (15)

guilty but mentally ill (GBMI) A finding that offenders are guilty of the criminal offense with which they are charged, but because of their prevailing mental condition, they are generally sent to psychiatric hospitals for treatment rather than to prison. Once they have been declared cured, however, such offenders can be transferred to correctional facilities to serve out their sentences. (6)

habitual offender statute A law intended to keep repeat criminal offenders behind bars. These laws sometimes come under the "three strikes and you're out" rubric.

hacker   A person who uses computers for exploration and exploitation. (14)

hard determinism   The belief that crime results from forces that are beyond the control of the individual. (4)

hate crime   A criminal offense in which the motive is hatred, bias, or prejudice based on the actual or perceived race, color, religion, national origin, ethnicity, gender, or sexual orientation of another individual or group of individuals. Also called *bias crime*. (2)

Hate Crimes Sentencing Enhancement Act   A federal law (28 U.S.C. Section 994) enacted in 1994 as part of the Violent Crime Control and Law Enforcement Act that required the U.S. Sentencing Commission to increase the penalties for crimes in which the victim was selected "because of [his or her] actual or perceived race, color, religion, national origin, ethnicity, gender, disability, or sexual orientation."

hedonistic calculus   The belief, first proposed by Jeremy Bentham, that behavior holds value to any individual undertaking it according to the amount of pleasure or pain that it can be expected to produce for that person. Also called *utilitarianism*. (4)

heritability   A statistical construct that estimates the amount of variation in a population that is attributable to genetic factors. (5)

heroin signature program (HSP)   A Drug Enforcement Administration program that identifies the geographic source of a heroin sample through the detection of specific chemical characteristics in the sample peculiar to the source area. (13)

homicide   The killing of one human being by another.

household crime (NCVS)   An attempted or completed crime that does not involve confrontation, such as burglary, motor vehicle theft, and household larceny.

human agency   The active role that people take in their lives; the fact that people are not merely subject to social and structural constraints but actively make choices and decisions based on the alternatives that they see before them. (8)

human development   The relationship between the maturing individual and his or her changing environment, as well as the social processes that the relationship entails. (8)

human smuggling   Illegal immigration in which an agent is involved for payment to help a person cross a border clandestinely.[13] (15)

human trafficking   See **trafficking in persons.**

hypoglycemia   A medical condition characterized by low blood sugar. (5)

hypothesis   An explanation that accounts for a set of facts and that can be tested by further investigation. Also, something that is taken to be true for the purpose of argument or investigation.[14] (3)

id   The aspect of the personality from which drives, wishes, urges, and desires emanate. More formally, the division of the psyche associated with instinctual impulses and demands for immediate satisfaction of primitive needs.[15] (6)

identity theft   The unauthorized use of another individual's personal identity to fraudulently obtain money, goods, or services; to avoid the payment of debt; or to avoid criminal prosecution. (14)

illegitimate opportunity structure   Subcultural pathways to success that the wider society disapproves of. (7)

impression management   The intentional enactment of practiced behavior that is intended to convey to others one's desirable personal characteristics and social qualities. (8)

incapacitation   The use of imprisonment or other means to reduce the likelihood that an offender will be capable of committing future offenses. (4)

individual rights advocate   One who seeks to protect personal freedoms in the face of criminal prosecution.

inferential statistics   Statistics that specify how likely findings are to be true for other populations or in other locales. (3)

informed consent   The ethical requirement of social scientific research that research subjects be informed as to the nature of the research about to be conducted, their anticipated role in it, and the uses to which the data they provide will be put. (3)

infrastructure   The basic facilities, services, and installations needed for the functioning of a community or society, such as transportation and communications systems, water and power lines, and public institutions, including schools, post offices, and prisons.[16] (15)

insanity (legal)   A legally established inability to understand right from wrong or to conform one's behavior to the requirements of the law. (6)

insanity (psychological)   Persistent mental disorder or derangement.[17] (6)

insider trading   Equity trading based on confidential information about important events that may affect the price of the issue being traded. (12)

institutional robbery   Robbery that occurs in commercial settings, such as convenience stores, gas stations, and banks. (10)

instrumental crime   A goal-directed offense that involves some degree of planning by the offender. (10)

instrumental Marxism   A perspective that holds that those in power intentionally create laws and social institutions that serve their own interests and that keep others from becoming powerful. (9)

integrated theory   An explanatory perspective that merges (or attempts to merge) concepts drawn from different sources. (1)

interactional theory   A theoretical approach to exploring crime and delinquency that blends social control and social learning perspectives. (8)

interactionist perspective   See **social process theory.**

interdiction   An international drug control policy that aims to stop drugs from entering the country illegally. (13)

internal validity   The certainty that experimental interventions did indeed cause the changes observed in the study group. Also, the control over confounding factors, which tend to invalidate the results of an experiment. (3)

international terrorism   The unlawful use of force or violence by a group or an individual who has a connection to a foreign power or whose activities transcend national boundaries against people or property to intimidate or coerce a government, the civilian population, or any segment thereof in furtherance of political or social objectives.[18] (15)

Internet   The world's largest computer network. (14)

intersubjectivity   A scientific principle that requires that independent observers see the same thing under the same circumstances for observations to be regarded as valid. (3)

intimate-partner assault   A gender-neutral term used to characterize assaultive behavior that takes place between individuals involved in an intimate relationship. (10)

irresistible-impulse test   A standard for judging legal insanity that holds that a defendant is not guilty of a criminal offense if the person, by virtue of his or her mental state or psychological condition, was not able to resist committing the crime. (6)

jockey   A professional car thief involved regularly in calculated, steal-to-order car thefts. (11)

joyriding   An opportunistic car theft, often committed by a teenager seeking fun or thrills. (11)

Juke family   A well-known "criminal family" studied by Richard L. Dugdale. (5)

just deserts model   The notion that criminal offenders deserve the punishment they receive at the hands of the law and that punishments should be appropriate to the type and severity of crime committed. (4)

justice model   A contemporary model of imprisonment in which the principle of just deserts forms the underlying social philosophy. (4)

Kallikak family   A well-known "criminal family" studied by Henry H. Goddard. (5)

Kefauver Committee   The popular name for the federal Special Committee to Investigate Organized Crime in Interstate Commerce, formed in 1951. (12)

Kriminalpolitik   The political handling of crime. Also, a criminology-based social policy. (Epilogue)

labeling   An interactionist perspective that sees continued crime as a consequence of limited opportunities for acceptable behavior that follow from the negative responses of society to those defined as offenders. Also, the process by which a negative or deviant label is imposed. (8)

La Cosa Nostra   See **Cosa Nostra.**

larceny   The unlawful taking or attempted taking of property (other than a motor vehicle) from the possession of another, by stealth, without force or deceit, with intent to permanently deprive the owner of the property.

larceny-theft (UCR)   The unlawful taking, carrying, leading, or riding away of property (other than a motor vehicle) from the possession or constructive possession of another. Attempts are included. (2)

latent crime rate   A rate of crime calculated on the basis of crimes that would likely be committed by those who are in prison or jail or who are otherwise incapacitated by the justice system. (2)

law and order advocate   One who suggests that under certain circumstances involving criminal threats to public safety, the interests of society should take precedence over individual rights.

Law Enforcement Assistance Administration (LEAA)   A federal program, established under Title 1 of the Omnibus Crime Control and Safe Streets Act of 1967, designed to provide assistance to police agencies.

learning theory   A perspective that places primary emphasis upon the role of communication and socialization in the acquisition of learned patterns of criminal behavior and the values that support that behavior. (8)

left realism   A conflict perspective that insists on a pragmatic assessment of crime and its associated problems. Also called *realist criminology.* (9)

left-realist criminology   An approach to the subject matter of criminology based on ideas inherent in the perspective of left realism. (9)

legalization   Elimination of the laws and criminal penalties associated with certain behaviors—usually the production, sale, distribution, and possession of a controlled substance. (13)

liberal feminism   A perspective that holds that the concerns of women can be incorporated within existing social institutions through conventional means and without the need to drastically restructure society. Criminal laws, such as the Violence against Women Act, for example, have been enacted in order to change the legal structure in such a way that it becomes responsive to women's issues. (9)

life course   Pathways through the age-differentiated life span. Also, the course of a person's life over time. (8)

life course criminology   A developmental perspective that draws attention to the fact that criminal behavior tends to follow a distinct pattern across the life cycle. (8)

lifestyle theory   Another term for the routine activities approach of Lawrence Cohen and Marcus Felson. See **routine activities theory.** (4)

Mafia   See **Cosa Nostra.** (12)

mala in se   Acts that are thought to be wrong in and of themselves. (4)

mala prohibita   Acts that are wrong only because they are prohibited. (4)

Marxist criminology   A perspective on crime and crime causation based on the writings of Karl Marx (9)

masculinity hypothesis   (1) A belief (from the late 1800s) that criminal women typically exhibited masculine features and mannerisms. (2) In the late 1900s, the belief that, over time, men and women will commit crimes that are increasingly similar in nature, seriousness, and frequency. Increasing similarity in crime commission was predicted to result from changes in the social status of women (for example, better economic position, gender role convergence, socialization practices that are increasingly similar for both males and females, and so on). (5)

mass murder   The illegal killing of four or more victims at one location within one event. (10)

mesomorph   A body type described as athletic and muscular. (5)

meta-analysis   A study of other studies about a particular topic of interest. (3)

metatheory A theory about theories and the theorizing process.

misdemeanor A criminal offense that is less serious than a felony and is punishable by incarceration, usually in a local confinement facility, typically for a year or less.

M'Naughten **rule** A standard for judging legal insanity that requires that offenders not know what they were doing, or if they did, that they not know it was wrong. (6)

modeling theory A form of social learning theory that asserts that people learn how to act by observing others. (6)

money laundering The process of converting illegally earned assets, originating as cash, to one or more alternative forms to conceal such incriminating factors as illegal origin and true ownership.[19] (12)

Monitoring the Future A national self-report survey on drug use that has been conducted since 1975. (2)

monozygotic (MZ) twins Twins that develop from the same egg and that carry virtually the same genetic material. (5)

moral enterprise The efforts made by an interest group to have its sense of moral or ethical propriety enacted into law. (8)

mores Behavioral proscriptions covering potentially serious violations of a group's values. Examples include strictures against murder, rape, and robbery. See also **folkways**. (4)

motor vehicle theft (UCR) The theft or attempted theft of a motor vehicle. According to the Federal Bureau of Investigation, this offense category includes the stealing of automobiles, trucks, buses, motorcycles, motorscooters, and snowmobiles. (2)

murder An unlawful homicide.

National Advisory Commission on Criminal Justice Standards and Goals A federal body commissioned in 1971 by President Richard Nixon to examine the nation's criminal justice system and to set standards and goals to direct the development of the nation's criminal justice agencies.

National Crime Victimization Survey (NCVS) A survey conducted annually by the Bureau of Justice Statistics that provides data on surveyed households that report they were affected by crime. (2)

National Incident-Based Reporting System (NIBRS) A new and enhanced statistical reporting system that will collect data on each single incident and arrest within 22 crime categories. (2)

National Survey on Drug Use and Health (NSDUH) A national survey of illicit drug use among people 12 years of age and older that is conducted annually by the Substance Abuse and Mental Health Services Administration. (13)

National Violence against Women (NVAW) Survey A national survey of the extent and nature of violence against women conducted between November 1995 and May 1996 and funded through grants from the National Institute of Justice and the U.S. Department of Health and Human Services' National Center for Injury Prevention and Control. (10)

National Youth Survey (NYS) A longitudinal panel study of a national sample of 1,725 individuals that measured self-reports of delinquency and other types of behavior. (2)

natural law The philosophical perspective that certain immutable laws are fundamental to human nature and can be readily ascertained through reason. Human-made laws, in contrast, are said to derive from human experience and history—both of which are subject to continual change. (4)

natural rights The rights that, according to natural law theorists, individuals retain in the face of government action and interests. (4)

negative affective states Adverse emotions that derive from the experience of strain, such as anger, fear, depression, and disappointment. (7)

negligent homicide The act of causing the death of another person by recklessness or gross negligence. (2)

neoclassical criminology A contemporary version of classical criminology that emphasizes deterrence and retribution, with reduced emphasis on rehabilitation. (4)

neurosis A functional disorder of the mind or of the emotions involving anxiety, phobia, or other abnormal behavior. (6)

No Electronic Theft Act A 1997 federal law (Public Law 105–147) that criminalizes the willful infringement of copyrighted works, including by electronic means, even when the infringing party derives no direct financial benefit from the infringement (such as when pirated software is freely distributed online). In keeping with requirements of the NETA, the U.S. Sentencing Commission enacted amendments to its guidelines on April 6, 2000, to increase penalties associated with electronic theft. (14)

nonprimary homicide Murder that involves victims and offenders who have no prior relationship and that usually occurs during the course of another crime such as robbery. (10)

nothing-works doctrine The belief popularized by Robert Martinson in the 1970s that correctional treatment programs have little success in rehabilitating offenders. (4)

nurturant strategy A crime control strategy that attempts "to forestall development of criminality by improving early life experiences and channeling child and adolescent development" in desirable directions.[20]

occasional offender A criminal offender whose offending patterns are guided primarily by opportunity. (11)

occupational crime Any act punishable by law that is committed through opportunity created in the course of an occupation that is legal.[21] (12)

offense A violation of the criminal law or, in some jurisdictions, a minor crime, such as jaywalking, sometimes described as "ticketable."

offense specialization A preference for engaging in a certain type of offense to the exclusion of others. (11)

Office of Juvenile Justice and Delinquency Prevention (OJJDP) A national office that provides monetary assistance and direct victim-service programs for juvenile courts.

Office of National Drug Control Policy (ONDCP) A national office charged by Congress with establishing policies, priorities, and objectives for the nation's drug-control program. ONDCP is responsible for developing and disseminating the *National Drug-Control Strategy*. (13)

omertà   The informal, unwritten code of organized crime, which demands silence and loyalty, among other things, of family members. (12)

Omnibus Anti-Drug Abuse Act   A federal law (Public Law 100–690) enacted in 1988 that substantially increased federal penalties for recreational drug users and created a new cabinet-level position (known unofficially as the drug czar) to coordinate the drug-fighting efforts of the federal government.

Omnibus Crime Control and Safe Streets Act   A federal law enacted in 1967 to eliminate the social conditions that create crime and to fund many anticrime initiatives nationwide.

operant behavior   Behavior that affects the environment in such a way as to produce responses or further behavioral cues. (6)

operationalization   The process by which concepts are made measurable. (3)

opportunity structure   A path to success. Opportunity structures may be of two types: legitimate and illegitimate.

organized crime   The unlawful activities of the members of a highly organized, disciplined association engaged in supplying illegal goods and services, including gambling, prostitution, loan-sharking, narcotics, and labor racketeering.[22] (12)

Panopticon   A prison designed by Jeremy Bentham that was to be a circular building with cells along the circumference, each clearly visible from a central location staffed by guards. (4)

paradigm   An example, a model, or a theory. (5)

paranoid schizophrenic   A schizophrenic individual who suffers from delusions and hallucinations. (6)

Part I offenses   The crimes of murder, rape, robbery, aggravated assault, burglary, larceny, and motor vehicle theft, as defined under the FBI's Uniform Crime Reporting Program. Also called *major crimes*. (2)

Part II offenses   Less serious offenses as identified by the FBI for the purpose of reporting arrest data. (2)

participant observation   A strategy in data gathering in which the researcher observes a group by participating, to varying degrees, in the activities of the group.[23] (3)

participatory justice   A relatively informal type of criminal justice case processing that makes use of local community resources rather than requiring traditional forms of official intervention. (9)

patriarchy   The tradition of male dominance. (9)

peace model   An approach to crime control that focuses on effective ways for developing a shared consensus on critical issues that could seriously affect the quality of life. (9)

peacemaking criminology   A perspective that holds that crime control agencies and the citizens they serve should work together to alleviate social problems and human suffering and thus reduce crime. (9)

penal couple   A term that describes the relationship between offender and victim. Also, the two individuals most involved in the criminal act: the offender and the victim.

persistence   Continuity in crime. Also, continual involvement in offending. (8)

persistent thief   One who continues in common-law property crimes despite no better than an ordinary level of success. (11)

personal robbery   Robbery that occurs on the highway or street or in a public place (and that is often referred to as "mugging") and robbery that occurs in residences. (10)

pharmaceutical diversion   The process by which legitimately manufactured controlled substances are diverted for illicit use. (13)

phenomenological criminology   The study of crime as a social phenomenon that is created through a process of social interaction.

phenomenology   The study of the contents of human consciousness without regard to external conventions or prior assumptions.

phishing   Pronounced "fishing." An Internet-based scam to steal valuable information such as credit card numbers,

social security numbers, user IDs, and passwords.[24] (14)

phone phreak   A person who uses switched, dialed-access telephone services for exploration and exploitation. (14)

phrenology   The study of the shape of the head to determine anatomical correlates of human behavior. (5)

piracy   See **software piracy.**

pluralist perspective   An analytical approach to social organization that holds that a multiplicity of values and beliefs exists in any complex society but that most social actors agree on the usefulness of law as a formal means of dispute resolution. (9)

positivism   The application of scientific techniques to the study of crime and criminals. (4)

postcrime victimization   Problems that tend to follow from initial victimization. Also called *secondary victimization*.

postmodern criminology   A brand of criminology that developed following World War II and that builds on the tenets inherent in postmodern social thought. (9)

power-control theory   A perspective that holds that the distribution of crime and delinquency within society is to some degree founded upon the consequences that power relationships within the wider society hold for domestic settings and for the everyday relationships among men, women, and children within the context of family life. (9)

primary deviance   Initial deviance often undertaken to deal with transient problems in living. (8)

primary homicide   Murder involving family members, friends, and acquaintances. (10)

primary research   Research characterized by original and direct investigation. (3)

professional criminal   A criminal offender who makes a living from criminal pursuits, is recognized by other offenders as professional, and engages in offending that is planned and calculated. (11)

Project on Human Development in Chicago Neighborhoods (PHDCN)   An intensive study of Chicago neighborhoods employing longitudinal evaluations to examine the changing circumstances of people's lives in an effort to identify personal characteristics that may lead toward or away from antisocial behavior. (8)

proletariat In Marxist theory, the working class. (9)

prosocial bonds Bonds between the individual and the social group that strengthen the likelihood of conformity. Prosocial bonds are characterized by attachment to conventional social institutions, values, and beliefs. (8)

prostitution The offering of one's self for hire for the purpose of engaging in sexual relations, or the act or practice of engaging in sexual activity for money or its equivalent. (13)

protection/avoidance strategy A crime-control strategy that attempts to reduce criminal opportunities by changing people's routine activities, by increasing guardianship, or by incapacitating convicted offenders.[25]

psychiatric criminology Theories that are derived from the medical sciences, including neurology, and that, like other psychological theories, focus on the individual as the unit of analysis. Psychiatric theories form the basis of psychiatric criminology. See also **forensic psychiatry.** (6)

psychiatric theory A theory derived from the medical sciences, including neurology, and that, like other psychological theories, focuses on the individual as the unit of analysis.

psychoactive substance A substance that affects the mind, mental processes, or emotions. (13)

psychoanalysis The theory of human psychology founded by Sigmund Freud on the concepts of the unconscious, resistance, repression, sexuality, and the Oedipus complex.[26] (6)

psychoanalytic criminology A psychiatric approach developed by Sigmund Freud that emphasizes the role of personality in human behavior and which sees deviant behavior as the result of dysfunctional personalities.

psychological profiling The attempt to categorize, understand, and predict the behavior of certain types of offenders based on behavioral clues they provide. (6)

psychological theory A theory derived from the behavioral sciences that focuses on the individual as the unit of analysis. Psychological theories place the locus of crime causation within the personality of the individual offender. (6)

psychopath An individual who has a personality disorder, especially one manifested in aggressively antisocial behavior, and who is lacking in empathy. Also called *sociopath.* (6)

psychopathology Any psychological disorder that causes distress, either for the individual or for those in the individual's life.[27] Also, the study of pathological mental conditions—that is, mental illness.

psychopathy A personality disorder characterized by antisocial behavior and lack of affect.

psychosis A form of mental illness in which sufferers are said to be out of touch with reality. (6)

psychotherapy A form of psychiatric treatment based on psychoanalytical principles and techniques. (6)

public policy A course of action that government takes in an effort to solve a problem or to achieve an end.

punishment An undesirable behavioral consequence likely to decrease the frequency of occurrence of that behavior. (6)

pure research Research undertaken simply for the sake of advancing scientific knowledge. (3)

qualitative method A research technique that produces subjective results, or results that are difficult to quantify. (3)

quantitative method A research technique that produces measurable results. (3)

quasi-experimental design An approach to research that, although less powerful than experimental designs, is deemed worthy of use when better designs are not feasible. (3)

Racketeer Influenced and Corrupt Organizations (RICO) A statute that was part of the federal Organized Crime Control Act of 1970 and that is intended to combat criminal conspiracies. (12)

radical criminology A perspective that holds that the causes of crime are rooted in social conditions that empower the wealthy and the politically well organized but disenfranchise the less fortunate. Also called *critical criminology; Marxist criminology.* (9)

radical feminism A perspective that holds that any significant change in the social status of women can be accomplished only through substantial changes in social institutions such as the family, law, and medicine. Radical feminism argues, for example, that the structure of current legal thinking involves what is fundamentally a male perspective, which should be changed to incorporate women's social experiences and points of view. (9)

randomization The process whereby individuals are assigned to study groups without biases or differences resulting from selection. (3)

rape (NCVS) Carnal knowledge through the use of force or the threat of force, including attempts. Statutory rape (without force) is excluded. Both heterosexual and homosexual rape are included. (2)

rape (UCR) See **forcible rape.**

rape myth A false assumption about rape such as "When a woman says no, she really means yes." Rape myths characterize much of the discourse surrounding sexual violence. (10)

rape shield law A statute providing for the protection of rape victims by ensuring that defendants do not introduce irrelevant facts about the victim's sexual history into evidence. (10)

rational choice theory A perspective that holds that criminality is the result of conscious choice and that predicts that individuals choose to commit crime when the benefits outweigh the costs of disobeying the law. (4)

reaction formation The process by which a person openly rejects that which he or she wants or aspires to but cannot obtain or achieve. (7)

realist criminology See **left realism.**

recidivism The repetition of criminal behavior. (4)

recidivism rate The percentage of convicted offenders who have been released from prison and who are later re-arrested for a new crime, generally within five years following release. See also **dangerousness.** (4)

reintegrative shaming A form of shaming, imposed as a sanction by the criminal justice system, that is thought to strengthen the moral bond between the offender and the community. (8)

relative deprivation A sense of social or economic inequality experienced by those who are unable, for whatever reason, to achieve legitimate success within the surrounding society. (7)

replicability A scientific principle that holds that valid observations made at one time can be made again later if all other conditions are the same. (3)

research The use of standardized, systematic procedures in the search for knowledge.[28] (3)

research design The logic and structure inherent in an approach to data gathering. (3)

restitution A criminal sanction—in particular, the payment of compensation by the offender to the victim.

restorative justice A postmodern perspective that stresses "remedies and restoration rather than prison, punishment and victim neglect."[29] (9)

retribution The act of taking revenge upon a criminal perpetrator. (4)

reward A desirable behavioral consequence likely to increase the frequency of occurrence of that behavior. (6)

risk analysis See **threat analysis.**

robbery (UCR) The taking of or attempting to take anything of value from the care, custody, or control of a person or persons by force or threat of force or violence or by putting the victim in fear. (2)

routine activities theory A brand of rational choice theory that suggests that lifestyles contribute significantly to both the volume and the type of crime found in any society. Also called *lifestyle theory.* (4)

scenario writing A technique intended to predict future outcomes, that builds upon environmental scanning by attempting to assess the likelihood of a variety of possible outcomes once important trends have been identified. (Epilogue)

schizoid A person characterized by schizoid personality disorder. Such disordered personalities appear to be aloof, withdrawn, unresponsive, humorless, dull, and solitary to an abnormal degree. (5)

schizophrenic A mentally ill individual who is out of touch with reality and who suffers from disjointed thinking. (6)

secondary deviance Deviant behavior that results from official labeling and from association with others who have been so labeled. (8)

secondary research New evaluations of existing information that had been collected by other researchers. (3)

secondary victimization See **post-crime victimization.**

second-degree murder Criminal homicide that is unplanned and that is often described as "a crime of passion." (2)

securities fraud The theft of money resulting from intentional manipulation of the value of equities, including stocks and bonds. Securities fraud also includes theft from securities accounts and wire fraud. (12)

selective disinhibition A loss of self-control due to the characteristics of the social setting, drugs or alcohol, or a combination of both. (10)

selective incapacitation A social policy that seeks to protect society by incarcerating the individuals deemed to be the most dangerous. (6)

self-control A person's ability to alter his or her own states and responses.[30] (6)

self-report survey A survey in which anonymous respondents, without fear of disclosure or arrest, are asked to confidentially report any violations of the criminal law that they have committed. (2)

separation assault Violence inflicted by partners on significant others who attempt to leave an intimate relationship. (10)

serial murder Criminal homicide that involves the killing of several victims in three or more separate events. (10)

sex trafficking The recruitment, harboring, transportation, provision, or obtaining of a person for the purpose of a commercial sex act. (15)

sibling offense An offense or incident that culminates in homicide. The offense or incident may be a crime, such as robbery, or an incident that meets a less stringent criminal definition, such as a lover's quarrel involving assault or battery. (10)

simple assault (NCVS) An attack without a weapon, resulting either in minor injury or in undetermined injury requiring less than two days of hospitalization. See also **aggravated assault.** (2)

situational choice theory A brand of rational choice theory that views criminal behavior "as a function of choices and decisions made within a context of situational constraints and opportunities."[31] (4)

situational crime prevention A social policy approach that looks to develop greater understanding of crime and more effective crime prevention strategies through concern with the physical, organizational, and social environments that make crime possible.[32] (4)

snitch An amateur shoplifter. (11)

social bond The link, created through socialization, between individuals and the society of which they are a part. (8)

social capital The degree of positive relationships with others and with social institutions that individuals build up over the course of their lives. (8)

social class Distinctions made between individuals on the basis of important defining social characteristics. (9)

social contract The Enlightenment-era concept that human beings abandon their natural state of individual freedom to join together and form society. In the process of forming a social contract, individuals surrender some freedoms to society as a whole, and government, once formed, is obligated to assume responsibilities toward its citizens and to provide for their protection and welfare. (4)

social control theory A perspective that predicts that when social constraints on antisocial behavior are weakened or absent, delinquent behavior emerges. Rather than stressing causative factors in criminal behavior, control theory asks why people actually obey rules instead of breaking them. (8)

social development perspective An integrated view of human development that examines multiple levels of maturation simultaneously, including the psychological, biological, familial, interpersonal, cultural, societal, and ecological levels. (8)

social disorganization A condition said to exist when a group is faced with social change, uneven development of culture, maladaptiveness, disharmony, conflict, and lack of consensus. (7)

social disorganization theory A perspective on crime and deviance that sees society as a kind of organism and crime and deviance as a kind of disease or social pathology. Theories of social disorganization are often associated with the perspective of social ecology and with the Chicago School of criminology, which developed during the 1920s and 1930s. (7)

social ecology An approach to criminological theorizing that attempts to link the structure and organization of a human community to interactions with its localized environment. (7)

social epidemiology The study of social epidemics and diseases of the social order.

social learning theory A psychological perspective that says that people learn how to behave by modeling themselves after others whom they have the opportunity to observe.

social life The ongoing and (typically) structured interaction that occurs between persons in a society, including socialization and social behavior in general. (7)

social pathology A concept that compares society to a physical organism and that sees criminality as an illness. (7)

social policy A government initiative, program, or plan intended to address problems in society. The "war on crime," for example, is a kind of generic (large-scale) social policy—one consisting of many smaller programs. (1)

social problems perspective The belief that crime is a manifestation of underlying social problems, such as poverty, discrimination, pervasive family violence, inadequate socialization practices, and the breakdown of traditional social institutions. (1)

social process The interaction between and among social institutions, individuals, and groups. (7)

social process theory A theory that asserts that criminal behavior is learned in interaction with others and that socialization processes that occur as the result of group membership are the primary route through which learning occurs. Also called the *interactionist perspective*. (8)

social relativity The notion that social events are differently interpreted according to the cultural experiences and personal interests of the initiator, the observer, or the recipient of that behavior. (1)

social responsibility perspective The belief that individuals are fundamentally responsible for their own behavior and that they choose crime over other, more law-abiding courses of action. (1)

social structure The pattern of social organization and the interrelationships among institutions characteristic of a society. (7)

social structure theory A theory that explains crime by reference to some aspect of the social fabric. These theories emphasize relationships among social institutions and describe the types of behavior that tend to characterize groups of people rather than individuals. (7)

socialist feminism A perspective that examines social roles and the gender-based division of labor within the family, seeing both as a significant source of women's subordination within society. This perspective calls for a redefinition of gender-related job status, compensation for women who work within the home, and equal pay for equal work regardless of gender. (9)

socialization The lifelong process of social experience whereby individuals acquire the cultural patterns of their society. (1)

sociobiology "The systematic study of the biological basis of all social behavior."[33] (5)

sociological theory A perspective that focuses on the nature of the power relationships that exist between social groups and on the influences that various social phenomena bring to bear on the types of behaviors that tend to characterize groups of people. (7)

sociopath See **psychopath.** (6)

soft determinism The belief that human behavior is the result of choices and decisions made within a context of situational constraints and opportunities. (4)

software piracy The unauthorized and illegal copying of software programs. (14)

somatotyping The classification of human beings into types according to body build and other physical characteristics. (5)

specific deterrence A goal of criminal sentencing that seeks to prevent a particular offender from engaging in repeat criminality. (4)

spousal rape The rape of one spouse by the other. The term usually refers to the rape of a woman by her husband. (2, 10)

stalking A course of conduct directed at a specific person that involves repeated visual or physical proximity; nonconsensual communication; verbal, written, or implied threats; or a combination thereof that would cause a reasonable person fear. Also, a constellation of behaviors involving repeated and persistent attempts to impose on another person unwanted communication and/or contact. (10)

state-organized crime Acts defined by law as criminal and committed by state officials in the pursuit of their work as representatives of the state. [34]

statistical correlation The simultaneous increase or decrease in value of two numerically valued random variables.[35]

statistical school A criminological perspective with roots in the early 1800s that seeks to uncover correlations between crime rates and other types of demographic data. (2)

statute A formal, written enactment of a legislative body.[36] (1)

statutory law Law in the form of statutes or formal, written strictures made by a legislature or governing body with the power to make law. (1)

stigmatic shaming   A form of shaming, imposed as a sanction by the criminal justice system, that is thought to destroy the moral bond between the offender and the community. (8)

strain theory   A sociological approach that posits a disjuncture between socially and subculturally sanctioned means and goals as the cause of criminal behavior. Also called *anomie theory.* (7)

strategic assessment   A technique that assesses the risks and opportunities facing those who plan for the future. (Epilogue)

structural Marxism   A perspective that holds that the structural institutions of society influence the behavior of individuals and groups by virtue of the type of relationships created. The criminal law, for example, reflects class relationships and serves to reinforce those relationships. (9)

subcultural theory   A sociological perspective that emphasizes the contribution made by variously socialized cultural groups to the phenomenon of crime. (7)

subculture   A collection of values and preferences that is communicated to subcultural participants through a process of socialization. (7)

sublimation   The psychological process whereby one aspect of consciousness comes to be symbolically substituted for another. (6)

substantial-capacity test   A standard for judging legal insanity that requires that a person lack the mental capacity needed to understand the wrongfulness of his or her act or to conform his or her behavior to the requirements of the law. (6)

superego   The moral aspect of the personality; much like the conscience. More formally, the division of the psyche that develops by the incorporation of the perceived moral standards of the community, is mainly unconscious, and includes the conscience.[37] (6)

supermale   A male individual displaying the XYY chromosome structure. (5)

superpredator   One of a new generation of juveniles "who are coming of age in actual and 'moral poverty' without the benefits of parents, teachers, coaches and clergy to teach them right from wrong and show them 'unconditional love.' "[38] The term is often applied to inner-city youths who meet the criteria it sets forth.

survey research   A social science data-gathering technique that involves the use of questionnaires. (3)

tagging   The process whereby an individual is negatively defined by agencies of justice. Also called *labeling.* (8)

target hardening   The reduction in criminal opportunity for a particular location, generally through the use of physical barriers, architectural design, and enhanced security measures. (4)

techniques of neutralization   Culturally available justifications that can provide criminal offenders with the means to disavow responsibility for their behavior. (7)

TEMPEST   A standard developed by the U.S. government that requires that electromagnetic emanations from computers designated as "secure" be below levels that would allow radio receiving equipment to "read" the data being computed. (14)

terrorism   Premeditated, politically motivated violence perpetrated against noncombatant targets by subnational groups or clandestine agents, usually intended to influence an audience.[39] (15)

test of significance   A statistical technique intended to provide researchers with confidence that their results are, in fact, true and not the result of sampling error. (3)

testosterone   The primary male sex hormone. Produced in the testes, its function is to control secondary sex characteristics and sexual drive. (5)

Thanatos   A death wish. (6)

theory   A series of interrelated propositions that attempt to describe, explain, predict, and ultimately control some class of events. A theory gains explanatory power from inherent logical consistency and is "tested" by how well it describes and predicts reality. (1, 3)

threat analysis   A complete and thorough assessment of the kinds of perils facing an organization. Also called *risk analysis.* (14)

three-strikes legislation   Criminal statutes that mandate life impirsonment for criminals convicted of three violent felonies or serious drug offenses. (4)

total institution   A facility from which individuals can rarely come and go and in which communal life is intense and circumscribed. Individuals in total institutions tend to eat, sleep, play, learn, and worship (if at all) together. (8)

trafficking in persons (TIP)   The exploitation of unwilling or unwitting people through force, coercion, threat, or deception. (15)

transnational organized crime   Unlawful activity undertaken and supported by organized criminal groups operating across national boundaries. (12, 15)

trend extrapolation   A technique of futures research that makes future predictions based on the projection of existing trends. (Epilogue)

trephination   A form of surgery typically involving bone, especially the skull. Early instances of cranial trephination have been taken as evidence for primitive beliefs in spirit possession. (4)

truth in sentencing   A close correspondence between the sentence imposed upon those sent to prison and the time actually served prior to prison release.[40] (4)

Twelve Tables   Early Roman laws written circa 450 B.C., which regulated family, religious, and economic life. (4)

unicausal   Having one cause. Unicausal theories posit only one source for all that they attempt to explain. (1)

Uniform Crime Reporting Program (UCR)   A Federal Bureau of Investigation summation of crime statistics tallied annually and consisting primarily of data on crimes reported to the police and on arrests. (2)

utilitarianism   See **hedonistic calculus.** (4)

variable   A concept that can undergo measurable changes. (3)

verstehen   The kind of subjective understanding that can be achieved by criminologists who immerse themselves in the everyday world of the criminals they study. (3)

victim-impact statement A written document that describes the losses, suffering, and trauma experienced by the crime victim or by the victim's survivors. In jurisdictions where victim-impact statements are used, judges are expected to consider them in arriving at an appropriate sentence for the offender.

victimization rate (NCVS) A measure of the occurrence of victimizations among a specified population group. For personal crimes, the rate is based on the number of victimizations per 1,000 residents aged 12 or older. For household crimes, the victimization rates are calculated using the number of incidents per 1,000 households.

victimogenesis The contributory background of a victim as a result of which he or she becomes prone to victimization.

victimology The study of victims and their contributory role, if any, in crime causation.

victim-precipitated homicide A killing in which the victim was the first to commence the interaction or was the first to resort to physical violence.

victim precipitation Contributions made by the victim to the criminal event, especially those that led to its initiation. (10)

victim proneness An individual's likelihood of victimization.

Victims of Crime Act (VOCA) A federal law enacted in 1984 that established the federal Crime Victims Fund. The fund uses monies from fines and forfeitures collected from federal offenders to supplement state support of local victims' assistance programs and state victim compensation programs.

victim-witness assistance program A program that counsels victims, orients them to the justice process, and provides a variety of other services, such as transportation to court, child care during court appearances, and referrals to social service agencies.

Violence against Women Act (VAWA) A federal law enacted as a component of the 1994 Violent Crime Control and Law Enforcement Act and intended to address concerns about violence against women. The law focused on improving the interstate enforcement of protection orders, providing effective training for court personnel involved with women's issues, improving the training and collaboration of police and prosecutors with victim service providers, strengthening law enforcement efforts to reduce violence against women, and increasing services to victims of violence. President Clinton signed the reauthorization of this legislation, known as the Violence against Women Act 2000, into law on October 28, 2000. (10)

Violent Crime Control and Law Enforcement Act A federal law (Public Law 103–322) enacted in 1994 that authorized spending billions of dollars on crime prevention, law enforcement, and prison construction. It also outlawed the sale of certain types of assault weapons and enhanced federal death penalty provisions.

Violent Criminal Apprehension Program (VICAP) The program of the Federal Bureau of Investigation focusing on serial murder investigation and the apprehension of serial killers. (10)

virus See **computer virus.**

white-collar crime Violations of the criminal law committed by persons of respectability and high social status in the course of their occupation. (12)

Wickersham Commission Created by President Herbert Hoover in 1931, and officially known as the *Commission on Law Observance and Enforcement,* the mandate of this commission was to develop "objectives to improve justice system practices and to reinstate law's role in civilized governance." The commission made recommendations concerning the nation's police forces and described how to improve policing throughout America.

workplace violence The crimes of murder, rape, robbery, and assault committed against persons who are at work or on duty. (10)

Notes

1 American Board of Forensic Psychology, World Wide Web site, http://www.abfp.com/brochure.html (accessed November 22, 2006).

2 This and other computer crime–related terms are adapted from Donn B. Parker, *Computer Crime: Criminal Justice Resource Manual* (Washington, DC: National Institute of Justice, 1989).

3 Michael L. Benson, Francis T. Cullen, and William J. Maakestad, *Local Prosecutors and Corporate Crime* (Washington, DC: National Institute of Justice, 1993).

4 James A. Inciardi, *The War on Drugs II* (Mountain View, CA: Mayfield, 1992), p. 79.

5 Bryan Vila, "A General Paradigm for Understanding Criminal Behavior: Extending Evolutionary Ecological Theory," *Criminology,* Vol. 32, No. 3 (August 1994), pp. 311–359.

6 Adapted from Federal Bureau of Investigation, *FBI Policy and Guidelines: Counterterrorism,* http://www.fbi.gov/contact/fo/jackson/cntrterr.htm (accessed January 15, 2007).

7 BJS, *Drugs, Crime and the Justice System* (Washington, DC: U.S. Department of Justice, December 1992).

8 *American Heritage Dictionary and Electronic Thesaurus* (Boston: Houghton Mifflin, 1987).

9 George F. Cole, "Criminal Justice in the Twenty-First Century: The Role of Futures Research," in John Klofas and Stan Stojkovic, eds., *Crime and Justice in the Year 2010* (Belmont, CA: Wadsworth, 1995).

10 Society of Police Futurists International, *PFI: The Future of Policing* (brochure), no date.

11 Teresa C. LaGrange and Robert A. Silverman, "Low Self-Control and Opportunity: Testing the General Theory of

Crime as an Explanation for Gender Differences in Delinquency," *Criminology,* Vol. 37, No. 1 (1999), p. 41.

[12] Adapted from "Globalization," *Encyclopedia Britannica, 2007,* Encyclopedia Britannica Premium Service, http://www.britannica.com/eb/article?eu5369857 (accessed July, 23, 2007).

[13] Raimo Väyrynen, "Illegal Immigration, Human Trafficking, and Organized Crime," United Nations University/World Institute for Development Economics Research, Discussion Paper No. 2003/72 (October 2003), p. 16.

[14] *American Heritage Dictionary and Electronic Thesaurus.*

[15] Ibid.

[16] Adapted from Dictionary.com, http://dictionary.reference.com/search?1q=infrastructure (accessed January 10, 2003).

[17] *American Heritage Dictionary and Electronic Thesaurus.*

[18] Adapted from Federal Bureau of Investigation, *FBI Policy and Guidelines: Counterterrorism.*

[19] Clifford Karchmer and Douglas Ruch, "State and Local Money Laundering Control Strategies," *NIJ Research in Brief* (Washington, DC: National Institute of Justice, 1992), p. 1.

[20] Vila, "A General Paradigm for Understanding Criminal Behavior."

[21] Gary S. Green, *Occupational Crime* (Chicago: Nelson-Hall, 1990), p. 12.

[22] The Omnibus Crime Control Act of 1970.

[23] Frank E. Hagan, *Research Methods in Criminal Justice and Criminology* (New York: Macmillan, 1993), p. 103.

[24] "Phishing," TechWeb's *TechEncyclopedia,* http://www.techweb.com/encyclopedia/defineterm?term=phishing (accessed July 30, 2007).

[25] Bryan Vila, "Human Nature and Crime Control: Improving the Feasibility of Nurturant Strategies," *Politics and the Life Sciences* (March 1997), pp. 3–21.

[26] *American Heritage Dictionary and Electronic Thesaurus.*

[27] Laurence Steinberg, "The Juvenile Psychopath: Fads, Fictions, and Facts," *National Institute of Justice Perspectives on Crime and Justice: 2001 Lecture Series,*

Vol. V (Washington, DC: National Institute of Justice, 2002), pp. 35–64.

[28] Abraham Kaplan, *The Conduct of Inquiry: Methodology for Behavioral Science* (San Francisco: Chandler, 1964), p. 71.

[29] Fay Honey Knopp, "Community Solutions to Sexual Violence: Feminist-Abolitionist Perspectives," in Harold Pepinsky and Richard Quinney, eds., *Criminology as Peacemaking* (Bloomington: Indiana University Press, 1991), p. 183.

[30] Roy F. Baumeister and Julie Juola Exline, "Self-Control, Morality, and Human Strength," *Journal of Social and Clinical Psychology,* Vol. 19, No. 1 (April 2000), pp. 29–42.

[31] Ronald V. Clarke and Derek B. Cornish, eds., *Crime Control in Britain: A Review of Police and Research* (Albany: State University of New York Press), p. 8.

[32] David Weisburd, "Reorienting Crime Prevention Research and Policy: From the Causes of Criminality to the Context of Crime," *NIJ Research Report* (Washington, DC: National Institute of Justice, June 1997).

[33] Edward O. Wilson, *Sociobiology: The New Synthesis* (Cambridge, MA: Harvard University Press, Belknap Press, 1975).

[34] William J. Chambliss, "State-Organized Crime—The American Society of Criminology, 1988 Presidential Address," *Criminology:* Vol. 27, No. 2 (1989), pp. 183–208.

[35] *American Heritage Dictionary and Electronic Thesaurus.*

[36] Henry Campbell Black, *Black's Law Dictionary,* 6th ed. (St. Paul, MN: West, 1990), p. 1410.

[37] *American Heritage Dictionary and Electronic Thesaurus.*

[38] See John J. DiIulio, Jr., "The Question of Black Crime," *Public Interest* (fall 1994), pp. 3–12. The term *superpredator* is generally attributed to DiIulio.

[39] U.S. Department of State, *Patterns of Global Terrorism, 2001* (Washington, DC: U.S. Government Printing Office, 2002), http://www.state.gov/s/ct/rls/pgtrpt/2001 (accessed January 2, 2003).

[40] Lawrence A. Greenfeld, "Prison Sentences and Time Served for Violence," *Bureau of Justice Statistics Selected Findings,* No. 4, April 1995.

Name Index

Subject Index

Criminology-Related Websites

Academy of Experimental Criminology (AEC)
http://www.crim.upenn.edu/aec/about.htm
The Academy of Experimental Criminology was founded in 1999 to recognize successful randomized, controlled field experiments in criminology. The Academy publishes the Journal of Experimental Criminology.

American Society of Criminology (ASC)
http://www.asc41.com
The ASC is an international organization concerned with scholarly, scientific, and professional knowledge concerning the etiology, prevention, control, and treatment of crime and delinquency

Australian Institute of Criminology (AIC)
http://www.aic.gov.au
The Australian Institute of Criminology serves as the national center for the study of crime and criminal justice in Australia and for the dissemination of information in the areas of criminology and criminal justice. AIC makes its Trends & Issues in Crime and Criminal Justice Series available through its website. The series provides studies and information for decision makers to assist in the promotion of justice and the prevention of crime.

Balanced and Restorative Justice (BARJ) Project
http://www.barjproject.org
The Balanced and Restorative Justice (BARJ) project is a national initiative of the Office of Juvenile Justice and Delinquency Prevention (OJJDP). It works with communities and criminal justice agencies to provide training, education, technical assistance, evaluation, and research on emerging law enforcement and restorative justice practices. Its website contains PDF versions of project newsletters, as well a listing of project publications.

British Society of Criminology (BSC)
http://www.britsoccrim.org
The Society is Britain's major professional criminology organization, working to further the interests and knowledge of both academic and professional people engaged in any aspect of teaching, research, or public education about crime, criminal behavior, and the criminal justice system in the United Kingdom.

Campbell Collaboration's Crime and Justice Coordinating Group (CCJG)
http://www.campbellcollaboration.org/CCJG
The Crime and Justice Coordinating Group is an international network of researchers that prepares, updates, and rapidly disseminates systematic reviews of high-quality research conducted worldwide on effective methods to reduce crime and delinquency and improve the quality of justice.

Center for Restorative Justice and Peacemaking
http://rjp.umn.edu
The Center is "committed to the development of community-based responses to crime and violence that strengthen social harmony and individual healing through dialogue, repair of harm, and peace-building by providing technical assistance, training, and research in support of restorative dialogue practices." Its website provides the full text of several of the Center's publications as well as an annotated bibliography of restorative justice materials.

Center for the Study and Prevention of Violence (CSPV)
http://www.colorado.edu/cspv
The CSPV, a research program of the Institute of Behavioral Science at the University of Colorado at Boulder, was founded to provide informed assistance to groups committed to understanding and preventing violence, particularly adolescent violence.

Computer Crime and Intellectual Property Section (U.S. Department of Justice)
http://www.cybercrime.gov
The Computer Crime and Intellectual Property Section (CCIPS) of the U.S. Department of Justice is responsible for implementing the Department's national strategies in combating computer and intellectual property crimes worldwide.

Crime Library, Court TV
http://www.crimelibrary.com
Court TV's Crime Library is a rapidly growing collection of more than 600 nonfiction feature stories on major crimes, criminals, trials, forensics, and criminal profiling by prominent writers. The stories focus mostly on recent crimes, but an expanding collection also delves into historically notorious characters, dating back to the 1400s and spanning the globe.

Crime Mapping Research Center
http://www.ojp.usdoj.gov/nij/maps
The Mapping and Analysis for Public Safety (MAPS) program at the National Institute of Justice supports research into spatial aspects of crime, spatial data analysis, mapping, and analysis for evaluating programs and policy, as well as development of mapping, data sharing, and spatial analysis tools.

Crime Times
http://www.crime-times.org
An electronic journal fostering the effort to learn about the brain dysfunction that underlies much delinquency and criminality. The site provides research reviews and information on biological causes of disordered, criminal, and psychopathic behavior.

Critical Criminology Division of the ASC
http://www.critcrim.org
The ASC Division on Critical Criminology fosters research and theory development in the field of critical criminology, which is widely recognized as one of the major paradigms in criminology. The division also provides access to the online edition of the journal The Critical Criminologist.

Domestic Violence and Sexual Assault Data Resource Center
http://www.jrsa.org/dvsa-drc
The Domestic Violence and Sexual Assault Data Resource Center provides information on state-collected data. Funded by the National Institute of Justice, the center's website includes national summaries, state-by-state information, lists of related reports, and a list of national and state contacts.

Drug and Alcohol Services Information System (DASIS)
http://oas.samhsa.gov/dasis.htm
DASIS is the primary source of national data on substance abuse treatment. It has three components available online: National Survey of Substance Abuse Treatment Services (N-SSATS), Treatment Episode Data Set (TEDS), and Inventory of Substance Abuse Treatment Services (I-SATS).

European Society of Criminology
http://www.esc-eurocrim.org
The European Society of Criminology, founded in 2000, works to bring together persons actively engaged in research, teaching, and/or practice in the field of criminology.

Financial Crimes Enforcement Network (FinCEN)
http://www.fincen.gov
The Financial Crimes Enforcement Network is designed to help in the fight against money laundering. The FinCEN works to maximize information sharing among law enforcement agencies and its other partners in the regulatory and financial communities.

Homicide Research Working Group (HRWG)
http://www.icpsr.umich.edu/HRWG
The HRWG provides a clearinghouse for homicide research from many disciplines. It was created by homicide experts from criminology, public health, demography, geography, medicine, sociology, criminal justice, and a variety of other disciplines.

Identity Theft Resource Center (ITRC)
http://www.idtheftcenter.org
The ITRC is a nonprofit program dedicated exclusively to solving the problem of identity theft. Its website includes information on current laws that address the issue of identity theft, up-to-date studies, and links to relevant organizations.